THE MIDDLEGAME

by

Dr. M. Euwe & H. Kramer

ALGEBRAIC EDITION

Translated from the Dutch by W. H. Cozens

Editor: Lou Hays

BOOK TWO

DYNAMIC & SUBJECTIVE FEATURES

Hays Publishing, *Dallas*

Original English translation of *The Middle Game – Book Two* by W. H. Cozens

Authors: Dr. Max Euwe, Hans Kramer

Editor: Lou Hays

Typeset: Lou Hays

Computer file creation: John Hall, Lou Hays

Cover: Carolyn Hoefelmeyer

Proofreaders: John Hall, David Sewell, Jude Acers, Sid Pickard

PRINTED IN THE UNITED STATES OF AMERICA

Published in the United States and Canada by special arrangement with B. T. Batsford, Ltd., *London*

Hays Publishing

P.O. Box 797623

Dallas, Texas 75379

ISBN 1-880673-96-7

TABLE OF CONTENTS

FOREWORD

Once my opening and endgame series were completed it was natural that I should consider a book on the middlegame. It was obvious that this would involve entirely different problems, for ready knowledge and established facts play a far more important role in the openings and endings than in the middlegame. The theory of the middlegame is a very difficult thing to tackle, and this explains why it has been so long in preparation. Ten years ago, however, I was already exchanging ideas about a middlegame book with my former collaborator Hans Kmoch. In fact, this book really has not two authors, but three. Kmoch and I prepared a scheme at that time for the treatment of this missing phase, the middlegame, which has received such inadequate treatment in chess literature.

In the years just after the war we found no opportunity of working out this scheme and, when Mr. Kmoch said farewell to the Netherlands for good, I lost a valuable helper, to whom is due much of the merit of the opening and endgame books.

I count myself lucky to have found one of the leading players of the Netherlands, Mr. H. Kramer, willing to collaborate with me in writing this middlegame book on the basis of the previously drafted plan.

I warmly welcome the publication of an English edition of *Het Middenspel,* as I have many friends among British chess players. I have played in more than twenty tournaments in England and, indeed, my real chess career began at Hastings.

Dr. M. Euwe

January, 1964

INTRODUCTION TO BOOK TWO

Our general introduction, in Book One, called attention to the fact that middlegame theory can be handled in more ways than one. Throughout Book One we adopted the **static** approach, in which our starting point was always some persisting characteristic of the *position,* usually associated with the pawn skeleton.

In Book Two we take up the **dynamic** approach, in which we are concerned with what actually happens on the board. This is clearly very much a matter of practical *example,* and it may be difficult or even impossible to formulate general principles. Nevertheless, even in the heat of battle there will often be an opportunity to pause and weigh things up, and apply some of the positional considerations which have been dealt with in Book One.

Several of these will be arising in the course of the next few chapters. We discuss them now, however, from an entirely different standpoint. We shall be concerned not with the origin of these situations, but with the initiative which may result from them, and we shall occasionally make deliberate use of games already discussed in previous chapters.

PART SIX
THE INITIATIVE
INTRODUCTION

What do we really mean by the initiative in chess? We can make it clear by comparison with the concept of attack. An attack has a specific target, which has already emerged from the peculiarities of the position. The initiative has as yet no definite object, but instead looks for general goals, such as gaining control of maneuvering space, maintaining the tension, keeping the opponent busy, and reserving plenty of attacking options for oneself. This means the idea of initiative applies mainly to positions in which the balance of material has not been yet upset, as so often is the case with a direct attack. Initiative can arise, for example, from a lead in development, or having one's pieces positioned more actively than those of the opponent's; but if the initiative is successfully followed up, it can grow into a full-scale attack. One might liken it to a phase of reconnoitering, before the real battle is joined.

A considerable amount of opening theory can be acquired by diligent study; endgame technique can be learned up to a certain point, and so can the technique necessary for the conduct of various attacks, such as the minority attack, and a number of standard methods against the castled King. However, in the handling of the initiative the natural ability of the player is displayed. It is largely a matter of creating difficulties for the opponent, giving him chances to go wrong.

This explains why it is the phase of the game which typically requires so much time on the clock. As soon as one passes from the initiative to the attack, far less thought is necessary, for the position itself now dictates the direction and manner of the attack, so that quite suddenly the number of possibilities being examined becomes much more restricted.

CHAPTER 23
THE ACTIVITY OF THE PIECES

Once the development stage of the opening is completed there must inevitably come the moment when the players are thrown upon their own resources. The first priority of this phase of the game is to get the pieces placed as actively as possible. This may be called the second stage of development. Some of the pieces must push farther afield – particularly the Knights; the castled position must be put into a state of preparedness, and behind the lines the Rooks must be seeking the spot from which they can best make their weight felt. In the Ruy Lopez we meet the typical maneuvers Nbd2-f1-e3-d5; or Nbd2-f1-g3-f5; or Bb5-a4-b3-c2. It is often a difficult matter to decide precisely where a piece should go, especially if it stands reasonably well already. All sorts of refinements are involved here, and it is precisely these subtleties which decide whether one player or the other will be able to take the initiative.

We have read how Grandmaster X succeeds in making something out of nothing. But this "nothing" in fact usually consists of "something"– specifically, the superior activity of the pieces. The result of this is an initiative which can keep confronting the opponent with little threats, first here, then there, until in the end he commits some small inaccuracy and begins to slide downhill.

Now let the play speak for itself:

(Lasker's celebrated Rook-maneuver; from the 4th match-game, Tarrasch-Lasker, 1908).

1.e4 e5 2.Nf3 Nc6 3.Bb5 Nf6 4.O-O d6 5.d4 Bd7 6.Nc3 Be7 7.Re1 exd4 8.Nxd4 Nxd4 9.Qxd4 Bxb5 10.Nxb5 O-O 11.Bg5 h6 12.Bh4 Re8 13.Rad1 Nd7 14.Bxe7 Rxe7

POSITION 1

This position is closely balanced, but White's control of more space gives him reason to seek the initiative.

15.Qc3

Attacking the c-pawn and vacating d4 for the Knight with gain of tempo. Also, the Queen occupies the long diagonal, with possibilities of attack against g7. If Black now tries 15...Ne5 – not a good move, but an instructive one for the purposes of our argument – the continuation would be 16.Nd4, and White would be threat- ening to win the exchange by 17.f4 and 18.Nf5. In any case he would keep Black busy with new threats, and this, as we have explained above, is typical of the initiative.

15...Re5!

Lasker has no wish to be forced on the defensive. He fights for the initiative himself, and from the sequel it is evident that he was willing to run considerable risks to get it.

16.Nd4 Rc5!

A strange way of deploying a Rook, for a Rook without an open file behind it is highly vulnerable. Lasker means to call the tune at any price. The explanation of this move which he later gave was: *The Rook must expose himself to attack so as to draw the enemy fire.*

17.Qb3 Nb6 18.f4

Cutting off the Rook's retreat. If 18.Re3 Lasker would have played 18...Qe8 and if 19.Nf5, then 19...Kh7.

18...Qf6 19.Qf3 Re8

White's f4 has weakened his e-pawn, giving Black's other Rook a target.

20.c3 a5 21.b3 a4 22.b4 Rc4 23.g3

Protecting the f-pawn and so eliminating the chance of a Black breakthrough by 23...c5 24.Nb5 d5! 25.exd5 Rxf4.

23...Rd8!!

Again Black is threatening to rescue his Rook-by 24...c5 25.Nb5 cxb4, etc.

24.Re3

An attempt to prevent 24...c5 by combinative means.

24...c5! 25.Nb5 cxb4 26.Rxd6 Rxd6 27.e5

Tarrasch had relied on this move when he played 24.Re3. If the Rook were still at e1, then Black could now play 27...Qe7 and after 28.Nxd6 then 28...Rxc3 would be advantageous for Black. Lasker, however, has seen a flaw in White's designs.

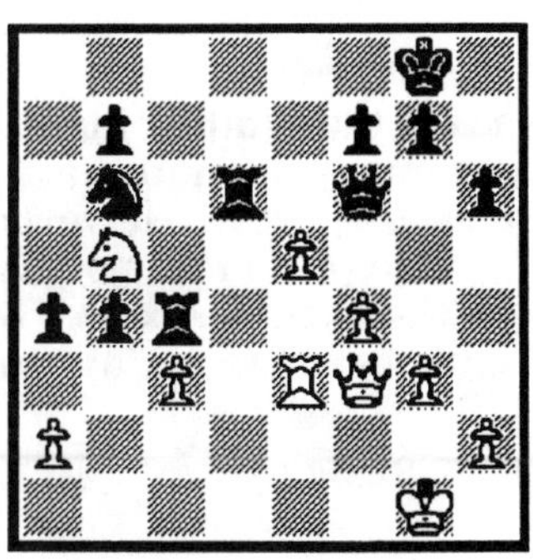

27...Rxf4!!

The brilliant refutation.

28.gxf4 Qg6+ 29.Kh1? Qb1+ 30.Kg2 Rd2+ 31.Re2 Qxa2 32.Rxd2 Qxd2+ 33.Kg3 a3 34.e6 Qe1+ 35.Kg4 Qxe6+ 36.f5 Qc4+ 37.Nd4 a2 38.Qd1 Nd5 39.Qa4 Nxc3 40.Qe8+ Kh7 41.Kh5 a1=Q White Resigned.

POSITION 2

(Fight for the initiative, from the game Alekhine-Keres, Salzburg, 1942).

1.e4 e5 2.Nf3 Nc6 3.Bb5 a6 4.Ba4 Nf6 5.O-O Be7 6.Qe2 b5 7.Bb3 d6 8.c3 O-O 9.Rd1 Na5 10.Bc2 c5 11.d4 Qc7 12.Bg5 Bg4 13.dxe5 dxe5 14.Nbd2 Rfd8

We looked at this game in Book One (Position 130) under the heading of the focus formation – the d5 square being the focus. Our first object there was to show the vulnerability of this square; now we investigate how the pieces can develop maximum activity. In this respect Black just missed an opportunity: 14...Nh5! 15.h3 Bxf3 16.Nxf3 Bxg5 17.Nxg5 Nf4 would have been a stronger line.

15.Nf1

Aiming for the weak point d5 via e3.

15...Nh5

Black grasps at the initiative; now after the obvious continuation 16.Bxe7 Qxe7 17.h3 Nf4 he would indeed have accomplished his object.

16.h3! Be6

Black could make the best of a bad bargain here by 16...Bxf3 17.Qxf3 Bxg5 18.Qxh5 Qe7. Then if the troublesome Knight shows itself at e3, Black promptly takes it off. The move chosen, however, is quite promising, as it puts another guard on d5, and constrains White to reckon with 17...Bc4.

17.Ne3 f6

The struggle for the initiative is in full swing. After 18.Bh4 Nf4 Black again achieves his aim.

18.Nh2! g6

He has no desire for the wild combination 18...Bf7 19.Nd5 Rxd5 20.exd5 fxg5 because after 21.d6 Bxd6 22.Qe4 and 23.Qxh7+ the initiative is firmly in White's hands. It looks, however, as though this is going to be the case anyway.

19.Bh6 Bf8

The consequent move. Black hopes that by exchanging the dark-squared Bishops he may yet make himself master of f4.

20.Bxf8 Kxf8?

This was the moment for Black to play 20...Nf4!. Probably he was under the impression that the move could not now be prevented.

21.g3!

This move disillusions him, and again a little combination is involved: 21...Bxh3 22.Nd5 Qa7 23.g4 Nf4 24.Nxf4 exf4 25.Qf3 winning the Bishop.

21...Rxd1+

With his ...Nf4 scheme knocked on the head, Keres deems it time to go for the draw.

22.Bxd1! Rd8 23.a4

The Rook is activated.

23...Nc4 24.axb5 axb5 25.Nd5!

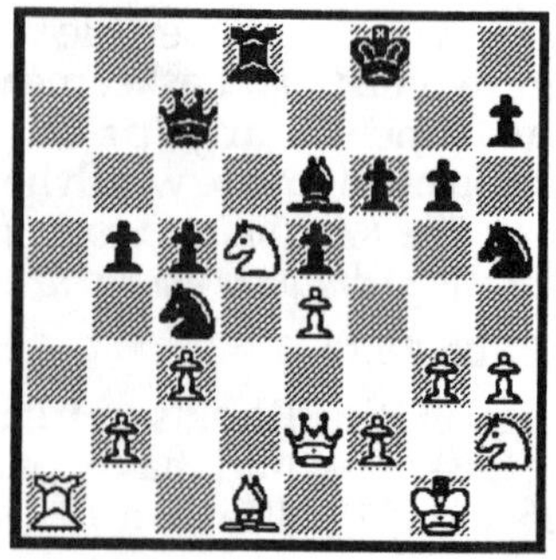

With this surprising continuation Alekhine introduces us to a stratagem which is of the utmost importance in gaining or holding the initiative – the long range pawn sacrifice.

25...Qb7

Acceptance by 25...Bxd5 26.exd5 Rxd5 would not give White any immediate win, but would provide him with increased opportunities to press the initiative; e.g. by 27.Qe4 followed by 28.Bxh5; or by 27.b3 Nd6 28.Qe3, with all sorts of troublesome little threats. Black discreetly declines the offer.

26.b3 Nd6 27.c4 bxc4 28.bxc4 Bxd5 29.exd5

This is the situation we met in Book One (Chapter 11): the White pawn majority has produced a protected passed pawn. One of the Black Knights is already on blockading duty, and has an ideal post. However, the other Knight is poorly placed, and Black must seek above all to get it back into play.

29...Ng7 30.Ng4 Qe7

At this point the White initiative at length becomes a genuine attack. Black's best line would have been 30...N7e8 31.Qe3 Qc7! (but not Fine's suggested 31...Nxc4 32.Qxc5+ Ncd6 33.Ra7 Qb8 because then comes 34.Nh6!).

31.Bc2 Nge8 32.h4 e4

Less committal would have been 32...Ng7.

33.Ne3 Qe5

Abandoning his second rank to the enemy. How serious this is we saw in our chapter devoted to the subject of open lines. 33...Rb8 would have been much better; or perhaps 33...f5 34.Ng2, and then ...Rb8.

34.Ra7! Kg8

After 34...h5 35.Ng2 the Knight penetrates powerfully via f4.

35.Ng4 Qd4

After 35...Qh5 36.Bxe4 f5, White can play 37.Bd3! threatening 38.Qe6+.

36.Bxe4!

Based on the fact that the Knight on d6 is tied to the defense of f7 and cannot simultaneously defend e4. In fact after 36...Qxe4 37.Qxe4 Nxe4 38.Nh6+ Black has the choice between 38...Kh8 39.Nf7+ and 40.Nxd8, and 38...Kf8 39.Rf7#.

36...f5 37.Nh6+

According to Fine, White could also win by 37.Bxf5 Nxf5 38.Qe6+ Kh8 39.Ne5.

37...Kh8 38.Bc2

Good enough, but 38.Bd3 would have saved a tempo: see White's 43rd move.

38...Qf6 39.Qe6 Qxe6 40.dxe6 Rc8 41.Nf7+ Nxf7 42.exf7 Nd6 43.Bd3 Kg7 44.f8=Q+ Kxf8 45.Rxh7 Kg8 46.Rd7 Ne8 47.h5

This is decisive, unleashing the full strength of the Bishop.

47...gxh5

Or 47...Nf6 48.Rd6 Kf7 49.hxg6+ Kxg6 50.g4! winning the f-pawn.

48.Bxf5 Ra8 49.Be6+ Kh8 50.Rd5 Nf6 51.Rxc5 Kg7 52.Kg2 Ra2 53.Bf5 Ra3 54.Rc7+ Kh6 55.f4 h4 56.g4 Black Resigned.

POSITION 3

(The proverbial "making something out of nothing" consists, in fact, of superior piece activity; from the game Kramer-Busek, Vienna 1955).

1.d4 d5 2.c4 c6 3.Nf3 Nf6 4.e3 g6 5.Nc3 Bg7 6.Qb3 O-O 7.Bd2 e6 8.Bd3 Nbd7 9.O-O b6 10.cxd5 exd5 11.e4 dxe4 12.Nxe4 Nxe4 13.Bxe4 Nb8

White is ahead in development, but if the position retains its closed character he will not be able to make anything out of it. Black will automatically make up his leeway; and in fact he already threatens ...Be6 and ...Bd5, blockading the isolated d-pawn.

14.d5!

Playing to dissolve the isolated pawn and reach an open game.

14...Bb7 15.Bg5 Qd7 16.dxc6

Played in accordance with the rule that an advantage in development is best exploited in an open game. After 16.Rad1 on the other hand Black plays 16...c5 and the position retains some of its closed character.

16...Bxc6 17.Rfd1 Qb7 18.Bd5!

The only move to keep the initiative. After 18.Bxc6 Nxc6 Black would have gained an important tempo as compared with the line played.

18...Bxd5 19.Rxd5 h6

If 19...Bxb2 20.Qxb2 Qxd5 21.Bh6 f6 22.Bxf8 Kxf8 23.Qxf6+ and White's initiative has become a real attack. The chosen move however is a weakening which has grave consequences later. All the same, Black would not get far without this move, for if, say, 19...Nc6 White would play 20.Rad1, threatening to invade the seventh rank.

20.Be3 Nc6

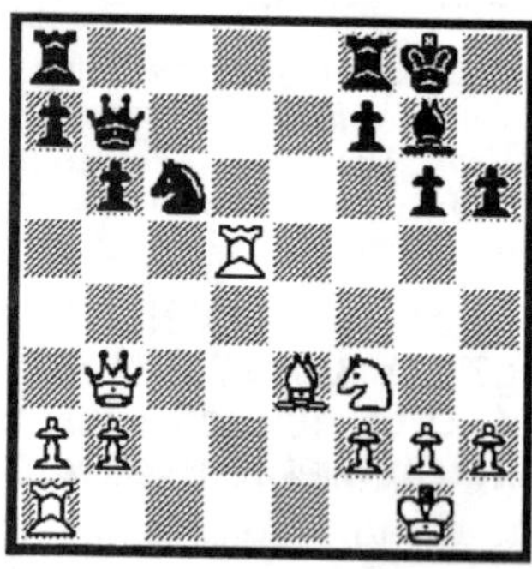

(Black is threatening to reach full equality by 21...Rad8; how can White retain the initiative?)

21.Rd6!

Showing that 19...h6 really was a weakening move. White threatens 22.Rxg6.

21...Kh7

After 21...Rad8 22.Rxg6 Na5 White would have to sacrifice the Exchange by 23.Rxg7+ Kxg7 24.Qc3+. He would still have an attack full of promise.

22.Qb5!

Now the Knight cannot very well move away, as then the White Rook would invade the seventh rank.

22...Rac8 23.Rad1 Rfd8

Black has achieved his immediate aim–the neutralizing and subsequent exchange of Rooks. But White's initiative continues unabated.

24.h4! Rxd6 25.Rxd6 Bf8

A necessary preparation for the exchange of the remaining pair of Rooks.

26.Rd1 Bg7

Or 26...Rd8 27.Rxd8 Nxd8 28.h5, with problems similar to those of the actual game.

27.h5 Qe7

Now after 27...Rd8 28.Rxd8 Nxd8 the penetration of the White Queen to e8 would be very strong.

28.b3 Rd8 29.Rxd8 Nxd8 30.Qd5

Powerful centralization of the Queen.

30...Ne6

The Black pieces lack support points. If 30...Nb7 31.hxg6+ fxg6 32.Nd4. Now Black would be practically forced to play ...Bxd4, leaving his Kingside disastrously weak.

31.hxg6+ fxg6 32.a4

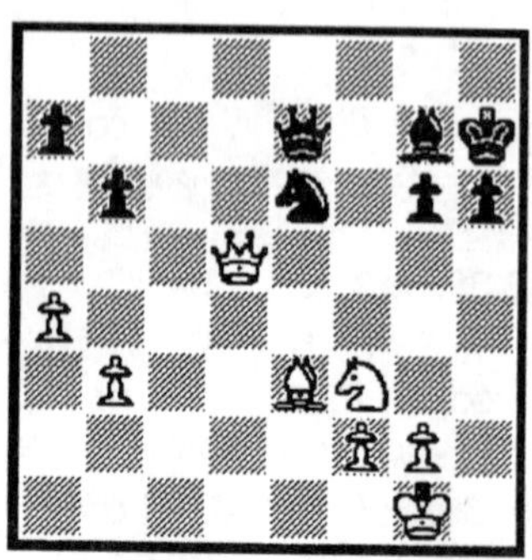

White's initiative has now gathered decisive momentum, as the following variations demonstrate: 32...Nc5 33.a5 Qd7 34.Qxd7 Nxd7 35.axb6 and now–

1) 35...Nxb6 36.Bxb6 axb6 37.Kf1 Kg8 38.Ke2 Kf7 39.Kd3 Ke6 40.Kc4 Kd7 41.Kb5 Kc7 42.Nh4 g5 43.Nf5.

2) 35...axb6 36.Kf1 Kg8 37.Ke2 Kf7 38.Kd3 Ke6 39.Kc4 followed by 40.Kb5.

32...Bf6 33.a5 Ng5

This loses a pawn, but neither 33...bxa5 34.Qxa5, nor 33...Nc5 34.b4 Na4 35.Qc6, is any better.

34.axb6 Nxf3+ 35.Qxf3 axb6 36.Qc6 Bg5 37.Bxb6 Qe1+ 38.Kh2 Qe5+ 39.g3 Bf6 40.Qc7+ Kg8 41.Qxe5 Bxe5 42.Kg2 Kf7 43.Kf3 Ke6 44.Ke4 h5 45.b4 Bb8 46.Be3 and **Black Resigned.**

The end might have been 46...Bd6 47.b5 Be7 48.f4 h4 49.g4! followed by 50.Kf3, 51.g5, and 52.Kg4.

POSITION 4

(From initiative to attack; from the game Skold-Fred, Stockholm, 1956).

1.e4 e5 2.Nf3 Nc6 3.Bb5 a6 4.Ba4 Nf6 5.O-O Be7 6.Re1 b5 7.Bb3 d6 8.c3 O-O 9.h3 Na5 10.Bc2 c5 11.d3 Qc7 12.Nbd2 Rd8 13.Qe2 Bb7 (No.4) **14.Nf1 Re8**

Evidently the intention is to have e5 well guarded, with the idea of an eventual ...d5. For example, if White continues with the obvious 15.Ne3, Black could now seize the initiative with 15...d5, since 16.exd5 Nxd5 17.Nxd5 Bxd5 18.Nxe5? fails to 18...Bd6.

15.Ng3 g6

It is understandable that Black does not permit the Knight to go to f5. But 15...d5 was still to be considered. True, Black would get into trouble after 16.exd5 Nxd5? 17.Qxe5! Bd6 18.Qxe8+, but 16...Bxd5 would have been perfectly playable: 17.Nxe5? Bd6 18.Bf4 Nd7! etc.

16.Bg5 Nc6

Now 16...d5 would have been answered by 17.b4! cxb4 18.cxb4 Nc6 19.a3, with White intending to become very active by Bb3 and Rac1. Black now tries another tack.

17.Nh2!?

Intending to force things by f4, but he ought to have played 17.h4, for after the text move Black can seize the initiative himself.

17...Nh5!

A tactical finesse, based on the unprotected state of White's Bg5. Now if 18.Nxh5, Black can reply 18...Bxg5.

18.Bxe7 Nf4!

The point of the previous move. On the other hand 18...Nxg3 would suit White admirably, for after 19.fxg3 he has his wish-the open f-file-without further ado.

19.Qf1 Qxe7 20.Ne2 Nh5?

Now White does achieve his objective, and the initiative falls into his hands again. Black had various ways of foiling White's plans. For instance, he could have played 20...Bc8; after which White's 21.g3 is prevented because of the pressure on h3; or simply 20...Nxe2+ 21.Rxe2 g5 22.Ng4 Qe6 23.Ne3 Ne7 after which the weak squares at d5 and f5 are adequately covered.

21.f4 exf4 22.Nxf4 Nxf4 23.Qxf4 Qe5 24.Qh4 h5

A serious weakening of his Kingside. Black had to do something about the threat of 25.Ng4, but 24...Bc8 would have been less committal.

25.Rf1 Bc8

So as to meet 26.Bb3 with 26...Be6.

26.Nf3 Qg7 27.Qf4 Ne5

An attempt to prevent the advance d4 by vigorous counteraction.

28.Rad1

Not 28.d4? right away, because of 28...cxd4 29.cxd4 Nxf3+ followed by 30...Qxd4+.

28...Be6 29.Ng5 Rac8

Again preventing d4.

30.Rf2!

On one hand protecting the Bishop, and so threatening d4 again; on the other hand preparing to triple on the f-file.

30...Rc7 31.d4 cxd4 32.cxd4 Nc4 33.Bb3 Rd8 34.Kh1!

White's initiative has now brought him a decisive positional advantage. He controls the center and the half-open f-file, as well as enjoying the greater freedom of movement. What follows now is not so much a matter of initiative as direct attack, for which 34.Kh1 was a fine preparation.

34...Re7 35.Rdf1!!

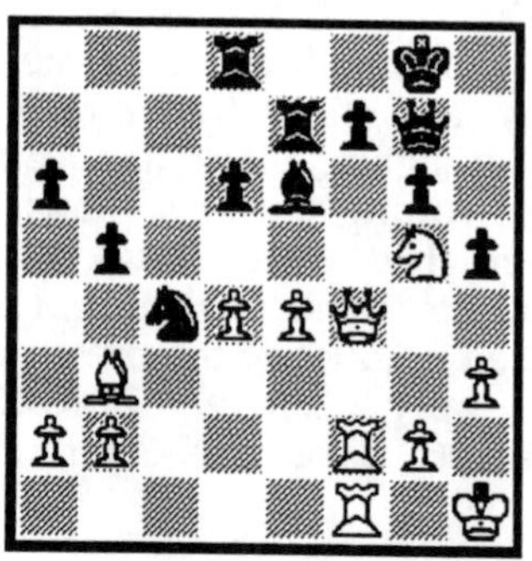

Threatening to conquer f7 by means of 36.d5.

35...Qxd4

Or 35...d5 36.e5 a5 37.g4! with a powerful attack.

36.Nxe6 fxe6 37.Qg5 Qg7 38.Bxc4 bxc4 39.Rf6

Decisive, for the threat of 40.Rxg6 is unanswerable. Even 39...Kh7 does not prevent it.

39...Kh8 40.Rxg6 Rf8 41.Qxh5+ Black Resigned.

CHAPTER 24
THE SECURITY OF THE KING

While trying for the initiative the security of one's own King is a matter of paramount importance. Until the King has found a safe place it is rather risky to undertake anything at all. The beginner is taught that it is prudent to get his King castled into safety as soon as possible; to do so is a part of normal development. Yet even the strongest masters regularly sin against this rule in tournament play–not through carelessness, but by deliberate intent. To understand this we shall have to go a little farther into the matter.

In modern chess the struggle begins from the first move. It is not a case of both players getting their pieces out somewhere or other, then castling, and only then beginning to think of making contact with the enemy. Modern chess is like modern war; important positions must be seized immediately, and right from the start every obstacle must be placed in the enemy's way. If the enemy is already preparing an attack on one flank it stands to reason that the King will not go to that side. He will be better off castled on the other side, or even in the middle. It is no simple matter to decide which will be the safest place; certainly the center will be the most dangerous place if the position is open, but it may be an appropriate place for the King if the center is closed.

Another very difficult matter to judge is just when the King should be shifted out of a danger zone. It may be advisable without delay, but it can also happen that some other measures are even more pressing–for instance the execution of one's own counterattack, or the prevention of some particular move of the opponent. If such tactics succeed it will be said that the player concerned has played a cool and masterly game; if they fail he can expect adverse criticism.

Here are some interesting examples:

POSITION 5

(Black's attempt to take the initiative misfires; from the game Lasker-Pirc, Moscow, 1935).

1.e4 c5 2.Nf3 Nc6 3.d4 cxd4 4.Nxd4 Nf6 5.Nc3 d6 6.Be2 e6 7.O-O a6 8.Be3 Qc7 9.f4

Here Black's prospects lie mainly in his possession of the c-file. As we have seen in Chapter 14 of Book One his best chance of making something out of this consists in carrying out a minority attack comprising the advance of his two Queenside pawns combined with ...Na5-c4.

Black's next move is therefore quite understandable; the only query is whether it might not have been more prudent to complete his development first by ...Be7 and ...O-O.

9...Na5 10.f5

White also makes an effort for the initiative. In view of his lead in development it is a matter of the greatest importance for him to open the position.

10...Nc4

When this game was played it was generally held that a backward pawn must be a serious disadvantage; but we explained in Chapter 22 of Book One how opinion on this subject has been modified. No modern master would have any scruples about playing 10...e5, with the probable continuation 11.Nb3 Nc4 12.Bxc4 Qxc4 13.Qf3 h6.

11.Bxc4 Qxc4 12.fxe6 fxe6?

Still frightened of the backward pawn. After 12...Bxe6! there would have been no cause for despair.

13.Rxf6!

With this splendid Exchange sacrifice, Lasker demonstrates how vulnerable the Black King is here.

13...gxf6 14.Qh5+ Kd8

Other King moves are no better: **1)** 14...Kd7 15.Qf7+ Be7 16.Nf5!! and wins, since 16...Re8 fails against 17.Nxd6! **2)** 14...Ke7 15.Nf5+!! exf5 16.Nd5+ Kd8 17.Bb6+ Kd7 18.Qf7+ Kc6 19.Qc7+ Kb5 20.a4+ and wins.

15.Qf7 Bd7

The more obvious move 15...Be7 is also insufficient: 16.Nf5 Qc7 (or 16...Re8 17.Bb6+ Kd7 18.Nxd6!) 17.Na4 and Black is helpless against the threat of 18.Bb6; e.g. 17...Rf8 18.Qxh7 Ke8 19.Bb6 Qd7 20.Qh5+ and mate in a few moves.

16.Qxf6+ Kc7 17.Qxh8 Bh6

Black had been counting on this move, but an elegant refutation puts an end to his hopes.

18.Nxe6+ Qxe6 19.Qxa8 Bxe3+ 20.Kh1 Black Resigned.

(The presence of the Black King in the middle enables White to take the initiative; from the game Lasker-Reti, New York, 1924).

1.e4 e6 2.d4 d5 3.Nc3 Nf6 4.Bg5 Bb4 5.Nge2 dxe4 6.a3 Be7 7.Bxf6 gxf6 8.Nxe4 f5 9.N4c3 Bd7 10.Qd2 Bd6 11.O-O-O Qe7

POSITION 6

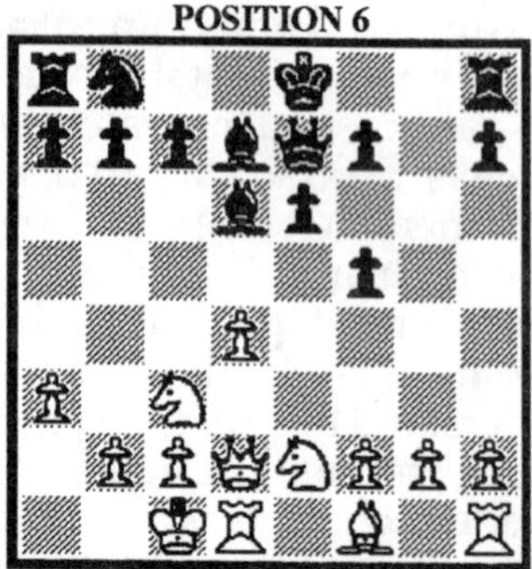

It is clear that Black's formation is not a particularly fortunate one. After accepting the doubled f-pawn his first obligation was to take steps against a possible d5 by White. The simplest way would have been by means of ...b6 and ...Bb7, followed by ...c6; and the indicated place for the King was on the Queenside.

12.Ng3

Threatening 13.Nxf5 exf5 14.Re1 Be6 15.d5, after which the open center files would portend grave peril for the Black King.

12...Qh4 13.Qe1!

Not only defending against Black's threat of 13...Bf4, but also renewing his own threat of 14.Nxf5.

13...Nc6?

According to Alekhine in the tournament book, 13...Qf4+ 14.Kb1 Nc6 would have been somewhat better.

14.Nxf5! Qf4+ 15.Ne3 Nxd4 16.g3 Qe5

17.Bg2 Nc6

After 17...Bc6 Alekhine gives the following forcing variation: 18.f4 Qg7 19.Bxc6+ Nxc6 20.Nf5 Qf8 21.Nxd6+ cxd6 22.Nb5 O-O-O 23.Qc3! and White wins a pawn (23...Kb8 24.Nxd6!).

18.f4 Qg7 19.Nb5!

In order to meet 19...Qf8 with 20.Nf5, forcing the win of a pawn. The order of moves, incidentally, is very important here. An immediate 19.Nf5? would be a serious mistake, because of the reply 19...Bxf4+!.

19...O-O

At long last the Black King finds a safer place, but at the cost of a pawn, and White now holds the advantage positionally.

20.Nxd6 cxd6 21.Rxd6 Rfd8 22.Qd2 Be8 23.Rd1 Rdc8

With some remote hope of counterplay on the c-file, but White's attack on the other flank is much too fast.

24.f5!

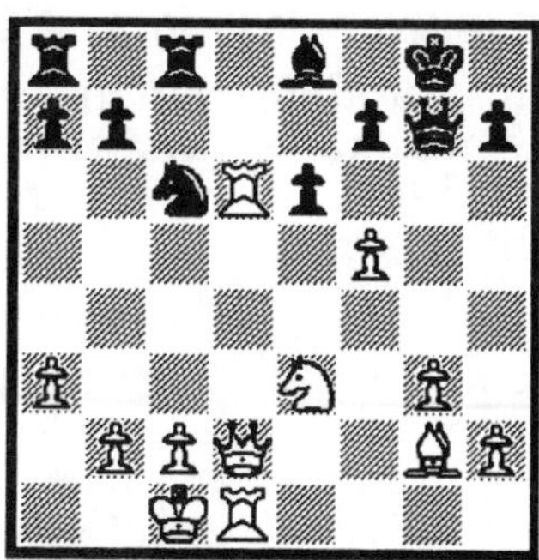

24...e5 25.f6 Qf8 26.Nf5 Kh8 27.Qg5 Rc7

Equally hopeless would have been 27...Rd8 28.Rxd8 Rxd8 29.Rxd8 Nxd8 30.Ne7 winning a second pawn.

28.Bxc6! Rxc6

Or 28...Bxc6 29.Rd8! and wins.

29.Rd8 Rcc8 30.Qg7+ Qxg7 31.fxg7+ Kg8 32.Ne7+ Black Resigned.

POSITION 7

(By means of an Exchange sacrifice Black punishes White's premature initiative; from the game Tolush-Botvinnik, Leningrad, 1939).

1.d4 Nf6 2.c4 g6 3.Nc3 d5 4.Bf4 Bg7 5.e3 O-O 6.Rc1 c5 7.dxc5 Qa5 8.cxd5 Rd8 9.Qd2 Nxd5 (No.7) **10.Bc7**

The more obvious move 10.Nxd5 leaves Black with a winning attack after 10...Qxd2+ 11.Kxd2 Rxd5+ 12.Kc2 Bf5+ 13.Kb3 Rd2.

10...Qxc7 11.Nxd5 Rxd5!

This Exchange sacrifice, forced incidentally, allows Black to seize the initiative.

12.Qxd5 Be6 13.Qd2 Nc6 14.Rd1?

The threat of 14...Rd8 was difficult to parry; e.g. 14.Bd3 Rd8 15.Qe2 Ne5 16.Rd1 Qa5+ 17.Kf1 Rxd3! 18.Rxd3 Bc4. The best plan would have been to return the exchange forthwith, by 14.Rc3.

14...Rd8 15.Qc1 Qa5+

Now the wretched position of the White King brings its retribution.

16.Rd2 Rd5

Threatening to turn the board into a slaughter-house by 17...Rxc5 18.Qb1 Bxa2 19.Qa1 Nb4.

17.Ne2 Rxc5 18.Nc3 Bxc3 19.bxc3 Rxc3 20.Qb2 Ra3

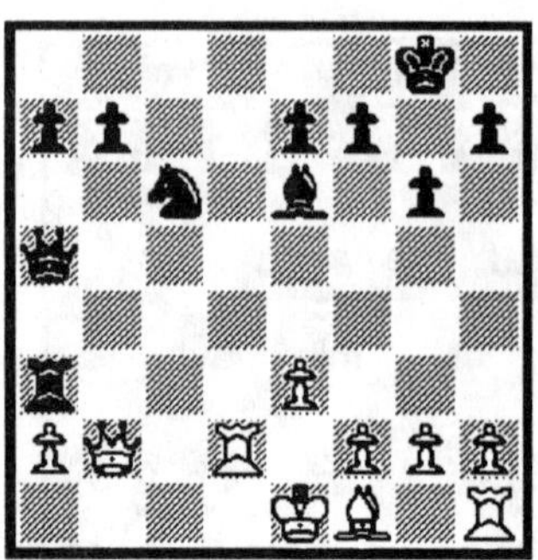

A sorry situation for White, and a drastic demonstration of the consequences of having one's King caught in the middle. Hard pressed by threats from all directions, he is still unable to complete his development, and far from enjoying the advantage of the Exchange, he finds himself in effect two pieces short on the Kingside.

21.Qb5 Qc3 22.Qb2 Qc5 23.Qb1

Or 23.Be2 Rxa2 24.Qb1 Qc3 25.Qd1 Nb4 and wins.

23...Bxa2! 24.Rxa2 Qa5+ 25.Rd2 Ra1 26.Bd3 Rxb1+ 27.Bxb1 Ne5

Even now White could put up a respectable fight if only he could castle and get his King into safety. But Black holds on to his advantage with an iron hand.

28.Ke2 Qb5+ 29.Bd3 Nxd3 30.Rxd3 a5 31.Rhd1 Qc4 32.Kf3

At last the Rooks are free to cooperate, and the King is not in immediate danger; but now, with Black's united passed pawns advancing irresistibly, it is all too late.

32...b5 33.Rd7 b4 34.Ra7 a4 35.Rd8+ Kg7 36.Rda8 a3 37.g3 Qb5 White Resigned.

(White's operations refuted by a powerful counterstroke; from the game Robatsch-Larsen, Moscow, 1956).

1.Nf3 f5 2.e4 fxe4 3.Ng5 e5 4.d3 e3 5.Bxe3 Nc6 6.Qh5+ g6 7.Qf3 Qf6 8.Qg3 Nge7 9.Nc3 h6 10.Nge4 Qf7

POSITION 8

11.Nb5

Threatening not only 12.Nxc7+ but also 12.Nd6+ cxd6 13.Nxd6+ winning Black's Queen.

11...Nf5 12.Qf3 d5! 13.Nf6+

He might as well press forward, for a retreat would be to admit that his earlier aggression was not justified. If 13.Ng3 Black calmly plays 13...a6.

13...Qxf6 14.Nxc7+ Kd8 15.Nxa8 e4!

With this sudden counterattack Black demonstrates very convincingly that White's King is in more danger than his own.

16.dxe4

White opens the d-file as another possible avenue of attack against the Black King. In any case 16.Qd1 would also have been insufficient: 16...Nxe3 17.fxe3 Qxb2 18.Rb1 Bb4+ 19.Kf2 Rf8+ 20.Kg1 Bd2!! and wins.

16...Qxb2 17.Qd1

No better was 17.Rd1 because of 17...Bb4+ 18.Bd2 Ncd4 19.Qd3 Nxc2+.

17...Nxe3 18.fxe3 Qc3+ 19.Kf2 Bc5! and **White Resigned,**

After 20.Qxd5+ Bd7 he is helpless against the threatened 21...Qxe3# (e.g. 22.Bd3 Qd2+, etc.).

POSITION 9

(By means of a central breakthrough, White takes advantage of Black's insecure King position in the middle; from the game Keres-Taimanov, U.S.S.R. Championship, 1955).

1.d4 Nf6 2.c4 e6 3.Nc3 Bb4 4.Nf3 b6 5.Bg5 Bb7 6.e3 h6 7.Bh4 g5 8.Bg3 Ne4 9.Qc2 Bxc3+ 10.bxc3 d6 11.Bd3 f5

Now if White continues normally with 12.O-O, Black seizes the opportunity to consolidate by ...Nbd7-f6. Instead White sacrifices a central pawn to blast open lines and exploit Black's King position.

12.d5! exd5 13.cxd5 Bxd5 14.Nd4 Nd7

After 14...Qf6 White plays 15.f3 Nxg3 16.hxg3, etc., or even 15.Nxf5 Qxf5 16.f3.

15.f3 Nxg3 16.hxg3 Qf6 17.Bxf5 O-O-O

Thus Black hopes to safeguard his King, but it rapidly becomes apparent that White has chances for a vigorous attack.

18.Qa4! a5 19.Kf2 h5 20.Rab1 h4 21.e4

In the tournament book Keres gives 21.gxh4 gxh4 22.Rb5 as a better line. Then after 22...Bb7 23.Qc4! there are powerful Exchange sacrifices in the air; e.g. 23...d5 24.Rxd5! or 23...Kb8 24.Nc6+ Bxc6 25.Qxc6 Nc5 26.Rxc5!.

21...Bb7 22.gxh4 gxh4 23.Ne6 Ne5?

If 23...Rdg8, 24.Nxc7! wins an important pawn, but Black's best chance was 23...Qxc3. Keres would then have continued with 24.Qd1, threatening 25.Rc1; not however 24.Rhc1 at once, because of the following fantastic line given by Keres: 24...Qd2+ 25.Kg1 h3!! 26.Rxc7+ Kb8 27.Rxb7+ Ka8 28.Bxh3 Qe3+ 29.Kh2 Rxh3+!! and suddenly it is Black who has the winning attack.

24.Qd4

Black had apparently reckoned only with 24.Nxd8+ Kxd8 25.Qd4. The move played is much stronger.

24...Rdg8 25.Nxc7+!

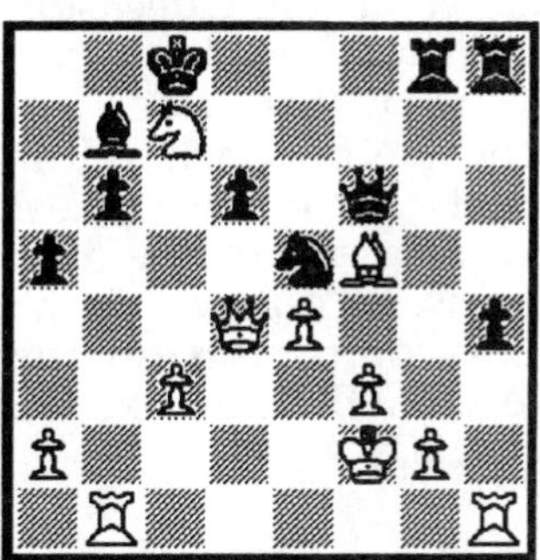

Now like a house of cards the Black King's position falls apart.

25...Kb8 26.Qxb6 Nd3+ 27.Kf1 Nb4 28.Rxb4

A convincing finish.

28...axb4 29.Nb5 Black Resigned.

(How White brought his King into safety in the game Muhring-Jaurequi, Moscow 1956).

1.d4 d5 2.c4 dxc4 3.Nf3 Nf6 4.e3 g6 5.Bxc4 Bg7 6.O-O O-O 7.Qe2 Nfd7 8.Rd1 Nb6 9.Bb3 Bg4 10.h3 Bxf3 11.Qxf3 Nc6 12.Nc3 e5 13.d5 Na5 14.Bc2 Nac4 15.e4 Qe7 16.a4 a5 17.Ne2 Rad8 18.Qb3 Nd6 19.Be3 Nd7

20.f3 f5 21.Bd3 f4 22.Bf2 Bf6 23.Rac1 Rc8 24.Rc3 Qg7 25.Rdc1 Bd8

POSITION 10

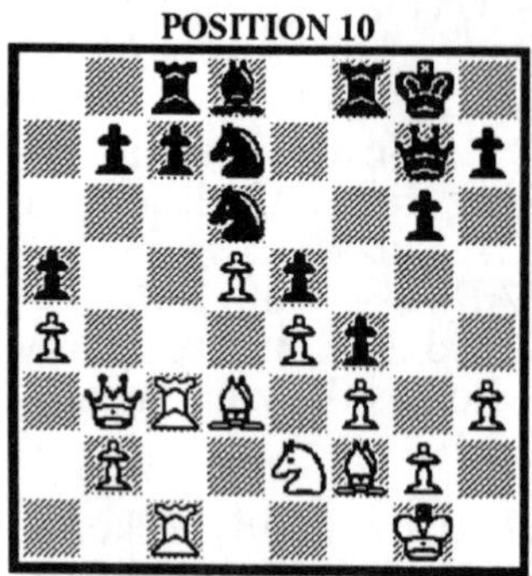

In positions in which one player has the initiative on the Queenside and the other on the Kingside, the odds are usually with the one who is pressuring the opponent's King. In the present case White's Queenside advantage (pressure against the semi-backward c-pawn) is hardly sufficient compensation for the initiative which Black can build up on the other flank.

26.Kf1!

Taking the bull by the horns: since the effectiveness of Black's play on the Kingside depends largely on the presence of the White King there, White runs his King straight across to the other side.

26...g5 27.Ke1 h5 28.Kd1 Rf6

The direct 28...g4 29.Kc2 gxf3 30.gxf3 Qg7? would lose immediately to 31.Rg1.

29.Kc2 Rh6 30.Kb1 g4 31.R3c2 Nf6?

This gives the opponent a chance to seize the initiative by a surprising move.

32.Nxf4! exf4 33.e5 Nfe8 34.exd6 Nxd6 35.Bc5 Qd7 36.Re2!

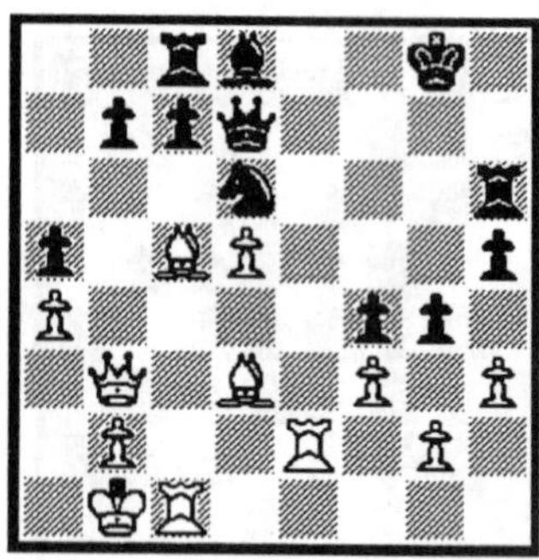

Now it becomes clear that Black's Kingside activities have imperiled his own King; for instance, he dares not win a pawn at h3: 36...gxh3 37.gxh3 Qxh3 38.Re6 Rxe6 39.dxe6 Be7 40.Rg1+, and White has a winning attack.

36...Rf6

A better chance was 36...g3. After the text move White opens the h-file and later uses it to great effect for a Rook penetration.

37.hxg4 hxg4 38.fxg4 Qxg4 39.Re6!

The direct attack on the Black King begins to take place.

39...Rxe6 40.dxe6 Be7 41.Bxd6 Bxd6 42.e7+ Kg7 43.Rh1

With every White piece in action the issue is beyond doubt. Notice that in a direct attack the presence of Bishops of opposite colors is an advantage rather than a disadvantage for White. We have already mentioned this peculiarity in Book One.

43...Kf6 44.Rh7 Qg8

There is no saving move. If 44...Ke5 45.Rf7 wins.

45.Qc3+ Be5 46.Rh6+

Black Resigned. The last finesse is 46...Kg5 47.Rg6+ Qxg6 48.Qxe5+!.

POSITION 11

(A snapshot from the 6th match-game Smyslov-Geller, 1955).

1.d4 Nf6 2.c4 g6 3.Nc3 Bg7 4.e4 d6 5.f3 O-O 6.Be3 e5 7.Nge2 c6 8.d5 cxd5 9.cxd5 Ne8 10.Qd2 f5 11.h3 Nd7 12.g3 Nb6 13.b3

White has deferred castling too long, and no wonder; for Kingside castling was hardly to be considered in view of the advancing Black f-pawn, while Queenside castling appears distinctly unhealthy in view of the c-file. Nonetheless White should have castled–on the Queenside–at move 11.

13...f4! 14.gxf4 exf4 15.Bd4

The exposed position of White's King prevents him from capturing the f-pawn: 15.Bxf4 Bxc3 16.Qxc3 Rxf4 17.Nxf4 Qh4+, etc. Now the Black pieces will obtain access to e5.

15...Nd7! 16.h4 Ne5 17.Bg2 Bd7 18.Bf2

White still cannot take the f-pawn: 18.Nxf4? Rxf4 19.Qxf4 Nd3+ and wins.

18...Rc8 19.Nd4 Qa5 20.Rc1 Nc7 21.Rc2 Na6 22.O-O

At last! But meanwhile Black's advantage has become overpowering. We give the rest merely for the sake of completeness.

22...Nc5 23.Nce2 Qxd2 24.Rxd2 Nxe4 25.fxe4 f3 26.Nxf3 Nxf3+ 27.Bxf3 Rxf3 28.Bxa7 Rh3 29.Bf2 Be5 30.Nd4 Bg4 31.Be1 Re3 32.Bf2 Rxe4 33.Re1 Rxe1+ 34.Bxe1 Rc1 and **White Resigned.**

POSITION 12

(Snapshot from the game D. Byrne-Fischer, New York, 1956).

1.Nf3 Nf6 2.c4 g6 3.Nc3 Bg7 4.d4 O-O 5.Bf4 d5 6.Qb3 dxc4 7.Qxc4 c6 8.e4 Nbd7 9.Rd1 Nb6 10.Qc5 Bg4 (No.12) **11.Bg5?**

White was of course well aware that his best line would have been 11.Be2 and 12.O-O. But he realized that after 11.Be2 Nfd7 12.Qa3 Bxf3 13.Bxf3 e5 14.dxe5 Qe8 Black would have attained a good game; hence this attempt to prevent the liberating move 11...Nfd7.

11... Na4!!

This is based on the alternative continuations: 12.Nxa4 Nxe4 13.Qxe7 Qxe7 14.Bxe7 Rfe8, or 13.Qc1 (instead of 13.Qxe7) 13...Qa5+ 14.Nc3 Bxf3.

12.Qa3 Nxc3 13.bxc3 Nxe4 14.Bxe7 Qb6 15.Bc4

On 15.Bxf8 Bxf8 16.Qb3 Black continues with 16...Nxc3! (17.Qxc3? Bb4) with good compensation for the exchange.

15...Nxc3! 16.Bc5

Of course 16.Qxc3 would be answered by ...Rfe8; but the text move appears to refute Black's play completely.

16...Rfe8+ 17.Kf1 Be6!!

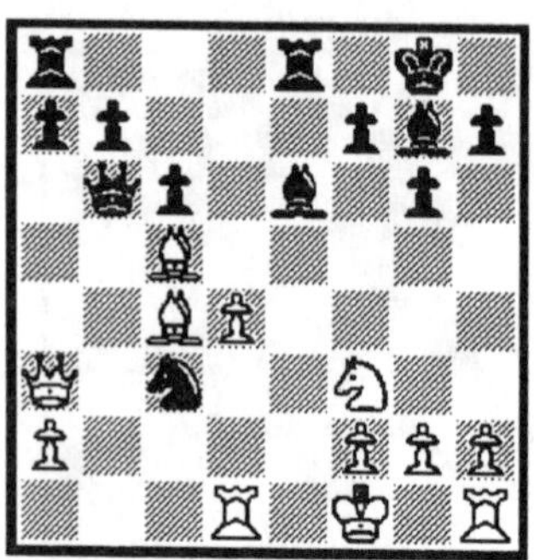

The uncommonly beautiful point of the combination.

18.Bxb6

Other possibilities were:

1) 18.Qxc3 Qxc5! 19.dxc5 Bxc3. **2)** 18.Bxe6 Qb5+! 19.Kg1 Ne2+ 20.Kf1 Ng3+ 21.Kg1 Qf1+ 22.Rxf1 Ne2#.

18...Bxc4+ 19.Kg1 Ne2+ 20.Kf1 Nxd4+ 21.Kg1 Ne2+ 22.Kf1 Nc3+ 23.Kg1 axb6 24.Qb4 Ra4 25.Qxb6 Nxd1

The issue of the game is settled. For the Queen Black has two Bishops and a Rook, not to mention the White pawns which are going to fall like ripe apples. The game ended as follows:

26.h3 Rxa2 27.Kh2 Nxf2 28.Re1 Rxe1 29.Qd8+ Bf8 30.Nxe1 Bd5 31.Nf3 Ne4 32.Qb8 b5 33.h4 h5 34.Ne5 Kg7 35.Kg1 Bc5+ 36.Kf1 Ng3+ 37.Ke1 Bb4+ 38.Kd1 Bb3+ 39.Kc1 Ne2+ 40.Kb1 Nc3+ 41.Kc1 Rc2#.

(Snapshot from the game Smyslov-Kottnauer, Groningen, 1946).

1.e4 c5 2.Nf3 d6 3.d4 cxd4 4.Nxd4 Nf6 5.Nc3 a6 6.Be2 e6 7.O-O b5 8.Bf3 Ra7 9.Qe2 Rc7 10.Rd1 Nbd7 11.a4 bxa4 12.Nxa4

POSITION 13

12...Bb7?

Just as in the previous game the opportunity to get castled is neglected. Urgently necessary here was 12...Be7, followed by 13...O-O. True, Black now threatens to assume an initiative with 13...Ne5, but the following breakthrough cuts right across his plans.

13.e5! Nxe5

Nor does the Black King find safety after 13...dxe5 14.Bxb7 exd4 15.Bxa6 Bc5 16.Nxc5 Nxc5 17.Bb5+ Ke7 18.Bf4.

14.Bxb7 Rxb7 15.Qxa6 Qb8 16.Nc6 Nxc6 17.Qxc6+ Nd7 18.Nc5!!

Thus White forces a decision as elegant as it is speedy.

18...dxc5

There is no choice. If 18...Rc7, then White wins with 19.Nxd7.

19.Bf4! Bd6

The consequences of 19...Qxf4 would have been equally fearful: 20.Qc8+ Ke7 21.Qxb7 Kf6 22.Rxd7 Kg6 23.g3 Qf5 24.Ra7 and wins.

20.Bxd6 Rb6 21.Qxd7+ Black Resigned.

After 21...Kxd7 22.Bxb8+ he is a piece down.

CHAPTER 25
TO MAKE THE EXCHANGE OR PERMIT THE EXCHANGE?

Time and again the chessplayer is confronted with the decision of whether or not to exchange or leave that option to his opponent. This concerns not only pawn exchanges, but the pieces as well. Finding the correct answer to this problem usually requires a considerable amount of thought, since it can also involve the question of who is going to have the initiative.

It is of course impossible to lay down any general rule for such cases; every case must be decided on its merits. To make the exchange may perhaps be judged less effective than leaving it to the opponent; but this is only the broadest of generalizations, and it refers in particular to pawns. For that matter the pawns always have an important role in the fight for the initiative, for it is through them that tension is maintained. The examples which we treated in Book One under the heading of "Tension Form" showed that exchanging pawns is likely to slacken the tension, whereas leaving the exchange to the opponent may eventually create a central superiority; and it is this consideration which leads to all the tension formations, for instance in the Queen's Gambit, King's Indian and Ruy Lopez.

The present chapter however is by no means a recapitulation of the section mentioned above. There we were concerned with the tug-o'-war with respect to the pawn structure, while our present examination of the question whether or not to exercise our option of exchanging will be related instead to its possible effects on the initiative. Moreover we have a much wider field, for we consider not only pawns but the problem of whether or not to exchange any pieces at all.

All these points will now be dealt with in practical examples.

POSITION 14

(An example of tension from the game Bronstein-Sliwa, Moscow, 1956).

1.e4 e5 2.Nf3 Nc6 3.Bb5 a6 4.Ba4 d6 5.c3 Bd7 6.d4 Be7 7.O-O Bf6 8.Be3 Nge7 9.Nbd2 O-O

As far as the central pawn configuration is concerned, two points are abundantly clear: **1)** White would achieve nothing by exchanging on e5. **2)** Black can hardly exchange on d4, since the recapture with the c-pawn would give White too strong a center. Moreover the advance d5 by White would be convenient for Black after 10.d5 Nb8 11.Bc2 a5, etc.

10.a3! Ng6 11.b4

From now on Black must reckon seriously with the possibility of d5, since White is ready to follow up with c4 and c5.

11...Re8 12.Bc2 h6 13.Nb3

White is in no hurry to play d5 since

he has other ways of strengthening his position.

13...Bg5?

With such a constricted position Black's policy must be to exchange pieces. The text move does achieve this, but it could have been done more economically by 13...Bg4 14.h3 Bxf3 15.Qxf3 Bg5.

14.Nxg5 hxg5 15.g3!

This nullifies Black's control of f4, and intends to answer 15...Bh3 with 16.Qh5! Bxf1 17.Rxf1, with a powerful attack.

In return for the sacrificed Exchange White would have: **1)** A pawn (for Black's front g-pawn would be untenable). **2)** Greater maneuvering space. **3)** The Bishop pair. ...and these, as we explained in Book One, Chapter 4, would add up to more than sufficient compensation for the slight material deficit.

15...f6 16.Qh5 Nce7 17.Nc5!!

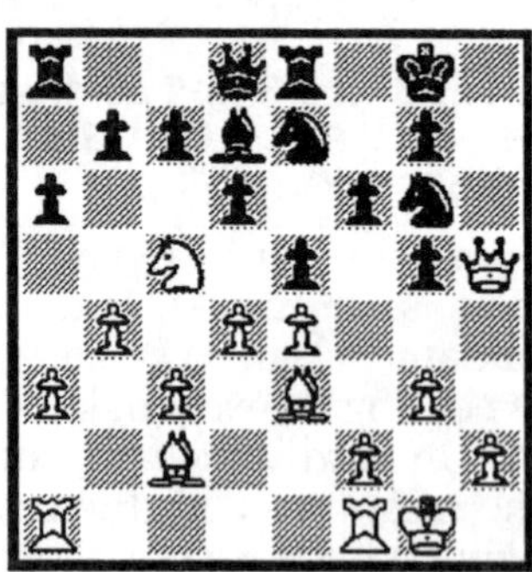

A superb way of profiting from the weakness of the Black castled position. This fierce Knight can hardly be captured, for after 17...dxc5 18.Bb3+ Kf8 19.dxe5! fxe5 20.Bxc5 Black can resign. Nor is there any salvation in the interpolation 18...c4; for after 19.Bxc4+ Kf8 20.dxe5 Bb5 there comes 21.Ba2!.

17...Bc6 18.Bb3+ d5 19.Rad1!

Once again the strongest move is to refrain from exchanging.

19...b6 20.Nd3 exd4

Forced, as White was threatening 21.dxe5.

21.Bxd4 Kf7 22.f4 Rh8 23.Qe2 gxf4 24.Nxf4 Nxf4 25.Rxf4 Qc8

Other moves are no better.

26.exd5 Bxd5 27.Bxf6!

A fitting finish to this pretty game.

27...gxf6 28.Rxd5 Nxd5 29.Bxd5+ Black Resigned.

POSITION 15

(Black tries to force his opponent into clearing up the central situation; from the game Lasker-Henneberger, Zurich, 1934).

1.d4 Nf6 2.c4 e6 3.Nc3 Bb4 4.Nf3 Bxc3+ 5.bxc3 d6 6.g3 O-O 7.Bg2 Qe7 8.Ba3 Nbd7 9.Nd2 e5 10.O-O Re8 11.e3

We have now reached the Wyvill Formation, the pawn formation we discussed in Book One, Chapter 9, Section 3. The conclusion reached there was that White ought to hold his pawn formation intact as long as possible, meanwhile building up his attack behind the lines, a strategy which is similar to the play of the previous example. Black for his part should try to force White to play d5.

11...c5 12.Rb1 Nb6?

This is quite in accordance with the positional requirements outlined above, for Black will now be able to play ...Be6, putting pressure on White's c-pawn so as to induce him to advance d5. Nevertheless 12...Rb8 or even 12...e4 would have been better, simply because White now gets the initiative.

13.dxc5! dxc5 14.Rb5!

Defense of the c-pawn would now require ...Nfd7, after which Black would have great difficulty completing his development. He therefore decides to let the pawn go.

14...Bd7 15.Bxc5 Qe6 16.Rb4 Bc6 17.Bxb6 Bxg2 18.Kxg2 axb6 19.Qc2

Although White is now a pawn up the situation is far from clear, in view of the pawn weaknesses in both camps. Black's best would have been 19...e4.

19...Red8 20.f3 Rd6 21.Rf2 Rad8 22.Ne4 Nxe4 23.Qxe4

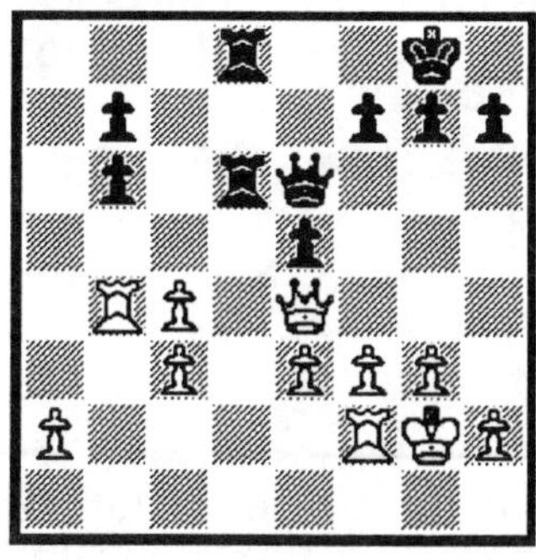

(Black controls the d-file, but White still holds the initiative).

23...Qd7

Intending to answer 24.Qxe5 with 24...Re8 25.Qf4 Rf6 26.Qg5 h6; and 27...Rxe3. Too hasty would be 23...Rd2 because of 24.Qxb7 Rxf2+ 25.Kxf2 Rd2+ 26.Ke1.

24.Rbb2 f6 25.c5 bxc5 26.Rxb7 Qe6 27.g4!

White prevents ...f5; the invasion 27...Rd2 would now be neutralized by the fine reply 28.Ra7!.

27...Rd3 28.c4 g6 29.Rb8!

Forcing off a pair of Rooks.

29...Kg7 30.Rxd8 Rxd8

Merely by maintaining the initiative White has succeeded in creating a sound extra pawn out of his rickety pawn formation. The rest is technique-interesting enough in itself, but not essential to our theme.

31.Rb2 Kh6 32.Kg3 Rd1 33.h4 Rg1+ 34.Kh2 Rd1 35.Kg3 Rg1+ 36.Rg2 f5 37.Qd5 Rxg2+ 38.Kxg2 Qa6 39.Qg8 Qxa2+ 40.Kh3 Qa7 41.Qf8+ Black Resigned.

POSITION 16

(Exchange at d5 usually achieves nothing against the Stonewall Defense; from the 12th match-game Flohr-Botvinnik, 1933).

1.d4 e6 2.c4 f5 3.g3 Nf6 4.Bg2 Be7 5.Nc3 d5 6.Nf3 c6 7.O-O O-O 8.b3 Qe8 9.Bb2 Nbd7 10.Qd3 Qh5 (No.16) **11.cxd5**

This exchange on d5 often gives some initiative in such positions, for it enables White to start a minority attack on the Queenside (see Book One, Chapter 14). The present position, however, is an exception which provides us with a welcome chance of giving a warning against superficial thinking. How is it that the minority attack gives White such a promising initiative in many variations of the Queen's Gambit Declined? The reason must be that the b4-b5 of the minority attack is a means of breaking the half-open c-file fully open. But this is not the whole explanation. The essential point is that Black, who has the half-open e-file, cannot be so prompt with his counterattack. His thematic advance is ...f5-f4, and this needs preparation. Preparation however needs time, and White can use this time to push forward his b-pawn without delay.

In light of these considerations the difference between the present diagram and the more normal Queen's Gambit positions, in which the minority attack has legitimate expectations of success, is clear enough. Black has already played ...f5, and so will probably be able to play ...f4 before White can play b5 on the other flank. In short, Black's minority attack gets in first.

11...exd5 12.Nd2?

Better was 12.Ne1 and if 12...Ne4 then 13.f4.

12...Ne4 13.f3

Now 13.f4 would be answered by 13...Nxd2 14.Qxd2 Nf6 and Black works with gain of tempo – a typical proof that he holds the initiative.

13...Nxc3! 14.Bxc3 f4!

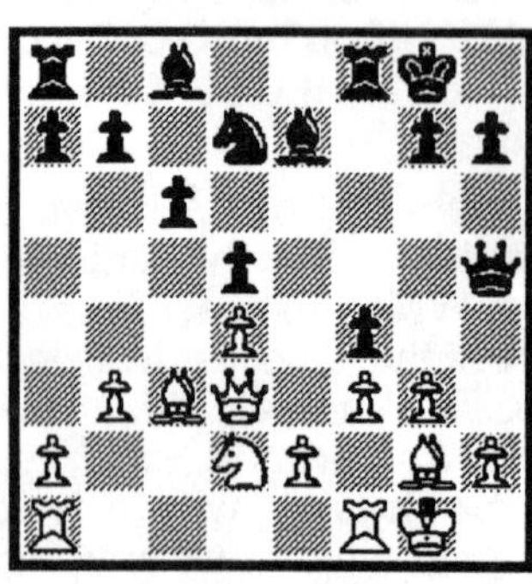

It is evident that Black has taken charge. Little or nothing will come of White's minority attack.

15.Rfe1

Perhaps slightly better would have been 15.Rfd1, in order to be able to bring reserves to the threatened Kingside by Nf1 and Be1.

15...Bd6 16.Nf1 Rf7!

Freeing f8 for the Knight, so that he can develop his Queenside pieces without relaxing the pressure on White's position.

17.e3

Forcing Black to exchange on e3 or g3. It might have been better to play 17.Bd2, to meet 17...Nf8 by capturing twice on f4, and only then playing e3.

17...fxg3 18.Nxg3

If 18.hxg3 Qg5 19.Kf2 Nf6 is strong for Black.

18...Qh4 19.Nf1 Nf6

In the altered circumstances the Knight naturally does better to go to f6 rather than f8.

20.Re2 Bd7 21.Be1 Qg5 22.Bg3 Bxg3 23.Nxg3

After 23.hxg3 Nh5 would be unpleasant (24.Kh2 Nxg3!).

23...h5!

The storm troops advance–a sure sign that the phase of initiative is giving way to the phase of real attack.

24.f4 Qg4 25.Rf2

Giving Black his chance of a pretty combination. 25.Rf1 h4 26.Bf3 would have been better.

25...h4 26.Bf3

Nor was there much hope in 26.h3 Qe6 (26...Qxg3 27.Rf3 costs the Queen!) 27.Nf1 Ne4.

26...hxg3!! 27.Bxg4 gxf2+ 28.Kg2 Nxg4 29.h3 Nf6 30.Kxf2 Ne4+

and **White Resigned,** for he loses another pawn (31.Kg2 Bxh3+ 32.Kxh3? Nf2+).

POSITION 17

(Black plays ...Nb6 in an attempt to force White to clarify the central situation; from the game Capablanca-Botvinnik, Moscow, 1936).

1.Nf3 f5 2.g3 Nf6 3.Bg2 e6 4.c4 Be7 5.O-O O-O 6.d4 d5 7.Nc3 c6 8.Qb3 Kh8 9.Ne5 Nbd7 10.Nxd7 Nxd7 11.Rd1 (No.17) **11...Nb6!**

Forcing White to make up his mind about the c-pawn.

12.cxd5

Practically forced. After 12.c5 Nd7 the initiative is with Black; e.g. 13.Qa4 e5! or 13.f4 b6!.

12...exd5 13.Na4 Nc4 14.Nc5 b6?

Definitely the sharpest choice, but nonetheless it is inferior. Capablanca quite rightly indicated that after 14...Qb6! Black would have seized the initiative.

15.Nd3 Bf6 16.Qc2! Bd7

If 16...Bxd4 the continuation would be 17.Nb4 Qf6 18.Nxc6! Bxb2 19.Bxb2 Nxb2 20.Rxd5.

17.e3 Nd6 18.a4 a5 19.b3 Re8 20.Ba3 Ne4

In the end this Knight finds itself on f7, so it might as well have gone there immediately.

21.f3 Ng5 22.Ne5 Rc8

Not 22...Bxe5 23.dxe5 Rxe5? 24.f4.

23.Rac1 Kg8 24.Qd3 Nf7 25.f4 Be7 26.Bxe7 Qxe7 27.Rc3 Nxe5

This exchange was practically unavoidable, since White threatened to double Rooks. Now White, with a protected passed pawn and a good Bishop, has decidedly the better of it.

28.dxe5 Qb4 29.Rdc1

Threatening 30.e6! Rxe6 31.Bxd5! cxd5 32.Rxc8+.

29...Rb8 30.Qd4

Here we break off our commentary, as the rest of the game falls outside the scope of our theme. Although White seems to hold the advantage at this point he had to be content with a draw, after the following moves:

30...b5 31.Ra1 Ra8 32.axb5 Qxb5 33.Rc5 Qxb3 34.Rxd5 Be6 35.Rd6 c5 36.Qxc5 (better was 36.Qd2!) **Rec8 37.Qb6 Rab8 38.Qxb3** (38.Qd4! Rc4 39.Qd1!) **Bxb3 39.Bc6** (39.e4!) **a4 40.g4 fxg4 41.Kf2 Kf8 42.Kg3?** (42.Ra3!) **Rb6 43.Be4 Rxd6 44.exd6 Rd8 45.Bxh7 Rxd6 46.Kxg4 Rh6 Draw.**

POSITION 18

(Black delays the capture at e4; from the game Boutteville-Kramer, Moscow 1956).

1.c4 Nf6 2.g3 e6 3.Bg2 d5 4.d4 Be7 5.Nf3 O-O 6.O-O c6 7.b3 Nbd7 8.Bb2 b6 9.Nbd2 Bb7 10.Qc2 Rc8 11.e4 (No.18)

11...Qc7

After an immediate exchange of the e-pawn White gains ground, and has the initiative.

12.Rac1

The advance e5 usually gains nothing in such positions, as we shall show later (Example 27, Cortlever-Rabar, Dubrovnik, 1950).

12...dxe4!

Now this is satisfactory, for if 13.Nxe4 Nxe4 14.Qxe4 Black plays 14...c5! with gain of tempo.

13.Ne5

An attempt to seize the initiative.

13...c5 14.Nxd7 Qxd7 15.dxc5

Thus White hopes to obtain good chances, for if 15...Bxc5 then 16.Bxf6, while after 15...bxc5 16.Nxe4 Nxe4 17.Bxe4 Bxe4 18.Qxe4, White will have a slight but persistent initiative.

15...e3!

This interpolation quite upsets his calculations. The first point is the variation: 16.Bxb7? exd2! 17.Bxc8 dxc1=Q 18.Bxd7 Qxc2 and Black wins.

16.fxe3 Bxg2 17.Kxg2 Ng4!

This is the second point, and it depends, like most tactical finesses, on a number of seemingly fortunate possibilities: e.g. 18.Qc3 Bf6; or 18.Qe4? Qxd2+; or 18.Kf3 Nxh2+.

18.Rf3 Bxc5 19.Qc3 f6 20.b4 Be7 21.Rf4

If 21.h3 Ne5 22.Rf4 Nd3! winning the exchange.

21...e5 22.Rf3

No better is 22.R4f1 because of 22...Rfd8 23.Rfd1 Qd3!.

22...Rfd8 23.Nf1 Qc6 (see next diagram) **24.c5 b5 25.Qb3+ Kh8 26.h3 Nh6 27.Qc2 Rd7 28.e4 Rcd8 29.Re1 Nf7! 30.h4 Nh6! 31.Qe2 Ng4 32.Rf5 g6 33.Rf3 h5 34.Bc1 Rd4 35.Nh2 Rxb4**

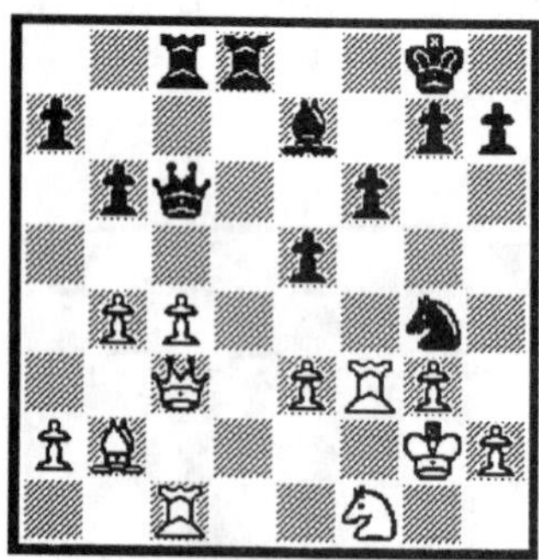

After 23...Qc6

36.Rd3 Rxd3 37.Qxd3 Rd4 38.Qb3 Rxe4 White Resigned.

POSITION 19

(White also gets the initiative if Black waits too long with the capture ...dxe4; from the game Cortlever-Trott, Beverwijk, 1953).

1.Nf3 Nf6 2.g3 d5 3.Bg2 Nbd7 4.d4 e6 5.O-O Be7 6.b3 O-O 7.Bb2 b6 8.c4 c6 9.Nbd2 Bb7 10.Qc2 Rc8 11.e4 Qc7 12.Rac1 Qb8 13.Rfe1 Rfd8 14.Qb1

This position could also have arisen out of Example 18. However Black has delayed too long the capture on e4 and this allows White to gain the initiative.

14...Nxe4 15.Nxe4 dxe4 16.Rxe4 c5 17.d5!

Due to the unprotected Be7, White is now able to maintain the central tension.

17...Bf6!

Killing two birds with one stone. The Bishop removes itself from the line of fire, and at the same time nullifies White's dangerous QB.

18.Rg4 exd5 19.cxd5 h5?

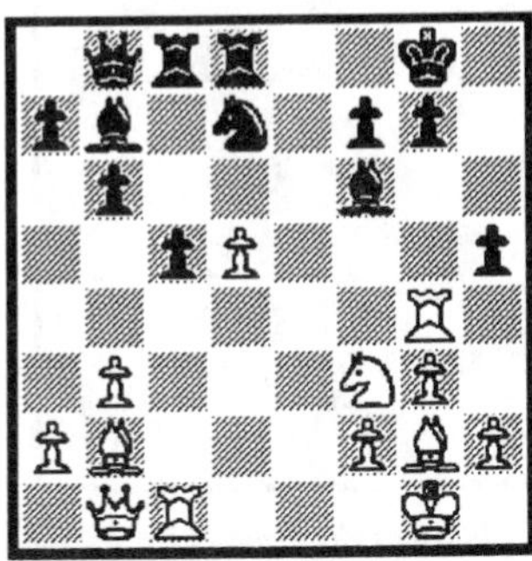

It is true that Black could not take the d-pawn: 19...Bxd5? 20.Ng5 Bxg5 21.Rxg5, but he could have set up a reasonable defense by 19...Bxb2 20.Qxb2 f6 21.Rd1 Kh8, etc.

20.Ng5!

The real point of White's previous moves.

20...hxg4?

Black unwisely takes up the gauntlet. He had better chances of holding out by 20...Nf8 21.Bxf6 hxg4 22.Bxd8 Rxd8 23.Qf5 Qc7!.

21.Qh7+ Kf8 22.Re1 Ne5 23.Bxe5 Bxe5 24.Qh8+ Ke7 25.Qxg7 Rf8

There is no better defense against the primary threat 26.Qxf7+ Kd6 27.Qe6+ Kc7 28.Qe7+ Rd7 29.Ne6#.

26.Rxe5+ Kd7 27.Nxf7 Rg8 28.Qf6 Black Resigned. If 28...Rde8 there follows 29.Qf5+ Kc7 30.d6#.

(Whether or not to exchange Knights; from the game Pirc-Christoffel, Yugoslavia-Switzerland Match 1949).

1.c4 Nf6 2.Nf3 c6 3.d4 d5 4.e3 Bf5 5.Nc3 e6 6.Bd3 Bg6 7.Ne5 Nbd7 8.f4 Be7 9.O-O Qc7 10.Qc2 Bxd3 11.Qxd3 Rd8 12.Bd2 O-O 13.Rac1

POSITION 20

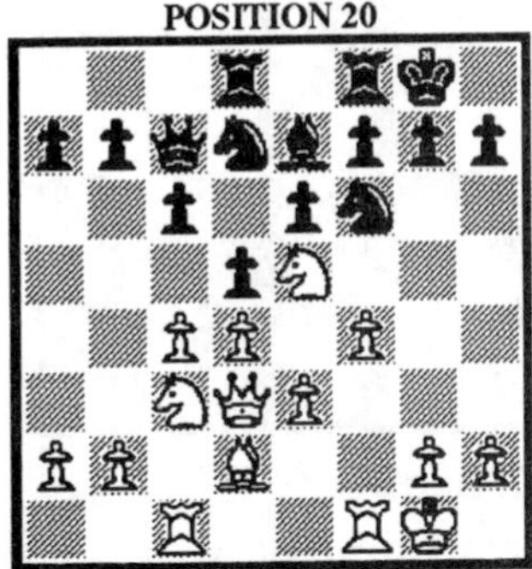

In this position White is retaining all options-the best method of keeping a persistent initiative. He can begin a Queenside advance by b4 followed by either c5 or cxd5; in the center he has the thrust e4 available; while even a sort of bayonet attack on the Kingside by g4 is a distinct possibility. All these opportunities arise mainly from the influence of the Knight on e5, and Black's main headache is to decide whether or not to take it off.

13...Nxe5

He decides to cut the knot.

14.fxe5 dxc4 15.Qxc4 Nd7?

The Knight should have gone to d5, for then 16.e4 fails against 16...Nb6 17.Qd3 Qxe5! while 16.Ne4 is met by 16...f6 17.exf6 gxf6.

16.Ne4 c5

Black wants to prevent White from playing 17.Bb4, with exchange of Bishops and subsequent occupation of d6 with the Knight, but he is jumping out of the frying pan into the fire.

17.Bb4!

This forces the following pawn move, after which the Black Knight cannot get into play via b6.

17...b6 18.Bc3 Qc6

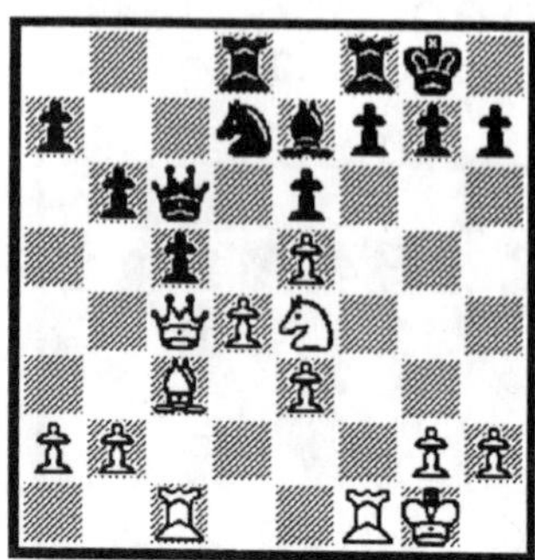

19.dxc5! Bxc5

The real point of White's move would have been revealed if Black had captured with the Knight instead, for then comes: 20.Nf6+!! gxf6 21.exf6, and now 21...Bd6 fails to 22.Qg4+ and mate next.

20.Nxc5 Qxc5

The other possibilities were: **1)** 20...bxc5 21.b4 Rc8 22.Bd4 Qc7 23.bxc5 Nxe5 24.Qc3! f6 25.Bxe5, and White's position is decisively superior. **2)** 20...Nxc5 21.Bd4! (not however 21.b4? Qe4!).

21.Bd4!

Thus White obtains control of the c-file by force, securing a great positional advantage.

21...Qc8 22.Qc7 Qa8 23.b4

With the same idea as the 17th move – namely to deprive the Black Knight of available squares.

23...Qe4 24.Qc6! Qd3 25.Qf3 Qb5

Not playable is 25...Rc8 because of 26.Rxc8 Rxc8 27.Qxf7+.

26.Rc7 a6

If 26...Nxe5, then 27.Bxe5 Qxe5 28.Rxf7.

27.Qc6 Qxc6 28.Rxc6

At last White has his favorable ending. The rest is, as they say, a matter of technique.

28...Rc8 29.Rfc1 Rxc6 30.Rxc6 Rb8 31.Rc7 Rd8 32.Ra7 g6 33.Rxa6 Rc8 34.Ra7 Nf8 35.Bxb6 Rc4 36.Bc5 Kg7 37.a4 g5 38.Rc7 Re4 39.a5 Ng6 40.a6 Black Resigned.

POSITION 21

(The problem of the Knight exchange in the so-called Pillsbury Position; from the game Pillsbury-Marco, Paris, 1900).

1.d4 d5 2.c4 e6 3.Nc3 Nf6 4.Bg5 Be7 5.e3 O-O 6.Nf3 b6 7.Bd3 Bb7 8.cxd5 exd5 9.Ne5 Nbd7 10.f4

About this time Pillsbury was getting some striking results with this system, characterized by the Knight on e5 with the strong reinforcing pawn formation d4-e3-f4. The cause of these successes lay in the fact that nobody had yet found the right answer to the problem of whether or not to exchange the Knights.

10...c5?

Black assumes the Knight must not be taken, but this premise is false. By 10...Ne8 11.Bxe7 Qxe7 12.O-O Nxe5! 13.fxe5 f6! Black can achieve strong counterplay, as Teichmann demonstrated later.

11.O-O c4?

Trading Knights is still indicated. Black starts a Queenside attack instead, but before this has time to become dangerous the White Kingside initiative becomes a hurricane.

12.Bc2 a6 13.Qf3 b5 14.Qh3

Threatening 15.Nxd7 and thereby forcing Black to weaken his King's position.

14...g6 15.f5!

White opens the f-file, and at once the energetic final attack is under way.

15...b4

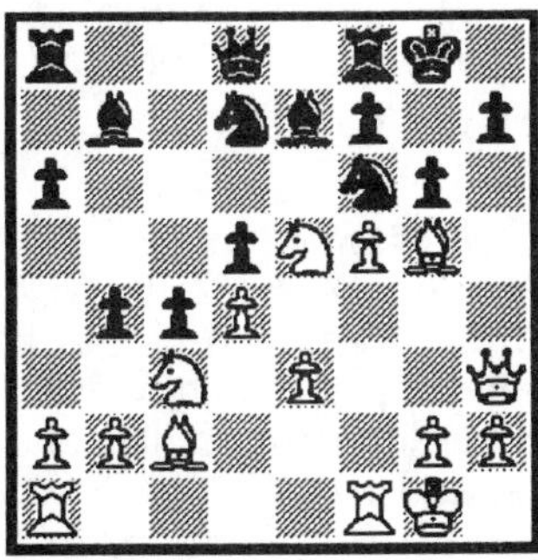

16.fxg6! hxg6

After 16...bxc3 White wins by 17.Bxf6 Nxf6 18.Rxf6 hxg6 19.Bxg6!.

17.Qh4! bxc3 18.Nxd7 Qxd7 19.Rxf6 a5

An attempt to bring succor to the scene of operations by ...Ra6; but it is all too late.

20.Raf1 Ra6 21.Bxg6!

A superb finish.

21...fxg6 22.Rxf8+ Bxf8 23.Rxf8+! Kxf8 24.Qh8+ Kf7 25.Qh7+ Black Resigned.

POSITION 22

(Whether or not to exchange Knights; from the game Teichmann—Dus-Chotimirsky, Prague, 1908).

1.d4 d5 2.c4 e6 3.Nc3 c5 4.e3 Nf6 5.Nf3 Nc6 6.a3 a6 7.dxc5 Bxc5 8.b4 Bd6 9.Bb2 dxc4 10.Bxc4 b5 11.Bd3 Bb7

Tarrasch stated, in his excellent book *Die Moderne Schachpartie*, that in symmetrical positions such as this one that the advantage goes to the player who can get in Ne4 first (this is from White's point of view; from Black's point of view the equivalent move is ...Ne5). Hence White should have followed this rule by playing 12.Ne4.

12.O-O? Ne5! 13.Nxe5

If White had let the Knight stay, and played 13.Be2 instead, Black would still have the initiative, 13...O-O being his simplest continuation.

13...Bxe5 14.Qe2 O-O 15.Rad1 Qe7 16.f4

With this and his next move White makes a bid for the initiative by means of a central pawn advance; but it soon transpires that these are the very moves which give Black attacking chances.

16...Bc7 17.e4 Bb6+ 18.Kh1 Rfd8 19.Bb1 Rac8 20.Rxd8+ Qxd8

Tarrasch gives his approval of this move on the grounds that 20...Rxd8 would have been strongly answered by 21.Qc2, with the threat of 22.e5. Here, however, he is under a misapprehension, for after 20...Rxd8 21.Qc2 Ng4! 22.e5? Qh4 it is White who can resign.

21.Rd1 Qe7 22.e5?

This advance is still wrong. Better was 22.h3.

22...Nd5 23.Nxd5 Bxd5 24.Qg4

This threatens 25.Rxd5; nevertheless the simple move 24.Be4 was preferable.

24...Qb7! 25.f5

Otherwise Black continues with 25...Be4.

25...Rc4 26.Qg3 Rf4!

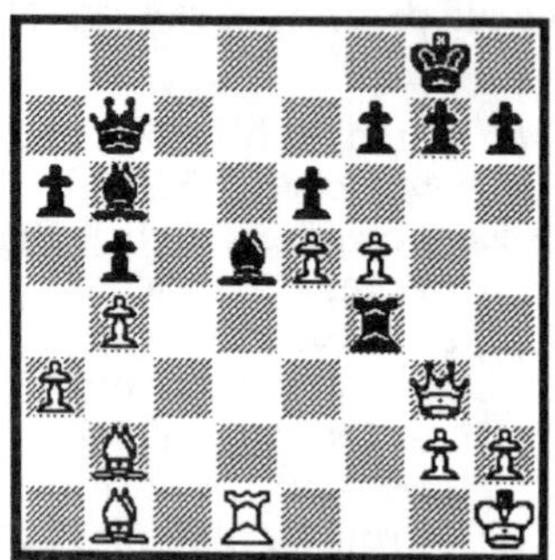

And suddenly White is defenseless against invasion at f2.

27.f6 g6 28.Ba2 Rf2 29.Bxd5 Qxd5 30.Rc1

There is no defense: 30.Qg4 is met by 30...h5, and 30.Rb1 by 30...Rxb2.

30...Rxb2 White Resigned.

POSITION 23

(Whether or not to exchange Bishops; from the game Yates-Reti, New York, 1924. See also position 168 in Book One).

1.e4 c6 2.d4 d5 3.Nc3 dxe4 4.Nxe4 Bf5 5.Ng3 Bg6 6.Nf3 Nd7 7.c3 Ngf6 8.Bc4 e6 9.Qe2 Be7 10.O-O O-O 11.Re1 Nd5 12.Bb3 a5 13.a3 Qc7 14.c4 Nf4 15.Bxf4 Qxf4 16.Rad1 Bf6 17.Bc2

The question of whether to trade Bishops here or leave them to be exchanged by the opponent is really a matter for the openings theorist, and in this middlegame book we only consider it in passing. Speaking very generally one may say that a Bishop exchange is not usually the way to hold or gain the initiative. There was a very instructive move in the game Kramer-Busek, Vienna, 1955 (see Example 3) namely 18.Bd5!. In the present game we have what appears to be a very simple case.

17...Rfd8?

In the tournament book Alekhine recommended 17...Bxc2 18.Qxc2 Qc7 as a continuation giving Black full counterplay. It seems however that Black was determined to take the initiative, and that 17...Bxc2 was not sharp enough to suit him. Be that as it may, in a few moves he will have cause to regret that he did not make the exchange.

18.Bxg6! hxg6 19.Ne4 Nb6 20.b3 Be7 21.Rd3! Bxa3?

This Bishop was urgently needed for Kingside defense. Alekhine recommended 21...Nd7; but the really logical continuation was the thrust 21...a4.

22.Ne5?

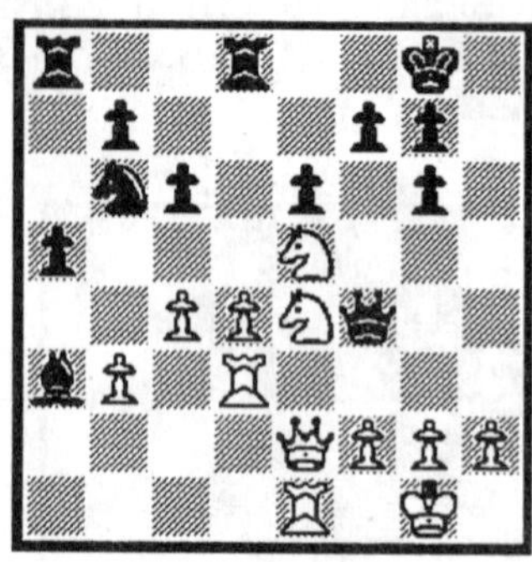

The tournament book shows that 22.Nfg5! was the move to win. Then after 22...f5 23.Nf6+! is possible; while after 22...Rd7 23.g3 Qf5 White has a decisive maneuver in the curious step-wise Rook movement 24.Rf3 Qg4 25.Qe3, followed by26.Rf4.

22...Qh4?

This loses quickly and conclusively. By sacrificing the Exchange with 22...Rxd4 23.Rxd4 Qxe5 Black could have avoided disaster.

23.Rh3 Qe7 24.Ng5! Black Resigned.

Now 24...f6 fails to 25.Nxg6, while 24...Qxg5 loses the Queen after 25.Rh8+! Kxh8 26.Nxf7+; otherwise he has no defense against 25.Qg4-h4.

POSITION 24

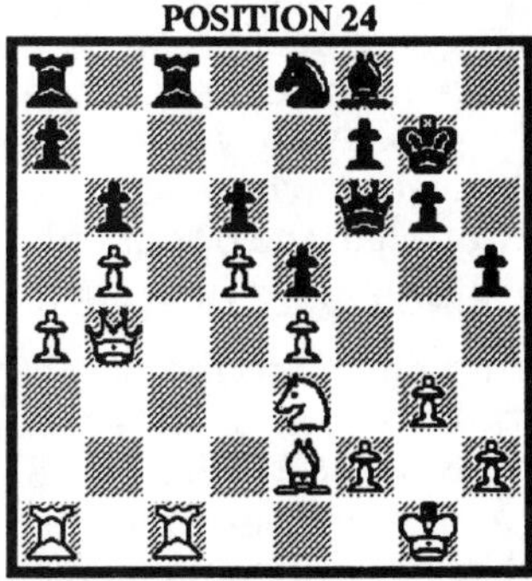

(Whether or not to exchange Rooks; from the game Petrosian-Pilnik, Amsterdam, 1956).

1.d4 Nf6 2.c4 c5 3.d5 e5 4.Nc3 d6 5.e4 g6 6.Nf3 Bg7 7.Bg5 Na6 8.Be2 Nc7 9.Nd2 Bd7 10.a4 b6 11.Nb5 Bxb5 12.cxb5 O-O 13.b4 h6 14.Bxf6 Qxf6 15.O-O Rfd8 16.Nc4 Bf8 17.g3 cxb4 18.Qb3 Kg7 19.Rfc1 h5 20.Ne3 Ne8 21.Qxb4 Rdc8 (No.24) **22.Rc6!**

Following the principle which we met in our discussion of play on the files: play a Rook to the farthest available square on the open file. It is now practically impossible for Black to exchange Rooks. If 22...Rxc6 White has a choice of powerful continuations in 23.bxc6 followed by 24.a5; or 23.dxc6 followed by 24.Nd5.

22...Qd8 23.Rac1 Nf6 24.Bf1

This Bishop, although very much hampered by its own pawns, espies a chance of great activity outside the pawn chain. If 24...Nd7 then 25.Bh3 would be just about decisive.

24...Rcb8

What else is there?

25.Bh3 a6 26.Re1 axb5 27.axb5 Nh7 28.Nc4 Ra2 29.Bg2

Stronger would have been 29.Qb3. White was under time pressure, however, and was content for the moment to merely maintain his grip.

29...Qf6 30.Rf1 Ng5 31.Qb3

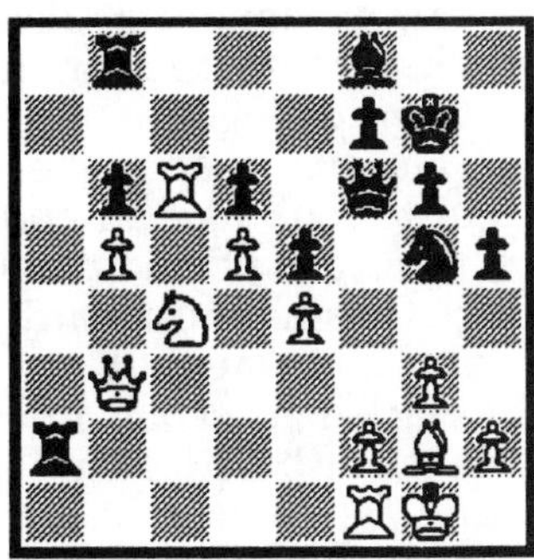

Now Black is bound to lose a pawn.

31...Rba8 32.h4 Nh7 33.Rxb6 Ra1 34.Rc6 R8a2 35.Qe3 Qd8 36.Rxa1

White could have won more quickly by leaving the Rooks on the board and playing 36.b6!.

36...Rxa1+ 37.Kh2 Nf6 38.f3 Qb8 39.Qb3 Nd7 40.b6 Nc5 41.Qb2 Ra4 42.Qb5 Ra2 43.Rc7 g5 44.Ne3 gxh4 45.Nf5+ Kg8 46.gxh4 Ra6 47.b7 Ra7 48.Rc8 Qxb7 49.Qe8 Nd7 50.Nxd6 Black Resigned.

(Whether or not to exchange Queens; from the game Landau-Dunkelblum, Brussels, 1939).

POSITION 25

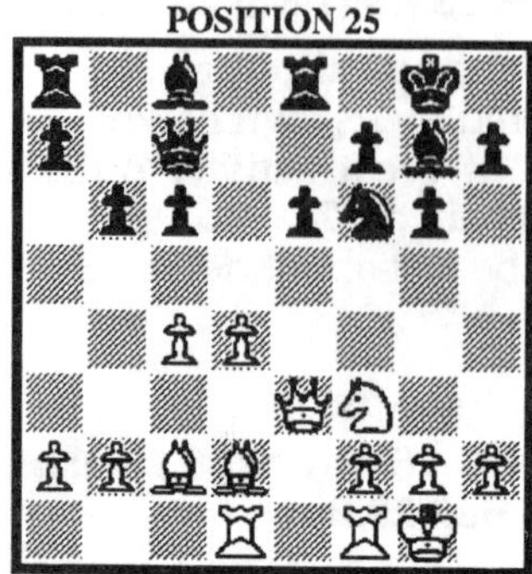

1.d4 d5 2.c4 c6 3.Nf3 Nf6 4.e3 g6 5.Nc3 Bg7 6.Qb3 O-O 7.Bd2 e6 8.Bd3 Nbd7 9.O-O Qe7 10.e4 dxe4 11.Nxe4 Nxe4 12.Bxe4 Re8 13.Rad1 Nf6 14.Bc2 Qc7 15.Qe3 b6

Whereas an exchange of Bishops often marks the transition from opening to middlegame, the exchange of Queens often makes the game begin to look like an ending. However there are positions which even though Queenless can hardly be classed as endgames. If, in the diagram, Black had fallen in with White's plans, the best description of the resulting play would have been middlegame without Queens.

16.Qe5! Qb7

Black is quite right to avoid the exchange of Queens, for after 16...Qxe5 17.dxe5 Nd7 18.Bc3, White, with the open d-file under his control, would possess a decisive positional advantage. However, after the move played White also gets the advantage.

17.Bg5 Nd7 18.Qd6 f6 19.Be3 Nf8 20.h4!

Black was threatening to consolidate by ...Bd7 and ...Rad8 followed by ...Bc8: White hastens to work up Kingside threats.

20...Bd7 21.h5 gxh5

If 21...Rad8 22.hxg6 hxg6 23.Qg3 followed by Nh4, and White maintains the pressure.

22.Qh2 Re7 23.Qxh5 Be8 24.Qh3 Bg6

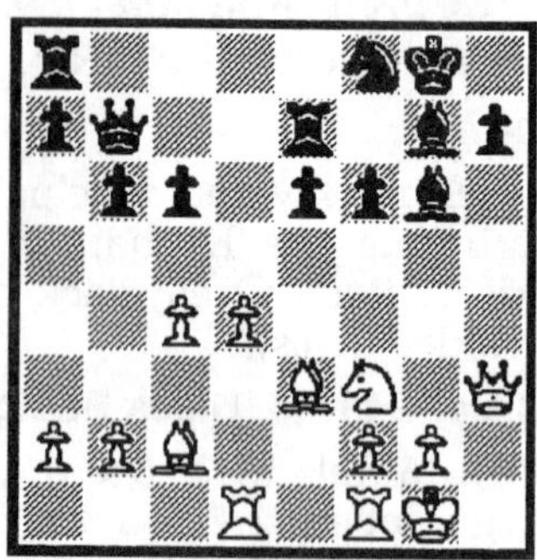

25.Bb3!

White stands to gain nothing either by exchanging Bishops at g6 or by letting Black make the exchange. It is generally good policy to avoid exchanging pieces whenever one has more terrain than the opponent.

25...Bf7 26.Nd2 e5 27.Nf3 Ng6

Resigning himself to the weakening of his pawns, since after either 27...exd4 28.Nxd4, or 27...e4 28.Nh4 the appearance of an enemy Knight at f5 would be very uncomfortable.

28.dxe5 Nxe5 29.Nxe5 fxe5 30.Bc2!

The Bishop reverts to its former post, because under the new circumstances a Bishop exchange at g6 would weaken Black still more: 30...Bg6 31.Bxg6 hxg6 32.Qg4; and now if 32...Kh7 33.Rd6 is very strong, while if 32...Kf7; the White attack goes sweetly with 33.f4! e4 34.f5.

30...e4 31.Bg5 Re6

Somehow or other the Black Rooks must defend the e-pawn as well as prevent the invasion Rd7.

32.Rfe1 Rae8 33.c5!

Threatening 34.Bb3 Rg6 35.Rd7.

33...h6 34.Bc1 bxc5 35.Bb3 R6e7 36.Bxh6 Bxb3 37.axb3 Bd4

The Black King is already bereft of pawns, and now the Bishop must also be situated to block a Rook invasion.

38.Qg4+ Kh7 39.Be3! Qd7 40.Qh5+

It goes without saying that exchange of Queens is not to be considered at this stage.

40...Kg8 41.b4

A bull's-eye!

41...Re5 42.Qg6+ Qg7

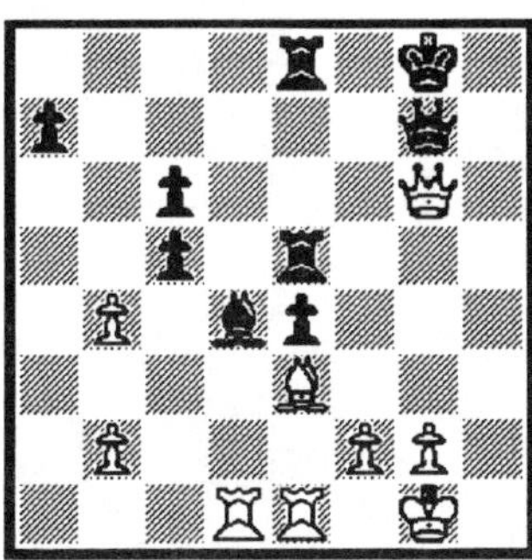

43.Qxg7+

The exchange of Queens is now the shortest road to victory.

43...Kxg7 44.Rxd4! cxd4 45.Bxd4 Kg6 46.Bxe5 Rxe5 47.Ra1 Rb5

If 47...Re7 48.Ra6 Rc7 49.b5 and wins.

48.Ra4!

A fine move, based on the fact that the Black King cannot set foot on his fifth rank because of 49.Ra5.

48...Kf6 49.Kf1 Ke6 50.Ke2 Rg5. Black Resigned without waiting for a reply.

White has a virtually forced win by 51.g3 Rb5 52.b3! Kd6 53.Ke3 Rf5 54.Ra2! Rf3+ 55.Kxe4 Rxb3 56.Rd2+ Ke6 57.Rd4, and the united passed pawns will roll irresistibly onward.

(Middlegame without Queens; from the game Sundberg-Kramer, Goteburg, 1952).

1.d4 Nf6 2.Nf3 e6 3.Bg5 c5 4.e3 Qb6 5.Qc1 Be7 6.Nbd2 d5 7.c3 Nc6 8.Be2 h6 9.Bh4 Bd7 10.Qc2 Rc8 11.Qb3

POSITION 26

11...Qxb3?

Exchanging in this position is an error; Black should have played 11...c4, and then if White exchanges with 12.Qxb6 axb6 13.O-O, he could seize the initiative by 13...b5.

12.axb3 g5?

A needless weakening. The right course was 12...cxd4 and if 13.exd4 g5 14.Bg3 Nh5; or if 13.Nxd4 then 13...a6.

13.Bg3 cxd4 14.Nxd4 a6 15.b4 O-O 16.h4

Now White has the initiative on both wings.

16...Ne4 17.Nxe4 dxe4 18.hxg5 hxg5 19.Nb3 Na7

Preventing both 20.b5 and 20.Nc5, and preparing 20...Bb5 on his own account.

20.Be5! f6 21.Bd4 Nc6 22.Bc5 f5 23.O-O-O Be8

He has no option, for if either Rook protects the Bishop there follows 24.Bb6.

24.Bxe7 Nxe7 25.Nc5

White has a won game, but the desperate efforts which Black makes require special attention.

25...a5 26.Nxe6 Rf6 27.Nxg5 axb4 28.Rd4!

Instead of trying to hold his winnings White quite rightly plays for the attack. He now threatens 29.Bc4+.

28...b5 29.Bd1! bxc3 30.Bb3+

Suddenly, like the parts of a well-oiled machine, all the White pieces are working smoothly together against the Black King.

30...Kg7 31.Ne6+ Kg6 32.Rh3! cxb2+ 33.Kxb2 Nc6 34.Rd6 Ne5

Also hopeless was 34...Bf7: 35.Rg3+ Kh6 36.Rd1!.

35.Nf8+ Kg7 36.Rh7+ Kxf8 37.Rxf6+ Black Resigned.

CHAPTER 26
THE AVOIDANCE OF EXCHANGES

Several times already we have shown that the side which possesses the greater freedom of movement does well to keep the pieces on the board. Space advantage automatically allows one to find good posts for one's pieces, while the opponent, hampered by a lack of space, has to make do with a more modest development of his forces. His pieces often get in each other's way, a state of affairs which usually ties him down to passive play.

Pawn exchanges can be avoided in one way only; namely by pushing past. This however usually has the effect of limiting one's choice of lines of play, and this in turn, as we have seen, will not be conducive to establishing an initiative. The solidifying of the pawn structure requires very careful consideration, and it is useful to be familiar with the ins and outs of the typical formations. We refer the reader at this point to the discussions of the various blocked-oblique formations, especially in Book One, Chapters 7, 9 and 11, and shall content ourselves now with a few examples.

The avoidance of piece exchanges is a frequent occurrence, and the problem begins to arise right out of the opening; e.g. 1.e4 c6 2.d4 d5 3.Nc3 dxe4 4.Nxe4 Nf6 5.Ng3, or 5.Nc3. Another familiar example of the avoidance of piece exchanges is 1.e4 c5 2.Nf3 Nc6 3.d4 cxd4 4.Nxd4 g6 5.c4 Bg7; and now 6.Nc2!.

Now for a few middlegame examples.

POSITION 27

(Pushing past with a pawn restricts one's own opportunities; from the game Cortlever-Rabar, Dubrovnik, 1950).

1.Nf3 Nf6 2.g3 d5 3.Bg2 e6 4.O-O Be7 5.d4 O-O 6.b3 Nbd7 7.Bb2 c6 8.c4 b6 9.Qc2 Bb7 10.Nbd2 Rc8 11.Rac1 Qc7 12.Rfd1 Qb8 13.e4 Rfd8

Examples 18 and 19 showed the kind of position that results when White maintains the tension in the center. The present example shows how the game develops when White avoids the exchange.

14.e5

An obvious and tempting advance. On the one hand White gains some terrain; on the other hand he limits his own opportunities.

14...Ne8 15.cxd5

Otherwise Black frees himself by ...c5.

15...cxd5 16.Qd3 Rxc1

In accordance with the principle that the side with the less available space should seek simplification.

17.Rxc1 Rc8 18.Nb1

It would be no good to play 18.Rd1 in the hope of avoiding further exchanges. Black would simply respond with 18...Qc7, threatening 19...Qc2.

18...Rxc1+ 19.Bxc1 Qc8 20.Qc3

After 20.Be3 Ba6 Black also gets plenty of elbow room. It is now very clear that White has accomplished nothing; he has had to allow the exchange of all the Rooks, and his space advantage has lost all meaning.

20...Qxc3 21.Nxc3 Ba6 22.Bf1 Bxf1 23.Kxf1 Nc7 24.Nb1.

So as to play 25.Ba3 And force the exchange of Black's good Bishop.

Draw

POSITION 28

(White avoids piece exchanges; from the game Keres-Botvinnik, Moscow 1956).

1.e4 c5 2.Nf3 Nc6 3.d4 cxd4 4.Nxd4 Nf6 5.Nc3 d6 6.Bg5 e6 7.Qd2 h6 8.Bxf6 gxf6 9.O-O-O a6 10.f4 h5 11.Kb1 Bd7 12.Be2 Qb6

White holds an advantage in space; Black has the Bishop pair. The doubled pawn in the Black set-up could become a liability, but it might also turn out to be an advantage. In an ending the doubling, although devaluing the pawns themselves, could enhance the activity of the Bishop pair.

13.Nb3!

White could have retained some initiative by 13.Rhf1 Nxd4 14.Qxd4 Qxd4 15.Rxd4 with an eye on a raid against the h-pawn by Rf3-h3; nevertheless, the move played is the most logical solution to the problem. By this avoidance of exchange, White poses Black the perpetual question of how to get some play for his pieces – a problem which is particularly troublesome here in view of Black's serious lack of space.

13...O-O-O 14.Rhf1 Na5

Going for simplification. This time White cannot very well avoid it, for 15.Nd4 Nc6 would lead only to an eventual repetition of moves.

15.Rf3!

From here the Rook can operate on either flank.

15...Nxb3 16.axb3 Kb8 17.Na4!

Now it is clear that White has a firm hold on the initiative. He has no cause to fear the exchange of this Knight, for this would mean Black giving up his only trump card, the Bishop pair. Moreover, after 17...Bxa4 18.bxa4, the b3 square would be available for the Rook, enabling it to join in a powerful attack on the Black King.

17...Qa7 18.f5!

The direct attack begins.

18...Be7 19.fxe6 fxe6

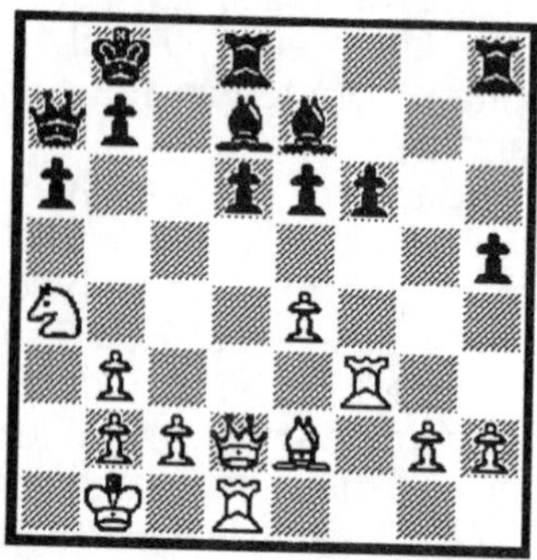

20.Rxf6!

A splendid combination which nets White a pawn.

20...Rh7

That 20...Bxf6 loses to 21.Qxd6+ and 22.Nb6+ is easy enough to see. Not so easy to work out however is the variation 20...b5, which White would have answered by 21.Rf7. Then there could follow 21...Be8 22.Rg7! bxa4 23.Qb4+ Ka8 (or 23...Kc8 24.Rxe7! Qxe7 25.Bxa6+ and mate next) 24.e5! Bc6 25.exd6 and wins.

21.Rg6 b5 22.Nc3 Qc5 23.Na2 Rf8 24.Nb4 Ka7 25.Bf3 h4 26.h3 Bc8 27.Nd3 Qc7

Against 27...Qd4 there is a powerful reply in 28.c3 Qb6 29.e5!, after which 29...d5 fails against 30.Bxd5.

28.Nf4 Rf6 29.Bg4 Rxg6

There is no salvation in 29...Rhf7 30.Nxe6! Bxe6 31.Bxe6 Rxg6 32.Bxf7.

30.Nxg6 Bb7 31.Bxe6 Bd8 32.Bd5 Bxd5 33.Qxd5 Rf7 34.e5 Black Resigned.

POSITION 29

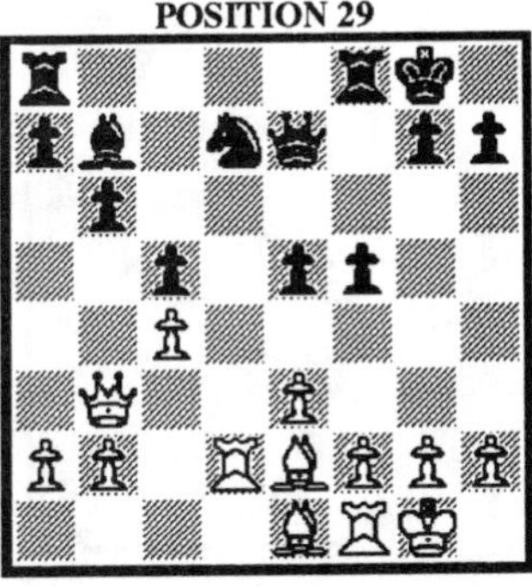

(Black leaves the open d-file to his opponent in order to avoid exchanges; from the game Vidmar-Nimzowitsch, New York 1927).

1.d4 Nf6 2.Nf3 e6 3.c4 Bb4+ 4.Bd2 Qe7 5.Nc3 O-O 6.e3 d6 7.Be2 b6 8.O-O Bb7 9.Qc2 Nbd7 10.Rad1 Bxc3 11.Bxc3 Ne4 12.Be1 f5 13.Qb3 c5 14.Nd2 Nxd2 15.Rxd2 e5 16.dxe5 dxe5 (No.29) **17.f3**

With the intention of meeting 17...Nf6 with 18.Bh4, followed by doubling Rooks on the d-file.

17...g5!

A brave and unprejudiced attack pattern.

18.Bf2 Nf6 19.Rfd1

It is certainly no exaggeration to say that nine out of ten players in Black's shoes would now have played to exchange all the Rooks on the open d-file.

19...Rae8!

Nimzowitsch, who so often "went his own way", avoids exchanges in the interests of forming a Kingside attack; the basis for this is his Kingside space control and the excellent scope of the QB on the long diagonal.

20.Qa4

Alekhine, whose excellent tournament analyses we a partially following here, suggested 20.Bg3 as some improvement.

20...Ba8!

Protecting the a-pawn and parrying the threat 21.Rd7.

21.Rd6 Qg7!

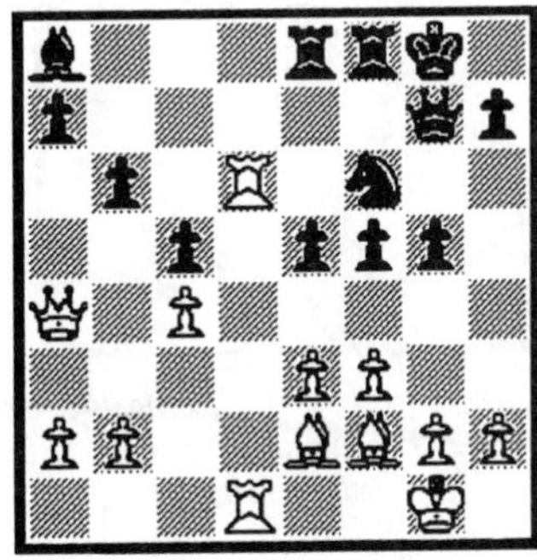

Black must operate with some circumspection. An immediate 21...e4 for instance would allow White to gain some dangerous counterplay by 22.f4 gxf4 23.Bh4 f3 24.Bxf6.

22.Bf1?

Now Black's courage is rewarded. Stronger was 22.Be1. Then if 22...e4 White would have the powerful response 23.Bc3, while after 22...g4

23.fxg4 Nxg4 White could at least defend himself by 24.Bxg4.

22...e4! 23.Be1

If 23.fxe4 Nxe4 24.Rd7 Qxb2; while if 23.Be2 exf3 24.gxf3 g4 25.f4 Black gets a destructive attack along the diagonal by 25...Qb7!.

23...exf3 24.Bc3 Qe7!

Prettily refuting White's last few moves.

25.R6d3

Forced, for 25.Bxf6 loses to 25...Qxe3+ 26.Kh1 fxg2+ 27.Bxg2 Qe1+ and mate next.

25...fxg2 26.Bxg2 Bxg2 27.Bxf6

Or 27.Kxg2 Qe4+ with a quick win.

27...Qe4! 28.R1d2 Bh3 29.Bc3 Qg4+ White Resigned. It is mate in two more moves.

POSITION 30

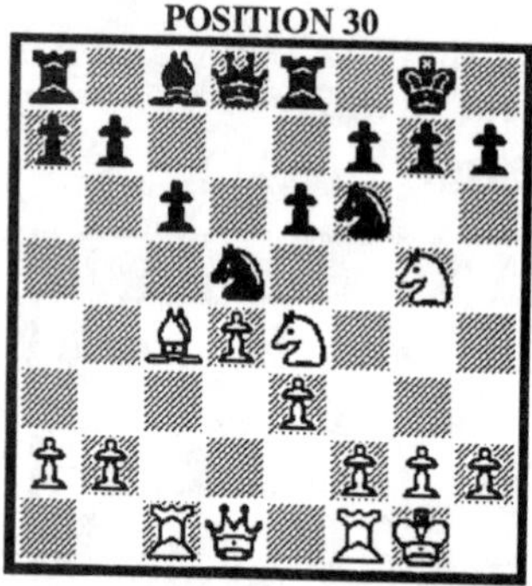

(Avoidance of Knight exchange enables White to keep the initiative; from the game Alekhine-West, Portsmouth, 1923).

1.d4 Nf6 2.c4 e6 3.Nf3 d5 4.Nc3 Be7 5.Bg5 Nbd7 6.e3 O-O 7.Rc1 c6 8.Bd3 Re8 9.O-O dxc4 10.Bxc4 Nd5 11.Ne4 Bxg5 12.Nfxg5 N7f6 (No.30) **13.Ng3!**

Just as in Example 28 (13.Nb3!) White is avoiding a Knight exchange in order to confront his opponent with maximum difficulty in his development.

13...h6 14.Nf3 Nb6 15.Bb3 Nbd7

Black aims for the freeing advance ...e5.

16.e4 e5 17.dxe5 Ng4 18.e6!

Thus White ensures himself a definite advantage. The Black pawn on e6 will be not only weak, but also an obstacle.

18...fxe6 19.Nd4 Nde5 20.h3 Nf6 21.f4 Nf7 22.Kh1

With Black unable to undertake anything of importance, White prepares a Kingside attack at his leisure.

22...a5 23.Rc3 Qb6 24.e5 Nd5 25.Nh5!

Beginning the decisive assault. If now 25...Nxc3 then 26.Qg4 g5 27.Nf6+ Kf8 28.bxc3.

25...Re7 26.Rg3 Nh8 27.Qd3 Qc7

In his famous book *My Best Games of Chess 1908-23* Alekhine gives the following beautiful variation: 28.Bd1 Nb4 29.Qh7+!! Kxh7 30.Rxg7+ Rxg7 31.Nf6+ Kg6 32.Bh5#. However, since the move 28...Nb4 is not forced he chose the text move – less elegant it is true, but a swift and certain win.

28.Bxd5! exd5 29.Nf6+ Black Resigned.

If 29...Kf8 then 30.Qh7 wins; or if 29...Kf7 then 30.Rxg7+ forces mate.

POSITION 31

(Avoidance of Bishop exchange; from the game Capablanca-Maroczy, Carlsbad, 1929).

1.d4 Nf6 2.c4 e6 3.Nf3 d5 4.Bg5 Be7 5.e3 O-O 6.Nc3 Nbd7 7.Rc1 c6 8.Qc2 h6 9.Bh4 a6 10.cxd5 Nxd5 (No.31) **11.Bg3!**

Since the Black position is somewhat cramped, White avoids exchanging; this will give the best chance to maintain some pressure.

11...Qa5 12.Nd2 Nxc3 13.bxc3 c5

By 13...b5 Black could have prevented White's next move.

14.Nc4 Qd8 15.Rd1 cxd4

Or 15...b5 16.dxc5 Bxc5 17.Nd6, and White maintains the initiative.

16.Rxd4 Bc5

A better continuation is the line given by Prins: 16...b5! with the point 17.Nd6 Bf6 18.Rd2 Qa5! 19.Nxc8 Raxc8 20.Rxd7 Rxc3 21.Qd2 Rxe3+! – a possibility based on White's still uncastled King. (See Chapter 24).

17.Rd2 Qe7 18.Be2 b6

Not so good is 18...b5 because of 19.Na5, so Black must be content with this more modest development of his Queenside.

19.Nd6 Nf6 20.O-O

Prins devoted a very thorough analysis to this game. For White's correct order of moves here he suggested 20.Bf3 Ra7 21.O-O. As actually played Black could have secured his best position in simple fashion by 20...Nd5! 21.Ne4 Bb7!.

20...Ra7 21.Bf3 Bd7

The attempt to force the Knight exchange by 21...Rd8 costs a pawn after 22.R1d1 R7d7 23.Nxc8 Rxc8 24.Rxd7 Nxd7 25.Bb7; while after 22...Bxd6 23.Bxd6 White's two Bishops give him a distinct pull.

22.Rfd1 e5

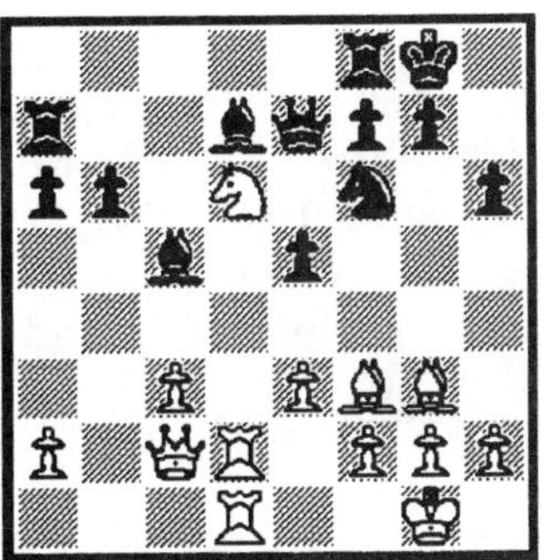

23.Bh4

To provoke the following weakening.

23...g5

It isn't easy for Black. Both 23...Qe6 24.Be2, and 23...Rc7 24.Nf5 leave White very much in control.

24.Bg3 Kg7 25.Be2 b5 26.h4 Rc7

By 26...Bxd6 27.Rxd6 Rc8 Black might have held out a little longer. After the text move his defensive lines cave in very rapidly.

27.hxg5 hxg5 28.Nf5+ Bxf5 29.Qxf5 Black Resigned.

Not only does he lose a pawn, but he is exposed to a withering attack: 29...Re8 30.Qxg5+ Kh8 31.Qh6+ Nh7 32.Bd3 f6 33.Bxh7, etc.

(Black cunningly preserves his Bishop from exchange; from the game Euwe-Van den Hoek, Amsterdam, 1942).

POSITION 32

1.d4 Nf6 2.c4 e6 3.Nc3 Bb4 4.Qc2 Nc6 5.e3 e5 6.d5 Ne7 7.Bd3 O-O 8.Nge2 a5 9.O-O d6 (No.32) **10.a3 Bc5!**

Quite correct. White's main strategy is based on playing for f4, and after the obvious 10...Bxc3 11.Nxc3, this move would have followed with great effect.

11.Na4 Ba7 12.b4 axb4 13.axb4 b5! 14.Nac3 bxc4 15.Bxc4 Bf5!

To provoke White into the following advance, which gives maximum scope to the Bishop on a7.

16.e4?

White falls in with his opponent's plans. The right move was 16.Bd3.

16...Bg6 17.Bg5 Ng4 18.Ba6 f5!

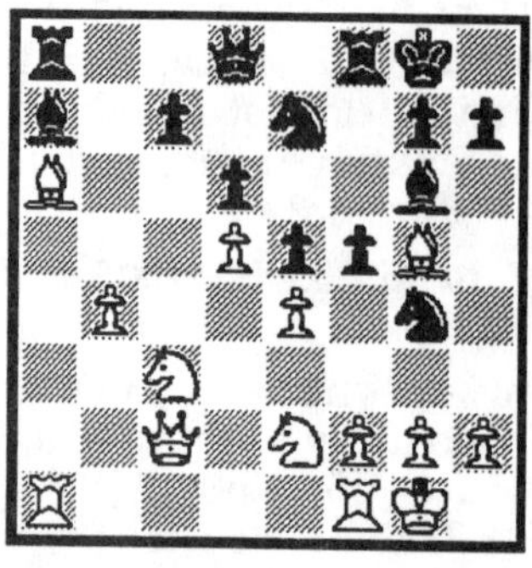

(The attack on f2 reaches its climax)

19.Bh4 fxe4 20.Nxe4 Qd7 21.Bb7

There is no satisfactory defense. If 21.h3 then 21...Nf5 22.hxg4 Nxh4 wins.

21...Bxf2+ 22.Bxf2 Rxa1 23.Rxa1 Nxf2 24.N2g3 Nxe4 25.Nxe4 Qg4 26.Re1 Rf4 27.h3 Rxe4 28.Rc1 Re2! White Resigned.

PART SEVEN
ATTACKING THE KING
INTRODUCTION

Ever since chess began, direct attack on the King has been the focus of interest; and no wonder, for there is nothing in chess so eloquent as the mating attack which leads to the downfall of the enemy King. There used to be a distinction drawn between win by mate, and win by extra amount of material. In this latter case the side with more material left on the board was considered to be the winner, but this win was worth less than a win by checkmate.

Over a period of time, and in particular during the last hundred years, a great deal of experience has been gained in the art of direct attack. More than ninety per cent of the theory of the tactical side of the middlegame would seem to be based on this accumulated experience. We can be sure, for instance, that the first player who ever sacrificed his Bishop on h7 was universally acclaimed. Who that may have been we have no idea; his name is lost forever in the mists of time. What we do know is that since his day many thousands of Bishops have been sacrificed at h7, with the consequence that today's players can usually decide blindfolded whether this sacrifice is sound or not. What was once a brilliant and original sacrifice has become a routine technique. Yet this very sacrifice, hackneyed though it is, exemplifies in a sense the inexhaustible riches of the game; for even today there might still be in the position some little peculiarity which, although at first sight insignificant, may yet have far-reaching consequences.

This h7 sacrifice is just one of the many standard mating attacks which are part of the stock-in-trade of the modern player. In the next three chapters we propose to set out these typical methods, with illustrative examples. In many cases the reader will find it easy to supplement these examples from his own play, or from chess magazines and books. In this way he will acquire for himself a technique which will prove to be of great value in his future play.

CHAPTER 27
ATTACK AGAINST THE KING CASTLED KINGSIDE

In the great majority of games the King castles into a stronghold on the Kingside. Accordingly we must give most of our attention to attacking this kind of formation. It is a diffuse and extensive field of study, and we have had to adopt some sort of classification in order to keep the theme in sight. We start with well-known stock examples and proceed from these to less familiar and more difficult types.

The piece sacrifice with which many attacks begin is like a hand grenade thrown into the enemy lines; this kind of attack we shall call an explosion.

A. Explosion on h7

We read somewhere of a wealthy old man who stipulated in his will that his sons would receive their inheritance only after they had made a correct sacrifice on h7. It is indeed true that the chess novice cannot even begin to speak of Kingside attack until he has successfully accomplished the renowned h7 combination.

Pieces are sacrificed at h7 very frequently indeed-sometimes successfully, sometimes not. It is advisable to take careful note of every little accidental circumstance which may prove vital in the assessment of the correctness of the offer.

It would not be possible to make a systematic examination of every possible variation of the Bishop sacrifice on h7 within the compass of this book. We shall have to limit ourselves to some of the most typical forms.

POSITION 33

(From the game Colle-O'Hanlon, Nice 1930).

1.d4 d5 2.Nf3 Nf6 3.e3 c5 4.c3 e6 5.Bd3 Bd6 6.Nbd2 Nbd7 7.O-O O-O 8.Re1 Re8 9.e4 dxe4 10.Nxe4 Nxe4 11.Bxe4 cxd4 (No.33) **12.Bxh7+!**

The full consequences of this sacrifice are difficult to assess in this position, as the sequel shows.

12...Kxh7 13.Ng5+ Kg6?

Into the thick of the battle. The only real alternative was 13...Kg8, whereupon White would play 14.Qh5, threatening 15.Qxf7+ Kh8 16.Qh5+ Kg8 17.Qh7+ and mate in a few moves. We now turn our attention to a detailed analysis of Black's defensive resources after 13...Kg8 14.Qh5:

1) 14...Nf6? 15.Qxf7+ Kh8 16.Re4! and now: a) 16...Nxe4 17.Qh5+ Kg8 18.Qh7+ Kf8 19.Qh8+ Ke7 20.Qxg7#. b) 16...Bxh2+ 17.Kxh2 Nxe4 18.Qh5+ Kg8 19.Qh7+ Kf8 20.Qh8+ Ke7 21.Qxg7+ Kd6 22.Nf7+, winning the Queen. **2)** 14...Ne5 and now: a) 15.Rxe5 Bxe5 16.Qxf7+ Kh8 17.Qh5+ and White must take a perpetual check. b) 15.Qh7+ Kf8 16.Ne4 Ng6 17.Nxd6 Qxd6 18.h4 Ke7 19.h5 Rh8

20.Bg5+ Ke8! (not 20...Kf8? 21.hxg6! Rxh7 22.gxh7) 21.Qxg7 Rxh5 22.Qf6 Qe7! and Black has the better of it.

3) 14...Qf6 15.Qh7+ Kf8 16.Ne4 Qe5 17.cxd4 and now: a) 17...Qd5? 18.Qh8+ Ke7 19.Qxg7, and White's attack continues with undiminished violence. b) 17...Qxd4 18.Qh8+ Ke7 19.Bg5+ and wins. c) 17...Qxh2+ 18.Qxh2 Bxh2+ 19.Kxh2 with about even chances.

The conclusion of all this is that White's combination was sound enough to ensure a draw, but that Black need not have lost.

14.h4!

A fine continuation, threatening 15.h5+ Kf6 16.Qf3+.

14...Rh8

The most plausible defense. After 14...f5 15.h5+ Kf6 16.Qxd4+ Be5 17.Qh4 g6 18.f4, White slices through the Black position like a knife through butter.

15.Rxe6+!!

This magnificent move is the point of White's previous one. If Black takes the Rook White wins by 16.Qd3+ Kf6 17.Qf3+ Kg6 18.Qf7+ Kh6 19.Nxe6+.

15...Nf6 16.h5+

One surprise after another. Now 16...Rxh5 is answered by 17.Qd3+ Kh6 18.Qh7#.

16...Kh6 17.Rxd6 Qa5 18.Nxf7+ Kh7 19.Ng5+ Kg8 20.Qb3+ Black Resigned.

POSITION 34

(From the game Bueno-Subiza, Larache, 1943).

1.e4 e6 2.d4 d5 3.Nc3 Nf6 4.e5 Nfd7 5.Nf3 b6 6.Bd3 Be7 7.Be3 O-O 8.h4

White now threatens the Bishop sacrifice in its most effective form: 9.Bxh7+ Kxh7 10.Ng5+ with the following characteristic possibilities: **1)** 10...Kg8 11.Qh5. **2)** 10...Kg6 11.h5+. **3)** 10...Kh6 11.Nxe6+. **4)** 10...Bxg5 11.hxg5+ followed by 12.Qh5+.

8...f6?

This is primarily to keep White's pieces off of g5 while pressuring the White e-pawn; also Black hopes to eventually open the f-file. The first aim, as we shall see, is not achieved. The alternative 8...g6 would also have been bad, since it enables White to open the h-file at once by 9.h5. The only defense was 8...f5! closing the diagonal of the dangerous Bishop. If 9.exf6 then Black recaptures with the Knight and thus strengthens h7.

9.Bxh7+! Kxh7

If Black refuses the sacrifice by 9...Kh8, then White continues 10.Ng5 Qe8 11.h5! fxg5 12.Bg6 and 13.h6.

10.Ng5+! fxg5

Other possibilities are:

1) 10...Kg6 11.h5+ and wins. **2)** 10...Kg8 11.Qh5 fxg5 12.hxg5 Rf5 13.Qh7+ Kf8 14.g6 Ke8 15.Qxg7 and wins.

11.hxg5+ Kg8

Forced, for if 11...Kg6 12.Qh5+ Kf5 13.g4#. After the text move White can transpose into the variation given above by 12.Qh5; but he has a still more forcing line.

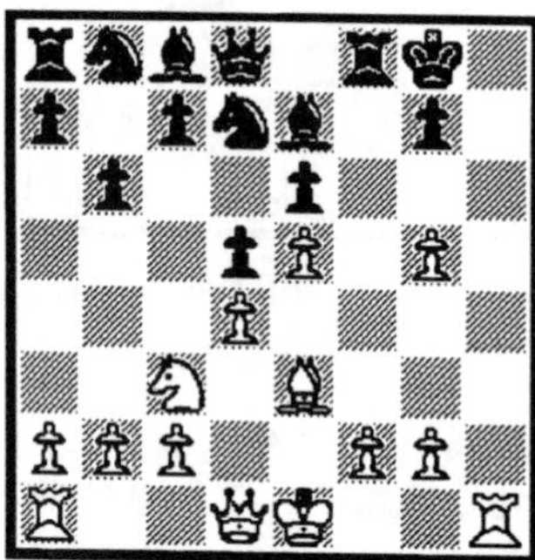

12.Rh8+ Kxh8 13.Qh5+ Kg8 14.g6

Mate cannot be averted, even by 14...Nf6, because of 15.exf6.

POSITION 35

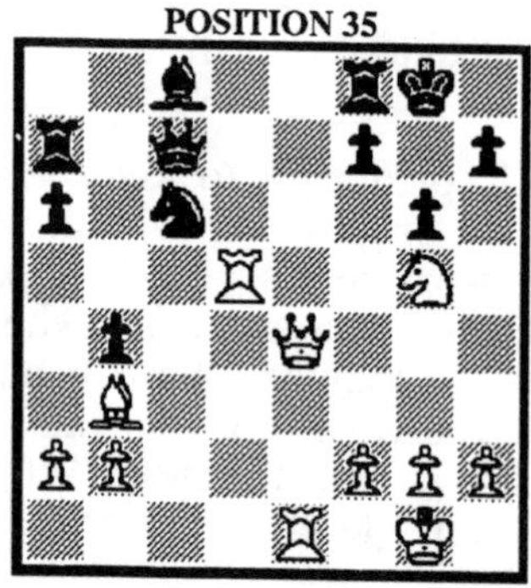

(An example of a Knight sacrifice at h7; from the game Christoffel-Canal, Zurich, 1952).

23.Nxh7 Kxh7 24.Rh5+ Kg7

The only move, for on 24...Kg8 24.Qxg6#.

25.Qh4!!

The magnificent point of White's combination.

25...gxh5 26.Qg5+ Kh7 27.Qxh5+ Kg7 28.Qg5+ Kh7 29.Re4 Black Resigned.

B. Explosion on g7

Piece sacrifices at g7 are quite common in practice, though not quite so common as the Bishop offer at h7. Here are a few striking examples.

POSITION 36

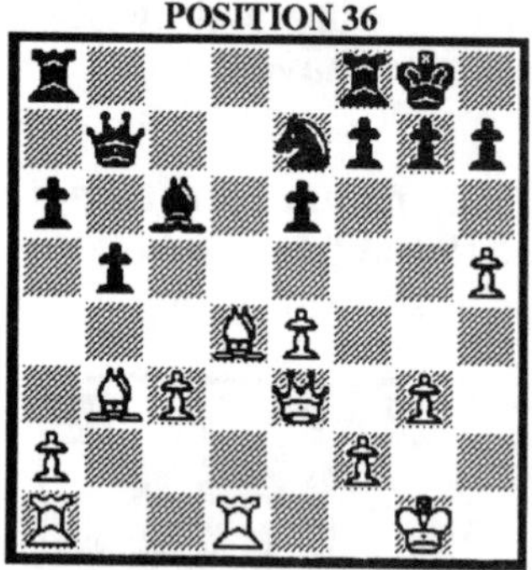

(The Bishop sacrifice at g7 in its elementary form; from the game Spielmann-Grunfeld, Carlsbad, 1929).

21.Bxg7! Kxg7 22.Qg5+ Ng6

After 22...Kh8 23.Qf6+ Kg8 24.h6 with mate to follow.

23.h6+ Black Resigned.

After 23...Kg8 24.Qf6 and mate can't be stopped.

POSITION 37

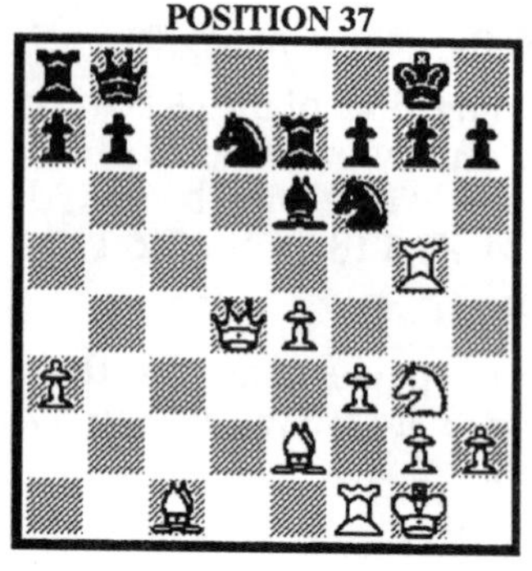

(A slightly more complicated Rook sacrifice at g7; from the game Botvinnik-Keres, The Hague, 1948).

21.Rxg7+! Kxg7 22.Nh5+! Kg6

After 22...Kg8 23.Nxf6+ Nxf6 24.Qxf6, with the double threat of 25.Qxe7 and 25.Bh6.

23.Qe3!

The devastating final point. **Black Resigned.**

POSITION 38

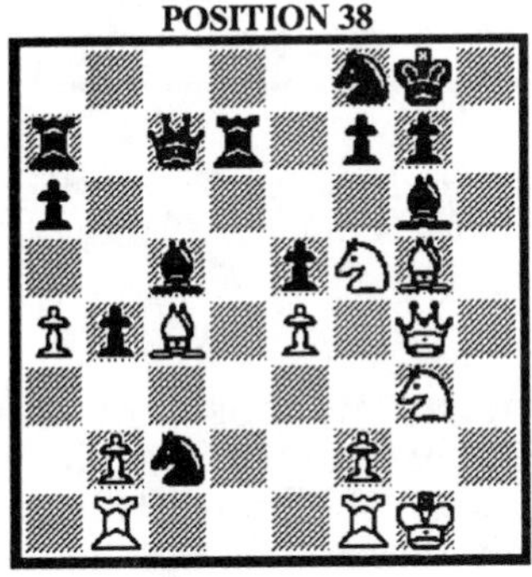

(An intricate Knight sacrifice at g7; from the game Smyslov-Konig, Radio match U.S.S.R. vs. Great Britain, 1946).

31.Nxg7!!

The question of whether or not Black can accept this offer is not easily answered. Smyslov gave the following analysis after 31...Kxg7 32.Nf5+ **1)** 32...Kg8 33.Bf6 Rd6 34.Nh6+ Kh7 35.Qh4 Rxf6 and now, instead of Smyslov's 36.Ng4+ Kg8 37.Nxf6+ Kg7 38.Ne8+, which, it is true, wins material, White has the direct hammer blow 36.Nxf7+! mating by force. **2)** 32...Bxf5 33.exf5 Rd4 34.f6+! Kh7 35.Bf4! Ne6 36.Qh5+ Kg8 37.Kh2 and the attack is decisive.

31...Bxf2+ 32.Rxf2 Qxc4 33.Ne8 Nh7 34.Nf6+ Kg7?

Here it was essential for Black to give up the exchange by 34...Nxf6 35.Bxf6 Rd6 36.Qh4 Rxf6 retaining some counterchances. The text move allows another explosion, this time on h6.

35.Bh6+!

Now on 35...Kxh6 White wins with 36.Nf5+! Bxf5 37.Rh2#.

35...Kh8 36.Nxd7 Qd4 37.Nxe5 Black Resigned.

C. Explosion on f7

At the beginning of a game f7 is the weakest point on the array, and numerous possibilities of raiding this point occur right from the start. There are also some standard combinations available in the middlegame; here are some examples.

POSITION 39

(From the famous blindfold game Alekhine-Feldt, Tarnopol, 1916).

1.e4 e6 2.d4 d5 3.Nc3 Nf6 4.exd5 Nxd5 5.Ne4 f5 6.Ng5 Be7 7.N5f3 c6 8.Ne5 O-O 9.Ngf3 b6 10.Bd3 Bb7 11.O-O Re8 12.c4 Nf6 13.Bf4 Nbd7 14.Qe2 c5 (No.39) **15.Nf7!! Kxf7 16.Qxe6+!! Kg6**

After 16...Kxe6 White has the piquant 17.Ng5#, and 16...Kf8 loses to 17.Ng5.

17.g4! Be4 18.Nh4#.

(A King hunt from the game Kramer-Ploegh, Leeuwarden, 1954).

POSITION 40

13.Nxf7! Kxf7 14.Qxe6+ Kg6

Compare this position with the next, in which the Black King has a flight square on e8.

15.Bd3+ Kxg5 16.Qe3+ Kg4 17.Qh3+ Kg5

Or 17...Kf4 18.Qg3#.

18.f4#.

POSITION 41

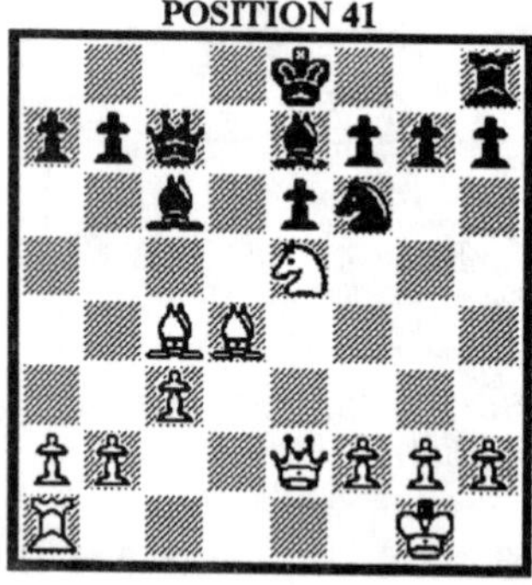

(Flight to the back rank is usually no better; from the game Donner-Hempson, Whitby, 1957).

1.Nxf7! Kxf7 2.Qxe6+ Ke8

If 2...Kg6 then White wins with 3.Bd3+ Kh6 4.Re1 Re8 5.Re3.

3.Rd1 Rf8

The threat was 4.Qf7+, and it would be useless to play 3...Bd7 in view of 4.Qf7+ followed by 5.Bxf6 and 6.Be6.

4.Be5 Qb6 5.Qc8+ Bd8 6.Bd6 Rf7 7.Qe6+ Re7 8.Bxe7 Black Resigned.

POSITION 42

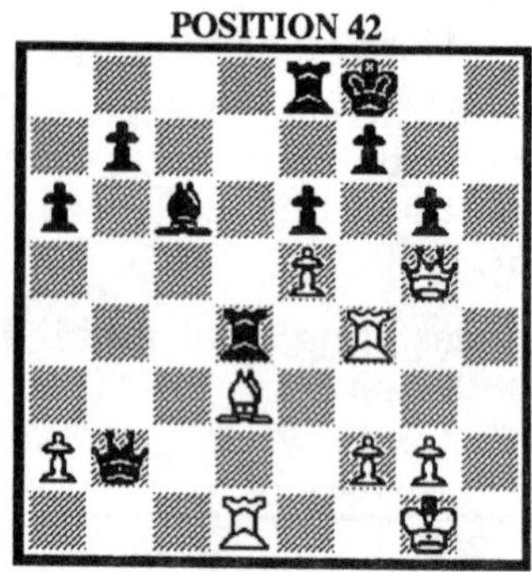

(A Rook explosion on f7; from the game Gligoric-Tolush, Leningrad 1957).

1.Rxf7+

Although this position differs considerably from the foregoing ones the decision is still brought about by a destructive sacrifice at f7.

1...Kxf7 2.Bxg6+ Kg8

White wins more rapidly after 2...Kf8 3.Qf6+.

3.Bh5+ Kh7 4.Qg6+ Kh8 5.Qf6+ Black Resigned.

It is mate in every variation:
1) 5...Kg8 6.Bf7+ and now: a) 6...Kh7 7.Qg6+ Kh8 8.Qh6#. b) 6...Kf8 7.Bg6+ Kg8 8.Qf7+ Kh8 9.Qh7#.
2) 5...Kh7 6.Bg6+ Kh6 7.Bf7+ Kh7 8.Qg6+ Kh8 9.Qh6#.

POSITION 43

(A famous Bishop sacrifice at f7; from the game Teichmann-Schlechter, Carsbad, 1911).

1.Bxf7+! Kxf7 2.Ng5+ Kg8

Alternatives are no better:

1) 2...Kg6 3.Qg4 h5 4.Nxe7+ and now: a) 4...Qxe7 5.Qf5+ Kh6 6.Nf7+, etc. b) 4...Rxe7 5.Qf5+ Kh6 6.Qh7+ Kxg5 7.h4+ Kxh4 8.Qg6 and 9.Qg3#. c) 4...Nxe7 5.Qe6+ Kxg5 6.h4+ Kxh4 7.Re3 Bc8 8.Rh3+ Kg5 9.Rg3+ Kh4 10.Kh2! Bxe6 11.Rxg7, and mate by 12.g3.

2) 2...Kf6 3.Nxh7+ Kf7 4.Qh5+ g6 5.Ng5+ Kf6 6.Qh7 gxf5 7.Qf7+ Kxg5 8.Qg7+ and mate follows.

3.Qh5 Nxf5 4.Qxh7+ Kf8 5.Qxf5+ Kg8 6.Qg6!!

This superb quiet move is the key to the combination. This sort of move is extremely difficult to foresee.

6...Qd7 7.Re3 and in view of the threat 8.Qh7+ Kf8 9.Rf3+ **Black Resigned.**

D. Explosion on h6

We now come to Kingside attacks characterized by an explosion on the sixth rank. In general these will be one square farther from the enemy King, and this fact usually confers a slightly less forcing character to the combination. The defender has somewhat more terrain at his disposal, and this fact sometimes allows him to bring up reserves to the threatened sector.

POSITION 44

(A long-term Bishop sacrifice; from the game Bronstein-Keres, Goteborg, 1955).

1.d4 Nf6 2.c4 e6 3.Nc3 Bb4 4.e3 c5 5.Bd3 b6 6.Nge2 Bb7 7.O-O cxd4 8.exd4 O-O 9.d5 h6 10.Bc2 Na6 11.Nb5 exd5 12.a3 Be7 13.Ng3 dxc4 (No.44) **14.Bxh6!!**

The consequences of this move are hardly calculable over the board. This is not so much a combination as a genuine sacrifice. The definite aspect of a combination is the fact that all the variations can be concretely visualized; a real sacrifice on the other hand is to a large extent based on general considerations. In addition to precise calculation, feeling for the position now plays an important part. In the present instance it seems that White had calculated only that he was certain to win a second pawn on h6. For the rest, it was a matter of instinct.

14...gxh6 15.Qd2 Nh7

Here are some other possibilities:

1) 15...Kg7? 16.Nf5+, and White wins. **2)** 15...Ng4? 16.h3, and now: a) 16...Bg5? 17.f4 Bh4 18.Nf5, recovering the sacrificed piece with a winning position. b) 16...Ne5 17.Qxh6 Ng6 18.Nh5 Bf6 19.Rad1 d5 20.Rd4!, etc. **3)** 15...Re8 16.Qxh6 Bf8 17.Qg5+ Kh8 18.Nd6, followed by 19.Nh5! with an annihilating attack. **4)** 15...Nc5 16.Qxh6 Nce4 17.Rae1 d5 18.Nf5 Ne8 19.Bxe4 dxe4 20.Re3, and again the White attack is too strong.

16.Qxh6 f5

Thus Black gains himself some elbow room, but he is still unable to put together a satisfactory defense.

17.Nxf5 Rxf5

After 17...Rf6 White wins by 18.Nxe7+ Qxe7 19.Bxh7+; while if 17...Rf7 then 18.Nfd6 Bxd6 19.Nxd6 is conclusive.

18.Bxf5 Nf8 19.Rad1

The issue is already beyond doubt. White has regained his sacrificed material, and meanwhile the Black King's defenses have been utterly destroyed. The rest presents no great difficulty.

19...Bg5 20.Qh5 Qf6 21.Nd6 Bc6 22.Qg4 Kh8 23.Be4 Bh6 24.Bxc6 dxc6 25.Qxc4 Nc5 26.b4 Nce6 27.Qxc6 and **White won** easily.

POSITION 45

(A simpler example of an h6 explosion; from the game Geller-Papapavlou, Amsterdam, 1954).

1.d4 Nf6 2.c4 e6 3.Nc3 d5 4.Nf3 c6 5.e3 Nbd7 6.Bd3 Bd6 7.e4 dxe4 8.Nxe4 Nxe4 9.Bxe4 Nf6 10.Bc2 O-O 11.O-O c5 12.Bg5 cxd4 13.Qxd4 Be7 14.Qh4 h6 (No.45) **15.Bxh6**

Almost an automatic move in this and similar positions.

15...gxh6 16.Qxh6 Qa5

The Queen is trying to get across to help the Kingside defense, forestalling the threat 17.Rad1 and 18.Rd4.

17.Ng5 e5 18.Bh7+ Kh8 19.Be4+ Kg8 20.Rae1 Bg4 21.Re3 Rad8 22.Rg3 Rd4 23.Ne6!!

A problem move, which wins outright. (23...fxe6 24.Rxg4+). **Black Resigned.**

POSITION 46

(From the game Euwe-Maroczy, Zandvoort, 1936).

1.d4 d5 2.c4 e6 3.Nc3 Nf6 4.Bg5 Be7 5.e3 O-O 6.Nf3 Nbd7 7.Rc1 c6 8.a3 h6 9.Bf4 a6 10.h3 dxc4 11.Bxc4 b5 12.Ba2 Bb7 13.O-O c5 14.Ne5 c4 15.Bb1 Re8 16.Qe2 Nxe5 17.dxe5 Nh7 18.Qh5 Nf8 19.Rcd1 Qc7 (No.46) **20.Bxh6! gxh6 21.Rd4 f5**

If Black returns the piece immediately with 21...Bg5 then there follows 22.h4 Qxe5 23.hxg5 hxg5 24.Rg4 f6 25.Rg3, threatening both 26.f4 and 26.Rh3.

22.exf6 Bxf6 23.Rg4+ Bg7 24.Qxh6

Although White has only two pawns for the piece, and Black's pieces are quite well deployed, the following moves will show that the exposure of Black's King is too much to overcome.

24...Rad8 25.Ne2 e5 26.Ng3

It is important now to notice that 26...Rd6 fails to 27.Rxg7+ Qxg7 28.Qxg7+ Kxg7 29.Nf5+.

26...Re6 27.Qh4

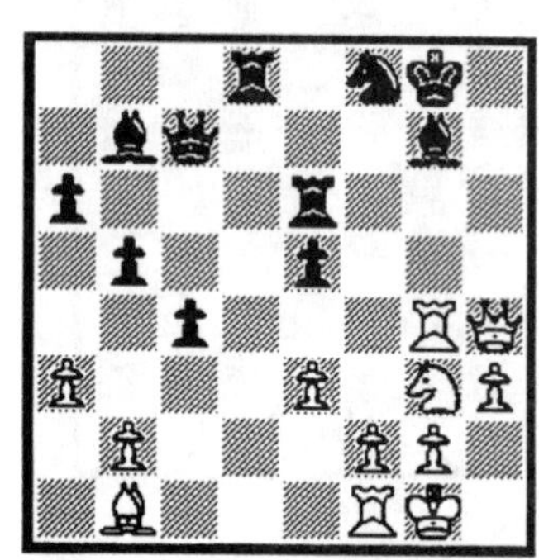

27...Rd3

Here are some other possibilities: **1)** 27...Qe7? 28.Rxg7+ and wins. **2)** 27...R8d6 28.Nf5 Ng6 29.Qg3 Rb6 30.h4, and there is no defense against the threat of 31.h5. **3)** 27...e4 28.Nxe4 Bxe4 29.Bxe4 Rxe4 30.Rxe4 Bxb2 31.f4, and now: a) 31...Rd7 32.Rf3 Rh7 33.Rg3+ Bg7 34.Re7! Qb6 35.Qg5 Ne6 36.Qg6 and wins. b) 31...c3 32.Qg5+ Kf7 33.f5 c2 34.f6 Ne6 35.Qh5+ Kf8 36.Rxe6 c1=Q 37.Qh8+ Kf7 38.Re7+ Qxe7 39.Qg7+ Ke6 40.Qxe7+ Kd5 41.Qxd8+ and wins.

28.Nf5 Ng6 29.Qh5!

Much stronger than 29.Rxg6 Rxg6 30.Ne7+, which allows Black the surprising defense 30...Qxe7! 31.Qxe7 Rxg2+ 32.Kh1 Rxf2+ 33.Qxb7 Rxf1+, etc.

29...Qf7 30.h4 Bf8 31.Nh6+ Bxh6 32.Qxh6 Qh7 33.Qg5 Kf7 34.Bxd3 cxd3 35.Qf5+ Black Resigned.

The continuation might have been 35...Ke7 36.h5 Nf8 37.Qxh7+ Nxh7 38.Rg7+; or 35...Rf6 36.Qd7+ Kg8 37.Qe8+ Kg7 38.Qe7+ Rf7 39.Qxe5+ Kf8 40.Qd6+ Kg7 41.Qd3.

POSITION 47

(A highly unusual explosion on h3; from the game Averbakh-Kotov, Zurich, 1953).

30...Qxh3+!! 31.Kxh3 Rh6+ 32.Kg4 Nf6+ 33.Kf5

The King unwillingly goes to the front of his troops.

33...Nd7

Threatening mate in three, by 34...Rf8+ 35.Kg4 Rg8+ 36.Kf5 Rf6#.

34.Rg5 Rf8+ 35.Kg4 Nf6+ 36.Kf5 Ng8+ 37.Kg4 Nf6+

Black repeats moves to gain time.

38.Kf5 Nxd5+ 39.Kg4 Nf6+ 40.Kf5 Ng8+ 41.Kg4 Nf6+ 42.Kf5 Ng8+ 43.Kg4 Bxg5 44.Kxg5

Nor does 44.Rh1 let the Black King escape: 44...Rxh1 45.Kxg5 Rh6! 46.Kg4 Nf6+ 47.Kf5 Ne8+ 48.Kg5 Rg8+! 49.Kxh6 Nf6 and 50...Rg6#.

44...Rf7

Threatening to carry out the execution by 45...Rg7+ and 46...Rf6#.

45.Bh4 Rg6+ 46.Kh5 Rfg7 47.Bg5

The only defense against 47...Rh6#.

47...Rxg5+ 48.Kh4 Nf6 49.Ng3 Rxg3 50.Qxd6 R3g6 51.Qb8+

The familiar spite check.

51...Rg8 White Resigned.

E. Explosion on g6 (or g3)

A sacrifice at g6 usually blows up the entire Kingside, with deadly results.

POSITION 48

(A classic example; from the game Lasker-Bogolyubov, Zurich, 1934).

30...Bxg3!

The point of this combination is the following variation: 31.hxg3 Qxg3+ 32.Kh1 Rxe1+! 33.Qxe1 Bg2+! 34.Kg1 Bxf3+ 35.Kf1 Qh3+ and mate next move.

31.Re2 Bxh2+!

Now if 32.Rxh2 then Black wins with 32...Qg3+ 33.Ng2 Bxg2 34.Rxg2 Re1+.

32.Kh1 Rxe2 33.Qxe2 Bd6 and **Black won** easily.

POSITION 49

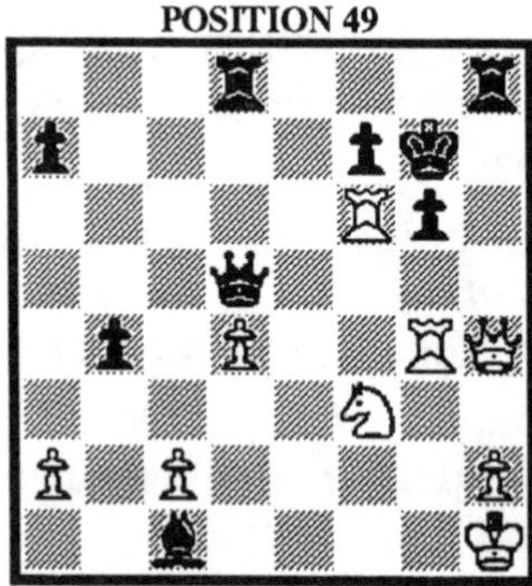

(A double explosion on g6; from the game Saunders-Winter, London, 1934).

1.Rfxg6+

Not only obvious, but forced.

1...fxg6 2.Qe7+ Qf7

Other moves allow White to force mate.

3.Rxg6+ Kxg6 4.Ne5+ and **White won** easily.

POSITION 50

(An elementary example of a Bishop sacrifice at g6; from the game Marshall-Burn, Paris, 1900).

1.d4 d5 2.c4 e6 3.Nc3 Nf6 4.Bg5 Be7 5.e3 O-O 6.Nf3 b6 7.Bd3 Bb7 8.cxd5 exd5 9.Bxf6 Bxf6 10.h4 g6 11.h5 Re8 12.hxg6 hxg6 13.Qc2 Bg7 (No.50) **14.Bxg6**

This is no sacrifice; more like an execution.

14...fxg6 15.Qxg6 Nd7

Black rushes help toward the King, but it is too late.

16.Ng5 Qf6 17.Rh8+ Kxh8 18.Qh7#.

POSITION 51

(A complicated sacrifice at g6; from the game Matanovic-Kieninger, Hamburg, 1955).

1.e4 e5 2.Nf3 Nf6 3.d4 exd4 4.e5 Ne4 5.Qxd4 d5 6.exd6 Nxd6 7.Bd3 Nc6 8.Qf4 Qe7+ 9.Be3 g6 10.Nc3 Be6 11.O-O Bg7 12.Rfe1 O-O 13.Bc5 b6 14.Ba3 Bxc3 15.bxc3 Qd7 16.Rad1 Na5 17.Qh6 f6 (No.51) **18.Bxg6!**

Taking advantage of the circumstance that the Black Queen will not be able to interpose on g7, because it must defend the Bishop on e6.

18...hxg6 19.Qxg6+ Kh8 20.Bxd6 cxd6 21.Rxe6!

This new sacrifice, in conjunction with White's next move, forms the basis of the whole combination.

21...Qxe6 22.Rd4 Qc4

The only way to stop mate by Rh4.

23.Rxc4 Nxc4 24.Qh5+ Kg7 25.Qg4+

Now it all goes like clockwork; White wins the Knight as well. Without this little tailpiece to the combination White's game with Queen against two Rooks might yet have been not too easy to win. **Black Resigned.**

POSITION 52

(A long-term offer at g6; from the game Idigoras-Panno, Mar del Plata, 1955).

23.Nxg6!!

This Knight sacrifice comes like the proverbial thunderclap out of a clear sky.

23...fxg6

No better would have been 23...Bxg5 24.Nxe7+! Kg7 25.f4 Bh6 26.dxc5, and the White Bishops dominate the board.

24.Be6+ Kg7 25.f4 Nd8

Trying to rush reserves to the threatened Kingside.

26.d5 Bc8 27.Rh2 Bxe6

This removes a dangerous piece from White's attack. Nevertheless Black remains remarkably helpless.

28.dxe6 Qa6 29.Qg4 Rh8

In order to unpin the Knight by 30...Kf8; but White's reply spoils his plan.

30.Nf3 Qd3 31.e4 c4 32.bxc4 Qxc4?

Stronger would have been 32...Rc8; then 33.f5 could have been answered by 33...Be3+.

33.f5! g5 34.Qh5!

Even stronger than 34.Nxg5, to which Black's reply would also have been 34...Kf8.

34...Kf8 35.Qg6 Bg7

Forced, for White was threatening not only 36.Rxh6, but also 36.Bxf6.

36.Rxh8+ Bxh8 37.Nxg5 Bg7 38.Nh7+ Kg8

Or 38...Nxh7 39.Bxg7+ Kg8 40.Bh6+ Kh8 41.Qg7#.

39.Bxf6 exf6 40.Nxf6+ and mate next move.

F. Explosion on f6 (f3)

The Knight sacrifice on f6 is part of the repertoire of every advanced player. Quite frequently this sacrifice is made possible by a pawn on e5.

POSITION 53

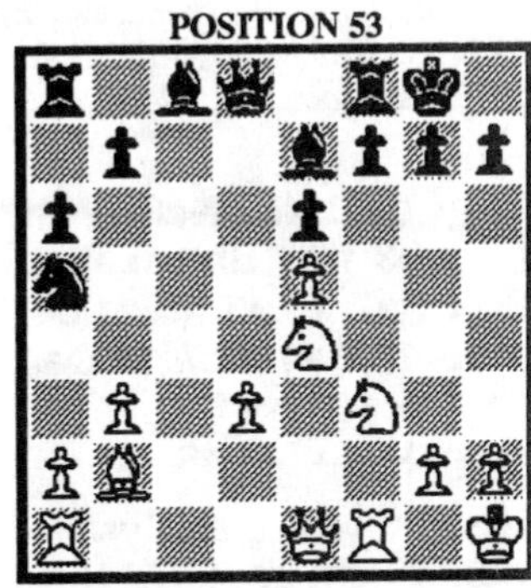

(A characteristic Knight sacrifice on f6; from the game Alexander-Szabo, Hilversum, 1947).

21.Nf6+ gxf6

After 21...Bxf6 22.exf6 gxf6 White can force the win with 23.Qg3+ Kh8 24.Qh4 e5 (24...Kg7 25.Qg5+) 25.Bxe5! fxe5 26.Ng5. Nor can Black decline the offer by 21...Kh8 since then White has 22.Qe4 Bxf6 23.exf6 g6 24.Qh4 Rg8 25.Qh6 Qf8 26.Ng5! Qxh6 27.Nxf7#.

22.Qg3+ Kh8 23.exf6 Bxf6 24.Ne5!

The point. White threatens 25.Rxf6 Qxf6 26.Nc4, winning the Queen.

24...Bxe5

On 24...Bg7 Black is annihilated by 25.Rxf7! Rg8 26.Ng6+ hxg6 27.Qh3+ with mate to follow.

25.Bxe5+ f6 26.Rxf6! Black Resigned. On 26...Rxf6 27.Qg5.

POSITION 54

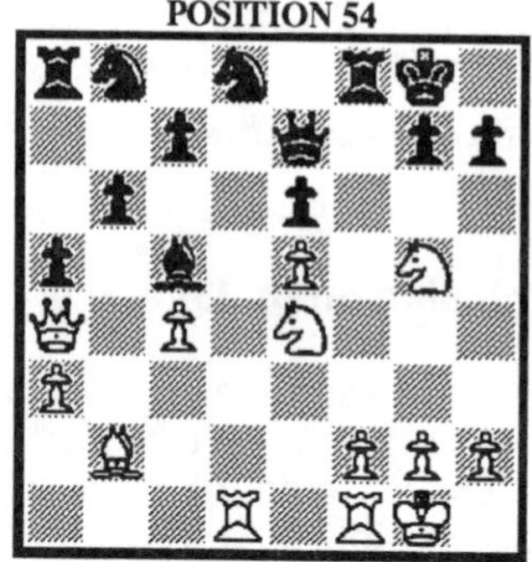

(One f6 explosion in the game, and another in the analysis; from the game Trifunovic-Bondarevsky, Saltsjobaden, 1948).

1.d4 e6 2.e4 d5 3.Nd2 Nc6 4.Ngf3 Nf6 5.e5 Nd7 6.b3 f6 7.Bb2 fxe5 8.dxe5 Bc5 9.Bd3 Qe7 10.a3 a5 11.c4 dxc4 12.bxc4 b6 13.Be4 Bb7 14.Qa4 Nd8 15.O-O Bxe4 16.Nxe4 O-O 17.Rad1 Nb8 18.Nfg5! (No.54) **h6**

Now we follow the analysis of Pirc in the tournament book. At this point he refutes 18...Nf7 by the following sparkling combination: 19.Nxh7! Kxh7 20.Nf6+!!, and now:

1) 20...gxf6 21.exf6 Qe8 22.Qc2+ Kh6 23.Bc1+ Kh5 24.Qh7+ and mate to follow. **2)** 20...Kh8 21.Qc2 gxf6 22.exf6 Qe8 23.Qg6 Rg8 24.Qh5+ mating.

19.Nf6+!! gxf6

Refusal of the sacrifice is no help either: 19...Kh8 20.Qc2 gxf6 21.exf6 Rxf6 22.Bxf6+ and wins.

20.exf6 Rxf6

A vital link in this combination is the possibility 20...Qe8 21.Rxd8!!, to be followed if 21...Qxa4 by 22.f7#!; or if 21...Qxd8 by 22.Qc2 Qd7 23.Qg6+ and mate follows.

21.Bxf6 Qxf6 22.Qe8+ Bf8 23.Ne4

Decisive. The rest of the game is routine.

23...Qe7 24.Qxd8 Qxd8 25.Rxd8 Kf7 26.a4 Bg7 27.f4 Ke7 28.Rfd1 c5 29.R1d6 Bd4+ 30.Kf1 Be3 31.g3 Bd4 32.Rc8 Black Resigned.

POSITION 55

(An unusual Knight sacrifice at f6; from the game Fertoszegi-Vecsey, played in a Hungarian tournament in 1954).

20.Nf6+!!

Beginning a very pretty combination –a Knight sacrifice based on a second Knight sacrifice.

20...gxf6 21.Qxh6 Qc8

Rushing to help the King *via* f8, and so refute the combination, but now White plays his second trump.

22.Ng5!!

Threatening Qh7+ and mate next move.

22...fxg5 23.Qxg5+ Kf8

Compulsory; any other King move would be met by 24.Qh5+, and White gets in at f7.

24.Qh6+ Kg8

Again there is no choice; 24...Ke8 is tantamount to resignation (25.Qh8+).

25.Re3 Bf5

There is nothing better to be found against the deadly threat of Rg3+. If 25...Be6 then 26.Rg3+ Ng6 27.Rxg6+ fxg6 28.Qxg6+ Kf8! 29.Qf6+ Ke8 30.Bxe6, and wins.

26.exf5 Nxf5

Or 26...Qxf5 27.Rg3+ Ng6 28.Rxg6+ and wins.

27.Qg6+ Kh8 28.Qh5+ Kg7 29.Qxf7+ Kh8 30.Qf6+ Kh7 31.Be6! Black Resigned.

POSITION 56

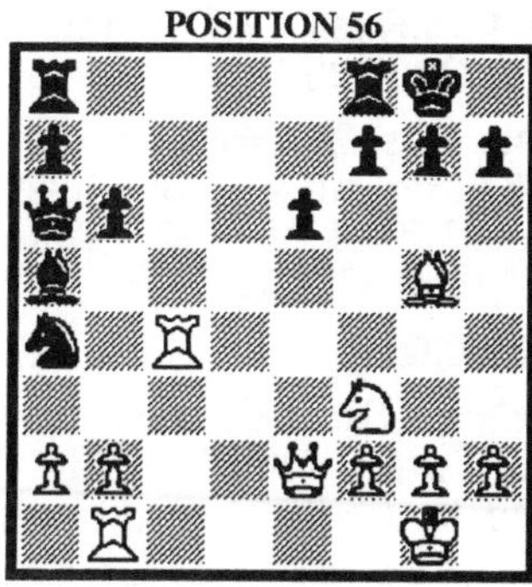

(A time-bomb on f6; from the game Alekhine-Sterk, Budapest, 1921).

23.Bf6!

The really surprising point about this move is not the obvious fact that 23...gxf6 loses the Queen to 24.Rg4+, but rather the following move.

23...Rfc8 24.Qe5!! Rc5

The main line is 24...Qxc4 25.Qg5 Kf8 26.Qxg7+ Ke8 27.Qg8+ Kd7 28.Ne5+ Kc7 29.Qxf7+, winning the Queen. Also, if 24...gxf6 then 25.Rg4+ Kf8 (or 25...Kh8 26.Qxf6#) 26.Qd6+ Ke8 27.Rg8#.

25.Qg3 g6 26.Rxa4 and wins.

POSITION 57

(An original f3 explosion; from the game Fuchs-Szilagyi, Sofia, 1957).

39...Qxf3+!! 40.Rxf3 Rxf3

A most remarkable position. In spite of White's large advantage in material, he has no defense to the invasion of Black's Rooks.

41.Qe1 Rf2+ 42.Kh1 R8f3 43.Qxf2

The threat was 43...Rxh3+ 44.Kg1 Rd2+! 45.Kf1 Rh1#.

43...Rxf2 44.Nd2 Kg7

White Resigned here, perhaps prematurely, for he can safely play 45.Rf1! since then 45...Rxd2? 46.Rf7+! leaves White with a stalemate defense. It is more or less by accident that Black can still win by 45...Re2! 46.Nf3 Kg6 47.Nxe5+ dxe5 48.Rf6+ Kg7 49.Rf7+ Kg8 50.Rg7+ Kf8 51.Rf7+ Ke8 and Black escapes from the checks of the White Rook, thanks to the intervention of the Bc5.

G. Sacrifice on g5, in reply to h6

The sacrifice of a minor piece for two pawns on g5, a widely known elementary combination, occurs only occasionally in contemporary tournament practice. The reason probably lies in the fact that this offer no longer comes as a surprise.

Consequently any player who feels the need to relieve the pin on his Nf6 by ...h6 and ...g5 will likely have judged closely whether or not his opponent can successfully undertake this type of piece sacrifice. Here is one example:

POSITION 58

(From the game Ragozin-Lilienthal, Leningrad, 1939).

1.e4 e5 2.Nf3 Nc6 3.Bb5 a6 4.Ba4 Nf6 5.O-O Be7 6.Re1 b5 7.Bb3 d6 8.c3 O-O 9.d4 Bg4 10.Be3 exd4 11.cxd4 Na5 12.Bc2 Nc4 13.Bc1 c5 14.b3 Na5 15.Nbd2 Nc6 16.Bb2 Nxd4 17.Bxd4 cxd4 (No.58) **18.h3 Bh5 19.g4 Nxg4!**

This sacrifice is really necessary as the retreat 19...Bg6 runs into 20.Nxd4, threatening both 21.f4 and 21.Nc6.

20.hxg4 Bxg4 21.Qe2

Another line would be 21.Kg2, to which Black would reply 21...Bf6 and on 22.Bd3 Rc8 followed by 23...Rc3.

21...Rc8 22.Bd3 Bg5!

The effect of this pin is very strong. Black threatens 23...B5xd2 and 23.Qf1 would be no remedy, in view of 23...B5xd2 24.Nxd2 Qg5.

23.e5

Looking for counterplay. After 23.Nf1 Rc3 24.N1h2 Bh5 White is bound hand and foot.

23...Bxd2 24.Qe4

White hopes this sharp interpolation will save him.

24...g6

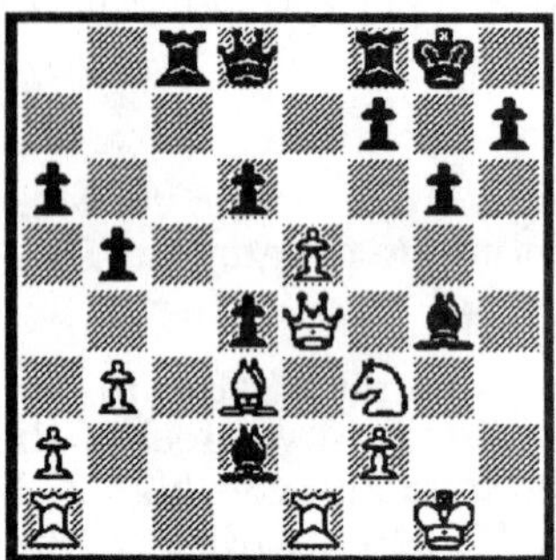

25.Qxg4

After 25.Nxd2 Bf5 26.Qe2 Qg5+ 27.Kh2 Qh4+ 28.Kg1 Bxd3 29.Qxd3 Rc3 30.Qe2 dxe5, Black has four pawns for the piece, and his attack still persists.

25...Bxe1 26.Rxe1 dxe5 27.Rxe5 Re8 28.Rxe8+ Qxe8 29.Kg2

No better is 29.Qxd4 in view of 29...Rd8, and now if 30.Qe4 then 30...Qxe4 31.Bxe4 Rd1+ 32.Kg2 Ra1; or if 30.Qc3 then 30...Qd7 31.Be2 Qg4+.

29...Qd8 30.Qf4

On 30.Nxd4 Rc5! threatening both ...Rg5 and ...Rd5; while 30.Qxd4? loses a piece to 30...Qxd4 31.Nxd4 Rd8.

30...Rc5

Thus Black definitely preserves his d-pawn, leaving White, with two minor pieces against Rook and three pawns, at a decisive disadvantage. The rest of this game is not relevant to our theme.

31.Qe4 Kg7 32.a4 bxa4 33.bxa4 a5 34.Bb5 Rd5 35.Bc4 Rc5 36.Bb5 Rd5 37.Bc4 Rd6 38.Qe5+ Qf6 39.Qxa5 d3 40.Qd2 Qf5 41.Qc3+ Rf6 42.Qxd3 Qg4+ 43.Kf1 Qxf3 44.Qxf3 Rxf3 45.a5

Rc3 46.Be2 Ra3 47.a6 h5 48.Kg2 h4 49.Bc4 g5 White Resigned.

H. Open h-file

It goes without saying that the open h-file is a very important factor in the conduct of a Kingside attack. This is abundantly demonstrated by examples seen in various parts of this book.

Since very early times, the open h-file has been an integral part of attacking the King; the number of games won by it is beyond all estimate. Here are a few from various periods.

POSITION 59

(The 18th century; from the game Smith-Philidor, London, 1790).

29...Rxh2+ 30.Kxh2 Rh8+ 31.Nh5 Rxh5+ 32.Kg3 Nh3+ 33.Kg4? Rh4#.

POSITION 60

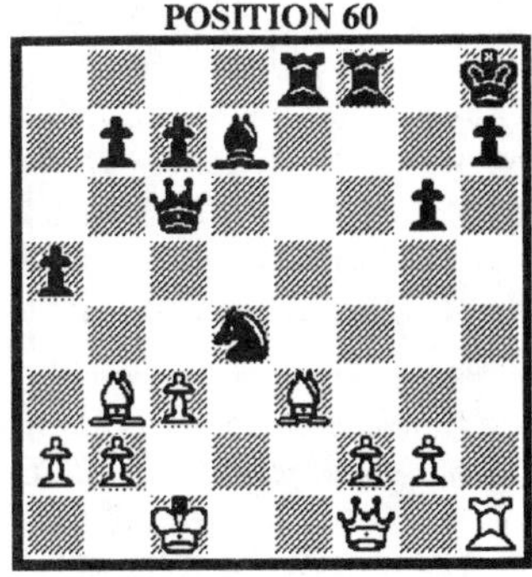

(The 19th century; from the game Steinitz-Chigorin, Match, 1892).

24.Rxh7+ Kxh7 25.Qh1+ Kg7 26.Bh6+ Kf6 27.Qh4+ Ke5 28.Qxd4+ Kf5 29.g4#.

POSITION 61

(The 20th century; from the game Filip-Badilles, Moscow, 1956).

1.Rxh7 Kxh7 2.Qh2+ Kg8 3.fxg6 Rf7

Forced, to stop the threatened 4.Qh7#. If 3...Rf3, then 4.Qh7+ Kf8 5.Qh8#.

4.gxf7+ Kxf7 5.Qh5+ Kg7 6.Qh6+ Kf7 7.g6+ Ke8 8.Qh8+ Bf8 9.g7 Black Resigned.

POSITION 62

(A typical h-file attack; from the game Karaklaic-Nedelkovic, Yugoslav Championship, 1957).

1.e4 c5 2.Nf3 d6 3.d4 cxd4 4.Nxd4 Nf6 5.Nc3 g6 6.Be3 Bg7 7.f3 O-O 8.Qd2 d5 9.e5 Nfd7 10.f4 Nb6 11.O-O-O Nc6 12.Nf3 e6 13.h4 h5 14.Bc5 Ne7 15.Nb5 a6 16.Nbd4 Nd7 17.Bd6 Re8 18.Ng5 Nf8 19.Be2 Nc6 20.Nxc6 bxc6 (No.62)

21.g4! hxg4 22.h5!

An energetic breakthrough prying open the h-file and allowing the Rooks to enter decisively. If 22...f6 White plays 23.h6! fxg5 24.hxg7 Kxg7 25.fxg5, followed by 26.Rh6 and 27.R1h1.

22...gxh5 23.Rxh5 f6

A vain attempt to stem the coming flood.

24.exf6

Threatening 25.f7# – no less.

24...Bxf6 25.Be5 Ng6

Slightly better was 25...Ra7, though White would have a winning attack anyway.

26.Qd3! Nxe5

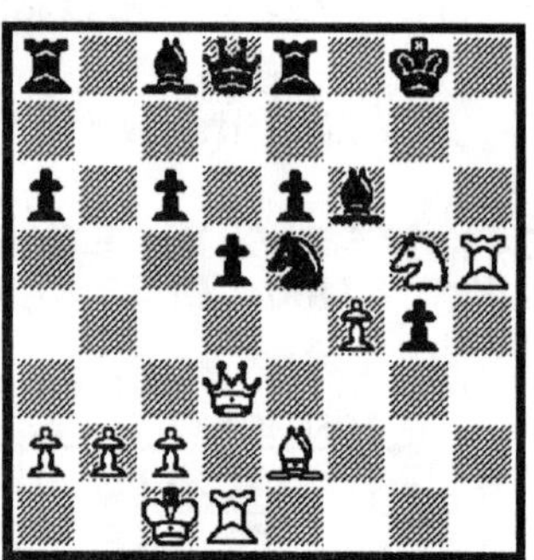

27.Rh8+!! Bxh8 28.Qh7+ Kf8 29.Qxh8+ Ke7 30.Qg7+ Nf7

This stays the execution for only one move.

31.Qxf7+ Kd6 32.Ne4#.

I. Open g-file

What we said about the h-file is largely true also for the utilization of the g-file. We now give a few of many available examples.

(A g-file combination; from the game Jaurequi-Szapiro, Moscow, 1956).

POSITION 63

1.Rxg6!

Tactical chances must be seized at first opportunity. If White delays here by 1.Bb3, Black gets counterplay by 1...Be6.

1...cxd5 2.Qxd5 Be6 3.Rxg7+!

The point. Black may have thought that White can get no more than perpetual check. If so, the next moves disillusion him.

3...Kxg7 4.Qg5+ Kh7 5.Qh6+ Kg8 6.Bd4 f6 7.Qg6+ Kh8 8.Kd2

Clearing the road for the Rook. Now on 8...Bh3 White wins with 9.Qh5+ and 10.Rg1+. **Black Resigned.**

POSITION 64

(A piece sacrifice to open the g-file; from the game Eliskases-Grunfeld, Mahrisch-Ostrau, 1953).

1.Nf5!

A surprising piece sacrifice whose main aim is to open the g-file for further tactical operations.

1...gxf5

Black could not keep the g-file shut by 1...Nxf5 2.gxf5 g5 because of the continuation 3.h4!.

2.gxf5 Qe8 3.Qg2 Qd7

It seems that Black can give sufficient protection to the g7 square, but White will show otherwise.

4.Rxg7+ Rxg7 5.Bxg7 Qxg7 6.Qc2!

This is the justification of the original Knight sacrifice on f5.

6...Ng6 7.fxg6 h6 8.Qf5 and White had an easy win.

POSITION 65

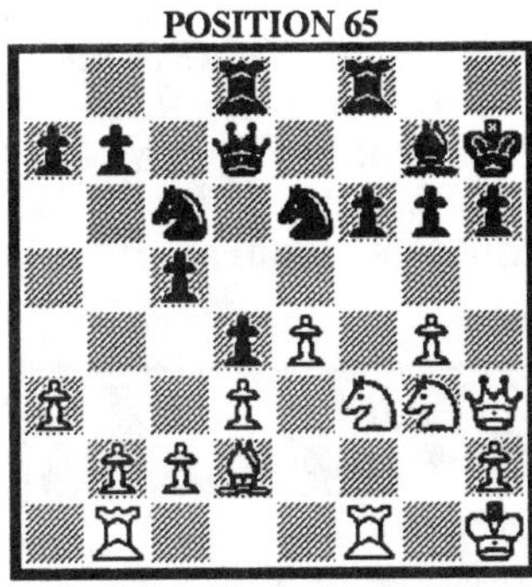

(A long-term Knight sacrifice on f5; from the game Smyslov-Kotov, Moscow, 1943).

24.Nf5!!

Just as in Example 64, this Knight sacrifice is used to open up an attack along the g-file; but it is far a more intricate example, with no immediate objective in view.

24...gxf5 25.gxf5 Nc7

Of course if 25...Ng5 then White can play 26.Bxg5 fxg5 27.Nxg5+ Kg8 28.Ne6.

26.Rg1 Ne8

The threat was 27.Rxg7+. Then if 27...Qxg7 28.Rg1; or if 27...Kxg7 then 28.Rg1+ Kf7 29.Qh5+ Ke7 30.Rg7+. Smyslov, in his notes indicated that 26...Rh8 would be met by 27.Bxh6!, e.g.– **1)** 27...Kg8 28.Rxg7+ Qxg7 29.Rg1. **2)** 27...Bxh6 28.Rg6 Qg7 29.Rxg7+ Kxg7 30.Qg3+, and 31.Qxc7.

27.Rg6 Rf7 28.Rbg1 Kg8 29.Rxh6 Kf8

Hoping to run the King out of the danger zone.

30.Rh7 Ke7 31.Qh5! Kd6

Still striving to escape. Another way would have been 31...Rc8 to create a flight square on d8. This would have been refuted prettily by 32.Ng5! fxg5 33.Bxg5+, and now: **1)** 33...Nf6 34.Rxg7 Rxg7 35.Bxf6+ Kxf6 36.Qh6+ Ke5 37.Rxg7 Qe8 38.Rg6. **2)** 33...Kd6 34.Bf4+ Ke7 (34...Ne5 35.f6!) 35.f6+! Nxf6 36.R1xg7 Nxh5 37.Rxf7+ Ke6 38.Rxd7 Nxf4 39.Rxb7 and wins.

32.Bf4+ Ne5

A logical try. In any event, 32...Ke7 is met by 33.Ng5! fxg5 34.Bxg5+ with variations much the same as those in the previous note.

33.Bxe5+ fxe5

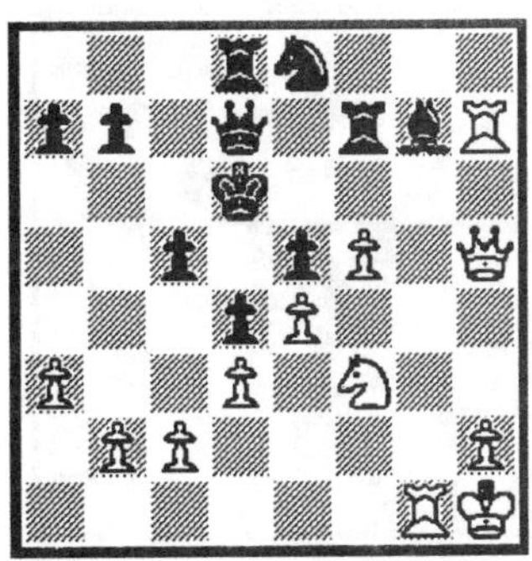

34.f6!!

A splendid move, beginning the final attack.

34...Nxf6 35.Qxe5+ Kc6 36.Rhxg7!

Regaining the sacrificed piece at last as 36...Rxg7 is met by 37.Qxf6+.

36...Kb5 37.Nxd4+ Kb6 38.b4 Rc8

Or 38...cxd4 39.Qa5+ Kc6 40.Qc5#.

39.Rxf7 Qxf7 40.Qd6+ Rc6 41.Nxc6 Nxe4 42.bxc5+ Black Resigned.

POSITION 66

(The g-file opened in very curious fashion; from the game Gomes-Neto, Rio de Janeiro, 1942).

1...Rg8! 2.c3

The attempt to neutralize the pin by Nb1-d2 fails: 2.Nb1 Nh4+!! 3.gxh4 g5 4.Nbd2 g4!, etc.

2...Nh4+!! 3.gxh4 g5 4.Rg1 Bxf3+ 5.Qxf3 gxh4+ White Resigned.

POSITION 67

(The g-file opened by a pawn storm; from a correspondence game Kramer-Kingma, 1936).

20.h4

With the intention of breaking open the g-file by g4-g5.

20...Ne8 21.g4 Qg6 22.h5

This is the correct way; after 22.g5 Black could play 22...h5!.

22...Qf6 23.Qg2 Qe7 24.g5

Now this does lead to the desired opening of a file for the Rooks.

24...Kh7

This allows White to launch his backward f-pawn into the attack as well; but it was the only way to defend h6. Exchanging at g5 would have been even worse.

25.f4! Nd6

Evidently 25...exf4 would not do after 26.e5+ Kh8 27.Qe4 and Black is helpless.

26.f5

This is much superior to capturing on e5. That way White would win a pawn with 26.Nxe5 Nxe5 27.fxe5 since Black could not play 27...Qxe5 due to 28.Bb2, etc., but with 27...Nb5 Black could get some counterplay.

26...Rg8

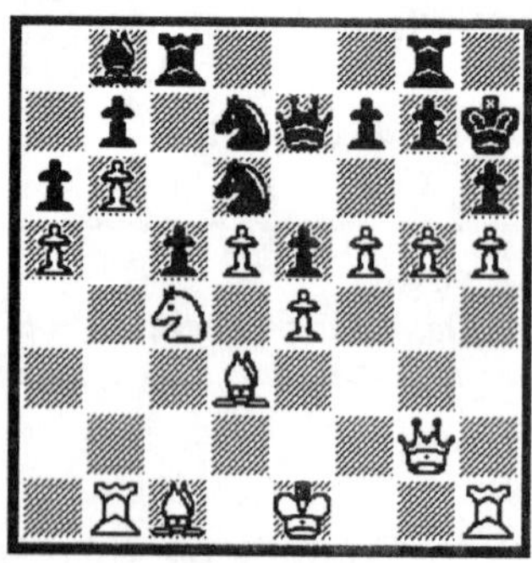

(A file for the Rooks to use on the Kingside is broken open by force).

27.f6!

The decisive breakthrough.

27...gxf6 28.g6+ fxg6

Forced, for if 28...Kg7 then White has 29.Bxh6+ Kxh6 30.Qd2+ Kg7 31.h6+ Kh8 (31...Kxg6 32.h7; or 31...Kf8 32.g7+)

32.g7+ Kh7 33.Qf2, and White has the winning threat of 34.Nxd6 and 35.Qf5#.

29.hxg6+ Rxg6 30.Rxh6+

Now if Black captures twice on h6, White would settle the issue by 32.Ke2, threatening 33.Rh1#.

30...Rxh6 31.Bxh6 Nxc4

Intending to follow up with 32...Rg8, which could not be played immediately because of 32.Qh3 Kh8 33.Bf8+ Qh7 34.Qxh7+ Kxh7 35.Bxd6.

32.Qh3 Kh8 33.Ke2!

This threatens 34.Bg7+ Kxg7 35.Rg1+ Kf7 36.Qh5+ and mate in two.

33...Rg8

Or 33...Qh7 34.Bg7+ Kxg7 (34...Kg8 35.Qe6+, etc). 35.Qxd7+ Kg6 36.Rg1+ and wins.

34.Bg7+! Kxg7 35.Rg1+ Kf8 36.Qh6+

The final point. Black must interpose his Queen now, for 36...Rg7 fails against 37.Qh8+, and 36...Kf7 against 37.Qh7+.

36...Qg7 37.Rxg7 Rxg7 38.Bxc4 Bd6 39.Qh8+ Rg8 40.Qh3! Rg7 41.Qe6! Bb8 42.d6 Black Resigned.

After 42...Rg2+ 43.Kf3 Rg7 44.Kf2, no Black piece can stir without immediate loss.

J. Open f-file

The f-file often plays an important part in an attack against the Kingside castled King. Some characteristic examples follow.

POSITION 68

(Exchange sacrifice on f6; from the game Taimanov-Nedelkovic, Leningrad, 1957).

18.Rxf6

The possession of the Bishop pair can compensate for the loss of the exchange – as we saw in Book One, Chapter 4 – but in the present case, of course, Black's ruined pawn formation provides additional compensation.

18...gxf6 19.Qf2 f5?

A stronger defense would have been 19...Kg7 20.Rf1 Qd8!.

20.e4! fxe4 21.Ng4 Rd6

Black must return the exchange since 21...R7d8 22.Qf6! is an immediate loss because 22...h5 is met by 23.Qxg6+.

22.dxc5 Re6 23.Bxe6 fxe6 24.Nh6+ Kg7 25.c4+ e5 26.Qe3

In such a dynamic position a deficit of a pawn is insignificant. The important thing is that the Black King is in an exposed position. The presence of opposite colored Bishops favors the White attack-a circumstance which we have already had occasion to mention.

26...Nd4!

Now White can't capture twice on d4 because of the loose Knight on h6.

27.Ng4! Qxc5 28.Kh1!

Threatening 29.Nxe5, which is impossible at the moment because of the reply 28...Ne2+.

28...Kg8 29.Rd1 b6 30.Qg5! Nf5

Other moves are no better. If 30...Ne6 then 31.Nh6+ Kg7 32.Bxe5+ wins; while on 30...Rc8 White plays 31.Nxe5 Ne6 32.Qh6 winning.

31.Nf6+ Kg7 32.Nd7 Qe3 33.Bxe5+ Kg8 34.Qg4

In this depressing position Black exceeded the time limit.

POSITION 69

(Queenside operations leading to a Kingside decision via the open f-file; from the game Gligoric-Petrosian, Belgrade, 1954).

27.b4

By means of this breakthrough White unhinges Black's Queenside, and as a result is able to undertake decisive operations on the f-file.

27...cxb4 28.c5! h5!

Taking the c-pawn would evidently cost a piece.

29.Qg3!

Best. After 29.Qf3 Black would have the liberating answer 29...Nb5; while after 29.Qxh5 Qxh5 30.Bxh5 Rxe4, it is Black who stands somewhat better.

29...Rxe4 30.c6!

Driving away the Nd7, the greatest obstacle to White's ambitions on the f-file.

30...Rxe2 31.Qxd6 Nb5?

As Gligoric later indicated, Black's best chance was 31...Qe7, although with correct play even this would not have been good enough. There could follow: **1)** 32.Qxe7 Rxe7 33.Nxb4 Nb5 34.cxd7 Rxd7. **2)** 32.Qxc7! Qe3+ 33.Kh1 Qxd3 34.Qxd7 Qe4 35.R5f3 g4 36.c7! and now 36...gxf3 will not do because the reply 37.gxf3 threatens 38.Rg1+.

32.Qxb4 Nb8

The best chance was still 32...Qe7.

33.Rxg5+ Kf7 34.Rxf6+!

Destruction down the f-file.

34...Kxf6 35.Qxf8+ Kxg5 36.h4+!! and mate next move.

K. Smothered Mate

The smothered mate stands beside the sacrifice of the Bishop on h7 among the standard, classically dramatic elements of combinative play. It has been known for centuries, and still occurs quite often – especially between ill-matched players.

POSITION 70

(Smothered mate in elementary form; from the game Atkins-Gibson, Southport, 1924).

1.Qg8+ Rxg8 2.Nf7#.

POSITION 71

(A rather more complicated example; from the game Reyss-Klaarwater, Rotterdam, 1932).

1.Rc8

Based on the idea 1...Rxc8 2.Qxe6+ Kh8 3.Nf7+ Kg8 (3...Rxf7 4.Qxc8+) 4.Nh6+ Kh8 5.Qg8+ Rxg8 6.Nf7#. The combination is unsound however, for Black can reply 1...Ne3! 2.fxe3 fxe5, and the threat of 3...Qf1# compels White to retreat.

POSITION 72

(Smothered mate as the denouement of a combination; from the game Kramer-Jaasma, Leeuwarden, 1953).

1.Ng5! Bxd3

The actual game continued 1...Kg8 2.Qf3 Bg6 3.Bxg6 fxg6 4.Qf7+ Kh8 5.Bxe7 Nxe7 6.Rxe7! and Black Resigned.

2.Qh5+ Kg8 3.Qxf7+ Kh8 4.Ne6 Rg8

This cuts off the Black King's flight square, but there was no choice.

5.Qh5+ Bh7 6.Ng5 Qf5 7.Qxh7+ Qxh7 8.Nf7#.

POSITION 73

(Smothered mate threats in the air; from the game Jezek-Boleslavsky, Vienna, 1957).

1... Qh3

For the moment there is no question of smothered mate. Mate is threatened at g2, and now if 2.Rf2, Ng4 wins for Black, as does 2.Qf2 Bxg2+ 3.Qxg2 Qxh4.

2.Rg1 Ng4! 3.Bg3 Bf6 4.Ne4

If 4.Qxd6 then 4...Qxh2+! 5.Qxh2 Nf2#. Also, after 4.Qf4 Be5 Black must win: **1)** 5.Be4 Qh5 6.Qf3 Bxg3 7.Qxg3 Qxh2+ 8.Qxh2 Nf2#. **2)** 5.Ne4 Bxe4 6.Bxe4 Qh5 7.Qf3 Bxg3 8.Qxg3 Qxh2+ 9.Qxh2 Nf2#.

4...Bxe4 5.Bxe4

If 5.Qxe4, then 5...Qxh2+ 6.Bxh2 Nf2#.

5...Qxg3! White Resigned. He must lose a piece.

L. The Double Bishop Sacrifice

This combination is rather rare today, but it nevertheless must rank among the standard procedures against Kingside castling. As far as is known its first occurrence was in the famous Lasker-Bauer game from the Amsterdam Tournament of 1889. Since then it has appeared from time to time, but is still no commonplace matter. A game won by this combination will still go round the world, for no editor of chess column or magazine would miss the chance of publishing it.

We now review a few excerpts from games by way of illustration.

(From the famous game Lasker-Bauer, Amsterdam, 1889; the game in which the double Bishop sacrifice originated).

POSITION 74

1.Nh5 Nxh5 2.Bxh7+ Kxh7 3.Qxh5+ Kg8 4.Bxg7!

Now Black must accept this second offer of a Bishop since 4...f5 5.Rf3 Qe8 6.Qh6 Rf6 7.Bxf6 wins for White.

4...Kxg7 5.Qg4+ Kh7 6.Rf3 e5 7.Rh3+ Qh6 8.Rxh6+ Kxh6 9.Qd7

Winning another piece. Were it not for this last point, it might have been problematic for White to win. **Black Resigned.**

POSITION 75

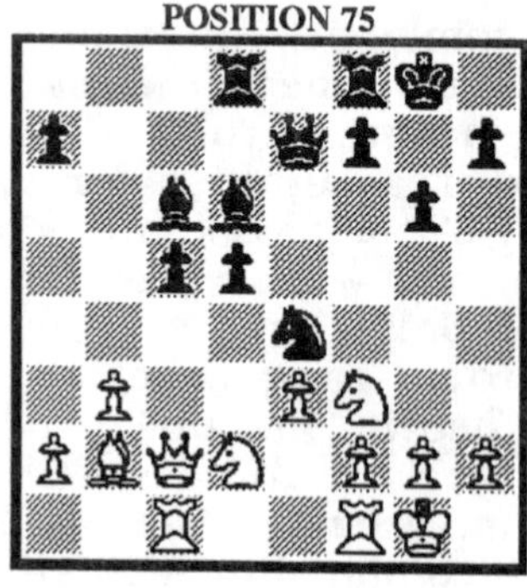

(From the game Nimzowitsch-Tarrasch, St Petersburg, 1914).

1...Nxd2

Although piece exchanges are usually considered to be undesirable to the owner of hanging pawns (See Book One, Chapter 20), the exchange is very strong here due to tactical possibilities.

2.Nxd2

If 2.Qxd2, Black follows up with 2...d4, threatening 3...Bxf3.

2...d4! 3.exd4 Bxh2+ 4.Kxh2 Qh4+ 5.Kg1 Bxg2 6.f3

The only chance. After 6.Kxg2 Qg4+ 7.Kh2 Rd5 there is no defense against the crushing threat of 8...Rh5#.

6...Rfe8!

This quiet move cuts off the White King's flight via the e-file.

7.Ne4

Parrying Black's most dangerous threat: 7...Re2 and mate on h1. If 7.Qd3 then Black wins with 7...Qg3 8.Ne4 Rxe4 9.fxe4 Bf3#.

7...Qh1+ 8.Kf2 Bxf1

Now White cannot recapture on f1 without losing the Queen to 9...Qh2+.

9.d5

A dangerous counteraction along the long dark-squared diagonal

9...f5! 10.Qc3 Qg2+ 11.Ke3 Rxe4+

Leading to a pretty and forceful finish.

12.fxe4 f4+ 13.Kxf4 Rf8+ 14.Ke5 Qh2+ 15.Ke6 Re8+ 16.Kd7 Bb5#.

POSITION 76

(From the game Koltanowski-Defosse, Belgian Championship, 1936).

1.Bxh7+ Kxh7 2.Qh5+ Kg8 3.Bxg7 Kxg7

Koltanowski gives the following interesting variations: **1)** 3...f6 4.Qh8+ Kf7 5.Bxf8 Bxf8 6.Qh5+ Ke7 7.Qh7+ Kd6 8.Rxe6+, and Black loses his Queen. **2)** 3...f5 4.Qh8+ Kf7 5.Qh7! Qd7 6.Rd3 f4 7.Rxd5 Bxd5 8.Bd4#.

4.Qg5+ Kh7

After 4...Kh8 White wins with 5.Rd4 f6 6.Rh4+ Qh7 7.Rxh7+ Kxh7 8.Qh5+ Kg7 9.Rxe6.

5.Rd4 Bh2+ 6.Kh1 Qf4 7.Rxf4 Bxf4 8.Qxf4 Rg8 9.Re5 Black Resigned.

POSITION 77

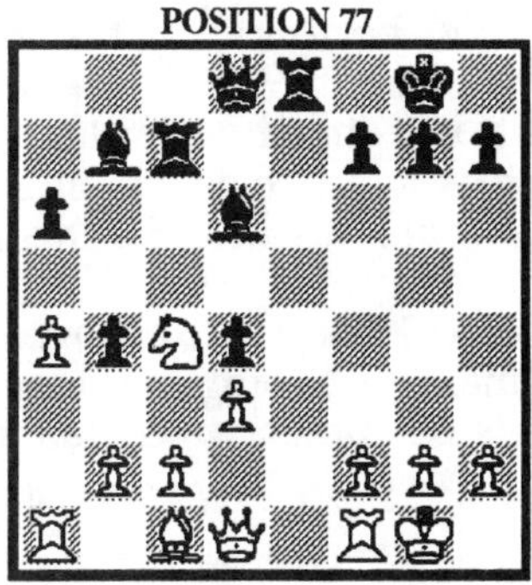

(From the game Kirilov-Furman, U.S.S.R. Championship, 1949).

1...Bxh2+ 2.Kxh2 Qh4+ 3.Kg1 Bxg2 4.Kxg2

Declining the Bishop is no better: **1)** 4.f4 Qg3! and wins. **2)** 4.f3 Qg3 5.Bf4 Qxf4 6.Kxg2 Qg5+ 7.Kf2 Qh4+ 8.Kg2 Rc6 winning.

4...Rc6 5.Bf4

If instead 5.Qf3 then play would proceed 5...Rg6+ 6.Qg3 Re2! 7.Qxg6 hxg6 8.Bd2 Rxd2! 9.Nxd2 Qg5+ and Black must win in the long run.

5...Qxf4 6.Rh1 Rf6!

A fine interpolation.

7.Rh2

To give his King the h1 square for refuge. Other possibilities: **1)** 7.Qd2 Qf3+ wins. **2)** 7.f3 Rg6+ 8.Kf1 Qg3 9.Qd2 Qxf3+ forces mate.

7...Rg6+! 8.Kh1 Re1+! 9.Qxe1 Qf3+ 10.Rg2 Qxg2#.

M. The b1-h7 Diagonal

The dangerous aspect of the b1-h7 diagonal to the enemy King is by no means necessarily connected to a Bishop sacrifice on h7, either with or without a supplementary sacrifice on g7. There are other dangers, perhaps less direct but no less deadly in their effects.

POSITION 78

(From the game Euwe-Fischer, New York, 1957).

1.d4 Nf6 2.c4 e6 3.Nc3 d5 4.cxd5 exd5 5.Bg5 Bb4 6.e3 h6 7.Bh4 c5 8.Bd3 Nc6 9.Nge2 cxd4 10.exd4 O-O 11.O-O Be6 12.Bc2 Be7 13.Nf4 Qb6 (No.78) **14.Bxf6! Bxf6 15.Qd3 Rfd8**

Forced, for an attempt to keep the diagonal closed by ...g6 would lead to an explosion on g6; 16.Nxg6 fxg6 17.Qxg6+ Bg7 18.Qxe6+, winning.

16.Rae1

Threatening 17.Qh7+ Kf8 18.Nfxd5 and wins. 16...Qxd4 doesn't help matters because of 17.Qh7+ Kf8 18.Rxe6!.

16...Nb4

16...g6 is still no good because of 17.Rxe6!

17.Qh7+ Kf8 18.a3!

The Bishop has done his duty on the diagonal, and can now be spared.

18...Nxc2 19.Ncxd5! Rxd5 20.Nxd5 Black Resigned.

POSITION 79

(From the game Szabo-Kotov, Groningen, 1946).

1.d4 Nf6 2.c4 e6 3.Nf3 d5 4.Nc3 c5 5.e3 Nc6 6.a3 Be7 7.dxc5 Bxc5 8.b4 Bb6 9.Bb2 O-O 10.Be2 dxc4 11.Bxc4 Qe7 12.O-O a6 13.Qc2 Bc7 (No.79) **14.Ng5!**

This motif is typical of a tactical operation utilizing the b1-h7 diagonal. If now 14...h6 then 15.Nd5! exd5 16.Bxf6 wins.

14...Bxh2+?

Better was 14...Ne5. Compare our discussion of a similar situation in Example 22.

15.Kh1!

Of course 15.Kxh2 would be answered by 15...Ng4+ and 16...Qxg5.

15...h6?

Losing by force. The indicated line was 15...Be5 16.f4 Bxc3 17.Bxc3 g6. This would repulse the attack on the b1-h7 diagonal, though at the cost of increasing the dangers on the a1-h8 diagonal instead.

16.Nd5 exd5 17.Bxf6 Bf5 18.Qxf5 g6

All forced. Now White could win quite simply by 19.Bxe7 gxf5 20.Bxf8. In the game he chose a more complicated method, which for that matter also wins quickly enough: 19.Qxg6+ fxg6 20.Bxd5+ Rf7 21.Bxe7 hxg5 22.Kxh2 Nxe7 23.Bxf7+ Kxf7 24.Rac1, etc.

N. The a1-h8 Diagonal

The dangers which face the King on the a1-h8 diagonal occur quite often in modern tournament practice. The reason is to be found in fashion – dating from about 1920-of developing the Bishops on the flanks. The fianchetto is standard development in the Indian defenses, in Reti's Opening and the English. As soon as a fianchettoed Bishop is exchanged off there remains a gaping weakness in the King's position-a welcome target for many a raid.

POSITION 80

(A famous surprise attack; from the game Spielmann-Honlinger, Match Game, 1929).

1.Nf5

Now if 1...gxf5, then White wins by 2.Bxf5 f6 3.Bxe6+ Kh8 4.Bxc8.

1...Qc5 2.Re5 Bd5 3.Ne7+!

The Knight is sacrificed for no other reason than that it is in the way.

3...Qxe7 4.Qxh7+! Kxh7 5.Rh5+ Kg8 6.Rh8#.

POSITION 81

(A typical example; from the game Defosse-Frank, Brussels, 1942).

1...Qh4! 2.Nf3

After 2.gxh4 Black wins with 2...Rg6+ 3.Kh1 Nxf2#. Of course 2.f3 allows 2...Qxh2#.

2...Ng5! 3.gxh4

There is no good defense. On 3.Nxh4 Nh3#.

3...Nxf3+ 4.Kg2 Ne1+ 5.Kg3 Rg6+ 6.Kf4 Rg4+ 7.Ke5 Nf3#.

POSITION 82

(The danger of the long diagonal elucidated in the game Donner-Larsen, Wageningen 1957).

1.d4 Nf6 2.c4 g6 3.g3 Bg7 4.Bg2 O-O 5.Nc3 d6 6.Nf3 Nc6 7.O-O a6 8.d5 Na5 9.Nd2 c5 10.Qc2 Rb8 11.b3 b5 12.cxb5 axb5 13.Bb2 b4 14.Nd1 Ba6 15.Re1 Bh6 16.e4 Bxd2 17.Qxd2 c4 (No.82) **18.e5!**

White makes good use of the a1-h8 diagonal, which has been seriously weakened by the exchange of Black's dark-squared Bishop. Now if Black continues with 18...c3 then White plays 19.Nxc3! bxc3 20.Bxc3 and recovers his piece with a great advantage.

18...Ne8 19.Qd4! c3

Black tries to block the dangerous diagonal. After 19...dxe5 20.Qxe5 f6 White wins with 21.Qe6+ while 20...Nf6 loses to 21.d6!!.

20.Nxc3 bxc3 21.Bxc3 f6

The only way; 21...dxe5 transposes into the previous note.

22.Qa7!

The point of the whole combination is that if now 22...Ra8 then White plays 23.Bxa5!.

22...Nxb3 23.axb3 Ra8 24.Ba5! Rxa7 25.Bxd8 fxe5 26.f4!

White could also have won a pawn by 26.Bf1 Rd7 27.Bxe7, but his actual choice is sharper and more consequent.

26...Ng7 27.Bb6 Raa8 28.fxe5 Nf5

Not 28...dxe5 29.d6! and wins.

29.exd6 exd6 30.Bf2 Rfb8

It begins to look as though Black is going to save himself after all. However, White hammers away at the weakness of that a1-h8 diagonal and quickly forces the game.

31.g4! Nh6 32.Re7 Nxg4

White is operating with all sorts of venomous finesses. Here, for instance, if 32...Rb7 33.Rxa6!.

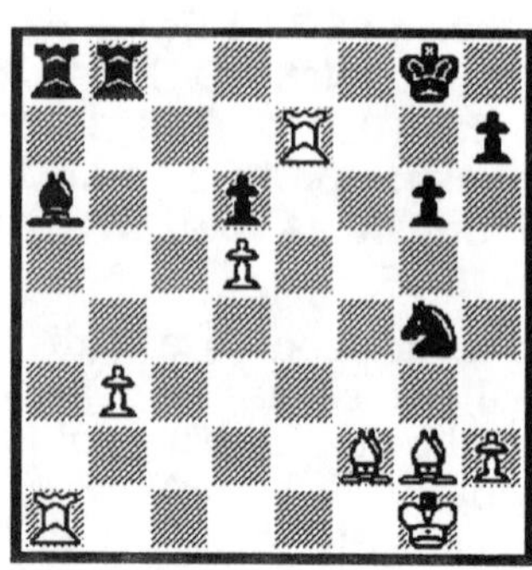

(The same deadly diagonal, even in the endgame).

33.Bd4 Rb4

Should Black try to close the diagonal by 33...Ne5 White continues 34.Bxe5 dxe5 35.d6! Bb7 36.Rxa8 Bxa8 37.d7! Kf8 38.Re8+ winning a piece.

34.Rg7+ Kf8 35.Rxh7! Bb7 36.Rf1+ Ke8 37.Bg7!!

Triumph of the long diagonal: White threatens 38.Rf8+ Ke7 39.Bh6#.

37...Rd8 38.Rf8+ Kd7 39.Bf6+! Black Resigned.

O. Some Complex Examples

We end this long chapter with some examples of the attacking methods against Kingside castling, already discussed, combined in various ways.

POSITION 83

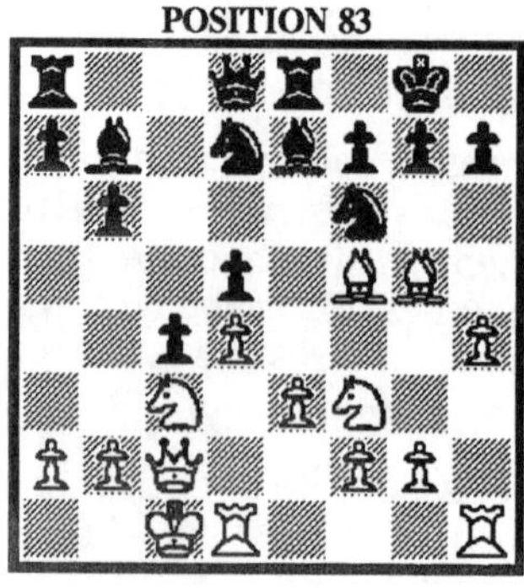

(A pawn-storm against the Black King; from a match Rubinstein-Teichmann, 1908).

1.d4 d5 2.c4 e6 3.Nc3 Nf6 4.Bg5 Nbd7 5.e3 Be7 6.Nf3 O-O 7.Qc2 b6 8.cxd5 exd5 9.Bd3 Bb7 10.O-O-O c5 11.h4 c4 12.Bf5 Re8 (No.83) **13.Bxf6**

In view of the fact that the players have castled on opposite sides, it might seem that this game belongs in the next chapter, but in fact Black's attack never has a chance to get going at all.

13...Nxf6 14.g4 Bd6 15.g5 Ne4

Black hopes this move will help to halt White's attack. White, however, calmly pushes on.

16.h5! Qe7

Black is not going to open a file voluntarily for the White Rooks. After 16...Nxg5 White has a quick win with by 17.Nxg5 Qxg5 18.Bxh7+ Kf8 19.h6! gxh6 20.Rdg1.

17.Rdg1 a6

With the evident intention of starting a pawn-storm on his own account by ...b5-b4. The start is as far as it gets.

18.Bxh7+!

An explosion on h7, but quite different in character from those we dealt with in Section A.

18...Kxh7 19.g6+ Kg8

Hans Kmoch, in his excellent book *Rubinstein Gewinnt*, gives the following pretty variation: 19...fxg6 20.Nxe4 dxe4 21.Ng5+ Kh6 (or 21...Kg8 22.Qxc4+)22.hxg6+ Kxg6 23.Nxe4+ Kf7 24.Qxc4+ and wins.

20.Nxe4

Seizing the precise moment to remove the Knight. Black cannot retake with the Queen because of 21.gxf7+ Kxf7 22.Ng5+.

20...dxe4 21.h6

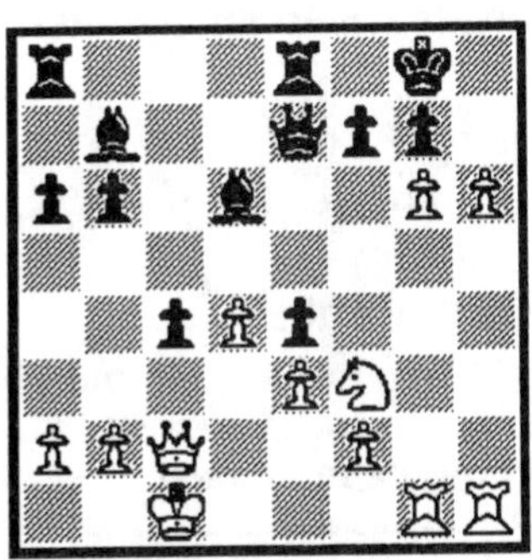

(The open file at all costs)

21...f6?

After 21...exf3 White would have won by 22.gxf7+ Qxf7 23.hxg7!. After 21...fxg6 however, the win would not have been so simple. Kmoch gives 22.Nh4! g5 23.Ng6 Qf6 24.h7+ Kf7 25.h8=Q Rxh8 26.Nxh8+ and Black has fighting chances. But after the actually played move the Black position collapses like a house of cards.

22.hxg7! exf3 23.Rh8+ Kxg7 24.Rh7+ Kg8 25.Qf5!

The White Queen has the last word, threatening both 26.Qh5 and 26.g7.

25...c3 26.Rxe7

Here Black surrendered. After 26...Bxe7 White wins by 27.Qe6+. The only move would be 26...Rxe7 whereupon 27.Qxf6 Bb4 28.Rh1 Rg7 29.Qe6+ forces mate.

POSITION 84

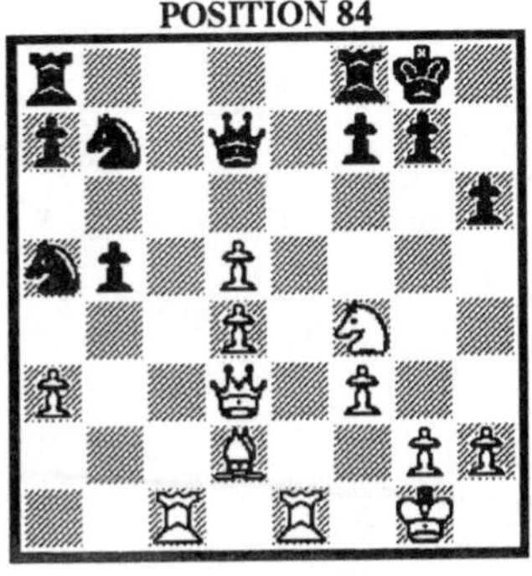

(An assault with pieces against the Black King's position; from a Match Game, Euwe-Van den Bosch, 1934).

1.d4 Nf6 2.c4 e6 3.Nc3 Bb4 4.a3 Bxc3+ 5.bxc3 O-O 6.f3 d5 7.e3 c5 8.cxd5 exd5 9.Bd3 b6 10.Ne2 Ba6 11.O-O Bxd3 12.Qxd3 Nc6 13.e4 cxd4 14.cxd4 Qd7 15.Bg5 Ne8 16.Rac1 Nd6 17.exd5 Na5 18.Bd2 Ndb7 19.Nf4 h6 20.Rfe1 b5

After a temporary pawn sacrifice at d5, Black has shifted the main part of his forces toward the Queenside. This allows White the opportunity of getting in his blow on the opposite wing.

21.Nh5

Threatening to win by 22.Bxh6 as 22...gxh6? loses to 23.Nf6+.

21...Qxd5 22.Re5 Qa2 23.Nxg7! Nb3

If Black had accepted the offer, the sequel would have been 24.Bxh6+! Kxh6 25.Rh5+! Kxh5 26.Qh7+ Kg5 27.Qg7+ Kf5 28.g4+ Ke6 29.Qe5+ Kd7 30.Rc7+ Kd8 31.Qe7#. For that matter 25.Qe3+ (instead of 25.Rh5+) would also have led to mate.

24.Nh5!

This is decisive in every variation: **1)** 24...Qxd2 25.Nf6+ Kg7 26.Qh7+ Kxf6 27.Rc6+ forcing mate. **2)** 24...Nxc1 25.Nf6+ Kg7 26.Qh7+ Kxf6 27.Qxh6#. **3)** 24...f5 25.Rxf5 Nxc1 26.Rxf8+ Kxf8 27.Bb4+ Ke8 28.Qxb5+ Kd8 29.Qxb7 wins. **Black Resigned.**

POSITION 85

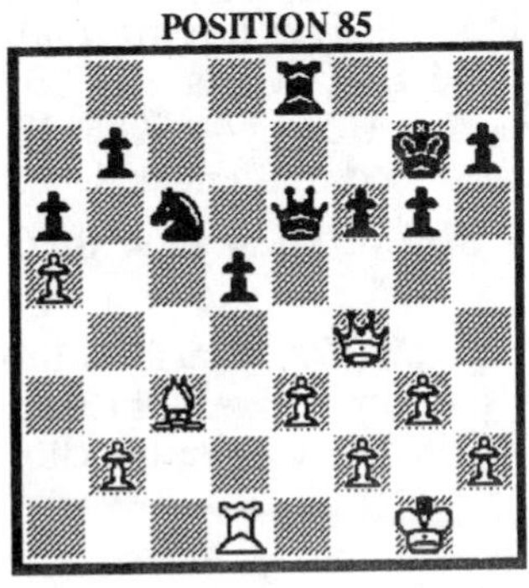

(Another sudden raid with pieces; from the game Fine-Shainswit, New York 1944).

29.Rxd5!!

In itself this sacrifice is obvious enough, but over the board it is impossible to calculate that it leads to a forced win for White.

29...Qxd5 30.Qxf6+ Kh6 31.Qg7+

White repeats moves to gain time on the clock. In practice a player has to contend not only with the problems on the board, but also with his clock; that is to say he must keep an eye on how much time he has in hand.

31...Kg5

After 31...Kh5 32.Qxh7+? Kg4 33.Qxg6+ Kf3! the Black King would slip through the mesh. But instead of 32.Qxh7+? White would play 32.h3!! and win; for after 32...Ne5 33.Qxh7+ Kg5 34.f4+ Kf5 35.fxe5! Qd1+ 36.Kf2 Qc2+ 37.Ke1! Qc1+ 38.Ke2 Qc2+ 39.Bd2 and White will win.

32.Qf6+ Kh6 33.Qf4+

The strongest continuation.

33...Qg5

Fine, who declared that the present combination was the deepest he ever made, gave the following lines in answer to 33...g5 34.Qf6+ Kh5 35.h3! and now: **1)** 35...Re4 36.Qg7! h6 37.g4+ Rxg4+ 38.hxg4+ Kxg4 39.Qxh6 and White will win this ending, though it would require careful, accurate play. **2)** 35...Qe6 36.g4+ Kh4 37.Qf3 Qd6 38.Kg2! forcing mate. **3)** 35...Ne5 36.Bxe5 wins. **4)** 35...g4 36.hxg4+ Kxg4 37.Qf4+ Kh5 38.g4+ Kh4 39.Bf6+ and mate next.

34.Bg7+ Kh5 35.Qf3+ Qg4 36.Qd5+ Qf5?

On 36...g5 37.Qf7#. Black had to try 36...Ne5! as after 37.Bxe5 Qf5 38.Qd1+ Kh6 39.Bc3 White has a rather difficult task to convert his advantage into a win.

37.Qd1+ Qg4

There is no choice, for if 37...Kg5 38.h4#.

38.f3 Qe6 39.g4+ Kg5

The Black King tiptoes around the edge of the abyss. After 39...Kh4 40.Qe1+ would be mate next.

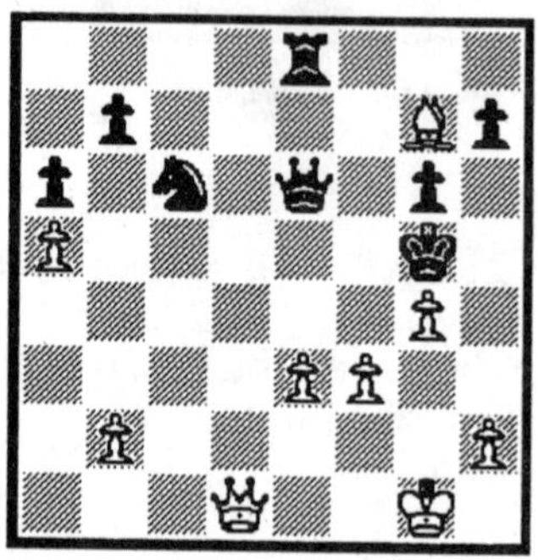

(The net finally closes)

40.Kg2!!

A quiet move with deadly effect.

40...Qxe3

Or 40...h5 41.h4+ Kxh4 42.Qh1+ Kg5 43.f4+ Kxg4 44.Qh3#.

41.h4+ Kxh4

Now mate is forced. But after 41...Kf4 42.Bh6+ Black could resign.

42.Qh1+ and mate next move.

CHAPTER 28
ATTACK AGAINST THE KING CASTLED QUEENSIDE

After the detailed discussion in the previous chapter concerning the attack against the King castled Kingside, we can deal much more briefly with the attack against Queenside castling. It goes without saying that all the standard combinations, the attacks along open files and diagonals, and the execution of bayonet attacks in the shape of pawnstorms, apply equally to castling on either flank. However, there are some differences in both attack and defense, which we discuss in the following examples.

There is one obvious fact which confronts the defender with new problems – his defensive line is one square longer, and to that extent more vulnerable. The attacker can find more points of contact. From either point of view it is easy to see why Queenside castling is not very common in practice.

We now examine an example which can be considered characteristic in attacking the Queenside castled position.

POSITION 86

(The Queen sacrifice on c6; from the game Taube-Finotti, Hamburg, 1939).

1.e4 e5 2.Nf3 Nf6 3.Nxe5 d6 4.Nf3 Nxe4 5.Qe2 Qe7 6.d3 Nf6 7.Bg5 Be6 8.Nc3 Nbd7 9.d4 d5 10.O-O-O c6 11.Kb1 h6 12.Bf4 O-O-O (No.86) **13.Qa6!**

Now if 13...bxa6 then follows the piquant 14.Bxa6#.

13...Nh5?

Overlooking White's next. The only chance was 13...Qb4 14.Qxa7 Bd6 15.a3 Qb6 16.Qa8+ Nb8. On the other hand 13...Nb8 would lose almost as quickly as the text, e.g., 14.Qxa7 Nfd7 15.Na4 and 16.Nb6+.

14.Qxc6+!

A combination worth remembering!

14...bxc6 15.Ba6#.

POSITION 87

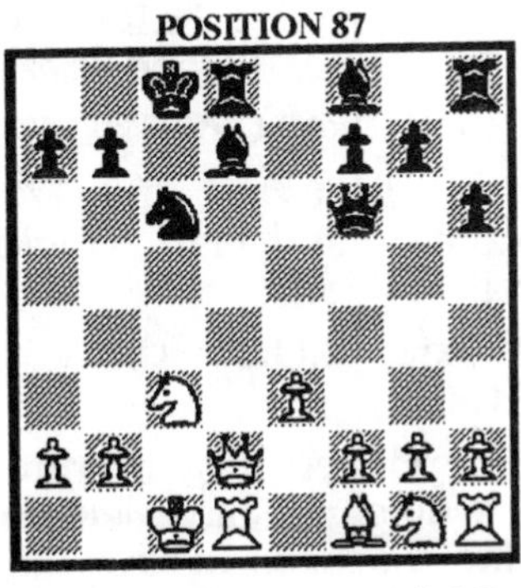

(A raid against the King castled Queenside; from the game Pirc-Alekhine, Bled 1931).

1.d4 d5 2.c4 e6 3.Nc3 c5 4.cxd5 cxd4 5.Qa4+ Bd7 6.Qxd4 exd5 7.Qxd5 Nc6 8.Bg5 Nf6 9.Qd2 h6 10.Bxf6 Qxf6 11.e3 O-O-O 12.O-O-O (No.87) **Bg4 13.Nd5 Rxd5!**

This is obvious enough since Black will be able to regain the exchange at once. Alekhine, however, has deeper plans than this!

14.Qxd5 Ba3!!

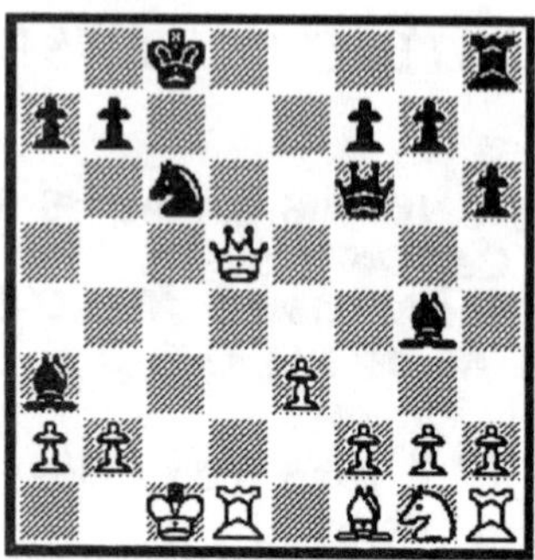

Also good would have been 14...Bxd1 15.Qxd1 Qxf2, but Black's play is even stronger, and more in line with our present theme.

15.Qb3

The real point of the combination consists of the following forcing variation: 15.bxa3 Qc3+ 16.Kb1 Rd8 17.Qxd8+ Nxd8 threatening both 18...Bxd1 as well as 18...Bf5+. Of if 15.Rd2, the consequences would be similar: 15...Bxb2+! 16.Rxb2 Qc3+ 17.Kb1 Qe1+ 18.Kc2 Rd8 and Black wins.

15...Bxd1 16.Qxa3 Qxf2 17.Qd3 Bg4!

Keeping a firm grip. After 17...Rd8 on the other hand Black would get some relief by 18.Nh3!.

18.Nf3 Bxf3 19.Qf5+ Kb8 20.Qxf3 Qe1+ 21.Kc2

Alekhine pointed out at the time that 21.Qd1 would not have lengthened the game much: 21...Qxe3+ 22.Qd2 Qe6! 23.Kb1 Rd8 24.Qf4+ Ka8, etc.

21...Rc8 22.Qg3+ Ne5+ 23.Kb3 Qd1+ 24.Ka3 Rc5!

This intervention of the Rook puts an end to it. There are three possibilities: **1)** 25.Kb4 Qd2+! 26.Kxc5 b6+ 27.Kb5 Qa5#. **2)** 25.b4 Rc3+ 26.Kb2 Qc1#. **3)** 25.b3 Ra5+ 26.Kb4 Qd2#. **White Resigned.**

(A pawn sacrifice for the sake of an open file; from the game Najdorf-Panno, Brazil, 1957).

POSITION 88

1.e4 c6 2.Nf3 d5 3.Nc3 dxe4 4.Nxe4 Nf6 5.Nxf6+ gxf6 6.d4 Bg4 7.Be2 Qc7 8.h3 Bh5 9.Nh4 Bxe2 10.Qxe2 Nd7 11.O-O e6 12.c4 O-O-O (No.88) **13.b4!**

When the two players have castled on opposite sides of the board the most important thing is to seize the attack as quickly as possible. This old rule is as valid today as it was in the "good old days". In the present case Black already has an open file for his Rooks, so it is up to White to obtain an open file for his Rooks as soon as possible. He chooses the best method.

13...Bxb4

If Black does not take, White will push on to b5.

14.Rb1 c5 15.Qf3 Qc6 16.d5 Qa6 17.a3 Ba5 18.Bf4! Bc7 19.Bxc7 Kxc7 20.Rfd1 Rhe8 21.Qf4+ Kc8

Forced, for 21...Qd6 loses to 22.Rxb7+, while 21...e5 22.Qe4 leads to a decisive weakening of the Black pawns.

22.Nf3 e5

An attempt to free himself by giving back his extra pawn.

23.Qe4 f5 24.Qxf5 Qxc4 25.Ng5! f6

This loses the exchange, but 25...Rf8 26.Nxf7! Kb8 27.Qe6! was no better.

26.Nf7 Qa6 27.Nxd8 Kxd8 28.Qxh7 b5 29.Qe4 Qb7 30.h4 Rh8 31.g3 a6 32.Qf5 Qb6 33.Qe6 Kc7 34.d6+!

In an endgame, Black might have had considerable counterchances, based on united passed pawns. White prefers to pursue his attack against the King.

34...Kc8 35.Rdc1 Qc6 36.a4 Kb7 37.Rb2 Kb6 38.axb5 axb5 39.Rcb1 b4 40.Qc4!

The beginning of the final phase. White can afford to give up the d-pawn.

40...Kb7

White was threatening to win outright by 41.Rxb4+ cxb4 42.Rxb4+.

41.Ra1! Qxd6 42.Qe4+ Kb6 43.Rba2 Nb8 44.Qa8 Rd8 45.h5!

White is not satisfied to win the Queen by 45.Ra6+, etc.

45...Qd3 46.Qa5+ Kc6 47.Rc1 Rd5 48.Qa8+ Black Resigned.

POSITION 89

(A characteristic attack with pieces against the Black castled position; from the game Bernstein-Piotrowski, Berlin 1902).

1.e4 e5 2.Nf3 Nc6 3.Bc4 Bc5 4.c3 Nf6 5.d4 exd4 6.O-O Nxe4 7.cxd4 Bb6 8.Re1 d5 9.Bxd5 Qxd5 10.Nc3 Qh5 11.Rxe4+ Be6 12.d5 O-O-O (No.89) **13.Bg5! f6**

Clearly the Black Rook cannot leave the d-file and, as the following variations demonstrate, both ...Rd7 and ...Rd6 have their dangers: **1)** 13...Rd7 14.Qb3 Na5 15.dxe6! Nxb3 16.exd7+ Kxd7 17.axb3, and with three minor pieces for the Queen White has the better of it. **2)** 13...Rd6 14.Qe2! Bxd5 15.Re8+ Rxe8 16.Qxe8+ Nd8 17.Nb5 Rd7 18.Ne5 wins.

14.Rxe6 fxg5 15.Qa4 Nb8 16.Rc1 Rd7 17.Rxb6!

Removing Black's best defensive piece is of overriding importance for the attacker, even though it costs material.

17...axb6 18.Ne5 Re7 19.Nb5!

The decisive strengthening of the attack.

19...Rxe5

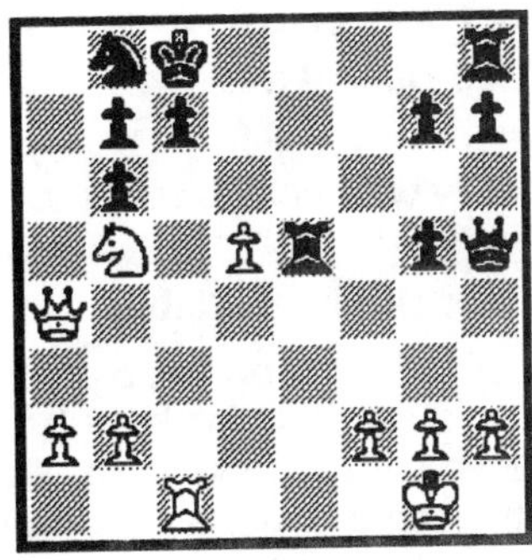

(A pointed interpolation brings the decision)

20.g4!!

The superb climax to the combination. On the other hand, 20.Qa8 would be hasty because of 20...Re7 21.d6 Qe8!.

20...Qh6

Or 20...Qh3 21.Nd6+ Kd8 22.Nf7+ regaining his sacrificed material with great advantage.

21.Rxc7+ Kd8 22.Qa8 Black Resigned.

POSITION 90

(Diamond cut diamond; from the game Boleslavsky-Mikenas, U.S.S.R. Championship, 1957).

1.e4 c6 2.Nf3 d5 3.Nc3 Bg4 4.h3 Bxf3 5.Qxf3 e6 6.d3 Nf6 7.g3 Bb4 8.Bd2 d4 9.Nb1 Bxd2+ 10.Nxd2 Qa5 11.a3 Nbd7 12.Qe2 h5 13.h4 Ng4 14.Bh3 Ndf6 15.O-O O-O-O (No.90) **16.Nc4 Qc7 17.e5 Ne8 18.a4!**

After 18.Bxg4 hxg4 19.Qxg4 , Black wins the pawn back at once by 19...b5 20.Nd2 Qxe5.

18...f5 19.exf6 Nexf6 20.b4!

In accordance with the requirement of the position that both sides must pursue the attack with maximum vigor. In such positions a pawn more or less means nothing, and White doesn't capture on e6 as the opened e-file would only help Black.

20...Rhf8 21.b5 Kb8

The attempt to keep the position closed by 21...c5 would be met by 22.a5 Qf7 23.a6 b6 24.f3, and White wins at least a pawn while holding a powerful initiative.

22.bxc6 Qxc6 23.Bg2 Qc7

On 23...Nd5 White plays 24.Rab1 since 24...Nc3 is strongly countered by 25.Qe1!.

24.Rab1

In Chapter 18 of Book One we emphasized the importance of converging lines. The point where the open file and open diagonal cross – b7 – is now under heavy pressure.

24...Nd5 25.Qxe6

At precisely the right moment. White is not interested so much in winning the pawn as in the resulting attack against d5.

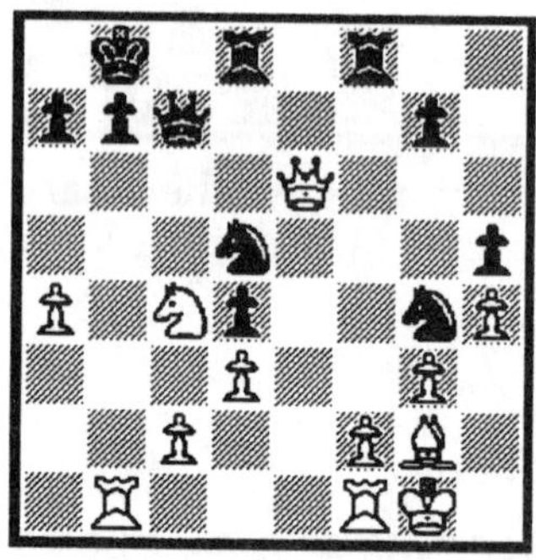

(Black sets his counterattack into motion).

25...Rxf2 26.Rxf2 Qxg3 27.Rf3! Qh2+ 28.Kf1 b6

Necessary, for after 28...Qxh4 the combined force of all the White pieces against the Black King would be irresistible: 29.Rxb7+! Kxb7 30.Rf7+ Kb8 31.Qc6 Nde3+ 32.Ke2 and wins.

29.a5! Nf4

The drama reaches its climax. Unless there is a forcing line now, White will have to take perpetual check.

30.Rxb6+ axb6 31.Qxb6+ Kc8 32.Qc6+ Kb8 33.Qb5+ Kc7

The only square for the Black King. After 33...Ka7 34.Qb6+ and 35.Qxd8+ wins. Or if 33...Ka8 then 34.Rxf4+ wins, and on 33...Kc8 34.Qf5+ wins.

34.Rf2!

Combining attack and defense. White threatens 35.Qb7#, and the reply 34...Nxg2 is met by 35.Rf7+.

34...Rd5 35.Qb6+ Kc8

Again the only square. If 35...Kd7 36.Qb7+ Ke8 37.Qb8+ followed by 38.Qxf4 wins.

36.Qc6+ Kd8

Or 36...Kb8 37.Qe8+ Kc7 38.Qf7+ wins.

37.Qa8+ Ke7

Or 37...Kc7 38.Qa7+.

38.Qb7+ Rd7

There is no satisfactory flight square left for the Black King. If he goes to the back rank 39.Qb8+ is conclusive, while 38...Kf6 39.Qxd5 Nxf2 40.Qd6+ Kf7 41.Ne5+ is no more attractive.

39.Qe4+ Ne6 40.Re2 Kf8 41.Qxe6

The game was adjourned here, but **Black Resigned** later without resuming play. The continuation might have been: 41...Qf4+ 42.Bf3 Qxf3+ 43.Ke1 and now: **1)** 43...Nf6 44.Ne5 Qg3+ 45.Kd1 Re7 46.Ng6+! **2)** 43...Qf7 44.Qxf7+ Kxf7 45.Ne5+ Nxe5 46.Rxe5 and the Rook and pawn ending would be easy to win.

POSITION 91

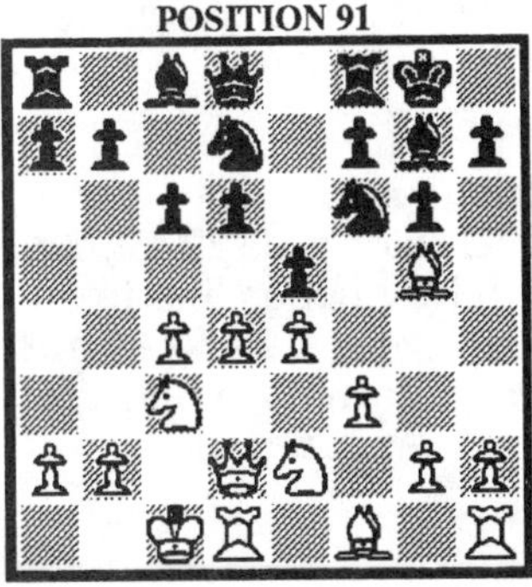

(Sacrificial attack by Black against the White King castled Queenside; from the game Muhring-Johannessen, Moscow, 1956).

1.d4 Nf6 2.c4 g6 3.Nc3 Bg7 4.e4 d6 5.f3 e5 6.Nge2 O-O 7.Bg5 c6 8.Qd2 Nbd7 9.O-O-O (No.91) **9...a6**

White will attack on the Kingside; Black on the Queenside. Black's move is very much to the point.

10.Kb1

Better chances were afforded by 10.d5 c5 11.g4! Qa5 12.Ng3 and 13.h4.

10...b5 11.d5 b4 12.Na4 cxd5 13.cxd5 Qa5 14.b3 Nb6 15.Nb2.

After 15.Nxb6 Qxb6 Black gets his attack in first, as he is ready for ...a5-a4.

15...Nfxd5!!

A very surprising Knight sacrifice which in any event gives Black excellent attacking chances.

16.exd5 Bf5+ 17.Ka1 Rfc8

Threatening 18...Rc2. White must reckon with a possible ...e4.

18.Ng3

This prevents 18...Rc2 since after 19.Nxf5! Rxd2 20.Ne7+ Kf8 21.Rxd2 f6 22.Nc6, retaining Rook and two minor pieces for the Queen. Nonetheless, 18.Rc1 would probably have been a better move. Black would then have had the choice of capturing on d5 – either with or without a preliminary ...Rxc1+ – or by playing 18...e4 with unfathomable complications.

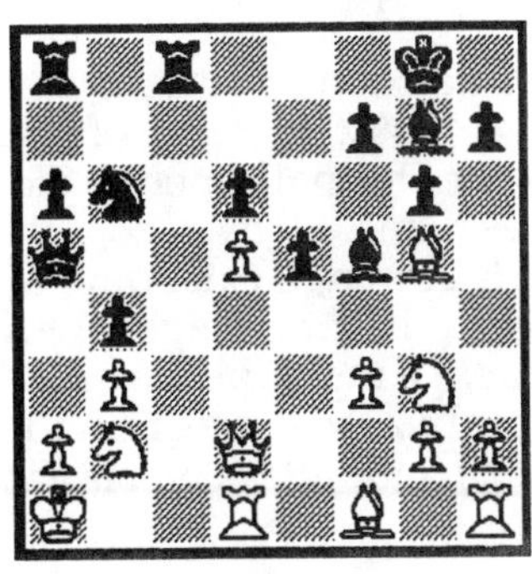

18...Bc2!

Even stronger than 18...Rc2. If now 19.Rc1 then 19...Bxb3.

19.Bc4 Rxc4!

Based on the latent strength of the Bishop lurking on g7. The White Knight dares not leave b2; e.g., 20.Nxc4? e4+ 21.Nb2 Bxb3 winning.

20.bxc4 Bb3

Now Black's attack is overwhelming.

21.Na4 e4+ 22.Kb1 Nxa4 23.axb3 Nc3+ 24.Qxc3

There is no option, for if 24.Kb2 Qa2+ 25.Kc1 Qb1#.

24...bxc3 25.Nxe4 Rb8 26.Kc2 Qa2+ 27.Kd3 Rxb3 White Resigned.

POSITION 92

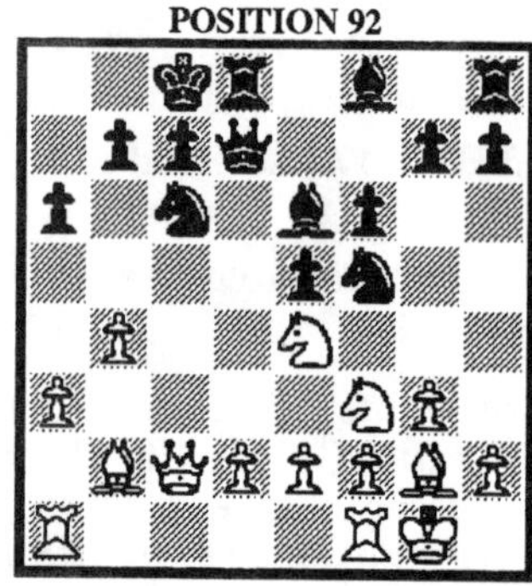

(From the game Olafsson-Duckstein, Wageningen, 1957).

1.c4 e5 2.Nc3 Nf6 3.g3 d5 4.cxd5 Nxd5 5.Bg2 Ne7 6.Nf3 Nbc6 7.O-O Nf5 8.b4 a6 9.Bb2 Be6 10.Ne4 f6 11.a3 Qd7 12.Qc2 O-O-O

Black's decision to castle Queenside was very risky, in view of White's control of the half-open c-file, the weakness created by ...a6, and the White Bg2's range extending all the way down the long diagonal toward the Black King's new residence. Presumably he reckoned on neutralizing the attack on his King by exerting pressure in the central sector. The sequel, however, fails to justify his hopes.

13.Rfc1 Nfd4 14.Bxd4!

Quite correct. The QB is not needed in the coming attack on Black's King.

14...exd4

After 14...Nxd4 15.Nxd4 exd4 White continues 16.Nc5 Bxc5 17.Qxc5 Kb8 18.b5! axb5 19.Rab1 c6 20.a4!, with a strong attack. But now if 15.Nc5, Black can reply 15...Bxc5 16.Qxc5 Bd5!; and White's KB is shut out of the attack.

15.Qb2 d3 16.e3 Kb8 17.Rab1!

White could also have played b5 at once, but the threat is stronger than the execution. In any case, White now threatens b5 with even greater force.

17...Na7 18.Nc5 Bxc5 19.bxc5!

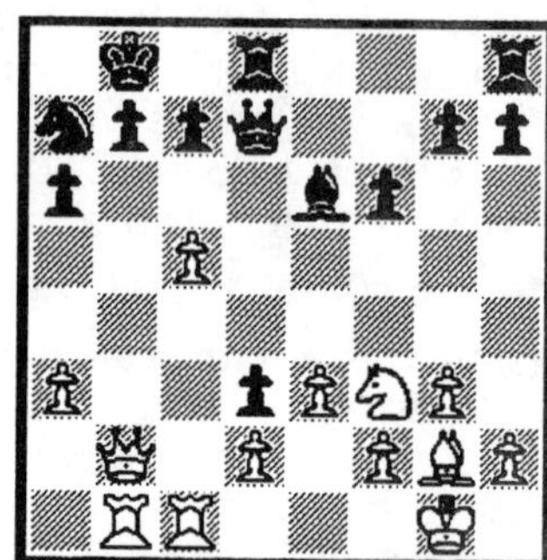

(Once more it is b7 which has to suffer).

19...c6

The obvious 19...Bd5 would be prettily refuted by 20.Ne5!! fxe5 21.c6! Qc8 22.Bh3! and wins.

20.Nd4 Bf7

He still cannot play ...Bd5, e.g., 20...Bd5 21.Bxd5 cxd5 22.c6!, etc. Black had a slightly better line in 20...Bg4; but then comes 21.Rc4! and the pressure against the Black King becomes overwhelming.

21.Qb6!

Threatening to the left 22.Qxa6, and to the right 22.Nxc6+.

21...Ka8 22.Bh3! Nc8

Or 22...Qe7 23.Nf5 Qd7 24.Nd6 and wins.

23.Bxd7 Nxb6 24.Bxc6!

Winding up with a powerful blow. If the Knight moves away the b-pawn falls, while 24...bxc6 25.Rxb6 would be hopeless. **Black Resigned.**

CHAPTER 29
ATTACK AGAINST THE UNCASTLED KING

From the previous chapters one might naively conclude that since the King is exposed to such varied dangers when he castles Kingside, and since castling Queen seems to be an even riskier undertaking, it would be better to not castle at all. Nothing could be farther from the truth. The most perilous situation of all for the King is to be left in the middle. Of course there will be rare cases where this is not so, but exceptions do not invalidate the rule.

This is not difficult to explain. Castling is always part of the mobilization of the pieces-usually an indispensable link in the scheme which aims at getting all of one's forces working together like the parts of a well-oiled machine.

Without castling one cannot connect the Rooks, and there is a likelihood of finding oneself with an army only partly in action facing a fully developed enemy. In this sort of situation, not surprisingly, the King comes in for the hardest knocks.

In Chapter 24 we saw that the presence of the King in the middle often permits the opponent to seize the initiative. To avoid a lot of repetition we could content ourselves here with a glance back at the examples given in that chapter. However, it would not be proper to finish this section on methods of attacking the King without just a few examples of attacking him in the center.

(Open e-file; from the game Colle-Euwe, Antwerp, 1926).

POSITION 93

1.c4 Nf6 2.d4 g6 3.Nc3 Bg7 4.e4 O-O 5.f4 d6 6.Nf3 c5 7.d5 e6 8.Bd3 exd5 9.cxd5 (No.93) **9...Qb6**

With this move Black prevents White from castling, as this would be met by ...c4+ winning a piece.

10.Bc2

After 10.Nd2 Ng4 11.Nc4 Qd8 White still cannot castle, for example, on 12.O-O? Qh4 13.h3 Bd4+ 14.Kh1 Qg3! wins. White's best move is Pachman's 10.Qb3.

10...c4 11.Qe2 Re8 12.Ba4

This only helps Black develop; better was 12.Rb1 in order to play 13.Be3.

12...Bd7 13.Bxd7 Nbxd7 14.Nd2

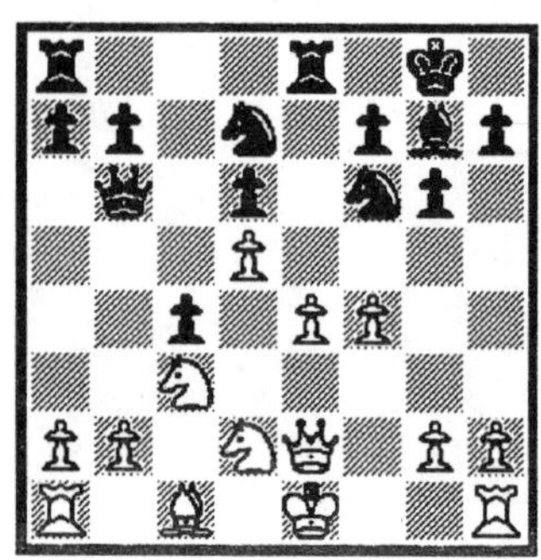

Or 14.Qxc4 Nxe4! 15.Nxe4 Nf6 16.Nd2 Nxe4 17.Nxe4 f5 with a winning attack for Black.

14...Nxe4! 15.Ncxe4

On 15.Ndxe4 the simplest continuation is 15...Bxc3+ 16.bxc3 Nc5.

15...Rac8

Since White has no time to get both his King and Queen into safety, Black permits himself the luxury of protecting his c-pawn. This pawn becomes very important in the attack.

16.Kf1 f5 17.Nxc4 Rxc4! 18.Nf6+

A distress signal. After 18.Qxc4 Black continues 18...Rxe4 19.Qc8+ Nf8 20.Qc2 Bd4 21.Qd3 Nd7 22.g4 Nc5 and the attack crashes through. After White's actual move the attack is even more rapid.

18...Nxf6 19.Qxc4 Ng4

Instantly decisive. If White attends to the mating threat at f2 by 20.Qc2, Black forces mate in a few moves by 20...Qb5+. **White Resigned.**

POSITION 94

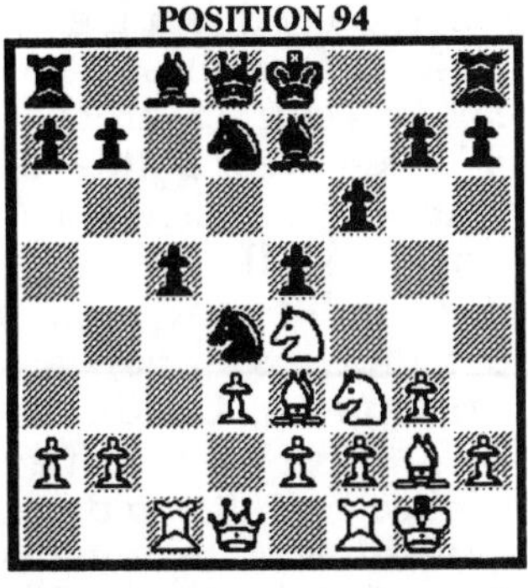

(Open diagonals; from the game Kramer-Soultanbeieff, Terwinselen, 1947).

1.c4 c5 2.Nf3 Nf6 3.Nc3 d5 4.cxd5 Nxd5 5.g3 Nc6 6.Bg2 Nb6 7.O-O e5 8.d3 Be7 9.Be3 f6 10.Rc1 Nd4 11.Ne4 Nd7 (No.94) **12.b4!**

This pawn sacrifice is aimed at liquidating the Black outpost on d4, and make it difficult for Black to castle.

12...Nxf3+ 13.Bxf3 cxb4 14.Qb3 a5

This not only protects the b-pawn, but also prepares to develop the Rook via a6. After 14...f5, or 14...Nf8 White has the powerful 15.Nc5.

15.Qe6!

Threatening mate in two by 16.Nd6+ and 17.Qf7#.

15...Nf8!

The only move. After 15...Nc5 White plays 16.Bh5+! g6 17.Nxf6+ Kf8 18.Bh6#, while 15...Ra6 is met by 16.Nxf6+! Nxf6 (not 16...gxf6 17.Bh5+ and mate next) 17.Qxc8.

16.Nd6+ Qxd6 17.Rxc8+ Rxc8 18.Qxc8+ Bd8 19.Bxb7

White has regained his pawn and still has excellent attacking chances in view of Black's uncastled King.

19...Nd7

There is nothing better. Before Black can get his pieces cooperating White's attack is bound to crash through. For example: **1)** 19...Kf7 20.Rc1 Ng6 21.Qc4+! and wins. **2)** 19...Ne6 20.Rc1 Kf7 21.Rc6 Qe7 22.Ra6, etc.

20.Rc1 O-O

Too late!

21.Bc6 Nb6

On 21...Nb8 White wins with 22.Bc5 Qxc6 23.Bxf8!

22.Qa6!

White still must be precise; after 22.Qb7, Black can still resist by 22...Rf7!.

22...Nd7 23.Qb7

Now this is decisive, for if 23...Rf7 then 24.Bd5.

23...Nb8 24.Bd5+ Kh8 25.Bc5 Black Resigned.

PART EIGHT
THE ART OF DEFENSE
INTRODUCTION

In discussing positional play we availed ourselves of various characteristics, mostly concerned with the placement of the pawns. Combination play we classified under various more-or-less familiar standard operations against the enemy King. In the matter of defense there is a complete lack of such features. The sole characteristic feature of defensive play is the fact that one or even both of the opponents is in danger, and this can be in any sort of position, no matter what the positional or material factors may be.

Until now we have been viewing things from the perspective of the player who has the better game-seeing how he converted his chances into a win or, when he did not follow the correct line, noting how he could have done better. Now we are going to be looking at things from the other side of the issue, alongside the player who is in trouble. We shall realize immediately that it is much harder to conduct a defense accurately than to carry out an attack. In defense the smallest fault may be fatal, whereas a slip on the part of the attacker may do no more than slacken the pace of the attack, or at worst lead to a draw.

Failure in defense is remarkably common, even among the strongest players, and successful defenses are surprisingly rare.

This is not exclusively due to the actual difficulties on the board-the problem of picking one's way through the various dangers. Experience shows that the usual trouble is that the defender sees dangers that are not really there; and being in no fit state to distinguish a real threat from an imaginary one, he becomes confused and eventually loses his head completely.

Anyone who wants to be a successful defender first of all needs nerves of steel. He must be capable of cool deliberation and exact calculation. Staying power is also very important, for the defender must not relax for even a single moment. Only if these requirements are met will he be capable of refuting an enemy attack, or finding a sufficient defense, or deciding which line will give him the best practical chances. Moreover only the cool-headed will be able to make proper use of past experience in organizing his defense.

The number of defensive artists is extremely small. Wilhelm Steinitz was the first to lay down the correct procedure for defense-in so far as one can speak of "correct procedure". Emanuel Lasker went a little farther than Steinitz. So confident was he in his defensive skill that he often assumed an indifferent position in order to tempt his opponent into premature attacks. Lasker scored many of his wins by punishing such attacks. Since Steinitz and Lasker must be regarded as the founders of defensive technique – a technique which, incidentally, still needs development-we devote our next two chapters to a discussion of their ideas on this subject.

CHAPTER 30
WILHELM STEINITZ AS DEFENDER

Steinitz lived at a time when the whole conception of positional play was very vague. The one idea of the average player in those days was-attack at any price. The more pieces sacrificed for the attack, the prettier the game was considered; and whoever got his attack in first was a long way towards winning the game. Quite frequently, one of the players, instead of completing his development, was darting about the board with his Queen in order to grab up enemy pawns. The attack which followed this sort of adventure usually sliced through the position like a knife through butter.

It was Steinitz who first determined a system of methods for conducting positional play by establishing definite principles. If the game is built up in accordance with these principles, particularly with regard to the harmonious development of the pieces, the formation of the center, and the strong and weak points in the position, then we may be certain that in due course attacking chances will be possible. Steinitz also emphasized, however, that defense must be conducted economically. If, for instance, the King's side is threatened there must be enough, but not too many pieces available for the defense. Too few pieces will be unable to stem the assault, but too many, on the other hand, will only get in each other's way. Moreover, they will be needed elsewhere.

Another important principle for the defender is the avoidance of weaknesses. In practice, of course, this is not always practicable, but the damage should be limited as far as possible. Only when it is unavoidable should weaknesses be created. However, elementary this thinking may appear, the records demonstrate that sins against this rule have always been, and still are today, rather frequent.

Steinitz was quite logical in applying his principles in practice. His efforts to avoid creating weaknesses sometimes resulted in most of his pieces retreating to the back rank. If this happens in a modern game, we still call it a "Steinitzian" position-proof that his teachings are still held in high regard.

Here are some examples from the games of Steinitz.

POSITION 95

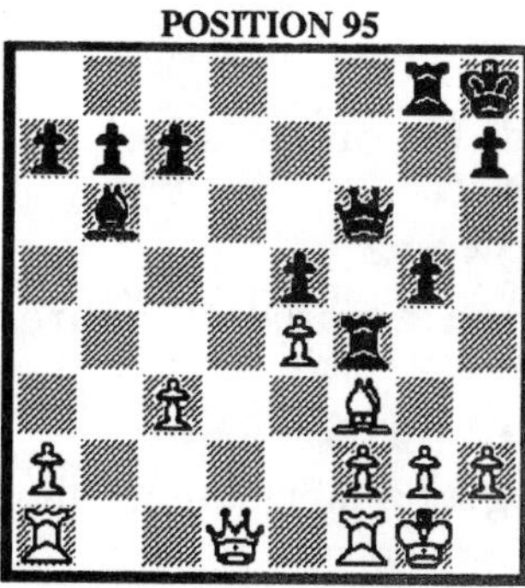

(The avoidance of weakening moves; from a consultation game Chigorin and Ponce vs. Steinitz and Gavilan, Havana, 1889).

Clearly White is on the defensive. Black's last move was ...Rg8, which threatens to push the g-pawn with decisive results: 1...g4 2.Be2 g3 3.hxg3 Rxf2 4.Rxf2 Qxf2+ 5.Kh1 Qxg3.

1.h3?

This is obvious, but in fact a fatal mistake! With 1.h3? White weakens an already seriously compromised position. Steinitz himself gave the correct move to defend for White:

1.Kh1 and if 1...g4 then 2.Be2 Rxf2 3.Rxf2 Qxf2 4.Bxg4; or if 2...Rxe4 then 3.f3! is strong. The real point of the defense is the line 1...g4 2.Be2 Bxf2 3.g3!; then on 3...Rxe4 White has 4.Kg2, while the seemingly strong move 3...Qh6 (4.gxf4? g3!) is met by the counterattack 4.Qd5 Bxg3 5.Qxe5+ Rg7 6.Qe8+, with a draw by perpetual check.

Now let us return to the game to see the move actually played, which contravenes the theory of Steinitz.

1...g4!

A bullseye! Now if 2.Bxg4, Black wins outright with 2...R8xg4 3.hxg4 Rxf2 4.Rxf2 Qxf2+ and mate next move.

2.hxg4 h5!

This pawn cannot be taken because of 3...Rxf3.

3.g5

Forced. He cannot allow Black to play ...hxg4.

3...Rxg5 4.Kh2

Directed against the threat of 4...Rxf3.

4...Rh4+ 5.Kg1 Qf4 6.Re1

Making a flight square for the King at f1.

6...Rxg2+! White Resigned.

He will be mated in a few moves.

POSITION 96

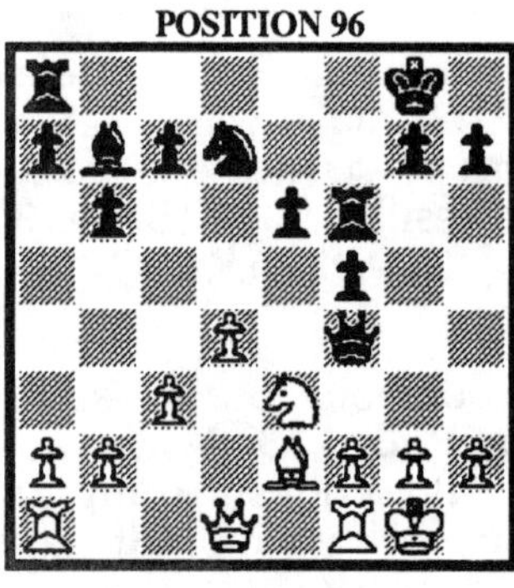

(The defender must be ready to make concessions; from the 2nd Match Game Steinitz-Vasquez, Havana, 1888).

1.e4 e6 2.d4 d5 3.Nc3 Nf6 4.Bg5 dxe4 5.Nxe4 Be7 6.Nxf6+ Bxf6 7.Bxf6 Qxf6 8.Nf3 O-O 9.c3 b6 10.Ne5 Nd7 11.Ng4 Qf4 12.Be2 Bb7 13.O-O f5 14.Ne3 Rf6

Whether Steinitz overlooked something in the opening stages, or whether he purposefully invited his opponent to attack, we shall never know. Certain it is that in the diagramed position, Black's attack has assumed very dangerous proportions. Against this must be set the fact that White has not weakened his position in any way. White must proceed with care; for instance, the attempt to change the state of affairs by the seemingly energetic 15.d5 would react to his disadvantage, as the following variation shows: 15...Rg6 16.dxe6? Qxe3!! 17.fxe3 Rxg2+ 18.Kh1 Rxe2+ 19.Kg1 Rg2+ 20.Kh1 Rxb2+ 21.Kg1 Rg2+ 22.Kh1 Rxa2+ 23.Kg1 Rg2+ 24.Kh1 Rg3+, etc.

15.Re1!

This is in full accord with the Steinitz theory of defense. It avoids the weakening moves h3 or g3, and prepares to answer 15...Rh6 with 16.Nf1.

Meanwhile White is beginning to focus on the weak pawn on e6.

15...Rh6 16.Nf1 Nf6

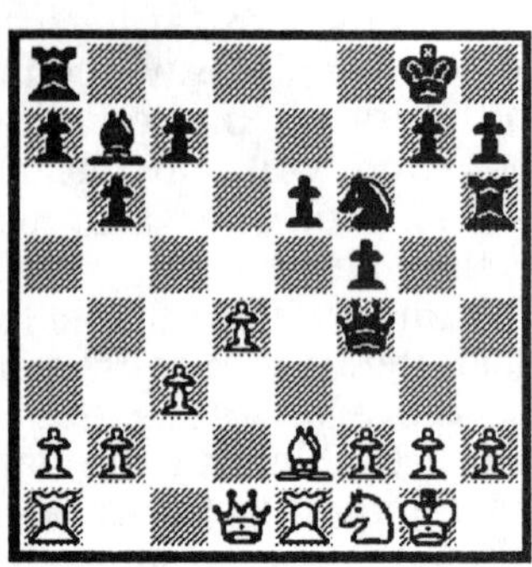

Threatening to force a weakness after all by 17...Ng4.

17.Bf3!

An important decision. Steinitz makes a concession, allowing his opponent to weaken his pawn structure with 17...Bxf3. Then 18.Qxf3 Qxf3 19.gxf3 and Black would no longer have a Kingside attack, and as compensation for the doubled and isolated f-pawn – which is not easy to get at anyway – he would be able to operate against Black's backward e-pawn.

17...Ne4

Black chooses to keep more pieces on the board to maintain attacking chances. Against the sharp move 17...Ng4 White could choose either the safe line 18.h3 Bxf3 19.Qxf3 Qxf3 20.gxf3 Nf6 21.Rxe6, or else the cold-blooded 18.Bxb7 Qxf2+ 19.Kh1, meeting 19...Nxh2 by 20.Nxh2 Qh4 21.Kg1, and 19...Rxh2+ by 20.Nxh2 Qh4 21.Qxg4! fxg4 22.Bxa8 g3 23.Kg1.

18.Re3 Rf8 19.Qa4

The Queen can now be spared from the royal guard, for anything like 19...Nd2 20.Bxb7 Nxf1 21.Kxf1, is not worth considering.

19...a5 20.Rae1

Building up the latent pressure against the e-pawn.

20...Rd8

The Black attack has already passed its peak. After 20...Ba6 21.g3 Qg5 22.Bxe4 Bxf1 23.Bf3! White wins the e-pawn.

21.Ng3

Now the time has come for White to begin his counterattack, and the first step is to remove Black's outpost on e4. This, however, means that White will have to weaken his King's position after all, and this will automatically give Black some renewed attacking prospects.

21...Qh4 22.h3

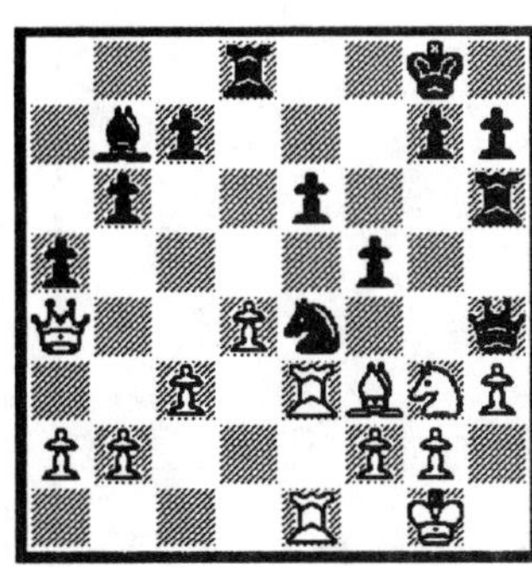

(The defender comes under fire again, but his counterattack saves the day).

22...Nxf2

This is the logical continuation of the attack. The other possibility, 22...f4, would be well-met by 23.Rxe4 Bxe4 24.Rxe4.

23.Bxb7

If 23.Kxf2, Black would reply with 23...Bxf3 and then 24...f4.

23...Nxh3+ 24.gxh3 Rg6?

Bachmann, in his book *Schachmeister Steinitz,* claims that 24...f4 was Black's correct line. Against this 25.Rxe6 would lose to 25...Rxe6 26.Rxe6 Qxg3+ 27.Bg2 f3 28.Re8+ Kf7!. According to Bachmann the only answer – albeit not an unsatisfactory one – to 24...f4 is 25.Bg2.

25.Bg2 Rf8 26.Qc4!

The tables are turned. Steinitz himself is now making threats, and they look like they are more powerful than those of his opponent.

26...Kh8 27.Qxc7 f4 28.Rf1 Rxg3

The only reasonable move, his Rook on f8 being unprotected.

29.Qd6!

Preparing for the execution.

29...Rd8 30.Rxf4!! Black Resigned.

His position bursts like a bubble.

POSITION 97

(Steinitz punishes a pawn sacrifice; from the game Steinitz-Golmayo, Havana, 1889).

1.e4 e5 2.Nc3 Bc5 3.f4 d6 4.Nf3 Nf6 5.fxe5 dxe5 6.Nxe5 Qd4 7.Nd3 Bb6 8.Qf3 Nc6 9.Be2 Bg4 10.Qf4 Bxe2 11.Kxe2 O-O-O

Characteristically, Steinitz has indulged in a risky-looking pawn grab. His King is unsafe, and how to complete development is a real problem.

12.Ne1

Unquestionably the best move, protecting the c-pawn and preparing d3.

12...Nb4

An attempt to cross White's plans. Now if 13.d3 Black plays 13...Nxc2 and White's wall of protecting pawns crumbles.

13.a3! Rhe8!?

Black feels sure he can smash the White position with a few powerful blows. However, things do not turn out that way; Steinitz plays a level-headed defense, not weakening his position any further.

14.axb4 Nxe4 15.Qf5+

An important intermediate check, bringing his Queen to a safer spot.

15...Kb8 16.Nxe4 Rxe4+ 17.Kd1 Rf4 18.Qh3 Re8

Nor could Black carry out his attack through by 18...Qxb4, e.g., 19.d3 Rf2 20.Be3 Qxb2 21.Bxf2 Qxa1+ 22.Ke2 Re8+ 23.Kf1 Qf6 24.Qf3, etc. The White position is not weakened, and Black lacks points of contact.

19.c3 Qc4 20.Kc2 Rf2 21.Nd3 Rfe2

The defense is running smoothly. After 21...Qe4 22.Re1 would enable White to force simplification.

22.b3 Qc6

On 22...Qe4 23.Qf3 would still be the answer.

23.Qf3 Qg6 24.Rf1! R8e3 25.Qf5 Qc6 26.b5 Qd6 27.Nf4!

Retribution is near.

27...Re5 28.Qxf7 R2e4 29.d3

At last!.

29...Re2+ 30.Nxe2 Rxe2+ 31.Bd2 Black Resigned.

POSITION 98

(The punishment of a premature attack; from the game Pillsbury-Steinitz, New York, 1894).

1.d4 d5 2.c4 dxc4 3.Nf3 e6 4.e3 c5 5.Nc3 Nc6 6.Bxc4 Nf6 7.O-O cxd4 8.exd4 Be7 9.Bf4 O-O 10.Rc1 Qb6 (No.98) **11.Nb5**

This appears to be promising, with the threat of 12.Bc7 Qa6 13.Nd6.

11...Ne8

Typical Steinitz! Rather than weaken his pawns (after 11...Nd5 12.Bxd5 Qxb5 13.Bxc6) he is willing to retreat to the back rank.

12.Re1 Na5 13.Bd3 Bd7 14.Nc7 Rc8

Forced, for 14...Nxc7 15.Bxc7 Qb4 16.a3 would lose a piece.

15.Nd5

The point of White's play.

15...exd5 16.Rxe7

White has obtained two advantages: the Bishop pair, and a Rook on the 7th rank. From the sequel it appears that in fact that neither of these is any real advantage at all. The Bishops cannot do much for the time being, and the Rook on e7 is in some danger of being cut off by Black's ...Be6. Meanwhile White has to cope with direct attack down the b-file, and on the other flank with a possible attack on his d-pawn by ...Bg4.

16...Nf6

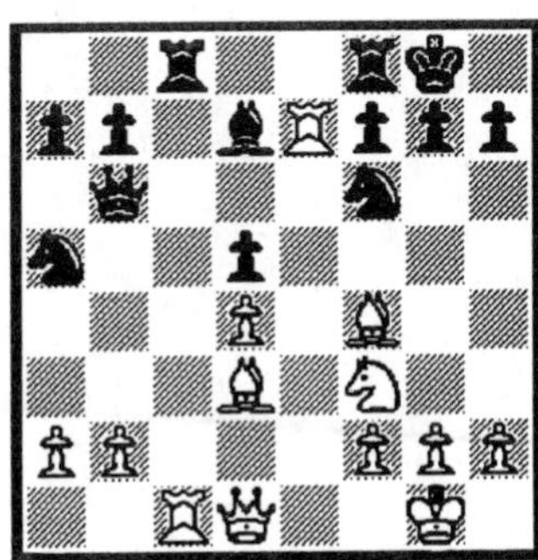

(White needs to push on with his attack)

17.Ng5

The defensive move 17.Re2 is hardly to be considered here. After 17...Bg4 18.R2c2 Rxc2 19.Rxc2 Bxf3 20.gxf3 Nc6 Black would have all the chances. The actually played move involves threats of 18.Nxh7 or 18.Bxh7+, since the Black Knight on f6 is overloaded with the task of defending the Bishop as well as the h-pawn.

17...Bg4 18.Bxh7+

The only way to avoid the loss of a pawn. The d-pawn falls after either 18.f3 Qxd4+ or 18.Qd2 Rxc1+ 19.Qxc1 Qxd4.

18...Nxh7 19.Qxg4 Rxc1+ 20.Bxc1 Nf6 21.Qd1 Nc6 22.Re1 Qxd4

From now on the leading role in the game will be played by Black's isolated but passed d-pawn.

23.Nf3

Fighting for the blockade square at d4. After 23...Qxd1 24.Rxd1 Rd8 25.Nd4 the passed pawn is stopped.

23...Qb6 24.Bg5! Qxb2 25.Re2?

Here White should have been content to clear up the position by 25.Bxf6 Qxf6 26.Qxd5. He tries for more, based on the weakened Black King's position.

25...Qb5! 26.Bxf6 gxf6 27.Rd2 Rd8 28.Nh4

White persists with attacking moves; there was more chance of holding out by28.Nd4, after which the passed pawn really is blockaded.

28...d4!

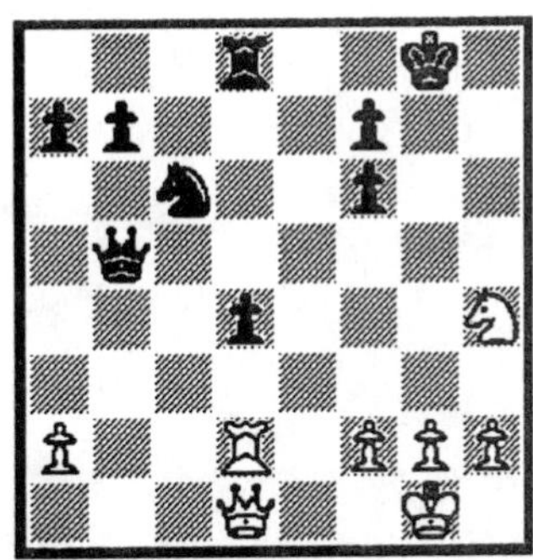

(Because of his superiority in maneuvering space, Black can easily defend his King).

29.Rd3 Ne5 30.Rb3 Qc6 31.Rg3+ Kf8 32.Qd2 Rc8

Steinitz is not worried about the White attack, which will consist merely of a few checks. He himself is now threatening to put an end to the whole business by 33...Qc1+.

33.Qh6+ Ke7 34.Nf5+ Kd7 35.h4 Qc1+ 36.Qxc1 Rxc1+ 37.Kh2 d3

This wins a piece. **White Resigned.**

Let us emphasize the principle laid down in this chapter: *The defender should not weaken his position unless absolutely compelled to do so.* It is all too easy to sin against this rule through taking the obvious line of play. In Example 95, for instance, it is an instinctive reaction to eliminate Black's threatening ...g4 by playing h3. The idea being to avoid the threat of that advance hanging over our head move after move. False reasoning, alas; false reasoning!

CHAPTER 31
EMANUEL LASKER AS DEFENDER

Some of Lasker's contemporaries accused him of black magic. Others believed that he practiced hypnotism on his opponents. These allegations were not taken seriously, of course, but on one thing there was general agreement: Lasker was lucky! He was so lucky that he could get into atrocious positions and still win in the end. There were plenty of most convincing examples to be quoted: against so-and-so, Lasker had won after his opponent had really had all the winning chances; against another Lasker had escaped when his opponent had him practically at his mercy.

Looking back from now, we realize that most of Lasker's contemporaries had no inkling of his remarkable talents. Even the present generation may not have grasped it fully. The real reason behind Lasker's success was his exceptional defensive technique. Whereas Steinitz had based his play primarily on the events on the board, Lasker went one step farther – or, let us say, a step to one side. He was guided by his philosophy of struggle, and was always striving to force his opponents into a fight. From the earliest days of his career he realized that this could best be accomplished by a policy of provocation. He played moves which were intended to goad his opponent into playing for a win, and so unconsciously taking risks which were not strictly necessary.

Lasker made a careful study of his opponents, and his great strength lay in his ability to cause them to believe that they had the better position. If, for instance, a certain player was known to have a predilection for the Bishop pair, then Lasker was quite happy to let him have them. This opponent might then begin to overestimate his chances and avoid drawish lines, only to find presently that his game was deteriorating, his position going from bad to worse, until in the end he was forced to give up in the face of the iron logic of Lasker's play. It is clear that such a style often involved maneuvering on the edge of a precipice; but this was just what Lasker wanted, and it explains the belief, so widely held at the time, that Lasker was a lucky player.

Lasker founded no school. The style he made his own was simply the style of the strongest player. Lasker won because he was much stronger than most of his contemporaries. Not even the strongest player can win all the time, especially if his opponent will take no risks. As a result Lasker was always provoking not only his opponent but also himself – his opponent by voluntarily surrendering to him the better chances, so as to delude him into thinking that he really had a significant advantage; himself because his natural will to survive then drove him into just those double-edged positions which he desired: and so it was war to the bitter end.

Here now are some examples of Lasker's defensive skill.

POSITION 99

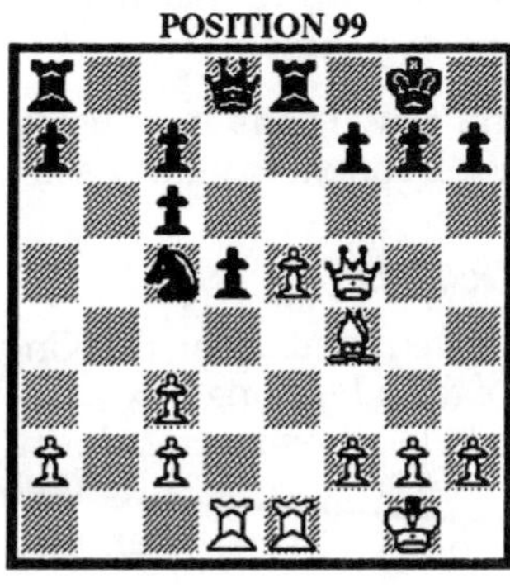

(Lasker goes for a pawn win on the Queenside, regardless of the danger looming against his King; from the game Winawer-Lasker, Nuremberg. 1896).

1.e4 e5 2.Nf3 Nc6 3.Bb5 Nf6 4.O-O Nxe4 5.d4 Be7 6.Qe2 Nd6 7.Bxc6 bxc6 8.dxe5 Nb7 9.Nd4 O-O 10.Nc3 Bc5 11.Nf5 d5 12.Qg4 Bxf5 13.Qxf5 Re8 14.Bf4 Bd4 15.Rfe1 Nc5 16.Rad1 Bxc3 17.bxc3 (No.99) **Qc8**

The White pawn structure is more seriously weakened than Black, and the endgame after 18.Qxc8 Raxc8 19.Rb1 Rb8 clearly favors Black.

18.Qh5

White has greater freedom on the Kingside, chiefly because of his 4-3 pawn majority. It is therefore logical to play for the attack.

18...Qa6 19.Re3 Qxa2

It has been said that anyone who makes this sort of pawn snatch must be either a beginner or a great master. The former captures out of ignorance; the latter, although quite aware of the dangers which exist, reckons that his counterchances will be adequate.

20.Rc1 Qc4 21.Rf3 Ne6 22.Bd2 Re7 23.Rh3 Qe4 24.f3

Tarrasch says in the tournament book this loses too much time. A stronger line is 24.f4 Qg6 25.Qh4 Rd7 26.g4.

24...Qg6 25.Qh4 Rd7 26.f4 Qe4 27.g4

Now, however, Tarrasch prefers 27.Rd3 and 28.Re1 to this advance.

27...Nf8 28.Qf2 a5!

The extra pawn puts in a word, and forces the opponent to make haste with his attack.

29.Re3 Qc4 30.f5

White pushes his attack on the Kingside in view of the advancing a-pawn on the other flank. He does not fear losing the g-pawn: after 30...Qxg4+ 31.Rg3 White's chances would be better than they are now, for the open g-file would be available for his Rooks.

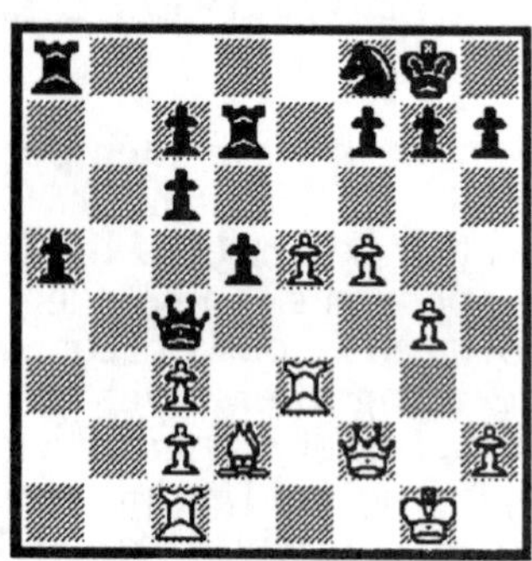

30...a4!

Lasker has conducted the game on correct Steinitzian principles: his castled position has not been weakened, and the condition that defensive resources should be economically deployed is fully satisfied, with one Rook and Knight operating defensively, and the Queen and other Rook offensively. It goes without saying that counter-attack – in the form of a steadily advancing passed pawn-is also not to be forgotten.

31.Rf1

The obvious move, 31.e6, would be met by 31...fxe6 32.fxe6 Nxe6 33.Rxe6 Qxg4+ winning. The line given by Dr. Tarrasch, 31.h3, would fare no better after 31...a3 32.e6 fxe6 33.fxe6 Re7 34.Qf5 a2 35.Rf1 Qxf1+! and again Black wins.

31...a3 32.Ree1 a2 33.h3 c5 34.Kh2

Black's a-pawn is an essential part of the defense of his King, as the following possibility shows: 34.e6 fxe6 35.fxe6 Nxe6! 36.Rxe6 a1=Q winning.

34...d4 35.Qf3 c6 36.e6

At last the long-awaited attack, but it comes too late. The counterattack is too far advanced.

36...fxe6 37.fxe6 Nxe6 38.Qxc6 Rda7 39.Ra1 Rf8

The roles are reversed. Now it is Black who attacks on the Kingside.

40.Rfe1 Nd8 41.Qb6 Raf7 42.Bg5 Rf2+ 43.Kg3

If 43.Kg1 then 43...Qd5 forces mate.

43...Qxc3+

White Resigned. After 44.Kh4 Qxh3+! 45.Kxh3 R8f3+ 46.Kh4 Rh2#.

POSITION 100

(Lasker in a tight corner; from the game Lasker—Dus-Chotimirski, Moscow, 1925).

1.e4 e5 2.Nf3 Nc6 3.Bb5 a6 4.Ba4 Nf6 5.O-O Be7 6.Re1 b5 7.Bb3 d6 8.c3 Na5 9.Bc2 c5 10.d3 O-O 11.Nbd2 Re8 12.Nf1 Qc7 13.Bg5 Rb8 14.a3 Be6 15.h3 h6 16.Bd2 Nc6 17.Qe2 Bf8 18.a4 b4 19.c4 Nd7 20.Be3 g6 21.N3d2 f5 22.exf5 gxf5 23.Qh5 Nf6 24.Qg6+ Qg7 25.Qxg7+ Bxg7 (No.100) **26.f4**

Lasker later admitted that this was a bad continuation. Yet even this bad move displays Lasker's fighting instinct. The fact is that the relatively less bad move 26.f3 would have certainly led to eventual loss, as then White would have no counterplay.

26...Nd7 27.Rad1

In order to meet 27...exf4 28.Bxf4 Bxb2 with 29.Bxd6.

27...Bf7 28.Nb3

What else? 28.b3 is refuted by 28...exf4 29.Bxf4 Nd4.

28...exf4 29.Bxf4 Nd4

It would seem that with this move and Black's next, White's game is doomed.

30.Nxd4 Bxd4+ 31.Kh2 b3!

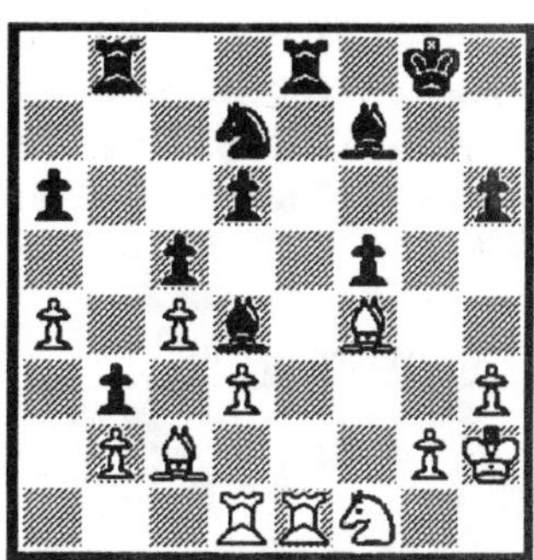

32.Rxe8+

Interpolating an important check. The reply 32...Rxe8 would allow 33.Bxb3.

32...Bxe8 33.Bb1 Ne5 34.Ng3! Bg6

The first piece of negligence. The Bishop would have been more actively placed on d7, retaining the possibility of a subsequent capture of the a-pawn. Bogolyubov's suggested continuation in the tournament book is 34...Bd7 35.Rd2 Nf7 36.a5 Re8 37.Ne2 Bf6.

35.Rd2 Rb4

This looks crushing; nevertheless, Black should have given preference to 35...Nf7.

36.Ne2 Rxa4?

Now 36...Nf7 was essential. White could have then continued with 37.Nc1!.

37.Nxd4! cxd4 38.c5! Ra1 39.cxd6 Nd7 40.Rd1

There is venom in every move. White threatens 41.Bc2! Rxd1 42.Bxb3+! and 43.Bxd1.

40...Bf7 41.Re1 a5?

Missing his last opportunity. According to Bogolyubov he might just have held out by 41...Ra5 42.Re7 Nf8.

42.Re7 Nc5 43.Be5! Ra4

After 43...Rxb1 White would play the same next move.

44.Rc7! Ne6 45.d7 Rb4 46.Rc8+ Kh7 47.Rh8+ Kg6 48.Re8! Rb6 49.Bf4! Nxf4 50.d8=Q Rc6 51.Re7 Black Resigned.

POSITION 101

(Lasker wins a lost game; a famous Match Game Lasker-Janowsky, 1910).

1.d4 d5 2.c4 e6 3.Nc3 c5 4.cxd5 exd5 5.Nf3 Be6 6.e4 dxe4 7.Nxe4 Nc6 8.Be3 cxd4 9.Nxd4 Qa5+ 10.Nc3 O-O-O

One of the most famous "won" positions in the history of chess. Dr. Tarrasch wrote, in his book *Die Moderne Schachpartie* "the White Knight on d4 stands badly, and this must be White's undoing". It is rather sad to think that a world champion–and such a world champion–should get into such a hopeless position by move 10 with the White pieces.

11.a3

Apparently to prevent ...Bc5.

11...Nh6?

Black has several good moves here, each of which should be good enough to win.

The strongest of all would be 11...Bc5! with the point 12.b4 Bxd4! 13.bxa5 Bxc3+ 14.Bd2 Rxd2 15.Qxd2 Bxd2+ 16.Kxd2 Nxa5 and Black wins. No improvement for White is 13.Bxd4 in view of 13...Qg5 14.Nb5 a6.

12.b4 Qe5 13.Ncb5 Nf5!

Black correctly intensifies his pressure against d4. Incidentally he already had an opportunity here to become a victim of a typical Lasker trap: after the obvious move 13...a6 White would have 14.Qc1! axb5 15.Nxc6 bxc6 16.Qxc6+ Qc7 17.Qa6+ Qb7 18.Rc1+ Kb8 19.Bf4+ and wins.

14.Rc1

White must throw everything into a counterattack. The fact that he loses a pawn in the process is of secondary importance.

14...Nxe3 15.fxe3 Qxe3+ 16.Be2 Be7

The reserves arrive. Still Black cannot force the issue with 16...a6 as then White would play 17.Na7+ Kc7 18.N7xc6 bxc6 19.Nxe6+ and White's attack would be as dangerous as Black's.

17.Rc3!

Lasker finds the best moves. The tempting 17.Nxa7+ leads to a win for Black after 17...Kb8 18.N7xc6+ bxc6 19.Nxc6+ Kb7 20.Nxd8+ Rxd8 21.Qc2 Rc8.

17...Bh4+!?

This interpolated check has been much praised. A simpler method would have been 17...Qxc3+! 18.Nxc3 Nxd4 and Black would have all the chances.

18.g3 (see next diagram) **18...Qe4**

Many of Lasker's contemporaries claimed that Black could have clinched the game here by 18...Qxc3+ 19.Nxc3

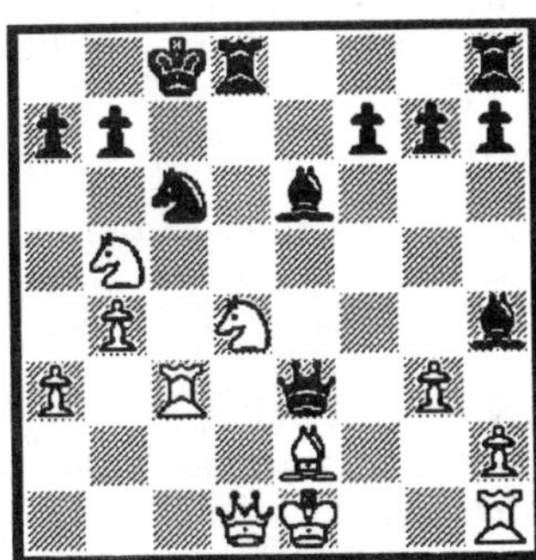

After 18.g3

Bf6 20.O-O Bxd4+ followed by 21...Bxc3. Tarrasch gave the alternative 20.N3b5 (instead of 20.O-O) Nxd4 21.Nxd4 Bxd4 followed by Rhe8.

Later on Lasker had something to say about all this in his well-known manual. After 18...Qxc3+ 19.Nxc3 Bf6 20.N3b5! Nxd4 he remarks that White had a much better move in 21.Qc1+, for then on 21...Kb8 22.Qf4+ Ka8 23.Nc7+ Kb8 24.Na6+ Ka8 25.Qb8+! Rxb8 26.Nc7#. A better move than 20...Nxd4 is 20...Bxd4; but even then after 21.Nxd4 Nxd4 22.Kf2! White is by no means lost.

19.O-O Bf6 20.Rxf6!

This sacrifice is forced, but it leads to a winning attack.

20...gxf6 21.Bf3 Qe5 22.Nxa7+ Kc7

Forced, for if 22...Kb8 23.N7xc6+ bxc6 24.Nxc6+, and the Black Queen will be taken with check.

23.N7xc6 bxc6 24.Rxc6+ Kb8 25.Rb6+ Kc8

If 25...Ka7, he is mated by 26.Rb7+ and 27.Qa4+.

26.Qc1+ Kd7 27.Nxe6 fxe6 28.Rb7+ Ke8 29.Bc6+ Black Resigned.

If 29...Kf8 then 30.Qh6+ forces mate.

(Both sides defend and both sides attack; from the game Lasker-Alekhine, St. Petersburg, 1914).

POSITION 102

1.d4 d5 2.c4 e5 3.dxe5 d4 4.Nf3 Nc6 5.a3 Bg4 6.Nbd2 Qe7 7.h3 Bxf3 8.Nxf3 O-O-O 9.Qd3

This move protects the gambit pawn indirectly: 9...Nxe5 10.Qf5+ Nd7 11.Nxd4.

9...h6 10.g3 g6 11.Bg2 Bg7

Black could have regained the gambit pawn by 11...Nxe5, but after 12.Nxe5 Qxe5 13.Bf4, White would have a strong initiative.

12.O-O Nxe5 13.Nxe5 Bxe5 14.b4!

Until this point the game has been a textbook example of the proper reaction to a gambit. The guiding principle should not be to try to hold on to the gambit pawn, but instead willingness to return it. Here we see Lasker applying this idea. In similar fashion he found an adequate defense to the once dreaded Evans Gambit.

14...f5

Certainly not 14...Nf6? as then 15.f4 Bd6 16.c5 wins the Bishop.

15.c5!

This is in agreement with the principle established in our discussion of open diagonals in Chapter 17. These pawns will now reinforce the action of the KB on the long diagonal.

15...Qe6 16.c6 Ne7!

The best defense under the circumstances; if Black's own pawns do not give an adequate defense for their King then the King will take shelter behind the enemy pawns.

17.cxb7+ Kb8

18.Bb2?

Now Black gets time to start his counterattack. A more incisive method was 18.b5!, followed by a4-a5; then Ba3-c5, and eventually the powerful breakthrough with b6.

18...Rd6 19.Rac1 Rhd8 20.Rc2 f4 21.gxf4 Bxf4 22.Rd1 Nf5 23.Bc1

Lasker always had his weather eye open for tactical pitfalls. He most likely knew exactly what he was doing when he rejected 23.Qe4 Qb3 24.Bc1, which some annotators claimed would have won. However, the highly unpleasant 24...d3! would have put a very different complexion on the game, with Black winning at least the Exchange.

23...Ne3! 24.Rc5!

As usual Lasker is at his best when it comes to a scrimmage.

24...Qf6

Certainly not 24...Nxd1 25.Bxf4 Nb2 because of 26.Bxd6!, threatening 27.Bxc7#.

25.Qe4 Nxd1 26.Bxf4 Nc3?

This fails against Lasker's diabolical continuation. By 26...Nxf2!! on the other hand, attack and defense might yet have remained in equilibrium (27.Bxd6 Rxd6!).

27.Bxd6!! Qxd6

For if 27...Nxe4 then 28.Bxc7+ Kxb7 29.Bxe4+ Ka6 30.b5#!

28.Qe5

Thus Black's attack is repulsed and now White's material advantage gives him an easy win.

28...Qb6 29.Qe7 Qd6 30.Re5 d3 31.exd3 Qxd3 32.Re3 Qd1+ 33.Kh2 Nb5 34.Re6 Nxa3 35.Rf6 Black Resigned.

POSITION 103

(A laborious defense; from the game Lasker-Janowsky, New York 1924).

1.e4 e5 2.Nf3 Nc6 3.Bb5 a6 4.Ba4 Nf6 5.O-O d6 6.Re1 Bg4 7.c3 Be7 8.h3 Bh5 9.d3 Qd7 10.Bxc6 Qxc6 11.Bg5 Bg6 12.Nbd2 h6 13.Bxf6 Bxf6 14.Nf1 O-O 15.Ne3 Rae8

Black has an excellent position. He has the Bishop pair, while White's Knights can find no support points. Apart from the state of affairs on the board, however, there are other factors to be weighed in a game between two chessmasters. In the present case Lasker is very well aware of the fact that Janowsky was a great advocate of the two Bishops. In addition Janowsky's natural optimism was notorious. If he stood a little better he thought he had a won game; if he had some considerable advantage he confidently expected his opponent to strike his colors. All of Lasker's fighting instincts have been aroused by his somewhat unfavorable opening. He has voluntarily conceded the two Bishops to his opponent, prevented any immediate assault by ...g5-g4, and so forced Janowsky into positional warfare.

16.Qb3

As Lasker cannot undertake much himself he concentrates for the moment on thwarting Black's plans, This move prevents on the one hand ...Qd7 followed by ...c6 and ...d5; and on the other hand an eventual ...f5.

16...Bd8

Alekhine, whose excellent analyses in the tournament book we shall now be borrowing, condemned White's next move, which permits Black to play ...f5 without more ado. He suggested instead 17.a4 Kh8 18.a5, so as to be able to play 19.Ra4 if required.

17.Qd5?! Qxd5 18.Nxd5 f5 19.Nd2 Bf7!

Black forestalls 20.exf5 followed by 21.Ne4.

20.Ne3 f4 21.Nec4 Bf6 22.a4 Rd8 23.Na5 Rb8 24.Nf3 g5 25.Nh2 h5 26.Nc4 Be6 27.f3

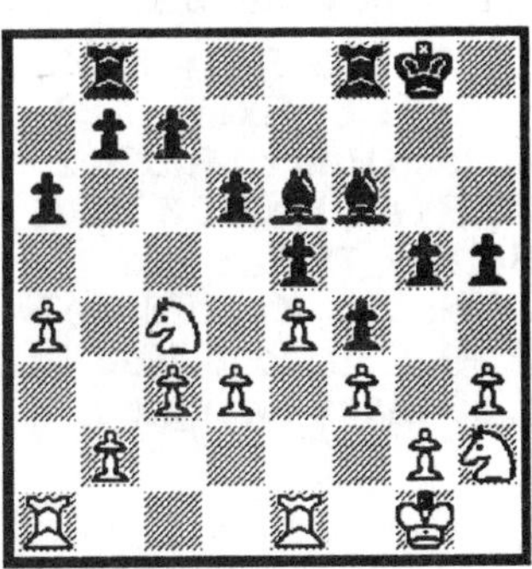

White must prevent ...g4, but in doing so he has to assume a passive structure on the Kingside.

27...Rfd8

Correct. The breakthrough ...d5 is now the indicated method of increasing his advantage.

28.Re2 Kf7 29.a5 Rg8

Black is in no hurry. This move makes room for the other Rook on d8 so as to have not only ...d5 but also ...g4 as possibilities.

30.Ra4 Rbd8 31.Rb4

Putting pressure on Black's one and only weakness.

31...Bc8 32.b3 Rh8

Janowsky is reluctant to give up the idea of direct attack on the White King. Now it seems that he means to double Rooks on the h-file and then play for the decisive trump ...g4.

33.Nb2

Help for the threatened Kingside. The Knight heads for f2 via d1, in order to prevent ...g4.

33...d5!

This is serious!

34.exd5 Rxd5 35.Rc4 c6 36.b4!

Typical Lasker. He shuts in his own Rook in order to induce his opponent to attack it.

36...Bf5 37.Rd2 Rhd8 38.Kf2 Rb5?

Now Black is wandering from the correct path. The proper play was 38...Bxd3 39.Nxd3 Rxd3 40.Rxd3 Rxd3 41.Ke2 e4! 42.Rxe4 Rxc3 and Black has a sound extra pawn.

39.Ke2 Rbd5

Now Black sees that 39...Be6 is no threat at all, for after 40...Bxc4 41.dxc4 the Black Rook is lost, leaving Black a piece down.

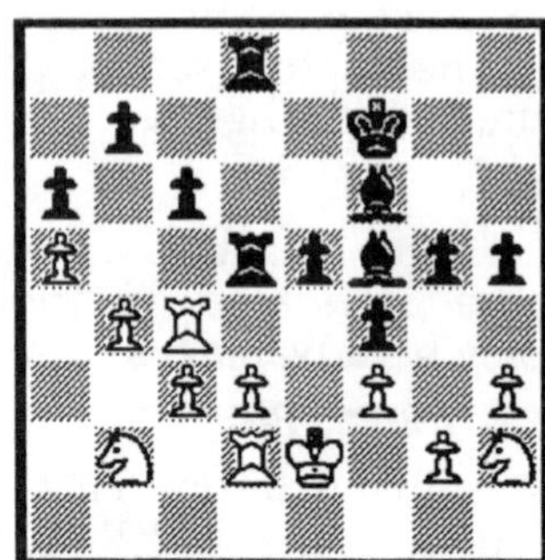

40.Kd1 Ke6?

Again Janowsky misses the right continuation. Correct was 40...Bxd3 41.Nxd3 Rxd3 42.Rxd3 Rxd3+ 43.Kc2 e4! 44.Nf1 exf3! 45.Kxd3 fxg2 and wins.

41.Kc2 Be7

There is no direct decision in sight, but Black still has a won game.

42.Nf1

Now if 42...g4 he can reply with 43.hxg4 hxg4 44.fxg4 Bxg4 45.Ng3.

42...c5

Threatening to roll up the White position by 43...cxb4 44.cxb4 Rb5 45.Kb3 Rd4.

43.bxc5 Bxc5 44.Ra4 R8d7 45.Rd1 Ba7 46.Ra3 g4 47.hxg4 hxg4 48.c4

Mindful of the Steinitz principles Lasker makes concessions only when he must. This move is necessary to let the Rook on a3 defend the d-pawn, and so allow the Nb2 to get into the game at last.

48...R5d6 49.Nd2 Be3?

Alekhine gives 49...Bd4 50.Ne4 Bxb2 51.Kxb2 Bxe4 52.fxe4 Rh7. Another good move was 49...Rh7. White's unexpectedly tenacious resistance is sapping Janowsky's patience.

50.Rh1 gxf3 51.gxf3 Rg7 52.Rh2 Bg1

If 52...Rg3 53.Rb3 Rd7 54.Na4!, with counterplay.

53.Re2 Rg3

Better was 53...Rd8 followed by ...R8g8.

54.Nd1! Rd7 55.Rb3 Rdg7 56.Nc3!

From this point it may be said that equilibrium has been restored. The correctness of this move depends on a pretty indirect defense of White's f-pawn.

56...Be3

Not possible is 56...Rg2 because of 57.Rxb7!.

57.Nd5 Rg2

Black cannot win the f-pawn by 57...Bxd2 58.Rxd2 Rxf3 because of 59.Rb6+! and Black loses a piece.

58.Rxe3! fxe3 59.Rb6+ Kd7

The attempt to refute White's combination by 59...Kf7 fails after 60.Nxe3 Re2 61.Nxf5 R7g2 62.Nd6+ and 63.Ne4.

60.Nxe3 Kc7?

Now 60...Re2! was forced. Then after 61.Nxf5 R7g2 would be powerful. White would have nothing better than 61.Rxb7+ Kc6 62.Rxg7 Rxe3 63.Ne4 Rxf3 and it is not clear how White can make anything out of the extra pawn.

61.Nxf5 Rh7 62.Nd6 Rhh2 63.N6e4

Now, with two Knights and a pawn against a Rook, White has an easy task. The game continued:

63...Rh1 64.Kc3 Rc1+ 65.Kb4 Rd1 66.Nb3 Rxd3 67.Rxb7+ Kc8 68.Rf7 Rb2 69.Nec5 Rd6 70.Rf5 Re2 71.Ne4 Rd3 72.Rxe5 Rb2 73.Nec5 Rxf3 74.Re8+ Kc7 75.Re6 Rc2 76.Nxa6+ Kb7 77.Nac5+ Ka7 78.Re7+ Ka8 79.Na4 Rh2 80.Nbc5 Kb8 81.Rb7+ Kc8 82.a6 Black Resigned.

CHAPTER 32
DEFENSE IN GENERAL

Almost all there is to say about defensive chess can be demonstrated by examples from the games of Steinitz and Lasker. What others have achieved in this sphere after them – no matter how phenomenal – amounts to no more than a return to the conceptions of these two world champions. The games of Steinitz exemplify mostly the so-called passive method of defense, while those of Lasker provide more examples of active defense, in agreement with the idea of struggle which was integral to his philosophic views of chess (and life in general).

In modern tournament chess, so far as one can speak of defense at all, the preference is for active defense, combined with a striving for counter-attack. With masters there is almost always a tendency to avoid defense. Capablanca, as we know, used to steer for simplification as soon as danger threatened.

There is no point in trying to classify defense under various headings. We devote this chapter to a series of defensive actions, some more successful than others. The accent will be on attacks skillfully parried; after all, there is no shortage of unsuccessful attempts at defense; examples are all too plentiful.

POSITION 104

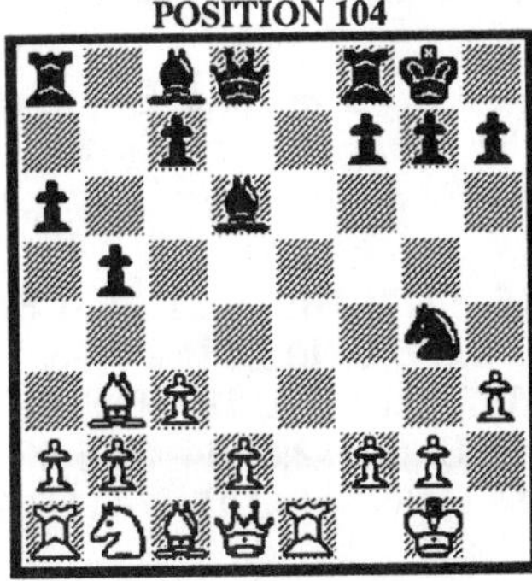

(A famous example of cool-headed defense; from the game Capablanca-Marshall, New York 1918).

1.e4 e5 2.Nf3 Nc6 3.Bb5 a6 4.Ba4 Nf6 5.O-O Be7 6.Re1 b5 7.Bb3 O-O 8.c3 d5 9.exd5 Nxd5 10.Nxe5 Nxe5 11.Rxe5 Nf6 12.Re1 Bd6 13.h3 Ng4!

A very dangerous situation for White has arisen: most of his pieces are undeveloped, and Black is pressing an extraordinarily vigorous attack out of the early opening.

14.Qf3

The Queen must come into action to help defend her King. The capture of the Knight would give Black an overwhelming attack: 14.hxg4 Qh4 15.Qf3 Qh2+ 16.Kf1 Bxg4 17.Qxg4 Qh1+ 18.Ke2 Rae8+ 19.Kd3 Rxe1 20.Qh3 Rxc1; all this according to Capablanca. Later it was found that in this variation White could dramatically switch roles by playing 19.Be6!! (instead of 19.Kd3). However, after 14.hxg4 Qh4 15.Qf3, Black has the winning line 15...Bh2+ and then on 16.Kh1 Bxg4 wins, or if 16.Kf1 then 16...Bxg4 17.Qe4 Bf4! 18.g3 Qh5! wins.

14...Qh4 15.d4

White must find a way to develop his Queenside. Any hasty attempts at counterattack are doomed to failure. Tartakower gave the following variations: **1)** 15.Re8? Bb7! 16.Rxf8+ Rxf8 17.Qxg4 Re8! 18.Kf1 Qe7 19.Qd1 Qe4 20.f3 Qe5 21.d4 Qh2 with a winning attack. **2)** 15.Re4 h5 16.d4 Bb7 17.Rxg4 hxg4 18.Qxb7 Rae8 19.Nd2 Re1+ 20.Nf1 gxh3 and Black wins.

15...Nxf2!

A brilliant continuation of the attack. If now 16.Qxf2, there follows not 16...Bg3? 17.Qxf7+! Rxf7 18.Re8#, but 16...Bh2+!! 17.Kf1 Bg3 and now 18.Qxf7+ fails because Black recaptures with check. After 18.Qe3 Bxh3! 19.gxh3 Rae8 Black has an annihilating attack.

16.Re2!

A fine defensive move, forcing the Knight to a decision since 16...Bg3 is again impossible because of 17.Qxf7+! Rxf7 18.Re8#.

16...Bg4

The try 16...Nxh3+ is poor because of 17.gxh3 Bxh3 18.Re4!, while 16...Bxh3 17.gxh3 Nxh3+ also leads to nothing after 18.Kf1. According to Tartakower, however, 16...Ng4 was well worth consideration. After 17.Re8! Nf6 18.Rxf8+ Kxf8 19.Nd2 Rb8 20.Nf1 Bb7 21.Qf2 the chances would be about even.

17.hxg4!

Forced, for on 17.Qxf2 Bg3 18.Qf1 Bxe2 19.Qxe2 Rae8 Black would win.

17...Bh2+

On 17...Nxg4 there follows simply 18.Bf4.

18.Kf1 Bg3 19.Rxf2

Afterwards Capablanca said that 19.Ke1! would have been more exact.

19...Qh1+ 20.Ke2

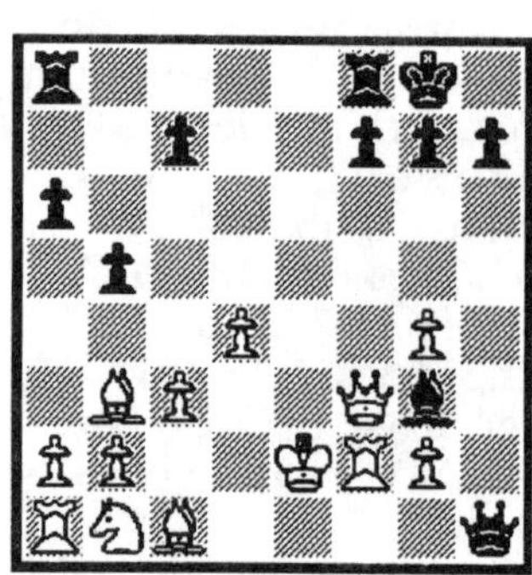

20...Bxf2?

After this White will win easily. The stronger line was 20...Qxc1 21.Qxg3 Qxb2+ 22.Kd3 Qxa1 23.Kc2 b4 24.g5 bxc3 25.Qxc3 after which White's advantage would be only slight.

21.Bd2 Bh4 22.Qh3

The idea of simplification, especially by the exchange of Queens, is one of the oldest and most obvious methods of defense.

22...Rae8+ 23.Kd3 Qf1+ 24.Kc2

And now, with his King in safety, there remains only one problem for White – the development of his Queenside.

24...Bf2 25.Qf3! Qg1

The direct attack by 25...Re2 still permits simplification by 26.Na3 Rxd2+ 27.Kxd2 Qxa1 28.Qxf2 Qxb2+ 29.Nc2. Or White could try to develop his Rook by26.a4, e.g., 26...Qe1 27.axb5 Be3 28.Bc4! Rxd2+ 29.Nxd2 Qxd2+ 30.Kb3 and now 30...axb5 fails against the already familiar 31.Qxf7+!.

26.Bd5! c5 27.dxc5 Bxc5 28.b4 Bd6 29.a4

The last problem is solved, and the issue of the game is no longer in doubt.

29...a5 30.axb5 axb4 31.Ra6 bxc3 32.Nxc3 Bb4 33.b6 Bxc3 34.Bxc3 h6 35.b7 Re3 36.Bxf7+!

Forcing mate in all variations.

36...Rxf7 37.b8=Q+ Kh7 38.Rxh6+ Kxh6 39.Qh8+ Kg6 40.Qh5#.

(Black's attack meets a fine refutation; from the game Rubinstein-Lasker. St Petersburg, 1909).

1.d4 d5 2.Nf3 Nf6 3.c4 e6 4.Bg5 c5 5.cxd5 exd5 6.Nc3 cxd4 7.Nxd4 Nc6 8.e3 Be7 9.Bb5 Bd7 10.Bxf6 Bxf6 11.Nxd5 Bxd4 12.exd4 Qg5 13.Bxc6 Bxc6 14.Ne3 O-O-O 15.O-O Rhe8

POSITION 105

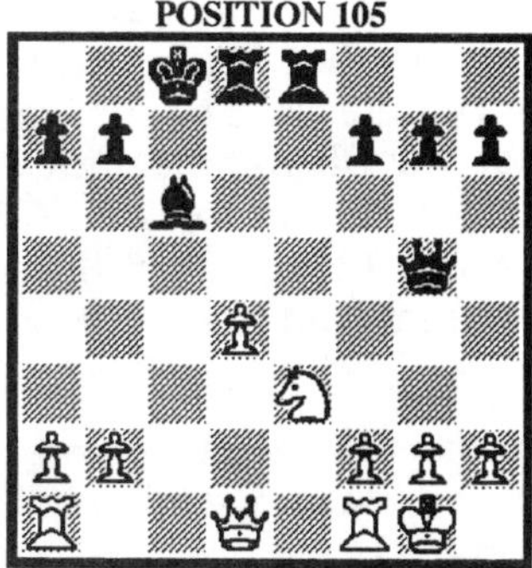

16.Rc1!!

Threatening to assume the attack by 17.Rc5 and 18.d5. There is more to it than that: the text move is part of a highly refined defense, as the sequel demonstrates.

16...Rxe3

Lasker showed in the tournament book that Black would also be in difficulties after 16...Kb8 17.Rc5 Qf4 18.d5 Rxe3 19.Qc1 Re4 20.dxc6 bxc6 21.Qc3.

17.Rxc6+ bxc6 18.Qc1!!

The deep point behind White's 16th move.

18...Rxd4

A better chance was 18...Re5 19.Qxc6+ Kb8 20.dxe5 Qxe5. This variation depends on the two defensive resources 19.f4 Rc5! and 20.f4 Re6!.

19.fxe3 Rd7 20.Qxc6+ Kd8 21.Rf4!

Now he threatens to win by direct attack with Qa8+ followed by Re4+ or Rc4+.

21...f5 22.Qc5 Qe7

After 22...Rd1+ 23.Kf2 Rd2+ 24.Ke1 Qxg2 White wins the Rook by 25.Qa5+. The text leads to a lost ending.

23.Qxe7+ Kxe7 24.Rxf5

And White won as follows:

24...Rd1+ 25.Kf2 Rd2+ 26.Kf3 Rxb2 27.Ra5 Rb7 28.Ra6 Kf8 29.e4 Rc7 30.h4 Kf7 31.g4 Kf8 32.Kf4 Ke7 33.h5 h6 34.Kf5 Kf7 35.e5 Rb7 36.Rd6 Ke7 37.Ra6 Kf7 38.Rd6 Kf8 39.Rc6 Kf7 40.a3 Black Resigned.

POSITION 106

(In a manner analogous to that of Example 105 Rubinstein refutes the attack of another World Champion; from the game Rubinstein-Capablanca, San Sebastian, 1911).

1.d4 d5 2.Nf3 c5 3.c4 e6 4.cxd5 exd5 5.Nc3 Nc6 6.g3 Be6 7.Bg2 Be7 8.O-O Rc8 9.dxc5 Bxc5 10.Ng5 Nf6 11.Nxe6 fxe6 12.Bh3 Qe7 13.Bg5 O-O (No.106) **14.Bxf6 Qxf6 15.Nxd5! Qh6**

On 15...exd5, 16.Qxd5+ wins, as does 15...Bxf2+ 16.Kg2.

16.Kg2 Rcd8 17.Qc1!!

The sparkling point of White's 14th move. Compare the move 18.Qc1!! of the previous example.

17...exd5

No good is 17...Rxd5 as White plays 18.Qxh6 gxh6 19.Bxe6+.

18.Qxc5 Qd2 19.Qb5 Nd4 20.Qd3!

Forcing a favorable liquidation

20...Qxd3 21.exd3 Rfe8 22.Bg4

The translation of White's material advantage into a win is now strictly a matter of technique. Rubinstein won as follows:

22...Rd6 23.Rfe1 Rxe1 24.Rxe1 Rb6 25.Re5!

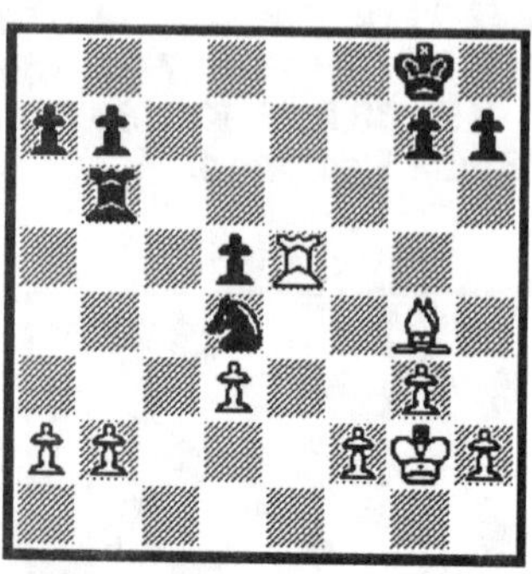

25...Rxb2 26.Rxd5 Nc6 27.Be6+ Kf8 28.Rf5+ Ke8 29.Bf7+ Kd7 30.Bc4 a6 31.Rf7+ Kd6 32.Rxg7 b5 33.Bg8 a5 34.Rxh7 a4 35.h4 b4 36.Rh6+ Kc5 37.Rh5+ Kb6 38.Bd5 b3? *(38...Rxa2!! with counterplay–Capablanca)* **39.axb3 a3 40.Bxc6 Rxb3 41.Bd5 a2 42.Rh6+ Black Resigned.**

POSITION 107

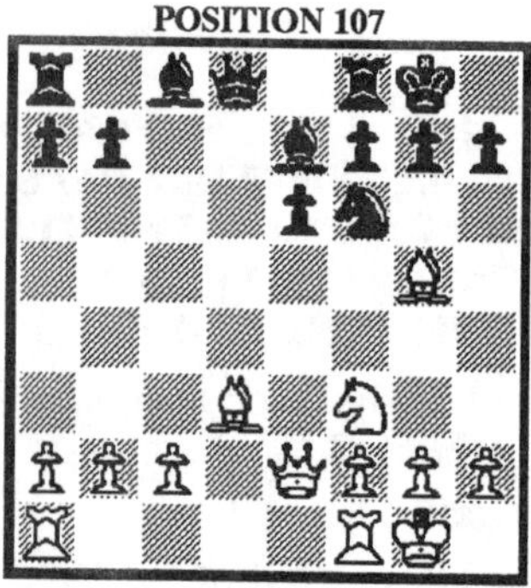

(Rubinstein following in the footsteps of Steinitz; from the game Maroczy-Rubinstein, Karlsbad, 1907).

1.e4 e6 2.d4 d5 3.Nc3 dxe4 4.Nxe4 Nd7 5.Nf3 Ngf6 6.Nxf6+ Nxf6 7.Bd3 c5 8.dxc5 Bxc5 9.O-O O-O 10.Bg5 Be7 11.Qe2

A familiar sort of position. White has the advantage due to his Kingside attacking chances as well as a Queenside pawn majority, which can be important in the ending. We shall see how Rubinstein begins to build a satisfactory defense. The first task is to develop the QB; but the immediate 11...b6 fails tactically to 12.Bxf6 Bxf6 13.Qe4, and if 12...Bd7 then the same continuation would win the b-pawn.

11...Qc7

This protects the b-pawn and thus prepares to develop the QB on d7.

12.Rad1 Rd8

This further preparation for ...Bd7 is perhaps superfluous. It is true that White could answer the immediate 12...Bd7 with 13.Bxf6 Bxf6 14.Bxh7+ Kxh7 15.Qd3+ g6 16.Qxd7. Whether he would have any advantage after 16...Qxc2 is doubtful. The text move seems overcautious, and preference should have been given to 12...Bd7, especially as it would have enabled d8 to be occupied by the QR instead of the KR.

13.c4!

Not only beginning to mobilize the Queenside majority, but also depriving Black of his use of d5.

13...Bd7 14.Bd2

This brings to light another advantage of White's previous move. The Bishop is going to take up an ideal post at c3, from which post it can play an active role in a Kingside attack.

14...Rac8 15.Bc3 Be8

Thus Black has completed his development.

16.Qc2

White "sacrifices" two tempi in order to force a weakening of Black's Kingside, but how important this weakening will be, compared to the loss of time, is difficult to say. White said afterwards that he should have played 16.Ne5.

16...h6 17.Ne5

With such an advanced post as this, it is routine to be able to build up a Kingside attack.

17...Nd7

This is the correct method of defense. The outpost Knight must be removed.

18.Nxd7

Otherwise the Knight goes to c5.

18...Bxd7 19.Qe2!

In spite of the exchange of Knights, which must be considered a minor success for the defense, Black's situation is far from easy. The threat now is 20.Qg4 Bf8 21.Bf6 Re8 22.Qe4 and Black will have to weaken his King position further. We know from Steinitz that weaknesses must be avoided if at all possible.

19...Bc6 20.Qg4

The immediate 20.f4! was stronger.

20...Bf8 21.f4

White threatens to reinforce the attack by f5.

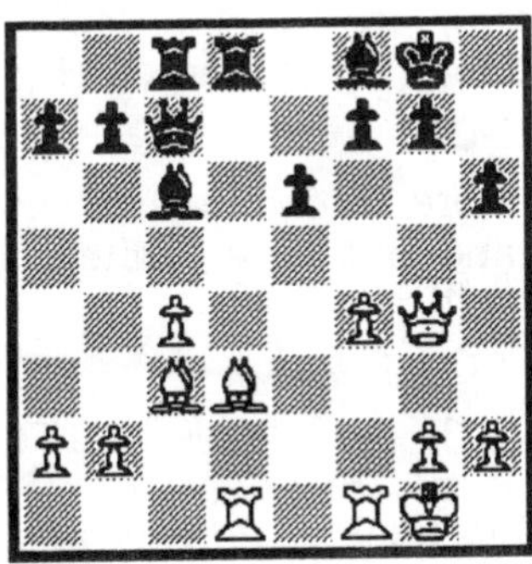

21...Rxd3!

At precisely the right moment Black plays his trump card. For the sacrificed Exchange he gets a pawn and retains the Bishop pair, while at the same time one of White's most dangerous attacking pieces is annihilated. We discussed this sort of exchange sacrifice in Chapter 4.

22.Rxd3 Be4 23.Rd2

It is now White's turn to think of defense. The attempt to keep the attack going by 23.Rg3 would end badly. Maroczy gave the following variation: 23...Qxc4 24.Bxg7? Bf5 25.Qh5 Bxg7 26.Qxh6 Bg6 27.Qg5 Bd4+ and the defense triumphs.

23...Qxc4 24.Rfd1 Bd5

With the fall of the c-pawn, Black has the d5 square again available for his pieces.

25.h3 f5 26.Qg6 Qxf4

Certainly not 26...Qxa2 because of 27.Rxd5 exd5 28.Qe6+ winning.

27.Rxd5!

The Bishop is too powerful, and White is glad enough to give back the exchange.

27...Qe3+! 28.Kh1 exd5 29.Qxf5 Rd8 30.Rxd5 Qc1+ 31.Kh2 Bd6+ 32.Be5 Bc7!

The last defensive move in this game. Black's troubles are now over.

33.Rxd8+ Bxd8 34.Qd7 Qg5 35.Bg3

After 35.Bxg7 Black can give perpetual check beginning with 35...Qf4+.

35...Qe7 36.Qxe7 Bxe7 37.Be5 Kf7 38.Kg3 g6 39.Kf4 Ke6 40.Ke4 h5 41.b3 and the players agreed to a **Draw**.

POSITION 108

(Defense against a gambit; from the game Mieses-Maroczy, Monte Carlo, 1903).

1.e4 e5 2.d4 exd4 3.c3 dxc3 4.Bc4 cxb2 5.Bxb2 d6 6.Ne2 Nc6 7.O-O Be6 8.Bd5 Nf6 9.Qb3 Qc8 10.Nf4

At the time this game was played gambits were still very popular, since most players felt uncomfortable when having to defend. As a rule the player who had won one or more pawns tried stubbornly to hold on to them, arguing that if he could parry the enemy attack without conceding any material his advantage would give him a certain win in the ending. Before the endgame the gods have placed the middlegame, as Dr. Tarrasch used to preach in those days. What he meant by that is drastically shown in the game Mieses-Marshall, Monte Carlo, 1903, which continued as follows: 10...Nd8 11.Bxf6 gxf6 12.Nh5 c6 13.Re1 Be7 14.Qf3 Rg8 15.Nxf6+ Bxf6 16.Qxf6 cxd5 17.exd5 Rg6 18.Qh8+ Kd7 19.Nc3 Bxd5? (Black should have gone in for the drawing combination 19...Qc4! 20.dxe6+ Nxe6 21.Qxa8 Rxg2+! 22.Kxg2 Qg4+; now White must acquiesce to a draw by perpetual check with 23.Kh1 Qf3+ since after 23.Kf1 Black has the attack after 23...Qh3+ 24.Ke2 Nf4+ 25.Kd2 Qd3+, etc). 20.Qe8+ Kc7 21.Nxd5+ Kb8 22.Rac1 Nc6 23.Rxc6! bxc6 24.Rb1#.

The present game was played a few rounds later in the same tournament, and we shall see Maroczy's approach to the problem of this defense.

10...Bxd5! 11.exd5 Ne5 12.Re1 Be7!

Black voluntarily returns one of the pawns, and in doing so is determined to catch up in development. Simple and obvious though this may seem to us today, it must be remembered that this game was played in another era. The principle – brand new at the time – which Black applies here is in general a good remedy for all gambits. It is just this willingness to return the material won whenever it seems proper which has damped the enthusiasm of today's players. This principle of Maroczy's is of the greatest import to the defender.

13.Bxe5 dxe5 14.Rxe5

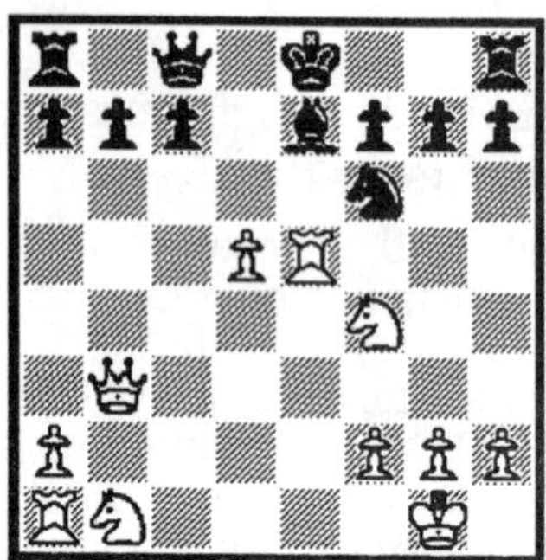

14...Qd7!

Consistent play. Black offers a second gambit pawn as well. After 15.Qxb7 O-O, Black will have completed his development, and with such moves as ...Bd6 will at once go over to a powerful counterattack.

15.Qg3

An attempt to keep the attack going.

15...O-O-O!

Once more Black offers the gambit pawn, and this time White may as well take it.

16.Qxg7 Qd6! 17.Qg5

Forced; 17.Nd3 loses to 17...Nd7 followed by ...Bf6; while 17.Rf5 Qb4! leaves Black with a decisive attack.

17...Rhe8

The counterattack is now in full swing. The end of this game shows once again that the counterattack that follows a successfully conducted defense is very often overwhelming.

18.Nd2 Nd7 19.Rxe7 Qxe7 20.Qg3 Qb4! 21.Nf3 Rg8 22.Qh4 Qc3 23.Rb1 Qxf3 24.Qh6 Nb6 White Resigned.

POSITION 109

(The principle of returning the gambit pawn applied more recently by Smyslov; from the game Penrose-Smyslov, Munich, 1958).

1.e4 e5 2.Nf3 Nc6 3.d4 exd4 4.c3 dxc3 5.Nxc3 Bb4 6.Bc4 d6 7.O-O Bxc3 8.bxc3 Nf6 9.Ba3 Bg4 10.Bb5 O-O 11.Bxc6 bxc6 (No.109) **12.e5 Nd5 13.Qd3?**

An attempt to maintain the initiative; but White should have strived to attain equality by 13.exd6 cxd6 14.c4. As in the previous example Black is prepared to give back his extra pawn, in the conviction that he will at least have some endgame advantage.

13...Re8 14.exd6 Nf4

Quite in the spirit of Maroczy. Without hesitation the defender leaps upon the attacker at the right moment.

15.Qc4 Ne2+ 16.Kh1 Bxf3 17.gxf3 cxd6 18.Qxc6

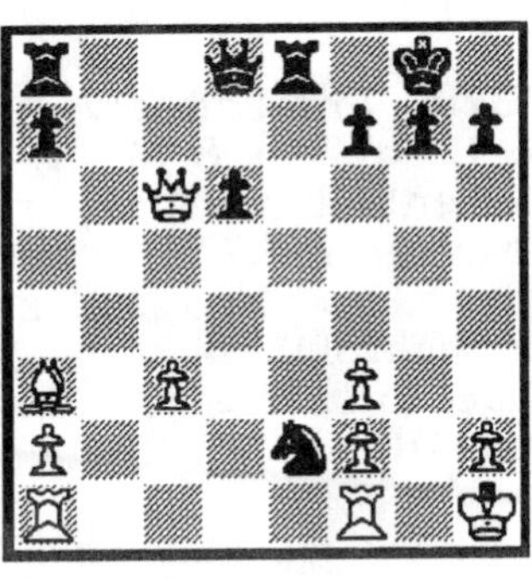

18...Rc8! 19.Qxd6 Qh4!

With the White pawn position ruined, Smyslov plays for mate.

20.Rfd1

Black threatens 20...Qh3, so White intends to meet it with 21.Rd3.

20...Qxf2 21.Rf1 Qh4 22.Rad1 Re6

The heavy artillery goes into action, as Tartakower used to say.

23.Qd7 Ng3+ 24.Kg1

Also insufficient was 24.Kg2; there would follow 24...Re2+ 25.Rf2 Rxf2+ 26.Kxf2 Ne4+ 27.Ke3 Rxc3+!.

24...Rce8 25.Rf2

On 25.hxg3 Black mates with 25...Qxg3+ 26.Kh1 Rh6#.

25...Ne2+ White Resigned.

If 26.Kf1 then 26...Qh3+ 27.Ke1 Nd4+ 28.Kd2 Re2+ and White's Queen is lost.

POSITION 110

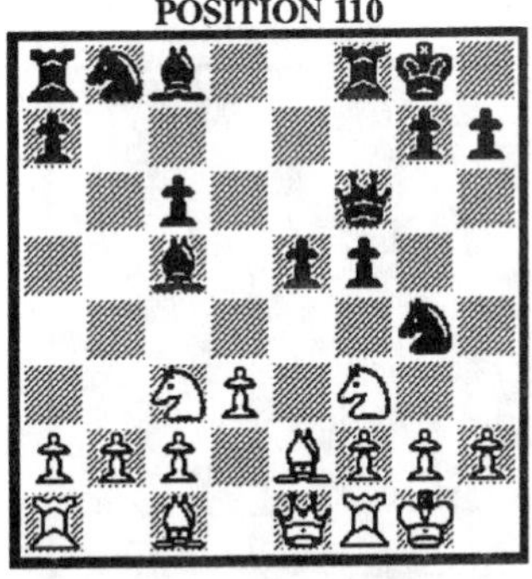

(Defense artist Maroczy in action again; from the game Maroczy-Helling, Dresden, 1936).

1.e4 d5 2.exd5 Nf6 3.Bb5+ c6 4.dxc6 bxc6 5.Be2 e5 6.d3 Bc5 7.Nf3 Ng4 8.O-O f5 9.Nc3 Qf6 10.Qe1 O-O (No.110) **11.h3**

Faithful to the principles of Steinitz, White has so far avoided weakening his King's position. He has deferred h3 until Black has himself castled Kingside, for to have played it while the opponent could have replied with h5 would have suited Black down to the ground.

11...h5?

Now that Black no longer has a Rook on h8, this move is not so threatening as it would have been before castling. Nonetheless, Black's attack is still quite dangerous-underlining yet again the importance of the Steinitzian principle.

12.hxg4 hxg4 13.Ng5 g3

If now 14.Nh3, then 14...Qh4 15.Bg5 Qh7 16.Kh1 f4 17.fxg3 Bxh3 and Black wins.

14.Na4!

Taking the bull by the horns.

14...Bxf2+ 15.Rxf2 f4

After the obvious 15...gxf2+ 16.Qxf2 Black has a shortage of material and no attack.

16.Ne4 Qh4

17.Nxg3 fxg3 18.Rxf8+ Kxf8 19.Bf3!

The same idea as in the two previous examples. White freely returns all his material gains in order to stop the enemy attack. The counterattack then sets in all the more forcibly; e.g., 19...Qxa4 20.Qxe5, and Black is busted.

19...Nd7 20.Qe4 Qh2+ 21.Kf1 Nf6 22.Qxc6 e4

Not 22...Rb8 because of 23.Qd6+; however White should not play 23.Qxa8 as after 23...Qh1+ 24.Ke2 exf3+ Black still has some chances.

23.dxe4 Qh1+ 24.Ke2 Ba6+ 25.Qxa6 Rd8 26.Bf4

Maroczy is consistent to the very end.

26...Qxa1 27.Bd6+ Kf7 28.Qc4+ Kg6 29.e5 Qg1 30.Qc5 Qc1 31.exf6 gxf6 32.Be4+ Kh6 33.Qf5 Black Resigned.

POSITION 111

(A follow-up to the previous game; from the game Reshevsky-Euwe, Amsterdam 1950).

1.d4 Nf6 2.c4 e6 3.Nc3 Bb4 4.Qc2 c5 5.dxc5 O-O 6.Nf3 Na6 7.Bd2 Nxc5 8.a3 Bxc3 9.Bxc3 b6 10.Ng5 (No.111) **10...Re8!**

The only defense against the threatened 11.Bxf6 and 12.Qxh7#. The defense10...g6 is insufficient after 11.b4 Na6 12.h4 h6 13.h5 with a winning attack.

11.b4

If 11.Bxf6 immediately, then 11...Qxf6 12.Qxh7+ Kf8 13.Qh5 Ke7 and suddenly Black has strong counterplay since 14.Qf3 is met by 14...Qxg5 15.Qxa8 Nb3! and Black wins. The flight of the Black King can be compared to that of the White King in Example 110.

11...h6!

Black must conduct his defense as vigorously as possible. After the passive 11...Na6 White could strengthen his position undisturbed.

12.h4

We saw this type of Knight sacrifice also in Example 110. There is, however, the important difference that after acceptance in the present case the attacker will have immediate control of the h-file.

12...hxg5

The logical continuation. After 12...Na6 13.Rd1 Bb7 14.f3! White controls the whole board.

13.bxc5

The obvious continuation of the attack is 13.hxg5. Then play could proceed with 13...N6e4 14.bxc5 Bb7 15.f3 Nxg5 16.O-O-O bxc5 17.e4 and White would have very good chances. However, Black has the better line 14...Nxc3 (instead of 14...Bb7). Then play could continue 15.Qh7+ Kf8 16.Qh8+ Ke7 17.Qxg7 Ne4 18.g6 Rf8 19.Qe5 Bb7 and Black is holding his own.

13...gxh4

In general it is not wise for the defender to open files for the enemy Rooks. Therefore the move 13...g4 suggests itself, but after 14.h5 e5 15.f3, White would retain excellent chances.

14.Rxh4 bxc5 15.Qd3!

15...d6

Threatening to put an end to White's attack by 16...e5. The more obvious 15...d5 would lead to an endgame favorable for White after 16.Qh3 Kf8 17.cxd5 exd5 18.Rh8+ Ke7 19.Bxf6+ gxf6 20.Qe3+ Be6 21.Qxc5+, etc.

16.g4!

White continues the attack with this sharp riposte. The natural defense 16...Kf8 isn't good enough after 17.g5 Ng8 18.Rh8, threatening the destructive 19.Qh7.

16...Bb7!

We know from earlier examples that the defender must not hesitate to give back some of his gains, or even put himself on the debit side of the material balance sheet. Viewed in this light it is therefore of considerable importance for the defender to be a pawn in hand.

17.g5 Ne4 18.Rxe4 Bxe4 19.Qxe4 Qxg5

The air has cleared. Black has broken the direct attack, but this is not to say that all danger of defeat is over. The position indeed is such that White's two Bishops may well be worth more than Black's Rook and two pawns. An analysis of this endgame, however, would fall outside our scope. We give it in brief.

20.Qg2 Qh6 21.Qh3 Qxh3 22.Bxh3 Rab8 23.Bg2 Kf8 24.Kd2 Ke7 25.f4 f6 26.Kc2 Rh8 27.Bf3 Rh4 28.Rg1 Kf7 29.f5? Rxc4 30.fxe6+ Kxe6 31.e4 g5 32.Rh1 Rxc3+! 33.Kxc3 Ke5 34.Rf1 Rf8 35.Bg2 f5 36.exf5 Rxf5 37.Re1+ Kf6 38.Kc4 Rf4+ 39.Kc3 Draw.

(Counterattack is the best form of defense; from the game Panno-Rosetto, Rio de Janeiro, 1957).

1.c4 Nf6 2.Nc3 e6 3.d4 Bb4 4.e3 O-O 5.Bd3 d5 6.Nf3 c5 7.O-O Nc6 8.a3

Bxc3 9.bxc3 dxc4 10.Bxc4 Qc7 11.Bb2 e5 12.h3 e4 13.Nd2 Ne7 14.a4 Ng6 15.Ba3 b6 16.Qe2 Nh4 17.dxc5 bxc5 18.Rab1 Re8

POSITION 112

With the advanced Black e-pawn, and the menacing Knight on h4, the White Kingside is under considerable pressure. Having no way to further strengthen his Kingside position, White strives for counterplay elsewhere.

19.Rb5 Bxh3!?

A promising sacrifice, which sets White some nasty problems. The more obvious move 19...Re5 would have allowed White the powerful counterstroke 20.f4 exf3 21.Nxf3 Nxf3+ 22.Qxf3.

20.gxh3 Qd7 21.f3!

The liquidation of the Black e-pawn is a matter of life and death for White. After 21.Rfb1 Qxh3 22.Qf1 Qg4+ 23.Kh1 Rad8 Black would have many chances.

21...Rad8 22.Rb2!

Strengthening the 2nd rank, and at the same time threatening 23.Bb5.

22...exf3 23.Nxf3 Qxh3 24.Bxf7+

Signaling a clear refutation of Black's attack.

24...Kh8 25.Bxe8 Qg4+ 26.Kh2 Rxe8 27.Nxh4 Qxh4+ 28.Kg1 Qg5+ 29.Qg2 Qxe3+ 30.Qf2 Qg5+ 31.Kh1 h6

Threatening 32...Re4, but it never gets beyond a threat.

32.Qf5 Qe3 33.Bxc5 Qxc3 34.Rc2 Qb3 35.Rcf2 Black Resigned.

POSITION 113

(How Botvinnik won a prize for best defense; from the game Szabo-Botvinnik, Budapest, 1952).

1.d4 e6 2.c4 f5 3.g3 Nf6 4.Bg2 Be7 5.Nf3 d5 6.O-O O-O 7.b3 c6 8.Ba3 Nbd7 9.Qc1 Ne4 10.Nbd2 Bxa3 11.Qxa3 b6 12.Rac1 Bb7 13.Rfd1 Qf6 14.cxd5 exd5 (No.113) **15.Ne1!**

In the Stonewall formation, which we discussed in Chapter 9, the placing of the White Knights on f3 and d3 is the most effective way of exploiting the weakness of the e5 square.

15...a5

Before mobilizing his Rooks Black must protect the a-pawn.

16.Ndf3 f4

Black starts his counterplay at the right moment. If he had waited one more move, White would have taken the opportunity to play Nd3, after which Black would not have found it so easy to advance his f-pawn.

17.Nd3 fxg3 18.hxg3 Rae8

Preventing 19.Nde5, which would now be answered by 19...Nxe5 20.dxe5 Rxe5! 21.Nxe5 Qxf2+ leaving Black with full compensation for the sacrificed material.

19.Rc2

Preparing to double Rooks on the half-open c-file, after which Black will have new difficulties to face.

19...Qh6 20.Qc1

In the endgame White could easily make use of his positional superiority; for in that case Black's attacking chances, which to a certain extent compensate for White's advantages, would be much reduced.

20...Qd6 21.Bh3!

In the context of the struggle for control of e5, the Black Knight on d7 is an important piece, and must be liquidated.

21...Rf6 22.Kg2

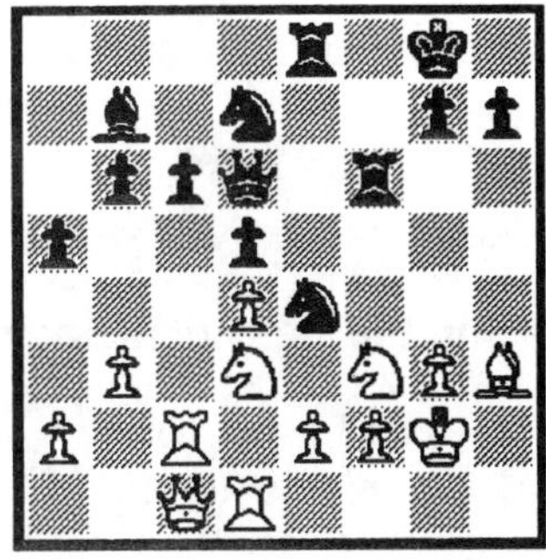

(White wins control of the advance post at e5, and Black defends by counterattack)

The immediate 22.Bxd7 Qxd7 23.Nde5 would allow the strong 23...Qh3!. The King move also forestalls an eventual Knight sacrifice on g3.

22...c5

Black is playing for tactical possibilities based on his Bishop on the long diagonal.

23.Bxd7 Qxd7 24.Nfe5

The dangerous diagonal must be kept closed. After 24.dxc5 bxc5 25.Nxc5 Nxc5 26.Rxc5 d4!, suddenly Black has counterplay.

24...Qd6 25.f4!

Still playing logically to strengthen his support point at e5. On the other hand, 25.f3 would be poor in view of 25...cxd4! 26.fxe4 dxe4 and the Black Bishop becomes terribly active.

25...cxd4 26.Rc7!

At move 20 we remarked that the exchange of Queens would enable White to profit from his positional advantage undisturbed. The same consideration underlies the text move. White is willing to part with the Exchange to get rid of the Queens, and thus brings Black to the very edge of the abyss.

26...Nc5 27.Rxc5 bxc5 28.Qxc5 Qxc5

If Black refuses the exchange of Queens, White would take the front d-pawn and then, with his powerfully placed Knights, would have full compensation for the Exchange. (See Book 1, Chapter 4).

29.Nxc5 Ba8 30.Rxd4 Rc8 31.Ncd3 Rc2 32.Ra4 Rxe2+

After 32...d4+ 33.Kf2 Rh6 34.Ng4 Re6 35.N3e5 h5 36.Rxa5 White has good chances.

33.Kf3 Rc2 34.Rxa5 Rf8 35.Ke3

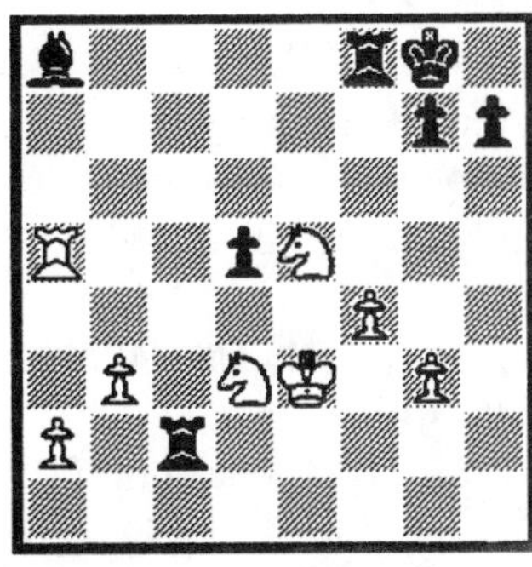

(Black sacrifices a pawn which is only an obstruction to him).

35...d4+!

Black must get the utmost activity from his pieces, and he cannot permit 36.Kd4. The d-pawn is only dead weight, which considerably reduces the scope of his Bishop.

36.Kxd4 Rd8+ 37.Ke3 Rg2 38.g4 Rc2

Up to the 40th move both sides were in time pressure.

39.b4 Bd5 40.a4 Bh1

The last move before the fall of the flag. It would have been better to play the Bishop to g2, so as to have Bf1 in hand.

41.Ra7 Ra2 42.b5 Ra3 43.a5?

By leaving the b-pawn momentarily unprotected, White allows Black a little counter combination which eliminates the worst danger. Stronger was 43.b6, e.g., 43...Bg2 44.a5 Bf1 45.b7 Bxd3 46.Ra8 Ba6+ 47.Kf2 Ra2+ 48.Kg3 Ra3+ 49.Kh4, and White wins.

43...g5! 44.f5

After 44.b6 gxf4+ 45.Kxf4 Rd4+ 46.Kf5 R4a4 47.b7 Bxb7 48.Rxb7 Rxa5 Black draws easily.

44...Rd5

With the double threat of 45...Rxe5+ and 45...Rxb5.

45.Re7 Rxb5 46.f6!

Threatening 47.Re8#. Black is faced with a new crisis.

46...Rxe5+

The only move. If 46...Rb8 47.Nd7 wins.

47.Rxe5 Kf7 48.Rf5 Bb7 49.Kd2 (see next diagram)

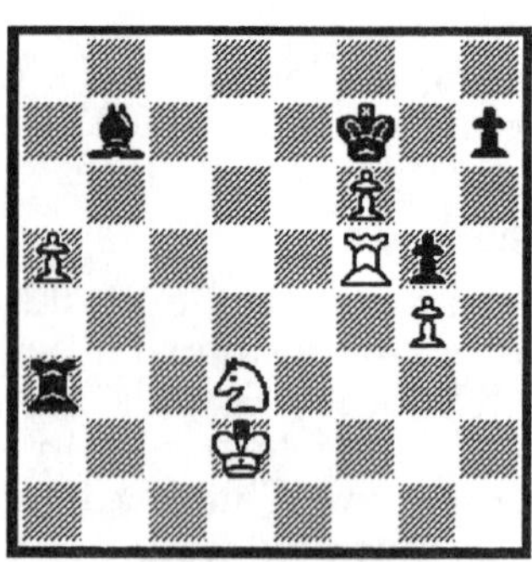

After 49.Kd2

Now White is threatening 50.Ne5+, e.g., 49...h6 50.Ne5+ Kf8 51.f7 Bc8 52.Ng6+ and wins.

49...Bc8! 50.Ne5+ Kf8 51.Rxg5 Rxa5!

The climax of Black's defense. In sacrificing the Exchange Black succeeds in annihilating his opponent's last pawn. Incidentally this is the third exchange sacrifice in this game!.

52.Nd7+

Also possible is 52.Ng6+ and so is 52.f7 Rxe5 53.Rxe5 Bxg4, the consequences being the same in each case.

52...Bxd7 53.Rxa5 Bxg4

Knowledge of the endgame, and judgment in going in for it, are vital matters for the defender. Endgame theory shows that the present position would be drawn even without Black's h-pawn. Many a narrow escape is attributable to the endgame knowledge of the defender. (See for instance Examples 123 and 124).

54.Ke3 Be6 55.Kf4 Bc4 56.Ra7 h5 57.Kg5 h4 58.Kxh4 Draw.

POSITION 114

(Increasing pressure against Black's Kingside; from the game Alekhine-Euwe, Amsterdam, 1936).

1.e4 e5 2.Nf3 Nc6 3.Nc3 Nf6 4.Bb5 Bb4 5.O-O O-O 6.d3 d6 7.Ne2 Ne7 8.c3 Ba5 9.Ng3 c6 10.Ba4 Ng6 11.d4 Re8 12.Bb3 exd4 13.cxd4 (No.114) **13...Be6**

The defender's first priority is to parry the opponent's threats. At this point 14.Ng5 was a decidedly unpleasant one; e.g., 13...Nxe4 14.Nxe4 Rxe4 15.Ng5! (this is stronger than 15.Bxf7+ Kh8) Re7 16.Qh5 h6 17.Qxg6 hxg5 18.Bxg5, and White has a crushing attack.

14.Ng5 Bxb3 15.Qxb3 Qd7

Parrying the two threats of 16.Qxb7 and 16.Qxf7+.

16.f3

The aggressor also needs to make a defensive move. The e4 square needed this extra protection, in view of the threat 16...h6 17.Nh3 Nxe4.

16...h6 17.Nh3 Re6

More accurate was 17...Bb6!, to force White to play 18.Be3.

18.Nf4 Nxf4 19.Bxf4 Bb6 20.Rad1

Compare the previous note. Now that White is able to defend his d-pawn with the QR he has in effect gained an important tempo.

20...Rae8 21.Kh1 d5 22.e5 Nh7

An interesting position. White has a useful 4-to-3 pawn majority on the Kingside, while Black has a corresponding majority on the Queenside. White's majority is more advanced, which gives him definite chances of attack against the Black King. Black has positional compensation for this in that his Bishop is "good" (not obstructed by his own pawns) while White's Bishop is somewhat hampered in this respect.

23.Nf5 f6

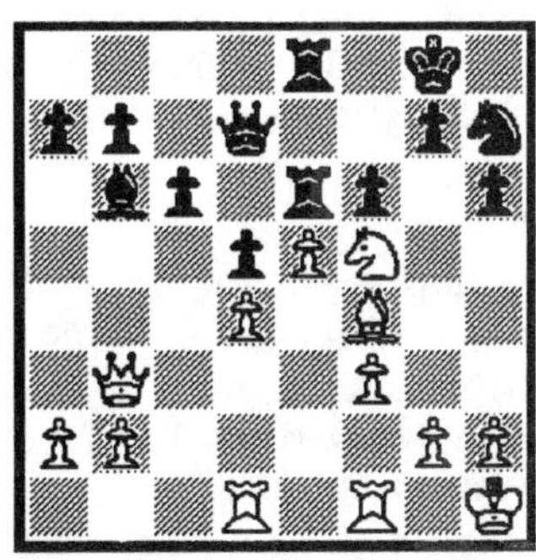

A familiar motif: striking at the opponent's advanced post.

24.g4!

Black's defense was based primarily on taking the sting out of the threat 24.Nd6, which he was planning to meet with 24...fxe5, and then if 25.Nxe8 then 25...exf4; or if 25.dxe5 then 25...Rf8. The text creates new problems.

24...fxe5 25.Bxe5 Nf6

Hoping to shake off the pressure by 26...Bc7. If then 27.Qxb7, Black has 27...Bxe5 28.Qxd7 Nxd7 29.dxe5 Rxe5; or if 27.Bxf6 Rxf6 28.Qxb7 Rb8 29.Qxa7 Rxb2 and Black has a promising counteraction.

26.Qd3

Stops 26...Bc7 which is met by 27.Nxh6+! gxh6 28.Qg6+ Qg7 29.Qxg7+ Kxg7 30.Bxc7, winning a pawn.

26...Kh8

Neutralizing the threat.

27.Rg1

After the direct 27.g5 hxg5 28.Rg1, Black counters with 28...Rxe5 29.dxe5 Bxg1 30.exf6 Bb6 31.fxg7+ Kg8.

27...Bc7

According to plan.

28.f4!

The strength of this move lies in the fact that Black is unable to occupy the newly weakened e4 square. If 28...Ne4 then 29.Bxg7+ Qxg7 30.Nxg7 Nf2+ 31.Kg2 Nxd3 32.Nxe6; while 28...Bxe5 29.dxe5 Ne4 loses to 30.Qxe4!.

28...Qf7

By removing the Queen from the d-file Black now threatens 29...Bxe5 30.dxe5 Ne4. Moreover, against the attempt 29.Nxg7 Black has 29...Rxe5! 30.fxe5 Ne4 up his sleeve.

29.Rdf1 Bxe5 30.fxe5 Ne4!

An important trump in the hand of the defender. Now if 31.Nxh6 Black responds 31...Nf2+ 32.Kg2 Rxh6 33.Rxf2 Rxh2+!.

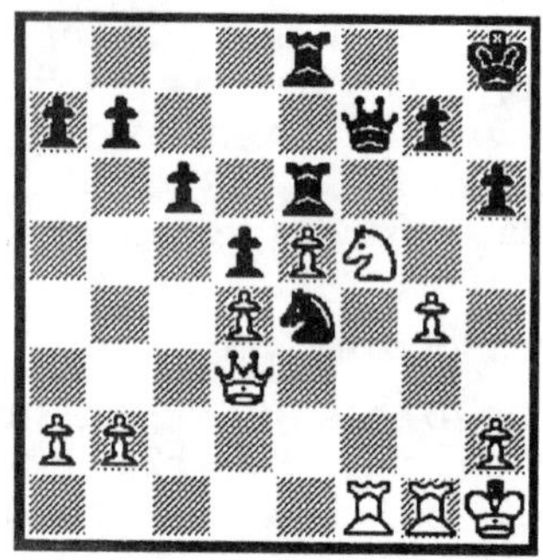

(Attack and defense in equilibrium)

31.g5

White is not content with the drawish line 31.Nd6 Qg6 32.Nxe4 Qxe4+ 33.Qxe4 dxe4 34.Re1 c5. With the text move White has in mind side-stepping this line.

31...hxg5 32.Nd6

If 32...Qg6 then White plays 33.Qh3+!.

32...Nf2+ 33.Kg2 Nxd3 34.Nxf7+ Kg8 35.Nxg5 Rg6

Now not only has Black overcome his difficulties, he even has the initiative.

36.h4

Stronger would have been 36.Kf3 and 37.Kg4.

36...c5! 37.dxc5

After 37.Rf3 c4 Black's Queenside majority would be menacing.

37...Rxe5 38.Kh3

White should be looking for the draw. It is too late for 38.b4 Re4!.

38...Nxc5 39.Rc1 Rc6 40.Rge1 Ne4 41.Rxc6 bxc6 42.Rc1?

Here White could have just held the draw by 42.Nxe4 Rxe4 43.Rxe4! dxe4 44.Kg4 Kh7 45.Kf4 Kg6 46.Kxe4 Kh5 47.Kf5.

42...Nxg5+ 43.hxg5 Re6

And Black won as follows:

44.Kg4 Kf7 45.Rc3 a5 46.Kf3 Kg6 47.Ra3 Kxg5 48.Rxa5 Kf5 49.a4 g5 50.Ra8 Re4 51.Rf8+ Ke5 52.Re8+ Kd4 53.Rb8 c5 54.b4 c4 55.a5 Re3+ 56.Kf2 Ra3 57.Rg8 c3 58.Rxg5 Ra2+ 59.Kf3 c2 60.Rg1 and **White Resigned** without awaiting his opponent's reply.

POSITION 115

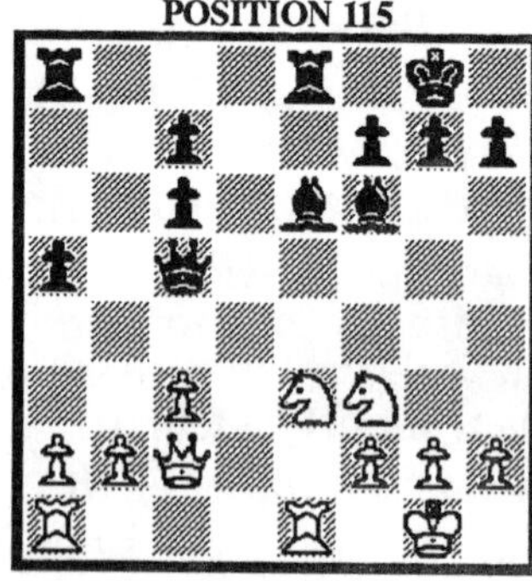

(Combinative defense; from the game Kramer-Van Doesburg, Hilversum, 1940).

1.e4 e5 2.Nf3 Nc6 3.Bb5 Nf6 4.O-O Nxe4 5.d4 Be7 6.dxe5 O-O 7.Qe2 d5 8.exd6 Nxd6 9.Bxc6 bxc6 10.Be3 Bf6 11.c3 Re8 12.Rd1 Qe7 13.Nbd2 Nf5 14.Nf1 a5 15.Qc2 Nxe3 16.Nxe3 Qc5 17.Re1 Be6

The White Knights will be hard pressed to hold their own against Black's far-ranging Bishops. Since

Black is threatening further progress by ...a4-a3, White goes in for the following combinative liquidation.

18.Nd4! Bxd4 19.cxd4 Qxd4 20.Qxc6 Qxb2 21.Nd5

Black was threatening to gain a powerful outside passed pawn by 21...Bxa2.

21...Rac8 22.Nxc7!

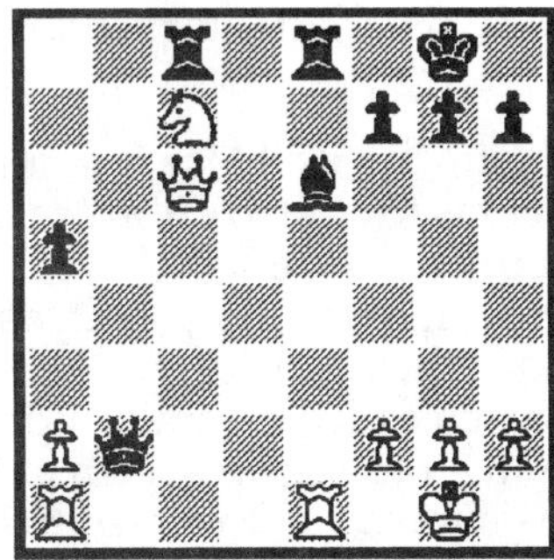

(The elusive Knight)

This is the clever point of the defense. Now no matter what Black tries he cannot prevent the Knight from escaping or White obtaining full compensation by tactical means.

22...Re7

The simplest variation is 22...Red8 23.Nxe6 Rxc6 24.Nxd8 Re6 25.Nxe6. The attempt to improve on this line by 22...Qb8 23.Rec1 Red8 leads to our main line: 24.Rab1 Qa7 25.Nb5! Rxc6 (or 25...Qe7 26.Qe4) 26.Nxa7 Rxc1+ 27.Rxc1 Bxa2 28.Nc6 and now 28...Rc8 loses to 29.Ne7+, while on 28...Ra8 White has 29.Nxa5! just the same. Meanwhile, from the diagram White is threatening to put an end to all danger by 23.Qa4.

23.Nd5! Rxc6 24.Nxe7+ Kf8 25.Nxc6 Bxa2 26.Nxa5 g6 27.Rac1 Draw.

(Active defense; from the game Penrose-Larsen, Hastings, 1956- 57).

POSITION 116

1.e4 c6 2.Nc3 d5 3.Nf3 dxe4 4.Nxe4 Nf6 5.Nxf6+ gxf6 6.b3 Rg8 7.Bb2 Bh6 8.Qe2 Bg4 9.O-O-O Nd7 10.h3 Bh5 11.g4 Bg6 (No.116) **12.h4**

Now it seems that Black is in real trouble; White threatens to win the Bg6 by 13.h5, and there is no evident defense. A whisper went around the tournament room that Larsen's game was lost.

12...Nc5!!

Now if 13.h5, Black has the answer 13...Be4. This solution seems quite temporary and rather shaky. Now if White tries the obvious 13.b4 it appears that Black is once again in the lurch. After the game Larsen revealed that he would have responded 13...Na6! and then 14.h5 Bxc2 15.Kxc2 Nxb4+ followed by 16...Rxg4; he would then have three pawns for the piece and attacking chances, the net result being that Black would be better.

13.Kb1

Unpinning the d-pawn in the belief that Black has nothing better than 13...Be4 after which 14.d4 Bxf3 15.Qxf3 Ne6 16.d5 gives White a tremendous attack.

13...Qd5! 14.d3

Controlling the e4 square. Note that if 14.b4 then 14...Ne6 15.h5 Be4 would be fine for Black.

14...O-O-O!

Now on 15.h5 the saving clause is 15...Be4 because of the pin on the d-pawn. Also 16.Bg2 would be met with 16...Bf5! 17.gxf5 Rxg2.

15.Bh3?

A little stronger was 15.Bg2; then if 15...Bf5 16.Bh3 Bxg4 17.Bxg4+ Rxg4 18.Qxe7.

15...Ne6

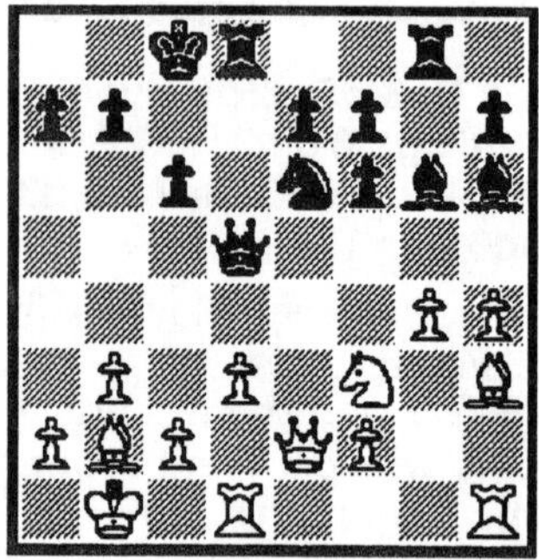

16.g5?

White could still have held the game by 16.h5!, e.g., 16...Nf4 17.Qxe7! Qxf3 18.hxg6 fxg6 19.Qxf6 Rgf8 20.g5+! Nxh3 21.Qe6+, etc.

16...Bh5!

The Bishop which was virtually written off suddenly becomes a trump card.

17.Bxe6+ fxe6 18.Rh3 fxg5 19.hxg5 Rxg5 20.Bc1 Rf5 21.Bxh6 Bxf3 White Resigned.

POSITION 117

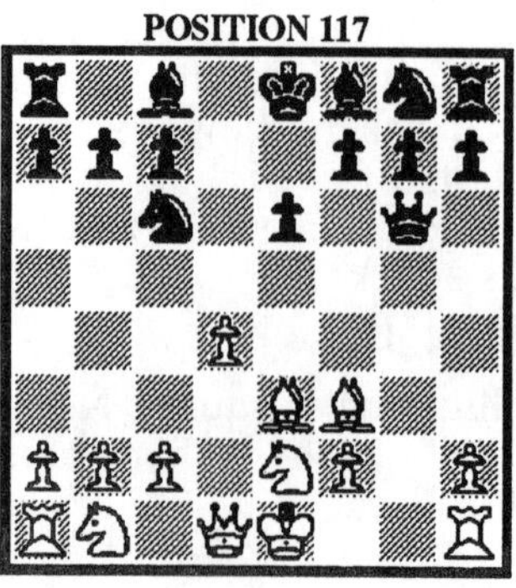

(Nimzowitsch as defender; from the game Brinckmann- Nimzowitsch, Berlin, 1927).

1.e4 Nc6 2.d4 d5 3.exd5 Qxd5 4.Be3 e6 5.Be2 Qxg2 6.Bf3 Qg6 7.Ne2

As compensation for his sacrificed pawn White has a considerable lead in development, and this can lead to a direct attack if he can open up the position. This can be achieved only one way-by the central thrust d5.

7...Nb4

Typical Nimzowitsch! He is going to maneuver his Knight to d5, in order to assert control over the vital d5 square-thus making d5 problematic. This is the strategy which Nimzowitsch called centralization. A player of the old stamp – such as Dr. Tarrasch – would have reacted to this move with undisguised horror.

It is a flagrant violation of the well-known rule: *Do not play any piece twice in the opening.*

8.Na3 Nd5 9.Nc4

We now make use of some of the excellent notes given by Nimzowitsch himself in his book *Chess Praxis*. Here he prefers 9.Nb5, and gives the continuation 9...c6 10.Nf4 Nxf4 11.Nc7+ Kd7 12.Nxa8 Ng2+, with unfathomable complications.

9...Qf6 10.Ng3 Qd8!

Black explains his last two moves by the need to "overprotect" the central point d5. This is another of the ideas he introduced into practice. *Strategically important points,* said Nimzowitsch, *must be overprotected.* The pieces which take part in this overprotection will thereby be well-placed, and as soon as the strategic point concerned finds itself in the front line, the overprotecting pieces will automatically attain maximum activity. Anyone who takes the trouble to glance back at the

Steinitz chapter may come to the conclusion that Steinitz and Nimzowitsch perhaps stand closer together than a superficial examination might suggest.

11.Qd2 Ngf6 12.Ne5 c6!

With iron consistency Nimzowitsch perseveres with his overprotection.

13.O-O

After 13.O-O-O, Black would play 13...Bb4, and after 14.c3 Be7 followed by ...Qc7 and ...Bd7 would still make for the White King.

13...Bd6 14.Kh1 Qc7

Castling is still deferred. If Black castled KR at the present moment he would run into a dangerous attack on the half-open g-file.

15.c4 Nxe3 16.Qxe3 c5!?

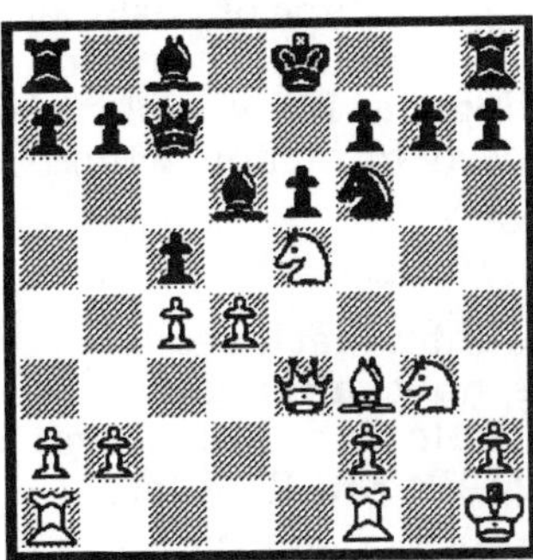

With the intention of opening a counterattack in the center – dangerous tactics while the opponent is better developed. Nimzowitsch correctly concluded that 16...Nd7! would have been stronger than the actually played move.

17.Qg5

Here Nimzowitsch gives two stronger lines for White: **1)** 17.Rae1 cxd4 18.Qxd4. **2)** 17.Nd3 cxd4 18.Qxd4. To these we add another: **3)** 17.Rfe1 cxd4 18.Qxd4, followed by 19.Rad1, which leads to a more harmonious development of the White position. This third possibility, not given by Nimzowitsch, is probably best of all.

17...cxd4

The point being that after 18.Qxg7 Rg8 19.Qxf6 Bxe5 Black has the best of it.

18.Rae1 Kf8!

The natural 18...O-O would allow White possibilities of a violent attack. Here is one pretty variation: 19.Rg1 h6 20.Qf4 Bxe5 21.Rxe5 Nd7 22.Nh5! Qxe5 23.Qxh6 g6 24.Rg5 Qh8 25.Rxg6+!, forcing mate.

19.Rg1 h6 20.Qf4 Bxe5 21.Qxe5

On 21.Rxe5 Black has the strong 21...Nd7.

21...Qxe5 22.Rxe5 Nd7

It would have been wiser to return one of the extra pawns here. After 22...g6! 23.Rd1 Ke7 24.Rxd4 Rd8 Black would win easily.

23.Rb5?

More resourceful would have been 23.Ra5, making Black's task more challenging.

23...a6 24.Rb3

Also losing is 24.Rb4 Ne5 25.Bg2 Nd3!.

24...Nc5 25.Ra3 Rb8

The rest is easy. Black converted his material advantage as follows.

26.b4 Nd7 27.c5 Ne5 28.Re1 Nxf3 29.Rxf3 Bd7 30.Rd3 Rd8 31.Kg1 Bb5 32.Rd2 Rd5 33.Ne4 Ke7 34.Nd6? Rg5+ 35.Kh1 Bc6+ and **White Resigned.**

(Defense in a lost position; from the game Fine-Capablanca, AVRO, 1938).

1.e4 e6 2.d4 d5 3.Nc3 Bb4 4.e5 c5 5.Bd2 cxd4 6.Nb5 Bxd2+ 7.Qxd2 Nc6 8.Nf3 f6 9.Qf4 Nh6 10.Nd6+ Kf8 11.Bb5

POSITION 118

11...Nf7?

This move is a serious error which should lose eventually. The best chance was 11...Nxe5! 12.Nxe5 Ke7 13.Nxc8+ Rxc8 14.Bd3 Qa5+ 15.Kd1 fxe5 16.Qxe5.

12.Nxf7 Kxf7 13.Bxc6 bxc6 14.exf6 gxf6

After 14...Qxf6 15.Qc7+ Qe7 16.Ne5+ Kf8 17.Qxe7+ Kxe7 18.Nxc6+ and 19.Nxd4, with a winning endgame.

15.Ne5+ Kg7

Or 15...Ke8 16.Nxc6 Qd7 17.Nxd4. Also, 15...Kg8 16.Qg3+, transposing into the actual game. Black always comes out a pawn down.

16.Qg3+ Kf8 17.Nxc6 Qd7

There is no choice, since the White Queen must not be allowed into d6. After 17...Qb6 18.Qd6+ Kf7 19.O-O-O e5 20.f4!, and White has a powerful attacking position.

18.Nxd4 e5

A pawn down, and with an insecure King, Black is definitely lost. In the circumstances passive play would be quite hopeless; the only chance is to adopt an active policy. Here, as in so many cases, the best method of defense is attack!

19.Nb3 Qf5 20.Qd3 d4

It may seem surprising that Black makes no attempt to avoid the exchange of Queens. The point is that, with the Queens off, the exposure of the Black King would be less serious, while White's other advantage, the extra pawn, would become problematical since in an endgame the far striding Bishop would be more than a match for the White Knight.

21.O-O Rg8

Exchange of the Queens on d3 would create a closed type of position, with White's d-pawn more or less restraining the Black center pawns. This closed formation would favor the Knight.

22.f4 Bb7

The counterattack really becomes serious now: after 23.Qxf5 Black would mate in a few moves with 23...Rxg2+ 24.Kh1 Rg6+, etc.

23.Rf2 Be4 24.Qd2 Kf7!

Very craftily parrying White's threatened 25.fxe5, which would now be met by25...Rxg2+ 26.Rxg2 Bxg2 and now: **1)** 27.Kxg2 Rg8+ forcing mate. **2)** 27.Qxg2 Rg8 winning the Queen. **3)** 27.Nxd4 Qxe5 28.Kxg2 Rg8+ 29.Kf1 Qe4 30.Re1 Qg4! and Black's attack is still dangerous. **4)** 27.e6+ Qxe6 28.Nxd4 Qg4! and Black has enough counterplay.

25.Re1! Rg4 26.Nc5?

A mistake which could have been disastrous. The right move was 26.fxe5 and if 26...Rxg2+ then 27.Rxg2 Bxg2 28.e6+!, or if 26...Qxe5 then

27.h3! Rh4 28.Qxd4 Qxd4 29.Nxd4 Bxg2 30.Nf5, etc.

26...Bxg2!

A pretty combination, which turns the tables.

27.Rxg2 Rag8! 28.Re2 exf4!

With the double threat of 29...f3 and 29...Qxc5.

29.Nb7 Qd5

Preventing 30.Nd6+, and maintaining both threats.

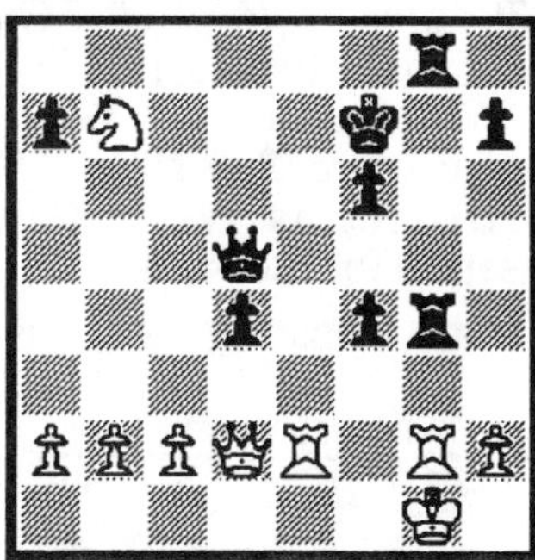

30.Rxg4

The Knight is lost. Now it is White who is struggling to hold the game.

30...Rxg4+ 31.Rg2 Rxg2+ 32.Qxg2 f3! 33.Qh3

Still protecting the Knight indirectly since 33...Qxb7?? loses to 34.Qxh7+.

33...Qg5+ 34.Qg3

Forced, since 34.Kf2 loses after 34...Qe3+ 35.Kf1 Qe2+ 36.Kg1 f2+.

34...Qc1+ 35.Kf2 Qe3+ 36.Kf1 Qe2+ 37.Kg1 Qd1+ 38.Kf2 Qxc2+ 39.Kxf3 Qc6+ 40.Ke2 Qxb7

From the last diagram right down to here, every move was forced. The success achieved by Black in this phase shows that even in apparently lost positions there can be practical chances-a fact that Lasker repeatedly used in many of his wins, as we saw in Chapter 31.

41.b3 Qe4+ 42.Kd2 Qe5?

Not best. Correct was 42...f5!.

43.Qh3 Qg5+

And here 43...Qe4 would still give very good chances to win.

44.Kd3! Draw.

POSITION 119

(A premature Resignation; from the game Popiel-Marco, Monte Carlo, 1902).

Marco Resigned in this position, under the impression that he must lose a piece due to the pin on the Bd4. There is something to be said for resigning a hopeless position, and saving oneself unnecessary brain-racking. In this position, however, there was no need to resign; on the contrary! By playing **1...Bg1!** Black could have not only saved the game but actually won it. This case of premature resignation is a classic example for the advocates of the motto: *No game was ever won by resigning it.*

POSITION 120

(A defense that failed; from the game Kramer-Waling Dijkstra, Leeuwarden, 1954).

1.Nxg5!?

This looks promising as after 1...fxg5 White plays 2.Rxc5+, while 1...Na4 can be met by interpolating 2.Qa3 and then 2...Qe5 is followed by 3.Rc7+, the Rook being immune to capture due to the Knight fork on e6. 1...Na4 2.Qa3 Qxa3 3.Ne6+ Kg8 4.Rxa3 Rdc8 5.Rfa1 Nb6 6.Rxa8 Rxa8 7.Rxa8+ Nxa8 8.Kf1 Nb6 9.Nc5 Nc4 10.Nxb7 Be8 11.Bxc4 dxc4 12.Nd6.

In the actual game Black Resigned at this point. All very neat. Subsequent analysis showed that 1.Nxg5!? is in fact a losing move. For example, after 1.Nxg5!? Na4 2.Qa3, Black should have played 2...Qe5! and after the "finesseful" 3.Rc7+ there are three paths: **1)** 3...Kh6? 4.Rxh7+! Bxh7 5.Nf7+ winning for White. **2)** 3...Kh8? 4.Rxh7+! Kg8 5.f4! and again White wins. **3)** 3...Kg8!! 4.Qe7 Qxe7 5.Rxe7 fxg5 6.Rxb7 and White has only slender chances to draw.

POSITION 121

(Another unsuccessful defense; from the game Pachman-Neikirch, Portoroz, 1958).

1.Bxh7+ Kxh7 2.Qh5+ Kg8 3.Bxg7

This is the celebrated double Bishop sacrifice, the technique of which we saw in Examples 74-77.

3...f5!

The best defense. After 3...f6 Pachman gives 4.Bxf6! and if 4...Rxf6 then 5.Rg5+ Qg7 6.Rd3!, while if 4...Qxf6 then 5.Rg5+ Qxg5 6.Qxg5+ Kf7 7.f5 with a decisive attack.

4.Be5!?

The only way to continue the attack. After 4.Bxf8 Kxf8 5.Rd3 Ba6 6.Rg3 Qf7! White has no good move.

4...Nc4??

In *Fide Review* (4/1958) Pachman gave 4...Qh7, stating that after 5.Qg5+ Kf7 6.d5! (after 6.Qf6+ Ke8 7.Qxe6+ Qe7 Black wins) Bxd5 7.R5xd5 exd5 8.Rxd5 White will win. With the surprising resource 8...Ke8!, it is Black who will win, as White has no compensation for the Rook.

5.Qg6+ Black Resigned.

POSITION 122

(The attacker also can slip up; a miraculous triumph for the defense from the game Czerniak-Eliskases, Mar del Plata, 1940).

1.a7+?

This looks like a clever winning move, but appearances are deceptive. The correct move was 1.d5.

1...Nxa7 2.Rxa7

Now in view of the threat of Ra8+ it looks like it's high time for Black to Resign. But...

2...Rb6!! 3.Qxb6 Rxg3+ 4.fxg3 Qe3+

The White King has no escape from perpetual check.

POSITION 123

(Attack and defense hold one another in equilibrium; from the game Alekhine-Reti, Vienna, 1922).

1.e4 e5 2.Nf3 Nc6 3.Bb5 a6 4.Ba4 Nf6 5.Nc3 b5 6.Bb3 Bc5 7.Nxe5 Nxe5 8.d4 Bd6 9.dxe5 Bxe5 10.f4 Bxc3+ 11.bxc3 O-O (No.123) **12.e5**

Now it's clear that Black can't play ...Ne4 because of 13.Qd5. Also the passive 12...Ne8 is uninviting, while after 12...Re8 13.O-O, the Black Knight has no flight squares.

12...c5!!

Counterattack is the only good defense; after 13.exf6, Black would obtain the better game with 13...Re8+ and 14...c4.

13.Ba3!

Preventing 13...c4 and seemingly refuting Black's last move.

13...Qa5!

One surprise after another.

14.O-O Qxa3 15.exf6 c4

Once more the picture has changed. Black now seems to have the upper hand, but...

16.Qd5!

With the powerful threat of 17.Qg5 g6 18.Qh6 and mate on g7. There is also the crude threat 17.Qxa8.

16...Qa5!

Meeting both threats: 17.Qg5 Qb6+ and 18...Qxf6; or if 17.Qxa8 then 17...Qb6+ and 18...Bb7, winning the Queen.

17.fxg7 Qb6+ 18.Kh1 Kxg7

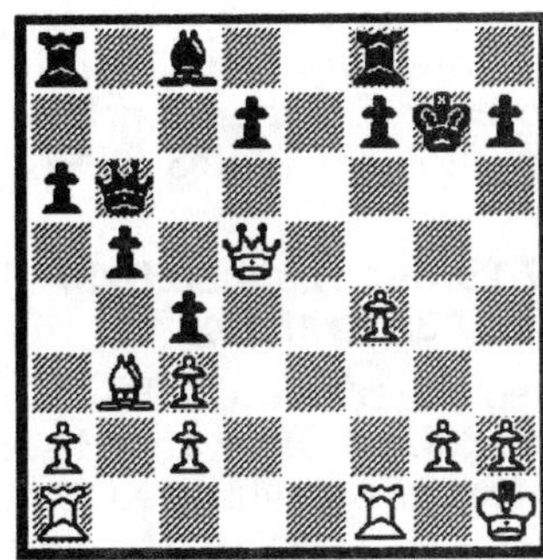

19.Bxc4!

Yet another surprising combination. If 19...bxc4 then 20.Qxa8 Bb7 21.Rab1! and White wins as 21...Qxb1 loses to 22.Qxf8+.

19...Bb7 20.Qe5+ Qf6 21.Bd3 Rfe8!

If Black plays 21...Qxe5 instead, then after 22.fxe5 the endgame is very much in White's favor; e.g., 22...Rac8 23.Rf4 Rxc3 24.Rg4+ Kh8 25.Rh4.

22.Qh5

Still attacking. On the other hand 22.Qxf6+ Kxf6 23.Bxh7 would be fine for Black in view of the line 23...Re2 24.Rg1 Rf2! and White can't respond with 25.Raf1 because of 25...Bxg2+!.

22...h6 23.Qg4+ Kh8 24.Qxd7 Re7 25.Qd4 Qxd4

Black decides to enter a critical endgame. The decision whether an ending is won or drawn is often more a matter of intuition than calculation. In this case it seems that Black has scant compensation for his two lost pawns; however, Reti, who was a celebrated composer of endgame studies, has decided otherwise.

26.cxd4 Rd8 27.f5 f6

Simpler would have been 27...Rxd4, for after 28.f6 Re6 29.Rae1 Rg4! Black would be better, while 27...Rxd4 28.Kg1 f6 29.Rae1 Rg7 transposes into the actual game.

28.Rae1

Black's pieces are starting to demonstrate vigorous activity. If White tries 28.Rf4 then Black would have 28...Rg7 29.Bf1 Rc8 30.Rf2 Rc3 and 31...Bd5.

28...Rg7 29.Be4 Rxd4 30.Bxb7 Rxb7 31.Re6 Kg7 32.Rxa6 Rc4

Even stronger would have been 32...Ra4 33.Rxa4 bxa4 and 34...Rb2, but the text is also sufficient to hold the game. The rest of the ending, which is very interesting, went as follows:

33.Rf3 Rxc2 34.h3 Kf7! 35.Rg3 Rf2 36.Rg6 Rxf5 37.Rxh6 Kg7 38.Rh4 b4 39.Rg4+ Kf7 40.Rg3 Rfb5 41.Rb3 Kg6 42.Kh2 Rc5 43.Ra4 Rcb5 44.h4 R5b6 45.Kh3 Rb8 46.g3 f5 47.Ra5 Rc8 48.Rf3 Rf6 49.Kg2 Rc3 50.Ra8 Rxf3 51.Kxf3 Rc6 52.Rg8+ Kf6 53.Rf8+ Kg6 54.Rb8 Rc4 55.Rb6+ Kg7 56.h5 Rd4 57.Rc6 Re4 58.Rg6+ Kf7 59.g4 Rxg4 60.Rxg4 fxg4+ 61.Kxg4 Kg7 Draw.

POSITION 124

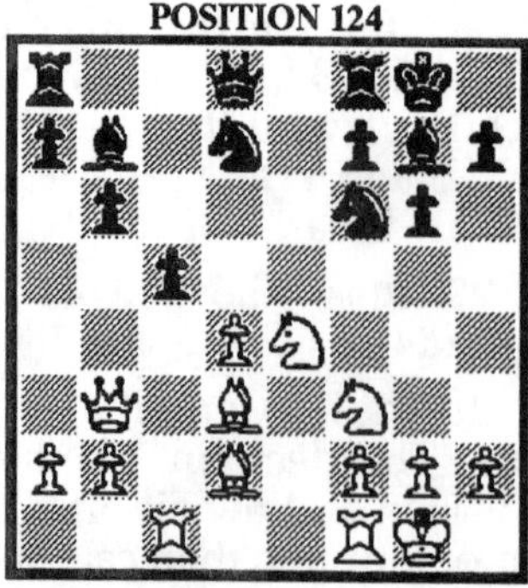

(Another defense based on going over to the endgame; from the game Kramer-Padevsky, Munich, 1958).

1.Nf3 Nf6 2.d4 g6 3.c4 Bg7 4.Nc3 d5 5.e3 O-O 6.Qb3 e6 7.Bd2 b6 8.Rc1 Bb7 9.Bd3 c6 10.O-O Nbd7 11.cxd5 exd5 12.e4 dxe4 13.Nxe4 c5

Now both 14.Nd6 Bxf3 and 14.Bg5 h6 would be poor for White. Also if White tries 14.Nxf6+ Qxf6 15.Bg5 Qd6 16.Rfe1, then Black gets a great advantage by 16...Bxf3 17.gxf3 Bxd4 18.Be7 Bxf2+!; or if 17.Be7 then 17...Qf4, etc.

14.Rfe1

Relatively best, but Black still retains the advantage.

14...cxd4 15.Bb4 Nxe4!

Not 15...Re8 because of 16.Nd6. If White meets the text move with 16.Bxf8, then Black plays 16...Qxf8 17.Bxe4 Bxe4 18.Rxe4 Nc5.

16.Bxe4 Bxe4 17.Rxe4

White hopes to surmount his difficulties with this course. He can now answer 17...Re8 with 18.Rf4! Bh6 19.Rxf7!, while 17...Nf6 allows 18.Rxd4.

17...Nc5! 18.Bxc5 Rc8!!

White's strategy has failed. If now 19.Nxd4 then 19...Bxd4 20.Rxd4 Qxd4! 21.Bxd4 Rxc1+ mating. Or if 19.Qa3 then 19...Qd5 20.R4e1 bxc5 21.Qxa7 c4 and Black's center pawns are dangerously mobile.

19.Bxf8!

A pawn sacrifice in order to force a barely tenable ending.

19...Rxc1+ 20.Re1 Rxe1+ 21.Nxe1 Bxf8 22.Nd3

The Knight's blockade on the light-squares will be the key to White's drawing strategy.

22...Qd7 23.a4 Qe6

Although usually a Queen trade facilitates the exploitation of the extra pawn, in this case it seems that Black would have done better to keep the Queens on the board.

24.Qxe6 fxe6 25.f4

We give the rest without comment. Black's extra pawn proves to be without significance.

25...Kf7 26.Kf2 Ke7 27.Kf3 Kd6 28.Ke4 Bg7 29.b3! a5 30.g4 Bf6 31.h3 Kc6 32.Nf2 Bh8 33.Nd3 b5 34.axb5+ Kxb5 35.h4 h5 36.g5 Bg7 37.Kf3 a4 38.bxa4+ Kxa4 39.Ke4 Kb3 40.Nc5+ Kc2 41.Nd3 Kc3 42.Nf2 Kc4 43.Nd3 Draw.

PART NINE
THE TECHNIQUE OF MANEUVERING
INTRODUCTION

Up to now we have been dealing throughout the book with subjects more or less interesting to players of a very wide range of playing strengths. Our present subject however – methodical maneuvering – is one which many players will find rather uninteresting, or even boring. This in no way invalidates the fact that maneuvering is an important matter; in a sense it plumbs the deepest secrets of chess skill.

It appears that some players have no need whatever to study the technique of maneuvering; the innate talent of Sultan Khan is a case in point. Others – Spielmann, for instance, never grasp the essence of maneuvering. To these players "maneuvering" is just another name for what the Germans refer to as *Sitzfleisch* (a rough translation of which would be to "sit in place").

Maneuvering may be the only way to use the initiative. When one has a certain advantage which cannot be exploited by direct procedures, one must tack about, and approach one's goal by "sailing a zig-zag course". There must, however, be a definite advantage, no matter how small for maneuvering to be practical.

As a requirement for maneuvering, Nimzowitsch suggested that one should have an advantage in space plus at least one or more enemy weaknesses. The advantage must be at least twofold. If, for instance, the one and only weakness is a weak e-pawn, one cannot maneuver against it. One can put pressure on it, of course, but we do not speak of maneuvering unless it is possible to switch suddenly from one target to another; e.g. transferring the pressure to some other weak point, or training one's pieces on the enemy King. Such a Kingside attack may perhaps become possible only as a result of the fact that the enemy forces have been diverted away to defend some other weakness elsewhere. It is frequently the case that the pieces cannot be regrouped quickly enough to meet the second threat.

The theory of maneuvering is still not fully worked out. It may indeed be that it is not subject to any definite laws, since it is all so much a matter of practice. Tarrasch in his day was already making use of maneuvering techniques, which he used to call "cat-and-mouse-play". The only person to make a real study of the subject was Nimzowitsch. We shall go into his ideas in detail, for he must be considered the real founder of the technique of maneuvering. At any rate he was the first to attempt to classify his ideas into some sort of system.

Maneuvering is not a phenomenon exclusively characteristic of the middlegame; it is, if anything, even more important in the endgame. Endgame theory provides a number of cases where the winning scheme has to be based on alternating operations. In endings with Knight vs. Bishop especially this device is constantly cropping up.

Important as this subject is, we must beware of exaggerating it. If the basis for maneuvering is lacking, and one plays on and on, merely in the hope that the opponent will make a mistake sooner or later, this is not maneuvering; it is woodshifting. We return to this point in the game Cohn-Nimzowitsch in Chapter 36.

CHAPTER 33
TYPICAL MANEUVERING

To demonstrate exactly what we mean by maneuvering we now plunge straight into a long game, which will explain our meaning better than words could do.

This game is a five-act play:

Act I The opening, in which White secures a slight advantage.

Act II The first part of the middlegame, in which White's advantage takes concrete form, but in which the game takes on a completely closed character.

Act III The second part of the middlegame, in which, after prolonged maneuvering, White at last achieves the best possible layout for his pieces and then goes over to the attack.

Act IV After the breakthrough several weak spots in the Black position are exposed to attack.

Act V With a surprising turn White wins a pawn, and then converts the material advantage into a win.

(A typical game of maneuver: Petrov-Reshevsky, Semmering-Baden, 1937-Act I. Of only secondary importance for our purpose).

1.d4 d5 2.Nf3 Nf6 3.c4 c6 4.e3 Bf5 5.Bd3 Bxd3 6.Qxd3 dxc4 7.Qxc4 e6 8.Nc3 Be7 9.O-O O-O 10.e4 Nbd7 11.Bg5 h6 12.Bh4 Nb6 13.Qe2 Nfd7

In accordance with the principle that the side with less freedom should seek piece exchanges. A better method of doing this would have been 13...Nh7! planning 14...Ng5, which would begin to put pressure on White's d-pawn as soon as possible.

14.Bg3!

An idea we have seen in Chapter 26. Avoidance of piece exchanges can be of great significance in maintaining the initiative.

14...Bb4 15.a3 Bxc3 16.bxc3

POSITION 125

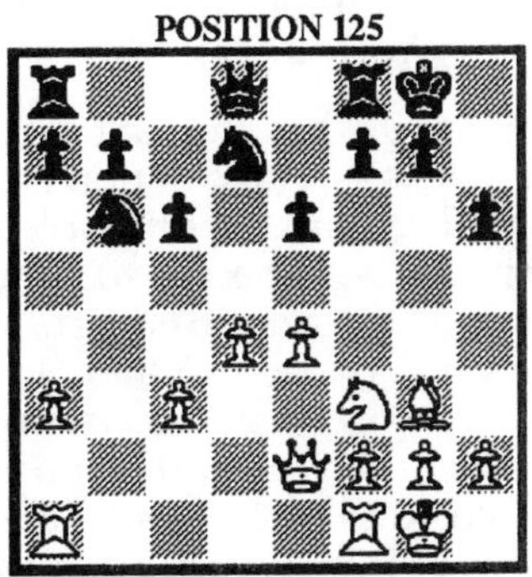

(The beginning of Act II).

White has several advantages. He controls more central space, he has the half-open b-file at his disposal, and his Bishop is beautifully placed.

16...Qe7 17.a4 a5

Black can't allow the further advance of the White a-pawn. Now, however, the half-open b-file takes on an even greater value, since the Black b-pawn has become backward.

18.Rfb1 Rfc8 19.Ne5!

Very strong. Now White threatens 20.Nxd7, winning the b-pawn. If Black plays 19...Nxe5 then 20.Rxb6 also wins the b-pawn after 20...Ng6 21.Qb2 Ra7 22.Rb1.

19...Ra6

The only move.

20.Nc4 Nxc4 21.Qxc4 Nb6 22.Qd3 Rd8 23.c4 e5 24.d5

Not 24.Bxe5? Qxe5 winning a piece.

24...f6 25.Rc1

Threatening 26.c5 and 27.d6.

25...Qc5 26.Kf1!

Again, very well-played. White plans f3 and Bf2.

26...Nd7

Otherwise White will succeed in playing c5 and d6. Black cannot exchange pawns without leaving White in full command of the c-file.

27.f3 Qf8 28.Bf2 c5

This move finishes the first stage of the middlegame. The position is now closed, and on general principles the Knight might be expected to be more valuable than the Bishop. (See Chapters 1-3 of Book One). In the present case, however, it is not so since White: **1)** has a good Bishop (his own pawns on light squares, Bishop on dark squares). **2)** can exert positional pressure on the b-file. **3)** will be able to prepare a breakthrough on the Kingside.

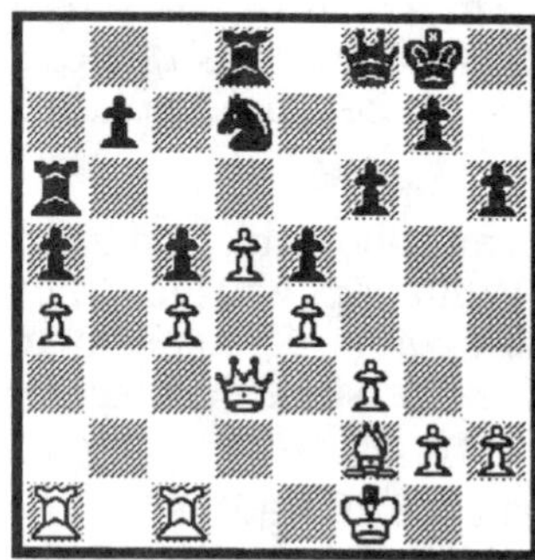

(The beginning of Act III)

Now comes a long series of moves which may seem insignificant taken separately, but which, seen as a whole, exemplify typical maneuvering technique. White gradually builds up the most favorable arrangement of his pieces, always with the Kingside breakthrough in mind. He can allow himself the luxury of making moves – or even conducting whole operations – for the sole purpose of gaining time. Meanwhile Black can do absolutely nothing.

29.Be1 b6 30.Bc3 Qd6 31.Ke2 Raa8 32.Kd2 Rf8 33.Kc2 Rf7 34.Re1 Kf8 35.Re2 Kg8

Black has adopted a passive policy. He has little choice, for the scheme of playing the Knight from d7 to b8-a6-b4 would allow White an immediate central breakthrough. For example, 35...Nb8 36.f4! exf4 37.e5, etc.

36.Rae1 Re8 37.Kb3 Kf8 38.g3

White is making steady progress. His King is in a safe spot on the Queenside, while the rest of his pieces are now so placed that the important advance f4 cannot be long delayed.

38...Ke7

This allows White to play f4 immediately. However, the Black King could not remain on this side of the board much longer. Like his opposite number, he seeks safety on the Queenside.

39.f4!

Black cannot meet this with 39...exf4 because of 40.e5! fxe5 41.Bxe5 and wins.

39...Kd8 40.Qf3 Ref8 41.Qg4 Re7 42.f5

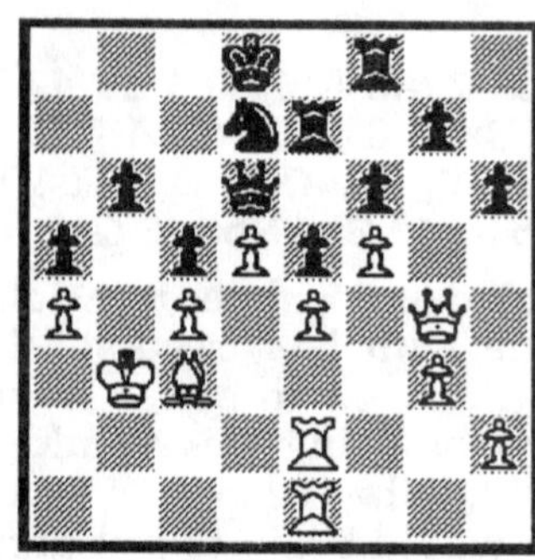

White has made further headway. The Black f-pawn is now fixed, and preparations can begin for the breakthrough by g5.

42...Kc7 43.Qf3 Ree8 44.h4 Rh8 45.g4 Reg8 46.Bd2 Qf8 47.Ka3

White's last few moves have clearly been intended as preparation for g5. Now, however, there follows a series of moves with which White does not seem to be doing anything in particular.

47...Kd6 48.Rg2 Qa8 49.Reg1 Rh7 50.Rg3 Rgh8

If White plays g5 now, Black would control the open h-file. Thus the g5 breakthrough is temporarily prevented.

51.Rh1 Qc8 52.Rgh3 Qg8 53.Qb3 Qd8 54.Rb1

Here White could have proceeded with the g5 break, but it would have led to the exchange of all four Rooks. Therefore, before committing himself White decides to continue maneuvering in the hope of finding a more favorable opportunity.

54...Qa8 55.Rbh1 Qd8 56.Qb5 Qa8 57.R1h2 Qc8 58.Rd3 Qa8 59.Rh1 Rd8 60.Rdh3 Rdh8 61.Kb3 Qc8 62.Kc2 Qa8 63.Kd3 Qc8 64.Be3 Qc7 65.R3h2 Qc8 66.Qb1 Qc7 67.Qg1 Qd8 68.g5!

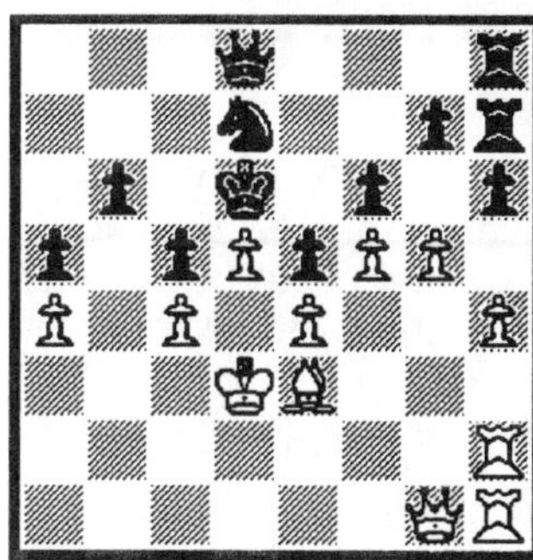

(The beginning of Act IV).

At long last White opens a file. As this move threatens both 69.g6 winning a Rook, and 69.gxh6 gxh6 70.Rg2, controlling the g-file, Black has no option but to take.

68...hxg5 69.hxg5 Rxh2

Black has also placed his pieces to the best advantage, and he can now take off all four Rooks. Nevertheless, White retains a strong initiative.

70.Rxh2 Rxh2 71.Qxh2 fxg5

Black cannot allow 72.g6. For example, 71...Qf8 72.g6 Ke7 73.Qh7, threatening74.Bh6!, but after the text move Black is left with an isolated, backward pawn on g7. His gain of a pawn is only temporary.

72.Qh5 Qg8 73.Bxg5 Nf6 74.Qh4 Kd7

If White now captures twice on f6, Black would draw by perpetual check.

75.Ke2 Ne8

Trying to post the Knight on the fine blockading square d6. However, White immediately prevents this.

76.Qh2! Qf7 77.Kd3

Threatening 78.Qxe5, which could not have been played at once because of 77...Qh5+.

77...Kd6 78.Qb2 Qb7 79.Bd2!

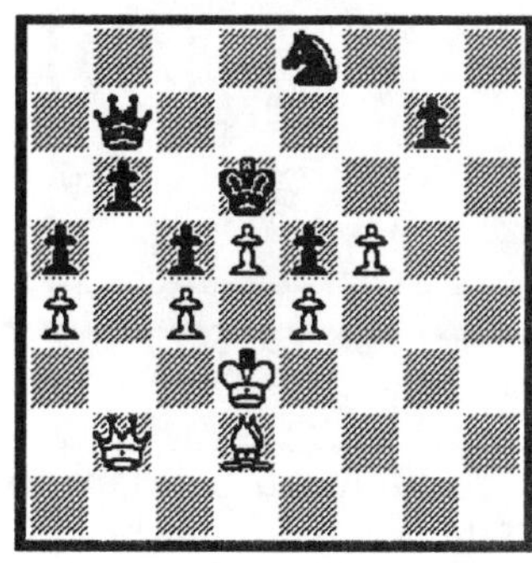

(Act V begins).

With this move White prettily forces the win of a pawn. He threatens not only 80.Bxa5 but also 80.Bc3, attacking the e-pawn. Black cannot defend against both of these threats because his Queen cannot leave either b6 or c6 unprotected. White's advantage is now decisive.

79...Nf6 80.Bxa5 Nd7 81.Qb5 Qc7 82.Bd2 Qc8 83.Bg5 Qa8 84.Kc2 Qc8 85.a5 bxa5 86.Qxa5 Qb8 87.Qd8

Now, in view of the threat Be7#, Black must allow the exchange of Queens, leaving a Bishop vs. Knight ending which is easy to win.

87...Qxd8 88.Bxd8 Nf8 89.Bg5 Kc7 90.Kb3 Nd7 91.Be7 Kb6 92.Bd8+ Kb7 93.Kc3 Kc8 94.Be7 Kc7 95.Kd3

The White King heads for g6 to clinch the win.

95...Kc8 96.Ke3 Kc7 97.Kf3 Kc8 98.Kg4 Nb6 99.Bxc5 Nxc4 100.Bb4 Nb2 101.Kg5 Nd3 102.Kg6 Black Resigned.

After 102...Nf2 103.Kxg6 Nxe4 104.f6, he must give up his Knight for the pawn; or if 102...Nxb4 103.Kxg7, and the f-pawn walks right in.

POSITION 126

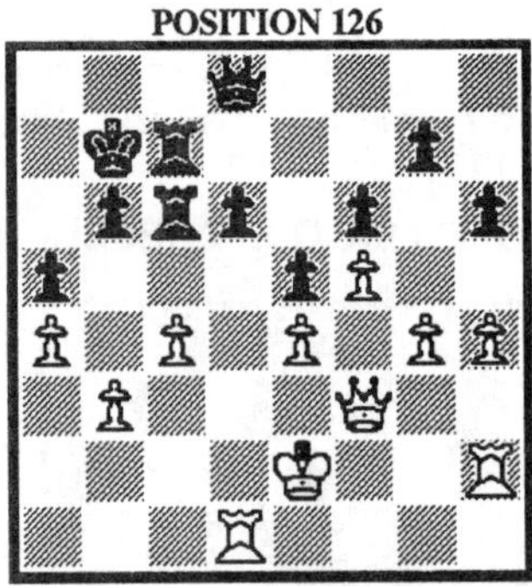

(A snapshot from the 6th Match Game Keres-Euwe, January, 1940).

In this position – a pendant to the previous game – Black has just played 34...f6. Clearly White will now maneuver for the pawn breakthrough with g5, but first he seeks to position his pieces into their best locations to support the breakthrough.

35.Rg2 Rc8 36.Rg3 Qd7 37.Qd3 Qf7 38.Rh1 Rh8 39.Rhh3

Here one might have expected 39.R3h3 followed in due course by g5, a procedure analogous to that of the previous game.

39...Rcc8

Indirectly defending the d-pawn. Now if 40.Qxd6 there follows 40...Rhd8 41.Qa3 (or 41.Qe6 Qxe6 42.fxe6 Rd4) Rd4 and Black has a powerful counterattack.

40.g5!?

This gives no clear result. From an objective point of view it would have been better to continue maneuvering for a more favorable opportunity, with Rooks doubled on the h-file.

40...hxg5 41.hxg5 Qc7 42.Qd5+ Ka7 43.Rd3

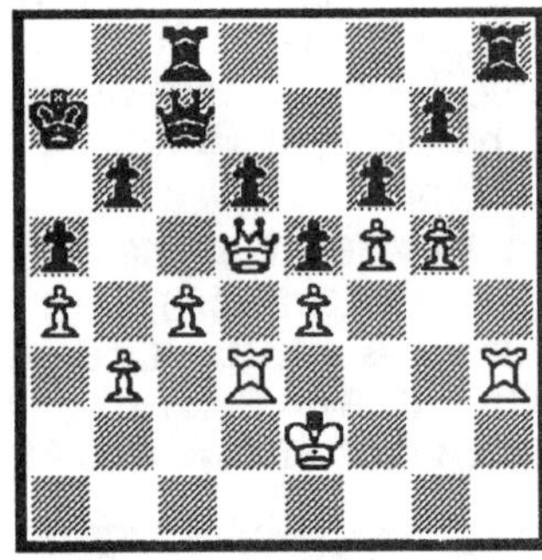

43...Rxh3?

This allows White to achieve his goals. Much better was 43...fxg5 44.Rxh8 Rxh8 45.Qxd6 Qxd6 46.Rxd6 Rh4 47.Ke3 Rh3+ with excellent drawing chances.

44.Rxh3 fxg5 45.Rh7 Qe7

Preventing 46.f6.

46.Kf3 Rf8 47.Kg4 Rf7

The strong position of the White King made 48.Qe6 a serious threat. After Black's ...Rf7, however, 48.Qe6 Qxe6 49.fxe6 Re7 50.Kf5 Kb7 and White would have some problems making progress.

48.b4!

Opening up a second front. This theme will be cropping up continually in connection with maneuvering. This new breakthrough leads to a strong attack against the Black King.

48...axb4 49.a5 Qb7

Black attempts to keep the b-pawn in the hope of making counterchances with it. There was no hope in 49...bxa5 50.Qxa5+ Kb7 51.Qxb4+ Kc7 52.Qa5+ as the decisive entry of the White Rook cannot be prevented

50.axb6+ Kxb6 51.Qxd6+ Ka7 52.Qxe5 b3 53.Rh3!

Now 53...b2 fails against 54.Ra3+. There is moreover a threat of 54.Qa5+.

53...Rf6 54.Qd4+ Rb6

Or 54...Qb6 55.Qd7+ Ka6 56.Qa4+, and the b-pawn falls.

55.Rxb3 Black Resigned.

CHAPTER 34
HOW TARRASCH MANEUVERED

As far as we know, the first player to make conscious use of maneuvering technique in tournament play was Dr. Tarrasch. Cat-and-mouse play was his term for it, and he employed it in positions in which his opponent could do nothing. Tarrasch discovered that this is precisely the situation in which the opponent is likely to commit inaccuracies. By his own apparently pointless shuffling to and fro, he was in fact providing the opponent with opportunities to go wrong. To familiarize the reader with Tarrasch's lines of thought we now analyze one of his games from the Nuremberg tournament of 1888, making grateful use of his own notes from his well-known book *Dreihundert Schachpartien*.

POSITION 127

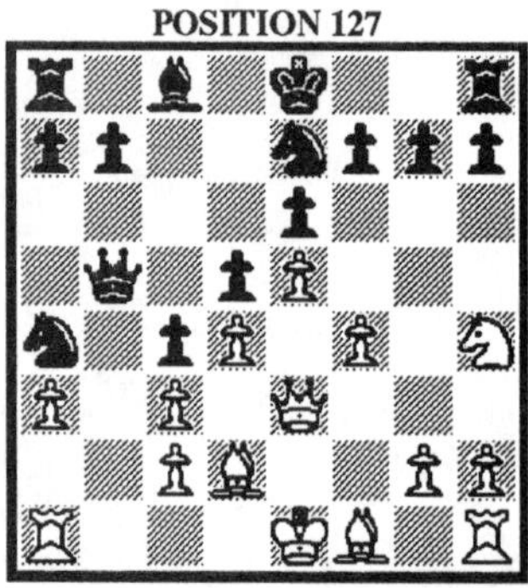

(Gottschall-Tarrasch, Nuremberg, 1888).

1.e4 e6 2.d4 d5 3.Nc3 Bb4 4.e5 Ne7 5.f4 c5 6.a3 Bxc3+ 7.bxc3 c4 8.Nf3 Qa5 9.Qd2 Nd7 10.Nh4 Nb6 11.Qe3 Na4 12.Bd2 Qb5

This last move provoked much criticism at the time. Von Gottschall considered the move weak, and another critic stated that Black could have won the front c-pawn by ...a6 followed by ...Nc6-a7-b5. Tarrasch disagreed, defending his move with the argument which really boiled down to the fact that it spoiled nothing. Black can take the liberty here of deliberately losing moves, leaving his opponent to guess what he is really up to. In any case, as Black pointed out, White can defend his c-pawn by Nf3-g1-e2.

13.Be2 Ng6

After 13...Qb2 14.O-O Black cannot take on c2 as then 15.Bd1 wins.

14.Nf3 Ne7 15.Nh4

White wants to stop Black from playing ...Nf5.

15...Ng6 16.Nf3 Ne7 17.Nh4 Ng6 18.Nf3 Qa5 19.O-O Qd8 20.Qf2 Ne7 21.Nh4 Ng6 22.Nf3 Ne7 23.Nh4 Ng6 24.Nf3 Bd7 25.Kh1 Nb6

Intending to work this Knight around to f5 via c8 and e7. However, this plan never comes off.

26.Rae1 Qe7 27.Bc1 Na4 28.Qe3 h6

Black does not permit 29.Ng5, as the Knight could not then very well be driven away by 29...h6 because of the answer 30.Nxe6!, followed by, if 30...fxe6 31.Bh5, or if 30...Bxe6 31.f5, etc.

29.g3 Rc8

"Weak" declared White at the time. "Not at all" replied Black in his notes. "The Rook can now proceed *via* c6 and b6 to b1".

30.Ng1 h5!

Otherwise White plays 31.Bh5!, threatening 32.f5! exf5 33.e6!.

31.Nh3 Qf8 32.Bf3 Ne7 33.Bg2 Nf5

Here, and for the next few moves, Tarrasch is "tacking". At this point, however, 33...Rc6! was preferable.

This was, after all, the intention of his 29th move.

34.Qd2 Qe7 35.Ng5 Qd8 36.Bh3 g6 37.Bxf5 gxf5 38.Re3 Qe7 39.Qg2 Kd8

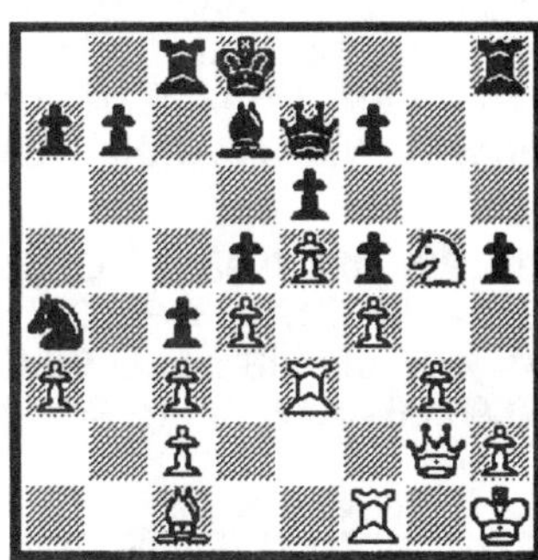

This move was sharply criticized by Tarrasch himself after the game. The right plan was feasible in the following stages: **1)** Play the Rook from c8 to c6-b6-b1. **2)** Play the Knight around to b5, first advancing the a-pawn to a4. **3)** Winning the a-pawn.

40.Bd2! Kc7 41.Ra1 Kb8 42.h4?

An error by which White deprives himself of the chance for counterplay with a later g4.

42...Rc6

At last; but less effective now that the White a-pawn is adequately protected.

43.Ree1 Rb6 44.Kg1 Be8 45.Kh1 Rb5 46.Kg1 Nb6 47.Qe2 Ra5 48.Bc1 Ra4 49.Bb2 Na8 50.Reb1 Nc7 51.Ra2 Nb5 52.Rba1 Bd7 53.Kg2 Kc8 54.Qe3 Kd8 55.Kf2

There is nothing White can do. Meanwhile the Black King is going to take over the protection of the h-pawn, thereby allowing the Rh8 to engage in action against the a-pawn.

55...Ke8 56.Kg2 Kf8 57.Kf2 Kg7 58.Kg2 Kg6 59.Nf3 Rc8 60.Nd2 Rc6 61.Nb1

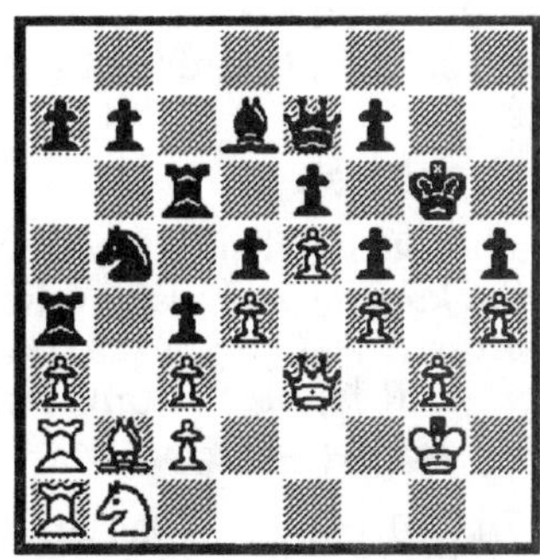

Protecting the pawn a fourth time. Since Black can get no farther in this way he must again resort to maneuvering.

61...Rc8 62.Nd2 Kh6 63.Nf3 Nc7 64.Kf2 Nb5 65.Kg2 Rc6 66.Nd2 Rca6 67.Nb1 R4a5 68.Kf2 Nc7 69.Nd2 Ba4 70.Bc1 Nb5

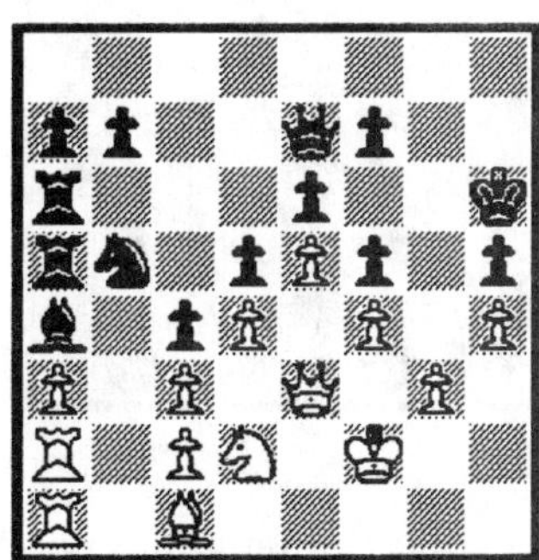

The struggle seems to have reached a dead end, with all the threatened points defended as many times as they are attacked. With Black's next move the game suddenly enters an entirely new phase.

71.Kg2 Bxc2!!

Most surprising. Black gets only two pawns for the piece, but the sacrifice must nevertheless be considered to be correct as White will still be devoid of any real counterplay. His Knight has no way to become active, and meanwhile the advance of Black's Queenside pawns will eventually produce a pair of united passed pawns.

72.Rxc2 Nxa3 73.Bxa3

But not 73.R2a2? because of the shot 73...Nc2!.

73...Rxa3 74.Rxa3

Tarrasch gives 74.Rb1 as better. But after 74...Qc7 75.R2b2 Qa5 76.Rb4 b5 77.Rxb5 Qxc3 78.Qxc3 Rxc3 79.R1b2 Raa3 80.Nf1 Rd3, Black dominates.

74...Qxa3 75.Qe1 b5 76.Nb1

After 76.Qb1 comes ...Qa4 and then if 77.Qb4 then 77...Qxb4 78.cxb4 Ra4, and Black must win. Instead of 77.Qb4 White might have tried 77.Rb2!.

76...Qb3 77.Qc1 Ra2 78.Rxa2 Qxa2+ 79.Kf3

79...Kg7!

A very fine maneuver. The threat now is simply ...a5 and ...b4; but if Black had pushed 79...a5 immediately, then White could force the draw with 80.Qa3!, e.g., 80...Qxa3 81.Nxa3 b4 82.Nc2 b3 83.Na3, etc., or if 80...Qxb1 then 81.Qf8+ with perpetual check.

80.Qa3

Seeing no hope in marking time, White makes one last attempt at perpetual check.

80...Qxb1 81.Qe7 Qf1+! 82.Ke3 Qe1+ 83.Kf3 Qxc3+ 84.Kg2 Qd2+ 85.Kh3 Qa5

By guarding d8 Black allows his own King to escape the coming checks.

86.Qf6+ Kf8 87.Qh8+ Ke7 88.Qf6+ Ke8 89.Qh8+ Kd7 90.Qf8 Qd8! 91.Qc5

The game cannot be saved. After 91.Qd6+ Ke8 92.Qc6+ Qd7 93.Qa8+ Ke7 94.Qh8 Qe8! 95.Qf6+ Kd7 the Black King escapes the checks, while if 91.Qxf7+ Qe7 92.Qxh5 b4 the last word is with Black's united passed pawns.

91...Qb8 92.Qb4 Ke8 93.Qc5 Qb7 94.Qa3 b4 95.Qf3 b3 96.Qxh5 b2 97.Qh8+ Kd7 98.Qf8 b1=Q 99.Qxf7+ Kc6 100.Qxe6+ Kb5 White Resigned.

POSITION 128

(After Black's 39th move in the game Muller-Tarrasch, Manchester, 1890).

Tarrasch commented in *Dreihundert Schachpartien* that in positions of this sort he liked to move to and fro on principle, to induce his opponent to weaken his position, or, failing that, at least convince him of his helplessness. The game continued:

40.Nfd2 Qg7 41.Nf1 Qd7 42.Nfd2 b3

Winning the Exchange, though a difficult struggle lies ahead as the White Knights are well-suited to a closed position like this.

43.Rc3 Bb4 44.Nf1!

Quite right: after 44.axb4 axb4 Black would win easily as his Rooks would have the a-file for the invasion of White's position.

44...Bxc3 45.Nxc3 h6!

The only way to obtain an open file for his Rooks.

46.gxh6 Kh7

Not 46...Qh7 because after 47.Na4! the Knight would become very active.

47.g4! Kxh6 48.g5+ Kg7 49.Qd2 Bd5

Black cannot allow the advance d5.

50.Ng3 Rh8 51.Rh1 Rxh1 52.Nxh1 Rc8 53.Kg1 Rh8 54.Qg2 Kf7

The King moves across to guard the Bishop, releasing the Queen for duties on the open h-file.

55.Nf2 Kf8 56.Qg3 Bc6 57.Kg2 Qh7

Now Black is not afraid of d5, the White position being such that the advanced d-pawn could be easily won.

58.Kg1 Qh5 59.Kg2 Kf7 60.Kg1 Ke6 61.Kg2 Kd6 62.Kf1 Qf3 63.Qxf3 exf3 64.Kg1

Now comes the most attractive part of the game. Tarrasch maneuvers so that the Knights are slowly but surely restricted in their activities.

64...Bb7 65.Nb5+ Kd7 66.Nc3 Ba8 67.Na4

White can move only this Knight. If 67.N2d1 Rh1+! 68.Kxh1 f2+ wins.

67...Be4! 68.Nc3

After either 68.Nb6+ Ke6 69.Nxc4 Rc8!, or 68.Nc5+ Kc6 69.N5xe4 fxe4 70.Nxe4 Re8 the Black Rook forces entry into the White defenses.

68...Bc2

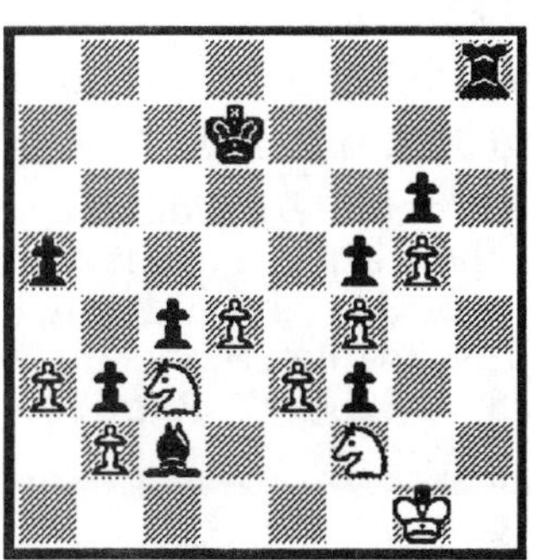

Now White is in *zugzwang:* if 69.Na4 Kc6 70.Nc3 Re8 71.N3d1 Bxd1 72.Nxd1 c3 73.bxc3 Rxe3 and wins.

69.Nh1 Rh3 70.Nf2 Rg3+ 71.Kf1 Bd3+ 72.Ke1 Rg1+ 73.Kd2 Rf1 74.Nxd3

If 74.N3d1 Bc2 75.Kc1 Bxd1, or if 74.N2d1 f2! followed by 75...Rxd1+.

74...cxd3 75.Kxd3 Rc1 and **White Resigned.**

CHAPTER 35
LASKER'S MANEUVERING SKILL

When we compare the maneuvering of Tarrasch with that of Lasker it appears that, whereas Tarrasch regarded the process as a sort of cat-and-mouse game with a helpless opponent, Lasker made it an integral part of his fighting approach to chess. Tarrasch scored his greatest successes in a chess world in which the majority of the players had no conception – or at best an imperfect one – of the elements of positional play; but Lasker had to do battle time and again with players who, by studying the excellent books written by Tarrasch, knew a great deal about positional play. As a result, he frequently found himself in situations in which, although he had achieved some positional advantage – e.g. a space superiority, or better pawn position – there was not yet a direct way of forcing a decision. His method then, as he himself said, was to keep starting up new attacks until he had thrown the enemy ranks into disorder, and then suddenly to switch back to his main offensive. The following game is a good example of his methods.

(Lasker-Salwe, St. Petersburg, 1909).

1.e4 e5 2.Nf3 Nc6 3.Bb5 d6 4.d4 Bd7 5.Nc3 Nf6 6.O-O Be7 7.Bg5 exd4 8.Nxd4 O-O 9.Bxc6 bxc6 10.Qd3 Re8 11.Rae1 c5 12.Nb3 Ng4 13.Bxe7 Rxe7 14.f4 Rb8 15.h3 Nh6 16.f5

Lasker said afterwards that White should have played 16.g4. The move played has in any case the disadvantage of giving Black free use of e5 and g5.

16...f6 17.Nd5 Re8 18.c4 Nf7 19.Qc3 Re5 20.Nd2 c6 21.Nf4 Qb6 22.b3 Rbe8 23.Qg3 Kh8 24.Nh5 Rg8 25.Rf4 Qd8 26.Nf3 Re7

POSITION 129

The weakness of the Black d-pawn is balanced by the weakness of the White e-pawn, so that White's only real advantage is some spatial superiority. The attack on the enemy King soon comes to a full stop.

27.Rh4

After 27.Rg4 Black plays 27...Qf8 with an adequate defense, according to Lasker.

27...Qe8 28.Qf2

Now a typical phase of tacking begins. The attempt at direct attack by 28.Nf4 would get nowhere because of 28...Nh6.

28...Rf8 29.Qd2

Not quite as innocent as it looks.

29...Qb8 30.Kh1 Rfe8 31.Rg4 Rg8

The best defense. Incidentally, there was a chance for a pretty tactical sequence by 31...Nh6 and now White can play either 32.Nxf6! Nxg4 33.Nxe8, or 32.Rxg7! Rxg7 33.Qxh6

Rf7 34.Nxf6 R8f8 35.Ng5, winning in both cases.

32.Rd1

Strengthening the pressure against the d-pawn.

32...Qb4

Searching for counterplay. It appears from the sequel, however, that the Queen would have done better to stay at home. Therefore, 32...Qe8 deserved preference.

33.Qf2 Qc3 34.Qh4 Nh6 35.Rf4 Nf7 36.Kh2 Rge8 37.Qg3 Rg8

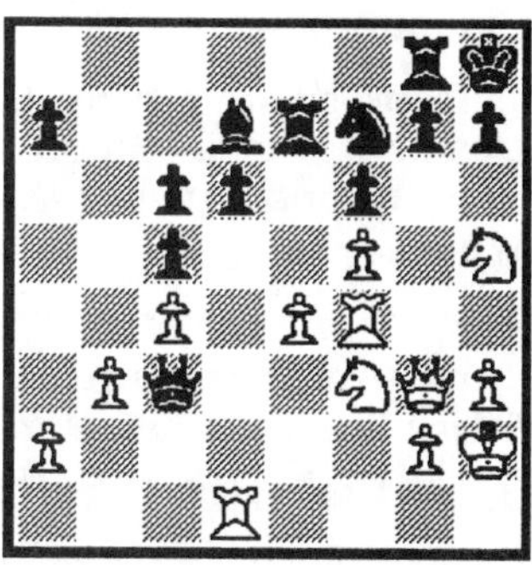

Compare this diagram to the previous one. The only Black piece to have changed position is the Queen, and in such a way that she can no longer, in a single move, defend the critical square d6. In the tournament book Lasker points out that 38.Rg4 Nh6 39.Rh4, could now be answered by 39...d5 40.cxd5 cxd5 41.Rxd5 Bc6: a counterattack clearly based on the weakness of White's e-pawn.

38.Rh4!

This prevents 38...d5, for now White could play 39.cxd5 cxd5 40.Nf4 winning. In any event 39.Nf4 is a threat, for 39...Nh6 no longer works in view of 40.Rxd6.

38...g5 39.fxg6

Lasker says that 39.Rg4 fails to 39...Be8.

39...Rxg6 40.Qf2 f5

Otherwise White plays 41.Rf4, and the Black f-pawn would soon come under heavy pressure.

41.Nf4 Rf6 42.Ne2 Qb2 43.Rd2 Qa1 44.Ng3 Kg8

There was a threat of 45.exf5 Bxf5 46.Nxf5 Rxf5 47.Rxh7+! Kxh7 48.Qh4+ Kg7 49.Qxe7. Black's King move does not parry the threat.

45.exf5 Bxf5

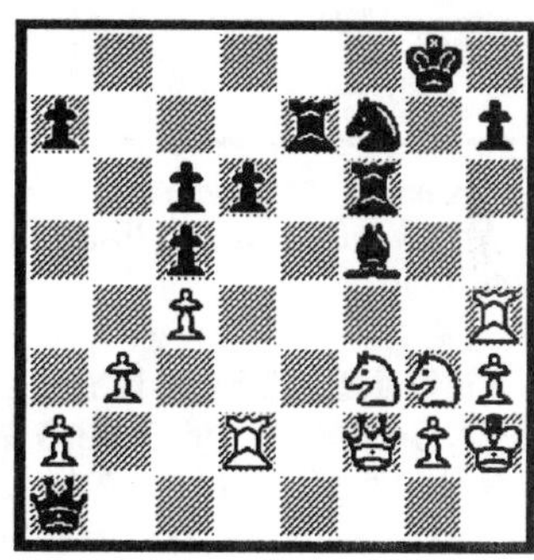

46.Nd4!

This is better than 46.Nxf5 Rxf5 47.Rxh7, after which Black has either 47...Qf6 or 47...Rxf3 with complications.

46...cxd4 47.Nxf5 Kf8 48.Qxd4 Qxd4 49.Nxd4 Ne5 50.Rh5 Ref7 51.c5

Lasker plays the ending with great skill. This move leads to a four Rook ending, and such endings routinely allow many drawing chances; Lasker has seen, however, that in the present case his advantage will quickly prove decisive.

51...dxc5 52.Rxe5 cxd4 53.Rxd4 Rf2 54.Rd8+ Kg7 55.Ra5 Rc2 56.a3!

In order to avoid losing the a-pawn after 56...R7f2.

56...c5 57.Rc8 Rb2 58.Rb5 Rff2 59.Rb7+ Kg6 60.Rc6+ Rf6 61.Rxc5 Ra6 62.a4!

Now 62...Rxa4 fails after 63.Rc6+ Kf5 64.Rb5+ Ke4 65.bxa4!.

62...Rf6 63.Rc3 a6 64.Rg3+ Kh6 65.Rgg7 Black Resigned.

POSITION 130

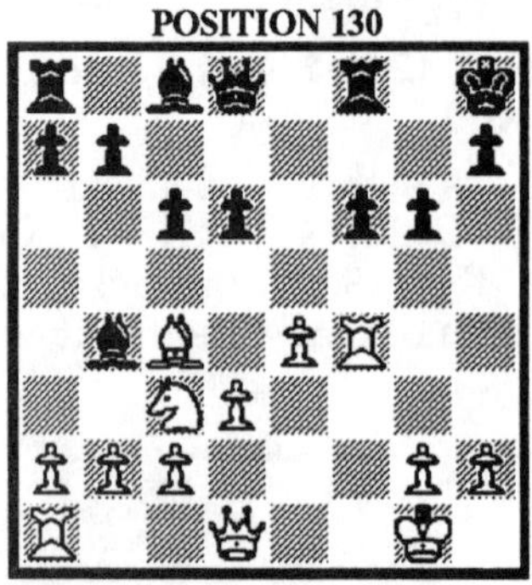

(Another example of Lasker's maneuvering skill – this from his later years; Tylor-Lasker, Nottingham, 1936).

1.e4 e5 2.Nf3 Nc6 3.Nc3 Nf6 4.Bb5 Bb4 5.O-O O-O 6.d3 d6 7.Bg5 Ne7 8.Nh4 c6 9.Bc4 Kh8 10.f4 exf4 11.Bxf6 gxf6 12.Rxf4 Ng6 13.Nxg6+ fxg6 (No.130) **14.Bb3**

To prevent Black from playing ...d5 with a gain of tempo, which would have been the case, for instance, after 14.d4 Bxc3 15.bxc3 d5!.

14...Qe7 15.Ne2 Ba5 16.c3 Bd7 17.Ng3

With an eye on the two Black Bishops, White would like to see the position assume a closed character. He therefore takes steps to discourage Black from playing ...f5, even though in doing so the Knight is not very well placed on g3.

17...Bc7 18.Rf2 Kg7 19.Qd2 Rae8 20.Raf1 Be6!

An important decision: Black gives up the Bishop pair. The point is that the White Bishop is so active that it would be dangerous for Black to open up the position. Also, as the rest of the game shows that Black's remaining Bishop will outperform the White Knight.

21.Qc2

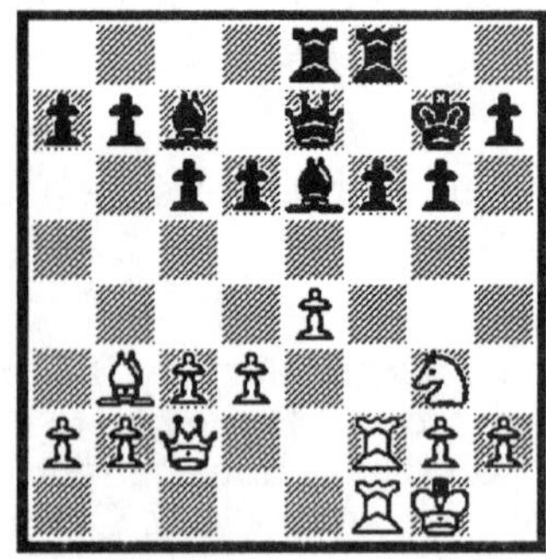

(Black forces a weakening of the enemy e-pawn, and then proceeds to put it under fire)

21...Bb6 22.d4 Bc7

The Bishop promptly returns to its former position. The intention was solely to force d4 and thereby weaken the e-pawn.

23.Kh1 h5!

Threatening to win the e-pawn by 24...h4 25.Ne2 Bc8 26.Rf4 g5.

24.Re1 Qf7 25.Rfe2 Bxb3 26.axb3

It is quite possible that after 26.Qxb3 Qxb3 27.axb3 Re7 28.Kg1 R8e8 White's endgame might be tenable, though it would not be a pleasant task. Black would continue to maneuver, keeping White under constant nagging pressure.

26...Qd7 27.Nf1 Re7 28.Qd3 Rfe8 29.Nd2 d5!

The game enters a new phase. Black has laid siege to the weak e-pawn, but since White has no other weaknesses, he can easily defend it. Therefore, Black opens up the position so that the Bishop can demonstrate its superiority over the Knight.

30.exd5 Rxe2 31.Rxe2 Rxe2 32.Qxe2 Qxd5 33.Qe7+ Qf7 34.Qe4

The ending favors Black in any case, for in addition to the far-ranging Bishop he has the better pawn position. It is therefore understandable that White prefers to keep the Queens on the board.

34...Qd7 35.Nf3 Kf7!

Intending to continue with 36...Qe6 37.Qc2 Qe3. Against 36.Nh4, Black has the powerful reply 36...Qg4! up his sleeve.

36.c4 Qe6 37.Qd3

If 37.Qxe6+ Kxe6 38.Kg1 Kf5 39.Kf2 Ke4 40.Ke2 g5! and Black will soon win a pawn.

37...Bf4!

A powerful post for the Bishop, mainly because of its potential access to c1, e.g., 38.Kg1 Qe3+ 39.Qxe3 Bxe3+ 40.Kf1 Bc1.

38.g3 Qe3! 39.Qc3

Nor would 39.Qd1 be any better due to 39...Qc1!.

39...Bh6 40.c5

White has little choice. Either he must exchange Queens, or he must allow the Black Queen to penetrate into his position. He is hoping that Black will now exchange Queens at c3, but Lasker is no longer content with that.

40...Qf2 41.Qc4+ Kg7 42.Qd3 Be3 43.Qd1

43...a5!

Placing White in *zugzwang*. After 44.d5 cxd5 45.Qxd5 Black has 45...Qf1+ mating.

44.b4 axb4 45.b3 Kh6 and **White Resigned.**

CHAPTER 36
THE TEACHINGS OF NIMZOWITSCH

Nimzowitsch was the only Grandmaster who ever undertook a systematic study of the subject of maneuvering. In his famous books *My System* and *Chess Praxis* he provided a precise definition of the process of alternation and a description of its various aspects. The ideas of Nimzowitsch are so fundamental that he must be considered the greatest pioneer of all in this domain.

The first prerequisites for maneuvering, according to Nimzowitsch, are enemy weaknesses and a space advantage of one's own. He emphasizes that the space advantage is the most vital aspect, since the weaknesses will usually arise as an automatic consequence of the pressure which the advantage in space makes possible. His method is to put the enemy weaknesses under attack successively, and at a gradually increasing tempo. His extra freedom of movement enables him to regroup his pieces faster than his opponent can. When the opponent finally fails to keep up the pace, his fatal moment has come.

Nimzowitsch applied and studied his maneuvering methods in many games. In the course of these he realized that facility in regrouping by the side which controlled the better lines of communication nearly always depended on the use of one particular central square. This square he called the pivot of the maneuvers, and he typically decreed that as far as possible this square should be given extra protection. This is the famous "overprotection" we saw in Chapter 32. The pieces which provide this extra protection will, according to Nimzowitsch, automatically be well-placed.

We now examine several Nimzowitsch games to see how he puts his theories into practice.

POSITION 131

(The game Holzhausen-Nimzowitsch, Hanover, 1926).

1.e4 Nc6 2.Nf3 e6 3.d4 d5 4.exd5 exd5 5.Bg5 Be7 6.Bxe7 Qxe7+ 7.Qe2 Bf5 8.c3 Be4 9.Nbd2 O-O-O 10.O-O-O Nh6 11.Ne5 Nxe5 12.dxe5 Bg6

Nimzowitsch, whose annotations in *Chess Praxis* we now follow in part, states that Black is already preparing to maneuver. The weaknesses are the e-pawn and the b1-h7 diagonal; the pivot point is the e4 square.

13.Nf3 Rhe8 14.Qe3 Kb8 15.Qf4 Be4

The value of this square is already apparent.

16.Re1 Qc5 17.Nd2 Bg6 18.Nb3 Qb6 19.Qd4 f6 20.f4 fxe5 21.fxe5

Not 21.Rxe5 Rxe5 22.Qxe5 Re8 winning.

21...Be4

Now the e-pawn must fall; but afterwards is when the maneuvering begins in earnest.

22.Nd2 c5 23.Qe3

This is better than 23.Qa4 Rxe5 24.Nxe4 dxe4 25.Rxe4, after which

Black gets a winning attack with 25...Qe6! 26.Rxe5 Qxe5.

23...Rxe5 24.Qg3 Qc7 25.Bd3 Rde8 26.Bxe4 dxe4 27.Nc4 R5e6 28.Qxc7+ Kxc7 29.Ne3!

The Knight reaches an ideal blockading square. As we have already learned, such a Knight is the perfect counter to a passed pawn.

29...Nf7 30.Kc2 Nd6 31.c4 Kc6 32.Rhf1

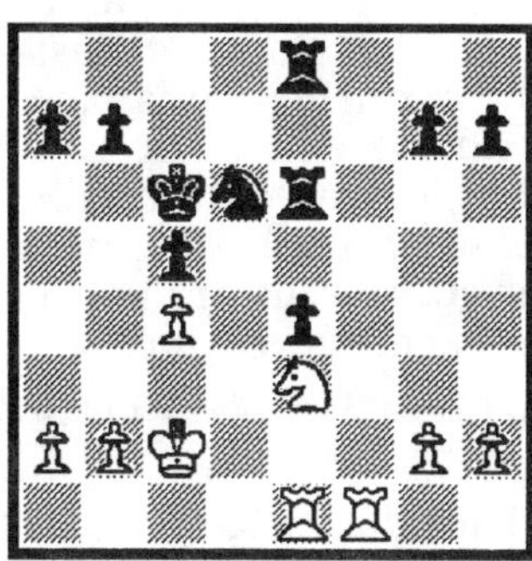

32...Rh6!

A typical tacking maneuver. Black forces a weakening of the enemy pawn structure which, although apparently insignificant now, will later become a matter of decisive importance.

33.h3 Rg6 34.Re2 a6

Play on both flanks: the advance ...b5 will lead at least to an increase in Black's space control.

35.Rf4 b5 36.b3 Rg5 37.g4 Rge5 38.Kc3 a5

Intending to play ...a4 and then ...axb3 and ...bxc4, thus opening two Queenside files for his Rooks.

39.Ref2 a4 40.bxa4 bxc4!

A temporary pawn sacrifice; after 41.Nxc4 Nxc4 42.Kxc4 Ra8 Black regains his pawn, at the same time removing the blockade of his passed pawn.

41.Rf8 R5e7

Safety first. Under no circumstances will Black tolerate an enemy Rook operating behind his lines.

42.Rxe8 Rxe8 43.Nxc4

Otherwise 43...Ra8 follows.

43...Nxc4 44.Kxc4 Ra8

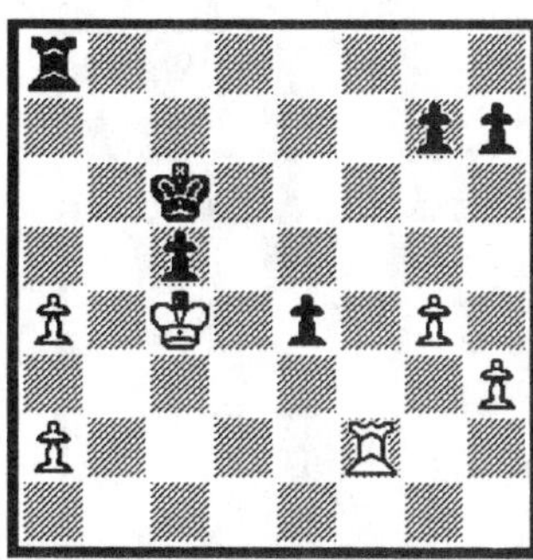

Comparing this diagram to the previous one it is clear that Black's alternating maneuvers have created progress. The Black Rook will now force an entry on the Queenside and then proceed to threaten the White pawns on the Kingside.

45.Rf7

As usual in Rook endings the best defense is counterattack. In any case 45.Kb3 Kd5 followed by the advance of the passed e-pawn would lead to a quick loss for White.

45...Rxa4+ 46.Kb3 Rb4+ 47.Kc3 Rb7 48.Rf5 Ra7

Threatening not only 49...Rxa2, but also 49...Ra3+ followed by 50...Rxh3.

49.Kc4 Ra4+ 50.Kb3 Rd4 51.Re5 Kd6 52.Re8 Rd3+ 53.Kc4 Rxh3 54.Rxe4 Ra3!

This marks the culmination of the alternating maneuvers against the two weaknesses. White can no longer protect them both at the same time.

55.Re2 Ra4+ 56.Kb5 Rxg4

The rest of the game is purely technical; Black wins easily.

57.a4 Rb4+ 58.Ka5 h5 59.Rd2+ Kc6 60.Re2 Rg4 61.Re6+ Kd5 62.Re8 h4 63.Rd8+ Kc4 64.Kb6 h3 65.Rd1 Kb4 66.Rb1+ Kxa4 67.Kxc5 g5 68.Rh1 Rg3 69.Kd4 g4 70.Ke4 Rg2 71.Kf4 h2 White Resigned.

POSITION 132

(Nimzowitsch-Buerger, London 1927)

1.c4 Nf6 2.Nc3 d5 3.cxd5 Nxd5 4.g3 Nxc3 5.bxc3 g6 6.Bg2 Bg7 7.Qb3 c6 8.d4 O-O 9.Ba3 Nd7 10.Bh3 Re8 11.f4 Qc7 12.Nf3 Nf6 13.Bxc8 Raxc8 14.O-O e6 15.Rad1 (No.132) **15...b6**

With the obvious intention of freeing his game by ...c5. Nimzowitsch now applies what he termed "prophylaxis". He takes measures to discourage this freeing advance – for the time being by occupying the d-file.

16.c4 Red8 17.Rd3 Bf8

Now 17...c5 would be well-met by 18.dxc5 bxc5 19.R1d1.

18.Bb2

Nimzowitsch plans to maneuver, and avoids exchange of pieces. But it appears that he is getting nowhere.

18...Bg7 19.Ba3 Bf8 20.Bxf8

After all! Without this exchange Black would easily achieve c5.

20...Rxf8 21.Qb2

Again preventing c5, which would fail to 22.dxc5.

21...Qe7 22.Ne5 Rfd8 23.Rfd1 Ne4

Black tries another path. Not particularly inviting is 23...c5 because of 24.Qa3 Qc7 25.d5.

24.Qc2 f6 25.Nf3 b5 26.c5 f5 27.Re3

After 27.Nd2, Nimzowitsch gave 27...Nxd2 28.R3xd2 Rd5 29.e4 fxe4 30.Re2 Qf6 31.Rxe4 h5! as a likely continuation, the chances being about equal.

27...a5 28.Ne5 Rc7 29.a3 Kg7 30.Kg2

Intending to play g4-g5 and then h4-h5. Since this would at least give White an enduring initiative, it is understandable that Black does not permit the g-pawn to advance; but the weakness which his next move creates on g6 is the justification for the following exchange sacrifice.

30...h5 31.Rxe4! fxe4 32.Qxe4 Qf6 33.Nxc6 Rd5

Giving back the Exchange brings no relief: 33...Rxc6 34.Qxc6 Rxd4 35.Qc7+!, and then if 35...Kg8 36.Rb1! or if 35...Kh6 36.Rxd4 Qxd4 37.Qd6! – a very dangerous raid.

34.Ne5 Qf5 35.Qd3! Qxd3 36.Rxd3 Rd8 37.Kf3 Rb8 38.Rb3 b4 39.a4 Rd8 40.Ke4 Rcc8

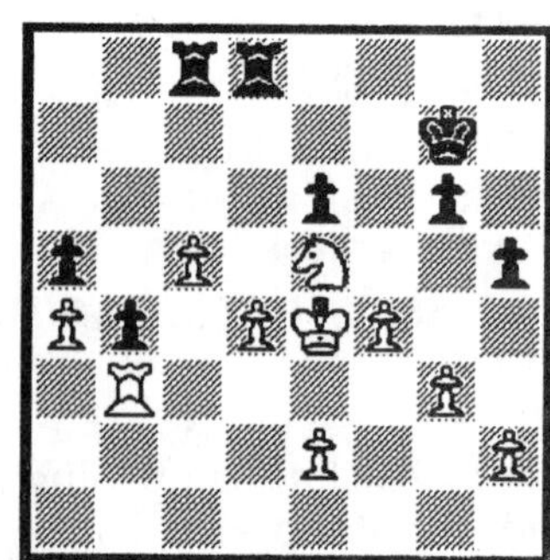

White now plans to create two united passed pawns by e4 and d5. To achieve this goal several conditions must be met: **1)** The c-pawn must be solidly defended. **2)** Black's protected passed b-pawn must be blockaded. **3)** The White King must be posted on c4.

41.Nc4 Ra8 42.Re3 Kf6 43.Nd2 Ke7 44.Nb3

The ideal post for the Knight.

44...Ra6 45.Kd3 Rd5 46.h4 Ra8 47.Kc4 Kd7 48.Rd3 Kc7

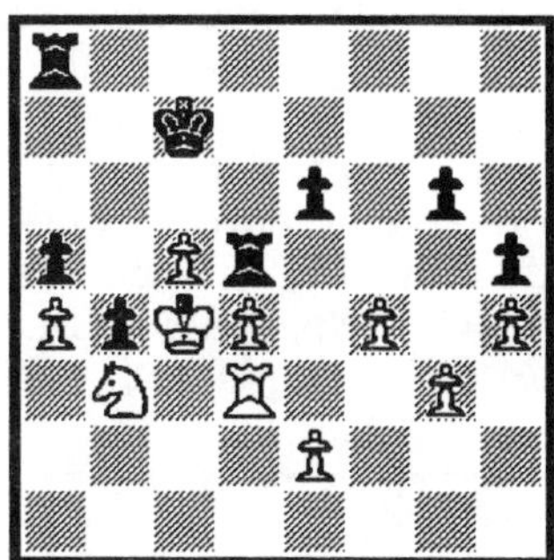

49.Rd1

Nimzowitsch carries his love of maneuvering to excess. The direct 49.e4 could have been played immediately; for example 49...Kc6 50.Nxa5+! (not 50.exd5+?? exd5#!) 50...Rxa5 51.exd5+ exd5+ 52.Kxb4.

49...Rd7 50.Rg1 Rf7 51.Rb1 Kb7

Black can do nothing.

52.Nd2 Kc6 53.Nf3 Kc7 54.Ne5 Rg7 55.Rb3

Now we are virtually back to move 40, but with the White King on c4 instead of e4.

55...Rb8 56.e4 Rgg8 57.d5

The goal is reached. White's united passed pawns slice through the Black position like a knife through butter.

57...exd5+ 58.exd5 Rbc8 59.d6+ Kd8 60.Kd5 Rg7 61.c6 Black Resigned.

(Maneuvers in a Queen-and-pawn ending; from the game Nimzowitsch-Antze, Hanover, 1926).

In this ending the pivot for White's alternating maneuvers will be d4, and to a smaller extent e5 and f6 as well.

White's broad strategy will be to create a passed pawn on the Queen-side. Another important idea is to invade with the White King via h5. Black's counterplay lies in harrying the White King with checks, and in his passed h-pawn.

POSITION 133

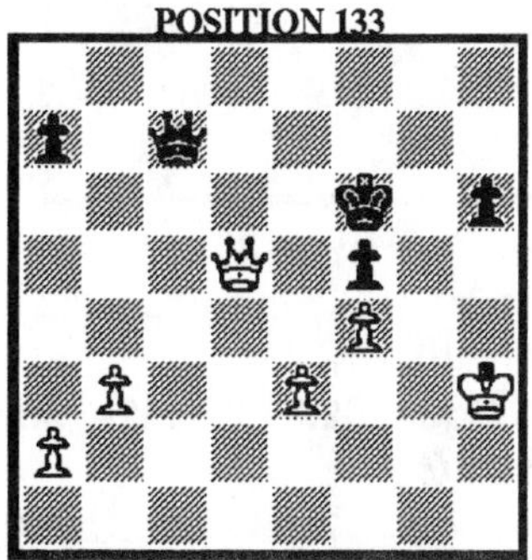

44.Qd4+ Kg6 45.Qd2 Kf6 46.Qb2+ Kg6 47.b4 Qc4 48.Qd2 Kh5

Not 48...Qf1+ because 49.Qg2+ forces off the Queens with a simple win for White. This tactic constantly arises in this type of ending and thus must be constantly watched for.

49.a4 a6 50.Kg3 Qg8+ 51.Kh2 Qc4 52.Qb2 Qd3 53.Qg2

Indirect protection of the e-pawn. (53...Qxe3 54.Qh3+).

53...Qc4 54.Kg3 Qg8+

After 54...Qxb4 55.Qe2+ Kg6 56.Qxa6+ White would have a powerful passed a-pawn.

55.Kh3 Qc4 56.Qf3+ Kg6 57.Kh4!

Step by step White is encroaching. Now 57...Qxb4 loses to 58.Qc6+ Kg7 59.Kh5!.

57...Kg7 58.Qb7+ Kg6 59.Qb6+ Kh7 (see next diagram)

60.Qf6!

An important step towards the win; Black now has to protect not only his a-pawn, but also the f-pawn.

60...Qd5

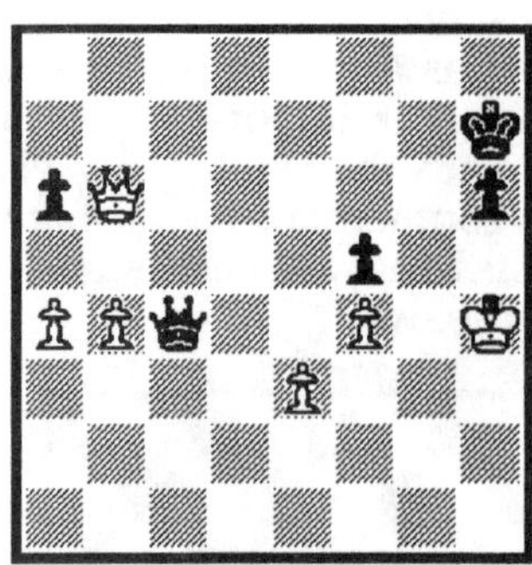
After 59...Kh7

Threatening perpetual check starting with 61...Qh1+.

61.Kg3 Qg8+ 62.Kh2 Qa2+ 63.Kh3 Qd5 64.Qe7+

After 64.Qxa6 Qf3+ 65.Kh2 Qf2+ 66.Kh1 Qf3+ Black escapes with a draw by perpetual check.

64...Kg6 65.Qe8+! Kh7

In reply to 65...Kf6 Nimzowitsch gave 66.Kg3 Qd3 67.a5 Qf1 68.Qe5+ Kg6 69.Qe6+ Kg7 70.Qxf5 Qg1+ 71.Kf3 Qf1+ 72.Ke4 Qc4+ 73.Ke5 Qb5+ 74.Ke6 winning.

66.Kg3 Qb3 67.a5! 67...Qb1

This allows White to win the a-pawn after which the game is as good as over. The best defense was 67...Qd3! 68.Qf7+ Kh8 69.Qf6+ Kh7 70.Qd4! (the pivot!) and then: **1)** 70...Qf1 71.Qd7+ Kg6 72.Qe6+ Kg7 73.Qxf5 and White wins. **2)** 70...Qb1 71.Qd7+ Kg6 72.Qc6+ Kg7 73.Qb7+ Kf8 74.Qxa6, etc., as in the actual game.

68.Qd7+ Kg6 69.Qc6+ Kg7 70.Qb7+ Kf8 71.Qxa6 71.Qe1+ 72.Kf3 Qd1+ 73.Qe2 Qd5+ 74.Kf2 Qd8 75.a6 Qh4+ 76.Kg2 Qe7 77.Qf3 Qc7 78.b5 Qg7+ 79.Kf2 Qb2+ 80.Qe2 Qa1 81.b6 and **Black Re- signed.**

(From the game E. Cohn-Nimzowitsch, Karlsbad, 1911).

The position with which we end our discussion of Nimzowitsch raises an interesting question. Can the methods he employs here really be classified as maneuvers, or is he merely marking time?

According to the tournament book the position diagrammed here could have been agreed drawn forthwith; but according to Nimzowitsch any such suggestion was quite out of the question, the difficulties which the opponent had to contend with being quite sufficient to justify the decision to play on.

POSITION 134

63...a5

The idea is to clear the a7 square for the King. Long-term planning!

64.h4 Kg6 65.Kh2 h5 66.Kg2 Kh6 67.Rf2 g6

Black plays with great patience – typical of a maneuvering scenario.

68.Rf1 Kg7 69.Rf2 Kf7 70.Kh2 Ke7 71.Re2 Qc1

Black has a lot of freedom, but as yet cannot create meaningful threats. This game exemplifies the fact that maneuvering amounts to a "slow" initiative.

72.Qf2 Kd7 73.Re1 Qc6 74.Kg2 Rg4

There are two weaknesses in the White pawn position – e3 and g3. The characteristic alternating procedure is to first put one weakness and then the other under attack.

75.Rf1

Could White, by means of 75.Re2 have prevented the Black King from crossing the c-file to the Queenside home at a7? Nimzowitsch gave 75...Re4 76.Kh2 Qc1 77.Kg2 Qd1 78.Kh2 Qd3 after which White is tied to the defense of the e-pawn, and consequently cannot prevent Kb7.

75...Qc7 76.Qf3 Kc8 77.Qf2 Kb8 78.Kh3 Ka7

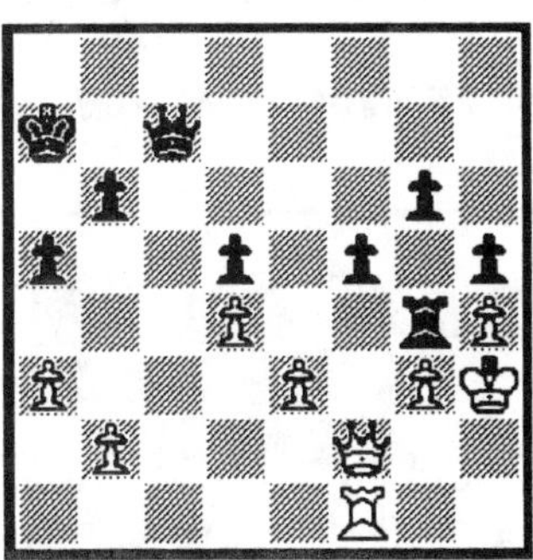

A comparison to the previous diagram shows that Black has traveled his King across from h7 to a7, and has meanwhile fixed the Kingside pawns. The consequence of this fixing is that White now has permanent weaknesses at g3 and e3. Black's maneuvering axis consists of the support points e4 and g4. White's two weak points are close together, and therefore should be easy enough to defend. The question is whether Black, by combining his concentrated attack on these two weaknesses with a breakthrough by ...g5, or with an invasion down the c-file, will be able to crack White's defenses

79.Rg1 Qd7 80.Kh2

Black threatened 80...f4!.

80...Qd6 81.Kh3

Now the threat was 81...Rxh4+.

81...Qc6 82.Re1 Qe6 83.Kh2 Qe4

Now White has to seriously watch for the possible breakthrough 84...g5 85.hxg5 h4.

84.Kh3 Qe6 85.Kh2 Qe7 86.Kh3 Qe4 87.Rg1 Qe6 88.Kh2 Re4

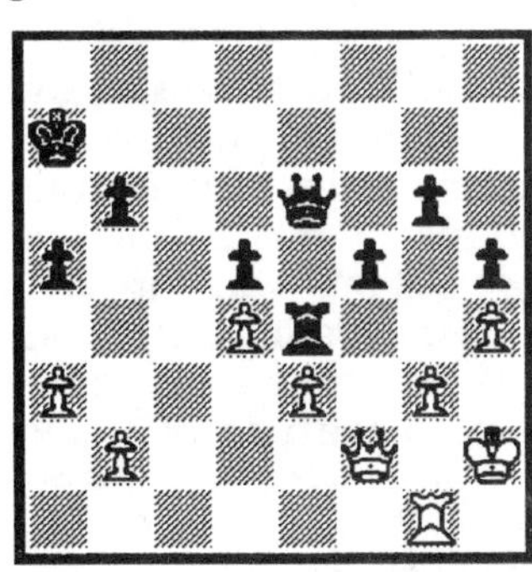

89.Rc1?

White gives up the e-pawn in the hope of getting counterchances. He was afraid that 89.Re1 would be strongly met by 89...g5. Nimzowitsch gave 90.hxg5 h4 91.gxh4 f4 92.g6 f3 leaving his readers to decide about the outcome. Certainly Black would have had dangerous attacking chances, but after 93.g7 it is, to say the least, doubtful whether they would be sufficient to win.

89...Rxe3 90.Qf4 Re2+ 91.Kh3 Ka6 92.b4 axb4 93.axb4 Kb5

Now, with the White Queen unable to move for fear of discovered check, the end is in sight.

94.Rc7 Qe4

Forcing the trade of Queens because of the mates threatened on both h1 and g2. If 33.Qf1 then 33...Qg4#.

95.Qxe4 Rxe4 96.Rg7 Re6 97.Rd7 Kc4 98.Kg2 Kxd4 99.Kf3 Kc4 100.b5 d4 White Resigned.

CHAPTER 37
CAPABLANCA MANEUVERED ONLY WHEN NECESSARY

The fame of Capablanca as a player did not rest on any great accomplishments in the realm of maneuver. His tremendous talents usually led to winning positions without having to resort to maneuvering techniques. His style was so direct and profoundly motivated that the types of positions he usually created did not lend themselves to maneuver. Nonetheless, Capablanca scored several victories by means of maneuvering skill, and we give two of them here. In both cases we see him operating on both flanks, using maneuvers which envelop practically the whole board.

POSITION 135

(The game Capablanca-Michell, Ramsgate, 1929).

1.c4 e5 2.Nc3 Nf6 3.g3 Nc6 4.Bg2 g6 5.d3 Bg7 6.Bd2 Ne7 7.Nf3 d6 8.O-O O-O 9.Qc1 Nh5 10.Bh6 f5 11.Bxg7 Kxg7 12.e3 h6 13.Ne2 Be6 14.Qc3 Kh7 15.Nd2 c6 16.Rae1 Qd7 17.f4 exf4 18.Nxf4 Nxf4 19.gxf4 Rae8 (No.135) **20.Rf3**

With this and his next move Capablanca begins to exert pressure on the g-file. Black reacts with operations in the center.

20...Ng8 21.Rg3 Nf6 22.Bf3 d5 23.b3 Rd8 24.d4

A necessary advance. The threat was 24...dxc4, etc.

24...Ne4 25.Nxe4 fxe4 26.Be2 Qe7 27.Rf1 Rf7

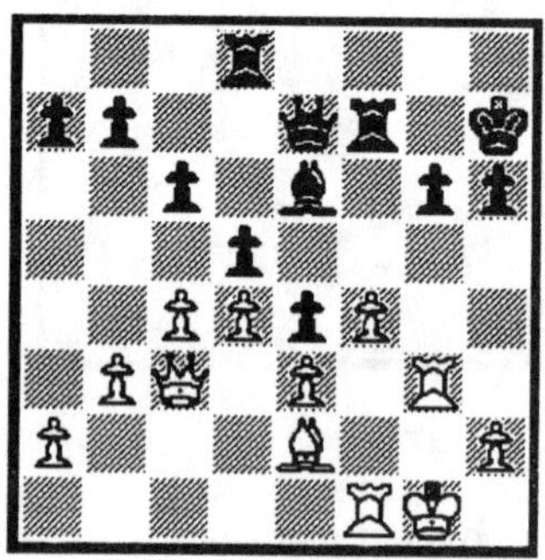

28.Qa5

In order to induce a weakening of Black's Queenside. Another possibility, of course, would have been 28.c5, followed by b4-b5; but in the current situation this would not have had any great effect.

28...a6 29.Rf2 Bf5 30.Rfg2 Rd6 31.Bg4

The struggle is coming to a dead end, and Capablanca now attempts to put new life into the position by exchanging his good Bishop for Black's bad Bishop. The "bad" Black Bishop is in fact an important defensive piece.

31...Bxg4 32.Rxg4 Qd7 33.h4 Rf5

Black prevents h5.

34.c5

Now that Kingside operations have come to a halt, White tries to do something on the Queenside.

34...Rdf6 35.a4 Qe7 36.Qb6 Re6 37.Qa5 Rh5 38.Qe1 Rf6 39.b4 Qd7 40.Qg3 Qe6

41.Rb2

At last the moment has arrived when White can force his opponent into weakening his Queenside.

41...Rhf5 42.Qg2 Rf7 43.b5 axb5 44.axb5 Rc7 45.Kh2 Qf6 46.Qf1 h5

A difficult decision. This move forces White to play Rg5, after which Black exchanges a pair of Rooks and at the same time plugs the weakness on g6. At the same time, however, he relieves White of his weak h-pawn. There is much to be said for retaining the possibility of ...g5, or even trying ...g5 at once. On the other hand Black's plan of getting the position clarified at last is not to be wholly condemned.

47.Rg5 Rxg5 48.hxg5 Qf5 49.Qh3! Qxh3+?

A serious mistake, giving White the chance to resume his alternating attacks on both flanks with great effect. The correct line was 49...Kg7! 50.Qxf5 gxf5 51.bxc6 bxc6 52.Rb8 Ra7 and the counterattack against the White e-pawn gives Black excellent drawing chances.

50.Kxh3 Kg7 51.Kh4 Kf7 52.bxc6 bxc6 53.Rb8 Re7

The attack on the e-pawn would now come too late: 53...Ra7 54.Rc8 Ra3 55.Rc7+ Kg8 56.Rxc6 Rxe3 57.Rxg6+.

54.Rc8 Re6 55.Rc7+ Kg8 56.Kg3 Kf8

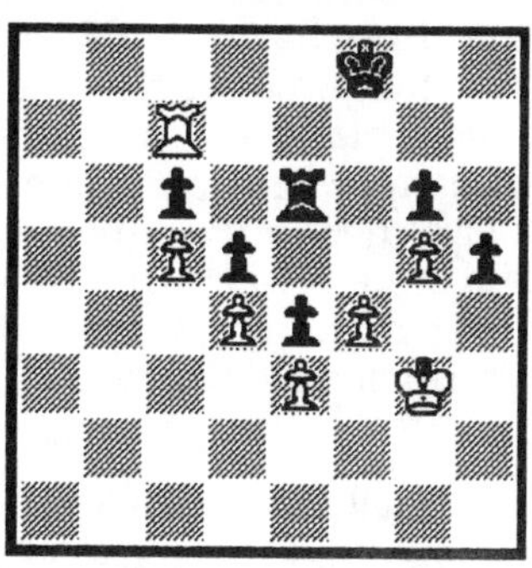

57.f5!

The decisive breakthrough.

57...gxf5 58.Kf4 Re7 59.Rxc6 h4 60.Rh6 Rg7 61.Rxh4 Black Resigns.

POSITON 136

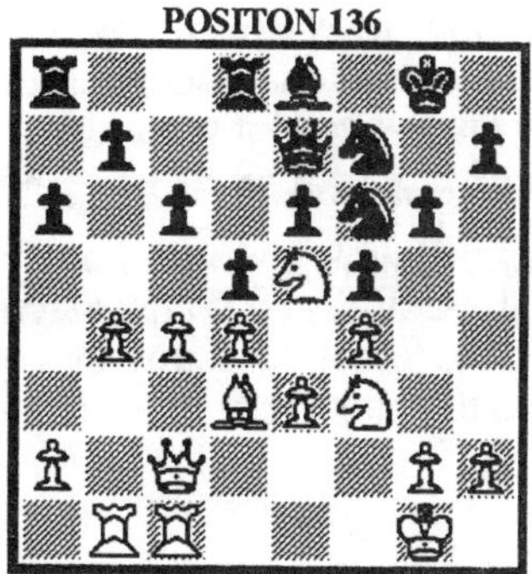

(The game Capablanca-Treybal, Carlsbad, 1929).

1.d4 d5 2.c4 c6 3.Nf3 e6 4.Bg5 Be7 5.Bxe7 Qxe7 6.Nbd2 f5 7.e3 Nd7 8.Bd3 Nh6 9.O-O O-O 10.Qc2 g6 73 11.Rab1 Nf6 12.Ne5 Nf7 13.f4 Bd7

Black should have tried 13...Nxe5 14.dxe5 Ng4!.

14.Ndf3 Rfd8 15.b4 Be8 16.Rfc1 a6 (No.136) **17.Qf2**

White has already begun an attack on one flank, but this move gives notice that he intends to keep Black busy on the other flank as well.

17...Nxe5 18.Nxe5 Nd7 19.Nf3!

In dealing with the subject of the initiative in Chapters 23-26 we established the principle that the side with an advantage in space should avoid exchanges. The fact that we see this principle here during the process of maneuvering is not surprising, for alternating maneuvers are, as we know, a form of initiative.

19...Rdc8

Now Black will be completely hemmed in. Better was 19...dxc4 20.Bxc4 Bf7 followed by ...Nf6 or ...Nb6.

20.c5 Nf6 21.a4 Ng4 22.Qe1 Nh6 23.h3 Nf7 24.g4

White has the initiative on both sides of the board. The art of maneuvering now is to use the greater speed with which he can switch his forces from one flank to the other to stretch Black's cramped defenders to the breaking point.

24...Bd7 25.Rc2 Kh8 26.Rg2 Rg8 27.g5

Not 27.gxf5, which would have been fine for Black. White could not leave this pawn on the fourth rank any longer, as Black was threatening to free himself by ...g5.

27...Qd8 28.h4 Kg7

After 28...h5 29.gxh6 Nxh6 the g6 square would have been too weak.

29.h5

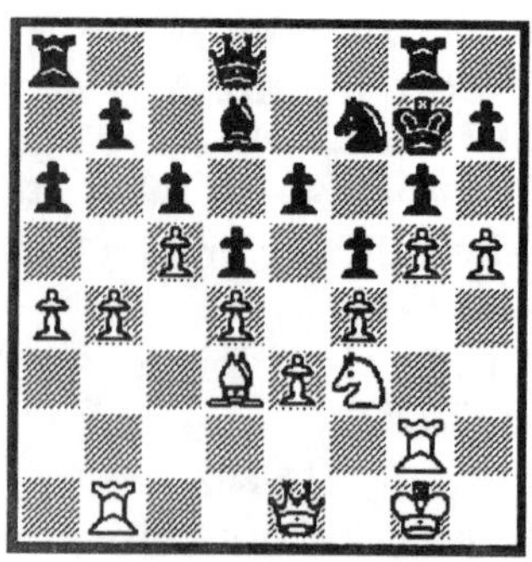

White has attained an ideal maneuvering position. At any favorable moment he can open a file for his Rooks on whichever flank he chooses.

29...Rh8 30.Rh2 Qc7 31.Qc3 Qd8

Black is completely passive.

32.Kf2 Qc7 33.Rbh1 Rag8 34.Qa1 Rb8 35.Qa3

Here and the next few moves Capablanca rather surprisingly rejects the thematic line Rh3, R1h2, and Qh1, trebling on the h-file.

35...Rbg8 36.b5!

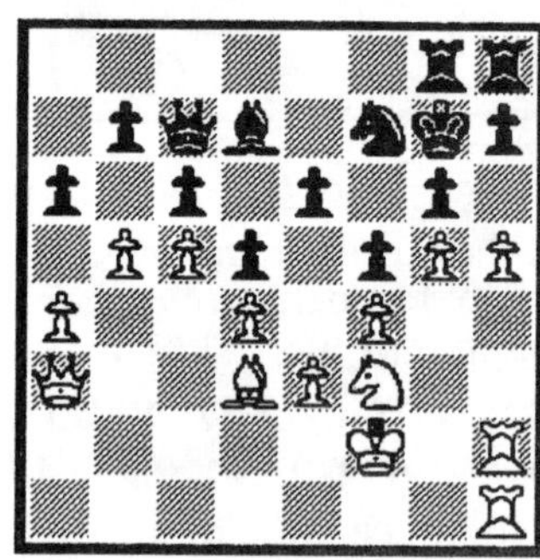

Based on the finesse 36...cxb5 37.h6+! Kf8 38.c6+ winning a piece.

36...axb5 37.h6+

An extremely important moment, in which the actions on the two flanks seem to converge. If instead of this White had played 37.axb5, Black could have obtained counterchances by 37...gxh5! 38.Rxh5 Ra8.

37...Kf8 38.axb5 Ke7 39.b6

Now Black is completely encircled.

39...Qb8 40.Ra1 Rc8 41.Qb4 Rhd8 42.Ra7

The play on both flanks is at an end, and now White can bring every piece over to the Queenside. The only vulnerable spot in Black's position is at b7. How can White possibly get at it? In spite of the terrible grip exerted by White's remarkable V-formation of pawns, the answer is not easy to see.

42...Kf8 43.Rh1 Be8 44.Rha1 Kg8 45.R1a4 Kf8 46.Qa3 Kg8 47.Kg3

The Knight will have to be brought via d2 and b3 to a5 to intensify the pressure on the b-pawn. Before embarking on this maneuver White must rule out the possibility of ...e5 by Black. If 47.Nd2 at once then Black could cause some trouble by 47...e5 48.fxe5 Nxe5.

47...Bd7 48.Kh4 Kh8 49.Qa1 Kg8 50.Kg3 Kf8 51.Kg2 Be8 52.Nd2 Bd7 53.Nb3 Re8

Or 53...Be8 54.Na5 Rd7 55.Nxb7 Rxb7 56.Ra8 winning.

54.Na5 Nd8

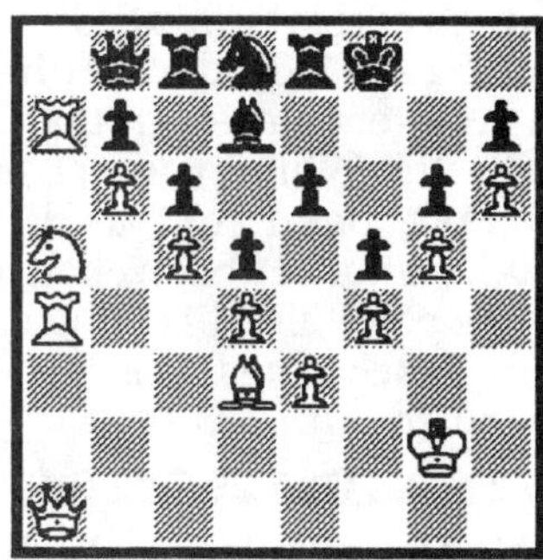

55.Ba6!!

The brilliant conclusion which Capablanca must have foreseen long ago.

55...bxa6 56.Rxd7 Re7

After 56...Kg8, 57.Nb3 wins the a-pawn.

57.Rxd8+ Rxd8 58.Nxc6 Black Resigned.

CHAPTER 38
ALEKHINE'S DYNAMIC MANEUVERING

Alekhine's games of maneuver generally took a livelier course than those of his contemporaries. He possessed a dynamic style which pervaded even his maneuvering. Time and time again we find his prolonged positional efforts interwoven with tactical complications. Here we show some examples of the dynamic qualities of his maneuvering methods.

POSITION 137

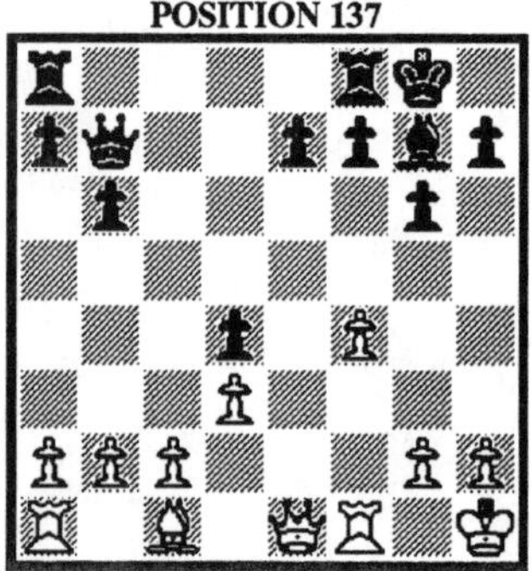

(The game Sir George Thomas-Alekhine, Baden-Baden, 1925).

1.e4 Nf6 2.d3 c5 3.f4 Nc6 4.Nf3 g6 5.Be2 Bg7 6.Nbd2 d5 7.O-O O-O 8.Kh1 b6 9.exd5? Qxd5 10.Qe1 Bb7 11.Nc4 Nd4 12.Ne3 Qc6 13.Bd1 Nd5 14.Nxd4

This leads to a serious weakening of the c-pawn. Stronger would have been 14.Nxd5 Qxd5 15.Rf2.

14...cxd4 15.Nxd5 Qxd5 16.Bf3 Qd7 17.Bxb7 Qxb7 (No.137) **18.c4**

The is no other way to secure the c-pawn; for example, 18.Rf2 Rac8 19.a4 Rc5 and White will be forced into such tortuous moves as 20.b3 Rfc8 21.Qd1 Qc7 22.Ra2. It would have been an improvement, however, to play 18.Bd2 Rac8 19.c4 dxc3 20.Bxc3. The pawn structure would be exactly the same as in the game, but by trading the Bishops White could obtain more chances of counterplay against Black's weakened Kingside.

18...dxc3 19.bxc3 Rac8 20.Bb2

A little better was 20.Bd2.

20...Rfd8 21.Rf3 Bf6 22.d4

This fixes both center pawns on the same color as their Bishop. Considered from the practical point of view 22.Qe2 Qa6 23.c4 would have offered the best counterchances. In that case admittedly the White pawn position would have been just as badly weakened; but after the exchange of Bishops the possibility of counterplay against the Black Kingside is certainly not to be ruled out.

22...Qd5 23.Qe3 Qb5 24.Qd2 Rd5

Here Nimzowitsch would have observed that the axis for Black's maneuvers is formed by the support points at d5 and c4.

25.h3 e6 26.Re1 Qa4

Reminding the opponent that he also has a weakness at a2.

27.Ra1 b5 28.Qd1 Rc4

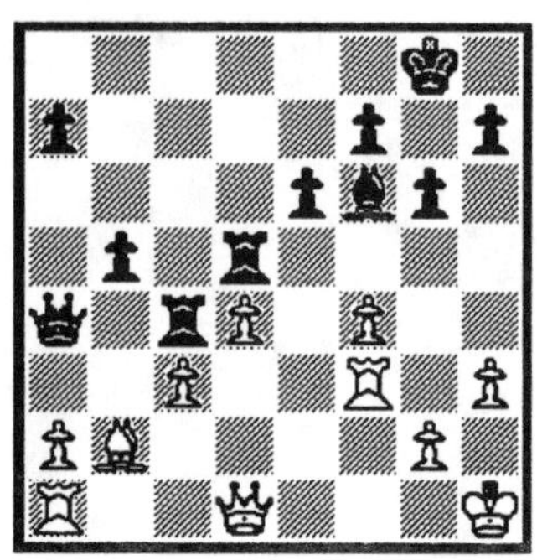

29.Qb3 Rd6 30.Kh2 Ra6 31.Rff1 Be7 32.Kh1 Rcc6 33.Rfe1 Bh4

Forcing the Rook off the e-file, for if 34.Re2 Black wins by 34...Qxb3 35.axb3 Rxa1+ 36.Bxa1 Ra6 37.Bb2 Ra2 38.Kh2 a5 and ...a4.

34.Rf1 Qc4

In typical maneuvering style. The scheme now is ...Ra4 followed by ...R6a6. Exchange of Queens can no longer be avoided.

35.Qxc4 Rxc4 36.a3

Forced, for White was threatened with the possibility of 36...b4.

36...Be7 37.Rfb1 Bd6

Black pauses to force yet another White pawn onto the same color as his Bishop.

38.g3 Kf8 39.Kg2 Ke7 40.Kf2 Kd7 41.Ke2 Kc6 42.Ra2

Now that the Black King is reinforcing the defense, White must be ready to meet 42...Rca4.

42...Rca4 43.Rba1 Kd5 44.Kd3 R6a5 45.Bc1 a6 46.Bb2

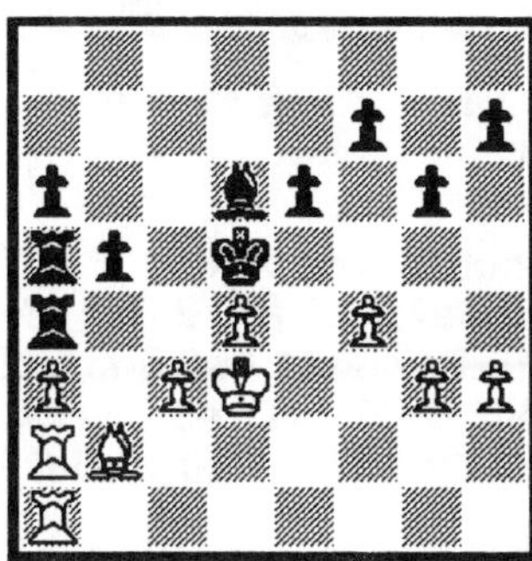

Black has accomplished all his aims; all that remains is the execution.

46...h5!

Threatening to unhinge White's whole game by 47...h4.

47.h4 f6 48.Bc1 e5 49.fxe5 fxe5 50.Bb2

Or 50.dxe5 Bxe5 51.Bf4 Bxf4 52.gxf4 Ke6 and ...Kf5.

50...exd4 51.cxd4 b4

Sealing the fate of the a-pawn.

52.axb4 Rxa2 53.bxa5 Rxb2 White Resigned.

POSITION 138

(The game Rubinstein-Alekhine, Dresden, 1926).

1.d4 Nf6 2.Nf3 e6 3.Bf4 b6 4.h3 Bb7 5.Nbd2 Bd6 6.Bxd6 cxd6 7.e3 O-O 8.Be2 d5 9.O-O Nc6 10.c3 Ne4 11.Nxe4 dxe4 12.Nd2 f5 13.f4 g5 14.Nc4 d5 15.Ne5 Nxe5 16.dxe5 Kh8 (No.138) **17.a4?**

At first sight White's position looks quite good. He has the better Bishop, and is threatening to take the initiative on the Queenside with a5. The sequel seems to show, however, that he is being too optimistic, and that he would have been wiser to play 17.g3 and if 17...Rg8 then 18.Kh2.

17...Rg8 18.Qd2 gxf4!

Based on the tactical finesse 19.exf4 Qh4 20.Kh1 Rxg2! 21.Kxg2 Rg8+ and Black wins quickly.

19.Rxf4 Qg5 20.Bf1 Qg3

Beginning to maneuver. The threat is 21...Qxh3

21.Kh1 Qg7! 22.Qd4 Ba6

Dashing White's only hope, for he must now give up his good Bishop for Black's bad one.

23.Rf2 Qg3 24.Rc2 Bxf1 25.Rxf1 Rac8

All the time Black operates with threats.

26.b3 Rc7 27.Re2 Rcg7 28.Rf4 Rc7 29.Rc2 Rcg7 30.Re2

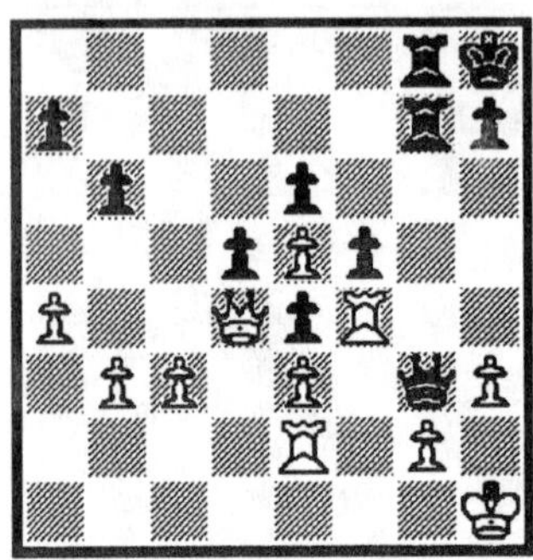

In the process of maneuvering it frequently happens that moves, even whole sequences, are repeated. In the present case the game has not reached an impasse, as one might think. Black's primary aim is to gain time, which was probably running short on his clock.

30...Rg6!

With the terrible threat of 31...Rh6 followed by ...Rxh3+.

31.Qb4

Alekhine, whose excellent annotations we are gratefully using, showed that if White had made the more natural move 31.Qd1 he would have found himself in *zugzwang* after Black's reply 31...Rh6: **1)** 32.Rf1 Qxe5. **2)** 32.Qf1 Qg7! and the e5 pawn is lost. **3)** 32.b4 Qg7 33.Qd4 Rxh3+!. **4)** 32.c4 d4! and wins.

31...Rh6 32.h4 Qg7!

Disdaining the obvious gain of the h-pawn, Black goes after bigger game.

33.c4

Or 33.Qd6 Rg6 34.R4f2 f4! 35.exf4 e3 36.Rxe3 Rxg2 and wins.

33...Rg6 34.Qd2 Rg3!

For the last time Black occupies the g3 support point, which in this game has functioned as the "Nimzowitchian" pivot square.

35.Qe1

There is no longer any defense against the threat of 35...Rh3+ 36.Kg1 Qg3; for instance 35.Kg1 d4! 36.exd4 e3 37.Qc2 Rh3 38.Qd3 Qg3 and wins. As we see, everything depends on the g3 square.

35...Rxg2 White Resigned.

POSITION 13

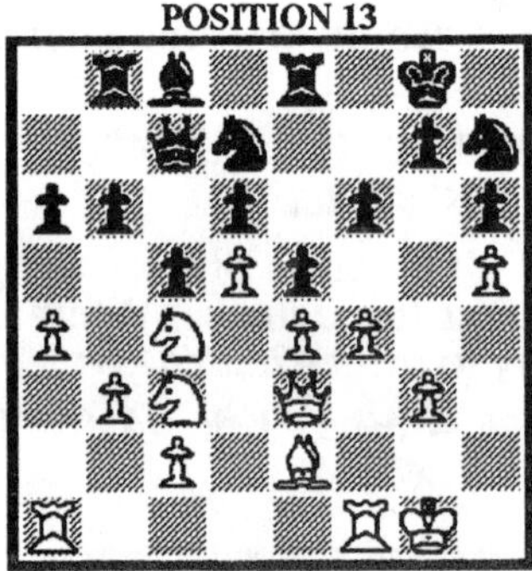

(The game Alekhine-Castillo, Buenos Aires, 1939).

1.d4 c5 2.d5 e5 3.e4 d6 4.Nc3 Ne7 5.g3 Ng6 6.h4 Be7 7.h5 Nf8 8.Bb5+ Nbd7 9.a4 a6 10.Be2 h6 11.Be3 Bg5 12.Qd2 Nh7 13.Nf3 Bxe3 14.Qxe3 O-O 15.Nd2 b6 16.Nc4 Qc7 17.f4 Re8 18.O-O Rb8 19.b3 f6

White has more space, and thereby the better chances. It is difficult, however, for him to strengthen his position any further, since it is hard to find a way to conveniently open a file. Moreover, White must be somewhat cautious as his own King position is a bit drafty for him to undertake anything reckless. In these circumstances there is only one possibility left: he must maneuver. Black, for his part, has just as little chance of opening a file without disadvantage. For instance, if 19...b5 then 20.axb5 axb5 21.Na5 would be very favorable for White. Black, therefore, must maneuver, but his pieces have less room in which to do it.

20.Qf2 Kh8 21.Kh2 Ndf8 22.Ne3

Otherwise Black could have played 22...b5 23.axb5 axb5 24.Na5 Bd7!.

22...Ra8 23.Rh1 Bd7 24.Qf1 Qb7 25.Kg2 Re7

Until now Black's moves have appeared to follow a regular pattern, with the aim of enforcing ...b5. This last move, however, does not fit into the pattern. Apparently Black has decided that ...b5 is not practicable.

26.Bd3 Be8 27.Qf3 Qc7 28.Rhf1 Qc8 29.Nc4 Qc7 30.Kh2 Qd8 31.Be2 Raa7 32.Rab1 Qc7 33.Rf2 Rb7 34.Ra1 Bd7 35.Ne3 Ra7 36.Raf1 Qb8 37.Ra1 Bc8 38.Qg2 Re8 39.Qf1 Qc7 40.Nc4 Qd8 41.Qd1 Rae7

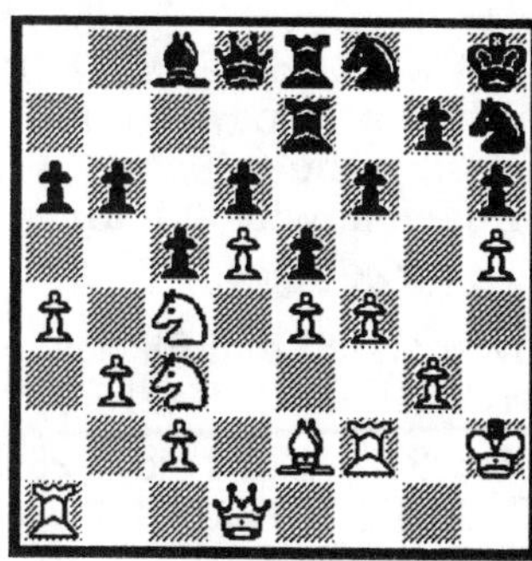

42.Bg4!

All this has looked like aimless woodshifting, but now suddenly it appears that White has achieved something. He threatens 43.Bxc8 Qxc8 44.Nxd6, while the exchange at e5 also portends danger for Black.

42...exf4?

A familiar occurrence after prolonged maneuvering: the opponent is losing his patience, and feels obliged to take some definite action.

43.gxf4 f5

With an eye on the open position of the White King. After either 44.exf5 Re3; or 44.Bxf5 Bxf5 45.exf5 Re3, Black would suddenly have a powerful attack.

44.Bh3!

This surprising riposte poses insoluble problems for Black, for 44...fxe4 fails against 45.Bxc8 Qxc8 46.Nxd6, while if Black does not take the e-pawn he has no good answer to the advance e5.

44...b5 45.axb5 axb5 46.Nxb5 Rxe4 47.Nbxd6 Qh4 48.Qf3 Nf6 49.Nxe8 Ng4+ 50.Kg2 Rxe8 51.Bxg4 fxg4 52.Qg3 Qxh5 53.f5! Bb7

Not 53...Bxf5 as 54.Nd6 wins.

54.Rd1 Ng6

A last desperate attempt to save the day.

55.fxg6 Bxd5+ 56.Rxd5 Qxd5+ 57.Kg1 Re1+ 58.Rf1 Rxf1+ 59.Kxf1 Qf5+ 60.Qf2 Qxg6 61.Qf8+ Kh7 62.Ne3 Qa6+ 63.Kf2 Qa7 64.Qf5+ g6 65.Qxg4 h5 66.Qf4 Qd7 67.Qe5 Black Resigned.

CHAPTER 39
INDIAN STYLE MANEUVERS: SULTAN KHAN

During the years 1928-32 a remarkable figure appeared in European tournaments – the Indian Mir Sultan Khan. He disappeared as suddenly as he had come, but during those few years his accomplishments were amazing.

It is a striking fact that although Sultan Khan must be regarded as a natural player, with no pretensions to knowledge of theory, yet he was an outstandingly skillful exponent of the art of maneuvering. It is thus reasonable to assume that the art of maneuver is an innate talent. Apparently it can be to some extent be assimilated by careful study, but is, in the final analysis more an intuitive ability than a learned methodology. Here we present Sultan Khan's most celebrated piece of maneuvering.

(The game Sultan Khan-Capablanca, Hastings, 1929-30).

1.Nf3 Nf6 2.d4 b6 3.c4 Bb7 4.Nc3 e6 5.a3 d5 6.cxd5 exd5 7.Bg5 Be7 8.e3 O-O 9.Bd3 Ne4 10.Bf4 Nd7 11.Qc2 f5

Stronger was 11...Ndf6.

12.Nb5 Bd6?

According to Dr.Tartakower, who analyzed this game in detail in his book *Neue Schachsterne,* the right defense was 12...a6!, the point being 13.Qxc7 is met by 13...axb5 14.Qxb7 Ndc5 15.dxc5 Nxc5 followed by 16...Nxd3+. Another important possibility is 13.Nxc7 Rc8 14.Ne6 Rxc2 15.Nxd8 Rxb2! 16.Nxb7 Nxf2, etc.

13.Nxd6 cxd6 14.h4 Rc8 15.Qb3 Qe7 16.Nd2 Ndf6 17.Nxe4 fxe4 18.Be2

POSITION 140

18...Rc6

With the obvious idea of doubling on the c-file.

19.g4! Rfc8

The d-pawn cannot be saved: 19...Qe6 20.g5 Nd7 21.Bb5 Rc7 22.Qb4 and Black must lose material.

20.g5 Ne8 21.Bg4!

Rather than play 21.Qxd5+ Kh8 22.Qb3 Rc1+ 23.Kd2 Rxa1 24.Rxa1 Qc7, which wins a pawn, but at the price of losing the initiative, White steers for the following liquidation.

21...Rc1+ 22.Kd2 R8c2+.

Tartakower stated that Black should have tried 22...Rxa1 23.Rxa1 Rc4.

23.Qxc2 Rxc2+ 24.Kxc2 Qc7+ 25.Kd2 Qc4 26.Be2 Qb3 27.Rab1 Kf7

After this Black will be totally devoid of counterplay. He had to try 27...b5 followed by ...b4, or else 27...Bc6 28.Rhc1 Bb5 29.Rc3 Qa4.

28.Rhc1 Ke7 29.Rc3 Qa4 30.b4! Qd7

White was threatening to put the Queen out of play by 31.b5.

31.Rbc1

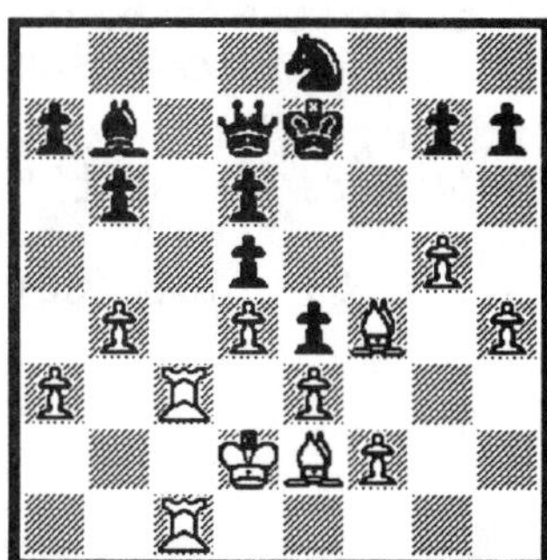

Although it is clear that White has the advantage, both materially and positionally, the fact remains that no direct win is possible. Hence White commences maneuvering.

31...a6 32.Rg1 Qa4 33.Rgc1 Qd7

The threat was 34.Rc7+ Nxc7 35.Rxc7+ and 36.Rxb7.

34.h5 Kd8 35.R1c2 Qh3

The Queen is still active, but can achieve nothing.

36.Kc1 Qh4 37.Kb2

Before proceeding with serious maneuvering White places his King in a safe corner, just as we have seen in the games of Nimzowitsch.

37...Qh3 38.Rc1 Qh4 39.R3c2 Qh3 40.a4 Qh4 41.Ka3 Qh3 42.Bg3 Qf5

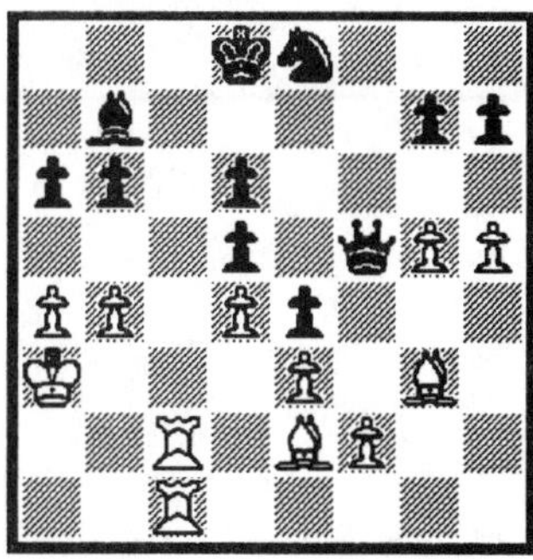

43.Bh4

Suddenly White introduces a small finesse. Now if Black plays 43...Qh3 then White has 44.g6+! Qxh4 45.gxh7 and the pawn promotes. Nor is 43...Kd7 playable, for White could reply 44.Rg1! threatening 45.Bg4. These lines demonstrate the exploitation of the exposed Black King.

43...g6 44.h6

What has White achieved by this little intermezzo? In the first place his h-pawn is no longer vulnerable, and secondly the Black Knight is now completely immobilized.

44...Qd7

On 44...Qh3 White has 45.Bg3 Qf5 46.Bf4.

45.b5 a5

Black cannot allow the opening of diagonals. After 45...axb5 46.Bxb5 followed by 47.Bxe8, the White Rooks penetrate down the c-file.

46.Bg3 Qf5 47.Bf4 Qh3 48.Kb2 Qg2 49.Kb1

The f-pawn is indirectly protected: 49...Qxf2 50.Bh5 Qh4 51.Rh2 trapping the Queen.

49...Qh3 50.Ka1 Qg2 51.Kb2 Qh3 52.Rg1!

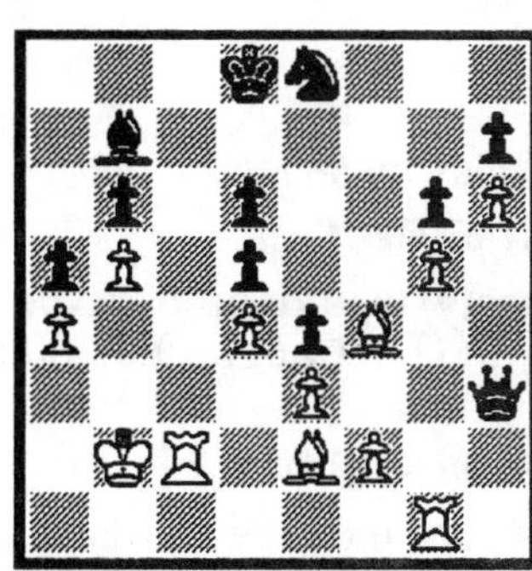

The decisive phase is rapidly approaching, with direct threats beginning to appear. Black now must defend against the threat of 53.Bg4 Qh4 54.Be6 followed by 55.Bg8 – not to mention 53.Bg4 Qh4 54.f3! exf3 55.Bxf3 Qh3 56.Bg4 Qh4 57.Rh2 trapping the Queen.

52...Bc8

The retreat of the Queen is no better, as the following variations given by H. Johner in the *Neue Zuricher Zeitung* demonstrate: **1)** 52...Qe6 53.Bg4 Qf7 54.Rgc1 Qg8 55.Rc8+! Bxc8 56.Rxc8+ Ke7 57.Rb8 Qh8 58.Rb7+ Kf8 59.Be6 and wins. **2)** 52...Qd7 53.Bg4 Qe7 54.Rgc1 Qf7 55.Rc3 Qg8 56.Rc8+! and wins.

53.Rc6! Qh4

As Tartakower pointed out, there was also the possibility 53...Bb7 54.Bg4! Qh4 55.Rc2, and the Queen hunt is on.

54.Rgc1 Bg4

The continuation 54...Bb7 would only have led to the exchange of the worthless White f-pawn for the valuable Black b-pawn: 55.Rxb6 Qxf2 56.Rc2 Bc8 57.Rb8 Nc7 58.Bg4 and wins.

55.Bf1! Qh5

Even with check, Black cannot take the f-pawn: 55...Qxf2+ 56.R6c2 Qg1 57.Rg2 Qh1 58.Rh2 Qg1 (58...Qf3 59.Be2 Qxe2+ 60.Rxe2 Bxe2 61.Rc6) 59.Be2, etc.

56.Re1

Otherwise Black gets some counterplay by 56...Be2.

56...Qh1 57.Rec1

Too hasty would be 57.Rxb6 Bh3 58.Rc6 Bxf1 59.R6c1 Qf3! 60.Rxf1 Qe2+.

57...Qh5 58.Kc3! Qh4

White's last move prevents 58...Be2. For example 59.Kd2! Bxf1 60.Rxf1 Qf3 61.Bg3 Qg4 62.Rfc1 Qxg5 63.Rxb6 Qxh6 64.Rb8+ Ke7 65.Rxe8+ Kxe8 66.b6 and wins.

59.Bg3! Qxg5 60.Kd2 Qf5 61.Rxb6

The fall of this pawn robs the Black position of all cohesion. Against the furious activity of the White pieces there is nothing to be done.

61...Ke7 62.Rb7+ Ke6 63.b6 Nf6 64.Bb5 Qf3 65.Rb8 Black Resigned.

The end might have been: **1)** 65...Nd7 66.Re8+ Kf7 67.b7! Bh5 68.Re1 Bg4 69.Bxd7, or **2)** 65...Nh5 66.Re8+ Kf7 67.Rc7+ Kf6 68.Rf8+.

CHAPTER 40
MORE RECENT GAMES OF MANEUVER

We conclude our survey of the art of maneuver by exemplifying its use in modern tournament games. We shall see that the ideas developed from Nimzowitsch and others have lost none of their validity.

(The game Averbakh-Neikirch, Portoroz, 1958).

1.e4 e5 2.Nf3 Nc6 3.Bb5 a6 4.Ba4 Nf6 5.O-O Be7 6.Re1 b5 7.Bb3 O-O 8.c3 d6 9.h3 Na5 10.Bc2 c5 11.d4 Qc7 12.Nbd2 Nc6 13.dxe5 dxe5 14.Nf1 Bd6 15.Nh4 Ne7 16.Qf3 Rd8 17.Ne3 Qc6?

POSITION 141

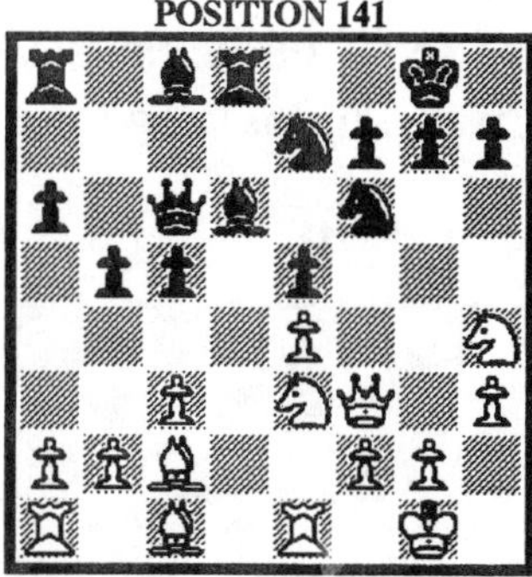

18.c4

White plays for control of d5. Admittedly this weakens d4, but this is only of academic importance while Black has no way of occupying it.

18...Ne8

Hoping to reach d4 by way of c7 and e6.

19.Bb3

Threatening 20.cxb5 axb5 21.Qxf7+ mating, and so forcing Black's reply.

19...b4 20.Nd5 Qb7?

This allows White to post the Bishop actively on a4. The tournament book gives 20...a5 as better and if 21.Bg5 then 21...Ra7.

21.Ba4 Nc7 22.Bg5!

22...Ncxd5

The natural 22...Ne6 fails to 23.Bxe7 Bxe7 24.Bc6!. Also, the interpolation 23...Nd4 does not help after 24.Nf6+ Kh8 25.Qh5 and White wins. Finally, 22....f6 is poor because of 23.Nxf6+ gxf6 24.Qxf6 with a terrific attack.

23.cxd5 f6 24.Be3 Bd7

Now the siege of Black's c-pawn begins. 24...c4 25.Rac1 is no improvement.

25.Bxd7 Qxd7 26.Rac1 Rdc8 27.Rc4 Rab8 28.b3 Rc7 29.Rec1 Rb5 30.g4!

The familiar motif: with most of the Black forces tied to the defense of the c-pawn, White opens a second front on the other side of the board.

30...g5 31.Ng2 Kg7 32.h4 h6 33.h5!

Denying Black the use of g6.

33...a5 34.Ne1 Qc8 35.Nd3 (see next diagram) **35...f5**

A rather desperate attempt to get some counterplay. Black is totally tied up by the need to defend the c-pawn. It is sufficiently protected now, but

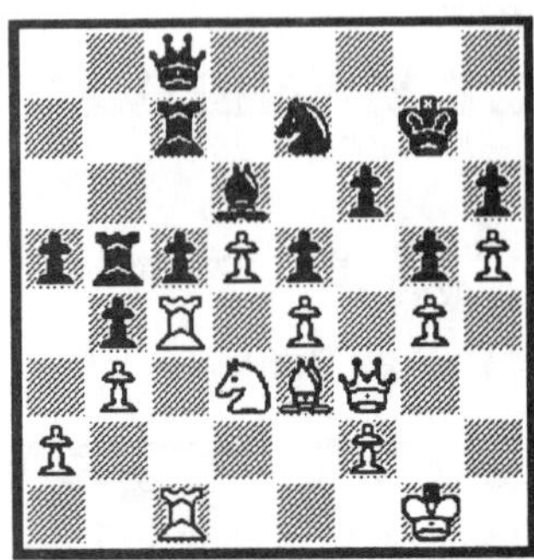

After 35.Nd3

after White plays Qe2, f3, and Qf2 it would be lost anyway.

36.exf5 Ng8 37.Re1

Now the Black e-pawn is going to suffer.

37...Nf6 38.Bc1! Rf7

No better is 38...e4 in view of 39.Rcxe4 Nxe4 40.Qxe4 and 41.Bb2+.

39.Bb2 Qc7 40.Rce4!

Beautifully decisive.

40...Nxe4 41.Qxe4 Kf6 and **Black Resigned** without waiting for 42.Nxe5.

POSITION 142

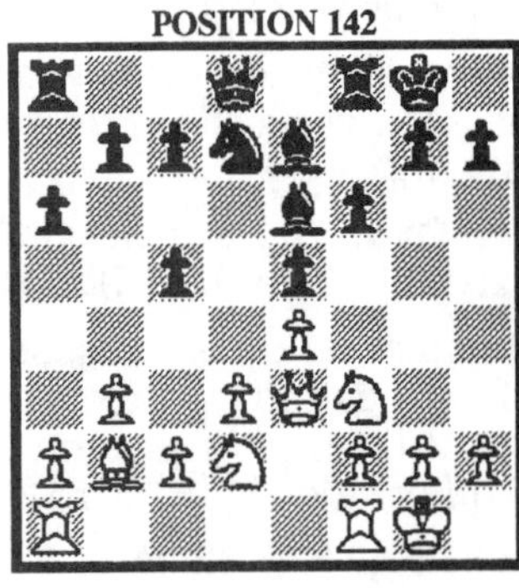

(The game Blau-Keres, Zurich, 1959).

1.e4 e5 2.Nf3 Nc6 3.Bb5 a6 4.Ba4 Nf6 5.O-O Be7 6.Bxc6 dxc6 7.Qe1 Be6 8.d3 Nd7 9.b3 c5 10.Bb2 f6 11.Nbd2 O-O 12.Qe3 (No.142) **12...Nb8**

The Knight is heading for d4 via c6. At d4 it may be exchanged, in which case Black dissolves his doubled pawns by the recapture; or if it is driven back by c3 the White d-pawn is left weakened.

13.Rfd1 Nc6 14.c3 Qe8 15.Rac1 Rd8 16.Nf1

White could have advanced his backward d-pawn, but this advance, of course, has the drawback of allowing Black to get rid of his doubled c-pawns. Also, the position would be opened up for the two Bishops. For example, 16.d4 cxd4 17.cxd4 exd4 18.Nxd4 Nxd4 19.Bxd4 Qh5! and now 20.Rxc7 loses to 20...Bd6. So, one way or another it seems best for White to continue maneuvering.

16...Rf7 17.Ng3 Bf8 18.Rd2

White passes up his last good chance to play d4.

18...Rfd7 19.Rcd1

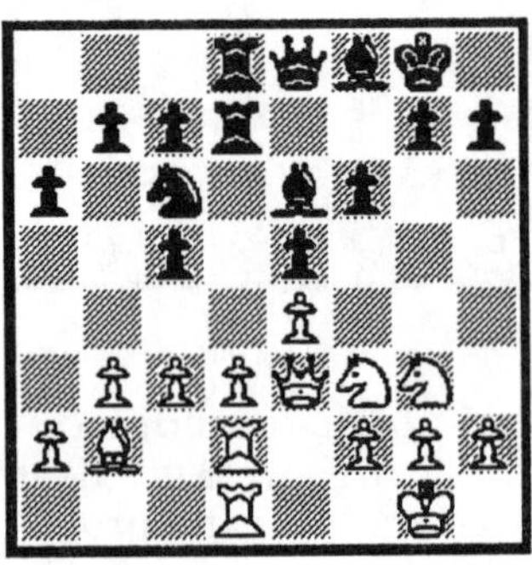

19...a5!

Now that the d-pawn has been definitely relegated to the status of backward pawn (for 20.d4 would be answered by 20...cxd4 21.cxd4 exd4 22.Nxd4 Bc5), it is a weakness. Black therefore loses no time in seeking to create a second weakness in White's position.

20.Ne2 a4 21.bxa4

The passive 21.Nf1 axb3 22.axb3 Na5 was no better, but an immediate 21.c4 was worth consideration.

21...Ra8! 22.Nc1

Now 22.d4 could be answered by 22...cxd4 23.cxd4 Bb4.

22...Rxa4 23.c4

Not an easy decision, but White had only unpleasant choices here. On 23.Ba1 Black has 23...Qa8, while 23.a3 is no improvement either.

23...Nd4 24.h3 g6 25.Bxd4 cxd4 26.Qe2 Qa8 27.Rc2

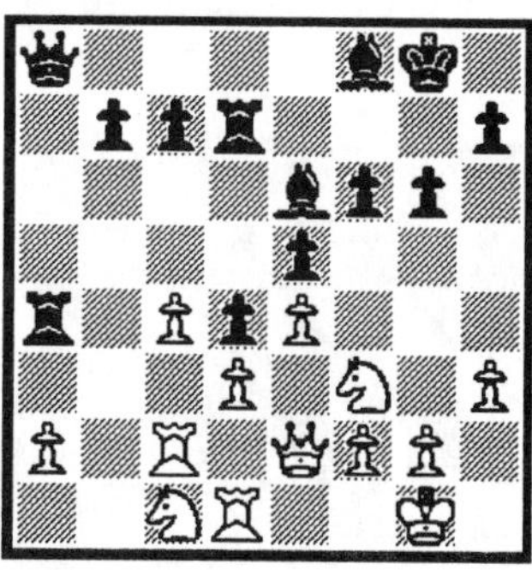

27...Rd6

Now the game acquires a new aspect, and Black begins to maneuver in earnest against the enemy weak points.

28.Nd2 Rb6 29.Ndb3 Ra3 30.Kh2 c5 31.g3

In order to play f4 later, but he is never able to get it in.

31...Qc8 32.Qf1 Bh6 33.Qg2 Bd7 34.Re2 Qc7 35.Rde1

White prevents ...f5 by putting indirect pressure against the Black e-pawn.

35...Re6 36.Qf3

Again restraining ...f5.

36...Kg7 37.Rc2 Ba4 38.Rb2 Rb6 39.Ree2? Rb4?

Time pressure; both players overlooked the win of the exchange by 39...Bxc1 40.Nxc1 Bd1.

40.Qg2

Up until now White's defensive lines have held up under heavy pressure. All the same he has had to concede terrain, and his pieces have been forced back all along the line. In the closing phase of the game Black decides to give up the two Bishops, as in this way he is able to facilitate the attack on the d-pawn.

40...b5! 41.cxb5 Bxc1 42.Nxc1 Rc3 43.Qf1 Bxb5 44.Rec2 Ba4 45.Nb3

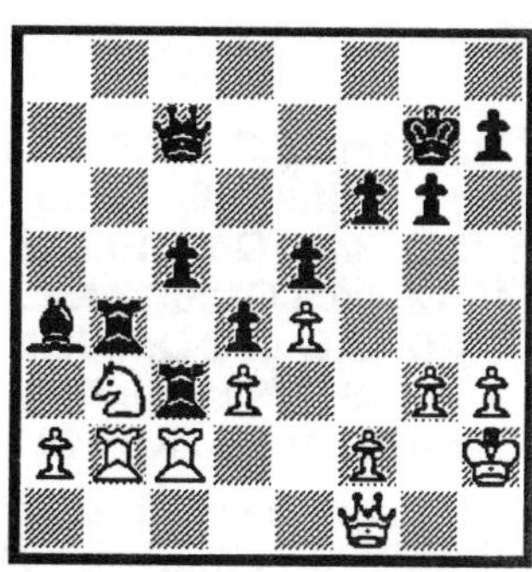

Hoping for 45...Rxc2 46.Rxc2 Bxb3 47.axb3 Rxb3 48.Qc1! with counter-chances. For that matter, White had nothing better; if 45.Rxc3 Rxb2 46.Ra3 Black continues 46...Qa5, while 45.Rxb4 cxb4 46.Rxc3 allows the strong reply 46...Qxc3.

45...Qb6! 46.Qc1 Bxb3 47.axb3 Rbxb3 48.Ra2

After 48.Rxb3 Qxb3 49.Rxc3 dxc3 50.Qa1 c2 51.Qa7+ Kh6 52.Qxc5 Qxd3 53.Qf8+ Kg5 54.h4+ Kg4! Black wins.

48...Rxd3 49.Rxc5 Rdc3 50.Rxc3 dxc3 51.Rc2 Rb2 52.Kg2 g5 53.h4 Qb7 54.Rxc3

The e-pawn cannot be saved. If 54.f3 then 54...Qb3 wins, or if 54.Kf3 g4+ 55.Ke3 Qb6+ 56.Kd3 Qd4+ and wins. And if White tries 54.Rxb2 then Black wins with either recapture.

54...Qxe4+ 55.Rf3 Rb3 56.Qd1 Qxf3+ 57.Qxf3 Rxf3 58.Kxf3 gxh4 59.gxh4 f5 White Resigned.

POSITION 143

(The game Olafsson-Alster, Wageningen, 1957).

1.d4 f5 2.Nc3 d5 3.Bg5 g6 4.h4 Bg7 5.Qd2 Nc6 6.Nf3 Nf6 7.Bh6 Bxh6 8.Qxh6 Be6 9.e3 Qd7 10.Bb5 Ng4 11.Qf4 a6 12.Bxc6 Qxc6 13.Ne5 Nxe5 14.Qxe5 Kd7 15.O-O-O Qd6 16.Ne2 c6 17.Nf4 Rhg8 18.Rd3 b6 19.Rb3 Rab8 20.Nd3 Qxe5 21.Nxe5+ Kd6 22.f4 c5

To close our study of the techniques of maneuvering we examine a position which one might have expected to find in a book on the ending. We repeat that the art of maneuvering is by no means peculiar to the middlegame. It is precisely in the ending that typical alternating tactics are frequently necessary in order to turn some definite advantage into a win. We have in mind in this case the common ending with Knight against bad Bishop which often arises out of the French Defense, with White pawns on d4, e5, and f4 against Black pawns on d5, e6, and f7. The present position is of this type. The presence of four Rooks means that it retains some middlegame character, but even so the Knight is stronger than the bad Bishop. For the time being, however, this advantage is not a decisive one. White has the initiative and uses it to carry out the following maneuvers.

23.Ra3 Ra8 24.Rd3

White avoids having his Rook cut off from play by Black's ...c5-c4.

24...Kc7 25.Rh3 Rad8 26.Rd1 Rg7 27.Rg3 Rdg8 28.Rh1 Kd6 29.Kd2 Bc8 30.Ke2 Be6 31.Kf2 Bf7

In the tournament book Bouwmeester gives two other possibilities: **1)** 31...h5 and now: a) 32.Rg5 Bd7 33.Rh3 c4 34.Rhg3 Be8 and White is getting nowhere on the Kingside. b) 32.c3 c4 33.Rb1 and White transfers the zone of battle to the Queenside. **2)** 31...h6 and now 32.h5 can be met by 32...g5. In this case also, White will have to try his luck on the other flank. He will, however, have to be continually alert for a possible Black ...g5.

32.h5!

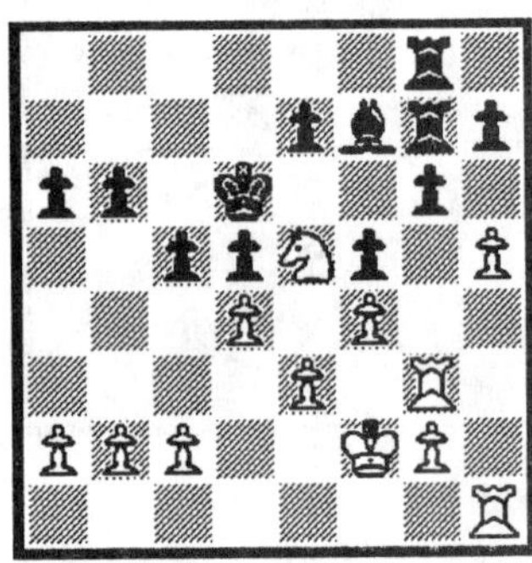

Since 32...gxh5 loses to 33.Nxf7+, Black has to allow a weakening of his pawns.

32...Rf8

White threatened 33.h6.

33.hxg6 Bxg6

Forced, for 33...hxg6 loses a pawn to 34.Rh6.

34.Rh6 Rfg8 35.Nf3

En route for g5 to put pressure on the weak h-pawn.

35...e6 36.Ng5 Rc7 37.c3 c4 38.Nf3

Since 38.Rgh3 gets nowhere after 38...Rgg7, White begins to maneuver, with the goal of creating a second weakness.

38...b5 39.Ke1 b4

A clever counterthrust, with the idea of 40.cxb4 c3 41.bxc3 Rxc3 42.Kd2 Rgc8.

40.Kd2 bxc3+

Better was 40...a5, maintaining the tension.

41.Kxc3 Rb7 42.Ne5 Rbg7

After 42...Rgb8 43.Nxg6 hxg6 44.Rgxg6 Rxb2 45.Rxe6+ White wins.

43.b3 cxb3 44.axb3 Rb8 45.Nd3

On 45.Nxg6 Black has the simple reply 45...Rbg8.

45...Re7 46.Rh1

White has forced the second weakness. Now he fastens on the Black a-pawn.

46...a5 47.Ra1 Ra8 48.Nc5 Raa7 49.Ra2 Kc6 50.Rh3 Kb5 51.Rh1 Be8 52.Rb1 Kc6

White was threatening 53.b4 axb4+ 54.Rxb4+ Kc6 55.Rxa7 Rxa7 56.Nxe6.

53.Kd3 Kb5 54.Kc3 Kc6 55.Rbb2 h5 56.b4

Since White is getting no farther with his attack on the Black a-pawn, he decides to exchange it for his own destitute b-pawn. This, however, is simplification which improves Black's drawing chances.

56...axb4+ 57.Kxb4 Kd6 58.Kc3

Now White threatens 59.Rb6+ Bc6 60.Rxa7 Rxa7 61.Nxe6! forcing a won ending: e.g., 61...Ra3+ 62.Kd2 Ra2+ 63.Kd3 Rxg2 64.Nd8 Kc7 65.Rxc6+ Kxd8 66.Rd6+ and wins, as given by Bouwmeester in the tournament book.

58...Bc6 59.Kd2

Before understanding anything further White transfers his King to the other flank.

59...h4 60.Ke1 Rxa2

This is inevitable in the long run, for otherwise White will bring his King to h3.

61.Rxa2 Rh7 62.Ra6 h3!

Indirectly protecting his e-file, and at the same time dissolving one of his weaknesses.

63.gxh3 Rxh3 64.Kf2 Rh2+ 65.Kg3 Rh6 66.Nd3

Threatening 67.Ne5 or 67.Nb4. The squares e5 and c5 form what Nimzowitsch would have called the axis of White's operations.

66...Kc7 67.Ra7+ Kd8?

This is the final mistake. The correct play was 67...Kd6 68.Ne5 Be8 after which it is not clear how White could have gotten any farther.

68.Nc5

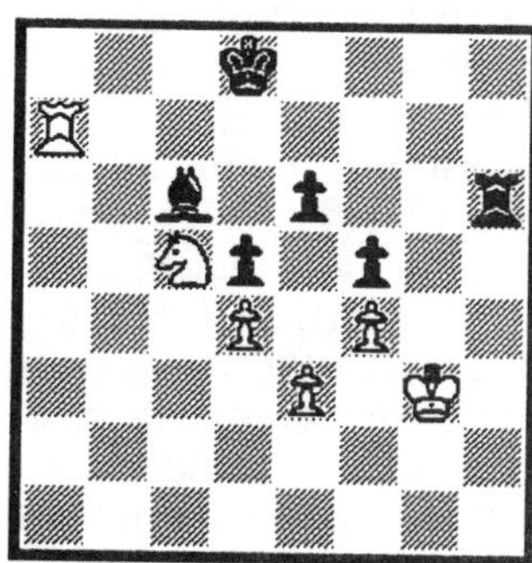

Now that the Black King can no longer protect the e-pawn, this duty must be permanently undertaken by the Rook. This allows His White Majesty to enter the front line in person.

68...Be8 69.Kf2 Rh2+ 70.Ke1 Rh6 71.Kd2 Bh5 72.Kc3 Ke8 73.Kb4 Bf7 74.Nd7

Now White can attack the Black position with his Knight at one end of the axis (e5) and his King at the other end (c5). Against this invasion there is nothing to be done; e.g., 74...Rh3 75.Ne5 Bh5 76.Kc5 Rxe3 77.Kd6 Kf8 78.Kxe6 Re4 79.Kf6 Kg8 80.Rg7+ Kh8 81.Rg3! Bg4 82.Ra3! Kg8 83.Ra8+ Kh7 84.Nf7 and wins. **Black Resigned.**

PART TEN
LIQUIDATION
INTRODUCTION

Dr. Tarrasch once remarked that there is nothing more difficult than to win a won game. This pronouncement could well serve as the motto for our next four chapters. We hasten to add, however, that liquidation is not seen only in the middlegame. It often occurs as a means of transition from the middlegame to the ending; there are plenty of examples of it in the opening.

The problem of liquidation is to choose the exact moment when pieces, or some particular piece, should be exchanged. The tempting idea of forcing a win or draw by trading off all the enemy pawns or pieces is difficult to realize in practice. Judicious liquidation involves steering a median course between the one extreme of premature simplification and the other extreme of interminable "woodshifting". Knowledge of the ending plays an outstandingly important role, for without this knowledge it is difficult and sometimes impossible to assess the correctness of a possible liquidation.

The transition from opening to middlegame is quite often associated with the exchange of one or more pieces; while the transition from middlegame to ending can occur only by means of liquidation in some form or other. During the middlegame itself there are two main reasons to exchange pieces. The first motive is one of defense: when under attack, one strives to exchange off dangerous enemy pieces. This is basically a security measure. The other motive for exchanging pieces arises when one has some distinct advantage. Then it is natural to play to consolidate this advantage in the endgame, thus eliminating the possibility of sudden counterattacks by the opponent.

Far and away the most interesting chapter of this section is Chapter 44: Combinative Liquidation. At the beginning of the liquidation or at the end, or during the actual process, there suddenly comes an unexpected move, a stroke of inspiration, which converts mere automatic simplification into an attractive combination.

In addition to the reasons given above for going in for liquidation there remains one other very important motive which applies to a certain class of players – they just prefer simplified positions. It is no accident that this section contains so many examples drawn from the games of Capablanca, for in such positions Capablanca was absolutely in his element – like a fish in water.

CHAPTER 41
LIQUIDATION IN THE OPENING

Everyone must have met the sort of game in which the Queens are exchanged at the very outset-usually with the idea of preventing the opponent from castling.

From the theoretical point of view this would usually lead to a small advantage. Since the King cannot be castled into safety the King would be relegated to staying in the center, which, as we well know, can become dangerous. Moreover, even if the chances of direct attack on the King should not be especially dangerous (and this is usually the case, since the most dangerous attacking piece has just been exchanged off) yet this kind of exchange of Queens can still lead to trouble. The point is that it is often more difficult to unite the Rooks, since one must first find a haven for the King. A familiar example of this type of liquidation is the variation: 1.d4 Nf6 2.c4 d6 3.Nc3 e5 4.dxe5 dxe5 5.Qxd8+ Kxd8.

Even when loss of castling is not involved, the trade of Queens in the opening may still yield an enduring initiative; this is shown in our next game.

(The game Rossolimo-Euwe, Beverwijk, 1953).

1.e4 e5 2.Nf3 Nc6 3.Bc4 Be7 4.d4 d6

POSITION 144

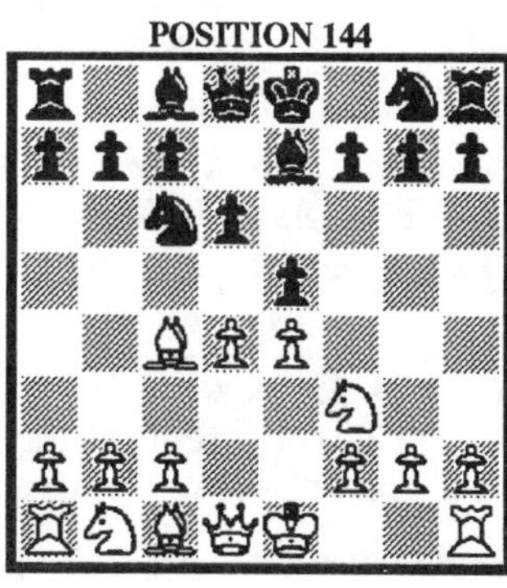

5.dxe5 dxe5 6.Qxd8+ Bxd8 7.Nc3

White's liquidation has simplified the position, but Black's game is not easy. He could play 7...Nf6 and then castle, but after 8.Bb5 Bd7 9.O-O O-O 10.Re1 Re8 11.Bg5 a6 12.Rad1 he would find himself in trouble.

7...f6

Protecting the e-pawn, so that Black can now threaten to drive the Bc4 off of its important diagonal by 8...Na5.

8.a3 Na5 9.Ba2 b6 10.Be3 Nb7

The consequent move 10...Ba6 would be met by 11.Nd2! with the powerful threat of 12.b4.

11.O-O-O Nd6 12.Nd2

Black has been losing time, therefore White avails himself of the chance to improve the placing of his pieces. This move casts an eye towards the c4 square while also making f4 a possibility.

12...Ne7 13.Nc4 Nxc4?

This is a typical mistake: Black thinks he is easing his defense by exchanging. He should have played ...Nf7, overprotecting his e-pawn, an important precaution in the event of a White f4.

14.Bxc4 c6 15.Ne2

Worth a thought was 15.b4, with the idea of continuing with 16.b5, obtaining a support point on d5.

15...Bc7 16.h3 Bd7?

Now 17.Bf7+ Kxf7 18.Rxd7 would not help, for Black would continue 18...Rac8 and 19...Rhd8. White need not hurry with the liquidation.

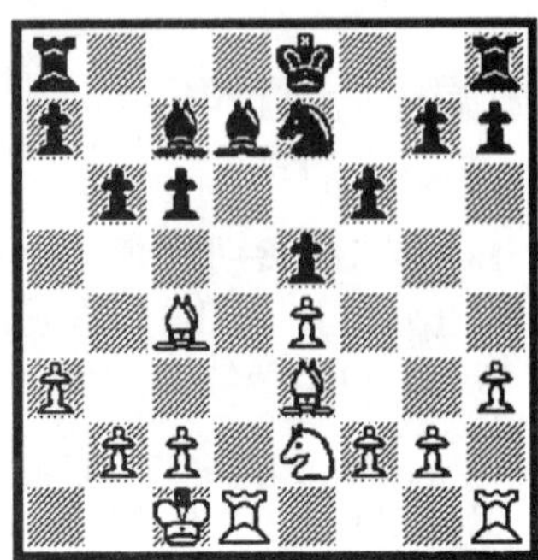

(White still defers liquidation).

17.Ng3!

Threatening 18.Nh5. If Black parries with 17...g6 White can continue with 18.Bh6! and win the Exchange – a clear demonstration of the strength of the Bishop on c4. On the other hand if Black continues with the natural 17...Rd8 and on 18.Nh5 Kf8 to evict the Knight by ...Be8, the surprising sequel would be 19.Rd2 Be8 20.Nxf6! gxf6 21.Bh6#!.

17...h5

Practically forced.

18.Bf7+ Kxf7 19.Rxd7 Rac8 20.Nf5!

Forestalling for the time being the possibility of having the Rook forced off by Black's ...Rhd8.

20...Rhe8 21.Rhd1 Kf8 22.Nd6 Bxd6 23.R1xd6

White's advantage is now decisive.

23...Ra8 24.a4

Such moves as this are characteristic of the theme of Chapter 17 – *The Struggle for the Diagonals.* White strives to bring his Bishop back to life by opening a diagonal.

24...c5

Temporarily closing the diagonal.

25.Re6 Kf7 26.Red6

Also good would have been 26.Rc6. White maneuvers in search of a better plan.

26...Kf8 27.Kd2!

Here is one great advantage of liquidation in the opening: the King himself can play an active part in the fight.

27...Rec8 28.Kc3 Nc6 29.Kc4 Nd8

There would be no point in playing to d4, for White would simply play 30.c3.

30.c3 Nf7 31.Rd2

Stronger would have been 31.Re6; but under time pressure, White is taking no risks.

31...Ke8 32.Kb5 Rd8

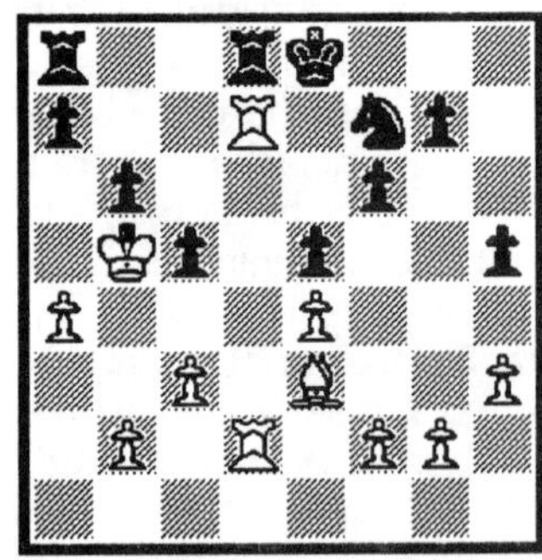

(Now White must liquidate further).

33.Rxd8+ Nxd8

33...Rxd8 is quite hopeless, for after 34.Rxd8+ Black loses quickly after 34...Nxd8 35.a5, or 34...Kxd8 35.Ka6.

34.a5! Rb8 35.axb6 Rxb6+

Black must lose a pawn; after 35...axb6 White plays 36.Rd6.

36.Kxc5 Nb7+ 37.Kd5 Ra6 38.b4 Kd7 39.Kc4+

Operating at the head of his troops, the King does not feel altogether safe. He therefore retires in order to prepare for c4. It is clear that this move could not be played forthwith!.

39...Nd6+ 40.Kb3 Kc7 41.f3

The rest is simple technique.

41...Ra1

On 41...Nb5 White plays 42.Rd5!.

42.Bc5 Ne8 43.Kb2 Ra6 44.Rd1 Kc8 45.Kb3 Nc7 46.c4 Ne6 47.Be3 Nf4 48.b5 Re6 49.Bxf4 exf4 50.Rd5 g6 51.c5 Kc7 52.Kc4 Re8 53.Rd6 f5 54.Rxg6 fxe4 55.Rg7+ Kb8 56.fxe4 Rxe4+ 57.Kd5 Re8 58.c6 Re2 59.Rb7+ Ka8 60.Rf7 Kb8 61.Rb7+ Ka8 62.Rf7 Kb8 63.Rxf4 Rxg2 64.Rf8+ Kc7 65.Rf7+ Kb8 66.Rb7+ Ka8 67.Rh7 Rg5+ 68.Kd6 Black Resigned.

POSITION 145

(How an early exchange of Queens can sometimes lead to a strong attack on the King. From the game Prins-Kotov, Amsterdam, 1954).

1.d4 Nf6 2.c4 d6 3.Nc3 e5 4.dxe5 dxe5 5.Qxd8+ Kxd8 6.Bg5 Be7 7.Nf3 Nbd7 (No.145) **8.Bh4**

A multi-purpose move. White clears g5 for occupation by a Knight, and at the same time prepares to plant the Bishop on g3, attacking the e-pawn. In itself this attack is nothing unusual, but the presence of the Bishop on g3 has an ulterior significance. The structure of the position will sooner or later require Black to play ...c6, and the ideal post for his King would typically be on c7, after which he could complete his development. However, it is clear that the existence of a White Bishop on g3 would defeat Black's ideas. As a result the Black King will be relegated to staying in the center, with all the dangers that implies.

8...c6 9.O-O-O

More exact than 9.Bg3, which would permit 9...Bd6!.

9...Ng4

If Black persists with 9...Kc7 there follows 10.Bg3 Bd6 11.c5! Nxc5 12.Nxe5; or if 10...Ng4? then 11.h3.

10.Bg3 f6

In this way Black tries to build a barrier against the enemy Bishop while solidly protecting the e-pawn.

11.Nh4 Nh6 12.e4 Bb4 13.Be2!

This is logical. Since White means to take advantage of the insecurity of Black's King in the center, he does not shrink from the doubling of his c-pawn which would arise after ...Bxc3. This exchange would open up more lines against the Black King.

13...Ke7 14.f4!

The indicated means of freeing the Bishop.

14...exf4 15.Bxf4 g5?

After 15...Nf7 16.Nf5+ would be strong; but 15...Ne5! would have been better than the move played. Exchange on h6 by White would only ease Black's game.

16.Be3 Ne5 17.Nf3 Nhg4 18.Bg1 Be6 (see next diagram) **19.Nd4!!**

It seemed that Black, with his last move, had reached the end of his troubles; but this reply of White's demonstrates otherwise.

19...Bxc3

It is easy enough to see that 19...Nxc4 would fail to 20.Nxe6 Kxe6 21.Bxc4+.

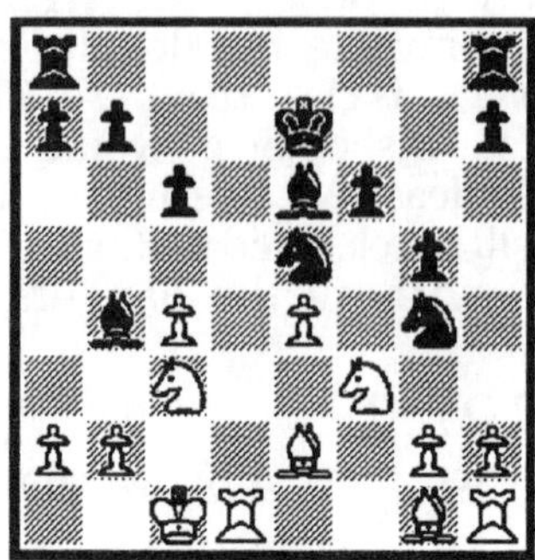

After 18...Be6

Less easy to reckon out are the consequences of 19...Bxc4 20.Nf5+. For instance: **1)** 20...Ke6 21.h3! Bxc3 22.Rd6+ Kf7 23.Bxc4+ Nxc4 24.Rd7+ Ke8 25.Re7+ Kd8 26.bxc3 (or 26.hxg4) and White dominates. **2)** 20...Kf7 21.h3 Bxc3 22.Nd6+ Ke7 23.Nxc4 winning a piece. **3)** 20...Kf8 21.h3 Bxc3 22.Bc5+ Kg8 23.Bxc4+ Nxc4 24.Rd7, etc. These variations make it clear that the Black King is exposed to all sorts of dangers in the middle, in spite of the exchange of Queens.

20.bxc3 Nh6

Still bad is 20...Bxc4: e.g., 21.Nf5+ Ke6 22.Rd6+ Kf7 23.Bxc4+ Nxc4 24.Rd7+ and wins.

21.Nxe6 Kxe6 22.c5 Rhd8 23.Bd4

Obviously White avoids further liquidation. His one aim now is to keep the pieces on the board; otherwise his attack would fizzle out.

23...Nhf7 24.Rhf1 Ke7 25.Rf2 Rf8 26.Bh5!

Threatening to thin out to a won Rook ending by 27.Bxf7 Rxf7 28.Bxe5 fxe5 29.Rxf7+ Kxf7 30.Rd7+.

26...Nh8 27.Bxe5 fxe5 28.Rf5!

Forcing a further exchange.

28...Rxf5 29.exf5 Rf8 30.g4 b6

After 30...Nf7 31.Bxf7 Rxf7; the White Rook penetrates to d6.

31.Rd6 Rf6 32.Rxf6 Kxf6 33.Kd2?

A serious error, allowing Black to seize the draw with 33...bxc5 34.Kd3 Ng6 35.fxg6 hxg6 36.Bxg6 Kxg6, etc. The right move for White was 33.cxb6.

33...Ng6?

Black misses his chance; now White forces the win with accurate play.

34.fxg6 hxg6 35.cxb6! axb6 36.c4 gxh5

Forced, for after 36...c5 37.Bxg6 Kxg6 38.Kd3 White wins easily.

37.c5! b5 38.gxh5 g4 39.Ke3 Kg5 40.Ke4 Kxh5 41.Kxe5 Kh4 42.Kf6!

The winning idea. Before going after the c-pawn White must get rid of the Black g-pawn or else win a tempo.

42...Kh5

Or 42...Kh3 43.Kg5 and wins.

43.a3 Black Resigned.

The end would have been 43...Kh6 44.Ke6 Kh5 45.Kd6 Kh4 46.Kxc6 Kh3 47.Kxb5 Kxh2 48.c6 g3 49.c7 g2 50.c8=Q g1=Q 51.Qh8+ Kg2 52.Qg8+, etc.

Many of these well-known liquidations in the opening are rather difficult to evaluate. In both the examples just given the exchange of Queens enabled White to take the initiative without any drawbacks. It often happens, however, that such liquidation can be made only at the cost of a positional concession; for example in the variation 1.d4 g6 2.c4 Bg7 3.Nc3 d6 4.e4 e5 5.dxe5 dxe5 6.Qxd8+ Kxd8; the liquidation has produced a situation very different from that seen in the game Prins-Kotov.

The point is that Black has a better pawn structure, since the d4 square is somewhat vulnerable. The same thing happens in the familiar King's Indian line 1.d4 Nf6 2.c4 g6 3.Nc3 Bg7 4.e4 d6 5.f3 e5 6.dxe5 dxe5 7.Qxd8+ Kxd8. In both instances the evaluation depends mainly on the relative importance of White's initiative – based on Black's inability to castle – and Black's positional advantage in the form of a stronghold on d4. We studied this sort of position in detail in Book One, Chapter 11.

Another familiar type of early liquidation is based on the theme: the Bishop pair versus the better pawn structure. The best-known example is the endgame which arises from the Exchange Variation of the Ruy Lopez: 1.e4 e5 2.Nf3 Nc6 3.Bb5 a6 4.Bxc6 dxc6 5.d4 exd4 6.Qxd4 Qxd4 7.Nxd4. White has four pawns to three on the Kingside, whereas Black's Queenside majority has been made practically worthless because of the doubled c-pawns. However, Black has the Bishop pair, and experience has shown that Black has very satisfactory play. The liquidation from the Caro-Kann: 1.e4 c6 2.d4 d5 3.Nc3 dxe4 4.Nxe4 Nf6 5.Nxf6+ exf6 6.Bc4 Bd6 7.Qe2+ Qe7 8.Qxe7+ Bxe7 produces a pawn position very similar to the Lopez position given above, but with this fundamental difference: that Black has no compensation for the weakened pawns, as both players retain their Bishops.

Although these liquidations are not really middlegame stratagems at all-the game going straight from the opening to the ending-yet they do still provide some fighting play. There is a third type of liquidation in which this quality is absent. We mean the liquidation which seeks only to emasculate the position with a quick draw in view. The Exchange Variation of the French Defense (1.e4 e6 2.d4 d5 3.exd5 exd5) is notorious in this respect.

The same sort of thing happens in various openings; e.g. the Four Knights: 1.e4 e5 2.Nf3 Nc6 3.Nc3 Nf6 4.Bb5 Nd4 5.Nxd4 exd4 6.e5 dxc3 7.exf6 Qxf6 8.dxc3 Qe5+ 9.Qe2 Qxe2+; or the Scotch: 1.e4 e5 2.Nf3 Nc6 3.d4 exd4 4.Nxd4 Nf6 5.Nc3 Bb4 6.Nxc6 bxc6 7.Bd3 d5 8.exd5 cxd5 9.Qe2+ Qe7 10.Qxe7+.

We close this chapter with a game in which White employs a liquidation which is not easy to assess, leading as it does to a somewhat uncommon kind of weakened pawn structure.

(The game Fine-Alekhine, AVRO, 1938).

1.e4 e5 2.Nf3 Nc6 3.Bb5 a6 4.Ba4 d6 5.O-O Bd7 6.c3 g6 7.d4 Bg7

POSITION 146

(An unusual liquidation into the endgame).

8.dxe5 Nxe5 9.Nxe5 dxe5 10.f4

A surprising advance. One might expect that the weakening of White's e-pawn would prove to be a serious matter in the subsequent play, but the fact is that it is Black who has great difficulties because of the open f-file.

10...Bxa4

Much later Romanovsky found an improvement here for Black: 10...Bb5! 11.Bxb5+ axb5 12.Qb3 Qd7 13.fxe5 Bxe5 14.Na3 c6. However, by 15.Bf4 White still gets good play.

11.Qxa4+ Qd7

After 11...b5 12.Qb3, the Black Queenside is seriously weakened.

12.Qxd7+ Kxd7 13.fxe5 Ke6 14.Bf4

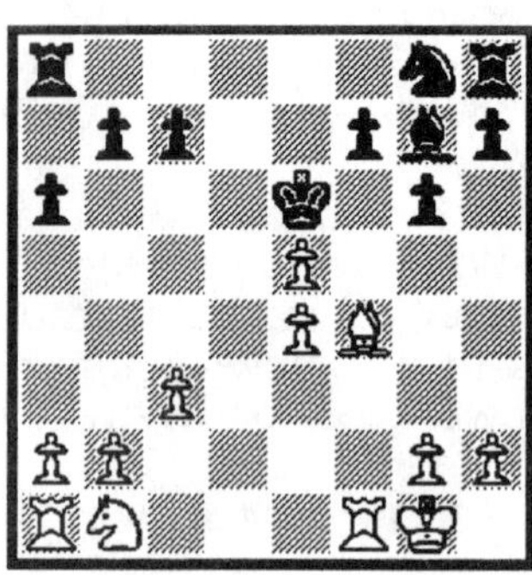

(The result of the liquidation).

This is the position at which White was aiming when he played 10.f4. Clearly, Black cannot win back the pawn at once, since if he captures on e5, he leaves the f-pawn unprotected. It is also clear that the White e-pawn cannot be held indefinitely. Fine has sized up the situation very acutely. The recapture of the e-pawn will cost precious time which White will be able to put to good use. Despite the relatively reduced material, the position of the Black King in the center will be a focal point of key tactical blows later.

14...Rf8 15.Nd2 Bxe5 16.Nb3 Bxf4 17.Rxf4

Not 17.Nc5+ Kd6 18.Nxb7+ Kc6 19.Na5+ Kb5 for Black wins a piece.

17...b6

Now Nc5+ must be prevented.

18.a4! Ke5?

He had to try 18...a5.

19.g3!

Black very likely overlooked the force of this innocent looking move. Apparently he had reckoned only with 19.Raf1, whereupon 19...f5 20.g4 Ne7 would have followed.

The advantage of White's actual move is that his QR remains on its own file – a very important point in view of the threatened a5.

19...Nf6

Now 19...g5? would have been fatal, for after 20.Rf5+ Kxe4 21.Raf1, the Black King is in a mating net. Nor is there time now for 19...a5 because of 20.Nd4!, after which 20...Nf6 fails against 21.Nf3+! Ke6 22.Ng5+ Ke5 (or ...Ke7) 23.Raf1, winning the f-pawn.

20.Nd2 Nh5

The Knight is out of play here. A little stronger was 20...Nd7.

21.Rf2 Ke6

Black now realizes that 18...Ke5 was an unfortunate choice. On 21...a5 White has the strong reply 22.b4.

22.a5! Ra8

There is no choice; if 22...b5 then White has 23.Nb3 with the threat of Nc5+.

23.Raf1

Now if Black defends the f-pawn with either Rook. White would have 24.g4 Ng7 25.axb6 cxb6 26.Rf6+ winning the b-pawn.

23...Rhd8

Indirectly defending the f-pawn.

24.Nf3

Threatening not only 25.Ng5+ but also 25.Nd4+, e.g., 24...f6 25.Nd4+ Kd7 26.g4.

24...Ke7 25.axb6 cxb6 26.Ng5 h6

Or 26...f6 27.Nxh7 Rd6 28.g4, etc.

27.Rxf7+ Kd6 28.Nf3 g5 29.Nd4

The rest is only a matter of technique.

29...Re8 30.Rh7 Rh8 31.Rff7 Rxh7 32.Rxh7 Rf8 33.Rxh6+ Nf6 34.Nf3 Ke7 35.Nd2 g4 36.Rg6 Nd7 37.Rxg4 Ne5 38.Rg5 Kd6 39.Rf5 Rd8 40.Nf3 Nd3 41.Rd5+ Ke7 42.Rxd8 Kxd8 43.b3 Ke7 44.Nd2 a5 45.Kf1 b5 46.Ke2 Black Resigned.

CHAPTER 42
LIQUIDATION FOR DEFENSIVE REASONS

The idea of using liquidation to nip in the bud a threatening attack is associated particularly with the name of Capablanca, who used to employ it with great skill. As soon as any unpleasantness threatened, Capablanca was happy to simplify. He was not primarily playing for the draw; in the new simplified position he would make new attempts to win. These tactics of Capablanca should not be confused with liquidation prompted by fear. In games between players of considerably different playing strength, it commonly happens that the weaker player, through understandable fear, exchanges off everything he can lay his hands on, in the hope of achieving a draw. This policy is seldom successful, but the weaker player can console himself with the thought that he would have been no more likely to obtain a win or draw out of the stronger player by any other means. Early liquidation may even have the advantage of making the game last longer, so that there will be ample time to ponder on how to play better next time!

Here is an illustration of liquidation for defensive purposes.

(The game Spielmann-Capablanca, New York, 1927).

1.e4 c6 2.d4 d5 3.Nc3 dxe4 4.Nxe4 Nf6 5.Ng3 Bg4 6.Qd3 Nbd7 7.h3 Bh5 8.Nxh5 Nxh5 9.Nf3 e6 10.g3 Bd6 11.Bg2 O-O 12.O-O Qc7 13.b3 Nhf6 14.Bb2 (No.114) **14...e5**

POSITION 147

Capablanca plays for exchanges, apparently on the grounds that White, if undisturbed, could build up a strong position by Rfe1 followed in due course by c4.

15.dxe5 Nxe5 16.Qf5

The idea behind this move is to prevent Black taking the sting out of the White Bishop pair by playing ...Nxf3+ followed by ...Be5.

16...Rfe8 17.Rfe1 Nxf3+ 18.Bxf3 Rxe1+ 19.Rxe1 Re8 20.Rxe8+ Nxe8

Black has exchanged a lot of material, but he is still under some pressure, mainly due to the White Bishop pair.

21.Bg4

With the nasty threat of 22.Qc8.

21...Qe7

Counterattack: 22.Qc8 can now be met by 22...Qe1+ 23.Kg2 Bc5.

22.Kf1 Bb4 23.c3 Nd6 24.Qd3 Ba5 25.Ba3

Alekhine recommended 25.b4 Bc7 26.c4 as somewhat stronger.

25...Bc7 26.c4 Qe5 27.Qe2 Qxe2+

28.Kxe2 b6

In this position the players agreed to a draw. According to Alekhine in the tournament book, White still had the better of it. He could have maintained a promising initiative, either by 29.c5 Nb5 30.cxb6; or by 29.Kd3 c5 30.b4.

POSITION 148

(Liquidation from the game Marshall-Lasker, St. Petersburg, 1914).

White has just played his Queen from f2 to h4. Black could now exchange on d3, but after 21...Nxd3 22.Rxd3 Bb5, White has the resource 23.Rb3.

21...Ba4!

Attacking the Rook, with the point that if now 22.b3, then 22...Nxd3 23.Rxd3 Bb5 would be very effective. Or if White should play 23.bxa4 (instead of 23.Rxd3) then 23...Nb2 followed by 24...d3+ would be strong.

22.Bxg6

Leading to a remarkable liquidation.

22...hxg6 23.Bd8 Qxd8 24.Ng5 Qxg5 25.Qxg5 Bxd1 26.Qxg6

Yet another White threat: 27.Rf7.

26...Bc2!

One of the basic principles of good defense is the willingness to give back any material gained. (See Chapters 30-32).

27.Qxc2 d3 28.Qd1 a5

Now with Rook and two minor pieces, together with a powerful passed pawn, Black has more than sufficient compensation for the Queen.

29.Qg4 Rf8 30.Rd1 Rae8 31.Qg6 Re2 32.Rf1

After 32.Rxd3 Black wins with 32...Nxd3 33.Qxd3 Re1+ 34.Kh2 Be5+.

32...d2 33.Rxf8+ Kxf8 34.Qxd6+ Kg8 35.Qd8+ Kh7 36.Qh4+ Bh6 White Resigned.

POSITION 149

(By means of liquidation White forestalls the threatened attack on his King; from the game Bronstein-Panno, Amsterdam, 1956).

1.c4 Nf6 2.Nc3 g6 3.d4 Bg7 4.e4 d6 5.f3 e5 6.Nge2 c6 7.Be3 O-O 8.Qd2 Qa5 9.O-O-O b5 (No.149) **10.cxb5 cxb5 11.dxe5 dxe5 12.Nd5!**

The point of the liquidation. After 12...Qxa2, White replies Nc7, winning the Exchange. The Black Queen alone cannot do much harm.

12...Qxd2+ 13.Rxd2 Nxd5 14.exd5

White has not only stopped the threatened attack against his castled position, but also secured the better game, his passed d-pawn being an especially strong asset.

14...b4 15.Ng3 f5 16.Bg5 Nd7 17.Bb5 Rb8 18.Bc6 Kf7 19.Rc2

We stop at this point since the issues of primary interest in this liquidation process have been clarified. White has an ongoing initiative.

POSITION 150

(A futile liquidation; from the game Sterner-Boleslavsky, Sweden vs. U.S.S.R. Match, 1954).

1.e4 c5 2.Nf3 Nc6 3.d4 cxd4 4.Nxd4 Nf6 5.Nc3 d6 6.Be2 e5 7.Nb3 Be7 8.O-O O-O 9.Be3 Be6 10.f4 a5 (No.150) **11.fxe5**

Played, presumably, out of fear of the opponent's world-class ranking. Fear, however, is a poor counselor. In view of the nature of Black's position – backward d-pawn and consequent weakness on d5-the indicated procedure here was 11.f5 Bc8 12.Bc4.

11...dxe5 12.Qxd8 Rfxd8 13.Rfd1

Possibly it had been White's original intention to play 13.Nc5, but on second thought he was afraid of 13...Bxc5 14.Bxc5 Nd4. The sequel might have been 15.Bd3 Nd7 16.Ba3 Rac8; or 15.Be7 Nxe4! 16.Bxd8 Nxc3 17.bxc3 Nxe2+ 18.Kf2 Rxd8 19.Kxe2 Bc4+. The last variation is an example of combinative liquidation – a subject which we take up in Chapter 44.

13...Nb4 14.Rxd8+ Bxd8 15.Bd3 a4 16.Nd2

16.Nc5 would be answered by 16...Bb6.

16...a3 17.b3 Ng4 18.Bc5

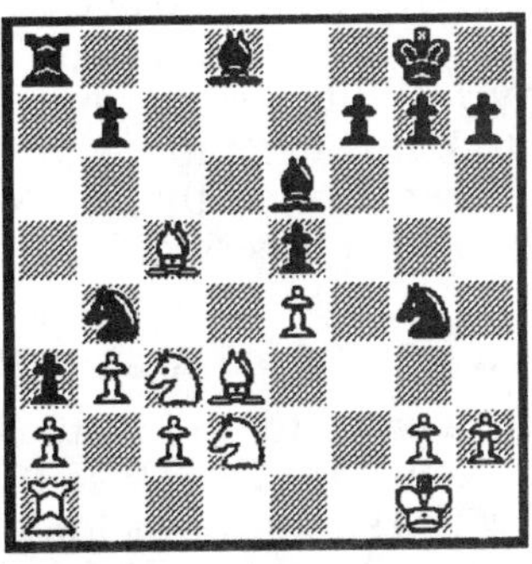

Other possibilities were: **1)** 18.Nf1 Rc8 19.Bd2 Bb6+ and wins. **2)** 18.Nd1 Nxe3 19.Nxe3 Bb6 20.Nf1 Bd4 and the a-pawn falls.

18...Nxd3 19.cxd3 Rc8 20.Bb4

The only alternative was 20.d4, against which Boleslavsky gives 20...b6 21.Bb4 Ne3 and then if 22.Nd5 exd4 23.Ne7+ Bxe7 24.Bxe7 Rc2 25.Bb4 Rb2; or if 22.d5 Nc2 23.Rc1 Nxb4 24.dxe6 Bg5 25.exf7+ Kf8, etc.

20...Bb6+ 21.Kf1 Ne3+ 22.Ke2 Nc2 and **White Resigned.**

POSITION 151

(Capablanca liquidates in order to repel an attack; the game Marshall-Capablanca, New York, 1918).

1.d4 d5 2.Nf3 Nf6 3.c4 e6 4.Nc3 Nbd7 5.Bg5 Be7 6.e3 O-O 7.Rc1 c6 8.Qc2 dxc4 9.Bxc4 Nd5 10.Bxe7 Qxe7 11.O-O Nxc3 12.Qxc3 b6 13.e4 Bb7 14.Rfe1 Rfd8 15.d5 (No.151)**15...Nc5!**

To have taken the d-pawn would have opened the e-file, which would have given White a strong initiative. Now Black threatens to destroy the White pawn center by 16...Nxe4! 17.Rxe4 cxd5 answering 18.Rg4 by 18...f5.

16.dxe6 Nxe6 17.Bxe6 Qxe6 18.Nd4!

Offering a pawn to try for attacking chances. Now if 18...Qxa2 then 19.Nf5 f6 20.e5 with a strong attack for White after either 20...fxe5 21.Rxe5 or 20...Qe6 21.Nxg7 Kxg7 22.exf6+ Qxf6 23.Re7+.

18...Qe5!

Capablanca sidesteps any White attacking chances with this brilliant liquidation, by which he gains excellent counterplay at the cost of a pawn.

19.Nxc6 Qxc3 20.Rxc3 Rd2

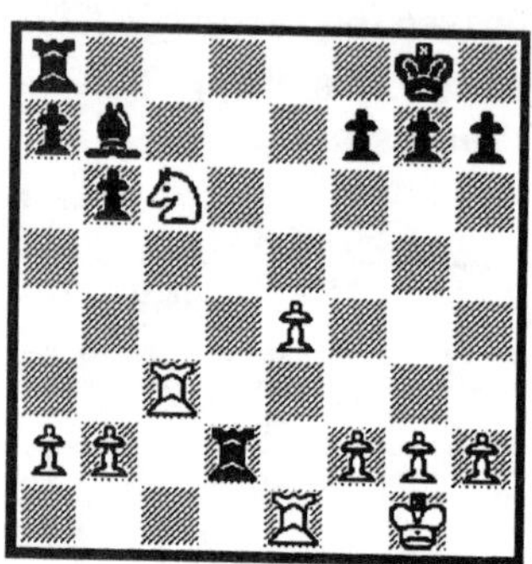

At his 18th move Capablanca must, of course, have considered 21.Ne7+ Kf8 22.Rc7. Then if 22...Bxe4 23.f3, and the game is in White's favor. However, Black can do better with 22...Re8! 23.Rxb7 (23.Ng6+ fxg6 24.Rxb7 Rxe4!) 23...Rxe7 24.Rb8+ Re8 25.Rxe8+ Kxe8 with an ending which is a theoretical draw, since Black's active Rook offsets the extra pawn. This variation should be considered to be the main line of the liquidation.

21.Rb1 Re8 22.e5

On 22.f3 Black plays 22...f5 for if 23.exf5 R8e2.

22...g5!

Preventing f4 while giving air to the King.

23.h4 gxh4

To answer 24.f4 with 24...Re6 followed by ...Rg6, putting the g-pawn under pressure.

24.Re1 Re6 25.Rec1

The Knight has to stay on c6 to screen the g-pawn. 25.Nxa7 Rg6 would do no good.

25...Kg7 26.b4 b5

To allow b5 would, of course, relieve White considerably.

27.a3 Rg6 28.Kf1 Ra2

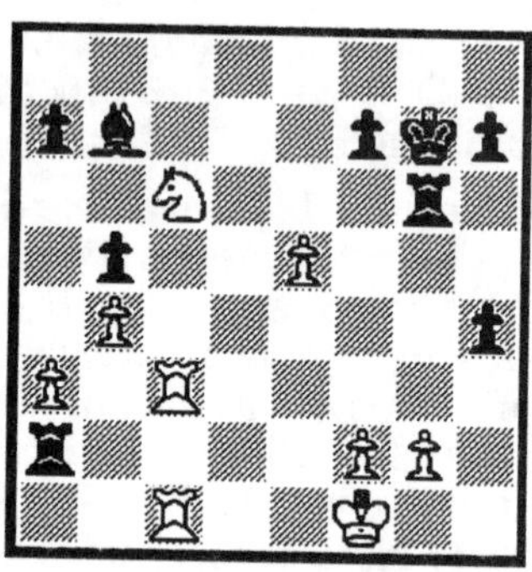

29.Kg1

White is in *zugzwang!*

29...h3 30.g3 a6 31.e6 Rxe6 32.g4

White is still in *zugzwang*. If 32.Nd4 h2+ 33.Kxh2 Rh6+ 34.Kg1 Rh1#.

32...Rh6 33.f3

On 33.g5 Black has the winning liquidation 33...h2+ 34.Kh1 Rxc6 35.Rxc6 Rxf2.

33...Rd6 34.Ne7 Rdd2

Rooks doubled on the seventh rank – every chessplayers dream!

35.Nf5+ Kf6 36.Nh4 Kg5 37.Nf5 Rg2+ 38.Kf1 h2 39.f4+ Kxf4 White Resigned.

CHAPTER 43
LIQUIDATION TO PRESERVE AN ADVANTAGE

Far and away the most important type of liquidation in chess is that which aims to convert a definite advantage into a clear win. This sort of liquidation means transition from the middlegame to the ending, or at least into a simpler position in which the win will be obtained in a more straightforward fashion. Knowledge of the endgame is generally very important at this point; without it a correct evaluation of the resulting position is rather difficult.

The simplest form of liquidation for converting, say, an extra pawn into a won endgame is to exchange off all the pieces and then win the pawn ending. Against a resourceful player, however, this is not easily done; chess is not so easy as that. The player who is a pawn short will usually throw everything into the task of creating counterchances. From our chapters on defense (30-32) we know that the player with some material advantage is wise to not strive too stubbornly to hold on to the extra material. The initiative is often worth more than a pawn.

In practice it often happens that the moment comes when one has a choice of liquidating into various forms of endgames. It might be, for example, that an extra pawn could be safely carried forward into a Rook ending; but it might also be possible to liquidate into a Bishop ending, or a Knight ending. Which would be best? Or would it perhaps be best to maintain the tension a little longer in order to attempt to secure some further concession from the opponent first? To these questions no general answer can be given; it all depends on the position. In one position the transition to a Rook ending might be the proper procedure; in another it might be well the worst choice. Only through experience can one acquire the familiarity which leads to the right judgment.

We now review a few examples, the study of which will lead to a better developed instinct for liquidation.

POSITION 152

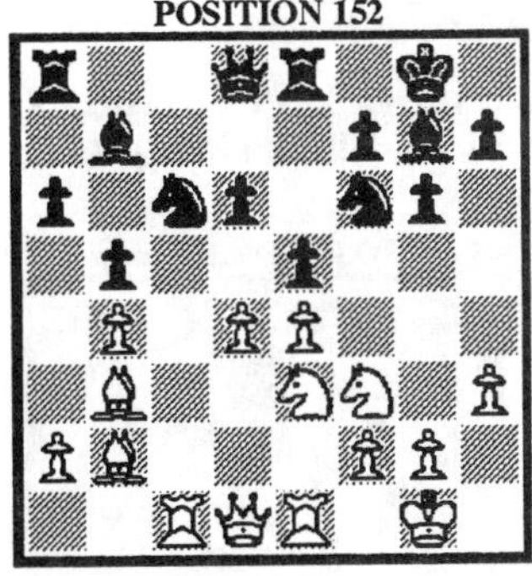

(A forcing liquidation; from the game Toran-Donner, Beverwijk, 1957).

1.e4 e5 2.Nf3 Nc6 3.Bb5 a6 4.Ba4 Nf6 5.O-O Be7 6.Re1 b5 7.Bb3 d6 8.c3 O-O 9.h3 Na5 10.Bc2 c5 11.d4 Qc7 12.Nbd2 Re8 13.Nf1 g6 14.Ne3 Bf8 15.b4 cxb4 16.cxb4 Nc6? 17.Bb2 Bb7 18.Bb3 Bg7 19.Rc1 Qd8 (No.152) **20.dxe5 Nxe5**

After 20...dxe5 21.Nd5! White is clearly on top.

21.Bxe5!

A surprising exchange of the strong Bishop on b2; however this is the point of the liquidation. White will force through an attack against f7.

21...dxe5 22.Qxd8 Raxd8 23.Rc7 Rd7

All forced.

24.Rxd7 Nxd7 25.Ng5

The attack on f7 is decisive.

25...Re7

After 25...Rc8 26.Nxf7 Kf8 27.Nd6 White wins easily.

26.Rc1

Now there is no defense against the threat of 26.Nxf7 Rxf7 27.Rc7.

26...Bh6 27.Nxf7 Bxe3 28.fxe3 Kg7 29.Rc7 Bxe4

Or 29...Ba8 30.Nd6 Kf6 31.Rc8 Nb6 32.Rb8 winning.

30.Nd6

Threatening 31.Nc8, and 30...Bf5 fails to 31.g4. **Black Resigned.**

POSITION 153

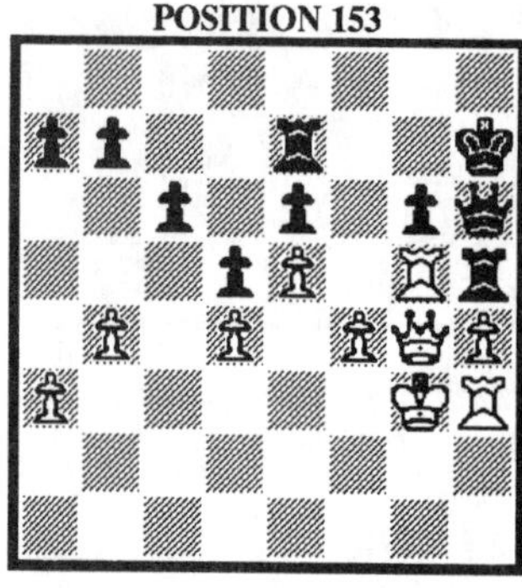

(Liquidation into a won Rook and pawn ending; from the game Capablanca-Eliskases, Moscow, 1936).

White has just played his Rook from h2 to h3. Black replied:

1...Kg7 2.Rxh5 Qxh5 3.Qxh5 gxh5 4.f5!

This pawn sacrifice allows the decisive entry of White's King.

4...exf5 5.Kf4 Re6

No improvement is 5...Rf7 as White plays 6.Rg3+ and 7.Rg5 winning

6.Kxf5 Rg6

Thus ruling out White's threat of Rg3-g5; but now White's King enters with effect.

7.e6 Rg4 8.Ke5 Re4+ 9.Kd6 Rxd4 10.Re3 Black Resigned.

Now returning to the original diagram we consider whether Black could have defended better by 1...Re8 (instead of 1...Kg7). Then the liquidation 2.Rxh5 gxh5! gives White nothing, so he must try some preliminary maneuvers. He could play 2.Kf3 Re7 3.Rg3 Rxh4 4.Rxg6 Rxg4 5.Rxh6+ Kxh6 6.Rxg4. Now even though Black can hold on a little longer, he would still lose in the end. For example, 6...Rg7 7.Rh4+ Kg6 8.Rh8 Re7 9.Kg4 Kg7 10.Ra8 a6 11.Kg5 and Black loses because it's *zugzwang*.

POSITION 154

(Black takes the initiative and uses it to force more and more liquidation; from the game Jager-Troger, Bad Neuenahr, 1957).

1.d4 Nf6 2.Nf3 e6 3.e3 d5 4.Bd3 Nbd7 5.Qe2? Bd6 6.Nbd2 O-O 7.O-O e5 8.dxe5 Nxe5 9.Nxe5 Bxe5 10.f4? Bd6 11.e4 Bg4 12.Qe1 dxe4 13.Nxe4 (No.154) **13...Re8**

The poor position of the White Queen allows Black to seize the initiative.

14.Nxf6+ Qxf6 15.Qg3 Qd4+ 16.Kh1 Be2!

Trying to invade the seventh rank.

17.Bd2!

A resourceful reply. White threatens 18.Bc3 and if Black tries 17...Qxb2 then there follows 18.Bc3! Qxc3 19.Bxh7+ winning.

17...Bb4! 18.Bxe2

Since 18.Bc3 Bxc3 leaves his pawns badly weakened, White has to liquidate further.

18...Rxe2 19.Bxb4 Qxb4 20.Qd3 Rae8 21.Rad1

Indirectly defending the b-pawn: 21...Qxb2? 22.Qxe4! Rxe4 23.Rd8+ mates.

21...h6 22.b3 Qe4

Forcing by simple means a winning ending.

23.Qxe4 R8xe4 24.c4

White cannot avoid the loss of a pawn. After 24.Rc1 Rd2! threatening 25...R4e2 Black has a winning position.

24...Rxa2 25.Rd8+ Kh7 26.Rd7 Rxf4! 27.Rg1 Rb2 28.h3 Rxb3 29.Rxc7 h5 White Resigned.

POSITION 155

(A forceful liquidation; from the game Clarke-Szabo, Wageningen, 1957).

Clearly Black has a much better game, with control of the open c-file as well as chances of Kingside attack by virtue of the half-open h-file. Szabo finds a forceful means of liquidating into a won ending.

1...Ng4+! 2.Kh1 Qd4!

Forcing the following liquidation.

3.Qxd4

The tournament book suggested 3.Qf3 as a better chance to resist.

3...exd4 4.Nb3 Ne3 5.Nxd4

A forlorn effort to fend off impending defeat. If 5.Nxe3 dxe3 6.Rc1 then 6...e2 wins; or if 5.Rf3 Nxg2 6.Kxg2 Bxh3+! 7.Kxh3 Bd2+ winning.

5...Nxf1 6.Bxf1 Bc1 7.Nxb5 Bxb5 8.Bxb5 Bxa3 9.Ne3 Bxb4 10.Rb1 Bc5 11.Nc4 Rxh3+ 12.Kg2 Rch8 White Resigned.

POSITION 156

(A less successful liquidation; from the game Vidmar-Capablanca, New York, 1927).

1...Nxd3?

In the tournament book Alekhine analyses the liquidation which this move begins. He recommended 1...Ba4 as a stronger move, for example: **1)** 2.Qd2 Qxd2 3.Rxd2 Nxd3 4.Rxd3 Rc4 or ...Rc2, followed by doubling Rooks and bringing the King to d7. **2)** 2.Rd2 Nxd3 3.Qxd3 Rc3, and Black has the initiative.

2.Qxd3 Qc3

Now either 2...Ba4 of 2...Rc3 are well-met by 3.Bd2!.

3.Be3 Qxd3 4.Rxd3 a5 5.a4 Rc4 6.f3

In this position a **Draw** was agreed. White stands slightly better, for after 6...Bxa4 7.Bb6 Black loses his a-pawn, and then White's protected passed d-pawn is superior to Black's b-pawn. Nonetheless, with opposite colored Bishops this advantage is a purely theoretical one.

POSITION 157

(A faulty liquidation; from the game Olafsson-Szabo, Portoroz, 1958).

1.Qxb6

In the tournament book Matanovic and Gligoric point out that instead of liquidating this way, White could have won quickly by 1.Qc8!, threatening 2.Re8+ Bxe8 3.dxe8=Q+ Rxe8 4.Qxe8#.

1...axb6 2.Rb1

The point being that if 2...Bxb1 White mates by 3.Re8+.

2...Ne5

This allows White to win directly. Much better was 2...Nd4.

3.Rxe5 fxe5 4.Rxb6 Be4

The alternative, 4...c3 loses after 5.Rxb7 c2 6.Rc7 h6 7.Rc8 Kh7 8.a4 or 8.Kf1.

5.Re6 Bc6 6.Rxe5 Kg8

Not 6...Bxd7 when White wins with either 7.Rd5 or 7.Bxd7 Rxd7 8.Re8#.

7.Rc5 Kf7 8.Rxc4 Ke7 9.f4 Ra8

Liquidation is the recurring theme here. On 9...Bxd7 there follows 10.Rc7 and the general exchange on d7 wins.

10.Rd4 Kd8 11.Be6 Ra3 12.f5 Re3 13.Rg4 g6 and **Black Resigned** without waiting for 14.fxg6.

POSITION 158

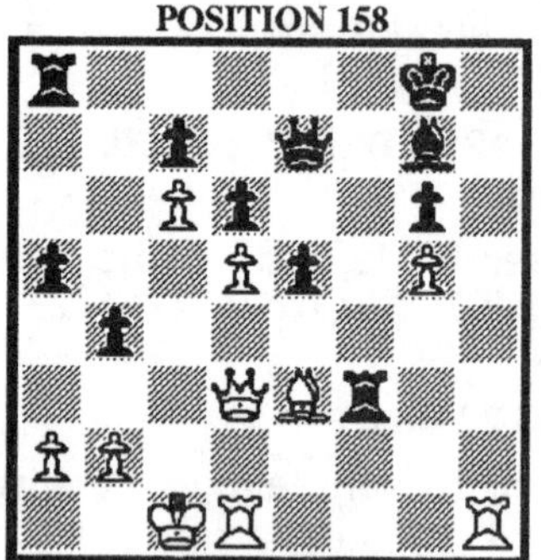

(A world champion liquidates; from the game Botvinnik-Alexander, Munich, 1958).

1.Qxg6! Kf8

In the *British Chess Magazine* (January, 1959) Alexander gave the following lines: **1)** 1...Rxe3 2.Rdf1! winning. **2)** 1...Qf7 2.Qh7+ Kf8 3.g6! Qf6 4.Bh6! Bxh6+ 5.Qxh6+ Qg7 6.Qh8+! wins. **3)** 1...Raf8 2.Qh7+ Kf7 3.Qh5+ Kg8 4.g6 R8f5 5.Qh7+ Kf8 6.Bh6 Bxh6+ 7.Qxh6+ Qg7 8.Qxg7+ Kxg7 9.Rdg1! and the threat of 10.Rh7+ wins for White.

2.Qe4! Qf7 3.g6 Qf5 4.Qxf5+ Rxf5 5.Rdf1

The key move. White reaches f7 with a gain of tempo.

5...Rxf1+ 6.Rxf1+ Kg8 7.Rf7 Rc8 8.Kc2 e4

Otherwise White plays 9.Kd3.

9.b3 Bc3 10.Kd1 Be5

Black's position is hopeless, because he cannot exchange off the Rooks: after ...Rf8 White plays Rxf8+ and after ...Kxf8, Bb6! wins.

11.Ke2 Bc3 12.Ba7! Black Resigned.

White's King strolls to victory via e3, e4 (winning the Black e-pawn as he goes) f5 and e6, etc.

POSITION 159

(Black has a choice of liquidations; from the game Durasevic-Milic, Belgrade, 1954).

1.Qe1?

Hoping for 1...Qxe1+ 2.Rxe1 Rxe1 3.Kxe1 Ne6 4.Nf5 with winning chances.

1...Nh3+!

Spoiling White's fun.

2.Kg3

Forced. After 2.gxh3 Qh4+ it's all over.

2...Qg5+

Winning the Exchange by 2...Qxe1+ 3.Rxe1 Rxe1 4.Kxh3 leads to a tricky ending. Black prefers to win the White Queen, but even here there are technical problems. It seems that winning the Exchange may have been the wiser course.

3.Kxh3 Rxe1 4.Rxe1 Be6+

A further forcing liquidation – logical as the Knight was stronger than the Bishop.

5.Nxe6 fxe6

The end of the liquidation – the only question is whether White can somehow hold on to draw. We leave this a moot point; suffice it to say White's task is difficult.

6.Bb4 d5 7.g3 Kf7 8.Re2 Qf5+ 9.Kg2 Qd3 10.Kf2 d4 11.Ba5 Qd1 12.cxd4 Qxd4+ 13.Kg2 Qd1 14.Rd2 Qa4 15.Bc3 b4 16.Rd4 Qc2+ 17.Rd2 Qb3 18.Be5 g5 19.g4 Qe3 White Resigned.

POSITION 160

(Accurate liquidation from the game Reshevsky-Pachman, Buenos Aires, 1960).

1.d4 Nf6 2.c4 e6 3.Nc3 Bb4 4.e3 O-O 5.Nge2 d5 6.a3 Be7 7.cxd5 Nxd5 8.Qc2 Nxc3 9.Nxc3 c5 10.dxc5 Bxc5 11.Be2 Nc6 12.O-O Qe7 13.b4 Bd6 14.Rd1 Bd7 15.Bb2 Rfd8? (No.160) **16.Ne4!**

The strength of this move is seen in the following lines: **1)** 16...Be5 17.Bxe5 Nxe5 18.Qc7!. **2)** 16...Be8 17.b5 Nb8 18.Nxd6 Rxd6 19.Rxd6 Qxd6 20.Qc8, etc.

16...Bb8 17.b5 Ne5 18.Qc5!

A powerful shot. Now after 18...Qxc5 19.Nxc5 b6 20.Nxd7 Rxd7 21.Rxd7 Nxd7 22.Bf3 White wins.

18...Kf8

Hoping for 19.Bxe5 Qxc5 20.Nxc5 Bxe5 21.Nxd7+ Rxd7 22.Rxd7 Bxa1 23.Rxb7 with drawing chances a pawn down, due to the opposite colored Bishops.

19.Rac1!

White is in no hurry. He quietly builds up the pressure.

19...f6 20.a4 Nf7 21.Ba3 Qxc5

Black is now forced to liquidate to a losing position.

22.Nxc5 Ke8 23.Nxb7

It's over now.

23...Rc8 24.Rxc8+ Bxc8 25.Bf3 Black Resigned.

POSITION 161

(White goes into an ending with opposite colored Bishops; from the game Botvinnik-Pachman, Leipzig, 1960).

With his last move (...Qf8-d6) Black offers the exchange of Queens expecting to draw the ending because of the unlike Bishops.

1.Kf3 Kg7

Clearly 1...Qxd5 2.exd5 would only help White with a passed pawn and use of e4.

2.Qxd6 Bxd6

Black had hoped to hold this ending; he has even given up a pawn for it. Botvinnik's excellent play shows the way to victory.

3.Ke2 Bb4

Otherwise a5 is a possibility.

4.Kd3 Kf6 5.Kc4 Be1 6.Kd5 Bb4 7.Bd7 Be1 8.Be8 Bc3 9.Kc6!

The only way to win. Pachman now **Resigned.** Let us examine three other moves which only draw: **1)** 9.h3 Be1. **2)** 9.h4 gxh4 10.gxh4 g5!. **3)** 9.g4 Bb4 10.Bxg6 Kxg6 11.Kxe5 Kf7! 12.Kxd4 Ke6. After 9.Kc6! Black gets into *zugzwang*. Pachman resigned because it was adjourned here and he was certain that Botvinnik would find the following winning line: 9.Kc6! Ba5 10.Kc7! Kg7 11.Kd6 Kf6 (or 11...Bc3 12.Ke6 followed by Bc6-d5- c4-d3 and Kxe5) 12.Bxg6! Kxg6 13.Kxe5 Kf7 14.h4 g4 15.Kf5 Be1 16.h5 Bd2 (or 16...Bxg3 17.Kxg4 Be1 18.Kf5, etc). 17.e5 Ke7 18.Ke4! Ke6 19.a5! Bxa5 20.h6 and wins.

POSITION 162

(Another liquidation into an ending with unlike Bishops; from the game Keres-Tal, U.S.S.R. Championship, 1957).

1...Ba4!

The liquidation 1...Bxe5 2.dxe5 Qxe5 gives nothing after 3.Bxa7 Qxe2 4.Bxe2 attacking the Bishop.

2.Re1 Bxe5 3.dxe5 Rd8 4.b4

If 4.Bb1 then ...Bd1 follows; while on 4.Bc2, then 4...Bxc2 5.Qxc2 Nc6 is excellent for Black.

4...Bc6! 5.f3 Qxd3 6.Qxd3

Even the greatest masters go astray in the judgment of endings of unlike

Bishops. Here Keres had to try 6.bxa5 Qxa3 7.a6! with drawing chances.

6...Rxd3 7.bxa5 Rxa3 8.Bxa7 Rxa5 9.Bd4 Ra2 10.Rb1 Rd2 11.Bc3 Rc2 12.Bd4 Kf7

This ending is an instructive win in all lines. It differs from Example 161 in two ways: the extra pawn is passed and there are Rooks on the board to inhibit the drawing tendencies of unlike Bishops.

13.h4 Kg6 14.Rb4 h6 15.Rb2 Rxb2

Now even with the Rooks off, it's a win.

16.Bxb2 Kh5 17.Ba3 Kxh4 18.Bf8 Kg3 19.Bxg7 h5 20.Bh6 Bxf3! 21.gxf3 Kxf3 22.Kf1 b5 23.Bd2 h4 24.Bb4 h3 25.Kg1 Ke2 White Resigned.

POSITION 163

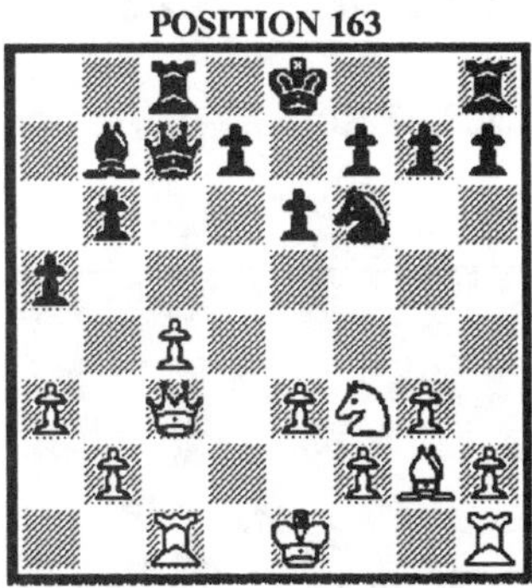

(Liquidation from the game Aguilera-Capablanca, Barcelona, 1929).

1.d4 Nf6 2.c4 e6 3.Nc3 Bb4 4.Qb3 c5 5.dxc5 Nc6 6.Nf3 Qa5 7.Bd2 Qxc5 8.a3 Bxc3 9.Bxc3 Na5 10.Bxa5 Qxa5+ 11.Qb4 Qc7 12.e3 b6 13.g3 Bb7 14.Bg2 a5 15.Qc3 Rc8 16.Rc1 (No.163) **16...d5!**

Well-timed. Now the c-pawn is attacked and if 17.b3, then 17...dxc4 18.bxc4 Bd5. Nor is 17.Nd2 good after 17...dxc4 18.Bxb7 Qxb7 attacking the White Rook.

17.cxd5

White goes in for a liquidation-but this type of play was Capablanca's strongest suit.

17...Qxc3+ 18.Rxc3 Rxc3 19.bxc3 Bxd5

Now Capablanca has his favorable ending because of the weakened White pawns.

20.Nh4 Bc4!

Avoiding the liquidation 20...Bxg2 21.Nxg2 Ne4 seemingly winning a pawn. After 22.Ke2! Nxc3+ 23.Kd3 Nd5 24.Rb1! f5 25.Nf4 and White will regain the pawn.

21.Kd2 g5 22.Bc6+

Forced. After 22.Nf3 Ne4+ wins.

22...Ke7 23.Ng2 Rc8 24.Bb7 Rb8 25.Bc6 Rd8+ 26.Kc2 Rc8 27.Ba4

Black's Rook maneuvers have not been without point. For example 27.Bb7 Rc7 28.Ba8 Bd5 29.Bxd5 Nxd5 and the c-pawn falls; note that 25...Rd8+ forced 26.Kc2 which blocks the possible defense by 30.Rc1.

27...Bd5 28.Rg1 Ne4 29.Kb2 Nxf2 30.Ne1 Ng4 31.Bc2 Nxe3 White Resigned.

On 32.Bxh7 Rh8 and 33...Rxh2+.

POSITION 164

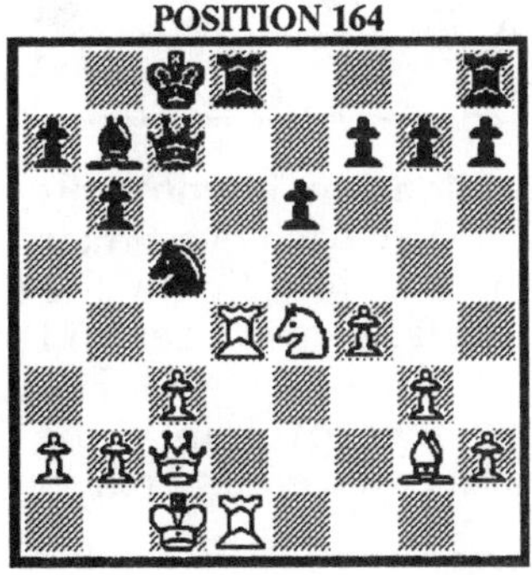

(Liquidation into a Queen ending; from the game Maroczy-Betbeder, Hamburg, 1930).

1.e4 e6 2.d4 d5 3.Nc3 Nf6 4.Bg5 dxe4 5.Nxe4 Be7 6.Bxf6 Bxf6 7.c3 Nd7 8.Qc2 Qe7 9.O-O-O b6 10.f4 Bb7 11.g3 O-O-O 12.Bg2 c5 13.Nf3 cxd4 14.Nxd4 Bxd4 15.Rxd4 Nc5 16.Re1 Qc7 17.Red1

White has slightly more space, but no more. Black decides to liquidate.

17...Rxd4 18.Rxd4 Nxe4 19.Bxe4 Rd8 20.Qd3!

White could win a pawn here: 20.Bxb7+ Qxb7 21.Rxd8+ Kxd8 22.Qxh7 but then comes22...Qh1+ 23.Kc2 Qg2+ 24.Kb3 Qd5+ 25.c4 Qf3+ 26.Kb4 a5+ 27.Kb5 Kb7 and White cannot win.

20...Rxd4 21.Qxd4 f5

Black has to concede something. If 21...g6 then 22.Qh8+ Kd7 23.Bc2! h5 24.Qf8 is very strong for White. However, Black should have tried 21...Bxe4 22.Qxe4 g6.

22.Bxb7+ Qxb7

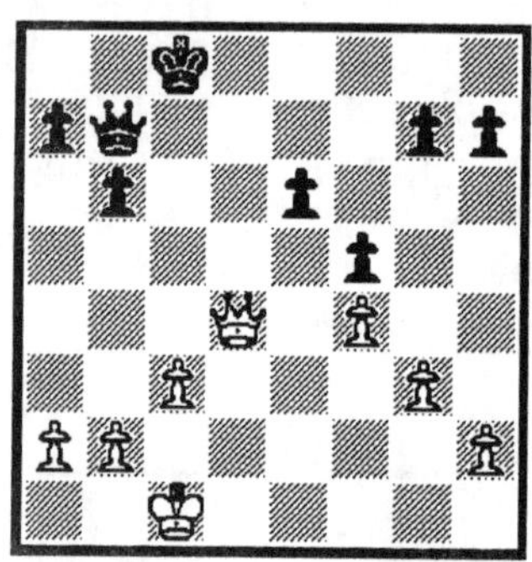

The liquidation is complete, and both sides have achieved their aims. Black it is true, has slightly the worst of it, but he feels this Queen and pawn ending must be drawable. However, Maroczy was probably the best Queen and pawn ending player of all time.

23.Kc2!

Seeing that 23...Qg2+ 24.Kb3 Qxh2 25.Qxg7 helps only White.

23...Qa6

To answer 24.Qxg7 with 24...Qe2+ drawing by perpetual check.

24.a4 Qb7 25.Kb3 h5

After 25...Qd5+ 26.Qxd5 exd5 27.c4! dxc4+ 28.Kxc4 Kc7 29.Kd5 White is winning.

26.Qd6 Qf7 27.Ka3 Kb7 28.h4 a5 29.b4 axb4+ 30.cxb4 Qg6 31.Qd7+ Kb8 32.Qd3 Qf6 33.Kb3 Qa1 34.a5!

The winning motif: White uses an outside passed pawn to force the win.

34...bxa5 35.Qb5+ Kc8

Or 35...Kc7 36.Qxa5+ Qxa5 37.bxa5 and the outside passer wins handily.

36.Qc6+ Kb8 37.Qb6+ Kc8 38.Qxe6+ Kd8 39.Qd5+ Ke7 40.bxa5 Qb1+ 41.Ka4 g6 42.a6 Qa1+ 43.Kb5 Qb2+ 44.Kc6 Qf6+ 45.Kc7 Qc3+

Or 45...Qxa6 46.Qd7+ and 47.Qd6+ winning.

46.Qc6 Qe3 47.Kc8! Black Resigned.

POSITION 165

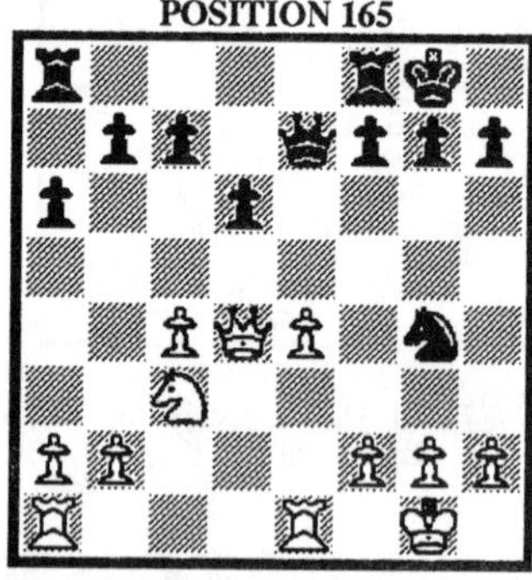

(The game Tarrasch-Vogel, Nuremberg, 1910).

1.e4 e5 2.Nf3 Nc6 3.Bb5 d6 4.d4 Bd7 5.Nc3 Nf6 6.O-O Be7 7.Re1 exd4 8.Nxd4 Nxd4 9.Qxd4 Bxb5 10.Nxb5 O-O 11.Bg5 Ng4 12.Bxe7 Qxe7 13.c4 a6 14.Nc3 (No.165)

With 14...Qe5 Black can force an ending; but who then stands better?

14...Qe5 15.Qxe5 dxe5

This looks better than 15...Nxe5 16.b3 though after 16...c6 Black's position is not too bad; e.g., 17.Rad1 Rad8 18.f4 Ng6 19.g3 b5!.

16.Nd5

Dr. Tarrasch in his superb book *Die Moderne Schachpartie* claims that White obtains the advantage with this move.

16...c6

Better was 16...Nf6. Then if 17.Nxc7 Rac8 or if 17.Nxf6+ gxf6 18.Rad1 Rad8 White's edge is small.

17.Ne7+ Kh8 18.Nf5

Otherwise ...g6 hems in the Knight.

18...Rad8 19.Rad1 g6 20.Nd6

With the double threat of Nxb7 and Nxf7+.

20...Rd7 21.c5 Kg8

In order to double Rooks-21...R8d8 loses to 22.Nxf7+!.

22.Nc4!

Decisive; Black's only choice is between losing a pawn or giving up the d-file.

22...Rfd8

Or 22...Rxd1 23.Rxd1 f6 24.Rd7 Rf7 25.Rxf7 Kxf7 and now White wins a pawn by 26.Na5 or 26.Nd6+.

23.Rxd7 Rxd7 24.f3 Nh6

Tarrasch pointed out 24...Nf6 25.Re2 Re7 26.Rd2 Rd7 27.Rxd7 Nxd7 28.b4 followed by 29.Na5 with a won Knight ending.

25.Nxe5 Rd2 26.Nc4 Rc2 27.b3 Rxa2 28.Rd1

Black now faces a decisive incursion down the d-file.

28...a5 29.Rd8+ Kg7 30.Ra8 a4 31.Rxa4 Rxa4 32.bxa4 Ng8 33.Nd6 Kf6 34.Nxb7 Ke5 35.a5 Ne7 36.Nd6 Kd4 37.a6 Black Resigned.

POSITION 166

(The 3rd Match Game Lasker-Janowsky, 1909).

1.e4 e5 2.Nf3 Nc6 3.Bb5 a6 4.Bxc6 dxc6 5.d4 exd4 6.Qxd4 Bg4 7.Nc3 Qxd4 8.Nxd4 O-O-O 9.Be3 Bb4 10.Nde2

With a double exchange of pieces Black can weaken the White pawn position.

10...Bxe2

This exchange, in combination with the next one, forces a weakening of the White pawns.

11.Kxe2 Bxc3 12.bxc3

White now has an isolated a-pawn and doubled c-pawns. From the defensive point of view, however, these pawns are very strong, for three of them are blocking four opposing ones. And since Black has no good way to attack these pawns, the net result of the liquidation is that White virtually has an extra pawn on the Kingside.

12...Nf6 13.f3 Nd7 14.Rad1 Ne5 15.Rd4 b6

To drive away the Rook by 16...c5, but 15...b5 followed by ...Nc4 was stronger.

16.f4!

Now Black cannot play ...Nc4 without first undoubling White's c-pawns.

16...Nd7 17.Rhd1 c5 18.R4d3 Nb8 19.Kf3 Rde8

Putting pressure on the e-pawn.

20.f5!?

Typical Lasker!

20...f6

Tarrasch criticized this, suggesting 20...Nc6 21.Bf4 Re7 and 22...Rhe8.

21.g4 Re7 22.Bf4 Rhe8 23.Re3 Nc6 24.g5 Na5?

Weak. Correct was 24...fxg5 25.Bxg5 Ne5+.

25.h4 Nc4 26.Re2 Rf7 27.Rg1 Kd7 28.h5! Nd6

Not 28...Ne5+ 29.Bxe5 Rxe5 30.g6 hxg6 31.fxg6 Rf8 32.Rh2 and h6.

29.h6 fxg5 30.Rxg5 g6

Losing a pawn, but things were bad anyway.

31.fxg6 hxg6 32.Rxg6 Ref8 33.Rg7!

Refuting White's 30th move.

33...Rxg7 34.hxg7 Rg8 35.Rg2 Ne8 36.Be5 Ke6 37.Kf4 Kf7 38.Kf5

Now if 38...Nxg7+ then 39.Bxg7 Rxg7 40.Rxg7+ Kxg7 41.Ke5 Kf7 42.Kd5 wins easily, while 38...Nd6+ 39.Bxd6 cxd6 40.Rb1 presents no great difficulty. **Black Resigned.**

POSITION 167

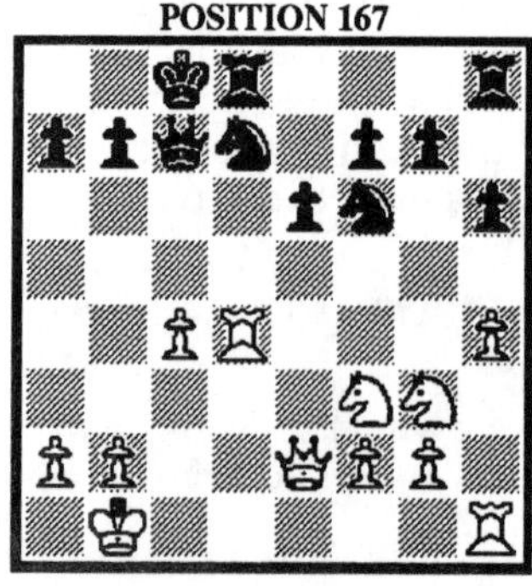

(Black forces a favorable liquidation; from the game Pogats-Portisch, Budapest, 1961).

1.e4 c6 2.d4 d5 3.Nc3 dxe4 4.Nxe4 Bf5 5.Ng3 Bg6 6.Nf3 Nd7 7.h4 h6 8.Bd3 Bxd3 9.Qxd3 Qc7 10.Bd2 Ngf6 11.O-O-O e6 12.c4 O-O-O 13.Bc3 c5 14.Kb1 cxd4 15.Bxd4 Bc5 16.Qe2 Bxd4 17.Rxd4 (No.167) **17...Nb8!**

Clearing the way for liquidation on the d-file. Moreover the exchanges prepared by this move are given an especially forceful character by the vigorous reentry of the Knight at c6.

18.Rhd1 Nc6 19.Rxd8+ Rxd8 20.Rxd8+ Qxd8 21.Qd2?

An error, leading to a poor Knight ending. Correct was 21.b3 Nd4 22.Nxd4 Qxd4 23.h5 after which it is not certain Black could increase his advantage.

21...Ng4 22.Ne4

Defense by counterattack.

22...Qxd2 23.Nfxd2 Kc7!

Maintaining the tension. 23...f5 24.Nc5 e5 25.Ne6 only gives White counterplay.

24.Nf1

On 24.f3 the e3 square is weakened and ...Ne3 is then strong.

24...Nd4

Protecting e6 and thereby preparing ...f5.

25.f3 Ne5 26.b3 Ng6!

Now White must lose material.

27.h5 Nf4 28.Ne3

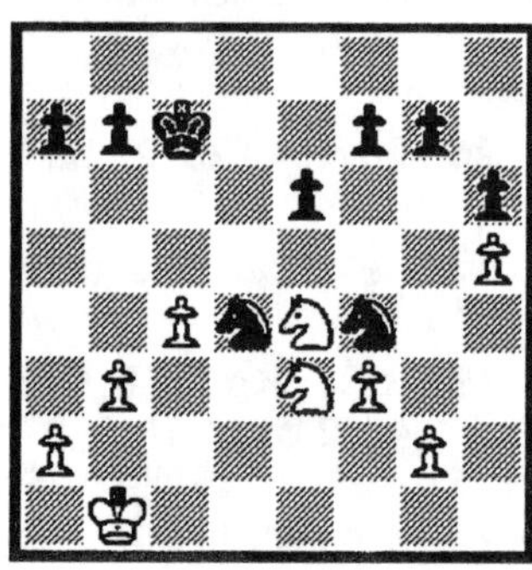

(Instead of capturing the h-pawn, Black finds a way to liquidate further).

28...Nf5

Black plays to win the g-pawn rather than the h-pawn, thus leaving White with isolated and vulnerable pawns. White resists this plan, but still must lose.

29.Nxf5 exf5 30.Ng3 g6!

Black nears the goal. The g-pawn is lost.

31.Kc2 Nxg2 32.Kd2 Kd6 33.hxg6 fxg6 34.Ke2 Ke5 35.Kf2 Nf4 36.Ke3 Nd5+!

Now on 37.cxd5 Black wins with 37...f4+.

37.Kd2 Nb4 38.a3 Nc6 39.Ke1

To answer 39...Kf4 with 40.Kf2. Of course, 39.Ke3 loses to 39...f4+.

39...Nd4 White Resigned.

CHAPTER 44
COMBINATIVE LIQUIDATION

The concept of liquidation is commonly identified with transition from middlegame to ending, as we saw in the last chapter. We come now to a theme which has a typically middlegame character – the combination whose object is to force a liquidation. The result, of course, is still a transition to the endgame, but the method employed differs from that exemplified in Chapter 43.

There it came about simply by the exchange of several pieces; in combinative liquidation on the other hand, some surprising point suddenly emerges. This may be the beginning of the combination, as for instance in the pseudo-sacrifice which often crops up in the openings; but it can also occur at the end of the combination. In this latter case the combination begins with the exchange of a few pieces and then suddenly the position flares up.

The simplest form of combinative liquidation occurs in the opening: 1.e4 e5 2.Nf3 Nc6 3.Bc4 Nf6 4.Nc3 Nxe4 5.Nxe4 d5, and Black regains the piece. The same combination occurs in many openings; e.g. 1.e4 e5 2.f4 exf4 3.Nf3 Be7 4.Bc4 Nf6 5.Nc3 Nxe4 6.Nxe4 d5; or 1.e4 e5 2.Nc3 Nf6 3.Bc4 Nxe4 4.Nxe4 d5. The liquidation here functions, in fact, as a transition from opening to middlegame.

Here is an example of another sort of liquidating combination in the opening:

(Combinative liquidation in the opening).

1.e4 c5 2.Nf3 Nc6 3.d4 cxd4 4.Nxd4 Nf6 5.Nc3 d6 6.Be2 e5 7.Nb3 Be7 8.Bg5

POSITION 168

8...Nxe4! 9.Bxe7

After 9.Nxe4 Bxg5 10.Nxd6+ Ke7 the White Knight must move, whereupon Black can exchange Queens.

9...Nxc3 10.Bxd8 Nxd1 11.Rxd1

Not 11.Bc7 Nxb2, leaving Black a pawn up. Notice that this liquidating combination is possible only because White's b-pawn is undefended, and because the Knight can escape via a4.

11...Kxd8 12.Rxd6+ Ke7

The combination is over, and Black has fully freed his position. Moreover in the resulting ending he has the initiative.

POSITION 169

(A liquidating combination of doubtful value; from the game Unzicker-Stahlberg, Moscow 1956).

1.e4 c5 2.Nf3 Nc6 3.d4 cxd4 4.Nxd4 Nf6 5.Nc3 d6 6.Bg5 e6 7.Qd2 Be7 8.O-O-O O-O 9.f4 h6 10.Bh4 (No.169) **10...Nxe4**

Black could have chosen another way of liquidating here: 10...Nxd4 11.Qxd4 Qa5 12.e5 dxe5 13.Qxe5 Qxe5 14.fxe5 Nd5 15.Bxe7 Nxe7.

Subsequent experience showed that Black could hold his own in the ending. The line actually played is a combinative liquidation aiming at a quick draw. The Russian Grandmaster Geller has used this system a number of times, and with considerable success. The present game, however, casts doubt on the value of this liquidation.

11.Bxe7

Black would have no trouble after 11.Nxe4 Bxh4 12.Nxc6 bxc6 13.Nxd6 Be7.

11...Nxd2 12.Bxd8 Nxf1 13.Nxc6 bxc6 14.Be7 Re8 15.Rhxf1 Rxe7 16.Rxd6 Bb7

This position is critical to the validity of this combinative liquidation. An important point is the possibility 17.Re1 c5 18.g3 Rc8 with a quick draw (Szabo-Geller, Amsterdam, 1956). Another variation giving equal chances is 17.Ne4 c5 18.Nxc5 Bxg2.

17.g3! c5 18.Rfd1

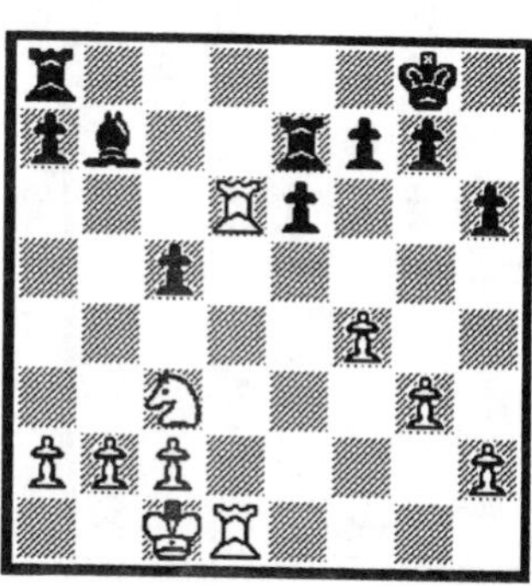

(The result of the liquidating combination initiated at the previous diagram)

White has a slight but definite pull. He is master of the open d-file, and the Black pawn structure has been weakened.

18...g5?

After 18...Kf8 White can achieve a won Knight vs. Bishop ending: 19.Rd8+ Rxd8 20.Rxd8+ Re8 21.Rxe8+ Kxe8 22.Nb5!. But Black's best chance would have been18...g6!.

19.Re1! gxf4 20.gxf4 Kf8 21.Re5 Rc7

According to the tournament book, 21...Rc8 would have been a little better.

22.Nb5 Rcc8 23.f5! exf5

After 23...a6 White would transfer the Knight via a3 to the important blockade square c4.

24.Rxf5 Be4 25.Rf4 Bh7 26.Rdf6

Also good would be 26.Rxh6 Kg7 27.Ra6 Rab8 28.Rxa7!.

26...Bg8 27.Nd6 Rc7 28.Rxh6 Rd8 29.Nf5 Rcd7 30.b3 Rd1+ 31.Kb2 Rg1 32.Rc6 Rg2 33.h4 Bh7 34.Rxc5

Now followed **34...Bg6 35.Rc7 Rh2 36.h5! Bxh5 37.Nh6 Rdd2 38.Nxf7 Kg7 39.Ng5+ Kh6 40.Nf3 Rdf2 41.Rf6+** and **Black Resigned.**

After 41...Bg6 comes 42.Nxh2 Rxf6 43.Ng4+ the last little combinative liquidation.

POSITION 170

(Another combinative liquidation from the Sicilian; the game Spassky-Rabar, Goteborg, 1955).

1.e4 c5 2.Nf3 Nc6 3.d4 cxd4 4.Nxd4 Nf6 5.Nc3 d6 6.Bg5 e6 7.Qd2 a6 8.O-O-O Bd7 9.f4 h6 10.Bh4 (No.170)

This position is very similar with the previous one at the same stage. In combinative liquidation the slightest discrepancy may make all the difference.

10...Nxe4

We now recognize some variations which also appeared in the previous game: 11.Bxd8 Nxd2 12.Bh4 Nxf1; or 11.Nxe4 Qxh4 12.Nxc6 Bxc6 13.Nxd6+ Bxd6 14.Qxd6 Qe7 or ...Rd8.

11.Qe1! Nf6 12.Nf5 Qa5 13.Nxd6+ Bxd6 14.Rxd6 O-O-O 15.Rd1!

An excellent move, the strength of which is in the fact that it prevents any further liquidation on the d-file. For instance, after 15.Bxf6 gxf6 16.Qd2 Ne7 17.Be2 Bc6 followed by ...Qc7 there would be a general exchange on the d-file.

15...Qc7 16.Qf2 Ne7 17.Bd3 Bc6 18.f5! e5 19.Rhe1 Ned5 20.Nxd5 Rxd5 21.Qg3

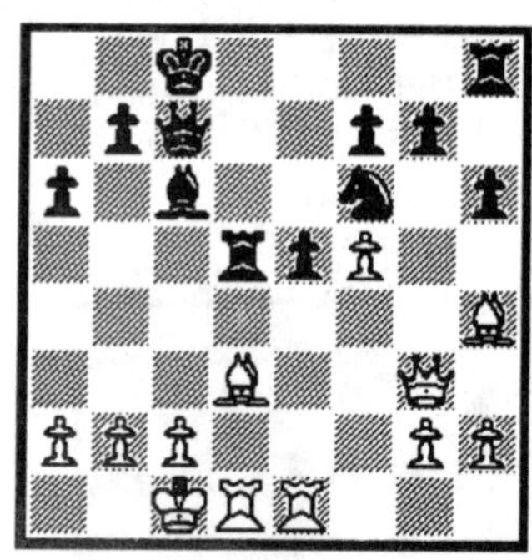

(A new liquidating combination).

21...e4

The tournament book points out that 21...Ne8 22.Bc4 Rxd1+ 23.Rxd1 f6 24.Qa3! also favors White.

22.Qxc7+

Bad would have been 22.Qxg7 because of 22...Qf4+ 23.Kb1 Qxh4 24.Qxh8+ Rd8 25.Qg7 exd3, etc.

22...Kxc7 23.Bxf6

After 23.Bxe4 Black's combination goes smoothly: 23...Rxd1+ 24.Kxd1 Nxe4.

23...exd3 24.Bxg7 Rhd8

This is better than 24...Rg8, after which White gets the better of it by 25.f6 dxc2 26.Rxd5 Bxd5 27.Kxc2.

25.Be5+ Kc8 26.cxd3 Rxd3?

This leaves White with a sound extra pawn, in an ending which is a win, in spite of the Bishops of opposite colors. Black had a much better line in 26...Rc5+ 27.Kb1 Bxg2, splitting up the White pawns so that the extra one would carry very little weight.

27.Rxd3 Rxd3 28.Kc2 Rd8 29.g4

It would take us too far afield to go into the problems of this ending. It went as follows:

29...Re8 30.Kd2 Kd7 31.Re3 Rg8 32.Rg3 Ke7 33.Ke3 f6 34.Bc3 Kf7 35.Kf4 Re8 36.Rd3 Re4+ 37.Kg3 Re2 38.h3 Ke7 39.Kh4 Be4 40.Rd2 Re3 41.Bd4 Re1 42.Bf2 Rf1 43.Bc5+ Kf7 44.Rd7+ Kg8 45.Rd6 and Black Resigned.

POSITION 171

(Combinative liquidation in a familiar variation of the Orthodox Queen's Gambit; the game Capablanca-Rossolimo, Paris, 1938).

1.d4 Nf6 2.c4 e6 3.Nc3 d5 4.Bg5 Be7 5.e3 O-O 6.Nf3 Nbd7 7.Rc1 c6 8.Bd3 h6 9.Bh4 dxc4 10.Bxc4 b5 11.Bd3 a6 12.a4 b4 13.Ne4 (No.171) **13...Nxe4 14.Bxe7 Nxf2!**

The point of the combination. The obvious 14...Qxe7 15.Bxe4 would by contrast lose a pawn immediately.

15.Bxd8

Also playable is 15.Kxf2, but after 15...Qxe7 16.Rxc6 e5! Black would have a fine game.

15...Nxd1 16.Kxd1 Rxd8 17.Rxc6 Bb7?

Better was 17...e5!; e.g. 18.d5 e4 19.Bxe4 Nf6.

18.Rc7 Bxf3+

Further simplification. If Black attempts to retain this Bishop from exchange by 18...Rab8 White still has the better game after 19.Ke2 Bd5 20.R1c1 Bb3 21.a5.

19.gxf3 Nb6

Now 19...e5 would be ineffective, in view of 20.Be4 Rac8 21.Rxc8 Rxc8 22.Bb7.

20.Rc6

White has no time for 20.a5, because of 20...Nd5.

20...Nxa4 21.Kc2

Thus White not only saves his threatened b-pawn, but also regains the lost a-pawn, for he threatens not only 22.Bxa6, but also 22.Ra1 as well as 22.Kb3.

21...Rdb8 22.Ra1 b3+ 23.Kc1 Rb4 24.Bxa6 Nb6 25.Kd2

Playing to win a piece by 27.Kc3 after the preparatory move 26.Rd6. Then 27...Ra4 28.Rxa4 Nxa4+ 29.Kxb3 would win for White.

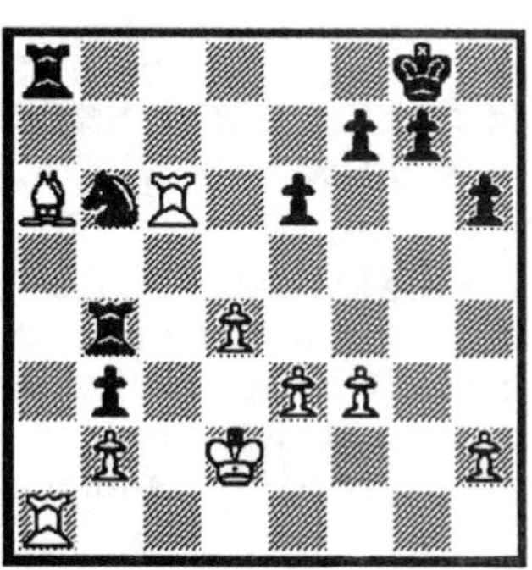

25...e5!?

Now 26.Kc3 could be met by 26...Nd5+.

26.dxe5 Nc4+

Based on two finesses: **1)** The unprotected Rook on a1, which prevents White from capturing twice on c4; and **2)** The interpolation which follows on his next move.

27.Kc3 Nxe5 28.Rc5 Rb6

Apparently Black is reckoning on 29.Rxe5 R8xa6 30.Rxa6 Rxa6 31.Kxb3 Ra1 and Black still has some play.

29.Bd3!

This is the complete refutation. Black cannot take the Rook without being mated on the back rank, and 29...Re8 fails to 30.Rxe5! Rxe5 31.Ra8+ with mate to follow. **Black Resigned.**

POSITION 172

(A snapshot from the 8th and 10th match games, Euwe-Capablanca, 1931).

1.d4 Nf6 2.c4 e6 3.Nf3 b6 4.g3 Bb7 5.Bg2 Bb4+ 6.Bd2 Bxd2+ 7.Qxd2 O-O 8.Nc3 Ne4 9.Qc2 (No.172) **9...Nxc3 10.Ng5!**

Winning the Exchange. Capablanca, however, was of the opinion that Black has full compensation, which explains why he went into this line both in the 8th and 10th games of this match.

10...Ne4

This is the strongest move. Not so good is 10...Qxg5 11.Bxb7 Nxe2 12.Qxe2 Nc6 13.Bxa8 and Black has little to show for the lost Exchange.

11.Bxe4 Bxe4 12.Qxe4 Qxg5 13.Qxa8 Nc6 14.Qb7 Nxd4 15.Rd1

An important point emerges about Black's combination in the variation 15.Qe4 Qa5+ 16.Kf1 Nb3 with the double threat of 17...Nxa1 and 17...Nd2+. Best of all for White, however, would have been 15.O-O! Nxe2+ 16.Kg2 f5 17.f4! with winning chances.

15...c5!

In the 8th game Black played 15...Qe5, and after 16.e3 Nc2+ 17.Ke2 d5 18.Rd2 Qxb2 19.cxd5 White had a clear advantage. After the text move, which Capablanca played in the 10th game, it is not easy for White to get any enduring advantage. The game continued:

16.e3 Nc2+ 17.Kd2 Qf5 18.Qg2 Nb4 19.e4 Qf6 20.Kc1 Nxa2+ 21.Kb1 Nb4 22.Rxd7 Nc6 23.f4 e5 with an early draw.

(Simple liquidation from the game Prokes-Capablanca, Budapest, 1929).

POSITION 173

1...Bxe5 2.Rxe5 Qc4!

The point: the Black Queen attacks not only the White a-pawn, but also the d-pawn, this being possible because White's Queen is unguarded. Black thereby wins a pawn. The game continued:

3.Qc1 Qxa2 4.Re1 a5 5.Kg2 a4 and Black won by weight of material.

POSITION 174

(A more complex liquidating combination from the game Euwe-Milic, Beverwijk, 1958).

1.Bxd6!

This can't be answered by 1...Bxd6 because of 2.Nf6+.

1...Nd7 2.Bxe7 Nxe7 3.Ncd6 Ne5

Black's last hope depends on this move.

4.Nf6+ Kh8 5.Nfe8!

By threatening mate at g7, White forces the following liquidation.

5...Nxf7 6.Nxf7+ Kg8 7.Nxd8

White has won a piece. If Black tries to regain it by 7...Ra8 then White wins by 8.Nxg7; e.g. **1)** 8...Kxg7 9.Rf7+ Kg6 10.Rxe7 Rxd8 11.Re5 Kf6 12.Re6+. **2)** 8...Rxd8 9.Ne6 Rxd5 10.Rf8+ Kh7 11.Rf7+.

In the game Black tried:

7...Nxd5 and the sequel was: **8.Nb7 Rb6 9.Nxc5 Rxb2 10.Rf3 Rb1+ 11.Kf2 Rb2+ 12.Kg3 Re2 13.Nd6 g5 14.Nce4 Nf4 15.Rf2 Re3+ 16.Kg4 Kh7 17.Kf5** and **Black Resigned.**

POSITION 175

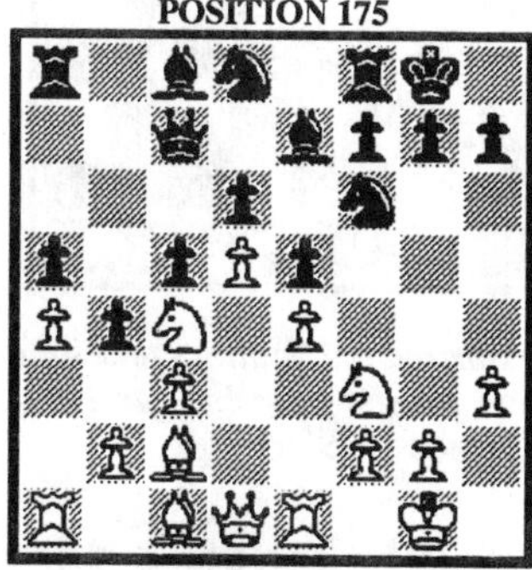

(Capablanca once more the liquidation artist; the game Capablanca-Vidmar, New York, 1927).

1.e4 e5 2.Nf3 Nc6 3.Bb5 a6 4.Ba4 Nf6 5.O-O Be7 6.Re1 b5 7.Bb3 d6 8.c3 Na5 9.Bc2 c5 10.d4 Qc7 11.Nbd2 O-O 12.h3 Nc6 13.d5 Nd8 14.a4 b4 15.Nc4 a5 (No.175) **16.Nfxe5!**

A celebrated liquidation combination. Alekhine expressed the opinion that it should not have led to a winning ending. In the tournament book he gives 16.Be3, and if Black plays 16...Nd7, then 17.Nfd2, as a more precise continuation. It is undeniable, however, that Capablanca's method leads in any case to an ending which is favorable; and this was all Capablanca usually needed in order to win.

16...Ba6

An interpolation which doesn't alter anything.

17.Bb3 dxe5 18.d6 Bxd6 19.Qxd6 Qxd6 20.Nxd6

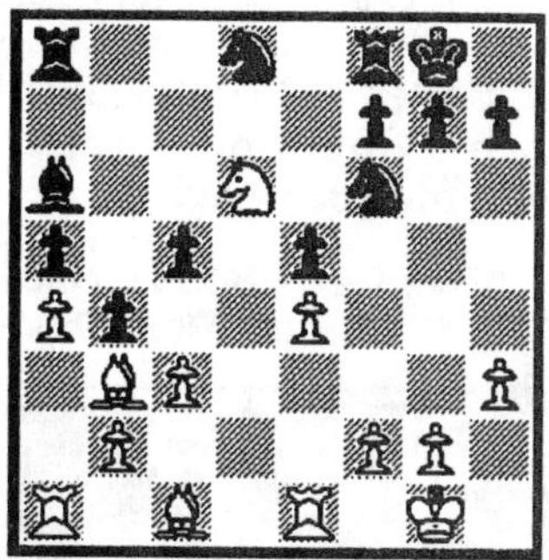

(This is the endgame for which Capablanca was playing).

20...Nb7?

This is the weak move, according to Alekhine. Why, he asks, should Black voluntarily leave his opponent the two Bishops? The obvious move was 20...Rb8, and if 21.Bc4, then 21...Bxc4 22.Nxc4 Nc6, and Black can defend himself. Golombek, however, in his book *Capablanca's Best Hundred Games of Chess*, shows that White could do much better with 21.Nb5! Then: **1)** 21...Bxb5 22.axb5 Rxb5 23.Bc4, followed by 24.Rxa5. **2)** 21...bxc3 22.bxc3 Bxb5 23.axb5 Rxb5 24.Bc4 and 25.Rxa5. In both cases the liquidation is very much in White's favor, with his two Bishops coming into their own and a White Rook penetrating the enemy lines.

21.Nxb7 Bxb7 22.cxb4 cxb4

Alekhine considered this another piece of negligence, and suggested 22...axb4 23.f3 Ba6 and eventually ...c4. but even in this case White still has the better of it: 23.Be3! after which 23...Nxe4 is not good enough because of 24.f3 Nf6 25.Bxc5, while 23...Rfc8 24.Rec1 Ra5 25.f3 Ba6 26.Bc4 leaves Black saddled with a seriously weakened Queenside.

23.f3 Rfd8

Once again Alekhine is not objective with his criticism. He accuses Black of planless play, and suggests 23...Nd7 24.Be3 Rfc8! 25.Red1 Rc7 as better play. But after 26.Rd6 R8c8 27.R1d1 (given by Golombek) the Black a-pawn cannot be saved.

24.Be3 h6 25.Red1 Bc6 26.Rac1 Be8 27.Kf2 Rxd1 28.Rxd1 Rc8 29.g4!

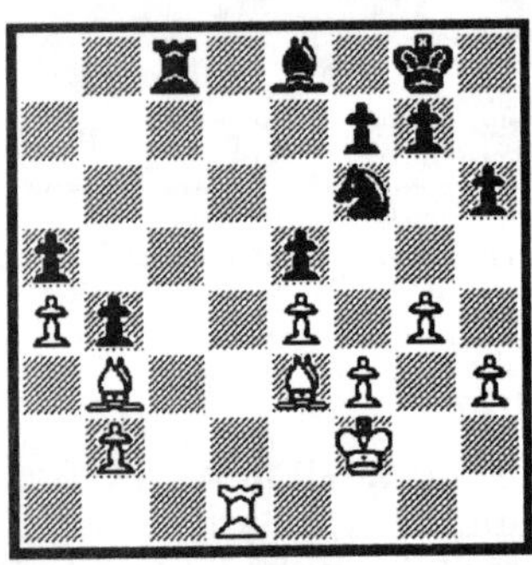

Threatening to drive the Knight away by h4 and g5, and then win a pawn by Rd5. On the other hand 29.Bb6 would be too hasty, because of 29...Nd7 30.Bxa5 Nc5.

29...Bd7

This loses rapidly, but a saving defense cannot be found.

30.Bb6 Be6

Loss of a pawn is unavoidable. If 30...Ra8 White wins by 31.Bc7.

31.Bxe6 fxe6

The interpolated check 31...Rc2+ does not help: 32.Ke3 fxe6 33.Rd2, etc.

32.Rd8+ Rxd8 33.Bxd8 Nd7 34.Bxa5 Nc5 35.b3!

The most accurate way, according to Alekhine in the tournament book. He adds, 35.Bxb4 Nxa4 36.b3 Nb6 37.Bd6 Nd7 38.Ke3 is also an easy win, of course.

This goes to show that even the greatest masters may easily be mistaken when they are not taking an unbiased view. Alekhine overlooks that 35.Bxb4 is a terrible blunder, for Black has the reply 35...Nd3+.

35...Nxb3 36.Bxb4 Nd4 37.a5 Black Resigned.

POSITION 176

(An assortment of familiar and unfamiliar liquidation motifs; from the game Jamsarat-Kramer, Moscow, 1956).

1.e4 c5 2.Nf3 Nc6 3.d4 cxd4 4.Nxd4 Nf6 5.Nc3 d6 6.Bc4 e6 7.Bg5 Be7 8.Qd2 a6 9.Bb3 h6 10.Bh4 O-O 11.O-O-O Bd7 12.g4 (No.176) **12...Nxe4!**

A liquidating combination which we have met before in this chapter. This time the consequences are ramified.

13.Nxe4

After 13.Bxe7 Nxd2 14.Bxd8 Nxd4 15.Rxd2 Nxb3+ 16.axb3 Rfxd8 17.Rxd6 Bc6 18.R1d1 Rxd6 19.Rxd6 Kf8; the endgame is in Black's favor, in view of the weakened state of White's Kingside.

13...Bxh4 14.Nxd6 Nxd4!

The point of the combination is the following variation: 15.Nxb7 Qb6 16.Qxd4 Qxd4 17.Rxd4 Bc6 and Black wins a piece.

15.Qxd4 Bc6 16.Rhg1 Qf6 17.Qxf6

Forced, for White cannot play 17.f4 (because of 17...Qxd4 18.Rxd4 Bf2) nor 17.Rd2 (17...Bg5).

17...Bxf6 18.f4 Rad8

It is now apparent that White's advanced cavalry post cannot be maintained. 19.g5 would be met by 19...hxg5 20.fxg5 Be5 21.Nc4 Bxh2. With the Bishop pair now in full cry it is clear that the liquidation which started at the diagramed position has worked out in Black's favor.

19.Rd3 Rd7 20.Ne4 Bd4 21.Rgd1 Rfd8 22.c3 Bb6

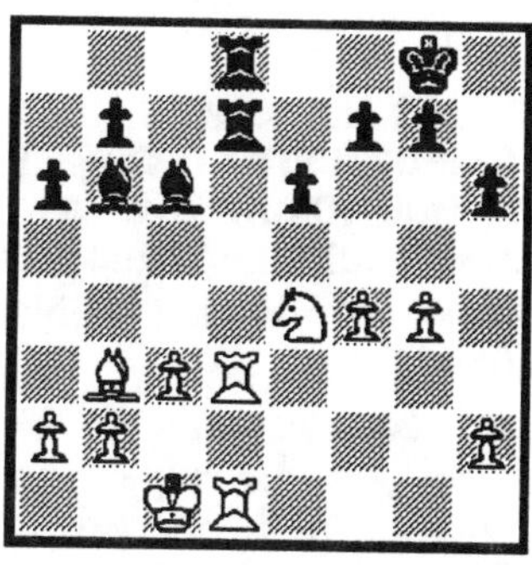

(A combination upsets White's intended liquidation).

23.Rxd7

It seems that White has overcome the worst of his difficulties, for if 23...Rxd7 24.Rxd7 Bxd7 25.Kd2, etc., but now comes a shock.

23...Be3+ 24.Kb1

After 24.R7d2 comes 24...Bxe4 25.Bc2 Bf3! and White, who has won the Exchange, will now lose a whole Rook.

24...Rxd7 25.Rxd7 Bxd7 26.Nd6 Bc6 27.f5 Bf4 28.Nc8

A last try. After 28...exf5 29.gxf5 Bxh2 30.Ne7+ Kf8 31.Nxc6, there would be an ending with opposite colored Bishops.

28...Be4+ 29.Bc2 Bxc2+ 30.Kxc2 Bxh2 and Black won as follows:

31.fxe6 fxe6 32.c4 Kf7 33.Kd3 Bc7 34.c5 Ke8 35.b4 Kd7 36.Nb6+ Bxb6 37.cxb6 g6 38.a4 Kc6 39.Ke4 h5 40.gxh5 gxh5 White Resigned.

POSITION 177

(Liquidation from the game Darga-Lehmann, Bognor Regis, 1961).

1.Bxc6 whereupon **Black Resigned**, for he faces the losing end of the liquidation after **1...Qxc5 2.dxc5 Rxd1+ 3.Rxd1 bxc6 4.Rd8+ Kg7 5.f6+!.**

POSITION 178

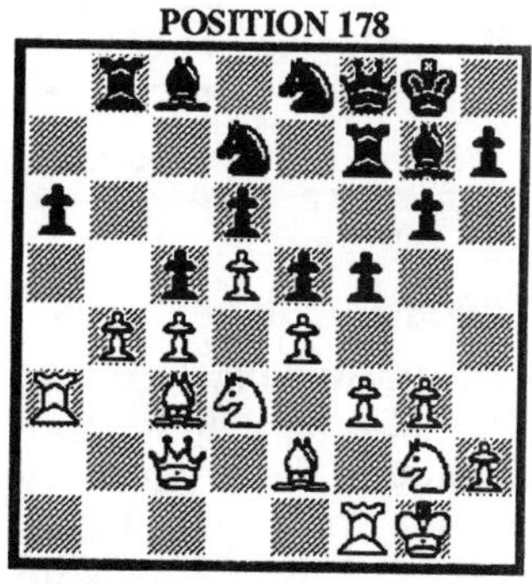

(Combinative liquidation from the game Korchnoi-Gurgenidze, U.S.S.R. Championship, 1960).

1.bxc5 dxc5 2.exf5 gxf5 3.f4!

With two important branches: **1)** 3...e4 4.Ne5!, and unless Black exchanges Knights, giving White connected passed pawns, he will lose the exchange after 5.Nc6. **2)** 3...exf4 4.Ngxf4 with several threats, e.g. Bh5, or Ne6.

3...Qe7 4.fxe5 Nxe5 5.Nxe5 Bxe5 6.Bxe5 Qxe5 7.Re3

Typical of this sort of combination. After several consecutive exchanges comes the deadly follow-up. Possibly Black had hoped, when embarking on this sequence of moves, that he would be able to defend himself at this point by 7...Qd4. Then, however, there follows not 8.Rf4 Qa1+, but simply 8.Rd1 Rb2 9.Rxd4 Rxb2 10.Rxe8+. **Black Resigned.**

POSITION 179

(From the game Honfi-Lengyel, Budapest, 1961).

1.Nxc5 Bxc5 2.Nc6!!

A fantastic move; Black cannot play 2...Bxe3+ 3.Kh1, as the Bishop is tied to the defense of the f8 square, where White is threatening mate, e.g. 3...Qg8 4.Qxg8+ Kxg8 5.Ne7+ Kh8 6.Rf8#.

2...bxc6 3.Bxc5 Bd7

No better is 3...h6 because of 4.Qg6 Bd7 5.Rf7.

4.Bd4 e5

Or 4...Qg8 5.Qxd7 Rd8 6.Bxg7+ and wins.

5.Bxe5 and **Black Resigned.**

POSITION 180

(The game Capablanca-Villegas, Buenos Aires, 1914).

1.d4 d5 2.Nf3 Nf6 3.e3 c6 4.Bd3 Bg4 5.c4 e6 6.Nbd2 Nbd7 7.O-O Be7 8.Qc2 Bh5 9.b3 Bg6 10.Bb2 Bxd3 11.Qxd3 O-O 12.Rae1 Qc7 13.e4 dxe4 14.Nxe4 Nxe4 15.Rxe4 Bf6 16.Qe3 c5 (No.180) **17.Ne5 cxd4**

Another course was 17...Nxe5 18.dxe5 Be7; but he hopes that his chosen move will lead to the more far-reaching liquidation 18.Bxd4 Nxe5 19.Bxe5 Bxe5 20.Rxe5 b6, followed by ...Rd8, Black getting in first with occupation of the d-file.

18.Nxd7!!

A magnificent combination. Now 18...dxe3 is answered by 19.Nxf6+, and then: **1)** 19...gxf6 20.Rg4+ Kh8 21.Bxf6#. **2)** 19...Kh8 20.Rh4 h6 21.Rxh6+! gxh6 22.Ne8+, and with two minor pieces for the Rook White has a winning advantage.

18...Qxd7 19.Bxd4 Bxd4?

Now White will achieve his objectives in full. Better would have been 19...Qe7.

20.Rxd4 Qc7 21.Rfd1 Rfd8 22.b4 Rxd4 23.Qxd4

White's positional advantage is now clear. His control of the d-file makes the Queenside majority a formidable weapon in his hand.

23...b6

A shade better would have been 23...a6, making it not quite so easy for White to create a passed pawn.

24.g3 Rc8 25.Rc1 Rd8 26.Qe3

Black's seizure of the d-file is only an apparent success. He will not be able to profit from the file, for at any moment White may play c5, creating a passed pawn which will tie down Black's pieces completely.

26...Kf8 27.c5 bxc5 28.bxc5 Rd5 29.Qe4! g6

Not 29...Rxc5 because of 30.Qb4.

30.c6 Kg7 31.a4 Rd6?

A blunder. The only possible way to hold out was 31...Rd8.

32.Qe5+ and **Black Resigned,** for he cannot prevent 33.Qxd6! Qxd6 34.c7, etc.

POSITION 181

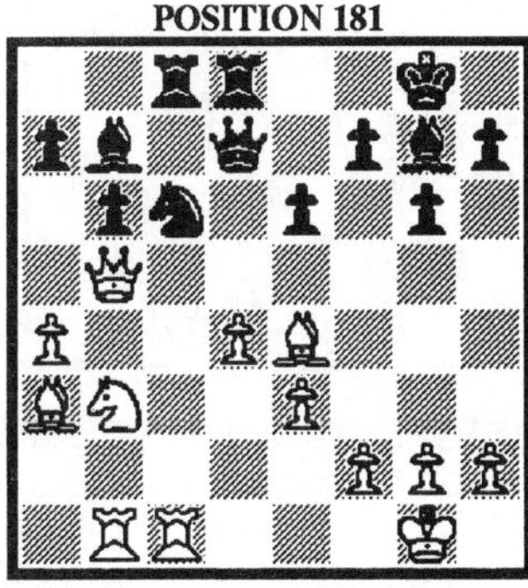

(A wild liquidation combination from the game Furman-Nezmetdinov, U.S.S.R. Championship, 1955).

1...Nxd4!?

Black hopes to free himself by tactical means.

2.Qxd7 Ne2+ 3.Kf1 Nxc1

Black has played for this position in the hope of 4.Qxd8+ Rxd8 5.Bxb7 Rd1#. Or if the White Queen should take the other Rook then 4...Ba6+ 5.Qxa6 Rd1#. Unfortunately the combination is unsound. Of course 3...Rxd7 would lose after 4.Bxb7 Rxc1+ 5.Nxc1 Nxc1 6.Rxc1.

4.Qxc8!

Anyway!

4...Ba6+ 5.Ke1! Rxc8 6.Rxc1

And a census reveals that Black is a piece short.

POSITION 182

(A successful liquidating combination, from the game Lombardy-Fischer, New York, 1961).

1.e4 c5 2.Nf3 d6 3.d4 cxd4 4.Nxd4 Nf6 5.f3 Nc6 6.c4 e6 7.Nc3 Be7 8.Be3 O-O 9.Nc2 d5 10.cxd5 exd5 11.Nxd5 Nxd5 12.Qxd5 Qc7 13.Qb5 Bd7 14.Rc1 (No.182) **14...Nb4! 15.Nxb4**

White takes up the gauntlet-unwisely, as the sequel shows.

15...Qxc1+ 16.Bxc1 Bxb5 17.Nd5

This was the tactical finesse that White was relying on when he went in for the liquidation. Black, however, has seen farther.

17...Bh4+!

The real point of Black's 14th move.

18.g3 Bxf1 19.Rxf1 Bd8

The combination is ended and Black has won the Exchange. True, White has some compensation – a pawn and advantage in space – but in the long run it will not be enough. The game ended as follows:

20.Bd2 Rc8 21.Bc3 f5! 22.e5 Rc5 23.Nb4 Ba5 24.a3 Bxb4 25.axb4 Rd5 26.Kf2 Kf7 27.h4 Ke6 28.Ke3 Rc8 29.Rg1 Rc4 30.Re1

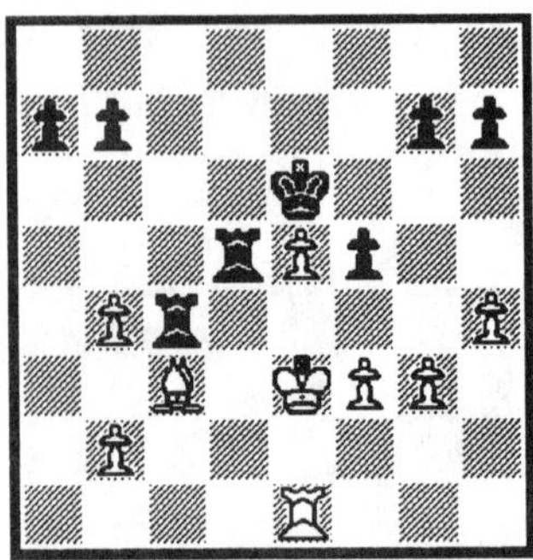

30...Rxc3+! 31.bxc3 Rxe5+ 32.Kd2 Rxe1 33.Kxe1

This liquidation has produced a pawn ending which is won for Black.

33...Kd5 34.Kd2 Kc4 35.h5 b6 36.Kc2 g5 37.h6 f4 38.g4 a5 39.bxa5 bxa5 40.Kb2 a4 41.Ka3 Kxc3 White Resigned.

POSITION 183

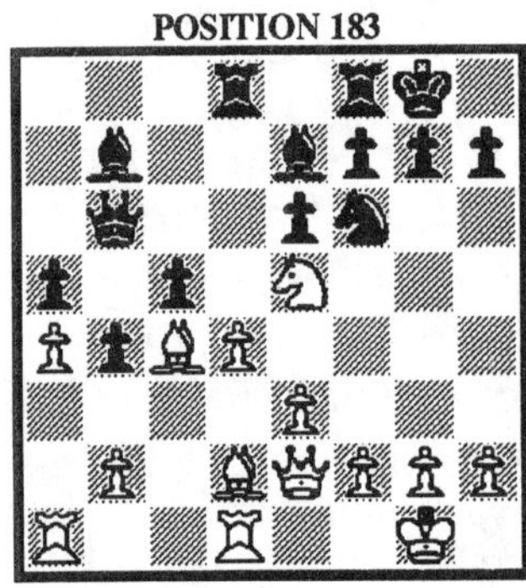

(The game Friedstein-Smyslov, Moscow, 1944).

1.d4 Nf6 2.Nf3 d5 3.c4 c6 4.Nc3 dxc4 5.e3 b5 6.a4 b4 7.Na2 e6 8.Bxc4 Be7 9.O-O O-O 10.Qe2 Bb7 11.Rd1 a5 12.Bd2 Nbd7 13.Nc1 Qb6 14.Nd3 c5 15.Nde5 Nxe5 16.Nxe5 Rad8 (No.183)

White offers a pawn.

17.Bb5

After 17.dxc5 Qxc5! White would get into difficulties. He therefore offers a pawn in order to try for counterplay on the d-file.

17...cxd4 18.exd4 Qxd4

According to Smyslov 18...Rxd4 19.Be3 Rxd1+ 20.Rxd1 Qc7 21.Nd7!, after which 21...Rd8 fails to 22.Bb6, while 21...Ra8 22.Nxf6+ Bxf6 permits the penetration of the Rook by 23.Rd7.

19.Nc4 Qd5!

Black plays for attack, and is not concerned about holding the extra pawn.

20.Qf1 Qh5 21.Nxa5

(Black essays a sparkling exchange combination).

21...Bf3!! 22.gxf3

If 22.Nc6, Black wins a pawn by 22...Bd6 23.h3 Bxc6 24.Bxc6 Qe5 25.g3 Qxb2.

22...Rxd2 23.Rxd2 Qg5+ 24.Kh1 Qxd2

The outcome of the combination is clear enough. White's King position is wrecked, and this fact now dictates the course of the game.

25.Qe2 Qf4 26.Nc4 Rc8 27.Rd1 Rc5 28.Ne3 g6

Smyslov pointed out that there is nothing in 28...Rh5 29.Nf1 Bd6 30.Qe3 Rxh2+ 31.Kg1!.

29.Ng2 Qc7 30.Ne3 b3! 31.Qd3 Qf4 32.Ng2 Qb4 33.Ne3 Qh4 34.a5 Rh5 35.Nf1 Qxf2 36.Rd2

Otherwise 36...Bc5 follows.

36...Qc5 37.Bc4 Qxa5 38.Bxb3 Kg7 39.Ng3 Rh4 40.Kg2 Rb4

Threatening 41...Rxb3.

41.Qc3 Qb5 42.Rd3 Bd6!

Breaking all resistance. After 43.Rxd6 Rxb3 the b-pawn falls.

43.Re3 Bf4 and **White Resigned** in view of the line 44.Rd3 Be5 45.Qc2 Nd5 46.Ne2 Rh4, by which Black wins at least another pawn.

PART ELEVEN
FAMILIAR FAILINGS
INTRODUCTION

In the previous ten parts we have been discussing the origins of positional features and examining their peculiarities. We have reviewed the various pawn formations, scrutinized their weaknesses and shown how attacks against Kingside or Queenside may be carried out. We have also gone into the subject of maneuvering, and have examined the nature of good defensive play. All these things are concerned – to a greater or lesser degree – with weaknesses in the layout of the pieces on the board. The weaknesses which we are going to discuss now are very different. They are not even exclusively concerned with chess, but are fundamental human weaknesses.

There was a time when chessplayers always captured whatever there was to be captured; to refuse a sacrifice was considered cowardly. The order of the day was the desire to win material, and this is the subject of Chapter 45.

In direct contrast to this is the desire for exchanges. In Chapter 46 we consider the type of player who – far from recklessly accepting every offer – is frightened of getting involved in any fight at all, and tries everything he knows to bring about exchanges in the hope of a quick draw.

Anyone who has made rapid progress at chess, and frequently has to meet inferior players, should take care not to cultivate too pretty a style of play. Unjustified Kingside attacks, unjustified checks – often from the simplest of motives – and also unjustified sacrifices are all symptoms of the failing which we discuss in Chapter 47 – the desire to always win by direct attack, and preferably in the most impressive way.

Finally we come, in Chapter 48, to the desire for a draw. Some players experience a kind of dread which shows itself in an exaggerated respect for the opponent – a determination not go get into any sort of combination or complication with a player who has any reputation as a tactician.

The failings depicted in these chapters are experienced by most players in their student days, and they are always liable to return during "off-form" periods. They are, in short, manifestations of our human limitations, and the effort to overcome them has to be renewed again and again.

CHAPTER 45
EAGERNESS TO WIN MATERIAL

The overrating of one's own chances as judged by material is to some extent a general phenomenon. It is true that the failing is most common in inexperienced players, but history shows that even leading players are guilty now and then.

In earlier times the attempt to win material was normal practice. Refusal to accept a proffered piece or pawn was considered a craven attitude. In such celebrated games as, for instance, Anderssen's *Immortal Game* the brilliant win was made possible by the fact that the loser was so keen on winning material. It was only under the influence of Steinitz that players came to realize the importance of achieving full development of the pieces before even thinking of winning material. Nevertheless, it happens even today that some players will snatch a pawn while still not fully developed, trusting that they will be able to weather the attack which follows. It is not to be wondered at if such an attack does often cut the enemy to pieces.

Here are some examples:

POSITION 184

(A classic example; The Immortal Game, Anderssen-Kieseritzky, London, 1851).

1.e4 e5 2.f4 exf4 3.Bc4 Qh4+ 4.Kf1 b5 5.Bxb5 Nf6 6.Nf3 Qh6 7.d3 Nh5 8.Nh4 Qg5 9.Nf5 c6 10.g4 Nf6 11.Rg1 (No.184) **11...cxb5**

We do not intend to present a comprehensive analysis of this famous game. We content ourselves with indicating the points at which Black is guilty of undue greed for material. This is the first such point; in return for the piece White obtains a big lead in development.

12.h4 Qg6 13.h5 Qg5 14.Qf3 Ng8

In Chapters 30-32, which we devoted to the subject of defense, we saw that the defender should be ready at any moment to return the material he has won. The text is motivated by precisely the opposite principle. In order to hold on to his extra piece Black is willing to deprive himself of what little development he has. He should have considered 14...Nxg4.

15.Bxf4 Qf6 16.Nc3 Bc5 17.Nd5 Qxb2 18.Bd6!

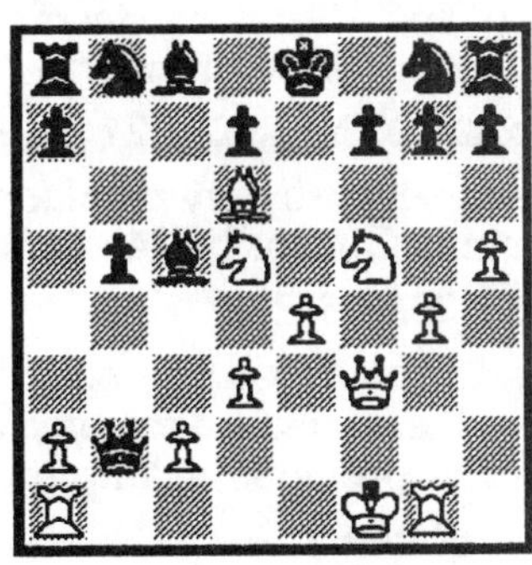

The finish of this game is very fine, and is justly famous – notwithstanding the fact that its earlier part, as Dr. Lasker said, is an affront to our susceptibilities.

18...Bxg1 19.e5 Qxa1+ 20.Ke2 Na6

With 20...Ba6, Black could have given White more trouble. Black's move is still motivated, albeit subconsciously, by the determination to not relinquish material. He rules out White's check at c7.

21.Nxg7+ Kd8 22.Qf6+! Nxf6 23.Be7#.

POSITION 185

(From the famous game Capablanca-Bernstein, San Sebastian, 1911).

This was the position after White's 22nd move – Knight from d4 to e2. It is apparent that White has an attack against the Black King's position but it is not so clear how to advance the attack. Black was evidently of the opinion that his King was secure enough and therefore deemed the time ripe for a little plundering.

22...Qxa2? 23.Neg3 Qxc2? 24.Rc1

Played mainly to prevent Black from exchanging Queens by 24...Qc5.

24...Qb2 25.Nh5 Rh8

After 25...g6 26.Qxh6+ Kg8 White pursues the attack in a manner which recalls the previous example: 27.e5! gxh5 28.gxh5, etc.

26.Re2 Qe5 27.f4 Qb5 28.Nfxg7

The correctness of this offer hinges on the question whether White's Knight will ever escape after 28...Nxg7 29.Nf6+ Kg6 30.Nxd7 f6.

The continuation 31.e5! Kf7 32.Nxf6 Re7 33.Ne4 dxe5 34.fxe5 gives an affirmative answer.

28...Nc5

This loses rapidly and hopelessly. In any case 28...Rd8 or 28...Qb6 would have been better.

29.Nxe8 Bxe8 30.Qc3 f6 31.Nxf6+ Kg6 32.Nh5 Rg8 33.f5+ Kg5 34.Qe3+ Black Resigned.

POSITION 186

(The 16th match-game Gunsberg-Steinitz, New York, 1891).

1.e4 e5 2.Nf3 Nc6 3.Bc4 Bc5 4.b4 Bxb4 5.c3 Ba5 6.O-O Qf6 7.d4 h6 8.Qa4 Bb6 9.Bb5 Nge7 10.Ba3 exd4 11.e5 Qg6 12.cxd4 Nd5 13.Re1 Nf4 14.g3 Qg4 15.Nbd2 Nh3+ 16.Kg2 Ng5 17.Bb2 Ne7 18.Be2 Ne6 19.Kh1 Qf5

Here Gunsberg picked up his KN with the clear intention of moving it to h4. He even placed it momentarily on that square, and then hastily retracted the move. After a while Gunsberg picked up the Knight again and played Nh4. As he did so he shook his head and shrugged his shoulders as if to say "I'm bound to move this piece and I can't find any better place to put it".

20.Nh4 Qxf2

Steinitz played this move without pausing to think. In view of what had happened he was quite convinced that his opponent had overlooked, until too late, that his f-pawn was unprotected.

21.Ne4

Rude awakening. The only square for the Black Queen is e3, but then comes 22.Bf1, and the Queen is snared in mid-board. **Black Resigned.**

We give this example to show that the instinct to win material can manifest itself in some strange ways. We must make it clear, however, that Gunsberg's tactics here are not to be condoned. After the game Steinitz pointed out that Gunsberg had himself been the victim of similar tactics, in a match-game with Chigorin, and that on that occasion Gunsberg had been extremely angry.

POSITION 187

(The game Reti-Marshall, New York, 1924).

1.Nf3 Nf6 2.c4 d5 3.cxd5 Nxd5 4.d4 Bf5 5.Nc3 e6 6.Qb3 Nc6 7.e4 Nxc3 8.exf5 Nd5 9.Bb5 Bb4+ 10.Bd2 Bxd2+ 11.Nxd2 exf5 12.Bxc6+ bxc6 13.O-O O-O 14.Qa4 Rb8 15.Nb3 Rb6 16.Qxa7 Qg5 17.Qa5 c5 18.Qxc5 Nf4 19.g3 Rh6

Alekhine, whose excellent analyses in the tournament book we shall follow in part, states that Black now has all sorts of threats, the foremost being 20...Qh5 21.h4 Qf3.

20.Qxc7?

Just like Black in the previous example, White is here guilty of material greed. He should have played 20.Qc2!, with the following variations: **1)** 20...Nh3+ 21.Kh1 f4 22.Qc5, and White will defend without difficulty. **2)** 20...Rxh2 21.Kxh2 Qh5+ 22.Kg1 Qf3 23.gxf4 Qg4+, drawing by perpetual check.

20...Ne2+ 21.Kg2 Qg4 22.Rh1 f4 23.f3

Nearly forced, for Black is threatening 23...f3+ 24.Kf1 Qh3+ 25.Ke1 Qg2 26.Rf1 Rxh2 followed by 27...Qxf1+!.

23...Qh3+ 24.Kf2

Now White hopes for 24...Nxg3 25.Qxf4! Nxh1+ 26.Rxh1 with chances of holding.

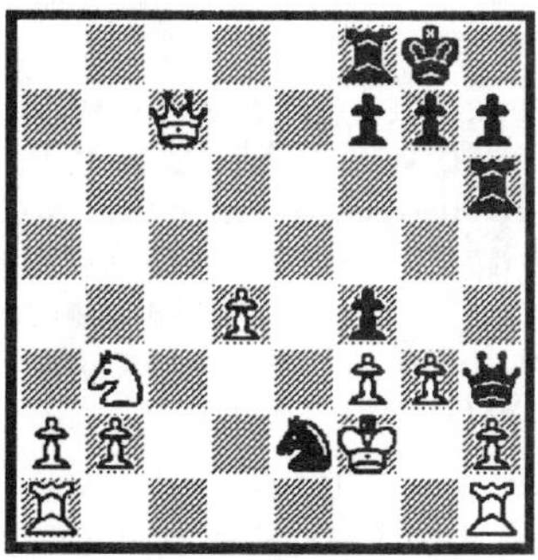

24...Rc8!

This is much stronger. The White Queen is forced to leave the vital dark-squared diagonal.

25.Qa5 Nxg3!

Now this sacrifice is decisive, for if White accepts it he loses as follows: 26.hxg3 Qxg3+ 27.Ke2 Qg2+ 28.Kd3 Rxh1 29.Rxh1 Qxf3+ and 30...Qxh1.

26.Rhg1 Qxh2+ 27.Rg2 Qh4 28.Rc1 Re8

Cutting off the King's flight to e1 and threatening 29...Re2+ and 30...Qh1#.

29.Qb5 Ne4+ 30.Kf1 Qh1+ White Resigned.

POSITION 188

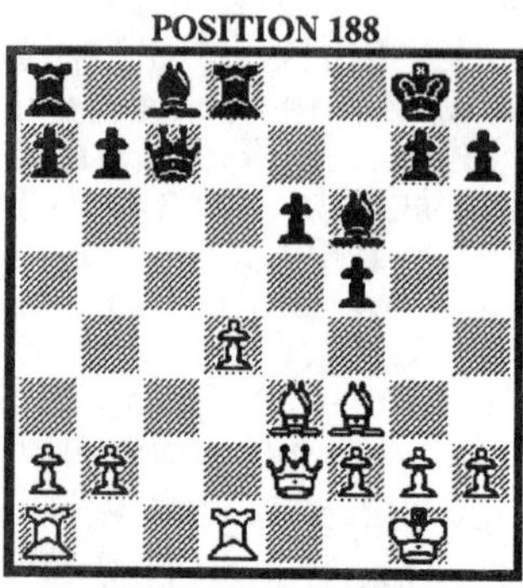

(The game Alekhine-Flohr, Berne, 1932).

1.d4 d5 2.Nf3 Nf6 3.e3 e6 4.Bd3 c5 5.c3 Nc6 6.Nbd2 Qc7 7.O-O Be7 8.Qe2 O-O 9.e4 dxe4 10.Nxe4 cxd4 11.Nxd4 Nxd4 12.cxd4 Nxe4 13.Bxe4 f5 14.Bf3 Bf6 15.Rd1 Rd8 16.Be3

The d-pawn is obviously weak, but in order to win it Black will have to weaken his position seriously. The sequel demonstrates that White will be able to take powerful advantage of this weakening, mainly because of his advanced development.

16...f4?

Better would have been 16...g5, though even so White would get a dangerous attack by 17.h3 Qg7 18.Rac1 f4 19.Bd2 Bxd4 20.Ba5.

17.Rac1 Qd6 18.Bd2 Bxd4

The attempt to develop the Queenside by 18...Rb8 leaves White a clear advantage after the continuation 19.a3 Bd7 20.Bb4.

19.Ba5! Rd7 (see next diagram)

Forced, for if 19...Re8 White wins a piece by 20.Qc4.

20.Rxd4!

The winning shot.

20...Qxd4 21.Qxe6+ Rf7

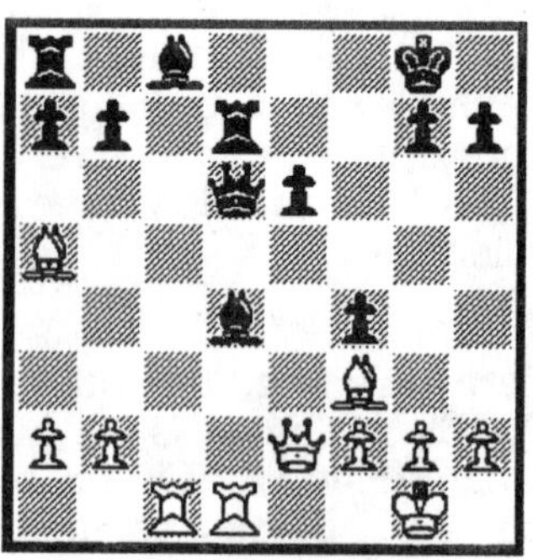

After 19...Rd7

After 21...Kf8 the quiet move 22.Re1! is devastating; e.g. 22...g6 23.Qe8+ Kg7 24.Bc3, winning the Queen.

22.Rxc8+ Rxc8 23.Qxc8+ Rf8 24.Qxb7 Re8

Investigating whether White may show symptoms of greed by 25.Bc3, and intending, if so, to cure him by 25...Qxc3!.

25.h3 Qc5 26.Bc3 Qe7 27.Bd5+ Kh8 28.Qxe7 Black Resigned.

POSITION 189

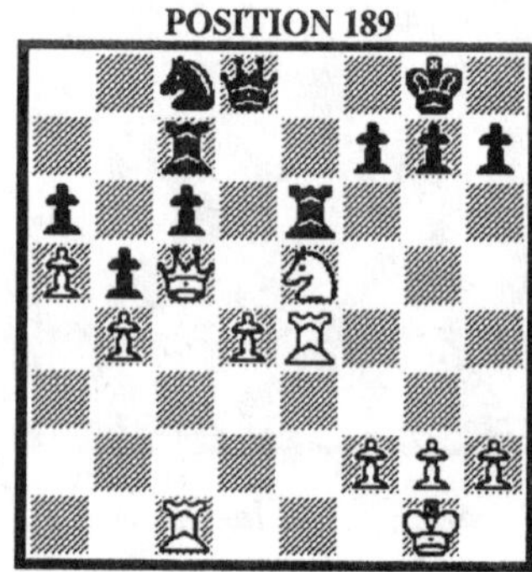

(From the game Euwe-Alekhine, Zurich, 1934).

1...f6?

Hoping to win a piece. The correct move, however, was 1...Ne7.

2.Nf7!!

The refutation. The Knight cannot be captured, as the following variation shows: 2...Kxf7 3.Qh5+ Ke7 4.Rxe6+

Kxe6 5.Re1+ Kd6 6.Qc5+ Kd7 7.Qf5+ Kd6 8.Qe6#.

2...Qe8 3.Rxe6 Qxe6 4.Nd8 Qe4 5.Nxc6

Instead of winning a piece Black has lost a pawn. The rest of the game – not important to our theme- went as follows:

5...h6 6.d5 Qd3 7.h3 Qd2 8.g3 Kh8 9.Kg2 Qd3 10.Re1 Kh7 11.Re3 Qd2 12.Re8 Qd3 13.Qd4 Qc4 14.Qe4+ Qxe4+ 15.Rxe4 Kg8 16.Nb8! Kf7 17.Nxa6 Rd7 18.Rd4 Ne7 19.d6 Nf5 20.Rd5 Nxd6 21.Nc5 Rd8 22.Ne4 Nb7 23.a6! Ke6 24.Rxd8 Black Resigned.

POSITION 190

(The game Kinzel-Duckstein, Vienna, 1958).

1.e4 e5 2.Nf3 Nc6 3.d4 exd4 4.Bc4 Nf6 5.O-O Nxe4 6.Re1 d5 7.Bxd5 Qxd5 8.Nc3 Qa5 9.Nxe4 Be6 10.Bd2 Bb4 11.Nxd4 Nxd4 12.c3 Qd5 13.cxb4 O-O 14.Rc1 Rad8 (No.190) **15.Rc5! Qxa2?**

It was necessary to try 15...Qd7. The reason will soon appear.

16.Bc3 Nb5

This does not trouble White; but it is questionable if there is a good defense now.

17.Nf6+! gxf6

If 17...Kh8 18.Qh5 wins.

18.Bxf6! Rd5

White was threatening 19.Rg5#.

19.Qd2! and **Black Resigned.**

POSITION 191

(Won by Koltanowski in a simultaneous blindfold exhibition, Antwerp, 1931).

1.e4 c6 2.d4 d5 3.Nc3 dxe4 4.Nxe4 Nf6 5.Bd3 Qxd4 6.Nf3 Qd8 7.Qe2 Bf5 8.Nxf6+ gxf6 9.Bxf5 Qa5+ 10.Bd2 Qxf5 11.O-O-O Qe6 12.Qd3! (No.191) **12...Qxa2?**

It must be mentioned that this game was played in an exhibition in which White was without sight of any of the boards or men. The opponent jumps to the conclusion that the blindfold player has overlooked something; hence the pawn grab. The refutation is immediate and shattering.

13.Qd8+! Kxd8 14.Ba5+ Ke8 15.Rd8#.

POSITION 192

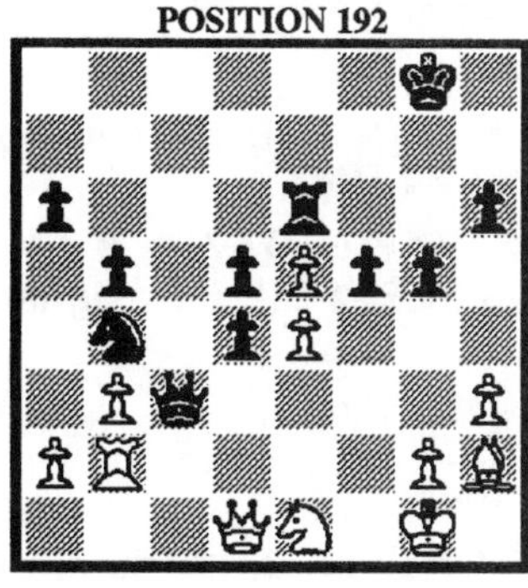

(From a game Spassky-Tal, Leningrad, 1959).

This position is quite different from the last one. It is a snapshot from a hard and serious game in which the contestants had been doing their best to outdo one another. By now both were likely in time trouble, and this would explain Black's next move. Or is the capture of the Rook under such circumstances rather to be considered a reflex action.

1...Qxb2?

Black should have taken not the Rook but the pawn. After 1...dxe4 he would undoubtably stand to win. With all the White pieces badly placed in contrast to the Black ones the Black pawn mass would surely decide the issue in the long run. The continuation might be 2.Rf2 e3! 3.Rxf5 d3 4.Nxd3 Nxd3 5.Qf1 Qc5 and wins. After the text the roles are reversed.

2.exf5 Rc6 3.Bg3!

More precise than 3.Qh5, which permits the strong reply 3...Qc3!.

3...d3

A possibility worth examining is 3...Nc2. There might follow: 4.Qh5! Nxe1 5.Qe8+ Kh7! 6.Qe7+ Kg8! 7.Bxe1, and now: **1)** 7...Qc1 8.f6 Qxe1+ 9.Kh2 Rxf6 10.Qxf6 Qe3 11.Qg6+, in White's favor. **2)** 7...Rc1 8.Qe8+! Kh7 9.f6 Rxe1+ 10.Kh2 wins.

4.Qh5 d2?

Now Black is lost. He could have held out by 4...Rc7.

5.Qe8+ Kg7 6.Qe7+! Kg8 7.f6 dxe1=Q+ 8.Bxe1 Black Resigned.

(The game Ilyin-Zhenevsky—Lasker, Moscow, 1925).

1.e4 c5 2.Nc3 e6 3.Nf3 d6 4.g3 Nf6 5.Bg2 Be7 6.O-O O-O 7.b3 Nc6 8.Bb2 Bd7 9.d4 cxd4 10.Nxd4 Qa5 11.Qd2 Rac8 12.Rad1 Kh8 13.Nce2

POSITION 193

13...Qxa2?!

After what we have been saying in the last few examples about greed for material, comment on this move seems superfluous, especially as it leads to the loss of the Black Queen in a few moves. Appearances can be deceptive. It is a safe assumption that Lasker is not just grabbing a pawn. Anyone who really knows his play will realize that Lasker is choosing this line of play purposely. Better than any other player Lasker understood human nature. He has assessed the position somewhat as follows. Any retreat of the Black Queen would be answered by 14.c4, giving White an excellent game, while 13...Qxd2 would give White the better ending. After the chosen move, on the other hand, Black's position is very sound. White's material advantage certainly gives him the better chances, but against this must be weighed the fact that the Queen sacrifice will upset White's equilibrium. He is sure to think that Lasker has made a bad blunder, and so will feel bound to play for a win.

14.Ra1 Qxb2 15.Rfb1 Qxb1+ 16.Rxb1 Rfd8 17.c4 Ne8 18.f4

In the tournament book Bogolyubov condemns this move as a weakening of the Kingside, and recommends 18.Nxc6 instead.

18...a6 19.Kh1 Nc7 20.Qe3 Rb8 21.Rd1 Nb4

Black's last few moves appeared to be preparing for the advance ...b5, but Lasker suddenly changes his plan and decides instead to exploit the strategic support point at b4.

22.Qc3 a5 23.Ra1

The Rook has no business here, as Bogolyubov correctly comments.

23...b6 24.Qe3?

A blunder which loses the Exchange.

24...e5! 25.Nf5 Bxf5 26.exf5 Nc2 27.Qc3 Nxa1 28.Qxa1 Bf6 29.Qg1 d5!

Thus Black assumes the initiative in the center.

30.cxd5 Nxd5 31.fxe5 Bxe5 32.g4 f6 33.h4 b5

Now Black's extra pawn on the Queenside brings a quick decision.

34.Nd4 Ne3!

Forcing a winning liquidation; the White Knight cannot move because of ...Rd1.

35.Qxe3 Rxd4 36.Bf3 a4 37.h5 a3 38.Qe2 Rbd8 White Resigned.

POSITION 194

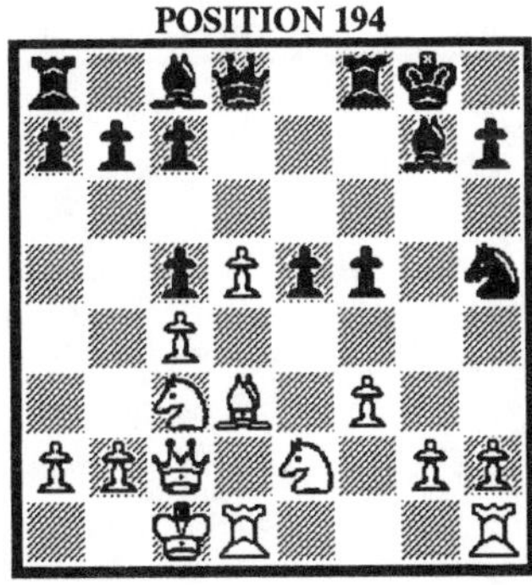

(The game Petursson-deGroot, Stockholm, 1937).

1.d4 Nf6 2.c4 g6 3.Nc3 Bg7 4.e4 d6 5.f3 O-O 6.Bd3 e5 7.d5 Nbd7 8.Nge2 Nh5 9.Be3 f5 10.exf5 gxf5 11.Qc2 Nc5 12.Bxc5 dxc5 13.O-O-O

White's last move was a preparation for g4, which would lead to a strong attack. Black refutes this scheme in a surprising manner.

13...Qg5+! 14.Kb1 Qxg2!

In the present circumstances this is not the kind of greed which we have seen in several of the previous positions in this chapter. Rather, it is a level-headed means of removing the sting out of the dangerous enemy pawns. From this point of view Black's tactics are comparable to those of Dr. Lasker in example 193. There are indeed certain resemblances between Dr. Lasker and Professor A.D. de Groot, who graduated in 1946 with a thesis on *Thought Processes of the Chessplayer* – a study in experimental psychology.

15.Rhg1 Qxf3 16.Ng3 Nxg3 17.Rxg3 Qh5 18.Rdg1 Rf7 19.Qg2 Qh6

Holding everything. Without the help of the sacrificed pawn White has no way of further strengthening his position.

20.Rh3 Qf6 21.Qe2 e4

Now that Black's united passed pawns begin to roll the day is won. White tries one more desperate offer, which Black accepts with the *sang-froid* as he did the two pawns earlier in the game.

22.Qh5 exd3 23.Qxh7+ Kf8 24.Rhg3 Qh6! 25.Qxh6 Bxh6 26.Rg8+ Ke7 27.Re1+ Kf6 28.d6

Threatening 29.Nd5#. If 28.R1e8, Black would have replied 28...Re7!.

28...Rf8 29.Nd5+ Kf7 30.Rgg1

Again threatening mate, this time by 31.Re7.

30...Be6 31.Nxc7 Rae8 32.b3 Bf4! 33.Nxe8 Rxe8 34.h4 Bxd6 35.h5 Rh8 36.Rh1 f4 37.h6 Bf5 38.Reg1 d2+ 39.Kb2 Be5+ 40.Ka3 Bc2 White Resigned.

We close this chapter with a striking example arising out of greed for material.

1.d4 d5 2.e4

The Blackmar-Diemer Gambit, enthusiastically embraced by Diemer.

2...dxe4 3.Nc3 Nf6 4.f3 exf3 5.Qxf3 Qxd4

Black grabs everything offered.

6.Be3 Qe5 7.O-O-O! Bg4?

This is refuted in sparkling style.

8.Qxb7! Qxe3+ 9.Rd2 Qe1+ 10.Nd1 Qxf1 11.Nf3!!

POSITION 195

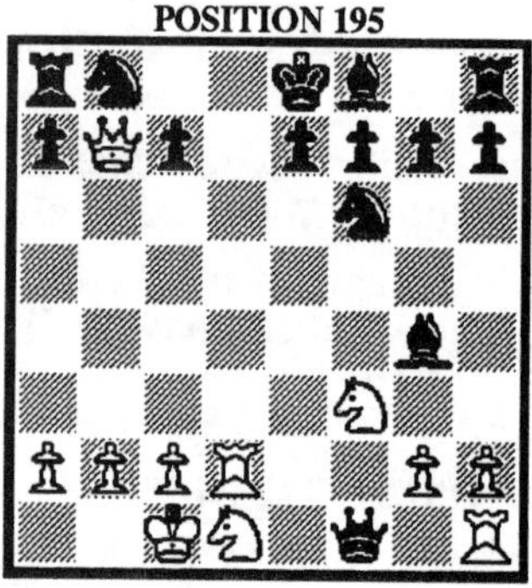

(A game won by Diemer, Bad Liebenzell, 1939).

Most surprising. Instead of contenting himself with the simple 11.Qxa8 White presents his grasping opponent with yet another piece.

11...Qxh1?

This is the condemned man's breakfast. He could have at least prolonged his life by the less greedy course: 11...Qa6 12.Qxa8 Qb6.

12.Ne5!

Threatening 13.Nxg4 followed by 14.Qc8#.

12...Bf5 13.Nc6! Bd7

The only way of parrying 14.Rd8#.

14.Qc8+! Bxc8 15.Rd8#.

CHAPTER 46
EAGERNESS TO EXCHANGE PIECES

The so-called drawing style of play is usually identified with the exchanging of as many pieces as possible. There is some justification for this, for prudent play – the desire to steer clear of all risks – usually does imply simplification. The subject of this chapter is the player who carries this idea to extremes. He has an exaggerated faith in the endgame, and seeks by every means to reach it, only to find all too often that when he gets there his opponent has the better chances. This may even happen without the endgame being reached.

This desire for exchange is the direct antithesis of the desire for material gain. The aim of the players in Chapter 45 was always to build up as big a material lead as possible in the shortest possible time; the inveterate exchanger would rather get rid of some pieces than win a pawn. The materialist plays to win; the exchanger to draw. All this, however, is not to be confused with the legitimate method of playing for a win employed by players whose playing strength shows itself to the full only in simple positions.

We illustrate the dangers of indiscriminate exchanging in this chapter.

POSITION 196

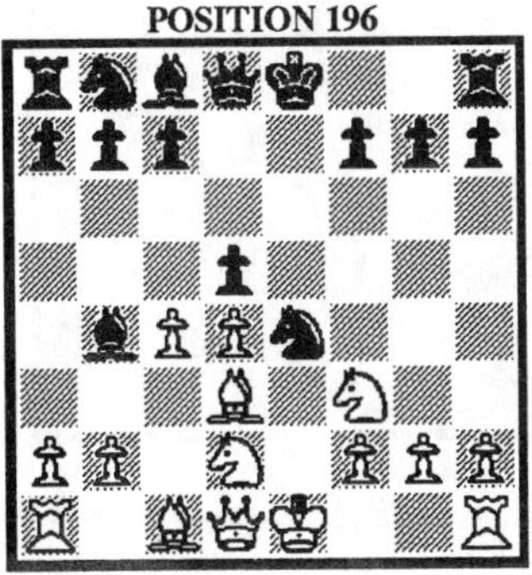

(The game Alekhine-Marshall, St. Petersburg, 1914).

1.e4 e5 2.Nf3 Nf6 3.Nxe5 d6 4.Nf3 Nxe4 5.d4 d5 6.Bd3 Bd6 7.c4 Bb4+ 8.Nbd2 (No.196) **8...Nxd2**

Natural, but inaccurate. Alekhine, in his excellent book, *My Best Games of Chess 1908-23*, stated that 8...O-O was correct, and then after 9.O-O Bxd2! 10.Bxd2 Bg4 Black would have good play.

9.Bxd2 Qe7+ 10.Qe2 Qxe2+

Black proceeds with his policy of exchanges. According to Alekhine, the exchange of Queens is a decisive mistake. The more accurate method would have been 10...Bxd2+ 11.Kxd2 Qxe2+ 12.Bxe2 dxc4 13.Bxc4 O-O, keeping White's advantage within bounds.

11.Kxe2 Bxd2 12.Kxd2!

The difference between this line and the one just now given emerges: if 12...dxc4 White can interpolate 13.Rhe1+!.

12...Be6 13.cxd5 Bxd5 14.Rhe1+ Kd8 15.Be4! Bxe4

Black may just as well continue to exchange now, for 15...c6 16.Bxd5 cxd5 17.Re5 would cost him a pawn.

16.Rxe4 Re8 17.Rae1 Rxe4 18.Rxe4 Nc6

Black is out to exchange nearly all the pieces as fast as possible, and if he only had time for ...Kd7 and ...Re8 this plan would have succeeded completely. A point in his favor is the fact that he can answer the seemingly strong 19.Ng5 by 19...Kd7! as 20.Nxh7 is met by 20...Rh8. All these exchanges, however, have left White

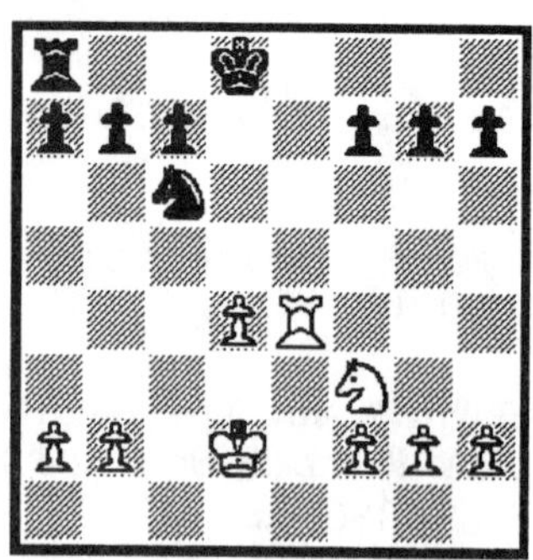

with a lead in development. True, there is not much material left, but it is enough to keep White in control.

19.Rg4! g6 20.Rh4! Ke7

Black must give up a pawn. If 20...h5 White has 21.g4! Kd7 22.gxh5.

21.Rxh7 Rd8 22.Rh4 Rd5 23.Re4+ Kf8

After 23...Kf6 24.Kc3 there is the unpleasant threat of 25.Re8.

24.Kc3 Rf5 25.Re2 a6 26.a3 Ne7

In order to occupy d5 with the Knight- a stratagem already known to us in the play against an isolated pawn.

27.Re5! Rf6

Black must now forgo exchanges, for after 27...Rxe5 28.dxe5 he would have no compensation at all for his pawn deficit.

28.Kd3 b6

Preventing 29.Rc5.

29.Re2! Nd5 30.Ke4 Nf4

There is nothing in 30...Re6+ 31.Ne5 Nf6+ 32.Kf3.

31.Rc2 Nxg2

Threatening to win a piece by 32...Rf4+, so White cannot take the c-pawn.

32.Ne5! Ke8

Now Black in his turn cannot protect the c-pawn because of the threatened 33.Nd7+.

33.Rxc7 Rxf2 34.Nc4! b5 35.Nd6+ Kf8 36.d5 f6 37.Nb7!

Preparing the decisive advance of the d-pawn.

37...Nf4 38.b4 g5 39.d6 Ne6

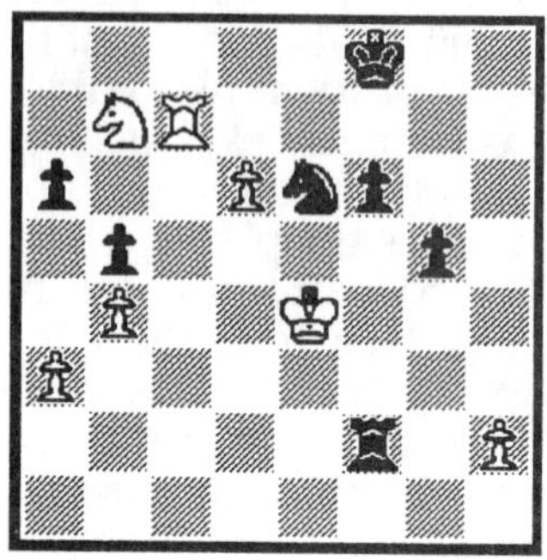

40.Kd5! Nf4+

If 40...Nxc7 41.dxc7 Rc2 42.Nc5 wins, or if 40...Re2 41.Kc6 Nd4+ 42.Kb6, etc.

41.Kc6 Rxh2 42.Nc5!

This prevents the enemy Knight from opposing the advance of the d-pawn. The rest presents no difficulty:

42...Rd2 43.Rc8+ Kf7 44.d7 Ne6 45.Nxe6 Kxe6 46.d8=Q Rxd8 47.Rxd8 g4 48.Re8+ Kf7 49.Re2 f5 50.Kd5 Kf6 51.Kd4 f4 52.Ke4 Kg5 53.Rc2 f3 54.Rd2 Kh4 55.Kf4 Black Resigned.

POSITION 197

(A match game Van Scheltinga-de Groot, 1936).

1.d4 Nf6 2.c4 g6 3.Nc3 Bg7 4.e4 d6 5.Nf3 O-O 6.Be2 e5 7.O-O Nfd7 8.Be3 Nc6 9.Qd2 (No.197) **9...exd4 10.Nxd4 Nxd4 11.Bxd4 Bxd4 12.Qxd4 Qf6**

Black's intention was apparently to obtain a quick draw after 13.Qxf6 Nxf6, or else by simplifying the position, to minimize the inconvenience which his space disadvantage might cause. White's next move, however, makes it clear that the foregoing moves have led only to a weakening of the Black position.

13.Qd2! Qe5!?

After 13...c6 White would win a pawn by 14.Rad1. Now Black intends to meet 14.Nd5 with 14...c6!, but he would have done better to choose 13...Nb6.

14.f4! Qc5+ 15.Kh1 Nf6

Now it looks as though Black has solved all his problems, for 16.Nd5 is met by 16...Nxe4.

16.b4!! Qxb4?

Losing outright, but after 16...Qc6 17.Qd4 Black is in dire straits.

17.Qd4! Black Resigned. After 17...Kg7 18.Nd5 Qc5 19.Qxf6+ mates, while 17...Nd7 (or 17...Ne8) loses to 18.Nd5, with the double threat of 19.Ne7# and 19.Nxb4.

POSITION 198

(The game Tarrasch-Marco, Leipzig, 1894).

1.e4 e5 2.Nf3 Nc6 3.Bb5 a6 4.Ba4 Nf6 5.Nc3 Bb4 6.Nd5 Be7 7.d3 d6 8.c3 O-O (No.198) **9.Nxf6+!**

Not every exchange is made just for the sake of trading down some pieces. In his famous book *Dreihundert Schachpartien*, Tarrasch awards himself an exclamation mark – most probably because Black would otherwise have made the exchange himself, and then, after ...Nb8, have advanced with ...f5.

9...Bxf6 10.O-O Ne7 11.Be3 Ng6 12.d4

Tarrasch attached great importance to occupying the center with pawns.

12...Bg4 13.h3

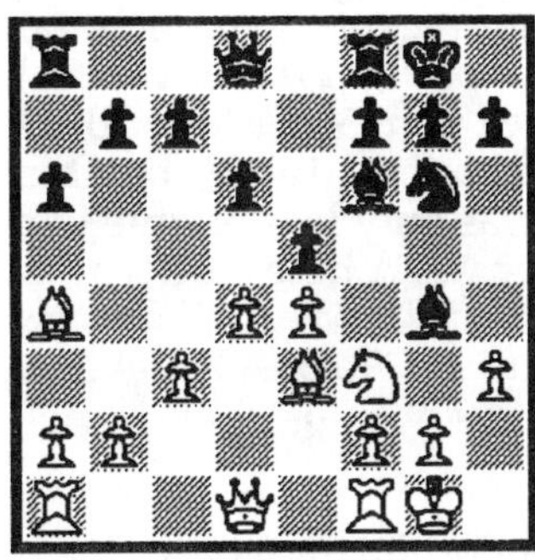

13...Bxf3?

Black is too anxious to exchange pieces. The Bishop should have been retired to e6 or d7, according to Tarrasch.

14.Qxf3 Bg5 15.g3

Preventing 15...Nf4.

15...Bxe3 16.fxe3!

Quite correct: the open f-file guarantees White an enduring initiative.

16...Kh8 17.Rf2 c6 18.Bb3 f6 19.Be6 Re8

After 19...Qe7 White could continue with 20.d5, but after the move played he can't maintain the Bishop on e6, for

20.d5 would be met simply by 20...Nf8.

20.Bf7 Re7 21.Bxg6 hxg6

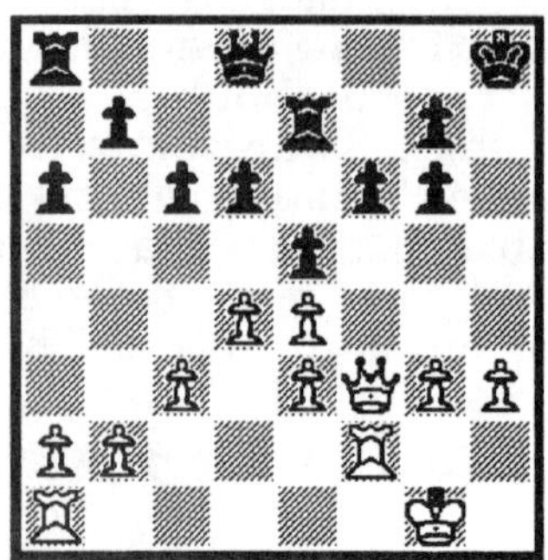

The results of the respective strategies of both players is now clear: White's exchange at move 9 prepared to obtain a central space advantage, and that on the 21st move weakened the Black King's position. Black also has exchanged twice, but his 13th move was only loss of time while his 15th gave White control of the half-open f-file. We shall now see how instructively Tarrasch develops his advantage.

22.h4!

An important move, for otherwise Black would get a satisfactory pawn structure by ...g5.

22...Qe8 23.Re1

Black threatened ...exd4, winning the e-pawn.

23...Kg8 24.Rd2!

The purpose of this move is to prepare to play d5, so as to close the center before resuming with his Kingside attacking ideas.

24...Qf7 25.d5 c5 26.Rf1 Qe8 27.Rh2

White's plan consists of h5 and then if ...g5, the breakthrough with h6 follows.

27...Rd8 28.Qg4

The immediate 28.h5 would be premature: 28...gxh5 29.Rxh5 Qg6!.

28...b5 29.Kg2!

Still preparing the advance of the h-pawn. After 29.h5 g5 30.Qf5 Qd7 31.Qg6 Black would have the chance to counterattack with 31...Qg4.

29...b4 30.c4 Qa4 31.h5!

Much stronger than 31.Qxg6 Qxa2, etc.

31...g5 32.h6 Qc2+ 33.Rf2 Qxc4 34.hxg7 Kxg7 35.Qf5 Kg8 36.Qxf6 Qxe4+ 37.Kg1 Black Resigned.

POSITION 199

(The game Beem-Van Scheltinga, Amsterdam, 1935).

1.e4 e5 2.Nf3 Nc6 3.Bc4 Bc5 4.Nc3 Nf6 5.d3 d6 6.Be3 O-O (No.199) **7.Bxc5?**

This move and White's next form an ill-motivated attempt to rapidly simplify the game by exchanges.

7...dxc5 8.Nd5 Qd6 9.Nxf6+ Qxf6

White's exchanges have only given the initiative to Black.

10.h3

White must prevent the pinning ...Bg4.

10...Bd7 11.O-O Ne7!

The Knight moves toward the Kingside to help in the attack. The continuation 11...Nd4 12.Nxd4 would only help White's chances.

12.Nh2 Ng6 13.Ng4 Qg5 14.Qf3 Nf4

Threatening to win at least a pawn by 15...h5.

15.Kh2 Kh8 16.Ne3 c6!

Otherwise White would force more exchanges by 17.Nd5.

17.Rg1 Rad8 18.Rae1 Bc8! 19.g4 Rd6!

Very much to the point. Now the Rook is poised to invade the Kingside with effect.

20.Nf5

The attempt to challenge the Black Knight by 20.Ng2 would lose to 20...Nxh3!, and White has the Trojan horse within his walls.

20...Bxf5 21.gxf5 Qh5 22.Qxh5

White gladly avails himself of the chance to exchange Queens as well. This leads him straight into a lost ending, as the Bishop is no match for the Knight here. Whether 23.Qg3 g6 would have been better is an open question.

22...Nxh5 23.Rg5 g6 24.fxg6?

Somewhat better was 24.Reg1.

24...fxg6 25.Reg1

If 25.Rxe5 Rxf2+ 26.Kg1 Rdf6; or if 25.Rg2 Rdf6 26.Kg1 Rf3. In either case Black would have a crushing attack.

25...b5 26.Bb3 Rxf2+ 27.R1g2 Rxg2+ 28.Kxg2 a5 29.a4 Nf4+ 30.Kg3?

Another mistake; a better defense was 30.Kh2 though even so 30...c4! would be very strong.

30...Nxd3 31.cxd3 Rxd3+ 32.Kf2 Rxb3 33.axb5 cxb5 White Resigned.

POSITION 200

(The game Rubinstein-Schlechter, San Sebastian, 1912).

1.d4 d5 2.Nf3 Nf6 3.c4 e6 4.Nc3 c5 5.cxd5 Nxd5 6.e4 Nxc3 7.bxc3 cxd4 8.cxd4 Bb4+ 9.Bd2

As the opening comes to an end and the middlegame phase begins one often has to decide whether or not to initiate exchanges. The familiar rule that the side with less freedom of movement does well to seek exchanges is not infallible. In the present case White has a great superiority in terrain and by the above mentioned rule Black should have welcomed the exchange of Queens; but as we shall see, this is the very exchange which favors White.

9...Qa5?

Experience has shown that Black's best chance is 9...Bxd2+ 10.Qxd2 O-O 11.Bc4 Nc6 with about even chances.

10.Rb1! Bxd2+

Not good is 10...Nc6 because of 11.Rxb4! Nxb4 12.Qb1 Qxa2 13.Qxa2 Nxa2 14.Bc4 winning.

11.Qxd2 Qxd2+ 12.Kxd2!

Black's object has been obtained, but it is White who is left with an advantage in development sufficient to give him a powerful initiative.

12...O-O

One would have expected Black to keep his King in the center. Therefore, 12...Ke7 would have given better chances of survival.

13.Bb5!!

An uncommonly fine move, the object of which is to force the weakening which follows.

13...a6

This is unavoidable if Black is to get his Queenside pieces out.

14.Bd3 Rd8 15.Rhc1 b5

Permitting the invasion; but 15...Nc6 16.Ke3 Kf8 17.Rb6 is no more attractive.

16.Rc7 Nd7 17.Ke3 Nf6 18.Ne5 Bd7

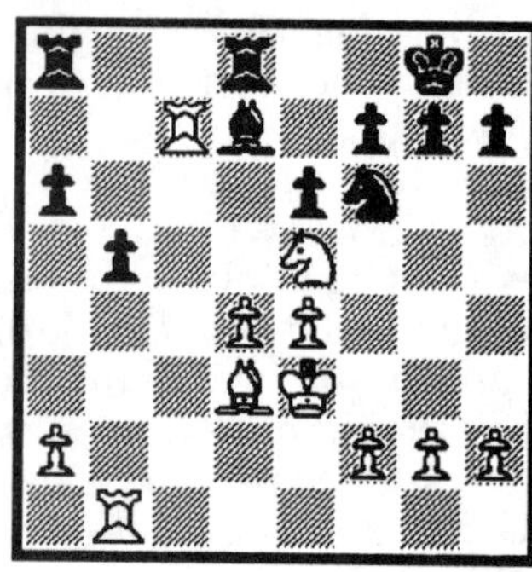

19.g4!

White begins the attack. The threat is to win a piece with 20.g5.

19...h6

In the tournament book this move is given a question mark, and 19...g5 is suggested as stronger. Kmoch has shown that White also gets the advantage in that case by 20.h4 h6 21.hxg5 hxg5 22.f4 gxf4+ 23.Kxf4, threatening 24.g5.

There remains the question whether Black can avoid the weakening by 19...Be8. The following analysis by Kmoch, from his book *Rubinstein Gewinnt*, shows that White still retains the advantage: 20.g5 Nh5 (not 20...Nd7? 21.Nc6) 21.Be2 f6 22.gxf6, and then; **1)** 22...gxf6? 23.Bxh5 fxe5 24.Bxe8 exd4+ 25.Kd3 Rxe8 26.Rg1+ Kh8 27.Kxd4!, etc. **2)** 22...Nxf6 23.Rg1 g6 24.h4, and White has both a positional advantage and a Kingside attack as well.

20.f4 Be8 21.g5 hxg5 22.fxg5 Nh7

On 22...Nd7 White still wins with 23.Nc6, while 22...Nh5 is strongly met by 23.Be2.

23.h4 Rdc8 24.Rbc1 Rxc7 25.Rxc7 Rd8 26.Ra7

Now Black's only defense for the a-pawn would be 26...Rd6, but then White plays 27.Ra8 Kf8 28.Nxf7! Kxf7 29.g6+! winning.

26...f6 27.gxf6 gxf6 28.Ng4 Bh5 29.Nh6+ Kh8 30.Be2!

Taking advantage of the fact that Black's Bishop is tied to the defense of f7.

30...Be8 31.Rxa6

This settles it. The rest is not difficult.

31...Kg7 32.Ng4 f5 33.Ra7+ Kh8

After 33...Kg6, Black may even be mated; e.g. 34.h5+ Kg5 35.Rg7+ Kh4 36.exf5 exf5 37.Nh6 Nf8 38.Nxf5+ Kh3 39.Bf1+ Kh2 40.Rg2+ Kh1 41.Ng3#.

34.Ne5 fxe4 35.Bxb5! Nf6 36.Bxe8 Rxe8 37.Kf4 Kg8 38.Kg5 Rf8 39.Kg6

Threatening 40.Rg7+ followed by 41.Nf7+. **Black Resigned.**

(From a blindfold exhibition by H. Kmoch at Leeuwarden, 1933).

1.e4 c6 2.d4 d5 3.exd5 cxd5 4.Bd3 Nc6 5.Nf3 Bg4 6.c3 Nf6 7.Bf4 Qb6 8.Qb3 (No.201) **8...Qxb3?**

POSITION 201

This exchange plays into White's hands. The a-file is opened for White's Rooks, and Black's a-pawn becomes fatally weak.

9.axb3 e6

Black hesitates to play 9...Bxf3 which would give White the two Bishops as well. The weakening of White's pawns would not affect the result.

10.Nbd2 Be7 11.b4! O-O 12.b5 Nb8 13.Ra2 Nbd7 14.O-O Bd8

To protect the a-pawn from b6.

15.Bd6 Re8 16.Ne5 Nxe5 17.dxe5 Nd7 18.Nb3 Bb6

Black should have tried for counterplay by 18...f6.

19.Na5 Bxa5 20.Rxa5 Nb6 21.Rfa1 Nc8

22.b6!

Based on lines like 22...Nxb6 23.Rxa7 Rxa7 24.Rxa7 Ra8 25.Rxb7! or 22...a6 23.Bxa6! Rxa6 24.Rxa6 bxa6 25.b7 Nxd6 26.exd6 followed by27.Rxa6.

22...Rd8 23.Bc7 Rd7 24.Bb5 Rxc7

There is nothing better.

25.bxc7 Kf8 26.Bd7 a6 27.Rb5! b6 28.Bxc8 Rxc8 29.Rxb6 Rxc7 30.Rbxa6 Be2 31.Ra8+ Ke7 32.R8a7 Black Resigned.

POSITION 202

(The game Wade-Kottnauer, Beverwijk, 1961).

1.d4 Nf6 2.c4 e6 3.Nc3 d5 4.Bg5 Be7 5.Nf3 O-O 6.e3 h6 7.Bh4 b6 8.cxd5 Nxd5 9.Bxe7 Qxe7 10.Rc1 Bb7 11.Be2 Rc8 12.O-O c5

Black has obtained a fully satisfactory game, but as of yet there is little significant play in the position. The line which suggests itself is 13.Nxd5 exd5 14.dxc5 bxc5, giving Black the so-called hanging pawns (See Book One, Chapter 8). Instead of this, however, White decides to get rid of a few pieces, apparently in the expectation of a quick draw.

13.dxc5 Rxc5 14.Qd2 Nxc3 15.Rxc3 Nd7 16.Rfc1 Rac8 17.Rxc5 Rxc5 18.Rxc5 Nxc5

The first part of White's plan (the simplification) is successfully completed. The second part (the draw) is not going to be so easy.

Black has several microscopic advantages; a flight square for his King, control of e4, and a more active placing of his minor pieces.

19.h3 Bd5 20.Nd4

Now Black can't capture the a-pawn because of 21.b4. White prefers this indirect protection of the a-pawn to 20.a3, which would weaken b3, and to 20.b3, which would fix that pawn on the same color as his Bishop and invite Black to attack by ...a5-a4.

20...Ne4 21.Qc2?

The right move was 21.Qc1. Then 21...Bxa2 is met by 22.Qc8+ Kh7 23.Qc2 f5 24.b3; or if 22...Qf8 then 23.Qa6.

21...Qb4!

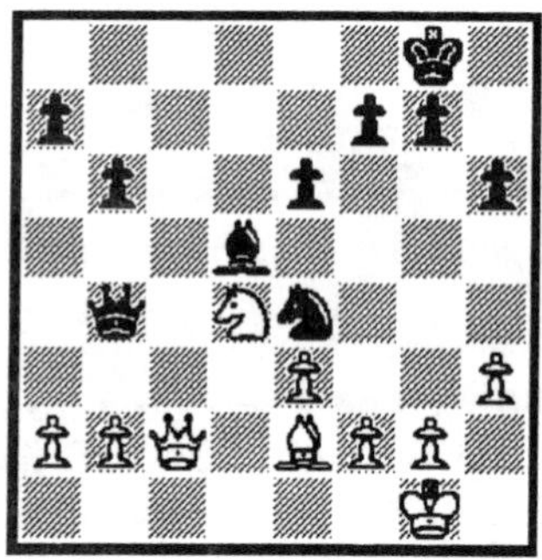

22.Bf3

Black threatened not only 22...Qe1+ but also 22...Bxa2. In *Schakend Nederland*, March 1961, Kottnauer gave the following possibilities: **1)** 22.Kf1 Nd2+ 23.Kg1 Bxa2. **2)** 22.a3 Qe1+ 23.Bf1 Nd2 24.Qd3 Bc4. **3)** 22.Qb1 Nc3 23.a3 Qxd4!. **4)** 22.Nb3 Bxb3 23.axb3 Qe1+ 24.Bf1 Nd2 25.Qd3 Qc1 and Black wins at least a pawn. **5)** 22.Bd3 Qe1+ 23.Kh2 Nc5. In all of the previous variations Black's advantage is clear. **6)** 22.Bf1! This possibility, not given by Kottnauer, is the best chance, e.g. 22...Qe1 23.Nf3 Qa1 24.a3 g6 25.Nh2, and White plans to escape the bind by 26.f3 followed by Kf2.

22...Qe1+ 23.Kh2 Nd2!

An unexpected move. White had hoped for 23...Nxf2, after which he hoped to hold the draw by 24.Bxd5 exd5 25.Qc8+ Kh7 26.Qf5+, with perpetual check.

24.Qc8+

The threat was 24...Nf1+ 25.Kg1 Nxe3+ winning the Queen; there was no relief in 24.Kg3 because of 24...Nf1+ 25.Kf4 g5+ 26.Ke5 Nxe3!.

24...Kh7 25.Bxd5 Nf1+ 26.Kg1 Nxe3+ 27.Kh2 Nf1+!

Far better than 27...Nxd5 28.Qc2+, after which Black, even with a sound extra pawn, is faced with a difficult technical task.

28.Kg1 Nd2+ 29.Kh2 Qe5+ 30.Kg1 Qxd4!

Illustrating a fact that Capablanca had pointed out – that in Queen endings a Knight cooperates better than a Bishop, especially when there is a chance of a mating attack. Kottnauer's conduct of this game prettily supplements our treatment of the subject of liquidation in Chapters 41-44.

31.Qc2+ g6 32.Qc7 Kg8

Not falling for the trap 32...exd5 33.Qxf7+ Qg7 34.Qxd5 Qxb2 35.Qd7+ after which it is very doubtful whether Black can do more than draw.

33.Qc8+ Kg7 34.Bxe6 fxe6 35.Qxe6 Qd8 36.Qe5+ Kh7 37.Qf4 Qd7 38.h4 h5 39.b3 Nb1 40.Qb4 Qc7 41.g4 Nc3 42.g5 Qc5 White Resigned.

(The 6th match-game Smyslov-Botvinnik, 1957).

1.d4 Nf6 2.c4 g6 3.Nc3 d5 4.Nf3 Bg7 5.Qb3 dxc4 6.Qxc4 O-O 7.e4 Bg4 8.Be3 Nfd7 9.O-O-O Nc6 10.h3 Bxf3

11.gxf3 Nb6 12.Qc5 f5 13.Ne2 Qd6 14.e5

POSITION 203

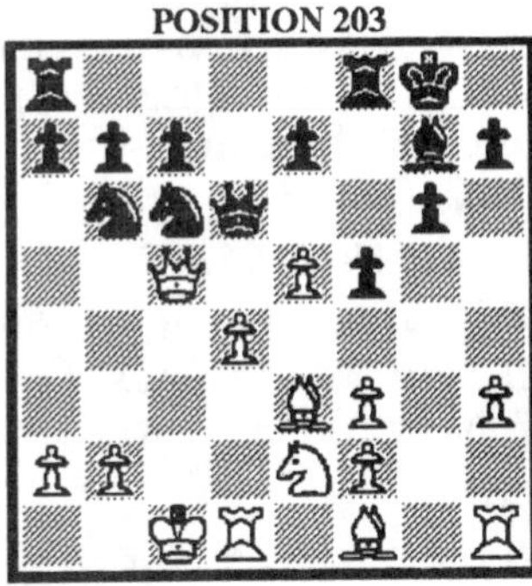

14...Qxc5+

This gives White a big advantage in the ending. After the game it was generally agreed that 14...Qd5 was the correct move. Here are some possible continuations: **1)** 15.Nc3 Qxc5! (and not 15...Qxf3 16.Be2) 16.dxc5 f4! 17.cxb6 fxe3 18.bxc7 Bxe5 with good play for Black. **2)** 15.Qxd5 Nxd5 16.Nc3 Nxe3 17.fxe3 f4 18.e4 Rad8. **3)** 15.b3 Rfd8! (but not 15...Qxf3 16.Nf4 followed by 17.Bg2) 16.Nf4 Qxc5 17.dxc5 Rxd1+ 18.Kxd1 Nd7 19.Ne6 f4! 20.Bxf4 Ndxe5. **4)** 15.Kb1 Rad8 (if 15...Qxf3 the answer now would be 16.Nc3! and if 16...Qxh1? then 17.Bc4+) 16.Bg2 Qxc5 17.dxc5 Nd5 18.f4 e6 19.Bxd5 Rxd5 20.Nc3 Rxd1+ 21.Rxd1 a6 22.a3 Rd8 23.Rxd8+ Nxd8. In all these variations Black gets a much better endgame than he does in the actual game.

15.dxc5 Nc4 16.f4 Nxe3 17.fxe3 Rfd8 18.Bg2

Now White has clear positional advantages: his Bishop is active while Black's is shut in, and White controls all the good squares in the center. For our purposes the rest of the game is relatively less important.

18...Nb4 19.Bxb7 Rab8 20.c6! Kf7 21.Nd4 e6 22.Nb5 Nd5

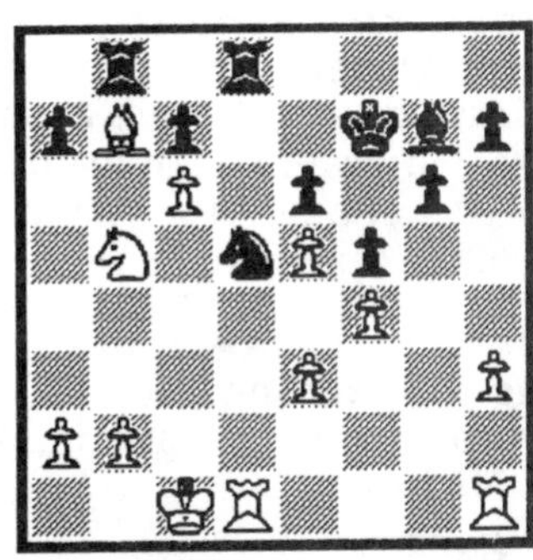

23.Rxd5! exd5 24.Nxc7 Rbc8 25.Bxc8 Rxc8 26.Nxd5 Rxc6+ 27.Kd2 Ke6 28.Nc3 Black Resigned.

POSITION 204

(From the game Euwe-Averbakh, Zurich, 1953).

Black has a Queenside majority, while White has a central majority. Black's protected passed pawn at b3 can be a strong asset, but for the time being it is securely blockaded. White's central pawn position is, on the other hand, in a dynamic state and hence White currently holds the initiative.

1.exf5

This move and White's next are not merely unmotivated exchanges, for White must find a way to free his Queenside pieces.

1...Bxf5 2.Bxf5 Nxf5 3.Rae1

Perhaps 3.Re5, avoiding the exchange of Queens and playing for attack instead, might have been the best idea. However, the move played is also good enough, for White is in control of the open e-file.

3...Qd8

Forcing the exchange, for 4.Qd2 is hardly possible: 4...Qh4 and if 5.Nf4? then 5...Nxd4.

4.Qxd8 Rxd8

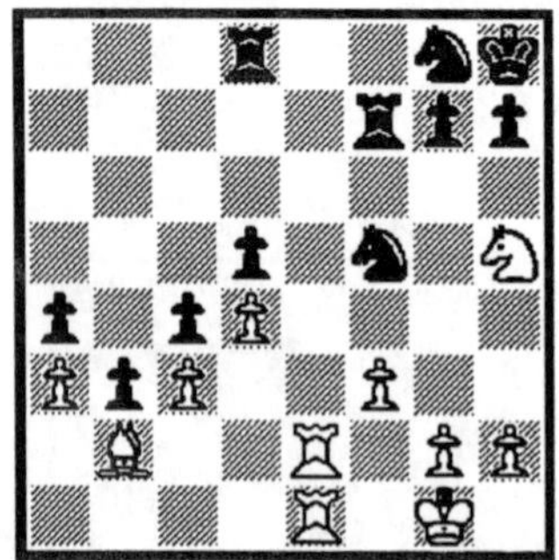

5.Re8?

This leads to the exchange of all the Rooks, after which Black suddenly finds himself better off. The correct move was 5.Re6! with favorable play for White, who will be able to attack the enemy pawns from behind.

5...Rxe8 6.Rxe8 Re7!

This move had been overlooked by White in his previous calculations. He must now permit the exchange of his other Rook, for otherwise Black will play 7...Re2.

7.Rxe7 Ngxe7 8.Kf2 Kg8 9.g4 Nd6 10.Ke3 Nb5

One Black Knight has taken up an ideal post, and it is becoming clear that in this minor piece ending Black's protected passed pawn is a formidable factor.

11.f4?

Understandably striving to advance his Kingside majority as rapidly as possible, but creating an incurable weakness at e4, which in turn enables his opponent to strengthen his game decisively. The best line was 11.Nf4 and 12.Ne2.

11...Nc8 12.f5 Ncd6 13.Nf4

In the hope that the attack on the d-pawn will force Black to play 13...Nc7. Now comes a surprise.

13...Nxa3!

Thus Black creates a pair of united passed pawns on the extreme Queen's flank.

14.Bxa3 Nb5 15.Bc1 Nxc3 16.Ne2

No better is 16.Kd2 due to 16...Nb1+ 17.Kd1 a3.

16...Nb1 White Resigned.

POSITION 205

(The game Capablanca-Mieses, Kissingen, 1928).

1.d4 Nf6 2.c4 e6 3.Nc3 d5 4.Bg5 Be7 5.e3 Nbd7 6.Nf3 O-O 7.Rc1 a6 8.cxd5 exd5 9.Qb3 c6 10.Bd3 (No.205) **10...Nh5?!**

The usual procedure in this sort of position, as we saw in Chapter 14, is for both sides to initiate minority attacks – White by b4-b5, and Black by ...f5-f4. From this point of view the text move seems to be strategically correct, as the f-pawn is no longer blocked. It soon becomes clear, however, that Black does not have a minority attack in mind; he is instead playing for exchanges.

11.Bxe7 Qxe7 12.O-O Nhf6

Thus Black has lost two moves in order to exchange his good Bishop for White's bad one. Black's strategically correct move here was ...f5, preceded if necessary by ...g6.

13.Na4 Ne4 14.Bxe4 Qxe4

After the more natural 14...dxe4 15.Nd2 Nf6 White gets the advantage by 16.Nc5 Re8 17.Nc4. Black's best line is apparently 14...dxe4 15.Nd2 Kh8!.

15.Qb4!

After this move Black will sorely miss his dark-squared Bishop which he spent precious time in exchanging off! The dark squares in his position are now painfully weak.

15...Qg6

The tournament book gives 15...f6 16.Nd2 Qe6 17.Nb3 Re8 18.N3c5 Nxc5 19.Nxc5 Qe7 as a better defense.

16.Qe7 f6 17.Rc3 Qe8

Seeking further simplification.

18.Qd6 Rf7 19.Rfc1 Qf8 20.Qxf8+ Kxf8

Black is distinctly uncomfortable. The natural 20...Nxf8 is not possible because of 21.Nb6 Rb8 22.Nxd5.

21.Ne1!

The Knight heads for Black's besieged Queenside, where the decision is bound to come.

21...Ke8 22.Nd3 Rb8

Not 22...b5 because of 23.Rxc6 Bb7 24.Rc7

23.f3 Re7 24.Kf2 Nf8 25.Rb3 Nd7

Black's joy was brief. White was threatening 26.Rxc6 and if 26...Bd7 then 27.Nac5 threatens 28.Nxa6.

26.g4 b5

Black weakens his position still more; but what was he to do?

27.Nac5 Nb6

Now, too late, Black discovers that exchanging does not relieve his troubles: after 27...Nxc5 28.Rxc5 Bb7 29.Ra3 Ra8 30.Ra5 Rc7 31.Nb4 Kd7, White forces the game by 32.Rc3 and Rca3.

28.Nb4

What follows now is not pretty.

28...Bb7 29.Nxb7 Rbxb7 30.Rxc6 a5 31.Rxb6 axb4 32.Rxb7 Rxb7 33.Rxb4 Black Resigned.

We close the chapter with a few drastic examples of ill-judged exchanging.

POSITION 206

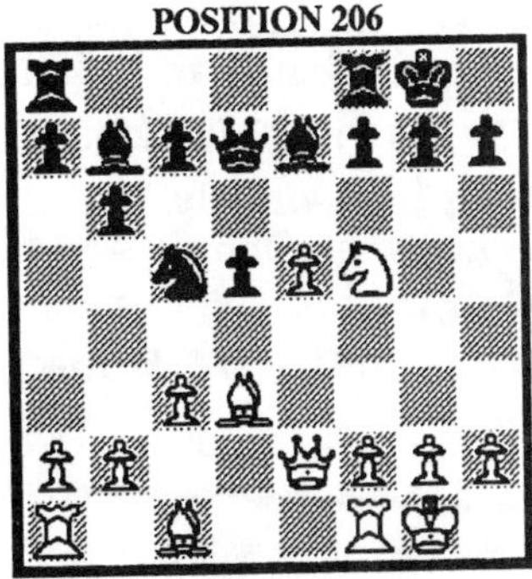

(The game Bogolyubov-Hussong, Karlsruhe, 1939).

1.d4 Nf6 2.Nf3 b6 3.e3 Bb7 4.Bd3 d6 5.Nbd2 Nbd7 6.e4 e5 7.c3 Be7 8.Qe2 O-O 9.Nf1 d5 10.Nxe5 Nxe5 11.dxe5 Nxe4 12.Ng3 Nc5 13.O-O Qd7 14.Nf5 (No.206) **14...Nxd3? 15.Qg4!**

Suddenly there is no defense to the double threat of 16.Qxg7# and 16.Nh6+ followed by 17.Qxd7. **Black Resigned.**

POSITION 207

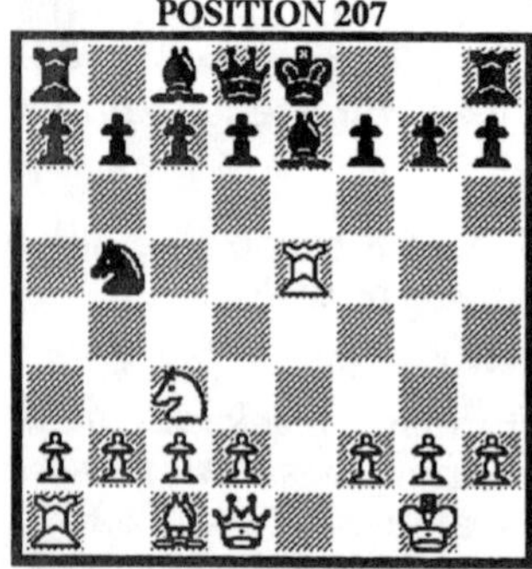

(The game Bachmann-Fiechtl, Regensburg, 1887).

1.e4 e5 2.Nf3 Nc6 3.Bb5 Nf6 4.O-O Nxe4 5.Re1 Nd6 6.Nxe5 Nxe5?

Correct was 6...Be7, but Black is determined to exchange everything.

7.Rxe5+ Be7 8.Nc3 Nxb5? (No.207)

Continuing the same tactics. He should have castled.

9.Nd5! d6

Or 9...O-O 10.Nxe7+ Kh8 11.Qh5, threatening 12.Qxh7+ and 13.Rh5#.

10.Rxe7+ Kf8 11.Qf3 f6 12.d3 c6

This loses immediately, but 12...f5 is also hopeless: 13.Qh5 Qxe7 14.Nxe7 Kxe7 15.Bg5+.

13.Qxf6+! gxf6 14.Bh6+ Kg8 15.Nxf6#.

(The game Szabo-Reshevsky, Zurich, 1953).

1.d4 Nf6 2.c4 e6 3.Nf3 d5 4.Nc3 c5 5.cxd5 Nxd5 6.e3 Nc6 7.Bd3 Nxc3 8.bxc3 Be7 9.Qc2 g6 10.h4 h5 11.Rb1 Rb8 12.Be4 Qc7 13.O-O Bd7 14.d5 exd5 15.Bxd5 Bf6 16.Ng5 Nd8 17.c4 Bc6 18.Ne4 Bg7 19.Bb2 O-O (No.208)

We end this chapter with an astonishing example showing that even world class masters may be troubled by over eagerness to exchange. In this example it amounts to chess blindness. This seems to have been a bad day for both these Grandmasters; it occasionally happens to all of us. At times like this we know we are likely to make wrong decisions at critical moments, and for want of inspiration it is only natural to make exchanges automatically. Such must have been the circumstances which produced the following remarkable sequence of moves.

20.Nf6+

POSITION 208

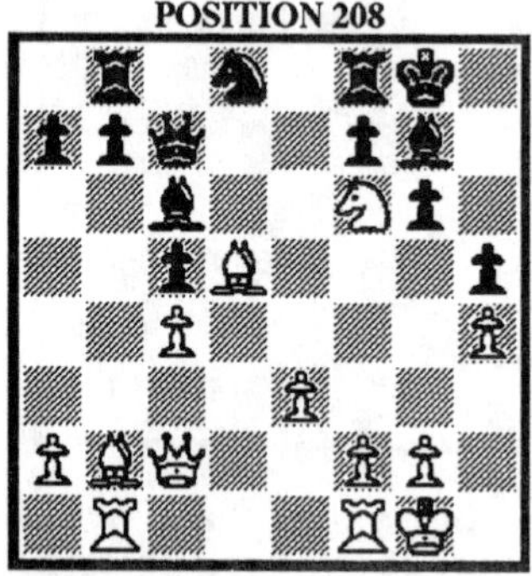

20...Bxf6? 21.Bxf6?

Amazing. By 21.Qxg6+ White can mate.

21...Bxd5

He has spotted the mate threat.

22.cxd5 Qd6 23.Qc3 Qxd5 24.Rfd1 Qf5 25.e4 Qe6 26.Bg7 b6 27.Bxf8

By 27.Bh6! f6 28.Qg3 White would win a whole Rook.

27...Kxf8 Draw agreed.

CHAPTER 47
EAGERNESS TO CHECKMATE

The chessplayer's one objective is admittedly to checkmate the opposing King; experience has shown, however, that for achieving this aim the sensible policy is to content oneself at first with more modest objectives. Going directly for checkmate from the first move may, it is true, lead to some successes against weaker players; but against equal or stronger opponents this policy is more likely to bring some sad disappointments.

Even among the stronger players, however, there remain some champions of the direct mating attack. Their choice of opening – King's Gambit, Blackmar-Diemer Gambit, etc. – signifies their intention. The results of the adherents of this style of play are subject to violent fluctuations; surprising wins against stronger opponents alternate with equally surprising losses to weaker ones. We devote this chapter exclusively to the subject of this unjustified playing for mate, including under this same heading the giving of pointless checks (on the principle that it might be mate!) and the making of unjustified sacrifices. We subdivide as follows:

A. Unjustified Kingside Attacks
B. Unjustified Checks
C. Unjustified Sacrifices

A. Unjustified Kingside Attacks

There was a time when players would start an attack with a single piece; if often happens in the games which have come down to us from the days of Morphy and Anderssen. Those days are gone.

Today the most inexperienced beginner soon gets to know that it is essential to bring the pieces into play before contemplating any attack.

Certain features must be present in a position before it is ripe for Kingside operations. If these features are lacking, the prospects for the Kingside attack are not very good. We elucidate this point now with the help of some examples.

(The game Tartakower-Lasker, New York, 1924).

1.c4 e5 2.a3 Nf6 3.e3 Be7 4.Qc2 O-O 5.Nc3 d6 6.Nf3 Re8 7.Be2 Bf8 8.O-O Nc6 9.d4 Bg4 10.d5 Ne7 11.h3 Bd7 12.Nh2 Qc8 13.e4 Ng6

The pawn formation suggests a Queenside attack by White, based on b4 and eventually c5. Black's plan, on the other hand, should be the advance ...f5, with Kingside attacking chances. For a detailed examination of such positions we refer the reader to our discussion of various pawn formations.

14.f4!? (see next diagram)

As we just mentioned in our above comment, White's usual strategy here would be the advance b4 and c5. The advance 14.f4 in this and similar positions is normally anti-positional since after 14...exf4 Black obtains a strong outpost square on e5 and the half-open e-file with which to press on the now backward e-pawn. However, this position is exceptional in that White can "get away" with the usually anti-positional advance f4. This is because he will obtain strong pressure on the newly opened f-file, which, in conjunction with the concentration of his minor pieces on or near the Black Kingside, will provide enough pressure to compensate for the aforementioned positional liabilities. In this game Tartakower utilizes these factors well, until a critical moment when he misses a chance for a double exchange sacrifice which would have forced Black to work hard to achieve the draw. Having missed his chance he winds up in a seriously compromised position, which Lasker quickly exploits to his advantage.

POSITION 209

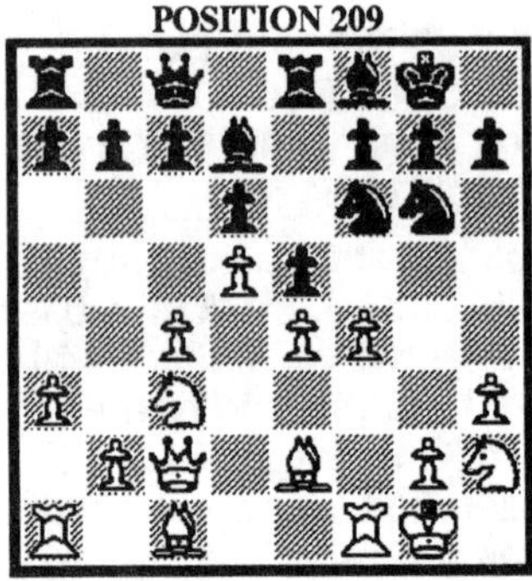

14...exf4 15.Bxf4 Nxf4 16.Rxf4 Be7!

Showing very fine positional sense. The weakening of e5, consequent to the advance 14.f4, has given Black the chance to occupy the outpost at e5. The purpose of the text move is to prepare to occupy e5 by a coordinated sequence of moves. Incidentally, the text also prevents the possibility of White pushing e4–e5; now if 17.Nf3 then 17...Nh5 and White loses the Exchange.

17.Raf1 Rf8 18.Qd3 Be8

Vacating d7 for the Knight (...Nd7-e5).

19.Qg3?

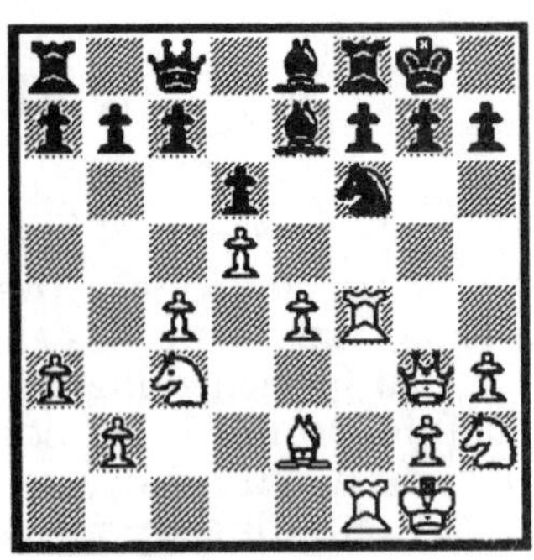

After this Black is able to occupy e5 and repulse White's attack. As Tartakower later commented, he and a group of strong Berlin players analyzing this position found that a brilliant double Exchange sacrifice would have maintained the pressure and forced Black to defend resourcefully to hold the game. The right sequence for White was 19.Rxf6!! Bxf6 20.Rxf6! gxf6 and the shattered Black Kingside must be defended with great care. Their analysis is very long so we omit it here, merely contenting ourselves with pointing out the proper culmination of White's pressure on the f-file.

19...Qd8

White threatened the obvious 20.Rxf6 now.

20.Nd1 Nd7 21.Ne3

Now Black wins material. White should have tried 21.Nf3, though Black would retain a definite positional grip by 21...Bf6.

21...Bg5 22.Rg4

If 22.Rf5 Black wins the Exchange by 22...Bh4 followed by 23...Ne5 and/or ...g6.

22...f6

Threatening ...h5.

23.Qf2 h5 24.Rg3 h4!

Much stronger than 24...Bh4 which would allow 25.Rxg7+! Kxg7 26.Qxh4.

25.Rg4 Bh5

White's attack has been thoroughly refuted. The game continued: **26.Nf5 Bxg4 27.Nxg4 Qe8 28.Bf3 Ne5 29.Nxe5 Qxe5 30.Nxh4 Bxh4 31.Qxh4 f5 32.exf5 Rxf5 33.Re1 Qxb2 34.Bg4 Qd4+ 35.Kh2 Raf8 36.Qe7 Qf4+ 37.Kh1 Re5 38.Rxe5 dxe5 39.Qxc7 e4 40.Qe7 Qf6 41.Qxb7 Qa1+ 42.Kh2 Qe5+ 43.Kg1 Rb8 44.Qd7 Rb1+ 45.Kf2 e3+ 46.Ke2 Rb2+ 47.Ke1 Qc3+ 48.Kf1 Qc1+** and mate next move.

POSITION 210

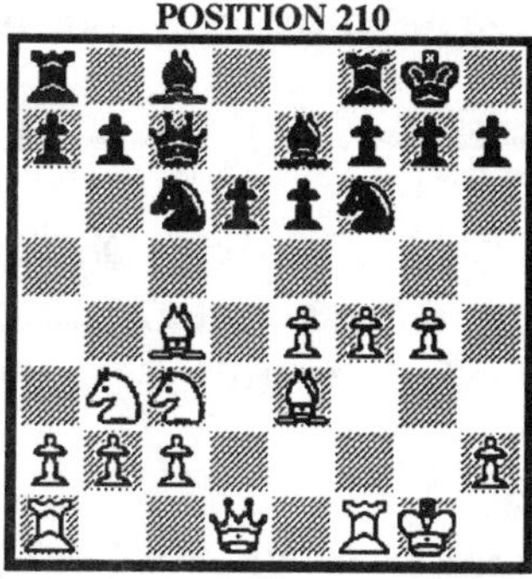

(The game Cardoso-Benko, Portoroz, 1958).

1.e4 c5 2.Nf3 Nc6 3.d4 cxd4 4.Nxd4 Nf6 5.Nc3 d6 6.Bc4 Qb6 7.Nb3 e6 8.O-O Be7 9.Be3 Qc7 10.f4 O-O 11.g4?

This sharp advance repeatedly occurs in similar positions in the Sicilian. In this case, however, it is premature. The attack has point when it leads to the opening of a file by g5 (e.g. when Black has played ...h6 and White has castled on the other side) or when it succeeds in driving back the enemy pieces. Even in such cases it needs very careful preparation, for the advance g4-g5 is bound to create weaknesses in one's own camp. A sudden counterattack may prove devastating, and in practice this is quite frequently what happens.

11...d5!

Hitting the nail on the head. White can hardly play 12.exd5 because of 12...Nb4 13.Be2 N4xd5 and the Black counterattack is in full swing.

12.Bd3 dxe4 13.Nxe4 Nd5 14.Bd2 a5

Black has completely taken over the initiative; and it is now clear that White was only beating the air with his 11th move.

15.c3 Rd8 16.g5 a4 17.Nc1 Qb6+ 18.Kh1 Ne3

The pawn grab 18...Qxb2 was quite possible, but Black is not going to be sidetracked into expeditions in search of plunder (see Chapter 45). He prefers to concentrate logically on the weaknesses which White's unjustified attack has created.

19.Bxe3 Qxe3 20.Qf3 Qxf3+ 21.Rxf3 b6! 22.Bc2 Bb7 23.Ne2 Na5 24.N2g3

If White tries to forestall the coming invasion by 24.b3 there follows 24...axb3 25.axb3 Nxb3! 26.Rxa8 Bxa8 27.Bxb3 Bxe4.

24...Nc4

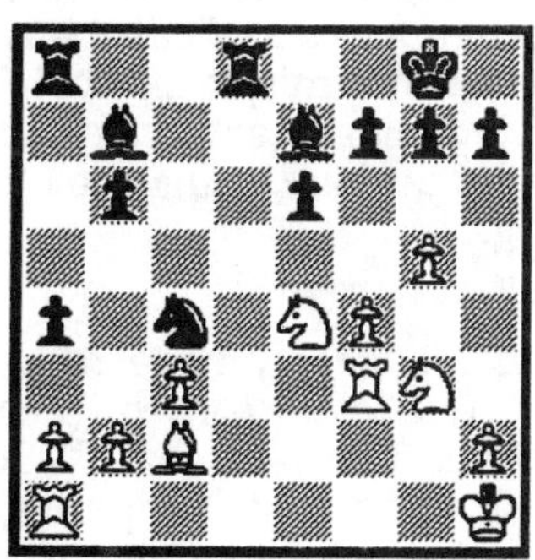

25.Rd1

Now 25.b3 would fail against 25...axb3 26.Bxb3 Nd2.

25...Rxd1+ 26.Bxd1 Nxb2 27.Be2 Bd5 28.f5 exf5 29.Rxf5 Bxa2 30.Rb5 a3 31.Nf5 Bc4!

So strong is the passed a-pawn now that Black can coolly permit Nxe7+.

32.Bxc4 Nxc4 33.Rb1 a2 34.Ra1 Bc5 35.Nd4 Ne3 36.Nb3 Nc2 37.Ned2 Nxa1 38.Nxa1 Re8 39.Ndb3 Re2 40.h4 g6 and **White Resigned.**

POSITION 211

(The game Bhend-Petrosian, Zurich, 1961).

1.e4 c5 2.Nf3 d6 3.d4 cxd4 4.Nxd4 Nf6 5.Nc3 e6 6.Be2 a6 7.O-O Qc7 8.a4 Nc6 9.Kh1 Be7 10.f4 O-O 11.Nb3 b6 12.Bf3 Bb7 13.Qd2 Rab8 14.g4

The position is similar to Example 210, but the advance g4 has been much better prepared. Only the White Queen is rather misplaced, blocking the Bc1; but this is a temporary matter, and White can now bring the Queen to f2 or g2.

14...d5!?

Black could hardly have reckoned out all the detailed consequences of this move. The fact that White's Queen is at present hampering his development, and the fact that the weakening of his Kingside by g4 may prove to be serious were probably the considerations which most influenced him in choosing this dynamic pawn sacrifice.

15.exd5 Nb4 16.dxe6 Bxf3+ 17.Rxf3 Qb7

Just as in the previous game the long White diagonal plays an important part. The point of this move is the variation: 18.Qg2 Nxc2! 19.Rb1 Ne1 and wins.

18.Kg2 Nxg4 19.Qe2 f5 20.Nd1

White's first task is to drive back the enemy cavalry by c3 and Nf2.

20...Rf6! 21.c3 Rg6!

Extraordinarily well conceived. If the White King now gives up his protection of the Rook by 22.Kh1 the Black Knight will penetrate into White's game with decisive power via c2.

22.cxb4 Ne5+ 23.Kf2 Bh4+ 24.Rg3 Ng4+ 25.Kg1

Not 25.Kf1 Bxg3 26.hxg3 Qh1#.

25...Bxg3 26.hxg3 Qd5! 27.Ra3

On 27.e7 there follows simply 27...Re8.

27...Rh6

This makes it clear why Black interpolated 26...Qd5!. White cannot now play 28.Qg2, being tied to the defense of the Knight on d1.

28.Nf2 Nxf2 and **White Resigned.**

If 29.Qxf2 allows mate by 29...Qh1, while 29.Kxf2 loses the Queen by 29...Rh2+.

B. Unjustified Checks

The giving of pointless checks is mostly confined to inexperienced players, but the greatest masters are occasionally guilty, too. Their likeliest time for this to occur is during time pressure, when there are several moves to be made in a few seconds.

Some checks are absolutely meaningless; e.g. 1.e4 e6 2.d4 Bb4+. On the other hand after 1.d4 Nf6 2.c4 e6 3.Nf3 b6 4.g3 Bb7 5.Bg2, there is some point in 5...Bb4+; 6.Bd2 Be7, as the White

Bishop often proves to be in the way at d2. It is not easy to draw the line between the legitimate and the unwarranted check. For instance after 1.e4 e6 2.d4 d5 3.Nc3 Nf6 4.Bg5 dxe4 5.Nxe4 Be7 6.Bxf6 gxf6 7.Nf3 b6 there seems to be no need for 8.Bb5+ c6 9.Bd3, for if White plays, for example 8.Bc4 (instead of 8.Bb5+) Black will soon have to play ...c6 anyway, in order to prevent d5. There is no doubt at all about the shortsightedness of the check in the following example:

POSITION 212

(The game Van-Steenis-Wechsler, Hastings, 1946-47).

1.e4 e6 2.d4 d5 3.Nc3 Bb4 4.exd5 Qxd5 5.Qg4 Ne7 6.Qxg7 (No.212) **6...Qe4+**

Black wants to guard the h-pawn, so that after 7.Ne2, or 7.Be2, he can safely play 7...Rg8. However:

7.Kd1!

Now suddenly Black finds not only his Rook *en prise,* but his Queen as well, and there is nothing to do but **Resign.**

(From the game Filip-Darga, Bled 1961).

POSITION 213

1.Qd8+

This obvious check is not an error, it is the quickest way to win.

1...Kg7 2.h4

This still wins, but White is afraid of a few checks which a level-headed examination would show to be quite harmless. The direct win is 2.Rc1 Bd7 3.Rc7, for after 3...Qb1+ 4.Kg2 Qe4+ 5.f3 Black's checks have run out.

2...Qf3! 3.Rc1 Bb7

Threatening mate and still "hanging in there". Black is still lost though.

4.Rc7+ Kg6 5.Qg8+ Kf5

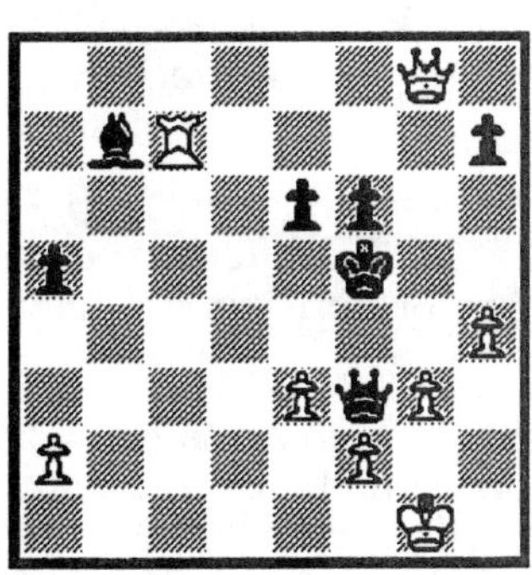

6.Qxh7+??

This check is not only not necessary, it is suicide. Even now White can win by 6.g4+ Ke5 7.Rc5+ Kd6 8.Qf8+ Kd7

9.Qf7+ Kd8 10.Qc7+ Ke8 11.Qb8+ followed by 12.Rc7+.

6...Kg4! and **White Resigned,** for whether he plays 7.Rxb7 or 7.Qg6+, Black's reply is 7...Kh3 and mate cannot be stopped.

POSITION 214

(From the game Anderssen-Bird, Vienna, 1873).

1.d5?

A serious mistake. Now Black could win by 1...Re8 2.dxc6+ Kc7 3.Be3 Bc5!. Instead he played:

1...Bc5+?

This check is useless and allows White to regain the attack.

2.Kh1 b5

Now 2...Re8 would not help: 3.dxc6+ Kc7 4.Bf4+, the difference being that the White Bishop does not get pinned.

3.Bf4!

Taking full advantage of Black's error on the first move. The point is in the variation given in the tournament book: 3...bxa4 4.Qe5 Rc8 5.d6 Re8 6.Qxc5 Re2 7.Qxa7+ Ke6 8.Qg1 and wins. Notice that 3...Re8 loses to 4.dxc6+.

3...Qh5 4.dxc6+ Kxc6 5.Bd1 Rd8 6.a4!

Now the position is broken open and the Black King finds himself in the line of fire.

6...Qd5 7.axb5+ Bxb5 8.Kg2 g5 9.Bc2 Kb6 10.c4!

The complement to White's 6th move.

10...Qd7 11.Qa5+ Kb7 12.Be4+ Bc6 13.Qa6+ Black Resigned.

C: Unjustified Sacrifices

There can scarcely be any facet of chess which displays the weakness of human nature more starkly than the subject to be discussed now. Ever since chess began players have been sacrificing unjustifiably; and no doubt it will always be the same.

The reasons are various. One player is over optimistic; another cannot resist letting fly, even in time trouble, only to find a boomerang coming back at his own head; some players want to win too prettily; others suddenly lose all power of self-criticism.

The remedy? Apart from the usual advice to weigh up everything carefully and to practice self-control, the best advice was given by *"Woodshifter"* a regular contributor to the old American *Chess Review* —"Sit on your hands!."

We now give a series of examples of players who at the critical moment were *not* sitting on their hands.

POSITION 215

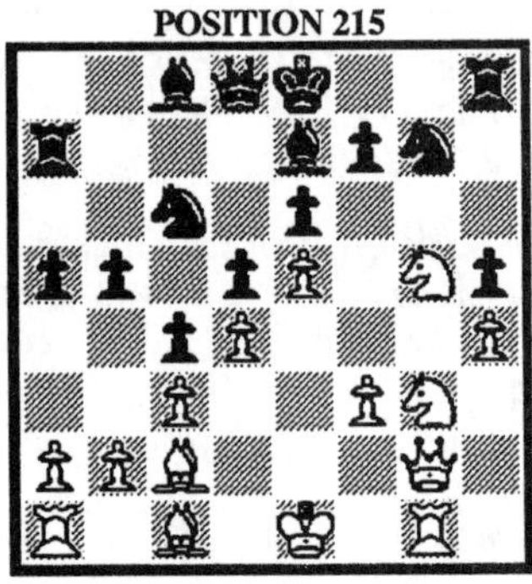

(From the game Spielmann-Nimzowitsch, New York, 1927).

1.Nxf7!?

A correct sacrifice according to Alekhine, whose excellent annotations in the tournament book we shall be using in some of the following notes. However, there is a more convincing first move for White; the accurate course begins with 1.Ke2!, after which the Knight sacrifice will occur with increased effect. Also, after 1.Ke2!, White would then have the possibility of 2.Nh7! and 3.Nf6+ (e.g. in reply to 1...Bf8).

1...Kxf7 2.Nxh5?

The first Knight sacrifice was good enough, but this second one is certainly not. The capture of the h-pawn is all the more curious in view of the several good alternatives White had available: 2.Bg6+, 2.Ne4, 2.Nf5, or 2.Ne2 – this last being Alekhine's choice as the best of all. The sequel might have been 2...Bxh4+ 3.Kd1 Kg8 4.Nf4 Rf7 5.Ng6 Be7 6.Nxh8 Kxh8 7.Qg6!, with mate in a few moves.

2...Bxh4+ 3.Ke2 Nxh5 4.Bg6+ Ke7 5.Bxh5 Kd7!

Spielmann had apparently reckoned only with 5...Rxh5 6.Qg7+ Ke8 7.Qg6+. Black's method brings his King into safety, and leaves him with a winning superiority in material.

6.Qg7+ Be7 7.Bf7 Rh2+ 8.Kd1 Kc7 9.Bf4 Rxb2 10.Qh7 Kb6 11.Rg8 Qc7 12.Qh8 Nd8 13.Bg6 Rg2

Still simpler was 13...b4.

14.Qh1 Rxg6 15.Rxg6 b4 16.Rg7 Qc6 17.Qh8 Qa4+ 18.Ke1 Nc6!

Black returns his extra piece in the interests of a rapidly decisive counterattack.

19.Qxc8 Bh4+ 20.Bg3 Rxg7 21.Bxh4 Qc2 22.Bd8+ Nxd8 23.Qb8+

Or 23.Qxd8+ Kb7 and wins.

23...Nb7 White Resigned.

POSITION 216

(From the game Euwe-Smyslov, The Hague, 1948).

In this position White has the following straightforward win, given by Smyslov: 1.Qg4 (threatening to sacrifice at g6) 1...Nf6 2.Qg3 (maintaining the threat) 2...Nxe4 3.Qe3! and now, whether Black retreats the Knight or protects it with 3...f5, the reply 4.Nexg6 is crushing.

1.Nexg6

This sacrifice is also correct, and incidentally more attractive than the above method.

1...fxg6

Of course not 1...Bxe2 2.Nf8#!.

2.Nxg6?

Just as in the previous example it is the second Knight sacrifice which is wrong. By 2.Qg4 White should win without difficulty; e.g. **1)** 2...Qf7 3.e5 Ne7 4.e6 Qe8 5.Nh5 Ng8 6.Ng7! and the Black Queen must give up her protection of g6. **2)** 2...Ne7 3.e5 Bf7 4.h4! Qc6 5.e6 Be8 6.h5, etc. **3)** 2...Bf7 3.e5 Bg5 4.e6 Bxf4 (or 4...Be8 5.Nxg6 Bxg6 6.Qf5! Qg7 7.Qf7!! Qxf7 8.exf7 Bxb1 9.f8=N#!) 5.Qxf4 Bxe6 6.Qe5 wins. **4)** 2...Bg5 3.Nxg6! Kxg6 4.Qf5+ forcing mate.

2...Kxg6

If 2...Qf7, intending to answer 3.Nf8+ with 3...Qxf8 4.e5+ Kh8 5.Qe4 Qg7 6.e6 Nf6!, there follows instead 3.Qd1!, after which 3...Qxg6 fails against 4.e5.

3.e5+

Better, but in the long run still insufficient, would have been 3.Qf3 Be6 4.Qf8! Kh7 5.Qxd8 Nc6 and then: **1)** 6.Bf6 Bf5!! and the White attack can get no farther. **2)** 6.Qd5 Qd7 7.Qxb5 Nxd4 8.Qxd7+ Bxd7 9.cxd4 Ne7 10.d5 Kg7 and Black will eventually consolidate to win.

3...Kf7 4.Qh5+ Kf8 5.f4

Nor would 5.Bc5+ help after 5...Be7 6.Qf5+ Ke8 7.Qg6+ Bf7.

5...Bb6 6.Qf5+ Ke7 7.Qh7+ Kd8

Very fine: now if 8.Qxb7 then Black interpolates 8...Bxd4+ before recapturing.

8.Bxb6+ Qxb6+ 9.Kh2 Qe3 10.Qf5 Nc6 and White Resigned.

POSITION 217

(From the game Kramer-O'Kelly, Beverwijk, 1946).

The main theme of this position involves a Rook sacrifice on g6. Indeed after 1.Bxf7!! Black would have no good defense, for if 1...Qxf7 then 2.Qh4! (even stronger than Rg6+ at once, as Black must now prevent 3.Qg5#) 2...Ne6 3.Rg6+ and Black can resign. Or if 1...Nf3 2.Rxf3 Qxf7 3.Qh4!. In the tournament book Kmoch remarks that after 1.Bxf7 the combination 2.Rg6+ becomes a real threat, for after 2...Rxg6 3.hxg6+ Kg7 4.gxh7+ would be decisive, and after 2...hxg6 3.hxg6+ Kg7 4.Qxh8+! the pawn would promote.

Instead of all this, White played:

1.Rg6+? fxg6! 2.hxg6+ Kg7 3.gxh7+ Rg6!

White had not foreseen this, but reckoned only on 3...Kf8 4.Rg8+ and mate next move.

4.Rxg6+ Kxg6 5.Bg8 Kg7 6.Qg2+ Kf8 7.Qh3 Qg7 8.Qh4 Qg1+! White Resigned.

POSITION 218

(The game J. Littlewood-Botvinnik, Hastings, 1961-62).

1.e4 c5 2.Nf3 d6 3.d4 cxd4 4.Nxd4 Nf6 5.Nc3 g6 6.Be3 Bg7 7.f3 a6 8.Bc4 b5 9.Bb3 Bb7 10.Qd2 Nbd7 11.O-O-O Nc5 12.Kb1 Nxb3 13.cxb3 O-O 14.Bh6 Bxh6 15.Qxh6 b4

According to Flohr White could have forced a draw here by the line 16.Nd5 Nxd5 17.exd5 Bxd5 18.Nf5 gxf5 19.Rxd5 e6 20.Rxd6!, and it is perpetual check after 20...Qxd6 21.Qg5+, etc.

16.e5

Intending to meet 16...Nd7 with 17.exd6 bxc3 18.Nf5 gxf5 19.Qg5+ Kh8 20.dxe7.

16...Nd7!

Nevertheless he plays it! The point is that if 17.exd6, Black has the strong reply 17...e5!.

17.h4 bxc3 18.h5 dxe5 19.hxg6

After 19.Ne6 fxe6 20.hxg6, Black defends himself by 20...c2+ 21.Kxc2 Qc7+ followed by ...Nf6.

19...Nf6 20.bxc3

Black's defense is based on the important finesse 20.Nf5 c2+! It is not always easy to demonstrate that an attack is premature.

20...exd4 21.gxh7+ Kh8 22.Rxd4 Qa5 23.Qe3 Nd5 24.Qd2 Nxc3+ 25.Ka1 Rad8 26.Rc1 Qxa2+ 27.Qxa2 Nxa2 28.Rxd8 Rxd8 White Resigned.

POSITION 219

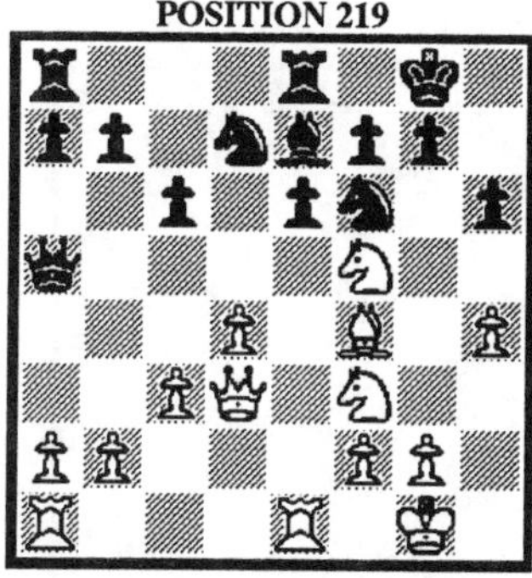

(The game Tal-Keres, Bled, 1959).

1.e4 c6 2.d4 d5 3.Nc3 dxe4 4.Nxe4 Bf5 5.Ng3 Bg6 6.h4 h6 7.Nf3 Nd7 8.Bd3 Bxd3 9.Qxd3 Ngf6 10.Bf4 Qa5+ 11.c3 e6 12.O-O Be7 13.Rfe1 O-O 14.Nf5 Rfe8

In this position White has a simple way to secure a slight space advantage: 15.Nxe7+ Rxe7 16.Bd6 R7e8 17.Ne5, but in view of Black's solid position it would not lead to much.

15.Nxg7!?

This sacrifice must be considered unsound, but the refutation is not easy to find.

15...Kxg7 16.Ne5

Threatening 17.Qg3+ Kh7 18.Nxf7, with at least three pawns for the sacrificed piece.

16...Rh8 17.Qh3

Now threatening to decisively strengthen the attack by sacrificing the second Knight at f7.

17...Rh7!

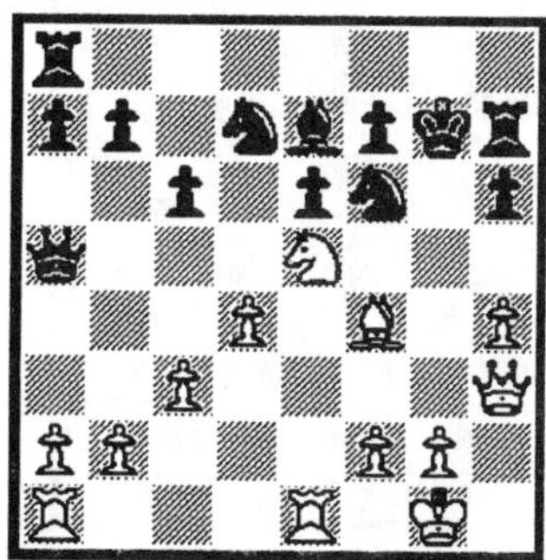

A fine defense. If instead 17...Raf8, White could, if he wished, force a draw by 18.Qg3+ Kh7 19.Qd3+. Or he could choose the neat line 18.Qg3+ Kh7 19.Bxh6, whereupon 19...Kxh6 fails against 20.Qg5+ Kh7 21.Nxd7 Qxg5 22.Nxf8+.

18.c4

After 18.Nxf7 Kxf7 19.Qxe6+ Kf8 20.Bxh6+ Rxh6 21.Qxe7+ Kg8 the attack is spent.

18...Nf8 19.Rad1 Rd8 20.Bd2 Qb6 21.Bc3 Kg8 22.Re3 Ne8

In order to expel the White Knight from its dominating position by ...f6.

23.Rg3+ Ng7 24.Rdd3 f6 25.Ng6 Nxg6 26.Rxg6 Kf7 27.h5 Qa6

The counterattack begins.

28.b3 Qxa2 29.d5

The last fling.

29...cxd5

Good enough, but 29...Qb1+ 30.Kh2 Bd6+ would have settled matters at once.

30.cxd5 Rxd5 31.Rxd5 exd5 32.Qd3

Black was threatening 32...Nxh5! 33.Qxh5 Qb1+ 34.Kh2 Qxg6.

32...Qa6 33.Qxd5+ Qe6 34.Qf3 Rh8 and Black won without difficulty.

POSITION 220

(The 10th match-game, Botvinnik-Bronstein, 1951).

1.d4 e6 2.Nf3 Nf6 3.c4 b6 4.g3 Bb7 5.Bg2 Be7 6.O-O O-O 7.b3 d5 8.cxd5 exd5 9.Bb2 Nbd7 10.Nc3 Re8 11.Ne5 Bf8 (No.220) **12.Rc1**

This pawn sacrifice is not without basis: White reckons on seriously weakening Black's castled position.

12...Nxe5 13.dxe5 Rxe5 14.Nb5 Re7 15.Bxf6 gxf6 16.e4?

Ill-judged. There was a better continuation in 16.Qd4! c6 (or 16...Bh6 17.e3) 17.Qg4+ followed by 18.Nd4, with good chances for White.

16...dxe4 17.Qg4+ Bg7 18.Rfd1 Qf8!

Bronstein gives back one of his two extra pawns. This is a first principle of good defense. See Chapters 30-32 on this subject.

19.Nd4 Bc8 20.Qh4 f5 21.Nc6

Stronger was 21.Bh3; e.g. 21...Bxd4 22.Rxd4 Be6 23.Rxc7! Rxc7 24.Qg5+ Qg7 25.Rd8+. Even in this variation Black would still have good chances by playing 23...Rae8! (instead of 23...Rxc7).

21...Re8 22.Bh3 Bh6 23.Rc2 e3 24.fxe3 Bxe3+ 25.Kh1 Be6 26.Bg2 a5 27.Bf3 Kh8 28.Nd4 Rad8 29.Rxc7

Here White has a choice of two other variations, neither of them quite satisfactory: **1)** 29.Qf6+ Qg7 30.Qxg7+ Kxg7 31.Nxe6+ fxe6 32.Rxc7+ Kf6!, and despite the presence of opposite colored Bishops, Black has good winning chances. **2)** 29.Nxe6 Rxd1+ 30.Bxd1 Rxe6, and Black must win in the long run.

29...Bd5!

30.Re1

Nothing comes from 30.Qf6+ Kg8. On the other hand 30.Rf1 Qd6 raises some difficult problems. A possible continuation could be 31.Nxf5 Bxf3+ 32.Rxf3 Qd1+ 33.Kg2 Rd2+ 34.Kh3 Rxh2+! 35.Kxh2 Qg1+ 36.Kh3 Qh1+ 37.Kg4 Rg8+ 38.Kh5 Rg5+ 39.Kh6 Rxg3+ 40.Rxe3 Rg6+ 41.Kh5 Qd1+ with mate to follow.

30...Qd6 31.Rc2

If 31.Rc3, there follows – not 31...Re4 because of 32.Rcxe3! Rxh4 33.Re8+ Kg7 34.Nxf5+ – but 31...f4!.

31...Re4! 32.Bxe4 Bxe4+ 33.Qxe4 fxe4 34.Nf5 Qb4 35.Rxe3 Rd1+ 36.Kg2 Rd2+ 37.Rxd2 Qxd2+ 38.Kh3 Qf2 39.Kg4 f6

Depriving the White King of the g5 square, and so threatening ...h5+. **White Resigned.**

(The game Van den Bosch-Kramer, Leeuwarden, 1941).

1.d4 Nf6 2.Nf3 g6 3.Nc3 d5 4.Bf4 c6 5.Qd2 Bg7 6.Bh6 O-O 7.h4 Bf5

Black's opening play has been risky, and his task now would not be easy if White proceeded with 8.Ne5! followed by f3 and g4.

POSITION 221

8.O-O-O?!

This is much too venturesome.

8...Bxh6 9.Qxh6 Ng4 10.Qd2 Nxf2 11.e4 Nxh1

Too dangerous for Black would be 11...Nxe4 12.Nxe4 dxe4 (or 12...Bxe4 13.Qh6) 13.Ne5 with a strong White attack.

12.Qh6

After 12.exf5 Ng3 Black would have no difficulty; but now White threatens 13.Ng5.

12...f6 13.exf5 Qe8 14.h5

The idea of this pawn sacrifice is to keep the Black Queen away from g6.

14...gxh5

If 14...gxf5, White could continue with 15.Qf4 e6 16.Nh4, followed by Be2, winning the Knight on h1.

15.Ne4!?

A new sacrifice, which can hardly be accepted in view of the continuation 15...dxe4 16.Bc4+ Kh8 17.Nh4! Rg8 18.Bxg8 Kxg8 19.Rxh1. At the same time White deprives the outlying Black Knight of its escape squares, and also threatens 16.Nc5. Decidedly a many-sided move.

15...Nd7 16.Bc4!?

It is rare indeed for a player to "fork himself" in this way. This unique position deserves a diagram.

16...dxc4 17.Rxh1 Qf7 18.Rh3

With the aim of preventing 18...Qg7.

18...Kh8 19.Nh4 Rg8 20.Ng6+ Rxg6 21.fxg6 Qxg6 22.Qe3 Qxg2

The attack is broken and Black's advantage in material must win the game. "Sacrificing is easy enough;" a chessmaster once remarked, "the problem is how to win your material back!".

23.Rxh5 Rg8 24.Nf2 Qf1+ and **White Resigned.**

(From the game Schlechter-Salwe, St. Petersburg, 1909).

POSITION 222

The unsoundness of a sacrifice is not by any means always easy to prove. The diagram illustrates a case in point: Schlechter played:

1.dxe5

and the game continued:

1...Rxa6 2.exf6 gxf6 3.Nd5 Bxd5 4.exd5 Kg7 5.Nh4 Re8 6.h3 Qd8 7.Re3 Ng6 8.Nf5+ Kf8 9.Re6!

White scored an impressive win, which received the first brilliancy prize of the tournament.

Tarrasch, in his book *Die Moderne Schachpartie,* appended a question mark to the move 1...Rxa6. "This is greediness", he wrote. "It is self-evident that Black should not accept this exchange sacrifice, for it leaves his Kingside broken open and gives White a powerful attack. Black must play 1...dxe5, and then after 2.Qd6 Qxd6 3.Rxd6 Ra2 he would still have equality."

Lasker however, in his famous manual, sees it differently. After the first move he comments: "The introduction to a combination which received the brilliancy prize. This, however, was a dubious award. It is clear enough that after 1...Rxa6 White will lay the Black Kingside in ruins by 2.exf6. This makes the Black Nf6 a desperado. The whole combination is therefore refuted by 1...Nxe4!, for after 2.Bxe4 Rxa6 3.exd6 Rxd6 Black wins material with no danger at all."

CHAPTER 48
OBSESSION WITH THE DRAW

In direct contrast to the player who makes reckless sacrifices there is the one who is over-anxious to draw. His trouble is not boldness but timidity. His play is altogether too prudent. He will involve himself in no complications whatsoever, but is always on the lookout either for the draw or for his opponent to blunder – and this without ever taking the slightest risk himself. Unlike the player of the last chapter – the one who sacrificed on the slightest pretext – this one persistently chooses the quiet line of play, so that his whole approach to the game becomes unjustifiably passive.

This obsession with the draw is not to be confused with the quality of *solidity*. The solid player avoids unreasonable risks, and seeks to steer the game into positional channels. When circumstances so require he will also seize his chances inexorably. This is quite in accordance with the theories laid down by Steinitz and developed by Lasker – theories which really boil down to this: that every position must be treated on its merits.

If, for instance, the position calls for an attack then that attack must be undertaken – not *may* but *must*. Anyone who shrinks from this obligation, said Lasker, ceases to be a fighter, and will go under.

It is wrong to suppose that this preoccupation with the draw is peculiar to inexperienced players; it affects everyone at times – even the greatest masters. An example of this is the first World Championship match between Tal and Botvinnik. Tal was known to be a brilliant tactician – the combinative player *par excellence*.

Botvinnik decided to counter his methods by keeping the game as simple as possible all the time, and in consequence he found himself declining sacrifices on principle. Under such circumstances it is very difficult to achieve the golden mean. Botvinnik had to play a second match before he found it.

Now some examples.

POSITION 223

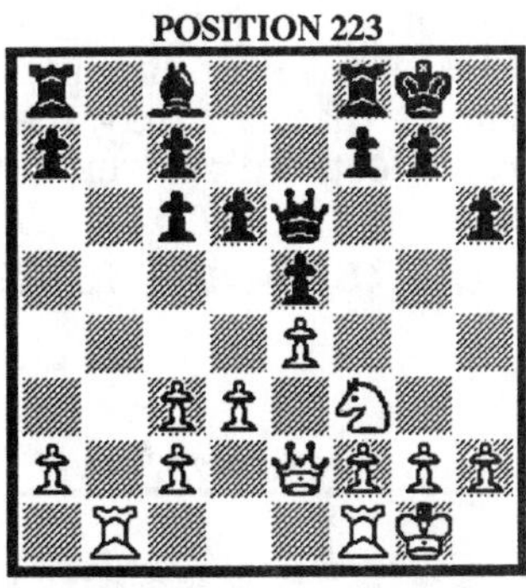

(The game Marshall-Vidmar, New York, 1927).

1.e4 e5 2.Nf3 Nc6 3.Nc3 Nf6 4.Bb5 Bb4 5.O-O O-O 6.d3 Bxc3 7.bxc3 d6 8.Bg5 Qe7 9.Bxc6 bxc6 10.Rb1 h6 11.Bxf6 Qxf6 12.Qe2 Qe6 (No.223) **13.Nh4**

This offer of the a-pawn is unsound, and as such could have been placed in the previous chapter. We have placed it here, however, because of Black's answer, which is played in characteristic drawing style.

Marshall's decision to offer the sacrifice is understandable, as Black was threatening not only to capture at a2, but also to seize the initiative with ...f5.

13...Qf6?

This move is prompted by groundless fear. Black could take the a-pawn without any qualms, as Alekhine showed in the tournament book: 13...Qxa2! 14.c4 (otherwise the Queen simply returns to e6) 14...Qa5 15.f4 exf4 16.Rxf4 Qg5 17.R1f1 a5 and White has no compensation for the passed a-pawn.

Why did the normally cool and calculating Vidmar refuse the pawn? Probably he had not yet played himself into form. This was his first round game, and he did not relish the idea of plunging straight into the fray by grabbing a pawn from so redoubtable an attacking player as Marshall. Be that as it may, the game was drawn forthwith by repetition of moves:

14.Nf3 Qe6 15.Nh4 Qf6 16.Nf3 Qe6 Draw

POSITION 224

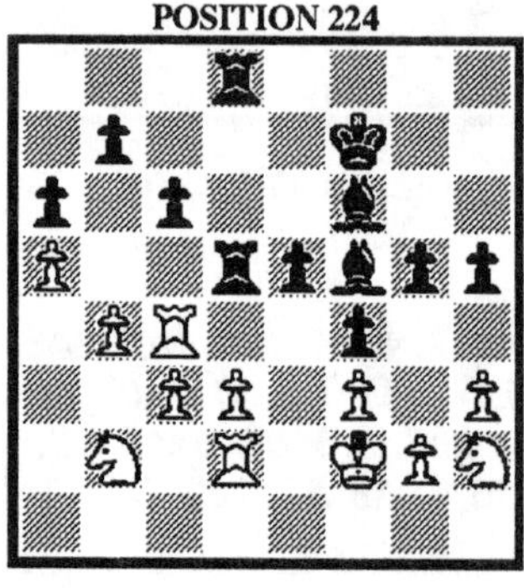

(Black refuses the gift of the d-pawn; from the game Lasker-Janowsky, New York, 1924).

In this position Black played:

1...Rb5? 2.Ke2 Rbd5 3.Kd1 Ke6? 4.Kc2

White has now protected his d-pawn, Black having refused to capture it on two occasions. The tournament book analysis shows that he could have taken it on the first move: 1...Bxd3 2.Nxd3 Rxd3 3.Rxd3 Rxd3 4.Ke2 e4 5.Rxe4 Rxc3; and Black has a sound extra pawn. Again at the third move Black could have captured: 3...Bxd3 4.Nxd3 Rxd3 5.Rxd3 Rxd3+ 6.Kc2 e4! 7.fxe4 Rg3, etc.

POSITION 225

(From the 3rd match-game Tal-Botvinnik, 1960).

The question is whether or not Black should capture the h-pawn. The answer is more difficult to determine than the answer to the questions posed by the two previous examples. Botvinnik thought better of his intention to take the h-pawn and played:

1...Ng7

The game continued:

2.Bg5 h6 3.Bxh6 Nf5 4.Bf4 Rxh4 5.Rxh4 Nxh4 6.O-O-O

Now White gets counterplay on the open h-file. After the game, however, it was established that Black's best plan would in fact have been 1...Bxh4!. The main variation runs: 2.Rxh4 Qxh4 3.Bg5 Qh2 4.Qb4 f6 5.Qxb7 Rb8 6.Qxc6 fxg5 7.Qxe6+ Kd8 8.Nc5, and now, as Petrosian pointed out, 8...Nhf6!. If White does not offer the exchange but continues more quietly with 2.Bh6, Black plays 2...Be7 3.f4 Bf8 and retains the extra pawn.

POSITION 226

(Passive play, aiming at the draw; from the game Szabo-Filip, Portoroz, 1958).

1.Bd3 Rac8?

At this point the tournament book recommends the immediate capture at c3. Then after 2.Bb2 Qa5 3.f4 Qd5 4.f5 Rfe8; Black can defend himself adequately. Another good possibility is 1...Nxe5 2.dxe5 Nd7 (but not, too greedily, 2...Qxc3 3.exf6! Qxa1 4.Bb2, etc.).

2.f4 Qxc3

The exchange of Knights is now poor because White could recapture with the f-pawn. On the other hand Black cannot mark time any longer, for if White is allowed to play c4 his position will be overwhelming.

3.Bb2 Qc7 4.f5 Qd6 5.Rf4 Nd5 6.Rh4 N7f6 7.Rf1 Ne7

Sounder would have been 7...Rc7. The text move aims to force White to declare his intentions.

8.fxe6 fxe6 9.Rxf6! Rxf6 10.Bxh7+ Kf8 11.Bd3 Ng8?

This is too passive. Essential was 11...Nf5.

12.h3

Probably more accurate was 12.Rh8; but Black's situation is now so utterly passive that White can well afford the time to make a flight square for his King.

12...Bd5

Preventing 13.d5, which would have been a powerful reply either to 12...Nh6 or to 12...Rh6, giving White a direct attack against the King.

13.Rh8 Rf5 14.Qg4 Rc7 15.Qh4 Bb7 16.Qh7 Rc1+ 17.Kh2 Black Resigned.

POSITION 227

(From the 2nd match-game Janowsky-Marshall, 1905).

Black's hanging pawns at d5 and c5 are likely to be a weakness in the endgame, and, as we saw in Chapter 8, a priority for Black is to retain control of e5. He has just played his KR from h6 to e6, with the idea of driving the White Knight from its advanced post. Instead of reacting logically with f4 White suddenly begins to play timidly.

1.Nd3 Ba6 2.Rb1?

The obvious and strong continuation is 2.Nf4 Bxf4 3.gxf4 Bc4 4.b4!, and the White Bishop pair will become formidable.

2...Bc4 3.Nc1?

Clearly played to keep the Black pieces out of b3; but after the game Janowsky himself did not know why he had not played 3.b4 or 3.Nf4 instead.

3...Be5 4.Bxe5 Rxe5 5.b3?

Despite White's sequence of timid moves his position is still good for a draw – for instance by 5.Nd3, or 5.Bf1.

5...a5! 6.a4 Kf8 7.Nd3

At last!

7...Bxd3 8.Rxd3 c4 9.Rc3?

Fearing that if he plays 9.R3d1 Black will capture the b-pawn or play c3. Both these lines would be incorrect, as the following variations show: **1)** 9...cxb3 10.Rd3 Rb4 11.R3xb3 Rxa4 12.Rb8+ Kf7 13.Ra8, and White soon wins a pawn. **2)** 9...c3 10.Rdc1 Rc8 11.Kf1, and the c-pawn is more of a liability than an asset. But **3)** 9...Rb4! would retain Black's advantage.

9...Re6! 10.Rbc1

Otherwise Black plays 10...R6b6.

10...Rxb3 11.Rxb3 cxb3 12.Rb1 Rb6 13.Bf1

Intending 14.Bb5.

13...Rb4 14.Bb5 Nc8 15.Kf1 Nd6 16.Bd3 Nc4 17.Ke2 g6 18.f3 Nb6 19.Bb5 Nc4 and **White Resigned.**

PART TWELVE

PERSONAL STYLE

INTRODUCTION

In most positions there are likely to be several good moves available, and a diversity of schemes and possibilities to be weighed up. The actual choice of moves is usually made on subjective grounds. Even when there are very definite characteristics present, which largely predetermine the broad strategy, there usually remains a move-by-move choice of more or less equivalent continuations. A line of play which is good objectively (in theory) may not be so good subjectively (in practice).

Every chessplayer has his own aptitudes and peculiarities, and even these are subject to fluctuation from time to time. When there is a choice of continuations which, from the abstract point of view, are essentially equally good, a player has to decide which suits him best.

We all make mistakes; but the person who really knows his own capabilities and then aims as far as possible to avoid the type of position which doesn't suit him, will make fewer mistakes in the long run than one who tries to be utterly objective, setting himself problems which he is subjectively unfit to solve.

Although it would be out of the question to attempt to teach the subject of style in a book, the fact remains that there is great value in examining the styles of others and getting to know them. Therefore, we close this book with a series of games of the great masters, which should give the student some idea of the diversity of chess styles. The whole subject will have to be handled very briefly. The concept of style involves so many nuances that we have made no attempt at systematic classification, but have contented ourselves with an alphabetical arrangement; and we make no claim to completeness.

What we have done is to select some of the most celebrated players of yesterday and today, comment briefly on the stylistic character of each, and then append a few examples. The reader must therefore not expect a collection of brilliances and sparkling combinations; the chosen games are intended to be typical.

1. ALEKHINE (1892-1946)

Alekhine strove first and foremost to avoid passive positions. Above all he was an attacker, and for the sake of attack he would gladly take risks. Originality was a prominent feature of his play; although he usually avoided the well-known gambits he had a penchant for improvising his own. His style may be described as an amalgam of fantasy, science, and ambition.

In some respects Alekhine was diametrically opposed to Steinitz. For example, consider the variation 1.e4 e6 2.d4 d5 3.Nc3 Bb4 4.Bd2 (Speyer-Alekhine, Hamburg, 1910). Even so early Alekhine chose to not take the pawn. Steinitz would certainly have taken it, following his own motto "The only way to refute a gambit is to accept it". Then Steinitz was always content to accept a passive position, whereas Alekhine decidedly was not. Here are some examples of the way Alekhine liked to treat the openings.

(Alekhine-Fine, Hastings, 1936-37).

1.e4 e5 2.Nf3 Nc6 3.Bb5 a6 4.Ba4 Nf6 5.O-O Be7 6.Re1 b5 7.Bb3 d6 8.c3 Na5 9.Bc2 c5 10.d4 Qc7 11.Nbd2 O-O 12.Nf1 Bg4

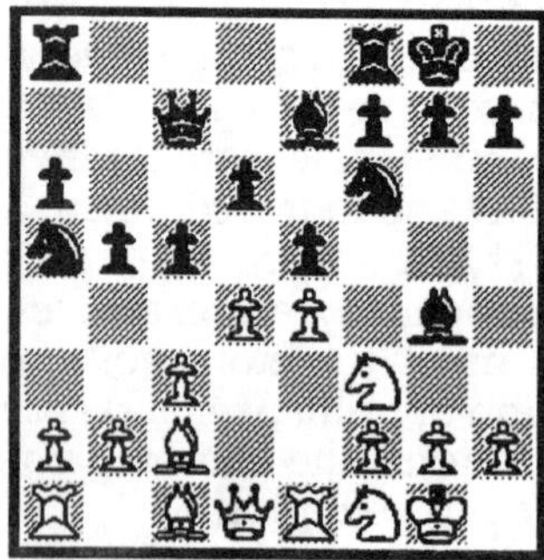

13.Ne3! Bxf3 14.Qxf3

Alekhine remarked that 14.gxf3 was also playable.

14...cxd4 15.Nf5

Later, Alekhine observed that a more accurate choice here was 15.cxd4 exd4 and only then 16.Nf5.

15...dxc3 16.Qxc3 and White has attacking chances.

(Alekhine-Euwe, 7th match-game, 1935).

1.e4 e6 2.d4 d5 3.Nc3 Bb4 4.Nge2 dxe4 5.a3 Be7 6.Nxe4 Nc6 7.g4

This much criticized move is typical of Alekhine's style.

7...b6

The best reply is 7...e5!,e.g., 8.d5 Nd4! 9.N2c3. Alekhine thought that 7...Nf6 was best.

8.Bg2 Bb7 9.c3 Nf6 10.N2g3 O-O

Too risky; Black could still get a reasonable game with ...Qd7 followed by Queenside castling.

11.g5 Nxe4 12.Nxe4 Kh8 13.Qh5

With excellent attacking chances for White.

(Alekhine-Flohr, Nottingham, 1936).

1.e4 e6 2.d4 d5 3.Nc3 Bb4 4.Bd2 dxe4 5.Nxe4?

Better was 5.Qg4 Qxd4 6.Nf3, as Alekhine later recommended. However, it was later shown that Black can respond effectively with 6...Nh6! 7.Qf4 e5!. The correct way for White to get attacking chances is 6.O-O-O! (instead of 6.Nf3). Therefore, the preferred path for Black after 5.Qg4 is 5...Nf6 6.Qxg7 Rg8 7.Qh6 Nc6.

5...Qxd4 6.Bd3 Bxd2+ 7.Qxd2 Qd8?

This cautious retreat is poor. Correct was the "greedy" 7...Qxb2 as after 8.Rd1 Nd7 Black can consolidate eventually. This line conforms to Steinitz's dogma that a gambit can be refuted only by accepting it.

8.O-O-O Qe7 9.Nf3 Nf6 10.Rhe1 Nxe4 11.Rxe4 Nd7 12.Rg4 f5 13.Rf4 Nf6 14.Re1 and White has the initiative (14...g6 15.h3 followed by g4).

EXAMPLE 228

(The game Alekhine-Reshevsky, Kemeri, 1937).

1.e4 Nf6 2.e5 Nd5 3.Nf3 d6 4.d4 Bg4 5.c4 Nb6 6.Be2 dxe5 7.Nxe5

In the 29th match-game Alekhine-Euwe, 1935, White played 7.c5.

There followed 7...e4 8.cxb6 exf3 9.Bxf3 Bxf3 10.Qxf3. Now, instead of 10...Nc6!, Black chose the weaker move 10...axb6.

7...Bxe2 8.Qxe2 Qxd4 9.O-O

Alekhine later stated that 9.Na3! would have been better. Then if 9...N8d7 10.Nf3, or if 9...e6 then 10.Nc2.

9...N8d7 10.Nxd7 Nxd7 11.Nc3 c6 12.Be3 Qe5 13.Rad1 e6 14.Qf3

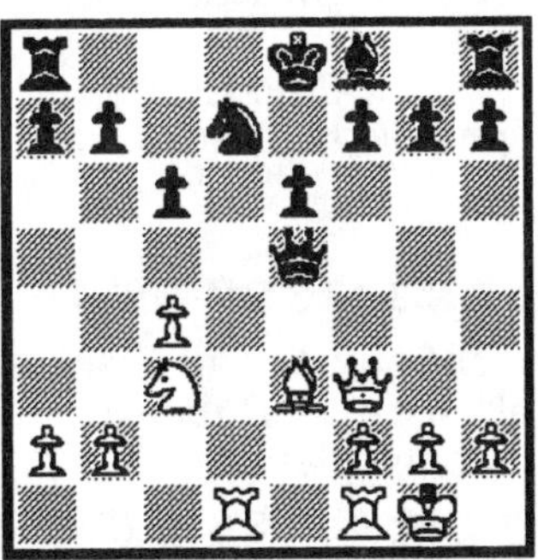

14...O-O-O 15.Bxa7 Qa5 16.Bd4 Qf5 17.Qg3

Another promising course was 17.Qxf5, but Alekhine is clearly bent on settling the issue in the middlegame.

17...e5 18.Be3 Bb4 19.Na4 Ba5 20.f4!

Directed against 20...Bc7 and 21...e4.

20...Bc7 21.b3 f6 22.fxe5 Qe6 23.h3

The main idea here is to meet 23...Nxe5 with 24.Nc5 without allowing 24...Qg4.

23...Rhg8 24.Bd4 Nxe5

Better was 24...fxe5: 25.Qe3 e4 26.c5 Rde8.

25.Qc3

With the double threat 26.Nc5 and 26.Nb6+. Upon 25...Kb8 26.Nc5 Qd6 there follows 27.Qb4!, with a winning attack.

25...Nd7 26.c5! Rge8 27.b4!

Now if 27...Qxa2 then 28.Ra1 Qe6 29.b5 threatening 30.Nb6+.

27...Nb8 28.Nb6+ Bxb6 29.cxb6 Qxa2 30.Qg3!

Now on 30...Qf7, Alekhine gives 31.Ra1 Rxd4 32.Ra8 Re5 33.Qxe5.

30...Rd7 31.Bc5

Alekhine did not spare himself in his notes. Here he indicated later that 31.Bxf6 gxf6 32.Rxd7 Kxd7 33.Qc7+ Ke6 34.Re1+ would have been simpler.

31...Qf7 32.Ra1 Qg6 33.Qh2 Re5 34.Ra8 Rd2

Or 34...Qe8 35.Qg3 and 36.Qa3.

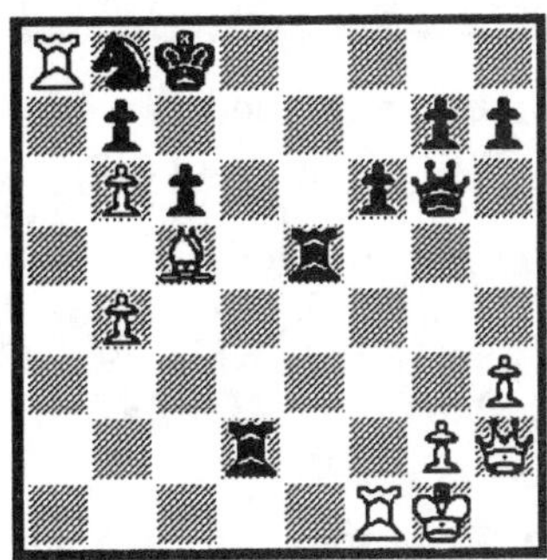

35.Rxb8+ Kxb8 36.Qxe5+ fxe5 37.Rf8+ and mate follows.

2. ANDERSSEN (1818-1879)

The style of Adolf Anderssen is distinguished by sheer fantasy and by a tireless striving after beauty, but not so much by cold reason. His immortal game (see example 184) is universally known. Here we give another example of his style.

EXAMPLE 229

(The game Rosanes-Anderssen, Breslau, 1863).

1.e4 e5 2.f4 exf4 3.Nf3 g5 4.h4 g4 5.Ne5 Nf6 6.Bc4 d5 7.exd5 Bd6 8.d4 Nh5 9.Bb5+

Anderssen gave 9.O-O as the best move. Interesting is the fact that 20th century opening theory agrees with him.

9...c6! 10.dxc6 bxc6 11.Nxc6 Nxc6 12.Bxc6+ Kf8 13.Bxa8 Ng3 14.Rh2?

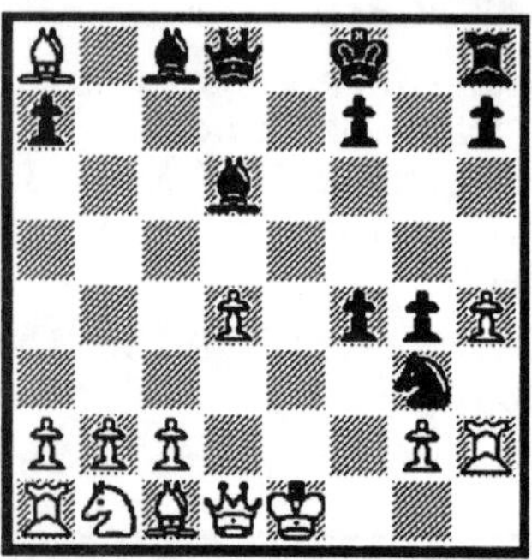

A serious error. Better was 14.Kf2 after which Anderssen gave 14...Nxh1+ 15.Qxh1 Bf5; a century later Keres suggested 15...g3+ 16.Ke1 Qe7+ 17.Kd1 Bg4+, apparently envisaging 18.Bf3 Bxf3+ 19.gxf3 Rg8 20.Qg2 Qxh4 21.Ke2 Qh2 22.Kf1 h5.

14...Bf5

There were two stronger choices: 14...Ba6 (Pachman), or 14...Qe7+ 15.Kf2 Ne4+ (Keres).

15.Bd5 Kg7

Making room for the Rook.

16.Nc3 Re8+ 17.Kf2 Qb6

Threatening 18...Bc5!.

18.Na4 Qa6

Threatening mate in four, starting with 19...Qe2+.

19.Nc3

Or 19.c4 Qxa4! 20.Qxa4 Re2+ 21.Kg1 Re1+ 22.Kf2 Rf1#.

19...Be5 20.a4 Qf1+!! 21.Qxf1 Bxd4+ 22.Be3 Rxe3 23.Kg1

Otherwise 23...Re2#.

23...Re1#.

3. BLACKBURNE (1842-1921)

Blackburne had an unpretentious style, but was nevertheless a very remarkable player. One of his great assets was an incredible skill in spotting opportunities which seem to be more or less accidental. Add to this the fact that he possessed an iron nerve and we have the dreaded "natural player". Blackburne played many brilliant games. As a positional player, however, he is not to be ranked with Steinitz or Tarrasch.

EXAMPLE 230

(The game Blackburne-Charousek, Berlin, 1897).

1.d4 d5 2.Nf3 e6 3.Bf4 Bd6 4.Bxd6

Unpretentious, but in Blackburne's "natural" style. A Rubinstein would certainly have played 4.e3.

4...Qxd6 5.Nbd2 Nf6 6.c3 Nbd7 7.Qc2 e5 8.e3 O-O 9.dxe5 Nxe5 10.Be2

He should have traded Knights first.

10...Bg4 11.h3 Bh5 12.Nxe5

Practically forced, otherwise Black will play 12...Bg6.

12...Bxe2!

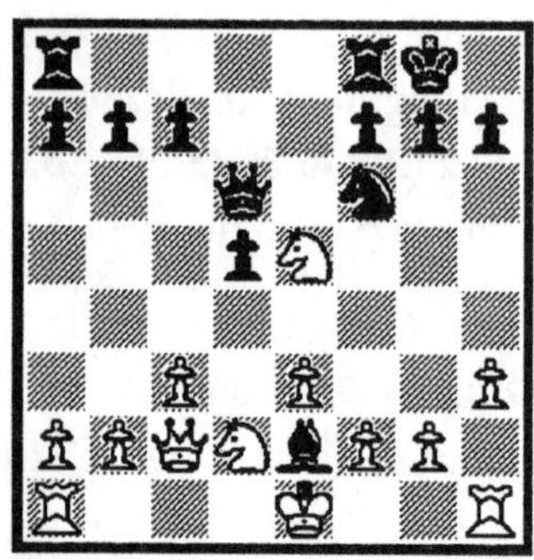

13.Nef3

White could win a pawn by 13.Nxf7, but after 13...Qa6 Black would have more than enough compensation.

13...Qa6 14.Nb3 Bd3 15.Qd1 b6 16.Nc1 Bc4!

The incisive way to continue the attack. After 16...Bg6 17.Qe2 White would be out of difficulties.

17.Ne5

Not 17.b3 because of 17...Qa5! 18.Qd2 Ba6, keeping up the pressure.

17...Rad8 18.Qc2 Qb7 19.Ne2 Rfe8 20.Nxc4 dxc4 21.O-O Qe4 22.Qxe4 Nxe4 23.Rfd1 g5

Reti pointed out 23...c5! 24.Nf4 Nd2! and White's position is in a terrible bind.

24.Nd4 Rd5 25.Nf3 Rd3

On 25...R8d8 White could play 26.Rd4!.

26.Ne1 Rdd8 27.Nf3 c5 28.Kf1 b5 29.a3 a5 30.Ke2 b4

White's position looks critical, but this was where Blackburne displays his remarkable resourcefulness.

31.axb4 axb4 32.Rxd8 Rxd8 33.cxb4

Now if 33...cxb4, White obtains the d4 square.

33...c3!

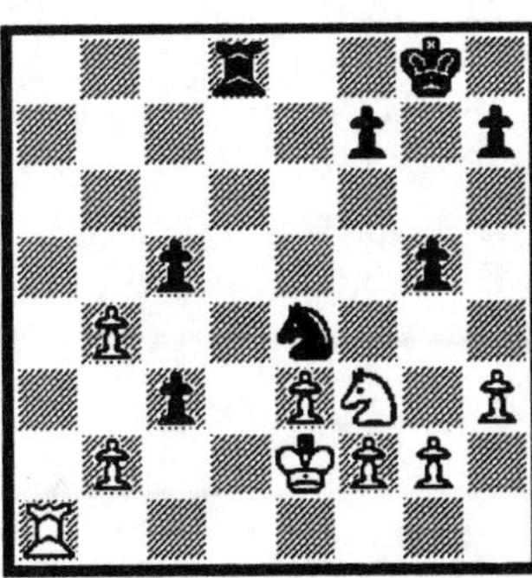

34.bxc3 Nxc3+ 35.Ke1 cxb4 36.Nd4 Rb8 37.Nb3 Kg7 38.Ra6 h5 39.g3 Rc8 40.Nd4 Rc5 41.Ra7 Kg6 42.Rb7 Ra5 43.Rxb4 Ra1+ 44.Kd2 Ne4+ 45.Ke2 Ra2+ 46.Kf3 Nxf2 47.Rb6+ f6 48.g4!

Not 48.h4 because of 48...g4+ 49.Kf4 Nh1 and Black is winning.

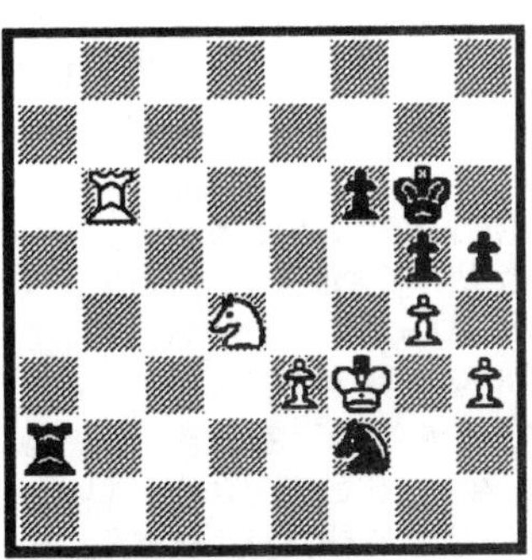

48...h4 49.Rb7 Nxh3 50.Ne6!

The obvious 50.Nf5 loses to 50...Ng1+ 51.Ke4 Ra4+

50...Ng1+ 51.Ke4 Ra4+ 52.Kd3 Ra8

Forced, otherwise he will be mated after 53.Nf8+ and 54.Rh7#. Even after 52...Rxg4 Blackburne would play 53.Nf8+ Kf5 54.Rb5#.

53.Rg7+ Kh6 54.Rf7 Rg8 55.Rxf6+ Rg6 56.Rf1! Draw

A narrow escape, but a very praiseworthy piece of work by White.

4. BOGOLYUBOV (1889-1953)

Bogolyubov was an attacking player, to be ranked with Anderssen, Marshall, and Spielmann. With subtle positional play he was less at home; though in his later years he did operate routinely on positional grounds while producing many fine endgames. Bogolyubov was an optimist. One of his famous aphorisms was "When I am White I have the advantage because I am White; when I am Black I have the advantage because I am Bogolyubov".

His aims, however, were apt to outrun his capabilities. His great talent was at times just not great enough, and the occasional gross errors in his play were due to this disharmony.

EXAMPLE 231

(The game Bogolyubov-Alekhine, Salzburg, 1942).

1.e4

Around 1928 Bogolyubov wrote a book on the d-pawn opening, under the title 1.d2-d4!. However, later in his career he usually preferred 1.e4.

1...c6 2.d4 d5 3.Nc3 dxe4 4.Nxe4 Nf6 5.Nxf6+ exf6 6.Bc4 Bd6 7.Qe2+ Be7 8.Nf3 Bg4 9.c3 Nd7 10.h3!

Demonstrating that the development of the Bishop to g4 has its drawbacks.

10...Bh5 11.g4! Bg6 12.Nh4! Nb6 13.Bb3 Nd5 14.Bd2!

After the seemingly energetic 14.f4 Black would get good counterplay by 14...f5 15.gxf5 Bh5!.

14...Qd6 15.Nf5!

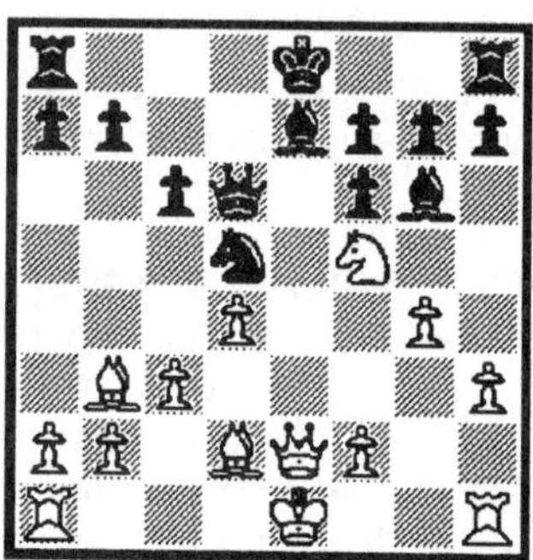

Forcing the following exchange, after which the Black doubled pawns are blockaded, while White retains the Bishop pair and g-file.

15...Bxf5 16.gxf5 g6 17.O-O-O O-O-O 18.Qf3 g5

Black must control f4, otherwise he could hardly hope to defend.

19.Rhe1 Rhe8 20.Re4 Bf8 21.Rxe8 Rxe8 22.Qh5!

Winning a pawn.

22...Qd7 23.Qxh7 Re4 24.Qh8 Qd8 25.Qh5 Qd7 26.Qh8 Qd8

White has repeated the position to gain time on the clock.

27.Re1!

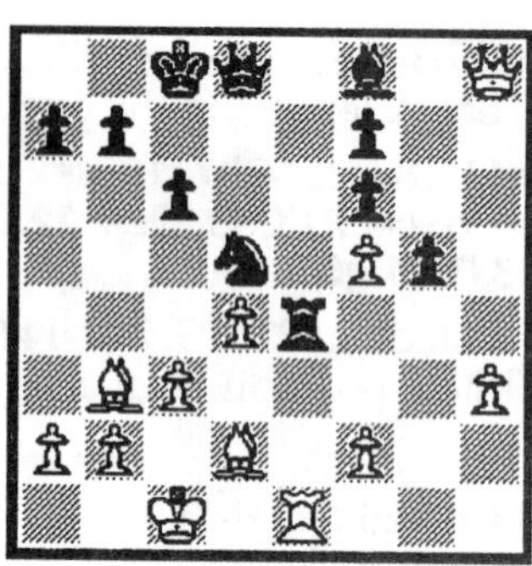

So that if 27...Rh4 then 28.Qg8 Rxh3 29.Qxf7 Ne7 (or 29...Be7 30.Bxd5 cxd5 31.Rxe7) 30.Qxf6.

27...Rxe1+ 28.Bxe1 Kc7 29.Bd2 Qe7 30.Qh5 Qd7 31.Qf3 Bh6 32.h4! Nf4 33.Bxf4+ gxf4

Now White no longer has the Bishop pair, and there are opposite colored Bishops. With Queens off the board, Black would have good drawing chances; but while the Queens are on the board White has good attacking prospects, as the presence of opposite colored Bishops favors the attack.

34.Qh5 Bf8 35.Bxf7 c5 36.Be6 Qd6 37.Qf7+ Be7 38.dxc5 Qxc5 39.h5

The passed h-pawn shows its worth.

39...f3 40.h6 Kb6 41.Bc4

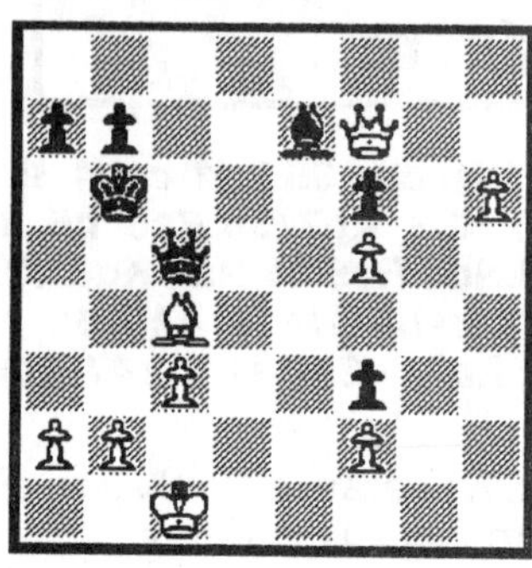

After 41.h7 Qxf2 42.h8=Q Qe1+ 43.Kc2 Qe2+ 44.Kb3 Qb5+ Black draws by perpetual check.

41...Bd6 42.Bd5 Qc8 43.Qe6 Qf8

If 43...Qxe6 44.fxe6 Bf4+ 45.Kc2 Bxh6 46.e7 wins.

44.h7 Ka5 45.Bxf3 Qh6+ 46.Kc2 Black Resigned.

5. BOTVINNIK (Born 1910)

In some ways Botvinnik was a disciple of Lasker. He was, like his great forerunner – first of all a great fighter. He revels in difficult positions, but when necessary he also plays simple positions with an accuracy which is scarcely surpassable. His mastery stems from the harmony which exists between his chess technique and his human attributes.

His style is distinguished by great originality. He never minds having his pawn position shattered, providing that he thereby obtains free play for his pieces.

In this respect he goes much farther than even Tarrasch, who spoke out in favor of having an isolated d-pawn. Botvinnik was not only unafraid of an isolated d-pawn; he quite frequently was prepared to accept doubled or even trebled pawns.

Botvinnik not only thirsts for battle: as a rule he is thoroughly prepared for it. Several times he lost matches in defense of the World Championship-first against Smyslov, then against Tal, and then against Petrosian. In two of these cases – against Smyslov and Tal – he had the opportunity for a return match, and both times he made such thorough preparations, and directed those preparations so accurately at the weaknesses of his opponents, that they were no match for him. His skill in the deep and exhaustive analysis of adjournment positions is scarcely rivaled.

He has adopted his own particular repertoire of openings, especially with the Black pieces. Against 1.e4 his first choice of defense used to be the French (1...e6 2.d4 d5 3.Nc3 Bb4) and then the Sicilian, in keeping with his preference for difficult positions. Later he often used the Caro-Kann, especially when he needed a solid defense against the ferocious attacking style of Tal.

Several of Botvinnik's variations with the White pieces exemplify his disregard of weakened pawn structures; e.g. 1.d4 Nf6 2.c4 e6 3.Nc3 Bb4 4.Qb3 c5 5.dxc5 Nc6 6.Bg5 h6 7.Bh4 Nd4 8.Qa4! Bxc3+ 9.bxc3 Nf5 10.Bxf6 Qxf6 11.Rc1. Or 1.d4 d5 2.c4 dxc4 3.Nf3 Nf6 4.e3 e6 5.Bxc4 c5 6.O-O a6 7.a4 cxd4 8.exd4. This latter variation occurred repeatedly in his match with Petrosian, the man who dethroned Botvinnik as World Champion in 1963.

EXAMPLE 232

(The game Botvinnik-Chekhover, Leningrad, 1938).

1.d4 Nf6 2.c4 e6 3.Nc3 Bb4 4.Nf3 O-O 5.Bg5 d6 6.e3

Another way is 6.e4,e.g., 6...h6 7.Bxf6 Bxc3+ 8.bxc3 Qxf6, but Botvinnik wishes to leave e4 open for occupation by his pieces.

6...Qe7 7.Be2 e5 8.Qc2 Re8 9.O-O Bxc3

This practically forces the doubling of the c-pawns, as 10.Qxc3 would be met by 10...Ne4 11.Bxe7 Nxc3. For that matter, Botvinnik was not afraid of doubled pawns when there is positional compensation (in this case the possibility of occupying d5 later).

10.bxc3 h6 11.Bh4 c5

Black hopes to induce White to play d5, but it doesn't work out well here. Botvinnik suggested 11...g5 followed by ...Nh5 as Black's best course.

12.Rfe1

To be able to play 18.Nd2.

12...Bg4 13.Bxf6 Qxf6 14.Qe4 Bxf3

After 14...Bc8 15.Qd5 is annoying to Black.

15.Bxf3 Nc6 16.dxc5

"A doubled pawn is a weakness which may perhaps be endured, but an isolated doubled pawn is a disadvantage which must lead to the loss of the game". Not long ago this was the accepted opinion, but Botvinnik's games have repeatedly demonstrated that this must be taken with a grain of salt.

16...dxc5 17.Rad1 Rad8 18.Rd5

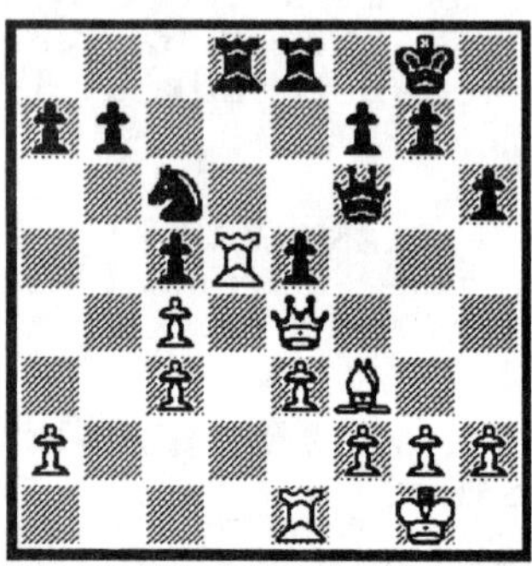

Here we see the doubled pawn as a support pawn in the exploitation of a strong square.

18...b6

Better was 18...Qe7 19.Red1 g6, with the idea of playing ...f5 as soon as possible.

19.Red1 Na5 20.h3 Rxd5 21.Rxd5!

Botvinnik declines to dissolve his doubled pawns by 21.cxd5. He would then have a protected passed pawn, but Black would have been able to favorably blockade it at once by ...Nb7-d6.

21...Qe7

Or 21...Rd8 22.Qd3 Rxd5 23.Qxd5 and White has excellent chances.

22.Bg4 Qb7 23.Bf5 Qb8

White was threatening 24.Rd7 Qxe4 25.Bxe4, and 26.Bd5. If 23...g6 White has 24.Bxg6 fxg6 25.Qxg6+ Kf8 26.Rd6 winning.

24.Rd7 Rd8

Black must surrender a pawn, in view of 25.Bh7+ Kf8 26.Qd5 Re7 27.Rd8+.

25.Qxe5!

Black can't take the Queen because of mate on the back rank.

25...Nxc4 26.Qxb8 Rxb8 27.Be4!!

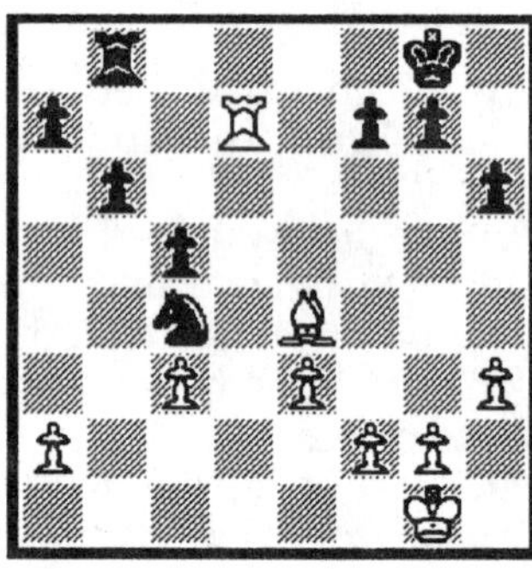

Iron logic. After the natural 27.Rxa7 Black would get counterplay by 27...Nd6 followed by ...c4 and ...Nb5. Now White's main threat is 28.Bd5, winning the f-pawn.

27...Na3 28.Bd5 Rf8 29.e4!

Still White resists the temptation to win material.

29... a5 30.c4! b5 31.cxb5 Nxb5 32.e5 a4

Or 32...g5 33.Rb7 Nc3 34.Bc4 and Black is lost.

33.f4

White's pawn majority in the center and Kingside will now yield a decisive passed pawn.

33...Nd4 34.Kf2 g5 35.g3 gxf4 36.gxf4 Ne6

After 36...Kg7 37.Ke3 Nf5+ 38.Ke4 Kg6 39.Bxf7+ Rxf7 40.Rxf7 Ng3+ 41.Kf3 Kxf7 42.Kxg3 c4 43.Kf2 c3 44.Ke2, White wins easily as he can stop the c-pawn.

37.Ke3 c4 38.f5

White still eschews material gain in order to proceed with his main strategy.

38...Nc5 39.Rc7 Nd3 40.e6 fxe6 41.fxe6 Black Resigned as White will play 42.e7+ and 43.Bc6.

6. BRONSTEIN (Born 1924)

Like Botvinnik, Bronstein is at home in difficult positions; the difference is that Bronstein will take far greater risks. From first move to last his games are usually struggles in which he devotes much of his time seeking original, creative lines of play. These tactics are motivated not only by the idea of forcing his opponent into prolonged thought, but also by his desire to win as brilliantly as possible.

His style has something of Alekhine (his pawn sacrifices and his instinct for breakthrough) but also something of Tartakower (the best move is not necessarily the strongest; preference may sometimes be given to a second-best move in order to confuse the opponent). The game Porreca-Bronstein, Belgrade 1954, provides a good illustration: 1.e4 c6 2.d4 d5 3.Nc3 dxe4 4.Nxe4 Bf5 5.Ng3 Bg6 6.h4 h6 7.Nh3 Bh7 8.Bc4 Nf6 9.Nf4 Nbd7 10.O-O Qc7 11.Re1, and now the very remarkable move 11...Bg8!!? to eliminate the possibility of a sacrifice on e6, which, after the normal 11...e6, would hang over the Black position like the sword of Damocles. The position deserves a diagram.

(Compare the Steinitz Chapter!).

EXAMPLE 233

(The game Bronstein-Medina, Goteborg, 1955).

1.d4 Nf6 2.c4 e6 3.Nc3 d5 4.cxd5 exd5 5.Bg5 Be7 6.e3 c6 7.Qc2 Nbd7 8.Bd3 Nf8

The main variation runs: 8...O-O 9.Nf3 Re8 10.O-O Nf8, after which White typically aims for the minority attack by 11.Rab1.

9.Nge2

Of course White could still play for the minority attack: 9.Nf3 Ne6 10.Bh4 g6 11.O-O Ng7 12.b4, but Bronstein often avoids routine paths.

9...Ne6 10.Bh4 g6

Now Black's plan has clarified: he intends ...Ng7, followed by ...Bf5, with a strategically desirable exchange of the light-squared Bishops.

11.O-O-O

Now the cards are on the table. Queenside castling usually foreshadows a pawn-storm on the other flank; here, however, it will become clear that this is an exceptional position.

11...Ng7 12.f3!

White prepares to activate his central pawn majority.

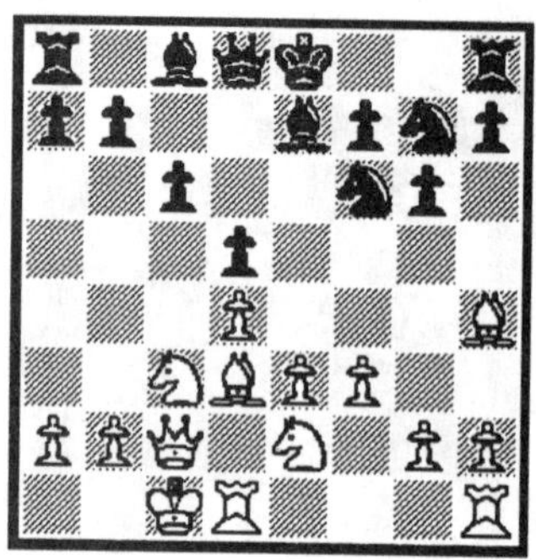

12...Nf5

After 12...Bf5 White has the powerful advance 13.e4.

13.Bf2 Qa5 14.Kb1 Be6 15.h3

White is in no hurry to advance in the center. If, for instance, Black now castles Kingside, White could obtain excellent chances by playing 16.g4.

15...O-O-O 16.e4! Ng7

Practically forced, as if 16...dxe4 17.fxe4 Ng7 White opens a violent assault by 18.d5.

17.Bg3

It is clear that White has the initiative, and his procedure is characteristic. First the Bishop is placed where it is most active.

17...Nge8 18.Be5 Rf8 19.Nc1

Suddenly the crisis arrives. White threatens to win Black's Queen by 20.Nb3.

19...dxe4 20.fxe4 Nd7 21.Bh2 Nb8 22.d5!

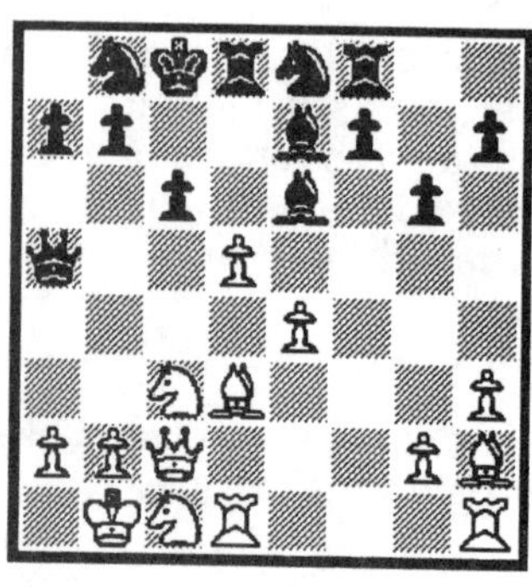

Starting an overwhelming attack. If 22...cxd5, White interpolates 23.Nb3 and then wins by 24.Nxd5+.

22...Bd7 23.Nb3 Qb6

After 23...Qb4 24.a3, and the Black Queen still has to go to b6.

24.d6! Black Resigned

After 24...Bxd6 25.Nd5 the Black Queen has no move.

7. CAPABLANCA (1888-1942)

Capablanca was the possessor of a virtually perfect technical style, but he was lazy, and had a degree of self-satisfaction which made him incline towards superficiality. He had little patience, and was seldom in the mood for hard work. Nevertheless, there was real inspiration in his ability to forsee possible danger, and in the way he could nip it in the bud long before it could amount to anything serious. As might be expected of such a superb technician, he had a particularly fine feeling for liquidation. All things considered, his was a style which tended more to defense than aggression.

Capablanca had no faith in principles, but only in good moves. Since he usually steered clear of trenchant lines of play he developed primarily into a specialist in the playing of simple positions. The following game is an illustration:

EXAMPLE 234

(From the game Capablanca-Steiner, Budapest, 1928).

1.d4 Nf6 2.c4 e6 3.Nc3 d5 4.Bg5 Nbd7 5.e3 Be7 6.Nf3 O-O 7.Rc1 c6 8.Bd3 dxc4 9.Bxc4 Nd5 10.Bxe7 Qxe7 11.O-O Nxc3 12.Rxc3 b6 13.Qc2 c5 (see next diagram)

The play from this point is typical of Capablanca's methods.

14.dxc5!

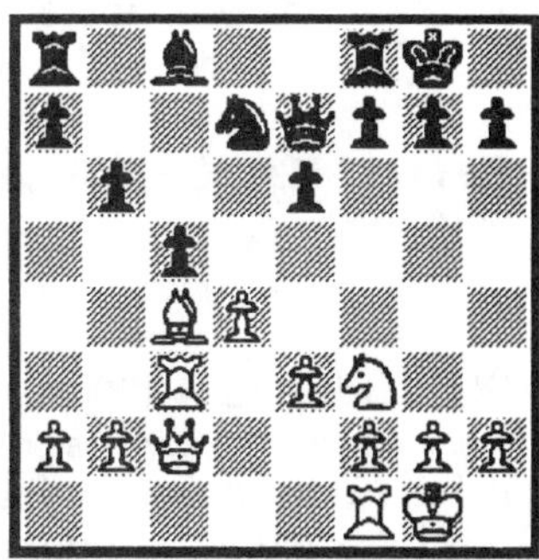

Another way is 14.Bb5 cxd4 15.Nxd4, but the move played is typical of Capablanca's methods.

14...Nxc5 15.b4 Na6 16.a3 Bb7 17.Bd3 h6 18.Rc1

White dominance of the c-file gives him a big advantage. Black can't challenge the c-file by 18...Rc8 because of 19.Rxc8 Rxc8 20.Qxc8+.

18...Rad8 19.Ne5 Qd6 20.f4 Nb8 21.Rc7 and Black's difficulties proved insuperable. Next we shall look at one of Capablanca's greatest performances.

EXAMPLE 235

(The 11th match-game Capablanca- Lasker, Havana, 1921).

1.d4 d5 2.Nf3 e6 3.c4 Nf6 4.Bg5 Nbd7 5.e3 Be7 6.Nc3 O-O 7.Rc1 Re8

Playable, but the standard 7...c6 is more reliable.

8.Qc2 c6 9.Bd3

Probably stronger is 9.a3, but Capablanca usually chose the simplest way.

9...dxc4 10.Bxc4 Nd5 11.Bxe7 Rxe7

The normal 11...Qxe7 12.O-O Nxc3 13.Qxc3 e5 was preferable.

12.O-O Nf8 13.Rfd1 Bd7 14.e4 Nb6?

More in keeping with the demands of the position would have been the exchange on c3: in a cramped position, as we know, it is good to exchange as many pieces as possible. Lasker was on the lookout for complications, knowing, better than anyone, that once the position has been simplified Capablanca would be at home like a fish in water.

15.Bf1 Rc8 16.b4!

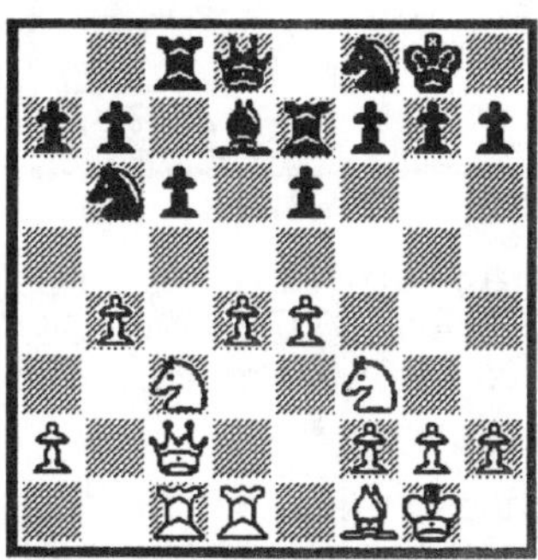

Restraining the freeing move ...c5.

16...Be8 17.Qb3 Rec7 18.a4 Ng6 19.a5 Nd7 20.e5!

Conceding Black the free use of d5, it is true, but in return obtaining for himself the superb point d6.

20...b6 21.Ne4 Rb8 22.Qc3

A superficial move which allows Black to place his Knight on d5 with a gain of tempo. Best would have been 22.Qa3.

22...Nf4 23.Nd6 Nd5 24.Qa3 f6

Somewhat more exact was 24...Qe7, drawing a bead on White's b-pawn.

25.Nxe8 Qxe8 26.exf6

This procedure may be compared to that in the game against Steiner (Example 234). Capablanca simplifies while firmly maintaining the initiative.

26...gxf6 27.b5 Rbc8 28.bxc6 Rxc6 29.Rxc6 Rxc6 30.axb6 axb6 31.Re1 (see next diagram)

Later analysis established that 31.Bb5 would have been still stronger.

31...Qc8 32.Nd2 Nf8

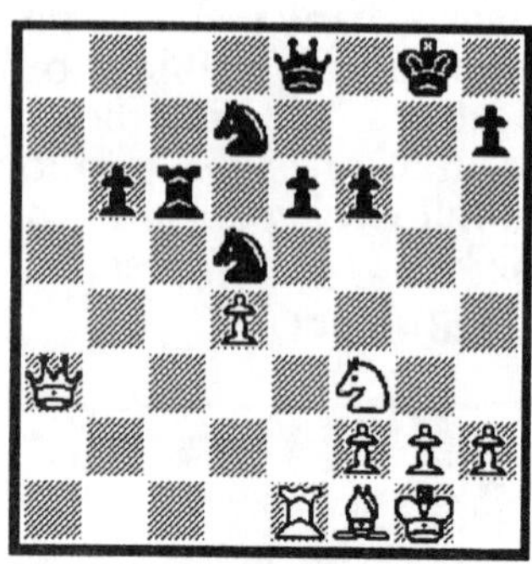

After 31.Re1

Bolstering up the King's position. After 32...Rc3 33.Qd6 Rc6 34.Qg3+ Kh8 35.Ne4 White's attack is decisive.

33.Ne4 Qd8 34.h4

Intending to meet 34...f5 with 35.Bb5 Rc7 36.Ng5. Black should now play 34...h6! with the idea of still getting in ...f5.

34...Rc7 35.Qb3 Rg7 36.g3 Ra7 37.Bc4 Ra5 38.Nc3 Nxc3 39.Qxc3 Kf7 40.Qe3 Qd6 41.Qe4 Ra4 42.Qb7+ Kg6

Or 42...Qe7 43.Qc6 Ra7 44.d5! and wins.

43.Qc8 Qb4 44.Rc1 Qe7

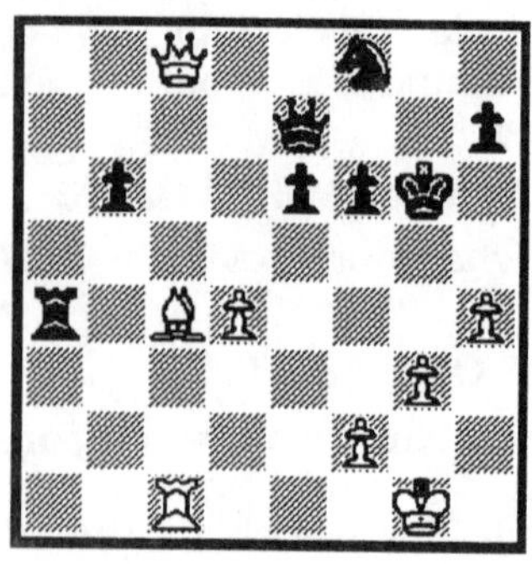

Nor does 44...Qa3 afford any salvation, for after the reply 45.Bd3+! the possibilities are: **1)** 45...Qxd3 46.Qe8+. **2)** 45...Kh6 46.Rc7. **3)** 45...f5 46.Qe8+ Kh6 47.Re1 Ra8 48.Rxe6+ Nxe6 49.Qxe6+ Kg7 50.Qe5+.

45.Bd3+ Kh6

After 45...f5 46.Bxf5+!, for then if 46...Kxf5 47.Qc2+, or if 46...exf5 47.Qc6+.

46.Rc7 Ra1+ 47.Kh2 Qd6 48.Qxf8+! Black Resigned.

8. CHAROUSEK (1873-1900)

Charousek died young, and his immense talent never was given a chance to fully ripen. It is said that as a schoolboy he found Bilguer's great *Handbuch* in a public library and copied out the whole thousand or so pages, memorizing much of it in the process. It is a strange story, but this Hungarian was a strange figure. His handling of the openings, his feeling for position and his flair for combination place him in the company of Morphy, Pillsbury, and Alekhine.

Although he lived at a time when the gambits offered fewer chances than had been the case in Morphy's day, he showed a marked liking for gambit play. Charousek's prime lasted only about two years (1896-97). The last three years of his life were a losing battle with tuberculosis.

EXAMPLE 236

(The game Charousek-Lasker, Nuremberg, 1896).

1.e4 e5 2.f4 exf4 3.Bc4 d5 4.Bxd5 Qh4+ 5.Kf1 g5 6.Nf3 Qh5 7.h4 Bg7

Black's treatment of White's opening shows clearly enough why the gambits went out of fashion at the end of the last century: Black has promptly returned the pawn in order to be able to develop his pieces.

8.Nc3 c6 9.Bc4 Bg4 10.d4 Nd7

In a later game Maroczy played 10...h6, preventing the following line.

11.Kf2!

11...Bxf3 12.gxf3 O-O-O 13.hxg5 Qxg5 14.Ne2

Winning the f-pawn. Black's only chance now is to make something out of the insecurity of the White King's position.

14...Qe7 15.c3 Ne5 16.Qa4 Nxc4 17.Qxc4 Nf6 18.Bxf4 Nd7 19.Qa4 a6 20.Qa5 Nf8 21.Ng3

Charousek keeps a firm grip on the game.

21...Ne6 22.Nf5 Qf8 23.Bg3 Rd7

There is no time for 23...Bf6 because of 24.d5 cxd5 25.exd5 Qc5+ 26.Qxc5 Nxc5 27.Nd6+ and wins.

24.Nxg7 Qxg7 25.Qe5 Qxe5 26.Bxe5 f6 27.Bxf6 Rf8 28.Rh6 Nf4 29.Ke3 Ng2+ 30.Kd2 Rdf7 31.e5 Nf4 32.Rah1

Since the diagramed position comment has been unnecessary– White wins without difficulty. This game – against the reigning world champion and the winner of the tournament – must have given Charousek great satisfaction.

32...Rg8 33.c4 Ne6 34.Ke3 Nf8 35.d5 Rd7 36.e6 Black Resigned.

9. CHIGORIN (1850-1908)

During his lifetime Chigorin was known as an ingenious exponent of attacking play. From his own comments it appears that he believed that his best talent was to be found in combinative play. The truth is that the brilliance of his combinative play was so great that it obscured the surprising fact that Chigorin lost more games through tactical mistakes than strategical ones. Nowadays he is recognized as the founder of the modern Russian school of chess.

Probably the best known of all strategic principles is that of keeping a foothold in the center. This is an idea which he sought to realize in a variety of ways. The main line of the Ruy Lopez is based on it: 1.e4 e5 2.Nf3 Nc6 3.Bb5 a6 4.Ba4 Nf6 5.O-O Be7 6.Re1 b5 7.Bb3 d6 8.c3 O-O 9.h3 Na5 10.Bc2 c5 11.d4 Qc7.

The same idea occurs in less familiar ways: 1.e4 e5 2.Nf3 Nc6 3.Bb5 Nf6 4.O-O d6 5.d4 Nd7; or 1.e4 e5 2.Nf3 Nc6 3.Bb5 a6 4.Ba4 Nf6 5.Nc3 d6 6.d4 Nd7 7.Ne2 f6. Some of Chigorin's opening experiments have become important parts of modern opening theory.

The strategic originality of the great Russian pioneer is exemplified in such lines as 1.e4 e6 2.Qe2, and 1.d4 d5 2.c4 Nc6. To the dogmatic thinking of Steinitz and Tarrasch, Chigorin opposed a freshness of ideas, a flair for seizing the tactical opportunity, and outstanding endgame technique.

Here is one of his games from his famous match with Tarrasch.

EXAMPLE 237
(Match-game (15) Tarrasch-Chigorin,1893).

1.e4 e5 2.Nf3 Nc6 3.Bb5 a6 4.Ba4 Nf6 5.Nc3 d6 6.d4 Nd7 7.Ne2 Be7 8.c3 O-O 9.Ng3 Bf6 10.h3

In order to not be forced into clearing up the center by 10...Nb6 11.Bb3 Bg4.

10...Ne7 11.O-O Ng6 12.Bb3 Re8 13.Qd3 Ndf8

These maneuvers behind the lines are typical of Steinitz. The Knight now threatens to come into play via e6.

14.Ne2 Qe7 15.Bc2

Tarrasch's aim, as shown in his analyses in his book *Dreihundert Schachpartien,* is to maintain his center pawns on e4 and d4. Chigorin, for his part, means to hold a pawn on e5. In the concentration of his pieces as far as possible on his own e-pawn we recognize the principle which was so enthusiastically championed later on by Nimzowitsch under the name "overprotection".

15...Bd7

Here Black could have freed his game by 15...d5. Presumably he preferred to not start simplifying yet; it is hardly likely that he was afraid of the continuation 16.dxe5 Nxe5 17.Nxe5 Qxe5 18.Ng3 dxe4 19.Nxe4, as given by his opponent.

16.Be3 Rad8

17.d5

Constricting the Black position – a strategy of which Tarrasch was a past master.

17...h6! 18.Kh2 Nh7 19.c4 Rf8

Black is playing for the counter-stroke ...f5, a method which to us, seventy years later, has become almost a matter of routine, for instance in the King's Indian.

20.Ng3 Ng5

If 20...Nf4 Tarrasch would have continued with 21.Bxf4 exf4 22.e5! fxg3+ 23.fxg3 g6 24.exf6. Black has a stronger move in 20...Rde8!, so as to meet 21.Nf5 with 21...Bxf5 22.exf5 e4!.

21.Nxg5 Bxg5 22.Nf5! Qf6

Forced, for 22...Bxf5 fails to 23.exf5 Nf4 24.Bxf4 Bxf4+ 25.g3 Bg5 26.f6, and White wins.

23.g3

Now the threat of 24.f4 forces some clearing of the situation.

23...Bxe3 24.fxe3! Nh8

24...Bxf5 would give White an overpowering advantage on the Kingside after 25.exf5 Ne7 26.g4.

25.Rf3 Rde8 26.Raf1 Bxf5

Now on 27.exf5? comes 27...e4.

27.Rxf5 Qe7 28.Bd1 g6 29.Rf6 Kg7

Threatening 30...Qxf6, and so stamping White's last move as a waste of time.

30.R6f2 f6

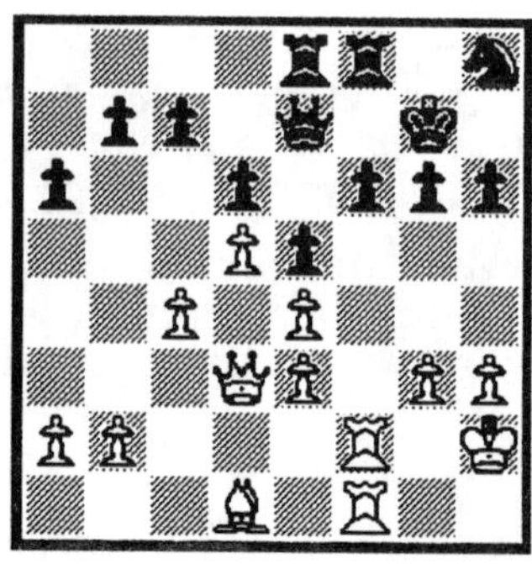

31.h4

Tarrasch gave this move a mark of disapproval, and expressed the opinion that 31.Bg4 instead would have given him a won game. His reasoning was as follows: the Black Knight can be kept away from g5 by h4, the advance of the Black f-pawn is prevented, and in due course White will bring about the decision by the Queenside advance b4 and c5. However, he gave no analysis to support this opinion, and we fail to see how it can be substantiated. For instance, after 31.Bg4 h5 32.Be6 c5 followed by ...Nf7 and ...Nh6, Black has enough counterplay.

31...h5! 32.g4

Still under the impression that he has the advantage.

32...hxg4 33.Kg3

If 33.Bxg4 there follows 33...f5 34.exf5 Qxh4+.

33...Nf7 34.Bxg4 Rh8 35.Rh2 Ref8 36.h5

This and White's next are still based on a wrong assessment of the position. He thinks he has the better of it, but the boot is on the other foot.

36...gxh5 37.Bxh5?

The temporary pawn sacrifice 37.Bf5 would have provided the best chance of counterplay.

37...Rfg8 38.Kf2 Kf8 39.Rfh1 Ng5 40.Ke2 Qh7

Laying bare the weakness of White's doubled pawn.

41.Rh4 Qg7 42.Qc2 Rh6 43.Qa4?

According to Tarrasch this move is the decisive mistake. After 43.Bg4! R8h8 44.Rxh6 Rxh6 45.Rxh6 Qxh6 46.Kd3 and 47.Bf5 he considered that White's game would be defensible. Tarrasch, however, was a dogmatist. Capablanca, who was above suspicion in this respect, said later that in endgames of Queen and Knight against Queen and Bishop the side with the Knight will have the better chances whenever threats are available, for these threats will not easily be repelled. In the present case, after 46...Qh1 47.Bf5 Nf3 Black has very definite threats.

43...Rxh5! 44.Rxh5 Nxe4 45.Qd1? Qg2+ White Resigned.

10. DONNER (1927-1988)

In many ways the style of Donner calls to mind that of Capablanca, especially as regards his handling of simple positions and his methods of liquidating.

There are points of dissimilarity, however. Donner was better acquainted with the openings; however, his endgame technique lacked the refinement of Capablanca's. Also his results showed much more fluctuation than that of the great Cuban in his day.

The following game might well have been played by Capablanca.

EXAMPLE 238

(The game O'Kelly-Donner, Beverwijk, 1963).

1.c4 Nf6 2.Nc3 e6 3.Nf3 d5 4.d4 Be7 5.Bg5 O-O 6.e3 b6 7.cxd5 Nxd5 8.Bxe7 Qxe7 9.Nxd5 exd5 10.Bd3 c5 11.dxc5 bxc5

Black has acquired hanging pawns- a center formation we discussed at some length in Chapter 20 *(The Middlegame, Book One).*

12.Qc2 g6 13.Rc1

13.O-O would have been safer.

13...Na6! (see next diagram)

14.a3

If White accepts the pawn sacrifice by 14.Bxa6 Bxa6 15.Qxc5, Black

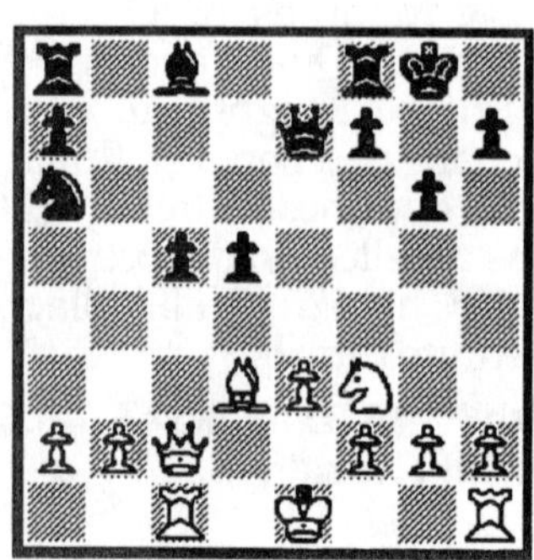

After 13...Na6!

continues 15...Qb7 and White, being unable to castle, finds his King wide open to a dangerous attack; e.g. 16.Qd4 Qb5 17.Qd2 Rac8.

14...c4! 15.Be2 Bf5 16.Qc3 Nc5 17.Nd4

Not 17.b4? because of 17...cxb3! 18.Qxc5 b2!.

17...Nd3+ 18.Bxd3 Bxd3 19.Nc6 Qe4 20.Qe5

Threatening 21.Ne7#, and so forcing off the Queens.

20...Rfe8! 21.Qxe4 dxe4 22.Rc3 a5!

Now 23.b3 fails against 23...Rac8! 24.Nxa5 cxb3 25.Rxc8 Rxc8 26.Nxb3 Rc3!.

23.a4 Ra6 24.Nd4 Rb6 25.Nb5 Re5 26.Ra3

Providing an answer to the threatened sacrifice of Rook for Knight and pawn. If now 26...Rexb5 27.axb5 Rxb5; White can play 28.Ra2 Bb1 29.Ra1 Rxb2 30.O-O Bd3 31.Rfc1 followed by Rc3 and Rca3.

26...h5! 27.h4 Rf5

Now Black threatens to win by 28...Rbf6.

28.g3 Kg7 29.Rh2 Kf6 30.Kd2

Without hope is 30.b3: 30...cxb3 31.Rxb3 Bxb5 32.Rxb5 Rfxb5 33.axb5 Rxb5.

30...Ke5 31.b3 Rbf6 32.Ke1 Kd5

If now 33.bxc4+ Kxc4, and the Black King forces a decisive entry into White's position.

33.Nd4

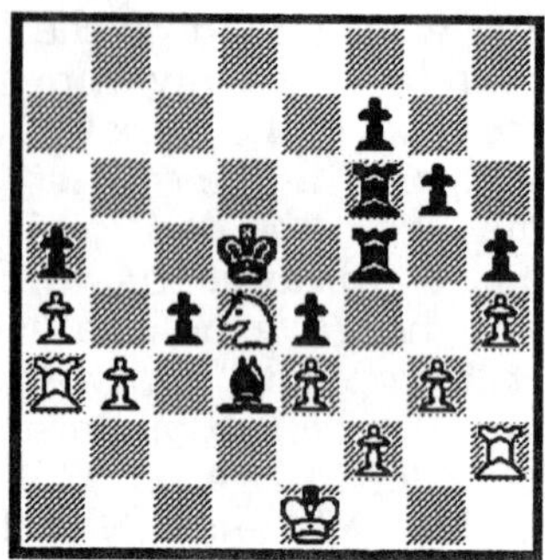

33...c3!!

Worthily crowning this game with a fine Exchange sacrifice.

34.Nxf5 Rxf5 35.Ra1 Kc5 36.Rd1 Rd5

To the immediate 36...Kb4 White could reply 37.f4.

37.f4 exf3 38.Rf2 Be2! White Resigned.

For after 39.Rxd5+ Kxd5 40.Rxe2 fxe2 41.Kxe2 Ke4 42.b4 axb4 43.a5 Kd5 the pawn ending is well and truly lost.

11. DURAS (1882-1957)

The Czech grandmaster was outstanding as a practical player. From the combinative viewpoint he was very strong; from the positional point of view he was less strong. This, of course, could be said of many players, but what particularly distinguished Duras was his ingenuity in bad positions. Only when his situation became critical did he really begin to play. Then all his fighting instinct was aroused and the idea of having a lost game rarely entered his head.

The consequence was that many a game which others might have resigned he miraculously saved.

EXAMPLE 239

(The game Teichmann-Duras, San Sebastian, 1912).

1.d4 Nf6 2.c4 b6 3.Nc3 Bb7 4.Nf3 d5

Black's opening play was nothing less than revolutionary when it was played. No one could have expected that it would one day become respectable as the Queen's Indian. At this point, however, we know that 4...e6 is the more appropriate choice.

5.cxd5 Nxd5 6.e3 e6 7.Bb5+ c6 8.Bd3 Bd6 9.O-O Nd7 10.Ne4 Bc7 11.Bd2 O-O 12.Rc1 e5 13.Ng3 exd4 14.exd4 Nf4?

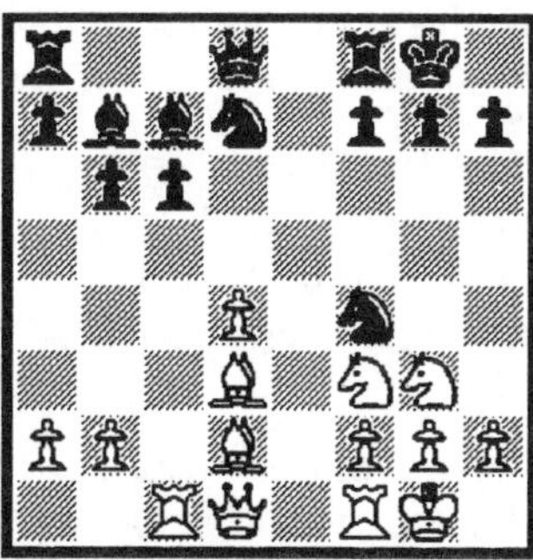

Duras is well on the way to overcoming his opening difficulties, but now, instead of seeking further simplification by 14...c5, he plays optimistically for the attack.

15.Be4 Rc8

Defending c6 indirectly: if 16.Bxc6 then 16...Ba6 17.Re1 Nd3, or if 17.Bxf4 Bxf4 winning the Exchange.

16.Qa4 Nb8 17.Rfe1

After 17.Bf5 Black has the resource 17...Ba6. All the time Black works with tactical finesses.

17...a5 18.Qc2 g6 19.Rcd1 Nd5 20.Bg5 Qd6 21.Qd2

The tournament book suggests 21.Bxd5 Qxd5 22.Ne4 as a better line.

21...f6 22.Bh6 Rf7 23.Bc2 Nd7 24.a3 Nf8 25.Bb3 Rd8 26.Qc2 Bc8 27.Rc1 Bb7

28.Ne4

Now it is clear that White has the better game. He has an alternative strong line here in 28.Ba4, to force the weakening 28...b5.

28...Qd7 29.Ba4 Rc8

Again c6 is defended indirectly: now 30.Bxc6 Bxc6 31.Qxc6 Bxh2+ wins for Black. Note that this would not be possible if White had not played 28.Ne4.

30.Nc3!

Threatening 31.Nxd5 Qxd5 32.Bb3.

30...Qg4 31.Nxd5 cxd5 32.Be8!

White advantage has assumed decisive proportions.

32...Bf4 33.Bxf7+ Kxf7 34.Qe2

Threatening not only 35.Qe7+ with mate next move, but also 35.Ne5+ winning the Queen. Black can think of resigning.

34...Bxh6 35.Ne5+ fxe5 36.Qxg4 Bxc1 37.dxe5?

According to the tournament book White could have forced the win by 37.Rxe5. After the move played, the chances are rather different.

37...Bxb2 38.h4 Ke8 39.Rb1 Rc4 40.Qg5 Bd4 41.Rd1

Here White overlooks the opportunity 41.Rb3.

41...Bc5 42.Rd2 Bxa3 43.Qf6 Rc6 44.Qg7 Be7 45.Rd3 a4 46.Rf3 Ne6 47.Qxh7 a3 48.Rf7

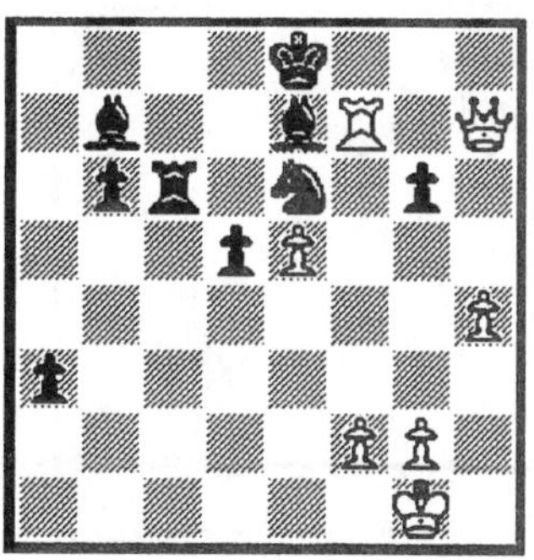

A last dangerous attempt; but the Black a-pawn is now too far advanced.

48...Rc7 49.Qxg6 a2! 50.Qxe6 a1=Q+ 51.Kh2 Qa4 52.f4 Qc6 53.Qf5 Qh6 54.Rh7 Qf8 55.Qg6+ Kd8 56.Rf7 Qh8 57.h5 Rc6

With the finesse 58.e6? Rxe6! 59.Qxe6 Qxh5+!.

58.Rh7 Qf8 59.Qg4 Bc8 60.Qf3 Qg8 61.Qd3 Bd7 and **White Resigned.** The miracle has happened!

12. EUWE (1910-1981)

One of the authors of this book would have preferred not to include this section dealing with himself, but the other one insisted, and there was no way out of it. However, we make no attempt at a stylistic analysis, but content ourselves with a game – one in which Euwe is seen fighting Alekhine with one of his own weapons, namely Alekhine's Defense. On principle this is good policy, but naturally opportunities are not frequent. The counter-gambit principle in the openings is based on the same idea; e.g. the Falkbeer: 1.e4 e5 2.f4 d5.

EXAMPLE 240

(The 29th match-game Alekhine-Euwe, 1935).

1.e4 Nf6 2.e5 Nd5 3.d4 d6 4.c4 Nb6 5.Nf3 Bg4 6.Be2 dxe5 7.c5 e4 8.cxb6 exf3 9.Bxf3 Bxf3 10.Qxf3

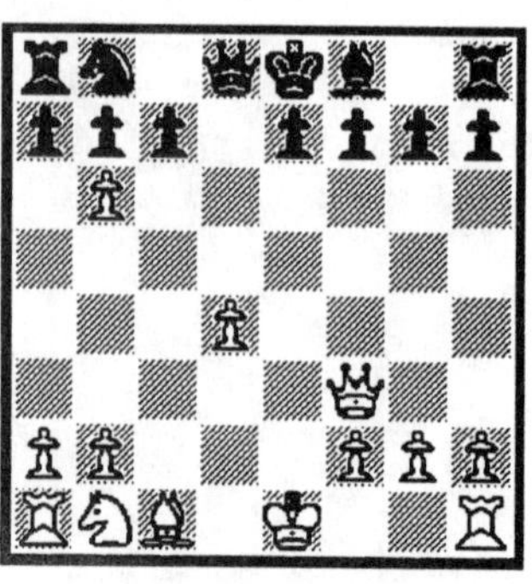

White is ahead in development, but also has the weaker pawn structure since the isolated d-pawn may become a liability.

A tempting idea here was to play 10...Nc6, attacking the d-pawn at once, but it would have achieved nothing; White would simply let the pawn go, by 11.O-O!, and then if 11...Nxd4? 12.Qxb7; or if 11...axb6 12.d5 with excellent attacking chances.

Black's choice in the diagram is more difficult than one might suppose, mainly because 10...c6 11.bxa7 Rxa7 12.O-O leaves Black very passively placed. In the actual game, in view of the above considerations, he sought freedom in a pawn sacrifice. Afterwards it emerged that the simplest line would have been 10...Nc6 11.O-O, and then 11...e6!.

10...axb6 11.Qxb7 Nd7 12.Bf4 e5!

The point.

13.Bxe5 Nxe5 14.dxe5 Bb4+ 15.Nc3 Bxc3+ 16.bxc3 O-O 17.O-O Qe7

The situation is completely reversed: the pawn sacrifice has produced an almost forced liquidation, removing all the minor pieces from the board. Black now has a slight pull in development, and White's weak pawns are ready made targets.

18.Rfe1 Qc5 19.Re3 Ra3 20.Qf3

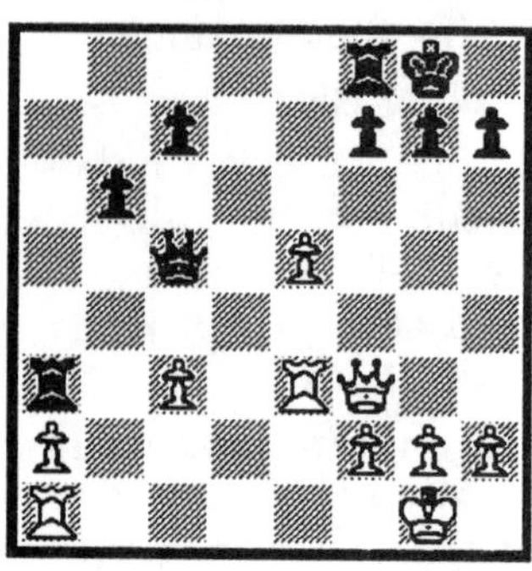

20...Re8?

After this Black has problems. By 20...Qc4! he could have recovered his pawn with immediate equality.

21.h3! Ra5

After 21...Rxe5 22.Rd1 h6 23.Rd7, White is attacking again.

22.Rd1 Qe7 23.Qc6!

Threatening 24.Rd7, and at the same time indirectly defending the e-pawn: 23...Rxe5? 24.Qxe8+! Qxe8 25.Rxe5, followed by R5d5 wins.

23...Rc5 24.Qd7 g6 25.f4 Rc4 26.Qxe7 Rxe7 27.Rd4 Rc5 28.Kf2 c6 29.a4 Ra7 30.Rb4 b5 31.axb5 cxb5 32.Kf3 Rac7

With 32...Ra3 Black could force an ending with three pawns against four, but under circumstances favorable to White. Black therefore decides to keep the Rooks on the board.

33.Rb3 Kf8 34.g4

White could have made things more difficult for his opponent by 34.Kg4.

34...Ke7 35.f5? gxf5 36.gxf5 f6!

This leads to the win of a pawn.

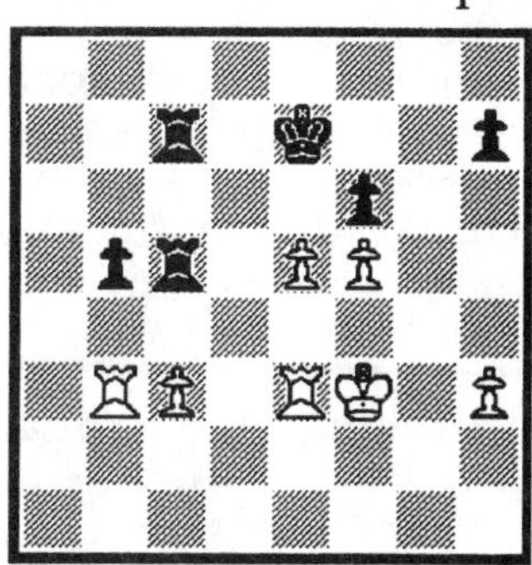

37.Kf4 fxe5+ 38.Rxe5+ Rxe5 39.Kxe5 Rc5+ 40.Ke4 Kf6 41.Ra3 Rc4+ 42.Kd3 Rh4 43.Rb3 Kxf5 44.Rxb5+ Ke6 45.c4 Rxh3+ 46.Kd4 Kd6 47.Rb6+ Kc7 48.Rf6 Rh5 49.Kc3 Kb7 50.Kb4 Kc7 Draw.

13. FINE (1914-1993)

The style of the Grandmaster Fine is best described as technically very good, but for the rest, relatively neutral. The truth is that he handled all sorts of positions well, without showing definite preference for any. His style was polished, his games streamlined. After the war Fine virtually withdrew from competitive chess. Here is a game in which he demonstrates the style which perhaps fitted his temperament best.

EXAMPLE 241

(The game Fine-Alekhine, Margate, 1937).

1.d4 e6 2.c4 f5 3.g3 Nf6 4.Bg2 Bb4+ 5.Bd2 Be7 6.Nc3 Nc6

With this move, the object of which is to induce complications, Alekhine had varying success. In this game Fine demonstrates its drawbacks.

7.d5! Ne5 8.Qb3 O-O 9.Nh3 Ng6 10.dxe6 dxe6 11.Rd1

Inferior is 11.Bxb7 Bxb7 12.Qxb7 Rb8 13.Qxa7 Rxb2 with counterplay for Black.

11...c6 12.O-O e5!?

The less trenchant 12...Kh8 would have been preferable.

13.c5+ Kh8 14.Ng5 Qe8 15.Ne6 Bxe6 16.Qxe6 Bxc5

After 16...Qc8 17.Qxc8 Raxc8 18.Bh3 White's two Bishops give him a clear advantage in the endgame.

17.Qxf5

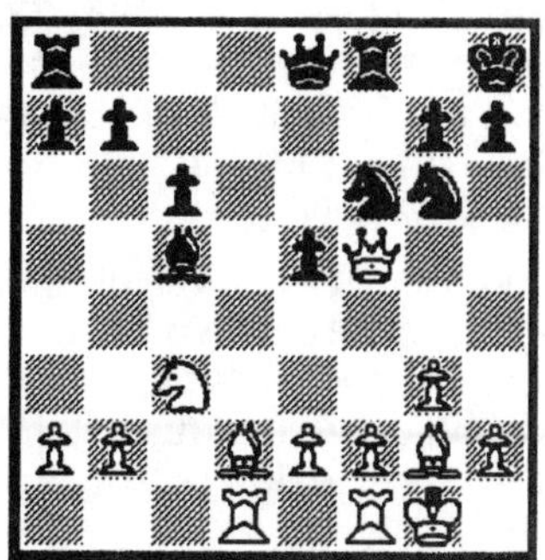

From a positional point of view, White has won the first round: he has the two Bishops and the better pawn structure.

17...Rd8 18.Qc2 Qe6 19.Na4 Be7 20.a3 Rd4

Now the obvious 21.Nc5 would lose: 21...Bxc5 22.Qxc5 R8d8 23.Qc2 Qd7 and Black wins a piece.

21.h3 b5

Black thinks he can go over to the offensive, but this move only weakens his pawn structure even more.

22.Nc3 a5 23.Be3 Rxd1 24.Rxd1 b4

Better would have been 24...Rd8.

25.axb4 axb4 26.Na4 Nd5 27.Bc5 Qf7 28.e3 Rc8

29.Qc4!

With the main threat of 30.e4.

29...Qf8

What else? After 29...Rf8 30.Rd2, or after 29...Bxc5 30.Nxc5 Rf8 31.Rd2, a pawn is bound to fall.

30.Bxe7 Ngxe7 31.e4 Nf6 32.Qxb4 Rd8 33.Rxd8 Qxd8 34.Nc5 Qd6 35.Qc3 h6 36.Nd3 Nd7 37.h4 Ng6 38.Bh3 Ngf8 39.b4 h5 40.Nc5 Nf6 41.Qc4 Qe7 42.Nb3!

The familiar maneuvering principle (See Part 9). The e-pawn has been kept under pressure as long as possible; now White switches his attention to Black's other weakness, the c-pawn.

42...Qd6 43.Na5 Qd2 44.Nxc6 Qe1+ 45.Bf1 Nxe4 46.Qe2

This settles it. The finish was:

46...Qxe2 47.Bxe2 g6 48.Nxe5 Nc3 49.Bd3 Kg7 50.f4 Nd5 51.b5 Kf6 52.Kf2 Nb6 53.Ke3 Na4 54.Kd4 Ne6+ 55.Kd5 Nc7+ 56.Kc6 Ne6 57.b6 Nd8+ 58.Kd7 Ne6 59.b7 Nac5+ 60.Kc8 Black Resigned.

14. FISCHER (Born 1943)

Usually the style of a chessmaster has to grow; it may take years before one may speak of any style at all. As a rule the young player begins with pure combination, and then in the course of time finds that he must add water to wine. He learns the methods of positional play, and develops endgame technique.

It is quite possible to begin as a combinative player – a tactician – and yet in maturing to acquire an out-and-out positional style of play.

The exceptional Grandmaster Fischer, however, is another and almost unique story in modern chess. At the age of twenty he already possessed a fully rounded style. He is both tactician and strategist, an openings expert without peer, and a virtuoso of the endgame.

The following game against Reshevsky is a good example of his super-class, technical style.

EXAMPLE 242

(The game Fischer-Reshevsky, New York 1963).

1.e4 c5 2.Nf3 d6 3.d4 cxd4 4.Nxd4 Nf6 5.Nc3 a6 6.h3 g6 7.g4 Bg7 8.g5 Nh5 9.Be2 e5 10.Nb3 Nf4 11.Nd5 Nxd5

A stronger line is 11...O-O 12.Nxf4 exf4 13.Bxf4 Bxb2 14.Bxd6 Re8.

12.Qxd5 Nc6 13.Bg4 Bxg4

Another inaccuracy; he should have played 13...Qe7 followed by ...Be6.

14.hxg4 Qc8 15.Qd1 Nd4 16.c3 Nxb3 17.axb3 Qe6 18.Ra5 f6 19.Qd5!

Now 19...Qxg4 would allow 20.Qxb7 O-O 21.gxf6!.

19...Qxd5 20.Rxd5 Kd7 21.gxf6 Bxf6

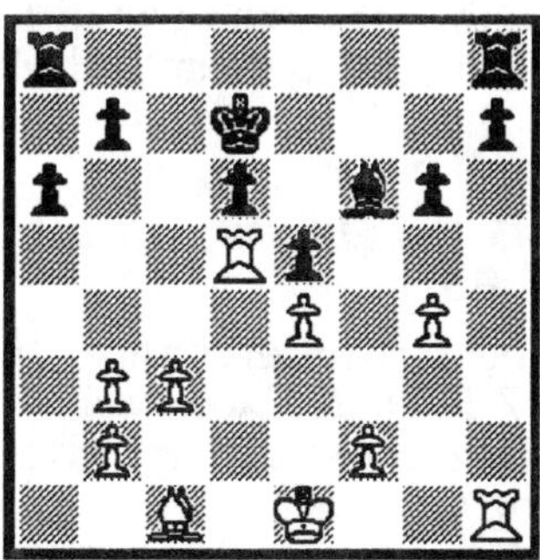

22.g5! Be7

Forced, for if 22...Bg7 White plays his Rook back from d5 to d3 and h3 to win the h-pawn.

23.Ke2 Raf8 24.Be3 Rc8 25.b4

Intending in due course to dissolve his doubled pawn by b5, and saddle Black with a weak pawn on the Queenside.

25...b5

This should have been avoided if possible. Black now has three vulnerable points– a6, d6, and h7. How to profit from a situation like this was the subject of Part 9- The Technique of Maneuvering. The present game prettily supplements the examples there given.

26.Rdd1! Ke6 27.Ra1 Rc6 28.Rh3

Threatening to win the h-pawn by Rah1.

28...Bf8 29.Rah1 Rc7 30.Rh4!

Putting Black in a state of *zugzwang*.

30...d5

Or 30...Rc4 31.f3 Rc7 32.R4h3!.

31.Ra1 Rc6

Not 31...dxe4 32.Rxa6+, after which 32...Kf5 allows 33.Rf6#, while 32...Kd5 loses a pawn to 33.Rxg6.

32.exd5+ Kxd5 33.Rd1+ Ke6 34.Rd8 Kf5

White threatened 35.Re8+ Kf5 36.Rxe5+! Kxe5 37.Bd4+ Kf5 38.Bxh8 Kxg5 39.Rxh7.

35.Ra8 Re6 36.Rh3

Black has no good defense against 37.Rf3+; e.g. 36...Kg4 37.Rg3+ Kh4 38.Rf3 Bg7 39.Ra7 Rg8 40.Rd7! and the Black King is in a mating net.

36...Bg7 37.Rxh8 Bxh8 38.Rxh7 Re8 39.Rf7+ Kg4

The best move was 39...Ke4, but there is no saving the game. If 39...Ke6 White wins by 40.Ra7.

40.f3+ Kg3 41.Kd3

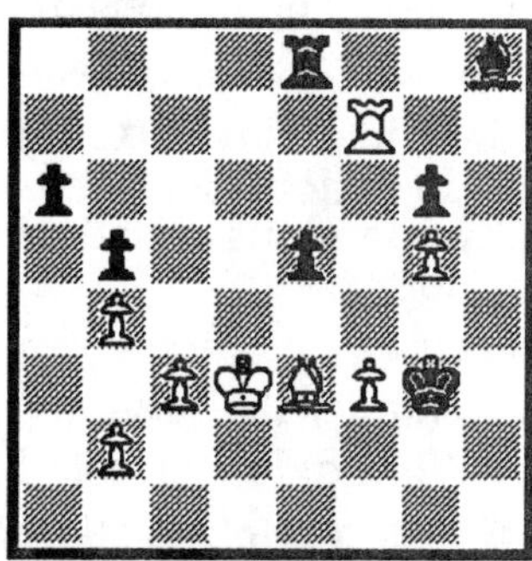

An aesthetic flaw. By 41.Kf1!, threatening 42.Bf2+ Kh3 43.Rh7#, White could force the game at once, for if 41...Kh4 42.Kg2 and White mates.

41...e4+ 42.fxe4 Rd8+ 43.Bd4 Kg4 44.Rf1 Be5

Or if 44...Kxg5 45.Rg1+ Kf4 46.Rxg6, White wins easily.

45.Ke3 Bc7 46.Rg1+ Kh5 47.Kf3 Rd7 48.e5 Rf7+ 49.Ke4 Rf5 50.e6 Bd8 51.Bf6 Bxf6 52.gxf6 Rxf6 53.Kd5 Rf2 54.Re1 Black Resigned.

15. FLOHR (1908-1983)

Flohr was a player of splendid positional style. He would hold on to the tiniest of advantages and exploit them with infinite patience and accuracy; but he was also a formidable tactician – in particular in his early years. About 1936 his style began to take on a defensive cast, and this was the main reason why this Grandmaster never became a serious threat to Alekhine.

Here is a fine example of Flohr's positional and tactical powers.

EXAMPLE 243

(The game Flohr-Donner, Beverwijk, 1960).

1.Nf3 c5 2.c4 Nc6 3.g3 g6 4.Bg2 Bg7 5.O-O a6 6.Nc3 Rb8

Preparing the advance ...b5, the object of which is to enhance the action of the Bg7 on the long diagonal.

7.d3 b5 8.cxb5 axb5 9.Be3 Nd4

If 9...d6 White plays 10.d4. Black's Queenside action has been rather premature, and its disadvantages begin to appear.

10.Rc1 d6

Better would have been 10...e6, to deprive White of his control of d5.

11.Bxd4 cxd4 12.Nd5 e6 13.Nb4!

Blocking the b-pawn. Black's Queenside attack has only weakened his position there.

13...Ne7 14.Qc2 Bh6?

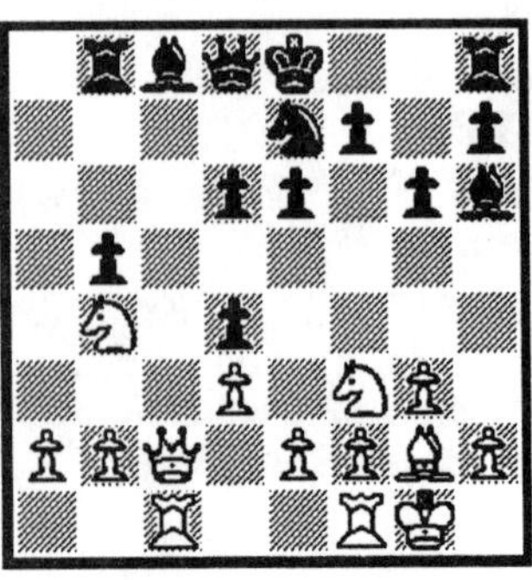

The idea is to expel White's Rook from the c-file; but Black's best hope of keeping his disadvantage to a minimum would have been 14...O-O 15.Qc7 Bb7.

15.Nxd4! Bxc1 16.Ndc6 Nxc6 17.Nxc6 Qc7 18.Qc3!

This is the point of White's 15th move. Now 18...Bxb2 would be met by 19.Qxb2 O-O 20.Nxb8 Qxb8 21.Bc6 b4 22.Ba4, followed by 23.Rb1, winning a pawn.

18...O-O 19.Nxb8 Qxc3 20.bxc3 Bd2 21.Rb1 Bb7!

The best counterchance. If now 22.Bxb7 Rxb8 23.Rxb5 Bxc3 and the opposite colored Bishops give Black drawing chances.

22.Nd7! Bxg2 23.Kxg2

23.Nxf8 would be an error; after 23...Bc6! the Knight has no escape.

23...Ra8 24.Rxb5 Ra7

Realizing that the normal 24...Rxa2 25.Nf6+ would be hopeless for Black: 25...Kg7 26.Ne8+ Kf8 27.Nxd6 Bxc3 28.Rb7 Rxe2 29.Rxf7+; or 25...Kf8 26.c4, and White's technical problem is not difficult.

25.Nf6+ Kg7 26.Ne8+ Kf8 27.Nxd6 Bxc3

Or 27...Rxa2 28.Rb7.

28.Rb8+ Kg7 29.Nb5 Black Resigned.

16. GLIGORIC (Born 1923)

Grandmaster Gligoric's style is reminiscent of Capablanca, Fine, and Flohr. In addition to his highly developed feeling for slight advantages and his excellent endgame skills, he has a very durable, tenacious temperament. His skill in holding on firmly to a positional advantage through all sorts of complications has made him a formidable opponent for even elite players of the world. It is very appropriate, therefore, that he was the first player to defeat Petrosian after he won the World Championship.

Example 244

(The game Gligoric-Petrosian, Los Angeles 1963).

1.e4 e5 2.Nf3 Nc6 3.Bb5 a6 4.Ba4 Nf6 5.O-O Be7 6.Re1 b5 7.Bb3 O-O 8.c3 d6 9.h3 Nb8

This variation has been tried repeatedly since the Second World War. The principle however is far from new: Steinitz frequently withdrew developed pieces to the back rank in order to redeploy them more effectively later.

10.d4 Nbd7 11.c4 c6 12.c5! Qc7 13.cxd6 Bxd6 14.Bg5 exd4!?

This raises a question which is perpetually debated: which is more important – active play for the pieces, or disruption of the pawn position? Here Black voluntarily permits the doubling of his f-pawn.

15.Bxf6 gxf6 16.Nxd4 Nc5 17.Nf5 Bxf5 18.exf5 Rad8 19.Qh5

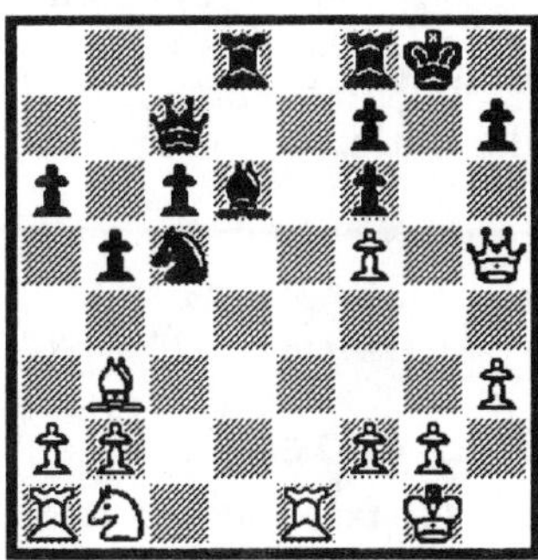

19...Be5

The critical moment. Black's pieces are active, and by 20...b4 21.Qe2 Bf4 he could have put considerable difficulties in the way of White's development.

20.Nc3 Rd4 21.Re3 Bf4 22.Re2 Bd2 23.Nd1 Bg5 24.g3 Qd6 25.Ne3 Bxe3

Black cannot allow this Knight to come nosing into his weakened King position.

26.Rxe3 Kg7 27.Bc2 Qd5 28.a3 Rd2 29.Qg4+ Kh8 30.Rd1!

Forcing Black into an endgame in which the activity of his pieces will count for less, while the weakness of his pawns will be accentuated.

30...Rxd1+ 31.Qxd1 Qxd1+ 32.Bxd1 Rd8 33.Bf3 Rd3

Black must play an active game, for after 33...Rd6 34.Rc3 Na4 35.Rc2! c5 36.b3 he would have no counterplay at all.

34.Re8+ Kg7 35.Bxc6 Rb3 36.Re7 Rxb2 37.Bd5 Kh6 38.Bxf7 Kg5 39.Be6!

And now, although nearly all the pieces have disappeared, White is threatening mate: 40.f4+ Kh6 41.Bg8, and mate on h7.

39...Nxe6 40.fxe6 Kf5 41.Rxh7 Kxe6 42.Ra7 Ra2 43.Rxa6+ Black Resigned.

17. JANOWSKY (1860-1927)

Janowsky was universally feared when he was on the attack; he produced many sparkling gems of combinative play. He had some conspicuous shortcomings, the most serious of which was his lack of self-control and self-criticism.

He always played to win, even when there was no justification for so doing, and this was often the very reason he lost. He was a typical "natural" player, with a fine instinct for the position but no knowledge of theoretical niceties.

He never shrank from any kind of complications, and never knew the meaning of fear.

Example 245

(The game Janowsky-Chajes, New York, 1918).

1.d4 Nf6 2.Nf3 d5 3.c4 e6 4.Bg5 Be7 5.e3 Nbd7 6.Nc3 c6 7.Bd3 dxc4 8.Bxc4 b5 9.Bd3 a6 10.O-O c5 11.Rc1 Bb7 12.Qe2 O-O 13.Rfd1

Janowsky has played the opening entirely without finesse, bringing his pieces into play in the customary manner.

13...Qb6 14.Ne5

This threatens 15.Nxd7, and Black can't stop this with 14...Nxe5 because of 15.dxe5 Nd5 16.Nxd5 and 17.Bxe7.

14...Rfe8 15.dxc5 Nxc5 16.Bxf6 Bxf6

17.Bxh7+!

The classic sacrifice on h7 again. See Chapter 27 A, the section on Kingside attacks.

17...Kxh7 18.Qh5+ Kg8 19.Qxf7+ Kh7 20.Nd7 Nxd7 21.Rxd7 Bc6 22.Ne4!

The brilliant point of White's combination. If now 22...Bxe4 there follows 23.Qxf6 Rg8 24.Qh4+ Kg6 25.Qxe4 and wins. And if 22...Bxd7 then 23.Nxf6+ wins immediately.

22...Bxb2 23.Ng5+ Kh6

Or 23...Kh8 24.Qh5+ Kg8 25.Qh7+, and mates.

24.g4! g6

If 24...Kxg5 25.Qh5+ Kf6 26.Rf7#.

25.h4 Rh8 26.Qh7+! Black Resigned.

18. KERES (1916-1975)

The Estonian Grandmaster Keres was a richly imaginative player in his youth – but not only in his youth: in his maturity the same description held good.

The difference is that in his early days his temperament ran ahead of his technique, so that sometimes his methods were too risky and his combinations not sound. In his later years Keres matured into a complete positional player, while acquiring a perfect knowledge of the openings. Add to this the fact that he had reached great heights in the endgame and we see Keres as the possessor of an ideal style.

Keres himself considered that combinative play best suited his personality. His great skill in dealing with complications was developed largely through correspondence play. In his postal games his one aim was to build up the tension, and he used to steer for complications right from the start. However, experience taught him that in the end the accumulation of small advantages pays better than always going for the attack at all costs.

Our illustration is one of his earliest games.

Example 246

(Keres-Laurentius, Correspondence, 1934/5).

1.e4 e6 2.d4 d5 3.e5

This used to be a favorite weapon of Keres against the French Defense.

3...c5 4.Nf3 Qb6 5.Bd3!? cxd4 6.O-O Nc6

This obvious move is not best. The accurate path is 6...Nd7!, reserving c6 for the other Knight.

7.Nbd2 Nge7

Black misses another opportunity; he should have played 7...f6!.

8.Nb3 Ng6 9.Qe2 Qc7 10.Nbxd4! Ngxe5 11.Nb5! Nxf3+ 12.Qxf3 Qd7

This strange-looking move aims to keep the possibility of playing ...Qf7 later, and reserving d8 for the King. After 12...Qd8 13.Bf4 e5 14.Re1 f6 15.Qh5+ the King would have to go to e7.

13.Bf4 e5 14.Rfe1 f6 15.Rad1!

A very fine move, powerfully completing White's development.

15...Be7

Black's best chance was to play 15...a6 16.Qh5+ Kd8 17.Be4 axb5 18.Rxd5 exf4 19.R1d1!, after which Black can at least defend himself better than in the game.

16.Bc4! d4 17.Be6! Qd8 18.Bxe5!

Keres is in his element. This sacrifice is based on two possibilities: 18...fxe5? 20.Qf7#, and 18...Nxe5 19.Rxe5 Bxe6 20.Rxe6, and Black defense is cracked.

18...Bxe6 19.Nc7+ Kf7 20.Nxe6

Since the Knight can't be taken because of 21.Bc7+ White has recovered all of his material, and in view of Black's insecure King, the game is as good as over. But Keres still has some pretty points to show us.

20...Qa5 21.Bxd4 Qxa2

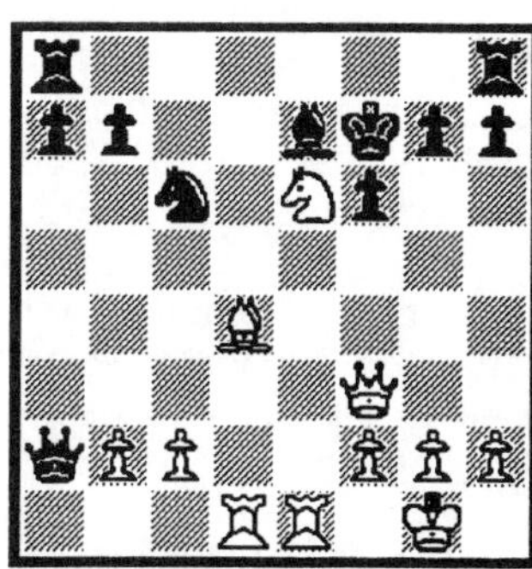

22.Bxf6!! Bxf6

He would have been no better off with 22...gxf6 23.Qh5+ Kg8 24.Qg4+ Kf7 25.Qg7+ Ke8 26.Nc7#.

23.Rd7+ Ne7

On any of the three King moves White still wins handsomely: **1)** 23...Kg8 24.Qxf6! gxf6 25.Rg7#. **2)** 23...Ke8 24.Rxb7!. **3)** 23...Kg6 24.Rxg7+! Bxg7 25.Qg4+ Kf7 26.Qxg7+ Ke8 27.Nc5+ forcing mate.

24.Rxe7+ Kxe7 25.Qxb7+

Or 25...Ke8 26.Ng5+ Kd8 27.Rd1+ Ke8 28.Qxa8+ Ke7 29.Qb7+ Ke8 30.Qc8+ Ke7 31.Rd7#.

25...Kd6 26.Qc7+ Kd5 27.Qc5#.

19. Em. LASKER (1868-1941)

The style of Emanual Lasker was unique. He had not quite the creative powers of Alekhine, nor quite such an intense will to win; but instead he possessed incomparable skill in provoking errors and remarkable ingenuity in exploiting them. His attentiveness, his powers of concentration and his tactical prowess were nothing short of miraculous. He also had very good nerves, evidenced by the fact that he made fewer nervous slips than almost any other world class player. (One of the very few instances on record was his famous loss to Torre, Moscow, 1925).

The layout of his games was generally quiet and unpretentious. One might describe him as lying in wait; but he was certainly not passive. His defense was superb. We devoted the whole of Chapter 31 to it, with varied examples.

In the openings he liked to create and maintain tension, and he never shrank from complications. In the wildest positions he seemed to know better than anyone the best plan of action, or – an even more difficult matter – which would be relatively best.

Lasker's name is associated with several opening lines. Lasker's Defense in the orthodox Queen's Gambit Declined (1.d4 d5 2.c4 e6 3.Nc3 Nf6 4.Bg5 Be7 5.e3 O-O 6.Nf3 Ne4) and Lasker's Defense to the Evans Gambit (1.e4 e5 2.Nf3 Nc6 3.Bc4 Bc5 4.b4 Bxb4 5.c3 Ba5 6.O-O d6 7.d4 Bb6!) have both had considerable effect on opening theory. Indeed, their influence extends beyond the opening into the sphere of middle-game style, for with these variations Lasker showed that a sound position could not be overrun.

Above all Lasker was a fighter. He probed the weak points in his opponents armory. Against the positional player he would introduce every tactical possibility; the combinative expert he would combat by positional means. In pursuit of these ends he would take great risks; there are instances on record in which he deliberately chose inferior lines for the sole purpose of getting his opponent into the sort of position in which he would feel ill at ease. Nor did Lasker content himself with seeking loopholes in his opponents' chess technique: he went so far as to play upon weaknesses in their actual mental make-up. He knew, for instance, that Janowsky set great store in the two Bishops, and that he possessed boundless optimism. The combination of these two factors meant that once Janowsky had the two Bishops he was apt to consider the game as good as won – a mental attitude from which Lasker profited more than once.

Example 247

(The game Janowsky-Lasker, St. Petersburg, 1914).

1.d4 d5 2.Nf3 c5 3.c4 e6 4.e3 Nc6 5.Bd3 Nf6 6.O-O Bd6 7.b3 O-O 8.Bb2 b6 9.Nbd2 Bb7 10.Ne5 Qe7 11.a3

To prevent 11...cxd4 12.exd4 Ba3.

11...Rad8 12.Qc2 dxc4 13.Ndxc4

Preferable was 13.bxc4. Black could then, if he wished, have given White the familiar hanging pawns by 13...cxd4 14.exd4.

13...cxd4 14.exd4 Rc8 15.Qe2 Bb8 16.f4 Nd5

Black takes advantage of the outpost on d5 afforded by White's isolated d-pawn.

17.Rae1 f5!

This weakens his own e-pawn, it is true, but it also limits much of White's attacking prospects on the Kingside.

18.Qd2

Janowsky was an attacking player, and he had no love for patient, long, drawn-out maneuvering – which is precisely what the present position requires.

18...Nxe5 19.Nxe5

In the tournament book Tarrasch said that White would have done better to recapture with the d-pawn. He was probably right, but Janowsky was evidently out to make something of his attack on the weak e-pawn.

19...a6 20.Bb1 Bd6 21.Nc4 b5 22.Na5 Ba8 23.b4

Thus White establishes his cavalry route via b3 to c5; but Black has an exactly corresponding route available.

23...Nb6 24.Nb3 Bd5 25.Nc5 Nc4 26.Qc3 Rf6!

This parries the threat of 27.Nxe6 Bxe6 28.d5, and indirectly protects the a-pawn too, for if 27.Nxa6 Bxg2 28.Kxg2 Qb7+ would be decisive.

27.Bc1 a5 28.Rf2 axb4 29.axb4 Ra8 30.Ba2 Qf7 31.Bxc4

This must have been a painful decision for Janowsky in view of his predilection for the two Bishops.

31...Bxc4 32.Bb2

To keep Black busy watching the possibility of d5.

32...Rg6 33.Ra1

After the exchange of Rooks which follows now, the White Bishop is unable to protect the f-pawn from c1- a fact which Lasker proceeds to put to good use. This is a piece of typical maneuvering technique.

33...Rxa1+ 34.Bxa1 Qc7! 35.Qe3 Rg4! 36.g3

An unavoidable weakening. 36.Nxe6 would have been bad, of course, because of the reply 36...Qe7.

36...g5!

In the manner of Steinitz, Lasker has accumulated a variety of small advantages. Now comes the moment to strike. As Lasker put it in his famous manual, it is no longer merely that Black *can* attack, but that he *must*. The player who does not attack in such positions, said Lasker, forfeits all his fighting spirit, and will go under.

37.d5

A very dangerous attack, but Lasker has reckoned it all out.

37...Bxd5 38.Qd4 gxf4 39.Qh8+ Kf7 40.Qxh7+ Ke8 41.Qh8+ Bf8 42.Be5 Qf7 43.Rxf4 Rxf4 44.Bxf4

So far everything has gone well for White, but now Lasker plays his ace.

44...Qg7! 45.Qh5+

Exchange of Queens would leave Black with a favorable endgame; while if 45.Be5 Black can even play 45...Qg4, for if 46.Bd6 White is mated by 46...Qd1+ 47.Kf2 Qd2+ 48.Kf1 Bc4+ 49.Kg1 Qe1+ 50.Kg2 Qf1#.

45...Kd8 46.Bg5+ Kc7 47.Bf4+ Bd6 48.Bxd6+ Kxd6 49.Qh4

There is no good defense left. If 49.Qd1 the reply 49...Qb2 is decisive.

49...Qa1+ 50.Kf2 Qb2+ 51.Ke1

Loses rapidly; but in the endgame after 51.Ke3 Qc1+ 52.Kd4 Qc4+ 53.Ke3 Qxh4 Black's united passed pawns would leave White in a hopeless state.

51...Qc1+ 52.Ke2 Bc4+ and **White Resigned,** for after 53.Kf2 Qd2+, the Black King is in a mating net: 54.Kf3 Bd5+; or 54.Kg1 Qe1+.

20. MAROCZY (1870-1951)

There was very little fantasy in the make-up of the Hungarian Grandmaster Maroczy, but he had an truly exceptional positional instinct, and inexhaustible patience. He was a precision player, who combined healthy ambition with perfect technique. He collected small advantages and knew well how to turn them to account at the right moment. One could call his style "cumulative".

He chose quiet openings, was an ingenious defender and a fine exponent of the endgame. His Queen endings in particular were models of endgame technique. In the matter of style Maroczy may be considered a disciple of Steinitz and a forerunner of Rubinstein.

Example 248

(The game Maroczy-Marco, Paris, 1900).

1.e4 e5 2.Nf3 Nc6 3.Bb5 a6 4.Ba4 Nf6 5.O-O Nxe4 6.d4 b5 7.Bb3 d5 8.a4 Rb8

The stronger move 8...Nxd4 was not known when this game was played.

9.axb5 axb5 10.dxe5 Be6 11.c3 Bc5 12.Nbd2 O-O 13.Bc2 Nxd2 14.Qxd2 Qd7 15.b4 Be7

The Bishop can't be spared from the defense of the Kingside. After 15...Bb6? 16.Qd3 g6 17.Bg5 Bf5 18.Qd2 Bxc2 19.Bf6! White's attack would be rapidly decisive.

16.Re1 f6 17.Qd3 g6 18.Bh6 Rfe8 19.Bb3 fxe5 20.Nxe5 Nxe5 21.Rxe5 c6 22.Ree1

White has obtained a slight but persistent advantage in his potentially mobile Kingside majority, while Black's Queenside majority is more or less static.

22...Bf6 23.Be3 Bf5 24.Qd2 Ra8 25.h3 Rxa1 26.Rxa1 Qe6 27.Bd4 Bxd4 28.Qxd4 Qe5 29.Qc5

The exchange of Queens promises nothing so long as Black can control the e-file with his Rook.

29...Qe6 30.Rd1!?

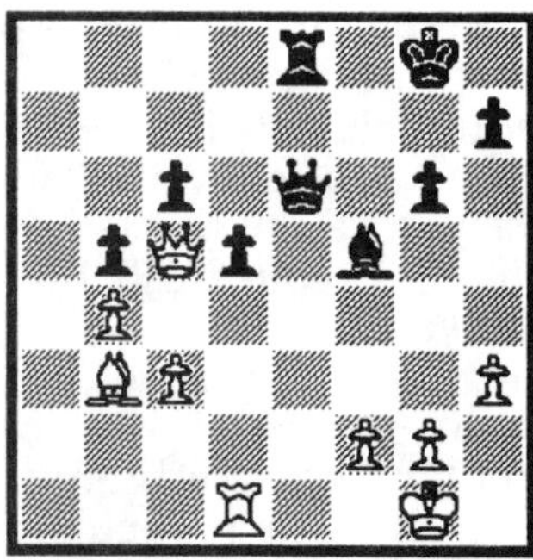

After 30.Ra6 Qe1+ 31.Kh2 Qe5+ 32.g3 Bd7 White would have the promising line 33.Rxc6! Bxc6 34.Qxc6.

30...Kg7 31.Ra1 Re7 32.Qd4+ Qf6 33.Ra7 Rxa7 34.Qxa7+ Qf7

Natural but bad. Black should have kept the Queens on the board, as now he gets a losing ending.

35.Qxf7+ Kxf7

White's advantage is twofold: he has the good Bishop (See Book 1, Part I-The Relative Worth of the Pieces) and an active pawn majority on the Kingside.

Black's corresponding majority on the Queenside is of far less value, as the pawns are practically blocked.

36.g4 Be4 37.f4 Ke6 38.Kf2 Kd6 39.Ke3 c5

Otherwise White plays Kd4, fixing the Black majority once for all.

40.Bd1 Bb1 41.Be2 d4+

If 41...Kc6 42.Bd3 Ba2 43.bxc5, and White must win in the end.

42.cxd4 cxb4 43.Bxb5 b3 44.Bd3 Ba2

Or 44...Bxd3 45.Kxd3 b2 46.Kc2 Kd5 47.f5! and wins.

45.Bc4 h5 46.f5 gxf5 47.g5! Black Resigned.

21. MARSHALL (1877-1945)

The name of Marshall is inseparably linked with the idea of attack – just like those of Anderssen and Spielmann. Marshall was a great tactician, and not usually over concerned about strategic niceties; a common circumstance with "natural" players. Sometimes his insistence on forcing an attacking position was his downfall. The public found his style attractive, if a little naive. He knew little about theory, and was weak from the point of view of technique.

Yet, in spite of all this, his enterprising methods and the shrewdness of his ideas made him a dangerous opponent for anyone.

Example 249

(The game Nimzowitsch-Marshall, Bad Kissingen, 1928).

1.d4 Nf6 2.c4 b6 3.Nc3 Bb7 4.Bg5 e6 5.Qc2 h6 6.Bh4 Be7 7.e4 O-O 8.e5

The natural 8.Bd3 is strongly answered by 8...Nc6; but White had better moves in 8.Nf3 and 8.f3.

8...Nd5! 9.Bg3

Marshall said that 9.Bxe7 was preferable.

9...Nb4 10.Qb3 d5 11.exd6 Bxd6 12.O-O-O

Here the White King soon finds himself in the crossfire of Black's pieces; but the weakness of his d4 leaves him little choice.

12...N8c6 13.Bxd6 Qxd6 14.a3

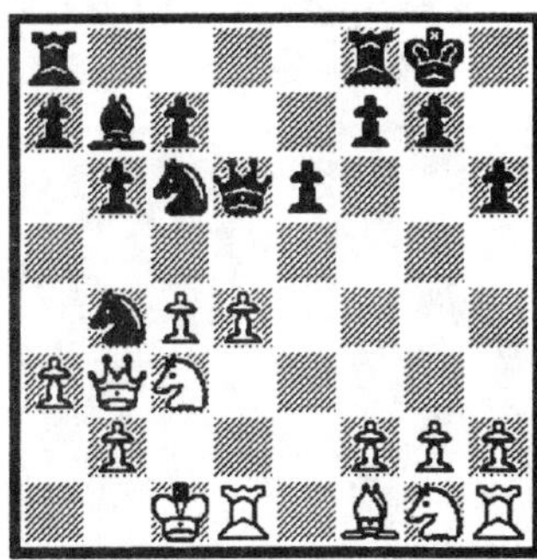

14...Nxd4!

Marshall reveled in this sort of position.

15.Rxd4

The alternative 15.Qxb4 would have the pretty sequel 15...c5 16.Qa4 Bc6; and then either 17.Qa6 Qf4+ 18.Kb1 Qxf2; or 17.Nb5 Qf4+ and 18...Nxb5, with a quick win for Black in both cases.

15...Qxd4 16.axb4 Qxf2 17.Qd1 Rfd8 18.Qe2 Qf4+ 19.Kc2 a5!

Mobilizing the Ra8. If now 20.b5 Black continues with 20...a4.

20.bxa5 Rxa5 21.Nf3 Ra1 22.Kb3 b5

The White King's wall of pawns is being annihilated.

23.Qe5

If 23.cxb5 Bd5+ 24.Nxd5 Qa4+ 25.Kc3 Rxd5; or if 23.Nxb5 Be4 followed by 24...c6.

23...bxc4+ 24.Kb4 Qc1 25.Nb5 c5+

Closing the mating net. If 26.Qxc5 Qxb2+ 27.Kxc4 Ra4+. **White Resigned.**

22. MORPHY (1837-1884)

Many people consider Morphy to be the greatest combinative player of all time. But Morphy owed his remarkable achievements not only to his admittedly tremendous combinative talents, but also to the fact that he was the first perfect positional player – insofar as one can speak of perfection in a human being. Moreover, he had excellent technique.

In the maturity of his positional insight, Morphy was half a century ahead of his time. While others racked their brains for the right procedure, Morphy simply knew what to do. Unlike his contemporaries who played for complications on the off chance of finding something, he struck only when the position was ripe. When he did strike, the blow was hard and often it settled the game outright.

Example 250

(The game Morphy-Riviere, Paris, 1863).

1.e4 e5 2.Nf3 Nc6 3.Bc4 Bc5 4.c3 Qe7

At the time when this game was played Morphy had already withdrawn from public chess. Arnous de Riviere was his personal friend and they played occasionally to investigate particular variations.

5.d4 Bb6 6.O-O d6 7.h3

Even today this move, which prevents Black from pinning the Knight, is still considered necessary to maintain the central tension as long as possible. The insertion of 7.a4 a6 and only then 8.h3 is now considered the most precise.

7...Nf6 8.Re1 h6

To prevent White from playing 9.Bg5- a move, however, which isn't a threat.The best line, according to Spielmann, is 8...O-O 9.b4 Nd8. Even so the move 8...h6 is still seen in contemporary play.

9.a4 a5

Better was 9...a6, so as to avoid weakening b5. The game might then continue 10.b4 O-O 11.Ba3 Nd7 12.b5 Nd8 13.Nbd2 Qf6 (Spielmann-Eliskases, match, 1936).

10.Na3

Morphy always brought every piece into play as quickly as possible. To playthe same piece twice in the opening was a breach of principle. Only under the influence of such players as Reti and Breyer, about 1920, was it realized that in some cases it can be good. The present position is such a case: White could obtain a definite advantage by 10.Bb5! Bd7 11.Na3 and 12.Nc4.

10...Nd8 11.Nc2 Be6 12.Ne3 Bxc4 13.Nxc4 Nd7 14.Ne3

The Knight comes powerfully into play now. If 14...c6 15.Nf5 Qf6 16.dxe5 dxe5 17.Nd6+.

14...g6 15.Nd5 Qe6

If 15...Qf8 White gets a big positional advantage by 16.Nxb6, for Black can't take with the Knight without losing his e-pawn.

16.Bxh6! f6

Black must prevent 17.Ng5, which would trap the Queen.

17.Bg7

According to Maroczy 17.Be3 was an even quicker win. The text move threatens not only 18.Bxh8 but also 18.Bxf6! Nxf6 19.Ng5, etc.

17...Rh5! 18.g4

White must press on like this, since Black threatens 18...Qf7.

18...Rxh3 19.Nxf6+ Nxf6 20.Ng5 Qd7

Maroczy, in his biography of Morphy, shows drawing chances for Black by 20...Qxg4+ 21.Qxg4 Nxg4 22.Nxh3 Kf7 23.f3 Kxg7 24.fxg4 exd4 25.Kg2 Ne6, etc.

21.Bxf6 Rh4 22.f3 exd4 23.cxd4 Rh6 24.Kg2 Nf7 25.Rh1 Nxg5

After 25...Rxh1 26.Qxh1 White also wins easily. As played, the rest is elementary.

26.Rxh6 Nh7 27.Qh1! Nxf6 28.Rh8+ Ke7 29.Rxa8 Bxd4 30.Qh6 Qc6 31.Rc1 Qb6 32.Rxc7+!

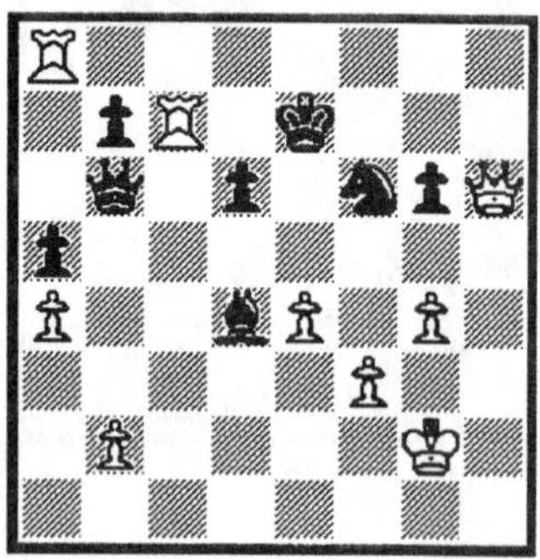

It would be unthinkable for a Morphy game to finish without fireworks.

32...Ke6 33.Re8+ Nxe8 34.Qxg6+ Ke5 35.Qf5#.

23. NAJDORF (Born 1910)

The strength of the Argentine grandmaster Najdorf lies mainly in the middle game and endgame. He admits that he plays the openings less well than his Grandmaster colleagues. His style is highly combinative, calling to mind the games of Alekhine. He makes snap decisions in keeping with his mercurial temperament. Positionally he has not reached the same heights as he has done in the field of tactics. In his early years in particular he lacked the composure and patience which are necessary for converting small positional advantages into a win.

Najdorf is a fine simultaneous player and one of the greatest blindfold experts the world has ever seen – perhaps the very greatest. The world record he holds – 45 simultaneous blindfold games- will be very difficult to surpass.

Here is Najdorf's immortal game.

Example 251

(The game Glucksberg-Najdorf, Warsaw, 1935).

1.d4 f5 2.c4 Nf6 3.Nc3 e6 4.Nf3 d5 5.e3

Too passive. Better is 5.g3.

5...c6 6.Bd3 Bd6 7.O-O O-O 8.Ne2 Nbd7 9.Ng5?

An elementary mistake, typical of mediocre opponents of the era of Anderssen and Morphy.

9...Bxh2+

With the point: 10.Kxh2 Ng4+ and 11...Qxg5.

10.Kh1 Ng4!

But this is the real refutation. If 11.Nxe6 Qh4.

11.f4 Qe8 12.g3 Qh5 13.Kg2 Bg1!! 14.Nxg1

In view of the threat to the e-pawn he has little choice. If 14.Rxg1 Black mates in two by 14...Qh2+ and 15...Qf2#.

14...Qh2+ 15.Kf3 e5!!

The climax of the combination.

16.dxe5 Ndxe5+ 17.fxe5 Nxe5+ 18.Kf4 Ng6+ 19.Kf3 f4!! 20.exf4

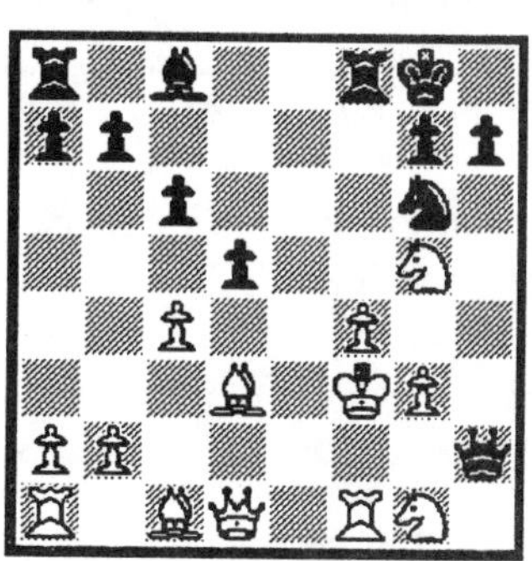

20...Bg4+! 21.Kxg4 Ne5+! 22.fxe5 h5#.

24. NIMZOWITSCH (1887-1935)

As a chess thinker Nimzowitsch is comparable to Steinitz. If Steinitz was the father of modern chess, Nimzowitsch was the formulator of the so-called hypermodern conceptions.

He was a man of excellent attributes- very witty, intelligent, a refined type of player with a splendid flair for all sorts of startling tactical and strategical details. On the other hand he was a curious individual, inclined to exaggerate and lose sight of the essentials. He developed his ideas in his books *My System* and *Chess Praxis*. We have already had occasion to elucidate his pioneer work in the domain of maneuvering (see Part 9) and have several times drawn attention to his doctrine of "overprotection".

Likewise in the openings Nimzowitsch made his mark. There is the Nimzowitsch Defence (1.e4 Nc6) and of course the very popular Nimzo Indian.

Example 252

(The game Bogolyubov-Nimzowitsch, San Remo, 1930).

1.d4 Nf6 2.c4 e6 3.Nc3 Bb4 4.Qb3 c5 5.dxc5 Nc6 6.Nf3 Ne4 7.Bd2 Nxc5 8.Qc2 f5

Control of e4 is vital for Black in the Nimzo Indian.

9.e3

Nimzowitsch was of the opinion that White's best line here is 9.a3 Bxc3 10.Bxc3 O-O 11.b4 Ne4 12.e3 b6 13.Bd3, with about even play.

9...O-O 10.Be2 b6 11.O-O-O

Kingside castling would have been less committal, though Black, with e4 in his possession, would have no problems.

11...a5! 12.a3 a4!

Very pretty; after 13.axb4? Nxb4 the White Queen can't go to b1 because of 14...Nb3#.

13.Nb5 Bxd2+ 14.Nxd2 Na5 15.Bf3 d5 16.cxd5 Ba6

Threatening to crush the White position completely, for 17.Nc3 would allow 17...Bd3.

17.Nc4 Bxb5 18.dxe6 Qc7

Nimzowitsch himself recommended the stronger line 18...Bxc4! 19.Rxd8 Raxd8!; for if 20.e7 Nab3+ 21.Kb1 Bd3; or if 20.Rd1 simply 20...Bxe6.

19.Bxa8 Bxc4 20.Bd5 Bxd5 21.Rxd5 Qc6 22.e7 Qxd5 23.exf8=Q+ Kxf8 24.Rd1 Qe5 25.h3 h5 26.g4 hxg4 27.hxg4 Nab3+ 28.Kb1 fxg4 29.Rg1 Qd5 30.Rd1

Not 30.Rxg4?, because Black would mate by 30...Qh1+,etc. The Black pieces are all well grouped in the middle of the board, in accordance with the principle of "centralization" set out by Nimzowitsch in his books.

30...Qe4 31.Rg1 Nd2+ 32.Kc1 Qd5! 33.Qh7

After 33.b4 Black wins as follows: 33...Ncb3+ 34.Kb2 Nc4+ 35.Ka2 Nd4 36.Qxa4 b5 37.Qa7 Na5+ 38.Ka1 Ndb3+ 39.Kb1 Qd3+ 40.Kb2 Nc4+ 41.Ka2 Qc2#. (Given by Nimzowitsch).

33...Nde4 34.Qh8+ Kf7 35.Kb1

The game is past saving. If 35.Rd1 Nb3+ 36.Kc2 Qc4+ 37.Kb1 Ned2+ 38.Rxd2 Qc1+ 39.Ka2 Qa1#.

35...Qd3+ and **White Resigned,** in face of 36.Ka2 Nc3+! 37.bxc3 Qc2+ 38.Ka1 Nb3#.

25. PETROSIAN (1929-1984)

In Petrosian, who dethroned Botvinnik in the 1963 World Championship, several styles converge. In the choice of opening he preferred hypermodern, stemming from Reti; he liked to play openings with fianchettoed Bishops (Reti's Opening, etc). His positional play reminds one of Nimzowitsch and Capablanca; and finally his defense is of the mold of Steinitz.

Petrosian built up his games along positional lines. He operated in a straightforward manner, neither courting complications nor going out of his way to avoid them. He also brought to his play a phenomenal endgame technique, great tactical alertness, and patience which is nearly inexhaustible. For years, although he certainly never avoided a contest, he hardly ever lost a game.

Example 253
(The game Petrosian-Tal, Moscow, 1963).

1.c4 Nf6 2.g3 e6 3.Bg2 c5 4.Nf3 d5 5.O-O Nc6 6.cxd5 Nxd5 7.d4 Be7 8.Nc3 O-O 9.Nxd5

Creating a weakening of the Black pawn position, since the recapture with the Queen gives White a favorable ending: 9...Qxd5 10.Ne5 Qxd4 11.Nxc6, etc.

9...exd5 10.dxc5 Bxc5 11.a3 a5 12.Bg5 f6 13.Rc1!

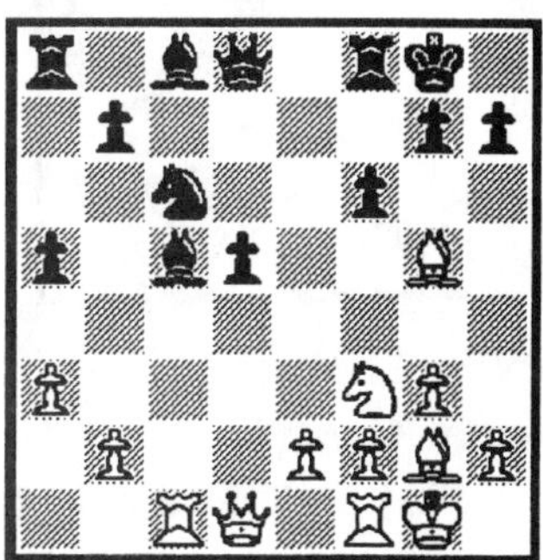

Petrosian has now provoked small weaknesses on both sides of the board. Here he operates with gain of tempo, for the tempting 13...Bxf2+ isn't good for Black: 14.Rxf2 fxg5 15.Nxg5! Qxg5 16.Qxd5+ Qxd5 17.Bxd5+ Be6 18.Bxe6+ and Black has not won a pawn but lost one.

13...Ba7 14.Bf4 Be6 15.Ne1 Re8 16.Nd3 Qe7 17.b4 axb4 18.Nxb4! Nxb4 19.Rc7

An interpolation as unexpected as White's 13th move.

19...Qd8 20.axb4 g5

True to his style, Tal reacts as sharply as possible.

21.Qd3

The third interpolation. The point of this one is the possibility 21...Bf7 22.Rxf7! Kxf7 23.Qxh7+ with a powerful attack.

21...Re7 22.Rxe7 Qxe7 23.Be3

All Petrosian's positional planning does not prevent him from keeping a weather eye on every little tactical pleasantry. Here, for example, Black can't play 23...Qxb4 because of 24.Bxa7 Rxa7 25.Qe3! Nor can he play 23...Bxe3 24.Qxe3 Qxb4 because the Be6 would be *en prise.*

23...d4 24.Bxd4 Rd8 25.e3 Bxd4 26.exd4 Qxb4 27.d5 Qd6 28.Be4 Bf7?

Although White's positional advantage is clear it is open to question whether he could have won the game after 28...Bxd5! 29.Rd1 Bxe4 30.Qxd6 Rxd6 31.Rxd6 Kg7. However, White's best chance after 28...Bxd5 would have been 29.Bxh7+ Kh8 30.Rd1!.

29.Bxh7+ Kg7 30.Be4 Qc5 31.Rb1 Rd7

Now 31...Bxd5? would lose the Exchange to 32.Rd1.

32.Qf3 Bg6 33.Bxg6 Kxg6 34.Qd3+ Kg7 35.Rb5 Qe7 36.Qf5

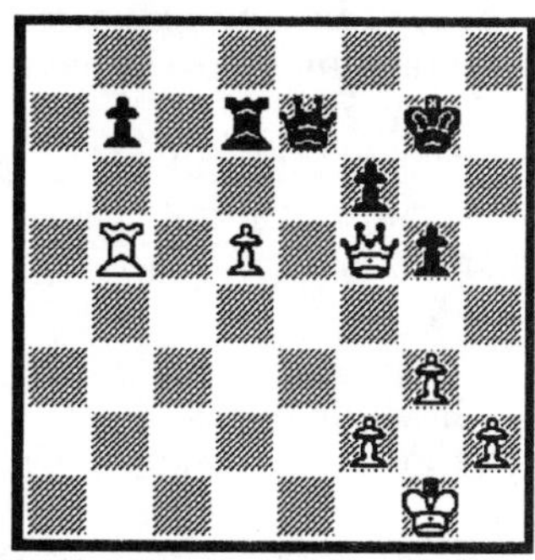

It is well known that in major piece endings it is no easy matter to convert an extra pawn into a win. In the present case, however, Black will soon be compelled to offer an exchange of Queens to prevent White from getting a direct mating attack. White's task will then be considerably lightened.

36...Rd6 37.Kg2 Qd7 38.Qxd7+ Rxd7 39.Kf3 Re7 40.Rb6 f5 41.d6 Rd7 42.h4 Kf6 43.hxg5+ Kxg5 44.Ke3 Kf6

Otherwise the White King goes to d5 or e5.

45.Kf4 Ke6 46.f3

All very simple: after 46...Rxd6 47.Rxd6+ Kxd6 48.Kxf5, White can either stop the b-pawn (48...b5 49.Ke4) or, if Black prevents this, promote his own g-pawn with check (48...Kd5 49.g4).

46...Kf6 47.Rb5 Ke6 48.Rxf5 Kxd6 49.g4 Ke6 50.Rf8 b5 and Black Resigned, without waiting for White's reply. The finish might have been: 51.Rb8 Rd5 52.Rb6+ Kf7 53.Ke4 Rc5 54.f4, etc.

26. PILLSBURY (1872-1906)

Pillsbury's healthy, robust style of play, and his preference for attack and combination are highly reminiscent of the methods of Alekhine and Marshall. However, Pillsbury was far superior to Marshall in accuracy and judgment of position; unfortunately, his life was too short to allow him the experience to reach Alekhine's level. He showed little inclination to maneuver, but this was natural in view of his youth. If his play seemed to lack refinement, this is due to the vigor of his approach.

Example 254

(The game Pillsbury-Lasker, Nuremberg, 1896).

1.e4 e6 2.d4 d5 3.Nc3 Nf6 4.e5 Nfd7 5.f4 c5 6.dxc5 Nc6 7.a3 Nxc5 8.b4 Nd7

In his famous manual, Lasker suggested that 8...d4 would have been stronger.

9.Bd3 a5

Lasker queried this move, instead suggesting 9...Nb6 followed by ...Bd7 and ...Rc8.

10.b5 Ncb8 11.Nf3 Nc5 12.Be3 Nbd7 13.O-O g6 14.Ne2 Be7

Lasker later preferred 14...Bg7.

15.Qe1 Nb6 16.Nfd4 Bd7 17.Qf2 Nba4

By preventing a4 Black has artificially isolated the White b-pawn.

18.Rab1 h5 19.b6 Nxd3 20.cxd3 Bxa3

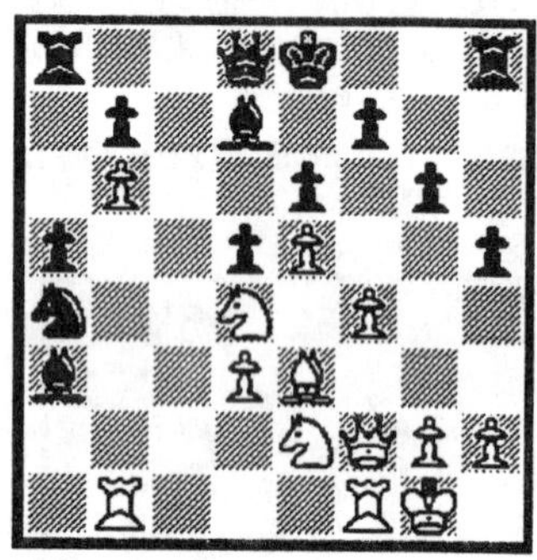

21.f5!! gxf5 22.Nf4

Threatening Qg3-g7.

22...h4 23.Ra1 Be7 24.Rxa4! Bxa4 25.Ndxe6!

Only this third sacrifice shows the deep tactical conception behind 21.f5!!.

25...fxe6 26.Nxe6 Bd7

After 26...Qc8 27.Qxf5 Qc6 28.Bg5! Qxb6+ 29.d4 Qb4 30.Qf7+ Kd7 31.Bxe7 Qxe7 32.Nc5+ Kd8 33.Nxb7+ Kd7 34.Nc5+ Kd8 35.Qxd5+ Kc7 36.Qb7+ Kd8 37.Qxa8+, and White wins.

27.Nxd8 Rxd8 28.Bc5 Rc8 29.Bxe7 Kxe7 30.Qe3 Rc6 31.Qg5+ Kf7 32.Rc1 Rxc1+ 33.Qxc1

The endgame is hopeless for Black since his Rook and Bishop can't match the Queen's superior mobility applied to Black's exposed King and scattered pawns.

33...Rc8 34.Qe1 h3 35.gxh3

Much better than 35.Qxa5 Rc1+ and ...Rc2+ giving Black some counterplay.

35...Rg8+ 36.Kf2 a4 37.Qb4 Rg6 38.Kf3 a3 39.Qxa3 Rxb6 40.Qc5 Re6 41.Qc7 Ke7 42.Kf4 b6 43.h4 Rc6 44.Qb8 Be8

Otherwise 45.h5 follows.

45.Kxf5 Rh6 46.Qc7+ Kf8 47.Qd8 b5 48.e6 Rh7 49.Ke5 b4 50.Qd6+ Black Resigned.

27. RESHEVSKY (1911-1992)

Although Reshevsky has introduced some good ideas in the openings, he was not really to be considered an expert in that field. nor did his greatest strength lie in positional play. He was certainly a great master of the endgame, but what really made him such a dangerous opponent for anyone is his patience and his great tactical skill. What seemed to have been a weak point in his armory – his habitual time pressure – became the very hunting ground in which he displayed his tactical virtuosity.

Example 255

(The game Reshevsky-Vasconcellos, Boston, 1944).

1.e4 e6 2.d4 d5 3.e5 c5 4.dxc5 Nd7 5.Nf3 Bxc5

Better was 5...Ne7 and ...Nc6 to pressure White's e-pawn as soon as possible. The c-pawn will not run away.

6.Bd3 Ne7 7.O-O Nc6 8.Bf4

Now White enjoys an excellent, centralized development. His e-pawn is well-protected (Nimzowitschian "overprotection"), and thus the pieces protecting it are well placed.

8...Qc7 9.Nc3!

Indirect protection of e5. Now if 9...Nxe5 then 10.Nxe5 Nxe5 11.Qh5 Bd6 12.Nb5 wins.

9...a6 10.Re1 Qb6

This is a dangerous expedition. Black ignores the dictum that warns against grabbing the opponent's b-pawn when one's position is under-developed.

11.Bg3 Qxb2 12.Nxd5! exd5 13.Rb1 Qa3 14.e6 Nf6

A better course was 14...fxe6 15.Rxe6+ Ne7.

15.exf7+ Kxf7 16.Bh4!

A nice idea. Reshevsky intends to remove Black's best defender, the Nf6.

16...Nb4?

A further error. Black had to try 16...Be7.

17.Ne5+ Kf8 18.Bxf6 Nxd3

After 18...gxf6 White wins brilliantly by 19.Qh5!! fxe5 20.Rxe5 Bd7 21.Qf3+, mating soon.

19.Bxg7+! Kxg7

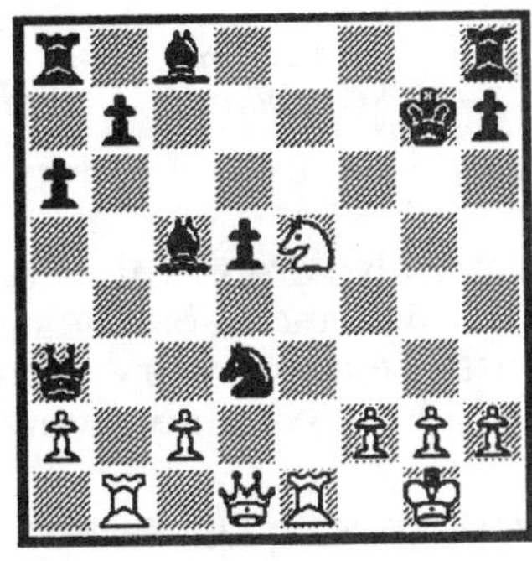

20.Rxb7+!!

A spectacular blow. Now if 20...Bxb7 then 21.Qg4+ Kf6 22.Qf3+ Kg7 23.Qf7+ Kh6 24.Qf6+ mates quickly.

20...Be7 21.Qh5!

With almost all of his attacking pieces under attack, Reshevsky weaves a pretty finale. Now if 21...Bxb7 then 22.Qf7+ Kh6 23.Ng4+ Kg5 24.Qg7+ Kh4 25.Qh6+! Kxg4 26.h3+ Kf5 27.g4#.

21...Rf8 22.Qg5+ Kh8 23.Ng6+!

The final point.

23...hxg6 24.Qh6+ Kg8 25.Qxg6+ Kh8 26.Rbxe7 Black Resigned.

28. RETI (1889-1929)

During and after World War I there emerged a group of young players who attempted to break completely with accepted opinion. Foremost among them was Reti. Instead of occupying the center with pawns these hypermoderns, with Reti as their leader, preferred to control the central territory by the action of their pieces. They developed their Bishops on the flanks and held back the center pawns as long as possible. In his innovations Reti eventually went too far. He overpressed his theories, as inexperienced players sometimes do, and was often the victim of practical difficulties.

Example 256

(The game Reti-Rubinstein, Karlsbad, 1923).

1.Nf3

Zukertort also frequently opened with this Knight move, but the system White uses here was worked out by Reti, and is quite rightly known as Reti's opening.

1...d5 2.g3 Nf6 3.Bg2 g6 4.c4 d4

This ambitious space-gaining move is virtually an attempt at refutation, but 4...c6 was more prudent.

5.d3 Bg7 6.b4!

A sophisticated stratagem; White anticipates the reinforcing move ...c5, undermining it in advance.

6...O-O 7.Nbd2 c5 8.Nb3 cxb4 9.Bb2 Nc6 10.Nbxd4 Nxd4 11.Bxd4

White's strategy has been completely successful. The center is under control by White's pieces – not pawns. Note that White has made no automatic developing moves; he has not yet castled. The hypermodern player does this only after some sophisticated preliminary strategical skirmishing.

11...b6 12.a3 Bb7 13.Bb2 bxa3 14.Rxa3 Qc7 15.Qa1

This doubling on the diagonal is an invention of Reti; it may be regarded as analogous to doubling heavy pieces on a file.

15...Ne8 16.Bxg7 Nxg7 17.O-O

Not 17.Rxa7? Rxa7 18.Qxa7 Ra8 trapping White's Queen.

17...Ne6 18.Rb1 Bc6

The threat was 19.Rxa7 Rxa7 20.Qxa7 Ra8 21.Qxb6.

19.d4

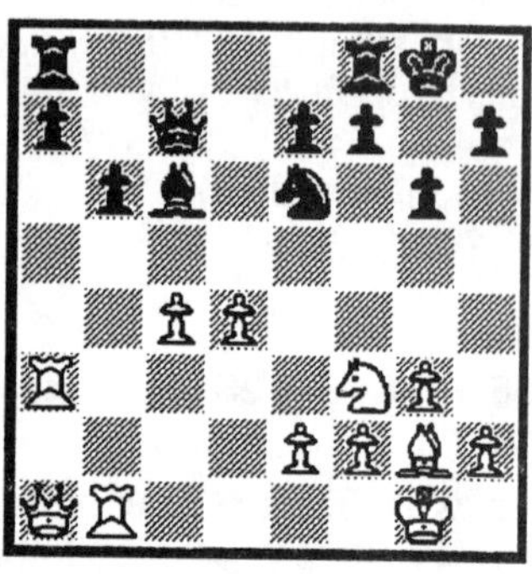

Only now do the center pawns come into action.

19...Be4 20.Rd1 a5 21.d5 Nc5 22.Nd4 Bxg2 23.Kxg2 Rfd8 24.Nc6 Rd6 25.Re3 Re8 26.Qe5 f6

Forced, because of the threat 27.Nxe7+. If 26...Rd7 then 27.Nxe7+

R8xe7 28.Qxc7 Rxc7 29.d6 Rxe3 30.dxc7 Re8 31.Rd8.

27.Qb2 e5 28.Qb5 Kf7 29.Rb1 Nd7 30.f3 Rc8 31.Rd3 e4

A last try. After 31...Nb8 32.c5! wins for White.

32.fxe4 Ne5 33.Qxb6! Nxc6 34.c5!

The point of White's previous move.

34...Rd7 35.dxc6 Rxd3 36.Qxc7+ Rxc7 37.exd3 Rxc6 38.Rb7+ Ke8 39.d4

White has acquired complete central domination. The following endgame is expertly handled by Reti, who was a noted composer of many fine endgame studies.

39...Ra6 40.Rb6!

Now after 40...Rxb6 41.cxb6 Kd7 42.e5 fxe5 43.dxe5 a4 44.e6+! Kxe6 45.b7, White wins.

40...Ra8 41.Rxf6 a4 42.Rf2 a3 43.Ra2 Kd7 44.d5 g5 45.Kf3 Ra4 46.Ke3 h5 47.h4

Preparing a decisive penetration of the White King.

47...gxh4 48.gxh4 Ke7 49.Kf4 Kd7 50.Kf5 Black Resigned.

29. RUBINSTEIN (1882-1958)

The style of the Polish grandmaster Rubinstein forms a bridge between Steinitz and the present day. He had a splendid grasp of the requirements of a position and was an exceptionally fine attacker when occasion demanded. However, in the field of the endgame many consider that his achievements will never be equaled.

In Rook endings in particular his play was simply phenomenal. Yet his play also had its deficiencies. Tactically he was more fallible, as his games against the great tactician Spielmann showed. For that matter there was nothing fanciful about any of his play, especially in the opening stages, where it tended rather towards monotony.

Example 257

(The game Tarrasch-Rubinstein, Mahrisch-Ostrau, 1923).

1.e4 e5 2.Nf3 Nc6 3.Nc3 Nf6 4.Bb5 Bb4 5.O-O O-O 6.d3 d6 7.Bg5 Bxc3 8.bxc3 Qe7 9.Re1 Nd8 10.d4 Bg4 11.h3! Bh5 12.g4 Bg6 13.d5

In the game Wolf-Rubinstein, Teplitz-Schonau, 1922, when Wolf chose 13.Nh4!, but after 13...h6 he overlooked the strong move 14.Bc4! (threatening 15.Nxg6). However, 13.d5 is no improvement.

13...c6 14.Bc4?

Better was 14.Bf1. On c4 the Bishop is exposed, as Black's next move shows.

14...Rc8 15.dxc6 bxc6 16.Bd3 Ne6 17.Bc1 Nc5 18.Nd2

From here on we are making a certain amount of use of Kmoch's analysis in his book *Rubinstein Gewinnt*. Kmoch showed that 18.Ba3 would not be good: 18...Ncxe4 19.Bxe4 Nxe4 20.Rxe4 Bxe4 21.Bxd6 Qd8 22.Bxf8 Qxd1+ 23.Rxd1 Bxf3 24.Rd3 e4 and Black wins.

18...h5!

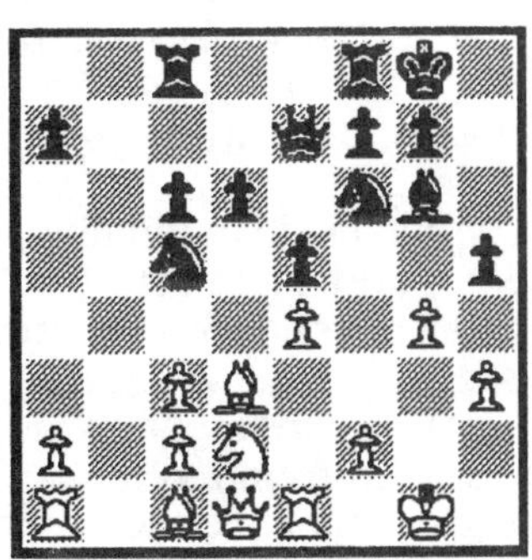

19.Ba3 Ne6 20.Nc4 c5

Practically forced as 20...Rfd8 fails to 21.Nxe5.

21.Bc1

Trying to find "greener pastures".

21...hxg4 22.hxg4 Nh7! 23.Kg2 Nhg5 24.f3 Rcd8 25.Nb2

Intending 26.Bc4.

25...d5!

But this timely central strike seizes the initiative.

26.exd5 Rxd5 27.c4 Rd4! 28.Be3

After 28.Rxe5 Qf6 29.Re1 Nf4+ 30.Bxf4 Rxf4 Black has a winning attack.

28...Rd6 29.Qe2 e4! 30.fxe4 Nxe4 31.Qf3 N4g5 32.Qg3 Qb7+ 33.Kf1 Rb6 34.Na4 Bxd3+ 35.cxd3 f5!

Prying open the f-file for a decisive attack on the King. He threatens not only 36...fxg4+, but also 36...f4.

36.Bxg5 fxg4+ 37.Kg1

Also losing is 37.Ke2 Nd4+ 38.Kd2 Rb2+! 39.Kc1 Ne2+.

37...Nxg5 38.Nxb6 Nf3+ 39.Kf2 Nxe1+

Now if 40.Kxe1 then 40...Qh1+ and 41...Qxa1; while if 40.Ke2 Re8+ 41.Kd2 Nf3+ is equally decisive. **White Resigned.**

30. SCHLECHTER (1874-1918)

The Austrian grandmaster Schlechter, though neither very deep nor particularly brilliant, was nevertheless an extremely strong player; his assets were his complete imperturbability, his skill in maintaining the equilibrium, and his mastery of the art of creating chances in critical situations.

Schlechter was extremely difficult to beat, as Lasker found out in 1910. Their ten game match ended with an even point total, but in the ninth game the score was 5-4 in favor of the Austrian. In the tenth game Schlechter, who was usually pacifism personified, spurned an easy draw – and with it the World Championship – in a determined bid to win.

Example 258

(The game Schlechter-Suchting, Karlsbad, 1911).

1.d4 d5 2.c4 c6 3.Nf3 Nf6 4.Nc3 Qb6 5.Qc2

More incisive is 5.c5 Qc7 6.g3.

5...Bg4 6.c5 Qc7 7.Ne5 Nbd7 8.Nxg4

Better was 8.Bf4 since now Black can achieve ...e5 under favorable conditions.

8...Nxg4 9.Qf5 h5! 10.e4 g6 11.Qf4 e5 12.dxe5 Bxc5

Now it is clear that Black has the better of it; but in this type of play Schlechter usually rose to the challenge with resourceful counterplay.

13.e6! Nde5 14.exf7+ Kd7?

A poor idea. Definitely better was 14...Kf8.

15.exd5 Nxf2 16.dxc6+ bxc6 17.Qa4 Nxf7?

Another error which allows White to dominate. Correct was Lasker's suggestion 17...Nxh1 with ...Nf2 to follow, which would stop White's Rook from reaching d1 later.

18.Be2 Nxh1 19.Bf4 Bd6 20.Rd1 Ke7 21.Rxd6 Nxd6 22.Ne4 Rad8 23.Qd4 Qa5+

Black only chance is to counterattack and hope.

24.b4 Qf5

In order to meet 25.Nxd6 with 25...Qb1+.

25.Bxd6+ Rxd6 26.Qxd6+ Kf7 27.Bc4+ Kg7 28.Qd4+ Kh7 29.Qxa7+!

Not 29.Nf6+, which would allow Black back into the game after 29...Kh6 30.Ng4+ hxg4! 31.Qxh8+ Kg5.

29...Kh6 30.Qe3+ g5 31.h4 Re8 32.Bd3 Kg7 33.Kd2 Qf4 34.hxg5

White liquidates to a winning ending.

34...Qxe3+ 35.Kxe3 Ng3 36.Kd4 Nxe4 37.Bxe4 Ra8 38.Bxc6?

An oversight. The right way was 38.Bb1 followed by 39.Kc5, winning.

38...Rxa2 39.b5 Kg6 40.b6

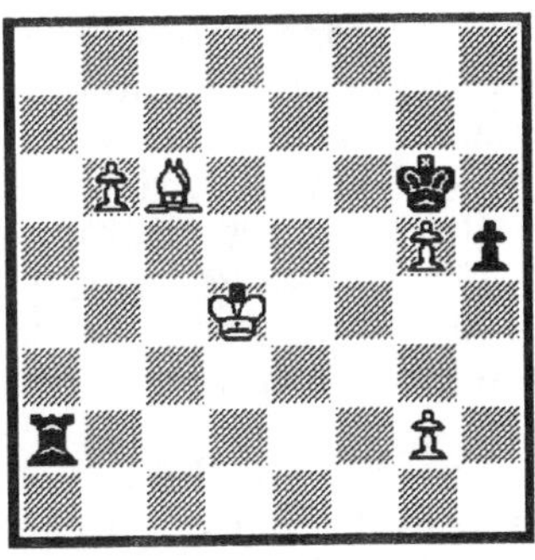

40...Kxg5?

Missing his chance. Lasker pointed out the following draw: 40...h4! 41.b7 Rb2 42.Kc5 Rxb7! 43.Bxb7 h3! 44.gxh3 Kxg5 and the Black King can run to h8 with a the well-known theoretical draw, because White's Bishop is the "wrong color" to help the h-pawn promote.

41.b7 Rb2 42.Kc5 Rc2+ 43.Kb6 Rb2+ 44.Bb5 Black Resigned.

31. SMYSLOV (Born 1921)

A study of Smyslov's games forces one to admit that it is not easy to say just where his special strength lies. This Russian grandmaster attaches little importance to complex opening variations. He builds up his games by simple means, and in the middlegame his play is just as simple and sound. This is not to say that he is averse to combinative play – there are many excellent examples of beautiful combinative games by Smyslov on record. But his greatest strength seems to be in the art of making "something out of nothing". He will maneuver patiently for hours at a time without ever relaxing for one moment; he seems to be stealthily stalking his opponent. There is indeed something of the assassin about him, for all at once, when least expected, he will strike. Since moreover his endgame technique is just about perfect, the smallest advantage in his hands is likely to win.

Example 259

(The game Smyslov-Botvinnik, Moscow, 1951).

1.e4 e5 2.Nf3 Nc6 3.Bb5 a6 4.Ba4 Nf6 5.O-O Be7 6.Re1 b5 7.Bb3 d6 8.c3 O-O 9.h3 Be6

Black essays an idea which originated from the great Russian Master Chigorin.

10.d4 Bxb3 11.Qxb3 Qd7 12.Bg5 h6 13.Bxf6 Bxf6 14.d5

White sets up a light-squared central pawn-chain in order to emphasize the limited scope of Black's Bishop.

14...Na5 15.Qc2 c6

Otherwise White will play Nbd2 followed by c4.

16.dxc6 Qxc6 17.Nbd2 Rac8 18.Rac1

Smyslov commented that this prevents b4 (which would be met by c4) overprotects c3, and prepares, if the opportunity presents itself, to play c4. These stratagems are in the style of Nimzowitsch.

18...Rfd8 19.Nf1 Nc4 20.b3 Nb6 21.Ne3 d5

Superficially, it would seem this central advance activates Black's game. But as we shall soon see, Smyslov has taken critical factors into account.

22.Ng4 d4

Best. After 22...dxe4 23.Nfxe5 Bxe5 24.Nxe5 Qb7 25.Rxe4! White is on top, e.g. 25...Rxc3 26.Qxc3 Qxe4 27.Qc7, or 25...Nd5 26.Rd4 Rxc3 27.Qxc3 Nxc3 28.Rxd8+ wins.

23.Nxf6+ Qxf6 24.Qb2 dxc3 25.Rxc3 Nd7 26.Rec1 Rxc3 27.Qxc3 Qd6! 28.Qc6 Nf6!

Black has defended well, but White still has the initiative.

29.Qxd6 Rxd6 30.Nxe5 Nxe4 31.f3 Ng5 32.f4 Ne6 33.f5 Nd8 34.Rc8 Kf8 35.Kf2 Ke7 36.Ke3

The line 36.Rxd8 Rxd8 37.Nc6+ would give Black chances to draw.

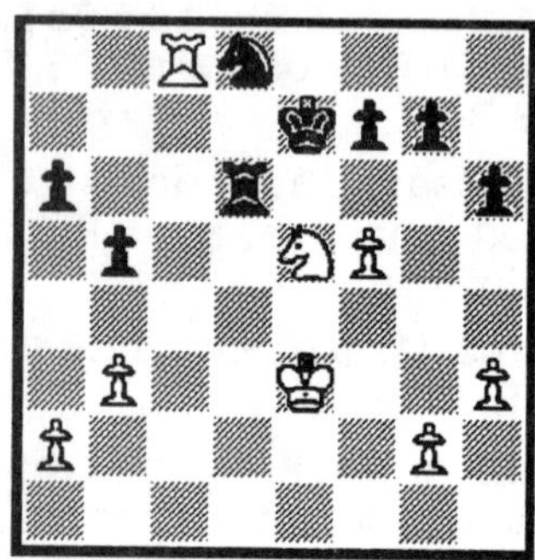

36...Rd1?

This is a serious mistake. He had to play 36...Rd5! 37.Ke4 Rd2.

37.Ra8! Kf6

If 37...Rd6 then White plays 38.Rxd8! as now 38...Rxd8 39.Nc6+ leads to a won King and pawn ending. However, he still had some drawing chances with 37...Re1+ 38.Kd4 Re2 39.Rxa6 Rxg2.

38.Nd3!

Now Black's position collapses.

38...Nc6 39.Rxa6 Black Resigned.

32. SPIELMANN (1883-1942)

Spielmann knew his own strength, but also his own weakness. "I can handle an attacking position just as well as Alekhine", he said, "but in actual play I cannot often achieve such a position". Spielmann was indeed a magnificent attacking player. The bravura with which he could carry an attack through to a brilliant conclusion appealed as much to the expert as it did to the public.

His main weakness was a lack of opening knowledge, and this deficiency revealed itself in an inability to build up the kind of position in which he could display his powers. On the other hand it may also explain the success of this Austrian master against, for instance, Rubinstein, whose way of building up his game also left something to be desired.

Spielmann's style calls to mind that of Chigorin. In sheer technique of combination he outdid the great Russian master, though he was not his equal in originality.

Example 260

(The game Rubinstein-Spielmann, Pistyan, 1912).

1.d4 c5 2.d5 d6 3.c4 g6

This line, the Benoni Defense, is a dynamic choice; both sides have chances in positions which are sharp both positionally and tactically. For a while this game follows Burn-Chigorin, Vienna, 1898.

4.e4 Bg7 5.Bd3 e6 6.Nc3 Ne7 7.Nge2 exd5 8.exd5

Tarrasch strongly censured this move, holding that 8.cxd5 was clearly best.

8...Nd7 9.f4 Nf6 10.Ng3?

The Knight will be a target here, as Black's next move demonstrates.

10...h5! 11.O-O h4 12.Nge4 Nxe4 13.Bxe4 Bd4+ 14.Kh1 Nf5

Threatening to win with 15...Ng3+!.

15.Bxf5 Bxf5 16.Re1+

Here, or at latest on the next move, White had to block the h-pawn's advance by playing h3.

16...Kf8 17.Qf3 h3! 18.g3

Rubinstein may have thought he could play 18.g4 here, overlooking the reply 18...Qh4, winning for Black.

18...Qd7 19.Bd2 Bg4 20.Qf1

On 20.Qd3 Black still plays 20..Qf5! as 21.Qxf5 allows 21...Bf3#. The far advanced h-pawn is clearly a thorn in White's side.

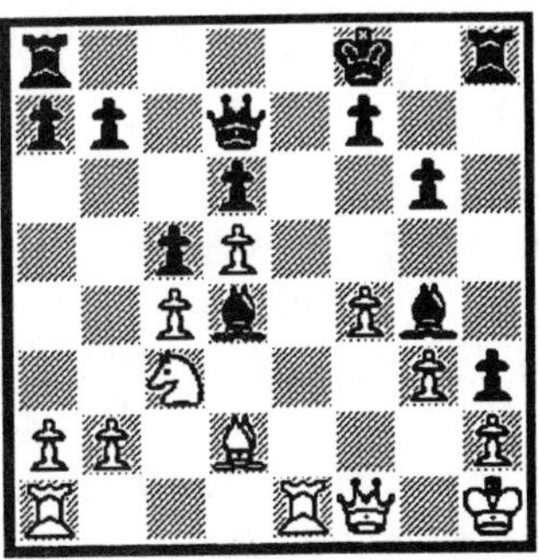

20...Qf5 21.Rac1 Kg7 22.Be3 Bf6 23.b3 Rhe8 24.Bf2

Otherwise Black will build up the pressure by doubling Rooks on the e-file.

24...Bf3+ 25.Kg1 Bg2 26.Rxe8 Bxf1!

The Queen will be stronger than the two Rooks in this position.

27.Rxa8 Qd3!

The point: if 28.Rxf1 then 28...Qf3 forces mate.

28.Re8

So that 28...Bxc3 can be met by 29.Re3. But Spielmann brilliantly forces the issue.

28...Qf3! 29.Kxf1 Qh1+ 30.Bg1 Qg2+ 31.Ke1 Qxg1+ 32.Kd2 Qxh2+

Now after 33.Ne2 Qg2 34.Rg1 Qxg1! 35.Nxg1 h2 the h-pawn Queens. **White Resigned.**

33. STEINITZ (1836-1900)

Steinitz was the first player who really understood Philidor, and especially Morphy. His games, and even more, his writings establish him as the father of modern positional play. Things which today are accepted without question – the occupation of the center, the strength of the two Bishops, the theory of weak squares, etc.- were revolutionary ideas in the days of Steinitz.

With all his gifts Steinitz had some definite weaknesses. Limited powers of combination hampered him in deciding between what was correct in theory and what was expedient in practice.

Steinitz was definitely of the materialistic attitude in chess. With intense will power and scientific argument he fought against the idea that a material deficit could be offset by positional advantages which were not in themselves decisive.

He was a great defender, but even here he carried his ides too far, sometimes imposing the role of defender upon himself quite deliberately, as in his famous Steinitz Gambit (1.e4 e5 2.Nc3 Nc6 3.f4 exf4 4.d4 Qh4+ 5.Ke2). He had many successes with this opening because his opponents reacted incorrectly to the position of the White King, whose exposure is in fact more apparent than real. On the other hand the Steinitz Defense to the Ruy Lopez, another of his creations, is a much more solid affair.

Much of his life's work was devoted to the demolition of gambits. "The only way to refute a gambit", said Steinitz, "is to accept it". The dangers he was willing to face in support of this dogma are shown in the following game.

Example 261

(The game Janowsky-Steinitz, Cologne, 1898).

1.e4 e5 2.f4 exf4 3.Bc4 Ne7 4.Qh5 Ng6 5.Nc3 Qe7?!

This may conflict with what Steinitz himself taught about the development of the pieces; no matter! Steinitz is determined to refute this gambit, and if he cannot do it with normal moves, he means to do it with abnormal ones.

6.d4 Nc6 7.Nf3 Qb4 8.Qd5 Nd8

Forced, but quite typical of Steinitz, who often withdrew his pieces to the back rank.

9.a3 Qe7 10.O-O d6

In order to force simplification, thus reducing White's pressure by playing 11...Be6 12.Qb5+ c6 13.Qb3 Bxc4.

11.Qh5 c6 12.Bd2 Ne6 13.Rae1

On 13.d5 Nc5 14.Rae1 Nd7 Black can use the excellent central outpost on e5.

13...Qc7 14.d5! Nd8 15.e5!

Black's opening experiment has been refuted; his situation is truly critical, such that many would be thinking of resigning. But in such positions Steinitz's defensive powers bordered on the miraculous.

15...dxe5 16.Nxe5 Bc5+ 17.Kh1 O-O 18.dxc6

Now on 18...bxc6 White plays 19.Nxg6 hxg6 20.Qxc5, ditto after 18...Nxc6. Also, after 18...Nxe5 19.Rxe5 Bd6 20.Nd5 Qxc6 21.Nf6+! gxf6 22.Rg5+! with a mating attack. Thus it seems that Black is on the verge of destruction.

18...Be3! 19.Nf3?

A poor choice. The correct way was 19.Bxe3! Qxe5! 20.Qxe5 Nxe5 21.cxb7 Bxb7 22.Rxf4 Nxc4 23.Rxc4 and despite the opposite colored Bishops, White has a winning ending. However, the ever over-optimistic Janowsky intends to force a "brilliant" middlegame victory.

19...Bxd2 20.Ng5 h6 21.Qxg6 hxg5 22.Nd5 Qxc6

Another good line was 22...fxg6 23.Nxc7+ Kh7 24.Nxa8 Bxe1 25.Rxe1 Nxc6.

23.Ne7+ Kh8 24.Qxg5

Now Black turns the tide. The right way was 24.Bxf7! Nxf7! 25.Nxc6 Bxe1 26.Ne7! Bd2 27.Qh5+ Nh6 28.Ng6+ Kg8 29.Nxf8 Kxf8 30.h4 with approximately equal chances, as Black could not play 30...gxh4 because of 31.Qc5+ Ke8 32.Qe5+ Kf8 33.Qd6+ and 34.Qxd2.

24...Qh6 25.Qc5

Threatening 26.Ng6+ and 27.Qxf8+, but this is easily defended.

25...Ne6 26.Bxe6 Bxe6 27.Re5 Be3! 28.Qb5 g6

Now it's becoming clear that Black is taking over the attack.

29.Qxb7 Kg7!

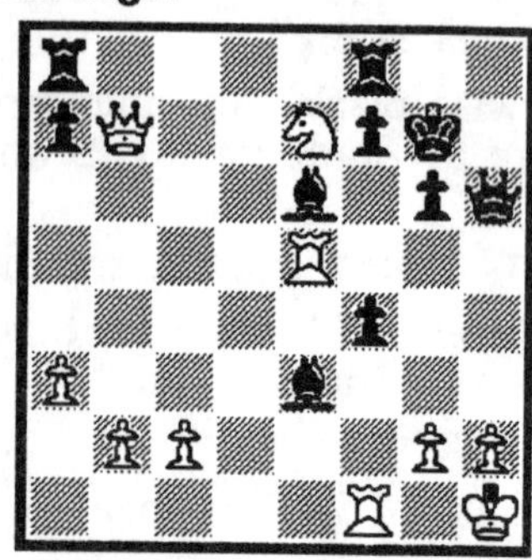

Threatening 30...Qxh2+ with mate to follow.

30.Qf3 Rad8 31.h3 Qh4 32.Nc6 Bg4 33.Qxg4

If the Queen moves away, then 33...Bxh3! wins.

33...Qxg4 34.hxg4 Rh8+ 35.Rh5 gxh5 White Resigned.

34. TAL (1936-1993)

The hazardous style of the Russian grandmaster Tal made a great impression on all chess lovers, both expert and amateur alike. He pounced on his opponents like a tiger; no risks would deter him. His great tactical gifts and his skill even in severe time pressure enabled him to scale the heights of Olympus in record time.

Tal, like every other chessmaster, had his vulnerable points. The return match with Botvinnik showed that in positional play and endgame technique he was no match for the man who both preceded and followed him as World Champion.

On the other hand it was true that in neither match was Botvinnik proof against Tal's lightning flash combinative genius.

Example 262
(The game Tal-Geller, Riga, 1958).

1.e4 e5 2.Nf3 Nc6 3.Bb5 a6 4.Ba4 Nf6 5.O-O Be7 6.Re1 b5 7.Bb3 O-O 8.c3 d6 9.h3 Na5 10.Bc2 c5 11.d4 Bb7

This main line of the Ruy Lopez has many times been the beginning of complex, intense battles, often spanning the board from Queenside to center to Kingside. Here Geller, who has a reputation for deep and original opening preparations, eschews the most traditional move, 11...Qc7 (Chigorin's move), in favor of less explored vistas.

12.b4

Tal, one of the most aggressive players in the history of chess, returns with an sharp reply.

12...cxb4 13.cxb4 Nc4 14.Nbd2 d5

Blowing open the center and leading to great complications.

15.exd5 exd4 16.Nxc4 bxc4 17.Qxd4 Bxb4

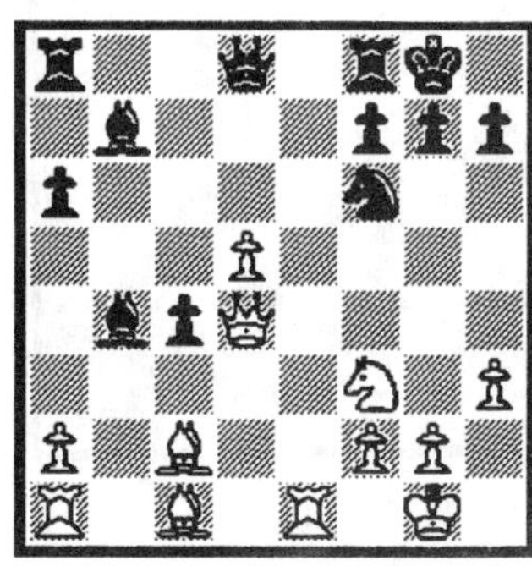

18.Rb1!! Bxe1

Black accepts the challenge. If 18...Nxd5 19.Bxh7+ Kxh7 20.Ng5+ Kg8 21.Qh4 Nf6 22.Rxb4 Qd5 23.Nf3 with White on top.

19.Rxb7 Re8

An alternative was 19...Qxd5 20.Qxd5 Nxd5 21.Nxe1 Rab8 with drawing chances in the ending.

20.d6 Qc8

Now if 21.Rc7 then there could follow 21...Qe6 22.Bg5 Nd5 with Black gaining the better of it.

21.Bg5!!

A startling sacrifice, typical of Tal's ferocious style.

21...Re2!

A fine counter. After 21...Qxb7 22.Bxf6 gxf6 23.Qh4 f5 24.Qg5+ Kf8 25.Qf6+ Kg8 26.Bxf5! White would have a winning attack.

22.Rc7 Qe6

Hoping for 23.Re7 after which Black would play 23...Bxf2+! 24.Qxf2 Rxf2 25.Rxe6 Rxc2.

23.Nxe1 Rxe1+ 24.Kh2 Rd8 25.Bxf6 gxf6?

The losing move. Tal pointed out the drawing line: 25...Qxf6 26.Qxf6 gxf6

27.d7 Kg7 28.Bf5 Re5 29.Rc8 Rxf5 30.Rxd8 Rd5.

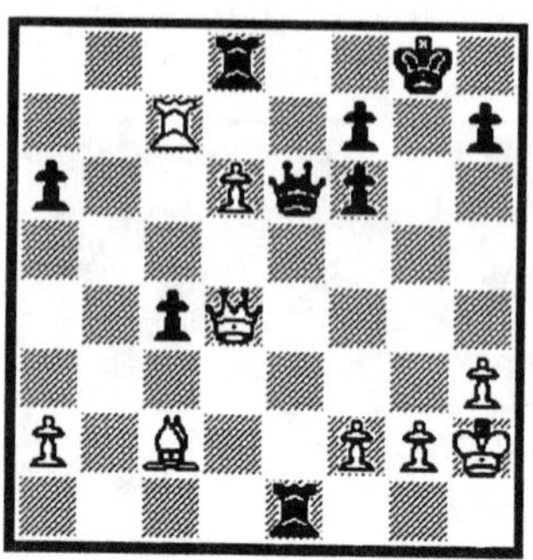

26.Re7!

This wins as now 26...Qxe7 fails to 27.Qg4+.

26...Qxd6+ 27.Qxd6 Rxd6 28.Rxe1

Now it's all over. It is remarkable how a player can thread his way through a maze of complex tactics for many moves and then fail to notice a relatively simple tactical point. The reason often is that time pressure caused by the preceding moves leads to a quick, but ill-fated move.

28...Rd2 29.Rc1 Rxf2 30.Be4 Rxa2 31.Rxc4 a5 32.Rc8+ Kg7 33.Rc7

With threats of 34.Bd5 and 34.Rxf7+ Kxf7 35.Bd5+ and 36.Bxa2. **Black Resigned.**

35. TARRASCH (1862-1934)

Tarrasch continued the work of Steinitz and made it readily available to everyone. His attitude toward actual play was a more practical one, if less courageous and perhaps less profound. His style might be described as "best-quality ready -made". In his later years he had to meet all the novel ideas put forward by such players as Reti and Breyer, and suffered many disappointments against younger players.

Through his writings Tarrasch did more than any man has done to reveal the secrets of good chess to players in general. The many rules he laid down have put many a moderate player on the right lines: *Do not play Knights to the edge of the board; occupy the center with your pawns; constricted positions contain the seeds of defeat; two Bishops are stronger than two Knights or Knight and Bishop; in the endgame the Rook should be placed behind the passed pawns; etc., etc.* But Tarrasch proclaimed only the rules, and ignored the many exceptions.

The influence of Tarrasch is still felt today, and will apparently continue to be. His dislike of constricted positions was so strong that he would accept a weakening of his pawn structure in preference. This explains why, in reply to 1.d4 he was such a convinced- even fanatical – champion of the defense 1...d5 2.c4 e6 3.Nc3 c5, regardless of the isolated d-pawn which can arise after 4.cxd5 exd5. After 1.e4 he considered 1...e5 2.Nf3 Nc6 3.Bb5 a6 4.Ba4 Nf6 5.O-O Nxe4 as just about the only correct defense. Such accepted defenses as the Orthodox Queen's Gambit Declined, and the Steinitz Defense to the Ruy Lopez found no favor with Tarrasch, as they lead to constricted positions. In this respect he differed from Steinitz, who had a distinct liking for defending constricted positions.

Example 263

(The game Breyer-Tarrasch, Goteborg, 1920).

1.d4 d5 2.e3 Nf6 3.Nf3 e6 4.Nbd2 Bd6 5.c4 b6

A preventative measure, designed to stop c5, which would seriously cramp Black.

6.Qc2 Bb7 7.c5?!

Now this is a strategical error, since White loses pawn control of the center. This opinion comes from

Tarrasch in his book *The Game Of Chess*. From this point on we use some of his notes.

7...bxc5 8.dxc5 Be7

Black has exchanged his b-pawn for White's d-pawn; i.e., a wing pawn for a central pawn.

9.b4 O-O 10.Bb2 a5 11.b5

Now White's c-pawn comes under fire. A better choice was 11.a3.

11...c6 12.a4 Nbd7 13.Bd4 Re8!

Black's intentions are clear: he is going to play ...e5.

14.Rc1 Bf8 15.Qb2 Ng4 16.h3 Nh6 17.Nb3 f6 18.Qa3 e5 19.Bc3 Qc7

The right moment, for now 20.b6 would be met by 20...Qxb6!.

20.Bb2 Rec8 21.Qa2!

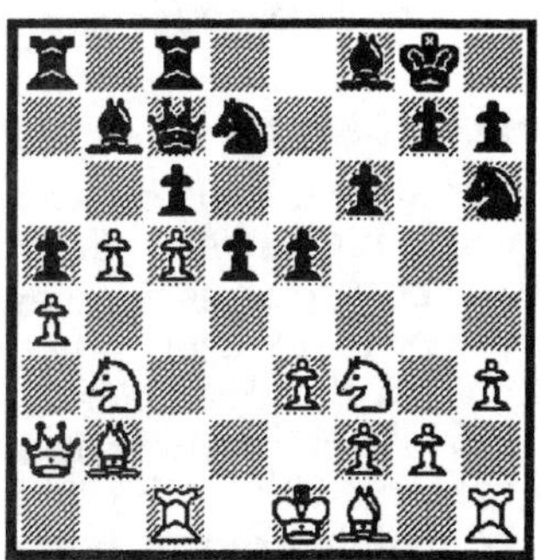

A tactical intermezzo. Now 21...cxb5? would lose a piece after 22.c6! Bxc6 23.axb5.

21...Qd8! 22.b6

The advance of White's Queenside majority has produced a protected passed b-pawn, but the c-pawn remains shakey.

22...Be7 23.Qb1 Qf8 24.Qc2 Nf7 25.h4 Nd8

Everything hinges on the c-pawn.

26.g3 Ne6 27.Bh3

Seemingly protecting the c-pawn indirectly.

27...Nexc5!

Sacrificing the Exchange to secure an overwhelming central pawn roller.

28.Nxc5 Nxc5 29.Ba3 Nd3+ 30.Qxd3 Bxa3 31.Bxc8 Rxc8 32.Ra1 Bb4+ 33.Nd2

Forced, otherwise Black plays ...e4.

To give some idea of Tarrasch's style of analysis and the clarity with which he could set out the essentials of the position, we give here his note on this position:

Black has far and away the better game. As regards material it is quite likely that in the endgame a Rook and two Bishops will turn out to be stronger than two Rooks and a Knight; furthermore the b-pawn is bound to fall. Black's center is very strong, and the advance of the d-pawn and c-pawn will produce a pair of united passed pawns. White is still uncastled, and Black can play to prevent Kingside castling by ...Ra8 and ...Ba6. The White's Rooks have not a single open file at their disposal, and the Knight is pinned. In reality White has only his Queen in play.

It is now up to Black to utilize his chances tactically. The simplest way, though perhaps not best, would be ...Qc5 followed by ...Qxb6 and then the advance of the c-pawn. Black plays however to prevent castling, to deprive the opponent of all good moves, to force all his pieces – especially the Knight-to unfavorable positions and finally to reduce him to desperation.

33...e4 34.Qb3

If 34.Qe2 then 34...Ra8 and 35...Ba6.

34...c5 35.Kd1 c4 36.Qa2 Qd6 37.Ke2 Ba6 38.b7 Rb8 39.Kd1 Rxb7

Tarrasch once said that there is nothing more difficult to do than win a won game, but in the present case he himself has given a very precise demonstration of how to do it.

40.f3 Kh8 41.fxe4 dxe4 42.Kc1 Qxg3 43.Nf1 Qe1+ 44.Kc2 Qc3+ 45.Kd1 Qd3+ 46.Kc1 Rd7

Now if 47.Qc2 then 47...Ba3+ 48.Rxa3 Qxa3+ 49.Qb2 Rd1+ 50.Kc2 Qd3#. **White Resigned.**

36. TARTAKOWER (1888-1956)

Despite the fact that Tartakower played so much chess and became so thoroughly experienced, his play was perpetually original. As a lawyer, he knew the art of defending a weak case; as a chessmaster nothing pleased him more than winning a game by means of a little known or inferior variation. His play showed a clear preference for the methods of Reti, Breyer and Capablanca without rejecting those of Steinitz or Rubinstein. This is clear also in the several excellent books he wrote. Tarrasch has written *Die Modern Schachpartie;* Tartakower responded with *Die Hypermodern Schachpartie* and *Die Zukunftseroffnung* (The Opening of the Future).

Example 264

(The 4th match-game, Tartakower-Sultan Khan, 1931).

1.d4 Nf6 2.g3

A very rare choice at this juncture, but Tartakower loved to play unusual, even bizarre-looking moves (though he was also an outstanding theorist).

2...d5 3.Nf3 c6 4.Bg2 Bf5 5.Nh4 Bg6 6.O-O e6 7.Nd2 Be7 8.Nxg6 hxg6 9.c4 Nbd7 10.Qb3 Qb6 11.Qxb6 axb6

The two Bishops are not an advantage in closed positions of this sort.

In any case, Sultan Khan often preferred Knights to Bishops, and as we shall see, soon trades off his remaining Bishop for the other Knight.

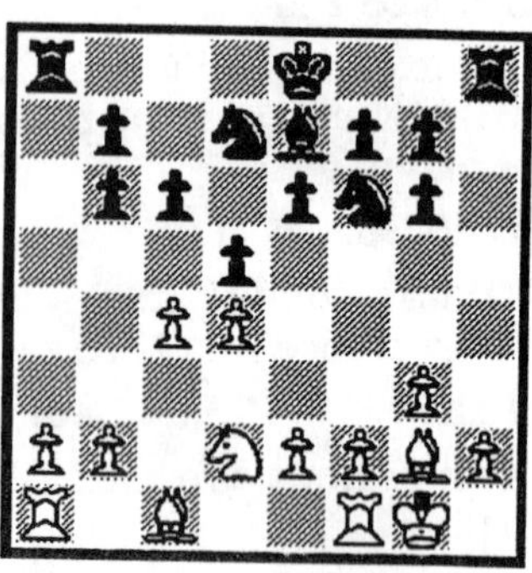

12.Rd1 Bb4

Better was 12...dxc4 13.Nxc4 b5, e.g., 14.Ne5 Nxe5 15.dxe5 Ng4.

13.cxd5 exd5 14.a3 O-O 15.Rb1 Bxd2

Showing his preference for Knights over Bishops.

16.Bxd2 Rfe8 17.Kf1 b5

Steinitz had shown that the way to fight against Knights is to deprive them of their best squares. However, if White plays f3 to keep out one Knight, then the other one maneuvers to c4 via b6. After his next move, White threatens 19.f3 Nb6 20.b3, keeping the Knights out of both c4 and e4.

18.Bb4 g5 19.h3

After 19.f3 Nf8 20.Kf2 Ne6 21.e3, the move 21...g4 is annoying.

19...Ne4 20.Bf3!

Tartakower adopts a new tack.

20...g6 21.Kg2 Kg7 22.e3 f5 23.Rh1 Re6 24.Rbg1!

Finally White's plan clarifies: he is going open a file on the Kingside.

24...Kf7 25.g4 Rh8

After 25...fxg4 26.Bxg4 Rf6 White must avoid 27.Bxd7??, allowing 27...Rxf2#.

However, by 27.f3 he would maintain the advantage.

26.Kf1 Ndf6

Slightly better was 26...f4 27.exf4 gxf4 28.h4 b6.

27.gxf5 gxf5 28.Bxe4! Nxe4 29.f3 Nf6 30.Rxg5 Rxe3 31.Rxf5!

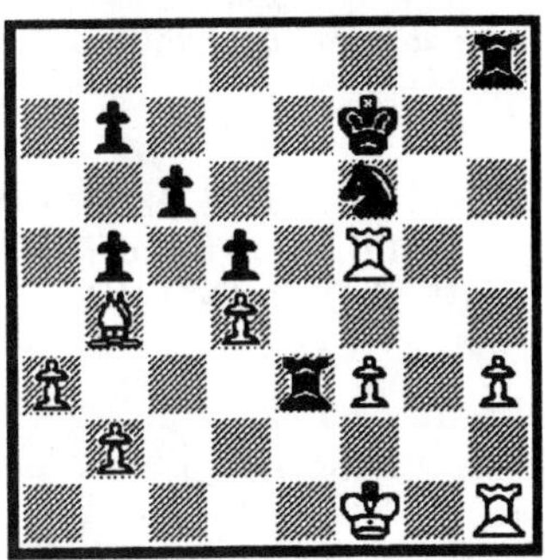

This depends on the finesse 31...Ke6 32.Kf2! (not 32.Rf4? Nh5) Rd3 33.Re5+.

31...Kg6 32.Rf4!

Now this is very strong, while 32.Kf2 would be poor because of 32...Rhe8.

32...Kg5? 33.Bd6 Re6

After 33...Rhe8 34.Rg1+ Kh5 35.Rf5+ White is winning.

34.Rg1+

White now takes advantage of the Black King's exposed position.

34...Kh5 35.Rf5+ Kh6

Or 35...Kh4 36.Bg3+ Kxh3 37.Rg5! and 38.Rh1#.

36.Bf4+ Kh7 37.Be5 Rf8 38.Rf4!. Black Resigned. Some idea of the strength of the opposition here is that Sultan Khan won this match 6.5–5.5.

37. TEICHMANN (1868-1925)

Although Teichmann was generally admitted to be an outstandingly capable player he seldom achieved the great things that were expected of him. The explanation was certainly not a lack of talent or of theoretical knowledge, but almost entirely in a casual attitude towards chess competition. Teichmann was lazy and all too ready to draw, but a mighty man if he ran into difficulties.

Example 265

(The 2nd match-game Mieses-Teichmann, 1910).

1.d3 d5 2.Nd2 e5 3.e4 c6 4.Qe2 Bd6 5.f4

A poor choice psychologically. This was just the kind of move to goad Teichmann out of his natural laziness.

5...exf4 6.exd5+ Ne7 7.dxc6

Otherwise, White will be a pawn down for nothing.

7...Nbxc6 8.Ne4 O-O 9.Qf2 Nd5 10.Bd2

Slightly better was 10.Be2.

10...Ne3!

Showing up the drawbacks of White's opening play.

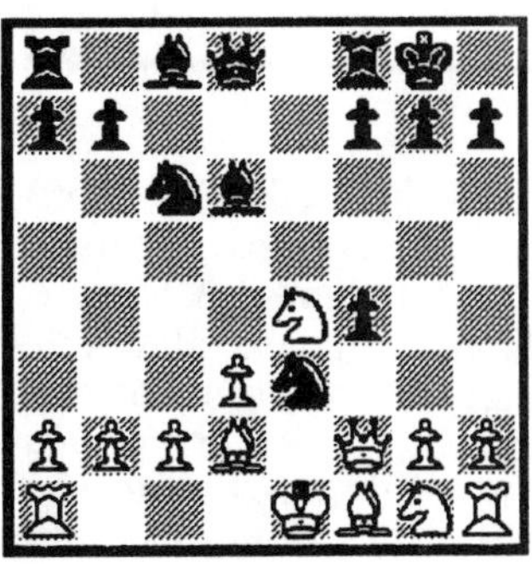

11.Bxe3 fxe3 12.Qxe3

This costs a piece, but 12.Qf3 Nd4 13.Qd1 would only appeal to a Steinitz.

12...Re8 13.O-O-O f5 14.Nf3 fxe4 15.dxe4 Qe7 16.Bc4+ Kh8!

After the obvious 16...Be6, White would have a chance for a winning combination: 17.Bxe6+ Qxe6 18.Ng5 Qxa2 19.Rxd6 Qa1+ 20.Kd2 Qxh1 21.Qb3+ Kh8 22.Nf7+ Kg8 23.Nh6+ Kh8 24.Qg8+ followed by the well-known smothered mate.

17.Ng5 Ne5 18.Bb3 Bg4 19.Rd5 h6 20.h4 Rf8 21.Nh3

Now the rest is easy.

21...Be6 22.Rdd1 Bxb3 23.Qxb3 Rac8 24.g3

One may ask why White is playing on. Perhaps Mieses had in mind the game Teichmann-Burn, Ostend, 1905, in which Teichmann was virtually presented with the Exchange, yet lost in the end by dilatory play – assuming that the game would win itself (he must have forgotten Tarrasch's dictum that there is nothing so hard to win as a won game).

24...Nc4 25.Rhe1 Be5 26.Nf4 Rxf4!

Direct and powerful.

27.gxf4 Bxf4+ 28.Kb1 Nd2+ 29.Rxd2 Bxd2 White Resigned.

38. ZUKERTORT (1842-1888)

Zukertort played thousands of games with the great Anderssen. This must have been a excellent education in the realm of combinative play- insofar as he needed any educating in that art. Zukertort was indeed a tremendously talented combination player; moreover, he avoided the common error of his day, which was to play too wildly. From the positional point of view, however, Zukertort never reached the same heights. In both his matches with Steinitz he was consistently outplayed in this sphere. His failure was in the finding of a plan appropriate to this requirements of the position. But once on the right plan, he was dangerous even to Steinitz.

Example 266

(The 2nd match-game, Steinitz-Zukertort, New York 1886).

1.e4 e5 2.Nf3 Nc6 3.d4 exd4 4.Nxd4 Nf6 5.Nc3 Bb4 6.Nxc6 bxc6 7.Bd3 d5 8.exd5 cxd5 9.O-O O-O 10.Bg5 c6 11.Ne2 Bd6 12.Ng3

Black threatened 12...Bxh2+ 13.Kxh2 Ng4+. Nonetheless, a better choice would have been the more active 12.Nd4.

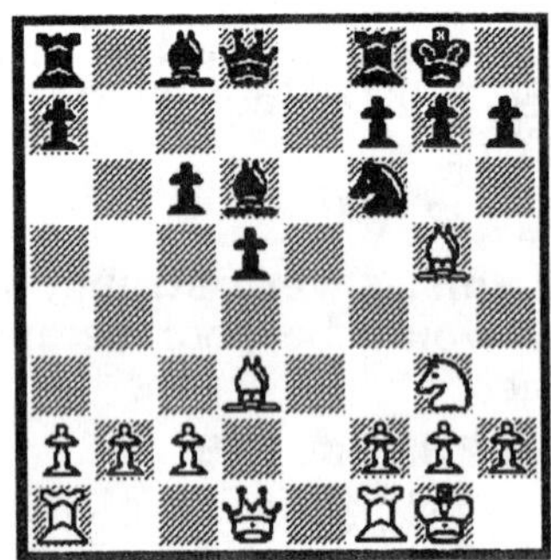

12...h6 13.Bd2? Ng4

Zukertort goes straight for the attack, threatening 14...Qh4. Now if 14.f3 then 14...Nxh2!, while 14.h3 fails to 14...Nxf2!.

14.Be2 Qh4 15.Bxg4 Bxg4 16.Qc1 Be2 17.Re1 Ba6 18.Bc3

Threatening 19.Bxg7 (19...Kxg7 20.Nf5+). If Black tries 18...d4, then White has 19.Re4. Steinitz held that White had a good game at this point.

18...f5 19.Re6 Rad8 20.Qd2

In order to meet 20...f4 with 21.Qd4.

20...d4!

21.Ba5 Rd7 22.Rxd6 Rxd6 23.Bb4 Qf6 24.Rd1?

Evidently, Steinitz didn't like 24.Nxf5 Re6 25.Bxf8 Qxf5; however, he should have tried 24.Re1.

24...Rd5 25.Bxf8 Qxf8 26.Nh5 Qe8 27.Nf4 Re5 28.h4 c5 29.h5?

Steinitz claimed that with 29.b4, he would still have had a good position.

29...Re4 30.c3 Qb8

This was the last move before time control. Apparently 30...Qe5 would have been better: 31.Nd3 Qd6 32.f3 Re3 33.Nf2 Rxf3 34.gxf3 Qg3+ 35.Kh1 Bb7.

31.g3

Had White tried 31.Nd3, Black would have 31...Rh4 32.g3 Rxh5 33.Nxc5 Qa8!.

31...Qe5 32.Ng6 Qd6 33.Nf4 d3!

Zukertort continues to work with tactical finesse. Now if 34.Nxd3 then Black has 34...Bxd3 35.Qxd3 Re1+!.

34.b3 c4 35.Rb1 Kh7 36.Kh2

More accurate was 36.Kg2.

36...Qb6

Threatening 37...Re2! 38.Nxe2 Qxf2+.

37.Kg1 Bb7 38.Rb2 Qc6 39.f3 Qc5+ 40.Qf2

If 40.Kh2 there follows 40...Re2+ 41.Nxe2 Qf2+ 42.Kh3 Qxf3! winning.

40...Re1+ 41.Kh2?

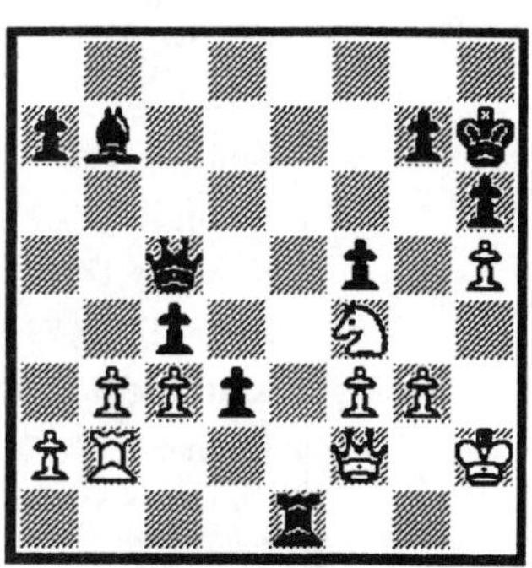

After 41.Kg2! the game could be held, according to Steinitz; e.g., 41...Re3 42.Ne6! Bxf3+ 43.Qxf3 Rxe6 44.bxc4, etc.

41...Qxf2+ 42.Rxf2 Bxf3!

Now on 43.Rxf3 then 43...d2 wins, while after 43.Ng2 Black has 43...Bxg2 44.Kxg2 cxb3 45.axb3 Rc1 46.c4 Rc2 47.Kf1 d2 48.Ke2 d1=Q+.

43.g4 Be2 44.Ng2 d2 45.Ne3 cxb3 46.axb3 Bxg4 White Resigned.

PLAYER INDEX

(References are to POSITION numbers)

OPENINGS INDEX

(References are to position numbers)

1.e4 e5

1.e4 Other

1.d4 d5

1.d4 Other

1.Other

medieval russia's epics, chronicles, and tales

St. George in the garb of a medieval Russian knight.
A sixteenth-century icon.

medieval russia's epics, chronicles, and tales

EDITED, TRANSLATED, AND WITH
AN INTRODUCTION BY

Serge A. Zenkovsky

Professor and Director of Russian Studies, Stetson University

NEW YORK
E. P. DUTTON & CO., INC.

Published simultaneously in Canada by
Clarke, Irwin & Company Limited,
Toronto and Vancouver.

ACKNOWLEDGMENTS

Grateful acknowledgment is made to the following for permission to quote from copyright material:

Selections from *The Russian Primary Chronicle* as translated by Samuel H. Cross in *Harvard Studies and Notes in Philology and Literature,* Volume XII, 1930, reprinted by permission of the Harvard University Press. Copyright, 1930, 1958, by The President and Fellows of Harvard College.

Selection from *The Correspondence between Prince A. M. Kurbsky and Tsar Ivan IV of Russia* translated by J. L. I. Fennell, 1955, reprinted by permission of the Cambridge University Press, London and New York.

LIBRARY OF CONGRESS CATALOG CARD NUMBER: 63-8606

SBN 0-525-47117-0

PREFACE

In preparing this volume for publication, I felt that at the present level of American and British scholarship in the field of Russian studies the time has come to offer readers and students a comprehensive anthology of Russia's medieval literature in translation. The works of modern Russian writers of the nineteenth century, especially those of the age of the great Russian novel as represented by Dostoevsky and Tolstoy, have long since become an inalienable part of American and British curricula of literary studies and of collections in public and school libraries. Also rather well known are the contemporary writings of Russia's Soviet period. Very different is the situation regarding the literature of previous centuries, especially that of the Russian Middle Ages, which lasted until the beginning of the eighteenth century. Indeed, there are available in English translation such masterpieces of medieval Russian letters as the *Primary Chronicle*, the *Lay of Igor's Campaign*, some adaptations and translations of the *Life*, or autobiography, of Avvakum, and of some other works written from the eleventh through the seventeenth centuries. Most of these translations, however, are either out of print or not readily available, having appeared in rare or expensive editions. Moreover, the tremendous remaining part of Russian medieval writings has never been translated either into English or into any other Western language.

The present anthology is therefore a pioneering effort to present to Western readers the finest works, a few in excerpt, of Russian literature from its very beginning, in the early eleventh century, through the seventeenth century, when Peter the Great forced Russia to rejoin the European family of nations and discard its medieval culture.

Russian medieval literature is very extensive. According to incomplete statistics, for example, there are over seven thousand versions of lives of saints written during Russia's Middle Ages, and many thousands of chronicles and tales. Therefore, the task of selecting for translation the most outstanding of these was not easy. I attempted to solve this problem by offering here as many recognized masterpieces of that period as possible, together with some lesser known works that also contribute to an understanding of the mentality, culture, and literary manners of Old Russia. My guiding principle was to offer entire works whenever possible, or at least complete narrative passages from such longer writings as the chronicles, in order to give the reader an opportunity to grasp the style and spirit of the Russians of that age. In a few cases—as, for instance, the long historical and polemical writings of the sixteenth and early seventeenth centuries—I decided, owing to the limitations of this volume, to include the most characteristic and interesting passages, in order to convey a more complete picture of the evolution of Russian letters.

When possible, already existing translations have been used; but the major part of the works published in this book appear for the first time in English. The translation of medieval Russian letters presents a number of technical difficulties. Their syntax, structure, and style are very different from the methods and devices of contemporary writers. Therefore, the translation of many passages required some adaptation to the mode of expression of modern English for them to be comprehensible to readers. For the sake of those who are not well acquainted with Russian medieval history, geography, and terminology, the words "prince," "city," or "river" have been added to avoid possible confusion. Since the Russian medieval calendar was 5,508 years behind the Western one, the corresponding Western dates have been supplied where necessary.

A customarily difficult problem is that of the transliteration of Russian names. For the titles of original Russian sources the system of the Library of Congress has been used, except for the diacritical signs. In the transliteration of Russian names and terminology, the Library of Congress system underwent some minor modification: for instance, the initial Russian soft vowels rendered by *ia* or *iu* have been changed to the more readable *ya* or *yu* (that is, "Yaroslav," not "Iaroslav"); the final *ii* and *yi* have been replaced by *y* (that is, "Kurbsky" instead of "Kurbskii"); and the final *iia* has been rendered by *ia* ("Dobrynia" in place of "Dobryniia"). Most of the proper names are given in their Russian form. Those of the clergy, such as "Theodosius" or "Sergius," are usually given in their original Greek or Latin version, and those of foreign rulers and writers in their original form, while common Christian names, such as "Alexander," "Nicholas," "Andrew," or "Helen," are given in the usual English manner.

Of the works previously translated into English and incorporated in the present collection, many have been revised against the original Russian texts and their transliteration of Russian names altered for the sake of consistency. It is my pleasant duty to acknowledge my gratitude to the following publishing houses, persons, and institutions for their permission to reproduce here the material listed:

1. to Harvard University Press, Cambridge, Massachusetts, for permission to reprint passages from *The Russian Primary Chronicle*, translated by Samuel H. Cross;

2. to G. P. Putnam's Sons, New York, and London, for permission to use portions of Leo Wiener's *Anthology of Russian Literature*;

3. to the Editorial Board of the *Slavonic and East European Review*, London, for permission to reprint *Adam's Address to Lazarus in Hell*, translated anonymously and published in Volume X (1932), pp. 145–152;

4. to Mr. Nicholas Zernov and The Society for the Promotion of Christian Knowledge, London, for permission to reprint *The Acts and Miracles of Our Dear and Holy Father, Sergius*, by Epiphanius the Wise, from *St. Sergius, Builder of Russia*, translated by Nicholas Zernov;

5. to Cambridge University Press, London and New York, for permission to reprint J. L. I. Fennell's translation of Prince Andrew Kurbsky's "First Epistle to Ivan IV," from *The Correspondence between Prince A. Kurbsky and Tzar Ivan IV of Russia*;

6. to Miss U. M. Lane and The Hogarth Press, Ltd., London, for permission to use *The Life of Archpriest Avvakum by Himself*, translated by Jane Harrison and Hope Mirrless.

In the preparation of this volume I was assisted by students in my graduate seminar on ancient Russian literature at the University of Colorado. The Reverend George Benigsen helped in translating *The Life of Yuliania Lazarevskyaya*, while Mr. Dan B. Chopyk translated Bishop Serapion's *Sermon on Merciless Heathens*. The remaining translations were made by myself in cooperation with my graduate student and assistant, Mr. Richard White. It is evident, however, that I am the only person responsible for all possible errors or shortcomings in selecting, translating, and commenting on the works in this book.

I am grateful to the Graduate School of the University of Colorado for financial help toward the completion of this volume when I was Professor of Slavic Languages and Literatures at that University.

Only I can fully appreciate the contribution made by my wife and colleague, Betty Jean, whose interest and editorial skill were so helpful in the planning and completion of *Medieval Russia's Epics, Chronicles, and Tales*.

SERGE A. ZENKOVSKY

CONTENTS

ILLUSTRATIONS

Maps

A page from the Gospel of Ostromir written in 1056.
It is the oldest Russian book in existence.

INTRODUCTION

The Literature of Medieval Russia

The term "Middle Ages" has a somewhat different connotation and time span for Russia than for Western Europe. In the West the Middle Ages began in the fifth century, when the Western Roman Empire fell under the blows of Germanic barbarians. They ended at the close of the fifteenth century or the beginning of the sixteenth, when Columbus discovered the New World, Luther broke the spiritual unity of the West, and secularized thought put an end to the "Age of Faith." The Russian Middle Ages began much later, only in the ninth century, and her Age of Faith came to an end in the early eighteenth century, when Russia adopted the secularized culture of Western Europe.

During the years that witnessed the fall of Rome, the Slavic tribes inhabiting the territory of present Russia were still in the age of prehistory. Only scattered data about the apparently Slavic "Antes" point to the inception of a loosely organized statehood in that area. Four additional centuries were needed for the appearance of a more solid national structure among the Eastern Slavs and for their emergence on the stage of history. The first indications of a firmly founded government among the Eastern Slavs, in the cities of Novgorod and Kiev, can be observed only in the ninth century when, in 862, according to legend, a certain Rurik became the prince of Novgorod. Since that time the word "Rus," or Russians, rapidly won a place in the pages of historical annals. In the tenth century the Kievan prince and conqueror Sviatoslav built a vast empire spreading from the Volga to the Dnieper and Danube rivers, and from Kiev to Novgorod. Despite these military and political successes, however, the culture of this early Russian state remained at a modest level. Only after the Christianization of Russia in 988 or 989 by Sviatoslav's son, Vladimir, did literacy and literature appear among these Slavs, and only from that time can historians observe the first blossoming of early Russian culture.

I. THE KIEVAN PERIOD (1030–1240)

1. Church Slavonic

Christianity came to Russia from Byzantium, or, as it was often called, the Eastern Roman Empire, at that time a powerful and highly developed nation culturally. Its flourishing capital, Constantinople, was still the most important political and cultural center of Europe and commanded a vast empire comprising the Balkan Peninsula, the Aegean Archipelago, all of Asia Minor, and parts of Italy. Its literary and state language was Greek; and Byzantium, as the preserver of both Christian thought and Greco-Roman arts and letters, was the main luminary of knowledge for still "dark" Western Europe. Despite Russia's conversion to Byzantine Christianity, however, Greek never won a position in Russia similar to that of Latin in the West, where for centuries Latin remained the exclusive liturgic and educational medium for medieval Catholic Europe. Indeed, from the very beginning of evangelization in Russia, the mass was read in Russian churches in Slavic, not in Greek. This does not mean that the Byzantine Greeks were not nationalists. To be sure, they always placed their language, the tongue of Homer, Plato, and the Gospel, above all others. Still, the wealth of the native cultures of non-Greek provinces of Byzantium compelled them at an early stage to permit the churches of the Middle East to use languages other than Greek. Later, when in 863 the Moravian prince Rostislav asked Constantinople to send missionaries for the Christianization of his realm—which occupied the present territories of Slovakia and Hungary—the Byzantine Church did not hesitate to permit the use of the Slavic tongue in the new churches.

The tasks of creating an alphabet for the Slavs and forming out of the primitive Slavic vernacular a suitable language for the mass and Gospel was entrusted to two brothers, Cyril and Methodius, Greek monks from the city of Saloniki. Linguists of genius, Cyril and Methodius created a Slavic alphabet (commonly called "Cyrillic") on the basis of the Greek one. They translated the ecclesiastic literature into one of the dialects of the Slavs of Macedonia, using Byzantine Greek stylistics and syntax. This new, somewhat artificial literary language—now called "Church Slavonic"—was perfectly Slavic in its vocabulary and grammar but rather Byzantine in its stylistic aspect.

Transplanted to Russia as a liturgic and literary language, Church Slavonic, which was very close to Old Russian, proceeded to absorb specific features of this Eastern Slavic language. Thus there developed a very interesting Russian literary language composed of Church Slavonic, with its original South Slavic linguistic features, interspersed with purely Russian characteristics. Surviving some periods of Russification, this adopted language remained the official literary language of Russia until the end of the seventeenth century, and the literary monuments written in it often have an elevated, solemn, even esoteric, coloration. As there were in medieval Russia no definite standards for the literary language, an erudite or sophisticated writer or cleric would couch his literary prose exclusively in Church Slavonic—which strongly reflected the refined and adorned stylistics of Byzantine letters—while in the same given period private correspondence, state documents, and even some simpler literary works were written in an almost pure and stylistically more naïve Old Russian vernacular. The possibilities for interweaving these two very close yet contrasting linguistic strata were innumerable and, since strict linguistic rules for the written language were established only in the eighteenth century, many Old Russian texts have a particular charm owing to a mingling of the vernacular with Church Slavonic. Unfortunately, this aspect of Old Russian literary monuments can not be reproduced at all in translation.

2. The Advantages and Limitations of Church Slavonic

The entire subsequent development of medieval Russian culture and literature was thus determined by the introduction and example of the Byzantine literary legacy in Church Slavonic translations. Initially, such adoption of a new culture in a linguistically comprehensible version offered a very considerable advantage for the Russians, who, contrary to the experience of the Catholic Germans or Poles, had not to learn a difficult foreign language, that is, Latin or Greek, in order to absorb the new religion and civilization. Byzantium's ecclesiastic and some of its secular literature, with all its stylistic patterns and genre models, became readily available to the Eastern Slavs in translation, and Russian letters were given a rapid start. Their beginning appears even spectacular when compared with the literary destinies of the Western Slavs—the Czechs and the Poles—who, having been Christianized by Rome, were obliged to adopt Latin in their mass and in their writing. Poland's first literary work in its native language did not appear until some three hundred years after its conversion to Christianity, and even five hundred years after evangelization the Poles continued to write in Latin more often than in Polish. A very similar delayed development can be observed among the Czechs. The first original Russian writings, however—some sermons by the Novgorodian and Kievan preachers, Bishop Luka Zhidiata and Metropolitan Hilarion—appeared as early as forty or fifty years after Russia's conversion. The *Primary Chronicle*, a significant work of literary, historical, and ideological interest came into being just a little over a century after the appearance in Kiev of Christian priests and Church Slavonic manuscripts, while the *Lay of Igor's Campaign*, Russia's greatest monument in the heroic epic tradition, had already been written within two centuries after her Christianization.

The spread of Byzantine culture to Russia in its Church Slavonic versions, however, also had negative aspects. Because Russian priests officiated in Church Slavonic, they were not obliged to study Greek, and the knowledge of this language and of antique, classical, culture for centuries remained extremely limited in Russia. While Western Europe did not forget Virgil and classical Latin even during the darkest years of its cultural dormance—the fifth to eighth centuries—during the Russian Middle Ages knowledge of the Greek language and acquaintance with Byzantine literature in the original was restricted to but a few representatives of the upper cultural strata. Numerous translations from Greek into Church Slavonic were made in Russia but most of these were of theological or historical works. Neither the wealth of pre-Christian Greek literature nor the entirety of Byzantine secular writings became known to medieval Russians. The Russian clergy was apparently afraid to translate and propagate the works of pagan writers, while the Greeks themselves were not especially interested in spreading education and their cultural heritage among the Slavs. It can be surmised that Byzantium was content to keep Russia as a cultural colony not expected to attain the level of civilization of its cultural "mother country." In any case, the Greeks sent to Russia neither teachers for the purpose of forming a sophisticated cultural elite nor the works of ancient Greece. Moreover, they preferred to appoint Greeks to the head of the Russian Church than to prepare Russians for such positions, and did very little to raise the intellectual standard of the native Russian clergy. Thus, the humanistic, scientific, and philosophic traditions of Byzantium put down no substantial roots in Russia, and Byzantium's influence remained limited primarily to the religious, political, and artistic spheres, while the bulk of classical Greek, as well as Latin, thought and letters remained almost unknown to Russians until the late seventeenth century.

3. Kievan Russia

As has been pointed out, the cultural history of Russia begins largely with its Christianization at the end of the tenth century. While an early Russian state had existed at least since the mid-ninth century, and some scattered information concerning the national-state organization of the Russian, or Eastern, Slavs can be traced from the seventh century after Christ, or even the fifth (the state of the Antes), disappointingly little is known about the life of the pagan Russians and their culture. Judging from the quick flowering of their letters, art, and architecture after Christianization in 988–989, it can be presumed that the earliest contacts of the Eastern Slavs with Greece, Byzantium, the Caucasus, and peoples of the Eurasian steppes led to the formation in Eastern Europe of a very definite cultural type even before Christianity and letters came there. The trade routes from Scandinavia to Byzantium, from Central Asia and the Far East to Western Europe, passed through the territory of this early Russian state and certainly contributed to its cultural growth. The city of Kiev was at the crossroads of these two important trade routes, and its rise as the capital of a Russian state was largely due to the prosperity brought it by merchants who traveled to or through the city. After the Russians' conversion to Christianity at the instance of the Kievan Prince Vladimir (ruled 978–1015), Byzantine culture in its Slavicized forms won the dominant position among the Russians for the next seven centuries, and the years from A.D. 1000 to 1700 can be called the medieval or "Byzantinized" period of Russia.

Kiev itself became one of the wealthiest and most animated cities of medieval Europe, richer and more brilliant than Paris or London of the time. It was adorned with innumerable churches, and by the time of the reign of Vladimir's son, Yaroslav (ruled in Kiev 1019–1054) there were already numerous schools, hospitals, and libraries. In the eleventh and twelfth centuries Russia was an integral part of Europe, and Kievan princes maintained close dynastic ties with the ruling houses of Western countries. Their children married the sovereigns or princesses of England, Germany, France, Sweden, Hungary, and Byzantium. A daughter of Prince Yaroslav, Anna, married King Phillip of France and was the only literate member of the French royal family, for whom she signed state documents herself. Prince Vladimir Monomakh (who ruled in Kiev from 1112 to 1125), the grandson of Yaroslav, married Princess Gita, daughter of the last Anglo-Saxon king, Harold, whose family had been obliged to abandon England after the Norman Conquest and to live as emigrés in Kiev, where there were many foreigners. Western chronicles often mention the wealth and beauty of this early Russian capital. The German chronicler, Tittmar of Magdeburg, remarks that, during a fire, over four hundred churches burned in Kiev. The city's main cathedral, St. Sophia (Holy Wisdom), was lavishly decorated with delicate frescoes and mosaics. Its marble pillars were brought from the Crimea, and even now, despite centuries of mutilation and restoration, the cathedral's proportions and dimensions produce a strong impression.

The Kievan era, however, was short-lived: from the late tenth century to the early thirteenth. Yaroslav's children and grandchildren sundered the unity of Kievan Russia by indulging in fratricidal feuds and Vladimir Monomakh was the last Kievan sovereign recognized as leader by all the Russian princes. After his death the Kievan state disintegrated into a number of large and small principalities that competed and fought with one another. In the face of increasingly frequent raids into the South Russian territories by Turkic nomads—Pechenegs and, later, Kumans (Polovetsians)—the Slavic population began to migrate from the southern area of Kiev to the forests in the north, or westward to the plains of Galicia and the Carpathian Piedmont. The prosperous merchant city of Novgorod in the northwest, Galich—the capital of Galicia—in the extreme southwest, and the cities of Suzdal and Vladimir—precursors of Moscow—in the northeast outgrew Kiev in prominence. With the conquest of the Holy Land and Constantinople by the Crusaders, new trade routes opened up from West to East and Kiev's importance as a trading center rapidly diminished. The Mongol (Tatar) invasion that took place in 1237–1240 under the leadership of the heirs of Genghis Khan dealt the final blow to the dying Kievan state. Kiev itself was sacked and burned, not to recover for centuries; most other Russian cities were also devastated, and some two-thirds of the Russian population perished. Thus weakened, most of western and southern Russia then fell to the Lithuanians and Poles, while the rest of Russia remained a vassal state of the Mongol (Tatar) Empire for the following two centuries.

4. The Byzantine Literary Heritage of Kievan Russia

When Russia was Christianized by Prince Vladimir, some Christian literature and several secular Byzantine works had already been translated from the Greek into Church Slavonic by Cyril and Methodius or by Bulgarians, who formed a powerful Slavic state in the Balkans in the ninth and tenth centuries. Bulgaria's proximity to Byzantium stimulated the knowledge of Greek among the Bulgarians and an active translation of Greek works into Church Slavonic, as well as the transmission of Byzantine literary patterns from the Greeks to the Slavs. These

South Slavic translations from Greek became the first writings available to the Russians. Later, a considerable number of Byzantine writings were translated in Russia itself. Among the former, of capital importance were, of course, the Gospel and parts of the Old Testament, particularly the Psalms, which in Church Slavonic were readily understandable to all Russians who attended the Church service. Many of the liturgic texts had been composed by Byzantine theologians who were at the same time talented religious poets, such as St. John Damascene. Their aesthetic perfection, so clearly reflected in the ornate beauty of the Russian Church service itself, greatly influenced the subsequent spiritual and artistic development of the Russian people, while the stylistic and compositional influence of patristic writings on all genres of ancient Russian literature remained very great.

Among the translated literature, of prime importance also were writings of the early Christian Fathers and the "lives," or *vitae* (*zhitie*), of early Christian and Byzantine saints. Of the former, the most popular in Russia were the writings of St. John Chrysostom, which were continually translated and recopied throughout the whole seven centuries of the Russian Middle Ages. The spirit of this great Antiochian preacher of Christian social teachings influenced Russian religiosity almost as much as the Gospel itself; in any case, much more than the Old Testament—which, with the exception of the Psalms, was not often read by Russians. A collection of St. John Chrysostom's sermons, *Marguerite* (*The Pearl*), was printed in the 1630's long before the publication of the first full text of the Bible.

Saints' lives, often enhanced by fictional elements, were compiled in special collections in which the *vitae* were arranged in the order of the calendar; they remained for centuries the most edifying reading for Russians. Even as late as the nineteenth century, Greek, Syrian, Egyptian, and Russian *vitae* found an echo in the works of Tolstoy, Dostoevsky, Leskov, Turgenev, and other Russian authors, while for early Russian writers, especially the compilers of the *vitae* of native Russian saints, translated Byzantine hagiography constituted the main source for stylistic and spiritual inspiration.

Of similar attraction for the Russian reader were the Apocrypha—writings on subjects of the Old and New Testaments not recognized by the Church as authentic or canonic, translated from Greek into Church Slavonic either in Bulgaria or in Russia. Among them the apocrypha on King Solomon—whose wisdom eclipsed for Russian minds that of Aristotle and Plate—as well as the apocryphal tale *Descent of the Virgin Into Hell*, particularly absorbed the Russian reader. The latter was apparently considerably reworked in Russia and, in its content, was something of an Eastern counterpart to Dante's *Divine Comedy*. Russians liked especially its spirit of compassion for sinners, shown by the Holy Virgin's intercession on behalf of the souls condemned to perpetual torment. The Jobian theme of man's discontent with his fate was treated, in the form of a dialogue, in the apocryphal tale *Adam's Address to Lazarus in Hell.* This theme was taken up some six centuries later in an autobiographical *vita* by Monk Epiphany, a follower of the famous martyred Archpriest Avvakum.

A few works from Byzantine scholarly literature became known in Kievan and, later, in Muscovite Russia, such as the historical chronicles of John Malalas and George Hamartolas and the *History of the Judaic War* by Joseph Flavius. The style and manner of these writers were followed by the early Russian chroniclers.

Secular tales received by Russia from Byzantium included the legends of *Barlaam* and *Josaphat* and *Digenis Arkritas*, as well as the *Alexandria.* The first, of Indian origin, gives an account of the life of Buddha, who is presented as Prince Josaphat, a fictitious Christian hero and saint. It was reworked in Byzantium and Russia many times, and in the sixteenth century a Russian hymnologist, Markel Bezborody, composed a poetic church service in honor of this prince. The legend of *Digenis Akritas* originated within the confines of Byzantium and Persia and related the heroic deeds of Christian knights fighting the infidels. Although this Byzantine forerunner of the Spanish epic of El Cid was almost the only knightly tale known to Kievan Russia, its entire romantic element was expurgated from it by the austere Church authorities.

None of the great works of pre-Christian Greek poets, playwrights, and philosophers apparently found their way to Old Russian readers. It is true that Homer was known to them, at least by name, and some passages from his works were translated, but it can not be definitely stated that larger portions of his writings were ever in the hands of the literate Kievan. Almost the same can be said of the writings of Plato and Aristotle. While occasional quotations and passages from the works of these philosophers can be found in some ancient collections, as, for instance, *The Bee*, none of their works was ever entirely translated into Church Slavonic.

5. Earliest Russian Sermons and Thought

In the cultural life of every newly converted land, the clergy always occupies a position of pre-eminence. Therefore there is nothing astonishing in the fact that the first Russian writers and learned men were predominantly representatives of the Church. In Novgorod, soon after his elevation to the bishopric there in 1036, Luka Zhidiata wrote his *Instruction*, which is usually considered the oldest dated work in Russian literature. This is a didactic, rather dry homily consisting of admonitions and reminders concerning Church ritual. It is written in very simple language and can hardly be considered an inspiring piece of rhetoric.

Of completely different intellectual and literary value are the sermons of Metropolitan Hilarion, the first Russian—not Greek—head of the Russian Church, elevated to this position in 1051 by Yaroslav the Wise. Hilarion was a well-trained theologian and skillful writer who apparently knew Greek and was well versed in Byzantine religious literature. His main work, the *Sermon on Law and Grace*, is especially pointed and convincing, and despite its elaborate allegorical language the thought is clear and readily understandable. It begins with a treatment of the problem of the spiritual superiority of the New Testament over the Old: of the teachings of Christ over the law of Moses. Hilarion then switches very astutely from this topic to the thesis of the equality of newly converted Russia with older Byzantium. He considers that Russia has gained an honorable position in the Christian world because the religion of grace, ". . . the fount of the Gospel . . . overflowed upon our land . . . and, together with all Christians, we glorify the Holy Trinity." Hilarion presents the destiny of Russia in the general framework of world history and interprets it in the light of the divine plan for the general salvation of mankind. Strangely enough, this earliest Russian metropolitan is rather a philosopher of history than a preacher of purely religious, moralistic truths, and the appearance of a thinker of such depth of historical vision in the first decades of Russian Christian history is one of the most amazing phenomena of the early development of Russian culture.

While Hilarion is primarily anthropocentric, more concerned in his writings with the fate of man on earth or of the nation than with purely theological problems, Cyril of Turov, a preacher of the mid-twelfth century, is entirely theocentric. A member of a rich noble family, Cyril preferred the life of a monk to a military or court career. He subsequently became bishop, but he always remained a man of contemplation, meditating on the mystical relation between God and man. Of his numerous works, his sermons won the particular admiration of his contemporaries and of later generations. Their main concern is the problem of salvation, which he treats with great erudition and oratorical skill. Perhaps he often exaggerates in the use of complex allegories and metaphors, but it is precisely this perfect command of ornate Byzantine stylistics that lends his writing great charm and elegance. For long centuries his sermons remained the best example of elevated rhetoric in Russian literature, and Cyril can be called, without exaggerating, the greatest preacher of medieval Russia.

A rather humanistic trend in the Russian sermon was represented by the works of Metropolitan Clement, a native of Smolensk who was elected to the metropolitan see in Kiev in 1147. His contemporaries accused him of quoting more often from Plato, Aristotle, and Homer than from the Bible or the Church Fathers. The only fragment of his works which has been preserved is an impressive example of early Russian scholarship in the best Byzantine tradition. Clement's knowledge of Byzantine Greek learning seems to be very extensive, and there is reason to believe that he completed his education not in Russia but in some Greek monastery or school.

Very close in his cultural background and spirit to these prelates of the Russian Church was Prince Vladimir Monomakh (died 1125), grandson of Yaroslav the Wise. Monomakh had a fluent command of five foreign languages, was well read, and left some significant writings. Among them, his *Instruction*, addressed to his children, stands out for its penetrating moral and spiritual portrayal of the author himself. The work of a wise layman, a stern though benevolent, indefatigable, and farsighted ruler, the *Instruction* was written for the practical purpose of advising his children. In his admonitions Vladimir shows himself to have a profound understanding of Christian teaching, and illustrates his advice with examples from his own life. According to Monomakh, humility, contemplation, and the examination of one's own mind and life are the main instruments in the hard task of the self-perfection of a ruler. He follows the general patterns of the instructions of Byzantine and even Anglo-Saxon rulers (it may be recalled that his wife was an Anglo-Saxon princess). His ideas concerning a prince's obligations to his people and to himself are, however, original, yet appropriate to the general framework of the developing Russian spirituality: a ruler should never forget the teaching of Christ, for humility is one of the outstanding qualities of a Christian man and prince.

Among the erudite men of Kievan Russia was also a certain Daniel, styled "the Exile," who was the author of a *Supplication* written circa 1200 and addressed to the prince of Suzdal, Yaroslav. More adroitly than any other stylist of the dawn of Russian writing, Daniel plays gracefully with quotations from the Bible and Greek writers, Russian folk sayings, and his own pointed witticisms. Apparently intended as a petition for patronage, Daniel's *Supplication* displays his superior command of literary Church Slavonic and contemporary learning.

6. Chronicles

The chronicle (*letopis*) forms the most important and sizable part of Russian literature of the Kievan Era. These chronicles—or, more precisely, annals, since they consist usually of annual entries organized chronologically—contain very heterogeneous material. Along with concise entries giving in one or several lines information on a ruler or an event in a city, there can be found various historical and diplomatic documents, treaties, and admonitions, as well as longer stories about the deeds, adventures, and campaigns of a prince or the prose recordings of heroic legends. The Russian chronicles were not the product of a single author but a complex and continuously maintained work that was copied, completed, and often re-edited by successive writers. The earliest Russian annals are the *Primary Chronicle,* or *The Tale of Bygone Years*—the most interesting and best written of them. There can be discerned various distinct layers in the *Primary Chronicle,* which was begun about 1040 and continued through 1118 by at least six different annalists, among whom the most remarkable were its first writer-editor, Monk Nikon, who worked on it in the 1060's, and Monk Nestor, one of its last editors and compilers, who practically completed the writing of this work. It is very difficult to determine now which of its various writers gave the chronicle its general tenor and main ideological line, but in any case this "collective" work, the compositional elements of which are so heterogeneous, still produces a very unified and sustained impression. The annalist, or annalists, consistently stress the necessity of preserving the unity of the Kievan state, appeal repeatedly to the princes to give up their fratricidal feuds and live in brotherly love because they are members of the same dynasty, "brothers who have the same father and the same mother," who are supposed to preserve, not destroy, the fruits "of the heavy labor" of their forefathers.

In the Prolegomenon to the *Primary Chronicle* the annalist studies the formation of different peoples and races, all of whom were the offspring of Noah, and succeeds in finding among them the Slavs, the descendants of Japhet, thus establishing an honorable biblical background for his own nation. Describing the legendary visit to Russia by the Apostle Andrew, the annalist does not fail to claim that this Disciple of Christ predicted the forthcoming blossoming of Christianity in Russia. Very cleverly interweaving the actual fabric of historical material with legendary accounts and reminiscences, the annalist succeeds in creating a religious and political tradition for his newly emerged country, and points out that Russia has won a respectable status among the other nations of the Christian world.

A considerable amount of historical information covering the centuries preceding the rise of Russia was evidently taken from Byzantine chronicles, but it is reworked stylistically and ideologically. The very structure of the Russian annals—their chronological yearly entries—is different from that of Byzantine historical works, which are usually organized into chapters covering the reigns of the emperors.

Stories and tales integrated into the historical entries convey considerable freshness and charm to the *Primary Chronicle*. Many of these accounts, as, for instance, of the death of Prince Oleg or the revenge of Princess Olga, have a clearly legendary background and were probably taken from the epic tradition. Others have the character of actual eyewitness accounts, as, notably, the dramatic story of the blinding of Vasilko, written by Priest Vassily, or the narratives about the life of the monks of the Kievan Crypt Monastery.

The *Primary Chronicle* was the earliest and most literary, but not the only, historical work of the Kievan period. Most leading cities, as well as certain branches of the Rurik dynasty, which then ruled Russia, maintained their own annals from the twelfth century. Among these, the *Galician-Volynian Chronicle* and the *Kievan Chronicle* (a continuation of the *Primary Chronicle*) are the more skillfully written, and contain many passages that were the work of gifted writers. Most of the chronicles were written by members of the clergy, mainly monks; only the *Galician-Volynian* and perhaps the twelfth-century *Kievan* chronicles, which emphasize details of army and court life, were composed probably by a member of the princes' retinue. The northern chronicles, on the other hand, especially those of the city of Novgorod, are much drier and more concise, and are characterized by their business-like, even abrupt, style.

The heroes of the chronicles are predominantly princes. Sometimes the chronicler mentions commanders, knights, or priests, but such characters are certainly secondary. The annalists of the Kievan Era gave simple yet impressive sculptural—even monumental, in the words of D. Likhachev—portrayals of their hero-princes, who are divided clearly into positive characters and villains. The portrayals are frequently stereotyped: a good prince is usually described as "a good man of war," "handsome of face," "mild of habits," or "detesting wrong and loving right." The main positive attributes are defense of the Russian land, protection of the Church, and generosity toward his subjects. Few feminine figures appear in the chronicles, indeed, in general, in all of early Russian literature. Those that do are either faithful wives or affectionate mothers, but never a participant in a romantic love intrigue. Contrary to the Western tradition, Russia's austere Middle Ages do not know any amorous or erotic themes such as can be found in the *chansons* of the troubadours, not to speak of such manuals on the art of love as *de Arte honesti amandi* (1170) or *La Clef d'Amour* (1250), which were completely unthinkable in Kievan and early Muscovite letters. No traces even of innocent romantic courtship can be found in Russian chronicles or tales until the seventeenth century. The only exception, the Tale of *Peter and Fevronia of Murom*, written in the fifteenth century, stands out strikingly in pre-seventeenth century Russian literature for its unusual love theme, but even here the motif is one of the affection and devotion between a husband and wife.

7. Kievan Vitae and Paterics

Narrative writing with extensive biographical, occasionally fictional or legendary, content can be found in Kievan literature in the *vitae* (*zhitie*, saints' lives or hagiography) and paterics (monk's lives). While these two genres, especially the *vitae*, adhered to strict compositional patterns, they were nevertheless often embellished with interesting details mirroring medieval psychology and the author's own imagination.

The tragic fate of the Princes Boris and Gleb, sons of Vladimir, Christianizer of Russia, who were killed in 1016 in a fratricidal feud by order of their elder brother, was described in *vita* form as well as in two other narratives. Written by Nestor, one of the authors of the *Primary Chronicle*, the *vita* version of the brothers' martyrdom is most detailed and realistic, and it places the fratricide within the framework of Russian religious history. In Nestor's eyes Boris and Gleb were martyrs for peace in Russia, preferring death to participation in internecine strife. Their pathos is heightened by the touching laments Nestor puts in their mouths in anticipation of their murder. The anonymous author of the *Legend* (*Skazanie*) about Boris and Gleb emphasizes less their desire to preserve peace in Russia than their voluntary acceptance of death after the example of Christ. Meditating just before his murder, Boris recalls, "The Lord resists the proud and gives his grace to the humble." In these lines, written toward the end of the eleventh century, appears for the first time one of the leading characteristics of Russian Christianity—humility and the acceptance of fate in imitation of the deeds of Christ. This idea can be traced through subsequent Russian literature even into the early twentieth century.

Another masterpiece of early Russian hagiography is the *Life of St. Theodosius*, co-founder of the Kievan Crypt Monastery. This work, also written by Nestor, is probably his best. He furnishes not only abundant material on the life of Abbot Theodosius, which makes the *vita* a vivid and realistic narrative, but also tries to convey the religious philosophy of this great Russian saint: simplicity in life, humility of attitude before God and people, and Theodosius' gentle, loving care toward the monks and his spiritual children.

The early *vitae* and stories of the paterics have many structural features in common, and usually consist of a number of episodes loosely woven into one continuous narrative. While both were intended as edifying religious literature for the Christian education of their readers, their final purposes are, however, different. The *vita* is the official biography of a saint, explaining his role in the development of Orthodox saintliness and the religious mind, and giving the reason for his canonization. It is always solemn, often begins and ends with a prayer or hymn, and, much more than the pateric narrative, stresses the spiritual aspect of its hero's life. The *vitae* were traditionally constructed according to a stereotyped pattern, with the ideal of sainthood outweighing an accurate presentation of the details of the saint's actual life, since the aim of the hagiographer was not to present the life story itself but rather the saintly example, for the edification of believers. The stories of the paterics, on the other hand, were simply instructive tales about the lives of monks, many of whom were never canonized. The pateric described the life and deeds of the monks of a given monastery, and consequently the name of the monastery was usually included in the title.

These two genres are not always clearly distinguishable, and some biographies of noncanonized monks are very similar to the hagiographic *vitae*. Toward the end of the Russian Middle Ages the *vita* lost its strict hagiographic purpose and developed into a new genre of secular biography. The narratives of the pateric, likewise, gradually assumed the form of a not strictly religious short story. Both the *vitae* and paterics were the most popular reading of medieval Russia, and innumerable versions of the lives of Russian saints were written and rewritten from the eleventh through the seventeenth centuries. Together with Byzantine paterics and hagiography, they formed the major part of the libraries of Russian monasteries and of private collections, since they were the medieval equivalent of modern short stories and novels and intermingled descriptions of everyday life, edification, and ebullient oriental phantasy.

8. The Epos

The greatest literary work of Kievan Russia is the *Lay of Igor's Campaign* (*Slovo o polku Igoreve*), which describes an unsuccessful raid by Russian princes against the nomadic Turkic tribe of Kumans, who, in the twelfth and thirteenth centuries, inhabited the plains north of the Black Sea. This raid, which took place in 1185 under the leadership of Igor, Prince of Novgorod-Seversk, became the subject of the only epic and purely poetic work of Kievan Russia, written probably within a year or two after Igor's return from Kuman captivity.

Against the rather uniform and undiversified background of the chronicles and religious literature of the Kievan period, the *Lay of Igor's Campaign* stands out as an exceptional specimen of strictly secular poetic letters. Its lyric pathos, rich imagery and symbolism, noble national spirit and pagan references contrast strikingly with the rest of the preserved wealth of early Russian literature. Literary historians usually classify the *Lay* as a typical example of epic poetry, but its loose structure, lyric and rhetorical digressions, and the author's addresses to his audience rather suggest its classification as a work of mixed genre in which the epic content is strongly diluted by lyric digressions and allusive admonitions.

The origins of the Russian epic tradition still remain in darkness despite decades of intensive research. Since the end of the eighteenth century a tremendous wealth of Russian epic songs, the *byliny*, have been discovered and collected. Much of this epic folklore deals with the time of Kievan Russia and the court of Prince Vladimir, "the bright sun," Christianizer of Russia, and his valorous knights—Ilia Muromets, Aliosha Popovich, Dobrynia

Nikitich, and many others—who formed around Vladimir a Russian counterpart of King Arthur's Round Table. Scholars, however, can not agree in their estimates of the actual age of the *byliny*. Indeed, Dobrynia was the real uncle of Vladimir, and is well known from the chronicles. The name of Ilia, "the Russian knight" or "cousin of Vladimir," can be found in Scandinavian and Lombardian epics penned as early as the eleventh and twelfth centuries. Moreover, while the oldest Russian work containing a reference to the *byliny* epics and their heroes dates only from the sixteenth century, the narrative parts of the *Primary Chronicle* itself, as well as such later works as, for instance, the *Tale of the Destruction of Riazan*, show very definite traces of the epic tradition. Hence, it is possible to assume that the Russian epic tradition goes back as far as the time of Kievan Russia, although their exact form and poetic devices can hardly be determined at the present stage of scholarship. It may only be surmised that at the time when the *Lay of Igor's Campaign* was written, the Russian poetic and epic tradition already had rather deep roots, especially since the *Lay* refers to the songs of a former bard, Boyan, who previously glorified the valor of Russian princes.

The subject and treatment of the *Lay* may be compared to some extent with the French *Chanson de Roland*. Both have for their topics a Christian army's fight for the honor of its country and its defeat by pagan warriors. Both treat nature as an almost animate participant in the military and national drama. Also, both use extensively fixed epithets in characterizing their heroes. A decade ago Roman Jakobson pointed out the *Lay*'s similarity to its contemporary Western counterpart in the use of pagan, pre-Christian motifs. He also showed the similarity of the poetic devices of the *Lay* to those studied and described by the Byzantine scholar Choiroboskos, whose treatise on poetic tropes and figures had been known in Russia since 1073. In view of these parallels with West European and Byzantine writings, it is possible to state that the *Lay* did not evolve exclusively from the Russian epic tradition but might also have been influenced by the general poetic environment of Western Europe and the Balkans, with which Russia was so closely connected at that time. In any event, the *Lay of Igor's Campaign* will probably continue to be an enigma for many more generations of scholars because it remains a unique specimen of unusually high quality in Kievan poetics.

The narrative part of the *Lay* is not very developed. Instead of reporting in detail the successive stages and episodes of the campaign, the author really only alludes to events and persons supposedly familiar to his audience or readers. Instead of communicating the minutiae of the battle, he impresses on his audience his own sorrow over the Russians' defeat and his desire to see Russia once again powerfully united in order to prevent further national calamity. The work strongly mirrors Russia's and the author's sorrow over the princes' feuds, their perpetual warring, and the political decline of Russian power.

The narrative structure given the *Lay* by its author, whose intent was apparently not so much to narrate as to warn his contemporaries of the perilous consequences of princely feuding, differs from that of most Western or later Russian epic works, whose usual purpose is to recall past deeds and glory. This might be explained by the fact that the *Lay* was composed almost immediately after Igor's stunning defeat, while the episodes of the campaign were still vividly preserved in the reader's memory.

The *Lay of Igor's Campaign* did not considerably influence Russian literature in the next decades and centuries. It was too different from the generally functional, didactic, and religious tenor of the other writings of the newly Christianized Russians. Its reference to the pagan Slavic gods, moreover, probably seemed to the clergy too hazardous to warrant any wide circulation, while the topic of defeat could not have been particularly popular among the princes, especially since in the very near future the relatively minor misfortunes of Igor's campaign were vastly overshadowed by a catastrophe of immensely greater magnitude. Therefore, it is not too surprising that the *Lay* was preserved only in a single manuscript and that only one other medieval Russian poetic work definitely reflects a strong stylistic and structural influence of the *Lay of Igor's Campaign*. This is *Zadonshchina*, written two hundred years later, on the occasion of the first major Russian victory, in 1380, over the nomads, Russia's historical enemy.

II. THE PERIOD OF THE TATAR YOKE AND FEUDAL DIVISION (1240–1478)

9. The Mongol Invasion

The foreboding of the author of the *Lay of Igor's Campaign* and his apprehensions for Russia's future were soon justified by historical events. In 1223 the vanguards of Genghis Khan's

Mongol army, after a successful Caucasian campaign, unexpectedly crossed the Don River and inflicted a crushing defeat on regiments of the South Russian princes at the Kalka River. At this time the Mongols did not proceed to the conquest of Eastern Europe but crossed the Volga and disappeared into the Central Asian plains. In 1237, however, exactly half a century after the writing of the *Lay*, the Mongol hordes reappeared on the Volga, and in the following three years subjugated and devastated all of Russia.

It might be expected that the Mongol, or Tatar, Yoke ("Tatar" was the name of one of the Mongolian tribes of the Horde but became applied by the Russians to all of these Asian nomads) left a widespread influence on Russian culture and letters. Apart from the fact that Russian civilization was set back two centuries, however, this was not the case. Russian spiritual, artistic, and literary development remained entirely immune to the culture of these illiterate horsemen, while only a few political and military patterns of the Mongol Empire modified the previous Russian organizational forms. The Asian nomads—cattlemen and shepherds—did not settle in the Russian territories, but preferred the nearly uninhabited plains and grazing lands of the eastern and southern confines of present Russia to the forests and marshes of its central and northern parts, where most of the Slavic population lived. The tremendous differences in language, religon, and way of life between the sedentary Christian Slavs and the pagan (only subsequently Moslem) Asian nomads prevented the Russians from indulging in any widespread commerce with their conquerors, and there were few intermarriages between Russians and Tatars in the Middle Ages.

The century following the invasion was one of marked cultural decline but hardly of any perceptible changes in the basic features of Russian civilization. Monasteries and palaces had been burned, and the cultural elite decimated or abducted into slavery, but the surviving representatives of the Russian clergy and aristocracy tried to preserve the remnants of Russian civilization and literature although they were hardly able to develop them. The cultural decline was further intensified by the conquest of Western Russia by Poles and Lithuanians and the splitting up of Russian territories under the Mongols into innumerable small principalities that competed and fought among themselves. Only northern Russia, the republic of wealthy Novgorod, preserved the integrity of its immense territory, and the city itself became the center for burgeoning new forms in the arts, especially of architecture and painting.

10. Military Tales

While no stylistic changes are perceptible in Russian writings of the first century after the Mongol conquest, their topics clearly evidence whether they were written before or after the collapse of Kievan Russia. One of the most popular subjects for thirteenth-century works was, of course, the Tatar invasion and therefore the military tale—already well known in Kievan literature, as seen from the *Lay of Igor's Campaign* and the chronicles—now became much more widespread. Of the new ones, two, the *Orison on the Downfall of Russia* and the *Tale of the Destruction of Riazan*, give an exceptionally artistic treatment of the invasion and the feelings of the survivors.

Still enigmatic in its origin, the *Orison on the Downfall of Russia* seems to be only an introduction to some now lost longer work. It speaks of the previous grandeur and glory of the realm founded by Vladimir and Yaroslav and is highly pathetic, but, unfortunately, the preserved fragments end exactly with the words that begin a description of the catastrophe.

Tales of the capture of various cities are poignant and numerous. Riazan, a city in the extreme southeast of Kievan territory, was the first to fall to the Tatar armies, and the description of its destruction is the most dramatic account of this type. The *Tale of the Destruction of Riazan* is a complex work in which four separate episodes and various genres are interwoven. The episode dealing with Evpaty Kolovrat, a *bogatyr* (knight) who challenged the Mongol army, has strong motifs of the oral epos, and is no less impressive than Western tales of heroic knightly deeds. Folklore elements can also be found in the laments of the princes. The narrative is considerably more vivid and dynamic than that of the *Lay of Igor's Campaign* or of earlier military tales. While some of the symbols and tropes have a close connection with those of the *Lay*, however, the *Tale* is far behind the *Lay* in its poetic and stylistic excellence. The dominant idea of the *Tale* is the juxtaposition of the Christian Russian army to the Tatar "infidels," and more than any other work of early Russian literature the *Tale* conveys the concept of Russia as the bulwark of Christian civilization against the hordes of pagan Central Asian nomads. Other military tales of the time deal with the conquest of Kiev and of other Russian cities that fell to the Tatars, as well as the first battle, in 1223, between Russians and Mongols on the Kalka River.

During these difficult years the Tatars were not the only conquerors of Russian lands. Poles and Lithuanians succeeded in occupying extensive regions in the west, from the Nemen to the Dniester rivers and from the Carpathian Mountains to Kiev and Smolensk. German knights of the Livonian Order took over present Latvia and Estonia and pushed against the ancient city of Pskov. Swedes appeared on the Neva River, attacking the confines of the territory of Novgorod. The defense of this northern border is the subject of many episodes of the *Life of Prince Alexander Nevsky* (called "Nevsky" for his defeat of the Swedes on the Neva River). In the manuscripts his *vita* usually follows the *Orison on the Downfall of Russia,* and some scholars even believe that the *Orison* was intended as an introduction to the life of this courageous prince who was so largely responsible for Russia's gradual rehabilitation after the Tatar conquest. Alexander, who died in 1263, was canonized primarily for his devotion to the cause of the Russian land and Church rather than for exceptional spirituality. Therefore, his *vita* is more a work of secular biography incorporating military tales than a piece of hagiography. The author widely used biblical portrayals and stylistics in Alexander's *Life*, and treated many events in the manner of the Byzantine chronicles and military stories. Alexander is compared to Roman emperors and biblical patriarchs. The *Life* ends with a touching miracle: when, during Alexander's burial, the metropolitan wanted to put in Alexander's hand a parchment remitting his sins, in accordance with Church ritual, the dead hero extended his hand to take it.

The defense of Pskov against the Lithuanians forms the background of the *Tale of Prince Dovmont*, written in the thirteenth century, while the miraculous deliverance of the city of Smolensk from the Tatars is related in the *Heroic Deeds of Mercurius of Smolensk*, written in the fourteenth, or even fifteenth, century. In no other Russian military tale does the miraculous element play such importance as in this story, which is treated in the hagiographic manner: beheaded by the Tatars, Mercurius returns to the city he had saved, holding his severed head in his hands.

The great battle in 1380 at the Don River, where the Russians inflicted their first decisive defeat upon the Tatars toward the end of the Tatar Yoke, supplied rich material for several literary works. *Zadonshchina* (*The Deeds Beyond the Don*), the best known of these, written by Sofony of Riazan, is to a large extent an inversion of the *Lay of Igor's Campaign*. Indeed, Sofony appropriated many of the compositional patterns and poetic devices of the *Lay*, and in places *Zadonshchina* adheres almost literally to the figures of speech and symbolism of the *Lay of*

Igor's Campaign. Like the author of the *Lay*, Sofony had recourse to poetic generalization rather than to a minute description of the details of battle, and let the lyric laments of Russian women express the sorrow of the Russian land at the losses suffered by the Russian army. Still, the narrative of *Zadonshchina* is somewhat more detailed, realistic, and sustained in plot than the great twelfth-century Russian lay. Its spirit is entirely Christian, and it lacks the pagan tendencies of the former. While not so adept poetically, Sofony was no less skillful in expressing his ideas than was the anonymous bard of Kiev. Both gave voice to Russia's hopes, sorrows, and expectations: the *Lay* deplored the princes' disunity; *Zadonshchina* praised their successful united effort to cast off the foreign yoke.

Two other works that treat the same Russian victory, less poetic but more informative than *Zadonshchina*, are the *Tale of the Battle on the Don* in the Simon and Ermolinsky chronicles and the *Legend* (*Skazanie*) of the *Rout of Mamai* (khan of the Tatar Horde). In the latter are some beautiful, highly poetic descriptions of the Russian army and of the night preceding the battle.

With *Zadonshchina* the era of the Kievan tradition in Russian literature came to a close. During the cultural revival that ensued in Russia in the late fourteenth and fifteenth centuries, new problems, topics, and literary methods came to the fore.

11. The Vita of Ornamental Formalism

At the end of the fourteenth century Russian letters came under the influence of a new spiritual and literary movement that had arisen among the monks of Byzantium and of the Slavic Balkan states. The participants in this movement, who called themselves "Hesychasts" (from *Hesychia*—quietude, silence, indirectly, contemplation), taught self-perfection and domination of the passions. According to their views, a believer could achieve direct vision of the Divine Light, a visual contemplation of the Creator. This teaching, which to a large extent was conditioned by renunciation of the passions and the pleasures of this world and led its followers away from the realities of this life, resulted in the field of literature in the development of a highly artificial and rhetorical style. At first primarily influencing hagiography, in the fifteenth and sixteenth centuries this style spread to other types of writing. For a Hesychast writer, not the recorded biography but the ideal truth of the saints' lives was important. Their *vitae* depict not the everyday deeds of the heroes but rather the supreme truth and eternal significance of the saints' actions. Like the modern impressionist or even contemporary abstract painter, the writer conveyed a portrayal of the saint as he visualized it and not as it necessarily was.

In their search for a medium worthy of describing spiritual perfection, the Byzantine and Balkan-Slavic Hesychasts developed a highly ornate language. Its elements were bookish words, compounds (*composita*) consisting of two or three words, complex syntactical structure with a multitude of subordinate clauses, numerous epithets, repetition of the same sound at the beginning of each rhythmic unit of the sentence, and archaic grammatical forms. These devices conveyed to the *vita* an especially elevated and solemn tone.

Callistos (Patriarch of Constantinople from 1350 to 1363) was the first writer to apply widely this formal, sophisticated, and ornate style which, from Byzantium, spread to Serbia and Bulgaria and, at the beginning of the fifteenth century, to Russia. The Balkan-Slavic writers of this period considerably reformed their literary language by reviving outlived ancient grammatical forms of Church Slavonic. When the Hesychast literary vogue came to Russia, it also became instrumental there in restoring to the literary language the archaic Church Slavonic grammar and phonetics. This "neo-Byzantine" literary influence in Russia, whose duration is referred to as the second Balkan, or South Slavic, period in Russian literature, dislodged from Russian letters purely East Slavic vernacular forms, renewing the archaic Church Slavonic. The outstanding Russian representative of this new ornamental formalism, which Russians termed "weaving of words," was Epiphanius, called "the Wise" for his writings (died in 1422). His masterpieces were the well-known *Lives* of St. Sergius and St. Stephen, evangelizer of Perm, a Finnic region west of the Urals. Despite his rich stylistics, Epiphanius successfully conveys a realistic portrayal of the saints, adorned with prayers, eulogies, and laments, and his writings remained for some two centuries the most imitated specimens of the formal, ornamental style in Russia. In the mid-fifteenth century his work was continued by Pachomius the Serb, an emigré from the Balkans who reworked some of Epiphanius' *vitae* and composed numerous new ones.

Ornamental formalism reigned in Russian literature until the seventeenth century. Not all the literary works of these two centuries were written in this style, but it became almost compulsory in hagiography, sermons, and historical writings. The result was the transformation of the *vita* into a uniform enumeration of the saint's virtues, and lengthy eulogies that frequently completely overshadowed the actual story of his life. In the mid-sixteenth century Metropolitan Macarius, tutor and adviser of the young Ivan IV, undertook a compilation (*Chetyi Minei*) of the finest in Russian spiritual literature, and at that time all the earlier *vitae* were reworked according to the exigencies of ornamental formalism.

Side by side with the erudite writers of rhetorical *vitae* and chronicles, however, there were other literary works of the late fourteenth and fifteenth centuries whose authors used a simple, almost vernacular, language without any particular embellishment. A good example of such unsophistication and even naïve narration are the early versions of the *vita* of St. Michael of Klopsko (its later versions were reworked by the Muscovite writers of ornamental style) in which the hagiographer concentrates rather on interesting episodes of the saint's life than on epithets and eulogies.

Also in the same unadorned, yet expressive, language is the *vita*-tale of Prince Peter of Murom and his wife, Fevronia. This is the only medieval Russian literary work with some romantic content, and it supplies many everyday details from the life of these saint-spouses. Fevronia, a peasant girl by origin, is placed against the background of rural life. The composition of this narrative is complex, containing legendary folklore motifs interwoven with the narrative. This charming story, which ends with a description of the hero's and heroine's death and posthumous miracles, may be considered a Russian counterpart of the Western legend of Tristan and Isolde.

12. Chronicles of the Fourteenth and Fifteenth Centuries

The writing of annals was almost completely interrupted by the Mongol invasion. Kiev and Vladimir, Russia's northern capital, were so thoroughly sacked by the invaders that cultural life there was entirely suspended. Therefore the main chronicles of the thirteenth and fourteenth centuries are those of Novgorod, Tver, and Rostov; in the fourteenth century, when Moscow arose as a new political rival, chronicle writing also commenced there. The transfer of the Russian metropolitan see to Moscow in 1325 made out of this previously insignificant princedom an important religious and cultural center. The Muscovite chronicles of the late fourteenth and early fifteenth centuries—the *Simon* and *Trinity* (*Troitsky*) chronicles—include the ancient *Primary Chronicle*, and use widely the annals of such other cities as Novgorod, Smolensk, Riazan, Tver, and others. They cultivate insistently the idea of Russian reunification under the aegis of the Muscovite prince. The fact that they are only compilations necessarily deprives them of inner unity and of the stylistic uniformity that characterizes the *Primary*, *Kievan*, and *Galician-Volynian* chronicles, and they often grow into tremendous codices, since they were supposed to contain ever-growing new material beside the wealth of early historical information. While the chronicler's task became increasingly difficult in these centuries, he continued to work according to the originally elaborated methods: yearly entries and the inclusion of heterogeneous material. Among the codices of the era the most important are the *Laurentian*, written in 1337 for Great Prince Dmitry of Suzdal and Nizhny-Novgorod; the *Hypatian*, compiled in the early fifteenth century; and the *Radzivil*, or *Königsberg*, completed in the late fifteenth century and given by Prince J. Radzivil to the Königsberg library. All of these contain the entire text of the *Primary Chronicle* and rich later material.

Since the late fifteenth century there developed in Russia a new type of historical work, the so-called chronograph, in which the material was organized into article-chapters in place of the customary yearly entries and in which surveys of world events were usually included along with events in Russian history. They were written in the new ornamental style with heavy panegyrics to the rulers and Church leaders, a style which spread to the chronicles themselves, whose compilation continued into the late seventeenth century.

13. Political Legends and Tales

From the mid-fourteenth to the mid-fifteenth century two principalities, Tver and Moscow, competed for supremacy and attempted to unify around themselves the central regions of Russia on the upper Volga and Oka rivers. The victor was Moscow, which subjugated Tver and won leadership over all central Russia. The subsequent unification of all of Great Russia was completed in 1478, when Ivan III (1462–1505), the founder of Muscovite power, forced Novgorod also to accept the suzerainty of Moscow.

Eager to justify their claims to the political leadership of Russia, the Muscovite dynasty and its ideologists elaborated, according to the medieval tradition, a number of political legends, most of which had their origin in Byzantine and Western historical myths. Among them, the *Legend of the Babylonian Kingdom* and the *Legend of the Princes of Vladimir* propagated the idea that only a powerful ruler could guarantee the security of the nation. The latter legend aimed, moreover, at providing the Muscovite princes with a respectable genealogy: according to this legend, the Muscovite dynasty descended not only from half-mythical Rurik but had its origins much deeper in history—its founder was said to be Prus, a wholly imaginary brother of the Roman Emperor Augustus.

The narrow purpose of the Muscovite political legends—to establish the prestige of the Muscovite dynasty and gain support for its political claims—to a large extent limited their circulation and popularity. More widely read was the Novgorodian *Tale of the White Cowl.* Novgorod, Moscow's main adversary, also sought historical tradition in defending its independence and republican institutions against encroachment by the Muscovite princes. The central idea of this tale is Russia's selection by God as the defender of Orthodoxy: the final kingdom of the Holy Spirit, which will replace both the Old Testamentary kingdom of law and the New Testamentary kingdom of grace, would become manifest in the Russian land. Novgorod and its archbishop are singled out in this legend as the heirs to one of the most sacred symbols of pure Christianity, the White Cowl, the possession of which endowed this old republican city with spiritual superiority and placed it on a level with Moscow in the sphere of Church tradition. The *Tale of the White Cowl* became particularly popular in the seventeenth century and had a profound influence on the subsequent development of Russian ideology. In connection with this legend there arose in the early sixteenth century the theory of Moscow, the Third Rome. This concept, however, differed considerably from that of the *Tale of the White Cowl*, which taught that the entire people of Russia, not only Moscow and its ruler, bore historical responsibility for the guardianship of true Orthodoxy.

III. THE MUSCOVITE PERIOD

A. MUSCOVITE RUSSIA'S FIRST CENTURY (1478–1598)

IN 1478 Ivan III, by annexing the tremendous territory of the Republic of Novgorod, completed the main stage of the unification of Russia, which for centuries had remained divided into small feudal principalities. Two years later the Russians shook off forever the Tatar Yoke, and the Golden Horde disintegrated. Some seventy years later, in 1547, Ivan IV was crowned the first Tsar of Russia by the wise and erudite Metropolitan Macarius. Feudal Russia, with its endless fratricidal feuds and princely warring, was replaced by one powerful, unified autocratic state. This process of unification and the rise of autocracy required considerable military effort to preserve the new unity and defend the young tsardom, as well as the further elaboration of a new political philosophy justifying this newborn power. It is therefore understandable that throughout the late fifteenth and sixteenth centuries, during the reigns of Ivan III (1462–1505). Vassily III (1505–1533) and Ivan IV (1533–1584), Russian literature was dominated by two basic genres: the military tale and political polemics.

14. The New Military Tale

In the late fifteenth century there appeared a new type of military tale—narratives about the siege and defense of fortresses or cities. One of the first of these was the *Tale of the Taking of Constantinople*, which fell to the Turks in 1453. It was written by a certain Nestor Iskander, a professional Russian soldier who had been captured by the Turks, forced to accept Islam, and to join the Ottoman army. He was a writer of considerable talent, and described colorfully as an eyewitness the siege and storming of the city. While he is highly rhetorical, he nonetheless conveys a realistic picture of the battles. His original narrative was apparently reworked by some Muscovite writer who added an ideological introduction and conclusion: after the conquest of the Balkans and the fall of the capital of Orthodoxy, Russia was to take over the role of protector of Orthodoxy and become responsible for its fate.

The siege of the Tatar capital, Kazan, which was taken in 1552 by Russian troops under Ivan IV, supplied the topic for two very different narratives on the subject. One, the *Kazan History*, was written in the 1560's by an anonymous Russian who, similarly to Nestor Iskander, became prisoner of the Tatars and spent two decades in Moslem captivity. He observed the military operations from within the city, on the Tatar side, and after the Russians' victory joined Ivan's army. His work, besides depicting the siege, covers an extensive period of time, studies Russo-Tatar relations, the life of Russians in Tatar captivity, and the preparations for war. His literary devices are patterned considerably after Iskander's tale. Although he depicts the heavy fighting and storming of Kazan in long and ornate sentences, he provides very lively descriptions. Particularly impressive is his account of the tsar's return to Moscow and the capital's jubilation. Another treatment of the same siege was given by Prince Andrew Kurbsky, one of Ivan's commanders, in his *History of Tsar and Grand Prince Ivan Vassilievich.* Kurbsky is much more matter of fact, and uses the rich stylistics of his era with great taste and economy.

The *Story of Stephen Bathory's Campaign Against Pskov* exceeds all previous military tales in the extended employment of intricate, ornamented stylistics, allegory, metaphors, and epithets. The author belonged to a particularly sophisticated current in Russia letters, and had perfect command of all the subtleties of ornamental formalism. The use of compound words, figures of speech, and elaborate sentences makes this tale one of the best specimens of the heavy, embellished style of early Muscovite literature.

15. Polemic Literature

Beginning in the early fifteenth century, polemics on theological and political problems form a prominent part of Russian letters of the early Muscovite era. The first polemic arose over the heresy of the Strigolniks, a movement for Church reform that denied the necessity of some sacraments and of an ordained clergy and that grew very strong in Pskov and Novgorod around 1400. A century later appeared the rationalistic Judaizers, who to some extent followed the teachings of the Strigolniks but also denied veneration of icons and the dogma of the Trinity, thus preceding by half a century the emergence of the West European Unitarianism of Servetus and Socinius. This movement spread to Moscow, and Ivan III himself was strongly suspected of being a secret sponsor of the sect. In any case, the main opponent of the Judaizers, Abbot Joseph of Volok, who finally won the struggle and succeeded in destroying the movement, clearly hinted at the "pernicious" role in Church affairs played by Ivan III, the founder of Russian political unity. The lively polemics for and against the heresy of the Judaizers lasted several decades and produced a number of important works.

The struggle against the Judaizers was not yet over when a new conflict arose between the supporters and opponents of monastic estates. Joseph of Volok once again came out forcefully in favor of the estates of the monasteries, which he called "the wealth of the poor" and which in his eyes were fundamental for maintaining and educating the clergy as well as for the Church's social work. In Joseph's opinion the Church was responsible for the souls and well-being of believers and was supposed to take the necessary action for preserving their spiritual condition. His adversaries were the contemplative hermit-elders from the hermitages of northern Russia beyond the Volga, who taught that the Church's wealth leads to corruption of the clergy and diverts the attention of the monks from their spiritual tasks. They opposed Church intervention in the inner life of believers, and considered that only a Christian's personal action may lead to his salvation. Their leader, Nil Sorsky, a pupil of the Greek Hesychasts, insisted that the way to God can be found only through suppression of the passions, self-perfection, and a believer's individual effort to understand and follow the divine commandments. His teaching in some respects also had certain points in common with later Western Protestantism, since he was against adornment of the Church and excessive ritualism, supporting a purely spiritual, nonsocial role for the clergy. The polemics between the followers of Joseph, called the "Josephites," and the Trans-Volga elders was largely a discussion of the necessity for discipline and the enforcement of Church law against spiritual freedom and an individual approach to God.

In the 1550's there arose in Moscow and northern Russia still another religious movement, this time under the very definite influence of the Western Reformation. Like the previous nonconformist sects, its leader disputed the value of the sacraments and the Church hierarchy. This new threat to Orthodoxy, however, was rapidly liquidated and did not leave many traces in Russian spirituality. The controversies around these various teachings led to the growth of a prolific polemic literature which, while neither fictional nor even particularly artistically written, is nonetheless an important witness to an intense spiritual and intellectual life in the first century of the Muscovite Era.

Purely political polemics are best seen in the *Story of Sultan Mehmed*, by Ivan Peresvetov, and in the correspondence between Ivan IV ("the Terrible") and Prince Andrew Kurbsky. In his story, written about 1550, Peresvetov describes conditions in Russia under the guise of those in the Ottoman Empire, and argues against the excessive power of the boyar aristocracy. He was a firm supporter of autocracy, in which he saw the best instrument for consolidating national power: "When the Tsar is gentle and weak, his Tsardom declines and his glory diminishes. When the Tsar is dread and wise, his Tsardom grows and his name is glorified on the earth," writes Peresvetov. It can be considered that the autocratic rule of Ivan IV was to a certain extent the result of Peresvetov's writings, in which the latter suggested breaking the power of the feudal lords.

Prince Andrew Kurbsky represented a completely different viewpoint. He defended the political role of princes, boyars, and aristocracy in general, which he regarded as the bearer of national stability, conservatism, and wisdom. According to Kurbsky, autocratic rule necessarily leads to excesses, and a proud ruler becomes instrumental in the decline of his nation. A well-trained dialectician and writer, Kurbsky cleverly and convincingly presents his views in his correspondence with Ivan IV. He appeals to the tsar to cease persecuting the aristocracy and to pardon the victims of his wrath. Ivan was hardly less erudite than the prince, but he did not command his passions and pen as well, and exploded in vituperative replies to Kurbsky, his former friend and commander in chief of the Russian armies. Ivan is sarcastic and biting, and does not shun using the most offensive language in speaking of his enemies. The tsar's strongest argument is the boyars' misrule, which he describes in recollecting his childhood. While Kurbsky is always concise and to the point, Ivan is verbose, accumulating one argument after another to prove his views. Very different in their respective styles, Prince Kurbsky and Tsar Ivan are certainly the most outstanding of Russian sixteenth-century polemists, and their letters are the best example of the Muscovite epistolary art.

16. Encyclopedic Works

The greatest literary undertaking of the reign of the dread Tsar Ivan IV were the encyclopedic compilations of various types of Russian writings initiated and conducted under the supervision of Macarius, Metropolitan of Moscow from 1543 to 1564. The most important of these works were the *Reading Meneae* (*Chetyi Minei*), a collection of *vitae* and other spiritually edifying readings arranged for each calendar day. Altogether, there are in these *Meneae* some thirteen thousand folio pages, the equivalent of thirty or forty modern volumes; most of the existing *vitae* were rewritten for this new compilation in the official style of ornamental formalism.

The other encyclopedic work, written in the same ponderous formal manner, was the *Book of Grades* (*Stepennaia kniga*), an extensive rewriting of the chronicles and chronographs in which special attention was paid to the biographies of Russian rulers. The main literary interest presented by this historical work consists in the small stories and anecdotes incorporated in them (often taken from oral folklore) which herald the nascence of the fictional short story. Both of these works abound in neological compounds, epithets, and long rhetorical constructions.

The third important encyclopedic work of this time was the *Nikon Illustrated Codex of Chronicles*, a monumental historical encyclopedia covering not only Russian but also world history as far as it was known to sixteenth-century Muscovites. It consists of twelve enormous volumes richly illustrated with over ten thousand miniatures.

The completion of these catenae apparently exhausted the energies of Russian writers of the late Byzantine tradition and the talent of the ornamental formalists. After codifying and rewriting nearly all of previous Russian literature in these series, it was difficult and almost purposeless to invent any new sophistications in the adorned and heavy style. Thus, the *Reading Meneae, Book of Grades,* and *Illustrated Codex* became the final monuments of the period of exclusive Byzantine domination over Russian literature. While ornamental stylistics lasted into the seventeenth century, undergoing a final blossoming in 1615–1630, new currents and literary genres began to appear.

This last century of the undisputed domination of Byzantine stylistics over Russian writing was simultaneously the last century of the Rurik dynasty, which, according to legend, had ruled in Russia since 862. After the death of Ivan IV, his son, the last offspring of this dynasty—Tsar Theodore—reigned for some fifteen years, but with his death in 1598, the Rurik dynasty was extinguished. During the following fifteen years (1598–1613), called the "Time of Troubles" (*Smuta*), Russians witnessed four legitimate tsars from three new dynasties, two tsar-impostors, grave social disturbances, the breakdown of central government and foreign intervention, all of which brought the nation to the verge of another complete catastrophe. Only in 1613 was a new tsar, Michael (ruled 1613–1645), elected. Tsar Michael was the first of the Romanov dynasty, which reigned for the next 304 years, disappearing only with the revolution of 1917. His task was to rehabilitate the state, put an end to Polish and Swedish intervention, and bring social order to the nation. These tasks were fairly soon accomplished and order restored, but Russian culture and letters survived this historical trial very considerably changed.

B. THE WANE OF MEDIEVAL RUSSIA (1598–1700)

EROSION of the traditional Byzantine patterns in ancient Russian literature becomes perceptible from the second part of the sixteenth century. In historical works authors tend to prefer narration of the mythical legend in the manner of the Polish chroniclers to the down-to-earth style of early Russian annalists. Prose becomes more and more frequently interspersed with fragments of rhymed couplets. Job, Russia's first patriarch (from

1589 to 1605), included even in his *vita* of Tsarevich Dmitry long versified passages. One of the best, but now almost completely forgotten, medieval Russian hymnologists, Abbot Markel Bezborody, soon after his retirement in 1557, wrote a memorial church service to the saints Barlaam and Josaphat in the unusual form of a dramatic poem with vivid dialogues. Many hagiographers, especially those who did not belong to the official school of ornamental formalism but who wrote in a simple, unadorned manner, began to include the autobiographical reminiscences of their heroes, thus conveying a more realistic tenor to their *vitae*. Even the writers of these *vitae* began to lift the veil of anonymity, providing the reader with more information about themselves. Along with the steady growth of autobiographical elements in both the *vita* and in historical narratives, the Western picaresque tale and knightly novel became translated into Russian for the first time. Finally, fictional characters and a satirical portrayal of Russian life make their appearance, as in the short tale of *Shemiaka's Judgment*, written probably around the end of the sixteenth century.

This inauguration of new ways in Russian letters and the passing of the old literary tradition were accelerated by the events of the Time of Troubles, when large numbers of foreigners—Poles, Lithuanians, Swedes, and German and French mercenaries—came to Russia in the ranks of invading armies. At the same time many representatives of Russian society became closely acquainted with Western modes of life during their captivity in Poland, Lithuania, and Sweden. The reunion of "Little Russia"[1] with Muscovy in 1653 intensified Western, especially Polish, cultural influences. Moreover, the alienation from the hierarchy and the state of the conservative, Old Believer wing of the Church[2] considerably weakened the influence of traditionalists with the government and the cultural elite, and facilitated the further secularization and modernization of the Russian state, its culture, and letters.

To be sure, many Russian writers still continued until the middle of the seventeenth century to use the previously established literary manners, methods, and devices, but the more important and interesting part of literary production comes now from writers seeking new ways of expression. From the beginning of this century the *vita* was gradually replaced by secular biography, autobiography, and first-person confession. Ever-

[1] The southern part of Russia, with Kiev, now called "the Ukraine."

[2] For more detailed information on this movement, see the introduction to *The Life of Archpriest Avvakum by Himself* in this volume.

growing attention is given to the psychology of the heroes, and purely fictional characters come into being. The occasional rhymed couplets and versified fragments grow into larger poetic works, and lyric and epic songs open a new era in the expression of feelings and emotions.

17. Historical Works of the Time of Troubles

During the decades immediately following the Time of Troubles, historical works describing the calamities of social disturbance and foreign intervention played a dominant role in Russian letters. Both old and new literary methods characterize this transitional period. While some seventeenth-century writers achieved a high perfection in the employment of ornate stylistics, behind their rhetorical facade can frequently be found detailed portrayals of the character and psychology of their contemporaries as well as analyses of the reasons for the great cataclysm. The best stylist of the time was the *dyak* (high official) Ivan Timofeev, author of the well-known *Vremennik* (*Book of the Times*). His sentences are often built of rhythmic units with occasional rhyme, and are extremely rich in epithets, compound words, and a symbolic interpretation of names: for instance, artillery becomes "artifacts for the destruction of walls"; boats—"transporters over the water"; Theodore—"the gift of God"; John—"the Grace." The abundance of stylistic devices and allegories makes a reading of this clever analytical work—his study of the time of Ivan IV is particularly penetrating—extremely difficult. Timofeev's ideology is strictly conservative, the Time of Troubles being, in his mind, the result of the disappearance of the ancient dynasty and the rise of new social groups. Still, his conservatism does not preclude a severe judgment of the boyars, the upper class of this semifeudal society, whom Timofeev accuses of political irresponsibility and lack of civic virtue.

Other authors of historical works on the Time of Troubles—Palitsyn, Khvorostinin, Katyrev-Rostovsky, Shakhovskoy—use predominantly the same literary devices but, being more modest in displaying their stylistic ability, their works are more accessible to contemporary readers and translators. The most distinguished of these works is the *Povest'* (*Story*) written by Prince I. Katyrev-Rostovsky around 1626. Despite frequent rhetorical digressions, effusions of sympathy and indignation, he provides a well-organized, clear, and rather simply written account of events of the Time of Troubles. His versified fragments are skillfully rhymed, and refresh the prose recital of events. He should be remembered as the first seventeenth-century writer to present physical and psychological depictions of his heroes, as well as descriptions of landscape. Palitsyn's *Skazanie* (*Narrative*), the main part of which deals with the siege of the Holy Trinity and St. Sergius Monastery near Moscow, is remarkable for its powerful and severe philippic against the ruling classes of Russia, which, in his eyes, neglected their Christian and patriotic duties and, instead of caring for the nation and Church, indulged in the accumulation of personal power and wealth. The works devoted to the Time of Troubles are so numerous that it is hardly possible even to enumerate them here, but at least one other such work should be mentioned, the *Tale on the Death of Prince Skopin-Shuysky*. It is notable for the touching laments uttered by the prince's relatives after his poisoning. The author made in these laments extended use of folklore motifs, cleverly weaving them into the fabric of his tale.

18. Late Muscovite Vitae and Autobiography

The drastic changes in the traditional genres are particularly visible in the seventeenth-century *vita*. One of the earliest of this century was written by K. Osoryin, who, soon after the death of his mother in 1604, Yuliania Lazarevskaia, wrote the story of her life. The matter-of-fact, simple, and realistic narrative style of this *vita* opened a new era in Russian hagiography. Yuliania, who later was canonized, is presented against a background of the everyday life of rural Russia. In place of the habitual eulogies and stereotyped enumeration of the saint's virtues, Osoryin supplies details of family relations, of his mother's daily household occupations, her generosity toward the poor and the sick, and her help to the peasants during the famine that struck Russia under Boris Godunov. Of course, there are in this *vita* some descriptions of miracles performed by St. Yuliania, but for the first time the heroine of a hagiographic work is neither a nun distinguished by her holy life nor a pious princess, but the simple and devout wife of a small nobleman. The story's language is simple and unadorned, very fitting for a description of the life of this charitable and unobtrusive woman.

Close to the realistic descriptions found in the *vita* of Yuliania Lazarevskaia are the *vitae* of St. Dionysius, Abbot of the Holy Trinity and St. Sergius Monastery, of Ivan Neronov, of Boyarina Morozova—the two latter being important leaders of the Old Believers—and of Theodore Rtischev, boyar and close friend of Tsar Alexis (1645–1676). Although they preserve some features of traditional hagiography, most of these works are secular biographies of people of exemplary religious life, particularly the last, the story of a boyar noted for his welfare work and his role in promoting enlightenment in Russia. These *vitae* are almost completely devoid of rhetorical stylistics, and frequently employ elements of the vernacular language.

In the 1670's leaders of the schismatic Old Believers wrote the first true Russian autobiographies. *The Life of Archpriest Avvakum by Himself* belongs among the most significant works of medieval Russian literature, and modern Russian literary historians are unanimous in considering Avvakum one of the greatest masters of the Russian tongue. Concise, expressive, biting, and sarcastic, Avvakum broke radically with the old formalist tradition and the centuries-long use of Church Slavonic as the written language of Russian letters. D. Mirsky feels that Avvakum was the only Russian writer to use satisfactorily a pure Great Russian vernacular (the spoken language of Muscovy, present central and northern Russia) for a literary purpose: "Avvakum molded it into a new form for his own purpose, revamped it, widened its use and gave to this language new, purely literary, importance. His style is active, original, literary, creative." Avvakum reduced the length of the sentence, renounced the use of subordinate clauses, participles and gerunds, multiple epithets and compounds. He saturated his short, dynamic phrases—usually some eight to twelve words in length—with nouns and verbs. This leader of the Old Believers was not only a consummate stylist and expressionist but also a master of psychological delineations, and from his pen issued concise, pointed characterizations of his contemporaries. When appropriate, however, Avvakum knew how to use rhetorical stylistics in descriptions of his co-believers, as, for instance, in that of Boyarina Morozova. While his *Life* was the best of his numerous works, in most of Avvakum's writings can be found his vivid, colorful, colloquial language and his unusual gift for observation.

Another outstanding autobiography, or, rather, confession, came from the pen of Avvakum's spiritual father, Monk Epiphanius, who recorded his martyrdom and spiritual experiences during the persecutions inflicted upon the Old Believers by the Church and government. While Avvakum's *Life* treats his sermons, tribulations, and struggle for the old faith, Epiphanius' *Confession* presents the powerful, moving story of the writer's inner life, his doubts and visions, mystical experiences, and spiritual recoveries. This "Jobian" monologue is the first instance in Russian literature of the "exposure of the soul," which later became so famous in the works of Dostoevsky and Tolstoy.

The emergence of secular biography, autobiography, and the literary confession signaled the end of the medieval literary patterns. With the secularization of life, literature turned away from purely religious-historical biography. New ways of life, together with freer cultural and spiritual criticism, demanded a new type of letters, greater realism, and a more penetrating portrayal of character and human psychology. A fictional hero replaced the historical or hagiographical one, and the novella and satirical tale made their appearance.

19. The Birth of Fiction

The rise of fiction was the most spectacular literary event of the last century of Muscovite Russia. Many literary historians classify all the fictional works of this time under the term *povest'* (tale, long story, or novella), but among these numerous works with fictional heroes and plots can be distinguished two different genres. One, of the novella type, centers upon the deeds of the main character. In the other, the satirical tale, the social aspect, and the criticism of conditions and mores, overshadow the narrative part and character delineation. Both of these types of *povest'* evidently arose under the influence of Western picaresque novels that were translated in the seventeenth century into Russian, as, for instance, *Peter of the Golden Keys, Brunswick, Prince Bova, Basil the Golden-Haired, Eruslan Lazarevich* (of Oriental origin), or the *History of Apollonius of Tyre*. The seventeenth-century Russian novella, however, has a simpler structure than Western picaresque novels. It is much more concise, contains fewer characters and adventures, and the narrative is provided a purely Russian socio–historical setting. The most interesting aspects of this new genre are its unexpectedly wide range of topics, its moral appraisals, linguistic facets, and manners of treatment.

The *Tale of Savva Grudtsyn,* which to some extent resembles the story of Dr. Faust's temptations, is probably the oldest Russian novella, the earliest version dating from the middle of the seventeenth century. Written in heavy Church Slavonic and interwoven with hagiographic motifs, the tale depicts Savva's amorous adventures, and its realistic, even naturalistic, depictions of the worlds of the merchant and soldier are strikingly novel. Savva's adventures are placed against an actual historical background, and even the name of this fictitious hero belongs to a well-known merchant family. The same theme—the downfall and moral recovery of a youth—is the basis of another charming novella, this one in verse form, *Misery-Luckless-Plight,* which, for its choice use of the vernacular, the extensive inclusion of figures of folk speech, and its impeccable structure, can be considered one of the finest works of late medieval literature.

Shifting still further away from the earlier literary manners is the *Tale of Frol Skobeev, the Rogue.* Any moral element is entirely absent from this work, and the author obviously enjoys relating the successful adventures of another new hero—a rogue from the lower nobility whose swindles finally open for him the door to the society of the upper aristocracy. While Savva Grudtsyn is the victim of his own passions and of sorcery, Frol Skobeev is simply an adroit, cynical scamp who cares nothing for true love and for whom the seduction of aristocratic Annushka is merely a means to social success. The tale's language shows a new stage in the development of literary Russian: in place of the heavy Church Slavonic of *Savva Grudtsyn,* the author of *Frol Skobeev* uses the vernacular extensively and does not shun vulgarity.

An intermediate stage among these three novellas is represented by the tale *Karp Sutulov,* the story of a merchant's virtuous wife who cleverly maintains her virtue during her husband's absence on a business trip. A contrasting evolution of amorous motifs can be found in a touching *Novel in Verse,* written probably toward the very end of the century, about a young girl whose father forces her to break with her true love and marry another man. This tale is rich in colorful details of everyday life during this culturally and socially transitional period. The *Tale of Solomonia, the Possessed,* on the other hand, is the most striking Russian medieval horror novella because of its demonological scenes. In most of these novellas the plots and characters are given a precise setting as to locale and time.

No less rich is seventeenth-century satire, often written in rhymed verse. Its oldest specimen, *Shemiaka's Judgment,* mentioned above, is charming for its naïve and abrupt style. The judicial system of medieval Russia suffered strongly from the partiality and graft of the judges, and supplied abundant material for satire. Shemiaka is the classic type of venal judge, and this story, which became extremely popular in seventeenth- and eighteenth-century Russia, is known in innumerable prose and verse versions. A similar theme appears in the various prose and verse versions of the satire *Yorsh Yorshovich* (*Ruff, Son of Ruff*): *Proceedings of a Suit Brought by the Bream Against the Ruff in the Case of the Lake and Rivers of Rostov.* This theme of the partiality or impartiality of judges goes far back into history, to Buddhist, Tibetan, and Indian legends, Arabic tales, or ballads on the judgments of Charlemagne. Similar tales were certainly popular in oral form in Russia for centuries, but only now, with the relaxation of state and Church control over literature and the breakdown of a purely spiritually oriented culture, did they become available in written form. Other satirical poems and prose narratives have as their heroes drunkards, corrupt clerics and monks (as, for instance, in the *Supplication of Kaliazin* and the *Novella of Priest Savva*); the virtuous man and the sinner (as in the *Legend of the Rooster and the Fox,* the rooster being the symbol of polygamic man); or the debauched aristocracy, a jealous husband, and inefficient administrators. The number of novellas and satires penned in the seventeenth century is extremely large, and they clearly reflect the secularization of Old Muscovy and the collapse of its traditional mode of life and mentality.

20. Poetry

In the nineteenth century the beginning of Russian poetry was usually ascribed to Simeon Polotsky (1629–1680), a West Russian scholar and poet of Polish training and culture who, after coming to Moscow in 1664, became the writer of odes to the court and tutor to Tsar Alexis' children. Later research has discarded Polotsky not only as the initiator of Russian poetry but even as the first poet of the syllabic school of versification. As early as 1608 a nobleman, Ivanets Frunikov, wrote an ironical versified epistle, full of puns and folk witticisms, the *Letter of a Nobleman to a Nobleman.* With this oldest dated Russian work in verse not only Russian rhymed poetry began, but also its satirical and ironic ramifications—which later, after the middle of the century, produced verse versions of such satirical tales as *Shemiaka's Judgment, Yorsh Yorshovich,* or *Foma and Erema.* All of them use the vernacular, folk witticisms, and the rhymed couplet of the *skomorokhs,* folk jesters and entertainers. As every product of folk poetics, which abound in rhymed puns, colloquial sayings and vulgarisms, such works, unfortunately, are hardly fitted for translation.

At the same time, also in the beginning of the seventeenth century, there appeared the so-called "presyllabic" versification, of a more formal type, which was characterized by a regular use of rhymed couplets in a line of undetermined length, vacillating usually between eight and sixteen syllables, but with no specific meter. Patriarch Job in his *vita* of Tsarevich Dmitry, mentioned above, used a wealth of such couplets for the first time in a hagiographic work. Numerous similarly versified fragments can be found in the historical writings of the Time of Troubles, especially those of I. Katyrev-Rostovsky and G. Shakhovskoy, as well as in *The New Story About the Glorious Muscovite Tsardom* (*Novaya povest*) written around 1610. One of these earliest poets was Prince Ivan A. Khvorostinin, who in 1624 wrote the first large, formal poetic work, *Epistle Against Blaspheming Heretics,* a monumental theological poem abounding in autobiographical digressions. Directed against the propagation in Russia of Western religious beliefs, Khvorostinin's *Epistle* numbers over three thousand versified lines. The vogue for versification (*stikhobesie*) spread rapidly to various genres of Muscovite letters, and Khvorostinin's example was followed by scores of Russian versifiers who complied their theological and political treatises in rhymed form. Even many of the Old Believers, usually the staunch enemies of all new spiritual and cultural currents, succumbed to the temptations of this new vogue and also wrote some of their protests in verse form.

An attractive aspect of seventeenth-century Russian poetry can be found in lyric verses in which writers gave expression to their feelings, hopes, and sorrows. The earliest of these were recorded, surprisingly enough, by an English traveler in Russia in 1619, a certain Richard James, in whose transcriptions have been preserved the oldest known specimens of Russian lyric verse. The above-mentioned *Novel in Verse,* a huge work organized in alphabetic form with each chapter beginning with a consecutive letter of the alphabet, is partially a novella, partially a love poem. To the same transitional type also belongs *Misery-Luckless-Plight.* Toward the end of the century some remarkable lyric songs were written or recorded by Peter Kvashnin, S. Pazukhin, and other poets of this new Muscovite school. Most of them show the strong influence of folklore and are in the meter of folk lyrics, although some use the rhymed endings that developed under Western poetic influence, and a rather novel and sophisticated vocabulary.

The final stage of seventeenth-century Russian poetry is represented by the appearance of "syllabic" versification, which had come into ascendance in Polish poetry and made its way to Russia. The prosodic foundations of syllabic verse were a fixed number of syllables in each line, exclusively feminine rhyme, and a *caesura,* or break, in the middle of each line. This method of versification, so perfectly suited to the Polish language because of its constant accent on the penultimate syllable, was hardly appropriate for Russian, with its unstable stress. Therefore syllabic verse lasted only a short time in Russia, and syllabic poetry completely disappeared from Russian letters in the second quarter of the eighteenth century leaving very few traces on Russia's further poetic development. It was important, however, for acquainting Russians with the formal techniques of prosody.

This syllabic versification came to Muscovy from western and southern Russia (the Ukraine), where scholars and poets during the century of Polish domination were strongly influenced by Polish culture. The earliest syllabic poems appeared in Russian as early as the 1650's, but the first significant Russian syllabic poet was S. Polotsky, mentioned above, who was also the first Russian poet whose poems were printed during his lifetime. An erudite scholar and accomplished technician of *ars poetica,* Polotsky was not a man of real poetic inspiration. His copious work falls into two categories: odes written in his capacity as court panegyrist, and didactic poems revealing to Muscovites either ancient mythology or some achievement of Western scholarship. Skillfully constructed and often formed in geometric shapes and figures, in accordance with the mode of the time, his verses are dry and uninspiring, and should be classified rather as the writings of a leader of the enlightenment than of a genuine poet.

From the point of view of the development of the Russian literary language, Polotsky's verses—written in an artificial admixture of the Muscovite and Kievan versions of Church Slavonic—were a step backward, away from the increasingly simple, vernacular language of the novellas, satires, and autobiographies. Polotsky's importance in Russian literature is primarily historical because his work, which belongs more to baroque than to medieval literature, in the periodization suggested by D. Chizhevsky, brought Russia entirely into the literary sphere of the West. In the baroque period of the late seventeenth century, which signaled the end of the centuries-long medieval tradition, a prominent literary role was played by Polotsky's Muscovite followers, K. Istomin, S. Medvedev, and K. Khonykov, and later in the eighteenth century by A. Kantemir. Their language is somewhat easier than that of Polotsky, and they reveal more genuine poetic inspiration than did their teacher, but they do not excel him in erudition and poetic techniques.

The emergence of poetry was one of the most obvious manifestations of the profound changes in Russian literature. Western modes of life and culture rapidly won a place in Russia, and

Muscovy, in the second half of the seventeenth century, was very different not only from what it had been in the sixteenth century, but even in the *first* half of the seventeenth. The reunion of southern, formerly Kievan, Russia with Muscovy in 1653, as well as the Russian-Polish War of 1653–1668, were both instrumental in effecting these changes, since thousands of Kievan and West Russian scholars, noblemen, and merchants moved to Moscow or to the northern and eastern cities of the empire, carrying new Polish and Western modes with them. The Russian court was quick to adopt them, and in 1673 the first theatrical troupe performed in the palace of the tsar. Fourteen years later, in 1687, the first institution of higher education, the Muscovite Slavo-Greco-Latin Academy, was founded, and when, at the beginning of the eighteenth century, Peter I introduced his reforms—many of which only continued further the trends that had been taking place in preceding years—he, in effect, merely legalized the transformation of medieval Muscovite Russia into a Westernized empire and European power.

Part I

The Kievan Period

(1030–1240)

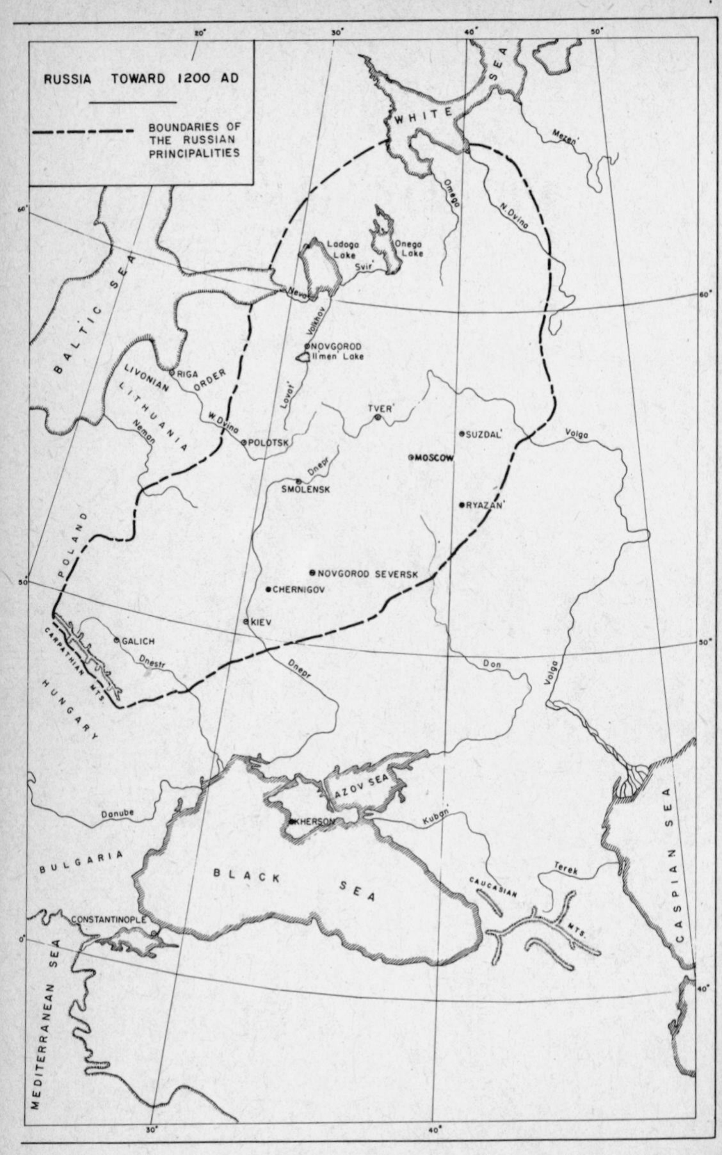

Russia Toward 1200 A.D.

THE PRIMARY CHRONICLE

THE *Primary Chronicle*, or, as it was called by its authors, *The Tale of Bygone Years*, is structurally a very complicated work compiled by various writers in the course of some three-quarters of a century, from about 1040 to 1118. Except for the introduction, which forms a prolegomenon to Russian history, the *Chronicle* starts with the year 852 (6360, according to the old Byzantine and Russian calendars) and is organized strictly on a yearly basis. Even when the chronicler had no event to record for a given year he recorded the year, leaving a blank space after it. Some of the entries are extremely laconic and are written in an almost telegraphic style, for example: "In the year 868(6376) Basil [Emperor of Byzantium] began to rule. In the year 869(6377) the entire Bulgarian land was Christianized. In the year 870 (6378) . . ." (no entry).

Besides these telegraphic entries, however, the *Chronicle* contains many colorful accounts of the deeds of the Russian princes, of legal documents—such as treaties between Russia and Byzantium, and the *Testament*, or *Instruction*, of Vladimir Monomakh—and lengthier descriptions of the feuds, wars, and other events that took place in old Russia.

According to the renowned Russian philologist A. A. Shakhmatov, which opinion is generally accepted by most contemporary investigators of *The Tale of Bygone Years*, the first draft of this chronicle was composed between 1037 and 1039. From 1060 to 1073 the task of its continuance was assumed by Nikon, a monk of the Kievan Crypt Monastery. Nikon recorded many events to which he was an eyewitness, and also re-edited the earlier entries. From 1093 to 1095 this version of the *Chronicle* was reworked in the Kievan Crypt Monastery, and the resulting redaction is usually referred to as the "Beginning Version" by literary historians. Around 1113 another monk of the Kievan Crypt Monastery, Nestor, rewrote the "Beginning Version," and it was probably he, also, who added the introduction with its historical and philosophical considerations. It was at this time, apparently, that the work received its present name, *The Tale of Bygone Years*. Nestor's version of the *Chronicle* also underwent redaction between 1117 and 1118, and this became the final form of the *Primary Chronicle*. As such, it was used as the initial part of most other Russian annals through the fourteenth and fifteenth centuries, as in the *Laurentian Chronicle*, the

Hypatian Chronicle, and the *Troitsky* (Trinity) *Chronicle*, the most important early Russian annals.

The text of the Prolegomenon and various stories taken from the *Primary Chronicle* are presented here in the translation by Samuel H. Cross. Some changes of geographical and historical names have been made for the sake of consistency in nomenclature and spelling throughout this volume.

◆ ◆ ◆

1. *Prolegomenon*

THIS IS THE TALE OF BYGONE YEARS: FROM WHENCE CAME THE RUSSIAN LAND, WHO FIRST RULED IN KIEV, AND FROM WHICH SOURCE THE RUSSIAN LAND HAD ITS BEGINNING

Let us begin this tale in this way: after the flood the sons of Noah—Shem, Ham and Japheth—divided the earth among them. To the lot of Shem fell the Orient, and his share extended lengthwise as far as India and breadthwise (from east to south) as far as Rhinocolura, including Persia and Bactria, as well as Syria, Media (which lies beside the Euphrates River), Babylon, Cordyna, Assyria, Mesopotamia, Arabia the Ancient, Elymais, India, Arabia the Mighty, Coelesyria, Commagene, and all Phoenicia.

To the lot of Ham fell the southern region, comprising Egypt, Ethiopia facing toward India, the other Ethiopia out of which the red Ethiopian river flows to the eastward, the Thebaid, Libya as far as Cyrene, Marmaris, Syrtis, Numidia, Massyris, and Mauretania over against Cadiz. Among the regions of the Orient, Ham also received Cilicia, Pamphylia, Mysia, Lycaonia, Phrygia, Camalia, Lycia, Caria, Lydia, the rest of Moesia, Troas, Aeolia, Bithynia, and ancient Phrygia. He likewise acquired the islands of Sardinia, Crete, and Cyprus, and the river Gihon, called the Nile.

To the lot of Japheth fell the northern and the western sections, including Media, Albania, Armenia (both little and great), Cappadocia, Paphlagonia, Galatia, Colchis, Bospore, Maeotis, Dervis, Sarmatia, Tauria, Scythia, Thrace, Macedonia, Dalmatia, Molossia, Thessaly, Locris, Pellene (which is also called the Peloponnese), Arcadia, Epirus, Illyria, the Slavs, Lychnitis, Adriaca, and the Adriatic Sea. He received also the islands of Britain, Sicily, Euboea, Rhodes, Chios, Lesbos, Cythera, Zacynthus, Cephallenia, Ithaca, and Corcyra, as well as a portion of the land of Asia called Ionia, the river Tigris flowing between the Medes and Babylon, and the territory to the north extending as far as the Pontus and including the Danube, the Dniester, and the Caucasian Mountains, which are called Hungarian, and thence even to the Dnieper. He likewise acquired dominion over other rivers, among them the Desna, the Pripet, the Dvina, the Volkhov, and the Volga, which flows eastward into the portion of Shem.

In the share of Japheth lie Russia, Chud, and all the gentiles: Meria, Muroma, Ves, Mordova, Chud beyond the hills, Perm, Pechera, Yam, Ugra, Litva, Zimegola, Kors, Setgola, and Liub. The Liakhs, the Prussians, and Chud border on the Varangian Sea. The Varangians dwell on the shores of that same sea, and extend to the eastward as far as the portion of Shem. They likewise live to the west beside this sea as far as the land of the Angles and the Italians. For the following nations also are a part of the race of Japheth: the Varangians, the Swedes, the Normans, the Rus [Russians], the Angles, the Gauls, the Italians, the Romans, the Germans, the Carolingians, the Venetians, the Genoese, and so on. Their homes are situated in the northwest, and adjoin the Hamitic tribes.

Thus Shem, Ham, and Japheth divided the earth among them, and after casting lots, so that none might encroach upon his brother's share, they lived each in his appointed portion. There was but one language, and as men multiplied throughout the earth, they planned, in the days of Yoktan and Peleg, to build a tower as high as heaven itself. Thus they gathered together in the plain of Shinar to build the tower and the city of Babylon round about it. But they wrought upon the tower for forty years, and it was unfinished. Then the Lord God descended to look upon the city and the tower, and said, "This race is one, and their tongue is one." So the Lord confused the tongues, and after dividing the people into seventy-two races, he scattered them over the whole world. After the confusion of the tongues, God overthrew the tower with a great wind, and the ruin of it lies between Assur and Babylon. In height and in breadth it is 5,433 cubits, and the ruin was preserved for many years.

After the destruction of the tower and the division of the nations, the sons of Shem occupied the eastern regions, the sons of Ham those of the south, and the sons of Japheth the western and the northern lands. Among these seventy-two nations, the Slavic race is derived from the line of Japheth, since they are the Noricians, who are identical with the Slavs.

For many years the Slavs lived beside the Danube, where the Hungarian and Bulgarian lands now lie. From among these Slavs, parties scattered throughout the country and were known by appropriate names, according to the places where they settled. Thus some came and settled by the river Morava, and were named Moravians, while others were called Czechs. Among these same Slavs are included the White Croats, the Serbs, and the Khorutanians. For when the Vlakhs attacked the Danubian Slavs, settled among them, and did them violence, the latter came and made their homes by the Vistula, and were then called Liakhs.[1] Of these same Liakhs some were called Polianians, some Lutichians, some Mazovians, and still others Pomorians. Certain Slavs settled also on the Dnieper, and were likewise called Polianians. Still others were named Derevlians, because they lived in the forests. Some also lived between the Pripet and the Dvina, and were known as Dregovichians. Other tribes resided along the Dvina and were called Polotians on account of a small stream called the Polota, which flows into the Dvina. It was from this same stream that they were named Polotians. The Slavs also dwelt about Lake Ilmen, and were known there by their appropriate name. They built a city which they called Novgorod. Still others had their homes along the Desna, the Sem, and the Sula, and were called Severians. Thus the Slavic race was divided, and its language was known as Slavic.

When the Polianians lived by themselves among the hills, a trade route connected the Varangians with the Greeks. Starting from Greece, this route proceeds along the Dnieper, above which a portage leads to the Lovat. By following the Lovat, the great lake Ilmen is reached. The river Volkhov flows out of this lake and enters the great lake Nevo. The mouth of this lake opens into the Varangian Sea. Over this sea goes the route to Rome, and on from Rome overseas to Constantinople. The Pontus, into which flows the river Dnieper, may be reached from that point. The Dnieper itself rises in the upland forest, and flows southward. The Dvina has its source in this same forest, but flows northward and empties into the Varangian Sea. The Volga rises in this same forest, but flows to the east, and discharges through seventeen mouths into the Caspian Sea. It is possible by this route to the eastward to reach the Bulgars and the Caspians, and thus attain the region of Shem. Along the Dvina runs the route to the Varangians, whence one may reach Rome, and go on from there to the race of Ham. But the

[1] Original Slavic name for Poles.

Dnieper flows through various mouths into the Pontus. This sea, beside which taught St. Andrew, Peter's brother, is called the Russian Sea.

2. *The Apostle Andrew Comes to Russia*

In the tenth or eleventh century the belief was held, based on the writing of Eusebius, that the Apostle Andrew, during his trip to the Greek colonies on the Black Sea, had visited the territories that were later to become Russia. This legend became very popular with the Russians and laid the foundation for the later-developed theory of Russia as the guardian of the Orthodox Christian faith. According to the *Primary Chronicle,* Andrew crossed through Russia from the mouth of the Dnieper River, passed the hills on which Kiev was later founded, and went as far north as the ancient city of Novgorod.

◆ ◆ ◆

When Andrew was teaching in Sinope and came to Kherson (as has been recounted elsewhere), he observed that the mouth of the Dnieper was nearby. Conceiving a desire to go to Rome, he thus went to the mouth of the Dnieper. Thence he ascended the river, and by chance he halted beneath the hills upon the shore. Upon arising in the morning, he observed to the disciples who were with him: "See ye these hills? So shall the favor of God shine upon them that on this spot a great city shall arise, and God shall erect many churches therein." He drew near the hills, and having blessed them, he set up a cross. After offering his prayer to God, he descended from the hill on which Kiev was subsequently built, and continued his journey up the Dnieper.

He then reached the Slavs at the point where Novgorod is now situated. He saw these people existing according to their customs, and on observing how they bathed and drenched themselves, he wondered at them. He went thence among the Varangians and came to Rome, where he recounted what he had learned and observed. "Wondrous to relate," said he, "I saw the land of the Slavs, and while I was among them, I noticed their wooden bathhouses. They warm them to extreme heat, then undress, and after anointing themselves with tallow, they take young reeds and lash their bodies. They actually lash themselves so violently that they barely escape alive. Then they drench themselves with cold water, and thus are revived. They think nothing of doing this everyday, and actually inflict such voluntary torture upon themselves. They make of the act not a mere washing but a veritable torment." When his hearers learned this fact, they marveled. But Andrew, after his stay in Rome, returned to Sinope.

3. *The Founding of the City of Kiev*

THE story of the founding of Kiev by three brothers, Kii, Shchek, and Khoriv, constitutes one of the oldest historical legends of Russia. An Armenian historian of the seventh century, Zenob Glak, knew of a similar legend concerning the founding of the city of Kuar (Kiev) in the land of Poluni (Polianians) by three brothers, Kuar, Mentery, and Kherean. It is possible that this legend arose from the actual merging of three settlements that archaeological evidence shows to have existed within the limits of present-day Kiev.

✦ ✦ ✦

The Polianians lived apart and governed their families, for thus far they were brethren, and each one lived with his gens on his own lands, ruling over his kinfolk. There were three brothers, Kii, Shchek, and Khoriv, and their sister was named Lybed. Kii lived upon the hill where the Borich trail now is, and Shchek dwelt upon the hill now named Shchekovitza, while on the third resided Khoriv, after whom this hill is named Khorevitza. They built a town and named it Kiev after their oldest brother. Around the town lay a wood and a great pine forest in which they used to catch wild beasts. These men were wise and prudent; they were called Polianians, and there are Polianians descended from them living in Kiev to this day.

Some ignorant persons have claimed that Kii was a ferryman, for near Kiev there was at that time a ferry from the other side of the river, in consequence of which people used to say, "To Kii's ferry." Now, if Kii had been a mere ferryman, he would never have gone to Constantinople. He was then the chief of his kin, and it is related what great honor he received from the emperor when he went to visit him. On his homeward journey, he arrived at the Danube. The place pleased him, and he built a small town, wishing to dwell there with his kinfolk. But those who lived nearby would not grant him this privilege. Yet even now the dwellers by the Danube call this town Kievetz. When Kii returned to Kiev, his native city, he ended his life there; and his brothers Shchek and Khoriv, as well as their sister Lybed, died there also.

4. *The Beginning of the Russian State and the Arrival of Rurik*

THE expansion of the Norsemen in the ninth and tenth centuries was not limited to northwestern Europe—Germany, France, and England. Long before the Vikings established themselves in France and, under William the Conqueror, in England, other Norse warriors from Norway, Sweden, and Denmark had penetrated to the Mediterranean Sea and built strong principalities in southern Italy and Greece. Some of these Norsemen entered the service of Byzantium in Constantinople. Simultaneously, another current of Norse expansion extended into eastern Europe. Skillfully utilizing the river systems of Russia, with the Dnieper playing the most important role, the Vikings—or, as the Russians called them, the Varangians—crossed through Russia and began to attack Byzantium, their bands being reinforced by Slavs.

According to both the *Primary Chronicle* and archaeological evidence, some of these Varangians settled in various places on Russian territory. It is difficult to determine now how important their role was in the subsequent organization of the Russian state, but the *Chronicle* records that Rurik, the leader of a group of Varangians, was invited to rule over Novgorod in 862, and legend has it that Rurik became the founder of both the Russian state and the dynasty that ruled Russia until 1598, when Fedor, the son of Ivan IV, died without an heir. The legend of Rurik's founding of the Russian state has been contested by many distinguished scholars and has divided most Russian historians into the Normanists, or "Norsemanists," who believe the legend to be true, and the anti-Normanists, who reject it and consider the Russian state to have been founded long before the arrival of Rurik.

◆ ◆ ◆

859 (6367) The Varangians from beyond the sea imposed tribute upon the Chuds, the Slavs, the Merians, the Ves, and the

Krivichians. But the Khazars imposed it upon the Polianians, the Severians, and the Viatichians, and collected a squirrel skin and a beaver skin from each hearth.

860–862 (6368–6370) The tributaries of the Varangians drove them back beyond the sea and, refusing them further tribute, set out to govern themselves. There was no law among them, but tribe rose against tribe. Discord thus ensued among them, and they began to war one against another. They said to themselves, "Let us seek a prince who may rule over us, and judge us according to the law." They accordingly went overseas to the Varangian Rus: these particular Varangians were known as Rus, just as some are called Swedes, and others Normans, Angles, and Goths, for they were thus named. The Chuds, the Slavs, and the Krivichians then said to the people of Rus, "Our whole land is great and rich, but there is no order in it. Come to rule and reign over us." They thus selected three brothers, with their kinfolk, who took with them all the Rus, and migrated. The oldest, Rurik, located himself in Novgorod; the second, Sineus, in Beloozero; and the third, Truvor, in Izborsk. On account of these Varangians, the district of Novgorod became known as Russian (Rus) land. The present inhabitants of Novgorod are descended from the Varangian race, but aforetime they were Slavs.

After two years, Sineus and his brother Truvor died, and Rurik assumed the sole authority. He assigned cities to his followers, Polotzk to one, Rostov to another, and to another Beloozero. In these cities there are thus Varangian colonists, but the first settlers were, in Novgorod, Slavs; in Polotzk, Krivichians; at Beloozero, Ves; in Rostov, Merians; and in Murom, Muromians. Rurik had dominion over all these districts.

With Rurik there were two men who did not belong to his kin, but were boyars. They obtained permission to go to Constantinople with their families. They thus sailed down the Dneiper, and in the course of their journey they saw a small city on a hill. Upon their inquiry as to whose town it was, they were informed that three brothers, Kii, Shchek, and Khoriv, had once built the city, but that since their deaths, their descendants were living there as tributaries of the Khazars. Oskold and Dir remained in this city, and after gathering together many Varangians, they established their domination over the country of the Polianians at the same time that Rurik was ruling at Novgorod.

863–866 (6371–6374) Oskold and Dir attacked the Greeks during the fourteenth year of the reign of the Emperor Michael.

When the emperor had set forth against the Saracens and had arrived at the Black River, the eparch sent him word that the Russians were approaching Constantinople, and the emperor turned back. Upon arriving inside the strait, the Russians made a great massacre of the Christians, and attacked Constantinople in two hundred boats. The emperor succeeded with difficulty in entering the city. The people prayed all night with the Patriarch Photius at the Church of the Holy Virgin in Blachernae. They also sang hymns and carried the sacred vestment of the Virgin to dip it in the sea. The weather was still, and the sea was calm, but a storm of wind came up, and when great waves straightway rose, confusing the boats of the godless Russians, it threw them upon the shore and broke them up, so that few escaped such destruction. The survivors then returned to their native land.

5. *Prince Oleg's Campaign Against Constantinople*

According to the *Primary Chronicle,* Rurik died in 879, leaving the conduct of state affairs to his relative, Oleg, in view of the infancy of Rurik's son, Igor. Oleg was the first nonlegendary ruler of Russia. In 882 he moved the capital from Novgorod to Kiev, and consolidated most of the Russian and Eastern Slavic tribes under his rule. A successful warrior and cautious ruler, Oleg became a popular figure in Russian historical tradition, and was called "the Seer" by his contemporaries. His campaigns against the Byzantine Empire, referred to by the writer of the *Chronicle* as the "Greek Empire," were particularly successful.

The tribes mentioned in the following text are primarily of Slavic origin. The Krivichians were a Slavic people who inhabited the entire northwestern Russian territory between the present cities of Moscow, Leningrad, and Minsk. The Chuds, Merians, and Ves were Finno-Ugric tribes of northern Russia.

◆ ◆ ◆

904–907 (6412–6415) Leaving Igor in Kiev, Oleg attacked the Greeks. He took with him a multitude of Varangians, Slavs, Chuds, Krivichians, Merians, Polianians, Severians, Derevlians, Radimichians, Croats, Dulebians, and Tivercians, who are Torks. All these tribes are known as Great Scythia by the

Greeks. With this entire force, Oleg sallied forth by horse and by ship, and the number of his vessels was two thousand. He arrived before Constantinople, but the Greeks fortified the strait and closed up the city. Oleg disembarked upon the shore, and ordered his soldiery to beach the ships. They waged war around the city, and accomplished much slaughter of the Greeks. They also destroyed many palaces and burned the churches. Of the prisoners they captured, some they beheaded, some they tortured, some they shot, and still others they cast into the sea. The Russians inflicted many other woes upon the Greeks after the usual manner of soldiers. Oleg commanded his warriors to make wheels, which they attached to the ships, and when the wind was favorable they spread the sails and bore down upon the city from the open country. When the Greeks beheld this, they were afraid, and sending messengers to Oleg, they implored him not to destroy the city, and offered to submit to such tribute as he should desire. Thus Oleg halted his troops. The Greeks then brought out to him food and wine, but he would not accept it, for it was mixed with poison. Then the Greeks were terrified and exclaimed, "This is not Oleg, but St. Demetrius, whom God has sent upon us." So Oleg demanded that they pay tribute for his two thousand ships at the rate of twelve *grivnas* per man, with forty men reckoned to a ship.

The Greeks assented to these terms, and prayed for peace lest Oleg should conquer the land of Greece. Retiring thus a short distance from the city, Oleg concluded a peace with the Greek emperors Leo and Alexander, and sent into the city to them Karl, Farulf, Vermund, Hrollaf, and Steinvith, with instructions to receive the tribute. The Greeks promised to satisfy their requirements. Oleg demanded that they should give to the troops on the two thousand ships twelve *grivnas* per bench, and pay in addition the sums required for the various Russian cities: first Kiev, then Chernigov, Pereiaslavl, Polotzk, Rostov, Liubech, and the other towns. In these cities lived princes subject to Oleg.

The Russians proposed the following terms: "The Russians who come hither shall receive as much grain as they require. Whosoever come as merchants shall receive supplies for six months, including bread, wine, meat, fish, and fruit. Baths shall be prepared for them in any volume they require. When the Russians return homeward, they shall receive from your emperor food, anchors, cordage, and sails, and whatever else is needful for the journey." The Greeks accepted these stipulations, and the emperors and all the courtiers declared: "If Russians come hither without merchandise, they shall receive no provisions. Your prince shall personally lay injunction upon such Russians as journey hither that they shall do no violence in the towns and throughout our territory. Such Russians as arrive here shall dwell in the St. Mamas quarter. Our government will send officers to record their names, and they shall then receive their monthly allowance, first the natives of Kiev, then those from Chernigov, Pereiaslavl, and the other cities. They shall not enter the city save through one gate, unarmed and fifty at a time, escorted by soldiers of the emperor. They may purchase wares according to their requirements, and tax-free."

Thus the emperors Leo and Alexander made peace with Oleg, and after agreeing upon the tribute and mutually binding themselves by oath, they kissed the cross, and invited Oleg and his men to swear an oath likewise. According to the religion of the Russians, the latter swore by their weapons and by their god Perun, as well as by Volos, the god of cattle, and thus confirmed the treaty.

Oleg gave orders that silken sails should be made for the Russians and linen ones for the Slavs, and his demand was satisfied. The Russians hung their shields upon the gates as a sign of victory, and Oleg then departed from Constantinople. The Russians unfurled their silken sails and the Slavs their sails of linen, but the wind tore them. Then the Slavs said, "Let us keep our canvas ones; linen sails are not made for the Slavs." So Oleg came to Kiev, bearing palls, gold, fruit, and wine, along with every sort of adornment. The people called Oleg "the Seer," for they were but pagans, and therefore ignorant.

6. *The Death of Oleg*

THE life of Oleg, the Seer, furnished material for several popular legends, one of which treats his death as predicted by the magicians.

◆ ◆ ◆

912 (6620) Thus Oleg ruled in Kiev, and dwelt at peace with all nations.

Now autumn came, and Oleg bethought him of his horse that he had caused to be well fed, yet had never mounted. For on one occasion he had made inquiry of the wonder-working magicians as to the ultimate cause of his death. One magician replied, "O, Prince, it is from the steed which you love and on which you ride that you shall meet your death." Oleg then reflected, and determined never to mount this horse or even to look upon it again. So he gave command that the horse should be properly fed, but never led into his presence. He thus let several years pass until he had attacked the Greeks. After he returned to Kiev, four years elapsed, but in the fifth he thought of the horse through which the magicians had foretold that he should meet his death. He thus summoned his senior squire and inquired as to the whereabouts of the horse which he had ordered to be fed and well cared for. The squire answered that he was dead. Oleg laughed and mocked the magician, exclaiming, "Soothsayers tell untruths, and their words are naught but falsehood. This horse is dead, but I am still alive."

Then he commanded that a horse should be saddled. "Let me see his bones," said he. He rode to the place where the bare bones and the skull lay. Dismounting from his horse, he laughed, and remarked, "Am I to receive my death from this skull?" And he stamped upon the skull with his foot. But a serpent crawled forth from it and bit him in the foot, so that in consequence he sickened and died. All the people mourned for him in great grief. They bore him away and buried him upon the hill which is called Shchekovitza. His tomb stands there to this day, and it is called the Tomb of Oleg.

7. *Igor's Death and Olga's Revenge*

After Oleg's death, Igor became the ruler of Russia. He was neither succcessful in his military enterprises nor popular with the people. A campaign undertaken by him against the Slavic tribe of Derevlians, who lived between Kiev and the present-day Polish border, resulted in his death. His clever widow, Olga, cruelly revenged the death of her husband. Folklore motifs are evident in this story of her revenge, which is one of the most colorful narratives of *The Tale of Bygone Years.*

◆ ◆ ◆

945 (6453) In this year, Igor's retinue said to him. "The servants of Sveinald are adorned with weapons and fine raiment, but we are naked. Go forth with us, O Prince, after tribute, that

both you and we may profit thereby." Igor heeded their words, and he attacked Dereva in search of tribute. He demanded an additional tribute, and collected it by violence from the people with the assistance of his followers. After thus gathering the tribute, he returned to his city. On his homeward way, he said to his followers, after some reflection: "Go forward with the tribute. I shall turn back, and rejoin you later." He dismissed his retainers on their journey homeward, but being desirous of still greater booty, he returned on his tracks with a few of his vassals.

The Derevlians heard that he was again approaching, and consulted with Mal, their prince, saying: "If a wolf comes among the sheep, he will take away the whole flock one by one, unless he be killed. If we do not thus kill him now, he will destroy us all." They then sent forward to Igor inquiring why he had returned, since he had collected all the tribute. But Igor did not heed them, and the Derevlians came forth from the city of Izkorosten, and slew Igor and his company, for the number of the latter was few. So Igor was buried, and his tomb is near the city of Izkorosten in Dereva even to this day.

But Olga was in Kiev with her son, the boy Sviatoslav. His tutor was Asmund, and the troop commander was Sveinald, the father of Mstikha. The Derevlians then said: "See, we have killed the Prince of Russia. Let us take his wife Olga for our Prince Mal, and then we shall obtain possession of Sviatoslav, and work our will upon him." So they sent their best men, twenty in number, to Olga by boat, and they arrived below Borichev in their boat. At that time, the water flowed below the heights of Kiev, and the inhabitants did not live in the valley, but upon the heights. The city of Kiev was on the present site of the palace of Gordiat and Nicephorus, and the prince's palace was in the city where the palace of Vratislav and Chud now stands, while the ferry was outside the city. Without the city there stood another palace, where the palace of the Cantors is now situated, behind the Church of the Holy Virgin upon the heights. This was a palace with a stone hall.

Olga was informed that the Derevlians had arrived, and summoned them to her presence with a gracious welcome. When the Derevlians had thus announced their arrival, Olga replied with an inquiry as to the reason of their coming. The Derevlians then announced that their tribe had sent them to report that they had slain her husband, because he was like a wolf, crafty and ravening, but that their princes, who had thus preserved the land of Dereva, were good, and that Olga should come and marry their Prince Mal. For the name of the Prince of Dereva was Mal.

Olga made this reply: "Your proposal is pleasing to me; indeed, my husband cannot rise again from the dead. But I desire to honor you tomorrow in the presence of my people. Return now to your boat, and remain there with an aspect of arrogance. I shall send for you on the morrow, and you shall say, "We will not ride on horses nor go on foot; carry us in our boat.' And you shall be carried in your boat." Thus she dismissed them to their vessel.

Now Olga gave command that a large deep ditch should be dug in the castle with the hall, outside the city. Thus, on the morrow, Olga, as she sat in the hall, sent for the strangers, and her messengers approached them and said, "Olga summons you to great honor." But they replied, "We will not ride on horseback nor in wagons, nor go on foot; carry us in our boat." The people of Kiev then lamented: "Slavery is our lot. Our prince is killed, and our princess intends to marry their prince." So they carried the Derevlians in their boat. The latter sat on the cross-benches in great robes, puffed up with pride. They thus were borne into the court before Olga, and when the men had brought the Derevlians in, they dropped them into the trench along with the boat. Olga bent over and inquired whether they found the honor to their taste. They answered that it was worse than the death of Igor. She then commanded that they should be buried alive, and they were thus buried.

Olga then sent messages to the Derevlians to the effect that, if they really required her presence, they should send after her their distinguished men, so that she might go to their prince with due honor, for otherwise her people in Kiev would not let her go. When the Derevlians heard this message, they gathered together the best men who governed the land of Dereva, and sent them to her. When the Derevlians arrived, Olga commanded that a bath should be made ready, and invited them to appear before her after they had bathed. The bathhouse was then heated, and the Derevlians entered in to bathe. Olga's men closed up the bathhouse behind them, and she gave orders to set it on fire from the doors, so that the Derevlians were all burned to death.

Olga then sent to the Derevlians the following message: "I am now coming to you, so prepare great quantities of mead in the city where you killed my husband, that I may weep over his grave and hold a funeral feast for him." When they heard these words, they gathered great quantities of honey, and brewed mead. Taking a small escort, Olga made the journey with ease, and upon her arrival at Igor's tomb, she wept for her husband. She bade her followers pile up a great mound, and when they had piled it up, she also gave command that a funeral feast should be held. Thereupon the Derevlians sat down to drink, and Olga bade her followers wait upon them.

The Derevlians inquired of Olga where the retinue was which they had sent to meet her. She replied that they were following with her husband's bodyguard. When the Derevlians were drunk, she bade her followers fall upon them, and went about herself egging on her retinue to the Massacre of the Derevlians. So they cut down five thousand of them; but Olga returned to Kiev and prepared an army to attack the survivors.

946 (6454) Olga, together with her son Sviatoslav, gathered a large and valiant army, and proceeded to attack the land of the Derevlians. The latter came out to meet her troops, and when both forces were ready for combat, Sviatoslav cast his spear against the Derevlians. But the spear pierced the ears of the horse, and struck the horse's foot, for the prince was but a child. Then Sveinald and Asmund said, "The prince has already begun battle; press on, vassals, after the prince." Thus they conquered the Derevlians, with the result that the latter fled, and shut themselves up in their cities.

Olga hastened with her son to the city of Izkorosten, for it was there that her husband had been slain, and they laid siege to the city. The Derevlians barricaded themselves within the city, and fought valiantly from it, for they realized that they had killed the prince, and to what fate they would in consequence surrender.

Olga remained there a year without being able to take the city, and then she thought out this plan. She sent into the town the following message: "Why do you persist in holding out? All your cities have surrendered to me and submitted to tribute, so that the inhabitants now cultivate their fields and their lands in peace. But you had rather die of hunger, without submitting to tribute." The Derevlians replied that they would be glad to submit to tribute but that she was still bent on avenging her husband.

Olga then answered: "Since I have already avenged the misfortune of my husband twice on the occasions when your messengers came to Kiev, and a third time when I held a funeral feast for him, I do not desire further revenge, but am anxious to receive a small tribute. After I have made peace with you, I shall return home again."

The Derevlians then inquired what she desired of them, and expressed their readiness to pay honey and furs. Olga retorted that at the moment they had neither honey nor furs but that she had one small request to make. "Give me three pigeons," she said," and three sparrows from each house. I do not desire to impose a heavy tribute, like my husband, but I require only this small gift from you, for you are impoverished by the siege."

The Derevlians rejoiced, and collected from each house three pigeons and three sparrows, which they sent to Olga with their greetings. Olga then instructed them, in view of their submission, to return to their city, promising that on the morrow she would depart and return to her own capital. The Derevlians re-entered their city with gladness, and when they reported to the inhabitants, the people of the town rejoiced.

Now Olga gave to each soldier in her army a pigeon or a sparrow, and ordered them to attach by a thread to each pigeon and sparrow a match bound with small pieces of cloth. When night fell, Olga bade her soldiers release the pigeons and the sparrows. So the birds flew to their nests, the pigeons to the cotes, and the sparrows under the eaves. Thus the dovecotes, the coops, the porches, and the haymows were set on fire. There was not a house that was not consumed, and it was impossible to extinguish the flames, because all the houses caught fire at once. The people fled from the city, and Olga ordered her soldiers to catch them. Thus she took the city and burned it and captured the elders of the city. Some of the other captives she killed, while she gave others as slaves to her followers. The remnant she left to pay tribute.

She imposed upon them a heavy tribute, two parts of which went to Kiev, and the third to Olga in Vyshegorod; for Vyshegorod was Olga's city. She then passed through the land of Dereva, accompanied by her son and her retinue, establishing laws and tribute. Her residences and hunting preserves are there still. Then she returned with her son to Kiev, her city where she remained one year.

8. *Sviatoslav's Campaigns and His Death*

PRINCE Sviatoslav, son of Igor and Olga, reigned from 956 to 971. He was a great warrior who built a mighty empire that comprised the Khazars, the Caucasian tribes of Yasians and

Kassogians, and all the Slavic tribes from Novgorod to Kiev, including the Viatichians. During his reign a horde of Pechenegs, an Asian tribe of Turkic origin, invaded the prairies of southern Russia and began raiding its agricultural lands.

In 968 the Byzantine emperor requested Sviatoslav's aid in subduing the Bulgarian kingdom in the Balkans. This led to a long war, first against the Bulgarians, and finally against Sviatoslav's original ally, Byzantium.

✦ ✦ ✦

956–964 (6464–6472) When Prince Sviatoslav had grown up and matured, he began to collect a numerous and valiant army. Stepping light as a leopard, he undertook many campaigns. Upon his expeditions he carried with him neither wagons nor kettles, and boiled no meat, but cut off small strips of horseflesh, game, or beef, and ate it after roasting it on the coals. Nor did he have a tent, but he spread out a garment under him, and set his saddle under his head; and all his retinue did likewise. He sent messengers to the other lands announcing his intention to attack them. He went to the Oka and the Volga, and on coming in contact with the Viatichians, he inquired of them to whom they paid tribute. They made answer that they paid a sliver piece per plowshare to the Khazars.

965 (6473) Sviatoslav sallied forth against the Khazars. When they heard of his approach, they went out to meet him with their prince, the Kagan,[1] and the armies came to blows. When the battle thus took place, Sviatoslav defeated the Khazars and took their city of Belovezha. He also conquered the Yasians and the Kassogians.

966 (6474) Sviatoslav conquered the Viatichians and made them his tributaries.

967 (6475) Sviatoslav marched to the Danube to attack the Bulgarians. When they fought together, Sviatoslav overcame the Bulgarians, and captured eighty towns along the Danube. He took up his residence there, and ruled in Pereiaslavetz, receiving tribute from the Greeks.

968 (6476) While Sviatoslav was at Pereiaslavetz, the Pechenegs invaded Russia for the first time. So Olga shut herself up in the city of Kiev with her grandsons, Yaropolk, Oleg, and Vladimir. The nomads besieged the city with a great force. They surrounded it with an innumerable multitude, so that it was impossible to escape or send messages from the city, and

[1] A Turkic word for emperor.

the inhabitants were weak from hunger and thirst. Those who had gathered on the other side of the Dnieper in their boats remained on that side, and not one of them could enter Kiev, while no one could cross over to them from the city itself.

The inhabitants of the city were afflicted, and lamented, "Is there no one that can reach the opposite shore and report to the other party that if we are not relieved on the morrow, we must perforce surrender to the Pechenegs?" Then one youth volunteered to make the attempt, and the people begged him to try it. So he went out of the city with a bridle in his hand, and ran among the Pechenegs shouting out a question whether anyone had seen a horse. For he knew their language, and they thought he was one of themselves. When he approached the river, he threw off his clothes, jumped into the Dnieper, and swam out. As soon as the Pechenegs perceived his action, they hurried in pursuit, shooting at him the while, but they did not succeed in doing him any harm. The party on the other shore caught sight of him, and rowed out in a boat to meet him. They then took him into their boat, and brought him to their company. He thus reported to them that if they could not relieve the city on the next day, the inhabitants would surrender to the Pechenegs.

Then their general, Pryetich by name, announced: "Tomorrow we shall approach by boat, and after rescuing the princess and the young princes, we shall fetch them over to this side. If we do not bring this to pass, Sviatoslav will put us to death." When it was morning, they embarked before dawn in their boats, and blew loudly on their trumpets. The people within the city raised a shout, so that the Pechenegs thought the prince himself had returned, and accordingly fled from the city in various directions. Thus Olga went forth with her grandsons and her followers to the boats. When the prince of the Pechenegs perceived their escape, he came alone to Pryetich the general, and inquired who had just arrived. Pryetich replied that it was a boat from the opposite bank. The prince of the Pechenegs inquired whether Pryetich was the prince himself. The general then replied that he was the prince's vassal and that he had come as a vanguard but that a countless force was on the way under the prince's command. He made this statement simply to frighten the Pecheneg. So the prince of the Pechenegs invited Pryetich to become his friend, to which request Pryetich assented. The two shook hands on it, and the prince of the Pechenegs gave Pryetich his spear, sabre, and arrows, while the latter gave him his own breastplate, shield, and sword. The Pechenegs raised the siege. and for a time the inhabitants could no longer water their horses at the Lybed on account of the retreating enemy.

But the people of Kiev sent to Sviatoslav, saying: "O Prince, you visit and observe foreign lands. But while you neglect your own country, the Pechenegs have all but taken us captive, along with your mother and your children as well. Unless you return to protect us, they will attack us again, if you have no pity on your native land, on your mother in her old age, and on our children." When Sviatoslav heard these words, he quickly bestrode his charger, and returned to Kiev with his retinue. He kissed his mother and his children, and regretted what they had suffered at the hands of the Pechenegs. He therefore collected an army, and drove the Pechenegs out into the steppes. Thus there was peace.

969 (6477) Sviatoslav announced to his mother and his boyars: "I do not care to remain in Kiev, but should prefer to live in Pereiaslavetz on the Danube, since that is the center of my realm, where all riches are concentrated: gold, silks, wine, and various fruits from Greece, silver and horses from Hungary and Bohemia, and from Russia furs, wax, honey, and slaves."

But Olga made reply, "You behold me in my weakness. Why do you desire to depart from me?" For she was already in precarious health. She thus remonstrated with him and begged him first to bury her and then to go wheresoever he would. Three days later Olga died. Her son wept for her with great mourning, as did likewise her grandsons and all the people. They thus carried her out, and buried her in her tomb. Olga had given command not to hold a funeral feast for her, for she had a priest who performed the last rites over the sainted princess.[1]

Olga was the precursor of the Christian land, even as the dayspring precedes the sun and as the dawn precedes the day. For she shone like the moon by night, and she was radiant among the infidels like a pearl in the mire, since the people were soiled, and not yet purified of their sin by holy baptism. But she herself was cleansed by this sacred purification. She put off the sinful garments of the old Adam, and was clad in the new Adam, which is Christ. Thus we say to her, "Rejoice in the Russians' knowledge of God," for we were the firstfruits of their reconciliation with him.

She was the first from Russia to enter the kingdom of God, and the sons of Russia thus praise her as their leader, for since her death she has interceded with God in their behalf. The

[1] By that time Olga had become a Christian.

souls of the righteous do not perish. As Solomon has said, "The nations rejoice in the praise of the righteous, for his memory is eternal, since it is acknowledged by God and men" (Proverbs, xxix, 2; Wisdom, iii, 4). For all men glorify her, as they behold her lying there in the body for many years. As the prophet has said, "I will glorify them that glorify me" (I Samuel, ii, 30). Of such persons David also said, "The righteous shall be had in everlasting remembrance, he shall not be afraid of evil tidings. His heart is fixed, trusting in Jehovah, his heart is fixed, and will not be moved" (Psalms, cxii, 7–8). And Solomon said, "The righteous live forever, and they have reward from God and grace from the Most High. Therefore shall they receive the kingdom of beauty, and the crown of goodness from the hand of the Lord. With his right hand will he cover them, and with his arm will he protect them" (Wisdom, v, 16–17). For he protected the sainted Olga from the devil, our adversary and our foe.

970 (6478) Sviatoslav set up Yaropolk in Kiev and Oleg in Dereva. At this time came the people of Novgorod asking for themselves a prince. "If you will not come to us," said they, "then we will choose a prince of our own." So Sviatoslav promised them that a prince should be designated, but Yaropolk and Oleg both refused, so that Dobrynia suggested that the post should be offered to Vladimir. For Vladimir was son of Malusha, confidante of Olga and sister of Dobrynia. Their father was Malk of Liubech, and Dobrynia was thus Vladimir's uncle. The citizens of Novgorod thus requested Sviatoslav to designate Vladimir, and he granted their request. The Novgorodians took Vladimir to be their prince, and he went forth to Novgorod with Dobrynia his uncle. But Sviatoslav departed thence to Pereiaslavetz.

971 (6479) Sviatoslav arrived before Pereiaslavetz, and the Bulgarians fortified themselves in the city. They made one sally against Sviatoslav; there was great carnage, and the Bulgarians came off victors. But Sviatoslav cried to his soldiery: "We seem to be conquered here already. Let us fight bravely, brothers and companions!" Toward evening, Sviatoslav finally gained the upper hand, and took the city by storm. He then sent messages to the Greeks, announcing his intention to march against them and capture their city, as he had taken Pereiaslavetz. The Greeks replied that they were in no position to offer resistance, and therefore begged him to accept tribute instead for himself and his soldiery, requesting him to notify them how many Russians there were, so that they might pay so much per head. The

Greeks made this proposition to deceive the Russians, for the Greeks are crafty even to the present day. Sviatoslav replied that his force numbered twenty thousand Russians. So the Greeks armed one hundred thousand men to attack Sviatoslav, and paid no tribute.

Sviatoslav advanced against the Greeks, who came out to meet the Russians. When the Russians perceived their approach, they were terrified at the multitude of the Greek soldiery, and Sviatoslav remarked: "Now we have no place whither we may flee. Whether we will or no, we must give battle. Let us not disgrace Russia, but rather sacrifice our lives, lest we be dishonored. For if we flee, we shall be disgraced. We must not take flight, but we will resist boldly, and I will march before you. If my head falls, then look to yourselves." Then his vassals replied, "Wherever your head falls, there we too will lay down our own!" So the Russians went into battle, and the carnage was great. Sviatoslav came out victor, but the Greeks fled. Then Sviatoslav advanced toward the capital, fighting as he went, and destroying towns that stand deserted even to the present time.

The emperor summoned his boyars to the palace, and inquired what they should do, for they could not withstand Sviatoslav's onslaught. The boyars advised that he should be tempted with gifts, to discover whether Sviatoslav liked gold and silks. So they sent to Sviatoslav gold and silks, carried by a clever envoy. To the latter they gave command to look well upon his eyes, his face, and his spirit. The envoy took the gifts, and went out to Sviatoslav. It was reported to the prince that Greeks had come bringing greetings, and he ordered that they should be introduced. They then came near and greeted him, laying before him the gold and the silks. Sviatoslav, without noticing the presents, bade his servants keep them. So the envoys returned before the emperor; and the emperor summoned his boyars. Then the envoys reported that when they had come before Sviatoslav and offered their gifts, he had taken no notice of them, but had ordered them to be retained. Then another courtier said, "Try him a second time; send him arms."

This suggestion was adopted, and they sent to Sviatoslav a sword and other accouterments which were duly brought before him. The prince accepted these gifts, which he praised and admired, and returned his greetings to the emperor. The envoys went back to the emperor and reported what had occurred. Then the boyars remarked: "This man must be fierce, since he pays no heed to riches, but accepts arms. Submit to tribute." The emperor accordingly requested Sviatoslav to approach no nearer, but to accept tribute instead. For Sviatoslav had indeed almost reached Constantinople. So the Greeks paid him tribute, and he took also the share of those Russians who had been slain, promising that their families should receive it. He accepted many gifts besides, and returned to Pereiaslavetz with great acclaim.

Upon observing the small number of his troops, Sviatoslav reflected that if haply the Greeks attacked him by surprise, they would kill his retinue and himself. For many warriors had perished on the expedition. So he resolved to return to Russia for reinforcements. He then sent envoys to the emperor in Silistria (for the emperor was then at that place) indicating his intention to maintain peaceful and friendly relations. When the emperor heard this message, he rejoiced, and sent to Sviatoslav gifts even more valuable than the former ones. Sviatoslav accepted these gifts, and on taking counsel with his retinue declared: "If we do not make peace with the emperor, and he discovers how few of us there are, the Greeks will come and besiege us in our city. Russia is far away, and the Pechenegs are hostile to us. So who will give us aid? Let us rather make peace with the emperor, for the Greeks have offered tribute; let that suffice. But if the emperor stops paying tribute, we shall once more collect troops in Russia in still greater numbers, and march again on Constantinople." His speech pleased his followers, and they sent their chief men to the emperor. The envoys arrived in Silistria, and reported to the emperor. He summoned them before him on the following day, and gave them permission to state their errand. They then replied, "Thus says our prince, 'I desire to maintain true amity with the Greek emperor henceforth and forever.'" The emperor rejoiced, and commanded his scribe to set down on parchment the words of Sviatoslav. One envoy recited all his words, and the scribe wrote them down. He spoke as follows:

"In accordance with the previous treaty concluded by Sviatoslav, Prince of Russia, and by Sveinald, with Johannes surnamed Tzimiskes, written down by Theophilus the secretary in Silistria during the month of July, in the year 971 (6479), the fourteenth of the indiction, I, Sviatoslav, Prince of Russia, even as I previously swore, now confirm by oath upon this covenant that I desire to preserve peace and perfect amity with each of the great Greek emperors, and particularly with Basil and Constantine, and with their successors inspired of God, and with all their subjects. In this resolve concur all Russians under my sway, both boyars and commons, forever. I will therefore contemplate no attack upon your territory, nor will I collect an army or foreign mercenaries for this purpose, nor will I incite any other foe against your realm or against any territory pertaining thereto, and particularly against the district of Kherson, or the cities thereto adjacent, or against Bulgaria. But if any other foe plans to attack your realm, I will resist him and wage war upon him. And even as I have given oath to the Greek emperors in company with my boyars and all my subjects, so may we preserve this treaty inviolate. But if we fail in the observance of any of the aforesaid stipulations, either I, or my companions, or my subjects, may we be accursed of the God in whom we believe, namely, of Perun and Volos, the god of flocks, and may we become yellow as gold, and be slain with our own weapons. Regard as truth what we have now covenanted with you, even as it is inscribed upon this parchment and sealed with our seals."

After making peace with the Greeks, Sviatoslav journeyed by boat to the cataracts of the Dnieper, and the general, Sveinald, advised him to ride around the falls on horseback, for the Pechenegs were encamped in the vicinity. The prince did not heed him, but went on by boat. The people of Pereiaslavetz informed the Pechenegs that Sviatoslav was returning to Russia after seizing from the Greeks great riches and immense booty but that his troop was small. When the Pechenegs heard this news, they ambuscaded the cataracts, so that when Sviatoslav arrived it was impossible to pass them. So the prince decided to winter in Belobereg, but the Russians had no rations, so that there was a severe famine, and they paid as much as half a *grivna* for a horse's head. But Sviatoslav wintered there nevertheless.

When spring came, in 972 (6480), Sviatoslav approached the cataracts, where Kuria, Prince of the Pechenegs, attacked him; and Sviatoslav was killed. The nomads took his head, and made a cup out of his skull, overlaying it with gold, and they drank from it. But Sveinald returned to Yaropolk in Kiev. Now all the years of Sviatoslav's reign were twenty-eight.

9. *Vladimir Christianizes Russia*

Vladimir, son of Sviatoslav, reigned from 980 to 1015, and solved the important problem of Russia's cultural orientation. He was faced with the need to choose a religion for his state, and vacillated between several: Islam, which had been carried to Central Asia by Arab armies and to the Upper Volga[1] by Arab missionaries; Judaism, to which belonged the upper class of the Khazars on the Lower Volga; the Christianity of the West, professed by the Germans; or the Christianity of the East, professed by Byzantium. Preachers of each of these religions were present in Kiev, and each tried to convert Vladimir to his particular faith. Finally, the Christianity of the East prevailed. This is not surprising, since for centuries Russia had been in close contact with Byzantium and, even earlier, with the Hellenic world. As early as the sixth and seventh centuries B.C., the Greeks had founded prosperous colonies in the Crimea, such as the important city of Kherson, and others at many places on the northern coast of the Black Sea, all of which became the focal point for Greek and, later, Byzantine, influence in eastern Europe. Lively trade relations between Kiev and Constantinople had been maintained for centuries, despite intermittent interruptions by Russian military campaigns against Constantinople —or, as the Russians of that time called it, "Tsargrad," the City of the Caesars.

◆ ◆ ◆

987 (6495) Vladimir summoned together his vassals and the city elders, and said to them: "Behold, the Bulgarians came before me urging me to accept their religion. Then came the Germans and praised their own faith; and after them came the Jews. Finally the Greeks appeared, criticizing all other faiths but commending their own, and they spoke at length, telling the history of the whole world from its beginning. Their words were artful, and it was wondrous to listen and pleasant to hear them. They preach the existence of another world. 'Whoever adopts our religion and then dies shall arise and live forever. But whosoever embraces another faith, shall be consumed with fire in the next world.' What is your opinion on this subject, and what do you answer?" The vassals and the elders replied: "You know, O Prince, that no man condemns his own possessions, but praises them instead. If you desire to make certain, you have servants at your disposal. Send them to inquire about the ritual of each and how he worships God."

Their counsel pleased the prince and all the people, so that they chose good and wise men to the number of ten, and directed them to go first among the Bulgarians and inspect their

[1] To the realm of the Volga Bulgarians, a Turkic state not to be confused with the Slavic Bulgarians of the Balkans.

faith. The emissaries went their way, and when they arrived at their destination they beheld the disgraceful actions of the Bulgarians and their worship in the mosque; then they returned to their own country. Vladimir then instructed them to go likewise among the Germans, and examine their faith, and finally to visit the Greeks. They thus went into Germany, and after viewing the German ceremonial, they proceeded to Constantinople where they appeared before the emperor. He inquired on what mission they had come, and they reported to him all that had occurred. When the emperor heard their words, he rejoiced, and did them great honor on that very day.

On the morrow, the emperor sent a message to the patriarch to inform him that a Russian delegation had arrived to examine the Greek faith, and directed him to prepare the church and the clergy, and to array himself in his sacerdotal robes, so that the Russians might behold the glory of the God of the Greeks. When the patriarch received these commands, he bade the clergy assemble, and they performed the customary rites. They burned incense, and the choirs sang hymns. The emperor accompanied the Russians to the church, and placed them in a wide space, calling their attention to the beauty of the edifice, the chanting, and the offices of the archpriest and the ministry of the deacons, while he explained to them the worship of his God. The Russians were astonished, and in their wonder praised the Greek ceremonial. Then the Emperors Basil and Constantine invited the envoys to their presence, and said, "Go hence to your native country," and thus dismissed them with valuable presents and great honor.

Thus they returned to their own country, and the prince called together his vassals and the elders. Vladimir then announced the return of the envoys who had been sent out, and suggested that their report be heard. He thus commanded them to speak out before his vassals. The envoys reported: "When we journeyed among the Bulgarians, we beheld how they worship in their temple, called a mosque, while they stand ungirt. The Bulgarian bows, sits down, looks hither and thither like one possessed, and there is no happiness among them, but instead only sorrow and a dreadful stench. Their religion is not good. Then we went among the Germans, and saw them performing many ceremonies in their temples; but we beheld no glory there. Then we went on to Greece, and the Greeks led us to the edifices where they worship their God, and we knew not whether we were in heaven or on earth. For on earth there is no such splendor or such beauty, and we are at a loss how to describe it. We know only that God dwells there among men, and their service is fairer than the ceremonies of other nations. For we cannot forget that beauty. Every man, after tasting something sweet, is afterward unwilling to accept that which is bitter, and therefore we cannot dwell longer here." Then the vassals spoke and said, "If the Greek faith were evil, it would not have been adopted by your grandmother Olga, who was wiser than all other men." Vladimir then inquired where they should all accept baptism, and they replied that the decision rested with him.

After a year had passed, in 988 (6496), Vladimir marched with an armed force against Kherson,[2] a Greek city, and the people of Kherson barricaded themselves therein. Vladimir halted at the farther side of the city beside the bay, a bowshot from the town, and the inhabitants resisted energetically while Vladimir besieged the town. Eventually, however, they became exhausted, and Vladimir warned them that if they did not surrender, he would remain on the spot for three years. When they failed to heed this threat, Vladimir marshaled his troops and ordered the construction of an earthwork in the direction of the city. While this work was under construction, the inhabitants dug a tunnel under the city wall, stole the heaped-up earth, and carried it into the city, where they piled it up in the center of the town. But the soldiers kept on building, and Vladimir persisted. Then a man of Kherson, Anastasius by name, shot into the Russian camp an arrow on which he had written: "There are springs behind you to the east, from which water flows in pipes. Dig down and cut them off." When Vladimir received this information, he raised his eyes to heaven and vowed that if this hope was realized, he would be baptized. He gave orders straightway to dig down above the pipes, and the water supply was thus cut off. The inhabitants were accordingly overcome by thirst, and surrendered.

Vladimir and his retinue entered the city, and he sent messages to the Emperors Basil and Constantine, saying: "Behold, I have captured your glorious city. I have also heard that you have an unwedded sister. Unless you give her to me to wife, I shall deal with your own city as I have with Kherson." When the emperors heard this message, they were troubled, and replied: "It is not meet for Christians to give in marriage to pagans. If you are baptized, you shall have her to wife, inherit the kingdom of God, and be our companion in the faith. Unless

[2] The city of Kherson was located in the Crimea.

you do so, however, we cannot give you our sister in marriage." When Vladimir learned their response, he directed the envoys of the emperors to report to the latter that he was willing to accept baptism, having already given some study to their religion, and that the Greek faith and ritual, as described by the emissaries sent to examine it, had pleased him well. When the emperors heard this report, they rejoiced, and persuaded their sister Anna to consent to the match. They then requested Vladimir to submit to baptism before they should send their sister to him, but Vladimir desired that the princess should herself bring priests to baptize him. The emperors complied with his request, and sent forth their sister, accompanied by some dignitaries and priests. Anna, however, departed with reluctance. "It is as if I were setting out into captivity," she lamented; "better were it for me to die here." But her brothers protested: "Through your agency God turns the Russian land to repentance, and you will relieve Greece from the danger of grievous war. Do you not see how much evil the Russians have already brought upon the Greeks? If you do not set out, they may bring on us the same misfortunes." It was thus that they overcame her hesitation only with great difficulty. The princess embarked upon a ship, and after tearfully embracing her kinfolk, she set forth across the sea and arrived at Kherson. The natives came forth to greet her, and conducted her into the city, where they settled her in the palace.

By divine agency, Vladimir was suffering at that moment from a disease of the eyes, and could see nothing, being in great distress. The princess declared to him that if he desired to be relieved of this disease, he should be baptized with all speed, otherwise it could not be cured. When Vladimir heard her message, he said, "If this proves true, then of a surety is the God of the Christians great," and gave order that he should be baptized. The Bishop of Kherson, together with the princess's priests, after announcing the tidings, baptized Vladimir, and as the bishop laid his hand upon him, he straightway received his sight. Upon experiencing this miraculous cure, Vladimir glorified God, saying, "I have now perceived the one true God." When his followers beheld this miracle, many of them were also baptized.

Vladimir was baptized in the Church of St. Basil, which stands at Kherson upon a square in the center of the city, where the Khersonians trade. The palace of Vladimir stands beside this church to this day, and the palace of the princess is behind the altar. After his baptism, Vladimir took the princess in marriage.

Those who do not know the truth say he was baptized in Kiev, while others assert this event took place in Vasiliev, while still others mention other places.

Hereupon Vladimir took the princess and Anastasius and the priests of Kherson, together with the relics of St. Clement and of Phoebus his disciple, and selected also sacred vessels and images for the service. In Kherson he thus founded a church on the mound which had been heaped up in the midst of the city with the earth removed from his embankment; this church is standing at the present day. Vladimir also found and appropriated two bronze statues and four bronze horses, which now stand behind the Church of the Holy Virgin, and which the ignorant think are made of marble. As a wedding present for the princess, he gave Kherson over to the Greeks again, and then departed for Kiev.

When the prince arrived at his capital, he directed that the idols should be overthrown and that some should be cut to pieces and others burned with fire. He thus ordered that Perun should be bound to a horse's tail and dragged along Borichev to the river. He appointed twelve men to beat the idol with sticks, not because he thought the wood was sensitive, but to affront the demon who had deceived man in this guise, that he might receive chastisement at the hands of men. Great art thou, O Lord, and marvelous are thy works! Yesterday he was honored of men, but today held in derision. While the idol was being dragged along the stream to the Dnieper, the unbelievers wept over it, for they had not yet received holy baptism. After they had thus dragged the idol along, they cast it into the Dnieper. But Vladimir had given this injunction: "If it halts anywhere, then push it out from the bank, until it goes over the falls. Then let it loose." His command was duly obeyed. When the men let the idol go, and it passed through the falls, the wind cast it out on the bank, which since that time has been called Perun's Shore, a name that it bears to this very day.

Thereafter Vladimir sent heralds throughout the whole city to proclaim that if any inhabitant, rich or poor, did not betake himself to the river, he would risk the prince's displeasure. When the people heard these words, they wept for joy, and exclaimed in their enthusiasm, "If this were not good, the prince and his boyars would not have accepted it." On the morrow the prince went forth to the Dnieper with the priests of the princess and those from Kherson, and a countless multitude assembled. They all went into the water: some stood up to their necks, others to their breasts, the younger near the bank, some of them holding children in their arms, while the adults waded farther out. The priests stood by and offered prayers. There was joy in heaven and upon earth to behold so many souls saved. But the devil groaned, lamenting: "Woe is me! how am I driven out hence! For I thought to have my dwelling place here, since the apostolic teachings do not abide in this land. Nor did this people know God, but I rejoiced in the service they rendered unto me. But now I am vanquished by the ignorant, not by apostles and martyrs, and my reign in these regions is at an end."

When the people were baptized, they returned each to his own abode. Vladimir, rejoicing that he and his subjects now knew God himself, looked up to heaven and said: "O God, who hast created heaven and earth, look down, I beseech thee, on this thy new people, and grant them, O Lord, to know thee as the true God, even as the other Christian nations have known thee. Confirm in them the true and unalterable faith, and aid me, O Lord, against the hostile adversary, so that, hoping in thee and in thy might, I may overcome his malice." Having spoken thus, he ordained that churches should be built and established where pagan idols had previously stood. He thus founded the Church of St. Basil on the hill where the idol of Perun and the other images had been set, and where the prince and the people had offered their sacrifices. He began to found churches and to assign priests throughout the cities, and to invite the people to accept baptism in all the cities and towns.

He took the children of the best families, and sent them to schools for instruction in book learning. The mothers of these children wept bitterly over them, for they were not yet strong in faith, but mourned as for the dead. When these children were assigned for study, there was thus fulfilled in the Russian land the prophecy which says, "In those days, the deaf shall hear words of Scripture, and the voice of the stammerers shall be made plain" (Isaiah, xxix, 18). For these persons had not ere this heard words of Scripture, and now heard them only by the act of God, for in his mercy the Lord took pity upon them, even as the Prophet said, "I will be gracious to whom I will be gracious" (Exodus, xxxiii, 19).

10. *Yaroslav the Wise*

FRATRICIDAL warring among the sons of Vladimir ended in 1016 with the victory of Prince Yaroslav, who established a firm rule over Russia for nearly forty years, from 1016 to 1054. This was the "golden age" of Kievan Russia, the age when material, intellectual, and artistic achievements were particularly brilliant. Prince Yaroslav, called "Yaroslav the Wise" by his contemporaries because of the peace and prosperity that marked his reign, maintained lively relations with Byzantium and Western Europe, and his children and grandchildren married the royalty of various western European nations. His daughter, Ann, became queen of France, and ruled that country in the name of her son after the death of her husband, Henry I, the Capet. It is of interest to note that Ann was the only literate member of the French royal family, and signed most of the state documents for her husband and son.

◆ ◆ ◆

1037 (6545) Yaroslav built the great citadel at Kiev, near which stand the Golden Gates. He founded there also the metropolitan Church of St. Sophia, the Church of the Annunciation by the Golden Gates, and also the Monastery of Sts. George and Irene. During his reign, the Christian faith was fruitful and multiplied, while the number of monks increased, and new monasteries came into being. Yaroslav loved religious establishments and was devoted to priests, especially to monks. He applied himself to books, and read them continually day and night. He assembled many scribes, and translated from Greek into Slavic. He wrote and collected many books through which true believers are instructed and enjoy religious education. For as one man plows the land, and other sows, and still others reap and eat food in abundance, so did this prince. His father Vladimir plowed and harrowed the soil when he enlightened Russia through baptism, while this prince sowed the hearts of the faithful with the written word, and we in turn reap the harvest by receiving the teaching of books. For great is the profit from book learning.

Through the medium of books, we are shown and taught the way of repentance, for we gain wisdom and continence from the written word. Books are like rivers that water the whole earth; they are the springs of wisdom. For books have an immeasurable depth; by them we are consoled in sorrow. They are the bridle of self-restraint. For great is wisdom. As Solomon said in its praise: "I (Wisdom) have inculcated counsel; I have summoned reason and prudence. The fear of the Lord *is the beginning of wisdom.* Mine are counsel, wisdom, constancy, and strength. Through me kings rule, and the mighty decree justice.

Through me are princes magnified and the oppressors possess the earth. I love them that love me, and they who seek me shall find grace" (Proverbs, viii, 12, 13, 14–17). If you seek wisdom attentively in books, you will obtain great profit for your spirit. He who reads books often converses with God or with holy men. If one possesses the words of the prophets, the teachings of the evangelists and the apostles, and the lives of the holy fathers, his soul will derive great profit therefrom. Thus Yaroslav, as we have said, was a lover of books, and as he wrote many, he deposited them in the Church of St. Sophia which he himself had founded. He adorned it with gold and silver and churchly vessels, and in it the usual hymns are raised to God at the customary seasons. He founded other churches in the cities and districts, appointing priests and paying them out of his personal fortune. He bade them teach the people, since that is the duty which God has prescribed them, and to go often into the churches. Priests and Christian laymen thus increased in number. Yaroslav rejoiced to see the multitude of his churches and of his Christian subjects, but the devil was afflicted, since he was now conquered by this new Christian nation.

11. *The Blinding of Vasilko*

LIKE the Middle Ages in western Europe, the feudal period in Russia was characterized by cruel power struggles among the princes of the ruling house. The first victims of such a struggle were Boris and Gleb, whose story was recorded in the entry for the year 1015. No less tragic was the struggle between Princes Sviatopolk and David against their cousin, Prince Vasilko, who ruled Volynia and Galicia in western Russia. The struggle ended with the blinding of Vasilko by his cousins. This story was told to the chronicler by the priest Vasily, and is one of the most dramatic narratives in *The Tale of Bygone Years.*

◆ ◆ ◆

1097 (6605) Satan now incited certain men to report to David son of Igor that Vladimir was conspiring with Vasilko against Sviatopolk and against himself. David gave credence to their false words, and endeavored to stir up Sviatopolk against Vasilko, saying: "Who killed your brother Yaropolk? Now he plots against me and against you, and has conspired with Vladimir. Take thought for your own head."

Sviatopolk was thus perturbed, and wondered whether these allegations were true or false. He was uncertain, and replied to David: "If you speak aright, may God be your witness. But if you speak from motives of jealousy only, God will punish you for it."

Sviatopolk was concerned for his brother and himself, and wondered whether the rumor were true. He finally believed David, who thus deceived Sviatopolk, and the two of them set out to plot against Vasilko. Now Vasilko and Vladimir were ignorant of this fact. David remarked, however, that if he and Sviatopolk did not seize Vasilko, neither of them could be sure of the domains they then held. And Sviatopolk believed him.

Vasilko arrived on November 4th, crossed over to Vydobychi and went to make his reverence to St. Michael in the monastery where he also supped. He pitched his camp on the Ruditsa. At evening, he returned to his camp. When it was morning, Sviatopolk urged him by messenger not to depart before his name day. Vasilko refused, urging that he could not wait that long or there would be disorder in his domain. Then David begged him not to depart, but rather to obey his elder kinsman. Vasilko, however, was still reluctant to comply.

Then David remarked to Sviatopolk: "See, he sets no store by you, though he is in your power. If he departs to his domain you shall see whether he does not seize your cities of Turov and Pinsk, and other towns which belong to you; then you will perhaps remember my words. Call the men of Kiev and take him prisoner; then deliver him over to me."

Sviatopolk followed his advice, and sent word to Vasilko, saying, "If you are unwilling to remain until my name day, at least come and embrace me now, and then we shall meet with David." Vasilko promised to go, and did not perceive the treachery which David was planning against him. Vasilko thus mounted his horse and rode off. One of his servants then met him and urged him not to go, because the princes were plotting to take him prisoner. But Vasilko heeded him not, as he thought to himself: How can they intend to take me prisoner? They joined me in the oath that if any one of us should attack another, the holy cross and all of us should be against him. Having thus reflected, he crossed himself, and said, "God's will be done."

He thus rode with a small escort to the prince's palace. Sviatopolk came out to meet him, and they went into the hall. David entered, and all sat down. Then Sviatopolk begged Vasilko to remain until the festival.

Vasilko replied, "I cannot remain, kinsman; I have already ordered my camp to move forward."

David sat silent as if struck dumb, till Sviatopolk invited Vasilko to breakfast with them, and Vasilko accepted. Then Sviatopolk said, "Remain seated here a moment while I go out and make certain dispositions." He thus went out, leaving David and Vasilko alone together. Vasilko tried to open a conversation with David, but there was no voice nor hearing in him, for he was afraid, and had treachery in his heart. After he had sat awhile, he inquired where his kinsman was. The answer was given that he was standing in the vestibule. David then rose and asked Vasilko to remain seated while he went in search of Sviatopolk. He thus stood up and went thence. When David had thus gone out, others seized upon Vasilko and fettered him with double fetters, setting guards over him by night. This treachery took place on November 5th.

In the morning, Sviatopolk assembled the boyars and the men of Kiev and informed them of what David had told him, to the effect that Vasilko had been responsible for his brother's death, was plotting with Vladimir against him, and intended to kill him and seize his cities. The boyars and the populace replied: "It behooves you, O Prince, to protect your own life. If David spoke aright, let Vasilko suffer the penalty. If David has spoken falsely, let him suffer the vengeance of God and answer before God."

When the priors heard of the circumstances, they interceded with Sviatopolk in Vasilko's behalf, but he protested that it was all David's affair. When David heard of all this, he urged that Vasilko should be blinded, on the ground that if Sviatopolk did nothing and released Vasilko, neither he himself nor Sviatopolk would be able to retain their thrones much longer. Sviatopolk was in favor of releasing him, but David kept close watch over him and would not consent.

During the night, they thus took Vasilko to Belgorod, which is a small town ten versts from Kiev. The transported him fettered in a cart, and after removing him from the vehicle, they led him into a small house. As he sat there, Vasilko saw a Tork[1] sharpening a knife, and then comprehending that they intended blinding him, he cried out to God with loud weeping and groaning. Then came the emissaries of Sviatopolk and David: Snovid, the son of Izech, the squire of Sviatopolk, and Dmitry, David's

[1] Torks were a Turkic tribe of southern Russia.

squire, and they laid a rug upon the floor. After they had spread it, they seized Vasilko and endeavored to overthrow him. He offered a violent resistance, so that they could not throw him. Then others came and cast him down. They bound him, and laid upon his chest a slab taken from the hearth. Though Snovid, the son of Izech, sat at one end and Dimitri at the other, they still could not hold him down. Then two other men came, and after taking a second slab from the hearth, they too sat upon him, and weighed upon him so heavily that his chest cracked. Then a Tork, Berendi by name, a shepherd of Sviatopolk, came up with his knife, and though intending to strike him in the eye, missed the eye entirely and cut his face. This scar Vasilko bears to this day. Afterward, however, he struck him in one eye, and took out the pupil, and then in the other eye, and also removed the pupil of the latter.

At that moment Vasilko lay as if dead. They raised him in the rug, laid him fainting in the wagon, and carried him off to Vladimir. While he was being thus transported, they happened to halt with him at a marketplace after they had crossed the bridge at the town of Zvizhen. They took off his bloody shirt, and gave it to a priest's wife to wash. After she had washed it, the woman put it on him while the others were eating, and she began to weep, for he was as if dead. He heard her weeping, and inquired where he was. They replied that the town was Zdvizhden. He then begged for water. They gave him some, and after he had drunk the water, full consciousness returned to him. He remembered what had occurred, and feeling his shirt, he lamented: "Why did you take it from me? I had rather have met my death and stood before God in this bloody shirt."

When they had eaten, they rode on swiftly in the cart with him, and over a rough road, for it was then the month of *Gruden*, called November. They arrived with him at Vladimir on the sixth day. David accompanied them, and behaved as if he had captured some prize. They quartered Vasilko in the Vakeev palace, and placed over him a guard of thirty men, as well as two servants of the prince named Ulan and Kolchko.

Blinded Prince Vasilko asks for water.
A miniature from the *Radzivil Chronicle* of the fourteenth century.

12. *Metropolitan Hilarion*
Sermon on Law and Grace

THE *Sermon on Law and Grace* is arranged in two distinct parts: "The Sermon on the Law of Moses Given to Him by God and on the Grace and Truth Brought to the Earth by Jesus Christ," and "The Eulogy to Our Kagan, Vladimir."

This famous sermon by Metropolitan Hilarion is one of the oldest Russian literary-philosophical works and is the earliest Russian sermon preserved. It was written several decades before the *Primary Chronicle* and the most ancient Russian *vitae*, probably between 1037 and 1050. Its author, Hilarion, became in 1051 the first Russian (non-Greek) head of the Russian Church and Metropolitan of the city of Kiev. He was one of the most erudite and brilliant Russian preachers and writers of the Kievan age. Despite his clearly Byzantine cultural background, he manifests the Russian national spirit.

Besides the *Sermon on Law and Grace*, there has also been preserved Hilarion's *Confession of Faith*, in which he emphasizes the Trinitarian foundation of Christian dogma and the dual nature of Jesus Christ. In this work he wrote, "He suffered for me as a man. . . . He revived as God, . . . and after three days he arose from the dead, as a victor, Christ, my King."

In his *Sermon on Law and Grace* Metropolitan Hilarion reveals himself to be an astute preacher. The central idea of the sermon is the juxtaposition of the faith of the Old Testament with that of the New Testament. For a biblical comparison, he uses the story of the two sons of Abraham: the first, Ishmael, who was not free, but the son of Hagar, Sarah's handmaid; the second, who was free, being the son of Abraham by his wife, Sarah. For Hilarion, Christianity is the faith of freedom and liberation, while the religion of the Old Testament was one of law, compulsion and strict obedience.

Hilarion's attitude toward the problem of salvation is very characteristic of early Eastern Christianity: salvation through "baptism and good deeds," through Christian mercy and charity. This is remote from Luther's and Calvin's teachings of salvation solely through faith and, concomitantly, moral behavior.

This sermon, despite its clear tendency to raise the prestige of the Russian nation and the Russian Church, was composed in a typical Byzantine style, and is saturated with repeated parallels between Hagar and the Old Testament, and between Sarah and the New Testament. When Hilarion wrote that "Divine Grace announced to God" and that "the Father did as he was told by Divine Grace," he apparently referred to "Holy Sophia," that is, the Divine Omniscience of the three hypostases of the Trinity. The teaching of "Holy Wisdom," or "Holy Sophia," was widespread throughout Byzantium and Russia at that time, and is attested to by the fact that cathedrals in Kiev, Constantinople, and Novgorod were dedicated to "Holy Sophia."

Having adroitly presented his point, which is the supreme nature of the Christian faith, Hilarion turned to the destiny of the Russian people. In his eyes, when the Russians adopted Christianity they became the equal of all Christian peoples, including the Greeks. He regarded the Russian Church as having the same dignity, status, and rights as the Byzantine Church. It must be remembered that both Yaroslav and Hilarion attempted to liberate the Russian Church from Byzantine supervision and that Hilarion was the first native Russian to head the Russian Church and to defend its autonomy from Constantinople.

Hilarion ends his sermon with a highly rhetorical panegyric to Prince Vladimir, whom Russians consider a saint for having Christianized Russia. Optimistic, bright, even triumphant notes can easily be discerned in Hilarion's treatment of history. Russia had become enlightened by the Christian faith, and therefore its future would lie in Christ's hands.

The following translation is based upon the text of Metropolitan Hilarion's sermon published by A. B. Gorskii in *Pamiatniki dukhovnoi literatury vremeni velikogo kniazia Yaroslava I-ogo*, Moscow, 1844.

◆ ◆ ◆

THE SERMON OF THE LAW OF MOSES GIVEN TO HIM BY GOD, AND OF THE GRACE AND TRUTH BROUGHT TO EARTH BY JESUS CHRIST

Blessed be the God of Israel, the God of Christianity who visited his people and brought them salvation. He did not disdain his creation which was for ages possessed by pagan darkness and by worship of the devil, but he enlightened the Children of Abraham by giving them his Law tablets, and later he saved all nations, sending them his Son, his Gospel, and his baptism, and by giving them resurrection to eternal life.

Law was the precursor and the servant of Grace and Truth. Grace and Truth were the servants of the future life and immortal life. Law led its people of the Old Testament toward the blessing of baptism, and baptism led its sons to the life eternal. Moses and the prophets announced the coming of Christ, but Christ and the Apostles announced resurrection and the future age.

And what could the Law achieve? And what could Grace achieve? First was the Law and then Grace. Hagar and Sarah are the pictures of Law and Grace: Hagar was a handmaid and Sarah was free. First comes the handmaiden and then the free woman may come. And he who reads (the Bible) must understand this. Abraham, since his youth, had Sarah for his wife and she was free and not a slave, and so God decided before all ages to send his Son into the world that Grace might appear through him (but sent him to man only later). But Sarah was restrained from bearing children, since she was unfruitful. But she was not actually unfruitful, but was chosen by divine Providence to bear in her old age. The wisdom of God was not revealed to anyone, but concealed from both angels and men. This wisdom was not shown, but was concealed to be revealed at the end of the age.

It was Sarah who said unto Abraham:

> "Behold now, the Lord has prevented me from bearing children; go in to my maid; it may be that I shall obtain children by her."

And so the divine Grace (of the Son) announced to God, the Father:

> "It is not yet my time for descending to the earth and to save the world. Descend to Mount Sinai and give them the Law."

And, just as Abraham did as Sarah told him and went into Hagar, so God, the Father, did as he was told by the divine Grace and descended to Mount Sinai.

And Hagar, the handmaid, bore from Abraham a servant (not a truly free man), and Abraham gave him the name Ishmael. And Moses brought from Mount Sinai the Law and not the Grace, the shade and not the Truth.

When Abraham and Sarah were old, God appeared to Abraham by the oaks of Mamre, as he sat at the door of his tent in the heat of the day. And he ran to meet him, and bowing lowly to the earth, he hastened into the tent (to Sarah). And so, when the end of the age was nearing, God appeared to the humankind, descended to the earth, and blessed the womb of the Virgin. And he was received by the Immaculate Virgin into the tent of the flesh. And the Virgin said to the angel:

> "Behold I am the handmaid of the Lord; let it be to me according to your word."

Once the Lord gave Sarah to bear a child, and she begat Isaac, and the free woman begat a free son. And, when once more our Lord visited the humankind, he appeared unknown and hidden from men and then was born Grace and Truth, but not the Law. And now it was the Son and not the servant.

And the child grew up and was weaned; and Abraham made a great feast on the day that Isaac was weaned. And when Christ was upon the earth Grace did not reveal Itself and Christ was hiding himself until he was thirty. And when he had grown and was weaned, then there, in the river Jordan, Grace was revealed by a man. And our Lord invited many and made a great feast and offered up the fatted calf of the age, His beloved Son, Jesus Christ, and God then called to this feast many of heaven and earth and they the angels and men into one (Church).

This blessed faith spreads now over the entire earth, and finally it reached the Russian nation. And, whereas the lake of the Law dried up, the fount of the Gospel became rich in water and overflowed upon our land and reached us. And now, together with all Christians, we glorify the Holy Trinity, while Judea remains silent.

THE EULOGY TO OUR KAGAN VLADIMIR

Rome, with voices panegyrical, praises Peter and Paul through whom they came to believe in Jesus Christ, the Son of God:

> Asia, Ephesus, and Patmus praise John the Theologian;
> India praises Thomas;
> Egypt, Mark.

All lands, cities, and men honor and glorify their teacher who brought them the Orthodox Faith. Thus, let us, through our own strength, humbly praise our teacher and mentor, the great Kagan of our land Vladimir, the grandson of Igor of yore and son of glorious Sviatoslav, who ruled in their day with courage and valor, becoming famed in many lands for their victories and fortitude. And they did not reign in a poor and unknown land, but in Russia, which is known and celebrated by all to the ends of the earth.

A good attestation of your devotion, blessed one, is the Holy Church of the Blessed Virgin, the Mother of God, which you build on the orthodox foundation and where your valorous body now lays at rest and awaits the archangel's trumpet.

A good and certain attestation is your son, George [Yaroslav's Christian name], whom God has made the heir to your throne,

who does not destroy your laws, but confirms them,
who does not diminish works of piety, but extends them,
who does not undo, but strengthens,
who finishes that which you have left unfinished
even as Solomon finished the works begun by David;
who has built a great and holy temple to God's omniscience
that it may hallow your city;
who has embellished with all manner of things beautiful,
with gold and silver and precious stones
and with sacred vessels;
so that the church is a wonder to all surrounding lands
and so that the like cannot be found in all the northern land,
nor in the east nor the west;
who has given your famous city of Kiev the crown of glory,
who has turned your city and its people
to all-glorious Mother of God,
who is always ready to succor Christians
and for whom he has built a church with doors of gold
in the name of the first holy day of the Lord of the Annunciation,
that the veneration, which the archangel will offer to the Virgin,
may also be upon this city.
To her he speaks, saying:
"Rejoice, Blessed One, the Lord is with you!"
And to the city he speaks, saying:
"Rejoice, faithful city, the Lord is with you!"

Arise from your grave, venerated prince,
Arise and shake off your sleep.
You are not dead,
but only sleep until the day of resurrection of all.
Arise! You are not dead,
for it is not right that you should die,
for you have believed in Christ,
the Sustainer of the whole world.
Shake off your deep sleep
and lift up your eyes
that you might see what honor the Lord has granted you,

and you still live upon this earth,
unforgotten through your sons.
Arise! Behold your child George,
Look upon your beloved one,
whom God has brought forth from your loins.
Behold him embellishing the throne of your land.
Rejoice and be of good cheer!
Behold the pious wife of your son, Irina.
Behold your grandchildren
and your great-grandchildren.
Behold how they live and how they are cared for by God.
Behold how they preserve devotion in your tradition,
how they partake of the Sacraments of the Holy Church,
how they glorify Christ,
how they venerate before his Holy Name.
Behold your city radiant with grandeur.
Behold your blossoming churches,
Behold Christianity flourishing.
Behold your city gleaming,
adorned with holy icons and
fragrant with thyme,
praising God and filling the air with sacred songs.

And beholding all this, rejoice and be of good cheer, and praise the Lord, the Creator of all which you have seen.

13. *Cyril of Turov*

Sermon on the First Sunday After Easter

Among Russian writers of the Kievan period, Cyril, Bishop of Turov, was probably the most accomplished master of Orthodox theology and the Byzantine style of writing. He had an excellent command of Greek and his literary achievements surpass those of any other Russian man of letters of that era. He wrote numerous epistles, prayers, and sermons, all of which are distinguished by their elegant and elaborate style. They show clearly the author's gift for composition and his extensive knowledge of the Bible and early Church history. In his works he quotes the patriarchs and prophets of the Old Testament with unusual adroitness for that time. Though full of symbolism and allegory, his writings are nonetheless lucid and fully comprehensible, and they gained the admiration of endless generations of Russians. Even as late as the seventeenth century, many of Cyril's stylistic patterns were still popular with writers of the conservative literary tradition. Of all his works, Cyril's triumphant description of spring as the symbol of the resurrection is the most popular.

Very little is known of the author's life except that he lived in the middle of the twelfth century and was Bishop of Turov. His best-known works are eight sermons delivered on the occasion of the eight Sundays beginning with Palm Sunday. The *Sermon on the First Sunday after Easter*, perhaps his most famous single composition, is offered here in a translation by Leo Wiener.

◆ ◆ ◆

The Church needs a great teacher and a wise orator to celebrate the holiday properly, but we are poor in words and dim in mind, not having the fire of the Holy Ghost—the enjoyment of words useful to the soul; yet for the love of my brethren who are with me, we shall say something about the renewal of the Lord's resurrection. In the past week of the Easter there were joy in heaven and terror in the nethermost regions, a renewal of life and liberation of the world, a destruction of hell and victory over death, a resurrection of the dead, and annihilation of the enticing power of the devil; a salvation of the human race by the resurrection of Christ; an impoverishment of the Old Testament and enslavement of the Sabbath; an enrichment of the Church of Christ, and enthronement of the Sunday.

Last week there was a change of all things, for the earth was opened up by heaven, having been purified from its satanic impurities, and the angels with their wives humbly served at the resurrection. All creation was renewed, for no longer are the air, the sun, the fire, the springs, the trees, thought to be gods; no longer does hell receive its due of infants sacrificed by their fathers, nor death its honors, for idolatry has come to an end, and the satanic power has been vanquished by the mystery of the cross. The Old Testament has become impoverished by the rejection of the blood of calves and sacrifices of goats, for Christ has given himself to the Lord as a sacrifice for all. And with this, Sunday ceased to be a holiday, but the Sunday was sanctified on account of the resurrection, and Sunday is now supreme, for Christ arose from the dead on that day. . . .

Today the heavens have been cleared from the dark clouds that enshrouded them as with a heavy veil, and they proclaim the glory of God with a clear atmosphere. . . .

Today the sun rises and beams on high, and rejoicing warms the earth, for there has arisen for us from the grave the real sun, Christ, and he saves all who believe in him. Today the moon descends from its high place and gives honor to the greater lights. The Old Testament, as had been prophesied, has stopped with its Sabbath, and with its prophets gives honor to the Testament of Christ with its Sunday. Today the winter of sin has stopped in repentance, and the ice of unbelief is melted by wisdom. Today spring appears spruce, and enlivens all earthly existence; the stormy winds blow gently and generate fruits, and the earth, giving nurture to the seed, brings forth green grass. For spring is the beautiful faith in Christ which, through baptism, produces a regeneration of man, and the stormy winds are the evil, sinful thoughts that, being changed to virtue through repentance, generate soul-saving fruits; but the earth of our being, having received the Word of God like a seed, and, passing through an ecstatic labor, through the fear of him, brings forth a spirit of salvation.

Today the newborn lambs and calves frisk and leap about joyfully and returning to their mothers gambol about, so that the shepherds, playing on their reeds, praise Christ in joy. The lambs, I say, are the gentle people from among the pagans, and the calves—the idolaters of the unbelieving countries who, having accepted the Law through Christ's incarnation and the teachings of the Apostles and miracles, and having returned to the holy Church, suck the milk of its teachings; and the teachers of Christ's flock, praying for all, praise Christ, the Lord, who had collected all the wolves and sheep into one herd.

Today the trees send forth buds and the fragrant flowers bloom, and behold, the gardens already emit a sweet odor, and the workers laboring in hope acclaim Christ the giver of fruits. We were before like the trees of the forest that bear no fruit, but today the faith of Christ has been grafted on our unbelief, and those who already held to the roots of Jesse have burgeoned with the flowers of virtue and expect through Christ a regeneration in heaven, and the saints who labor for the Church expect a reward from Christ. Today the plowman of the Word leads the oxen of the Word to the spiritual yoke, sinks the plow of baptism into the furrows of thought and deepening them to furrows of repentance plants in them the spiritual seed and rejoices in the hope of future returns. Today everything old has taken an end, and all is new for the sake of the resurrection. Today the apostolic rivers are full, and the pagan fish let out their broods, and the fishermen, having examined the depth of the divine incarnation, drag in full nets into the Church. . . . Today the industrious bees of the monastic order show their wisdom and set all to wonder, for living in the wilderness and providing for themselves, they astonish both angels and men, just as the bee flies upon the flowers and forms combs of honey in order to furnish sweetness to man and what is needed in the Church. . . .

Today there is a feast of regeneration for the people who are made new by the resurrection of Christ, and all new things are brought to God: from heathens, faith; from good Christians, offerings; from the clergy, holy sacrifies; from the civil authorities, God-pleasing charity; from the noble, care for the Church; from the righteous, humility; from the sinners, true repentance; from the unhallowed, a turning to God; from the hating, spiritual love.

THE LIVES OF SAINTS AND MONKS

14. *Nestor: The Martyrdom of Boris and Gleb*

After the death of Vladimir, a fratricidal struggle broke out among his sons. The eldest, Sviatopolk, seized power and began plotting the elimination of his brothers, Boris, Gleb and Yaroslav. The murder of Boris and Gleb is described in a touching manner by the chronicler: the two refused to take up arms against their elder brother in order to prevent further bloodshed. They decided to accept their fate passively, following the example of Christ. This was the earliest imitation in the Middle Ages of Christ as a humble martyr dying for the sins of man. In both Western and Byzantine Christianity at that time, Christ's image was that of a pantocrat: an awe-inspiring, omnipotent ruler of the universe, to be dreaded. The humble aspect of Christ was stressed neither in Byzantine nor in Western Christianity until the time of St. Francis, some two hundred years after the martyrdom of Boris and Gleb.

The text presented here is the Samuel H. Cross translation.

◆ ◆ ◆

Sviatopolk settled in Kiev after his father's death, and after calling together all the inhabitants of Kiev, he began to distribute largess among them. They accepted it, but their hearts were not with him, because their brethren were with Boris. When Boris returned with the army, after meeting the Pechenegs, he received the news that his father was dead. He mourned deeply for him, for he was beloved of his father before all the rest.

When he came to the Alta, he halted. His father's retainers then urged him to take his place in Kiev on his father's throne, since he had at his disposal the latter's retainers and troops. But Boris protested: "Be it not for me to raise my hand against my elder brother. Now that my father has passed away, let him take the place of my father in my heart." When the soldiery heard these words, they departed from him, and Boris remained with his servants.

But Sviatopolk was filled with lawlessness. Adopting the device of Cain, he sent messages to Boris that he desired to live at peace with him, and would increase the territory he had received from his father. But he plotted against him how he might kill him. So Sviatopolk came by night to Vyshegorod. After secretly summoning to his presence Putsha and the boyars of the town, he inquired of them whether they were wholeheartedly devoted to him. Putsha and the men of Vyshegorod replied, "We are ready to lay down our lives for you." He then commanded them to say nothing to any man, but to go and kill his brother Boris. They straightway promised to execute his order. Of such men Solomon has well said: "They make haste to shed blood unjustly. For they promise blood, and gather evil. Their path runneth to evil, for they possess their souls in dishonor" (Proverbs, i. 16–19).

These emissaries came to the Alta, and when they approached, they heard the sainted Boris singing vespers. For it was already known to him that they intended to take his life. Then he arose and began to chant, saying: "O Lord, how are they increased who come against me! Many are they that rise up against me" (Psalms, iii, 1). And also, "Thy arrows have pierced me, for I am ready for wounds and my pain is before me continually" (Psalms, xxxviii, 2, 17). And he also uttered this prayer: "Lord, hear my prayer, and enter not into judgment with thy servant, for no living man shall be just before thee. For the enemy hath crushed my soul" (Psalms, cxl, 1–3). After ending the six psalms, when he saw how men were sent out to kill him, he began to chant the Psalter, saying, "Strong bulls encompassed me, and the assemblage of the evil beset me. O Lord my God, I have hoped in thee; save me and deliver me from my pursuers" (Psalms, xxii, 12, 16, vii, 1). Then he began to sing the canon. After finishing vespers, he prayed, gazing upon the icon, the image of the Lord, with these words: "Lord Jesus Christ, who in this image hast appeared on earth for our salvation, and who, having voluntarily suffered thy hands to be nailed to the cross, didst endure thy passion for our sins, so help me now to endure my passion. For I accept it not from those who are my enemies, but from the hand of my own brother. Hold it not against him as a sin, O Lord!"

After offering this prayer, he lay down upon his couch. Then they fell upon him like wild beasts about the tent, and overcame him by piercing him with lances. They also overpowered his servant, who cast himself upon his body. For he was beloved of Boris. He was a servant of Hungarian race, George by name, to whom Boris was greatly attached. The prince had given him a large gold necklace which he wore while serving him. They also killed many other servants of Boris. But since they could not quickly take the necklace from George's neck, they cut off his head, and thus obtained it. For this reason his body was not recognized later among the corpses.

The desperadoes, after attacking Boris, wrapped him in a canvas, loaded him upon a wagon, and dragged him off, though he was still alive. When the impious Sviatopolk saw that he was still breathing, he sent two Varangians to finish him. When they came and saw that he was still alive, one of them drew his sword and plunged it into his heart. Thus died the blessed Boris, receiving from the hand of Christ our God the crown among the righteous. He shall be numbered with the prophets and the Apostles, as he joins with the choirs of martyrs, rests in the lap of Abraham, beholds joy ineffable, chants with the angels, and rejoices in company with the choirs of saints. After his body had been carried in secret to Vyshegorod, it was buried in the Church of St. Basil.

The impious Sviatopolk then reflected, "Behold, I have killed Boris; now how can I kill Gleb?" Adopting once more Cain's device, he craftily sent messages to Gleb to the effect that he should come quickly, because his father was very ill and desired his presence. Gleb quickly mounted his horse, and set out with a small company, for he was obedient to his father. When he came to the Volga, his horse stumbled in a ditch on the plain, and broke his leg. He arrived at Smolensk, and setting out thence at dawn, he embarked in a boat on the Smiadyn. At this time, Yaroslav received from Predslava the tidings of their father's death, and he sent word to Gleb that he should not set out, because his father was dead and his brother had been murdered by Sviatopolk. Upon receiving these tidings, Gleb burst into tears, and mourned for his father, but still more deeply for his brother. He wept and prayed with the lament, "Woe is me, O Lord! It were better for me to die with my brother than to live on in this world. O my brother, had I but seen thy angelic countenance, I should have died with thee. Why am I now left alone? Where are thy words that thou didst say to me, my brother? No longer do I hear thy sweet counsel. If thou hast received affliction from God, pray for me that I may endure the same passion. For it were better for me to dwell with thee than in this deceitful world."

While he was thus praying amid his tears, there suddenly arrived those sent by Sviatopolk for Gleb's destruction. These emissaries seized Gleb's boat, and drew their weapons. The servants of Gleb were terrified, and the impious messenger,

Goriaser, gave orders that they should slay Gleb with dispatch. Then Gleb's cook, Torchin by name, seized a knife, and stabbed Gleb. He was offered up as a sacrifice to God like an innocent lamb, a glorious offering amid the perfume of incense, and he received the crown of glory. Entering the heavenly mansions he beheld his long-desired brother, and rejoiced with him in the joy ineffable which they had attained through their brotherly love.

"How good and fair it is for brethren to live together!" (Psalms, cxxxiii, 1). But the impious ones returned again, even as David said, "Let the sinners return to hell" (Psalms, ix, 17). When they returned to Sviatopolk, they reported that his command had been executed. On hearing these tidings, he was puffed up with pride, since he knew not the words of David: "Why art thou proud of thy evildoing, O mighty one? Thy tongue hath considered lawlessness all the day long" (Psalms, lii, 1).

After Gleb had been slain, his body was thrown upon the shore between two tree trunks, but afterward they took him and carried him away, to bury him beside his brother Boris in the Church of St. Basil. United thus in body and still more in soul ye dwell with the Lord and King of all, in eternal joy, ineffable light, bestowing salutary gifts upon the land of Russia. Ye give healing to other strangers who draw near with faith, making the lame to walk, giving sight to the blind, to the sick health, to captives freedom, to prisoners liberty, to the sorrowful consolation, and to the oppressed relief. Ye are the protectors of the land of Russia, shining forever like beacons and praying to the Lord in behalf of your countrymen. Therefore must we worthily magnify these martyrs in Christ, praying fervently to them and saying: "Rejoice, martyrs in Christ from the land of Russia, who gave healing to them who draw near to you in faith and love. Rejoice, dwellers in heaven. In the body ye were angels, servants in the same thought, comrades in the same image, of one heart with the saints. To all that suffer ye give relief. Rejoice, Boris and Gleb, wise in God. Like streams ye spring from the fount of life-giving water which flow for the redemption of the righteous. Rejoice, ye who have trampled the serpent of evil beneath your feet. Ye have appeared amid bright rays, enlightening like beacons the whole land of Russia. Appearing in faith immutable, ye have ever driven away the darkness. Rejoice, ye who have won an unslumbering eye, ye blessed ones who have received in your hearts the zeal to fulfill God's only commandments. Rejoice, brethren united in the realms of golden light, i the heavenly abodes, in glory unfading, which ye through your merits have attained. Rejoice, ye who are brightly irradiate with the luminance of God, and travel throughout the world expelling devils and healing diseases. Like beacons supernal and zealous guardians, ye dwell with God, illumined forever with light divine, and in your courageous martyrdom ye enlighten the souls of the faithful. The light-bringing heavenly love has exalted you, wherefore ye have inherited all fair things in the heavenly life: glory, celestial sustenance, the light of wisdom, and beauteous joys. Rejoice, ye who refresh our hearts, driving out pain and sickness and curing evil passions. Ye glorious ones, with the sacred drops of your blood ye have dyed a robe of purple which ye wear in beauty, and reign forevermore with Christ, interceding with him for his new Christian nation and for your fellows, for our land is hallowed by your blood. By virtue of your relics deposited in the church, ye illumine it with the Holy Spirit, for there in heavenly bliss, as martyrs among the army of martyrs, ye intercede for our nation. Rejoice, bright daysprings, our Christ-loving martyrs and intercessors! Subject the pagans to our princes, beseeching our Lord God that they may live in concord and in health, freed from intestine war and the crafts of the devil. Help us therefore who sing and recite your sacred praise forever unto our life's end."

15. *Nestor*

The Narratives of the Kievan Crypt Monastery

THE Crypt Monastery, located on the hilly banks of the Dnieper River on the outskirts of the city of Kiev since its foundation in the eleventh century, became the main spiritual and cultural center of early Russia. Its founders, Sts. Antonius and Theodosius, were remarkable religious leaders whose lives and teachings inspired endless generations of the Russian people. Until the revolution of 1917, the Crypt Monastery remained the principal place for Russian devotional pilgrimages, and even now its churches and crypts attract numerous pilgrims.

Works describing life in the monastery are collected either in the *Primary Chronicle*, their author apparently being Nestor, a monk of this monastery, or in the *Kievan Crypt* (*Monastery*) *Paterikon* (the Greek word *paterikon* means a collection of lives of saints or stories about the life of monastery inhabitants). The *Kievan Crypt* (*Monastery*) *Paterikon* was written in the first quarter of the thirteenth century by Bishop Simon and Monk Polycarpe, both having been monks of this monastery. Later, more stories were added to the *Paterikon* by other writers. Despite the fact that Simon and Polycarpe lived some hundred and fifty years after Nestor, the style of their work differs very little from his. In both collections can be found historical accounts of life in the monastery, edifying tales about its inhabitants, some half-legendary stories with considerable mystic or fantastic elements, and finally demonological narratives describing the struggles of the monks with the devil.

The stories of the Kievan Crypt Monastery were entered by Nestor under the years 1051 and 1074. However, as often happens in the *Primary Chronicle*, these tales were not necessarily connected with the given year but describe life in the monastery over most of the second half of the eleventh century. Nestor himself belonged to the monastery, and witnessed many of the events described by him.

The text of this work is that of Samuel H. Cross as translated by him in the *Primary Chronicle*.

◆ ◆ ◆

THE FOUNDING OF THE CRYPT MONASTERY AND THE LIFE OF ST. ANTONIUS

1051 (6559) Yaroslav, after assembling the bishops, appointed Hilarion Metropolitan of Russia in St. Sophia.

Let us now relate why the Monastery of the Crypts bears this name. Prince Yaroslav was fond of Berestovoe and the Church of the Holy Apostles there situated. He gathered a large company of priests, among whom was a presbyter named Hilarion, a virtuous man, learned and ascetic. Hilarion used often to walk from Berestovoe toward the Dnieper to a certain hill, where the old Crypt Monastery now is, and made his orisons there. He dug a little crypt two yards deep, and often went thither from Berestovoe to chant the hours and offer his prayer to God in secret. Then God inspired the prince to appoint him Metropolitan in St. Sophia; and the crypt remained as it was.

Not many days afterward, there was a certain man, a layman from the city of Liubech, in whose heart God inspired the desire to go on pilgrimage. He made his way to Mount Athos,[1] beheld the monasteries there, and upon examining them and

[1] Mount Athos, or the "Holy Mount," has long been the most important monastic center of Eastern Christianity. It is located in Greece in the vicinity of the city of Saloniki.

being charmed by the monastic life, he entered one of the local monasteries, and begged the prior to confer upon him the monastic habit. The latter complied with his request and made him a monk, calling him Antonius, and after he had admonished him and instructed him in his monastic obligations, he bade him return to Russia accompanied by the blessing of the Holy Mount, that many other monks might spring from his example. The prior blessed him and dismissed him, saying, "Go in peace." Antonius returned to Kiev, and reflected where he should live. He went about among the monasteries and liked none of them, since God did not so will, and subsequently wandered about among the hills and valleys seeking the place which God should show him. He finally came to the hill where Hilarion had dug the crypt, and liked this site, and rejoiced in it. He then lifted up his voice in prayer to God, saying amid his tears, "O Lord, strengthen me in this place, and may there rest upon it the blessing of the Holy Mount and of the prior who tonsured me." Thus he took up his abode there, praying to God, eating dry bread all the day long, drinking water in peace, and digging the crypt. He gave himself rest neither day nor night, but endured in his labors, in vigil, and in prayer. Afterward good men noticed his conduct, and supplied him according to his necessities. Thus he acquired distinction as the great Antonius, and those who drew near to him besought his blessing.

When the Great Prince Yaroslav died, Iziaslav his son inherited his domain and settled in Kiev, while Antonius was celebrated throughout Russia. Iziaslav observed his manner of life, and came with his retainers to request his blessing and prayers. The great Antonius was thus remarked and revered by everyone. Brothers joined him, and he welcomed and tonsured them. Brethren thus gathered about him to the number of twelve. They dug a great crypt and a church, and cells, which exist to this day in the crypt under the old monastery. When the brethren had thus assembled, Antonius said to them, "God has gathered you together, my brethren, and ye are under the blessing of the Holy Mount, through which the prior at the Holy Mount tonsured me, and I have tonsured you also. May there be upon you first the blessing of God and second that of the Holy Mount." And he added this injunction: "Live apart by yourselves, and I shall appoint you a prior; for I prefer to go alone to yonder hill, as I formerly was wont when I dwelt in solitude." So he appointed Barlaam as their prior, and betook himself to the hill, where he dug a grotto, which is under the new monastery, and in which he ended his life, enduring in virtue, and for the space of forty years never issuing forth from the crypt in which his bones lie to the present day.

The brethren thus abode with their prior, and as the number of monks in the crypt increased, they considered the establishment of a monastery outside the original crypt. Thus the prior and the brethren approached Antonius and said to him, "Father, the brethren have increased in numbers, and we can no longer find room in the crypt. If God and thy prayers so direct us, we might build a small church outside the crypt." Antonius then bade them so to do. They obeyed him, and built a little chapel over the crypt and dedicated it to the Assumption of the Holy Virgin.

God continued to augment the number of the brotherhood through the intercession of the Holy Virgin, and the brethren took counsel with the prior as to constructing a monastery. The friars again visited Antonius, and said, "Father, our brethren increase in numbers, and we are desirous of building a monastery." Antonius rejoiced, and replied, "Blessed be God for all things, and may the prayers of the Holy Virgin and of the fathers of the Holy Mount be with you." Having thus spoken, he sent one of the brotherhood to Prince Iziaslav with the message, "My Prince! Behold, God strengthens the brotherhood, but their abode is small; give us therefore the hill which is above the crypt." When Iziaslav heard these words, he rejoiced, and sent his servant, and gave to them the hill. The prior and the brethren founded there a great church, and fenced in the monastery with a palisade. They constructed many cells, completed the church, and adorned it with icons. Such was the origin of the Crypt Monastery, which was so named because the brethren first lived in the crypt. The Crypt Monastery thus issued from the benediction of the Holy Mount.

ST. THEODOSIUS, ABBOT OF THE CRYPT MONASTERY

Now, when the monastery was completed during the priorate of Barlaam, Iziaslav founded the Monastery of St. Demetrius, and appointed Barlaam prior therein, since he intended, by virtue of his material wealth, to make it superior to the ancient monastery. Many monasteries have indeed been founded by emperors and nobles and magnates, but they are not such as those founded by tears, fasting, prayer, and vigil. Antonius had neither silver nor gold, but accomplished his purpose through tears and fasting, as I have recounted.

When Barlaam had departed to St. Demetrius', the brethren held a council, and then once more visited the ancient Antonius with the request that he should designate them a new prior. He inquired whom they desired. They replied that they desired only the one designated by God and by his own selection. Then he inquired of them, "Who among you is more obedient, more modest, and more mild than Theodosius? Let him be your prior." The brethren rejoiced, and made their reverence before the old man. Being twenty in number, they thus appointed Theodosius to be their prior. When Theodosius took over in the monastery, he began to practice abstinence, fasting, and tearful prayer. He undertook to assemble many monks, and thus gathered together brethren to the number of one hundred.

He also interested himself in searching out the monastic rules. There was in Kiev at the time a monk from the Studion Monastery named Michael, who had come from Greece with the Metropolitan George, and Theodosius inquired of him concerning the practices of the Studion monks. He obtained their rule from him, copied it out, and established it in his own monastery to govern the singing of monastic hymns, the making of reverences, the reading of the lessons, behavior in church, the whole ritual, conduct at table, proper food for special days, and to regulate all else according to prescription. After obtaining all this information, Theodosius thus transmitted it to his monastery, and from the latter all others adopted the same institutions. Therefore the Crypt Monastery is honored as the oldest of all.

While Theodosius lived in the monastery, following a virtuous life and the monastic rule, and receiving everyone who presented himself, I, a poor and unworthy servant, came to him, and he accepted me in my seventeenth year. Hence I have set down and certified what year the monastery came into being, and why it is named the Crypt Monastery; but to Theodosius' life we shall recur later.

1074 (6582) In this year the Church of the Crypts was founded by the Prior Theodosius and the Bishop Michael, while George the Metropolitan was absent in Greece and Sviatoslav was reigning in Kiev.

Theodosius, the Prior of the Crypt Monastery, passed away. We shall therefore supply a brief account of his assumption. When the Lenten season approached, upon the eve of Quinquagesima Sunday, Theodosius was accustomed, after he had embraced the brethren according to his practice, to instruct them how to pass the Lenten period in prayer by night and by day, and how to guard against evil thoughts and the temptations of the devil. "For," said he, "demons incite in monks evil thoughts and desires, and inflame their fancy so that their prayers are impaired. One must combat such thoughts when they come by using the sign of the cross and by saying, 'Lord Jesus Christ our God, have mercy on us, Amen!' With this end in view, we must practice abstinence from many foods, for evil desires develop out of excessive eating and immoderate drinking, and by the growth of such thoughts sin is caused. By this means," said he, "oppose yourselves to the influence of the demons and their malice, guard against laziness and too much sleep, be zealous in churchly song, in the traditions of the fathers, and in the reading of the Scriptures. For it befits monks above all things to have upon their lips the Psalter of David, and thereby to expel the weaknesses caused by the devil. It befits all young persons to show toward their elders love, obedience, and attention, and it behooves all older persons to offer the younger brethren their love and admonition, and to be an example by their continence and vigil, their self-restraint and humility, to counsel and console the youthful, and to spend Lent in such pursuits."

"For," he added, "God has given us these forty days in which to purify our souls. This is a tithe given to God by the body. For the days of the year are three hundred and sixty-five, and giving to God each tenth day as a tithe makes a fast of forty days, during which the soul is cleansed and happily celebrates the resurrection of the Lord as it rejoices in God. For the Lenten season purifies the heart of man. In the beginning, fasting was first imposed upon Adam, so that he should not taste of one tree. Moses fasted forty days to prepare himself to receive the law upon Mount Sinai, and then he beheld the glory of God. During a fast, Samuel's mother bore him. Through their fasting, the Ninevites averted the wrath of God. By his fasting, Daniel prepared himself for great visions. After his fast, Elijah was taken up to heaven to receive celestial sustenance. Through their fasting, the Three Children quenched the violence of the fire. And our Lord, by fasting forty days, made known to us the Lenten season. By means of their fasting, the Apostles rooted out the teaching of the devil. By virtue of their fasts, our fathers appeared to the world as beacons that continue to shine after their decease. They exhibited great labors and continence; for example, the great Antonius, Euthymius, Savva, and the other fathers. Let us imitate them, my brethren."

After thus instructing the brotherhood, he kissed them, calling each by name, and then left the monastery, taking with him but a few loaves of bread. He entered a crypt, closed the door behind him, and covered himself with dust. He spoke to no one, unless some object was needful to him, and in any case he conversed only on Saturday and on Sunday through a small window. Upon other days, he remained in fasting and in prayer, maintaining strict abstinence. He returned to the monastery on the eve of Friday, St. Lazarus' day. For on this day ends the forty days' fast, which opens on the first Monday after the week of St. Theodore and concludes on Friday, the feast of St. Lazarus. Holy Week is then observed as a fast on account of our Lord's passion. Theodosius thus returned according to his custom, embraced the brethren, and with them celebrated Palm Sunday.

When Easter Day came, he celebrated it brilliantly as usual, and then fell ill. When he was taken ill, and had been sick for five days, he bade them carry him in the evening down into the courtyard. The brethren laid him upon a sled and set him before the church. He then desired that the whole brotherhood should be summoned, so the brethren struck upon the bell, and all assembled together. Theodosius then said to them, "My brethren, my fathers, and my children! I now depart from you, for God made known to me, while I was in the crypt during the Lenten season, that I must now quit this world. Whom do you desire for your prior, that I may confer my blessing upon him?"

They made answer, "You have been a father to us all. Whomsoever you yourself select shall be our father and our prior, and we shall obey him even as we obey you." Then our father Theodosius said, "Go apart from me and designate him whom you desire, except the two brothers Nicholas and Ignatius: but choose from the rest whomever you prefer, from the eldest down to the youngest."

They obeyed his behest, and upon withdrawing a short distance in the direction of the church, they took counsel together, and then sent two of the brethren back to Theodosius to beg him to designate the one chosen by God and his own holy prayer, and who should be agreeable to Theodosius himself. Theodosius then made answer, "If you desire to receive your prior from me, then I will appoint him not so much from my own choice as by divine disposition," and he designated the presbyter James. This nomination did not meet with the approval of the brotherhood, who objected that James had not taken orders in the monastery, since he had come thither from Letetz with his brother Paul. They demanded rather Stephen the Cantor, who was then a pupil of Theodosius, and therefore said, "He has grown up under your hand and has served with you; appoint him as our prior."

Then Theodosius said, "By the commandment of God, I designated James, but you prefer that the appointment should coincide with your own wishes." He gave way to their desire, however, and appointed Stephen to be their prior, and blessed him, saying: "My son! I give over to you this monastery. Guard it with care, and maintain what I have ordained in its observances. Change not the traditions and the institutions of the monastery, but follow in all things the law and our monastic rule."

The brethren then raised him up, carried him to his cell, and laid him upon his bed. At the beginning of the sixth day, while he was seriously ill, Prince Sviatoslav came to visit him with his son Gleb. While the prince was sitting beside him, Theodosius said: "I depart from this world and entrust this monastery to your guardianship in the event that some disorder arises in it. I confer the priorate upon Stephen; desert him not in his hour of need."

The prince embraced him, and after promising to care for the monastery, departed from him. When the seventh day was come, while Theodosius was steadily growing weaker, he summoned Stephen and the brotherhood, and spoke to them these words: "Upon my departure from this world, if I have found favor with God and he has accepted me, then this monastery, after my decease, will grow and prosper through his help. In that event, know that God has accepted me. But if, after my death, the monastery begins to lose in membership and income, be assured that I shall not have found favor in the sight of God."

When he had spoken thus, the brethren wept, saying, "Father, intercede with God for us, for we know that he will not scorn your labors." They thus sat out the night with him, and at the beginning of the eighth day, being the second Saturday after Easter, in the second hour of the day, he commended his soul into the hands of God, upon May 3rd, in the eleventh year of the indiction. The brethren thus mourned for him.

Theodosius had given command that he should be buried in the crypt where he had performed many good works. He had also directed that his body should be buried by night, and they followed his injunction in this respect. When evening was come, the brethren took up his body and laid it in the crypt, after conducting it thither in all honor with hymns and candles to the glory of our God Jesus Christ.

BROTHER ISAAC AND THE DEMONS

There was also another monk, named Isaac. While still in

the world, he was very rich, since in the secular life he was by birth a merchant of Toropetz. But he resolved to become a monk, and distributed his fortune to the needy and to the monasteries. He then approached the great Antonius in the crypt, and besought him to receive him into the order. Antonius accepted him, and put upon him the monastic habit, calling him Isaac, for his secular name was Chern. Isaac adopted an ascetic mode of life. He wrapped himself in a hair shirt, then caused a goat to be bought, flayed it, and put on the skin over his hair shirt, so that the fresh hide dried upon him. He shut himself up in a lonely gallery of the crypt in a narrow cell only four ells across, and there lamented and prayed to God. His sustenance was one wafer, and that only once a day, and he drank but moderately of water. The great Antonius carried it to him, and passed it in to him by a little window through which he inserted his arm. Thus Isaac received his food. He subsisted thus for seven years without seeing the light of day or even lying down upon his side, for he snatched what sleep he could in a sitting posture.

Once, when evening had fallen, he had knelt till midnight singing psalms, as was his wont, and when he was wearied, he sat down upon his stool. As he sat there, and had as usual extinguished his candle, a light suddenly blazed forth in the crypt as if it shone from the sun, and strong enough to take away man's vision. Two fair youths then approached him. Their faces were radiant like the sun, and they said to him: "Isaac, we are angels; Christ is drawing near to you. Fall down and worship him."

He did not understand their devilish artifice nor remember to cross himself, but knelt before the work of the demons as if to Christ himself. The demons then cried out and said, "Now, Isaac, you belong to us."

They led him back into his cell and set him down. They then seated themselves around him, and both the cell and the aisle of the crypt was filled with them. One of the devils, who called himself Christ, bade them take flutes and lyres and lutes and play, so that Isaac could dance before them. So they struck up with flutes, lutes, and lyres, and began to make sport of him. After they had tormented him, they left him half alive, and went away when they had beaten him.

The next day at dawn, when it was time to break bread, Antonius came to the window according to his custom and said, "May the Lord bless you, Father Isaac." But there was no answer. Then Antonius said, "He has already passed away," so he sent into the monastery in search of Theodosius and the brethren. After digging out the entrance where it had been walled up, they entered and lifted him up, thinking him dead, and carried him out in front of the crypt. They then perceived that he was still alive, and Theodosius the prior said, "This comes from the devil's artifice." They laid him upon a bier, and Antonius cared for him.

About this same time it happened that Iziaslav returned from Poland, and was angry with Antonius on account of Vseslav, so that Sviatoslav caused Antonius to escape by night to Chernigov. When Antonius arrived there, he was attracted by the Boldiny hills, and after digging another crypt, he settled there. At that spot in the Boldiny hills, there is a monastery dedicated to the Virgin even to this day. When Theodosius learned that Antonius had fled to Chernigov, he came with his brethren, took Isaac, and bore him to his own cell, where he cared for him. For Isaac was so weakened in body that he could not turn from one side to the other, nor rise up, nor sit down, but he lay always upon one side, and relieved himself as he lay, so that numerous worms were caused under his back by his excrement. Theodosius washed and dressed him with his own hands, and for two years cared for him thus. It is wondrous and strange that he lay thus for two years, tasting neither bread nor water nor any other food nor fruit, nor did he speak with his tongue, but lay deaf and dumb for the whole two years.

Theodosius prayed to God in his behalf, and offered supplications over him by day and by night, until in the third year he spoke and heard, rose upon his feet like a babe, and began to walk. He would not go faithfully to church, but the brethren carried him thither by force; they also taught him to go to the refectory, but seated him apart from the rest of the brethren. They set bread before him, but he would not take it unless they placed it in his hand.

Theodosius then said, "Leave the bread before him, but do not put it in his hand, so that he can eat of his own volition."

For a week he ate nothing, but gradually he became aware of the bread, and tasted it. Thus he began to eat, and by this means Theodosius freed him from the craft of the devil.

Isaac then assumed severe abstinence. When Theodosius was dead and Stephen was prior in his stead, Isaac said: "Demon, you deceived me once when I sat in a lonely spot. I must not confine myself in the crypt, but must vanquish you while I frequent the monastery." He then clad himself in a hair shirt, and put on over this a sackcloth coat, and began to act strangely. He undertook to help the cooks in the preparation of food for the brotherhood. He went to matins earlier than the others, and stood firm and immovable. When winter came with its heavy frosts, he stood in shoes so worn that his feet froze to the pavement, but he would not move his feet till matins were over. After matins, he went to the kitchen, and made ready the fire, the water, and the wood before the other cooks came from the brotherhood.

There was one cook who was also named Isaac, who mocked at Isaac and said, "There sits a black crow; go and catch it." Isaac bowed to the ground before him, then went and caught the crow, and brought it back to him in the presence of all the cooks. They were frightened, and reported it to the prior and the brotherhood, who began to respect him. But not being desirous of human glory, he began to act strangely, and to play tricks, now on the prior, now on the brethren, and now on laymen, so that others dealt him blows. Then he began to wander through the country, acting like an idiot. He settled in the crypt where he had formerly lived, for Antonius was already dead. He gathered young men about him and laid upon them the monastic habit, so that he suffered blows from the Prior Nikon as well as from the parents of these youths. But he suffered these hardships, and willingly endured blows and nakedness and cold by day and by night.

One night he lit the stove in a cabin by the crypt. When the stove was heated, fire began to issue forth from the crevices, for it was old and cracked. Since he had nothing to put over the stove, he braced his bare feet against the flame till the stove burned out, and then left it. Many other stories were told about him, and I myself witnessed some such occurrences.

Thus he won his victory over the demons, holding their terrors and apparitions of as little account as flies. For he said to them: "You did indeed deceive me the first time in the crypt, since I did not perceive your craft and cunning. But now that I have on my side the Lord Jesus Christ and my God and the prayers of my father Theodosius, I hope to vanquish you." Many times the demons harassed him, and said, "You belong to us, for you have worshiped us and our leader." But he replied, "Your chief is Antichrist and you are demons," and signed his countenance with the cross. At this they disappeared. Sometimes, however, they came upon him again by night, and frightened him in his dreams, appearing like a great company with mattocks and spades, and saying, "We will undermine the crypt, and bury this man within it," while others exclaimed, "Fly, Isaac, they intend to bury you alive." But he made answer, "If you were men, you would have come by day; but you are darkness and come in darkness, and the darkness shall swallow you up." Then he made the sign of the cross against them, and they vanished.

On other occasions, they endeavored to terrify him in the form of a bear, sometimes as a wild beast and sometimes as a bull. Now snakes beset him, and now toads, mice, and every other reptile. But they could not harm him, and said to him, "Isaac, you have vanquished us!" He replied, "You conquered me in the image of Jesus Christ and his angels, of whose sight you are unworthy. But now you rightly appear in the guise of beasts and cattle or as the snakes and reptiles that you are, repulsive and evil to behold." Thereupon the demons left him, and he suffered no more evil at their hands. As he himself related, his struggle against them lasted for three years. Then he began to live still more strictly, and to practice abstinence, fasting, and vigil.

After thus living out his life, he finally came to his end. He fell sick in his crypt, and was carried in his illness to the monastery, where he died in the Lord upon the eighth day. The Prior John and the brethren clothed his body and buried him.

Such were the monks of the monastery of Theodosius, who shine forth like radiant beacons since their decease, and intercede with God in behalf of the brethren here below, as well as for the lay brotherhood and for those who contribute to the monastery in which to this day the brotherhood abides together in virtuous life amid hymns, prayers, and obedience, to the glory of Almighty God, and protected by the intercession of Theodosius, to whom be glory, Amen.

16. *Bishop Simon and Monk Polycarpe*

The Kievan Crypt Paterikon

THE narratives of this *Paterikon* come from the pen of Simon, Bishop of Vladimir and Suzdal, who apparently began his ecclesiastical career in the Crypt Monastery; and from the pen of Polycarpe, a monk of the same monastery. Simon, who became bishop in 1214 and died in 1226, wrote his narratives as an appendix to his epistle to Polycarpe. In this epistle Simon endeavors to reconcile Polycarpe, who was dissatisfied with his life in the monastery, with his brethren and abbot, and to convince him that the monastery was the spiritual center of the land.

Apparently Polycarpe wanted to become a bishop and his relations with the other monks were rather strained. That portion of the *Paterikon* written by Polycarpe was done some years later, when he had become reconciled with the monastery. It is addressed to Abbot Akindin, and has about the same structure as the first part—that is, an epistle with eleven tales about the lives of the monks, but is in a style less personal than the work of Simon. It was written for wide circulation both within and without the monastery, whereas the work of Simon was meant to be read only by Polycarpe.

In the thirteenth century both works were made into one, and to them was added the story of "The Brethren of the Crypt Monastery" (Damian, Jeremy, and Matthew) and "Isaac and the Demons" from the *Primary Chronicle* by Nestor. Later, more narratives were added to this *Paterikon,* and it became one of the most popular collections of this genre in Russia.

Bishop Simon wrote the first four stories of this collection, while the last one, "Marko the Gravedigger Who Was Obeyed by the Dead," is the work of Polycarpe. The translations here presented are based on the text published by D. Abramovich, *Kievo-Pecherskii paterik,* Kiev, 1931.

✦ ✦ ✦

Bishop Simon

PRINCE SVIATOSHA OF CHERNIGOV

This blessed and faithful Prince Sviatosha, called Nicholas after he became a monk, was the son of Prince David and the grandson of Prince Sviatoslav. This prince came to the conclusion that all things in this vain life are illusive and that everything on the earth comes to its end and passes away, but that the blessings of the future life are eternal and everlasting and that the Kingdom of Heaven, which God has prepared for those who love him, is unending. And he relinquished his princedom together with all his honor, glory and power, seeing no worth in all these things. And he came to the Crypt Monastery and became a monk. This happened in 1106 (6614) on the 17th day of February. All the monks who were living in the monastery at that time are witnesses to his virtuous life and his fulfillment of the vows of obedience.

For three years he remained in the kitchen working with his brethren. With his own hands he chopped wood for the preparation of meals, carrying it on his shoulders, often from the river

Dnieper. And his brothers, Iziaslav and Vladimir, were hardly able to keep him from such heavy labor. However, he asked and begged that they permit him to work at least one more year in the kitchen with his brethren. Thereafter, he was placed in charge of the monastery gates, for in every type of work he was skillful and diligent. He remained there, at the gates, for three years, never leaving except to attend church services. From there he was told to go and serve in the refectory. Finally, according to the will of the abbot and all the brethren, he was permitted to have his own cell, which he himself built. This cell is called Sviatosha's cell to this very day, and the vegetable garden, which he planted with his own hands, is also called after his name still. People say of him that no one has ever seen him idle. He was always occupied with some kind of work, and thus he earned his keep. On his lips permanently was a prayer to Jesus: "Jesus Christ, have mercy upon us." He never ate anything more than the monastery meals. He had considerable wealth, but he gave everything away to pilgrims and the poor and for the building of churches. Up to now there are many books given by him to your monastery. When he was still ruling, this blessed Sviatosha had a very skilled physician, Peter, who was from Syria. This Peter came with him to the monastery, but, seeing that the prince voluntarily accepted poverty and worked in the kitchen and at the gate, he left him and, settling in Kiev, became a doctor for many citizens of this city. This physician used to come often to Prince Sviatosha at the monastery and, seeing his bitter sufferings and endless fasting, tried to convince him to change his way of living, saying: "Prince, you should care for your health and not ruin your body with endless labor and abstinence. You will become so ill, that you will not be able to carry the burden which, for God's sake, you have voluntarily accepted. God does not desire unbearable fasting and labor, but only a humble and contrite heart. You are not accustomed to hardships such as you, working like a slave, must now endure. Your pious brothers, Iziaslav and Vladimir, feel that your poverty is a reproach to them. How could you turn away from such glory and honor to such wretchedness and how can you exhaust your body with such food? I wonder about your stomach; once sweet meals were too heavy for it, and now it accepts and endures simple herbs and dry bread. Beware, for sometime all your maladies will attack you at once, and you, deprived of resistance, will succumb, and I will not be able to help you. You will leave your inconsolable brothers to mourn after you. Also, your boyars, who once served you, hoped to become powerful and glorious with your help. Now they are deprived of your love, and they complain about you. They have built large houses for themselves, but they remain in them in great grief. You yourself have not even a place to lay your head, remaining in this backyard. They consider that you have become insane. Who among the princes has done anything of this nature? Did your blessed father, David, or your grandfather, Sviatoslav, do so? Or who among the boyars has acted in this way? Or who even intended to do anything similar, excepting Barlaam, who was the abbot here? And if you don't follow my advice, you will meet an untimely death."

So he used to talk with Prince Sviatosha, now Monk Nicholas, sitting with him in the kitchen or at the gate. And he was instructed to do so by Prince Sviatosha's brothers. But Prince Sviatosha answered him, saying: "Brother Peter, I have thought for a long time and I have decided not to spare my flesh so as to prevent it from arousing in me a new struggle. It is better to keep it submissive under the burden of heavy labor, for it is said: 'Strength is achieved through weakness,' and, 'These present temporary passions are nothing worse in comparison with the glory which will be revealed in us.' I thank God for he has liberated me from the slavedom of this world and made me the servant of his servants, these blessed monks. And my brothers had better look after themselves, for each man must bear his cross alone. They should be satisfied with having my patrimony—all of what I had: my wife and children, the house and power, brethren and friends, serfs and estates, I gave up for Christ's sake so as to inherit eternal life. I became poor for the sake of God, so that I might gain God's favor.

"And even yourself, when you treat people, don't you prescribe refraining from excessive eating? To die for Christ would be a real acquisition of fortune for me. And sitting here in the backyard next to the refuse heap is the winning of a real kingdom. It may be that no prince has done as I do now. Then I will be the first example for them. Perhaps one of them will want to imitate my example and follow in my footsteps. As far as my life is concerned, it should not be of concern to you, nor to those who have asked you to come to me."

When the blessed prince was sick, his physician, Peter, usually prepared some medicine for the illness, such as severe heartburn or other pains that had occurred to the prince. But before the physician could reach the prince, the prince was already cured. And he never permitted himself to be treated by a physician. And so it happened many times. Once, when the physician himself became ill, Prince Sviatosha sent him a messenger to say: "Don't take your medicine and you will be cured. And if you don't obey me, you will suffer bitterly."

But the latter, relying on his medical skills, drank the medicine, hoping to be cured of his illness; but instead of being cured, he almost died. And only the prayer of the blessed prince helped and cured him.

Another time the physician again became ill, and the blessed prince sent his messenger once more to say, "If you don't attempt to cure yourself, you will be completely recovered in three days."

The Syrian obeyed him, and on the third day he recovered, according to the words of the blessed prince. As soon as he had recovered, the blessed one asked him to come to the monastery, and there he enjoined the physician to become a monk, saying, "In three months from now, we shall part." With these words Prince Sviatosha predicted the death of the physician.

The Syrian misunderstood the prince's words, thinking that not his own death but that of the prince was nearing. He fell before the prince's feet and tearfully implored him, saying:

"Alas, woe is me, my lord and benefactor!
Who will help me, a foreigner?
Who will feed so many people who are hungry?
Who will be the intercessor of the offended?
Who will be merciful with the poor?
Have I not told you, my prince,
that you will be mourned by all your inconsolable brothers?
You cured me not only through the words and power of God,
but also with the help of your prayers.
Where will you depart to, my good pastor?
Tell me what fatal illness you have,
and I will cure you.
And, if I cannot,
then my head shall be given for your head,
and my soul for your soul.
Oh, my lord, don't leave me
without telling me how you learned of your death.
I would give my life for you.
If God has announced your passing away to you,
please pray to him that I might die in your place.
Where would I be able to mourn my loss,
if you leave me?

Should I do it here, at this refuse heap,
or at the gate where you live?
And what can you leave me if you die?
You yourself are almost naked, and when you die
you will be buried in your patched and tattered garments.
Help me through your prayers
as once Prophet Elijah gave Elisha his mantle
to get through paradise
under the shelter of the wonderful house of the Lord.
Even the beast knows where the sun will rise
before it goes to its lair.
And the bird knows how to find its abode
and the turtledove knows how to find the nest
where it raises its fledglings."

But the blessed one answered him: "It is better to place one's hopes in the Lord than to rely upon many; God knows how to feed his creatures and how to protect and save his poor. My brothers should not worry about me, but about themselves and their children. I never wanted any treatment by a physician during my life, because when the hour of death has come the physician cannot help." And the prince went with the physician down into the crypt and dug a grave for himself, and he asked the Syrian, "Which of us wants this grave the more?"

And the Syrian replied: "It should come to pass as each of us desires. But you should live, and I should be buried here."

And then the blessed prince told him, "Let it be as you do desire."

The Syrian physician became a monk, and passed three months weeping incessantly both day and night. The blessed one consoled him, saying, "Brother Peter, do you wish that I should take you with me?"

And the physician answered tearfully: "I want you to release me and let me die in your place. Please, pray for me."

And the blessed prince told the physician, "Prepare for death, my son, and in three days you will depart to the lord."

And after three days the physician took Holy Communion, lay down on his bed, adjusted his robes, stretched out his legs, and gave up his soul into the hands of the Lord, as it was predicted by Blessed Prince Sviatosha.

Prince Sviatosha lived after this for another thirty years, never leaving the monastery again. And when he died, almost the entire city of Kiev came to his burial. Learning of Blessed Sviatosha's death, his brother, Prince Iziaslav, sent a messenger to the abbot, asking that he be given the crucifix of Prince Sviatosha, his pillow, and the board upon which he had knelt.

The abbot gave them to the prince, saying, "It will renew your faith."

The prince accepted them and carefully preserved them at home. And he gave the abbot three pieces of gold so as not to receive this blessing of the abbot for nothing.

Once, this prince became so ill that all his family lost hope and, seeing that he was about to die, his wife, children, and boyars went to his chambers and remained with him. He raised up slightly and asked for some water from the well of the Crypt Monastery, and then he became mute.

In the meantime a messenger went to the monastery for the water. The abbot took Sviatosha's hair shirt,[1] put it first on the grave of St. Theodosius, and then gave it to the prince's messenger, telling him to put this shirt on Prince Iziaslav. Before the messenger had returned with the water and hair shirt, the ill prince suddenly uttered the words, "Go beyond the gates of the city and meet St. Theodosius and St. Nicholas."

And when the messenger returned with the water and the hair shirt, the prince exclaimed, "Nicholas–Nicholas Sviatosha!"

And the prince was given the water, and the hair shirt was placed on his body, and he recovered immediately. And everyone glorified God and his saints. And each time Iziaslav became ill, he would put on this hair shirt, and he always recovered. And in all battles he wore this hair shirt, and he remained unharmed. But once, a poor sinner, he dared not put on the hair shirt, and he was slain in battle. And he was buried in this hair shirt, as he had requested. And the brethren still remember other great deeds of the saint. Until this day the monks of the Crypt Monastery still hold Blessed Prince Sviatosha in their memory.

Bishop Simon

VIKING SHIMON AND ST. THEODOSIUS

The Building of the Church of the Holy Virgin of the Crypt Monastery

And now I will come to other stories. Everyone should know how, according to the will of God and the prayers and desires of the Holy Virgin, the beautiful and great Church of the Crypt

[1] Hair shirt–a shirt made of horsehair, and worn as a penance.

Monastery, dedicated to the Holy Virgin, was founded and built. This is the church of the great abbey of all the Russian land, the monastery of St. Theodosius.

There was in the land of the Vikings[2] a certain prince whose name was Africanus, the brother of Yakun, who, when he and Prince Yaroslav were fighting against evil Prince Mstislav, lost his gold-embroidered mantle when he was fleeing from battle. This Prince Africanus had two sons, Friand and Shimon. After Prince Africanus' death, his brother, Yakun, drove his nephews from their patrimonies. And thus Shimon came to our faithful Prince Yaroslav. And Yaroslav received him with honor and sent him to his son, Vsevolod, appointing him to be the senior counselor to Vsevolod. And through this position Shimon gained great influence. The reason for Shimon's devotion to the Holy Crypt Monastery is explained in the following narrative.

During the reign of Prince Iziaslav in Kiev, the Kumans came to the Russian land, this being in 1068 (6576). And the sons of Yaroslav, Princes Iziaslav, Sviatoslav, and Vsevolod, decided to attack them. And Shimon went with Prince Vsevolod. When they came to the great and holy Father Antonius and asked him for his blessing and prayers, the abbot opened his lips, which had been sealed for a very long time, and clearly foretold of their forthcoming demise. Then Shimon the Viking fell at the abbot's feet and begged him to tell how he, Shimon, might escape this fate.

And the blessed abbot told him: "My son, many of you will fall in battle, pierced by swords. And when many of you attempt to escape from the enemy, you will be pursued and struck down by weapons or drowned in the river. But you, my son, will escape, and later you will be buried in the church that you will build."

And the Russian regiments engaged in battle on the river Leta, and because of God's wrath the Christians were defeated and routed. And many *voevodas*[3] and warriors fell in battle. Among those who had fallen in battle lay Shimon, who was wounded. He raised his eyes to the heavens and there saw a great church, the same that he had seen once at sea. And, remembering the words of the Savior, he said, "Lord! Deliver me from bitter death through the prayers of your most holy Mother and the reverend fathers Antonius and Theodosius."

And at that moment a certain power took him from the

[2] Apparently Shimon came to Russia from Sweden.
[3] Military commanders.

clutches of death. He became cured of his wounds and soon found that all his family was safe and in good health.

And then he returned to the great Antonius and told him of this wonderful miracle, saying: "My father, Africanus, once made a cross on which was the figure of Christ with pieces of gold that weighed fifty grivnas.[4] And on his head he placed a golden crown. When my uncle, Yakun, drove me from my patrimony, I took with me the girdle and the crown from this image of Jesus. And when I did so, I heard coming from the cross a voice that was directed to me, and it said:

> " 'Man, never put this crown on your own head, but take it to the place that I have chosen. And there the Reverend Father Theodosius will erect a church in honor of my Mother. Place this crown in his hands and tell him to hang it over my altar.'

"And I fell to the ground, seized with awe, and I lay there motionless, as if dead, for a long time. Then I got up and went to a ship. When we were crossing the sea, there occurred a great storm, and we all feared for our lives. And I began to pray, 'Lord! Forgive me, for I am perishing because of the crown I took from your revered and holy image.'

"And I saw in the heavens a church, and I began to wonder what this vision meant. And then there came from above a voice that announced:

> " 'This is the church that should be built by the Reverend Father Theodosius in the name of the Mother of God. And in this church you are to be buried.'

And I saw the size and the height, and I measured it with the golden girdle and found it to be twenty feet wide and thirty feet high, and the walls and the roof were fifty feet. And we all glorified God and, becoming consoled, we experienced great joy at having escaped a bitter death. Until now, I did not realize where the church, shown me both at sea and at the river Leta where I was lying at death's door, was to be built. And then I heard from your revered tongue that I will be buried here in the church that will be erected."

And Shimon took out the golden girdle, and said, "Here are the measurements and the plan, and here is the crown that should be hung above the holy altar."

And Abbot Antonius glorified God, and told the Viking, "My child, from this day on you will never be called Shimon, but Simon."

[4] Old Russian unit of money.

And Antonius invited Blessed Father Theodosius to come to him, and he told him, "Here is Simon who wants to build such a church." And Antonius gave Theodosius the girdle, crown, and plans. And from that day Simon loved holy Theodosius very much, and he gave him his wealth and estate for the needs of the monastery.

Once Simon came to Blessed Theodosius, and after the usual talk he told the holy one, "Father, I ask you to give me a gift."

And Theodosius answered, "Oh, my child, what can you, a powerful man, ask from me, a humble one?"

And Simon answered, "The gift I ask of you is most important, and beyond my power to obtain."

And Theodosius replied: "My child, you know how poor we are and that often we don't even have enough bread for the daily meal. And I know not what else we may have."

But Simon said: "If you want to give me this gift, you can do so, thanks to the grace that you have received from God, who called you a 'Reverend Father.' When I had taken the crown from the head of Jesus, he told me:

> " 'Take it to the place that I have chosen. And there the Reverend Father Theodosius will erect a church in honor of my Mother.'

And so I now ask you to give me your word that your soul will bless me both during our lives and after our deaths."

And the saintly father answered: "What you ask me is beyond my power, but if the church is built, and if after my passing the rituals and traditions are preserved in this church, then know that I shall dare to ask God. But now I know not whether my prayers would be acceptable."

And Simon said: "God is my witness that I was told about you by the purest lips of his holy image. Therefore, I beg you, pray for me, for my son, George, and for his descendants, in the same way in which you pray for your monks."

The saint promised this to Simon the Viking, and then added: "I don't pray for my monks only, but for everyone who for my sake loves this holy monastery."

Then Simon bowed deeply to the earth, and spoke: "My father, I won't leave you until you have confirmed in writing what you have said."

Theodosius felt compelled to do so, since Simon loved him. And he wrote, "In the name of the Father, and of the Son, and of the Holy Ghost. . . ." And these words became the prayer which, from that time to this, is always placed in the hands of the dead. And since that time it has become the custom to put such letters in the coffins of the dead. No one did this before. And the following was written in the prayer:

"Remember, me, O Lord, when thou comest into thy kingdom, and when thou judgest everyone according to his deeds, then permit, O Lord, that thy servants Simon and George remain on the right side of thy glory, and hear thy blessed voice saying, 'Come, O blessed of my Father, and inherit the kingdom that has been prepared for you since time immemorial.'"

And Simon asked, "My father, please ask the Lord also to absolve the sins of my father and my relatives."

And Theodosius raised his hands to the heavens and said, "Be blessed by the God of Zion, and you, and everyone to the last of your line, shall view the beauty of Jerusalem."

Simon received this holy blessing and this prayer as a priceless gift. Once he was a Viking, and now, thanks to the grace of God, he became an Orthodox Christian. He was instructed by our holy father Theodosius, and, for the sake of the miracles performed by holy Antonius and Theodosius, he gave up his Western heresy and became a believer of the one true faith. And this he did with all his household and all his priests, and they numbered about three thousand. And Simon was the first to be buried in the church of the Crypt Monastery. Since that time Simon's son, George, also loved this holy place exceedingly. Prince Vladimir Monomakh sent George, the son of Simon, to the land of Suzdal, and entrusted to him his son, Yury. Many years later this Prince Yury became the ruler of Kiev, and he entrusted to George the land of Suzdal as if George were his own father.

Bishop Simon

THE COMING OF THE GREEK ICONOGRAPHERS FROM CONSTANTINOPLE TO ABBOT NIKON

Once, several Greek iconographers from Constantinople came to Abbot Nikon of the Crypt Monastery and began to complain, saying: "Bring before us the men who hired us. We wish to have a trial. They hired us to embellish a small church, and we made the agreement in front of witnesses, but this church is very large. Take back your gold (which we received as payment), and we'll return to Constantinople."

Abbot Nikon (not understanding of what they were speaking)

asked them, "Who were the people who made this agreement with you?"

And the Greeks described these people and gave their names as being Antonius and Theodosius.

But the abbot answered them, saying: "My children, we cannot bring them before you, for they departed this world ten years ago. But they still continue to pray incessantly for us; they steadily safeguard this church; they care for this monastery; and they protect all those who live in it."

Hearing these words, the Greeks were awestruck. However, they brought before the abbot numerous merchants, Greeks and Abkhasians,[1] who had traveled with them from Constantinople to Kiev. And the iconographers declared: "We made the agreement and accepted gold for payment from those who hired us in the presence of these merchants. But since you, Abbot, do not wish to bring to us those who commissioned us, or are unable to bring them here, then show us their images so that our witnesses can see them."

When the abbot brought them the icons of Sts. Antonius and Theodosius, the Greeks and Abkhasians, upon seeing them, bowed deeply and said: "Verily, they are their image! And we believe that even after death they still live and can protect, save, and succor those who turn to them for aid." And they decided to give the mosaic, which they had brought with them from Constantinople to sell, for the embellishment of the altar.

And the iconographers began to confess their sins: "When we arrived in our boats at the city of Kanev on the river Dnieper, we had the vision of a mountain on which was a large church. And we asked other travelers, 'What church is this?' and they answered, 'It is the church of the Crypt Monastery in which you are to paint the icons.'

"And, becoming angry,[2] we decided to go back, and started down the river. But that same night there occurred a severe storm on the river, and when we awoke the next morning we found that we were at the village of Tripole, farther up the river, and that a certain power was pulling us always up river. And only with great difficulty were we able to stop our boat. And we remained there the whole day, contemplating the meaning of this event, since in one night, and without any rowing,

[1] Abkhasians: a tribe in the western Caucasus.

[2] They were upset because having seen the size of the church they realized that their work would have to be much more extensive than they had expected.

we went up the river for a distance that usually requires three days of travel.

"The next night we again had the same vision of the church, and in the church was an icon of the Holy Virgin, and from this icon there came a voice announcing: 'Men! Why do you worry? Why do you not submit yourself to my will and that of my Son? If you do not obey, but try to escape, you, together with your boat, will be taken from this place and placed in the church. And know that you will never leave the monastery, but will there receive the tonsure, and will there end your days. But you will be granted mercy in the life eternal for the sake of the builders of the monastery, Abbots Antonius and Theodosius.'

"And the next day, when we awoke, we once more attempted to escape, and made a great effort to row downstream; but the boat moved continually upstream. And soon it landed at the shore under the monastery, and of its own accord."

After the Greeks had finished their narration, they and the monks glorified God, the miraculous holy icon of his most pure mother, and the holy fathers Antonius and Theodosius. And actually, having become monks, the iconographers and builders did end their days in the Crypt Monastery. And they were buried near the altar, and their robes still hang there and their books are preserved in the monastery for the commemoration of this miracle.

Bishop Simon

JOHN AND SERGIUS

There were two men from this great city (of Kiev) who were very close friends, and their names were John and Sergius. Once, both of them went into the Church of the Crypt Monastery, which was built by the will of God. And there they saw that from the icon of the Holy Virgin there emanated a bright light, even brighter than the rays of the sun. And so they decided to pledge themselves to become spiritual brothers.

Many years later John became very ill and was on his deathbed, leaving a son, Zacharias, who was only five years old. Before his death John called for the abbot of the Crypt Monastery, and gave him all his personal wealth for distribution to the poor. The part that belonged to his young son, which consisted of one thousand *grivnas* of silver, and one hundred *grivnas* of gold, he left in trust with his spiritual brother, Sergius. John also asked his spiritual brother to care for his son, Zacharias, telling Sergius, "Give this gold and silver to my son when he comes of age."

When Zacharias was fifteen years old, he wanted to obtain his gold and silver from Sergius. But Sergius, incited by the devil, decided to keep the money for himself, and in so doing to lose his soul. Therefore he told the youth: "Your father gave his entire estate to God, and you should ask God for your gold and silver. He owes it to you, and, being merciful, perhaps he will return it to you. But I don't owe your father even a single gold coin, for he, having lost his mind, gave away all his wealth and left you in poverty."

Hearing these words, the youth became sad and once more he begged Sergius for his money, but this time asking for only one-half of his money, letting Sergius keep the second half. But Sergius began to reproach the son and the son's father in strong words.

Zacharias then attempted to obtain from Sergius at least one-quarter or even one-tenth of his money; but seeing that he would not receive anything from Sergius, he spoke to him, saying, "Come and avow in the Church of the Crypt Monastery, before the miraculous icon of the Virgin, the same icon before which you pledged to be my father's spiritual brother, that you received no money from my father."

And Sergius promised to avow before the icon that he had received neither one thousand *grivnas* of silver nor one hundred *grivnas* of gold from John. But as Sergius approached the icon to avow, an invisible power prevented him from nearing it. And suddenly he began to shout: "Holy Angels and St. Theodosius! Enjoin this merciless angel not to slay me. Pray to the Holy Virgin to drive away the devils who attack me! Take your gold and silver! It is in a sealed vessel in my house!"

Everyone was seized with awe. And from that day it was forbidden to pronounce avowals on this icon. Men were sent to Sergius' house, and there they found the sealed vessel, and in it were two thousand *grivnas* of silver and two hundred *grivnas* of gold, for God had miraculously increased the fortune of the poor, knowing that Zacharias would give his fortune to the abbot of the Crypt Monastery. Zacharias remained at the monastery to the end of his days, and his fortune was used to erect the Church of St. John the Baptist. This church was dedicated to the memories of John and Zacharias, since their gold and silver had erected it.

Monk Polycarpe

MARKO THE GRAVEDIGGER WHO WAS OBEYED BY THE DEAD

We sinners imitate the ancient writings on the saints. But the ancient writers, with great difficulties, sought the saints in he wilderness, in the mountains, and in the abysses. Some of these authors have themselves seen these saints, while of other saints they have heard stories of their lives, works, miracles, and deeds, and have composed the *Paterikon*, which we read and in which we enjoy spiritual narrations. I, an unworthy one, have not yet been able to comprehend the truth of reason, and I have seen nothing of this kind. I tell only what I have heard. This narration was told to me by Bishop Simon, and I wrote it down for you, my reverend father. I have never been in holy places, nor have I seen Jerusalem nor Mount Sinai. Therefore I am unable to add anything to this narration for the purpose of embellishment, as is the habit of those who are clever with words. I do not want to praise anything but this Holy Crypt Monastery, the monks who live therein, and the lives and miracles of the latter. I shall rejoice when I remember them, for I, a sinner, hope that the saintly fathers will pray for me. And here I shall begin the narration concerning the gravedigger Marko.

St. Marko used to live in the crypt, and during his life there the body of our father, Theodosius, was taken from the crypt into the great holy church. This Marko dug graves in the crypt with his own hands, and carried the earth away on his shoulders. He worked hard all day and all night to do these pious deeds. Though he dug many graves for the burial of his brethren, he never accepted payment for doing so. If someone gave him money, he would take it and distribute it among the poor and crippled.

Once, according to his custom, he dug a grave and, laboring very much, became tired. However, the grave was not sufficiently wide. It so happened that this very day one of the brothers passed to God, and there was no grave available except this narrow one. The dead man was brought to the crypt, but because the grave was so very narrow he could not be placed in it. And the brethren began to grumble at Marko, for it was neither possible to adjust the dead man's robes nor to anoint him with holy oil. Marko, the monk of the cave, bowed to everyone with humility and said, "Forgive me, my fathers, but I could not finish the grave because of my poor health."

pride into humility, and God rejects neither the contrite he nor the humble man."

And Theophile answered him, saying: "I know, my fath that I should have fallen dead for my sins when you raised ı dead brother. But, because of prayers, the Lord gave me n life, hoping for my repentance. Now I beg you, please, eitl take me with you to the Lord or return my sight to me."

Marko replied: "There is no need for you to see this transito world. Pray to the Lord that you may see his glory in the ne world. Your hour will come, even if you do not wish it Nevertheless, I shall give you a foretoken of your passing. Thr days before your death, you will regain your sight. And, passin to God, you will there see endless light and unspoken glory And Blessed Marko passed to God, being buried in the crypt a grave he himself had dug.

This separation from Brother Marko added greatly to The phile's suffering and increased his weeping. He shed whole to rents of tears, and the tears continually increased. He had special vessel, and because his tears would always reappe when he began praying, he would put this vessel before himse so that his tears would fall into it. Some days this vessel woul be full of tears, since every day Theophile expected the end o his life as Blessed Marko had predicted. When Theophile fel that his day of passing to God was drawing near, he began t pray zealously, saying: "Our Lord who loves man, my God, my most holy King, you do not want the death of a sinner; you anticipate their conversion to righteousness. You know our weak nesses, our gracious Comforter. You are health to the ill and salvation for the sinner. You are succor for the exhausted and an uplifting for the fallen. O Lord, I, an unworthy one, pray to you in this hour to show me your amazing grace and to reveal to me the unfathomable depths of your mercy. Deliver me from temptation. Do not permit the enemy to overcome me in my ordeal, but give me strength for the sake of the prayers of your saints and our great fathers, Antonius and Theodosius, and for the sake of the prayers of all saints who have served you since the beginning of time."

And in this moment a beautiful youth appeared before him, and said, "You pray well, but why are you so saddened by the vanity of your tears?" And the youth, taking a vessel much larger than that which Theophile had, and which was filled with the fragrance of myrrh, said: "Here are the tears that have poured forth from your contrite heart during your prayers to

But the monks continued to reproach him still more. Then Marko addressed the dead man: "Brother, your grave is so narrow we cannot even anoint you with holy oil. Take the oil and anoint yourself."

The dead man raised up slightly, extended his hand, took the oil, and anointed his face and chest, making the sign of the cross. He then returned the vessel, adjusted his robes, lay down, and once more died. Awe and trembling seized everyone because of the miracle.

Some time later, after a long illness, another brother died. One of his friends cleansed the body with a sponge and went to the crypt to view the grave where his friend was supposed to lie. He asked Marko about the grave, and Marko answered, "Go to the dead brother and tell him, 'Wait until tomorrow, until I dig your grave, and then you can enter into rest.' "

But the brother, who had come to the crypt, said: "Brother Marko, I have already cleansed the dead man's body with a sponge. How can you now ask me to speak to him?"

Marko once again spoke to him: "You can see for yourself that the grave is not finished. I enjoin you to go and tell the dead man that sinful Marko tells him: 'Brother, live one more day, and then tomorrow you will pass to God in peace. When I have prepared a place for you, I will send for you.' "

The brother who had come to Blessed Marko obeyed. When he returned to the monastery, all the brothers were standing around the dead man and were singing the usual hymns. The monk stood before the dead brother, and said, "Brother Marko has told me to tell you that your grave is not ready and that you should wait until tomorrow."

Everyone was astounded by these words. But as soon as they were spoken by the monk who had returned from Marko, the dead brother's soul returned to his body. The whole day and night he remained with his eyes open, but talked with no one at all.

The next day his friends once more returned to the cave to find out if the place was ready. And Blessed Marko told them: "Go and tell the following to one who has become alive: 'Abandon this provisional life and pass into the life eternal. Here the place is ready for your body. Give your soul to God, and your body will be buried here with many holy brothers.' "

The brothers came and told all this to the dead one who had come alive. Immediately the latter, in the presence of all who had come to visit him, closed his eyes and passed away. And he was placed with honors in the new place in the cave. And everyone wondered about this miracle. How could it be that, with just one word from Blessed Marko, the dead would become alive, and then die once more after Marko ordered it?

Two other brethren in this great Crypt Monastery had since their youth been united by the great love in their hearts. They had the same thoughts and the same desires, which were directed to God. And they begged Blessed Marko to prepare them a common grave where they would be able to lie together when God should order them to do so. Many years later the elder brother, Theophile, left the monastery on business. In the meantime the younger brother became ill and died and was laid in the grave prepared for him. Theophile returned only some days after the burial. Having learned of the death of his brother, he became very sad and, taking some other monks, went to the cave to see in which place the deceased was laid.

Having noticed that his brother was buried in a place that was higher than the place reserved for himself, he was seized by wrath, and began to complain to Marko, saying: "Why did you put him there? I am the older, and therefore should be put in the higher place. But you have buried him in my place."

Marko, the monk of the cave, being a humble man, bowed to Theophile, and said, "Excuse me, my brother, I have sinned before you." Then he said to the deceased, "Brother, give your place to your elder brother and lie down in the lower place." And immediately after these words of Blessed Marko, the dead man got up in the presence of all the monks and lay down in the lower place. Everyone saw this terrible and awe-inspiring miracle.

Then brother Theophile, who had reproached Marko, fell to his knees and said: "Brother Marko, I have sinned by moving my brother from his place. Tell him to return to the original place."

But Blessed Marko told Theophile: "God ended the enmity between us. He did so because you complained and so that you might be prevented from lasting enmity and evil feelings toward me. Even this soulless body has demonstrated its love to you, respecting your seniority even after death. I should like you to make use of your seniority by not leaving this crypt, but by lying down in this place. But you are not ready for passing away. Therefore, go and care for your soul. In some days from now you will be brought to this place. The resurrection of the dead is the work of God, whereas I am only a miserable sinner.

Look on your dead brother, who was not able to bea[r the] reproaches with which you covered me. And he left you a[ny] of the place that was prepared for both of you. God can r[aise] the dead, but I cannot say, 'Go down and lie in the lo[wer] place,' and then say, 'Go up and lie in the higher place.' If y[ou] want him to go back to his former place, order it, and perhap[s] he will go back to the place he left before."

Having heard these words, Theophile became saddened, and he thought that he would be unable to walk back to the monastery. When he returned to his cell, he began to cry disconsolately. He distributed everything he had, and kept only his mantle and robe. From that time forth, he was in permanent expectation of death, and no one could bring an end to his bitter crying and no one could convince him to eat well.

At the beginning of the day he would say to himself, "I don't know whether I shall live till evening." When evening was approaching, he would cry and say: "What should I do? Shall I be able to live till morning? Many people who arose this morning were not able to live until evening, but were obliged to lie down and were unable to get up again. And what of me? For I was told by Blessed Marko that my end was very near." And he spent each day mortifying his flesh with fasting, praying, and incessant weeping, expecting each day that his final hour was approaching. The expectation that his soul would soon be separated from his body exhausted him to such an extent that it became possible to count his ribs. Many people wished to console him, but this made him weep only the more. Finally, because of his incessant tears, he became blind. And so Theophile spent his days in great abstinence, thereby winning the grace of God by his exemplary life.

When Marko learned the hour of his own passing to God, he asked Theophile to come, and he told him: "Brother Theophile, forgive me for having caused you great sadness, lo! these many years. Now I leave this world. Pray for me. If I receive God's mercy, I shall not forget you. Let us pray that we may see each other with our fathers, Antonius and Theodosius, in the next life."

And Theodosius answered tearfully: "Father Marko, why do you leave me here? Why don't you return my sight to me?"

Marko told him: "Brother, don't grieve. Thanks to God you have lost your physical sight, but you have won the insight for understanding him with your spiritual eyes. My brother, I was responsible for your blindness, for I prophesied your death. But I did so for the sake of your soul, for I wanted to turn your

God. All your tears that you dried neither with your hand nor with your robe nor with a cloth fell from your eyes to the earth. All of them, at the command of the Creator, I gathered and preserved in this vessel. Now I have been sent to you to announce tidings of joy. With joy will you go to the one who said, 'Blessed are they that mourn, for they shall be comforted.' Having spoken these words, the youth disappeared.

After this, Blessed Theophile asked the abbot to come to his cell, and he told him of the appearance of the angel and of the angel's words. He showed the abbot both vessels, one of which was filled with tears and the other with a fragrance that could not be compared to any other. And Blessed Theophile asked that the contents of both vessels be poured over his body after his death.

Three days later, Blessed Theophile passed to the Lord and was buried in the crypt near the grave of Marko the gravedigger. And when the contents of the angel's vessel were spread over his body, the entire crypt was filled with a wondrous sweet fragrance. And the monks also poured the contents of the vessel of tears over him, doing this so that he who had shed these tears might harvest the fruits of his labor.

APOCRYPHA

17. *The Descent of the Virgin into Hell*

AFTER the Christianization of Russia under Prince Vladimi canonical books, such as the Bible, liturgic texts, and the work of the early Church Fathers, circulated through the Russia land. In addition to these, a considerable number of apocrypha or noncanonical writings came to Russia. Patterned after th Bible and written at the time of the New Testament, they wer never recognized by the Church. Among such works, *The Descent of the Virgin Into Hell*, or, as it was called by Russians *The Visitation to the Torments by the Mother of God*, is th most distinguished owing to its concept of divine mercy and th originality of its composition. "A visit to hell" was a subjec common to both Eastern and Western Christianity, its mos famous version being, of course, Dante's great poem *The Divin Comedy*.

The juxtaposition of eschatological concepts with the concep of divine mercy, as presented in this work, greatly influence the Russian religious mind and was reflected in medieval Russian *vitae*, spiritual songs, and icons.

This translation is based on the text of a seventeenth-centur manuscript that was revised and corrected by Professor N. K Gudzy according to a twelfth-century manuscript, and it appeared in his *Khrestomatiia po drevnei russkoi literature*, Moscow, 1955, pages 92–98. Some portions of this translation follov that of Professor L. Wiener.

◆ ◆ ◆

The Holy Virgin wished to see the torments of the souls, an so she said to the archangel, Michael, "I ask that you tell m all things which are upon the earth." And the archangel answered, "I shall tell you all things which are upon the eart Blessed One, as you would have it." And the Holy Virgin aske him, "How many torments does the Christian race suffer?" An the archangel said, "Innumerable are those torments." And the the Holy Virgin replied, "Show me what is in heaven and upo the earth."

Then the archangel ordered the angels to come from th south, and Hell was opened. And she saw those that were su fering in Hell, and there were a great number of them and there was much weeping. And the Blessed Virgin asked the archangel: "Who are these that they suffer so?"

And the archangel answered: "These are those who did not believe in the Father, the Son, and the Holy Ghost, but forgot God and believed in those things which God created for our sakes. They called the sun and the moon, beast and reptiles, earth and water God. And they made gods out of the devils Troyan, Khors, Veles, and Perun, and they worshiped these evil devils. And even now they are possessed by evil darkness, and therefore they suffer such torments."

And the Holy Virgin saw great darkness in another place. And she asked, "What is this darkness and who are those who dwell therein?" And the archangel answered, saying, "Many souls dwell in this place." And the Holy Virgin said, "Let the darkness be dispersed that I may see the torment." And the angels who watched over the torment answered, "We have been enjoined not to let them see light until the coming of your blessed Son, who is brighter than seven suns." And the Holy Virgin was saddened, and she raised her eyes to the angels and looked at the invisible throne of her father and said: "In the name of the Father, and the Son, and the Holy Ghost! Let this darkness be dispersed that I may see this torment."

And the darkness was dispersed and seven heavens appeared and there was a great multitude of men and women. And there were loud weeping and wailing in this place. And seeing them, the Holy Virgin said, weeping: "What have you done, wretched and unworthy people? What has brought you here?" But there was no voice nor any answer from them. And the watching angels spoke, "Wherefore do you not speak?" And one who was tormented replied, "Blessed One! For ages we have seen no light and we cannot look up." The Holy Virgin, looking on them, wept bitterly.

And a tormented one, seeing her, said: "How is it, Holy Virgin, that you have visited us? Your blessed Son came upon the earth and did not ask us, nor did Abraham the Patriarch, nor Moses the Prophet, nor John the Baptist, nor Paul the Apostle, the favorite of the Lord. But you, most Holy Virgin, are an intercessor and protector for the Christian people. You have prayed to God for us, but how did it come to pass that you have visited us, wretched as we be?"

Then the Holy Virgin inquired what was the sin of these tormented ones, and Michael answered: "These are they who did not believe in the Father, the Son, and the Holy Ghost, nor in you, Holy Virgin! They did not want to proclaim your name, nor that from you was born our Lord Jesus Christ who, having come in the flesh, has sanctified the earth through baptism. It is for this that they are tormented in this place."

Weeping, the Holy Virgin spoke to them. "Wherefore do you live in error? Do you not know that all creation honors my name?" And when the Holy Virgin finished speaking, darkness once more fell upon them.

And Michael said to her: "Whither, Blessed One, do you wish to go now: to the south or to the north?" And when the Virgin replied that she would go to the south, there appeared cherubim and seraphim and four hundred angels who took the Holy Virgin to the south. And there the Holy Virgin saw a river of fire. There was a multitude of men and women who stood in this fiery river. Some stood in the river to their waists, some to their shoulders, some to their necks, and some above their necks. Seeing this, the Holy Virgin exclaimed in a loud voice, "Who are they that stand in the fire up to their waists?" And the Archangel answered, "They are those that have been cursed by their fathers and mothers, and being so cursed, they are tormented here." And when the Holy Virgin inquired who were those who stood in the fire to their shoulders, Michael replied, "They are those who have cursed and indulged in lechery, and therefore are tormented in this place." And the Virgin asked, "Who are those that are in the fiery flame up to their necks?" And Michael answered, saying: "They are those who have eaten human flesh. For this they are tormented here." And the Holy Virgin then asked, "Those who are immersed in the fiery flame above their heads, who are they?" Michael the Archangel replied: "They are those, Lady, who, holding the cross, have sworn falsely. Such is the power of the cross that it is worshiped with awe by the angels and they tremble before it. And so, when a man swears by the cross and then lies, he is punished by such a torment."

And then the Holy Virgin saw a man who was hanging by his heels, and worms were devouring him. And she asked the archangel who he was and what were his sins. And the archangel answered, "They are those who took interest on their silver and gold, and therefore they are tormented in this place."

And then she saw a woman who was hanging by one tooth, and various serpents came from her mouth and were devouring her. The Holy Virgin, seeing this, asked Michael: "Who is this woman? What is her sin?" And the archangel answered, "Lady, this one is she who used to say evil words and gossiped, which led to evil discourse among her neighbors, and therefore she is damned." And the Holy Virgin replied, "Blessed be the woman who does not give birth to such a sinner."

And then Michael said, "Holy Virgin, you have not yet seen the greatest torments." And the Holy Virgin replied: "Let us go and visit so that I may see all torments." And, when Michael inquired where she should like to go, the Holy Virgin asked to go to the north. And then seraphim and cherubim and four hundred angels took the Blessed One to the north where there was a great fiery cloud, and in this fiery cloud there were fiery places to lie down. In these places were a great many men and women. And the Holy Virgin, weeping, asked who these men and women were and what were their sins. And the archangel replied: "Lady, those are the ones who, during holy weeks, did not get up to attend the Easter Midnight Service, but lay in bed lazily as if dead. Therefore, they are tormented in this place." And the Holy Virgin asked, "And those who were not able to get up, are they also condemned as sinners?" And Michael answered, "Holy Lady, only those who cannot get up even when their house be in flame on all four sides do not sin when they do not go to church."

And the Holy Virgin saw a big iron tree with branches of iron on which there were iron barbs. On these barbs hung a great many men and women by their tongues. Seeing them, the Holy Virgin began to sob, and asked Michael who these people were and what was their sin. And the archangel replied, "These people are calumniators and gossipers who separate brother from brother and husband from wife."

And she saw women hanging by their fingernails, and fire came from their mouths and burned them. And serpents came out of the flames and tormented them. And they cried out, saying, "Be merciful unto us, for we are tormented beyond all other torments." And the Holy Virgin asked what were their sins. And Michael answered, "These are the widows of priests who did not revere the office of the priesthood, but married other men after the death of their priestly husbands."

And the Virgin saw other women who were lying in fire and were devoured by various serpents, and Michael said, "These are nuns from convents who sold their bodies for lechery, and therefore they are tormented."

And the archangel said to the Blessed Virgin, "Come hither, Holy Virgin, and I will show you the place where many sinners are tormented." And the Holy Virgin saw the river of flames. And the river appeared as if it were flowing blood and it covered the whole earth. In the middle of this river were a great many sinners. Seeing these, the Virgin wept, and asked, "What is their sin?" And the archangel Michael answered, "These are the whores and the adulterers, those who listen to gossip, the matchmakers and calumniators, the drunkards, merciless princes, bishops, and archbishops, tsars who did not fulfill the will of God, the usurers, who collected interest, and the lawbreakers." Hearing this, the Blessed Virgin wept, and said, "Oh, these evil sinners, it would have been better if they had never been born!"

And Michael asked her: "Wherefore do you weep, Holy One? Have you never seen such great torments before?" And the Blessed Virgin answered, "Take me farther, that I may see all torments that are." And Michael asked, "Where do you wish to go, Blessed One, to the east or to the west, to the right into paradise or to the left where are the greatest torments?" And as soon as the Virgin replied that she wished to go to the left, there appeared seraphim and cherubim and four hundred angels and they took the Most Holy One to the east, to the left. And in the vicinity of the river there was a great darkness, and in the river there came many men and women, and it appeared as if the water were boiling. And great waves broke upon the sinners, and when the waves rose they drowned the sinners in a thousand feet of water, so that they were not even able to utter, "Righteous Judge, be merciful unto us!" And there was much gnashing of teeth in this place, since the sinners were devoured by the worms.

And seeing the Holy Virgin, the host of angels that watched over the sinners exclaimed in unison: "Holy, Holy, Holy! Holy God and you, Holy Virgin, we bless you and the Son of God born of you. For ages we have not seen light, but now, praise be to you, we have seen the light." And once more all of them exclaimed: "Rejoice, Blessed Virgin. Rejoice, Source of Light Eternal. Rejoice, Holy Archangel Michael and pray to our Lord for the entire world, for we have seen the sinners who are tormented, and we are very saddened."

The Holy Virgin, seeing the angels saddened and filled with sorrow because of the torments of the sinners, began to weep. And all exclaimed in unison, saying: "It is good that you have come to this darkness, for now you have seen their torments. Most Holy Lady and Archangel Michael, pray for them." And she heard the sobs and voices of the sinners who raised their laments, saying, "God have mercy upon us!" And the Virgin said, "God have mercy upon them." And as soon as she had said this, the tempest on the river of fiery waves ceased. And the sinners gained the hope in a tiny mustard seed. And the Holy Virgin, seeing this, wept and said, "What is this river and of what are its waves?" And Michael answered: "This river is a river of hot pitch, and its waves are of flame. And the Jews are tormented here because they tormented our Lord, Jesus Christ. And those who were baptized in the name of the Father, the Son, and Holy Ghost and still believed in demons and rejected God and baptism are also tormented in this place. And those who committed lechery with their mothers and daughters, and those who murdered with poisons or who killed with weapons, or who strangled their children are tormented in this place. Because of such deeds they are tormented. And the Holy Virgin said, "They deserve this for their sins." And when she had said these words the fiery waves once again enveloped the sinners, and darkness betook them. And Michael said to the Holy Virgin, "There is no thought of God for those who are lost in darkness." And the Most Holy One said: "O evil sinners, the flame of this fire shall never become extinguished."

And then the Holy Virgin spoke, saying: "I have only one request. Let me also enter, that I may suffer together with the Christians, for they have called themselves the children of my Son." And the archangel said, "Rest yourself in paradise!" And the Holy Virgin replied, "I beg you, move the host of the angels that we may pray for the sinners, and God may accept our prayer and have mercy upon them."

The archangel replied, saying: "Great is the name of our Lord God. Seven times in the day and seven times in the night do we bring praises and worship our Lady for the sake of the sinners. And we hope that our Lord will listen to our prayers." And the Holy Virgin answered, "I beg you, order that the angelic host carry me to the heavenly height and take me before the invisible Father."

And the archangel so ordered, and there appeared cherubim and seraphim, and they carried the Blessed One to the heavenly height, and put her down at the throne of the invisible Father. She raised her hands to her Blessed Son and said: "Have mercy, O Lord, upon the sinners, for I have seen them, and I could not endure. Let me be tormented together with the Christians." And there came a voice to her which said: "I see nails in my Son's hands. How can I have mercy upon them?" And she said: "I do pray for the infidel Jews, but for the Christians I ask thy mercy." And a voice again came to her, saying: "I see how they have had no mercy upon my brethren, so I can have no mercy upon them."

And the Holy Virgin again spoke, saying: "Have mercy, O Lord, upon the sinners, the creation of thine own hands, who proclaim thy name over the whole earth and even in their torments, and who in all places say, 'Most Holy Lady, Mother of God, intercede for us.' And when a child is born people say, 'Most Holy Virgin, help us.' "

Then the Lord spoke to her: "Hear, Holy Virgin! There is not a human being who does not praise thy name. I will not abandon them, neither in heaven nor upon the earth." Then the Holy Virgin asked: "Where is Moses the Prophet? Where are all the prophets? And you, Fathers, who have never committed a sin? Where is Paul, God's favorite? Where is Sunday, the pride of the Christian? And where is the power of the pure cross through which Adam and Eve were delivered from their curse?"

Then the Archangel Michael and all the angels cried, "Have mercy, O Lord, upon the sinners!" And Moses wept aloud and said, "Have mercy upon them, O Lord, for I have given them thy Law!" And John wept and cried out, "Have mercy, O Lord, for I have preached thy Gospel to them." And Paul wept and said: "Have mercy, O Lord, for I carried thine epistles to the churches." [Here a fragment is missing, but it is apparent from the text that follows that God did not concede to the prayers of the Holy Virgin and the saints.] And the saints, hearing the voice of the Lord, did not dare to answer.

The Most Holy Virgin, seeing that she could not intercede and that God would neither listen to their pleas nor take mercy on the sinners, said: "Where is the Archangel Gabriel who announced to me, 'Rejoice, because you have heard the Father before all ages and he will take away his reproach among men?' . . . [fragment missing]. And where are the servants of the throne and where is St. John the Theologian? Wherefore did they not appear with us to pray for these Christian sinners? Don't you see that I shed tears for the sinners? Come, all angels which are in the heavens. Come, all righteous people acquitted by God, since you are given the right to pray for sinners. And come you, Michael, for you are the first incorporeal one and are next to the throne. Let us all pray to the invisible Father for mercy, and let us not move away as long as he will not have mercy unto the sinners."

And Michael bowed to the ground before the throne, and with him bowed all those who are in heaven and all the incorporeal angels. Then the Lord, seeing the intercession of the saints, became merciful for his Son's sake, and said, "Come down, my beloved Son, and listen to the prayers of the saints and appear before the sinners."

And the Lord came down from the invisible throne, and all sinners who were in the darkness exclaimed in unison, "Have mercy upon us, King of All Ages! Have mercy upon us, Son of God!"

And the Lord then said: "Hear all! I have planted paradise, and have created man in my own image, and made him lord over paradise, and gave him life eternal. But they have disobeyed me and sinned in their selfishness and delivered themselves unto death. And since I did not want to see deeds done by hands which were forced by the devil, I came to earth and became incarnate through the Virgin. And I was raised to the cross to free them from slavery and the original curse. And I asked for water, but I was given gall mixed with vinegar. My hand created man and man put me into the grave. I descended to Hell and defeated the enemy and raised the selected ones. And I blessed the river Jordan to save you from original sin, but you did not care to repent for your sins. You became Christians only in words, and did not keep my commandments. For this you find yourselves in the fire everlasting, and I ought not to have mercy upon you! But today, by the mercy of my Father who sent me to you, and through the intercession of my Mother who has wept much for you, and through Michael, the archangel of the Gospel, and through the multitude of martyrs who have labored much in your behalf, I give you from Good Thursday to Holy Pentecost, day and night, for rest and for praising the Father, and the Son, and the Holy Ghost!"

And they all answered, "Glory be to thy mercy!" Glory to the Father, and to the Son, and to the Holy Ghost, now and forever. Amen.

18. *Adam's Address to Lazarus in Hell*

Among early Russian writings that cannot be dated with certitude a very prominent place is occupied by *Adam's Address to Lazarus in Hell.* Its style and content indicate that this work was written in the Kievan era and probably in the same century as the *Lay of Igor's Campaign*, with which it has many parallels. Its content is definitely apocryphal, but it is still difficult to determine whether the original text is Byzantine or Russian. The topic of this work is Adam's address to Lazarus in hell before he had been raised from the dead by Jesus. The address consists of two rather different parts, the first being poetic and original, while the second is composed of quotations from the Gospel, and apparently has been corrupted by the scribes.

The final text has been established by M. Hruchevsky, who divided the work into poetic lines. The translation offered here was published anonymously in *The Slavonic Review*, Volume X, 1931, pages 246–252. Several stylistic corrections have been made by the present editor.

◆ ◆ ◆

Hear, heaven, attend, earth,
how speaks the Lord.
"I bore sons and exalted them,
and they have rejected me.
The ass recognizes his master's manger,
But my people have not recognized me.
And behold I will not give my glory to another
but will send my Word on earth
that I may save my people from the meshes of Satan."

"Brethren, let us today sing songs,
let us cast aside grief, and be full of joy,"
spoke David, seated in infernal Hell,
setting his eyed fingers on the live strings.
And he struck the lute and said:
"For now has come a joyful time,
for now has come the day of salvation.
For I hear shepherds
playing the reed in the cave,
And their voice passes the gates of Hell
and enters my ears.
And I hear the trampling of feet of Persian horses,
that carry the Magi with their gifts for him,
from their kings to the King of Heaven,
who has today been born on earth.
And him, brethren,
we have been awaiting for many days,
whose throne is heaven
and whose feet rest on the earth.
The maiden mother
wraps him in swaddling cloths

who wraps the heavens in clouds
and the earth in darkness.
And she speaks bending over him:
"O great and heavenly king,
how hast thou willed
to descend to us on the earth in poverty?
Hast thou desired this cave,
and this manger,
in which thou liest now?
And lo, how soon does the furious Herod
shake as he sharpens his sword against thee,
wishing to kill thee,
whose throne is heaven
and whose feet rest on the earth."
And Adam spoke,
to those that were with him in Hell:
"Come, ye prophets
and all ye just men,
let us send a message to the Lord,
into the living world,
to the Lord Christ
asking him with tears
whether he wishes
to release us
from these torments?"
And Isaiah and Jeremiah,
upbraiding Hell
and his impotent power,
said to David:
"But who can carry the message
from us to him?
Gates of brass,
posts of iron,
locks of stone,
solidly sealed."
Then David spake to them clearly:
"Isaiah, Jeremiah, Aaron,
Ezekiel, Solomon,
Adam, Abraham, Isaac,
Jacob, Samuel, Daniel,
and all the seventeen prophets
attend to my voice:
Tomorrow will go from us
Lazarus the four-dayed,

friend of Christ.
He from us
will carry the message."

And hearing this, Adam,
first-created of men,
began beating his face
with his hands.
Groaning heavily,
he exclaimed and said:
"Tell the Lord about me,
Lazarus, glorious friend of Christ:
Thus cries to thee
thy first-created Adam:
Was it for this, Lord, thou createdst me
to be on this earth
for but a short age
only to condemn me
to be tormented in Hell for many years?
Was it for this, O Lord, that thou madest the earth full?
For now thy beloved ones,
my grandchildren, lie in darkness
in the pit of Hell—tormented by pain
and finding their joy in their grief.
They wash their eyes with tears
and gladden their hearts with grief
and are downcast exceedingly.
For on this earth
but a short while did we know prosperity,
and now in this sorrow
many years are we in duress.

For a short while was I king
of all God's creatures,
and now for many days
am I slave to Hell
and captive to devils.

For a short while did I see thy light,
and now it is many a year
that I do not see thy bright sun
nor hear the stormy winds,
O Lord.

If I have sinned
worse than any man,

it is according to my deserts
thou hast assigned to me these torments,
I do not complain, O Lord.

But this is what fills me with pity–
I was created in thine image,
and now I am upbraided,
cruelly tormented by the devil,
who oppresses me, O Lord.

If I, Adam,
while I lived in nature,
broke thy divine commandment,
behold, O Lord,
Abraham, first patriarch,
and thy friend
who for thy sake was ready
to sacrifice his son,
his beloved Isaac,
but thou saidst:
Through thee, Abraham, all the generation on earth shall be blessed.
In what way has he sinned
that he should be tormented here in Hell
and sigh heavily?
Descend, O Lord, for the sake of Abraham,
or has Abraham, too, sinned unto thee, O Lord?

And behold thy servants
Isaac and Jacob his son
lying in thraldom in the infernal Hell.

And behold Noah, the just,
whom thou, O Lord,
deliveredst from fierce deluge,
and canst thou not deliver him from Hell?
Or maybe he too has sinned
like myself?

And behold thy great prophet Moses,
who led the Jews through the Red Sea,
and spoke with thee on the Mountain of Sinai
and in the burning bush face to face,
in what way, O Lord, has he sinned
that he too should lie with us in the darkness of Hell?
Or maybe, Moses, too, O Lord, has sinned unto thee?

And David, O Lord,
whom thyself exaltedst on earth
and gave him to reign over many men,
and he did make the psalter and lute,
in what way has he sinned, Lord?
But he too is tormented together with us in this Hell,
and sighs, as he groans frequently,
or maybe he too has sinned
in the same way as myself?

And here, O Lord, is thy prophet Isaiah,
who from his mother's womb was lifted to heaven
and then returned into his mother's womb,
like as thou too, O Lord, didst descend into the womb
of a maiden,
and he too, O Lord, is with us in Hell,
or maybe Isaiah, too, has sinned, O Lord?

And here is thy great prophet Daniel,
son of Ezekiel the prophet,
who carried about a wooden rack in a frame,
who prefigured thy divine passion,
who smote the golden body in Babylon
and was cast into the lions' den,
and he, Lord, is with us in Hell
or maybe Isaiah, too, has sinned, O Lord?

And here, Lord, is Solomon son of David
who erected for thee a house in Jerusalem
and cast two eagles of gold
like unto cherubim and seraphim,
and spake: If God is on earth,
the Holy Ghost will descend on the two eagles.
And the two eagles flew round the church
and ascended to heaven.

And here is John, great among prophets,
The Lord's Precursor, the Baptist,
who was born from the annunciation of Gabriel,
who from youth grew up in the wilderness,
eating wild honey.
In what way has he sinned, O Lord?
On earth he was dishonored by Herod,
and now together with us he is tormented in Hell.

And here thy prophets complain,
Elijah and Enoch who pleased thee
more than all just men on earth.
No longer, O Lord, do we see
Thy resplendent sun
nor thy gratifying light,
but instead are possessed by sorrow
and downcast with grief.
Or maybe the prophets too have sinned unto thee?

Is it for the sake of our sins that thou wilt not release
us?
or art thou biding thy time?
If thou willst descend thyself,
thou alone knowest it,
But we are yearning men
and thou art longsuffering and without malice.
Come to us soon,
release us from Hell and bind the devil,
that the mutinous Jews may know thee,
and we all may worship thee."

And hearing this the Lord went to Bethany, to Mary the sister of Lazarus and of Martha; and Mary and Martha, as soon as they heard that he was coming, hastened forth and falling at his feet and wiping his feet with their hair said, "Lord, if thou hadst been here, our brother Lazarus had not died." And the Lord said to Martha and Mary, "Your brother shall rise again."

And Hell spake to the devil:

"I hear.
My soul is sad at having to release Lazarus,
and I am sore pressed to cast forth Adam."

And the Lord said to Mary and Martha: Where have ye laid him? And they came to the grave, and the Lord told them to take away the stone from the entrance of the grave. And Mary and Martha said: Lord, by this time he stinketh, for he hath been dead four days. And the Lord said: If ye would believe, ye should see the glory of God. And he lifted up his eyes and said, Lazarus, come forth. And Lazarus rose at once, bound with grave clothes, and the Lord said, Loose him.

And when Lazarus had risen from Hell, he spake to the Lord: "Lord, thy prophets in Hell cry unto thee, Adam the first-created and Abraham the patriarch with Isaac his son and Jacob his grandson. David cries unto thee on behalf of Solomon his son, 'Lead us out of Hell.' "

And the Lord spake to Lazarus: "Had it not been for David my beloved servant, I would have destroyed Solomon in Hell." And the Lord descended to Hell in person, and a multitude of heavenly warriors with him, Semiel, and Raguel, and Ismael, and Nanael, Tartarus, Gabriel, Michael, and all the angels advanced with the cross against Hell, saying, "Lift the gates of eternity and let the gates of sorrow be taken, that the King of Glory may enter."

And the angels and the prophets spake: "The Lord is strong and terrible in battle, for he is the King of Glory. Let them be taken."

And the great king David spake: "When I was alive . . .[1] that the gates of brass be overthrown and the posts of iron be broken.

And then will the Lord overthrow the gates of brass and break the posts of iron."

And the Lord spake to Adam: "This hand created thee from the beginning of time, and the same will lead thee out of corruption."

And then Jesus arose and said to his apostles: "Go Forth, preach to all lands, baptising in the name of the Father, the Son, and the Holy Ghost, teaching to obey them . . ." And the Lord himself ascended to heaven and was seated on the right hand of the Father, and all over the earth is his glory, of Christ Jesus our Lord.

[1] An apparent lacuna.

MILITARY TALES

19. *The Lay of Igor's Campaign*

WRITTEN on the occasion of Prince Igor's unfortunate campaign against the Kumans in 1185, the *Lay of Igor's Campaign* (*Slovo o polku Igoreve*) is unanimously acclaimed as the highest achievement in Russian literature of the Kievan era.

Igor was himself a well-known historical personality, a prince of Novgorod-Seversk (not to be confused with Novgorod "the great," the metropolis of northern Russia). Novgorod-Seversk, now a small city on the border between the Russian and Ukrainian S.S.R.'s, was at that time one of the Russian strongholds against the Kumans, nomads of Turkic origin who inhabited the prairie of southern Russia. Prince Igor (1151–1202), one of the leaders of Russian political and military activities of that region, began his campaign in 1185 to drive out these nomadic invaders, who, every year, would raid Russian territories, burn the cities and take the inhabitants as slaves. Relying only on his own military forces and those of his relatives, Igor moved into the prairie with no support from the other Russian rulers. This campaign ended in defeat and in Igor's capture by the Kumans, although he later escaped from them.

Though much is known about Igor, practically nothing is known about the author of the *Lay of Igor's Campaign*. One can only presume that he belonged to Igor's court, was a warrior, and, as is evident from his *Lay*, was very familiar with the life and environment of the prairie. Even less can be said of the literary antecedents of the work and of the epic tradition previous to it. It is true that the writer of the *Lay* often mentions Boyan, a bard who apparently lived in the eleventh century, but no details are known either of his life or of his poetic works.

The *Lay* is a poetic masterpiece and a highly sophisticated literary work. The word "poetic" should not be understood here in its narrower sense, since the *Lay* is neither rhymed nor organized in verses, nor does it follow any metrical pattern. The rhythm and the length of the sentences to some extent replace verse organization. Beside rhythm, the poetic elements of the *Lay* comprise an extremely rich imagery constructed primarily on parallels with nature, symbolism, poetic address, and lyric lamentation. Among other devices, the author of the *Lay* employs the repetition of characteristic images, stylized descriptions of military action, assonance and alliteration. Unfortunately, the latter are impossible to reproduce in translation. The structure of the *Lay* is by no means that of a narrative poem and rather than being an epic tale, per se, it is much more a lament over the feudal discord in medieval Russia, a stern admonition to the princes responsible for the fratricidal feuds. The writer's forebodings of impending disaster in the Russian land proved to be true, for only fifty years after Igor's defeat and the writing of the *Lay*, Russia was subjugated by the Mongol-Tatars and lost her independence for two hundred years.

Three distinct structural planes can be discerned in the *Lay*. The first concerns the destiny of Prince Igor, his campaign, defeat, and escape from the Kumans. This plane, the narrative core of the work, is somewhat clouded by invocations to the late bard, Boyan, reminiscences of past glory, and the allusive atmosphere of foreboding. The second plane consists of portents and lamentations over the outcome of the campaign and Russia's fate, such as the dream of Prince Sviatoslav of Kiev and the lament of Yaroslavna, the wife of Igor. The final plane consists of the author's admonitions to the princes to unite, and his censure of their feuding.

Unfortunately, the *Lay* was preserved in only one copy, discovered at the end of the eighteenth century and first printed in 1800. This single copy, which was subsequently destroyed in a fire in Moscow during the Napoleonic invasion in 1812, was itself defective, and so the first edition of the *Lay* was an unsatisfactory one reflecting the low standard of scholarship and interpretation of ancient manuscripts of that time. Many portions were apparently misread or misinterpreted, and in some places inadequately deciphered. Despite the efforts of generations of scholars and voluminous research, several passages in the *Lay* still remain incomprehensible, and have lent themselves to contradictory interpretations. In the present translation such passages have been placed in brackets.

The text that was used for the present translation of the *Lay of Igor's Campaign* is that revised by S. D. Likhachev and published in the series *Literaturnye pamiatniki*, Moscow-Leningrad 1950. However, the present translator has made wide use of the text and interpretations of Professor Roman Jakobson of Harvard University, who offers numerous and extremely ingenious explanations of certain unclear passages, while others have been interpreted in the light of such research as that on nature symbolism by N. V. Charlemagne.

The *Lay's* complex symbolism, structure, imagery, and philosophy require a more detailed commentary than any other medieval Russian work. Notes on the symbolism of the *Lay* and on Russian literary tradition appear at the bottom of each page, as well as comments pertaining to historical and geographical names specific to the work. Finally, references of a more general type can be found in the Introduction and in the Glossary.

The typographical arrangement and the chapter and stanza form given here are in agreement with authoritative publications of the *Lay* and also reflect this editor's feeling that they contribute to readability. For the sake of better understanding, some explanatory words have been added in parentheses and proper names have been preceded by the words "prince," "river," or "city."

◆ ◆ ◆

I. Invocation

Might it not behoove us, brethren
to commence in ancient strains
the stern lay of Igor's campaign,
  Igor, son of Sviatoslav?
Then let this begin
according to the events of our time,
and not according to the cunning of Boyan.[1]
For he, Boyan the Seer,
when composing a song to someone,
soared in his thoughts over the tree (of wisdom[2]),
ran as a gray wolf over the land,
flew below the clouds as a blue-gray eagle.

When he recalled the feuds of former times
he would let loose ten falcons upon a flock of swans.
  And the first swan overtaken
  was the first to sing a song
  to old Yaroslav,[3]

[1] Apparently a bard who lived in the eleventh century and who composed songs in honor of the Russian princes.

[2] Apparently this refers to the tree of wisdom or thought, a common symbol of Eastern mythology.

[3] Prince of Kiev from 1019 through 1054. He is considered the greatest ruler of Russia during the Kievan era.

to brave Mstislav,[4]
who slew Rededia[5] before the Kasog regiments,
and to handsome Roman,[6] son of Sviatoslav.

Boyan, however, did not let loose ten falcons
upon the flock of swans.
But rather he lay his wise fingers
upon the living strings
and they sounded lauds to the princes.
Let us begin this narration, brethren,
from the old times of Vladimir[7] to this present time of Igor,
who strengthened his mind with courage,
who quickened his heart with valor
and, thus imbued with martial spirit,
led his valiant regiments
against the Kuman land
in defense of the Russian land.

II. Prince Igor Prepares His Campaign

Igor looked up at the bright sun,
and saw that all his warriors
became enveloped in darkness.[8]
And Igor spoke to his army:
"Brethren and warriors!
It is better to be killed in battle,
than to become a captive.
Let us mount our swift steeds, brethren!
Let us view the blue river Don."

And the prince's mind was seized by ambition.
And the desire to drink from the great river Don
concealed the evil omens from him.
And he spoke:
"I want to break a lance at the Kuman frontier.
I want, oh, my Russians,

4 Mstislav the Brave, the brother of Yaroslav the Wise and Prince of Tmutorakan, a principality located on the Caucasian shore between the Black and Azov seas.

5 A prince of the Kasogs, now called the Cherkess, who was slain by Mstislav.

6 Roman the Handsome, a prince of Tmutorakan who was killed by the Kumans in 1079.

7 Apparently Vladimir the Saint, the Christianizer of Russia.

8 The author probably meant that the sun was eclipsed. An eclipse of the sun occurred on May 1, 1185.

either to drink with you Don (water) from my helmet,
or to leave my head there."
Oh, Boyan, the nightingale of yore!
If you were to sing the glory of the (Russian) campaign,
like a nightingale would you soar over the tree (of wisdom),
soaring in your mind up under the clouds
and singing the glory of both these ages.[9]
You would race along the trail of Trojan,[10]
over the prairies and the mountains.
And the god Veles' grandson
would sing Igor's song (thusly),
"It is not a storm that has driven
the falcons over the wide prairies.
It is a flock of jackdaws
racing toward the great river Don."

Or you, Boyan the Seer, grandson of god Veles, would sing:
"Steeds neigh beyond the river Sula.
Glory resounds in the city of Kiev.
Trumpets blare in the city of Novgorod.
Banners fly over the city of Putivl."[11]
Igor awaits his dear brother, Vsevolod.
This fierce auroch, Vsevolod,[12] (comes to him and) speaks:
"My only brother, Igor,
you are my only bright light.
We are both the sons of Sviatoslav.
Brother, order the saddling of your swift steeds,
as my (swift steeds) are ready.
They were already saddled at the city of Kursk.
And my men of Kursk are famed as warriors.
They were swaddled under trumpets.
They were brought up under helmets.
They were fed at lance point.
The roads are known to them.
The ravines are familiar to them.
Their bows are taut,

[9] The glorious age of Vladimir and this age of Igor. (See "Invocation.")

[10] Trojan: the meaning of this word is not clear. It may refer to Trajan, Emperor of Rome (98–117), who campaigned in southern Russia, to a Slavic and Balkan deity, or the city of Troy.

[11] Novgorod-Seversk and Putivl: important cities in Igor's principality.

[12] Fierce auroch Vsevolod: Igor's brother, who died in 1196, was prince of Trubchevsk and Kursk.

their quivers are open,
their sabers have been sharpened.
They race into the prairie like gray wolves,
seeking honor for themselves
and glory for their prince."

III. The Omens

Then Prince Igor set his foot in the golden stirrup
and rode into the open prairie.
The sun barred his way with darkness[13]
and night, moaning with tempest, awoke the birds.
The whistling of the beasts arose.
And the Div[14] arose and from the treetops it cried,
enjoying unknown lands to listen:
the land of the Volga,
the land on the Azov Sea,
the land at the river Sula,[15]
the city of Surozh,
the city of Kherson,[16]
and you, the idol of the city of Tmutorakan.[17]

The Kumans hastened by untrodden ways
to the great river Don.
Their carts squeak at midnight,
one may say, as dispersed swans.
Igor leads his warriors to the river Don.
The birds in the forests of oak portend his misfortune.
The wolves conjure the tempest in the ravines.
The screeching eagles call the beasts to the feast of bones.
Foxes bark at crimson shields.

O Russian land! You are already far beyond the hills.

IV. The First Day of Battle: The Russians Are Victorious

Evening was fading late into the night.
Finally the glow of dawn faded.
Mist enveloped the prairie.

13 Again the author wishes to say that the sun was eclipsed.

14 A deity in the form of a bird that represented foreboding for the Russians.

15 A tributary of the river Dnieper.

16 Surozh and Kherson: Greek cities in the Crimea.

17 Idol of Tmutorakan: probably a colossal idol that was held in veneration by the Kumans.

The song of the nightingale had died out.
The daws have begun to caw.
Russian warriors barred the wide prairie
with their crimson shields.
They seek honor for themselves
and glory for their prince.

Early in the morning of Friday
the Russians trampled the infidel Kuman armies,
and, spreading like arrows over the prairie,
they galloped away with beautiful Kuman maidens.
And with them they took:
  golds and brocades,
  and costly velvets.
With cloaks and coats and fur mantles
and with all kinds of Kuman garments
they began to bridge their way over the swamps and marshes.
The crimson banner,
the white gonfalon,
the scarlet panache, and
the silver lance
were taken to brave Igor,
son of Sviatoslav.

Brave Oleg's[18] clan slumbers in the prairie.
They have strayed far, flying.
They were born to be offended
  neither by the falcon,
  nor by the gyrfalcon,
  nor by you, the black ravens,
  the infidel Kumans.
Khan Gza flees like a gray wolf.
Khan Konchak[19] shows him the way to the great river Don.

V. The Second Day of Battle: The Victory of the Kumans

Very early on the second morn
a bloody dawn announced the day.
Black clouds arise from the sea
and want to envelop the four suns.[20]
Blue lightning shows through the clouds.

[18] Oleg was Igor's grandfather and the prince of Chernigov, main city of the region in which Igor's domain was located.

[19] Gza and Konchak: Kuman khans.

[20] "Four suns" refers to the four princes who lead the Russian armies: Igor, Vsevolod, Oleg, and Sviatoslav.

There is to be a mighty thundering.
The rain of arrows will come from the great river Don.
Here, on the river Kaiala,[21]
here, on the great river Don,
lances will be broken
and swords will be dulled on Kuman helmets.
O Russian land! You are already far beyond the hills.

Here the winds, grandsons of god Stribog,
blow the arrows from the sea
against the regiments of brave Igor.
The earth groans.
The rivers become turbid.
Dust covers the prairie.
The pennants announce:
"The Kumans have come from the river Don
and from the sea.
They encircle the Russian regiments from all sides."
The devil's children bar the prairie with their battle cries.
The brave Russians bar it with their crimson shields.

Fierce auroch Vsevolod!
Your defense is firm,
Your arrows rain down upon Kuman warriors.
Your Frankish swords[22] clang on Kuman helmets.
Where you, fierce auroch, gallop gleaming in your golden helmet,
there will lie the heads of infidel Kumans.
There Avar helmets[23] are cloven at your hands,
fierce auroch Vsevolod.
What wound can matter, brethren,
to one who has forgotten honors and fortune,
and his father's golden throne in the city of Chernigov,
and the habits and ways of his dearly beloved
and beautiful wife,
the daughter of Prince Gleb?[24]

[21] The river at which Igor was defeated. Its location remains unknown but apparently it was a tributary of the Donets, itself a tributary of the river Don.

[22] Frankish swords or lances: weapons made of steel imported from Western Europe.

[23] Apparently helmets made in the Avar style. The Avars were nomads who in the seventh and eighth centuries lived in southern Russia and Hungary.

[24] The daughter of Prince Gleb, the ruler of Pereyaslavl-Seversk.

VI. Censure of the Princes' Feuds

There were the eras of Trojan.
There passed the years of Yaroslav.
And there were the campaigns of Oleg,
Oleg, son of Sviatoslav.[25]
That Oleg fostered feuds with his sword
and sowed the Russian lands with arrows.
In the city of Tmutorakan
he used to put his foot in the golden stirrup
and its clinking could be heard by great Yaroslav,
who lived long ago.
And Prince Vladimir, son of Vsevolod,
would stop his ears in the city of Chernigov.[26]

And the dubious glory of Prince Boris,[27]
son of Vyacheslav,
brought him to his final Judgment,
and he remained in eternal sleep
on a burial shroud of green grass
for offending brave and young Prince Oleg.

On the river Kaiala Sviatopolk ordered
that his father be taken between two ambling Hungarian horses
to be buried in the Cathedral of St. Sophia in Kiev.[28]

Then, in the era of Oleg, son of misfortune,
the feuding spread and grew.
The fortune of god Dazhbog's[29] grandson was destroyed.
Human lives became shortened through the princes' discord.
In those days the plowman spoke but rarely,

[25] Prince Oleg was responsible for the fratricidal warring among the Russian princes. Oleg Sviatoslavovich, previously mentioned as Igor's grandfather, whose feudal wars shattered the unity of Russia, was an antagonist of Vladimir Monomakh. He died in 1115.

[26] So that he might not hear the clinking of Oleg's stirrup.

[27] Boris, son of Vyacheslav, was the first Russian prince to fight other Russian princes in alliance with the Kumans. Boris was killed in this campaign, while his brother, Oleg, escaped to the Kumans.

[28] Sviatopolk's father was killed in battle in 1078 and was taken to Kiev for burial. Slain warriors were carried in a carpet between two horses.

[29] Dazhbog: an ancient Russian deity; Dazhbog's grandson refers to the Russians. Veles and Stribog were also pre-Christian deities.

and the ravens often cawed, dividing corpses among themselves.
And the daws talked in their own tongue,
before flying to feed on corpses.

VII. The Russian Defeat

And so it used to be.
There were battles and campaigns,
but there had never been such battle as this.
From early morning to night,
from evening to dawn
there flew tempered arrows,
swords rained down upon helmets,
Frankish lances resound,
and all this in the unknown prairie,
in the Kuman land.
The black earth under the hooves
was strewn with bones,
was covered with blood.
Grief overwhelmed the Russian land.

What noise do I hear?
What clinking comes to my ears
so early in the morning, before the dawn?
Igor turns about his troops.
He is saddened by the fate of his brother, Vsevolod.
They fought for one day.
They fought for another day.
At noon on the third day Igor's banners fell.
Here, on the shores of the swift river Kaiala,
the brothers parted.
The wine of this bloody banquet was drunk to the last drop.
The Russians gave their guests to drink from the same cup.
They died for the Russian land.
  The grass withered from sorrow,
  and the saddened trees drooped earthward.

VIII. The Author's Laments

And now, brethren, unhappy times have arrived.
The prairie overwhelmed the Russian forces.
Grief reigned over the forces of god Dazhbog's grandsons.
Grief, like a maiden, entered the land of Trojan.
She splashed her swan wings at the river Don,
by the blue sea,

The Kumans attack Prince Igor's army. The Russian horses fall from exhaustion. A miniature from the *Radzivil Chronicle* of the fourteenth century.

and splashing, she put an end to the times of good fortune.
The princes' fight against the infidel came to an end.
And brother said to brother:
"This is mine,
and that also is mine."
And the princes began to argue about trifles,
calling them important matters,
and began to create discord among themselves.
The infidels from all lands began to invade
the Russian land and to win victory.

Oh, too far toward the sea has the falcon flown, slaying birds!
And Igor's valiant regiments cannot be resurrected!
He is mourned by Grief and Sorrow,
and they spread across the Russian land.
[Shaking the embers in the flaming horn],[30]
the Russian women begin to lament, saying:
"No more, our dear husbands,
can you be envisioned in our thoughts,
nor can you reappear in our dreams,
nor can you be seen with our eyes,
and never again shall we jingle gold and silver."
And, brethren, the city of Kiev began to groan from grief,
and the city of Chernigov also, from their misfortune.
Anguish spread over the Russian land.
Deep sadness flew through the Russian land.
And the princes created discord among themselves.
The infidels, victoriously invading the Russian land,
levied a tribute of one vair from each household.

All this happened because Igor and Vsevolod,
two valiant sons of Sviatoslav,
once more revived evil forces
which were curbed by their cousin, (another) Prince
Sviatoslav.[31]
This stern prince of Kiev
held (everyone) in fear and awe,
for, as a tempest, his powerful regiments

30 A part of the mourning ritual (?)

31 Sviatoslav III, the great prince of Kiev (1177–1194) and theoretical ruler of all Russia. He was the cousin and godfather of Igor and Vsevolod. In 1183 he defeated Khan Kobiak on the shores of the Azov Sea and took him as a prisoner to Kiev.

and his Frankish swords defeated and attacked the Kuman lands.
They trampled under Kuman hills and ravines,
made turbid Kuman rivers and lakes,
dried out Kuman streams and marshes.
Like a tornado, he seized Khan Kobiak
from amongst his great iron regiments
on the shore of the sea bay.
And Kobiak fell in the city of Kiev,
in the hall of Prince Sviatoslav.

Now the Germans and the Venetians,
the Greeks and the Moravians
sing the glory of Prince Sviatoslav
and reproach Prince Igor,
who has lost his fortune on the bottom of the river Kaiala
and filled the Kuman rivers with Russian gold.
And here Prince Igor exchanged his golden saddle of a prince
for the saddle of a slave.
And the cities became saddened
and joy vanished.

IX. The Dream of Prince Sviatoslav of Kiev

Sviatoslav had a troubled dream
in Kiev, on the hills:
"Early this night I was clothed in a black shroud
upon a bed of yew.
They ladled out for me
a blue wine mixed with sorrow.
From the empty quivers of the infidel strangers
there poured large pearls into my lap.[32]
They comforted me.
And the beams of my gold-roofed palace
were already without girding.[33]
During the entire night, since evening,
the gray-blue ravens were croaking.
[And at the foothills of the city of Plesensk[34]

[32] Pearls were the symbols of forthcoming tears for the Russians.

[33] It was the custom among Russians to remove the girding of porches before removing the dead from a house.

[34] Plesensk was a fortified city in the Galician mountains. Probably the allusion here is to the funeral of the Galician warriors, countrymen, or Igor's wife, who was the daughter of the prince of Galicia.

appeared a sledge,[35]
and this sledge was racing to the blue sea."]
And the boyars told the prince:
"O Prince, sorrow has seized your mind.
There were two falcons who flew
From their father's golden throne,
either to conquer the city of Tmutorakan
or to drink the water of the river Don with their helmets.
But their wings were clipped by the sabers of the infidels,
and they themselves were put in irons.
It became dark on the third day.
The two suns[36] were eclipsed.
[Two purple columns[37] faded into the sea
Two young moons—Oleg and Sviatoslav—became enveloped in darkness,[38]
On the river Kaiala darkness overcame the light,[39]
and the Kumans, like a brood of panthers,
spread across the Russian land.
And great violence came from the nomads.]
Already shame has eclipsed glory.
Already violence has defeated freedom.
Already the Div has descended to earth.
And now beautiful Gothic maidens[40]
have begun their song on the shore of the blue sea.
They jingle Russian gold.
They sing of the foreboding time.
They glorify the revenge of Sharokan.[41]
And we, the army, are without joy."

And then great Sviatoslav let fall his golden words
mixed with tears, saying:
"Oh, my young cousins, Igor and Vsevolod,
too early did you begin to disturb
the Kuman lands with your swords, seeking glory,
but you won it without honor,

35 In ancient Russia sledges were used for funerals.

36 Igor and Vsevolod.

37 Apparently symbols of the two armies of Igor and Vsevolod.

38 Young Prince Sviatoslav, Igor's nephew, and Igor's son, Prince Oleg.

39 Darkness symbolizes the infidel Kumans, and light, the Russian army.

40 In the twelfth century the Goths still maintained settlements in the Crimea, where they penetrated in the third century.

41 Sharokan: a Kuman khan defeated several times by the Russians.

for you spilled the blood of the infidels
without winning glory for yourselves.
Your valiant hearts are forged of Frankish steel
and are tempered in valiance.
What have you done to my silver-gray hairs?
No longer do I behold my powerful
and wealthy,
and well-girded brother,
Yaroslav of Chernigov,[42]
nor his lords.
With his Moguts and Tatrans,
with his Shelbirs and Topchaks,
with his Revugas and Olbers.[43]
They used to defeat the regiments (of the infidels),
and without shields,
only with their knives and ancestors' war cries.
But you said:
'Let us be valiant.
Let us assume the glory of the past.
Let us divide amongs ourselves
the glory of tomorrow.'
What is there to wonder, brethren,
when an old man feels like a young one?
When a falcon molts, he chases birds high and away
and does not permit harm to come to his nest.
But there is great misfortune,
and the Russian princes are no help to me."

X. The Bard Appeals to the Russian Princes

THE APPEAL TO VLADIMIR, SON OF GLEB[44]

Gloomy times have arrived.
The Russians cry out at the city of Rim
under the Kuman swords.
Prince Vladimir is covered with wounds.
Grief and sorrow to you Vladimir,
son of Gleb.

[42] Prince of Chernigov and borther of Sviatoslav, Prince of Kiev.

[43] Moguts, Tatrans, Shelbirs, Topchaks, Revugas, and Olbers: apparently Turkic tribes, but their identification is not certain. They settled in the land of Chernigov; in the principality of Yaroslav.

[44] Vladimir, son of Gleb: In 1185 the Kuman Khans Gza and Konchak invaded the Russian land, destroying the city of Rim on the river Sula. During this invasion Vladimir Glebovich was mortally wounded.

THE APPEAL TO VSEVOLOD, PRINCE OF SUZDAL[45]

Great Prince Vsevolod!
Do you not intend to come from far away
to watch over your paternal golden throne?
For you, with the oars (of your fleet),
can scatter the river Volga into droplets.
With the helmets (of your army)
you can pour out the river Don.
If you were here, then (Kuman) slave girls
would go for a *nogata,*
and (Kuman) male slaves for only a *rezana.*
And you can shoot over the dry land
with the fiery arrows,
with the courageous sons of Gleb.

THE APPEAL TO PRINCES RURIK AND DAVID[46]

O valiant Rurik and David!
Was it not your warriors who swam through blood
under the gilded helmets?
Was it not your army that roared like aurochs,
wounded by tempered swords in the unknown prairie?
Lords, set your feet in the golden stirrups
to avenge the outrage of the present day,
of the Russian land,
of Igor's wounds,
wounds of the daring son of Sviatoslav.

THE APPEAL TO PRINCE YAROSLAV OF GALICH[47]

O Yaroslav of Galich,
the prince of eight senses!
You sit high on your throne wrought of gold.
Your iron regiments defend the Hungarian mountains.
You bar the way to the (Hungarian) king.

[45] Vsevolod was called "the great nest" because of his numerous and powerful family. He was prince of Suzdal, a powerful principality in the vicinity of present-day Moscow, the latter being at that time only a small village in the Suzdalian principality.

[46] Rurik and David: Princes of Belgorod and Smolensk who died in 1215 and 1198. They were known for their courage during the fratricidal wars.

[47] Yaroslav of Galich, Prince of Galicia (1152–1187). Igor's father-in-law, he was called *Osmomysl* (eight-sensed) apparently because of his qualities for ruling. His land bordered on the Kingdom of Hungary, and he practically controlled the river Danube.

You close the gates of the river Danube.
You hurl stones over the clouds.
Your law reigns up to the river Danube.
Your thunder resounds above the lands,
You keep the gates of Kiev open,
From your father's golden throne you shoot at the sultans
beyond the (Russian) lands.
Lord, shoot at Konchak, the infidel slave,
for the revenge of the Russian land,
for the wounds of Igor,
the wounds of the valiant son of Sviatoslav.

THE APPEAL TO PRINCES ROMAN OF VOLYNIA AND MSTISLAV OF GRODNO[48]

And you, daring Roman and Mstislav,
your courageous thoughts direct your minds to action.
In your bravery you soar to valiant deeds,
like a falcon over the winds,
which desires, in its daring, to surpass the bird.
Your iron men are under Latin helmets[49]
and they make the earth tremble,
and (they make) many nations (tremble):
  the Nomads,
  the Lithuanians,
  the Deremelas,
  the Yatvags,[50]
  the Kumans.
(All of them) have dropped their lances
and have bowed their heads under your Frankish swords.

But Prince Igor, the sunlight has already dimmed for you.
And, by misfortune, the tree lost its foliage.
The enemies have already divided amongst themselves
the cities of the rivers Ross and Sula.[51]
The valiant regiments of Igor will not be resurrected.
The river Don appeals to you, Prince,
and summons the princes to victory.
O valiant princes, grandsons of Oleg,
you are ready for the battle.

[48] Roman (died 1205) and Mstislav (died 1226): Princes of Volynia, a region east of Galicia.
[49] Refers to the helmets of Latin or Western origin.
[50] Deremelas and Yatvags: Lithuanian tribes who lived at the northwestern Russian border.
[51] Tributaries of the Dnieper.

THE APPEAL TO MSTISLAV'S SONS

Ingvar and Vsevolod and you three sons of Mstislav![52]
You are six-winged falcons[53] of no mean nest.
You have not won your patrimonies by deeds of victory.
To what avail are your golden helmets,
your Polish lances and shields?
Bar the gates of the prairie with your sharp arrows
  for the Russian lands,
  for the wounds of Igor,
  the wounds of the daring son of Sviatoslav.

EVOCATION OF PRINCE IZIASLAV'S[54] DEATH IN THE BATTLE OF GORODETS (1162)

No more do the silver streams of the River Sula
protect the city of Pereyaslavl.
And the river Dvina, which flows to Polotsk,
that city of stern men,
became turbid under the cries of the infidels.

Only Iziaslav, son of Vasilko,
rained his sharp arrows upon Lithuanian helmets
and tarnished the glory of his grandfather Vseslav.
And, having been worsted by the Lithuanian swords,
he fell upon the bloody grass
[(as if it were) the marriage bed,]
under the crimson shields.

And Boyan said:
  "Prince, the wings of birds cover your warriors
   and the beasts already have begun to lick their blood."

Neither his brother, Briachislav,
nor the other brother, Vsevolod, was there (in battle).
And (you, Iziaslav) remained alone.
And you let drop from your valiant body,
through the golden necklace of a prince,
the pearl of your soul,
and voices became saddened,

52 Princes of Volynia.
53 Some of the Russian falcons have wings that have three distinct sections, and are therefore called "six-winged falcons."
54 Prince Iziaslav was killed at Gorodets in a war between the Russians and Lithuanians.

and joy ceased to be,
And the trumpets mournfully resound at the city of Gorodets.

THE APPEAL TO PRINCE YAROSLAV OF CHERNIGOV AND VSESLAV'S[55] HEIRS

O sons of Yaroslav and the grandsons of Vseslav,
lower your banners!
Put your dented swords into their sheaths!
You do not deserve the glory of your ancestors,
since, through your feuding,
you brought the infidels into the Russian land,
into the domain of Vseslav.
Your warring brought Kuman violence (into Russia).

THE EVOCATION OF PRINCE VSESLAV THE SORCERER

During the seventh age of Trojan
Vseslav cast lots for the maiden he desired, and,
cunningly leaning on the lance,
he leaped to the city of Kiev and
touched the golden throne of Kiev
with the staff of his lance.
Like a fierce beast he leaped from Belgorod at midnight,
under the cover of blue mist.
[He managed to cast thrice a lucky lot:]
  he opened the gate of the city of Novgorod,
  he tarnished the glory of Prince Yaroslav, and
  he leaped like a wolf to Nemiga [from Dudutki].

On the river Nemiga they built haystacks of heads.
They are threshed with steel flails
and lives are left behind on the threshing floor.
Souls abandon their bodies.
The bloody shores of the river Nemiga
  were sown with misfortune,
  were strewn with the bones of Russia's sons.

Prince Vseslav used to judge the people.
And, as prince, he ruled over the cities.
But, in the night, he prowled like a werewolf.

[55] Vseslav (d. 1101): Prince of Polotsk who in 1067 attacked and burned Novgorod, but was defeated at the river Nemiga. In 1068 he became Prince of Kiev for seven months. The "maiden" he cast lots for was the city of Kiev. He was considered a sorcerer.

He was able to go from Kiev to Tmutorakan
before the cock could crow.
And, prowling as a werewolf, he crossed
the way of great god Hors.[56]
At the Church of St. Sophia of Polotsk
the bells tolled the matins for him,
and he could hear them in Kiev.
His magician's soul lived in a valiant body,
but he still often suffered miseries.
Of him Boyan the Seer said wisely in his refrains:
"Neither a crafty man,
nor a clever man,
nor a clever bird,
can escape divine judgment."

O Russian land, you must mourn,
remembering your early age, your early princes.
And Vladimir of yore
could not be retained by the hills of Kiev.[57]
But now Prince Rurik's banners stand in readiness,
and so do Prince David's (his brother's).
Thus, they are blown (by the wind) in different directions.

XI. Igor's Wife, Euphrosinia, Daughter of Prince Yaroslav of Galich, Laments of the Walls of Putivl

At the river Danube lances sing their song,
but it is the voice of Yaroslavna which is heard.
Since morning, she sings like an unknown seagull:[58]
"Like a seagull I will fly along the river Danube.
I will dip my beaver-trimmed sleeve into the river Kaiala.
I will cleanse the bloody wounds of my prince,
on his mighty body."

Since morning Euphrosinia has lamented on the walls
of the city of Putivl, saying:
"O wind, why do you, my lord wind,
blow so fiercely?
Why do you bring on your light wings
Kuman arrows against the warriors of my beloved?

56 God of the sun in ancient Russia.
57 Because he unceasingly campaigned against his enemies.
58 The seagull was considered to be the bird of mourning.

Isn't it enough for you to blow under the clouds,
to loll the ships on the blue sea?
Why, my lord, did you scatter my joy
over the feathergrass of the prairie?"

Since morning Euphrosinia has lamented on the walls of the city of Putivl, saying:

"O river Dnieper, son of Slovuta,
it is you who have broken through
the stone mountains[59] of the Kuman land.
You lolled the boats of Sviatoslav
(when he went to meet Khan Kobiak's army.
O my lord wind, loll my beloved
and (bring) him to me that I might not
send him my tears to the sea so early in the morning,
at dawn."

Since morning Euphrosinia has lamented on the walls of the city of Putivl, saying:

"O my bright and thrice bright sun!
For everyone you are warm and beautiful.
Why did you spread, my lord, your burning rays
upon the warriors of my beloved?
In the waterless prairie you parched their bows
and closed their quivers with misfortune."

XII. Prince Igor Flees from Kuman Captivity

The seas splashed at midnight
and the tornado rushes through the mist.
God shows the way to Igor,
the way from the Kuman land,
to the Russian land,
to his father's golden throne.

The glow of the sunset had faded.
Igor sleeps.
Igor keeps his vigil.
Igor's thoughts cross the prairie,
from the great river Don
to the small river Donets.

[59] Stone mountains: apparently a reference to the cataracts in the river Dnieper, and the surrounding rocky shores.

Beyond the river, Ovlur whistles,[60]
having caught a horse.
He warns the prince.
Prince Igor will not remain a prisoner.
The earth rumbled,
the grass rustled,
and the Kuman tents began to stir.
Prince Igor raced to reeds like an ermine,
like a white duck (he races) on the water.
He leaps to his swift steed.
He (later) springs from it, like a gray wolf.
He rushed toward the curve of the river Donets.
He flew under the clouds like a falcon
which kills geese and swans
  for lunch,
  for dinner,
  and for supper.

If Prince Igor flies like a falcon,
then Ovlur races like a wolf,
shaking off the chilling dew.
And both of them exhausted their swift steeds.

XIII. Igor Speaks with the River Donets

The river Donets speaks:
  "Oh, Prince Igor,
  there will be no small glory for you,
  but dislike for Konchak,
  and joy for the Russian land."

And Igor spoke:
  "Oh, my river Donets!
  There will be no small glory for you,
  for you have lolled the prince on your waves,
  for you have spread for him green grass
  on your silver shores,
  for you have enveloped him in your warm mists
  in the shadow of green trees,
  for your drakes watched over him on the water,
  and your seagulls on the streams,
  and your black ducks in the winds."

60 Ovlur was Igor's faithful servant.

But different words came to him from the river Stugna.
Its stream is weak.
It has swallowed up other brooks and rivulets,
[and, therefore, has grown wide at its delta.
It hid young Prince Rostislav.[61]
It concealed him on its bottom near its dark bank.]
And Rostislav's mother mourned the young prince.
Flowers withered from sorrow,
and the saddened trees dropped earthward.

XIV. The Kuman Khans Pursue Igor

It is not the magpies which have begun croaking,
it is Khans Gza and Konchak
who search for Igor's path.
At that time the crows did not caw.
The daws became silent and
the jackdaws did not chatter.
Only the snakes were crawling,
and the woodpeckers show the way to the river with their sounds.
The nightingale announces the dawn with its gay song.

And Khan Gza told Khan Konchak:
"If the falcon fly to his nest,
we will shoot at the falconet[62]
with our gilded arrows."

And Khan Konchak replied to Khan Gza:
"If the falcon flies to his nest,
we will enmesh the falconet
with the charms of a beautiful maiden."

And Khan Gza said to Khan Konchak:
"If we enmesh him with the charms of
a beautiful maiden,
we will have neither the falconet
nor the beautiful maiden,
and (their) birds will start fighting us
in the Kuman prairie."

[61] Prince Rostislav was drowned at the age of twenty-two in 1093, during a fording of the river Stugna, a tributary of the Dnieper.

[62] The term "falconet" refers to Igor's son, Vladimir, who remained a prisoner of the Kumans.

XV. Apodosis

And Boyan, [the bard of olden times,
said of the time of Sviatoslav,
of Yaroslav,
and of Kagan Oleg:]
"It is difficult for a head
to be without shoulders.
But it is also a misfortune
for the body to be without the head."
And so it is difficult for the Russian land
to be without Prince Igor.
The sun gleams in the sky.
Prince Igor is in the Russian land.
Maidens sing on the Danube.
Their voices reach across the sea to Kiev.
Igor rides along the Borichev[63]
to the Church of the Holy Virgin of Pirogoshch.
The lands are jubilant.
The cities rejoice.
Once the glory of the princes of yore was sung,
now glory will be sung for the young.
Glory to Igor, son of Sviatoslav,
to fierce auroch Vsevolod,
and to Vladimir, son of Igor.
Hail to the princes and the armies
who fight for Christendom against the infidel hosts.
Glory to the princes and to the army. Amen.

20. *Prince Roman, Khan Otrok, and the Wormwood*

The *Galician and Volynian Chronicle,* from which this tale is taken, gives a rather detailed account of the fate of southern Russia in the thirteenth century. The authors of the first part demonstrate an unmistakable talent for narration and some

63 Borichev: a location of the Dnieper shore in the vicinity of Kiev where a church was built in honor of the Holy Virgin of Pirogoshch. This name comes from the name of an icon in a tower (*pyrios* is Greek for "tower") in Constantinople.

poetic inclination. The present excerpt gives a short but poetic account of the circumstances under which Khan Otrok returned to his native land.

The text upon which this translation is based is to be found in N. K. Gudzy's *Khrestomatiia po drevnei russkoi literature*, Moscow, 1955.

◆ ◆ ◆

Great Prince Roman, the unforgettable ruler of all Russia, died. He was the one who conquered all the heathen nations and with wisdom fulfilled all the divine commandments. He would strike against the infidels (Kumans) like a lion. He could be as full of wrath with them as is a lynx. He annihilated them like a crocodile. Many were the times he crossed their lands like an eagle. He was as courageous as an aurochs. He continued the deeds of his grandfather, Prince Vladimir Monomakh, who destroyed the infidel sons of Ishmael, who are usually called Kumans. He drove Khan Otrok from the steppes to beyond the Iron Gates (of the Caucasian Mountains) into Abkhasia.[1] Only the horde of Khan Syrchan remained on the river Don, and he had only fish for food. It was that time when Prince Vladimir Monomakh drank water from the river Don with his golden helmet. He conquered the entire Kuman land and drove away these accursed sons of Hagar.[2]

After the death of Prince Vladimir Monomakh, Khan Syrchan sent his bard, Oria, to his brother, Khan Otrok, who was still in the land of Abkhasia. And Syrchan told Oria to tell his brother: "Vladimir is dead. Come back, brother; return to your native land." And he added to Oria: "Tell these words I have spoken to my brother and sing him our Kuman songs. But, if he does not want to return, let him smell the fragrance of our prairie grass that is called wormwood."

When Khan Otrok wanted neither to return nor to listen to the songs of his brother's bard, the bard presented him a bouquet of wormwood from the prairie.

And when Khan Otrok inhaled the fragrance of the prairie wormwood, he began to weep, and said: "It is still better to die in one's native land then to win glory in a foreign one." And thus Khan Otrok decided to return to his native land.

[1] A small nation on the eastern shores of the Black Sea.

[2] Following the Byzantine tradition, the Russians considered all nomads to be the descendants of Ishmael, the son of Hagar.

21. *Tales from the Novgorodian Chronicle*

In southern and central Russia the princes eventually established their undisputed rule over the Russian cities and principalities, and the ancient people's assembly, the *Veche,* which had played an important role in Russia before the eleventh and twelfth centuries, gradually declined in importance. But in the cities of Novgorod and Pskov, in northwestern Russia, the power of the princes was curbed and the *Veche* became the principal ruling institution. The princes, who served as commanders of the army, the *posadniks,* who headed the civil administration, other administrators, and the bishops were all elected by the *Veche,* and often removed by it if its members became dissatisfied with them. Like such European merchant cities as Venice, Genoa, Hamburg and Lubeck, both Pskov and Novgorod had a powerful merchant class. Novgorod became a member of the Hanseatic League and maintained lively trade relations with Germany and other nations of northern Europe.

The style of the *Novgorodian Chronicle* strongly reflects the commercial atmosphere that prevailed in these two cities. The entries tell little about political events, but furnish details concerning matters of commerce, such as the state of the harvest, the prices of merchandise, trade activities, and climatic conditions that might have a bearing on the economic situation. Most of the longer stories in these northern annals are of southern origin, and were taken from the Kievan or central Russian chronicles.

The translation of the *Novgorodian Chronicle* presented here is based on *Novgorodskaia pervaia letopis,* Second Version, published by the Academy of Science of the U.S.S.R., Moscow and Leningrad, 1950.

◆ ◆ ◆

LIFE IN THE CITY OF NOVGOROD

1128 (6636) Kiriak, the Abbot of St. George, died. In the same year John, son of Vsevolod, grandson of Mstislav, died on the 16th of April. In the same year Zavid Dmitrevich was made *posadnik* in Novgorod. This was a cruel year: an *osminka* of rye cost a *grivna;* the people ate lime leaves, birchbark; they ground wood pulp and mixed it with husks and straw; and some ate buttercups, moss, and horseflesh. And the corpses of those who had fallen from starvation were in the streets, the marketplace, the road, and everywhere. And they hired men to carry the dead out of town, for the serfs could not go out. Sorrow and misery befell all. Fathers and mothers would give their children as gifts to merchants or put them to death. And many people went to other lands. Thus a blight was brought upon our land for our sins. And this year the water of the river Volkhov was very high, and it carried away many houses. And Prince Boris Vsevolodovich of Polotsk died, and Zavid Dmitrevich, *posadnik* of Novgorod, died.

1143 (6651) All this autumn was rainy; from Our Lady's Day of Nativity until the winter solstice it was warm and wet. The water was very high in the river Volkhov, and it carried away hay and wood. The lake froze, and there was great coldness in the night. And the wind broke up the ice and carried it into the river Volkhov, where it broke the bridge and carried away four of the bridge piles. In the same year Sviatopolk married in Novgorod. He brought his bride from Moravia between Christmas and Epiphany. And in the same year the Korelians campaigned against the Yamians, but were forced to retreat.

1156 (6664) The Novgorodians expelled Sudila, the *posadnik* of the city, and he died five days later. And they gave the position of *posadnik* to Yakun Miroslavovich. In the same spring, on April 29th, Archbishop Nifont passed away. Before he died he went to Kiev to oppose the metropolitan bishop, but many people say that he went to Constantinople after having plundered the Cathedral (St. Sophia in Kiev). They say many things about him, but it is their sin for doing so. We should remember that he was the one who embellished the Cathedral (St. Sophia of Novgorod), who decorated the porches, who made the icon case, and who adorned the church on the outside. He also built the Church of the Holy Savior in Pskov and the Church of St. Clement in Ladoga. I believe that God, because of our sins, did not desire that we should have his grave for our consolation and so he sent him to Kiev, where he died. And he was buried in the Crypt Monastery.

In the same year the whole populace of the city gathered and decided to elect as bishop a holy man, Arkady, who was chosen by God. And all the people went to the Monastery of the Holy Mother of God and took him, Prince Mstislav, the entire clergy of the Cathedral of St. Sophia, and all the priests, abbots, and monks of the city and brought them to the court of St. Sophia. And they entrusted the bishopric to Arkady until the Metropolitan of Russia should arrive and consecrate him.

And in the same year the merchants from over the seas erected the Church of Good Friday on the market square.

1157 (6665) There was malice among the people, and they rose against Prince Mstislav Yurievich and began to drive him from Novgorod, but the merchants took up arms for him. And brother quarreled with brother. The bridge over the river Volkhov was seized. Guards took their stand on either side of the town gates, and it nearly came to the shedding of blood between them. And then Sviatoslav Rostislavich and David Rostislavich arrived. That very night Mstislav fled from Novgorod. And in three days Rostislav himself arrived. And the brothers came together, and no harm came of it.

In the spring Prince George died at Kiev, and the people of Kiev set Iziaslav Davidovich on the throne. In the same year Andrew, Abbot of the Church of the Holy Mother of God, died. And Alexis was appointed in his place. And in the fall the weather was fearsome with thunder and lightning, and on November 7th, at five in the night, there was hail of the size of apples.

NOVGOROD AT WAR WITH SUZDAL

The chronicle entries for the years 1169 and 1170 which follow below, give a clear picture of the struggle between the princes of Novgorod and those of central Russia. First the princes of Suzdal and later those of Moscow tried to unify all Russia and to bring the prosperous merchant city of Novgorod under their sway. The struggle described in these two entries is against the armies of Suzdal, led by the autocratic Prince Andrey, and their allies, led by Prince Roman and Prince Mstislav. At this time the troops of Novgorod were commanded by young Prince Roman. These entries are written in short, telegraphic style. For a better understanding of the text some explanatory notes have been added in parentheses.

◆ ◆ ◆

1169 (6667) Danislav Lazutinich went with his troops beyond the Volok[1] to collect tribute, but (Great Prince Andrew) sent his army against them. And it came to a battle. There were only four hundred men of Novgorod against seven thousand soldiers from Suzdal, but God helped the Novgorodians, and the Suzdalians suffered thirteen hundred casualties, while Novgorod lost only fifteen men. Novgorod retreated, but then

[1] Volok (Portage) was the name of the region which formed the watershed between the West Dvina and Dnieper.

returned and collected tribute (beyond the Volok), and received tribute also from the peasants of Suzdal. And all returned home in good health.

In this same year in the winter the army of Suzdal, under the command of the son of Prince Andrew, Prince Mstislav, and Prince Roman, and with troops from Smolensk, Toropetz, and Murom; the armies of Riazan led by two princes, the Prince of Polotsk with his armies, and men from the entire Russian land all approached the city of Novgorod. But the people of Novgorod were firmly behind their leader, Prince Roman, and their *posadnik*, Yakun. And so they built fortifications about the city. On Sunday (the emissaries of the princes of Suzdal) came to Novgorod to negotiate, and these negotiations lasted for three days. On the fourth day, Wednesday, February 25th, the Day of St. Tarasy, Patriarch of Constantinople, the Suzdalians attacked the city and fought the entire day. Only toward evening did Prince Roman, who was still very young, and the troops of Novgorod manage to defeat the army of Suzdal with the help of the holy cross, the Holy Virgin, and the prayers of the Right Reverend Bishop Elias. Many Suzdalians were massacred, many were taken prisoner, while the remainder escaped only with great difficulty. And the price of Suzdalian prisoners fell to two *nogatas*.

1170 (6678) There were high prices in Novgorod. A barrel of rye cost four *grivnas*, bread cost two *nogatas*, and honey ten *kunas* a pood. After deliberations, the Novgorodians decided to renounce Prince Roman. And they sent their emissaries to Great Prince Andrew Bogoliubsky (of Suzdal), suing for peace. They asked Prince Andrew to give them another prince who would preserve their liberties. In the same year on the 4th day of October, St. Erofey's Day, Prince Rurik Rostislavich (the prince sent to Novgorod by Prince Andrew) arrived in Novgorod. This same year the God-loving archbishop, Elias, and his brother, Gabriel, founded a monastery and erected the Church of the Annunciation of the Holy Mother of God. And this year Prince Mstislav Iziaslavich, the grandson of Vladimir, died. In the same year Prince Gleb Giorgivich died at Kiev, and (the Kievans) put in Vladimir Mstislavovich.

THE ELECTION OF ARCHBISHOP MANTURY, AND NOVGOROD WARS AGAINST THE UGRIANS

THE entry for the year 1193 gives an interesting account of the election and consecration of a new archbishop. The second part of the entry is concerned with the description of a Novgorodian campaign against the people of Ugra (kinsmen of the present-day Hungarians) who occupied the area both east and west of the northern Urals. The Novgorodians began building their colonial empire in what is now northern Russia. By the fifteenth century, when this empire was nearing its end, it extended into Siberia and covered an area the size of present-day France, Germany, and Italy combined.

◆ ◆ ◆

1193 (6701) The archbishop of Novgorod, Gabriel, passed away on May 24th, the Day of Our Holy Father St. Simon. And he was solemnly buried in the porch of the Cathedral of St. Sophia next to his brother whose name was George after he took the holy vows. And then the people of Novgorod, the abbots, the Chapter of St. Sophia, and the clergy began their deliberations as to who should be the new archbishop. Some wanted to elect Mitrofan, while others wanted to elect Mantury, and still others wanted Grichina in this office. There was a great feud among them, and they decided to cast lots after High Mass in the Cathedral of St. Sophia. And they prepared the lots, and after the service they sent for a blind man and he was given to them by God. And with the help of divine Grace the blind man cast, and Mantury was chosen. And they sent for Mantury and they brought him to the Court of the Archbishop.

And they announced his election to the Metropolitan of Kiev, and he sent for Mantury with great honors. And Mantury went to Kiev with the patricians of Novgorod. And he was received there with love by Prince Sviatoslav and the metropolitan. He was consecrated on the 10th day of December, the day celebrated for the deaths of the holy martyrs Mina, Hermogen, and Eugraph. And Mantury returned to Novgorod on January 16th, the Day of the Falling Off of the Fetters of the Holy Apostle Peter.

In the same year the Novgorodian troops under Voevoda Yadreik reached the land of Ugra and took a town. And they went to another town and besieged it. And they remained there five weeks, and the people of Ugra sent the Novgorodian forces a deceitful message saying the following: "We are collecting silver and sables and other valuables for you, so that you should neither destroy us nor your own tribute." And in the meantime the Ugrians began collecting their forces, and when their army had been gathered, the city sent a message to Voevoda Yadreik saying the following, "Come to the city bringing with you twelve men."

And Voevoda Yadreik went to the city, taking with him the priest John Legena and other leading men, and they were cut to pieces by the Ugrians on the eve of St. Barbara's Day. And then they took thirty of the best Novgorodian warriors prisoner and cut them to pieces. And later fifty more Novgorodian warriors were cut down by the Ugrians.

And then Savka (apparently a Novgorodian) came to the Ugrian prince and said: "Prince, if you don't kill Jacob Prokshenich (presumably the second-in-command of the Novgorodian forces), but let him live to reach Novgorod, he will bring more warriors and will devastate your land." And the Ugrian prince called Jacob Prokshenich before him and ordered that he be killed, but Jacob said to Savka: "Brother, God and Holy Sophia will judge you if you have in mind the spilling of your brothers' blood. And you will appear before us and God, and you will be responsible for our blood." And after he said this he was killed, for Savka had secret connections with the Ugrian prince.

And then the army of Novgorod was starving because they had remained for six weeks, being induced to do so by Ugrian deceit. And on the Holy Day of St. Nicholas they broke camp and were all cut to pieces by the Ugrian army. And there were sorrow and misery among those who remained alive, and there were only eighty of them. During the whole winter there was no word in the city of Novgorod as to whether the men of the army of Voevoda Yadreik were dead or alive. And in Novgorod the prince, the archbishop, and the entire people of the city grieved.

In the same year a son, Rostislav, was born to Yaroslav in Novgorod. And they built a wooden church called Zhivoglozha to the Holy Apostles, and another church to St. Joan the Merciful at the Gates of Resurrection.

THE BATTLE ON THE RIVER KALKA

In 1224 the Mongols, united under Ghenghis Khan, invaded southern Russia for the first time. They came there more or less accidentally, returning to Central Asia after conquests in Persia and the Caucasus. (The Mongols became known to Russians by the name Tatar. The Tatars were actually a Mongolian tribe from which were taken the shock troops for the advancing Mongolian army.) After having defeated the Russian princes and their allies, the Kumans—who joined with the Russians the better to resist the invasion—the Mongols disappeared into the Central Asian steppes and deserts. They returned twelve years later, and this time they held the Russian land for nearly two and a half centuries. The report of this first decisive battle on the river Kalka is apparently of southern origin, and was incorporated into the *Novgorodian Chronicle* under the year 1224.

◆ ◆ ◆

1224 (6732) In the same year, for our sins, there came unknown tribes. No one knew who they were nor what was their origin, faith, or tongue, and some people called them Tatars, while others called them Taurmens, and still others called them Pechenegs. Some say that these are the same people of whom Methodius of Patras spoke and that they came from the Yetrian Desert, which is between North and East. Methodius said that at the end of time there will appear those whom Gideon drove away, and they will conquer the whole land from the Tigris and Euphrates rivers to the Pontic Sea, with the exception of Ethiopia. Only God knows who these people are or from whence they came. The wise men, who understand the Books, know who they are, but we do not. Here we record them in memory of the misfortunes of the Russian princes that came about at their (the Tatars') hands. We have heard that they have conquered many lands and have killed many Yassians, Abkhasians, Kossogians,[1] and godless Kumans. And many Kumans were driven away and many others were killed, owing to the wrath of God and his Immaculate Mother. Much evil has befallen the Russian land at the hands of these Kumans, and therefore most merciful God desired that these godless Kumans, son of Ishmael, should die in order to revenge the Christian blood that was upon them, these lawless ones.

These Taurmens (Mongols) came across the whole Kuman land and came close to the Russian border. And the remnants of these godless Kumans under the leadership of Khotian and other princes came to the so-called Kuman Wall, where many were killed together with princes David Koviakovich and George. This Khotian was the father-in-law of Mstislav Mstislavich, the Russian Prince of Galich. And he (Khotian) arrived in Galich with greetings for his son-in-law, Mstislav Mstislavich, and all the other Russian princes. He brought them numerous presents: horses, camels, buffaloes, and girls. And he presented

[1] Yassians, Kossogians, and Abkhazians were Caucasian tribes.

these gifts to them, and said the following: "Today the Tatars took away our land and tomorrow they will come and take away yours." And Khotian begged his son-in-law (for help). And Mstislav Mstislavich began to beg his brothers, the Russian princes, saying, "Brethren, if we do not help them, they will turn to the Tatars, and so later they (the Kumans) will be more powerful."

And hence, having deliberated for some time, they decided to start a campaign, responding to the appeals of the Kuman princes. And the warriors began to gather in their respective regions, and began a march against the Tatars after the whole Russian land was united. Soon the Russian army came to a place called Zarub on the Dnieper.

The Tatars, learning that the Russian princes had begun to march against them, sent their envoys to them, saying: "We hear that you, having followed the advice of the Kumans, do march against us. But we have neither occupied your lands nor your cities and villages, and we are not campaigning against you. We came because God let us conquer the godless Kumans who are our slaves and cattle herders. You should make peace with us. If the Kumans came to you, fight them and take all their belongings. We tell you this because we understand that they have done much harm to you and that is why we fight them."

The Russian princes paid no heed to these speeches, but killed the envoys and marched against the Tatars. They set up camp on the Dnieper in the vicinity of Oleshie. And the Tatars once again sent envoys, and they said the following: "You have listened to the Kumans and have killed our envoys. Come, then, though we have not occupied your lands, and it will be an injustice against God and everyone." And the Russians permitted the envoys to go away.

And Prince Mstislav Mstislavich forded the Dnieper and charged the Tatar outpost and took it with a thousand warriors. The rest of the Tatars of this outpost escaped to the Kuman Hills under the command of Gwemia Beg. Since the Tatars found no assistance, they hid their leader, Gwemia Beg, underground so that he would not be killed. But they were attacked at that place by the Kumans, and Gwemia Beg was killed with the approval of Mstislav Mstislavich.

As soon as the other Russian princes learned of this action, they all crossed the Dnieper, and after nine days they came to the river Kalka. They sent the Kuman vanguard, under the command of Yarun, ahead, while the Russian princes and their armies set up camp. Yarun began fighting with the Tatars, but his Kuman warriors failed, and retreated in such haste that they galloped over the Russian camp and trampled it underfoot. And there was not time for the Russian forces to form ranks. And so it came to complete confusion, and a terrible slaughter resulted.

Mstislav, Prince of Kiev, having witnessed this misfortune, decided not to retreat, but took his position over the river Kalka. It was a rocky, rugged place on which he built a stockade and fought off the Tatars for three days. In this fortification with Prince Mstislav there remained his brothers-in-law, Andrew and Alexander of Dubrovich. The Tatar troops that besieged the fortification were led by Chigyz Khan and Teshu Khan. With the Tatars there were also a number of Brodniks[1] (Cossacks) under the command of Ploskyn. This accursed commander pledged by the holy cross that Prince Mstislav and his two brothers-in-law would not be killed, but released for ransom. But this accursed Ploskyn lied, and he bound the princes hand and feet and turned them over to the Tatars. The princes were taken by the Tatars and crushed beneath platforms placed over their bodies on the top of which the Tatars celebrated their victory banquet. And the fortified camp of Mstislav was taken, and all his warriors were slain.

The other princes were pursued to the Dnieper, and six of them were killed there: Sviatoslav of Yanev, Iziaslav, son of Ingvar, Sviatoslav of Shumsk, Mstislav of Chernigov and his son, and George of Nesvizh. But Prince Mstislav Mstislavich, Prince of Galich, escaped by crossing the Dnieper, and he cut loose the boats from the shore to ensure his escape. Only one Russian warrior in ten lived through this battle; in returning to their homelands, many of these were killed by the Kumans for their horses and clothes.

In such a way did God bring confusion upon us, and an endless number of people perished. This evil event came to pass on the Day of Jeremiah the Prophet, the 31st day of May. As for the Tatars, they turned back from the Dnieper, and we know neither from whence they came nor whither they have now gone. Only God knows that, because he brought them upon us for our sins.

[1] Russian outlaws and adventurers who lived in the prairie among the Kumans.

Part II

The Period of Feudal Divisions

(1240–1478)

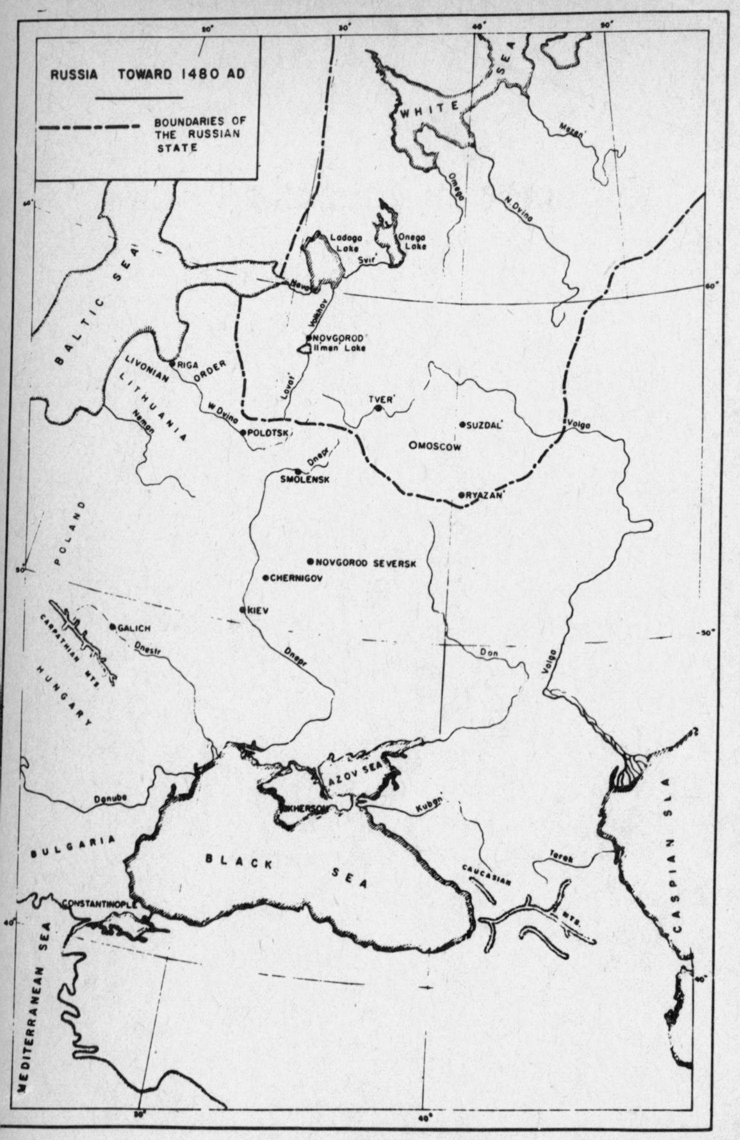

Russia Toward 1480 A.D.

MILITARY TALES

22. *Orison on the Downfall of Russia*

The *Orison on the Downfall of Russia* belongs to a well-known, but still obscure Russian thirteenth-century literary fragment. It is usually found in miscellanies that contain the *Tale of the Life and Heroic Deeds of the Great Prince Alexander Nevsky,* and always precedes it. However, its style differs strikingly from the tale of Alexander Nevsky. It is very probable that it is the beginning of a longer orison or lamentation bewailing the conquest of Russia by the Mongols. It ends abruptly with the indication that a catastrophe befell Russia. Its style is both rhetorical and pathetic, and reflects a strong nationalistic spirit embittered by the catastrophe. One can presume that a longer description of the Mongol invasion originally followed this introductory part.

Although this orison was not written in verse, it can easily be divided into short rhythmic units, many of which rhyme, as for instance, lines three to eleven. The rhythm and diction of this work have many features in common with those of the *Lay of Igor's Campaign.* Since the author mentions the ruler at the time of the orison's writing as being Yaroslav (Great Prince of Vladimir, 1238–1246), it can be concluded that this work was composed no earlier than 1237, the year the Tatars invaded Russia, and no later than 1246, the year of Yaroslav's death.

This translation is based on the Russian text edited by Kh. Loparev to be found in *Pamiatniki drevnei pismenosti i iskusstva,* Volume LXXXIV, St. Petersburg, 1892.

✦ ✦ ✦

O Russian land, brightest of the bright,
most beautifully adorned,
thou art marvelous to us, with thy many beauties.
Marvelous are thy numerous lakes,
thy rivers and venerated springs,
steep mountains, high hills,
oak forests, beautiful fields,
many beasts and countless birds,

great cities, wonderful villages, and monastery gardens,
honorable boyars and countless lords,
Christian churches and stern princes.
Thou, Russian land, art rich in wealth
and the Orthodox Christian faith.
Thou spreadest from Hungary to Poland and Bohemia,
from Bohemia to the land of the Yatvags,
from the land of the Yatvags to the Lithuanians and Germans,
from the land of the Germans to Karelia,
from Karelia to Ustiug
where live the pagan Toymians,
and beyond The Breathing Sea,[1]
and from the sea to the Bulgars,
from the Bulgars to the Burtasians,
from the Burtasians to the Cheremiss, and
from the Cheremiss to the Mordvians.
All these vast areas and the people that live on them
were subjugated by God to the Christian people (of Russia)
and to Great Prince Vsevolod
and to his father, Yury, Prince of Kiev,
and to his grandfather, Vladimir Monomakh,
with whose name the Kumans frightened
their children in their cradles,
and in whose reign the Lithuanians
did not dare show themselves from their swamps,
and in whose reign the Hungarians fortified
the stone walls of their cities with their iron gates
so that great Vladimir might not pass through.
And at that time the Germans did rejoice
in being so far (from the Russians) beyond the sea.
And the Burtasians, Cheremiss, Votiaks, and Mordvians
worked hard to pay tribute to Vladimir the Great.
And even the Emperor of Byzantium, Manuel,
fearing lest Vladimir the Great take Constantinople,
was sending rich presents to him.

And so it used to be.
But now a great misfortune has befallen the Russian land,
the land that was once ruled by the great Yaroslav and Vladimir,
and is now ruled by Prince Yaroslav
and his brother, Yury, Prince of Vladimir. . . .

[1] The White Sea and the Arctic Ocean, because of frequent fogs, were called "The Breathing Sea" by Old Russians.

23. *Tale of the Destruction of Riazan*

THE *Tale of the Destruction of Riazan* is one of the most interesting and best written accounts of the invasion of Russia by the Mongols under the leadership of Batu. Though the writer of this tale called Batu "tsar," meaning emperor, Batu was actually only a commander of the Mongolian armies that operated in Europe. The Mongolian emperor resided either in Mongolia or in northern China.

This story is contained in many manuscripts of the sixteenth and seventeenth centuries. Apparently it once formed a part of a miscellany that was composed and revised many times by the clergy of the Church of St. Nicholas of Zaraisk, which, according to legend, is located on the very spot where Princess Eupraxy killed herself. The composition of this account, which in our translation is divided into distinct parts, shows its heterogeneous origins. The first contains typical chronicle entries slightly embellished by the usual phraseology of old Russian military tales. The story of the knight, Eupaty Kolovrat, is one of the oldest examples of the Russian heroic tale and has several stylistic features to be found also in Russian *bylinas*, or heroic epic songs. Many features of this knightly epic resemble those of the deeds of medieval knights in western Europe. The joust between Eupaty and the Tatar knight, Hostovrul, and Batu's respect for the body of Eupaty Kolovrat and the survivors of his army, would fit perfectly well into the knightly tradition of western Europe. Other details seem to be patterned after the *Lay of Igor's Campaign*, such as the appeal by Great Prince Yury Ingvarevich to the princes of Riazan. In the last part, with its description of the mourning over and burial of the princes who fell on the field of battle, and in the remarkable lamentation of Prince Ingvar Ingvarevich, folkloric and biblical styles are skillfully blended.

It is evident that this is a fictionalized account of the destruction of Riazan and that it was actually written many years after the events occurred. The author apparently used for his source material a short account of the events and a list giving the names of the princes of Riazan but not the dates of their deaths. Therefore, the writer oversimplified the family relationships among the Riazan princes and also mentioned several princes who had actually died either before the battle or some time after: *i.e.*, Prince Vsevolod and Prince Oleg the Handsome are mentioned as heroic defenders of the Riazan land. Actually, Prince Vsevolod died in 1208 and Prince Oleg in 1258. Still, most of the facts and details given in this tale do not correspond to information provided in other documents and chronicles.

This translation is based on the Russian text published by V. P. Adrianova–Peretts in *Voinskie povesti drevnei Rusi*, Moscow and Leningrad, 1949, pages 9–17, 18, and 19.

✦ ✦ ✦

I. Batu Invades Russia

Within twelve years after bringing the miraculous icon of St. Nicholas from Kherson, the godless Emperor Batu invaded the Russian land with a great multitude of his Tatar warriors and set up camp on the river Voronezh in the vicinity of the principality of Riazan. And he sent his faithless envoys to the city of Riazan, to Great Prince Yury Ingvarevich, demanding tithes from everyone—from the princes and from all kinds of people. And they also demanded one-tenth of all the horses in the city. As soon as Great Prince Yury Ingvarevich learned of the invasion by godless Batu, he sent his people to the city of Vladimir, to the faithful and Great Prince George Vsevolodovich, asking that he either send succor against the godless emperor or come personally with his army. However, the great prince neither came personally nor sent help, since he had decided to fight Batu himself. And the Great Prince Yury Ingvarevich, having learned that he would receive no help from the Grand Prince of Vladimir, immediately sent to his kin for help, to Prince David Ingvarevich of Murom, to Prince Gleb Ingvarevich of Kolomna, to Prince Oleg the Handsome, and to Prince Vsevolod of Pronsk, and to other princes. And they started to deliberate as to how to satisfy the godless emperor with tribute. And the Great Prince Yury Ingvarevich decided to send his son, Fedor Yurevich, to Batu with many gifts and supplications that he not invade the land of Riazan.

Prince Fedor came to the Emperor Batu whose camp was on the river Voronezh. And he pleaded with the emperor. The godless, false, merciless emperor accepted the gifts and deceitfully promised not to launch a campaign against the principality of Riazan, but he bragged, and threatened to conquer all other Russian lands. And the emperor began to entertain the Riazan princes, and after this entertainment asked that they send their sisters and daughters to be his concubines. And one envious Riazan courtier told Batu that the wife of Prince Fedor belonged to the Byzantine Imperial Family and that she had a most beautiful body. Emperor Batu, who was false and merciless, became excited, and told Prince Fedor, "Prince, give me your wife so that I may enjoy her beauty."

But Prince Fedor laughed at Batu's suggestion, and said: "It is not our Christian custom to bring to you, the godless emperor, our wives so that your lust may be satisfied. If you conquer us, then you will be the ruler of our wives."

The godless Emperor Batu felt offended, and became angry. He ordered the immediate death of Prince Fedor, and commanded that his body be thrown in a field where it would be devoured by beasts and birds. And the retinue and the warriors of Prince Fedor were also put to death.

One of the servants of Prince Fedor, by name Aponitsa, managed to escape, and wept bitterly, seeing the body of his master. Having noticed that no one guarded the corpse, he took his beloved master's body and buried it secretly. Then he hurried to Princess Eupraxy and told her that Emperor Batu had killed her husband. At that moment the princess happened to be on the upper floor of the palace with her infant son, Prince Ivan. When she heard from Aponitsa that her husband had been slain, she was seized with grief, and threw herself from the window with the child in her arms. And so both were killed.

When Great Prince Yury Ingvarevich learned of his son's death and of the deaths of his son's retinue and warriors, he fell to mourning with Princess Agrippina. And for a long time there were lamentation and sorrow throughout the city. As soon as the great prince recovered from his bereavement, he began to gather an army and to groom his regiments. When Great Prince Yury Ingvarevich saw his kin, his boyars, and his voevodas fearlessly and bravely astride their horses, he raised his hands to the heavens and said with tears in his eyes: "Save us, God, from our enemies and those that march against us. And preserve us from the faithless and make their way dark and difficult."

And then he said to his men: "O my lords and brethren! Since we have received from God his blessing, we must also accept his punishment. It is better, through death, to win eternal glory than to be under the power of the heathen. And I, your brother, am ready to sacrifice my life for the holy divine Church, for the Christian faith, and for the country of our father, Great Prince Ingvar Sviatoslavovich."

And then he went to the Church of the Assumption of the Blessed Virgin, and prayed there. And he cried before the icon of the Blessed Virgin and prayed to the great worker of miracles, St. Nicholas, and to his holy kin, Sts. Boris and Gleb. And for the last time he kissed Great Princess Agrippina. And he received the blessings of the bishop and the priests.

II. Batu Defeats Prince Yury

And they marched against the infidel Batu, and meeting him on the border of the principality of Riazan, attacked and began to fight both fiercely and bravely. And it was a terrible and awesome battle, and many of Batu's regiments were defeated. And Emperor Batu, seeing how fiercely and bravely did the warriors of Riazan fight, became frightened. But who can resist the wrath of God? Batu's forces were innumerable and invincible. Each Riazan warrior had to fight with a thousand of the enemy. And every two Riazan warriors had to fight with ten thousand of the enemy. And Prince Yury Ingvarevich saw the slaying of his brother, David, and exclaimed in anguish: "O my kind brothers and dear warriors, the flower of Riazan's troops, be brave and resist mightily. Our dear brother, Prince David, was the first to drink the bitter cup to the dregs, and we shall do the same."

And the princes and the warriors changed horses and once again began to fight fiercely. And they cut through the many strong lines of the Tatar regiments, fighting bravely and fiercely. And all the Tatar regiments were struck with awe upon seeing the bravery and power of the Riazan armies. And they fought with such intensity that even the earth began to moan, and confusion reigned in the ranks of Batu's armies. The strong Tatar regiments were hardly able to overcome the Riazan offensive. In this battle were killed Great Prince Yury Ingvarevich, Prince David Ingvarevich of Murom, Prince Gleb Ingvarevich of Kolomna, Prince Vsevolod Ingvarevich of Pronsk, and many other brave Riazan princes, powerful voevodas, and warriors. Heroes and brave warriors, the flower of Riazan's army, all drank the same bitter cup to the dregs, and fell on the field of battle.* And Prince Oleg was taken prisoner half alive. All of this happened according to the will of God and because of our sins.

And the Emperor Batu, seeing that numerous regiments of his army had been defeated, was seized by awe and grief. He began conquering the Riazan lands, ordering that everyone and everything be cut down and burned without mercy. And he lay

* None of the men of Riazan deserted the battlefield; all were slain.

low the cities of Pronsk, Belgorod, and Izheslavets, killing everyone in these cities without mercy. And Christian blood flowed like a great river. And all this because of our sins.

When Emperor Batu saw Prince Oleg Ingvarevich, the most handsome and bravest of the Riazan princes, dying from his grievous wounds, he wanted to heal his wounds and win him over to his faith. But Prince Oleg began to reprimand Batu, and called him godless and the enemy of all Christendom. And fire came from the evil heart of Batu, and he ordered that Prince Oleg be cut to pieces. And so he became the second Stephen the Martyr, having received the crown of suffering from the all-merciful God. And he drank his bitter cup to the dregs with all his brethren.

III. The Taking of Riazan

The accursed Batu began the conquest of the land of Riazan, and soon approached the city of Riazan itself. They encircled the city and fought without surcease for five days. Batu changed his regiments frequently, replacing them with fresh troops, while the citizens of Riazan fought without relief. And many citizens were killed and others wounded. Still others were exhausted by their great efforts and their wounds. On the dawn of the sixth day the pagan warriors began to storm the city, some with firebrands, some with battering rams, and others with countless scaling ladders for ascending the walls of the city. And they took the city of Riazan on the 21st day of December. And the Tatars came to the Cathedral of the Assumption of the Blessed Virgin, and they cut to pieces the Great Princess Agrippina, her daughters-in-law, and other princesses. They burned to death the bishops and the priests and put the torch to the holy church. And the Tatars cut down many people, including women and children. Still others were drowned in the river. And they killed without exception all monks and priests. And they burned this holy city with all its beauty and wealth, and they captured the relatives of the Riazan princes, the princes of Kiev and Chernigov. And churches of God were destroyed, and much blood was spilled on the holy altars. And not one man remained alive in the city. All were dead. All had drunk the same bitter cup to the dregs. And there was not even anyone to mourn the dead. Neither father nor mother could mourn their dead children, nor the children their fathers or mothers. Nor could a brother mourn the death of his brother, nor relatives their relatives. All were dead. And this happened for our sins.

IV. Eupaty the Fearless

Seeing this terrible letting of Christian blood, the heart of godless Batu became even more hardened, and he marched against the cities of Suzdal and Vladimir, intending to conquer all Russian lands, to uproot the Christian faith, and to destroy the churches of God. At that time a Riazan lord, Eupaty Kolovrat, who was in Chernigov at the time of the destruction of the city of Riazan, heard of Batu's invasion. He left Chernigov with a small force and hurried to Riazan. When he came to the land of Riazan he saw it devastated and the cities destroyed, the rulers killed, and the people dead. And he rushed to the city of Riazan and found it destroyed, the rulers killed, and the people slaughtered. Some of them were cut down, while others were burned, and still others were drowned. And Eupaty wept with great sorrow and his heart became angry. He gathered a small force of seventeen hundred men who had been preserved by God outside the city. And they hurriedly pursued the godless emperor. And with difficulty they caught up with him in the principality of Suzdal, and suddenly fell upon his camp. And there began a battle without mercy, and confusion reigned. And the Tatars lost their heads from fear as Eupaty fought so fiercely that his sword became dull, and, taking a sword from a fallen Tatar, he would cut them down with their own swords. The Tatars thought that the Russians had risen from the dead, and Eupaty was riding through the ranks of the Tatar regiments so bravely that Batu himself became frightened.

With great effort the Tatars managed to capture five men from Eupaty's regiments, and then only because they were exhausted from their wounds. They were brought before the Tatar emperor, and he asked them, "Why do you cause me such evil?"

The warriors answered: "We are of the Christian faith, knights of the Great Prince Yury of Riazan, and from the regiment of Eupaty Kolovrat. We were sent by Prince Ingvar Ingvarevich to you, the powerful emperor, to honor you, to chase you away with honors, and to render unto you all honors. Do not wonder, Emperor, that we have not had time to serve up the bitter cup to your entire army." And the emperor admired their witty answers. And he sent his brother-in-law, Hostovrul, against Eupaty, and with Hostovrul went strong regiments. Hostovrul bragged to the emperor, and promised to bring back Eupaty alive.

Eupaty was encircled by Tatar troops because they wished to take him alive. And Hostovrul rode out against Eupaty, but

Eupaty was a giant, and with one blow he cleft Hostovrul to the saddle. And once more he began to cut down the Tatar troops, and he killed many of Batu's best knights. Some were cut down, while others were cleft to their waist, and still others were cleft to their saddles. The Tatars became afraid, seeing what a giant Eupaty was. And then they brought up catapults and began showering rocks upon him. And they finally killed Eupaty Kolovrat, but only with great difficulty.

Eupaty's body was brought before Batu, and the emperor sent for his princes, lords, and commanders, and all marveled at the courage, power, and bravery of the Riazan warriors. And the lords, commanders, and princes told Batu: "We were in many battles with many emperors in many lands, but never have we seen such courageous heroes, and even our fathers never told us of such. They are winged people. They do not think about death, and they fight bravely and courageously on their horses, one against a thousand, and two against ten thousand warriors. None of them would abandon the battlefield alive."

And Batu looked at Eupaty's body, and said: "O Kolovrat Eupaty, you have honored us with your courage, and you, with your small army, have killed many knights of my powerful horde and have defeated many of my regiments. If such a knight would serve with me, I would keep him very close to my heart." And he gave up Eupaty's body to the remainder of the Riazan force that had been captured on the battlefield. And Batu gave orders that the prisoners should be released and that no harm should come to them.

V. Prince Ingvar Buries the Dead

Prince Ingvar Ingvarevich (the brother of Great Prince Yury Ingvarevich of Riazan) returned from Chernigov, having been there with his relative, Prince Michael, at the time of the destruction of Riazan. And so he was preserved by God from the enemy of all Christendom. Prince Ingvar Ingvarevich found his fatherland devastated, and learned that all his brothers had been killed by the impure, lawbreaking Batu. And he came to the city of Riazan and found the city destroyed, and his mother and sisters-in-law, his relatives, and many other people lying dead. And he found the churches burned and all valuables taken from the common treasury of Chernigov and Riazan. When Prince Ingvar saw this great and enduring destruction he shrieked aloud in his sorrow, sounding as a trumpet summoning the army or as an organ resounding. And after these rending shrieks and horrifying lamentations, Prince Ingvar fell to the ground as if dead. With great difficulty and the help of water and a fresh breeze did he recover. And finally his soul did revive in his body.

Who would not so lament such a catastrophe? Who would not bewail the deaths of so many Orthodox people? Who would not mourn the death of so many rulers? Who would not mourn such a dispersion?

And Prince Ingvar searched through the bodies, and found the body of his mother, Princess Agrippina, and those of his brothers' wives. And he called a priest from villages that were preserved by God, and he buried his mother and the wives of his deceased brothers with great lamentations in place of the psalms and chants. And he cried and lamented terribly. And he buried the bodies of the other dead and he cleaned the city. And he had the city blessed by a priest and he gathered the few survivors and comforted them. And he lamented for a long time, thinking of his mother, his brothers, his relatives, and all the people of Riazan who had met such untimely deaths.

And all this happened because of our sins. There used to be the city of Riazan in the land of Riazan, but its wealth disappeared and its glory ceased, and there is nothing to be seen in the city excepting smoke, ashes, and barren earth. All churches and the cathedral were burned. And not only this city, but many others were conquered. There is neither the ringing of the church bells nor church services. And instead of joy, there are only uninterrupted lamentations.

And Prince Ingvar went to the place where his brethren were killed by the impious emperor Batu. Great Prince Yury of Riazan, Prince David of Murom, Prince Vsevolod of Pronsk, Prince Gleb of Kolomna, many other princes, boyars, voevodas, and warriors —indeed, all the best souls of Riazan—were lying on the barren earth and frozen grass. And they were covered with snow and ice, and no one cared for them. Beasts devoured their bodies, and a multitude of birds tore them to pieces. And they were lying together, even as they had fallen together. They all drank the same bitter cup to the dregs.

And when Prince Ingvar Ingvarevich saw this great number of corpses lying on the earth, he shrieked bitterly, like a trumpet resounding. He fell to the ground, and tears flowed from his eyes in a stream. And Prince Ingvar spoke in great sadness:

"O my dear brethren and warriors!
O my treasured lives!
How could you close your eyes

and leave me alone in such misfortune?
How could you disappear from my sight,
treasures of my life?
O my beautiful flowers!
O my unripened vineyard!
Why won't you speak to me, your brother?
Never again will you make my life sweet.
Why won't you look at me?
Why won't you talk with me?
How could you, fruitful gardens,
born of the same father,
and from the same womb of Great Princess Agrippina,
and fed by the same breast, forget me?
To whom have you forsaken me, your brother?
You did fade too early, my dear eastern stars.
You set so early, my dear suns.
You lie on this deserted land watched over by no one!
No one renders you honor or glory.
Indeed, your days of glory have dimmed.
Where is your power?
You, who used to be rulers of many lands,
now lie on this barren earth,
and your faces darken from decay.
O my dear brothers!
O my dear warriors!
Never again shall we share joys.
O my bright lights,
Why were you extinguished?
I have not had enough joy with you!
If God hears your prayers,
pray that I, your brother, might join you!
After days of joy have come those of tears and sorrow.
After pleasures and happiness,
have come lamenting and mourning.
O, why did I not die before you
so that I would not have had to see your deaths?
This is my bitter fate!
Do you hear my unhappy words that fall so sadly?
O mother earth!
O forest of oak, lament with me!
And how shall I describe these days
in which perished
so many rulers and warriors,
so many brave and dashing heroes of Riazan?

None returned,
but all drank the same bitter cup to the dregs.
My tongue does not obey me,
my lips close,
my sight darkens,
my strength ebbs,
for great is the sorrow of my soul."

And there was great sorrow and sadness, tears and sighs, fears and trembling, because of the evil ones that attacked our land. Great Prince Ingvar raised his hands to the heavens, and prayed tearfully:

"O Lord, my God,
I place my hope in thee.
Save and preserve me from my persecutors.
O my most holy Mother of Christ, my Savior,
don't forsake me in my hour of grief.
Boris and Gleb, our great martyrs and ancestors,
be of help to me in battle, lowly sinner that I am.
My brethren and warriors,
help me with your prayers in my struggles against the enemy,
these children of Hagar,
these grandchildren of Ishmael."

And then Prince Ingvar began to search among the bodies of the dead, and he took for burial the bodies of his brothers, Great Prince Yury, Prince Gleb of Kolomna, and of other princes related to him, as well as those of many other boyars and voevodas well known to him. And he transported the bodies to the city of Riazan, and buried them with honor. And the bodies of the others, which were lying on the devastated earth, he buried and had the last rites pronounced over them. Having buried all of them, Prince Ingvar then went to the city of Pronsk where he gathered the pieces of his slain brother, the peaceful and Christ-loving Prince Oleg. And he ordered the body returned to the city of Riazan, and he himself carried the venerable head of Prince Oleg to the city. And he kissed it with respect, and placed the body in the same coffin with the body of Great Prince Yury. In the vicinity of this grave were buried the remains of Princes David and Gleb in a single coffin. And then Prince Ingvar went to the river Voronezh where Prince Fedor Yurevich had been killed at the order of Batu. And

Prince Ingvar shed many tears over the body of Prince Fedor and he brought it to the city of Riazan, and in the vicinity of the icon of the great maker of miracles, St. Nicholas, he buried Prince Fedor together with his wife, faithful Princess Eupraxy, and his son, Prince Ivan. And he placed stone crosses over the graves. . . . [A fragment has been omitted.]

Then faithful Prince Ingvar, whose baptismal name was Cosmas, took the throne of his father, Ingvar Sviatoslavovich. And he restored the land of Riazan and he erected churches and monasteries. And he consoled the settlers and gathered his people together. And he was a great joy for the Christians who, with the help of God's strong hand, had escaped the godless infidel, Emperor Batu. And he put Prince Michael Vsevolodovich of Pronsk in his father's patrimony.

24. *Sofony of Riazan: Zadonshchina*

On September 8, 1380, Russian troops, under the command of the Great Prince of Moscow, Dmitry, defeated the Tatar armies, 300,000 strong, lead by Mamay, Khan of the Golden Horde. It was the first time, after one and a half centuries of Tatar domination over the Russian land, that the Russians defeated the Tatars. This battle did not bring an immediate end to the Tatar yoke, but it was a great victory for the Russians, both weakening the domination of the Tatars and fostering the unification of the Russian lands. Thus, it is not surprising that this important historical event is recorded in various literary works. Among them, the most interesting is the *Lay of Great Prince Dmitry Ivanovich and his Brother, Prince Vladimir Andreevich,* written by Sofony of Riazan. It is known in Russian as *Zadonshchina,* meaning "The Tale of Events Beyond the Don," because the battle took place not far from the Don River, on the Kulikovo prairie. *Zadonshchina* was the title used in one of several extant manuscripts by Sofony of Riazan.

The purpose of this poetic lay was not to give a detailed historical account of the background and development of this battle, one of the most memorable in Russian history. The author omitted a considerable number of events that were of importance to the final outcome of the conflict, while many others were consolidated for the sake of poetic unity. Instead, the author wished to give an epic account of the Russians' efforts, and to stress the importance of this, the first decisive victory over the Tatars.

For the basic patterns of this lay, Sofony of Riazan turned to the greatest poetic work of Kievan Russia, the *Lay of Igor's Campaign.* In many respects he imitated this work, using its symbolic parallelisms, metaphors, alliterative patterns, and poetic imagery. Some sentences are taken word for word from the text of the earlier *Lay* (*Slovo*). Still, Sofony of Riazan created a lay that is very different from that about Igor, not only in its historical perspectives and political conceptions but also in its structure and in the development of narrative line.

Like the author of the tale of Igor, Sofony of Riazan, in writing this work, had in mind not only a poetic account of the battle but also an appeal to Russian unity and Russian national feelings. But, whereas the *Lay of Igor's Campaign* is primarily a lyrical appeal, *Zadonshchina* has a very definite narrative scheme that gives a more realistic account of events. Unlike the *Lay*, the lyrical elements in this work are minimized, and the reminiscences of past feuds, so central to the *Lay*, are practically absent. *Zadonshchina*, like the *Lay*, was written not in verse but in rhythmic prose consisting of clearly distinguishable units.

The present translation is based on the text edited by V. P. Adrianova-Peretts, which is itself based on various medieval manuscripts of the work. This text was published in *Voinskie povesti drevnei Rusi*, in the series *Literaturnye Pamiatniki*, Moscow and Leningrad, 1949, pages 33–41. The division into chapters and stanzas, as well as the typographic arrangement, was made by the translator to facilitate reading.

◆ ◆ ◆

Proemium

Great Prince Dmitry Ivanovich, with his brother,[1] Prince Vladimir Andreevich, and his voevodas, attended a banquet at the house of Mikula Vasilievich. (And Prince Dmitry Ivanovich spoke, saying:)

"Do you know, dear brothers, that Emperor Mamai
invaded the Russian land at the swift river Don
and is advancing into the midnight land?
Let us go, brothers, into that midnight land,
the lot of Japheth, the son of Noah,

[1] Prince Vladimir was actually his cousin, but among close relatives it was customary to call each other "brother."

from whom has come most glorious Russia.
Let us ascend the mountains of Kiev
and view the glorious river Dnieper.
Let us view the entire Russian land
and beyond the east, the lot of Shem,
the son of Noah, from whom were born
the pagan nomads, the Moslem Tatars."

I. Exhortation

They have defeated the race of Japheth on the river Kalka.[2]
And since that time the Russian land has been sad.
And, from the battle on the Kalka to the defeat of Mamai,
the Russian land has been covered with grief and sorrow,
shedding tears and lamenting the loss of her children.
Princes, boyars, and all courageous men!
Let us leave our homes, our wealth, our women and children, our cattle,
that we may receive glory and honor in this world.
Let us lay down our lives for the Russian land and the Christian faith.
First, the sorrow of the Russian land did I describe,
as it has been done before in the books.
Then, I have described my sorrows and my glorifications
of the Great Prince Dmitry Ivanovich
and his brother, Vladimir Andreevich.
Let us come together, brothers, friends, and sons
of the Russian land.
Let us knit word after word.
Let us bring joy to the Russian land
and cast sorrow on the eastern country, the lot of Shem.
Let us sing of the defeat of Mamai, the infidel.
Let us sing glory to the Great Prince Dmitry Ivanovich
and to his brother, Prince Vladimir Andreevich.

Let us say the following words:
"It behooves us, brothers, to begin with new words
the telling of the glorious tale of the army of Prince Dmitry Ivanovich
and his brother, Prince Vladimir Andreevich, great-grandsons
of holy Prince Vladimir of Kiev."

2 In most of the manuscripts the river is called Kaiala, but Sofony apparently refers to the river Kalka, the site of the battle with the Mongols in 1223.

Let us tell the tale in the tradition of yore.
Let us race in thought across the lands.
Let us remember the deeds of former years.
Let us glorify wise Boyan, the great bard of Kiev,
for he, wise Boyan, would put his nimble fingers
on the living strings and would sing the glory of
the princes of Russia, of Igor Rurikovich, the first Great Prince of Kiev,
of Great Prince Vladimir Sviatoslavovich and
of Great Prince Yaroslav Vladimirovich.
So let us glorify with our melodies and powerful lyrics
this Great Prince Dmitry Ivanovich
and his brother, Prince Vladimir Andreevich,
great-grandsons of those princes who devoted all their
bravery and efforts to the Russian land and the Christian faith.

II. The Russians Prepare for the Campaign

Great Prince Dmitry Ivanovich and
his brother, Prince Vladimir Andreevich,
strengthened their minds with valor,
quickened their hearts with courage, and
imbued their thoughts with martial spirit.
And they gathered their regiments throughout the Russian land.
And they remembered the deeds of their great-grandfather,
Prince Vladimir of Kiev.

Skylark, joy of beautiful days!
Fly high into the beautiful blue sky.
Look on the powerful city of Moscow,
sing the glories of Great Prince Dmitry Ivanovich
and his brother, Prince Vladimir Andreevich.
The storm will bring the gyrfalcon
from the Russian lands into the Kuman prairie.
Steeds neigh in Moscow.
Glory rings out over all Russian lands.
Trumpets blare in Kolomna.
Drums resound in Serpukhov.
Banners are raised at the shore of the great river Don.
Bells resound in the great city of Novgorod,
but men of Novgorod remain in Holy Sophia, saying,
"O brethren, we shall not have time to help
Great Prince Dmitry Ivanovich."

It seems that eagles fly from the midnight land,
but they are not eagles.
They are Russian princes who fly together
to help Prince Dmitry Ivanovich and his brother,
Prince Vladimir Andreevich, telling them such words:
"Lord, Great Prince, the infidel Tatars have begun
advancing into our lands.
They take from us our patrimony.
They camp on the river Mech,
between the rivers Don and Dnieper.
Our lord, we will go beyond the swift river Dnieper.
We will win glory for our land in the tradition of old.
We will gain memories for our youth.
We will put our brave warriors to the test
for the Russian land and the Christian faith."

And then Prince Dmitry Ivanovich said:
"Brethren and princes of the Russian land,
we are all descendants of Prince Vladimir of Kiev.
Since our birth we have never permitted ourselves to be
offended,
neither by the falcon nor the gyrfalcon,
nor by the black raven nor by the infidel Mamai."

If only the nightingale could sing the glories
of the two brothers of the Lithuanian land,
Andrew and Dmitry, the sons of Olgerd,
and of Dmitry of Volynia,
for these courageous sons, gyrfalcons in time of battle,
our brave army captains,
were swaddled under trumpets,
were raised under helmets, and
were fed at lance point in the Lithuanian land.

And Andrew, son of Olgerd, spoke to his brother, Dmitry:
"We are two brothers, sons of Olgerd,
grandsons of Adiman, great-grandsons of Skolomend.
Let us gather together our dear brethren,
the nobles of brave Lithuania, bold and brave fellows.
Let us mount on swift steeds.
Let us view the swift river Don.
Let us drink the water of the Don from our helmets,
Let us test our Lithuanian swords on Tatar helmets,
and our German javelins on the armor of the Muslims."

And Dmitry, son of Olgerd, said to him:
"Brother Andrew, let us not spare ourselves
in defense of the Russian land and the Christian faith,
and in defense of the honor of Prince Dmitry Ivanovich.
Already, brother, thunder resounds and clamor raises in the stone city of Moscow.
But it is not thunder, brother.
It is the clamor of the powerful army of Dmitry Ivanovich.
The brave Russian warriors thunder in their gilded armor
and with their crimson shields.
Andrew, saddle your swift steed,
for mine has been long saddled.
Let us go, brother, into the open fields.
Let us go, brother, and view our regiments."

III. The Coming of the Tatars

Already from the sea there have begun blowing strong winds
into the mouth of the rivers Don and Dnieper.
And they have wafted great clouds over the Russian land,
and these clouds made the sunsets as crimson as blood,
and blue lightning flashes through these clouds.
There will be great clamor on the river Nepriadva,
between the rivers Don and Dnieper.
Many men will fall on the field of Kulikovo,
and blood will be shed on the river Nepriadva.

The carts (of the nomads) have begun to creak
between the Don and the Dnieper.
The Tatars march into the Russian land.
Gray wolves follow after them
from the mouths of the Don and the Dnieper.
They howl on the river Mech and
they wish to advance into the Russian land.
But they are not wolves.
They are the infidel Tatars who wish
to march into the Russian land and conquer it.

The geese have begun to cackle on the river Mech.
Swans have begun to flutter their wings.
But it is not geese that cackle
nor swans that flutter their wings.
It is the infidel Mamai who has entered the Russian land,
and he brought his warriors there.
These winged birds have been brought by misfortune.

They fly high under the clouds.
Ravens croak and magpies speak in their own speech.
The eagles screech menacingly, wolves howl,
and foxes bark, waiting for bones.
O, Russian land, you are far away beyond the hills.

IV. The Russian Army Marches to Battle

Already the falcon and the gyrfalcon
and the goshawks of Belozersk[3] race from the stone city of Moscow,
fly high under the blue sky,
ring their golden bells,[4]
and prepare to swoop down upon numerous flocks
of geese and swans.
And so the brave knights of Russia prepare
to strike the great armies of the infidel, Mamai.

Great Prince Dmitry Ivanovich sets in the golden stirrup
and takes his sword in his right hand.
The sun shines brightly from the east,
showing him the road (to victory).
What rumbles? What roars so early before the dawn?
It is Prince Vladimir Andreevich
who prepares his regiments for battle
and leads them to the great river Don.
And he speaks to his brother:
"Prince Dmitry, Great Prince, don't yield to these Tatars,
for these infidels destroy our fields and
invade our fatherland."
Prince Dmitry Ivanovich speaks to his brother:
"My dear brother, Vladimir Andreevich,
we are two brothers.
Our voevodas are appointed and our armies are well known to us.
We mount swift steeds and we wear gilt armor.
We have Circassian helmets and Muscovite shields.
We have German javelins and Frankish lances,
and our swords are made of steel.
The roads are known to us.
The rivers are prepared for fording.
The armies are eager to sacrifice their lives

[3] Allusion to the princes of Belozersk.
[4] Hunting falcons had small bells attached to their talons.

for the Christian faith.
Our banners flap in the wind,
and Russians seek honor and glory."

V. The Battle Begins

Already the falcons, the gyrfalcons, and
the goshawks from Belozersk swiftly cross the river Don.
And they strike against flocks of geese and swans.
They are Russian sons who strike against the great Tatar army,
And who, with their steel lances, clash against Tatar armors,
whose tempered swords sunder Tatar helmets,
on the field of Kulikovo,
at the small river, Nepriadva.

The earth became black from horse hooves.
The field became strewn with Tatar bones.
Much blood was spilled upon the field.
Strong regiments came together and clashed,
and they trampled the hills and the meadows.
The calm waters of rivers and lakes became stirred up.
The Div[5] called out in the Russian land,
calling all lands to listen.
And the glory of the Russian princes resounded,
from the roar of battle to the Iron Gates,
to Rome and to Kafa-on-the-Sea,
to Tyrnovo and to Constantinople.[6]
O great land of Russia.
you have defeated Mamai on the field of Kulikovo.

The storm clouds began to gather
and from them shone lightning,
and thunder roared mightily.
It was the clash of the sons of Russia
with the Tatar infidels, for they seek revenge for Tatar offenses.
The gilt armor of the Russian princes gleamed.
Their steel swords rained upon the Tatar helmets.
It is not aurochs that roar upon the field of Kulikovo.

[5] A god or bird of misfortune that was mentioned in the *Lay of Igor's Campaign*.

[6] Iron Gates: a narrow canyon on the lower Danube; Kafa-on-the-Sea: an Italian city in the Crimea; Tyrnovo: the capital of medieval Bulgaria.

It is the wailing of Russian princes, boyars, and voevodas of Prince Dmitry,
and the princes of Belozersk who were defeated at the swift river Don.
And there voevodas Fedor Semionovich, Timofey Valuevich,
Andrey Serkizovich, Mikhail Ivanovich,
and a great many warriors were cut to pieces by the Tatars.
And their bodies lie on the shore of the river Don.
And then a boyar of Briansk, Monk Peresvet,
was ordered to the place where he was fated to meet death.
And Monk Peresvet said to Prince Dmitry Ivanovich:
"It is better that we fall in battle
than become slaves of these infidels."
And Peresvet, galloping on his horse,
filled the air with his battle cry.
And his armor gleamed as he called
to his younger brother, Osliabia:
"Well, brother, it is time for those who are old
to feel young and for the young to win glory
by trying the arms of brave warriors."
And the brother, Monk Osliabia, answered:
"Brother Peresvet, I already see that there
will be heavy wounds on your body and
that your head will lie on the feathergrass.
I can see that my son, Jacob, will also lie in the green grass
on the field of Kulikovo and for the defense
of the Christian faith and revenge of the offenses
done to Great Prince Dmitry Ivanovich."

And at that time in the land of Riazan
at the river Don there was heard neither
the voice of the plowman nor of the shepherd.
Only the crows cawed and the cuckoos cuckooed,
circling above the corpses.
And it was awesome and bitter to look about,
for the grass was covered with blood
and the trees bowed down to the earth in their sorrow.

VI. The Lamentation of the Widows

The birds began to sing their songs of sorrow.
And the princesses and wives of the boyars and voevodas
began to lament the deaths of their husbands.
Maria Dmitrievna, the wife of Mikula,
cried early in the dawn on the fortress wall of Moscow:

"O river Don, my swift river,
mountains crumble before you, and
you flow to the land of the Kumans.
Oh, that you might bring me from there my lord, Mikula!"
And Fedosia, the wife of Timofey Valuevich, also lamented:
"Joy has abandoned the glorious city of Moscow.
Never again will I see my dear lord, Timofey Valuevich."
And Maria, the wife of Andrey,
and Xenia, the wife of Michael, lamented since dawn:
"For both of us the sun has set in the glorious city of Moscow.
News of our relatives has come from the swift river Don
and has brought great sorrow upon us.
Russian knights have dismounted their swift steeds
on the fateful field of Kulikovo."

And the Div cries under the Tatar sabers,
and there the wounded Russian knights weep.

And since dawn nightingales sing sadly
from the walls of the city of Kolomna.
But these sad songs are not sung by nightingales,
but by the wives of Kolomna who lamented:
"O Moscow, Moscow, our swift river,
why did you take our husbands from us to the Kuman land?"
And they addressed their great prince, saying:
"Oh, our Lord, why wouldn't you close
the river Dnieper with your oars?
Why wouldn't you empty the swift river Don
with the helmets of your warriors?
Why wouldn't you build a dam
on the river Mech from Tatar corpses?
Why wouldn't you close the gates of the river Oka,
that we might be preserved from the infidels,
for our husbands have succumbed in battle."

VII. The Defeat of the Tatars

Prince Vladimir Andreevich, with the Prince of Volynia,
threw seventy thousand warriors from his right flank against the infidels.
And they rapidly struck down the infidel Tatars,
their golden helmets gleaming,
their tempered swords raining on Tatar helmets.

And Prince Dmitry praises his brother:
"Brother, Prince Vladimir, you are our shield of iron
in this time of evil.
Don't let your regiments cease fighting.
Don't give in to these evil Tatars.
Don't pardon these traitors,[7]
for these infidels destroy our fields
and have killed most of our valorous army.
Oh, my brother, it is so sad to see
so much Christian blood spilled!"
And then Prince Dmitry Ivanovich addressed his boyars:
"Fellow boyars, voevodas, and sons of boyars,
This is not a banquet for drinking sweet Muscovite mead.
This is not a court in which to win higher ranks.
This is the place to win glory for your names.
This is the place where an old man must act as a young man,
and the young man must win glory."

And it seemed that a falcon flew to the swift river Don,
but it was not a falcon that flew beyond the swift Don.
Prince Dmitry galloped with his regiments beyond this river.
And Prince Dmitry said:
"Brother, Prince Vladimir,
now is the time to drink of the cup.
Let us attack the infidel army, brother,
with our strong regiments."

And the princes advanced onto the field of battle.
Once more tempered swords rained upon Tatar helmets.
Now the infidels can protect their heads only with their arms.
The infidels begin to retreat swiftly from the princes.
Banners flap in the wind.
The infidels flee while Russian cries of victory cover the field.
Their gilt armor gleams.
The aurochs have taken the stronger position.

Indeed, the tide turned, and the Russian
regiments began to cut the Tatars to pieces.
And despair seized the infidels.
Princes fell from their mounts,

[7] Apparently some of the Russian leaders hesitated in attacking the Tatars.

and Tatar corpses began to cover the field.
And blood flowed in a stream.
The infidels began fleeing on all sides.
They fled by impassable routes to the sea,
and they gnashed their teeth
and they clawed their faces in despair, saying:
"Alas, brothers, we shall never escape to our land.
We shall never again see our children.
We shall never again caress our wives,
but we must kiss the damp earth.
We shall never again campaign against Russia.
We shall never again receive tribute from the Russian princes."

And the Tatar lands began to mourn,
and sorrow and sadness covered the land.
And they lost their courage for campaigning against the Russian land.
Their joy disappeared.
The sons of Russia pillaged the Tatars of
cloths and silks, weapons and horses,
oxen and camels, wines and sugars,
jewelry and velvets, and they carried
the wealth of the Tatars to their wives.
Tatar gold jingled in the hands of Russian women.
Joy and happiness spread over the Russian land.
Russian glory was exalted,
while shame was brought upon the Tatars.
And the Div was enthroned, and the fear
of Russian princes spread over the earth.

Oh, great princes of Russia,
fight the enemy with your valorous army.
Fight for the Russian land and the Christian faith,
fight against the infidel emperor, Mamai.

And the infidels threw down their weapons,
and they bowed their heads to the Russian sword.
Their trumpets stopped sounding, and their voices became saddened.

VIII. The Escape of Mamai

Like a gray wolf, the infidel emperor, Mamai,
ran away with his guards.

And he came to the city of Kafa-on-the-Sea.
And the Italians asked him:
"Infidel Mamai, how did you dare to attack the Russian lands?
Once Tatar power spread over the Russian land of forest,
but the time of Emperor Batu has long passed.
Emperor Batu had four hundred thousand, and he conquered the whole Russian land,
the whole earth, from the east to the west.
And God punished the Russian land for its sins.
But this time you, Emperor Mamai,
came to the Russian land with a large army,
with nine hordes and seventy princes,
and yet you run away to the sea, and with only eight soldiers.
And there is no one to pass the winter with you in the prairie.
Did the Russian princes treat you so badly
that there are no longer princes or commanders with you?
Did they really become drunk with your own blood
on the field of Kulikovo, on the feathergrass?
Go away from us, infidel Mamai!
Go from us, as you went from the Russian forest!"

IX. Apodosis

We love the Russian land as a mother loves her dear child.
The mother caresses her child and praises it for good deeds,
but she also punishes it for bad deeds.
In the same way, our Lord God
was merciful unto the Russian princes
who fought between the Don and the Dnieper,
unto the Great Prince Dmitry Ivanovich,
unto his brother, Vladimir Andreevich.

And so Princes Dmitry Ivanovich and Vladimir Andreevich
remained victorious on the bone-strewn field of Kulikovo,
on the river Nepriadva.
And Prince Dmitry Ivanovich said:
"It is horrible, brethren, to see the earth
covered with the corpses of Christians,
even as the field is covered with haystacks.
And it is horrible to see that the river Don
has flowed blood-red for three days."

And then Prince Dmitry Ivanovich commanded:
"Count how many voevodas perished,
count how many young men were killed."
And Mikhail, a boyar of Moscow replied:
"Our lord, Great Prince Dmitry Ivanovich,
we are missing forty boyars from Moscow,
twelve princes from Belozersk,
thirty *posadniks* from Novgorod,
twenty boyars from Kolomna,
forty boyars from Serpukhov,
thirty magnates from Lithuania,
twenty boyars from Pereslavl,
twenty-five boyars from Kostroma,
thirty-five boyars from Vladimir,
eight boyars from Suzdal,
forty boyars from Murom,
seventy boyars from Riazan,
thirty-four boyars from Rostov,
twenty-three boyars from Dmitrov,
sixty boyars from Mozhaisk,
thirty boyars from Zvenigorod,
and fifteen boyars from Uglich.
And altogether 253,000 Russian men were
cut down by the infidel Emperor Mamai.[8]
But God was merciful to the Russian land,
and still more Tatars fell on the battlefield."
And then Prince Dmitry Ivanovich addressed the dead:
"Fellow princes, boyars, and sons of boyars,
you have found peace everlasting here, between
the Don and the Dnieper, on the field of Kulikovo.
Here you gave your lives for the holy Church,
for the Russian land and for the Christian faith.
Forgive me, brethren, and give me your blessing
for this life and for the life everlasting."

And then Prince Dmitry Ivanovich addressed his brother:
"Let us go, my brother, Vladimir Andreevich,
back to the Russian land,
back to the glorious city of Moscow.
And let us rule there on our throne,
for we have won glory and veneration.
Glory be to God!"

[8] Actually, the Russian casualties were barely higher than 100,000.

25. *Serapion of Vladimir*

Serapion of Vladimir is one of the outstanding Russian writers of the first century under the Tatar yoke. Probably of southern origin, Serapion was abbot of the Kievan Crypt Monastery at the time of the Tatar invasion, and later became Bishop of Vladimir, the capital city of the Vladimir-Suzdal principality. After the invasion, Vladimir became a new nucleus for Russian national life and culture. Bishop Serapion died in 1275.

The eloquent homilies of Serapion are distinguished by their highly rhetorical style, and are composed principally of short, rhythmic sentences. Very often these sentences are rhymed and show repetition of an initial word or syllable through several lines. These characteristics tend to convey a sense of poetic unity.

The first sermon is entitled *Sermon on the Merciless Heathens.* By the term "merciless heathens" Serapion refers to those Christians who do not follow the commandments of God and are not charitable to their fellowmen. In the second sermon, *Sermon on Omens*, Serapion speaks of God's wrath, which has manifested itself in earthquakes, conflagrations, and the Tatars' invasion of the Russian land.

The old Russian texts used as the basis for this translation can be found in *Serapion Vladimirskii, russkii propovednik XII veka* by E. V. Petukhov, St. Petersburg, 1888.

◆ ◆ ◆

SERMON ON THE MERCILESS HEATHENS

Let us contemplate, brethren, our Lord's love for men.
How does he try to bring us to himself?
What commandments does he place upon us?
What words does he chastise us with?
Yet, in spite of this, we do not turn to him.

He has seen our trespasses multiply.
He has seen us forsake his commandments.
Many admonitions have we heard from him.
Many fears has he inspired in us.

Many of his servants has he enlightened,
Yet what man has become the better for all this?

Then he released upon us the merciless heathens,
violent heathens, people having mercy neither
for the young,
for the weak and aged,
nor for infants.
The wrath of the Lord has descended upon us
even as David said: "He cast upon them the fierceness of his anger."

The sacred churches were destroyed.
The sacred vessels were defiled.
The saints were trodden upon.
The prelates were victims of the sword.
The bodies of holy monks became food for birds.
The blood of our priests and brothers,
as if it were water, soaked into the earth.
The strength of our princes and voevodas has disappeared.
Our valiant warriors, seized with great fear, have fled.
Many of our brothers and our children
have been led into captivity.
Weeds overgrow our villages.
Our pride has been humbled.
Our serenity has vanished.
Our wealth was taken from us by the heathens,
inheriting the fruits of our labors.
Our land has become the property of foreigners.
Our land taken from us,
we became the objects of the jibes
of those who live beyond our lands.

Then we realized that
God's wrath is like a torrent from heaven.
Yet we brought his anger upon ourselves.
His favor abandoned us,
and we became deprived of his merciful vigilance.
And now there is no misfortune which will pass us by.
And now we are punished without surcease.
Yet we do not turn to God.
We do not rue our trespasses.
We do not forsake our malevolent ways.
We do not cleanse ourselves of sin,

forgetting the awesome castigation meted out upon our land.
Being reduced to paucity, we act grandiosely.
And therefore evil forces will not cease to torment us.
Envy has increased and wickedness has overcome us.
Pride has turned our heads.
Hatred for friends has taken root in our hearts.
Avarice for possessions has enslaved us
and does not permit us to have mercy upon orphans,
nor does it permit us to be human beings.
We are predatory beasts desiring flesh to appease their hunger.
Nothing would prevent us from seizing the possessions of others,
even if it came to killing.
But even the beasts are satiated, after having eaten,
but we cannot appease our hunger,
for, when we have gained one thing,
we desire only another.

For wealth rightly come by, God will not be angered,
but as the prophet said:
"The Lord looked down from heaven
to see if they were any that did
understand and seek God."
And he saw that they had all gone astray.
"Have they no knowledge,
these evildoers who eat up my people
as if they eat bread?"

And Apostle Paul unendingly admonished:
"Brothers, refrain from evil and dark deeds,
for usurer-robbers will be judged with the idolaters."
And what did God say to Moses?
"You shall not afflict any widow or orphan.
If you do afflict them, and they cry out to me,
I will surely hear their cry;
and my wrath will burn,
and I will kill you with the sword."

And now that prophecy has been fulfilled,
for didn't we perish by the sword
and not once, but twice?
What can we do to end the evils which oppress us?
Remember the words of the Holy Scriptures:

to love each other,
to be charitable to all men,
to love thy neighbor as thyself,
to keep the body pure
so that it will not be defiled by lechery;
to cleanse the body with penitence,
if it has been defiled,
to be free of haughtiness,
to render good for evil.

No one does the Lord hate more than the rancorous,
for they will say: "Our Father, forgive us our trespasses,"
yet they themselves will not forgive others.
It is clearly written: "And with what measure you mete,
so shall it be measured to you again."

SERMON ON OMENS

The blessing of the Lord be with you!
Brethren, you have heard what the
Lord himself said in the Gospel:
"And there shall be signs in the sun,
and in the moon, and in the stars,
and there will be earthquakes in many places,
and famines."

This prophecy of our Lord
has now been fulfilled in our days.
Many times have we seen the sun extinguished,
the moon darkened,
and the stars disquieted.
And recently with our own eyes
have we seen the quaking of the earth.[1]
Now the earth, firm and immovable from time immemorial
by the will of God,
is today moved, quaking because of our sins,
unable to withstand our evil ways.

We have obeyed neither the Gospel
nor the Apostles,
nor the prophets,
nor those enlightened in God's ways:

1 According to the chronicles, an earthquake occurred in 1230, just six years before the Tatar invasion of Russia.

Basil and Gregory the Theologians,
John Chrysostom,
and the other blessed fathers
by whom the Faith was upheld,
the heretics were driven out,
and God made known to all the lands.
They have taught us without surcease,
but we are living in evil ways.

For this does God punish us,
bringing upon us calamities and earthquakes.
He no longer chastizes us with words,
but punishes us with afflictions.
God has castigated us in all ways,
yet he has not dispelled our evil ways.
Now he shakes the earth and makes it quake,
wishing to shake, like leaves from a tree,
our evil ways from the earth.
If any should declare that there have been earthquakes before,
I should not deny it.
But what has happened to us after the earthquakes?
Were there not famines, plagues, and numerous wars?
But we did not repent.
Thus, by the will of God,
there fell upon us a merciless people
who devastated our land,
took entire cities off to captivity,
destroyed our holy churches,
put our fathers and brothers to death,
and defiled our mothers and sisters.
Now, brethren, that we have experienced such calamities,
let us pray to the Lord, and repent,
lest we incur the wrath of God even more,
and thus bring upon us an even greater castigation.

Much is still wanting in our repentance and contrition.
If we turn from dissolute and merciless judgments,
if we turn from bloody usury,
and from greed, thieving, blasphemy, lies,
slander, malediction, denunciations, and other diabolical ways;
if we turn away from all these,
I know full well that good times will come to us,
both in this life and the next.

For the Lord himself has said:
"Turn unto me, and I will turn to you.
Refrain from all evil things,
and I will keep all afflictions from you."
When will we turn from sins?
Let us spare ourselves and our children.
When have we seen so many deaths?
Many were taken away before they could care for their houses.
Many lay down to sleep in the evening,
never to rise again.
Be fearful of such a sudden death, brethren.
If we follow the ways of God,
He will comfort us with his solace,
He will cherish us as his own children,
He will remove the burden of our earthly grief,
He will give us peace in the next life,
where we shall know elation and unending joy
with those who do the will of God.

I have told you many things, brethren and children,
but I perceive that our afflictions will neither lessen
nor change, for many take no heed,
acting as if they deemed themselves immortal.
I am afraid that the prophecy of the Lord
will come to pass for such people.
If I had not told them of God's ways,
they would not have sinned in their ignorance,
but I have told them, and now
there can be no pardoning of their sins.
And so I repeat again to you
that if we do not change our ways,
we shall have no pardoning before God.

I, your sinful pastor,
have followed the command of the Lord
in giving his word to you.

LIVES OF SAINTS AND BIOGRAPHICAL TALES

26. *Epiphanius the Wise*

THE names of Epiphanius the Wise, St. Stephen of Perm, St. Sergius of Radonezh, and the great painter Andrey Rublev signify the Russian spiritual and cultural revival of the late fourteenth and early fifteenth centuries. St. Sergius, and to some extent St. Stephen, gave a new impetus to Russian monasticism. St. Sergius became the holy patron of Muscovite Russia. His spirit of humility, his contemplation and unending prayers inspired and comforted the Russian people of the late Middle Ages. The wonderful icons and frescoes of Andrey Rublev offered a harmonius and colorful expression of the spirit of complete serenity and humility. For the Russian people these icons became the finest achievement of religious art and the highest expression of Russian spirituality. A contemporary of Andrey Rublev, Epiphanius the Wise, described the lives of St. Sergius and St. Stephen. In these works he made wide use of new literary devices, and perfected a completely new style of writing. Thus a new page in Russian literary history appeared.

Epiphanius gives a consistent, detailed, and well-organized account of the lives of these two saints. His main purpose in writing these biographical works was not to give an account of the life and deeds of each saint, but to portray an ideal type of sanctity. He endowed the heroes of his *vitae* with a number of general traits that he describes in lengthy panegyrics, containing a great number of epithets. The literary style that Epiphanius the Wise perfected was termed "weaving of words" (*pletenie sloves,* in Russian). In this style sentences are nearly deprived of verbs, consisting almost entirely of the adjectives and nouns that characterize the deeds and humility of the saints. Another feature of Epiphanius' "word-weaving" is the abundance of neologisms formed by nouns or combinations of nouns and adjectives, such as "songbeautifier," rather than "beautifier of songs."

Particularly representative of this style is the *Panegyric to St. Stephen of Perm.* Stephen of Perm was a well-known fourteenth-century missionary who converted the Finnic tribe of Permians to Christianity. He also created a Permian alphabet, thus becoming the founder of the Permian written tradition. The text of the present translation is based on the Russian text of the *Life of St. Stephen of Perm* published by V. G. Druzhinin in *Zhitie sv. Stefana episkopa Permskago, napisannoe Epifaniem Premudrym*, St. Petersburg, 1897.

The life of St. Sergius, which likewise abounds in epithets and lengthy panegyrics, was reworked in the fifteenth century by Pachomius the Serb. The present translation is taken from the work *St. Sergius, Builder of Russia* by Nicholas Zernov, and is based upon the simplified Russian text of G. P. Fedotov, who removed the panegyrics and especially cumbersome passages. Even though there have been some stylistic deletions, the overall meaning and continuity of the work remain.

◆ ◆ ◆

PANEGYRIC TO ST. STEPHEN OF PERM

My father, lord, and bishop, although you have passed away, I should like to sing your praises with my heart, with my tongue, and with my mind. When you were alive, I often was your annoyance, but now I am your panegyrist; and sometimes I would argue with you about happenings and works, about some verses or some lines, but now, remembering your enduring patience, your great reasoning, and your blessed humility, I humble myself; I cry, shedding tears.

And now, how shall I call you, my bishop?

How shall I name you?
How shall I appeal to you?
How shall I announce you?
How shall I regard you?
How shall I proclaim you?
How shall I praise you?
How shall I esteem you?
How shall I gratify you?
How shall I present you?
How shall I weave lauds to you?

Shall I call you a prophet,
since you prophesied prophetic prophecies,
and, like a prophet, explained the hopes of the prophets,
and among the people, faithless and unlearned,
you were a prophet?

Shall I call you an Apostle,
since you performed apostolic deeds
and, acting like an Apostle, following the examples of Apostles,
acted, following in the steps of the Apostles?

Shall I call you a lawgiver or a lawmaker,
since you gave the law to the lawless,
brought faith to the lawless,
and established the law among them?

Shall I call you the Baptist,
since you baptized many
who came to you to be baptized?

Shall I call you a preacher, since,
like a herald who announces in the town square,
you loudly preached the word of God to the heathens?

Shall I call you an evangelist,
since you proclaimed grace to them
and the Holy Evangel of Christ,
and performed many deeds of the annunciator of grace?

Shall I call you bishop,
since you were the great archbishop and the eldest bishop,
since you consecrated priests in your land,
and since you were above all other priests?

Shall I call you a teacher,
since you taught the heathens who had gone astray,
since you brought the faith to the heathens
and taught men who were unlearned?

Shall I call you a sufferer or a martyr,
since, like a martyr, you surrendered yourself
into the hands of men who were cruel in torturing,
since you were as a sheep among wolves,
since you accepted martyrdom, suffering, and torment?

And I, a great and unlearned sinner,
following the words that eulogize you,
do knit words and create words,

attempting to glorify you with words.
Gathering the words of praise,
and adding and weaving words,
I ask: How shall I eulogize you?
Shall I call you
  the pastor of those who have gone astray,
  the redeemer of those who have perished,
  the teacher of those who were enticed,
  the leader of those whose sight has been darkened,
  the cleanser of those who have been defiled,
  the guardian of the soldiers,
  the consoler of those who are afflicted,
  the nourisher of those who hunger,
  the provider for those in need,
  the punisher of those who are simpleminded,
  the sustainer of the offended,
  the one who prays for others fervently,
  the intercessor for the faithful,
  the savior of the heathen,
  the curser of demons,
  the breaker of idols,
  the destroyer of graven images,
  the servant of God,
  the upholder of wisdom,
  the lover of philosophy,
  the protector of chastity,
  the defender of the truth,
  the writer of books,
  the creator of Permian letters?

Many epithets have you received, O Bishop!
Many titles have you won!
Many gifts have you deserved!
Many blessings have enriched you!

THE LIFE, ACTS, AND MIRACLES OF OUR REVERED AND HOLY FATHER ABBOT SERGIUS

I. Childhood

Our holy Father Sergius was born of noble, Orthodox, devout parents. His father was named Cyril and his mother Mary. They found favor with God; they were honorable in the sight of God and man, and abounded in those virtues which are well-pleasing unto God.

Cyril had three sons, Stephen, Bartholomew, and Peter, whom he brought up in strict piety and purity. Stephen and Peter quickly learned to read and write, but the second boy did not so easily learn to write, and worked slowly and inattentively; his master taught him with care, but the boy could not put his mind to his studies, nor understand, nor do the same as his companions who were studying with him. As a result he suffered from the many reproaches of his parents, and still more from the punishments of his teacher and the ridicule of his companions. The boy often prayed to God in secret and with many tears: "O Lord, give me understanding of this learning. Teach me, Lord, enlighten and instruct me." His reverence for God prompted him to pray that he might receive knowledge from God and not from men.

One day his father sent him to seek for a lost foal. On his way he met a monk, a venerable elder, a stranger, a priest, with the appearance of an angel. This stranger was standing beneath an oak tree, praying devoutly and with much shedding of tears. The boy, seeing him, humbly made a low obeisance, and awaited the end of his prayers.

The venerable monk, when he had ended his orisons, glanced at the boy and, conscious that he beheld the chosen vessel of the Holy Spirit, he called him to his side, blessed him, bestowed on him a kiss in the name of Christ, and asked: "What art thou seeking, or what dost thou want, child?"

The boy answered, "My soul desires above all things to understand the Holy Scriptures. I have to study reading and writing, and I am sorely vexed that I cannot learn these things. Will you, holy Father, pray to God for me, that he will give me understanding of book-learning?"

The monk raised his hands and his eyes toward heaven, sighed, prayed to God, then said, "Amen."

Taking out from his satchel, as it were some treasure, with three fingers, he handed to the boy what appeared to be a little bit of white wheaten bread of the Holy Sacrament, saying to him: "Take this in thy mouth, child, and eat; this is given thee as a sign of God's grace and for the understanding of Holy Scriptures. Though the gift appears but small, the taste thereof is very sweet."

The boy opened his mouth and ate, tasting a sweetness as of honey, wherefore he said, "Is it not written, How sweet are thy words to my palate, more than honey to my lips, and my soul doth cherish them exceedingly?"

The monk answered and said, "If thou believest, child, more

than this will be revealed to thee; and do not vex thyself about reading and writing; thou wilt find that from this day forth the Lord will give thee learning above that of thy brothers and others of thine own age."

Having thus informed him of divine favor, the monk prepared to proceed on his way. But the boy flung himself, with his face to the ground, at the feet of the monk, and besought him to come and visit his parents, saying, "My parents dearly love persons such as you are, Father."

The monk, astonished at his faith, accompanied him to his parents' house. At the sight of the stranger, Cyril and Mary came out to meet him, and bowed low before him. The monk blessed them, and they offered him food, but before accepting any food, the monk went into the chapel, taking with him the boy whose consecration had been signified even before birth,[1] and began a recitation of the Canonical Hours, telling the boy to read the Psalms.

The boy said, "I do not know them, Father."

The monk replied, "I told thee that from today the Lord would give thee knowledge in reading and writing; read the Word of God, nothing doubting."

Whereupon, to the astonishment of all present, the boy, receiving the monk's blessing, began to recite in excellent rhythm; and from that hour he could read. His parents and brothers praised God, and after accompanying the monk to the house, placed food before him. Having eaten, and bestowed a blessing on the parents, the monk was anxious to proceed on his way. But the parents pleaded, "Reverend Father, hurry not away, but stay and comfort us and calm our fears. Our humble son, whom you bless and praise, is to us an object of marvel. While he was yet in his mother's womb three times he uttered a cry in church during holy Mass. Wherefore we fear and doubt of what is to be, and what he is to do."

The holy monk, after considering and becoming aware of that which was to be, exclaimed, "O blessed pair, O worthy couple, giving birth to such a child! Why do you fear where there is no place for fear? Rather rejoice and be glad, for the boy will be great before God and man, thanks to his life of godliness."

Having thus spoken the monk left, pronouncing a dark saying that their son would serve the Holy Trinity and would lead

[1] According to an introductory passage here omitted, the future spiritual life of St. Sergius was revealed to his mother shortly before his birth.

many to an understanding of the divine precepts. They accompanied him to the doorway of their house, when he became of a sudden invisible. Perplexed, they wondered if he had been an angel, sent to give the boy knowledge of reading. After the departure of the monk, it became evident that the boy could read any book, and was altogether changed; he was submissive in all things to his parents, striving to fulfill their wishes, and never disobedient. Applying himself solely to glorifying God, and rejoicing therein, he attended assiduously in God's church, being present daily at Matins, at the Mass, at Vespers. He studied holy scripts, and at all times, in every way, he disciplined his body and preserved himself in purity of body and soul.

Cyril, devout servant of God, led the life of a wealthy and renowned boyar, in the province of Rostov, but in later years he was reduced to poverty. He, like others, suffered from the invasions of Tatar hordes into Russia, from the skirmishes of troops, the frequent demands for tribute, and from repeated bad harvests, in conjunction with the period of violence and disorder which followed the great Tatar war. When the principality of Rostov fell into the hands of the Grand Duke Ivan Danilovich of Moscow, distress prevailed in the town of Rostov, and not least among the princes and boyars.[2] They were deprived of power, of their properties, of honors and rank, of all of which Moscow became the possessor. By order of the Grand Duke they left Rostov, and a certain noble, Vassili Kotchev, with another called Mina, were sent from Moscow to Rostov as voevodas. On arrival in the town of Rostov these two governors imposed a levy on the town and on the inhabitants. A severe persecution followed, and many of the remaining inhabitants of Rostov were constrained to surrender their estates to the Muscovites, in exchange for which they received wounds and humiliations, and went forth emptyhanded and as veriest beggars. In brief, Rostov was subjected to every possible humiliation, even to the hanging, head downward, of their governor, Averky, one of the chief boyars of Rostov. Seeing and hearing of all this, terror spread among the people, not only in the town of Rostov but in all the surrounding country. Cyril, God's devout servant, avoided further misfortune by escaping from his native town. He assembled his entire household and family and with them

[2] Grand Duke Ivan Danilovich of Moscow (1301–1341), called Kalita ("Moneybag"), was the actual founder of the Muscovite state. He spread his reign over a considerable part of the land between the Oka and Volga rivers. Rostov was an important city of the Volga.

removed from Rostov to Radonezh,[3] where he settled near the church dedicated to the Birth of Christ, which is still standing to this day.

II. The Hermitage

Cyril's two sons, Stephen and Peter, married, but his second son, Bartholomew, would not contemplate marriage, being desirous of becoming a monk. He often expressed this wish to his father, but his parents said to him, "My son, wait a little and bear with us; we are old, poor and sick, and we have no one to look after us, for both your brothers are married." The wondrous youth gladly promised to care for them to the end of their days, and from henceforth strove for his parents' well-being, until they entered the monastic life and went one to a monastery, and the other to a convent. They lived but a few years, and passed away to God. Blessed Bartholomew laid his parents in their graves, mourned for them forty days, then returned to his house. Calling his younger brother Peter, he bestowed his share of his father's inheritance on him, retaining nothing for himself. The wife of his elder brother, Stephen, died also, leaving two sons, Clement and Ivan. Stephen soon renounced the world and became a monk in the Holy Mother of God Monastery at Khotkov.

Blessed Bartholomew now came to him, and begged him to accompany him in the search for some desert place. Stephen assented, and he and the saint together explored many parts of the forest, till finally they came to a waste space in the middle of the forest, near a stream. After inspecting the place they obeyed the voice of God and were satisfied. Having prayed, they set about chopping wood and carrying it. First they built a hut, and then constructed a small chapel. When the chapel was finished and the time had come to dedicate it, Blessed Bartholomew said to Stephen, "Now, my lord and eldest brother by birth and by blood, tell me, in honor of whose feast shall this chapel be, and to which saint shall we dedicate it?"

Stephen answered: "Why do you ask me, and why put me to the test? You were chosen of God while you were yet in your mother's womb, and he gave a sign concerning you before ever you were born, that the child would be a disciple of the Blessed Trinity, and not he alone would have devout faith, for he would

[3] Radonezh was a village that belonged to St. Sergius' family and after which his family was named. This village, some nine miles from the Monastery of St. Sergius, is the present-day industrial city of Zagorsk.

lead many others and teach them to believe in the Holy Trinity. It behooves you, therefore, to dedicate a chapel above all others to the Blessed Trinity."

The favored youth gave a deep sigh and said, "To tell the truth, my lord and brother, I asked you because I felt I must, although I wanted and thought likewise as you do, and desired with my whole soul to erect and dedicate this chapel to the Blessed Trinity, but out of humility I inquired of you." And he went forthwith to obtain the blessing of the ruling prelate for its consecration. From the town came the priest sent by Theognost, Metropolitan of Kiev and all Russia, and the chapel was consecrated and dedicated to the Holy Trinity in the reign of the Grand Duke Simon Ivanovich,[4] we believe in the beginning of his reign. The chapel being now built and dedicated, Stephen did not long remain in the wilderness with his brother. He realized soon all the labors in this desert place, the hardships, the all-pervading need and want, and that there were no means of satisfying hunger and thirst, nor any other necessity. As yet no one came to the saint, nor brought him anything, for at this time, nowhere around was there any village, nor house, nor people; neither was there road or pathway, but everywhere on all sides were forest and wasteland. Stephen, seeing this, was troubled, and he decided to leave the wilderness, and with it his own brother the saintly desert-lover and desert-dweller. He went from thence to Moscow, and when he reached this city he settled in the Monastery of the Epiphany, found a cell, and dwelt in it, exercising himself in virtue. Hard labor was to him a joy, and he passed his time in ascetic practices in his cell, disciplining himself by fasting and praying, refraining from all indulgence, even from drinking beer. Alexis, the future metropolitan, who at this time had not been raised to the rank of bishop, was living in the monastery, leading a quiet monastic life. Stephen and he spent much time together in spiritual exercises, and they sang in the choir side by side. The Grand Duke Simon came to hear of Stephen and the godly life he led, and commanded the Metropolitan Theognost to ordain him priest and, later, to appoint him abbot of the monastery. Aware of his great virtues, the Grand Duke also appointed him as his confessor.

Our saint, Sergius, had not taken monastic vows at this time

[4] Grand Duke Simon Ivanovich the Proud (1323–1353) was the son of Ivan Kalita. Metropolitan Theognost, the former Metropolitan of Kiev, lived in Moscow and was one of the upholders of the rise of Muscovy.

for, as yet, he had not enough experience of monasteries, and of all that is required of a monk. After a while, however, he invited a spiritual elder, who held the dignity of priest and abbot, named Mitrofan, to come and visit him in his solitude. In great humility he entreated him, "Father, may the love of God be with us, and give me the tonsure of a monk. From childhood have I loved God and set my heart on him these many years, but my parents' needs withheld me. Now, my lord and father, I am free from all bonds, and I thirst, as the hart thirsteth for the springs of living water."

The abbot forthwith went into the chapel with him, and gave him the tonsure on the 7th day of October on the feast day of the blessed martyrs Sergius and Bacchus. And Sergius was the name he received as monk. In those days it was the custom to give to the newly tonsured monk the name of the saint whose feast day it happened to be. Our saint was twenty-three years old when he joined the order of monks. Blessed Sergius, the newly tonsured monk, partook of the Holy Sacrament and received grace and the gift of the Holy Spirit. From one whose witness is true and sure, we are told that when Sergius partook of the Holy Sacrament the chapel was filled with a sweet odor; and not only in the chapel, but all around was the same fragrant smell. The saint remained in the chapel seven days, touching no food other than one consecrated loaf given him by the abbot, refusing all else and giving himself up to fasting and prayer, having on his lips the Psalms of David.

When Mitrofan bade farewell, St. Sergius in all humility said to him: "Give me your blessing, and pray regarding my solitude; and instruct one living alone in the wilderness how to pray to the Lord God; how to remain unharmed; how to wrestle with the evil and with his own temptations to pride, for I am but a novice and a newly tonsured monk."

The abbot was astonished and almost afraid. He replied, "You ask of me concerning that which you know no less well than we do, O Reverend Father." After discoursing with him for a while on spiritual matters, and commending him to God, Mitrofan went away, leaving St. Sergius alone to silence and the wilderness.

Who can recount his labors? Who can number the trials he endured living alone in the wildnerness?

Under different forms and from time to time the devil wrestled with the saint, but the demons beset St. Sergius in vain; no matter what visions they evoked, they failed to overcome the firm and fearless spirit of the ascetic. At one moment it was Satan who laid his snares; at another, incursions of wild beasts took place, for many were the wild animals inhabiting this wilderness. Some of these remained at a distance; others came near the saint, surrounded him and even sniffed him. In particular a bear used to come to the holy man. Seeing the animal did not come to harm him, but in order to get some food, the saint brought a small slice of bread from his hut, and placed it on a log or stump, so the bear learned to come for the meal thus prepared for him, and having eaten it went away again. If there was no bread, and the bear did not find his usual slice, he would wait about for a long while and look around on all sides, rather like some moneylender waiting to receive payment of his debt. At this time Sergius had no variety of foods in the wildnerness, only bread and water from the spring, and a great scarcity of these. Often, bread was not to be found; then both he and the bear went hungry. Sometimes, although there was but one slice of bread, the saint gave it to the bear, being unwilling to disappoint him of his food.

He diligently read the Holy Scriptures to obtain a knowledge of all virtue, in his secret meditations training his mind in a longing for eternal bliss. Most wonderful of all, none knew the measure of his ascetic and godly life spent in solitude. God, the beholder of all hidden things, alone saw it.

Whether he lived two years or more in the wilderness alone we do not know; God knows only. The Lord, seeing his very great faith and patience, took compassion on him and, desirous of relieving his solitary labors, put into the hearts of certain god-fearing monks to visit him.

The saint inquired of them, "Are you able to endure the hardships of this place, hunger and thirst, and every kind of want?"

They replied, "Yes, Reverend Father, we are willing with God's help and with your prayers."

Holy Sergius, seeing their faith and zeal, marveled, and said: "My brethren, I desired to dwell alone in the wildnerness and, furthermore, to die in this place. If it be God's will that there shall be a monastery in this place, and that many brethren will be gathered here, then may God's holy will be done. I welcome you with joy, but let each one of you build himself a cell. Furthermore, let it be known unto you, if you come to dwell in the wilderness, the beginning of righteousness is the fear of the Lord."

To increase his own fear of the Lord he spent day and night in the study of God's word. Moreover, young in years, strong and healthy in body, he could do the work of two men or more.

The devil now strove to wound him with the darts of concupiscence. The saint, aware of these enemy attacks, disciplined his body and exercised his soul, mastering it with fasting, and thus was he protected by the grace of God. Although not yet raised to the office of priesthood, dwelling in company with the brethren, he was present daily with them in church for the reciting of the offices, Nocturnes, Matins, the Hours, and Vespers. For the Mass a priest, who was an abbot, came from one of the villages. At first Sergius did not wish to be raised to the priesthood and especially he did not want to become an abbot; this was by reason of his extreme humility. He constantly remarked that the beginning and root of all evil lay in pride of rank, and ambition to be an abbot. The monks were but few in number, about a dozen. They constructed themselves cells, not very large ones, within the enclosure, and put up gates at the entrance. Sergius built four cells with his own hands, and performed other monastic duties at the request of the brethren; he carried logs from the forest on his shoulders, chopped them up, and carried them into the cells. The monastery, indeed, came to be a wonderful place to look upon. The forest was not far distant from it as now it is; the shade and the murmur of trees hung above the cells; around the church was a space of trunks and stumps; here many kinds of vegetables were sown.

But to return to the exploits of St. Sergius. He flayed the grain and ground it in the mill, baked the bread and cooked the food, cut out shoes and clothing and stitched them; he drew water from the spring flowing nearby, and carried it in two pails on his shoulders, and put water in each cell. He spent the night in prayer, without sleep, feeding only on bread and water, and that in small quantities; and never spent an idle hour.

III. The Humble Abbot

Within the space of a year the abbot who had given the tonsure to St. Sergius fell ill, and after a short while, he passed out of this life. Then God put it into the hearts of the brethren to go to blessed Sergius, and to say to him: "Father, we cannot continue without an abbot. We desire you to be our abbot, and the guide of our souls and bodies."

The saint sighed from the bottom of his heart, and replied, "I have had no thought of becoming abbot, for my soul longs to finish its course here as an ordinary monk." The brethren urged him again and again to be their abbot; finally, overcome by his compassionate love, but groaning inwardly, he said: "Fathers and brethren, I will say no more against it, and will

(*Above*) St. Sergius. A portrait worked in embroidery of about 1450. (*Below*) St. Sergius and his monks build a fence around the monastery. A sixteenth-century miniature from the *Life of St. Sergius.*

submit to the will of God. He sees into our hearts and souls. We will go into the town, to the bishop."

Alexis, the Metropolitan of all Russia, was living at this time in Constantinople, and he had nominated Bishop Athanasius of Volynia in his stead in the town of Pereiaslavl. Our blessed Sergius went, therefore, to the bishop, taking with him two elders; and entering into his presence made a low obeisance. Athanasius rejoiced exceedingly at seeing him, and kissed him in the name of Christ. He had heard tell of the saint and of his beginning of good deeds, and he spoke to him of the workings of the Spirit. Our Blessed Father Sergius begged the bishop to give them an abbot, and a guide of their souls.

The venerable Athanasius replied, "Thyself, son and brother, God called in thy mother's womb. It is thou who wilt be father and abbot of thy brethren." Blessed Sergius refused, insisting on his unworthiness, but Athanasius said to him, "Beloved, thou hast acquired all virtue save obedience."

Blessed Sergius, bowing low, replied: "May God's will be done. Praise be the Lord forever and forever." They all answered, "Amen."

Without delay the holy bishop, Athanasius, led blessed Sergius to the church, and ordained him subdeacon and then deacon. The following morning the saint was raised to the dignity of priesthood, and was told to say the holy liturgy and to offer the bloodless Sacrifice. Later, taking him apart, the bishop spoke to him of the teachings of the Apostles and of the holy fathers, for the edification and guidance of souls. After bestowing on him a kiss in the name of Christ, he sent him forth, in very deed an abbot, pastor, and guardian, and physician of his spiritual brethren. He had not taken upon himself the rank of abbot; he received the leadership from God; he had not sought it, nor striven for it; he did not obtain it by payment, as do others who have pride of rank, chasing hither and thither, plotting and snatching power from one another. God himself led his chosen disciple and exalted him to the dignity of abbot.

Our revered father and abbot Sergius returned to his monastery, to the abode dedicated to the Holy Trinity, and the brethren, coming out to meet him, bowed low to the ground before him. He blessed them, and said: "Brethren, pray for me. I am altogether ignorant, and I have received a talent from the Highest, and I shall have to render an account of it, and of the flock committed to me."

There were twelve brethren when he first became abbot, and he was the thirteenth. And this number remained, neither increasing nor diminishing, until Simon, the archimandrite of Smolensk, arrived among them. From that time onward their numbers constantly increased. This wondrous man, Simon, was chief archimandrite, excellent, eminent, abounding in virtue. Having heard of our Reverend Father Sergius' way of life, he laid aside honors, left the goodly city of Smolensk, and arrived at the monastery where, greeting our Reverend Father Sergius with the greatest humility, he entreated him to allow him to live under him and his rules in all submission and obedience: and he offered the estate he owned as a gift to the abbot for the benefit of the monastery. Blessed Sergius welcomed him with great joy. Simon lived many years, submissive and obedient, abounding in virtue, and died in advanced old age.

Stephen, the saint's brother, came with his younger son, Ivan, from Moscow and, presenting him to Abbot Sergius, asked him to give him the tonsure. Abbot Sergius did so, and gave him the name of Theodore; from his earliest years the boy had been taught abstinence, piety, and chastity, following his uncle's precepts; according to some accounts he was given the tonsure when he was ten years old, others say twelve. People from many parts, towns and countries, came to live with Abbot Sergius, and their names are written in the book of life. The monastery bit by bit grew in size. It is recorded in the *Paterikon* —that is to say, in the book of the early fathers of the Church— that the holy fathers in assembly prophesied about later generations, saying that the last would be weak. But, of the later generations, God made Sergius as strong as one of the early fathers. God made him a lover of hard work, and to be the head over a great number of monks. From the time he was appointed abbot, the holy Mass was sung every day. He himself baked the holy bread; first he flayed and ground the wheat, sifted the flour, kneaded and fermented the dough; he entrusted the making of the holy bread to no one. He also cooked the grains for the "kutia," and he also made the candles. Although occupying the chief place as abbot, he did not alter in any way his monastic rules. He was lowly and humble with all people, and was an example to all.

He never sent away anyone who came to him for the tonsure, neither old nor young, nor rich nor poor; he received them all with fervent joy; but he did not give them the tonsure at once. He who would be a monk was ordered, first, to put on a long, black cloth garment and to live with the brethren until he got accustomed to all the monastic rules; then, later, he was given full monk's attire of cloak and hood. Finally, when he was deemed worthy, he was allowed the "schema," the mark of the ascetic.

After Vespers, and late at night, especially on long dark nights, the saint used to leave his cell and go the round of the monk's cells. If he heard anyone saying his prayers, or making genuflections, or busy with his own handiwork, he was gratified and gave thanks to God. If, on the other hand, he heard two or three monks chatting together, or laughing, he was displased, rapped on the door or window, and passed on. In the morning he would send for them and, indirectly, quietly and gently, by means of some parable, reprove them. If he was a humble and submissive brother he would quickly admit his fault and, bowing low before St. Sergius, would beg his forgiveness. If, instead, he was not a humble brother, and stood erect thinking he was not the person referred to, then the saint, with patience, would make it clear to him, and order him to do a public penance. In this way they all learned to pray to God assiduously; not to chat with one another after Vespers, and to do their own handiwork with all their might; and to have the Psalms of David all day on their lips.

In the beginning, when the monastery was first built, many were the hardships and privations. A main road lay a long way off, and wilderness surrounded the monastery. Here the monks lived, it is believed, for fifteen years. Then, in the time of the Grand Duke Ivan Ivanovich,[5] Christians[6] began to arrive from all parts and to settle in the vicinity. The forest was cut down; there was no one to prevent it; the trees were hewn down, none were spared, and the forest was converted into an open plain as we now see it. A village was built, and houses; and visitors came to the monastery bringing their countless offerings. But in the beginning, when they settled in this place, they all suffered great privations. At times there was no bread or flour, and all means of subsistence was lacking; at times there was no wine for the Eucharist, nor incense, nor wax candles. The monks sang Matins at dawn with no lights save that of a single birch or pine torch.

One day there was a great scarcity of bread and salt in the

[5] Grand Duke Ivan Ivanovich, son of Ivan Kalita and brother of Simon the Proud, reigned from 1353–1359. His son, Dmitry, was the hero of the Battle of Kulikovo.

[6] The word "Christians" here refers to the Russians themselves; surrounded by Moslem, pagans, and unorthodox Christians, the Russians called themselves Christians. This is reflected in the Russian word for peasant—krest'ianin.

whole monastery. The saintly abbot gave orders to all the brethren that they were not to go out, nor beg from the laity, but to remain patiently in the monastery and await God's compassion. He himself spent three or four days without any food. On the fourth day, at dawn, taking an ax, he went to one of the elders, by name Danila, and said to him: "I have heard say that you want to build an entrance in front of your cell. See, I have come to build it for you, so that my hands shall not remain idle."

Danila replied, "Yes, I have been waiting it for a long while, and am awaiting the carpenter from the village; but I am afraid to employ you, for you will require a large payment from me."

Sergius said to him: "I do not require a large sum of money. Have you any mildewed loaves? I very much want to eat some such loaves. I do not ask from you anything else. Where will you find another such carpenter as I?"

Danila brought him a few mildewed loaves, saying, "This is all I have."

Sergius said: "That will be enough, and to spare. But hide it until evening. I take no pay before work is done."

Saying which, and tightening his belt, he chopped and worked all day, cut planks and put up the entrance. At the close of day, Danila brought him the sieveful of the promised loaves. Sergius, offering a prayer and grace, ate the bread and drank some water. He had neither soup nor salt; the bread was both dinner and supper.

Several of the brethren noticed something in the nature of a faint breath of smoke issuing from his lips, and turning to one another they said, "Oh, brother, what patience and self-control has this man!"

But one of the monks, not having had anything to eat for two days, murmured against Sergius, and went up to him and said: "Why this moldy bread? Why should we not go outside and beg for some bread? If we obey you we shall perish of hunger. Tomorrow morning we will leave this place and go hence and not return; we cannot any longer endure such want and scarcity."

Not all of them complained, only one brother, but because of this one, Sergius, seeing they were enfeebled and in distress, convoked the whole brotherhood and gave them instruction from Holy Scriptures: "God's Grace cannot be given without trials; after tribulations comes joy. It is written, at evening there shall be weeping but in the morning gladness. You, at present, have no bread or food, and tomorrow you will enjoy an abundance."

And as he was yet speaking there came a rapping at the gates.

The porter, peeping through an aperture, saw that a store of provisions had been brought; he was so overjoyed that he did not open the gates but ran first to St. Sergius to tell him. The saint gave the order at once, "Open the gates quickly, let them come in, and let those persons who have brought the provisions be invited to share the meal"; while he himself, before all else, directed that the *bilo* should be sounded,[7] and with the brethren he went into the church to sing the *Te Deum*. Returning from church, they went into the refectory, and the newly arrived, fresh bread was placed before them. The bread was still warm and soft, and the taste of it was of an unimaginable strange sweetness, as it were honey mingled with juice of barley and spices.

When they had eaten, the saint remarked: "And where is our brother who was murmuring about moldy bread? May he notice that it is sweet and fresh. Let us remember the prophet who said, 'Ashes have I eaten for bread and mixed my drink with tears.'" Then he inquired whose bread it was, and who had sent it. The messengers announced, "A pious layman, very wealthy, living a great distance away, sent it to Sergius and his brotherhood." Again the monks, on Sergius' orders, invited the men to sup with them, but they refused, having to hasten elsewhere.

The monks came to the abbot in astonishment, saying, "Father, how has this wheaten bread, warm and tasting of butter and spices, been brought from far?" The following day more food and drink were brought to the monastery in the same manner. And again on the third day, from a distant country. Abbot Sergius, seeing and hearing this, gave glory to God before all the brethren, saying, "You see, brethren, God provides for everything, and neither does he abandon this place." From this time forth the monks grew accustomed to being patient under trials and privations, enduring all things, trusting in the Lord God with fervent faith, and being strengthened therein by their holy Father Sergius.

According to an account by one of the elders of the monastery, Blessed Sergius never wore new clothing, nor any made of fine material, nor colored, nor white, nor smooth and soft; he wore plain cloth or caftan; his clothing was old and worn, dirty, patched. Once they had in the monastery an ugly, stained, bad bit of cloth, which all the brethren threw aside; one brother had it, kept it for a while and discarded it, so did another, and a third and so on to the seventh. But the saint did not despise it,

[7] Bilo: a wooden or iron rod used to beat a gong, gongs being used in Russia instead of bells.

he gratefully took it, cut it out and made himself a habit, which he wore, not with disdain but with gratitude, for a whole year, till it was worn out and full of holes.

So shabby were his clothes, worse than that of any of the monks, that several people were misled and did not recognize him. One day a Christian from a nearby village, who had never seen the saint, came to visit him. The abbot was digging in the garden. The visitor looked about and asked, "Where is Sergius? Where is the wonderful and famous man?"

A brother replied, "In the garden, digging; wait a while, until he comes in."

The visitor, growing impatient, peeped through an aperture, and perceived the saint wearing shabby attire, patched, in holes, and face covered with sweat; and he could not believe that this was he of whom he had heard. When the saint came from the garden, the monks informed him, "This is he whom you wish to see."

The visitor turned from the saint and mocked at him: "I came to see a prophet and you point out to me a needy-looking beggar. I see no glory, no majesty and honor about him. He wears no fine and rich apparel; he has no attendants, no trained servants; he is but a needy, indigent beggar."

The brethren, reporting to the abbot, said, "We hardly dare tell you, Reverend Father, and we would send away your guest as a good-for-nothing rude fellow; he has been discourteous and disrespectful about you, reproaches us, and will not listen to us."

The holy man, fixing his eyes on the brethren and seeing their confusion, said to them: "Do not do so, brethren, for he did not come to see you. He came to visit me." And, since he expected no obeisance from his visitor, he went toward him, humbly bowing low to the ground before him, and blessed and praised him for his right judgment. Then, taking him by the hand, the saint sat him down at his right hand, and bade him partake of food and drink. The visitor expressed his regret at not seeing Sergius, whom he had taken the trouble to come and visit; and his wish had not been fulfilled. The saint remarked, "Be not sad about it, for such is God's Grace that no one ever leaves this place with a heavy heart."

As he spoke a neighboring prince arrived at the monastery, with great pomp, accompanied by retinue of boyars, servants, and attendants. The armed attendants, who preceded the prince, took the visitor by the shoulders and removed him out of sight of the prince and of Sergius. The prince then advanced and, from a distance, made a low obeisance to Sergius. The saint gave him his blessing and, after bestowing a kiss on him, they both sat down while everyone else remained standing. The visitor thrust his way through, and going up to one of those standing by, asked, "Who is the monk sitting on the prince's right hand? Tell me."

The man turned to him and said, "Are you then a stranger here? Have you indeed not heard of Blessed Father Sergius? It is he speaking with the prince."

Upon hearing this, the visitor was overcome with remorse, and after the prince's departure, taking several of the brethren to intercede for him, and making a low obeisance before the abbot, he said: "Father, I am but a sinner and a great offender. Forgive me and help my unbelief."

The saint readily forgave, and with his blessing and some words of comfort, he took leave of him. From henceforth, and to the end of his days, this man held a true, firm faith in the Holy Trinity and in St. Sergius. He left his village a few years later, and came to the saint's monastery, where he became a monk, and there spent several years in repentance and amendment of life before he passed away to God.

IV. The Miracles

We shall now turn to the miracles God performs through his elect. Owing to lack of water near the monastery, the brotherhood suffered great discomfort, which increased with their numbers and having to carry water from a distance. Some of the monks even complained to the abbot, "When you set out to build a monastery on this spot, why did you not observe that it was not near water?" They repeated this query with vexation, often.

The saint told them: "I intended to worship and pray in this place alone. But God willed that a monastery such as this, dedicated to the Holy Trinity, should arise."

Going out of the monastery, accompanied by one of the brethren, he made his way through a ravine below the monastery, and finding a small pool of rainwater, he knelt down and prayed. No sooner had he made the sign of the cross over the spot, than a bubbling spring arose, which is still to be seen to this day, and from whence water is drawn to supply every need of the monastery.

Many cures have been granted to the faithful from the waters; and people have come from long distances to fetch the water and carry it away and to give it to their sick to drink. From the time it appeared, and for a number of years, the spring was called after Sergius. The wise man, not seeking renown, was displeased, and remarked: "Never let me hear that a well is called by my name. I did not give this water; God gave it to us unworthy men."

A certain devout Christian living close by the monastery, who believed in St. Sergius, had an only son, a child, who fell ill. The father brought the boy to the monastery, and entreated the saint to pray for him: but while the father was yet speaking the boy died. The man, with his last hope gone, wept and bemoaned, "It would have been better had my son died in my own house." While he went to prepare a grave, the dead child was laid in the saint's cell. The saint felt compassion for this man, and falling on his knees prayed over the dead child. Suddenly the boy came to life, and moved. His father, returning with preparations for the burial, found his son alive, whereupon, flinging himself at the feet of God's servant, he gave him thanks. The saint said to him, "You deceive yourself, man, and do not know what you say. While on your journey hither your son became frozen with cold, and you thought he had died. He has now thawed in the warm cell, and you think he has come to life. No one can rise again from the dead before the Day of Resurrection."

The man however insisted, saying, "Your prayers brought him to life again."

The saint forbade him to say this; "If you noise this abroad you will lose your son altogether." The man promised to tell no one and, taking his son, now restored to health, he went back to his own home. This miracle was made known through the saint's disciples.

Living on the banks of the Volga, a long distance away from the Lavra,[8] was a man who owned great possessions, but who was afflicted incessantly, day and night, by a cruel and evil spirit. Not only did he break iron chains, but ten or more strong men could not hold him. His relatives, hearing tell of the saint, journeyed with him to the monastery, where dwelt the servant of the Lord. When they came to the monastery the madman broke loose from his bonds, and flung himself about, crying, "I will not go, I will not. I will go back from whence I came." They informed the saint, who gave the order to sound the *bilo*, and when the brethren were assembled they sang the *Te Deum*

[8] Lavra was the name given a monastery which was independent of local bishops, being under the direct authority of the head of the Russian Church. There were four such monasteries in Russia.

for the sick. The madman grew calmer little by little, and when he was led into the monastery, the saint came out of church, carrying a cross, whereupon the sufferer, with a loud cry, fled from the spot, and flung himself into a pool of rainwater standing nearby, exclaiming, "O horrible, O terrible flame." By the grace of God and the saint's prayers he recovered, and was restored to his right mind. When they inquired what he meant by his exclamation, he told them, "When the saint wanted to bless me with the cross, I saw a great flame proceeding from him, and it seized hold of me. So I threw myself into the water, fearing that I should be consumed in the flame."

One day the saint, in accordance with his usual rule, was keeping vigil and praying for the brotherhood late at night when he heard a voice calling, "Sergius!" He was astonished, and opening the window of the cell he beheld a wondrous vision. A great radiance shone in the heavens; the night sky was illumined by its brilliance, exceeding the light of day. A second time the voice called: "Sergius! Thou prayest for thy children; God has heard thy prayer. See and behold great numbers of monks gathered together in the name of the Everlasting Trinity, in thy fold, and under thy guidance."

The saint looked and beheld a multitude of beautiful birds, flying, not only on to the monastery, but all around; and he heard a voice saying, "As many birds as thou seest by so many will thy flock of disciples increase; and after thy time they will not grow less if they will follow in thy footsteps." Anxious to have a witness of this vision the saint called aloud for Simon, he being the nearest. Simon ran to him with all haste, but he was not found worthy to behold this vision; he saw no more than a ray of its light, but even so was greatly astonished. Filled with awe and wonder at this glorious vision, they rejoiced together.

V. The Patriarchal Charter

One day some Greeks arrived from Constantinople, sent by the patriarch to visit the saint. Making a deep obeisance they said to him, "The all-powerful Patriarch of Constantinople, Philotheus, sends you his blessing," and they presented him with gifts from the patriarch, a cross and a "paramand," and also handed him a letter from him.

The saint asked: "Are you sure you have not been sent to someone else? How can I, a sinner, be worthy of such gifts from the most illustrious patriarch?"

They replied, "We have indeed been sent to you, holy

Sergius." The elder went then to see the metropolitan, Alexis,[9] and took with him the missive brought from the patriarch. The metropolitan ordered the epistle to be read to him. It ran: "By the Grace of God, the Archbishop of Constantinople, the Ecumenical Patriarch Philotheus, by the Holy Spirit, to our son and fellow servant Sergius. Divine grace and peace, and our blessing be with you. We have heard tell of your godly life dedicated to God, wherefore we greatly praise and glorify God. One thing, however, has not been established: you have not formed a community. Take note, Blessed One, that even the great prophet and our father in God, David, embracing all things with his mind, could not bestow higher praise than when he said, 'But now, however good and however perfect, yet, above all, is abiding together in brotherly love.' Wherefore I counsel you to establish a community. That God's blessing and his grace be always upon you." The elder inquired of the metropolitan, "Revered teacher, what would you have us do?" The metropolitan replied, "With all our heart we approve, and return thanks."

From henceforth life on the basis of community was established in the monastery. The saint, wise pastor, appointed to each brother his duties, one to be cellarer, others to be cooks and bakers, another to care for the sick, and for church duties, an ecclesiarch, and a subecclesiarch, and sacristans, and so forth. He further announced that the ordinances of the holy fathers were to be strictly observed; all things were to be possessed in common, no monk was to hold property of his own.

His community having been established with much wisdom, the numbers of his followers soon increased. Also, the larger the supply of offerings to the monastery, the more hospitality was extended. No person in need ever left the monastery empty-handed; and the saint gave orders that the poor and all strangers were to be allowed to rest in the monastery, and no suppliant to be refused, adding, "If you will follow my precepts and continue in them faithfully, God will reward you, and when I leave this life our monastery will prosper and continue to stand with the Lord's blessing for many years." And to the present day it has remained standing.

[9] Metropolitan Alexis (1353–1378), the son of a boyar from Chernigov in southern Russia, was an outstanding Russian Church leader. He became adviser to Prince Ivan II and Prince Dmitry. Following the policy set by Metropolitan Peter and Theognost, he supported Moscow as the main center of Russian political and spiritual life, and fostered the unification of all Russian lands around Moscow.

VI. The Dissensions

Before long dissension arose; the devil, hating goodness, put about the idea of disputing the authority of Sergius.[10] One Saturday, while Vespers were being sung, and the Abbot Sergius, wearing his vestments, was at the altar, his brother, Stephen, who was standing by the choir, on the left, asked the canonarch, "Who gave you that book?" The canonarch replied, "The abbot gave it to me." The other said, "What has the abbot to do with it? Did not I sit in that place before?" and adding other silly remarks.

Although the saint was standing by the altar, he heard what was said, but he kept silence. When they all came out of church he did not go to his cell; he walked away from the monastery, unknown to all. When he arrived at the monastery of Makrisch,[11] he asked the abbot, Stephen, if one of his monks could lead him to some desert place. Together they searched and finally discovered a beautiful spot close to a river called the Kerzhach. The brotherhood, hearing about the saint, took to visiting him, in twos and threes, and more. Our Father Sergius sent two of his followers to the Metropolitan Alexis, with the request for his blessing and permission to erect a church. Aided by divine favor, a church was erected in a short while, and many brethren gathered there.

Soon several monks from the Holy Trinity, unable any longer to bear the separation from their spiritual father, went to the metropolitan and said: "Holy Lord, we are living like sheep without a shepherd. Command our abbot to return to his monastery, that he may save us from perishing and dying of grief without him."

The metropolitan dispatched two archimandrites, Gerasim and Paul, to the abbot with the message: "Your father, Alexis the Metropolitan, sends you his blessing. He has rejoiced exceedingly to hear that you are living in a distant wilderness. But, return now to the monastery of the Holy Trinity; those persons who were dissatisfied with you shall be removed from the monastery."

Whereupon, hearing this, the saint sent reply, "Tell my lord

[10] These dissensions were apparently caused by St. Sergius' desire to introduce a more disciplined and strictly enforced communal life in the monastery, which was in disagreement with earlier Russian monastic tradition.

[11] Makrisch was another monastery situated about twenty miles from the Monastery of St. Sergius.

the metropolitan, all from his lips, as from those of Christ, I receive with joy and do disobey in nothing."

The metropolitan, glad at his prompt obedience, instantly dispatched a priest to consecrate the church to the Annunciation of the Immaculate and Blessed Virgin, Mother of God. Sergius selected one of his followers, called Romanus, to be the abbot of the new monastery, and sent him to the metropolitan to be raised to the priesthood. The saint then returned to the monastery of the Holy Trinity.

When the news reached the monastery that the saint was returning, the brethren went out to meet him. On beholding him it appeared as if a second sun were shining; and they were so filled with joy that some of the brethren kissed the father's hands, others his feet, while others seized his clothing and kissed that. There were loud rejoicing and glorifying God for the return of their father. And what of the father? He rejoiced with his whole heart at seeing this gathering of his flock.

VII. St. Stephen of Perm

Now Bishop Stephen,[12] a god-fearing and devout man, had for St. Sergius a deep spiritual affection. One day he was travelling from his episcopacy of Perm to the capital, Moscow. The road along which the bishop journeyed lay about seven miles from St. Sergius' monastery. When the godly bishop came opposite the saint's monastery, he stopped and said, bowing low toward the direction of the saint, "Peace be with thee, brother in God!" The saint, at this hour, was seated at table with his brethren. Perceiving in spirit what Bishop Stephen was doing, he rose from the supper table, stood for an instant in prayer, then bowing said aloud, "Be joyful, thou shepherd of Christ's flock; the peace of God be always with thee." At the end of supper his disciples inquired of him what he meant. He openly told them, "At that hour Bishop Stephen, going on his way to Moscow, did reverence to the Holy Trinity, and blessed us humble folk." He pointed out to them, also, where this had taken place.

One time, when Theodore,[13] son of Stephen, was with Blessed Sergius in the monastery, he was taking part in the divine liturgy which was being sung by the saint, and with aforenamed

[12] Bishop Stephen: refers to St. Stephen of Perm (see introductory commentary).

[13] Theodore was the son of Sergius' brother, Stephen. He later became the bishop of Rostov.

Stephen, the saint's brother. Of a sudden Isaac, who had taken the vow of silence, saw a fourth person serving at the altar with them, of a bright, shining appearance, and in dazzling apparel. Isaac inquired of Father Macarius, who was standing by his side, "What miraculous apparition is this?" Macarius replied: "I do not know, brother; I see a fearful and ineffable vision. But I think, brother, that someone came with the prince." (Prince Vladimir was at this time in the monastery.) One of the prince's attendants was asked whether a priest had come with him; but, no, they knew of no one.

When the divine Mass was at an end, seizing a favorable moment, one of the brethren approached St. Sergius and questioned him. But he, anxious not to disclose the secret, asked, "What wonder did you see, brother? My brother, Stephen, was saying the Mass; also his son, Theodore and I, unworthy as I am. No other priest whatever was serving with us." His disciples insisted, entreating the saint to reveal the mystery to them, whereupon he said, "Beloved brethren, what the Lord God has revealed can I keep secret? He whom you beheld was an angel of the Lord, and not only this time but every time I, unworthy as I am, serve with this messenger of the Lord. That which you have seen tell no one, so long as I am on this earth." And his disciples were astonished beyond measure.

VIII. St. Sergius and Russia

A rumor spread that Khan Mamai was raising a large army as a punishment for our sins and that with all his heathen Tatar hordes he would invade Russian soil. Very great fear prevailed among the people at this report. The puissant and reigning prince, who held the scepter of all Russia, great Dmitry,[14] having a great faith in the saint, came to ask him if he counseled him to go against the heathen. The saint, bestowing on him his blessing, and strengthened by prayer, said to him: "It behoveth you, Lord, to have a care for the lives of the flock committed to you by God. Go forth against the heathen; and upheld by the strong arm of God, conquer; and return to your country sound in health, and glorify God with loud praise."

The grand duke replied, "If indeed God assist me, Father, I will build a monastery to the Immaculate Mother of God." And with the saint's blessing he hurriedly went on his way. As-

14 Grand Duke Dmitry, reigned 1363–1385, was the hero of *Zadonshchina*, and the first Russian prince to defeat the Tatars in a major battle.

sembling all his armies, he marched against the heathen Tatars; but, seeing the multitudes of them, he began to doubt; and many of his followers, not knowing what to do, were overwhelmed with fear. Of a sudden, a courier from the saint arrived, in all haste, with the message. "Be in no doubt, Lord; go forward with faith and confront the enemy's ferocity; and fear not, for God will be on your side." Forthwith, the Grand Duke Dmitry and all his armies, were filled with a spirit of temerity; and went into battle against the pagans. They fought; many fell; but God was with them, and helped the great and invincible Dmitry, who vanquished the ungodly Tatars. In that same hour the saint was engaged with his brethren before God in prayer for victory over the pagans. Within an hour of the final defeat of the ungodly, the saint, who was a seer, announced to the brotherhood what had happened, the victory, the courage of the Grand Duke Dmitry, and the names, too, of those who had died at the hands of the pagans; and he made intercession for them to all-merciful God.

The Grand Duke Dmitry returned to his country with great joy in his heart, and hastened to visit holy, venerable Sergius. Rendering thanks for the prayers of the saint and of the brotherhood, he gave a rich offering to the monastery and, in fulfillment of his vow, expressed his wish to build at once the monastery of the Immaculate Mother of God. After searching for a favorable place, venerable Sergius fixed upon one by the banks of the river Dubenka, and with the consent of the grand duke a church to the Assumption of our Blessed Virgin Mother of God was consecrated by St. Sergius. As abbot, the saint appointed one of his followers, Sabbas by name, a man of exceeding great virtue. A community was formed, and many brethren joined it.

Once again the Grand Duke Dmitry entreated St. Sergius to come to Kolomna, to consecrate a site for the building of a monastery to be dedicated to the Holy Epiphany. It was the saint's custom to go everywhere on foot. Obedient to the grand duke, he went to Kolomna, consecrated the site, and a church was erected and, at the grand duke's request, he sent him one of his disciples for the founding of the monastery, a priest-monk, Gregory, a devout man and of great virtue. In time a stone church was built, which is standing to this day.

Another time the illustrious Prince Vladimir begged St. Sergius, likewise, to come to his part of the country, to the town of Serpukhov, and consecrate a place by the river Nar, and dedicate a church to the Conception of the Immaculate Mother of God. Once again the saint obeyed the request. This god-fearing prince also begged him to send one of his disciples, Athanasius by name. Although the saint found it hard to grant this request, love prevailed, and he consented. Athanasius being a man of rare virtue, exceedingly learned in Holy Scriptures—many valuable writings by his hand bear witness to him to the present day—the saint loved him dearly. To him the saint entrusted the founding of the monastery, and the forming of the community. Aided by the prayers of the saint, the monastery was built, wonderful and beautiful, and named "On the Height."

But why pursue further the saint's planting of ecclesiastical fruit? It is well known how many monasteries were founded by God's own chosen servant. And, offspring of his offspring, burning bright as stars, they are everywhere radiating a serene and wondrous life, and a blessing to all.

The Metropolitan Alexis, being old, and seeing his weakness increasing, sent for St. Sergius. While they conversed, the metropolitan asked to have the cross with the "paramand" adorned with gold and precious stones brought to him, to give it to the saint; but he, bowing low in great humility, refused it, saying, "Forgive me, Lord, I have worn no gold ornaments since childhood, wherefore all the more do I wish in old age to continue in poverty." The bishop insisted, and said, "I know, beloved, that thou art fulfilling a vow, but be obedient, and take this which we offer thee with a benediction." Further, he said to the saint: "Dost know why I sent for thee? I desire, while I yet live, to find a man able to feed Christ's flock. I have doubted of them all; thee alone have I chosen as worthy. I know with all certainty that, from the puissant prince to the lowliest of his people, thou art the one they want."

On hearing this the saint was deeply grieved, regarding honor for himself as a thing of naught, and he pleaded with the bishop: "Forgive me, Lord, but this of which you speak is beyond my powers, and you never will find it in me. What am I but a sinner, and the least of men?" The bishop quoted many sayings from Holy Scriptures, but the saint, unyielding in his humility, said, "Gracious Lord, if you do not wish to drive away my poverty from your Holiness, speak no more about my poor self, nor permit anyone else, for no one can make me otherwise."

The bishop, understanding that the saint would not yield, allowed him to return to his monastery. Before long the Metropolitan Alexis left this life, in the year 1378 (6885); and once more the princes implored the saint to accept the rank of bishop; but, firm as adamant, he would in no way consent. Then a certain archimandrite, Michael, was raised to the bishopric; but this man, with great presumption, not only invested himself with the episcopal robes but also proceeded to plot against the saint, in the belief that the venerable Sergius would put a check on his audacity, wishing to occupy the episcopal throne himself. Blessed Sergius, hearing of Michael's threats against him, remarked to his disciples that Michael, vaunting himself of his sacred appointment, would not obtain his wish, for, overcome by pride, he would not reach the imperial city. The saint's prophecy was fulfilled. On his way by boat to Constantinople,[15] Michael fell ill and died. Thereupon everyone regarded St. Sergius as one of the prophets.

IX. The Last Miracles and the Passing Away of St. Sergius

One day the blessed father was praying, as was his wont, before the image of the Mother of our Lord Jesus Christ. Having sung the "Magnificat" of the Blessed Virgin, he sat down to rest a while, saying to his disciple, Micah, "Son, be calm and be bold, for a wonderful and fearful event is about to happen." Instantly a voice was heard, "The Blessed Virgin is coming." Hearing this the saint hurried from his cell into the corridor. A dazzling radiance shone upon the saint, brighter than the sun, and he beheld the Blessed Virgin, with the two Apostles Peter and John, in ineffable glory. Unable to bear so resplendent a vision, the saint fell to the ground. The Blessed Virgin, touching the saint with her hand, said: "Be not afraid, mine own elect, I have come to visit thee. Thy prayers for thy disciples for whom thou prayest, and for thy monastery, have been heard. Be not troubled; from henceforth it will flourish, not only during thy lifetime but when thou goest to the Lord, I will be with thy monastery, supplying its needs lavishly, providing for it, protecting it."

Having thus spoken, she vanished. The saint, in ecstasy, stood in trembling awe and wonder. Returning slowly to his senses, he saw his disciple, terror-struck, lying on the ground, whereupon he raised him up; but the other flung himself down at the feet of the elder, saying, "Tell me, Father, for God's sake what miraculous vision was this? For my spirit almost loosed its bonds with the flesh from so resplendent a vision."

[15] From the beginnings of the Russian Church until 1448, the head of the Russian Church, who was first the Metropolitan of Kiev and later the Metropolitan of Moscow, was consecrated by the Patriarch of Constantinople. After 1448, the year the Byzantine Church concluded its union of short duration with the Church of Rome, the Russian Church broke away and became independent.

The saint, so filled with ecstasy that his face glowed therewith, was unable to answer other than a few words, "Wait a while, son, for I, too, am trembling with awe and wonder at this miraculous vision." They continued in silent adoration until, finally, the saint said to his disciple, "Son, call hither Isaac and Simon." When these two came, he recounted to them all that had happened, how he had beheld the Blessed Virgin with the Apostles, and what a wonderful promise she had given him. Hearing this their hearts were filled with indescribable joy, and they all sang the "Magnificat," and glorified God. All night long the saint remained in meditation on this ineffable vision.

After a while, a Greek bishop came from Constantinople to Moscow, but, although he had heard a great deal about the saint, his doubt about him prevailed, for, he reasoned, "How can such a light have appeared in this savage land, more especially in these latter days?" He therefore resolved to go to the monastery and see the saint. When he drew near to the monastery, fear entered his soul, and as soon as he entered the monastery and beheld the saint, blindness fell upon him. The venerable Sergius took him by the hand and led him to his cell. The bishop, with tears, confessed his doubts to the saint, and prayed for the recovery of his sight. The gentle lover of humility touched his blinded pupils, and, as it were, scales fell from his eyes, and instantly he recovered his sight. The bishop proclaimed to all that the saint was indeed a man of God and that in God's mercy he himself had been deemed worthy to behold a celestial man and an earthly angel.

A moneylender, living near the saint's monastery, and who, like the strong in all ages, oppressed the poor, ill-treated a certain poor orphan, and, moreover, carried off his pig which was being fattened, and without paying for it had it killed. The ill-used orphan went to the saint in great distress and, weeping, begged for help. The saint, moved by compassion, sent for the offender, convicted him of wrongdoing, and said, "My son, do you believe that God is a judge of the righteous and of sinners; a father to widows and orphans; that he is quick to avenge and that it is a fearful thing to come under the wrath of God?" Having reproached him and told him he must pay what he owed to the orphan, he added, "Above all, do not oppress the poor." The man, overcome by fear, promised to amend and to pay the orphan, then returned to his own house. Little by little the effect of the saint's rebuke grew faint, and he decided not to pay his debt to the orphan. And, thinking it over in his mind, he went as usual into his larder, where he found the pig half devoured and swarming with maggots, although it was midwinter. He was stricken with fear, and without delay paid the debt; and ordered the pig to be thrown to the dogs and birds to eat, but they would not touch it and clear the usurer of his offense.

Now, again, one day, the saint was reciting the divine liturgy with one of his disciples, venerable Simon, the ecclesiarch, of whom we have already spoken, when a wonderful vision was vouchsafed to Simon. While the saint was saying the liturgy, Simon saw a flame pass along the altar, illuminating it and surrounding the holy table; as the saint was about to partake of the Blessed Sacrament the glorious flame coiled itself and entered the sacred chalice; and the saint thus received Communion. Simon, who saw this, trembled with fear. The saint, when he moved away from the altar, understood that Simon had been deemed worthy of this miraculous vision, and telling him to approach, asked, "Son, why are you fearful?" The other replied, "Master, I beheld a miraculous vision; the grace of the Holy Spirit operating with you." The saint forbade him to speak of it: "Tell no one of this which you have seen, until the Lord calls me away from this life."

The saint lived a number of years, continually chastening himself with fasting, and working unceasingly. He performed many unfathomable miracles, and reached an advanced age, never failing from his place at divine service; the older his body grew, the stronger grew his fervor, in no way weakened by age. He became aware of his approaching end six months before, and assembling the brotherhood he appointed his dearest disciple to take his place, one perfect in all virtue, following his master in all things, small of stature, but in mind a continual blossoming, whose name was Nikon. The saint exhorted him to guide Christ's flock with patient care and justice. The great ascetic soon began to lose strength and in September was taken seriously ill. Seeing his end, he again assembled his flock and delivered a final exhortation. He made them promise to be steadfast in orthodoxy and to preserve amity among men; to keep pure in body and soul; to love truth; to avoid all evil and carnal lusts; to be moderate in food and drink; above all, to be clothed with humility; not to forget love of their neighbor; to avoid controversy, and on no account to set value on honor and praise in this life, but rather to await reward from God for the joys of heaven and eternal blessings. Having instructed them in many things, he concluded, "I am, by God's will, about to leave you, and I commit you to Almighty God and the Immaculate Virgin, Mother of God, that they may be to you a refuge and rock of defense against the snares of your enemies." As his soul was about to leave his body, he partook of the sacred Body and Blood, supported in the arms of his disciples and, raising his hands to heaven, with a prayer on his lips, he surrendered his pure, holy soul to the Lord, in the year 1393 (6900), September 25th, probably at the age of seventy-eight. After his death an ineffable sweet odor flowed from the saint's body.

The entire brotherhood gathered around him and, weeping and sobbing, laid on its bier the body of him who in life had been so noble and unresting, and accompanied him with psalms and funeral orisons. The saint's face, unlike that of other dead, glowed with the life of the living, or as one of God's angels, witnessing to the purity of his soul, and God's reward for all his labors. His body was laid to rest within the monastery of his own creation. Many were the miracles that took place at his death and after, and still are taking place, giving strength to the weaker members of the community, deliverance from the crafts and wiles of evil spirits, and sight to the blind. The saint had no wish during his life for renown, neither in death, but by God's Almighty Power he was glorified. Angels were present at his passing into the heavens, opening for him the gates of paradise and leading him toward the longed-for blessings, into the peace of the righteous, the ever-looked-for glory of the Blessed Trinity.

27. *Peter and Fevronia of Murom*

IN RUSSIAN medieval literature the tale of *Peter and Fevronia of Murom* is a unique instance of a work in which some romantic elements are presented. The love between Peter and Fevronia is considerably spiritualized, however, emphasizing their faithfulness to each other both in this life and in life after death. In this respect, the story of Peter and Fevronia resembles that of Tristan and Iseult, although deprived of any amorous background. This tale can be divided into composite segments, as has been done in this translation. The first, and the most fantastic, part, "The Story of the Evil Serpent," echoes the widely spread motif concerning the effect of the blood of an evil serpent, a motif which can be found in the *Nibelungenlied.* The second section treats the miraculous healing of Prince Peter by a wise and fair maiden, a theme also to be found in both Eastern and European legends and fairy tales. The third part, "The Intrigues of the Boyars," unlike the preceding sections, contains a political polemic attempting to prove that the autocratic rule of a prince is superior to the rule of an aristocracy that leads to its own self-destruction through dissension. The conclusion of this work has hagiographic colorations. Peter and Fevronia appear here as devout and just rulers who care for their subjects, helping the poor and supporting the Church.

Unusual for a work describing the lives of saints—Peter and Fevronia actually were venerated as the saintly patrons of the city of Murom—is their last testament: to remain together in the same casket after death. Here, the elements of the purity and sanctity of the family supersede the usual ascetic tradition of hagiographic works.

Peter and Fevronia, in its language, symbolism, and its use of riddles (as in the speech of Fevronia), clearly reflects a folklore origin. The name Agrica itself plainly shows this influence, for Agrica was an invincible mythological warrior of Russian folk epics who possessed a magic sword with which he slew evil serpents and monsters.

The exact background of this story is not well known. Peter and Fevronia had been venerated in Murom since the middle of the fifteenth century, and they were both canonized in 1547 by an All-Russian Church Council in Moscow. However, this narrative has never been included in the official collection of *vitae* nor was it read in the Church. There are some indications that the life of Prince David of Murom, who ruled there from 1203 to 1228, was the historical source for this work.

This translation is based upon the Old Russian text prepared by Professor M. O. Skripil and published in the collection *Russkie povesti XV–XVI vekov*, Moscow, 1958, pages 108–115.

◆ ◆ ◆

I. The Evil Serpent

There is in the Russian land a city called Murom. I was told that this city was once ruled by a good prince named Paul. The devil, hating everything good among men, sent a serpent to the palace of Prince Paul's wife to seduce and debase her. And when the princess was with the serpent, she saw him as he really was, while it seemed to others who visited the princess's palace that not a serpent, but Prince Paul himself was with the princess. Time passed, and the wife of Prince Paul decided that she could no longer hide her secret. She revealed what had happened to her husband, for the serpent had already debased her.

Prince Paul tried to think of what to do with the serpent, and finally he told his wife: "I cannot discern how I am to deal with this evil spirit. I don't know any means of killing it. But we shall do the following. When you talk with him, ask him cleverly whether he knows how he is destined to die. And when you learn this, tell me, and you will not only be rid of this evil spirit and its debauchery, of which it is disgusting even to speak, but also in the next life you will gain the mercy of our righteous Judge, Jesus Christ."

The princess became gladdened by her husband's words, and thought, It would be good if it would only happen so. And when the serpent came, she began to converse slyly and cleverly with it about various things, keeping in mind her intentions. When it began to brag, she asked humbly and with respect, "You certainly know everything, and so you must certainly know to what kind of death you are destined."

And the great deceiver was himself deceived by the deception of the faithful wife and unknowingly betrayed his secret, saying, "My death will come from Peter's hand and Agrica's sword." The princess, hearing this, concealed it firmly in her heart. After the departure of this evil being, she told her husband, the prince, what the serpent had said. The prince, hearing this, was unable to understand what was meant by the words "My death will come from Peter's hand and Agrica's sword." But, since he had a brother named Peter, he summoned him and told him what his wife had learned from the evil serpent. Prince Peter, learning from his brother that the serpent gave his namesake as the cause of his death, began to think bravely of how to kill this serpent. Yet he was confused by the fact that he did not know what was the sword of Agrica.

Prince Peter had the custom of going alone to church to pray. Once he came to the Church of the Elevation of the Holy Cross which belonged to a convent beyond the city wall. There he was approached by a youth who asked the prince if he wished to see the sword of Agrica. The prince, desirous of fulfilling his desire to kill the serpent, answered, "Certainly! Where is it?" And the youth asked Prince Peter to follow him, and he showed him a niche in the bricks of the altar in which a sword was lying. Faithful Prince Peter took the sword and went to his brother, Prince Paul, and told him everything. And from that moment Prince Peter began to wait for the opportunity to kill this evil serpent.

Each day he visited his brother and his sister-in-law. One day, after he had visited his brother, he went to the room of his sister-in-law, and there he once again found his brother, sitting with the princess. Leaving her room, he met a man from Prince Paul's retinue, and he asked him: "I was just in my brother's room and found him there. Then I went directly to my sister-in-law's room and once again I found him there. How is this possible?"

And the man answered: "It is not possible, my lord. Prince Paul has not left his room since you left him." He went to his older brother's room and asked him: "When did you return to your room? When I left you, I went to the chambers of the princess without losing any time. And yet, when I came there, I found you next to her. I can't understand how you could get there before me. Therefore, I left there, came back here, and now once more I see that you were faster than I in getting here. I don't understand it."

Then Prince Paul explained to Peter that he had not left his room nor had he been with the princess during this time. Then Prince Peter understood what had happened. "All this is the witchcraft of this evil serpent. In my presence he assumes your image for his own so that he would not be killed by me. Brother, do not leave this room, for I am now going to your wife's chambers to fight the evil serpent. I hope that I will be able to slay it with the help of God."

Prince Peter then took Agrica's sword and went to the princess's chambers, where he again found the serpent in the form of his brother. He struck it with the sword, and the evil spirit returned to its true form and died in convulsions. Before it died, however, its blood spilled on Prince Peter. The body of Prince Peter became covered with sores and ulcers from this blood, and the prince became gravely ill. He was attended by many physicians, but none were able to cure him.

II. The Healing of Prince Peter

Having heard that there were many physicians in the region of Riazan, Prince Peter told his servants to convey him there. Weakened by his illness, Prince Peter was no longer able to mount his horse. When he arrived in the land of Riazan, he sent all the men of his retinue to look for physicians.

One of the young men of his retinue came accidentally to a village called Charity. In this village he approached the gate of a house in which apparently no one was at home. He entered the house and found no one. Finally, he entered a room in which he found a beautiful maiden who was weaving. Before her a hare was jumping and playing about. The maiden said to the young soldier, "It is indeed unfortunate when the yard is without ears and the house without eyes."

The young man didn't understand the meaning of these words, but asked where the master of the house was. The maiden answered, "My father and mother have gone alone to weep so as to pay their debt in advance, and my brother has gone to view death between his feet."

Once more the young soldier did not understand the maiden's words, and things appeared to be strange to him. He again spoke to the maiden: "I came to your place and I saw you weaving and a hare jumping about before you. Now I hear strange words from your lips which I cannot understand. First you told me that it is unfortunate when a yard is without ears and a house without eyes. Then you told me that your mother and father have gone to weep alone so as to pay their debt in advance and that your brother has gone to view death between his feet. I have not understood a word that you have told me."

The maiden smiled, and said: "Well, it is not too difficult to understand. You came into the house and found me sitting here weaving and dressed in house clothes. If we had a dog, it might have heard you and started barking. In such a case the yard would have had ears. If my brother were at home, he might have seen you coming here and warned me. In this case the house would have eyes. I told you that my parents went to weep alone so as to pay their debt in advance. Actually, they went to a burial and wept there. Once death has come to them, others will weep after them, and therefore they weep now to pay their debt in advance. As for my brother, I told you that he had gone to view death between his feet. Actually, he and my father climb trees and collect pitch. He went just now to climb trees, and when he does so, he must watch his feet so that he will not fall. If he should fall, it would be his death. Therefore I said that my brother had gone to view death between his feet."

The young soldier then said to the maiden: "I see that you are very wise. Please tell me your name." Upon learning that the maiden's name was Fevronia, the young soldier explained why he had come there: "I have come here on behalf of my lord, Prince Peter of Murom. My prince is sick and covered with sores and ulcers. He received these afflictions from the blood of an evil serpent which he killed with his own hands. Since that time many doctors have treated him, but none have been able to cure him. Therefore, he ordered us to bring him to this land, for he heard that there are many physicians here. But we know neither where they live nor what are their names."

Fevronia answered, saying, "The only one who can cure the prince is the one who would order that your prince be brought to this place."

"Who would that be? What do you mean by these words?" the young man inquired. "The prince will lavishly reward the physician who will cure him. Tell me the name of such a physician—who he is and where he lives."

The maiden then told him: "Bring your prince to this place. If he is kind of heart and not proud in answering my questions, he will be cured." The young soldier listened to these words and then returned to Prince Peter and told him in detail all that he had seen and heard.

Prince Peter then enjoined his retinue to take him immediately to this wise maiden. And they took him to the house wherein lived the maiden. The prince sent a page to the maiden asking: "Tell me, maiden, who is the man who can cure me? Let him cure me, and he will receive a large part of my wealth!"

Without hesitation the maiden answered the page: "I am the physician who is able to cure your prince, but I do not desire any part of his wealth. However, if I do not become his wife, I shall have no reason to cure him."

The page returned to the prince and repeated to him the words of Fevronia. Prince Peter did not take her words seriously, thinking that it would be impossible for a prince to marry the daughter of a man whose station in life was as low as that of one who collects pitch. And he instructed his page to tell the maiden that she must cure him, and that if she did, she would become his wife. The page repeated these words to the maiden. She then took a small pitcher and scooped up some leaven from a barrel and told the page: "Prepare a steambath for your prince, and, after the bath, spread this leaven over the sores and ulcers on his body. But you must take care not to cover all of the scabs, but leave one uncovered. And then your prince will return to good health." The young man brought the ointment made from leaven to the prince, and the servants immediately prepared the steambath.

While the servants were preparing the steambath, the prince decided to learn how wise this maiden really was, for he had only the word of his servant in this matter. To this end he sent her a small bundle of linen, asking that she make him a shirt, towel, and pants from this linen while he was in the steambath, and if she were successful, she would thereby prove her wisdom.

A servant brought the bundle of linen to Fevronia and repeated the command of Prince Peter. Fevronia, without any hesitation, ordered the man to climb up on the stove and fetch down a piece of dry wood. When the servant gave her the piece of wood, she marked off a piece one foot in length and ordered the man to cut off this piece. When the servant had done so, she told him to take the block to his master and ask him to make from it a spinning wheel and a loom, while she was combing the linen in preparation for making the shirt, pants, and towel.

The servant took the block of wood to Prince Peter and repeated Fevronia's request. The prince laughed, and said: "Go to Fevronia and tell her that it is not possible to prepare so many things from so small a block in so short a time."

Fevronia had anticipated this answer, and told the servant: "Well, if your prince is unable to make a spinning wheel and a loom from such a small piece of wood in so short a time, how can I, in return, weave a shirt, pants, and a towel for him from such a small bundle of linen, while he takes a steambath?" When the page returned to the prince, he was astounded by the wisdom of her answer.

Then Prince Peter went into the steambath, and his servants applied the ointment over the sores and ulcers, leaving only one scab uncovered, as was ordered by Fevronia. When Prince Peter left the steambath, his pains left him, and the next morning all his body was clear and healed excepting the one scab that had been left uncovered. He marveled at the curing powers of Fevronia. However, since Fevronia was the daughter of one of lowly birth, Prince Peter did not wish to marry her. He did, however, send her luxurious gifts, but Fevronia would not accept them.

Peter returned to his native city of Murom with his body completely healed excepting the single scab. Soon afterward, however, more sores and ulcers began to spread from the single scab which had not been covered by the ointment. And then his whole body was once again covered with sores and ulcers. Seeing that his affliction had returned, Prince Peter decided to return to Fevronia once again to undergo the proven treatment.

He returned to Riazan and to Fevronia's house, and despite the fact that he was ashamed for not having kept his promise to marry her, he asked her to treat him once more. Fevronia was not the least bit angry, but said that she would treat him only ıngry, and clothed the naked. And they helped the poor in eir misfortune.

When death was nearing, Peter and Fevronia prayed to God ıat they both might die in the same hour. And they requested ıat they be buried in the same tomb and in a common coffin in vhich their bodies would be separated only by a partition. And ogether they took monastic vows, Prince Peter becoming Brother David, and Princess Fevronia, Sister Euphrosinia.

And it happened that, shortly before her death, Princess Fevronia was embroidering a figure of the saints on a coverlet for the chalice of the cathedral. And a messenger came from Prince Peter, now Brother David, saying, "Sister Euphrosinia, I am ready to die, and wait only for you, so that we may die together."

But Princess Fevronia, now Sister Euphrosinia, answered, "You should wait, my lord, until I finish the coverlet for the chalice of the holy cathedral."

Then Brother David sent another messenger, who announced, "I can wait for you only a short time." Shortly after, another messenger arrived, saying: "I shall soon depart this world. There is no time left for waiting."

Princess Fevronia was just finishing the embroidering of the coverlet, but, hearing these words, she placed the needle in the coverlet and wound up the thread she had been using. Doing so, she sent a message to Brother David saying that they would now die together. And, having prayed, they offered up their souls to God on Friday, the 20th day of June.

After their deaths, some of the people decided that Prince Peter should be buried in the Cathedral of the Holy Virgin, which was within the walls of the city of Murom, and that Princess Fevronia should be buried in the Church of the Elevation of the Holy Cross, which was outside the walls of the city. And they actually did so, saying that it was not becoming for a man and woman who had taken monastic vows to be buried in the same casket. The body of Prince Peter was put in a casket and was placed in the cathedral, where it was left overnight. The body of Princess Fevronia was put in another casket and placed in the church outside the city walls. A tomb, which had been carved from a huge rock as a resting-place for Peter and Fevronia, remained empty in the yard of the Cathedral of the Holy Virgin.

The next morning the people went to the caskets of Peter and Fevronia and found them empty. The bodies of the holy prince and princess were found together in the tomb of stone, which

if he decided to be her husband. This time the prince firmly promised that he would take her as his wife.

The maiden then prescribed the same treatment as before. And when he was healed again, Prince Peter took Fevronia for his wife. And in this way did Fevronia become a princess. And both of them went to Peter's native city of Murom, and there they lived extremely piously, closely obeying the commandments of God. Soon after their arrival in Murom, Prince Paul died, and Prince Peter became the sole ruler of the city.

III. The Intrigues of the Boyars

The boyars of the city of Murom did not find Princess Fevronia to their liking. They, under the influences of their spouses, resented the princess because of her common origin. However, because of her charitable deeds, she was extremely popular among the simple people, and they prayed to God for her. Once, one of the courtiers, wanting to bring strife between Peter and Fevronia, came to the prince and told him: "The princess usually gets up from the table when she is not supposed to do so. Moreover, before leaving the table, she picks up the crumbs as if she were hungry."

Prince Peter decided to see if these accusations were true. He ordered that Princess Fevronia sit beside him at the table. When dinner was over, Fevronia picked up all the crumbs and kept them in her hand as she was accustomed to doing since her childhood. Seeing this, Prince Peter caught her by the hand and told her to open her fist, but when she did so they found fragrant myrrh and incense in the palm of her hand. And from that day on, Peter never attempted to question his wife's deeds.

Many years later the resentful boyars came once again to Peter and said: "Our lord, we want to serve you honestly and want you as our ruler, but we do not want Princess Fevronia as our princess, nor do we want her to rule over our wives. If you are to remain, our lord, you must take another for princess. Fevronia may take her wealth and go away anywhere she may wish to go."

Blessed Prince Peter was of gentle nature and did not become angry, but promised to talk to Princess Fevronia to learn what she would say of this. The shameless courtesans then decided to organize a banquet. They became drunk at this banquet and began to talk arrogantly like loudly barking dogs. And they began to deny Fevronia's miraculous gift of healing, which she had received from God not only for this life but even for after death.

They began talking: "Our lady, Princess Fevronia, the whole city and all the boyars ask you to give back to us Prince Peter, because we want him."

Fevronia answered: "You can have him. Only speak with him."

Then the boyars all spoke at once, saying: "Our lady, all of us want Prince Peter to rule over us, but our wives do not want you to rule over them. Please, take as much wealth as you desire and go wherever you like."

Hearing these words, Princess Fevronia told them that she would do as they desired but that now she must ask them to do one thing that she desired. The boyars, who were not very clever, rejoiced, and thought that they would easily rid themselves of her. So they pledged to do as she asked. And Princess Fevronia said, "I want nothing from you but my husband, Prince Peter."

The boyars deliberated for a short while and then said, "If Prince Peter will have it this way, we will not contradict him."

They hoped that they would be able to choose another ruler if Prince Peter did not wish to break the divine commandment, for it is written in the Gospel of Apostle Matthew: "But I say unto you, that whosoever shall put away his wife, saving for the cause of unchastity, makes her an adultress." And Prince Peter, following the commandment of Jesus, gave up his rule over the city of Murom.

The evil lords prepared boats for Peter and Fevronia, for the city of Murom was situated on the river Oka. And so they went down the river in these vessels. On the princess' boat was a courtier who, despite the fact that he was accompanied by his wife, was tempted by evil spirits and began to stare at Princess Fevronia with shameful thoughts. The princess immediately discerned his evil thoughts and exposed them to the man. Approaching him, she ordered him to scoop up water from the river on one side of the boat and drink it. When the man had done so, she ordered him to go to the other side of the ship and do the same. When the man had drunk the water, Fevronia approached him, and asked, "Tell me, did you find that the water tastes the same on both sides of the ship, or was it perhaps sweeter on one side than on the other?"

The man answered: "No, my lady. The water tasted the same on both sides."

Then she replied: "And so is the nature of all women. Why then do you want to leave your wife and think about another woman?" The courtier then realized that the princess possessed

the gift of reading the minds of men. Becoming afraid, up his evil intentions.

In the evening the boats docked, and when the travel disembarking, Prince Peter became seized with doubt whether he was right in giving up his rule in the city of His sagacious wife perceived his doubts, and comfort saying: "Do not grieve, my Prince, for merciful God, our C who directs our life, will never forsake us to misfortune."

That same evening the servants began to prepare dinn the prince. They cut down branches of some trees and, m a spit, put the kettle on. Princess Fevronia, who was wa along the shore, came upon these branches that had been from the trees. Seeing them, she said, "Bless them, for be morning these branches will grow into great trees with foliage." And so it happened, for when the travelers got up the morning they found that these branches had grown i great trees with rich foliage.

And when the servants began to load the boats, there came lord from the city of Murom, saying: "My lord, Prince Peter, come to you in behalf of all the courtiers of the city of Muron They ask that you do not desert them, your poor orphans, bu that you return as ruler to your native land. Many lords of th city have perished by the sword. Each, wanting to become rule of the city, killed the other. Those lords who have survived and all the rest of the people beg you to come back, my lord, and rule over us. And we will neither anger nor irritate you again. Some of our ladies did not wish to be ruled by Princess Fevronia, but now these ladies have perished in the feud. Those of us who remain alive do love her, and we beg you not to leave us alone, your humble servants."

Thus Prince Peter and Princess Fevronia returned to the city of Murom, and they ruled according to the commandments of God.

IV. The Passing Away of Peter and Fevronia

Peter and Fevronia always helped their people with alms and prayers. They treated all as if they were their own children. They loved everyone equally, and disliked only those who were proud or who exploited the people. Peter and Fevronia lay up their treasures, not on earth, but in heaven. They were real pastors of their city. They always ruled with truth and humility, and never with anger. They gave shelter to pilgrims, fed the

they had ordered prepared for them. The people, not understanding the meaning of this event, once more placed the bodies in separate caskets. On the following day the bodies of Prince Peter and Princess Fevronia were once again found together in the tomb of stone. Since that time no man has dared to disturb their holy bodies, but left them in their common tomb in the yard of the Cathedral of the Holy Virgin, which is located in the city of Murom. And whoever touched with contrition the tomb wherein lie the holy relics of Peter and Fevronia always received comfort and healing.

28. *The Life of St. Michael, A Fool in Christ*

THE life of Michael of Klopsko was one of the most popular hagiographic works of northern Russia in the fifteenth and sixteenth centuries. Some seventy ancient manuscripts containing different versions of this *vita* have been preserved, and they have been rewritten, re-edited, and expanded upon by various medieval writers. Michael of Klopsko was an actual historical person, known not only from his *vita* but also from chronicles and documents. He lived in the first half of the fifteenth century, came to the Monastery of the Holy Trinity in Klopsko, near the city of Novgorod, between 1408 and 1412, and died there between 1453 and 1458. This was a period of intense struggle within the Muscovite ruling dynasty—specifically, between the Grand Prince of Moscow, Vasily II (or the "Blind"); his cousin, Prince Dmitry Shemiaka; and the latter's brother, Vasily the "One-Eyed." The epithets "the Blind" and "the One-Eyed" indicate the cruelty of this struggle, as each cousin was responsible for the other's mutilation. Shemiaka's memory has become notorious because of his cruelty and perfidy; in fact, the name Shemiaka has become a synonym for injustice. His story will be found in the tale of *Shemiaka's Judgment*. In addition to the struggle for power among these cousins, the *Life of St. Michael* also reflects the desire of the Muscovite princes to unify Russia under their leadership and to incorporate the Novgorodian Republic into the Russian state.

Michael of Klopsko was one of the first Russian *yurodivy*, or "fools in Christ," as certain people were called who devoted themselves entirely to the service of God. They accepted voluntarily the role of a fool in order to be able to teach people the truth of Christ and also to speak the truth to the powerful princes and lords. These "fools in Christ" usually wore coarse linen frocks throughout the whole year, ate the barest minimum of food, and walked barefoot, even in winter. In their prophecies they often spoke truths in the forms of parables, and interesting examples of such can be found in this work.

This *vita* consists of a number of episodes that have been placed under subtitles for easier reading. The style of this work clearly recalls the simple, clipped language of the *Novgorodian Chronicle*. Many sentences are so curt that they often require additional words for comprehension, and any such added words have been placed in parentheses. Similar also to the *Novgorodian Chronicle* is the use of "in this same year" to introduce a new topic or episode. The style of "Michael's Advice to the Novgorodian Republic," however, differs considerably from the anecdotal manner and abrupt, curt style of the rest of the story. One can surmise that this section was a late addition to this work and was of a political nature—that is, it was intended to show the people of Novgorod that God himself, speaking through the mouth of Michael, wished Novgorod to become incorporated into the Muscovite realm.

Some of these episodes are presented in the form of anecdotes, and are among the earliest examples of Russian satirical writing. Their language resembles that of later Muscovite satirical tales of adventure, especially *Shemiaka's Judgment*. Michael's *vita* offers an interesting instance of primitive biography written in simple, naïve language and consisting of disconnected episodes from the life of the saint.

This translation is based upon version B of the earlier text of the *Life of St. Michael of Klopsko* to be found in L. A. Dimitrieva's *Povesti o zhitii Mikhaila Klopskogo*, published by the Academy of Sciences of the U.S.S.R., Moscow and Leningrad, 1958, pages 99–110. The subtitles for the various episodes have been supplied by the translator.

◆ ◆ ◆

I. Michael's Arrival in Klopsko

St. Michael, a fool in Christ, came to the Church of the Holy Trinity in Klopsko in the time of Abbot Theodosius who later became archbishop of Novgorod.

St. Michael came to the monastery on the eve of St. John's Day. The priest Ignatius, who was officiating in the church, began to cense it during the ninth hymn. Then he went to cense the cells (wherein resided the monks). When the priest entered one cell, the door of which was open, he found there Monk Michael who was sitting in a chair before a burning taper. He was writing *The Acts of the Apostles.* Ignatius became alarmed (at the presence of this unknown monk), and returning to the church, informed Abbot Theodosius and the other monks of this. The abbot then took the cross and the censer and himself went to the same cell and found that the door of the porch of this cell was closed. Therefore the abbot went to the window and, looking in, also saw a monk who was sitting and writing inside the cell. The abbot then began to pray, saying: "O Lord, Jesus Christ, Son of God, be merciful unto us."

After he had said his prayers, the abbot addressed the monk: "Who are you, my son, a man or a devil?"

And Michael answered with the same words, "Are you a man or a devil?"

The alarmed abbot then ordered the tearing down of the porch roof and the door to gain entrance to the cell. When Abbot Theodosius entered the cell, he began to cense the icon and the monk with thyme; and the monk, attempting to protect himself with his hand from the incense, made the sign of the cross. Theodosius once more asked him: "Who are you? Why did you come to us? Where are you from? What kind of man are you?"

But Michael, instead of answering, only repeated the words of the abbot: "Who are you? Why did you come to us? Where are you from? What kind of man are you?" And so the abbot did not learn the name (of the newcomer).

A short time later, before the day of Christ's Transfiguration, Prince Constantine and his wife came to the monastery to take Holy Communion and to present a gift to the monastery on the occasion of the holy day. On that occasion Michael was asked to read from the Book of Job during the dinner given in the refectory. Hearing his voice, Prince Constantine turned toward him and, recognizing him, said, "Oh, is it you Michael, the son of Maxim?"

But Michael countered, "God alone knows who I am."

Then Abbot Theodosius questioned the monk: "Well, my son, why won't you reveal your name to us?"

But Michael simply replied, "God alone knows who I am." But then he revealed his name as being Michael, and so he was called by all from that day on. Prince Constantine, however, asked the abbot and the monks to care for Michael because he was his relative. From that time the abbot and the monks began to care for Monk Michael.

II. Michael Predicts the Everlasting Spring

In this same year and in the three that followed, there was a great drought and the river Veriazh was entirely dried up. Toward the end of these years of drought Abbot Theodosius went to this dried up river and noticed the following words written in the sand of the riverbed: "In this place will be the spring of everlasting water." Seeing this, the abbot asked Michael, who was accompanying him, "Tell me, son, what is that which is written here?"

And Michael answered: "Here will be the spring of water everlasting." And both Abbot Theodosius and Michael addressed their prayers of thanksgiving to God. And then they began to dig, and immediately water gushed forth from the earth. And since that time there has been a well in that place, and it still exists. As soon as the inhabitants of that region learned of it, they began to use it, and do so until this day.

III. Michael Predicts the Tonsuring of Prokhor

A short time later, Michael told Abbot Theodosius, "We shall have guests."

And Theodosius asked Michael, "Son, what kind of guests shall we have?" But Michael did not explain who the guests would be. But when Abbot Theodosius and Michael left the church, they found three men standing in the monastery yard.

Michael told the abbot, "Invite them to the refectory, Father, that they might break bread with us."

And Theodosius told the strangers, "Let us go, my children, into the refectory that we may break bread."

One of the strangers answered, "Father, there are other friends with us."

And Theodosius told the man, "One of you must go and invite your other friends to have the meal with us."

One of the strangers then went for their friends, and he returned with thirty men who were in armor and with weapons and javelins. And they entered the refectory to break bread.

Theodosius and Michael addressed them: "Sit down, children, and break bread." All but two began eating.

Then Michael addressed those who were not eating. "It will not come to pass as you believe it will."

Actually, almost immediately after, both strangers who were not eating became ill. After the meal everyone who had eaten got up from the table, glorifying God and the Holy Trinity. And one of the strangers gave the monastery one hundred squirrel furs[1] (for the meal). And he said the following: "Father, care for our ill comrades. We leave you in peace."

And the two strangers remained ill for five days. One of them wanted very much to become a monk, and since Theodosius hesitated to tonsure him, Michael said to the abbot, "Tonsure him, Father, and he will be our brother." And so he took monastic vows and received the name of Prokhor. And the other stranger recovered, and left the monastery.

IV. The Miracle of the Filled Granary

In this same year there was a famine throughout the land of Novgorod. And Theodosius and all his brothers became saddened, but Michael said to Abbot Theodosius: "Don't grieve, Father, but remember that our Lord fed forty thousand men, besides the women and children, in the wilderness." And he convinced Abbot Theodosius that the monks should commence cooking rye in kettles and distribute it to pilgrims and travelers. But the monks began to grumble about this, being dissatisfied with Abbot Theodosius and with Michael. But Theodosius and Michael suggested to the monks, "Let us visit our granary."

And they learned that the granaries were overflowing and that the amount of grain did not diminish (even though many were fed from this grain). And they ordered that more rye be prepared so that they might continue to distribute it to the people without hesitation. And they glorified God, the Holy Trinity, and the blessed saints.

V. The Building of the Church of the Holy Trinity

On the Saturday of St. Lazarus, Prince Constantine arrived at the Monastery of the Holy Trinity in Klopsko greatly saddened. And he told Abbot Theodosius and Monk Michael, "I am very sad now because my brothers do not wish to give me my share of the patrimony."

And Michael answered him: "Prince, don't grieve. You will yet come in possession of your estate. In a short time your brother will send for you. Pray to the Holy Trinity and build a stone church in its name, and in return the Lord will reserve a temple in heaven for you."

And then the prince asked Abbot Theodosius: "Do you have any craftsmen? I want to build a church of stone in honor of

[1] Squirrel furs, or, as they are sometimes called, vairs, were a monetary unit in ancient Russia.

the Holy Trinity, the source of all life, to commemorate the memory of my parents and myself."

Theodosius sent for craftsmen, and there came craftsmen by the names of John, Clement, and Alexis. And the prince ordered these master craftsmen: "Build a church of stone in the honor of the Holy Trinity, the source of all life, and embellish it in the manner of the Church of St. Nicholas in Latki."

And the craftsmen answered: "We can do so, Lord Prince. And we are ready to serve you if God and the Holy Trinity will aid us." And they laid the foundation of the church on the day of the Commemoration of our holy Father Theodore Sekiot, April 22, 1423 (6931). And they began bringing the stone, but a mighty storm hindered them in their work, and they were able neither to bring the stones by the river nor to work on the walls of the church.

Then Michael said to the masters, "Pray to God for help, because the invisible power of God builds churches." And even as Michael spoke, God sent a helpful wind to fill their sails as they were going for the stone and when they returned with the stone.

For the consecration of the church, Prince Constantine came with his princess and the boyars and brought plenty of food and drink, because he was very glad. And, on the Day of the Holy Martyr Tekla, September 24, 1425 (6932), this Church of the Holy Trinity was completed, thanks to the blessings of Abbot Theodosius and the prayers of St. Michael. And Prince Constantine said to Theodosius and Brother Michael, "Father, thanks to your prayers I received the news from my older brothers that they will give me my patrimony."

And Theodosius and Michael answered: "Go in peace, our child, and they will meet you with friendship. Only, don't forget, our child, this house of God, the Church of the Holy Trinity, the source of all life, as well as ourselves, your poor servants."

And the prince promised: "All my life I shall never forget this House of God, the monastery, the Church of the Holy Trinity, and you, my poor brothers, who have prayed for me."

VI. Michael Predicts Abbot Theodosius' Election to the Archbishopric

This same year Simon, Archbishop of Novgorod, passed away. And Michael predicted to Abbot Theodosius, "You will be elected to the chair of the archbishop and will rule for three years, but you will also be deposed before you have become consecrated."

VII. Michael's Miraculous Appearances

On Tuesday of Holy Week during Matins the brethren found that Michael was missing from the monastery. And at that very time he appeared during Matins in the sacristy of the Cathedral of Holy Sophia of Novgorod, and he was there recognized after Matins by Gregory, the *posadnik*, who addressed him, saying, "Come and break bread with us," and he ordered one of his men to attend him. And suddenly Michael was no longer there. But when in Klopsko the priest went that day to celebrate the liturgy in the monastery, Michael was already in the church. When the brothers left the church for the refectory, there arrived a man who was sent by the *posadnik* to inquire the whereabouts of Michael. And Michael was already there.

VIII. Michael Predicts Alfiry's Misfortunes

This very day there was an argument between Alfiry, son of John, and Ivan Loshinsky, son of Simon, over the possession of land. And Michael predicted to Alfiry, "You will remain without hands and feet and you will become mute." And when Alfiry came to the Church of the Holy Virgin in Kurechka, he met Ivan, and said, "Brother Ivan, this land is mine," and he clapped his hands and his gloves dropped to the floor. When he bowed down to pick them up, a stroke hit him. His hands, feet, and tongue became paralyzed, and he could no longer speak.

IX. Michael and Priest Nicephorius

And there was another prophecy made by Michael concerning a certain priest, Nicephorius, who had secretly stolen the venerable icon of the archbishop. And Michael said to this priest, "You will be dishonored." And from that time the priest lost his mind. And Michael ordered that they look in the stove, and there they found the venerable icon that had been stolen.

X. The Prophecy to the Archbishop

Archbishop Euthemius received the taxes due him from the monastery, but he wanted additional collections. And so he took a horse as black as a raven from the monastery. And Michael told the archbishop, "You will live but a short time, and you will leave everything behind." And soon the archbishop fell ill and passed away.

XI. Michael and Archbishop Euthemius II

In this same year, another Euthemius was elected to the archbishopric. For the three years that followed he was not consecrated. Once, the bishop came to Klopsko to help the monastery. During the meal at the table the archbishop asked Michael, "Dear Michael, pray to God for me that I should be invested by Great Prince Vasily."

The archbishop had a kerchief in his hand, and Michael snatched it suddenly from the bishop and placed it on the bishop's head, and said, "You will go to Smolensk and you will be consecrated to the archbishopric." And actually, the bishop did go to Smolensk and was there consecrated.

The bishop returned to Michael, and said, "God and the metropolitan of Moscow gave me their blessing."

And Michael once again spoke to the archbishop: "You will be summoned to Moscow, and you will go there and you will submit yourself to the Great Prince and to the metropolitan.

XII. The Punishment of Posadnik Gregory

And the Monastery of the Holy Trinity at Klopsko was heavily oppressed by *Posadnik* Gregory. Once, on Easter Sunday, this Gregory came to Mass at the Church of the Holy Trinity of this monastery. When the abbot finished celebrating the Mass, he and the *posadnik* left the church. The *posadnik* stopped the abbot and the monks in the monastery, and addressed them: "Abbot, do not let your horses and cows into the meadows in the summer, for that is my land. Also, don't hunt or fish along river Voriazh, or in the marshes, or in the vicinity of my estates. And if your people come there, I shall order that their arms and legs be broken."

And Michael replied to the *posadnik*, "You yourself will lose your arms and legs, and, more than that, you will nearly drown in the river."

Once the abbot and Michael sent their men to the river and to the marshes. As the men of the monastery were pulling in the nets, the *posadnik* went to the river. He went up to the men of the monastery and followed them into the water. Chasing the fishermen, he hit one of them with his fist, and wanted to hit another one, but he missed and fell in the water, and nearly drowned. When his people came, he was nearly drowned, and they carried him home because he was unable to use his arms and legs, as was predicted by Michael.

Early in the morning he was brought to the monastery, but Michael forbade him to enter it and he forbade the monks to pray for him, to light a candle for him, or to mention his name in the liturgy. And Michael added, addressing the *posadnik*, "Don't bring us any food or drink; only leave us in peace."

The abbot and the monks were afraid that they had made a mistake by not praying for the *posadnik* or by not mentioning his name in the liturgy. In the meantime the *posadnik's* men decided to complain, and said: "We are going to complain to the bishop and to the authorities of the city of Novgorod, for you would neither pray for the *posadnik* nor mention his name during Mass." And they went to the bishop and to the authorities of the city of Novgorod—to Jacob Andreianov, Fefilat Zakharin, and John Vasiliev to lodge their complaint. And the bishop sent his archpriest and his archdeacon to Michael and Abbot Theodosius, saying, "Do pray for the *posadnik* during Mass, and celebrate special services for his recovery."

But Michael replied to the archpriest and the archdeacon: "We pray to God for the entire world, and not only for Gregory." (And then he addressed Gregory:) "Go to the other monasteries and ask there God's forgiveness."

And the *posadnik* began his pilgrimages to the monasteries, and he began to make gifts to them, as well as to the churches in the cities. His pilgrimages to monasteries lasted a year and one and one-half months. But nowhere, in any of these monasteries, did he find God's forgiveness.

Thereafter (returning to Novgorod), he sent a man to the bishop, saying, "My lord and my father, nowhere in the monasteries could I find help."

(The bishop answered:) "Go now, my child, to the Monastery of the Holy Trinity, and ask there the mercy of the Holy Trinity and of Monk Michael." And the bishop sent a priest (to Michael), and the *posadnik* went there personally. It was decided to hold a special service to the Holy Trinity and to celebrate the Mass. The *posadnik* was brought into the church in a carpet, but he was not even able to make the sign of the cross. The celebration of the service to the Holy Trinity began. And when they began to sing the hymn, the *posadnik* was able to move his hands, even though he had not been able to move his hands and feet for one year and one and one-half months. When the priest began reading the Gospel, the *posadnik* was already able to make the sign of the cross and to sit down. In the middle of the service he was able to stand, and so he remained standing until the end of the service. After Mass, everyone went to the refectory, and the *posadnik* addressed the monks during the meal, "Holy brothers, I wish you health and appetite."

But Michael countered: "Those who live by the sword shall perish by the sword." In such manner did Michael teach a lesson to Gregory the *posadnik.* And Michael added, "My child, be good to Michael and to the monastery."

XIII. Michael and Dmitry Shemiaka

A short time afterward Prince Dmitry Shemiaka visited Novgorod, and he came to the monastery in Klopsko that he might receive Michael's blessing. (And he said to Michael:) "Dear Mikhailushka, I was chased away from my patrimony, and my enemies have driven me from the throne of the great prince."[2]

And Michael replied, "Every power is given by God."

"My dear Mikhailushka, pray to God to help me get back my patrimony, and to become once more the great prince," Shemiaka once again said to Michael.

But Michael answered only, "Prince, all you will get is a three-foot coffin." But Prince Dmitry, paying no heed to Michael's words, decided to begin another campaign to become great prince. But Michael said, "It is in vain, Prince, for you cannot receive that which God does not wish you to have." And God did not help Shemiaka, and he escaped once more to Novgorod.

On Friday of the week of Pentecost, Prince Shemiaka returned to the monastery at Klopsko to bring gifts. He gave the brothers much food and drink. And to Michael he gave his own fur coat. When Prince Dmitry, accompanied by the abbot and the monks, returned to his boat, Michael patted the prince's head, and said, "The damp earth is already awaiting you." And he repeated these words thrice.

And the prince said, "My dear monk, I want to return to the city of Rzhev to my patrimony in Konstantinov."

But Michael added: "Prince, your desire will not be fulfilled."

And so it came to pass, for the prince died soon afterward.

XIV. Michael Addresses the Novgorodian Republic

Once, *Posadnik* John Nemir came to the monastery, and he asked the *posadnik,* "Why do you travel?"

The *posadnik* answered, "I have been at my wife's grandmother, Euphrasinia, and now I come to you to receive your blessing."

And Michael asked, "Well, my child, what kind of problems do you try to solve with women?"

John Nemir answered: "We expect that that great prince (of Moscow) will start a campaign against us. But we expect help from Prince Michael of Lithuania."

[2] Shemiaka led a revolt against his cousin, the Great Prince of Moscow, and for a short time became the ruler of Muscovy.

But Michael retorted: "Your Lithuanian prince will not be a help, but worse than nothing at all. Send your envoy to the Great Prince of Moscow right now, and sue for peace. If you don't come to an agreement with the Great Prince of Moscow, he will come with all his forces to Novgorod, and you will have no divine help. And the Great Prince of Moscow will camp at Bureguy. He will display his army along the river Shelon, and he will jail many citizens of Novgorod. Some will be sent to Moscow, some will be executed, and some will be forced to pay tribute. And the Lithuanian prince will not fight for you, and you will receive no help from him. Better that you send your archbishop and *posadniks* to Moscow with a petition for peace to the Great Prince. Better to pay him tribute; otherwise the Great Prince of Moscow will return here, will take your city, and will deprive you of liberty, and God will help him."

And so it came to pass as Michael said.

XV. Michael's Death

Michael had a simple way of living. He lived alone in his cell and had neither a headboard and pillow nor a bed; neither sheets nor covers, but he slept on the earth. He heated his cell with dried horse manure and lived in the monastery for forty and four years. The entire week he ate only break and water.

Once Abbot Theodosius called Michael for Communion, and after it Michael said, "Father, I would receive the Divine Sacrament from you."

And the abbot answered, "Have it, my child, and once more take Holy Communion."

And all were astounded by these words. And Michael took the censer and thyme and went to his cell. When everyone went to the refectory, the abbot had food sent to Michael's cell. And when the monks came to his cell and entered in, they found the holy man lying as if asleep. And the fragrance of the thyme from the censer near Michael was rising from the earth to the heavens. On January 11th, the Day of Our Father, Theodosius of Jerusalem, Michael was buried in the Monastery of the Holy Trinity, the source of all life.

Glory be to God, now and forever more.

29. *The Heroic Deeds of Mercurius of Smolensk*

After having conquered central and northern Russia, the Mongolian commander, Batu, began his advance into western Russia in 1237. However, because of the spring floods he was unable to take the city of Novgorod, and thus turned southward to the city of Smolensk. For some reason that remains indiscernible from historical writings, the Tatar troops were unable to capture Smolensk. From this event developed the charming legend of St. Mercurius of Smolensk, the heroic defender of his city. Written in a simple style characterized by redundancy, this is probably the most "medieval" of Russian legends. Contrary to this narrative, however, upon leaving the region of Smolensk Batu marched into southern Russia, where he devastated Kiev and other cities, and in 1241 he invaded Hungary. Defeating the Hungarians, he left Hungary so that he might return to Mongolia and participate in the selection of a new khan. The killing of Batu by King Stephen of Hungary, as mentioned in this tale, is the product of the writer's imagination.

The subject of *The Heroic Deeds*—the fight of a pious Russian knight against the nomadic invaders—was a common theme in Russian medieval epics, and various details have been supplied from early Christian and Byzantine hagiography. Very likely this legend grew out of the life of Mercurius of Caesarea (now Kaisaria, Turkey) and from the writings of Dionysius Pseudo-Areopagite. It was probably written in the late fourteenth century, and absorbed a considerable amount of Russian folklore elements.

This translation is based on the Old Russian text, edited by Professor M. O. Skripil, found in *Russkie povesti XI–XVI vekov*, Moscow, 1958, pages 106–107.

◆ ◆ ◆

There used to live in the city of Smolensk a young man called Mercurius who was very pious, who studied God's commandments both day and night, who distinguished himself by his holy life, and who, because of his fasting and prayers, shown like the star which announced the birth of Christ to the entire world. He had a contrite soul and the gift of tears.[1] Often he would pray before the cross of our Lord for the whole world, and he lived in the St. Peter's part of the city.

At that time the evil emperor Batu had conquered the Russian land, had shed rivers of innocent blood, and had tortured the Christians. This emperor came with a great army to the pious city of Smolensk, camped at a distance of twenty miles, burned

[1] Eastern Christianity considered the capacity for incessant tears during prayers to be a divine gift.

many holy churches, killed many Christians, and began to prepare for the assault of the city. The people of the city were deeply grieved, and remained incessantly in the Cathedral of the Holy Mother of God. From all their hearts they prayed and worshiped. And, shedding tears, they asked Almighty God, the Holy Mother of God, and all the saints to preserve their city from evil. And God decided to preserve the city and its people.

In the Crypt Monastery, which was located in the vicinity of the river Dnieper outside the city, the sexton of the church had a vision of the most Holy Mother of God. And she addressed him, saying: "O servant of God! Go at once to the cross where my servant, Mercurius, prays. And tell him, 'The Mother of God beckons you to come.' "

The sexton, going there and finding Mercurius praying to God before the cross, called to him by name, "Mercurius."

Mercurius answered, "What do you wish, my lord?"

And the sexton replied: "Go at once, brother. The Mother of God beckons you to the Crypt Monastery."

And when Mercurius, who was made wise by God, entered the holy church, he saw the Most Holy Mother of God sitting on the golden throne with the Christ Child in her arms and surrounded by the host of angels. Seized by awe, he fell at her feet and genuflected low before her.

And the Holy Mother of God raised him, and said: "Mercurius, my chosen one, I send you to take revenge immediately for the Christian blood which has been spilled. Go and defeat the evildoing emperor Batu and all his armies. Afterward, there will come to you a man with a handsome face. Give him all your arms, and he will decapitate you. Then take your head in your hands and return to your city. And there you will pass away and will be buried in my church."

Mercurius was saddened by these words, and, beginning to weep, he said: "O Most Holy Mother of God. How can I, a poor sinner and undeserving servant, be strong enough for such a deed? Is it possible, my Lady, that the heavenly hosts are not enough to defeat this evildoing emperor?"

Thereafter, Mercurius received her blessing, took up weapons and, bowing to the earth, went from this church. Outside the church he found a spirited steed and, mounting it, he left the city. With the help of God and his Holy Mother, he came to the regiments of the evildoing emperor, defeated the enemy, gathered together the Christian prisoners and, sending them back to his city, he courageously galloped over the regiments of

Batu even as an eagle soars through the air. The evildoing emperor, seeing such a rout of his men, and being seized by great awe and fright, rapidly fled with a small retinue, not having achieved the smallest success in battle. From Smolensk, Batu fled to Hungary, and there this evildoer was killed by King Stephen.

And the handsome warrior appeared before Mercurius. The latter gave all his arms to him and bowed deeply before him. And the warrior severed his head from the body. Then the Blessed One took his head in one hand and, leading his horse with the other hand, returned to the city decapitated. The people of the city, seeing this, were astounded by God's design. And when Mercurius came to the Molokhov Gate, he met there a certain maiden who was going to fetch water. When she saw the Blessed One walking without his head, she began to abuse him vilely. But he lay down at this gate and offered up his most contrite soul to God. And his steed, at that moment becoming invisible, disappeared.

The archbishop of the city came with a large number of people carrying crosses and hoping to take the honorable body of this saint to the church, but they were unable to lift his body from the ground. Then there began a great wailing and weeping among the people because it was impossible to raise the body of the saint. Even the archbishop became greatly bewildered and began to pray to God. And there came a voice to him that announced: "O servant of God! Do not grieve. He will be buried by the Same who sent him to victory."

And the body of the saint remained there unburied for three days. In the meantime, the archbishop remained all these nights praying to God to explain to him this mystery. And he remained without sleep. Praying, he looked out through the window that faced the cathedral, and there he saw a great light as if it were the rising of the sun. And in this light the Most Holy Mother of God and the Archangels Michael and Gabriel came from the church. And, coming to the place where the body of St. Mercurius was lying, the Most Holy Mother of God raised the venerable body of the saint and brought it to her cathedral and placed it in a casket. And this body can still be seen there, attesting to the miracle and glory of Christ, our God, and spreading the fragrance of cedar.

The next morning, when the bishop went to Matins in the cathedral, he saw there the wondrous miracle, the body of the saint lying in its place. And the people flocked to the cathedral, and, seeing this miracle, they glorified God.

30. *The Story of Great John, Archbishop of Novgorod the Great; How, in One Night, He Was Taken from Novgorod to the City of Jerusalem, and Then Returned to Novgorod the Great That Same Night*

THIS is one of the oldest Novgorodian legends. Bishop John was a very popular Church leader in the middle of the twelfth century, and around him there arose a number of stories. When Novgorod was threatened with incorporation into the Muscovite realm in the middle of the fifteenth century, Bishop Euthemius II (1430–1458) began collecting the legends and tales concerning the city's history and the deeds of its most outstanding leaders. Most likely this account of Great John was re-edited by Pachomius the Serb after discovery of Bishop John's relics in 1439. Pachomius, one of the innovators of the literary style known as "weaving of words" (*pletenie sloves*), embellished this text with more biblical words, difficult and complex sentences, and its stylistic redundancy.

The motif of a demon confined in a vessel is found both in tales from the East, as for instance in *Tales of the Arabian Nights*, and in early Russian hagiography.

The story is not presented here in its entirety. It ends with an account of the procession of the people and clergy to the St. George Monastery to ask Bishop John to return. Bishop John forgives the people and returns to his see.

This translation is based on the text published by N. K. Gudzy in *Khrestomatiia po drevnei russkoi literature*, Moscow, 1955, pages 207–209.

◆ ◆ ◆

FATHER, MAY YOUR BLESSING BE WITH US

This story should not lapse into oblivion, for God Almighty, who placed John in the bishopric, permits people to be overcome by temptation. He does this to sanctify and glorify them, testing their mettle as one might test gold. God has said, "I will glorify those who glorify me." Wondrous is God among the host of his saints, and God himself glorifies them.

And Christ said, "I give you power over evil spirits."

Once, in the evening, John, Archbishop of Great Novgorod,

went to recite his evening prayers, as was his custom. At that time there was a vessel filled with water near his cell, and the Reverend Father used it for his oblations. Suddenly he heard someone struggling in the water of this vessel. Coming closer to the vessel, and realizing that this was the design of the devil, he read a prayer so as to confine the demon in the vessel. The devil wished to frighten the holy father, but he was defeated in this purpose by the firm adamant.[1] The devil wanted to get out of the vessel, but could not overcome this power. A short time later, the demon could no longer endure and so began to shriek: "Oh, what a miserable plight! I am burned by fire and cannot resist any longer. Let me go at once, O servant of God."

The bishop answered: "And who are you? How did you get in this vessel?"

This devil answered: "I am an evil demon and came to this place so that I might corrupt you, hoping that you would become frightened and cease your praying. But you confined me so cruelly in this vessel, and here I am burned terribly by the fire. O woe is me, a cursed one! How could I become tempted? How could I get in this vessel? I am bewildered! Release me now, you servant of God. I shall not return to this place again!"

And the evil demon shrieked so, that finally the bishop spoke, saying: "For your daring I order that you this very night take me from Novgorod the Great to the city of Jerusalem. And place me before the church wherein is the Lord's Sepulcher. And this very night you must bring me back to my cell, which you have dared to enter. And only then shall I release you."

The demon promised to comply with the will of the bishop, and said, "Please, only release me from confinement, you servant of God."

Without releasing the demon from the power of the cross, the holy bishop let the devil out of the vessel and said to him: "Ready yourself and appear before me as a horse. Then I will mount you and you will fulfill my request."

The devil, like a cloud of darkness, left the vessel and appeared as a horse before the cell door. The bishop went from his cell and, having armed himself with the cross and grace, mounted the demon and that very night arrived in the city of Jerusalem in which is located the Holy Sepulcher of the Lord and the Tree of Life. Retaining his power over the demon, the bishop forbade it to move from the spot where it stood. And

[1] Adamant was often used in Russian medieval literature as a symbol of firm strength, and in this case refers to the power of the cross.

the demon, remaining under the power of the cross, was unable to move away.

In the meantime the Reverend Father went to the Church of the Holy Resurrection and, standing before the door of this church, knelt and prayed. And the doors of the church opened of their own accord, while the tapers and censers of the Lord's Sepulcher began to burn. The bishop, shedding tears, thanked God. And he venerated and kissed the Holy Sepulcher and the Tree of Life and the other shrines. Then he left the church, having fulfilled his longing. And the church doors closed after him of their own accord.

The bishop found the demon standing in the form of a horse and in the same place, as he had been ordered. And mounting the demon, the bishop found himself that very night in his cell, in the city of Novgorod the Great.

Leaving the saint's cell, the devil said: "Oh, John, you forced me to labor, carrying you in one night to Jerusalem and that very same night carrying you back to Novgorod the Great. I was bound to do so, by the power of the cross, as if I were bound by shackles. I had to undergo many calamities. Reveal to no one what has happened this night. If you do, I will lead you into temptation. You will be tried and sentenced for lechery, abused, and put on a raft in the river Volkhov.[2]

To prevent the abuse of the demon, Bishop John made the sign of the cross.

The bishop had the custom of discussing problems of the spirit with the honorable abbots, most learned priests, and God-abiding men, since he considered it a necessity that he share his wisdom with others and open to them the sublimity of the Holy Trinity. He never tired of teaching men, and he often told to them the occurrences of his own life, describing them as those of another man. "I know," he told them once, "a certain man who happened to go from Novgorod to the city of Jerusalem in one night, worshiped there at the Lord's Sepulcher, and returned that very night to Novgorod the Great." The abbots and the others were astounded.

But from that time on, and with the permission of God, the demon began to lead the bishop into temptation. The people had the vision many times of a harlot leaving the cell of the bishop. Many officials of the city, who used to come to the bishop's cell to receive his blessing, would see there a woman's

[2] Novgorod was situated on the river Volkhov, and the placing of convicts on a raft in the middle of the river was a common punishment.

necklace of coins and also a woman's robe and sandals. And they felt sore offended, and wondered what to say of this. But all this was the design of this demon who expected that the people would rise up against the bishop, would speak unjustly of him, and would drive him from their midst.

The people took council with the officials, and declared: "It is unjust for such a bishop, who is a whoremonger, to occupy the apostolic seat. Let us go and drive him from our midst, for about such people King David said: 'And words will pour forth from the mouth of the flatterer and they will speak of righteousness, lowliness, pride, and destruction. This they do for they worship the devil, even before the assembly of Jews.'"

But let us return to the narration. When the people came to the cell of the bishop, the demon walked among the people, and they saw him as a girl, leaving the cell of the saint. And the people began to exclaim that she should be seized, but they could not do so, although they followed her for a long time.

The bishop heard the cries of the people and came out to them and said, "What has happened, my children?" But the citizens paid no heed to these words, and told him what they had seen, condemned him as a whoremonger, abused him, and, after wondering what should be done with him, they decided, "Let us put him on a raft in the middle of the river Volkhov so that he may float down the river and away from our city."

And so they took the ascetic, holy, and great bishop of God, John, to the great bridge which spanned the river Volkhov, led him down to the river, and put him on a raft. And so the dream of the evil demon was fulfilled. However, God's grace shone on the face of the bishop, and his prayers to God overcame the demon's design. The demon had begun to rejoice, but when John, the bishop of God, was put on the raft in the middle of the river Volkhov, the raft immediately began to move upstream, although it was not driven by anyone. The raft on which the bishop was sitting was pushed upstream from the great bridge to the Monastery of St. George, and against a strong current. The bishop was praying for the people on the raft, saying, "O Lord, forgive them this sin, for they know not what they do."

And seeing this, the demon was abashed, and began to weep.

The people of Novgorod, seeing this miracle, rent their garments, returned, and said: "We have sinned; we have committed an injustice to this father, and we have condemned our pastor. We now know that this has happened through the designs of a demon."

31. *The Tale of the White Cowl*

THE *Tale of the White Cowl,* which was to become the cornerstone of Russian national ideology, was written toward the end of the fifteenth century in Novgorod, apparently by Archbishop Genady and his co-worker and interpreter, Dmitry Gerasimov. The tale was conceived with the purpose of defending the sovereignty of the Novgorodian Church, in particular, and the Russian Church, in general, from encroachment by the Grand Duke of Muscovy, but the tale grew into an ideological work that glorified the prestige of Russian Orthodox Christianity. Later, in the sixteenth century, after the fall of Constantinople to the Turks, there developed from this work the theory of Moscow being the Third Rome, which theory was clearly and concisely formulated by Monk Philotheus (*circa* 1510–1540) when he wrote: "All Christian realms will come to an end and will unite into the one single realm of our sovereign, that is, into the Russian realm, according to the prophetic books. Both Romes fell, the third endures, and a fourth there will never be."[1] This theory defined Moscow as the sole staunch defender of the Eastern Orthodox Faith, which, in the minds of Greeks, Russians, Southern Slavs, and other Eastern Europeans, was the only true Christian doctrine.

The background of this concept is a rather eclectic one, and can be traced to the Book of Daniel (VII, 27), in which the prophet announced that the final kingdom of the one true faith will come about and will never be destroyed. This concept of Daniel's was taken up by the Chiliasts (from the Greek, *chiliad,* meaning "a thousand"), who proclaimed the forthcoming Kingdom of Christ which would last a thousand years.

In the Middle Ages the Irish philosopher John Scotus Erigena (ninth century) and the Italian theologian Joachim de Fiore (twelfth century) modified Daniel's original concept into the theory of the "three kingdoms," that is, the Kingdom of the Father who gave the Law (Old Testament), the Kingdom of

[1] The best discussion of the works of Monk Philotheus can be found in V. Malinin's *Starets Eleazarova Monastyria Filofey i ego Poslaniia,* Kiev, 1901. This quotation is to be found on page 45 in the appendix of Malinin's work.

the Son who brought Grace, and the final Kingdom of the Holy Spirit, of which the Apostles said: "Where there is the spirit of God, there is freedom." The theory of the final Kingdom of the Holy Spirit became known in Russia, and later formed the basis for both the *Tale of the White Cowl* and the Third Rome theory.

In the eyes of Archbishop Genady and Dmitry Gerasimov, Russia was predestined by God to be revealed as this last kingdom, the Kingdom of the Holy Spirit, which will endure until the Last Judgment. The authors of the *Tale of the White Cowl* combined this theocratic, utopian tenet with the Roman Catholic legend of the gift of the city of Rome to Pope Sylvester by Emperor Constantine (Emperor of Rome, 306–337). This legend lay the foundation for the secular power of the Pope of Rome and also for the independence of the pope from the emperor.

The *Tale of the White Cowl* underwent many revisions and is extant in several versions; however, its central theme remains the same in all: the White Cowl, the symbol of the radiant Resurrection and Orthodox Christianity, remained in Rome as long as the popes preserved the original teachings of Christ. But when the popes broke with the Eastern Church and developed their "Latin heresies,"[2] divine power gave the White Cowl to the patriarch of Constantinople, which the Greeks of that time called the "Second Rome." When the Greeks began to "multiply their sins" and even began negotiating with the Pope of Rome, God punished them by letting their land be overrun by Turks.[3] The tale states that a century before the fall of Constantinople, God, who had predestined the last Orthodox nation, after the fall of Byzantium, to be Russia, commanded that the White Cowl be taken to the Archbishop of Novgorod, Vasily.

The present translation is based on the Russian text published by G. Kushelov-Bezborodko in *Pamiatniki starinnoi russkoi literatury*, Volume I, St. Petersburg, 1860, pages 287–303.

Since the translation given here is not the complete tale, it is essential to present a synopsis of the narrative up to the point where the translation begins.

[2] The Byzantines, and later the Russians, called the teachings of the Western Church "Latin Heresies," since Rome proclaimed the primacy of the pope and used the Latin tongue exclusively for liturgical purposes.

[3] The actual conquest of Constantinople by the Turks took place in 1453, some thirty or forty years before the *Tale of the White Cowl* was written in Novgorod.

SYNOPSIS

The *Tale of the White Cowl* opens with the story of Emperor Constantine's illness, which could be cured neither by physicians nor by magicians. One such magician, who was violently opposed to Christianity, advised the emperor that in order to be cured he must bathe in the blood of three thousand infants killed expressly for that purpose. However, at the last minute Emperor Constantine, moved by the tears and wailings of the mothers of the children who were to be slain, canceled his plan, preferring to die rather than to kill children in order to restore his health. That very night the emperor had a vision of the Apostles Peter and Paul, who told him that Pope Sylvester, who was in hiding from his persecutors at that time, could show him a font of salvation, bathing wherein would cure him of this affliction. In recompense, the emperor was to grant new rights to the Christian Church and to support it as the national religion.

The tale continues that the emperor was cured, ended the persecutions of Christians, and even wished to grant the imperial crown to the pope. The pope most humbly refused to accept it. So the emperor gave him a white cowl, the symbol of the primacy of spiritual power over secular power and of the Resurrection, the color white representing the radiance of the Resurrection of Christ. Having given the supreme power in the city of Rome to the pope, Emperor Constantine then left the Eternal City and went to the ancient city of Byzantium, which was later renamed the "city of Constantine," or Consantinople. Thus did the Eastern, or Byzantine, Roman Empire come into being.

After the death of Pope Sylvester, the tale goes on to say, the White Cowl was highly revered by the popes of Rome. However, in the ninth century, when the West was ruled by Emperor Charlemagne and the papal see was ruled by Pope Formosus,[4] a schism arose between the Eastern and Western Churches. The Western Church, under the leadership of the pope, developed new teachings and doctrines that the Eastern Church considered to be "Latin heresies," particularly the doctrine of the primacy of the Pope of Rome over the entire Church. From that time on the popes ceased to revere the White Cowl, and finally decided to profane and destroy it. However, a miraculous power saved the White Cowl, and the pope was

[4] Pope Formosus reigned from 891 to 896. During his reign there began the first conflicts between Rome and Constantinople over the jurisdiction of the two branches of the Church.

forced to send it to the patriarch of Constantinople, the capital of the still-extant Eastern Roman Empire, or, as it is more often called, Byzantium.

The translation begins at this point in the tale—that is, with the arrival of the White Cowl in Constantinople.

◆ ◆ ◆

At that time the Patriarch of Constantinople was Philotheus,[5] who was distinguished by his strict fasting and his virtuous ways. Once, he had a vision in the night of a youth from whom emanated light and who told him:

"Blessed teacher, in the olden times the Roman Emperor, Constantine, who, through the vision of the Holy Apostles Peter and Paul, was enlightened by God, decided to give Blessed Pope Sylvester the White Cowl to glorify the Holy Apostolic Church. Later, the unfaithful popes of the Latin heresies wanted to profane and destroy this cowl, but I appeared to the evil pope, and now this pope has sent this cowl to you. When the messengers arrive with it, you must accept it with all honors. Then send the White Cowl to the Russian land, to the city of Novgorod the Great with your written blessing. And there this cowl will be worn on the head of Vasily, Archbishop of Novgorod,[6] so that he may glorify the Holy Apostolic Cathedral of Holy Sophia and laud the Orthodox. There, in that land, the faith of Christ is verily glorified. And the popes, because of their shamelessness, will receive the vengeance of God." And having spoken these words, the youth became invisible.

The patriarch awoke filled with awe and joy, and was unable to sleep throughout the remainder of the night. And he contemplated this vision. In the morning he ordered that the bells should sound the Matins, and when day came he summoned the Church council and revealed his vision. And all praised God, perceiving that a holy angel had appeared to the patriarch. Yet they did not fully understand the meaning of the message. When they were still in council and were filled with awe due to their great joy, there arrived a servant of the patriarch, and he announced to them that messengers had arrived from the Pope of Rome. The patriarch ordered that they be brought

[5] Philotheus was patriarch of Constantinople from 1353 to 1355, and from 1364–1376.

[6] Vasily was archbishop of Novgorod from 1330 to 1342. In 1946 his grave was discovered and opened. In it were found both the White Cowl and the vestments embroidered with crosses which are mentioned in this tale.

before him. The messengers came, bowed lowly to the patriarch, and gave him the message. The patriarch read the message and pondered it, praising God. He announced its contents to Emperor John who was reigning at that time and whose name was Kantakuzen.[7] And then he went with the entire council to meet the bringers of the divine treasure which lay in an ark. He accepted it with all honors, broke the seal, and took from the ark the Holy White Cowl. He kissed it with reverence, and looked upon it with wonderment both for its creation and for the wonderful fragrance that emanated from it.

At that time the patriarch had diseased eyes and constant headaches, but when he placed the White Cowl upon his head, these afflictions immediately ceased to be. And he rejoiced with great joy and rendered glory to Christ, our Lord, to Constantine's blessed memory for his creating this wonderful cowl for Blessed Pope Sylvester. And he put the Holy Cowl on the golden salver that was also sent by the pope. He placed them in the great church in an honorable place until he could make a decision with the emperor's counseling.

After the White Cowl was sent from Rome, the evil pope, who was counseled by heretics, became angered against the Christian faith and was driven to a frenzy, extremely regretting his allowing the White Cowl to be sent to Constantinople. And he wrote an evil letter to the patriarch, in which he demanded the return of the White Cowl on the golden salver. The patriarch read this letter and, understanding the pope's evil and cunning design, sent him a letter in return that was based on Holy Scripture, and in it he called the pope both evil and godless, the apostate and precursor of the Antichrist. And the patriarch cursed the pope in the name of our Lord, Jesus Christ, the Holy Apostles, and the Church Fathers. And this letter came to the pope.

When the pope had read the letter and learned that the patriarch intended to send the White Cowl with great honor to the Russian land, to the city of Novgorod the Great, he uttered a roar. And his face changed and he fell ill, for he, the infidel, disliked the Russian land and could not even bear to hear of this land where the Christian faith was professed.

Patriarch Philotheus, having seen that the White Cowl was illumined with grace, began to ponder how he might keep it in

[7] John VI Kantakuzen (or Cantacuzene) was Emperor of Byzantium from 1347 to 1354.

Constantinople and wear it on his own head. He consulted with the emperor about the matter several times, and wanted to write to the other patriarchs and metropolitans to summon them to a council. After Matins one Sunday, the patriarch returned to his chambers and, after the usual prayers, lay down to rest. But he slept but lightly, and in this sleep he saw that two men, who were unknown to him, came through the door. And from them there emanated light. One of them was armed as a warrior and had an imperial crown upon his head. The other wore a bishop's vestments and was distinguished by his venerable white hair.

The latter spoke to the patriarch, saying: "Patriarch! Stop pondering your wearing of the White Cowl on your own head. If this were to be, our Lord, Jesus Christ, would have so predestined it from the founding of this city. And for a long time did divine enlightenment come from heaven, and then God's voice came to me and I learned that Rome had to betray God and embrace their Latin heresies. That is the reason I did not wish to wear this cowl upon my head, and thus I instructed other popes not to do so. And this imperial city of Constantinople will be taken by the sons of Hagar[8] because of its sins, and all holy shrines will be defiled and destroyed. Thus has it been predestined since the founding of this city.

"The ancient city of Rome will break away from the glory and faith of Christ because of its pride and ambition. In the new Rome, which will be the City of Constantinople, the Christian faith will also perish through the violence of the sons of Hagar. In the third Rome, which will be the land of Russia, the Grace of the Holy Spirit will be revealed. Know then, Philotheus, that all Christians will finally unite into one Russian nation because of its orthodoxy. Since ancient times and by the will of Constantine, Emperor of the Earth, the imperial crown of the imperial city is predestined to be given to the Russian tsar.[9] But the White Cowl, by the will of the King of Heaven, Jesus Christ, will be given to the archbishop of Novgorod the Great. And this White Cowl is more honorable than the crown of the tsar, for it is an imperial crown of the archangelic spiritual order. Thus, you must send this Holy White Cowl to the Russian land,

[8] Both the Byzantines and the Russians called all nomads, whether they were Turks, Mongols, or Arabs, the sons of Hagar. "Hagar" refers to the handmaid of the biblical patriarch Abraham.

[9] The Russians of that time used only one word, "tsar," for the English words "king," "King of Heaven," "emperor," and even "kahn." Equally, the word "tsarstvo" was used to mean "realm," "empire," "tsardom," and the "Kingdom of God."

to the city of Novgorod the Great, as you were told to do in the vision of the angel. You should believe and trust in what I say. And when you send it to the Russian land, the Orthodox Faith will be glorified and the cowl will be safe from seizure by the infidel sons of Hagar and from the intended profanation by the Latin pope. And the grace, glory, and honor which were taken from Rome, as well as the Grace of the Holy Spirit, will be removed from the imperial city of Constantinople after its capture by the sons of Hagar. And all holy relics will be given to the Russian land in the predestined moment. And the Russian tsar will be elevated by God above other nations, and under his sway will be many heathen kings. And the power of the patriarch of this imperial ruling city will pass to the Russian land in the predestined hour. And that land will be called Radiant Russia, which, by the Grace of God, will be glorified with blessings. And its majesty will be strengthened by its orthodoxy, and it will become more honorable than the two Romes which preceded it."

And saying this, the man of the vision who was dressed in a bishop's vestment wished to leave, but the patriarch, seized by great awe, fell before the bishop and said: "Who are you, my lord? Your vision has seized me with great awe; my heart has been frightened by your words, and I tremble to my very bones."

The man in the bishop's vestments answered: "Don't you know who I am? I am Pope Sylvester, and I came to you because I was ordered by God to reveal to you the great mystery which will come to pass in the predestined time." Then, pointing to the other man in the vision, he added: "This is blessed Emperor Constantine of Rome to whom I gave rebirth in the holy font and whom I won over to the faith of our Lord, Jesus Christ. He was the first Christian emperor, my child in Christ, who created and gave me the White Cowl in place of the imperial crown." And saying this, he blessed the patriarch, and became invisible.

Waking up, the patriarch was seized with awe, remembering the words about the White Cowl and the conquest of Constantinople by the pagan sons of Hagar. And he wept for a long time. When the hour of the divine Mass arrived, the patriarch went to the church, fell before the icon of the Holy Mother of God, and remained lying there for some time. Then he arose, took the White Cowl with great reverence, kissed it piously, placed it upon his head, and then put it to his eyes and his heart. And his adoration for this cowl increased even more. And doing this, he wept. His clerics, who were around him and saw that he wept inconsolably, did not dare to inquire as to why he was weeping. Finally the patriarch ceased crying and told his clerics in detail of the vision of Pope Sylvester and Emperor Constantine. Having heard these words, the clerics wept sorrowfully, and exclaimed, "Thy will be done!"

The patriarch, mourning the forthcoming misfortunes of the city of Constantinople and fearing to trespass the divine will, told them that he must fulfill the will of the Lord and do with the White Cowl as he was commanded to do. After having deliberated with blessed Emperor John, he took the White Cowl and the golden salver, put them in the aforementioned ark, sealed it with his seal, and, as he was commanded by the holy angel and Blessed Pope Sylvester, put in his epistle with his blessings, and in it he commanded Archbishop Vasily and all other bishops who would follow Vasily to wear the White Cowl upon their heads. He added many other honorable and marvelous gifts from his clergy for the bishopric of Novgorod the Great. And he also sent vestments with their embroidered crosses[10] for the glorification of the Holy Apostolic Church. And all this was placed in another ark. And he gave these arks to a bishop named Eumeny, and sent him forth with both joy and sorrow.

In the bishopric of the city of Novgorod the Great was Archbishop Vasily who distinguished himself by his fasting and virtuous ways. Once, in the night, he prayed to God and then lay down to rest, but he slept but lightly, and had a dream in which he saw the angel of God. This angel of God, who had a handsome appearance and radiant face, appeared before him in the garb of a monk and with the White Cowl upon his head. With his finger he pointed to his head and in a low voice announced: "Vasily! This White Cowl which you see on my head is from Rome. In olden times the Christian Emperor Constantine created it in honor of Sylvester, Pope of Rome. He gave it to this pope to wear upon his head. But God Almighty did not pennit the White Cowl to remain there because of their Latin heresies. Tomorrow morning you must go from the city with your clergymen and meet the bishop and messengers sent by the patriarch. And they will bring an ark, and in this ark you will find the White Cowl upon a golden salver. Accept it with all honors, for this White Cowl symbolizes the radiant Resurrec-

[10] See footnote 4.

tion which came to pass on the third day. And from now, you and all other archbishops of this city will wear it on your heads. And I have come to you to assure you before hand that all is as God wills it and to assuage any doubts you may have." And saying this, the angel became invisible.

Waking up, Archbishop Vasily was seized with awe and joy, pondering the meaning of the vision. The next morning he sent his clerics outside the city, to the crossroads, to see whether the messengers really would appear. In the vicinity of the city the servant of Archbishop Vasily met a Greek bishop who was unknown to him and who traveled to the city of Novgorod. They made a low obeisance and returned to the archbishop and told them all they had seen. The bishop then sent his messenger into the city to summon the clerics and the entire population. And he ordered the tolling of the bells, and both he and his clerics donned their vestments.

The procession had not gone far from the Cathedral of Holy Sophia when they met the aforementioned bishop, sent by the patriarch and bearing the ark that had been sealed by the patriarch, and which contained the venerable gifts, came to Archbishop Vasily, made a low obeisance before him, and gave him the epistles of the patriarch. They blessed and greeted each other in Christ's name. Archbishop Vasily accepted the epistles of the patriarch and the arks bearing the venerable gifts. And he went with them to the Cathedral of Holy Sophia, the Wisdom of God. There he put them in the middle of the church in an honorable place, and ordered that the patriarchal epistles be read aloud. When the Orthodox people, who were in the cathedral, heard these writings read aloud, they rendered glory to God and rejoiced with great joy. Archbishop Vasily opened one of the arks and removed the cover. And a wonderful fragrance and miraculous radiance spread through the church. Archbishop Vasily and all present were in wonderment, witnessing these happenings. And Bishop Eumeny, who was sent by the patriarch, wondered about these blessed deeds of God that he had witnessed. And they all rendered glory to God, and celebrated the service of thanksgiving.

Archbishop Vasily took the White Cowl from the ark and saw that it appeared exactly like the one he had seen on the angel's head in his vision. And he kissed it with reverence. At that same moment there came a sonorous voice from the icon of the Lord, which was in the cupola of the church, saying, "Holy, holy." And after a moment of silence there came the same voice, which thrice announced, "Ispola eti despota."[11] And when the archbishop and all those present heard these voices, they were seized with awe and joy. And they said, "The Lord have mercy upon us!" And the archbishop then ordered that all present in the church be silent, and he revealed to them his vision of the angel and his words concerning the White Cowl. And he told of his vision as it had happened and in detail, even as it was told to him by the angel in the night.

Giving thanks to God for sending this cowl, the archbishop went forth from the church, preceded by the deacons in holy vestments carrying tapers and singing hymns. And they proceeded with serenity and piety. And the people crowded round, jostling each other and jumping so that they might see the White Cowl on the archbishop's head. And all were in wonderment. Thus, in this way, thanks to the Grace of our Lord, Jesus Christ, and to the blessing of his Holiness Philotheus, Patriarch of of Constantinople, the White Cowl became a symbol upon the heads of the archbishops of Novgorod. And Archbishop Vasily was overcome with great joy, and for seven days he feasted all priests, deacons, and clerics of the city of Novgorod the Great. And he also offered food and drink to the poor, to monks, and to prisoners. And he asked that the prisoners be released. During the divine service he placed the holy and venerable gifts of the patriarch in the Cathedral of Holy Sophia and with the blessings of all clerics. And the golden salver, on which the White Cowl was placed, was also deposited in the Cathedral of Holy Sophia during the Mass.

The messengers of the patriarch who brought the Holy White Cowl were also shown great honor and they received many gifts. The archbishop sent gifts to the Emperor and Patriarch of Constantinople and sent the messengers forth with great honors. Thereafter, multitudes arrived from many cities and kingdoms to look upon, as if it were a miracle, the archbishop in the White Cowl. And they were in wonderment about it, and told of it in many lands. This Holy White Cowl was created by the first pious Christian Emperor, Constantine, for Blessed Pope Sylvester in the year 297 (5805). And this is the history of the Holy White Cowl up to this day.

[11] *Ispola eti despota* is Greek for "Many years to the lord," or, more loosely translated, "Long live the bishop." The Russians used this expression during the Church service, and it was always pronounced in Greek.

Part III

The Muscovite Period

(1478–1700)

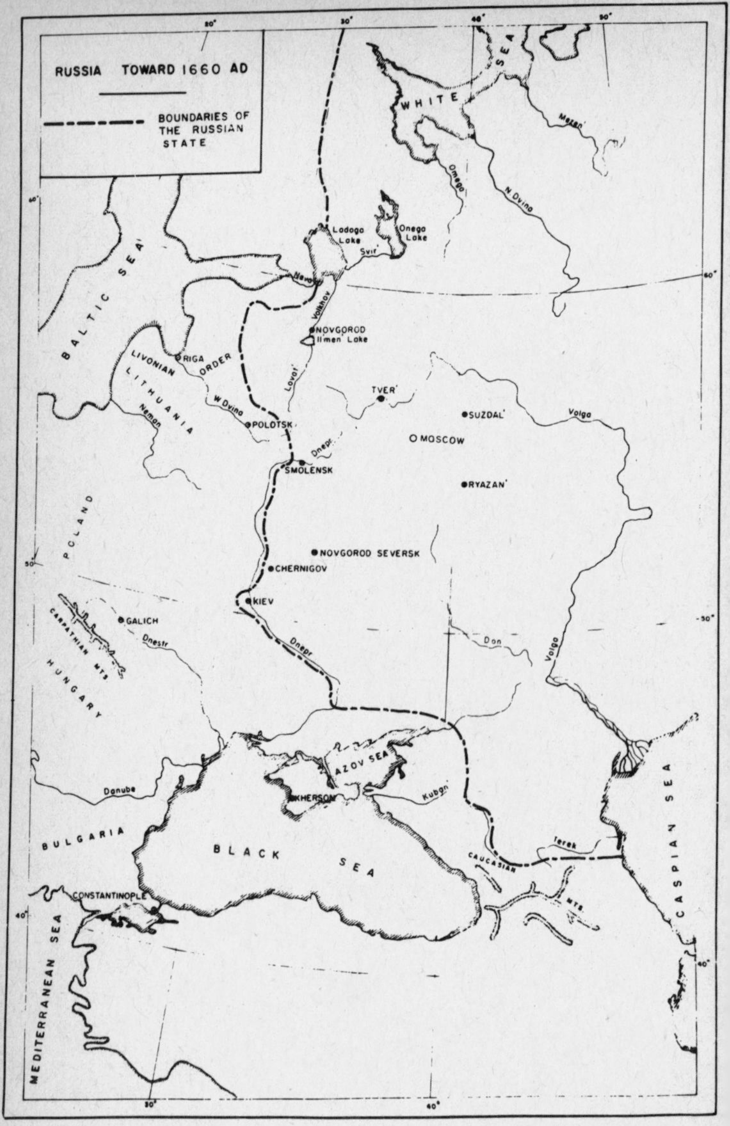

Russia Toward 1660 A.D.

32. *The Story of Stephen Bathory's Campaign Against Pskov*

FOR almost two centuries the primary objective of Muscovite Russia's foreign policy was to gain free access to the Baltic Sea in order to establish direct contact with the West and put an end to Russia's political and cultural isolation. On many occasions Russian armies had tried to capture the Baltic shores, which had been in the hands of the Teutonic Knights of the Livonian Order since the thirteenth century. In 1558 Ivan IV began a military campaign against this Order, and at first he was successful. When Sweden and the Polish-Lithuanian Empire came to the help of the Livonian Order, however, the Russian advance lost momentum. The war then became an exhausting, indecisive undertaking that lasted some twenty-five years. In its final stages Russia had to face the powerful coalition of Sweden, Denmark, Poland, Lithuania, and Hungary, the last three countries being united under the scepter of the energetic King of Hungary, Stephen Bathory.[1] After 1578 Russia lost most of the lands she had conquered earlier, and by 1581 King Stephen Bathory was able to begin an invasion of Russian territory. Polish, Lithuanian, and Hungarian troops, supported by some German mercenaries, invaded Russia and advanced on the city of Pskov, Russia's principal stronghold in the northwest. After a long siege and many attempts to subdue the city, King Stephen Bathory was forced to abandon his plans for conquest, for the heroic defense of Pskov and his failure to take the city had undermined both the strength and morale of his Polish-Lithuanian forces.

The *Story of Stephen Bathory's Campaign Against Pskov* was written in the form of an epic in the late sixteenth century by a talented and erudite anonymous writer who displays an excellent command of the traditional, ornamental stylistics of his

[1] Stephen Bathory was also elected King of Poland and Lithuania in 1575. His wife was Anna, the last princess of the Polish dynasty of Jagellons. The author of this work refers to Stephen as "King of Lithuania," although Poland, Lithuania, and Hungary were all united under his scepter.

time. His account is at once dramatic and ironic, picturesque, and varied. His metaphors and literary devices ideally serve his purpose to present a solemn account of the heroism of the Russian soldiers. With considerable mastery and pointed irony, the author describes King Stephen Bathory's campaign, his courageous, boastful courtiers and knights who, long before the final outcome of the battle was in sight, bragged that they would capture Princes Vasily and Ivan Shuysky, the valiant defenders of Pskov. This tale betrays the strong national fervor of the writer, who was firmly convinced that God would help the "only truly Christian" Russian army, and grant it final victory over the "infidel" invaders.

The excerpts that follow were taken from the early seventeenth-century Russian text published by V. I. Malyshev in *Povest o prikhozhdenii Stefana Batoriia na grad Pskov,* Academy of Sciences of the U.S.S.R., Moscow and Leningrad, 1952, pages 56, 57, 59, 60, and 65–78.

◆ ◆ ◆

Dreadful and cruel times have come. The Polish and Lithuanian king, Stephen Bathory, approached the borders of the Russian land with numerous forces. The rumor has spread to Pskov that this Lithuanian king has already invaded the land of Pskov and has occupied the city of Voronoch, located sixty miles from the city of Pskov.

Similar to insatiable hell which opens its jaws to swallow its victim, so also did the Polish-Lithuanian king prepare to take the city of Pskov in the pincers of his regiments. Always livelier and swifter, this king's army, like an ominous and great serpent wriggling from its cave, moved in columns to Pskov, and threatened the Russians with its campfires, guns, and smoke. The Lithuanian king boasted that he would swallow Pskov, even before he reached it. He boasted that he would satiate all the reptiles, snakes, and scorpions of his army with the rest of the booty. This ominous serpent leaped at Pskov, wanting to hurl it to the earth with its wings and to sting the Pskovian men to death with its stinger. He boasted that he would plunder all the spoils of Pskov and take them to Lithuania and that he would swallow up the Pskovian land, dragging on its tail all those who remained alive to the Lithuanian land. The serpent already flattered itself with thoughts of victory over Pskov.

Dark smoke rose from south of the God-protected city of

Pskov. The Lithuanian armies approached Pskov, and their black shadows, like a cloud, fell over the white stone walls of Pskov. Still, the whole Lithuanian land could not make the city black. Smoke began to rise from the enemy camp, which was three miles away from the city, on the river Cherekh. The tsar's officers, who scouted at this river, rushed to Pskov to inform the tsar's boyars and voevodas that the first Lithuanian troops were already at the river Cherekh. The tsar's boyars and voevodas ordered the tocsin sounded, and gave the command to burn the settlement beyond the Velikaia[2] River in order not to leave behind any quarters for the enemies. And so, on the day of the Holy Martyrs Frol and Lavr, on August 18, 1581 (7189), the siege of the God-protected city of Pskov began. The Lithuanian troops began crossing the river Cherekh, and soon afterward their regiments appeared at the gates of the city. The boyars and voevodas lead their men in a sortie against the enemy troops. But the enemy demonstrated their weakness in this skirmish, beginning the siege with methods of flight, and not daring to approach the city. And for them this was a bad omen. . . .

On Friday, September 8th, the day of the birth of the Holy Virgin, at five o'clock in the afternoon, the Polish and Lithuanian voevodas, captains, storm troops, and gaiduks[3] hurried joyfully and hopefully to storm the city of Pskov. The tsar's boyars and voevodas,[4] all warriors, and the citizens of Pskov saw from their walls that a large number of regiments were leaving the king's camp and moving toward the city with banners. The gaiduks were entering the trenches and tunnels, and the Russians understood that they were moving to storm the breaches in the fortress wall. The voevodas ordered that the tocsin, which was located on the city wall in the vicinity of the Church of Vasily the Great on the hill, be sounded to warn all people of Pskov that the Poles and Lithuanians had begun the storming of the city. The boyars and voevodas of the tsar, with all their warriors and streltsi, were ordered to their places, and stood in preparedness while the artillery received the command to open fire on the enemy regiments. The artillery fired incessantly on the enemy, destroyed many regiments, and killed many Lithuanians and Poles. And their corpses were covering the ground. Still the enemy was advancing to the fortress, fight-

[2] The city of Pskov is located on the Velikaia (Great) River.

[3] The Gaiduks were mercenary infantry and shock troops.

[4] The city of Pskov was under the command of Princes Ivan and Vasily Shuysky, and Prince Andrew Khvorostinin.

ing fiercely, daringly, and hopefully. The enemy advanced as if it were a great stream flowing toward the city. The enemy troops looked as terrifying as the waves of the sea. And an endless number of their sabers were glinting at the city as if they were lightning bolts.

In the Cathedral of the Life-Giving Trinity the clergy began the service, praying to God with tears and appealing to God for the deliverance of the city. The Pskovian men took leave of their wives and children, and hurried to the breaches of the fortress wall, prepared to stave off the enemy, and in their hearts they pledged to God that they would defend the Christian faith and die for each other, for the city of Pskov, for their homes, for their wives and children, and never surrender. And they did as they promised.

At six o'clock of this same day they heard a noise comparable to that of approaching gigantic waves or of powerful thunder. And the entire enemy army howled and ran to the breaches in the fortress wall, covering themselves with their shields, rifles, muskets, lances, and other weapons, and thus appearing to be under a roof. The tsar's boyars and voevodas appealed to God for help, encouraged the Russian warriors with their battle cries, and began fighting the enemies on the fortress walls. The innumerable Lithuanian troops rushed to the fortress wall like a rampaging stream. But our Christian warriors remained as firm as the stars in the sky, and did not permit the enemy to scale the walls. Like powerful thundering, there arose a din of shouts, noises of the shooting of artillery and gunfire, and battle cries of the great multitude of warriors from both armies.

The Pskovian army barred the way of the Lithuanian army, but these lawless Lithuanian warriors fiercely and daringly scaled the wall. The enemy artillery made such large breaches in the wall that even the cavalry could go through them. And at the Virgin's Veil and the Hog Gates there was not a single place safe from the enemy's artillery and guns. The Russians had begun building new wooden walls of many stories for artillery, but they could not complete them because of the heavy enemy artillery barrage. And only their foundations were completed. Thus many enemy warriors were able to climb the city walls. Many of their captains and gaiduks scaled the Virgin's Veil and Hog Towers with their banners, shooting at our defenders from the tower windows and from behind their shields. The first to scale the wall and to remain on it were the enemy's veteran soldiers who were clad in steel armor and armed with the best of weapons. The tsar's boyars and voevodas and the entire

Orthodox army resisted them firmly and unbendingly, fighting bravely and skillfully, and not letting the enemy into the city.

When the most glorified King Stephen saw that his choicest storm troops were on the walls of the city, that his captains and gaiduks had unfurled the banners of the Lithuanian army over the Virgin's Veil and Hog Towers, and that they opened fire against the city and against the Russian artillery to open the way for the taking of the city, his heart was filled with indescribable joy. And he looked hopefully forward to the taking of the fortress. He moved his headquarters closer to the city, into the church of Christ's great martyr, Nikita, which was situated one-half mile from the wall of Pskov.

His retinue, councilors, and beloved foremost aristocrats approached the king and spoke words of hope and praise to him: "Our lord and sovereign, you have done it. You are the conqueror and victorious ruler of the city of Pskov. Glory be to you. We beg you, extend your kindness to us and allow us to proceed to the fortress of Pskov, so that not only your captains and gaiduks will know the glory of having taken Pskov."

When the king heard how joyfully his noblemen and councilors expressed their readiness to fulfill his plans, joy overcame him. With a gay face and happy heart he told them, as if they were his brothers, "Well, my friends, if you show such intentions to fight, I shall also go with you and not stay behind, my friends."

But they answered: "Oh, our sovereign, King Stephen! You will make your triumphant and glorious entry into this great city of Pskov, in the same way as the great king, Alexander the Great, made his glorious and triumphant entry into the city of Rome.[5] And in the same way as Alexander's courtiers met him in the city, so also shall we, your servants, meet you in the city of Pskov with a hymn of glory. And we will prepare for you the spoils of the city. And we will meet you with the Russian commanders of Pskov, whom we shall capture! And for a particularly cherished treasure, we shall meet you with the two captured boyars and voevodas: the first commander of Pskov, Prince Vasily Shuysky, and the glorious, strong, invincible, great, and courageous second commander, Prince Ivan Shuysky. And we shall put them both in irons before you. And you, our sovereign, will do what you please with them in order that they be punished for their unruly resistance to you."

[5] Either the Polish nobles erred in their speeches or the author of this tale did, for Alexander the Great certainly was never at war with Rome.

Hearing this, the king permitted them to go to the walls of the fortress of Pskov with joy, telling them the following: "I knew, friends, that it always would happen as you used to predict, and so it will happen now. And you will accomplish what you intend to, for no one can resist you and your brilliant mind." And two thousand selected storm troops and personal guards of the king began the assault of the Hog Tower, which was already destroyed on their side, and they began shooting through the windows of the wall at the Christian people and at the Russian militia. Their bullets fell like drops of rain from a storm cloud, and flooded the Russian warriors. These bullets were killing the Christian people as if they were the stings of serpents. Other enemy troops stormed through the break in the Virgin's Veil Tower, and cleared the tower of Russian warriors, preparing the way for the final taking of the city.

The Russian voevodas, their soldiers, and the Pskovian militia firmly and courageously stood their ground. Some waited for the enemy with lances at the foot of the wall. The streltsy shot at the Poles with their muskets. Some of the noblemen shot with their bows, while still others hurled rocks or defended the city of Pskov in other ways. The artillery shot at the Russian army from the walls and the towers and, relieving tired ones with fresh troops, they shot incessantly and shouted, "Let's take the city of Pskov!"

The king often sent his messenger to them, inquiring whether the city had been taken, and ordered the commanders, captains, and the entire army to speed the taking of the city.

In the God-protected city of Pskov the voevodas and boyars of the tsar, with kindness and tears, urged their Christian warriors to fight heartily, and they, themselves, fought unyieldingly at the side of their troops. It was sad to see the heads of the Christian warriors falling to the earth like the ears of wheat torn from the ground and lying in one heap. Many soldiers fell from the many wounds inflicted by the enemy's weapons, from exhaustion, and from the incessant fighting. During the day it was extremely hot because of the burning sun. Only faith in God's protection and deliverance gave strength to the warriors.

In the city itself and in the Cathedral of the Life-Giving Trinity the clergy incessantly prayed with tears and moaning for deliverance of the city. When the clergy of the cathedral learned the news that the Lithuanians were already on the walls and in the towers, and that they had unfurled their banners and were shooting from the walls into the city, preparing their way, then Tikhon, the abbot of the Caves Monastery, and archpriest Luka, and all the deacons of the city began to weep with loud voices, extending their arms to the most holy icon. They fell to their knees. Like the streams of many rivers their tears covered the marble steps of the altar, and they began to pray with more fervor, asking the Holy Virgin to protect the city and its inhabitants. The noble ladies, who had gathered in the cathedral for the service, beat their breasts and prayed to God and the most Pure Virgin; they fell on the floor, beating the ground with their heads and crying for divine help. And in every house of the great and God-protected city of Pskov the women, infants, and children who remained at home fervently cried and prayed before the holy icons, beating their breasts and asking the Holy Virgin and all saints for help, and begging God for the forgiveness of their sins and deliverance of the city. And in all the streets of the city there was crying, moaning, and indescribable wailing.

The enemy troops were incessantly and steadily advancing. "Forward, friends!" shouted their officers. "Let us slay all the people of Pskov for their unsubmissiveness. Not even a memory of the Christian inhabitants of Pskov will remain. The shadow of death will engulf them, and nothing will be able to aid them in escaping from our hands."

But who can speak of the power of God? Who can praise his glory?
Blessed are those that fear God and follow his righteous ways,
and who honestly enjoy the fruits of their labors.
Listen, all people of the universe.
Listen all sons of man.
Listen all rich and poor.
Come all saints of Russia to the Christian land to aid the city of Pskov.
You have prayed for us and have helped us through your prayers to God.
You protected the city of Pskov,
which verily I say unto you is the God-protected city.
Let us glorify and declare together the power of the Holy Trinity.
God is our protection and power; God is our aid in the sorrow befallen us.
Therefore, I verily say unto you,
that we have no fear, as the voice of the prophet announced it.

Great is God and greatly is he glorified in this city of God.
We recognize God, who is on his holy mountain,
when we are in misfortune and when he intercedes for us.
For our humility God did not forsake us
when the kings of the earth gathered to march on Pskov, saying:
"God has abandoned that city. Let us hurry and take it."

O Lithuanian commander, Stephen Bathory!
Your tongue is cursed, and both you and your army are insanely proud.
How can you say that no one will deliver this city?
The power of God is with us!
Our Protector is the God of Jacob, the God of the Glorified Trinity,
the One God who has three names, but whom we worship as One,
the Father, the Son, and the Holy Ghost.
We place our hope in him and we rely upon him.
But you, Bathory, do not know him with your lawless Latin Heresies.
And you, Bathory, who place your own majesty before that of Heaven,
hope to conquer the city of Pskov, relying on your multitude of forces.
Wait, accursed one! You will see what happens to your forces!
You will see whether there is One who can deliver us!
And what is the worth of all your proud bragging about the taking of Pskov?
Because of your pride, you will now experience humiliation.
And from the heights of arrogance, you will descend to the hell of shame.
And so will it happen to your army,
for the Lord has remembered us for our humility
and has delivered us from our enemies.
And the Lord has heard the prayers of his servants
and through the miracle of his unfathomable compassion,
his mercy was revealed,
and he delivered his people and showed clemency to his servants.

A bomb from the great gun called the Leopard, which was placed upon the Praise Bastion, hit the Hog Tower squarely.

And the bomb killed a great many Polish and Lithuanian warriors. At about the same time, the tsar's boyars and voevodas ordered the exploding of a large quantity of black powder under this Hog Tower. And the overproud knights, courtiers, and nobles of the king, who had begged their king for permission to take the city of Pskov and bring in the Russian boyars and voevodas in irons, as it was previously mentioned, were blasted into the air according to God's design, and were thus slain by these Russian boyars and voevodas. And the corpses were so numerous that another tower might have been built with them. And the best of the royal nobles, who had boasted that they would bring the imprisoned Russian commanders to their king, remained under the ruins of the Hog Tower, prisoners of death until the Last Judgment. And the deep Pskovian moat was overflowing with their bodies.

The king learned this, when he asked, "Are my noblemen already in the castle?"

And his courtiers told him: "No, sire, they are under the walls of the castle."

And then the king asked, "Do my nobles fight behind the walls of the city and destroy the Russian forces?"

And they answered, "Sire, all your nobles have been killed in the Hog Tower or lie burned in the moat."

And the king was so bereaved that he wanted to run on his sword, as the pagans used to do, for his heart was bursting with sorrow. And he became wroth, and ordered his captains and storm troops who were fighting at the Virgin's Veil Tower to stand firm and take by any and all means the city of Pskov.

The tsar's boyars and voevodas, seeing the heavy and uninterrupted bombardment, the incessant storming, and realizing that many of their warriors had been killed or wounded, relied only upon the help of God. They sent for the holy and miracle-working icons and for the miracle-working relics of the faithful and great Prince Gabriel[6] who had once delivered the city of Pskov from the enemy. And they ordered that the icons be brought to the breach which had been made in the wall by the Poles. Once the holy icon of the Holy Virgin of Vladimir had protected the city of Moscow at the time of Tamerlane's invasion. Now another icon was brought to Pskov because of the invasion of King Stephen Bathory. Once the icon of the Virgin

[6] Prince Gabriel, as well as Prince Dovmont, mentioned in the following paragraph, were rulers of Pskov in the thirteenth and fourteenth centuries, and became known for their courageous defense of Pskov against the Teutonic Knights of the Livonian Order.

protected the city of Moscow from the infamous lame man [Tamerlane]. Now another icon of the Virgin, which had been brought from the Crypt Monastery,[7] helped and protected Pskov. At that time the holy icon of Vladimir was brought to Moscow on the day of the Assumption of the Holy Virgin, and Tamerlane was defeated because he became afraid of this icon of the Pure Virgin, and fled with all his army from Moscow and from Russia. This time the miracle happened in the glorious city of Pskov, on the very day of the venerable and glorious holy day of her birth.

When the holy, miracle-working icon of the Assumption of the Holy Virgin of the Crypt Monastery was brought from the Cathedral of the Holy Trinity with other icons, relics of Prince Gabriel, and other holy relics, divine protection invisibly appeared over the breach in the wall.

The Poles and Lithuanians were fiercely fighting against the Russians in the breaches of the wall and in the Virgin's Veil Tower. Together with the warriors, the Russian officers and commanders were fighting, preventing the enemy from breaking through into Pskov. And when the church procession moved from the cathedral with the icons, at the head of the procession, black-robed heralds rushed on their steeds; they were not soldiers, but the warriors of Christ. Among them were the cellarer of the Crypt Monastery, whose name was Arseny Khvostov; the treasurer of the Monastery of the Birth of the Holy Virgin in Snetegorsk, Jonah Naumov; and the abbot, Mantiry, who was known to everyone in Pskov. All three of these monks were aristocrats by birth and, before becoming monks, had been great warriors. Seeing the bloody battle, they rushed to the breach and, for the sake of God and their holy faith, called out in strong voices. And it seemed as if these voices were coming from the icons. They called to the commanders and to the whole Christian army: "Be not afraid. Let us stand firm. Let us charge against the Polish and Lithuanian forces. The Holy Virgin has come to our aid with all her mercy and protection, and with all the saints."

As soon as the words were heard that the Holy Virgin had come with all the saints to help the Russian commanders and warriors, they felt that the Holy Virgin really did give them her blessing and protection, and thus their weakening hearts became

[7] The Crypt Monastery mentioned here is west of the city of Pskov, and has preserved to the present its fortifications built by Ivan IV. The name of the monastery was apparently taken from the Kievan Cave (or Crypt) Monastery.

firm and they became ready for heroic deeds. In their hearts they accepted the aid of the Holy Virgin, and all commanders, warriors, and the aforementioned monks cried out in unison: "Oh, friends, let us die this day at the hands of the Lithuanians for the sake of Christ's faith and for our Orthodox tsar, Ivan of all the Russias! Let us not surrender to the Polish king, Stephen!" And they appealed also for the intercession of the holy protectors of Pskov, late Prince Gabriel, late Prince Dovmont, and Nicholas, the fool in Christ. And in their hearts they accepted their help, and the entire Russian Christian army stormed the enemy together, and they were fighting in the breach of the wall.

Thus, with God's and the Holy Virgin's help, and with the intercession of the holy miracle workers, the Russians expelled the Polish-Lithuanian forces from the breach and, where recently stood the feet of the enemy, now stood the firm feet of the Christian warriors. And they continued to defeat the enemy, going beyond the walls of the city, while others fought with the Lithuanian troops who remained in the Virgin's Veil Tower.

When the Lord demonstrated the Christian victory over Paul the Lithuanian, and when the Russian troops repulsed the Lithuanian warriors, captains, and gaiduks from the breach in the wall, this news of the blessing of Christ spread throughout the entire city of Pskov, and reached the women who had been left at home. And the word that the enemy had been stopped through divine help spread from house to house. And the women were ordered to go take the Lithuanian artillery and the remnants of the Lithuanian and Polish troops that remained in the city, and then to gather at the breach. And all the women of Pskov, who had remained in their homes in great sorrow, were seized with joy, forgot their womanly weaknesses, and gained the strength of men, hurried to the breach, and took from their homes weapons according to their strengths. Even before, at the beginning of the assault, some strong young women had been fighting against the enemy with arms. Now all, the young, the strong, and the weak, were running with ropes to pull the artillery pieces left by the enemy into the city. All of them rushed to the breach. And each woman wanted to surpass the others in her speed. A multiude of women gathered at the breach, and they were great help for the Christian warriors. Some of them, as I mentioned above, who were young and strong, fought with masculine courage against the Polish and Lithuanian forces, demonstrating their superiority over them. The others brought rocks so that the soldiers might hurl them at the Lithuanians both within and outside of the fortress. Others helped the warriors, and brought them water to quench their thirst, thus bringing back courage to their brave hearts.

This happened on Friday, on the holy day of the Holy Virgin's Birth. It was already evening, but the Polish and Lithuanians were still fighting in the Virgin's Veil Tower and were shooting against the Christian warriors in the city. Then the tsar's boyars and voevodas appealed to God for succor, called their troops together, and began the storming of the Virgin's Veil Tower. Men and women hurled themselves against the remaining enemy troops in the tower, fighting with all the arms given to them by God. Some shot muskets, while others were trying to smoke out the enemy from their hiding places. Others threw rocks at the Poles and Lithuanians, while still others poured boiling water upon them. Finally they put black powder under this tower also, and with God's help they blasted the remaining Lithuanians and Poles from the Virgin's Veil Tower. In this way, with the Grace of Christ, the stone wall of Pskov was cleansed of the evil Lithuanian feet. When night came, God sent light, and the remainder of the enemy was driven out from under the walls.

And then the Lithuanians and Poles began to flee from the fortress back to their camps. The Christian Russian warriors made sorties from the fortress, pursued them, cut them to pieces, and chased the others away. Those who remained in the moat were destroyed. Many were taken prisoner and brought back to the city, to the tsar's boyars and voevodas to be interrogated. Many enemy warriors were taken with banners, drums, and weapons. And many Russians returned to the city uninjured, and brought back with them enemy arms, special muskets, guns, and endless booty.

Thus, with God's blessing, through the infinite mercy of the Divine Trinity, and the prayers and intercession of the Holy Virgin, and in the honor of her glorious birth, and for the sake of the holy, great miracle workers, the great city of Pskov was delivered from the Poles and Lithuanians. And at three o'clock in the night the Lord gave a great victory to the Christian army over the proud and lawless enemy.

[The final part of this work describes the fighting around Pskov until February 4, 1582, the day when King Stephen Bathory lifted the siege of this fiercely embattled Russian fortress.]

33. *Prince Andrew Kurbsky: First Epistle Written to the Tsar and Grand Prince of Moscow in Consequence of His Fierce Persecution*

PRINCE Andrew Kurbsky's first epistle to Ivan IV is a strong protest against Tsar Ivan's autocratic rule. Wishing to destroy the old feudal system of Russia, by which the princes were practically independent rulers of their appanages, Ivan IV began a systematic purge of the aristocracy in the late 1550's and many nobles died on the scaffold or in prison.

An outstanding statesman and military leader, Prince Kurbsky was a close friend and adviser of Tsar Ivan IV until the latter began his cruel struggle against the Russian feudal aristocracy. Kurbsky then broke with the tsar and fled to Lithuania, where he settled for the rest of his life. Kurbsky had belonged to the intellectual elite of sixteenth-century Moscow and had been a pupil and friend of the famous and erudite scholar-monk, Maxim Trivolis, called Maxim the Greek, who had come to Russia in the early years of the sixteenth century. Living in Lithuania, Andrew Kurbsky became a writer and translator and participated in the revival of Russian Orthodox literature in the Russian parts of Poland and Lithuania. His best-known work is his correspondence with Ivan IV, in which he sharply criticized the tsar's autocratic policies and his persecution of the aristocracy.

This translation of the letter was made by J. L. I. Fennell and was published in *The Correspondence Between Prince A. M. Kurbsky and Tsar Ivan IV of Russia, 1564–1579*, Cambridge University Press, 1955, pages 3, 5, 7, 9, and 11.

◆ ◆ ◆

To the tsar, exalted above all by God, who appeared (formerly) most illustrious, particularly in the Orthodox faith, but who has now, in consequence of our sins, been found to be the contrary of this. If you have understanding, may you understand this with your leprous conscience—such a conscience as cannot be found even amongst the godless peoples. And I have not let my tongue say more than this on all these matters in turn; but because of the bitterest persecution from your power, with much sorrow in my heart will I hasten to inform you of a little.

Wherefore, O tsar, have you destroyed the strong in Israel and subjected to various forms of death the *voevodas* given to you by God?[1] And wherefore have you spilled their victorious, holy blood in the churches of God during sacerdotal ceremonies, and stained the thresholds of the churches with their blood of martyrs?[2] And why have you conceived against your well-wishers and against those who lay down their lives for you unheard-of torments and persecutions and death, falsely accusing the Orthodox of treachery and magic and other abuses, and endeavoring with zeal to turn light into darkness and to call sweet bitter? What guilt did they commit before you, O tsar, and in what way did they, the champions of Christianity, anger you? Have they not destroyed proud kingdoms and by their heroic bravery made subject to you in all things those in whose servitude our forefathers formerly were? Was it not through the keenness of their understanding that the strong German towns were given to you by God?[3] Thus have you remunerated us, [your] poor [servants], destroying us by whole families? Think you yourself immortal, O tsar? Or have you been enticed into unheard-of heresy, as one no longer wishing to stand before the impartial judge, Jesus, begotten of God, who will judge according to justice the universe and especially the vainglorious tormentors, and who unhesitatingly will question them "right to the hairs [roots?] of their sins," as the saying goes? He is my Christ who sitteth on the throne of the Cherubims at the right hand of the power of the Almighty in the highest—the judge between you and me.

What evil and persecution have I not suffered from you! What ills and misfortunes have you not brought upon me! And what iniquitous tissues of lies have you not woven against me! But I cannot now recount the various misfortunes at your hands

[1] The expression "the strong in Israel" echoes the current panegyrical political literature of the sixteenth century, extolling the absolution of the grand prince and the supremacy of Moscow, "the Third Rome," "the new Israel."

[2] A reference to the first wave of Ivan's persecutions which, according to Kurbsky (Skazaniia Kn. A. M. Kurbskogo, ed. N. Ustrialov [St. Petersburg, 1842], "Istoria . . ." Chapter VI, page 90) began "shortly after the death of Alexis Adashev and the banishment of Priest Sylvester," i.e., in 1560.

[3] The "proud kingdoms" destroyed by the "strong in Israel" in the fifties of the sixteenth century were the Tatar Khanates of Kazan (captured in 1552) and Astrakhan (captured in 1556). The "strong German towns" are the Baltic towns captured during the first three years of the Livonian War (1558–1560): Narva, Neuhausen, and Dorpat (1558); Marienburg, Ermes, and Fellin (1560).

which have beset me owing to their multitude and since I am still filled with the grief of my soul. But, to conclude, I can summarize them all [thus]: of everything have I been deprived; I have been driven from the land of God without guilt [*lit.* in vain], hounded by you. I did not ask [for aught] with humble words, nor did I beseech you with tearful plaint; nor yet did I win from you any mercy through the intercession of the hierarchy. You have recompensed me with evil for good and for my love with implacable hatred. My blood, spilled like water for you, cries out against you to my Lord. God sees into [men's] hearts—in my mind have I ardently reflected and my conscience have I placed as a witness [against myself], and I have sought and pried within my thoughts, and, examining myself [*lit.* turning myself around], I know not now—nor have I ever found—my guilt in aught before you. In front of your army have I marched—and marched again; and no dishonor have I brought upon you; but only brilliant victories, with the help of the angel of the Lord, have I won for your glory, and never have I turned the back of your regiments to the foe. But far more, I have achieved most glorious conquests to increase your renown. And this, not in one year, nor yet in two—but throughout many years have I toiled with much sweat and patience; and always have I been separated from my fatherland, and little have I seen my parents, and my wife have I not known; but always in far distant towns have I stood in arms against your foes and I have suffered many wants and natural illnesses, of which my Lord Jesus Christ is witness. Still more, I was visited with wounds inflicted by barbarian hands in various battles and all my body is already afflicted with sores. But to you, O tsar, was all this as nought; rather do you show us your intolerable wrath and bitterest hatred, and, furthermore, burning stoves.[4]

And I wanted to relate all my military deeds in turn which I have accomplished for your glory by the strength of my Christ, but I have not recounted them for this reason, that God knows better than man. For he is the recompenser for all these things, and not only for them, but also for a cup of cold water; and I know that you yourself are not unaware of them. And furthermore may this be known to you, O tsar; you will, I think,

[4] Evidently one of the commonest forms of torture employed by Ivan IV. Kurbsky speaks of Ivan's torture in his *History:* "Are not the various instruments of torture of the ancient torturers the same as those used by our new torturer [i.e. Ivan]? Pans and stoves? Cruel flogging and sharp nails? Red-hot pincers for lacerating human bodies? Needles to drive under the fingernails . . . ?" (p. 145)

no longer see my face in this world until the glorious coming of my Christ. Think not that concerning these things I will remain silent before you; to my end will I incessantly cry out with tears against you to the everlasting Trinity, in which I believe; and I call to my aid the Mother of the Lord of the Cherubims, my hope and protectress, Our Lady, the Mother of God, and all the Saints, the elect of God, and my master and forefather, Prince Fedor Rostislavich, whose corpse remains imperishable, preserved throughout the ages, and emits from the grave sweet odors, sweeter than aromatics, and, by the grave of the Holy Ghost, pours forth miraculous healing streams, as you, O tsar, know well.[5]

Deem not, O tsar, and think not upon us with your sophistic thoughts, as though we had already perished, massacred [though we are] by you in our innocence and banished and driven out by you without justice; rejoice not in this, glorying, as it were, in a vain victory; those massacred by you, standing at the throne of our Lord, ask vengeance against you; while we who have been banished and driven out by you without justice from the land cry out day and night to God, however much in your pride you may boast in this temporal, fleeting life, devising vessels of torture against the Christian race, yea, and abusing and trampling on the Angelic Form,[6] with the approbation of your flatterers and comrades of the table, your quarrelsome boyars, the destroyers of your soul and body, who urge you on to erotic deeds and, together with their children, act more [viciously] than the priests of Cronus. So much for this. And this epistle, soaked in my tears, will I order to be put into my grave with me, when I [shall be about to] come with you before the judgment of my God, Jesus Christ. Amen.

Written in Wolmar, the town of my master, King Augustus Sigismund, from whom I hope to receive much reward and com-

[5] Fedor Rostislavich, prince of Yaroslavl, Andrew Kurbsky's paternal grandfather to the ninth degree, ruled in Mozhaisk at the end of the thirteenth century. In 1294 he received the principality of Yaroslavl after marrying the daughter of Vasily Vsevolodovich, prince of Yaroslavl. He died in 1299 and was canonized in 1463.

[6] The Russian expression "to accept the Angel's form" is the equivalent of "to take monastic vows." In certain copies of the text there exists the following marginal note: "That is to say, he abuses the Angelic Form when he flies into a rage with certain people and then forces them to accept the monastic tonsure together with their wives and children, and condemns them to everlasting imprisonment in strong monasteries and dark cells, making the holy places fortresses of hell with the approbation of certain accursed and cunning monks."

fort for all my sorrow, by his sovereign grace, and still more with God's help.

I have heard from sacred writings that a destroyer will be sent by the devil against the human race, a destroyer conceived in fornication, the Antichrist, hostile to God; and now I have seen a counselor, known to all, who was born in adultery and who today whispers falsehoods in the ears of the tsar and sheds Christian blood like water and has already destroyed the strong and noble in Israel, as one in agreement with the Antichrist in deed.[7] It is not befitting, O tsar, to show indulgence to such men! In the first law of the Lord it is written: "A Moabite and an Ammonite and a bastard to the tenth generation shall not enter into the congregation of the Lord."[8]

34. *Ivan IV: Epistle of the Tsar and Sovereign to All His Russian Tsardom Against Those Who Have Broken the Pledge of Allegiance, Against Prince Andrew Kurbsky and His Comrades, Concerning Their Treacheries*

The epistle of Ivan IV, the Terrible, to Prince Andrew Kurbsky is one of the most impressive works defending the Byzantine-Russian concept of autocracy, which accepted the tsar as ruler by divine right. Ivan IV thus claimed the exclusive right to command the destinies of the state and his subjects, while considering himself responsible only to God for the fate of the state and its people. (Concerning Prince Andrew Kurbsky and the roots of this conflict, see the introduction to Prince Kurbsky's letter to Ivan.)

A cruel tyrant who was merciless to his enemies, Ivan IV was at the same time a great ruler whose policies helped determine the future of Russia. By breaking the power of the aristocracy he ended the feudal system of medieval Russia and thus laid the foundation for a unified Russian state. His successes against the Tatars opened to Russia the nearly limitless territories of the

[7] This is probably a reference to Fedor Alekseevich Basmanov, who was a favorite of Ivan's at that time. He was, indeed, renowned for his cruelty, and is alleged by Kurbsky to have murdered his father. There is, however, no confirmation of his illegitimacy.

[8] See Deuteronomy, 23: 2-3.

Tsar Ivan IV (the Terrible).
A late sixteenth-century Russian portrait.

Volga-Ural region and northern Asia, thus paving the way for future Russian expansion. Some one hundred and fifty years before Peter the Great, Ivan IV tried to open a window to Europe and to end Russia's isolation by winning an area on the Baltic shore from the Order of Livonian Knights.

Ivan IV was very well educated, was a forceful polemicist and writer, and even composed music. His style of writing is not restrained, but fierce, stinging and merciless, and he did not hesitate to insult his enemies.

These excerpts from Tsar Ivan's letter to Prince Kurbsky, which grew into a rather lengthy treatise, have been translated by Leo Wiener.

◆ ◆ ◆

Our God, the Trinity, who has existed since eternity but now as Father, Son and Holy Ghost, has neither beginning nor end; through him we live and move about, through him kings rule and the mighty write laws. By our Lord Jesus Christ the victorious standard of God's only Word and the blessed Cross, which has never been vanquished, have been given to Emperor Constantine, first in piety, and to all the orthodox tsars and protectors of orthodoxy and, insofar as the Word of God has been fulfilled, they, in eagle's flight, have reached all the godly servants of God's Word, until a spark of piety has fallen upon the Russian realm. The autocracy, by God's will, had its origin in Grand Prince Vladimir, who had enlightened all Russia through the holy baptism, and the great Tsar Vladimir Monomakh, who had received memorable honors from the Greeks, and the valiant great Tsar Alexander Nevsky, who had obtained a great victory over the godless Germans, and the praiseworthy great Tsar Dmitry, who had obtained a great victory over the sons of Hagar beyond the Don, then it passed to the avenger of wrongs, our ancestor, the great Tsar Ivan, the gatherer of the Russian land from among the ancestral possessions, and to our father of blessed memory, the great Tsar Vasily until it reached us, the humble scepter-bearer of the Russian empire.[1]

[1] Roman Emperor Constantine (306–337) granted the rights to the Christians, and summoned the first Ecumenical Council of the Christian Church. Prince Vladimir Christianized Russia in 988 or 989. Vladimir Monomakh was the last prince of Kiev (1112–1125) to be recognized as Grand Prince by all Russian princes of the Kievan era. Dmitry, Grand Prince of Muscovy, was the victor over the Tatars in 1380. "The great Tsar Ivan" is Ivan III, unifier of northern Russia (1462–1505) and grandfather of Ivan IV. Vasily—Vasily III (1505–1533)—was father to Ivan IV.

But we praise God for the great favor he has shown me in not permitting my right hand to become stained by the blood of my race: for we have not snatched the realm from anyone, but by the will of God and the blessing of our ancestors and parents, were we born in the realm, were brought up there and enthroned, taking, by the will of God and the blessing of our ancestors and parents, what belonged to us, and not seizing that which was not ours. Here follows the command of the orthodox, truly Christian autocrat, the possessor of many kingdoms—our humble Christian answer to him who was an orthodox, true Christian and a boyar of our realm, a councilor and a general, but now is a criminal before the blessed, vivifying cross of the Lord, a destroyer of Christians, a servant of the enemies of Christianity, who has departed from the divine worship of the images and has trodden underfoot all sacred commands, destroyed the holy edifices, vilified and trampled the holy vessels and images, who unites in one person Leo the Isaurian, Constantine Kopronymos and Leo of Armenia—to Prince Andrew Mikhailovich Kurbsky, who through treachery wanted to become a ruler of Yaroslavl.[2]

Wherefore, O Prince, if you regard yourself to have piety, have you lost your soul? What will you give in its place on the day of the terrible judgment? Even if you should acquire the whole world, death will reach you in the end! Why have you sold your soul for your body's sake? Is it because you were afraid of death at the false instigation of your demons and influential friends and counselors? . . .

Are you not ashamed before your slave Vaska Shibanov,[3] who preserved his piety and, having attached himself to you with a kiss of the cross, did not reject you before the tsar and the whole people, though standing at the gate of death, but praised you and was all too ready to die for you? But you did not emulate his devotion: on account of a single angry word of mine, have you lost not only your own soul, but the souls of all your ancestors: for, by God's will, had they been given as servants to our grandfather, the great tsar, and they gave their souls to him and served him up to their death, and ordered you, their children, to serve the children and grandchildren of our grand-

[2] Leo III the Isaurian (717–741), Constantine V Kopronymos (741–755), and Leo V, the Armenian, were Byzantine emperors who supported the heresy of the iconoclasts and were posthumously condemned by the Orthodox Church.

[3] Vaska (Vasily) Shibanov, a faithful servant of Prince A. M. Kurbsky who delivered his master's letter to Ivan IV, and died after long tortures without betraying the prince.

father. But you have forgotten everything and traitorously, like a dog, have you transgressed the oath and have gone over to the enemies of Christianity, and, not considering your wrath, you utter stupid words, hurling, as it were, stones at the sky. . . .

We have never spilled blood in the churches. As for the victorious, saintly blood—there has none appeared in our land, as far as we know. *The thresholds of the churches:* as far as our means and intelligence permit and our subjects are eager to serve us, the churches of the Lord are resplendent with all kinds of adornments, and through the gifts which we have offered since your satanic domination, not only the thresholds and pavements, but even the antechambers shine with ornaments, so that all the strangers may see them. We do not stain the thresholds of the churches with any blood, and there are no martyrs of faith with us nowadays. . . . Tortures and persecutions and deaths in many forms we have devised against no one. As to treasons and magic, it is true, such dogs everywhere suffer capital punishment. . . .

It had pleased God to take away our mother, the pious Tsarina Helen, from the earthly kingdom to the kingdom of heaven. My brother George, who now rests in heaven, and I were left orphans and, as we received no care from anyone, we laid our trust in the Holy Virgin, and in the prayers of all the saints, and in the blessing of our parents. When I was in my eighth year, our subjects acted according to their will, for they found the empire without a ruler, and did not deign to bestow their voluntary attention upon us, their master, but were bent on acquiring wealth and glory, and were quarreling with each other. And what have they not done! How many boyars, how many friends of our father and generals they have killed! And they seized the farms and villages and possessions of our uncles, and established themselves therein. The treasure of our mother they trod underfoot and pierced with sharp sticks, and transferred it to the great treasure, but some of it they grabbed themselves; and that was done by your grandfather Mikhaylo Tuchkov. The Princes Vasily and Ivan Shuysky took it upon themselves to have me in their keeping, and those who had been the chief traitors of our father and mother they let out of prison, and they made friends with them. Prince Vasily Shuysky with a Judas crowd fell in the court belonging to our uncle upon our father confessor Fedor Mishurin, and insulted him, and killed him; and they imprisoned Prince Ivan Fedorovich Byelsky and many others in various places, and armed themselves against the realm; they ousted metropolitan Daniel from the metropolitan see and banished him: and thus they improved their opportunity, and began to rule themselves.

Me and my brother George, of blessed memory, they brought up like vagrants and children of the poorest. What have I not suffered for want of garments and food! And all that against my will and as did not become my extreme youth. I shall mention just one thing: once in my childhood we were playing, and Prince Ivan Vasilievich Shuysky was sitting on a bench, leaning with his elbow against our father's bed, and even putting his foot upon it; he treated us not as a parent, but as a master . . . who could bear such presumption? How can I recount all the miseries which I have suffered in my youth? Often did I dine late, against my will. What had become of the treasure left me by my father? They had carried everything away, under the cunning pretext that they had to pay the boyar children from it, but, in reality, they had kept it back from them, to their own advantage, and had not paid them off according to their deserts; and they had also held back an immense treasure of my grandfather and father, and made it into gold and silver vessels, inscribing thereupon the names of their parents, as if they had been their inheritance. . . . It is hardly necessary to mention what became of the treasure of our uncles: they appropriated it all to themselves! Then they attacked towns and villages, tortured the people most cruelly, brought much misery upon them, and mercilessly pillaged the possessions of the inhabitants. . . .

When we reached the age of fifteen, we, inspired by God, undertook to rule our own realm and, with the aid of almighty God, we ruled our realm in peace and undisturbed, according to our will. But it happened then that, on account of our sins, a fire having spread, by God's will, the royal city of Moscow was consumed. Our boyars, the traitors whom you call martyrs, whose names I shall purposely pass over in silence, made use of the favorable opportunity for their mean treachery, whispered into the ears of a stupid crowd that the mother of my mother, Princess Anna Glinsky, with all her children and household, was in the habit of extracting men's hearts, and that by a similar sorcery she had put Moscow on fire, and that we knew of her doings.[4] By the instigation of these our traitors, a mass of insensate people, crying in the manner of the Jews, came to the apostolic cathedral of the holy martyr Dmitry of Saloniki, dragged out of it our boyar Yury Vasilevich Glinsky, pulled him

[4] Princes Shuyskys were members of an influential and wealthy aristocratic family who actually ruled in Moscow during Ivan IV's childhood.

inhumanly into the cathedral of the Assumption, and killed the innocent man in the church, opposite the metropolitan's place; they stained the floor of the church with his blood, dragged his body through the front door, and exposed him on the market-place as a criminal—everybody knows about this murder in the church. We were then living in the village of Vorobievo; the same traitors instigated the populace to kill us under the pretext, and you, dog, repeat the lie that we were keeping from them Prince Yury's mother, Princess Anna, and his brother, Prince Mikhail. How is one not to laugh at such stupidity? Why should we be incendiaries in our own empire? . . .

You say that your blood has been spilled in wars with foreigners, and you add, in your foolishness, that it cries to God against us. That is ridiculous! It has been spilled by one, and it cries out against another. If it is true that your blood has been spilled by the enemy, then you have done your duty to your country; if you had not done so, you would not have been a Christian but a barbarian—but that is not our affair. How much more ours, that has been spilled by you, cries out to the Lord against you! Not with wounds, nor drops of blood, but with much sweating and toiling have I been burdened by you unnecessarily and above my strength! Your many meannesses and persecutions have caused me, instead of blood, to shed many tears, and to utter sobs and have anguish of my soul. . . .

You say you want to put your letter in your grave: that shows that you have completely renounced your Christianity! For God has ordered not to resist evil, but you renounce the final pardon which is granted to the ignorant; therefore it is not even proper that any Mass shall be sung after you. In our patrimony, in the country of Lifland, you name the city of Volmir as belonging to our enemy, King Sigismund: by this you only complete the treachery of a vicious dog![5] . . .

Written in our great Russia, in the famous, imperial, capital city of Moscow, on the steps of our imperial threshold, in the year from the creation of the world 1564 (7072), the fifth day of July.

[5] The city of Volmir, actually Volmar, was conquered by Ivan IV during the first phase of the Livonian War (see introduction to Selection 32, the *Story of Stephen Bathory's Campaign Against Pskov*), and later was claimed by the Polish King Sigismund.

HISTORICAL WORKS FROM THE TIME OF TROUBLES

35. *Avraamy Palitsyn: Pseudo-Dmitry*

SOON after the death of Ivan IV, the Rurik dynasty, which had presided over Russia's destiny for seven hundred years, came to its end. Ivan had accidentally killed his eldest and favorite son, Tsarevich Ivan, and the throne was inherited by the physically and mentally debile Fedor. After reigning fourteen years, 1584 to 1598, Tsar Fedor died without leaving an heir to the throne. The dynastic crisis was aggravated by the fact that Ivan's youngest son, Dmitry, mysteriously perished in 1591. Rumors circulated that he had been slain at the order of Boris Godunov, Tsar Fedor's brother-in-law, a brilliant but ruthless statesman who wanted the throne for himself. Indeed, the Land Assembly, which was manipulated by Boris, elected him as Tsar of all the Russias in 1598. His reign was not a happy one, however, for Russia was plagued by famines and epidemics. Moreover, in 1602 a mysterious impostor appeared who claimed that he was Tsarevich Dmitry, the son of Ivan IV, declaring that he had escaped the knives of Boris' henchmen in 1590. The Poles, the age-old rivals and enemies of Russia, supported Dmitry and his claim to the Russian throne. He also received the blessing of the Pope of Rome, and in return Pseudo-Dmitry promised the Holy See that he would convert all Russia to the Roman Catholic faith. In 1604 he began his campaign against Tsar Boris, leading both Russian and Polish troops. Upon the unexpected death of Boris Godunov, Dmitry entered Moscow and became tsar in 1605. Hated by the boyars because of his sympathy for the Poles and by the Russian clergy for his rapprochement with the Catholic Church, Pseudo-Dmitry was murdered in the following year. For the next seven years anarchy reigned while Polish and Swedish armies occupied a good deal of Russian territory. Even Moscow fell to the Poles, in September of 1610. Only in 1613, after the election of Michael, the first tsar of the Romanov dynasty, did Russia begin its rehabilitation under a stable and legal government.

These nine years, 1604 to 1613, years of crisis, great unrest, and foreign intervention, are usually called the "Time of Troubles," and they left a deep and indelible impression on the mind of Russia. Many writers who lived through these dramatic events left memoirs and analyses concerning this period. In most of them can be found a feeling of offended nationalism and fierce hatred toward the foreigners who had invaded the Russian land during these turbulent years. These writers are especially bitter toward the Poles and Catholics, who supported Pseudo-Dmitry, hoping, through him, to dominate all of Russia.

Among such writers Avraamy Palitsyn, a monk and cellarer of the powerful Holy Trinity-St. Sergius Monastery, left one of the best accounts of the events of the time. A member of a wealthy aristocratic family, Averky (Avraamy was his monastic name) was born about 1555, and, like many aristocrats of the day, served both in the civil service and in the army. In 1588 the anti-Godunov faction forced him to take monastic vows, thus excluding him for a time from political activity. As cellarer of the Holy Trinity-St. Sergius Monastery he participated in the patriotic and counterrevolutionary revival of 1610 to 1613, and as an influential leader he wrote his history (*skazanie*), which became one of the most popular accounts of the Time of Troubles, surviving in over one hundred extant manuscripts from the seventeenth century alone. Palitsyn died in the Solovki Monastery on September 13, 1627.

The translations of Chapters V and VI of his work, *A Concise History Written in Memory of Past Generations*, are given here. These translations follow the text of *Skazanie Avraamiia Palitsyna*, edited by O. A. Derzhavina and E. V. Kolosova, Academy of Sciences, Moscow and Leningrad, 1955, pages 110–115.

✦ ✦ ✦

ABOUT THE DEFROCKED MONK GREGORY AND THE DEATH OF TSAR BORIS

In the year 1605 (7113) a certain monk, whose name was Gregory and who was a scion of the Otrepiev[1] family, and who had been an addict of occult books and other evils, left Russia and went to the Polish Kingdom. Living there, he began to write subversive proclamations, sending them to all parts of Russia, in which he declared that he was the real Dmitry, son of

[1] Pseudo-Dmitry remains one of the great enigmas of Russian history. His actual identity has remained unknown to this day. However, the government of Boris Godunov, as well as other opponents of the pretender, identified him as being Gregory Otrepiev, a scion of a wealthy and noble Muscovite family.

the tsar. He would go from city to city, hiding himself and causing disturbances among the people of both realms. Then he was joined by fugitives from western Russian and Polish cities, by serfs whose time had arrived according to the will of the evil spirit, and by one village after another, and by one city after another, and finally all were tempted. However, his scheme was evident to many. Yet, what a great amount of evil did they cause! And until this day Russia is unable to be rid of this yoke. He and his followers in evil have done so many base deeds in Russia that no one could describe them all, even if he wrote for many years. In two years this unfrocked monk Gregory succeeded in winning over one-quarter of the entire universe, the entirety of Europe; and even the Pope of Rome wrote on his behalf to the entire West, presenting Gregory as an exile from his fatherland. And the Pope ordered the Polish king, Sigismund III, to start a campaign against Russia in order to take revenge for the impostor. Gregory joined the Catholics, that eternal enemy of Christians, and he gave them a written promise that he would bring entire Russia under the blessing of the Antichrist,[2] thus delivering all Russians to eternal death through the abomination of the Catholic Communion. And he would have done this, if the Lord hadn't overthrown his evil design. To him refer the prophecies of Ezekiel, for it is written, "You shall be fuel for the fire and your blood shall be in the midst of the land" (21: 32).

Although Tsar Boris was not killed by this impostor, he died a sudden death in the summer of 1605 (7113) during the revolt brought about by Gregory, and all those upon whom Boris relied were dispersed along with his household.[3]

After Boris' death, this monk ascended the throne and called himself Tsar Dmitry. But from many witnesses we know that this Gregory was a simple monk, despite the fact that he wanted to become the Tsar of Russia. And he gathered together all the relatives of the murdered Tsarevich Dmitry[4] and many other people who had been deported by Tsar Boris. And those who

[2] In the sixteenth and seventeenth centuries the Protestant West and the Orthodox East often called the Pope of Rome the Antichrist, and they claimed that the Pope served Satan. The Catholics, in turn, called the Protestants the servants of Satan and the Antichrist.

[3] When Tsar Boris Godunov died, his son, Fedor II, became Tsar of Russia. However, he was soon murdered by the impostor's supporters, and Pseudo-Dmitry ascended to the throne of Muscovy.

[4] Maria Nagoy was the last wife of Ivan IV. After the killing of her son, Tsarevich Dmitry, Boris Godunov forced her to take monastic vows. She did so under the name of Marfa (Martha).

did not wish to join him, he won over through his gifts. In such manner did he win over the nun Marfa, the mother of Tsarevich Dmitry and the wife of Tsar Ivan Vassilevich, Tsar of all the Russias. And so she called this impostor her son. And many of the people of Uglich[5] who could have exposed him and even his real mother, Barbara, the wife of Bogdan Otrepiev, his brother's widow and son, and his uncle, Smirny-Otrepiev, did not. Therefore his uncle was sent to Siberia, and underwent many tribulations there. And there appeared many new martyrs: the nobleman Peter Turgenev, and Fedor Kolachev, who fearlessly exposed him, were beheaded in the central square of the imperial city of Moscow, after having undergone many tortures. When this Fedor Kolachev was led to the scaffold, he shouted to the crowd, saying: "You have accepted this servant of the Antichrist and you worship this messenger of Satan. But you won't understand this until you have perished because of it."

But the Muscovites only abused him and answered that he well deserved his execution. They paid no more heed to the execution of Peter Turgenev. Soon after these executions, Prince Vasily Shuysky[6] was also condemned to death on the scaffold for his exposures and intrigues, but the Poles, fearing his execution, asked the impostor to pardon him.

Soon after, following the evil impostor's advice, all metropolitans, archbishops, bishops, abbots, and all the leading clergymen with Patriarch Ignaty, as well as the princes and boyars with all the army commanders, obeyed him and signed the petition and sent ambassadors to the Polish Kingdom to ask the Lord of Sandomir to give his daughter to this impostor for his wife.[7] And all of them gave witness in their message that he was Dmitry, the real son of Tsar Ivan IV.

And even those who knew that he was Monk Gregory gave witness to this. Among them were Pafnuty, the Metropolitan of Krutitsa. When Pafnuty was abbot of the Miracle Monastery, this Gregory used to sing in his choir and then remained at the court of the Patriarch Job for one year, where he worked as a clerk. Soon after, he ran away to Lithuania because his heretical intrigues were exposed. And like a chariot of the pharaoh, he

[5] Tsarevich Dmitry was killed in the city of Uglich in 1591, so it is quite natural that in 1605 many inhabitants of this city could have testified that Pseudo-Dmitry was an impostor.

[6] After Pseudo-Dmitry's death, Prince Vasily Shuysky became Russia's tsar, ruling from 1606 to 1610.

[7] Marina Mnishek, a daughter of a voevoda of Sandomir, became the impostor's wife in 1606 in Moscow.

became involved in a plot, and after him the entire Russian state became insane, giving in to his temptations.

Now involved in this plot, this accursed, defrocked impostor got into a conspiracy with the voevoda of Sandomir when he lived at his house in Poland. And, following an evil path, this voevoda decided to give his own daughter, Marina, in marriage [to this pretender, and took her to Moscow] to the lawless celebration of her wedding, taking with him some six thousand selected troops. For the quartering of these Polish knights, not only were the houses of simple people taken, but even those of officials, courtiers, and the Nagoy family, the so-called relatives of the impostor. And in all good and noble places and houses heretical joy and violence spread.

This defrocked impostor, who was himself a sponsor of the crooked faith, feared that the same fate that befell Tsar Boris would befall himself. And therefore, coming and leaving the tsar's palace, and going to walk about the city, he surrounded himself with many guards. Before him and behind him there were marching armed soldiers with arquebuses, halberds, and other weapons. And this impostor would always walk in the center of them, while Russian courtiers and boyars had to follow far behind. Indeed, it was terrifying to behold so many glinting arms and shining armor. He selected his personal guardsmen, as well as the guards of his palace, only from among the Polish and German mercenaries. He permitted gamblers to gamble and cheat even in the tsar's palace. All his retinue and his common servants were clothed in finery as if they were bridegrooms, though no one knew what they had to celebrate. They loitered from street to street searching for pleasure and bedecked in purple finery and with gold and silver accouterments. And when they served the impostor, they adorned themselves with precious stones and pearls. And they did not want to look upon anyone who was humble. In such a way, the Poles were squandering the ancient treasures of Russia. And they used the silver vessels for carrying water and even in the bath, while they used silver and gold vessels for washing. And besides all this, they spread the seeds of the heretical dogma of Luther.

And no one dared to pronounce a word in the presence of the evil and fiercesome Cossacks.[8] And many an aristocrat shed tears, seeing the arrogance shown them by their serfs. The serfs could always claim that their masters had called Dmitry "an

[8] Many Don and Dnieper Cossacks, among whom were many runaway serfs, joined with Pseudo-Dmitry.

unfrocked impostor," and then such masters would always disappear. In all the Russian cities and in the venerated monasteries many laymen and monks perished. Some of them were imprisoned, while others were drowned, and the belly of a huge fish became their tomb. The impostor permitted both Jews and heretics to visit the holy and divine churches, and foreigners dared to enter the Cathedral of the Assumption of Our Holy and Honored Lady and to profane the miracle-working relics of the holy metropolitians, Peter and Jonas, leaning upon the reliquaries. And the unholy Poles entered the churches even with their weapons, but no one dared tell them a word, since resisting one of them could mean death.

Soon after, the accursed Roman pope sent a missal to the impostor reminding him of his promise to introduce into Russia the Roman Catholic form of Holy Communion and fasting on Saturday. This cursed, defrocked monk attempted to do as he was ordered, but when he wed his heretical bride, they were married in a divine Orthodox Church. But before marrying her, this cursed man corrupted many virgin nuns and even pious monks. And both he and the Poles were committing many shameful deeds. And the rebels and Cossacks who brought him to the throne enjoyed the fall of Christian virtues, seeing those shameful acts. And they offended people who were sad and grieved sorrowfully, calling them Jews and saying, "The tsar does as he wants, but, like Jews, you only complain about it." Even the Muscovites trod the path of perdition, did not repent before God, but enjoyed the gains from their speculations and, although bemoaning much, still cared primarily for the accumulation of wealth.

Becoming insanely proud, this defrocked monk and impostor ordered that his title be, "The most illustrious, invincible Caesar." This accursed man believed that by bearing the name of the Tsar he could win the highest and most sought-after of honors.

There was a high official at the court, whose name was Timothy Osipov, who was a person of pious behavior and disposition, and who gave little heed to this impostor's ambitions. This virtuous man saw that much harm was being done by this defrocked monk and his councilors. Seeing the unnatural and high title the impostor had given himself, this man realized that each man is mortal and possessed by passions and therefore should not call himself an "invincible Caesar," since only God is invincible. This Timothy Osipov was a man devoted to God, and he prayed piously and the fasts were strictly kept in his house. Once, after he had received the most wonderful and life-giving Communion—the pure flesh and blood of Christ, Our Lord, he went to the tsar's palace and daringly exposed the defrocked monk before the people, saying: "Verily, verily thou art Grishka Otrepiev, a defrocked monk, and not an 'invincible Caesar.' Thou art not Dmitry, the son of the tsar, but a slave to sin, and a heretic."

The defrocked impostor could not stand such a denunciation and shame, but ordered the man immediately executed. So ended the life and the heroic deed of this worthy martyr.

Once the impostor sent to the Khan of Crimea the most dishonorable of gifts. He ordered a fur coat made of swines' skins for the khan, and wrote him that he was preparing a campaign against the Crimea, the land of the southern sun, and that he himself would appear there soon to plunder the Crimean homes. And he ordered all Russians, as well as the Poles, to his service and to prepare the campaign against the city of Azov.[9] And he immediately sent a large corps of selected artillerymen to the city of Elets. He ordered that the army prepare to advance either by boats on the river Don or on land across the prairie. Rumors about these military moves spread to Constantinople, and the Turks began to prepare for the spilling of Christian blood. Some people claimed, I do not know whether it is true or not, that this defrocked monk wanted to arouse the Crimean Khan and the Turks, so that many Christian Russians would fall on the battlefield. It does appear that he was not really interested in victory over the sons of Hagar, but wanted rather to withdraw the Orthodox Russians in order that he might afterward settle the Muscovite realm with Poles. But the Lord himself did not allow this ambitious man's plan to come to fruition.

HOW THE DEFROCKED MONK PREPARED A PLOT WITH THE POLES TO KILL MUSCOVITES, BUT WAS HIMSELF KILLED BY THE MUSCOVITE BOYARS

This enemy, the defrocked monk, plotted with the heretics [the Poles] to massacre the Russian people of all ranks, beginning with the courtiers and ending with common officers. And he intended to have a great celebration with the shooting of artillery in the Pond Field at the Strelets Gate. And when the people went to this celebration, then he would order the gate to be closed and all would be slain.

[9] The city of Azov, located at the mouth of the river Don not far from the Azov Sea, was an important Turkish-Tatar fortress at that time.

But this base plot did not come to fruition because two days before the celebration was to have taken place, and ten days after his improper wedding, this accursed man died an evil death, having reigned for one year. He used to say of himself that he was thirty-four years of age, but his friends, the demons, didn't give him many more years of life. And so the writing of St. John Chrysostom, "Such is the honor which demons render to those who love them," was fulfilled.

After his death, the people of Moscow gave themselves to drinking in their joy, instead of rendering thanks to God. And everyone bragged about his deeds in murdering the impostor, Pseudo-Dmitry, and all boasted about their courage. But the people forgot to give thanks through prayer in the Church of the Holy Virgin for this most glorious victory. Once, a great miracle was performed by the Most Pure Holy Virgin in Constantinople, but this miracle against the Persians and the Scythians occurred on the sea and beyond the walls of the city, and not within the city walls.[10] In Moscow, however, the miracle occurred within the city. This accursed heretic was able to keep everyone firmly in tow, and he was loved by everyone. And yet, on that day, by the command of God, everyone rose against him. And a great amount of heretical [Polish] blood was spilled in the streets of Moscow. But, instead of rendering thanks to the Righteous Avenger, the people were seized by insanity and pride. And therefore the wrath of God did not subside; but we the Russians did not recognize the divine plan and designs, and were not able to realize from what evils the Lord had delivered us.

36. *Avraamy Palitsyn: Answer of the Defenders of the Holy Trinity–St. Sergius Monastery to the Polish Request of Surrender*

One of the most dramatic events of the Time of Troubles was the besieging of the Holy Trinity–St. Sergius Monastery by Polish and Lithuanian troops in 1609. After a long siege and many attempted stormings of the well-fortified monastery-fortress, the commanders of the Poles and Lithuanians, John Peter Paul Sapieha and John Alexander Lisowski, demanded

[10] The author refers to the so-called Miracle of the Holy Virgin's Veil which, according to the legend, protected the city of Constantinople against a Russian attack.

the monastery's surrender. The commanders of the Russian troops defending the monastery, Prince Gregory Dolgorukov and Alexis Golokhsvastov, together with Abbot Ioasaf and the leading elders, refused to capitulate, and answered the Polish and Lithuanian commanders in a letter that well reflects the bitterness, hatred, and fierce national feeling that reigned in both camps. For the defenders of this monastery, surrender to the Poles would not only have meant betrayal of the national cause but also betrayal of the Orthodox Faith. There are reasons to believe that the letter was written by Avraamy Palitsyn himself, as he was certainly the most skillful writer in the monastery at that time.

The present translation follows the text of the letter contained in *Skazanie Avraamiia Palitsyna* edited by O. Derzhavina and E. V. Kolosova, Academy of Sciences of the U.S.S.R. Moscow and Leningrad, 1955, pages 110–115.

◆ ◆ ◆

To the proud commanders Sapieha and Lisowski! Your dark majesties and your warriors are the opposers of God, the abomination of dissolution, and know that you attempt in vain to lead us, a flock of Orthodox Christians, into temptation. You should know that even a ten-year-old Christian youth from the Holy Trinity–St. Sergius Monastery would laugh at your request. And as far as your letter is concerned, we spit on it upon receiving it. What man would, at the expense of his soul, prefer darkness to light, a lie to the truth, honor to dishonor, and freedom to bitter slave labor? How could we forsake our eternal, holy, and true Orthodox Christian Faith of the Greek confession and submit ourselves to the new heretical law which betrays the Christian Faith and which was cursed by the four ecumenical patriarchs.[1] What would be our gain and honor in betraying our Orthodox sovereign and tsar[2] and submitting ourselves to our enemy, the impostor and rebel?[3] And you, people of the Latin faith, have become like Jews, and even worse, for the Jews didn't recognize the Lord and consequently crucified him. Yet how can we, who know our Orthodox sovereign, concede to your

[1] The four patriarchs refers to the four patriarchs of the cities of Constantinople, Antioch, Jerusalem, and Alexandria who broke with the Pope of Rome owing to the latter's claim for primacy.

[2] Sapieha and Lisowski fought in the name of the second impostor, that is, the second Pseudo-Dmitry, while the monastery refused to capitulate in the name of Tsar Vasily Shuysky (1605–1610).

[3] This refers to the second Pseudo-Dmitry.

request to forsake our Christian tsar despite the fact that our grandfathers were born in the vineyard of our true pastor Christ and under the rule of a Christian tsar? And how can you attempt to tempt us with false kindness, vain flattery, and ill-gained wealth. We shall remain faithful to the pledge we gave on the cross, for we do not care for all the wealth in the entire world.

37. *Prince Ivan M. Katyrev-Rostovsky*
A Description of the Tsars and Their Families

The Book of Annals, written by Prince Ivan M. Katyrev-Rostovsky, gives one of the best accounts of the Time of Troubles. Others who wrote about this first great national crisis in Muscovite Russia followed both the basic outline and the literary style found here. Since it gives a vivid description of this difficult time, the author remaining quite unbiased and keeping to the historical truth, it is an important source for historians. *The Book of Annals* is also significant for several innovations, such as the first literary portraits of the heroes of the narrative, especially of the tsars and their families. *The Book of Annals* was as well one of the first Russian works to describe nature and the changes of the seasons superbly; the account of the coming of spring is particularly noteworthy. The author often used rhymed passages, and there are many rhymed couplets to be found throughout the text.

The reader will find in this selection from *The Book of Annals* the portraits of the tsars and their families. The translation follows one of the earliest extant manuscripts, published in *Russkaia istoricheskaia biblioteka*, Volume 13, St. Petersburg, 1912.

◆ ◆ ◆

A SHORT DESCRIPTION OF THE MUSCOVITE TSARS, THEIR PHYSICAL APPEARANCES, STATURES, AND TEMPERAMENTS

[TSAR IVAN IV (THE TERRIBLE), REIGNED FROM 1533 TO 1584]

Tsar Ivan was physically unattractive, had gray eyes, a hooked and long nose, and was tall, lean, and with broad shoulders and chest. He had great physical prowess and was a person of great acumen, being well read, erudite, and very eloquent. He was fearsome to the enemy, and was always prepared to fight for the fatherland. He was cruel to his subjects given to him by the Lord, being always ready to spill their blood, and both merciless and daring at killing. He ordered that many people be slain, from infants to the aged; he laid waste to many of his own cities; and many clergymen were thrown into prisons and mercilessly executed at his orders. He committed many other evil deeds to his own people, deflowering many girls and women in his lust. This Tsar Ivan did many good things, however, and he cared very much for his armies, generously rewarding them from his treasury. Such was Tsar Ivan.

[TSAR FEDOR (IVAN'S SON) REIGNED FROM 1584 TO 1598]

Tsar Fedor was short of stature, and appeared as a man who constantly fasted. He was most humble, and greatly cared after his soul, standing before the icons and praying endlessly. He generously gave alms to the poor. He was not taken up with worldly matters, but concerned himself only with the salvation of his soul. And so, from his infancy to the very end of his days, his life was dedicated to matters of salvation; and thus God gave peace to his reign, brought his enemies in tow, and granted him a blessed epoch. Such was Tsar Fedor.

[TSAR BORIS (GODUNOV, BROTHER-IN-LAW OF TSAR FEDOR) REIGNED FROM 1598 TO 1605]

Tsar Boris shone in the full bloom of his handsome appearance, and he surpassed many people in his attractiveness. He was of average stature. He was a man of great intelligence, had a marvelous power of reasoning, and was a clever polemicist and eloquent orator. He was a faithful Christian, gave generously to the poor, and was a great builder. He spent much time on state affairs and he performed a great many marvelous deeds. He had, however, two great shortcomings, for he was not granted a certain virtue by God: he used to go too much to doctors, and he was obsessed by an insatiable desire for power. And he dared to slay those who should have been tsars before himself. And for such deeds he received divine retribution.

[TSAR FEDOR II, THE SON OF BORIS, WHO REIGNED SOME WEEKS IN 1605]

Tsar Fedor, the son of Tsar Boris, was a marvelous youth. He was so handsome that he blossomed like a flower in the meadow, having been created by God like a lily blooming in the fields. His eyes were large and black; his complexion was light and white as milk; his stature was average; and his body was slightly stout. He was brought by his father to the learned books, and he was clever and eloquent in polemics. And never did any senseless or coarse words come from his lips, but he was devoted to the faith and to the reading of books.

[TSAREVNA XENIA (DAUGHTER OF BORIS AND SISTER OF TSAR FEDOR II)]

Tsarevna Xenia, Tsar Boris's daughter, was a maiden of wonderful spirit, physically very attractive, of light complexion, and had beautiful rosy cheeks, red lips, and big black eyes. From her there radiated graciousness. Being sad and shedding tears, her graciousness would become particularly radiant. Her eyebrows were thick and joined, and her body was supple, while her skin was as white as milk. She was neither too tall nor too short; her hair was black and long, covering her shoulders. She was the most distinguished among maidens, and she was accustomed to reading books. She shone by her forceful and distinguished speech, and she did well in whatever she attempted. She had a fondness for beautiful voices, and loved to listen to church music.

[PSEUDO-DMITRY, REIGNED FROM 1605–1606]

This defrocked impostor was of very short stature, but was powerfully built and of great physical strength. His face did not have the distinction of a tsar, but it was very common and his body was covered with dark spots. But he was very witty and was rather learned. He was a daring and eloquent speaker, loved horseracing, was courageous in fighting the enemy, was brave and strong, and cared greatly for warriors.

[TSAR VASILY SHUYSKY (THE HEAD OF THE POWERFUL AND ARISTOCRATIC FAMILY OF BOYARS, HE ORGANIZED THE MURDER OF THE PRETENDER, PSEUDO-DMITRY, AND WAS THEREAFTER ELECTED BY THE BOYARS TO SUCCEED HIM) REIGNED FROM 1606 to 1610]

Tsar Vasily was short of stature, physically very unattractive, and had eyes that were dull, as if he were blind. He was rather cultured, and his reasoning was sound and pointed. He cared only for those people who brought him gossip and rumors about people, and he used to receive such persons with a joyful face, and with sweet pleasure, did he listen to them. He was given to sorcery, and cared little for the military.

38. *K. Druzhina-Osoryin*
The Life of Yuliania Lazarevskaia

THE *vita* of Yuliania Osoryin, called Lazarevskaia after the village of Lazarevo, where she lived and died, was written in the first quarter of the seventeenth century by her son, Kallistrat Druzhina-Osoryin. Although written with the purpose of glorifying her holy life, this work is very different from the typical *vitae* of saints of medieval Russia. With the exception of the descriptions of some miracles and the appearances of demons, Yuliania's biography much more resembles a narrative from a family chronicle than a hagiographic work. The biographer gives a detailed account of the domestic relations of Yuliania's family, and often remarks that the author, himself, and his family, witnessed her works and life. Yuliania was neither a nun who spent her life in a convent, nor a princess whose Christian charity and works gave her the halo of a saintly protectoress. She spent all her life with her family, and her biography is filled with the details of every-day events. While her life was one of prayer and Christian piety, the fact that she remained all her life with her husband and children as a devoted wife, mother, and daughter-in-law distinguishes this *vita* from the usual hagiographies dealing with heroes who performed miraculous deeds or defended the Orthodox Faith, and who were usually either hermits, church leaders, or pious rulers. With this *vita* there began to appear in Russia a realistic, secular biography.

This narrative is written in plain language, completely devoid of the panegyrics, lengthy epithets, and stylistic embellishments that characterize Russian lives of saints. The present translation follows an early seventeenth-century text published by M. Skripil in *Russkaia provest XVII veka*, Moscow, 1954, pages 39–47.

✦ ✦ ✦

In the days of the pious Tsar and Great Prince Ivan Vasilievich[1] of all Russia, there was at his imperial court a good and

[1] Ivan IV, or Ivan Vasilievich, usually called the Terrible or Dread, reigned over Russia from 1530 to 1584.

charitable man by the name of Yustin Nediurev, a housekeeper by rank.[2] He had a wife named Stefanida, equally devout and compassionate, daughter of a certain Gregory Lukin from the city of Murom. They led a pious and virtuous life, had several sons and daughters, and possessed considerable wealth and many serfs. To them was born this blessed Yuliania.

Her mother died when she was six years of age, and Yuliania was taken to the lands of Murom by her grandmother, who raised her in piety for six years. When the grandmother died, Yuliania's aunt, Natalia, wife of Putila Arapov, took, at the grandmother's behest, the young girl to her house. As the blessed Yuliania had loved God and the Holy Virgin since her very youth, she respected and honored her aunt and her aunt's daughters. She was humble and obedient, assiduous in prayer and fasting. Because of her fasting, she was much berated by her aunt and ridiculed by her cousins, who said, "O insane one! Why dost thou exhaust thy flesh and so ruin thy beauty, while thou art so young?" They urged her to take food and drink every morning, but she did not yield to them; rather she withdrew in silence, even though she accepted everything with gratitude and was obedient to all. She also refrained from laughter and games, as from her very childhood she was meek, silent, and obedient, and never rude or haughty. Although frequently urged by her companions to take part in games and frivolous songs, she did not comply, pretending confusion in order to conceal her virtues. Instead, she applied herself with great diligence to spinning and hoop embroidery, working late into the night. She also did all the sewing for orphans and ailing widows in the village, and supplied the sick and needy with all kinds of goods. Everyone admired her wisdom and devotion.

The fear of God dwelt in her. There was no church in the village, nor any closer than within two miles; so Yuliania had no chance to go to church in her maidenhood. Neither did she ever hear the reading of the Holy Scriptures, nor any preacher teaching salvation, but God himself instructed her in virtuous ways. When she was in her sixteenth year she was given in marriage to a virtuous and wealthy man, named Georgii Osoryin. They were married by a priest, Potapy, in the church of the righteous Lazar, in her husband's estate. This priest instructed them in the law of God according to the rules of the holy fathers, and she carefully listened to the teaching and instructions, carrying them out in her deeds. Her parents-in-law were

[2] The names of the relatives and other people mentioned in this *vita* are the names of real historical personages.

still alive and, when they saw her of mature age and accomplished in virtue, they commanded her to take charge of the whole household. She humbly obeyed them in all things, never contradicting them, but respecting them and fulfilling all their orders without fail, so that all marveled at her. Many people tested Yuliania in conversation and she gave a seemly and reasonable reply to every question, so that all wondered at her good sense, and glorified God. She prayed much every evening, and made one hundred and more genuflections. Upon arising each morning, she did the same, together with her husband. When her husband would be away in the tsar's service in Astrakhan[3] for a year or two, and sometimes even for three years, she went without sleep all night, praying or working, weaving or embroidering. She would sell her work and give the price to the poor or for the building of churches; she gave many alms in secret by night. During the day she managed the household and cared for widows and orphans as a true mother, ministering to them with her own hands and giving them to drink and to eat. She provided the serfs, both men and women, with food and clothing, and assigned them work according to their strength. She called no one a rude name, nor did she command anyone to pour water while she washed her hands, or to take off her shoes, but did all this herself. She instructed and corrected foolish serfs with meekness and humility, taking the blame upon herself and denouncing no one, but placing all her hopes in God and the Holy Virgin, She called for help upon the great wonder-worker Nicholas, and he assisted her.

One night in her husband's absence, as Yuliania arose for prayer, as was her wont, she was seized with fear and great terror by the attack of demons. Being young and inexperienced, she was frightened, lay down on the bed, and fell fast asleep. Then she saw many demons coming at her with weapons, saying, "If thou wilt not cease thy efforts, we will straightway destroy thee." She prayed to God and to the Most Holy Virgin and to St. Nicholas the wonder-worker. And St. Nicholas appeared to her, holding a large book; he dispersed the demons, so they disappeared like smoke. Lifting up his right hand, he blessed her, saying: "My daughter, take courage and stand firm and do not be afraid of the demons' threats! For Christ hath

3 All Russian nobles were supposed to serve either with the army or in the civil service. This service was not a permanent one, but each noble could be summoned into the service as soon as the necessity arose. The city of Astrakhan, where Yuliania's husband served, is located at the delta of the Volga in the vicinity of the Caspian Sea.

commanded me to guard thee from demons and from evil men." Then she straightway awoke from sleep and clearly saw the holy man leaving the chamber through the door, quick as lightning. Rising promptly, she followed him, and forthwith he became invisible; yet the anteroom of the chamber was securely locked. Taking this as a message, Yuliania rejoiced, praising God, and was more diligent in good works than before.

In a short time, for our sins God's wrath fell upon the Russian land, and a great famine occurred, and many starved to death. Yuliania gave many alms in secret; she began to accept food from her mother-in-law for morning and midday meals, and gave all to the poor and hungry. So her mother-in-law said to her: "How comes it that thou hast changed thy custom? When there was an abundance of bread, I was not able to make thee eat early and midday meals, and now, when there is a dearth of food, thou eatest!" Wishing to keep her secret, Yuliania answered, "When I did not bear children, I did not want to eat, but when I started to bear them I grew weak and I cannot eat my fill. Not only in the daytime, but many times in the night as well I am hungry, but I am ashamed to ask." The mother-in-law was glad to hear it, and sent her enough food not only in the daytime but also at night, for in their house there was an abundance of bread and of everything. However, while receiving food from her mother-in-law, Yuliania did not partake of it herself, but gave all to the poor. When anyone would die, she hired women to cleanse him, gave sheets to wrap the bodies, and money for the burial. When any deceased whatever were buried in their village, she prayed for the remission of their sins.

In a short time, there was a severe pestilence among the people and many died from the plague. Many locked their doors so that those who were afflicted would not enter their homes; and they would not even touch the garments of the ill. Yet, secretly away from her parents-in-law, Yuliania healed many of the afflicted, washing them in the bathhouse with her own hands; she prayed to God for their recovery, and if they died she prayed for their salvation, hired men to bury them, and ordered the forty days' prayer.[4] When her parents-in-law, after having been tonsured,[5] died in extreme old age, Yuliania buried them with honor: she gave many alms in their memory, and

[4] In the Orthodox Church special prayers are required for the dead for forty days after their death.

[5] It was the custom in medieval Russia, especially among the aristocracy, to take monastic vows shortly before the approach of death.

ordered many forty days' prayers. She also had the Mass celebrated for them and had meals served at her house for the priests, monks, and beggars every day during the forty days, and sent alms to the prisons. At that time her husband was serving for three years in Astrakhan, and she spent a great part of their wealth in almsgiving, not only in those days, but throughout these years, honoring the memory of her dead parents-in-law.

Having thus lived with her husband for many years in great virtue, according to God's commandments, Yuliania gave birth to sons and daughters. The devil, who hateth all good, sought to cause her strife, arousing frequent discord among the children and the serfs. Reasoning sensibly and wisely, Yuliania restrained them all, but the devil provoked a serf to slay the eldest son; then another son was killed in the service. Although she grieved, it was for their souls, and not because of their deaths. And she honored them with memorial Masses, prayers, and almsgiving. Then Yuliania begged her husband to give her leave to go to a nunnery. He did not let her go, but they agreed to live together yet have no bodily intercourse. She continued to prepare his bed as usual, yet she herself, after long evening prayers, would lie down on the stove without any bedding. She lay on firewood with the sharp edges against her body, and she put iron keys under her ribs, and on these she took little sleep until her serfs fell asleep. Then she would rise to pray throughout the night, until daylight, when she went to church for Matins and Mass. She occupied herself diligently with handiwork and managed her house in a manner pleasing to God. She provided her serfs with sufficient food, and appointed each of them a task according to their strength. She cared for widows and orphans, and helped the poor in all things.

Ten years after their bodily separation, Yuliania's husband passed away, and she buried him reverently, honoring him with memorial Masses, prayers, the forty-day service, and alms. From then on, she rejected even more all worldly things that she might better care for her soul and emulate the holy women of old and, in this way, to please God. She prayed and fasted, went every day to church, gave unending alms, so that ofttimes not a silver coin remained in her house and she had to borrow in order to give alms to the poor. When winter came, Yuliania borrowed silver from her children for warm clothing, but gave even this money to the poor and she herself passed the winter without any warm clothes. She wore her shoes over bare feet, using nutshells and sharp potsherds instead of inner soles so as to mortify the flesh.

Once the winter was so cold that the ground cracked from the frost, and for some time Yuliania did not go to church but prayed at home. It came to pass that once the local priest came alone to church very early and heard a voice from the icon of the Holy Virgin, which said: "Go and ask merciful Yuliania why she does not come to church and pray? Her prayers at home are also pleasing to God, but not so much as her prayers in church. However, let her be venerated, for she is already no less than sixty years of age, and the Holy Spirit resides within her!" The priest, being seized by awe, came forthwith to Yuliania, fell at her feet, asked her forgiveness, and told her of the vision. She treated him severely because he spoke of it in the presence of others. And she said, "Thou hast been tempted when thou spake of it; for how may I, a sinner, be worthy of such heavenly intervention?" And she adjured him not to tell anyone. Yet she herself went to church, prayed with warm tears, and venerated the icon of the Holy Virgin.

From then on, Yuliania even more devoted herself to God, going to church and praying every evening in the porch of the church, where there were icons of our Lady and of St. Nicholas. One evening she entered it to pray, as was her wont, and suddenly the chamber was filled with demons who wanted to kill her with various weapons. But she prayed to God with tears, and St. Nicholas appeared to her. He carried a club and chased the demons away, so that they disappeared like smoke. Yet he caught one of them, and tormented it. He blessed St. Yuliania with a cross, and forthwith became invisible. Still the demon screamed, crying: "I have always made trouble for thee: I have aroused strife amongst thy children and slaves. Yet I did not dare to come close to thee because of thy charity, humility, and prayer." (For Yuliania incessantly said Jesus' prayer with beads in her hands; and whether she was eating or drinking, or doing anything, she said the prayer incessantly; even when she was asleep, her lips moved and her soul was aroused to the praise of God; many times we saw her asleep, and her hand was moving the beads.) The demon ran away from her, screaming, "A great disaster befell me now because of thee, but I will make trouble for thee in thy old age: thou wilt starve, instead of feeding others!" But she blessed herself with the sign of the cross, and the demon disappeared. She came to us sore afraid and changed in the face. Seeing her perturbed, we questioned her, but she did not tell us anything. Yet, not too long later, she told us secretly, and bade us to tell no one.

Yuliania lived as a widow for nine years and showed great goodness to everyone. She gave away much property as alms, retaining only the essential for home needs; she rationed food year after year and gave all surplus to the needy. She lived even until the reign of Tsar Boris.[6] At that time there was a great famine in the whole land of Russia—such that, in dire need, many partook of unclean meats and of human flesh, and untold numbers starved to death. In Yuliania's house there was great scarcity of food and of all necessary supplies, for the sown spring rye never sprouted, and both horses and cattle died. She implored her children and serfs that they in no way touch anything belonging to others, nor steal, and whatever cattle and clothes and vessels were left, she sold for rye to feed the servants. She also gave considerable alms, for even in destitution she did not discontinue her customary charity, but let no one asking for help go away empty-handed. She herself came to extreme need, and not a grain was left in her house; yet she was not alarmed but placed all hope in God.

That year Yuliania moved to another village, called Vochnevo, in the confines of Nizhny-Novgorod, where there was no church closer than within two miles. Being afflicted with old age, and destitute, she did not go to church but prayed at home. That grieved her sorely, yet she remembered St. Kornily and other saints, and knew that praying at home did not harm them. When destitution increased in her house, she set the serfs free so they would not be exhausted by hunger. Those of them who were virtuous promised to endure with her, while others left, and she let them go with her blessing and prayers, being not the least angered. Then Yuliania commanded the remaining slaves to gather goosefoot and wood bark and, making bread therefrom, she lived on it with her children and the serfs. And through her prayers that bread was sweet. She continued to give to the poor and let no pauper go without; at that time the poor were innumerable. Her neighbors said to the beggars, "Why do you go to Yuliania's house? For even she herself is starving!" And the beggars told them, "We have walked through many villages and have received pure bread, but we did not relish it so much, for sweet is the bread of this widow." They called her this, for many did not know her name. And the neighbors, who

[6] Tsar Boris, brother-in-law of the last representative of the dynasty of Rurik, Tsar Fedor, ruled from 1598–1605. During his reign there were both plagues and great famines in Russia.

had plenty of bread, sent to Yuliania's house to ask for some of hers, to try it, and they also witnessed that her bread was very sweet. They marveled, saying to themselves, "Her servants are good at baking bread," for they did not understand that the bread was sweet through Yuliania's prayer. Yuliania endured this destitution for two years, and she neither grieved nor was troubled, nor complained, and did not sin with her lips, neither did she charge God foolishly. And she was not broken by poverty, but was more cheerful than in earlier years.

As her righteous passing drew near, Yuliania became ill on the twenty-sixth day of December and stayed abed for six days. In daytime she prayed as she lay in bed, and at night she arose to pray to God, standing without assistance and supported by no one, for, as she said, "Even from the sick God demands prayer." At daybreak on the second day of January, she summoned her confessor and received the last rites. Then, sitting up, she summoned her children and serfs and instructed them in love, prayer, charity, and in the other virtues. She added this also: "Since my youth and with all my heart I have desired to take monastic vows, but because of my sins and wretchedness this was not granted to me. I was not worthy, being a wretched and lowly sinner, God willing it so; glory be to His righteous judgment." She commanded that a censer be prepared and that incense be put in it; she kissed all those present and bade them peace and forgiveness. She lay down, crossed herself thrice, and, having wound the beads around her arm, she spake her last, saying, "Praise God in all things! Into Thy hands, O Lord, I commend my spirit. Amen!" And she surrendered her soul into the hands of God, whom she had loved since her youth. And all saw a golden halo around her head, such as is painted around the heads of the saints on icons. Having washed her, they laid her out in a storeroom, and that night they saw there light and burning candles, and a strong fragrance wafted from that storeroom. Having put her into an oaken coffin, they took her back to the confines of Murom, and buried her beside her husband at the wall of the church of the righteous Lazar, in the village of Lazarevo, which was three miles from the city. And this came to pass in the year 1604 (7112), on the tenth day of January.

They later erected over Yuliania a church in the name of Archangel Michael. A stove happened to be over her grave and, through the removal of ashes, the earth above her became thicker through the years. In the year 1615 (7123), on the eighth day of August, her son Georgii passed away, and they started to dig a grave for him in the porch between the church and the stove, for that porch had no floor. They found Yuliania's coffin intact and on top of the earth. It was in no way damaged, and they wondered whose it was, as for many years no one had been buried there. On the tenth day of the same month they buried her son Georgii next to her coffin, and went to his house to offer refreshments to the burial attendants. But the women who attended the funeral opened the coffin and saw it to be full of fragrant myrrh. Being seized with awe at that time, they did not reveal anything, but after the departure of the guests they related what had happened. Having heard this, we marveled. And when we opened the coffin, we saw even as the women had told us. We ladled out a small vessel of that myrrh and took it to the cathedral church of the city of Murom. In the daytime that myrrh looked like beetroot kvass, and at night it thickened, looking like crimson oil. We did not dare to open the grave and to view all the body. We saw only her legs and thighs intact, yet her head we did not see, because a log from the oven lay on the end of the coffin.

Next to the coffin there was an opening under the stove. In the night the coffin, by itself, moved toward the east. And, having gone the distance of two yards, it stopped at the church wall. This same night many people heard the ringing of the church bell. When they arrived, they saw nothing; only a fragrance emanated. Many people heard of it and came there to anoint themselves with the myrrh. And they received relief from various diseases. When all the myrrh had been distributed, a dustlike sand began to issue near the coffin. Those suffering of various ailments came and rubbed themselves with this sand and received relief. And even to this day they do so. And we would not dare to write this if there had been no witnesses.

39. *The Life of Archpriest Avvakum by Himself*

A SIMILAR fate befell the most unusual literary works of both the Kievan and Muscovite eras of Russian literature. Because of their nonconformity with the spirit of the Russian Church, both the *Lay of Igor's Campaign* and the *Life of Archpriest Avvakum by Himself* remained unavailable to the general reader, and therefore did not have a considerable influence on the further development of Russian literature. Once discovered, however, they fascinated the Russian reading public.

Born in 1621, Avvakum became a priest at the age of twenty. In the early 1640's he joined the revival movement of the Zealots of Piety, or Seekers After God (Bogoliubtsy), which attracted many representatives of the Russian Church at that time and which tried to breathe new life into Russian Orthodoxy. For several years both the government and the Church leaders supported this movement, but when the authoritarian and unbending Nikon became patriarch in 1652, he moved against this revival because he saw in its activities a threat to the authority of the hierarchy. Officially, the conflict arose over the re-editing of the missal and changes in the ritual, both of which Nikon revised to conform to those of the contemporary Greek Church. Avvakum and his followers advocated the ancient texts and rites which had originally been introduced into Russia from Greece, some seven centuries earlier. The real core of the conflict, however, was different. Nikon sought the unquestioning submission of the Church to the authority of the patriarch, and received the support of Tsar Alexis and the state, since they also desired stronger controls over the Church by both the central ecclesiastic offices and the state itself. Avvakum and his followers, who represented the lower clergy and their parishioners, felt that the parish priests and local laity should have a greater voice in Church affairs. Moreover, in opposition to domination and disciplining of the Church from above, they proposed a genuine religious regeneration of the Church on the local level.

In 1653 Patriarch Nikon succeeded in deporting Avvakum, Ivan Neronov, and other leaders of the reform movement, and thus Avvakum spent some nine years in Siberia. He was permitted to return to Moscow in 1662, but his fierce defense of his principles led once more to his deportation to northern Russia and, finally, to his censure by the Church council. In 1666 he was condemned for his opposition to the ecclesiastic authorities and for upholding the ancient traditions of the Russian Church. The next year this condemnation was reaffirmed by a larger Church council, in which not only the Russian hierarchs participated but also the Greek patriarchs of Alexandria, Antioch, and Jerusalem. This time Avvakum and his followers, Deacon Fedor (Theodore), the monk Epiphany, and the priest Lazar, were deported to Pustozersk, a small settlement and fort in the extreme northeast of European Russia, about a hundred miles from the Arctic Ocean. They remained there some fifteen years, and during that time Pustozersk became the spiritual center of the Old Believer movement, as it was called. It was there that Avvakum's autobiography and his many treatises and epistles were written. In 1682 the government, which was unable to curb the spread of this movement, ordered that Avvakum and his three comrades should be burned at the stake.

The autobiography of Avvakum is certainly not the first Russian work in which an author describes his own life and deeds, but it is the most important one in old Russian literature. Avvakum uses a simple but vigorous, clear, and laconic style in which there are hardly any of those stylistic devices of ornamentation which so characterized the literary works of his predecessors and contemporaries. His narration is dynamic, and reflects the active, unbending nature of the author. Avvakum rarely used the solemn Church Slavonic literary language, but turned to colloquial Russian. He does not hesitate to use crude folk sayings that lend expressiveness to his style. A keen observer and penetrating psychologist, he gives short, pointed, sometimes ironic portrayals of his contemporaries, among which perhaps the best are those describing his wife, Nastasia Markovna, and Tsar Alexis.

The *Life of Archpriest Avvakum by Himself* is given here in the translation by Jane Harrison and Hope Mirrlees, published by Leonard and Virginia Woolf at the Hogarth Press, London, 1924. This work is given in its entirety except for the introduction, which does not deal at all with Avvakum's life but consists rather of theological arguments and considerations, and also excepting the final section describing "The Healing of Those Possessed." For the convenience of the reader, the work has been divided into chapters by the editor of this anthology. The editor has also made some minor changes in personal and place names, and occasionally in wording, for a better understanding.

◆ ◆ ◆

I. Family Background

I was born in the Nizhny country, beyond the River Kudma, in the village of Grigorovo.[1] My father was given to strong drink; but my mother was given to fasting and prayer, and did most constantly instruct me in the fear of God. Now one day at a neighbor's I saw a dead ox, and that night, rising from my

[1] The village of Grigorovo is in the Nizhny-Novgorod (presently Gorky) region on the right shore of the Volga.

bed, I wept abundantly for my soul before the holy icons, pondering mortality and how I too must surely die; and from that day it became my custom to pray every night. Then my mother was left a widow, and I, young that I was, an orphan, and we were driven out by our kinsmen. My mother resolved that I should marry. And I prayed to the Mother of God that she would give me such a wife as should help me to win salvation. And in that village there was a maiden, she too was an orphan, who was wont to go continually to church, and her name was Anastasia. Her father was the blacksmith Marko, exceedingly rich, but when he died all his substance was wasted. So she lived in poverty and she would pray to God that he might so compass it that she should be joined to me in matrimony; and he willed that it should be so. At that same time my mother went to God, having first taken the veil, and died in the odor of sanctity. And I, because of persecution, moved to another place, and at the age of twenty I was ordained deacon and, after two years, priest. When I had been a priest eight years, I was raised to the rank of archpriest by Orthodox bishops, and this was twenty years ago. And it is thirty years in all that I have been in Holy Orders.

II. The Years of Mission with "Seekers After God" and Clashes with the Administration (1640–1652)

And when I was still but a parish priest I had many spiritual children—it would be five or six hundred souls in all. And never resting, I, miserable sinner, in churches and houses and at crossways, by towns and hamlets, even in the city of the tsar and in the country of Siberia, was diligent during a period of some twenty-five years in teaching and preaching the Word of God.

And in these days of my ministry a young woman came to confess to me, burdened with many sins, guilty of fornication and of all the sins of the flesh, and, weeping, she began to acquaint me with them all, leaving nothing out, standing before the Gospels. And I, thrice-accursed, though a leech, fell sick myself. I inwardly burned with a lecherous fire, and that hour was bitter to me. I lit three candles and fixed them to the lectern and placed my right hand in the flame, and held it there till the evil passion was burned out and, when I had dismissed the young woman and laid away my vestments, I prayed and went to my house, grievously humbled in spirit.

The time must have been midnight, and when I reached my house I wept before the icons so that my eyes swelled; and prayed diligently that God might remove from me my spiritual children, in that the burden was too heavy for me. And I threw myself upon the ground face downwards, sobbing bitterly. And as I lay I swooned and wist not how I was weeping, and in my fancy I was transported to the banks of the Volga and gazed at it with the eyes of my heart; and this is what I saw: On it were sailing two stately ships of gold, and their oars were of gold, and their masts were of gold and all was of gold; at the helm of each was sitting a man, and I said: "Whose are these ships?" They answered: "Luke's and Laurence's." Now these had been two of my spiritual children, and they had set me and my house on the path of salvation, and their end had been pleasing to God. And after that I saw a third ship, not adorned with gold, but pied with many and varied hues, red and white, and blue and black and ash, so that the mind of man would be hard put to grasp at the same time all its loveliness and excellence. And a young man, all shining, sat at the helm, and steered, and I called out to him: "Whose ship?" and he who was on her answered: "Thine. Sail away on her with thy wife and children, if thou wilt persist." And I was troubled not a little, and sitting there I pondered the meaning of the vision and of the sailing.[2]

And but a little time after this—as it has been written—*the sorrows of death compassed me, and the pains of hell gat hold upon me: I found trouble and sorrow*. A headman abducted her daughter from a widow, and I besought him to return the orphan to her mother; he scorned our prayers and raised up storms against me; he came to the church with a band of followers, and they crushed me to death. And I, having lain dead for half an hour and more, was brought to life by a wave of God's hand, and he was sore afraid and renounced the girl for my sake. Then the Devil prompted him: he came to the church, he beat me and dragged me, clad in my vestments, along the ground by the legs, and while he did it I was praying.

And likewise another headman at another time became as a wild beast against me. Breaking into my house, he beat me and gnawed the fingers of my hand, like a dog, with his teeth; and when his throat was full of blood, then he loosened his teeth from my hand and, throwing me aside, went to his house. But I, blessing God, wrapped up my hand in a cloth, and started for vespers; and on the way he leaped out on me again with two small pistols and, standing close to me, fired from one of

[2] The symbol of the ship is very common in Russian literature, and usually symbolized the life of a man. It has a biblical origin.

them and, by God's will, the powder exploded in the pan and the pistol missed fire. So he threw the pistol on the ground and in the same manner fired from the other, and God willed it should be in the same sort, for that pistol also missed fire. But I, praying diligently, with one hand signed him with the Cross and bowed low before him; then began he to snarl imprecations, but I said to him: "Out of thy mouth, Ivan Rodionovich, let blessings proceed." And next he took from me my homestead and drove me out with violence, seizing all my goods, leaving me not even a morsel of bread to eat on the road.

During that time my son Prokopy was born, the same that today lies a prisoner with his mother dug into a pit in the earth. So I took my staff and his mother took the unbaptized infant, and we set off on our wanderings, whither God should lead us, and on the way we baptized our son, even as Phillip of old baptized the eunuch.[3] And when in my wanderings I reached Moscow, I made straight for the tsar's chaplain, the Archpriest Stephen, and for Neronov, the Archpriest John, and they informed the tsar concerning me, and from that time began my acquaintance with the tsar.[4] And the reverend fathers sent me back whence I had come with royal mandates, and wearily I dragged myself home; but the walls of my house had been pulled down and I set to to rebuild them, and once again the Devil raised up a storm against me. There came to my village dancing bears with drums and lutes, and I, though a miserable sinner, was zealous in Christ's service, and I drove them out and I broke the buffoons' masks and the drums, on a common outside the village, one against many, and two great bears I took away—one I clubbed senseless, but he revived, and the other I let go into the open country. And after that Vasily Petrovich Sheremetiev,[5] who was sailing up the Volga to Kazan to take over the Governorship, took me on board, and he sternly reprimanded me and ordered me to bless his son who had a shaven face.[6] And when I saw that image of shame I would not bless him, but condemned him from the Scriptures. So my lord waxed terribly wrath and ordered that I should be flung into the Volga and,

[3] The episode described in the Acts of the Apostles, 8, 27-38.

[4] Archpriest Stephen Vonifatiev was the confessor of the tsar. He and Archpriest Ivan Neronov were the leaders of the Zealots of Piety.

[5] The Zealots of Piety energetically fought these buffoons, or *skomorokhs,* traveling actors, singers, and bear trainers whose performances and songs strongly reflected the pre-Christian mentality.

[6] The shaving of a beard was considered sinful in Muscovite Russia. Vasily Sheremetiev was a wealthy and influential aristocrat and high official.

having inflicted on me many hurts, they cast me aside, but in later years their rough handling turned to friendliness, for we were reconciled one to another in the antechamber of the tsar, and my youngest brother was his lady's confessor. Thus does God fashion the lives of his people.

Let us return to earlier days: again another headman became as a wild beast against me; he arrived with his folk at my homestead and attacked me, shooting from bows and muskets; and I, the while, prayed to the Lord, calling to him in a loud voice: "Lord God! Make his heart gentle, and reconcile him to me by whatsoever means thou choosest." And he fled from my yard, driven out by the Holy Ghost. And that very night his folk came running and they called out to me with many tears: "Little father! Euphemy Stepanovich is near his end and he is most inconveniently screaming; he strikes himself and groans, and of his own accord he says: 'I want parson Avvakum, God will punish me because of him.'" And I felt it to be a trap. And terror seized on the spirit within me and I prayed to God thus: "Thou, O Lord, who broughtest me out of my mother's womb, and out of nothing didst create me, if they are about to strangle me, then count me with Phillip, the Metropolitan of Moscow[7]; and if they are about to stab me, count me with the Prophet Zachariah[8]; and if they are about to drown me, then deliver me from their hands, as thou didst Stephen of Perm."[9] And praying the while I betook myself to the house, even to the house of Euphemy. And when they had led me into the yard, out rushed his wife, Neonila, and seized me by the hand, and she said: "Come in then, dearie, my lord, my father! Come in then, light of our eyes!" And I answered: "Strange! Before it was 'Son of a whore'! and now it's 'My Father!' Christ wields a crueler scourge than he. Your good man has not taken long to own himself in fault." She led me into the bedroom. Euphemy leaped out of the feather bed, fell down at my feet, and howled and blubbered confused words: "Forgive me, my lord! I have sinned before God and before thee"; and he was all of a tremble. And I said in reply: "Dost thou wish to be healed?" and he, lying on the ground, answered: "Aye, good father!" And I said: "Stand up, God pardons thee." But he, sorely stricken, could not rise by himself, so I lifted him and laid him on his bed, and con-

[7] Phillip, Metropolitan of Moscow, was imprisoned and then slain by the order of Ivan IV.

[8] According to biblical tradition, Prophet Zachariah was slain in 520 by his enemies whose immorality he denounced.

[9] For Stephen of Perm, see introduction to Selection 26.

fessed him and anointed him with sacred oil, and his sickness departed. So Christ willed it. And the next morning they sent me back with honor to my home, and he and his wife became my spiritual children, excellent servants of Christ. Thus doth the Lord harden his heart against the proud, but he showers blessings on the meek.

And but a little time after this I was once again driven out of this place, so I betook me to Moscow and by God's will the tsar was pleased to appoint me Archpriest of Yurievets-on-the-Volga.[10] But I did not stay there long, but a matter of eight weeks. The Devil prompted the priests and the peasants and the good wives; and they came to the patriarch's chancellery where I was occupied in business of the church and dragged me out of the chancellery (there would be nigh two thousand of them), and in the middle of the street they beat me with cudgels and stamped on me, and the good wives beat me with shovels; and, for my sins, they flung me into a corner of a house. The captain of the troops came rushing up with his soldiers, and seizing me they galloped on their horses to my little home; and the captain placed the soldiers round the house. But the folk came up to it, and raised an outcry through the town, especially the Jack priests and their Jills, whom I had rated for their whoring ways, and they howled: "Death to the thief, to the son of a whore, and we'll fling his body into the ditch, for the dogs." And, on the third day, by night, after a short rest, I left my wife and children and with two others made for Moscow by way of the Volga; I would have taken refuge in Kostroma,[11] but, lo! there too they had driven away their Archpriest, Daniel. Ah, lack-a-day! The Devil leaves no man in peace! I reached Moscow; and went to Stephen, the tsar's chaplain; and he grumbled at me: "Why," says he, "have you abandoned your minster church?" And more trouble was awaiting me. In the middle of the night the tsar came in to his chaplain for his blessing and he saw me there;—more vexation: "And why have you abandoned your town?" And there were my wife and children and household (some twenty souls in all) left behind in Yurievets and I not knowing if they were alive or dead—yet another burden on my heart!

[10] Yurievets-on-the-Volga used to be an important market city in the province of Nizhny-Novgorod.

[11] Kostroma was an important merchant city on the Volga. Archpriest Daniel was the leading member of the Zealots of Piety in that city, and he met with considerable difficulties there because he denounced the morality of the city's people.

III. Conflict with Nikon, and the Rout of the "Seekers After God" (1652–1653)

After that, Nikon, our friend, brought down the relics of the Metropolitan Phillip from the Solovki Monastery,[12] and before his arrival, Stephen, the chaplain, with the brotherhood[13] and I with them, passed a week in prayer and fasting, concerning the patriarchate, even that God might give us a shepherd fitted to the saving of our souls. And the Metropolitan of Kazan and I, we signed our names to a petition and gave it to the tsar and the tsarina, concerning the chaplain Stephen, that he might be made patriarch. But he did not wish it for himself and named the Metropolitan Nikon. And the tsar hearkened to him and wrote to Nikon to greet him on his arrival. "To Nikon, the Right Reverend Metropolitan of Novgorod and Velikie Luki and of all Russia, greetings,"[14] and so forth. And when he arrived he played the fox with us, and it was bowings and scrapings and "Good morrow to you!" For he knew that he was to be patriarch and wished to remove all obstacles thereto. But I'll not waste my time telling all these cunning machinations. And when he became patriarch he would not so much as allow his friends into the room of the Cross,[15] and now at last belched forth his venom.

In Lent he sent a pastoral letter to St. Basil's Church, to John Neronov. Now the latter was my spiritual father and I was lodging in his presbytery; and when he was absent I took the services; and at the time there was some talk of making me the successor to Silas, God rest his soul, at St. Saviour's, but God willed not that it should be so and I myself was not over eager concerning it; I was well content to continue at St. Basil's: I used to read godly books to the flock, and they would come in great numbers. Nikon inscribed his letter with the year and the date, "According to the tradition of the holy Apostles and the Fathers, it is not seemly to make obeisance in church to the knee, it should be no lower than the girdle, and moreover it behooves you to sign yourselves with three fingers."[16] We met

[12] In 1652 Tsar Alexis sent Nikon to bring the relics of Metropolitan Phillip from the Solovki Monastery to Moscow.

[13] When speaking of brotherhood, Avvakum refers to the main group of the Zealots of Piety in Moscow.

[14] Before becoming patriarch, Nikon was Metropolitan of Novgorod and Velikie Luki.

[15] Room of the Cross—the official reception room in the patriarchal palace.

[16] As previously mentioned, the conflict between the Zealots of

together and took counsel. It was as if winter was of a mind to come; our hearts froze, our limbs shook. Neronov entrusted his church to me and shut himself up in the Miracle Monastery, and he spent a week praying in a cell, and one day a voice came from the icon of the Saviour: "The hour of tribulation has come; it behooves you to suffer and be strong." And, weeping, he recounted these words to me and to Paul, the Bishop of Kolomna, the same that afterwards Nikon was to burn in the Novgorod country[17]; and then to Daniel the Archpriest of Kostroma, and also to all the brothers. Together with Daniel I wrote out excerpts from the Fathers concerning the manner to be used in crossing oneself and making obeisances, and we gave them to the tsar. And many were the excerpts we had made. But he hid them, we know not where; I am of opinion that he gave them to Nikon.

And a little later Nikon seized Daniel in the monastery outside the Tver Gates, and sheared him monk in the presence of the tsar, and tearing off his cassock and insulting him the while, had him taken to the Miracle Monastery and put in the bakehouse, and when he had suffered grievously there, he sent him to Astrakhan; and there they placed a crown of thorns on his head and cast him into a dungeon, where he died. After the shearing of Daniel, they seized another Daniel—he also was an archpriest, of Temnikov—and they confined him in the monastery of New St. Saviour's. And in the same way with the Archpriest Ivan Neronov, Nikon took off his biretta in church and had him confined in the monastery of Simon, and later banished him to Vologda, to the walled monastery of St. Saviour's, then to the fortress of Kola,[18] and in the end, after having suffered exceedingly, he recanted—poor soul; he signed himself with three fingers, and so died a heretic. Woe is me! Let every man stand firm and be ever on the watch lest his foot shall stumble. In the words of the Scriptures, these are surely evil days when even the elect yield to the blandishments of Antichrist. It behooves us to be exceeding strong in prayer to God, and he will save us and help us, for he is merciful and loves mankind.

Piety, which was later to grow into the movement of Old Believers, and Patriarch Nikon originally grew out of the latter's changes in the Russian rites and missals. One of the most controversial changes was that of the two-fingered sign of the cross to a three-fingered one.

[17] Bishop Paul of Kolomna was a staunch upholder of old traditions and a resolute enemy of Nikon. Nikon deported him to the Novgorod region, and, according to rumor, had him burned.

[18] The city of Vologda is located in northern Russia. The fortress Kola is located in the extreme north not far from the Arctic Ocean.

And I, too, while I was celebrating vespers, was arrested by Boris Neledinsky and his musketeers, and together with me they arrested nigh on sixty souls and took them off to prison, and me they fastened with a chain for the night in the patriarch's court. And when the Sabbath dawned they placed me in a cart and stretched out my arms and drove me from the patriarch's court to the monastery of Andronicus, and there they put chains on me and flung me into a black dungeon, dug into the earth, and there I lay for three days, and I had nothing to eat or to drink in the darkness, as I sat there bowing myself to the earth against my chains, though I knew not, as I made my obeisances, which was east and which was west. No one came to me but mice and black beetles, and the crickets chirped, and of fleas there was abundance. And on the third day I was famished, that is to say, I wanted to eat, and after vespers someone was standing before me, I knew not whether he was man or angel, and to this day I know not. I only know this that he said a prayer in the darkness and, taking me by the shoulder, led me on my chain to a bench and seated me on it and put a spoon into my hands and gave me a little bread and some cabbage soup to sup—Oh, but it was tasty!—and he said to me: "Enough, let that serve you as restorative." And, lo, he was gone! The door had not opened and yet he was gone! Were he a man, it were a miracle; but were he an angel? Then were there no cause for wonder, because for such as he there are no barriers. In the morning came the archimandrite[19] with the brothers, and they led me away; they spoke to me coaxingly, that I should yield to the patriarch, but I thundered against them from the Scriptures and snarled at them. They took off the big chain and put a small one on me in its place, and set a monk as jailer over me; they ordered that I should be dragged to church. In church they pulled my hair and poked my ribs and pulled at my chain, and spat in my eyes. May God forgive them in this life and the next! It was not they themselves that did it, but Satan in his malice. I remained there four weeks.

After me they next seized Login, the Archpriest of Murom. In the monastery church, in the presence of the tsar, they sheared him monk at mass. At the time of the carrying round of the Host, the patriarch seized the paten from the head of the Archdeacon and placed it on the altar, together with Christ's body and the chalice. Meanwhile, Therapont, the archimandrite of the Miracle Monastery, was standing outside the choir before

[19] This refers to Therapont, the archimandrite, or abbot, of the Miracle Monastery.

the King's Gates. Woe is me that Christ's body should be sundered, more impiously than ever by the Jews! When they had shorn him they tore from him his kaftan and his outer garment. But Login was consumed with the zeal of God's fire; and he defied Nikon and spat across the threshold to the altar straight into his eyes; loosening his girdle, he tore off his shift and flung it into the altar, into Nikon's face, and, oh, wondrous to tell, the shift spread itself out and fell on the altar in such way that it covered the paten as though it had been the corporals. And the tsarina was in church at the time. They put a chain on Login and, dragging him from the church, beat him with brooms and whips to the monastery of the Epiphany, and thrust him into a dungeon for the night and set musketeers to guard him strictly. But lo! in the night God gave him a new fur cloak and a biretta; and in the morning they told Nikon, and he, laughing, said: "*I* know that breed of sham saint!" and he took from him the hat, but left him the fur coat.

At that time they led me again from the monastery on foot to the court of the patriarch's palace; and then again, spreading out my arms and wrangling much with me, they took me away from there also. And on St. Nikita's day there was a procession with crosses, and as they were driving me in a cart we met the crosses. And they drove me to the monastery church, that they might shear me, and during Mass they kept me for a long time on the threshold. The tsar rose from his place and going up to the patriarch entreated him that he should not shear me, and they took me away to the Siberia Office and handed me over to the scribe, Tretiak Bashmakov, the same that today is suffering for Christ—the elder Savvaty (for he took the cowl), he lies in the monastery of New St. Saviour's in a dungeon dug into the earth: may God have mercy on his soul! and even in these days he entreated me kindly.

IV. Deportation to Tobolsk (1653–1655)

So they sent me then to Siberia with my wife and children, and of the many and great privations on the way, had I the time there would be much to tell. Dame Avvakum bore a child, and, she being unwell, we transported her in a cart to Tobolsk; it was a journey of 3,000 versts, and for some thirteen weeks we dragged along in carts and by water and half of the way in sledges.[20]

The archbishop got me a church in Tobolsk. And there in

[20] One verst is about five-eighths of a mile. The city of Tobolsk is located in western Siberia.

that church great afflictions found me out; in one and a half years five times were the *Tsar's Words*[21] called out against me, and a certain member of the archbishop's household, the scribe Ivan Struna, outraged me. The archbishop was away in Moscow, and in his absence he, taught by the Devil, fell on me. He was minded to torment without cause Anthony, the clerk of my church. He, Anthony, gave him the slip and fled to me, in church. But this Ivan Struna, having collected some others, came to me that same day in church—I was singing vespers—and came leaping into the church and seized Anthony in the choir by the beard. I, in the meantime, had shut the church doors and would let no one in, so Struna was alone and kept twirling round like an imp of hell; and I, when I had finished vespers sat him down, Anthony lending a hand, in the middle of the church on the floor and thrashed him soundly with a leather strap for having made a riot in church; and the other rogues, some twenty in number, fled, every man of them, driven away by the Holy Ghost. And Struna having declared that he repented, I let him go in peace. But Struna's kinsmen among the priests and monks raised the whole town against me, so that they might compass my death. And in the middle of the night they drove up in sledges to my homestead and broke into my house, being of a mind to take and drown me; but a terror from God fell upon them and drove them hence, and they fled away. For a month was I tormented by their tricks, for they would attack me in secret; and sometimes I would take refuge by night in the church, and sometimes with the governor, and I would beg that for safety I might be put in prison—but this they would not do. Matthew Lomkov—the same that as a monk was called Mitrophan, and later in Moscow was apparitor to the Metropolitan Paul—he kept close to my side; it was he that afterwards sheared me in the monastery church together with the deacon Afanasy: but at that time he was a just man, though the Devil has now swallowed him. Then the archibishop returned from Moscow, and, as was but meet considering his offense, thrust Struna into prison with chains on him. For a certain man had lain with his own daughter, and he, Struna, had accepted fifty kopeks from the fellow and had let him go without punishment. And the lord bishop ordered him to be fettered, and he bethought him of that affair with me. For he, Struna, went to the

[21] The expression "Tsar's Words" meant that one person accuses another and, pointing to him, claimed he was involved in a conspiracy against the tsar. It always led to the arrest of the accused man.

governor and his men in their office, and said the *Tsar's Words* against me. And the captain allowed a petty squire, Peter Beketov, to go bail for him. Woe is me! Misfortune entered the gates of Peter's dwelling place, and it grieves my soul. The archbishop took council with me, and, in accordance with the rubric, on the first Sunday in Lent he started cursing Struna for the sin of incest in the great church. And that same Peter Beketov came to church, and rated the archbishop and myself, and within an hour, on his way home from church, he went mad, and he died a bitter and an evil death. And his grace and I, we ordered his body to be flung into the street to the dogs, and the townsfolk mourned him and his sin; for three days they importuned God diligently that on the Day of Judgment he might be pardoned. Through pity for Struna he had brought this dire calamity upon himself, and on the third day his grace and I read the office over his body. But enough of this woeful business!

V. The Hardships of Traveling to Dauria (1655)

At this time an edict arrived, ordering that I should be taken from Tobolsk to the Lena, in that I had condemned Nikon from the Scriptures and pronounced him a heretic.[22] At that time a letter came from Moscow telling how two brothers, who lodged in the tsarina's apartments at the top of the palace, had both of them died of the plague, together with their wives and children, and many also of their friends and kinsfolk; God was pouring forth the vials of his wrath on the kingdom. But they, wretched men, knew not this and continued making disturbance in the church. Then Neronov spoke to the tsar, saying: "The visitation for schism is threefold: plague, the sword, and division." And thus has it come to pass in our days, even now; but the Lord is merciful. When he has punished us to bring us to repentance, than has he mercy on us and, driving away the ills of our souls and bodies, he giveth quietness. I preach Christ and my hope is in him; I confidently await his mercy and I believe in the Resurrection of the Dead.

So once more I got into the boat that had been assigned me —as I have said before—and sailed towards the Lena. And when I reached Eniseysk I was met by another edict, wherein I was ordered to get me to Dauria[23]—it would be more than twenty thousand versts from Moscow—and to give myself over to

[22] This was the result of Struna's *Tsar's Words* against Avvakum.

[23] Dauria was a region in eastern Siberia in the vicinity of Lake Baikal and which the Russians intended to conquer.

Afanasy Pashkov as chaplain to his troops that numbered six hundred men, and, for my sins, he was a fierce hard man, and it was ever his custom to burn folk and torture them, and beat them, and many times did I try to persuade him to desist, and now I was in his hands, and from Moscow came an order from Nikon that I was to be tormented.

On our journey from Eniseysk, it would be on the great Tunguska River, a storm sank my raft. It foundered completely in midstream and it was full of water and its sail was in tatters, only the deck remained above water, all the rest was under water. My wife, bareheaded[24] as she was, managed, I know not how, to drag the children out of the water on to the deck, but I, looking up at the sky, cried out: "O Lord! Save us! O Lord! Help us!" And by God's will we were driven to the shore; but why multiply words?

From another raft two men were wrenched away and drowned in the water. After that, when we were come to ourselves, we set out once more on our way.

VI. First Difficulties with Pashkov (1655–1656)

When we came to the Shaman rapids, diverse folk came sailing out to meet us, and with them were two widows; one of them was aged about sixty; and the other was older, and they were traveling by boat to a nunnery where they were to take the veil. And this Pashkov was minded to send them back, and to give them by force in marriage; and I said to him: "It is against the canons of the church to give such women in marriage." And in lieu of heeding my words and letting the widows go, he waxed angry and devised how he might torment me.

In other rapids—called the long rapids—he set about driving me from the raft. "You bring bad luck," says he, "to the raft. You're a heretic," says he; "off with you to the mountains! It is not for such as you to keep company with Cossacks." Alackaday! The mountains were high, the ravines impassable, there was a stone crag that stood there like a wall—you'd crick your neck before you saw its top. In these mountains great serpents were to be found, and in them dwelt geese and ducks with red feathers, and black crows, and grey jackdaws; in these mountains were also eagles, and hawks, and gerfalcons and guinea fowl and pelicans, and swans and other wild things in plenty, every variety of bird. Moreover, on these mountains many wild

[24] It was unseemly for a married woman to be without a kerchief on her head.

beasts wandered at liberty: wild goats, and deer and bison, and elk, and boars, and wolves, and wild sheep—clearly to be seen but not to be caught.

Pashkov was of a mind to turn me out into these mountains to live with beasts and birds, and I wrote him a little letter that began thus: "O man! Fear God who sits on the Cherubim and gazes into the abyss; before him tremble the celestial powers and every creature including man; thou alone despisest him and doest things that are not seemly," and so forth. It was a long letter; and I sent it to him. And some fifty men rushed on me; they seized my raft and hastened towards him, who was distant some three versts; and I stood there, boiling some porridge for the Cossacks and I fed them with it; and they, poor souls, ate of it and trembled, and some of them, looking at me, began to weep for me. They dragged up the raft; the executioners seized me and led me before him. He was standing with drawn sword, shaking with rage; he began to speak to me, saying, "What are you? A parson, or an unfrocked one?" And I answered, "I am Avvakum, the archpriest; speak! what is your business with me?" Then he roared like a wild beast, and struck me a great blow first on one cheek and then on the other, and then again on the head, and knocked me off my feet; and seizing his leather sword-strap struck me, where I lay, thrice on the back, and then, tearing off my shift, gave me seventy-two strokes on my naked back with the knout. And I kept saying, "O Lord Jesus Christ, Son of God! Help me!" And this I kept repeating without pause, so that it was bitter to him, in that I did not say, "Have mercy." At each stroke I said a prayer, but in the middle of the flogging I screamed to him, "You've beat me enough, I say"; so he ordered that it should stop. And I said to him, "Why do you beat me—do you know?" And he ordered them to beat me again on the ribs; and then they stopped; and I was trembling all over, and I fell. And he ordered them to drag me off to the raft that carried the money bags: they put fetters on my hands and feet and flung me on to the deck. It was autumn, the rain fell on me all night, and there was a pool where I was lying. When they were beating me it did not hurt because of the prayers I was saying; but now, as I lay, the thought came to me: "Son of God, why didst thou permit them to beat me so sorely? Look thee, Lord, I was championing the widow, consecrated to thee. Who shall judge between thee and me? When I was living as an evil man, thou didst not chastise me thus; but now I know not in what I have sinned." Ay! There was a righteous man for you, another dungfaced Pharisee, wishing, forsooth, to judge the Almighty! If Job spoke in that fashion it was because he was a perfect and an upright man; and, moreover, he knew not the Scriptures, for he dwelt outside the Law in a barbarian land, and it was through Creation, not through Revelation, that he learned to know God. But I, in the first place, was a sinful man, and, in the second place, I was learned in the Law and the Prophets and was fortified by the Scriptures in all my goings: "*We must, through much tribulation, enter into the Kingdom of God*"; and yet had I reached such a pitch of folly. Woe is me! How came it that the raft did not founder with me in the water? Then my bones began to ache, my veins to grow rigid, my heart to palpitate, verily, I was dying; the water began to splash into my mouth, then I heaved a sigh, yea, I repented before the Almighty, for, verily, the sweet Lord of compassion remembers not against us our former transgressions when once we have repented of them; and once more I ceased to feel the pain.

In the morning they flung me onto a small craft and carried me away. Then we came to the great rapids of the Padun, where the river is a verst in breadth, and there are three exceeding steep reefs stretching across the whole of the river, and, except you find the passages between them, your boat will be shattered into splinters. They brought me into the rapids: above was rain and snow, and they flung over my shoulders nought but a mangy little kaftan; the water flowed over my belly and my spine—my poor body was in sorry plight. The took me out of the raft and, skirting the rapids, they dragged me over the stones in fetters. Verily I was in a sad plight, but with my soul it was well; I was no longer peevish with God. Once again there came into my head the words spoken by the Prophets and the Apostles: "*My son, despise thou not the chastening of the Lord, nor faint when thou art rebuked of him.*

"*For whom the Lord loveth he chasteneth, and scourgeth every son whom he receiveth. If ye endure chastening, God dealeth with you as with sons; for what son is he whom the father chasteneth not?*"

And with these words I comforted myself.

And after that they brought me to the fortress of Bratsky, and flung me into a dungeon, and gave me straw to lie upon. And there I lay till Advent, in a freezing tower; these are the seasons when winter reigns, but God kept me warm, and that without garments. Like a poor dog I lay on the straw; and sometimes they fed me, and sometimes they did not; there were many mice and I would strike at them with my biretta—the fools had not given me a stick; I lay all the time on my belly, my back was covered with sores, and of fleas and lice there was abundance. I would fain have cried on Pashkov to pardon me; but it would have been contrary to God's will, it was ordained that I should endure. Then they moved me to a warm hut, and there I dwelt in fetters with hostages and dogs the whole winter; and my wife had been sent with the children some twenty versts away. And all the winter her serving-wench, Xenia, tormented her with her tantrums and complaints. After Christmas my son Ivan, who was still but a little lad, stole away from home that he might dwell with me; and Pashkov ordered him to be flung into the freezing dungeon where I lay; dear little lad, he spent the night there and was nigh froze to death; and in the morning Pashkov ordered him back to his mother and I saw him no more; it was all he could do to drag himself home to his mother from the frostbite on his hands and feet.

VII. The Dauria Campaign (1656–1662)

In spring we set out once more. There remained but scant provision, for the first store had all been robbed—books and garments and other sundries had all been taken; but the second store remained. I came near again to drowning on the lake of Baikal; I was made to pull a towing rope on the Khilok River, and upstream it was mighty hard going. And there was no time for eating nor for sleeping; for a whole year I suffered from the hardships of water-travel; the folk kept dying, and my feet and belly were blue. For two summers we journeyed by water and in the winter we were towed along by haulage. And, as I have said, on this same Khilok for the third time I came nigh to drowning. My boat was sucked by the current from the shore, and the boats of the other folk stayed where they were, but mine was caught up and carried away. My wife and children had remained on shore, and the boat bolted with the steersman and me! she was pitched and tossed on the swirling water, but I climbed onto her and cried out, "Help, Blessed Virgin! Thou art our Hope and Defense. Let me not be drowned!" Sometimes my feet would be in the water and sometimes I would scramble to the top; she was carried on for a verst and more, and then the folk stopped her and she was shattered to fragments. Ay, what could one do if Christ and the Immaculate Mother of God so willed it? And I climbed out of the water laughing, but the folk were weeping, and they spread out my garments on the bushes—cloaks of satin and taffetas, and sundry trifles: for I still had a store of such things in chests and coffers, but from that day they were rotted. But Pashkov was fain to give me another flogging. "You're making yourself a laughingstock," said he. And once again I importuned the sweet Mother of God: "Our Lady! Soothe thy fool!" And she, our Hope, did soothe him, and he began to concern himself about me.

Our next stage was the Lake of Irgen. There is there a haulage and in the winter we began hauling; he took from me my workmen, and would not permit me to hire others, and we had small children—many mouths and none to fill them; this poor hapless wretch of an archpriest set to fashion a dog-sleigh for himself and started hauling. That spring we began to sail down the Ingoda River—it was the fourth summer of my journey from Tobolsk. They were floating logs for the building of houses and towns. There began to be nothing to eat, the folk began to die of hunger and from ceaseless working in the water; shallow was the river, heavy were the rafts, merciless were the taskmasters, stout were the sticks, gnarled were the cudgels, cutting were the knouts, cruel were the sufferings—fire and rack; the folk were so spent with hunger that let him, Afanasy, but start tormenting one of them, and lo! he was dead on his hands. Ah, me! What a time! It would almost seem that he was out of his mind. There remained to Dame Avvakum one Moscow gown that had not been rotted with damp. It would have fetched twenty-five rubles and more in Moscow; but in these parts they gave us four sacks of rye for it, and we dragged on for another year, living on the Nercha River, and keeping ourselves alive with the roots and herbs that grew on the banks. One after another the folk died of hunger, and he saw to it that none of them ran away, and they were circumscribed within a small space, and they would wander over the steppes and fields, digging up grasses and roots, and we with them. And in winter we would live on fir cones, and sometimes God would send mare's flesh, and sometimes we found the bones of stinking carcasses of wild beasts left by the wolves, and what had not been eaten up by the wolves that did we eat; and some would eat frozen wolves and foxes—in truth, any filth that they could lay their hands on. A mare foaled, and, in secret, the starving folk devoured the foal together with the caul. And Pashkov got wind of it, and he flogged them with his knout to the point of death. And another mare died, and desperation seized them all, inasmuch as they had pulled the foal out of her, stealing a march on nature. When nought but the head had as yet emerged from the womb, they tore it out, yea, and they began to eat the blood that came away with it. Ah, me! What a time! And two of my little sons died from these sore straits, and roaming the hills and the sharp rocks with my children that survived, naked and barefoot, living on grass and roots, what did I not endure? And I, sinful man, partook willy-nilly of mare's flesh and foul carrion and the flesh of birds. Woe for my sinful soul! Who will pour water on my head and unseal for me the fountain of tears, even that I may weep for the poor soul that is mine, which I have been destroying with my daily appetites? But in Christ's name a great lady helped us, the captain's daughter-in-law, Eudokia Kirilovna, and also his, Afanasy's, wife, Thekla Semenovna; in secret they would give us some comfort against a death from starvation. Without his knowledge they would sometimes send us a piece of meat, sometimes a circular loaf, sometimes flour and oats, as much as ever they could, and sometimes one of them would save up ten pounds of flour and some coins and sometimes twenty pounds and hand it over to us, and sometimes she would rake out the chicken's food from the trough. My daughter, the hapless lass Agraphena, would go in secret under her window. And it was both pitiful and laughable! Sometimes, without the lady's knowledge, they would chase the child from the window, and sometimes she would come home burdened with a nice little store; at that time she was still but a child, but now she is twenty-seven. My poor little maid! She dwells unwed with her younger sisters by the Mezen, living from hand to mouth and weeping; and their mother and brothers lie buried in a dungeon in the earth. But what would you? Let every man endure great tribulation for Christ's sake! With God's help let even that which has been ordained come to pass, and let us suffer tribulation for the sake of the Christian faith. The archpriest used to love keeping company with the great but love in place of that, poor wretch, to endure even to the end; for it is written: *"Better is the end of a thing than the beginning thereof."* Enough of this: let us return to the previous matter.

We continued in the land of Dauria in dire straits some six or seven years, but during some of these years there would at times be some little balm, and he, Afanasy, slandering me, ceaselessly sought my death. And during these lean years he sent me of his own accord two widows—they were servants in his house and dear to him—Mary and Sophia, clothed about with an unclean spirit; many times had he tried spells and incantations upon them, but it had availed him nought; and tongues had begun to wag concerning the matter, whereupon the imp of hell would start tormenting them most cruelly, and they would twist themselves and shriek. He summoned me and, bowing to me, said, "I pray you take them home with you and physick them with prayer to God; God will hearken to you." And I answered him, "My Lord! What you ask of me is beyond my powers. By the prayers of the holy Fathers of our Church all things are possible to God." So I took the poor souls home—if it was presumptuous in me may I be forgiven. I had had some experience in such matters in Russia. Three or four persons possessed by an unclean spirit had, in former times, been brought to my house, and with the prayers of the holy Fathers I had cast out the imps of hell by the action and will of the living God and of our Lord Jesus Christ, Son of God, Light of the World. I had sprinkled them with tears and with water and anointed them with oil, chanting prayers the while, in the name of Christ, and the holy magic of these things had driven the imps out of these persons, and they had been healed—not by any virtue in me—by no means; but by their own faith. Of old time an ass was made the instrument by which a blessing came to Balaam,[25] and by a lynx a blessing came to Julian the martyr, and by a stag to Sisinius: they spoke with a human voice. God whensoever he chooses triumphs over Nature's laws. Read the life of Theodore of Edessa; there will you find that a harlot raised a man from the dead; in the *Christian's Pilot*[26] it is written: "*Not for all men are the gifts of the Holy Ghost, but all men can he leaven, excepting only heretics.*"

So they brought me these two women that were possessed; and I, as the custom is, myself fasted and would not let them eat, and I prayed and anointed them with oil and tried every remedy I knew. And the good wives returned to health and to their right minds; and I confessed them and administered the Sacrament to them; and they tarried in my house, praying to God, for they loved me and would not go home. And it came to his knowledge that they had become my spiritual daughters; and he was angered against me, more fiercely than before, and he was fain to burn me alive. "You have wormed out of them in the confessional," said he, "private matters concerning me." And how, forsooth, can one administer the Sacrament to a man if one has not first confessed him? And if you do not administer the Sacrament to the possessed, you'll in no wise succeed in casting out of them the imps of hell. A devil is not a mujik, forsooth, that he should fear the stick; what he fears is the Cross of Christ, and holy water and holy oil, but before the Body of

[25] See the Book of Numbers, Chapter 22.

[26] The *Christian's Pilot* was a Byzantine codex of canon law.

Christ he flies. Without the Blessed Sacrament I cannot heal; in our Orthodox faith there is no Communion without Confession; in the Roman faith they pay no heed to Confession; but to us, the Orthodox observers, this is not seemly, and for us the Sacrament of Penance must ever first be sought. And if in your need you cannot have a priest, then confess your sins to some discreet brother, and, beholding your contrition, God will pardon you; and then, having read through the Canon of the Mass before communicating, keep by you some reserved sacrament. And, whensoever you are away on a journey or engaged in traffic or whatever it may be that takes you far from a church, if you have first given sighs of contrition to the Lord and have confessed to your brother, as has been said above, then may you partake with a clear conscience of the Blessed Sacrament and all will be well, if you have first fasted and read through the Canon of the Mass: take then a little casket and spread a napkin in it, and light a candle, and pour a little water into a cup, and ladle some out in a spoon, and place with prayer a portion of Christ's Body in the water in the spoon, and sense it all with a censer; and weeping say out loud the whole of the prayer that begins: "O Lord! I believe and confess that thou art Christ, the son of the living God." (It is written in the Canon of the Mass.) Then, throwing yourself on the ground before the icon, ask for forgiveness and, standing up, kiss the holy image; and, having signed yourself, communicate with prayer, and drink a little of the water and pray again to God, saying, "Now glory to Christ!" Even if you die the minute after, it will be well with you. Enough of that matter, you yourselves know that it is good counsel. Now I shall go on with the story of the women.

Pashkov took the poor widows away from me, and in lieu of gratitude he gave me harsh words. He hoped that Christ had settled the matter once and for all; but they began to rave worse than before. He shut them up in an empty outhouse and allowed no one access to them; then he summoned a monk to them, but they flung logs at him, and he scuttled away. I sat at home weeping, and I knew not what to do. I did not dare to go up to the big house, for he was mighty wroth with me; so in secret I sent them holy water, and told them to wash themselves and drink a little of it, and, poor souls, their sufferings were eased a little. And in secret they stole off to me, and I anointed them with oil in the name of Christ, and once again God granted that they should be healed, and they returned home; and by night they would escape to me in secret to pray to God. And they became exceeding good churchwomen; they put aside vanities and began to follow all the observances of the Church; and afterwards in Moscow they went with their lady to dwell in the nunnery of the Ascension. Glory to God for them!

And then from the Nercha River we began to journey back to Russia; for five weeks we traveled on the naked ice in sledges. I was given two sorry nags for my children and my baggage, while myself and Dame Avvakum, we made our way on foot, stumbling over the ice. The country was barbarous, the natives were hostile, so we feared to get separated from the others, and yet we could not keep up with the horses—for we were a hungry, weary pair; and my poor old woman tramped along, tramped along, and at last she fell, and another weary soul stumbled over her, and he fell too; they both screamed, and were not able to get up. The man cried out, "Oh, good wife! Oh, my lady! Your pardon!" and my old woman answered, "Fie, gossip! Would you crush me to death?" And I came up, and she, poor soul, began to complain to me, saying, "How long, archpriest, are these sufferings to last?" And I said, "Markovna! till our death." And she, with a sigh, answered, "So be it, Petrovitch; let us be getting on our way."

VIII. The Story of the Black Hen

And we had a pet, a black hen, and she laid two eggs a day to feed the children, by God's will, helping us in our need; it was God's doing. But when they were carrying out the baggage to the dog sledge, she was crushed to death, for our sins, and to this day whenever I think of that hen my heart aches for her. I know not if it were a hen or miracle: all the year round she laid two eggs a day, and we would not have taken a hundred rubles for her—nay, we would have spat on them! mere dross! And that hen, God's living creature, fed us, and she would take her meals with us, pecking at the porridge of fir cones in the caldron, and pecking at the fish, and in exchange she gave us two eggs a day. Glory to God, who fashions all things well! And we had come by her in no ordinary way. My lady's hens had one after another turned blind, and they began to die, whereupon she gathered them into a basket and sent them to me. "And may it please you, Father," said she, "to pray over the hens." And I considered: she was a lady bountiful to us, she had children, and she had need of the hens. So I chanted a prayer and blessed some water and sprinkled the hens and censed them. Then I went to the forest and fashioned them a trough from which to eat, and sprinkled it with holy water, and sent the whole baggage back to her. And by a wave of God's hand the hens were healed, because of her faith. And it was from that same brood that our hen came; but enough of this matter; it was not the first miracle that Christ had brought to pass. Already Kosma and Damian had blessed and healed both men and cattle in the name of Christ.[27] God has a use for everything: cattle and fowls —they were created for the glory of his pure majesty, and also for the sake of mankind.

IX. At Lake Irgen

So we made our way back to Lake Irgen. My lady had pity on us and sent us a little basket of wheat, so we had our fill of frumenty. Eudokia Kirilovna was a lady bountiful to me, but the Devil set her quarreling with me in this manner: she had a son whose name was Simeon; he had been born in that place. It was I that had churched the mother and baptized the child, and every day they would send him to me for my blessing and I, having signed him with the Cross and sprinkled him with holy water, would kiss him and send him home; he was a fine healthy child and I loved him like my own. But the little lad began to ail, and I was away from home. And in a moment of pettiness of spirit she was vexed with me and sent the child to a medicine man. And I, when I learned of it, was angry with her, and a wide breach came between us; the little boy began to ail still more, and his right hand and foot dried up, so they were like little sticks. She grew ashamed; but she knew not what to do, and God oppressed her still further. The little one became sick unto death, and the nurses came to me weeping and I said to them, "If the goodwife is a baggage, then let her keep herself *to* herself." For I was waiting that she should repent. I saw that the Devil had hardened her heart, and I bowed down before the Lord God, praying that he might bring her to her right mind. And the Lord, the God of Mercy, softened the rich soil of her heart, and early next morning she sent to me her second son, Ivan; with tears he begged forgiveness for his mother, walking round the stove and bowing before me; and I was lying on the stove, naked, under a covering made from birch-bark, and Dame Avvakum was lying within the stove, and the children anywhere. It was raining at the time; we had no covering, and our winter quarters were dripping, so we were in sorry straits. And I said to him, bringing him low, "Tell your mother that she must ask forgiveness of Aretha, the medicine

[27] Kosma and Damian were considered the saintly protectors of men and cattle, and possessing miracle-working powers for healing.

man." Then she brought the sick child to me and I ordered her to lay him before me, and they were all weeping and bowing themselves. And I arose and got me my stole out from the mess and dirt and found some holy oil, and, praying to God, I censed the boy and signed him with the sign of the Cross. And God granted that the child was healed, both in his hand and foot. And I sprinkled him with holy water and sent him to his mother. Consider, thou who hearkenest to my story, what great things were compassed by a mother's penitence; it both physicked her own soul and healed her child. What then? It is not only today that God is with penitents. On the morrow she sent us fish and pies; and they were apt to our need, for we were starving; and that day we made our peace, she and I. When we had journeyed back from Dauria, she, sweet lady, died in Moscow, and I buried her in the nunnery of the Ascension.

And Pashkov himself learned of the affair with the boy, for she told him. I went to him and, bowing low before me, he, Pashkov, said, "God bless you! You have acted like a true priest; remember not our sins against us." And at that time he sent us no small store of food.

X. The Tribulations of the Mongolian Expedition (1661)

But in a very short space he was minded to torture me—hearken how it came about. He was sending his son, Eremy, off to fight in the kingdom of the Mongols, and with him some seventy-two Cossacks and some twenty natives. And he made a native to "*shamanit'*,"[28] that is to say, to tell their fortune, as to whether they would prosper and return home victorious. And in the evening that wizard—it was near my winter quarters—brought a live sheep and began to work magic over it: he rolled it to and fro for a long space and then he twisted its head and flung it away. Then he began to jump and dance, and invoke devils, and, giving great screams the while, he flung himself upon the earth, and foamed at the mouth; the devils were pressing him, and he asked them, "Will the expedition prosper?" And the devils said, "It will return with much booty, having gained a great victory." And the captains were glad; and all the folk, rejoicing, cried, "We will come home rich!" Oh, lackaday! It was bitter then, and even now it is not sweet to think upon. I, a bad shepherd, made my sheep to perish; from vexation of

28 *Shamanit'*: the Shamans were Siberian pagan priests and medicine men. Avvakum gives to this word a verbal infinitive ending, thus *shamanit'* means to perform pagan rites.

spirit I forgot the words of the Gospel, when the Sons of Zebedee counseled our Lord concerning the stubborn villagers, saying:—

"*Lord, wilt thou that we command fire to come down from heaven and consume them, even as Elias did?*"

But He turned and rebuked them, and said, Ye know not what manner of spirit ye are of.

For the Son of Man is not come to destroy men's lives, but to save them. And they went to another village.

But I, accursed, did not so. In my poor room I cried with a great cry to the Lord, "Hearken to me, my God! Hearken to me, King of Heaven! Sweet Lord! Hearken to me! Let not one of them return home; and dig a grave for every one of them yonder! Lay on them an evil fate, O Lord! Bring them to destruction, so that the Devil's prophecy may not be fulfilled." And many like words did I say, and in secret I prayed to God concerning it. They told him that I was praying thus, but he did but snarl abuses at me. Then he sent off his son with the captain; they rode off at night, directing their course by the stars. And I was seized with pity for them, for my soul foresaw that they would perish; nevertheless, I continued praying for their destruction, and some of them, as they passed, called out goodby to me, and I called back, "You will die yonder." And, as they rode off, the horses under them began to whinny, and the cows that were there to low, and the sheep and goats to bleat, and the dogs to howl, and the natives to howl, like the dogs. Terror seized them all. With tears Eremy sent me word, "that it may please my lord and spiritual father to pray for me." And I was seized with pity for him, for he had been my secret friend and had suffered for my sake. When his father was flogging me with the knout, he had tried to dissuade him, so that his father had chased him with drawn sword. And when they arrived after me, at other rapids, those of the Pandun, forty rafts all got through the straits in safety; but his, Afanasy's own raft, though her rigging was excellent and six hundred Cossacks had been set to build her, yet were they not able to get her through: the waters overcame them, or rather God was punishing him: all the crew were sucked into the water, and the raft was hurled against a rock; the waters splashed up against it, but did not flow into it. It is marvelous to watch God's lessons to the foolish! He himself was on the shore, and his lady was on the raft, and Eremy began to speak, saying, "Father! God will punish you for your sins; you flogged the archpriest with that knout unjustly; it is time to repent, my lord!" But he roared at him, like a wild beast, and Eremy, dodging behind a fir, clasped his hands and repeated the *Lord have mercy upon us*. But Pashkov, having seized a ringed musket, one that never missed, from an attendant, took aim at his son and pulled the trigger, and by God's will the weapon missed fire. Then, having adjusted the powder, he fired again, and again it missed fire. And he did the same a third time, and the third time, also, it missed fire. So he flung it on the ground, and the attendant picked it up and threw it out of the way, and it went off of its own accord.

And Pashkov sat him down on a chair and, leaning on his sword, he came to his right mind, and beginning to weep, he said, "I have sinned, accursed that I am, I have spilled innocent blood, I flogged the archpriest unjustly, God will punish me." It was strangely, strangely in accord with the words, *God is slow to anger and swift to hearken*. For because of his repentance the raft floated away from the reef; its prow was toward the water; and they pulled it from the shore and it leapt out into a lower level of the water. Then Pashkov called his son to him, and entreated him, saying, "Forgive me, Eremy, you spoke truly!" and he, running up, and bowing before his father, said, "It is God, my lord, that will forgive you; for I myself am guilty before God and before you." And he took his father's hand, and led him away. Eremy was a righteous-minded man, and a virtuous one; already was his own beard grey, and yet he honored his father exceedingly, and feared him, and according to the Scriptures it is seemly so to do, for God loves the children that honor their fathers. Come then, hearkener to my story! Is it not true that Eremy had suffered for my sake, and for the sake of Christ and his Law?

And all this was recounted to me by the helmsman of his, Afanasy's raft, by name Gregory Tielnoy. Let us return to the previous matter.

They went away, then, from me, and rode off to the wars; and pity seized me for Eremy, and I began to importune God Almighty that he might protect him. Time passed and they were expected home from the wars, and the day came fixed for their return, but they came not; and during three days Pashkov refused me admittance to his house. And at last he prepared a torture chamber, and had a fire kindled; he wished to torture me. And I was repeating prayers for my latter end, for I knew what manner of cook he was and that few came out alive from his roasting. And I sat waiting in my house, and I said to my wife, who was weeping, and to my children, "God's will be done! For whether we live, we live unto the Lord; and whether we die, we die unto the Lord." And lo! at that moment I saw two executioners come hurrying in to seize me. Marvelous are the acts of the Lord, and unspeakable the counsels of Almighty God! Suddenly Eremy himself, wounded, comes riding along by the little path that goes past my house and garden, and he calls out to the executioners, and makes them turn back with him; and he, Pashkov, left the torture chamber and came toward his son, staggering like a drunk man from grief. And Eremy, bowing low to his father, acquainted him with all that had taken place: how all his troops had been slaughtered, no single man surviving; and how a native had led him, through wild and lonely places, away from the Mongolian people; and how, without food, they had wandered over stony mountains and through the forest for seven days, having nought to eat but one squirrel; and how a man in my image had appeared to him in a dream and had shown him the path, and whither he must journey; and how he had leaped up and gone on his way rejoicing. When he had recounted all to his father, then I came in to greet him. But Pashkov rolled his eyes at me—the very spit of a white polar bear, and he would have gobbled me up alive, only the Lord did not grant that it should be so—and, drawing in his breath, he said, "What think you of your handiwork? How many men, think you, have you caused to perish?" But Eremy said to me, "Father Avvakum! for Christ's sake, get thee gone, and do not bandy words with him." And I went.

For ten years he had tormented me, or I him—I know not which. God will decide on the Day of Judgment.

A change of post came for him, and for me a letter; we were ordered back to Russia. He went away and did not take me with him, for in his heart he was saying, "If he travels back alone, then surely the natives will slay him." He and his guns and his folk, they sailed away on rafts, and, on my own journey back, I learned from the natives that they were a timid, trembling crew. And I, a month afterwards, having assembled the aged, and the sick, and the wounded, whatever there was there of useless folk (there would be ten of them, and I with my wife and children would bring it to seventeen), got into a boat, and, putting our trust in Christ and fixing the Cross to our prow, we started on our way, wherever God should lead us, fearing nothing. I gave the book, the *Christian's Pilot*, to the clerk, and he gave me a fellow for steersman in exchange; and he manumitted my friend Basil, the same that was wont to denounce folk to Pashkov and was the cause that much blood was shed, and he sought my life also. And at one time, having flogged me, he fastened me to the stake, but once again God kept me safe; and when Pashkov was gone the Cossacks wished to flog him to death, but I begged him off for Christ's sake and gave the money for his manumission to the clerk, and carried him back to Russia, from death to life. Poor soul, may he repent his sins! Ay, and I took back with me another lousy spy of the same kidney; him they did not wish to give up to me, and he fled from death to the forest, and, coming upon me on the path, he flung himself into my boat, for he was pursued and had nowhere to turn. And I, forgive me, acted cunningly. As Rahab, the harlot of Jericho, hid Joshua the son of Nun, so did I hide him, making him lie down at the bottom of a chest, and I flung a coverlet over him, and ordered my wife and daughter to lie on the top of him; they sought him high and low, but they would not disturb my wife from her place, and all they said was, "Rest in peace, Mother Avvakum! You have had enough to endure, as it is, my lady." And I—for God's sake forgive me—I lied that day, and I said, "He is not here"—I was loth to give him up to be slain. And when they had searched they went away empty-handed, and I carried him back to Russia. Elder and servant of Christ![29] Forgive me, then, in that I lied that day. How think you, it may be that it was not a very grievous sin? It would seem that Rahab the harlot did likewise, and the Scriptures praise her for it; give judgment, then, for God's sake: and if I acted sinfully, then pardon me; but if I acted in accordance with the traditions of the Church, then is it well. See, I have left a space for you, and do you, with your own hand, write in either forgiveness or penance for me and my wife and my daughter, for we all three shared in the cheat—we saved a man from death that he might repent before the Lord. Judge us then so that we shall not be judged for it by Christ on the Day of Judgment; write in a few words, I pray you:—

God pardons thee and blesses thee in this life and the life to come, together with thy helpmeet Anastasia, and thy daughter, and all thy house: thou hast acted rightly and justly. Amen.[30]

So be it then, my elder. God bless you for your graciousness. But enough of this.

The clerk gave us sacks of corn to the value of thirty silver pieces, and a cow, and five or six sheep, and dried meat, and

29 These words are addressed to Avvakum's cellmate and spiritual father, Epiphany.

30 This last passage is written into the manuscript by Epiphany, who read the manuscript and made some addenda.

this we fed on for the summer, as we sailed on our way. The clerk was a good soul; he had been sponsor to my daughter Xenia, who had been born in the days of Pashkov, but Pashkov would not give me myrrh and oil, so she had to stay long unchristened; but when he was gone I christened her (I myself churched my wife and baptized my children),[31] and the clerk and my eldest daughter were the gossips, and I was the parson. In this manner, then, I also christened my son Afanasy, and both confessed my own children and administered the Sacrament to them during the Mass I said at Mezen, and I myself communicated, but I did not administer it to my wife: there are instructions concerning this in the rubric, wherein we are bade so to do. But as to my excommunication, it came from heretics and, in Christ's name, I trample it under foot, and the curse written against me—why, not to mince my words, I wipe my arse with that; if the heretics curse me, the saints of Moscow—Peter, and Alexis, and Jonah, and Phillip—*they* bless me; and in accordance with their books, with a clear conscience I believe in and serve my God; but the apostates I loathe and curse: they are God's enemies and, living in Christ, I do not fear them. Were they to heap stones on me then, secure in the tradition of the Fathers, I would lie in peace beneath these stones—how much more so beneath the thorny, knavish curses of Nikon! Tush! Why multiply words? All we need do is to spit on their doings and their ritual, and on their newfangled books, then all will be well. Our following discourse will be pleasing to Christ and the Immaculate Mother of God, so enough of their knavery. Pardon me, good Nikonites,[32] for having abused you; live as ye will. As for me, I am now about to take up again my tale of woe, so go your ways in peace. For twenty years God has willed that I should be tormented by you, and should it be for twenty more, then will I endure it, in the name of the Lord our God and of our Saviour Jesus Christ. Enough of this. I have wandered, as it is, far enough from my story—let us return to it.

So I left Dauria; the food began to grow scarce, so I prayed together with my company, and Christ gave us a roebuck, a huge beast, and on him we lived till we reached Baikal. There, by the lake, we came on Russian folk—a settlement of sable-hunters and of fishermen; they were right glad to see us, dear souls, and we them, and they dragged us and our boat to shore, and led us far inland to the hills. There was a dear lad called

[31] Under ordinary circumstances, it was prohibited by the canons of the Orthodox Church to baptize one's own children.

[32] Nikonites: refers to the supporters of Nikon.

Terenty, and he and his comrades gazed on us, and we on them —dear souls—with tears of joy. And they snowed meat and drink on us, as much as ever we needed. They brought me some forty freshwater sturgeons, saying, "There, Father! God sent them into our fishery for you. Take them all." I, bowing to them, blessed the fish and bade them take them back, saying, "What need have I of so many?" They entertained me there and, from dire need, I accepted from them some provision. Then, having repaired our boat, we let out our sails, and prepared to cross the lake. But the lake grew rough, so we took to our oars. In that place the lake is very broad—it must be a hundred or at least eighty versts. When we stood to the shore there sprang up a tempest and we were forced to find a shelter from the waves on the shore. The place was surrounded by high mountains: I have wandered over the face of the earth 20,000 versts and more, but never have I seen their like. On their summit are tents and earthen huts, portals and towers, stone walls and courts, all neatly fashioned. Onions grow of them and garlic, bigger than the Romanov onion, and exceeding sweet to the taste; there also grows wild hemp, and in the gardens fine grass and exceeding fragrant flowers, and there is great quantity of birds—geese and swans that fly over the lake like snow. And there are fishes—sturgeon and trout, sterlet and salmon-trout and whiting and many other kinds; it is fresh water and in that mighty ocean lake there are sea-calves and great sea-hares. I saw none such during all the time that I was living on the Mezen,[33] and the fish in it are of a great weight, the sturgeon and salmon-trout are exceeding fleshy—they are not for frying, for it would be naught but fat. And all this has been fashioned by our sweet Christ for man, so that, with a mind at last at rest, he might give praise to God. But such is man that he is given to vanity, and his days go by like a shadow: he leaps, like a goat; he blows himself out, like a bubble; he rages, like a lynx; he seeks to devour, like a serpent; when he looks on the comeliness of his neighbour he neighs like a foal; he is crafty, like a fiend; when he has eaten his fill then, like an heathen, he falls asleep, without saying his prayers; he puts off repenting till his old age and then he vanishes; we know not where,— whether it be to light of darkness: it will be shown on the Day of Judgment. Forgive me; I myself have sinned more than other men.

[33] Mezen was a small city in northern Russia to which Avvakum was deported in 1664, remaining there until 1665.

XI. The Staunch Protopopitsa[34]

So we reached Russian settlements, and I was informed concerning the Church, and like Pilate, I saw that I "*could prevail nothing, but that rather a tumult was made.*" My mind was troubled and, sitting down, I began to ponder what I should do —should I continue preaching God's Word or should I hide myself? For I was tied by my wife and children. And seeing that I was troubled, my wife came up to me, timidly, delicately, and said, "How comes it, my lord, that you are troubled?" And I acquainted her with all my thoughts. "Wife! What must I do? The Winter of Heresy is at the door; am I to speak or to hold my peace? I am tied by you!" And she said to me, "Lord have mercy! What are you saying, Petrovitch? Have I not heard, have you not read, the words of the Apostle: *Art thou bound unto a wife? seek not to be loosed. Art thou loosed from a wife? seek not a wife.* I and the children, we give you our blessing, continue preaching the Word of God as heretofore, and take no thought for us until such time as shall seem good to God; when that times comes, remember us in your prayers; Christ is strong and he will not abandon us. Get thee gone, get thee gone to church, Petrovitch! Unmask the Whore of Heresy!" And I bowed myself to the earth before her, and shook myself free from the blindness of a troubled mind and began once more to preach and teach God's Word in the towns and in all places until such time as I could boldly tear the mask from the heresy of Nikon.

In Yeniseisk[35] I wintered, and having sailed through the summer again I wintered in Tobolsk; and on my way as far as Moscow I cried aloud in every town and in every village, in churches and in marketplaces, preaching the Word of God and teaching and laying bare the snares of the ungodly. And thereon I came to Moscow. Three years was I in coming from Dauria, and it took me five years traveling upstream. We journeyed ever eastward amid native tribes and habitations. Much might be said of that. Sometimes we fell into the hands of the natives; at Ob, the mighty river, in my presence they put to death twenty men who were Christians. And they were minded to do the like to me, but they let me go altogether. And again on the Irtysh River there was standing a company of them—they were lying in ambush for our men of Berezov to slay us—but I knew it not and I went up toward them. And when I was come up to

[34] Protopopitsa: the wife of a protopope, or archpriest.
[35] Yeniseisk: a Russian outpost and merchant city in central Siberia on the Yenisei River.

them I put in to the bank. In a moment they were round about me with their bows, and I, I tell you, went forth to embrace them as though they were monks and I spoke and said, "Christ be with me and with you too." And they entreated me kindly and they brought their wives to my wife. And my wife dissembled with them, as in the world they are wont to employ flattery; and the womenfolk were kindly and we felt it: when the womenfolk are good, then under Christ all is well. The men hid their bows and arrows. I bought some bear's flesh from them and they let me go free. As I was saying, I was come to Tobolsk. And the folk were astonished thereat, for Bashkirs and the Tatars were scouring all Siberia. But I, trusting in Christ, went through their midst. And when I had reached Verkhoturie,[36] Ivan Bogdanovitch, my friend, was astonished at me. "How did you ever get through, archpriest?" And I made answer, "Christ brought me through, and the all pure Mother of God brought me through. I fear no man, only Christ do I fear."

XII. Back in Moscow: Joys and Disputes (1664)

Thus did I come to Moscow, and as though I were an angel of God the tsar and all his boyars received me gladly. I went to see Theodore Rtishchev,[37] he came himself from his tent, received my blessing and began to speak of many things: for three days and three nights he suffered me not to go home, and thereafter he informed the tsar concerning me. His Majesty gave command to place me at his side and spake kindly to me. "Art thou well in health, archpriest?" said he. "God bade me see thee again." And I in answer kissed his hand and pressed it, and myself said, "God lives and my spirit lives, your Majesty! but for what is before us that God will ordain." And he sighed softly and went whither he had need. And other things happened, but what need to speak of it? That too passed by. He bade them place me in the guesthouse of a monastery in the Kremlin, and when he passed my door going out on expeditions he often gave me greeting, bowing low, and himself would say, "Bless me," said he, "and pray for me"; and one time he took

36 Verkhoturie was a Russian city in western Siberia almost in the foothills of the Ural Mountains.

37 Theodore (Fedor) Rtishchev was a statesman and personal friend of Tsar Alexis. He actively participated in church affairs and from 1645 to 1653 was a member of the Zealots of Piety. He remained faithful to Nikon after the latter's break with this movement. He was well known for his support of the arts, learning, and charitable activities.

his fur cap from his head and let it fall as he was riding on horseback. He used to slip out of his carriage to come to me and all his boyars kept bowing and scraping, crying, "Archpriest, bless us and pray for us." How shall I not grieve for such a tsar and such boyars? It grieves me to think how good they were, they gave me place wheresoever I wished, and they named me their confessor, that I might be made one with them in the faith. But I held all these things to be but vanity. And I gained Christ and was mindful of death, how all these things pass away.

And this was revealed to me in Tobolsk when I was half asleep. "Watch, I bid thee, that thou be not a branch cut off." I leaped up and fell before the icon in great terror, and I spake and said, "Lord, I will not go when they chant in newfangled fashion; my God." I was at early Mass in the cathedral on the name day of the tsarina. I was jesting with them in that Church in the presence of the officials, and from the moment of arrival I took notice whether they mixed the elements in triple or in twofold wise, and standing at the altar by the sacrificial table I abused them, and with time I got used to them, so I ceased from abusing them. Such was the bitter spirit of Antichrist that stung me.

Thus did our sweet Christ make me afraid and said to me, "After so great suffering wilt thou perish? Watch, lest I hew thee off as a dry branch." I went not to Mass, but I went to sup with the prince, and I told him all, every word. A kind boyar prince, Ivan Andrew Chelkov, began to weep. Woe is me, accursed one, that I forget so great mercy of God!

When I was at Dauria and I labored as a fisherman, I went in the winter to my children, and I went along the lake on snowshoes; there was no snow but great frosts, and the ice froze well-nigh the thickness of a man. I began to want to drink, and I suffered much from thirst. I couldn't go on, I was midway in the lake, I couldn't get to the water; the lake was eight versts. I began to look up to heaven and to say, "O Lord, thou didst cause water to flow in the desert for the thirsty people of Israel, then and now art thou; give me to drink by whatever means seem good to thee. O Lord my God! Woe is me. I know not how to pray, forgive me for the Lord's sake. Who am I, a dead dog?" The ice gave a crack beneath me and split up to either side across the whole lake and came together again, and a great mountain of ice rose up, and while this was going on I stood in my accustomed place, and looking toward the east, I bowed twice or thrice, pronouncing the name of the Lord in a loud voice from the depths of my heart. God had left me a small hole in the ice, and I, falling down, slaked my thirst. And I wept and was glad, praising God. After that the hole in the ice joined up and I, rising up, bowed down to the Lord and then again ran along the ice whither I must needs go to my children. And in my other wanderings it often happened to me like this. I was either walking along, dragging my sledge or catching fish or cutting wood in the forest, or whatsoever I might be doing, I always recited my office at the regular time, whether it was morning Mass or evening, at the hours it was the custom; if I chanced to be among other people none could hinder me, but I would stand upright and none of my companions with me, for they did not love my office, and when they were there it was impossible for me to carry it out, and I, going away from among men, would go through it in a shortened form, either under a hill or in a wood, beating with my head against the earth, and sometimes I would weep and feel wounded. But if there should be people with me I would place the icon on the sledge-rail and I would recite the office right through, and some would pray with me, but others would cook their porridge; and when I am going in my sledge on Sundays to the guesthouses I sing the whole church service, and on festival days when I am driving in a sledge I will sing, and often on Sundays as I go along I would sing. And when I do it very persistently, sometimes I would grumble though only a little, for my body was ahungered and would fain eat, and was athirst and would fain drink, and likewise my spirit, O Father Epiphany, desires spiritual food: It is not the hunger for bread that destroys a man nor the thirst for water, but the great hunger of a man when he lives without praying to God.[38]

If thou art not weary of listening to this thy servant of Christ, I, a sinner, will make known to thee this too, how often in the land of Daur, from loss of strength and from hunger I could not keep my rule, only a little of it could I keep, only the evening psalms and the midnight office at the first hour, but more than that I could not: I dragged myself about like a poor beast. I was grieved about that office of mine, but I could not take it up. You see by now I had got so weak. But sometimes I went to the forest for wood, and while I was away my wife and children would sit on the ground by the fire, my daughter with her mother, and they would both cry. Agraphena, my poor unhappy one, was then not yet grown up. I came back from the wood—

[38] Another direct address to Epiphany, Avvakum's confessor and fellow inmate in Pustozersk.

the child was sobbing hard. She could not speak for her tongue was fast bound, but she sat there and whimpered to her mother, and the mother looked at her and cried. But I breathed heavily and came near to the child with a prayer and said, "In the name of the Lord I bid thee speak to me and tell me why thou weepest." And she jumped up and bowed before me and began to speak clearly thus, "I do not know who it is, my Lord father, but there is a Shining One within me and he held me by my tongue and he would not let me speak to mother, and because of it I cried. But he said to me, 'Tell your father that he should recite his office as he used to do, and then ye all go forth again to Russia, but, if he does not keep his rule, about which he is himself troubled, then in this place ye shall all die, and he shall die with you.' " At that time another thing of that sort was said to her, that there would be an edict to fetch us, and how that many of our friends had perished in Russia; all this came to pass. I was to say to Pashkov that if he sang the morning and evening office then God would give fair weather, and the corn would grow and there would be constant rain, and they sowed wheat on a small plot a day or two before Peter's day, and immediately it sprouted and was all but rotted by the rains. I spoke to him about the evening and morning office and he set to do this. God sent fair weather, and the corn ripened immediately. What a miracle! It was sown late but it ripened early.

And again, poor man, he began to practice cunning arts about God's doings—the following year he sowed much, but an unwonted rain poured down, and the water overflowed from the river and drowned the plowed fields and washed everything away, and it washed away our hut, and until that time there had never been water there, and the natives wondered. Mark you, as he went his way, so God moved in his mysterious way. At first he laughed at the news, but afterward, when the child wanted to eat, he betook him to tears—and then I sought not to slacken about my office. Enough of this have I spoken; let us return to our first subject. We must needs remember all these things and not be forgetting them, so as not to lay aside any of God's doings in negligence and waste and not to alter them for the pleasure of this age of vanity.

Now I will tell of what was done at Moscow. They said that I was not at one with them. His Majesty bade Rodion Streshnev[39] persuade me that I should hold my peace. And I did his

[39] Rodion Streshnev: a relative of the tsar's wife and his councilor in Church affairs.

bidding. The tsar is set over us by God, and at this moment was kindly disposed towards me. So I hoped that little by little he would come to a better mind. They promised me on Simeon's day to place me at the printing office to correct books, and I was exceedingly glad, for that pleased me better than to be the tsar's confessor. I wanted something better than the confessional. I waited on him. He sent me ten rubles and the tsarina sent me ten. Luke, the confessor, sent me ten, and Rodion Streshnev also ten, and our old friend Theodore Rtishchev then ordered them to slip into my hat sixty rubles from his official salary, but about that I was to say nothing! Each man put his hand in his pocket and brought out every manner of thing. I lived in the house of my dear one, Theodosia Prokofievna Morozova,[40] and didn't go out inasmuch as she was my spiritual daughter. And her sister, Princess Eudoxia Prokofievna, was my daughter also. My dear ones, martyrs for Christ! And I was ever in the house of Anna Petrovna Miloslavskaia.[41] God rest her soul! And I went to Theodore Rtishchev's house to dispute with the apostles, and so lived about the space of half a year. And I saw that I prevailed nothing but that rather a tumult was made; again, I began to grumble, and I wrote to the tsar many things to the effect that he should earnestly seek for the ancient piety and defend from heresy our common mother holy Church, and on the patriarchal throne he should place a shepherd of the orthodox faith in place of the wolf and apostate Nikon, him that was an evildoer and a heretic. And when I had got ready the letter I had no more strength left in me: and I sent it forth on the journey to the tsar by my spiritual son Theodore, the Fool in Christ, which Theodore they strangled at Mezene, hanging him upon the gallows-tree. Now he in all boldness approached the tsar's carriage, and the tsar bade him sit down with the letter near the great entrance: he did not perceive that the letter was from me. And afterward, having the letter from him he bade let him go. And he—God rest his soul!—after staying a while with me again went into the church in the presence of the tsar and began to play the fool as though he was half-witted. The tsar was angry and bade them send him away to the

40 Theodosia Morozova—a lady-in-waiting to the tsarina, and widow of an influential boyar. She remained a faithful supporter of Avvakum. She and her sister, Eudoxia Urusova, were arrested in 1670 for their support of the Old Believer movement, and both died in prison in 1672.

41 Anna Miloslavskaia: a relative of the tsarina, and an influential supporter of Avvakum.

Miracle Monastery. There Paul the archimandrite bade them put fetters on him, and by the will of God the fetters brake to pieces upon his legs before the people. But he, God rest his soul! my friend! crept into the burning stove in the bakehouse after the loaves and sat on the grating with his naked rump and picked up the crumbs in the stove to eat of them. Then the monks were affrighted and told the archimandrite Paul that was now metropolitan. He acquainted the tsar with this, and the tsar came to the monastery and ordered them to let him go with honor. He again came to me, and from that day on the tsar began to look askance at me. He was ill pleased that I began again to speak. He would have liked me to hold my peace but that was not my way. And the bishops, like goats, began to leap up against me, and they plotted to send me in banishment from Moscow, for many of the Christians had come to me and perceiving the truth they would not walk in the service of a lie. And from the tsar there came to me the accusation, "They tell me that the bishops bring complaint against thee; they say because of thee the churches are empty. Go again," said he, "into banishment." Thus spake the boyar Peter Mikhailovich Saltykov.[42] And they brought me to Mezen, and many good people gave me this and that in the name of Christ. And everything remained, only they took me with my wife and my children and my household. From town to town I taught the people of God and denounced them, the spotted beasts. And they brought us to Mezen.

Having endured for half a year, they took me again without my wife to Moscow, and my two sons journeyed with me, Ivan and Prokopy. But my wife and the rest were all left at Mezen. And having brought us to Moscow they took us at first away to the Pafnutiev Monastery,[43] and there they sent us a letter, and they spake thus and thus: "Wilt thou so long vex us? be reconciled to us, dear old Avvakum!" But I refused as though they were devils. And they flew in my face.

Then I wrote them an answer with much violence of words, and I sent it by Kosma, a deacon of Yaroslavl, by the subdeacon of the patriarchal court—Kosma in public tried to overpersuade me, but in private he upheld me, speaking thus, "Archpriest, do not desert the ancient rites; a mighty man wilt thou be with Christ if thou wilt endure to the end—do not look to us for we

[42] Peter Saltykov was a boyar who energetically opposed Avvakum and his movement.

[43] Pafnutiev Monastery: a monastery in the vicinity of Moscow that often served as a prison for clergymen.

are ruined." And I to him made answer that he should again stand for Christ. And he said, "I cannot. Nikon has led me astray." And to speak shortly, he had denied Christ before Nikon, in that he had no strength to stand firm, my poor Kosma. I fell to crying; I blessed him, unhappy one—after that I had no more dealings with him; let God deal with him as seems good to him.

XIII. Preparations for the Trial (1664–1666)

Thus having remained ten weeks in Pafnutiev in chains, they took me again to Moscow, and in the room of the Cross the bishops held disputation with me. They led me to the Cathedral church, and after the Elevation of the Host they sheared me and the deacon Theodore, and then they cursed us and I cursed them back. And I was heavy at heart for the Mass. And after I had stayed for a time at the patriarchal court, they took us by night to Ugresha,[44] to the monastery of St. Nicholas—and the enemies of God shaved off my beard. What would you? It is like unto wolves not to pity the sheep; they tore at my hair like dogs and only left one forelock—such as the Poles wear on their foreheads. They did it carrying me not along the road to the monastery but by the marshes and the quagmires that people might not see me. They themselves saw that they were behaving as fools but they did not wish to cease from their folly; the devil had darkened their minds, why should one reproach them? It was not them or they would have been otherwise. The time had come spoken of in the Gospel. "*It must needs be that offences must come,*" and another Evangelist saith: "*It must needs be that offences come, but woe unto him by whom offence cometh.*" Look thou that readest! Our misery was of necessity, we might not escape it! For this cause God doth let loose offenses and even that the elect may be inflamed and that they may be made white, even that temptations be made manifest in us. Satan has asked and obtained from God our bright shining Russia, that he might purple it with martyr's blood. Well, hast thou imagined this, O devil, and to us it is sweet to suffer for our Sweet Lord.

They kept me at Nikolas's in a cold room for seventeen weeks. There I had a visitation from God; read of it in the letter to the tsar. And the tsar came to the monastery and paid a visit to my prison cell and gave a groan and then left the monastery; it seems from that that he was sorry for me, the will of God lay in that. When they had shorn me there was a very great dis-

[44] Ugresha: a village in the vicinity of Moscow.

turbance among them with the tsarina, God rest her soul! She, sweet lady, detected me at that time and asked to have me released from prison, as to which there is much to be said; God forgive them! As to my sufferings I do not hold them answerable, neither now nor hereafter; it sufficeth me to pray for them, be they alive or be they dead. The devil set discord between us but they were ever good toward me. Enough of this.

And poor Prince Ivan Vorotynsky[45] came there without the tsar to pray, and he asked to be admitted to my prison cell. But they would not let the hapless man in. I could only, looking through the window, weep over him. My sweet friend feared God, he was Christ's orphan. Christ will not cast him away. Thus always was Christ on our side, and all the boyars were good to us, only the devil was malicious and what could we have done if Christ had left us? They beat my dear Prince Ivan Khovansky[46] with rods and they burnt Isaiah,[47] and the lady Theodosia Morozova they brought to ruin, and they killed her son and tortured her and her sister Eudoxia, beating them with rods; and they parted her from her children and divorced her from her husband, and him they say, Prince Peter Urusov,[48] they married to another wife. But what was there to do? Let them torture those dear ones, they will go to their heavenly bridegroom. In every wise God will cause to pass this troublesome time and will call to himself the bridegroom to his heavenly palace, he the true Sun, our Light and our Hope. Let us turn again to the one first matter.

After this they took me again to the monastery of Pafnutiev, and there, having shut me up in the dark room, and put fetters on me, they kept me for well-nigh a year. There the cellarer Nikodemus was good to me at first, but he, poor fellow, smoked of tobacco more than that sixty poods the which they seized when they searched the house of the Metropolitan of Gaza,[49] and they seized a lute too and other hidden things of the monastery on the which they played and made merry withal. It is a

[45] Prince Ivan Vorotynsky: member of a wealthy aristocratic family who supported Avvakum and his movement.

[46] Prince Ivan Khovansky: a member of a conservative family that lent its support to Avvakum.

[47] Isaiah: the majordomo of the boyar, Peter Saltykov. He was burned for his faithfulness to the Old Belief.

[48] Prince Peter Urusov: the husband of Princess Eudoxia Urusova, and brother-in-law of Theodosia Morozova.

[49] Metropolitan Paisy of Gaza (Palestine): a Greek bishop who came to Russia in 1662 and became very influential at the court. He was the ideological leader of the opponents of Avvakum and the Old Believers, and was well known for his lack of scrupulousness and his participation in suspicious mercantile operations.

sin to speak of it, forgive me; it was not my business, let him look to it, to his own Lord he must stand or fall. This is just by the way. With them there were well-beloved teachers of Holy Writ. I asked of this Nikodemus, the cellarer, on Easter Day, in order that I might rest because of the holiday, that he would bid them open the door that I might sit on the threshold, and he abused me and refused me savagely as he willed. And after that he came into my cell he fell suddenly ill, they anointed him with oil and gave him the last sacraments and then and there he died. That was on Easter Monday, and before, on the night of Tuesday, there had come to him a man in the semblance of myself with a censer, and in shining vestments, and having censed him and taken him by the hand he moved himself and was healed. And he came to me with the servitor by night into the dungeon. And as he came he said, "Blessed is this dwelling—what a dungeon doth it contain—how blessed is this dungeon—what sufferings doth it hold! blessed are those bonds. . . ." And he fell before me and clasped my chain and said, "Forgive me, for God's sake! forgive, I have sinned before God and before thee. I have insulted thee, and for this God hath punished me." And I spake, "How hath he punished thee? Instruct me!" And he, "Thou thyself," said he, "didst come to me and didst cense me; thou didst have pity on me and didst raise me up. Why dost thou deny it?" And the servitor standing there said, "Yes, my Lord and Father, he took thee by the hand and led thee from the cell, and bowed down before thee, and thou didst go hence." And I charged him that he should say nothing to any man concerning this secret thing. And he questioned me how henceforth he might live for Christ. "Ah," said he, "dost thou charge me to go forth into the desert?" But I forbade him and would not suffer him to give up his stewardship, if only in secret he would preserve the ancient tradition of his fathers. And he bowed low and went away to his own place and on the morrow at meat he told it to all the brotherhood. And the people ceaselessly and with boldness pressed in to see me, asking for a blessing and for my prayers, and I taught them from Holy Writ and I healed them by the Word of God. At that time I had some enemies, but these were reconciled to me. Alas, when shall I quit this life of vanity? It is written: "Woe to him when all men speak well of him." In very truth I know now how I may endure to the end; of good deeds there are none now; but I glorified God. That he knows and with him it rests.

Thither there came to me in secret Theodore with his children; he that was strangled, God rest his soul! and he questioned me thus: "How wouldst thou have me walk? Shall I go in my shift in the old fashion or shall I put clothes upon me? The heretics," said he, "are seeking me, they would fain bring me to ruin. I," said he, "was at Riazan under guard at the archbishop's palace at the court, and he, Hilarion,[50] did grievously torment me: there was scarce a day when he did not beat me with cords and he kept me bound in iron fetters, compelling me to partake of the new communion of Antichrist. And I said, 'I could not,' and I prayed in the night and wept and spake, 'O Lord, if thou dost not save me, they will cause me to commit abomination and I shall perish. What can I do?' " And weeping much he said suddenly, said he, "My father, all my chains fell rattling from me, and the door was opened of its own motion. And I," said he, "bowed down to God, and I went forth. I came to the outer gates and the gates were opened. I went straight forth along the road to Moscow. It was scarce daylight," said he, "when they gave chase on horseback; three men passed quickly by me and they did not see me, and I," said he, "trusting in Christ, went on my way onwards. But," said he, "very soon they came upon me and they were snarling at me; said they, 'The son of a whore has escaped, where may one take him?' And again," said he, "they passed by me and did not see me. And I," said he, "again betook me to thee and asked whether I should go again to be tortured or whether I should don clothes and live in Moscow." And I, a sinner, bade him don clothes and not to hide himself from the hands of the heretics. They strangled him in Mezen, hanging him upon the gallows-tree. Eternal be his memory together with Luke Lavrentievich. My well-beloved children! They suffered for Christ. Glory to God for them. And Theodore accomplished an exceeding mighty deed above measure; by day he played the Fool of Christ, and all night long he wept and prayed. I know many good men, but I had never yet beheld such an ascetic. He lived with me in Moscow about half a year, but I was still ill—two of us lived in the same chamber with him and at the most he would lie an hour or two and then he would get up, and then he would go through a thousand genuflexions and would seat himself on the ground, or else, standing up, he would weep for some three hours; meantime I would continue lying and sometimes sleep, but sometimes I was restless, and when he had his fill of violent weeping then he would come up to me and say, "How long

[50] Hilarion, Bishop of Riazan: a former friend of Avvakum's who became a staunch supporter of Nikon and the modernists.

wilt thou continue lying? Come to thyself. Thou art a priest. How are thou not ashamed?" And I could not rise though he lifted me up saying, "Stand up, my sweet father!" And he pulled at me somehow or other. And he bade me say prayers as I sat, and he kept bowing down instead of me. He *was* my friend in very truth! He was sore vexed by his sufferings. At one time his intestine issued forth from him three yards in length, and at another five yards, and his guts were measureless—and it was both pitiful and laughable. At Ustiug for five years he froze barefoot in the frost with only his shift. I saw him myself. Then he became my spiritual son, and when I came from Siberia he ran up to my stall in the church in order to pray: he spoke thus: "When," said he, "one first began to thaw after the frost and get warm, my father, it was very hard to bear"; said he, "one stamps with one's feet on the brick floor as though they were wooden legs, and on the morrow they did not hurt."

He had with him there in his cell a psalter of those newly printed. He knew but little as yet of those newfangled things. But I told him all, word by word, concerning the new books—and he snatched at the book and hurled it into the stove. And he cursed all these newfangled ways. And he was exceeding zealous for the faith of Christ. But why speak many words? As he began, so he ended. And his great virtue lay not in idle words, as is with me, miserable man, for whom he died pleading to God.

A good man, too, was my dear old Afanasy, my spiritual son —his name in religion was Avraany—whom the apostates baked to death in Moscow on the fire, and like unto bread of sweet savor he was offered to the Holy Trinity. Until he took the cowl, he went about barefoot with only his shift, both winter and summer, only he was milder than Theodore and fell short of his asceticism. He dearly loved weeping, and weeping he would go about and with whomsoever he spoke his words were soft and sweet as though he wept. Theodore was very zealous and suffered much concerning the work of God. In every way he would weary himself to bring sin to light and to destroy it. But enough of them! As they lived, so they died, with Christ Jesus our Lord.

XIV. The Church Council of 1667 and the Final Schism

I will tell you yet more of my wanderings when they brought me out of the Pafnutiev Monastery in Moscow and placed me in the guesthouse, and after many wanderings they set me down in the Miracle Monastery, before the patriarchs of all Christendom, and the Russian Nikonites sat there like so many foxes. I spoke of many things in Holy Writ with the patriarchs. God did open my sinful mouth and Christ put them to shame. The last word they spoke to me was this: "Why," said they, "art thou stubborn? The folk of Palestine, Serbia, Albania, the Wallachians, they of Rome and Poland, all these do cross themselves with three fingers, only thou standest out in thine obstinacy and dost cross thyself with two fingers; it is not seemly." And I answered them for Christ thus: "O you teachers of Christendom, Rome fell away long ago and lies prostrate,[51] and the Poles fell in the like ruin with her, being to the end the enemies of the Christian. And among you orthodoxy is of mongrel breed; and no wonder —if by the violence of the Turkish Mohmut you have become impotent, and henceforth it is you who should come to us to learn. By the gift of God among us there is autocracy; till the time of Nikon, the apostate, in our Russia under our pious princes and tsars the Orthodox faith was pure and undefiled, and in the church was no sedition. Nikon, the wolf, together with the devil, ordained that men should cross themselves with three fingers, but our first shepherds made the sign of the cross and blessed men as of old with two fingers, according to the tradition of our holy fathers, Meletina of Antioch, Theodoret, the blessed Bishop of Cyrene, Peter of Damascus and Maxim the Greek;[52] and so too did our own synod of Moscow, at the time of the Tsar Ivan, bid them, putting their fingers together in that wise, make the sign of the cross and give the blessing, as of old the holy fathers Melety and others taught. Then in the time of Ivan, the tsar,[53] there were the standard-bearers, Gury and Varsanophy, wonder-workers of Kazan, and Phillip the Abbot of Solovki among the Russian saints."[54] And the patriarchs fell to thinking, and our people began to howl like wolf cubs and to belch out words against their fathers saying, "Our Russian holy men were ignorant, and they understood nothing, they are unlearned folk," said they. "How can one trust them? they have no letters." O Holy God! How hast thou suffered so great reviling of thy holy ones? I, miserable one, was bitter in my

[51] Here Avvakum quotes The *Tale of the White Cowl* (see Selection 31), which became one of the ideological foundation stones of the Old Believer movement.

[52] Maxim the Greek was a Greek scholar whose writings were often quoted by the Old Believers.

[53] This refers to Tsar Ivan IV.

[54] Sts. Gury and Varsanophy were Orthodox missionaries among the Tatars after the taking of Kazan. St. Phillip, Abbot of Solovki, later Metropolitan of Moscow.

heart, but I could do nothing. I abused them as hard as I could, and I spake as follows: "I am pure, and the dust that cleaves to my feet do I shake off before you, as it is written—'better one if he do the will of God than a thousand of the godless.'" Then louder than before they began to cry out against me: "Away with him, away with him; he hath outraged us all"; and they began to thrust at me and to beat me. And the patriarchs themselves threw themselves on me; about forty of them I think there must have been. Great was the army of Antichrist that gathered itself together. Ivan Uvarov seized me and dragged at me, and I cried aloud, "Stop, do not beat me!" Then they all sprang back and I began to speak to the interpreter, the archimandrite, thus: "Say to the patriarch, the Apostle Paul writes: 'For such an high priest became us, who is holy, harmless, and so forth,' but ye, having sorely mishandled a man, how then can ye straightway perform your office?" Then they sat down. I went away to the door and lay down on my side. "Ye sit down," I said to them, "but I lie down." At that they laughed. "The archpriest," said they, "is a silly fellow, and does not show honor to the patriarchs." And I said, "We are fools for Christ's sake. Ye are great and we without honor; ye are strong and we are weak." After that, again, the authorities came to me and began to talk with me on the question of the Alleluias: Christ put it in my heart and I put them to shame for their Romish heresy, through Dionysios the Areopagite, of whom mention has been made before. And Euphemy, the cellarer of the Miracle Monastery, spake: "Right art thou," said he, "there is no more to be said." And they took me along to chain me.

Then the tsar sent an officer with musketeers and they took me to the Vorobiev hills.[55]

There was the priest Lazar and the monk Epiphany, an elder.[56] They had been shorn and were ill treated as though they were village peasants, my dear ones. A wise man when he did but see them must needs fall aweeping when he looked at them. Well, let them suffer! Why grieve for them! Christ was better than them, and against him, our sweet Lord, evil was wrought by the forebears of the Nikonites, Annas and Caiaphas. No wonder, for they followed after an exemplar—we must grieve for

55 Vorobiev, or Sparrow Hills—hills in the vicinity of Moscow where Moscow University is now located.

56 Father Lazar and Monk Epiphany were condemned, together with Avvakum, by the Council of 1667. Both of them, as well as Avvakum and Deacon Fedor (Theodore), were deported to Pustozersk, and burned in 1682.

them, poor things! Woe to the hapless followers of Nikon! They have perished of their own wickedness and their stubbornness of soul!

Then they brought us from the Vorobiev hills to the guest-house of the Andreevsky Monastery to the Savin suburb, and as though we were robbers, followed after us and left us not, nay, even when we relieved nature. It was both pitable and laughable, as though the devil had blinded them.

Then again we were taken to the St. Nickolas Monastery at Ugresha. And there the tsar sent to me the officer Yury Lutokhin, that I might bless him, and we had much converse concerning this and that.

Then again they brought me to Moscow, to the guesthouse of the Nikolsky Monastery, and they demanded of us yet again a statement of the true faith. After that there were sent more than once to me gentlemen of the bedchamber, diverse persons, Artemon and Dementy.[57] And they spake to me in the name of the tsar: "Archpriest!" they said, "I see thy life that it is pure and undefiled and pleasing unto God, I and the tsarina and our children, be entreated of us." The envoy wept as he spake, and for him I weep always. I was exceeding sorry for him. And again he spake: "I beg of thee, hearken to me. Be thou reconciled with the patriarchs." And I said, "Even if God will that I should die, I will not be joined together with apostates. Thou art my tsar, but they, what have they to do with thee? They have lost their tsar and they have come here to gobble you up. I—say I—will not cease to uplift my hands to heaven until God give thee over to me."

The last word I got from the tsar was, "Wherever," said he, "thou shalt be, do not forget us in thy prayers." And I, sinful one, now, as far as I may, pray to God for him.

XV. Banishment to Pustozersk

After scourging my friends, but not me, they banished me to Pustozersk. And I sent from Pustozersk to the tsar two letters, the first not long but the other longer, what I had said to him, that I wrote also in the letters, and also certain signs of God, which had appeared to me in my prison. Who reads will understand. Also a letter written by the deacon was sent to Moscow by me and the brotherhood as a gift to the True Believers. The

[57] This refers to Artemon Mateev and Dementy Bashmakov, who were important bureaucrats and close councilors of Tsar Alexis. The latter was the head of *Tainy Prikaz* (Department for Secret Affairs) under Alexis.

book was an answer of the Orthodox and was a conviction of the heresy of the apostates—in it was written the truth concerning the dogmas of the Church. Further, two letters had been sent by the priest Lazar to the tsar and the patriarch, and of all this we got a present. In Mezen of my household they hanged two men, my spiritual children, the aforenamed Theodore, Christ's Fool, and Luke Lavrentievich, servants of Christ. Luke was a dweller in Moscow, the only son of his mother, who was a widow; he was of the guild of banners, a youth in years about fifteen. He came to Mezen, to his death, with my children. And when there was a general slaughter in my house, Pilate asked him, "And how do you, my man, cross yourself?" And he made answer with all temperance: "I do believe and do cross myself so, placing my fingers as doth my spiritual father, the archpriest Avvakum." And Pilate ordered them to put him in the dungeon, and there to put a noose round his neck, and he hanged him on a railing. And so he passed from earth to heaven. Greater than that what could they do for him? And if he were but a youth, he acted like an old man. He went his way to the Lord. Well were it even for an old man did he win through like that.

At this time the order was given to hang my two sons after the flesh, Ivan and Prokopy, but they, miserable ones, were weaklings and never thought them to lay hold on the crowns of victory. Being soon afraid of death they made submission, and so they buried them alive in the earth with their mother for third. There was a death without death for you. Repent as ye sit there, while the devil concocts something else! That death be terrible is not wonderful! Time was when even Peter, dear friend of Christ, made denial and went out and wept bitterly, and for his tears he was forgiven, and for my children it is not wonderful that, because of my sins, weakness was permitted them. Well and good! So be it! Christ is mighty to save us all and to have mercy upon us.

At this time the deputy, Ivan Elagin, was with us in Pustozersk, having come from Mezen, and he received from us a statement, and this was it: "Year and month," and again: "We keep the tradition of the holy Fathers unaltered, and we proclaim as accursed Paisy the Patriarch of Palestine with his fellows as an assembly of heretics," and besides there were said there a few words about Nikon, the fabricator of this heresy. For this they brought us to the scaffold, and when they had read the sentence they took me away without scourging me to the dungeon. They read me the edict: "Let Avvakum be put into an underground prison within the palisade and let there be given to him bread and water." But I spat on this and I desired to die, refraining from food, and I ate nothing for about eight days or more. But then my brethren bade me eat.

At the same time they took the priest Lazar, and cut out his whole tongue from his throat, but little blood flowed and soon stopped. And he spoke again without his tongue. Moreover, having placed his right hand upon the scaffold, they cut it off at the wrist, and the hand that had been cut off, lying upon the ground, of its own motion placed its fingers after the ancient use, and lying thus long time before the people, the poor thing made confession, and even unto death did not betray the sign of salvation. Even I am amazed at that; the lifeless thing convicts the living. And on the third day I felt in his mouth with my hand; it was all smooth, and there was no tongue, but it did not hurt. God had granted that with good hap it had healed up. In Moscow they had cut out his tongue and then there was some of it left, but now it was all cut away. But he spoke clearly for the space of two years as though he had a tongue. And when he had completed two years there was another wonder—in the space of three days his tongue grew again to its full size, but that it was a little stumpy, and again he spake, instantly praising God and railing at the apostates.

At this time they seized a hermit priest, an anchorite of strict rule, Epiphany, an elder, and cut out the whole of his tongue. And they cut off four fingers of his hand. And at first he spoke thickly, and at this time he prayed to the Virgin, the Mother of God, and there appeared to him in the air two tongues, that of Moscow and the present one. Now he, taking up one, put it in his mouth, and from that moment began to speak purely and clearly, and the whole tongue fitted itself into his mouth. Great are the works and unspeakable are the judgments of the Lord! He sendeth forth his judgments and again he healeth and hath mercy. But what availeth many words? God is an old hand at miracles. Out of nothing he brings life, and shall he not at the Last Day raise up all flesh in the twinkling of an eye; and who may discern concerning this thing? God is after this wise: he createth what is new and he reneweth that which is old. In all things glory be to him!

At this time they seized the deacon Theodore. They cut out the whole of his tongue, but left a little bit in his mouth, having cut it slantways across his throat. It healed just as it was at the time, but later on it grew again as it was before. It stuck out a little way from the lips, but stump-like. And they cut off his hand across the palm. By the gift of God it all healed, and he spake clearly and cleanly as before.

Then they covered us up with earth. There was a framework in the earth, and above the earth a second framework, and then again round the whole of it was a fence with four locks, and they set a watch to guard all the doors. Now we, both here and everywhere in dungeons, sing songs before the Lord Christ, the Son of God, such as Solomon sang when he beheld his mother Bathsheba: "*Thou art good, my fair one, thou art good, my beloved. Thine eyes burn like a flame of fire, thy teeth are as white as milk; the shining of thy face is brighter than the sun's rays, and altogether thou shinest like unto the day in its strength.*"

Then Pilate journeyed from us, and having settled his business at Mezen he returned to Moscow. And others of us were burned and baked. They burned Isaiah to death and afterwards burned Avraamy and other defenders of the Church—the most of them did he undo. God will count the number of them. A wonder is it that they would not come to their right mind. They think to establish the faith by fire or the knout and gallows-tree! Which of the Apostles taught them that? I know not. My Christ did not teach his Apostles that fire and knout and gallows-tree should lead to the faith. But it was said to the Apostle by the Lord thus: "*Go ye into all the world and preach the Gospel to every creature; he that believeth and is baptized, the same shall be saved.*" See now, my reader, Christ calls us to come if we will, but he does not bid the Apostles to burn with fire and to hang on the gallows-tree them that are disobedient. The Tatar god Mahmud[58] in his books wrote thus: "We bid ye lay low with the sword the heads of them that obey not our law and tradition." But Christ never gave such like command to his disciples, and these teachers, it is plain, are themselves Antichrists; they, who, leading men to the faith, destroy them and give them over to death—they bring forth works like unto their faith. It is written in the gospels: "*A good tree cannot bring forth evil fruit, neither a bad tree good fruit. Every tree is known by its fruit.*" But why speak many words? "No Cross, no Crown." He that will be crowned, for *that* he had not need to go to Persia. We have our Babylon at home. Come, True Believer! Name thou the name of Christ, standing in the midst of Moscow, cross thyself with the sign of the Saviour our Christ, with two fingers as we have received from the holy Fathers. Lo! here at home

[58] This refers to Muhammad, the Prophet of Islam.

for thee is thy Kingdom of Heaven. Glory to God! Suffer tortures for the placing of thy fingers, reason not much, but I with thee am ready to die for this and for Christ. If I am a foolish man and one without learning, yet this I know, that all the traditions of the Church, handed down to us by the holy Fathers, are holy and incorrupt. I keep them even unto death, as I received them. I will not falsify the eternal boundaries—that which was laid down before our days, let it so remain to all eternity, but, O thou heretic, do not tamper with things, touch not the sacrifice of Christ, lay not thine hand on the cross, nay, stir not even the corporals! And they have planned with the devil to misprint books and falsify everything, and to alter the sign of the cross in the church, and on the wafers. Within the altar they have banished the priestly prayers, they have altered the "Lord have mercy upon us," and in baptism they bid to invoke the Evil One. I would fain spit in his eyes and in theirs! And round about the font the Evil One leads them against the course of the sun, and in like fashion they consecrate the church, and when they solemnize marriage they lead the married counterclockwise; plainly they do this in hostility. And in baptism they do not abjure the Evil One. How should they? They are his children and they do not desire to abjure their father. But why multiply words? Woe is me for the True Believer! Every spirit that is exalted is brought low. As Nikon, the hound of hell, spake, so did he do. Print the books, Arsen,[59] anyhow, only not after the ancient fashion. And so he did! More than that, one cannot alter things. It behooves every man to endure for this, even unto death. May these damnable ones be accursed, with all their devilish imaginations: and to them whom they made to suffer in their souls, may theirs be threefold eternal remembrance.

For this I ask forgiveness of every True Believer. Some things that I have said were perhaps best unsaid—but I may read through the Acts of the Apostle and the epistles of Paul. The Apostles proclaimed concerning themselves that God was working through them. "*Not unto us but to our God be the praise.*" And I am of no account. So spake I again and again. I am a

[59] Arsen, a learned Greek, came to Moscow in 1649, and was invited to become a professor there. However, it was soon discovered that he had managed to become a Catholic three times, once a Moslem, and then, finally, Orthodox. For these successful conversions he was deported to Solovki Monastery. In 1652 Nikon invited him to revise the Russian missal, and this participation by Arsen in the re-editing of the holy books was largely responsible for the disrepute into which Nikon's reforms fell.

man that is a sinner. Wanton am I and a ravisher, a thief and a robber, the friend of publicans and sinners, and to every man am I a hypocrite accursed; forgive me and pray for me; to you who read me and who hearken am I bound more than to any. I know not how to live and what I am doing that I tell to men. What matter that they talk vanity of me, in the days of judgment they shall all know of my deeds, whether they be good or evil. But if I be unlearned in speech, yet am I not in thought; I am untaught in rhetoric and in dialectic and in philosophy, but the mind of Christ is our guide within us, as the Apostle saith, *though I be rude in speech yet not in knowledge.* [A fragment on "The Healing of the Possessed" has been omitted.]

XVI. Concluding Remarks to the Monk Epiphany

And now, my Elder, thou hast heard full much of my babbling, and I bid thee, in the name of the Lord, write thou also for thy servant in Christ, how the Mother of God kneaded this devil in her hands and gave him over to thee, and how the ants ate thee in thy secret parts, and how something devilish set fire to the Word and how the cell was burnt to ashes, but all within it were safe and sound. And how thou didst cry aloud to heaven: and other things thou dost remember to the glory of Christ and the Mother of God. Hearken to what I say; if thou dost not write to me I shall be sorely angered! Thou lovest to hear of me; of what thou art ashamed, tell me if even a little. The Apostles, Paul and Barnabas, were wont to set forth, in the assembly at Jerusalem, before all, what sights and wonders God had wrought by them among the Gentiles (see Acts 34 and 42), and the name of the Lord Jesus was magnified. And many who believed came to them, making confession and telling their deeds. And much of this is written by the Apostles and in the Acts. Fear not to tell me, only keep thy conscience straitly; seek not thine own glory, but speak thou for Christ and the Mother of God. Let thy servant in Christ read and rejoice. When we die, then shall this be read and we be remembered before God, and we will pray to God for them who read and who hearken. They shall be our people. They shall be there with Christ, and we shall be theirs for ever and ever. Amen.

40. *Shemiaka's Judgment*

Shemiaka's Judgment is one of the oldest Russian satirical stories with a purely fictitious plot. Indeed, the name "Shemiaka" can be traced back to the middle of the fifteenth century when Dmitry Shemiaka, prince of the northern city of Galych (not to be confused with Galich, capital of the southwestern province of Galicia), waged his endless feud against his cousin, Vasily III, Great Prince of Muscovy. The proper name "Shemiaka," however, subsequently became quite popular in Muscovite Russia, and there is no definite indication that the hero of the tale can be actually identified with Prince Dmitry Shemiaka or any other real historical figure.

The language and structure of the tale, its elements of popular satire and folk riddles, bring *Shemiaka's Judgment* somewhat closer to the oral folk tales (*skazki*) than to any literary narrative. Many Russian, Bielorussian, and Ukrainian tales and fairy tales about an unjust judge commonly employ the same motifs of crimes and court decisions that can be found in this tale. *Shemiaka's Judgment* satirizes Russian court mores of the sixteenth and seventeenth centuries, when judges often thought that their decisions should be a source of personal income. In those centuries this tale became extremely popular, and there have been preserved innumerable prose and verse versions of it.

The present translation follows the text of a seventeenth-century manuscript published by M. Skripil in *Russkaia povest XVII veka*, Moscow, 1954, pages 140–142.

◆ ◆ ◆

In a village of Russia there lived two peasant brothers. One was rich and the other poor. The rich one for many years lent money to his poor brother, but could not end his destitution.

Once the poor brother came to the rich one and asked him to lend him his horse because he hadn't one for bringing in wood. The rich brother did not want to give him the horse, and said, "On many occasions I have lent you money, but I cannot improve your condition." But he did lend him the horse, and then the poor brother asked to borrow the harness. The rich brother felt offended, and began to abuse his brother, saying: "You! You don't even have your own harness," and he didn't give him the harness. The poor man left the house of the rich brother, took his own sledge, and attached it to the horse's tail. He then went to the forest and later returned to his house, but he forgot to take out the gate spike. The sledge got caught on the spike and could not move. He flayed the horse with the knout, and the horse pulled with all its might, finally tearing away its own tail. When the poor brother brought back the horse and the rich brother saw that it no longer had a tail, he began to abuse his poor brother for having ruined his horse. And he refused to take the horse back, but went to the city to lodge a complaint with the judge, Shemiaka.

And the poor brother, seeing that his brother went to court, followed him, because he knew that if he did not come of his own volition, he would be obliged to pay an additional fee to the court messenger.

And both of them stopped for the night in some township not far from the city. The rich brother went to pass the night with the parson of the township because the parson was an acquaintance of his. The poor man also came to the parson's, and, arriving there, went to sleep in an upper bunk. The rich brother began to tell the parson about the misfortune concerning his horse, and explained why he was going to the city. And then the parson began to sup with the rich brother. The poor one, however, was not invited. As the poor hungry brother looked from the upper bunk to see what the parson and his brother were eating, he fell from the upper bunk, accidentally crashing onto the cradle of the parson's infant son, killing him.

And then the parson went with the rich brother to the city to sue the poor brother for the death of his infant son. As they came to the city wherein lived the judge, the poor one was following them. They were walking over a bridge to the city. At that time one of the inhabitants of the city was transporting his father in a cart to a steambath under the bridge in order to wash him. The poor brother, who knew that he must expect the worst from his rich brother and from the parson, decided to commit suicide. He jumped from the bridge into the moat in order to kill himself; but the moat was dry, and in jumping he accidentally fell on the old man and killed him. He was seized and brought before the judge.

The poor man began to think how to avoid the misfortune of a penalty and how to bribe the judge. But since he couldn't find anything in his pocket, he took a stone and wrapped it in a kerchief and put it in his hat and presented himself to the judge. And now the rich brother lodged his complaint against him, requiring a compensation for his horse, and began to explain the case to the judge. Shemiaka listened to the complaints, and told the poor man, "Answer." The poor brother didn't know what to say. He took out of his hat the wrapped stone and showing it to the judge, bowed deeply. The judge, thinking the poor man promised him a bribe, told his rich brother: "Since he tore away the tail of your horse, don't accept the horse from your brother as long as the tail will not grow back. But as soon as the tail grows back, at that time take from him your horse."

And then began the second trial. The parson began to sue the poor brother for the death of his infant son, because the poor man had crushed his son. The poor brother once more took from the hat the same bundle and showed it to the judge. The judge saw it, and thought that in the second trial the poor man promised another bundle of gold. And he told the parson: "Since he crushed your son, give him your wife until a child is born from him. And at that time take back from him your wife and the child."

And then began the third trial, for the crushing of the son's old father by jumping from the bridge. The poor one, taking the wrapped stone from his hat, showed it for the third time to the judge. The judge, hoping that the poor man was promising him a third bundle of gold for this, the third trial, told the son of the old man: "Go onto the bridge, while the man who killed your father remains under the bridge. And you must jump down from the bridge and kill him in the same way in which he killed your father."

When, after the trial, the plaintiffs left the court with the defendant, the rich brother began to claim his horse from the poor brother. But the latter told him: "According to the judge's decision, as he told you, I will return the horse to you when its tail grows back." So the rich one gave him five rubles in order to get back the horse, even though it had no tail. The poor brother accepted the five rubles, and returned the horse to him.

Then the poor one, according to the decision of the judge, claimed from the parson his wife in order to have a child with her, and having had the child, to return the wife with the child to the parson. But the parson began to beg him not to take his wife. For this concession the poor man took ten rubles from the parson.

Then the poor one told the third plaintiff: "According to the judge's decision, I will stand under the bridge while you go on the bridge and jump on me in the same manner in which I jumped on your father."

And the plaintiff thought, if I jump on him, probably I will not crush him but myself," and he began to plead with the poor man, and gave him some money in order not to be obliged to jump on him. In this way the poor man got money from all three of them.

The judge sent a servant to the defendant, ordering him to get from the latter the three bundles that had been shown him. The servant told him: "Give me that which you showed to the judge from your hat. He has ordered me to take it from you."

And the latter, taking the wrapped stone from under his hat, showed it to the servant. "Well, but that is a stone," said the servant.

The defendant said: "Yes, it is for the judge. I would have killed him if he hadn't tried me to my advantage."

The servant came back and told everything to the judge. And the judge, after listening to the servant, said: "I thank and praise God that I tried him to his advantage. If I had not done so, he would have killed me."

And the poor man returned home, being overjoyed and praising God.

41. *The Tale of Savva Grudtsyn*

The *Tale of Savva Grudtsyn* is a work characteristic of a transitional period when the new currents that were appearing in Russian literature modified previously well-established patterns. The story of Savva's life, which describes his adventures, his illicit affair with the wife of his father's close friend, and his military deeds during his service in regiments commanded by foreign soldiers according to Western tactics, reflects the new way of life and the new mentality of Muscovite Russia. Still, some elements of the earlier Russian hagiographic tradition persist, especially at the conclusion of the tale.

The basic theme of this work is the struggle between good and evil, illustrated by the fall of a man and his eventual redemption through repentance. Thus the *Tale of Savva Grudtsyn* has several thematic parallels with the poetic tale of *Misery-Luckless-Plight*. The style of *Savva Grudtsyn* is equally transitional, combining the solemn, archaic language and syntax with new, colloquial expressions and idioms.

It is worth noting that this tale begins in the Time of Troubles, when the Poles' intervention in Russia during the period 1605 to 1613 undermined the foundations of the old order in Russia. As in other Russian tales of the seventeenth century, most of the characters belong to well-known aristocratic and merchant families. The Grudtsyn-Usovs and the Vtorys were important merchants in northern Russia; the boyars Streshnev and Shein are well known from Russian history; and, finally, the tsar himself shows interest in Savva and actually influences the hero's destiny. The plot is certainly fictional and complex, but it does give vivid and realistic details of the life of a patriarchal Russian family of that time, of the life of the military, and of the mores of Muscovite society. The author was decidedly not a member of the literati of that period, for, despite the use of both archaic and colloquial expressions, his art is rather limited, and he often repeats word for word certain descriptions, speeches, and conceptions.

The translation follows an early eighteenth-century manuscript published, with some corrections, by M. Skripil in *Russkaia povest XVII veka,* Moscow, 1954, pages 82–102.

◆ ◆ ◆

This is a most truthful and true tale which has come to pass in these days and which reveals how God, who loves man, revealed his love to the Christian people. I wish to tell you, brethren, this most wonderful tale which is filled with awe and horror, which deserves inexplicable astonishment, and which explains the patience of our man-loving God who, awaiting our conversion, brings us to salvation through the most inexplicable of deeds.

On a day in 1606 (7114) God allowed, because of the multiplication of our sins, the God-offending apostate, heretic, and unfrocked monk Grishka Otrepiev[1] to attack the Muscovite state and to win the throne of the Russian land in a most robberlike, untsarlike manner. Also, at that time Russia was invaded by the

[1] Grishka, or Gregory, Otrepiev was a pretender to the Russian throne who claimed to be Prince Dmitry, the son of Ivan IV. See introduction to Selection 35. At that time Poland and Lithuania were united into one dominion, which explains the author's calling the foreign troops Polish in one case, Lithuanian in another.

increasing bands of faithless Lithuanians and Poles who performed all kinds of base deeds and who caused great misfortune to the Russian people in Moscow and in other cities. Because of these Lithuanian and Polish attacks, many people abandoned their homes and fled from city to city.

In the year 1606 (7114), in the city of Great Ustiug,[2] there lived a citizen named Foma, by surname, Grudtsyn-Usov, whose descendants still reside in that city. Seeing much anarchy and base deeds of the lawless Poles in Russia, this Foma decided to forsake the city of Great Ustiug, to live no longer in his home, but to migrate with his wife to the city of Kazan on the lower Volga, for in this city on the lower Volga there were no base Lithuanians or Poles.

And Foma and his wife lived in the city of Kazan until the beginning of the reign of the God-fearing sovereign, Grand Duke, and Tsar of All Russia, Michael Fedorovich. Foma had an only son, Savva, who was twelve years old. It was Foma's custom to make frequent business trips, traveling up and down the Volga, sometimes going to Solikamsk,[3] sometimes to the city of Astrakhan, and sometimes beyond the Caspian Sea to the land of Persia. He also taught his son, Savva, so that he might learn to attend to his business promptly and diligently, since after Foma's death his only son would inherit his estate.

After some time, Foma decided to sail to Persia and began the loading of his goods into the usual ships. He also loaded other boats with customary goods and ordered his son to sail to Solikamsk, there to learn the merchant's trade with all diligence. Having bidden farewell to his wife and son, Foma set out on his journey. Some days later, his son, Savva, sailed to Solikamsk in the ships his father had ordered loaded. Having reached the city of Orel, which is in the Usolsk region, he docked and, following his father's orders, went to live at the inn of a certain respectable man. The innkeeper and his wife, remembering the loving kindness of Savva's father, for he had done them many favors, cared with diligence for the son, rendering him many services and even treating him as their son.

In this city of Orel there lived a citizen, Bazhen Vtory by

[2] The city of Great Ustiug is located in northern Russia, between Moscow and the White Sea, and in the seventeenth century was an important merchant city.

[3] Solikamsk and Orel are located in the same region as Great Ustiug. The city of Atraskhan is located at the delta of the Volga, and was the main trading center for commerce with Persia and other countries of the Near East.

name, who was both famous and well known. He was already old in years and was known in many cities for his virtuous way of life and for his wealth. He had befriended and was well acquainted with Savva's father. Having learned that the son of Foma Grudtsyn had come to this city from Kazan, he thought to himself: Since his father and I share much love and friendship, why should I neglect the son by not inviting him into my home, to live with me and to eat at my table?

Having come to this conclusion, when Bazhen saw Savva walking in the street he invited him to his house, saying: "My dear friend, Savva, do you know that your father and I share much love and friendship? Why did you neglect me by not coming to abide in my home? This time, do not disobey me, but come and live in my house and break bread with me. And, for the love of your father, I shall receive you even as if you were my own son."

Hearing these words from Bazhen, Savva was very happy to be received into the house of such a famous man, and he bowed low before him, and made haste to move from the inn to Bazhen's house. And there he lived, enjoying all the comforts, and rejoicing.

This old man, Bazhen, had a young wife who had never been married before, but who was Bazhen's third wife. The Devil, that enemy who hates all things not vile in the human kind, having seen this man's virtuous way of life, decided to bring strife into his house by inducing Bazhen's wife to have sinful relations with the young man. Thus the wife began to seduce him into sin with tempting words. Human nature knows how to lead the mind of a young man into iniquity. And thus Savva, influenced by the flattery of this woman, or, better to say, by the Devil's envy, was led to the sin of adultery. They sinned endlessly, but still they were unable to satiate their desires. And Savva remained for a long time in such a sinful relation with her. They sinned even on Sundays and on holy days and, having forgotten all fear of God, they wallowed continuously, like swine, in the filth that is sin. And for a long time they remained in such insatiable lust, like beasts.

When the holy day honoring the Ascension of our Lord Jesus Christ neared, Bazhen Vtory took the young man and went to vespers in the holy church, this being on the eve of that holy day. Then they went home again and, after the usual supping, went each to his own bed, giving thanks to God. As soon as the God-loving man, Bazhen Vtory, had fallen soundly asleep, his wife, incited by the devil, got up secretly from her couch, went to the young man's bed, woke him, and compelled him to wicked adultery. Though young, Savva was seized by the fear of God, as if pierced by an arrow. And, fearing God's judgment, he began to ponder, asking himself, How could I do such a wicked deed and on such a great holy day?

And having thought thusly, he wished to be rid of her and, taking an oath, said to her, "I do not want to lose my soul forever by profaning my body on such a great holiday."

But she, in the grip of an insatiable carnal desire, tried to force him by her caresses and threats to submit to her. But try as she would, she could not force him to yield to her desire. And some kind of divine power helped him. When this evil woman saw that she could not bring the youth to do her bidding, she at once became seized by a wicked rage. Hissing like a fierce serpent, she went away from his bed. Then she began to ponder how she might destroy him through a magic potion. And she decided to fulfill her evil intention of destroying him without delay.

And she did as she had decided. When the bells announced matins, God-loving Bazhen quickly got up from his bed, woke the young man, Savva, and went with him to the morning service to glorify God. They listened to the liturgy with attention and with the fear of God, and then they returned home. When the hour of the sacred liturgy arrived, they returned to the holy church with joy so that they might hear the glorification of God. In the meantime, this accursed woman carefully prepared a magic philter for the youth, for she, like a serpent, wanted to spit poison at him.

When the holy liturgy was ended, Bazhen and Savva left the church, intending to go home. However, the voevoda of the city invited Bazhen to take dinner with him. And he asked, concerning the youth, "Whose son is this and where is he from?"

Bazhen answered that he was Foma Grudtsyn's son from Kazan. Thereafter, the voevoda invited the young man to his home, for he had known Savva's father well. So they went to the voevoda's house and, as was the custom, ate together with the others, and afterward returned home.

Arriving home, Bazhen ordered that wine be brought out so that they might drink in his home to honor the holy day. He was not in the least aware of his wife's evil scheme. When the wine had been brought in, she poured it into a cup and offered it to her husband. He drank it and gave thanks to the Lord. Then she poured more and drank it herself. Then she poured out the poisoned philter she had prepared, and offered it to Savva. He drank this base potion without any apprehension or hesitation, for he expected no evil deed from her, thinking that she harbored no ill will toward him. But as soon as he had drunk it, a fire began to burn in his heart. And he thought to himself: I have drunk many drinks in my father's house, but never such a wine as this one.

When he had finished the drink, he began to grieve in his heart and to long for a woman. The wife, like a fierce lioness, looked furiously at Savva and showed him not the least friendliness. But she began rather to slander the young man to her husband, saying base words and ordering her husband to drive the youth from their house. God-fearing Bazhen, although he took pity on the young man, was finally ensnared by his wife's cajolery and ordered the youth out of his home, accusing him of various failings. And the youth went away from the house with great sorrow and grief in his heart, lamenting and grieving the evil deeds of that woman.

He went back to the house of the innkeeper where he had previously lived, and the innkeeper asked him by what fault he had left Bazhen's house. And Savva answered, "I did not wish to live longer with those people, for I did not have enough to eat."

But he continued to grieve for and long after this woman. And, because of his grief, his handsome face began to wane and his flesh to waste away. Seeing the youth so grieving and lamenting, the innkeeper could not ascertain what had happened.

Now in the same city there was a magician who, through sorcery and charms, could tell why and to whom sorrow had come. He was also able to divine who would live and who would die. The innkeeper and his wife, who were sensible and cared greatly for the young man, summoned this sorcerer secretly, for they wished to learn why the youth grieved so. The sorcerer came and, consulting his book of magic, told them the truth: "The youth has no sorrow for himself, but longs only for the wife of Bazhen Vtory, since he has fallen into sinful adultery with her. But he became ashamed of her, and since that time he has grieved, longing for her."

The innkeeper and his wife, hearing this from the sorcerer, did not believe him, because they knew Bazhen Vtory to be a pious and God-fearing man who could not be involved in such an affair. Savva, however, continued to lament incessantly and to long for that accursed woman. And from day to day he wasted away, as if he were afflicted by some overwhelming bereavement.

Once, Savva left the city and went into the fields, wishing to take a walk to alleviate his longings and grief. He went walking alone, seeing no one before him nor no one behind him, and thinking of nothing in particular, but only grieving and lamenting his separation from that woman. Then there came into his mind an evil thought, and he said to himself: "If someone, man or devil, would do something so that I might take sexual pleasure with this woman, then would I serve even the Devil."

And coming to such an idea, as if he had lost his mind, he continued walking through the field, but a short distance behind him he heard a voice that called him by name. He turned around and saw a youth who was dressed in fine garments and was running swiftly toward him, entreating him with his hand to wait. And the youth came up to Savva. It must be said that this was not a youth, but the Enemy and the Devil who searches for ways to destroy human souls.

The youth came up to Savva and, after they had bowed to each other, said: "Brother Savva. Why did you run from me? I have awaited you a long time, hoping that you would come to me and would have brotherly love for me. I have known you for a long time, and I know that you are of the Grudtsyn-Usov family of the city of Kazan. And if you wish to know me, I may say that I am also from the city of Great Ustiug. And since, by birth, I can be considered your brother, you should become my brother and friend from this time on. And never leave me, so that I can be of help to you in all things."

Savva, hearing such words from his false brother, that is to say, from the Devil, became very happy to find a relative in such a distant and unknown land. And they kissed each other with love and went together through the wilderness. And the Devil said to Savva: "Brother Savva, wherefore do you grieve? Why do you destroy your youthful beauty?"

Savva avoided the questions, however, telling him that he was afflicted by a malady.

The Devil cunningly smiled and said: "Why do you conceal the truth from me? I know your ailment, but what would you give me if I were to cure you of it?"

And Savva answered: "If you actually know the affliction I bear in my heart, then I shall believe that you can help me."

The Devil replied: "In your heart you long for the wife of Bazhen Vtory, since you are deprived of her love. What would you give me if I once more united you with her and she once more loved you?"

Savva answered: "In such a case, I shall give you all the merchandise and wealth of my father and all my profits! Only cause me to be once more with this women."

The Devil laughed and retorted: "Why do you tempt me? I know that your father actually is very rich. But you are not aware that my father is seven times richer than yours. What are your goods to me? Only give me a short note, and I shall fulfill your desire."

The youth was very happy, thinking to himself: The wealth of my father will remain intact, and I shall give him the letter and write whatever he wants.

The youth did not know what misfortune he was bringing upon himself. Actually, he did not read or write well. Oh, the madness of youth! Thus he was ensnared by a woman's treachery and, for her sake, he was going to the Devil.

Hardly had the Devil spoken these words about the letter, when the youth happily promised to give him the letter. The false brother, that is to say, the Devil, quickly took paper and ink from his pocket, gave them to the youth, and ordered him to write the letter. Savva still did not fully know what he was writing, but began to write senselessly. And by this letter Savva renounced Christ, the True God, and gave himself in the service of the Devil. Having written the letter in which he rejected God, he gave it to the Devil, his false brother.

Thus, they both arrived in Orel. Then Savva asked the Devil, "Tell me, my brother, where you live, so that I may know your house."

The Devil laughed, and said: "I have no particular house anywhere, but wherever it is convenient, there do I spend the night. However, if you wish to see me often, look always for me in the Horse Market, since I sometimes live there when buying horses. Now, go to the shop of Bazhen, and I know that you will be gladly invited to live in this house."

Savva, following the words of his brother, the Devil, happily ran to Bazhen's shop. Bazhen, upon seeing Savva, eagerly invited him into his house, say to him: "Master Savva! What a wrong I have done you? Why did you leave my house? I pray you, come back now and live in my house. I am truly happy, for the love of your father, to have you here as if you were my own son."

Hearing such words from Bazhen, Savva was overcome with joy, and quickly entered Bazhen's house. And when the youth had entered, the wife, being incited by the Devil, met him with joy and greeted him, giving him a welcoming kiss. The youth was ensnared in the woman's flattery, that is to say, by the Devil, and was once more drawn into the sinful net with that accursed woman. From that time on, he remembered neither the holy days nor Sundays. He lost his fear of God, and wallowed with her constantly in the sin of lechery, as if he were a swine.

After quite a time had passed, there came a rumor to Savva's mother in the city of Kazan to the effect that her son was living an unrighteous and sinful life and that the father's wealth that was with him had all been squandered in lechery and drunkenness. Hearing such things about her son, the mother began to grieve profoundly, and wrote him a letter in which she urged him to return to his father's house in the city of Kazan. When the letter arrived, he read it, and laughed, paying it no heed. The mother sent him a second and a third letter in which she besought and entreated him to return home immediately from Orel to the city of Kazan. Savva, however, did not obey his mother's commands and entreaties, but, paying no heed to anything, continued only to persevere in his sinful passions.

Some time later, the Devil took Savva and went with him beyond the city of Orel into the fields of the countryside. As soon as they had left the city, the Devil said to Savva: "Do you know who I am? You were fully convinced that I am of the Grudtsyn family, but it isn't so. Now, out of love, I shall reveal the truth to you. Don't be afraid, and be not ashamed to call me your brother, for verily I do love you as a brother. But if you wish to know who I am, I am the son of a king. Let us go farther, and I shall show you my glory and the wealth of my father!"

Having said these words, he lead Savva to a certain hill and showed him a fine city a short distance away. Its walls and roofs were of pure gold, and gleamed.

And the Devil said to Savva: "This city is the work of my father. Let us go and bow down before my father. And now, take the letter you gave to me and present it to my father, and you will be given a great honor by him."

And having said these words, the Devil returned the letter in which Savva had renounced God.

Oh, the madness of youth! Didn't he know that there was no kingdom near the Muscovite state that was not under the sway of the tsar? If only he had made the sign of the cross, then all these devilish temptations would have vanished like a shadow.

When they approached this chimerical city and came up to

the city gates, they were met there by youths with dark faces and in vestments and belts decorated with gold. These youths bowed to them, rendering honor to the king's son, who was actually the Devil, and also greeting Savva. When they entered the courtyard of the Kings' palace, they were met there by more youths, who wore still more brilliant raiment than the first ones they had met. And these youths also bowed to them. Then they entered the King's palace and were met by still more youths, who surpassed each other in their proud dignities and their magnificent vestments. And they also rendered honors to the King's son and to Savva.

Entering the palace, the Devil said: "Brother Savva, wait here for me awhile. I shall go and announce you to my father, and I shall later take you to him. When you appear before him, think of nothing and have no fears; only give him the letter." Having said this, he passed into the inner chambers, leaving Savva alone. In a short while he returned, came to Savva, took him by the hand, and let him before the Prince of Darkness. The Prince of Darkness was sitting on a high throne embellished with gold and jewels. He was distinguished by his proud glory and his magnificent raiment. Round his throne, Savva noticed a large number of winged youth, the faces of some being blue, while the faces of others were red, and still others had faces as black as pitch. Savva appeared before the King, fell to the floor, and genuflected before him.

The King asked him: "From whence do you come? What is your plight?"

The senseless youth presented him with his God-rejecting letter, and said, "I have come, great King, to serve you."

That ancient serpent, Satan, accepted the letter, read it, turned toward his dark-faced warriors, and said, "Although I accept this youth, I know not whether he will remain faithful to me." Then he summoned his son, Savva's false brother, saying to him, "Go to another room, and have dinner with your brother."

Both bowed to the King, went to another room, and began to dine. They were served unimaginably aromatic dishes, and the same kind of drink. Savva marveled, and said that he had never partaken of similar dishes or of similar drinks in his own father's house.

After the meal, the Devil took Savva, and together they left first the King's courtyard and then the city. And Savva asked his brother, the Devil, "Tell me, brother, who were those winged youths who surrounded your father's throne?"

The Devil smiled and answered: "Aren't you aware that many nations serve my father—the Indians, the Persians, and many, many others. Don't wonder about this and don't hesitate to call me your brother. From now on I will be your younger brother. However, when I tell you to do something, you must obey me. And I shall render you all kinds of good deeds."

Savva promised to be obedient, and the Devil became so confident that, when they had arrived back in the city of Orel, he left Savva alone and went away. Savva still went to the house of Bazhen Vtory and continued to indulge in his sinful lechery.

In the meantime, Savva's father, Foma Grudtsyn, returned to Kazan from Persia, having been very successful in his business. As usual and as is due, he gave a kiss to his wife and then inquired about their son, asking whether he were still alive. And she answered him, saying: "I have heard from many people about him. After you left for Persia, he went to Solikamsk, and from there to the city of Orel. And since then, he sins and, as people say, has squandered all our wealth and has dissipated his health in drunkenness and in lechery. And on many occassions I have written him asking that he return home from there. But not once has he answered my letters, and so I don't know whether he is alive or not."

Hearing this from his wife, Foma was in a quandry. Then he sat down and penned a letter to Savva, beseeching him to return without delay to the city of Kazan. "I would like, my child," he wrote, "once again to see your handsome face, for I haven't seen you in a long time."

Savva, having received and read the letter, paid it no heed and did not even think of returning to his father. He wished only to indulge in his insatiable lust. Foma, seeing that his letter had accomplished nothing, ordered boats and goods prepared for sailing, and began his travels to Solikamsk, telling his wife, "I shall myself look for our son, and bring him back to our home."

As soon as the Devil learned that Savva's father was traveling to Solikamsk, he decided to take Savva to Kazan. So he told Savva: "Brother Savva, how long are we going to remain in this small town? Let us visit other cities and have a good time there. Then we can return here."

Savva did not contradict him, but said: "You are right, brother. Let us go. But we should wait for a short while, since I want to obtain some money for my merchandise."

But the Devil prevented him from doing so, and said: "Haven't you looked upon my father's glory? Aren't you aware that he has estates everywhere? Wherever we go, we shall have as much money as we need."

Thus they left the city of Orel, and their departure was known to no one, neither to Bazhen Vtory nor to Bazhen's wife. In one night Savva and the Devil covered the distance of two thousand miles, from the city of Solikamsk to the city of Kozmodemiansk[4] on the river Volga. And the Devil said to Savva: "In case you should meet someone you know, and this person should ask from whence you have come, you should answer that you came from Solikamsk and have spent three weeks traveling to this place." And Savva did as he was told, following the Devil's order.

They passed several days in the city of Kozmodemiansk, and then the Devil and Savva covered the distance from the city of Kozmodemiansk to the village of Paul's Ferry (Pavel's Perevoz) on the river Oka in one night. They arrived there on Thursday, which was the market day. Walking through the market, Savva noticed a very old beggar who stood dressed in repulsive rags. This man observed Savva carefully, and then began to weep. Savva left the Devil's side for a short time and went up to the old man, wishing to learn what caused him to cry. Approaching the old man, Savva asked him: "Wherefore do you grieve? Why do you weep so incessantly?"

And the beggar, who was a holy elder, answered: "My child, I cry because you have lost your soul. You don't realize that you have lost it, but you have voluntarily turned to the Devil. Do you know, my child, with whom you walk and whom you call your brother? It is not a man, but the Devil who walks with you and who hopes to bring you to the very pit of hell."

As soon as the old man had spoken these words, Savva turned toward his false brother, or, better to say, to the Devil. The Devil was standing a short way from him and was threatening Savva and gnashing his teeth. The youth left the holy elder and went up to the Devil. The Devil began abusing him, and said: "Why do you talk with such an evil destroyer of souls? Aren't you aware that this base elder has brought many people to their downfall? He noticed your Sunday clothes and wanted to win you by flattery, to take you away from the crowd, and then to strangle you with a cord and steal your clothes. You will be lost without me, if I abandon you."

After saying these words, the Devil took Savva from that

[4] The city of Kozmodemiansk is located on the Upper Volga, north of Moscow.

village. He went with him to a city called Shuya,[5] and they remained there together for a time.

In the meantime, Foma Grudtsyn came to the city of Orel and began inquiring about his son's whereabouts, but no one was able to give him any information. Everyone had seen his son in the city before Foma had arrived, but then he suddenly disappeared without telling anyone of his departure. Some said that the son was frightened by the father's arrival, because he had squandered his father's wealth, and had therefore disappeared. Especially astounded by Savva's departure were Bazhen Vtory and his wife. And Bazhen told Foma: "He spent the night at our place and the next morning he went away. We waited for him to come to dinner, but since that morning he has not reappeared in this city. And neither myself nor my wife knows where he has disappeared to."

Foma shed many tears, and lived for a time in Orel waiting for his son, but since his expectations went unrequited, he returned home. And he told of the unhappy case to his wife. Together they grieved and lamented the disappearance of their only son. Foma Grudtsyn grieved for a long time, and then he entered into his Father's House. And his wife remained a widow.

While the Devil and Savva were living in the town of Shuya, the pious and great sovereign, Tsar, and Grand Duke, Michael Fedorovich, the Autocrat of All the Russias, sent his army against the city of Smolensk[6] to fight the King of Poland. According to the tsar's decree, soldiers were to be recruited throughout all Russia. For the recruiting of such soldiers, Stolnik Timothy Vorontsev was sent from the city of Moscow to Shuya. And he recruited soldiers and drilled them everyday according to military regulations. Savva and the Devil used to go and watch the drills. Once the Devil told Savva: "Brother Savva, would you like to serve the tsar? Let us volunteer for the army."

Savva answered: "Well, brother, you are right. Let us serve." And so they joined the ranks of the army and began to go together for drilling. The Devil gave Savva such a talent for

[5] The city of Shuya is located between Moscow and Nizhny-Novgorod (which is now called Gorky).

[6] The city of Smolensk, some 250 miles west of Moscow, was an important fortress on the Russian-Polish frontier in the seventeenth century. It was lost to Poland during the Time of Troubles. In the years 1632 to 1634, Russia was at war to win back this important city. The Russian armies were under the command of Boyar B. M. Shein. The author erroneously called him Feodor Ivanovich Shein. Tsar Michael Fedorovich, the first Romanov to be tsar, reigned from 1613 to 1645.

The siege of Smolensk by the Poles, 1604–1610. An early seventeenth-century engraving.

military studies that he very soon surpassed the old soldiers and even the commanders. The Devil himself served as Savva's orderly, and cared for Savva and carried his weapons.

When these recently recruited soldiers were transferred from Shuya to Moscow, a German colonel continued their training.[7] When this colonel came to inspect the newly recruited soldiers during drill, he noticed a very young man who behaved most properly, who acted by the regulations, and who was faultless in his military deportment, and who surpassed many old soldiers and commanders in his studies. He was astounded by Savva's acumen, called him aside, and inquired about his background. Savva told him the whole truth. The colonel took a liking to Savva, called him his own son, and gave him his hat, decorated with precious stones, from off his head. And he entrusted to Savva three companies of recruits. And so Savva began to drill and to instruct them in place of the colonel.

The Devil secretly approached Savva and hold him: "Brother Savva, in case you don't have sufficient money to pay your soldiers, tell me and I shall bring you as much as you need, so as to prevent complaints and dissatisfaction among your troops."

And all Savva's soldiers were always quiet and peaceful, while in other companies there were complaints and disorder because the soldiers were dying of starvation and from the lack of clothing and provisions. Among Savva's troops the soldiers were peaceful and well organized, and everyone marveled at Savva's acumen.

Once, the tsar himself learned of Savva. At that time in Moscow was the very powerful boyar and brother-in-law of the tsar, Simeon Streshnev.[8] When this boyar learned of Savva, he ordered that he be brought to him.

When Savva came, Boyar Streshnev asked him, "My youth, do you want to be received in my house and to receive considerable honors from me?"

Savva bowed and replied: "I have a brother, my lord; I will

[7] Since the sixteenth century, the Russians had begun hiring foreign instructors to drill and equip their armies according to the requirements of contemporary military science. They preferred to hire German and English instructors because they were Protestants and not Roman Catholics. They preferred Protestants because Russia was constantly at strife with Poland, which for centuries had been an outpost of Catholic expansion.

[8] Boyar Simeon Streshnev was a well-known Russian statesman of the second half of the seventeenth century. The author of this tale erroneously ascribed to him an active part in the first half of the seventeenth century.

ask him. If he orders me to do so, I will serve you with pleasure." The boyar had no objections, and permitted Savva to go and ask his brother.

When Savva came and told everything to his false brother, the Devil, the Devil answered him angrily, saying: "Why do you wish to disregard the tsar's service and become a servant of the tsar's servant? You are now in an important position and you have become favorably known to the tsar. No, you mustn't do this, but let us rather serve the tsar. When the tsar learns of your faithful service, you will be promoted by him to the higher ranks."

By the order of the tsar, all recruits were distributed among the regiments of streltsy[9] in order to swell their ranks. Savva was quartered in the city at the house of Jacob Shilov, a streltsy captain of the Zimin regiment. His house was located in the Istretenka neighborhood of the Earthen City. This captain and his wife, who were pious and decent people, highly respected Savva for his acumen.

The regiments were readied in Moscow for the campaign, when one day the Devil came to Savva and told him: "Brother Savva, let us go ahead of the regiment to Smolensk to see what the Poles are doing there, how they have fortified the city, and what kind of weapons they have." In one night they went from Moscow to Smolensk. Coming there, they remained in the city for three days and three nights, being invisible. There they saw and inspected all things and saw how the Poles were fortifying the city and how they were placing grenades in the places of possible storming. On the fourth day in Smolensk, the Devil revealed himself and Savva to the Poles. Upon seeing them, the Poles became alarmed and began to chase after them, trying to catch them. The Devil and Savva escaped from the city, fled to the river Dnieper, and the river parted before them and they crossed the river as if it were dry. The Poles opened fire on them, but did not succeed in injuring them. And they marveled, saying, "They, who have sojourned in our city, are demons in men."

However, Savva and the Devil returned to Moscow and once again were quartered with this same Captain Shilov. When, at the tsar's command, the regiments marched from Moscow against Smolensk, this Savva and his brother went with the soldiers. The commander over all regiments was Boyar Feodor Shein.

[9] Streltsy (sing., strelets) were professional infantrymen who were armed with muskets, halberds, and sabers. This standing infantry was first organized by John IV.

On the way to Smolensk, the Devil told Savva: "Brother Savva, when we arrive in Smolensk a giant Polish knight will ride out from the city, and will challenge one of our soldiers to a joust. Don't fear him, but go against him. I know and I assure you that you will defeat him. The next day there will come another giant from the Polish ranks who will seek to joust. Once again you must go against him, and I know that you will defeat him also. When the third day comes, the third Polish knight will ride forth from Smolensk. Don't fear him, but go against him, and you will defeat him. You will be wounded by him, but I shall cure you of your wounds." So Savva was advised. And the regiments came to the city of Smolensk and set up camp in a good place.

As the Devil had said, there rode forth from the city of Smolensk a most terrifying warrior who rode on his horse and looked through the Muscovite ranks for an adversary. But no one dared to oppose him. But then Savva announced that he would do so, saying: "If I had a good, spirited steed, I would go to fight against this enemy of the tsar." And when his friends heard of this, they told his intentions to the boyar. The boyar ordered that Savva be brought before him and that he be given a good steed and a weapon, but the boyar thought that the youth would perish at the hands of such a terrifying giant. Then Savva, as he was ordered by his brother, the Devil, galloped against this Polish knight, quickly defeated him, and brought him and his horse to the Muscovite regiments. And Savva was praised by all.

The next day there rode forth from Smolensk another glorious warrior who was in search of an adversary among the Muscovite armies. And once more Savva rode out, and defeated the knight. And everyone was stunned by his daring. However, Boyar Shein became wroth with Savva, but he concealed his rage in his heart.

On the third day, there once more came a warrior from the city of Smolensk, and this knight was more glorious than the previous two, and was looking for an adversary. Although Savva was afraid to ride against such a terrifying warrior, he followed the Devil's order and immediately rode against him. And then this Pole furiously charged Savva and wounded him in his left thigh with his lance. Savva recovered, however, charged this Pole, killed him, and brought his body and horse into the Russian camp. He terrified the Poles in Smolensk, while the entire army was stunned. Then the Polish sortie commenced, army clashed against army, and the battle began. And the flank of the Russian army, in which Savva fought with his brother, was winning, and the Poles turned their backs, and fled. The Devil and Savva killed an endless number of Poles, but they themselves were not injured by anyone.

When Boyar Shein learned of the courage of this youth, he could no longer conceal the wrath in his heart, but summoned Savva to his tent, and asked him, "Tell me, my youth, from which family are you and whose son are you?" And when Savva told him that he was the son of Foma Grudtsyn of Kazan, the boyar began to abuse him with all kind of crude words, and told him: "Why did you need to take part in such mortal combat? I know your father and your relatives. They are immensely wealthy. What is the reason for your forsaking your parent's home to come here? Was it persecution or poverty? I tell you, don't delay any longer, but return to the house of your parents and remain there, living in abundance with your parents. If you don't obey, and I hear about you once more and learn that you have remained here, then you will perish without mercy. I will order that you be beheaded!" Saying this to the youth, the raging boyar left him. And the youth left the tent in great sadness.

When he had left the tent, the Devil asked him: "Why are you troubled about this? If people do not want our services here, we shall return to Moscow and live there." And soon after, they left Smolensk for Moscow, and there they continued to live in the house of Captain Jacob Shilov. The Devil spent the day with Savva, while in the evening he would go to his abode in hell where he dwelt according to the ancient evil customs.

After a considerable length of time, Savva fell ill, and his illness was so severe, he was at death's door. The wife of the captain was a wise, God-fearing woman. She cared for Savva and told him on many occasions that he should summon a priest so that he might take Holy Communion and confess his sins. "You should do this," she said, "for you may die suddenly without having had the last rites."

Savva rejected her advice because, as he said, "My illness is certainly grave, but not fatal." His condition worsened from day to day, and the captain's wife incessantly urged him to take the last rites, because, as she said, "You may die without having taken them."

Finally Savva was forced by this God-loving woman to summon a priest. The captain's wife sent for a priest from the Church of St. Nicholas which is located in the Rooks' neighborhood. The priest came to the ill man without delay. He was of a mature age, with great experience, and was very devout. When he came to the bedside of the ill man, he began to pronounce prayers before confession, as is the custom. When the other people had left the room, the priest began to confess the sick man.

Suddenly Savva noticed that the room had become filled with a multitude of demons. His false brother, who was actually the Devil, came with these demons, but this time he was not in the image of man, but in his true bestial form. The Devil, who remained behind the crowd of demons, was in a frenzy of rage, gnashing his teeth, and showing Savva the God-rejecting letter Savva had given him in the vicinity of Solikamsk. And the Devil told the ill man: "Look at this, you perjurer, do you realize what it is? Did you write this or do you believe that by repenting you can escape us? Oh, no, don't think that, for I will move against you with all my forces." And the Devil told him this and other evil threats. The sick man evidently heard them and was as first frightened, but later he relied upon the power of God and confessed everything in great detail to the priest. The priest, although he was a man of the holy life, also became frightened, since no one but he and Savva were in the room. And he was deafened by the great uproar that came from the multitude of demons, and only with great difficulty did the priest finish confessing the sick man. Then he left for home without saying anything to anyone.

After the confession, the evil spirit assaulted Savva and began to torture him mercilessly. One minute the Devil was beating him against the wall; another minute he was throwing him from the couch to the floor; then he throttled him until Savva began to gasp and foam came from his mouth; then he tortured him with many different kinds of torture. The aforementioned captain, who was also a pious man, saw with his wife that the youth was assaulted and tormented by the Devil. And they grieved and bemoaned the fate of the youth, but were unable to help him in any way. From day to day the assaults and torments of the Devil became fiercer, and those who witnessed them were terrified.

The master of the house, who saw the unusual fate of this youth and who realized that, because of his courage, the youth was known to the tsar himself, decided with his wife to inform the tsar. They hoped that there might be some relative of the youth in the tsar's palace. As soon as the man had decided this,

Portrait of a Russian boyar.
A seventeenth-century painting.

he sent his wife to her relative, telling her to inform the relative about everything and asking that she inform the tsar immediately. And he added, "In case the young man dies in such miserable plight, there may be litigation for not having informed the tsar."

His wife, without delay, hastened to her relative and told her exactly what she was ordered to say by her husband. Hearing these words, her relative was profoundly moved, grieved over the fate of the youth, and became sad at the situation of her relatives, fearing that this matter might bring them trouble. Therefore, without any delay, she went from her house to the tsar's palace and told the members of the tsar's court of these happenings. When the tsar heard about this youth, he showed mercy on him. He told the courtiers who were before him to send two sentries to the house of the captain where the sick man lay, whenever the daily changing of the sentries took place.

The tsar said, "They should watch over this youth with care so as to prevent him from killing himself by throwing himself into the fire or into the water, when he loses his senses because of the demons' torments."

And the pious tsar ordered that meals be sent daily to the sick man, and asked that the sick man appear before him in his palace as soon as he was cured. And so it was done. However, the sick man remained for a long time under the Devil's sway.

The first of July arrived, and on those days the youth was particularly tormented by the Devil. Finally he fell asleep, and while he was sleeping he began to talk as if he were awake and he shed tears from his exhausted eyes. And he said: "O Most Merciful Lady, Queen and Holy Virgin, have mercy upon me, our Lady, the Queen of Queens. I do not lie, I do not lie, but I shall do as I pledge."

The members of the captain's household and the sentries who watched him were astounded when they heard these words spoken by sick Savva, and they said, "He has a vision."

When the sick man woke from the sleep, the captain came to him, and said, "Tell me, Lord Savva, what kind of words did you speak while shedding tears in your sleep?"

And tears flowed steadily from Savva's eyes, and he said: "I saw that my couch was approached by a Lady from whom emanated light, and who shone with indescribable grace, and who was wearing a purple vestment. With her were two men distinguished by their venerable white hair. One of them was in an archbishop's vestment, while the other was wearing the robes of an Apostle. And I believe that they were none other than the Holy Virgin, the Friend of the Lord, John the Theologian, and Metropolitan Peter, the ever vigilant guardian of our city, Moscow, and the most glorious archbishop of bishops. I know well their images from the icons. And the Lady from whom emanated light said: 'What has happened to you, Savva? Why are you so full of sorrow?'

"And I said to her: 'I am full of sorrow, my Lady, because the Son of our God is wroth with me, and because you, the Intercessor for the Christians, are wroth with me.' And, smiling on me, she said: 'What do you think? How can you escape such a plight? How can you get your God-rejecting letter from hell?' And I told her: 'It cannot be done, my Lady, except with the succor of your Son and through your infinite mercy.' And she told me: 'I shall implore my Son and God in your behalf; only, you must follow to the word what I shall tell you. I shall deliver you from this misfortune, if you will decide to take monastic vows.'

"And so I vowed to her tearfully in my dream, and these were the words that you heard. And then she told me: 'Listen, Savva! On the holy day of my icon in my cathedral of the icon of Kazan, come to my church that is on the main square in the vicinity of the Rag Market. And then I shall perform a miracle for you in the presence of all.' And after this, she became invisible."

The captain and the sentries who kept watch over Savva marveled greatly upon hearing his words about his vision. And the captain and his wife began to ponder how they should inform the tsar of this vision, and decided to send their relative to inform the courtiers in the tsar's palace and let them tell of the vision to the tsar. When the aforementioned relative came to the captain's house, they told her of Savva's vision. When she learned of this, she went immediately to the tsar's palace in order to inform the courtiers in the tsar's palace and to let them inform the tsar of Savva's vision. When the tsar learned of it, he marveled greatly.

When, on July 8th, the holy day of the Icon of the Blessed Virgin of Kazan arrived, there was a church procession with holy icons and sacred crosses from the Cathedral of the Assumption of the Holy Virgin to the Holy Virgin of Kazan. In this procession participated the great sovereign, tsar, and grand duke, Michael, the holy patriarch, with the bishops, and a great many courtiers. And the tsar ordered that sick Savva be brought to this church. Then, by the tsar's order, the ill man was rapidly brought on a carpet to the Church of the Holy Virgin of Kazan and was laid before the entrance to the church.

When the holy Mass begun, ill Savva was assaulted by the evil spirit, and the Devil began to torment him ferociously, and Savva called in a loud voice, "Help me, my Lady and Holy Virgin! Help me, my Queen of Queens, the Mother of God!" And when the choir began to sing the Song of the Cherubim, people heard a sound like thunder, and there came a voice announcing: "Savva! Get up and come into my church!"

Then he got up from the carpet on which he had been brought, as if he had never been ill. He quickly came into the church, fell on his knees before the Icon of the Most Holy Virgin of Kazan, and prayed, shedding tears. At the same moment there fell from the cupola of the church the God-rejecting letter of Savva that he had given to the Devil at Solikamsk. And all writing was erased from the letter, as if nothing had ever been written there. And then the same voice repeated: "Savva! Here is the letter you wrote, and now fulfill my commandment, and don't commit the sin of disobedience." And he arose, picked up the letter, and, shedding tears, spoke in a loud voice before the icon: "Oh, Most Blessed Mother of God, Intercessor for all Christians, who prays for us to her Son and to our God, absolve me of my sins and save me from the very pit of hell. And I will fulfill what I have pledged."

When the tsar, the patriarch, and all who were there heard this and witnessed this most marvelous miracle, they thanked God and His Most Holy Mother, and greatly marveled about such divine mercy that had delivered him from the very pit of hell. And, after the divine liturgy, they began to glorify God, and the entire clergy gave a service of thanksgiving for the miracles that were performed before all.

Thereafter, the church procession with the holy icons and sacred crosses left the church and went to the cathedral. And the tsar returned to his palace rejoicing over this miracle, and thanking God. And Savva returned in good health to the house of the aforementioned Captain Shilov, and never again did he suffer from his disease. The captain and his wife saw this, marveled greatly, and thanked God for his great mercy for all men.

Savva remained living for a short time in the house of the captain. Then he distributed all his wealth to the poor and to the churches, and left for the Monastery of the Miracle of Archangel Michael, which is called the Miracle Monastery and which is located in the vicinity of the Cathedral of the Venerable and Glorious Assumption of the Most Holy Virgin. There he took his monastic vows, and remained laboring, fasting, and praying incessantly and thus pleasing God. There he lived for many years, and passed to the Lord in peace. And he was buried in this monastery.

42. *Frol Skobeev, the Rogue*

HARDLY any work of Russian seventeenth-century literature reflects so strikingly the drastic changes in both the way of life and the mentality of the Muscovite Russian as does the tale of *Frol Skobeev, the Rogue.* This story reveals the thorough secularization of Muscovite writings and the break with the traditions of the Age of Faith. The religious and moralistic tone in literature have vanished altogether. The solemn, ornate style, with an abundance of archaic Old Church Slavonic words, has given place to colloquial Russian and simple, short sentences. The subject itself of a rogue portrayed against the background of everyday Russian life was completely novel in Russian literature at that time, and the description of Frol Skobeev's life lacks the traditional clichés that dominated earlier biographical and hagiographic works. Amorous and erotic motifs now make their appearance. This work is a bitter satire on the new man who is shown as a rogue and cunning operator, and whose final success announced a new age for both Russian society and literature.

In some versions of this tale, the action takes places around 1680, the time when the customary barriers between the old, aristocratic boyars and the new gentry were crumbling, and the anonymous author gave the names of actual historical personages to his characters. The Skobeevs were small provincial squires of that time. Lovchikov actually did belong to the court and was a *stolnik* in the 1670's and 1680's. Only the name of Ordyn-Nashchekin, a famous statesman and diplomat during the reign of Tsar Alexis Mikhailovich, was slightly modified to Nadrin-Nashchekin. Still, it appears that the plot does not depict actual happenings, but reflects rather the new atmosphere and social trends in Muscovite Russia.

The present translation follows the oldest extant version of this tale, a manuscript written in the late seventeenth century and published by N. Skripil in *Russkaia Povest XVII veka*, Moscow, 1953, pages 155–166.

Some interesting passages indicating the further development of satirical and erotic themes in later versions of this tale have been interpolated from a manuscript published by N. K. Gudzy in *Khrestomatiia po drevnei russkoi literature*, Moscow, 1956, pages 415–425. These interpolated passages have been placed in brackets.

✦ ✦ ✦

In the district of Novgorod there lived the nobleman Frol Skobeev. In the same district were the estates of Stolnik[1] Nadrin-Nashchekin; and the stolnik's daughter, Annushka, was living at these Novgorodian estates.

Frol Skobeev, learning about the stolnik's daughter, came to the decision that he should have a love affair with her. But since he could not get to meet her, he decided to become acquainted with the steward of estates of Nadrin-Nashchekin. And so he began to visit him at his home. Some time later, Frol Skobeev happened to be at the steward's home when Annushka's nurse came to this steward. Frol Skobeev learned that the nurse lived with Annushka. When the nurse left to return to her mistress' home, Frol followed her and gave her a present of two rubles. And the nurse said to him, "My lord Skobeev, the favor you show me is beyond my service, for I haven't yet rendered you any service." And returning home to her mistress, the nurse said nothing to her of this matter. Frol spent a time at the steward's house, and then went home.

When the time of the Christmas holidays arrived, during which there is much merrymaking and the girls often have pretexts to pass the time gaily, the daughter of Stolnik Nadrin-Nashchekin, Annushka, told her nurse to go to all noblemen who had young daughters and whose estates were in the vicinity and ask them to come to Annushka's party and have some fun. The nurse went and asked all the daughters of noblemen, and they all promised to come to Annushka's party. Since the nurse knew that Frol Skobeev had a young sister who was unmarried, she went to Frol's house and asked his sister to come to Stolnik Nardin-Nashchekin's house, to Annushka's party. The sister told

[1] Stolnik: an important rank at the Russian court in Moscow. At official banquets and receptions the stolniks served the tsar at the table. They usually were members of the aristocracy, and were often high officials in various governmental agencies or commanders in the army.

the nurse: "Wait a moment and I will go and ask my brother. Then I will tell you what he has decided."

The sister went to Frol and told him: "The nurse of Stolnik Nadrin-Nashchekin's daughter has arrived, and asks that I come to Annushka's party."

Frol Skobeev told his sister: "Go and tell this nurse that you will go, but with another girl, a nobleman's daughter."

The sister pondered on what her brother had told her to tell the nurse. However, she did not dare to disobey her brother, and told the nurse that she would go that very evening with the daughter of another nobleman. Then the nurse returned to her mistress, Annushka.

In the meantime Frol Skobeev began to speak with his sister, saying, "Well, sister, it is time for you to get dressed to go to the party." When his sister began to don feminine attire, Frol ordered her: "Sister, bring me also a girl's attire. I shall don it, and we shall go together to Annushka, the stolnik's daughter."

The sister was very much afraid that people might recognize him, and then certainly there would be much trouble for her brother, for the stolnik was much liked by the tsar. Still, she did not dare to disobey her brother, and she brought him the attire of a girl. Frol, having dressed himself as a girl, went with his sister to Annushka, the stolnik's daughter.

There had already gathered many daughters of noblemen, but no one was able to recognize Frol in his feminine attire. Then the girls began to play parlor games, and enjoyed themselves. Frol also played the games, and was not recognized by anyone. Finally Frol left the room for his needs, and was accompanied through the corridor by the nurse, who carried a taper. On leaving, he told her, "Oh, my dear nurse, there are many girls here, and many of them ask services of you, but none of them would give you any gift for such services." Still the nurse did not recognize him. Then Frol gave her five rubles, which she accepted gratefully.

Seeing that the nurse still did not recognize him, Frol fell on his knees and explained to her that he was a nobleman, Frol Skobeev, and that he had come in feminine attire so that he might marry Annushka. When the nurse realized that he really was Frol Skobeev, she became frightened and did not know what to do. Still, remembering both of his generous gifts, she said to him, "Well, my lord Skobeev, I am ready to do everything you may ask, in view of your gracious generosity."

Returning to the place where the girls were enjoing themselves, she spoke not a word about Frol Skobeev, but soon after she told her mistress: "Well, girls, you have had enough of these games. I suggest you play another game, one that was played when I was young."

Annushka did not wish to disobey her nurse, and said only: "Well, my dear nurse, we shall play the games according to your desires."

And the nurse told them of her game, saying: "Please, dear Annushka, play the role of the bride." Pointing to Frol Skobeev, she said: "And this girl will be the bridegroom." And then she led the two into a nice chamber, to the bed, as a bride and bridegroom are usually led after the wedding. The girls accompanied them to the bedroom and then, leaving the two alone, went to the rooms in which they had been playing their parlor games. And the nurse ordered the girls to sing loudly so that they might not hear any cries coming from the bedchamber. And Frol Skobeev's sister was very much afraid, fearing that her brother might get into trouble.

Lying with Annushka on the bed, Frol told her that he was a nobleman, Frol Skobeev, from the district of Novgorod, and not a girl. Annushka was seized by great fright. But Frol, despite the fact that he was himself afraid, became daring and forced her to submit to his will. Thereafter, Annushka begged Frol not to bring shame upon her by telling of this to others. Later on, when the nurse and the girls returned to the chamber where Frol and Annushka were, they realized from Annushka's expression that something had happened. [Annushka had undergone a tribulation she had never before experienced.] However, the girls still did not recognize Frol Skobeev, for he was again in feminine attire. But Annushka took her nurse by the hand, led her away from the girls, and said to her: "What have you done to me! The one who was with me was not a girl. He is a man, Frol Skobeev."

However, the nurse answered: "I tell you the truth, my gracious lady, when I say that I was not able to recognize him. I thought that he was a girl like the others. If he has committed such a shameful deed, we can kill him and hide his body in some secret place, for we have plenty of servants."

But Annushka took pity on Frol Skobeev [because she had begun to care for him, having lain with him in the bedchamber]. And she told the nurse, "Well, nurse, let it be this way, for never again shall I regain my chastity."

Thereafter, all the girls, as well as Frol Skobeev, went to the reception room, and all enjoyed themselves until late into the night. Afterward, all the girls went to bed. And Annushka went to bed with Frol Skobeev [telling herself, "I wouldn't be able to find a better girl with whom to sleep." And they enjoyed themselves throughout the night with carnal pleasures. And since that time a profound pity for Frol Skobeev dwelt in Annushka's heart. And only with great sorrow did she part from Frol Skobeev.]

In the morning, when everyone had got up, the girls returned to their homes. Frol Skobeev also wanted to leave with his sister, but Annushka, who permitted all the others to go, kept Frol Skobeev in her house. Frol Skobeev remained at Annushka's house for three days, always in feminine attire, so that he might not be recognized by the house servants. And he and Annushka enjoyed themselves, and only after three days did Frol go home with his sister. Before leaving, Annushka gave Frol three hundred rubles. Frol [returned home, overjoyed, and from that time the destitute Skobeev became richer, and began to live like a wealthy man and] began to have banquets with his fellow noblemen.

Sometime thereafter, Stolnik Nadrin-Nashchekin wrote from Moscow that Annushka should come to Moscow because there were many noble young men, sons of stolniks, who were seeking her hand in marriage. [Although Annushka was most unwilling to do so,] she did did not want to disobey her father. And so she soon left for Moscow. And when Frol Skobeev learned that she had gone to Moscow, he became confused, knowing not what he should do. Although he was a nobleman, he was quite poor, and made his living working in Moscow soliciting litigations at the court.[2] He decided [to mortgage his estate, which was just a wasteland, and] to go to Moscow in order to take Annushka as wife. He began to make preparations for his trip to Moscow, although his sister was greatly grieved, not wanting him to go.

Frol Skobeev [took leave of his sister and] said: "Dear sister, don't grieve over anything. Maybe I will lose my life, but I will not give up Annushka. I will be either a colonel or a corpse. If things happen according to my plans, I will not leave you in

[2] These solicitors were not formally trained, for there were no formally educated lawyers in Muscovite Russia. The functions of lawyers were performed by professional legal solicitors who represented their clients at the court and in governmental agencies. Many of these solicitors, however, gained positions of great influence in government administration.

need. However, in case misfortune occurs, please don't forget me in your prayers." And having made all the preparations, Frol went to Moscow.

Arriving in Moscow, he took quarters in the vicinity of Stolnik Nardin-Nashchekin's mansion. The next day Frol Skobeev went to Mass, and in the church he met Annushka's nurse. After the liturgy was over, Frol Skobeev left the church and awaited the nurse. When the nurse came out from the church, Frol Skobeev approached her, bowed deeply, and asked her to announce his arrival in Moscow to Annushka. [The nurse promised to support him.] Coming home, she told Annushka about Frol's arrival. Annushka became very happy, and told her nurse to take him twenty rubles when he went to Mass the next day. And the nurse did as she was told.

Stolnik Nadrin-Nashchekin had a sister who had taken vows in the Maiden's Convent.[3] Once the stolnik went to visit his sister in the convent. When he came there, the sister met him with all due honors. And the stolnik passed a long time with his sister. They had many conversations, and once the sister asked the brother to permit her niece to visit her, since she had not seen her niece in many years. Stolnik Nadrin-Nashchekin promised to permit his daughter to visit her at the convent. The sister added: "I would only ask you to give the necessary order in your home so that your daughter may come whenever I send my carriage, even if you yourself are not at home."

Some time later, Stolnik Nadrin-Nashchekin and his wife had to go to visit some friends, and he ordered his daughter: "In case my sister, your aunt, should send her carriage from the convent, please go to her." And he then went with his wife to visit the friends.

Annushka asked her nurse to go immediately to Frol Skobeev and to tell him that he should procure a horse and carriage as soon as possible and come to her house, saying that he was sent from the Maiden's Convent by the stolnik's sister for Annushka. The nurse went to Frol Skobeev and repeated the commands of her mistress.

When Frol Skobeev heard this, he didn't know what to do and whom to deceive in order to obtain a carriage, for all noble aristocrats knew that he was a poor nobleman and a great cheat, able only to solicit litigations. But he thought of a certain stolnik named Lovchikov who had always been very kind to

[3] The Maiden's Convent: the proper name of a convent in the vicinity of Moscow.

him. Therefore he went to this Lovchikov and had a long talk with him. Finally Frol began to beg Lovchikov to lend him his carriage and horses [so that he might go and look for a fiancée. Giving in to his requests, Lovchikov lent him his carriage and a coachman.] Frol went to his quarters and gave the coachman drinks until he was completely stupefied. Then he dressed himself in the lackey's clothes, sat on the coachbox, and went in the carriage to the home of Stolnik Nadrin-Nashchekin to get Annushka. There he was recognized by Annushka's nurse, who told Annushka that her aunt had sent her carriage for her from the convent. Annushka readied herself, sat in carriage, and went to Frol's quarters.

In the meantime Lovchikov's coachman had awakened, and Frol, realizing that the coachman was not sufficiently drunk, gave him more to drink. He then put him in the carriage, sat on the coachbox, and returned to Lovchikov's mansion. Arriving there, Frol opened the gate, drove the carriage into the yard, and left it there. When Lovchikov's servants found the carriage in the yard and the coachman inside, stupefied from drink, they went to Lovchikov and told him that the carriage was in the yard and that the coachman was dead drunk. Yet no one could learn who had brought the carriage and horses into the yard. Stolnik Lovchikov ordered the putting up of the horses and carriage in the stables, and added: "It's all right. At least the horses were not sold. What can one expect from Frol Skobeev?" In the morning Lovchikov asked the coachman where he went with Frol Skobeev, and the man answered, "I remember that we went to his quarters, but I do not actually know where I drove and what I did."

Soon afterward Stolnik Nadrin-Nashchekin returned from his friends and asked to see his daughter. He was told by the nurse that Annushka, by his order, had gone to the convent to his sister, since the sister had sent her carriage for her. Nadrin-Nashchekin answered, "Well, that's all right."

Thinking that his daughter lived with his sister in the convent, Nadrin-Nashchekin did not go for a while to his sister. In the meantime Frol and Annushka married. When Nadrin-Nashchekin finally did go to see his sister at the convent, and passed some time there without seeing his daughter, he remarked to his sister, "Well, sister, I haven't seen Annushka here." The sister answered: "Brother, don't joke. What can I do if you don't honor my requests? I asked you to send her to me, but apparently you don't trust me. As for myself, I haven't had time to send my carriage for her."

Stolnik Nadrin-Nashchekin replied: "My dear lady and sister, of what are you speaking? I don't understand a thing you have said, because Annushka left for your convent a month ago when you sent the carriage and horses after her. At that time I was visiting friends with my wife. She was permitted to go, as I ordered it so."

But the sister explained: "Brother, I have not sent a carriage and horses for her, and neither has Annushka ever been in this place."

Nadrin-Nashchekin grieved profoundly for his daughter, and cried bitterly, for she had vanished without leaving the slightest trace. Returning home, he told his wife that Annushka had disappeared and was not at the convent with his sister. And then he began to question the nurse, asking who had come and with whom Annushka had left. The nurse answered: "A coachman came with a carriage and said that he had come from the Maiden's Convent for Annushka. And Annushka left with him, according to your order."

The stolnik and his wife were greatly grieved, and wept bitterly. The next morning the stolnik went to the tsar to tell him that his daughter had vanished into thin air. The tsar ordered that the disappearance of the stolnik's daughter be made public, and he made the following pronouncement: "In case someone is keeping her secretly and does not come forward and admit it, this man will be sentenced to death when she is found."

Hearing this, Frol Skobeev didn't know what to do. Finally he decided to go to Stolnik Lovchikov, for this stolnik had always been good and kind toward him. When Frol came to Lovchikov, they had a long conversation during which Lovchikov asked, "Have you taken a bride?" And when Frol answered that he had, the stolnik asked, "And did you marry a wealthy wife?"

Frol answered, "Up to now I haven't seen much wealth, but we shall see what the future holds."

And Stolnik Lovchikov told Frol: "Well, Mr. Skobeev, now you must start living in upright ways. Stop soliciting. It would be much healthier if you were to live in your own domain." Thereafter, Frol began begging Stolnik Lovchikov to intervene for him.

Lovchikov answered: "Well, if it is a decent cause I shall intervene for you, but if it is something dishonest, don't be angry with me."

Frol then revealed to Lovchikov that he had married Stolnik

Nadrin-Nashchekin's daughter and that she was staying at this place.

Lovchikov answered, "You did this on your own, so accept the responsibility for it on your own."

But Frol threatened: "If you don't intervene for me, you also may be made responsible! I can testify against you, since you lent me the carriage and the horses to take her away. If you hadn't lent them to me, I wouldn't have been able to do it."

Lovchikov became very confused, and answered: "You are a real rogue! What are you trying to do to me? How can I intervene for you?" And then he suggested that Frol should go on the next day to the Cathedral of the Assumption of the Holy Virgin, for Nadrin-Nashchekin would be there for the Mass.[4] "After the Mass," he continued, "all of us will be standing together at St. John's Square. In this moment come and fall before the feet of Nadrin and tell him about his daughter. And I shall try to intervene on your behalf."

Frol Skobeev went the next morning to the Cathedral of the Assumption of the Holy Virgin and saw that Stolnik Nadrin-Nashchekin and several other stolniks were praying there. All of them, as was their wont, gather after Mass before the Bell Tower of John the Great[5] in John's Square. Nadrin-Nashchekin talked of his bereavement caused by the disappearance of his daughter. Lovchikov discussed the matter with him and was trying to convince him that he should be merciful no matter what happened. While they were talking, Frol Skobeev approached them and bowed to the stolniks, as was his custom, since they all knew him. Paying no heed to the others, Frol Skobeev fell to the feet of Nadrin-Nashchekin and began begging for forgiveness, saying: "My merciful lord and the first of the stolniks! Forgive me my guilt as if I were your humble slave who had daringly made an altercation with you!"

Nadrin-Nashchekin was already of advanced age and therefore had poor eyesight, and so could not recognize the man before him. He then drew Frol up with the handle of his cane, and asked: "Who are you? Tell me about yourself. What do you want from us?"

[4] In the seventeenth century the Cathedral of the Assumption of the Holy Virgin, which is located in the Kremlin, was in the center of the area of Muscovite governmental agencies.

[5] The Bell Tower of John the Great is the highest of the campaniles in the Kremlin. It was built by John IV, and, like the Cathedral of the Assumption of the Holy Virgin, was in the center of the area of governmental agencies.

But Frol repeated only, "Absolve me of my guilt."

Lovchikov came nearer, and said, "Before you stands Frol Skobeev, a nobleman who asks you to absolve him of his guilt."

Then Nadrin-Nashchekin exclaimed: "Get up, you rogue! For a long time have I known you, you rogue and knave! Tell me what has happened, you scoundrel! So you have once more got yourself into a predicament. If it is not too bad, I will help you. But if it is really base, then do as you want. For a long time I have told you, rogue, to live decently. Now get up and tell what is your evil-doing."

Frol got up from before the stolnik's feet and informed him that his daughter was at his place and that he had married her. Having heard that his daughter was Frol's wife, the stolnik began to sob, and lost consciousness. When he had slightly recovered himself, he began to rage: "What have you done, rogue? Do you know who you are? Who are you? Your evil-doing cannot be forgiven. How could you, such a rogue, dare to wed my daughter? I will go to the sovereign and ask that he punish you for this offense which is such a great affliction for me, you rogue!"

Lovchikov, for the second time, came near Nadrin-Nashchekin and tried to convince him not to go to the tsar, saying: "You had better go home and explain this to your spouse and then do your best as you both shall decide. You cannot undo what is already done. And he, Frol Skobeev, can find no shelter from your wrath."

Stolnik Nadrin-Nashchekin followed the advice of Lovchikov, and took his carriage and went home. In the meantime Frol Skobeev went to his house and told Annushka: "Well, Annushka, I don't know what will become of us. I have told your father of our marriage."

Stolnik Nadrin-Nashchekin came home, went to his wife's chambers, and, bitterly weeping and sobbing, told her: "My wife, my wife! Do you know what? I have found Annushka!"

And the wife asked him: "And where is she, Father?"

And Nadrin-Nashchekin told his wife: "That thief, rogue, and knave, Frol Skobeev, has married her."

When his wife heard these words, she knew not what to do, but only grieved deeply for her daughter. And both of them began to weep bitterly and to reprove their daughter. And knowing not what they should do, they cursed their daughter. When they had become calm, they began to ponder, and they deeply regretted the fate of their daughter. Finally they decided: "We must send a servant to learn where this rogue lives and if Annushka is still alive or not." And so they summoned a servant and ordered him to find the house of Frol Skobeev and to learn about Annushka and whether she was still alive and eating well.

When the servant came to the house of Frol Skobeev and Frol noticed that a man from his father-in-law's house had come into the yard, Frol told his wife to go to bed and to behave as if she were very ill. Annushka did as her husband willed. When the man, who was sent by her parents, entered the house and bowed deeply, as was the custom, Frol asked him, "What man are you and what is your business?" The man told Frol that he was sent by Stolnik Nadrin-Nashchekin to find out whether Annushka was in good health or not.

And Frol Skobeev told him: "Do you see, my friend, what kind of health she enjoys? This is the result of her parents' wrath, for, as you know, they reprimand her and curse her. They should at least give her their blessing."

The man bowed, left Skobeev, and returned to his master, Stolnik Nadrin-Nashchekin. And the stolnik asked him: "Did you find their quarters? Did you find Annushka? Is she alive or not?" The man answered that Annushka was very ill and would hardly remain alive much longer. And he asked them to send their blessings to their daughter. The stolnik and his wife grieved deeply and pondered what they should do with this rogue and knave.

Finally, the mother spoke: "Well, my friend, there is little we can do. Apparently God himself has willed that such a rogue be our daughter's husband. We, my friend, must send them the icon with our blessings. When our hearts become more merciful, then we shall see them." And they took down from the wall an icon decorated with gold and precious stones that were worth five hundred rubles. And they sent it with a servant, directing him to tell Annushka to pray to it and to tell Frol Skobeev not to sell the icon and then squander the money.

The servant took the icon and went to Frol Skobeev's house. Frol Skobeev saw the man coming, and told his wife: "Get up Annushka!" She got up and sat down with Frol. The servant entered the room and gave the icon to Frol. The latter accepted it, put it in a new place, and told the servant: "Such is the power of parental blessings. As soon as they had sent their blessings, God helped Annushka, and she recovered. And now, thanks be to God, she is in good health."

The servant returned to his master, told him that he had given the icon to Annushka, that her health had much improved, and that Annushka thanked her parents. The man then went to his lodgings.

Stolnik Nadrin-Nashchekin began to deliberate with his wife concerning their daughter. And they became sorry for her. The mother asked: "What should we do, my friend? Certainly this rogue will starve Annushka. How can this dog provide for her, when he himself is hungry? We must send her some provisions in a six-horse carriage." And so they sent provisions and a list of such to Frol Skobeev. Frol ordered that the provisions be put in an appropriate place without looking at the list. And he ordered the stolnik's servant to thank the parents for such gifts.

And from that time, Frol Skobeev lived like a wealthy man, and often visited important personages. And everyone wondered about Frol Skobeev and how he could have dared to carry through this affair.

Only a month later did the hearts of the parents become merciful to Frol and his wife. And they sent a man to them asking that they come to their house for dinner. And the man came and asked that they come that very day for dinner. And Frol answered the man, saying, "Report to the father that we are ready to come today to his grace." Frol and his wife dressed and went to the house of Frol's father-in-law, Stolnik Nadrin-Nashchekin. And when they came to the father-in-law's house, Annushka went to her father and fell before the feet of her parents. When Nadrin-Nashchekin and his wife saw their daughter, they began reprimanding her and visited their parental wrath upon her. But looking upon her, they began to weep bitterly because she had married against the will of her parents. Finally, their wrath subsided and they forgave her and ordered that she sit with them. But to Frol Skobeev they said: "And you, rogue, why are you standing? Sit down here. How can you, such a rogue, be married to our daughter?"

But Frol answered only: "Well, my lord and father, it was the will of God." And all sat down at the table, but Stolnik Nadrin-Nashchekin ordered the servants not to admit any visitors to the house, saying: "In the event that someone does come and asks if the stolnik is home, tell them that he is not, since I do not want to have other people see that we are eating with our son-in-law, that knave and rogue, Frol Skobeev."

After the meal, the stolnik asked, "Well, rogue, how will you make your living?"

And Frol answered: "Well, you know that better than I. I know only how to make my living by soliciting litigations."

And the stolnik told Frol: "Well, rogue, stop your soliciting.

In the district of Simbirsk I have an estate on which there are three hundred peasant families. You, rogue, can have it for your own, and live there permanently." Then Frol Skobeev and his wife bowed deeply and thanked the parents for this gift. But the stolnik said: "Don't bow, rogue. Better that you prepare the deeds to this domain."

Frol and Annushka remained only a short while longer at the parents' home, and then left. But on their way, Stolnik Nadrin-Nashchekin ordered that they return, and asked: "Well, rogue, how will you get supplies? Do you have any money?"

Frol answered: "Well, my father, you yourself know what kind of money I have, but perhaps I should sell the peasants on this estate."

Stolnik Nadrin-Nashchekin replied, saying: "No rogue, don't sell them. I shall give you some money. Take it." And he ordered that three hundred rubles be given to him. Frol Skobeev took the money and returned to his quarters.

Sometime later he received the deeds to this estate. Stolnik Nadrin-Nashchekin eventually was to make Frol Skobeev the heir of all his capital and domains. After the death of his father, Frol Skobeev married off his sister to the son of another stolnik, while Annushka's nurse remained living with Annushka and her husband in great honor to the end of her days.

43. *Misery-Luckless-Plight*

THE origin of *Misery-Luckless-Plight* has not been exactly determined, and it is of mixed genre. Found in a single copy that apparently was prepared in the eighteenth century, this tale-poem, in its content, philosophy, and language, belongs to the middle of the seventeenth century, when the problem of religious regeneration became so acute during the period of the movement of the Seekers After God (see Selection 39) and the Great Schism. Its theme is the salvation of a sinner. The story is in blank verse, and seems to have been written by a man well acquainted with both the ancient Russian tradition and oral folk poetry. The use of recurrent descriptions, its imagery, and repetition of traditional nature symbols and metaphors (for example, "The youth flew as a falcon," or "Misery after him as a gray hawk") relate the work to both the written and folklore traditions. The meter of four stresses is close to that of the historical *bylina,* while the psychological depiction of the prodigal young man seems to indicate that the author was familiar with religious literature. The writer's originality lies in the fact that his portrayal of the youth is distinctly different from the stereotyped characterizations of hagiographic writers.

For the present edition Leo Wiener's translation of the poem has been used. For readability, however, it has been divided into songs and stanzas, and the original Russian verse form has been retained. The translation has been partially revised.

◆ ◆ ◆

I. The Nature of Man

By the will of the Lord, our God, and our Savior,
Jesus Christ, Almighty
from the beginning of the age of man.
In the beginning of this passing age
God created heaven and earth,
God created Adam and Eve.
He ordered them to live in holy paradise,
and gave them this divine command:
He told them not to eat the fruit of the grapevine,
from the great tree of Eden.

But the human heart is unthinking and unruly,
and Adam and Eve were tempted.
They forgot God's command,
ate of the fruit of the grapevine,
from the great and wonderful tree,
and for that great transgression of theirs,
God's wrath rose against Adam and Eve.
And God drove Adam and Eve from the holy paradise of Eden.
He settled them upon the lowly earth,
blessed them that they might grow and multiply,
and told them to appease their hunger through their own labor
from the fruits upon earth.

God gave them this commandment:
there should be weddings and marriages
for the propagation of the race of men,
and for having beloved children.

But the human heart was senseless and disobedient;
from the very start it was not submissive,
looked with disdain at the father's instruction,
did not obey the mother,
was untrue to the advice of friends.

Then there came a weak and wretched race
that turned to reckless deeds
and began to live in turmoil and wrong,
and discarded humility of spirit.
And God grew wroth with them,
and imposed great calamities upon them,
and permitted that great misery be accorded to them,
and immeasurable shame,
evil plight,
fiendish visitations.
and evil, immeasurable nakedness,
and endless poverty and extreme want.
And he did it to humble us, to punish us,
to lead us on the path of salvation.
Such is the nature of man from his very birth from father
and mother.

II. Parents' Admonition

The youth had reached the age of discretion and absence of
wantonness.
His father and mother loved him much,
and they began to teach and instruct him,
to prepare him for good deeds:

"Dear child of ours,
listen to your parents' instruction,
listen to their saws,
good and cunning and wise,
and you will not be in want,
you will not be in great poverty.
Go not, child, to feasts and carousings;
do not seat yourself on a high place;
drink not two beakers at once;
be not tempted by good, beautiful women, fathers'
daughters.

Lie not down in the back yards.
Fear not the wise man;

fear the fool
lest the fools lay hands on you
and take off your costly garments,
and cause you great shame and dishonor,
and expose you to the scorn and empty prattle of men.
Go not, my child, to the dice-players and innkeepers,
and keep no company with tavern-goers.
Make no friends with the foolish and simple.
Steal not, rob not,
nor deceive, nor tell a lie, nor do wrong.
Be not tempted by gold and silver;
collect not unrighteous wealth.

Be not a witness to false swearing,
and think no evil of father and mother
or any other man—
that God may protect you from all evil.
Dishonor not, child, the rich and the poor,
but regard them all alike.
Keep company with the wise and sensible,
and make friends with friends you may rely upon,
who will not deliver you to evil."

III. The Emancipation

The youth was then young and foolish,
not in his full senses, and imperfect in mind;
he was ashamed to submit to his father
and bow before his mother,
but wanted to live as he listed.
If the youth earned fifty rubles,
he found easily fifty friends,
and his honor flowed like a river;
the youth gained many friends for himself,
and they accounted themselves of his race.

And the youth had a trusted friend:
he named himself his plighted brother,
and he tempted him with tempting words;
he called him to the tavern yard,
led him into the hall of the inn,
brought him a cup of good wine,
handed him a beaker of heady beer,
and spoke to him the following words:

"Drink, my bosom friend, brother of mine,
to your joy and happiness and health.
Empty the cup of good wine
and follow it by a glass of sweet mead.
And if you drink, brother, until you be drunk,
lie down to sleep where you have drunk—
depend upon me, your plighted brother.
I shall sit down and keep watch over you:
at your head, dear friend,
I shall place a beaker of sweet mead,
by your side I shall place good wine,
and near you I shall place heady beer,
I shall watch well over you, dear friend,
and shall take you back to your father and mother."

At that time the youth depended
on his plighted brother; he did not wish to disobey him.
He settled himself near the heady drinks,
and emptied a cup of green wine,
followed it by a glass of sweet mead,
and he drank also the heady beer.
He drank until he lost his senses,
and where he had drunk, there he fell asleep;
he depended upon his plighted brother.

The day was inclining toward night
and the sun was in the west,
when the youth awoke from his sleep.
The youth looked all around him;
all the costly garments had been taken from him,
his shoes and stockings were all gone,
his shirt even was taken from him,
and all his property was stolen.
A brick was lying under his unruly head;
he was covered with a tavern sackcloth,
and at his feet lay ragged shoes;
at his head his dear friend was no more.

And the youth stood up on his bare feet
and began to clothe himself:
he put on the ragged shoes,
covered himself with the tavern sackcloth,
covered his white body
and washed his white face.

Sorrow entered the youth's heart,
and he spoke the following words:

"Though God has granted me a good life,
I have now nothing to eat or drink!
Since my money is gone,
even the last half-farthing,
I have not a friend,
not even half a friend.
They no longer account themselves of my race,
all my friends have disappeared!"

IV. The Expatriation

The youth felt ashamed to show himself
before father and mother,
and his race and family,
and to his former friends.
He went into a strange, distant, unknown land.
He found a court, a town in size,
and a house in that court, a palace in height.
In that house was given a splendid feast;
the guests drank, ate and made merry.

The youth came to the splendid feast,
made the sign of the cross over his white face,
bowed before the miraculous icons,
made his obeisance to the good people
on all four sides.

And when the good people saw the youth,
how well he made the sign of the cross,
how he acted according to the written rule,
they took him by the hands,
seated him at the oaken table,
not in the best place, nor in the worst,
they seated him in a middle place,
where the younger guests were seated.

And the feast was a merry one,
and all the guests at the feast were drunk and merry and boastful;
but the youth sat, not merry at all,
gloomy, sorrowful, joyless,

and neither ate, nor drank, nor made merry,
nor boasted of anything at the feast.
Said the good people to the youth:

"Wherefore, O good youth,
do you sit, not merry at the feast,
gloomy, sorrowful, joyless;
you neither drink, nor make merry,
nor boast of anything at the feast.
Or has the cup of good wine not reached you,
or is not your seat according to your father's worth?
Or have small children insulted you?
Or are our children not kind to you?
Or foolish and unwise people made light of you, youth?

But the good youth remained sitting, and said:

"My lords and good people!
I will tell you of my great misfortune,
of my disobedience to my parents,
of my drinking at the inn, about the cup of mead,
the tempting drinking of heady wine.

When I took to drinking the heady wine,
I disobeyed both father and mother;
their blessing departed from me;
the Lord grew wroth with me
and to my poverty were added
many great and incurable sorrows
and sadness without comfort,
want, and misery, and extreme wretchedness.

Want has tamed my flowery speech;
sadness has dried up my white body.
For this my heart is not merry,
and my white face is sad, and my eyes dim.
I have lost my paternal honor,
any my youthful valor has left me.
My lords and good people!
Tell me and teach me how to live in a strange land,
among strange people,
and how to find dear friends!"

Said the good people to the youth:

"You are a sensible youth!
Be not haughty in a strange land;
submit to friend and foe,
bow to old and young,
tell not of the affairs of others,
neither what you hear nor see.
Flatter not friends nor enemies;
have no tortuous fits,
nor bend as a cunning snake;
be humble before all
but withal keep to truth and right—
and you will have a great honor and glory.
When people will find you out
they will respect and honor you
for your great truth,
your humility and wisdom—
and you will have dear friends
who will call themselves your plighted brothers."

V. Temptations of Misery-Luckless-Plight

And the youth went hence into a strange land
and began to live wisely,
and through his great wisdom acquired greater wealth than before.
He looked out for a bride according to custom,
for he wished to marry.
The youth prepared a splendid feast,
according to his father's worth
and as best he knew,
and invited the honored guests and friends.
But through his own sin,
by God's will and the devil's temptation,
he boasted before his honored guests
and friends and plighted brothers.
A boastful word is always rotten,
and self-praise brings the destruction of man.
"I, a youth, have gained more possessions than ever!"

Misery-Luckless-Plight heard the young man's boasting
and spoke the following words:

"Young man, boast not of your fortune,
praise not your wealth!
I, Misery, have known people

who were wiser and richer than you,
but I, Misery, have outwitted them.
When a great misfortune befell them,
They struggled with me unto their death;
they were worsted by their luckless plight—
could not get away from me, Misery,
until they took their abode in the grave,
and I covered them forever with the earth.
Only then they were rid of nakedness,
and I, Misery, left them,
though luckless plight remained upon their grave."

And again it cawed ominously:

"I, Misery, attached myself to others,
for I, Misery-Luckless-Plight,
cannot live empty-handed; I, Misery,
wish to live among people
from whom I cannot be driven away with a stick;
but my chief seat and paternal home
is among the carousers!"

Spoke gray Misery the miserable:

"How am I to get at the youth?"

and evil Misery devised cunningly
to appear to the youth in his dream:

"Young man, renounce your beloved bride,
for you will be poisoned by your bride;
you will be strangled by that woman;
you will be killed for your gold and silver!
Go, young man, to the tsar's tavern,
save nothing, but spend all your wealth in drink;
doff your costly dress, put on the tavern sackcloth.
In the tavern Misery will remain,
and evil Luckless-Plight will stay—
for Misery will not gallop after a naked one,
nor will anyone annoy a naked man,
nor has assault any terrors for a barefooted man."

The young man did not believe his dream,
but evil Misery again devised a plan,

appeared as the archangel Gabriel,
and stuck once more to the youth for a new plight:

"Are you not, youth,
acquainted with poverty and nakedness,
with hopes and security?
What you buy for yourself is money spent,
but you are a brave fellow
and can live without expense!
They do not beat, nor torture naked people,
nor drive them out of paradise,
nor drag them down from the other world;
nor will anyone annoy a naked man,
nor has assault any terrors for a naked man!"

VI. The Last Trial

The young man believed that dream:
he went and spent all his wealth in drink;
he doffed his costly dress,
put on the tavern sackcloth,
covered his white body.
The youth felt ashamed to show himself to his dear friends.
He went into a strange, distant, unknown land.
On his way he came to a swift river.
On the other side were the ferrymen
and they asked for money to ferry him across;
but the youth had none to give,
and without money they would not take him across.
The youth sat a whole day,
until evening, and all that day until compline
the youth had nothing to eat,
not even half a piece of bread.
The young man arose on his swift feet,
and standing, he fell to grieving,
and he spoke the following words:

"Woe to me, miserable Luckless-Plight!
It has overtaken me, young man,
has starved me, young man, with a hungry death.
Three unlucky days have I passed,
for I, young man, have not eaten half a piece of bread!
I, young man, will jump into the swift river:
swallow my body, swift river!
And eat, O fish, my white body!

And that will be better than my shameful life;
will I ever be able to escape the hands
of Misery-Luckless-Plight?"

At that hour Misery leaped from behind a rock
near the swift river;
Misery was barefooted and naked
and there was not a thread upon it,
and it was girded with a bast thong,
and it called out with a mighty voice:

"Wait, young man, you will not escape from me, Misery!
Jump not into the swift river,
nor be in your misery doleful!
Though you live in misery, you need not be doleful,
and you should even let your dolefulness die in misery!
Remember, young man, your former life;
how your father spoke to you, and your mother
instructed you!
Why did you not then obey them?
You would not submit to them,
and were ashamed to bow to them,
but wanted to live as you listed!
But he who will not listen to the good teaching of
his parents
will be taught by me, Misery-Luckless-Plight!

Luckless-Plight spoke the following speech:

"Submit to me, impure Misery;
bow before me, Misery, to the damp earth,
for there is no one wiser in the whole world than I,
Misery;
and you will be ferried across the swift river,
and the good people will give you to eat and drink."

The young man saw his inevitable calamity,
and he submitted to impure Misery,
bowed before Misery to the damp earth!

The good fellow went ahead with a light step over the steep,
fair bank,
over the yellow sand.
He went happy, not at all doleful,

for he had appeased Misery-Luckless-Plight.
And as he went, he thought a thought.
"Since I have nothing,
I need not worry about anything!"
And as the youth was not sorrowful,
he started a fair song,
a mighty, sensible song it was:

"Sorrowless mother has borne me:
with a comb she combed my little locks,
dressed me in costly garments,
and stepping aside shaded her eyes
and looked at me:
'Does my child look well in costly garments?
In costly garments my child is a priceless child!'
Thus my mother always spoke of me!
And then I learned and know it well,
that a costly gown cannot be made without a master,
nor a child be comforted without a mother,
nor a drunkard ever become rich,
nor a dice-player be in good renown,
and I was predestined by my parents to be a well-dressed boy
who was born devoid of everything."

The ferrymen heard the good fellow's song,
took the young man across the swift river,
and took nothing from him for the ferrying.
The good people gave him to drink and to eat,
took off his tavern sackcloth,
gave him peasant's clothes.
And these good people spoke to him:

"You are a good fellow,
so go to your home,
to your beloved, respected parents,
to your father and mother dear,
greet your parents, father and mother,
and receive from them the parental blessing!"

From there the youth went to his home.
When he was in the open field,
evil Misery had gone before him;
it met the youth in the open field,
and began to caw above the youth,

like an ill-omened crow above a falcon.
Misery spoke the following words:

> "Wait! you have not gone away from me, good fellow!
> Not merely for a time have I, Misery-Luckless-Plight,
> attached myself to you;
> I shall labor with you to your very death!
> And not I, Misery, alone, but all my relatives,
> and there is a godly race of them:
> we are all gentle and insinuating,
> And he who joins our family will end his days among us!
> Such is the fate that awaits you with us.
> Even if you were to be a bird of the air,
> or if you went into the blue sea as a fish,
> I would follow you at your right hand."

The youth flew as a clear falcon,
and Misery after him as a white gyrfalcon;
the youth flew as a steel-blue dove,
and Misery after him as a gray hawk;
the youth went into the field as a gray wolf,
and Misery after him with greyhounds;
the youth became the feathergrass in the field,
and Misery came with a sharp scythe,
and Luckless-Plight railed at him:

> "You, little grass, will be cut down;
> you, little grass, will lie on the ground,
> and the boisterous winds will scatter you!"

The youth went as a fish into the sea,
and Misery after him with close-meshed nets,
and Misery-Luckless-Plight railed at him:

> "You, little fish, will be caught at the shore,
> and you will be eaten up and die a useless death!"

The youth went on foot along the road
and Misery at his right hand.
It taught the youth to live as a rich man by killing and robbing,
so that they might hang the young man for it,
or might put him with a stone in the water.

The youth bethought himself of the road to salvation
and at once the youth went to a monastery to be shorn a monk,
and Misery stopped at the holy gates—
no longer clung to the youth.

And this is the end of the story:
Lord, preserve us from eternal torment,
and give us, O Lord, the light of paradise!
Forever and ever, amen!

44. *Poems From the Collection of Baccalaureus Richard James*

IN 1619 a young British scholar, baccalaureus Richard James, visited Russia and brought back to England six short poems, or songs, which he had transcribed phonetically in Russian, using Latin letters. F. Buslaev, the first scholar to study and publish them, believed that they were specimens of Russian folklore, but contemporary scholars believe that all of the poems were written by an unknown Russian poet of the early seventeenth century. The use of rhymed verses, completely uncharacteristic of Russian folklore of the time, their vocabulary—which betrays an author well-versed in the Russian literary language—as well as their subjects strongly confirm the latter opinion. The poems reflect political events of the time, and one of them, "Ode on the Return to Moscow of Patriarch Filaret," even deals with an event that occurred in the same year as the transcription of these poems.

The first is about the second raid against Moscow by the Khan of Crimea, Devlet Girey. In 1571 the Tatars of Crimea, under Khan Devlet, cleverly circled Russian armies guarding the access to Moscow and attacked and burned the Russian capital. Over a million Russians perished during this raid, while hundreds of thousands of prisoners were captured by the Tatars, later to be sold on the Middle Eastern and Mediterranean slave markets. In 1572 Devlet repeated his raid, but was defeated by Russian troops under Prince M. Vorotynsky. Out of a hundred and twenty thousand Tatar warriors, only twenty thousand returned home. The poem depicts the Tatars' hope of inflicting a final blow on Moscow and of conquering the other Russian cities. The "seventy Apostles" mentioned in the poem are the Muscovite churches, dedicated to seventy pupils of Christ, while the expression "Holy Fathers" refers to the churches dedicated to the three theologians of the early Christian Church: St. Basil the Great, St. Gregory the Theologian, and St. John Chrysostom (Golden Mouth).

The second poem voices the feelings and lament over her fate of Princess (Tsarevna) Xenia, the daughter of Tsar Boris

Godunov. After the death of Tsar Boris, when the impostor, Pseudo-Dmitry, seized Moscow and became tsar, he abused the daughter of his enemy and then sent her to a convent in Ustiuzhna-Zheleznaia, in northern Russia, where she was forced to take monastic vows.

The last of the poems offered here from the James Collection is an ode glorifying the return from a Polish prison of Metropolitan Filaret (who soon became Patriarch), father of Michael Romanov, the first tsar of the dynasty which was to rule Russia until the revolution of 1917. Fedor (Filaret was his monastic name) Nikitich Romanov had been captured along with other Russian aristocrats by the Poles during the Time of Troubles, and only after the Russian-Polish armistice of 1618 was he permitted to leave the Polish-Lithuanian Condominium and return to Moscow.

The text of the *Raid of the Crimean Tatars* and *Ode to the Return of Filaret Romanov* follow the translations of Leo Wiener, while the text of *Song of Princess Xenia* is taken from W. R. Morfill's *Story of Russia*, New York and London, 1890. All three texts have been revised by the present editor.

✦ ✦ ✦

RAID OF THE CRIMEAN TATARS

Not a mighty cloud has covered the sky,
Nor mighty thunders have thundered:
Whither travels the dog, Crimea's khan?—
To the mighty Tsardom of Muscovy.
"Today we will go against stone-built Moscow,
But coming back, we will take Riazan."
And when they were at the river Oka,
They began their white tents to pitch.
"Now think a thought with all your minds:
Who is to sit in stone-built Moscow,
And who is to sit in the city of Vladimir,
And who is to sit in the city of Suzdal,
And who will hold the old city of Riazan,
And who will sit in the city of Zvenigorod,
And who will sit in the city of Novgorod?"
There stepped forward Divi Murza, son of Ulan:
"Listen, our lord, Crimea's khan!
You, our lord, shall sit in stone-built Moscow,
And your son in Vladimir,

And your nephew in Suzdal,
And your relative in Zvenigorod,
And let the equerry hold old Riazan,
But to me, O lord, grant Novgorod:
There, in Novgorod, lies my luck."
The voice of the Lord called out from heaven:
"Listen, you dog, Crimea's khan!
Know you not the Tsardom of Muscovy?
There are in Moscow seventy Apostles,
Besides the three Holy Fathers.
And there is in Moscow still an Orthodox tsar."
And you fled, you dog, Crimea's khan,
Not over the highways, nor the main road,
Nor following the black banner.

SONG OF PRINCESS XENIA, DAUGHTER OF TSAR BORIS GODUNOV

There weepeth a little bird,
A little white quail:
"Alas, that I so young must grieve!
They wish to burn the green oak,
To destroy my little nest,
To kill my little ones,
To catch me, quail."
In Moscow the Princess weepeth:
"Alas that I so young must grieve!
For there comes to Moscow the impostor
Grishka Otrepiev, the defrocked monk,
Who wants to take me captive,
And having captured make me a nun,
To send me into the convent.
But I do not wish to become a nun,
To go into a monastery:
I shall keep my dark cell open,
To look at the fine fellows.
O our beautiful corridors!
Who will walk over you
After our life as the tsar's family
And after Boris Godunov?
O our beautiful palace halls!
Who will be sitting in you
After our life as the tsar's family
And after Boris Godunov?"

And in Moscow the Princess weepeth,
The daughter of Boris Godunov:
"O God, our merciful Savior!
Wherefore is our Tsardom perished–
Is it for father's sinning,
Or for mother's not praying?
And you beloved palace halls!
Who will rule in you,
After our life as the tsar's family?
Fine stuffs of drawn lace!–
Shall we wind you around the birches?
Fine gold-worked towels!
Shall we throw you into the woods?
Fine earrings of hyacinth
Shall we hang you on branches,
After our life as the tsar's family,
After the reign of our father,
Glorious Boris Godunov?
Wherefore comes to Moscow the defrocked monk,
And wants to break down the palaces,
And to take me, princess, captive,
And to send me to Ustyuzhna Zheleznaia,
To make me, princess, a nun,
To place me behind a walled garden?
Why must I grieve,
As they take me to the dark cell,
And the abbess gives me her blessing?"

ODE TO THE RETURN OF FILARET ROMANOV, FATHER OF TSAR MIKHAIL, TO MOSCOW

The Tsardom of Muscovy was happy
And all the holy Russian land.
Happy was the sovereign, the Orthodox tsar,
The Grand Duke Mikhail Fedorovich,
For he was told that his father had arrived,
His father Filaret Nikitich,
From the land of the infidel, from Lithuania.
He had brought back with him many princes and boyars,
He had also brought the boyar of the tsar,
Prince Mikhail Borisovich Sheyn.
There had come together many princes, boyars, and dignitaries,

In the mighty Tsardom of Muscovy:
They wished to meet Filaret Nikitich
Outside the famous white stone-built Moscow.
'Tis not the beautiful sun in its orbit—
'Tis the Orthodox tsar that has gone out,
To meet his father dear,
Lord Filaret Nikitich.
With the tsar went his uncle,
Ivan Nikitich the boyar—
"The Lord grant my father be well,
My father, lord Filaret Nikitich."
They went not into the palace of the tsar,
They went into the cathedral of the most Holy Virgin,
To sing a holy Mass.
And he blessed his beloved child:
"God grant the orthodox tsar be well,
Grand Duke Mikhail Fedorovich!
And for him to rule the Tsardom of Muscovy
And the holy Russian land."

45. *Prince Ivan Khvorostinin: Autobiographical Verses*

PRINCE Ivan Khvorostinin (1585? to 1625) was one of the most controversial Russian writers of the first quarter of the seventeenth century. Scion of an ancient noble family and the son of the valiant defender of Pskov against King Stephen Bathory, Ivan Khvorostinin appeared at the Muscovite court quite early. He later became one of the intimate friends of Pseudo-Dmitry, who became tsar in 1605. After the fall of this impostor, Khvorostinin was banned from Moscow, but some years later he reappeared as commander of one of the armies that fought against the Poles in southwestern Russia. It seemed at the time that this talented aristocrat had a brilliant career before him, but his debauchery, dissoluteness, and unorthodox behavior caused him difficulty once more. He was apparently very unhappy in Moscow society, for he often criticized his surroundings, and complained that there weren't any clever people there, nor anyone worth being acquainted with. In one of his satirical verses, he claimed:

"These Muscovite people
cultivate much rye,
but live only by the lie."

Such verses aroused the indignation of the court, and a new investigation of his case showed that he wanted to flee to the West, to Italy, and that he denied such basic dogmas of the Orthodox Church as resurrection after death, and the Trinity. He apparently followed the teachings of the Unitarians. This early Russian Westernizer was then sent to the Monastery of St. Cyril where, in 1623, he decided to recant, and was then permitted to return to Moscow. Soon after his return he wrote his monumental *Exposition Against the Blaspheming Heretics*, in which he ambitiously attacked both the Roman Catholic and Protestant churches. This exposition, which is about 1,333 verses long, is written in rhymed couplets. His verses have no meter, and the line varies from six to fourteen syllables. This first Russian poem of considerable length deserves attention not only because of its size, but also because of the great variations in rhyme and the autobiographical elements of its final part. In this last section Prince Khvorostinin bitterly complained of the unfaithfulness of his servants and friends, who apparently informed the government of his unorthodox behavior and thinking. Besides this religious poem, he was the author of a number of other historical and polemical works in which he displayed a skillful command of contemporary literary devices and in which he often introduced rhymed passages.

The following translation of the final part of the *Exposition Against the Blaspheming Heretics* is based on the text published in *Letopis zaniatii arkheograficheskoi komissii*, Volume XVIII, St. Petersburg, 1907, pages 77–80.

◆ ◆ ◆

Look, reader, upon the Roman mores
and be faithful to God's glories.
Do not look for truth in any foreign creeds.
Do not betray the holy fathers' deeds.
Take care, for the Western Church's revelations
can certainly destroy our foundations.[1]
The Western Church is dark both day and night,
and bitter fruits grow like a blight.

[1] Under the expression "Western Church" Prince Khvorostinin means both the Catholic and the Protestant churches.

Their Eighth Council[2] did many wrong deeds,
betraying many of the holy fathers' creeds.
They want to condemn us to evil torments,
and they give their warriors heretical armaments.
The wave of their wrath is great,
but ever shall I their teachings berate.
I have wanted to bequeath something to my nation,
which is built upon a holy and Christian foundation.
But there were many evil doers,
who have confused our blessed rulers.
I have wanted to lend my hand to the work of salvation,
and for the destruction of their heretical creation.
But in place of ink, I had to use tears
and in irons I found the end of my career.
In prison I passed many days,
for a long time I did not see the sun's rays.
I have wanted to escape their evil gold,
and for such, never have I my soul sold.
I was forced to hide from treacherous detestation,
and thus could not continue my affirmation.
As an army commander I was always brave,
not wanting to bring my friends to the grave.
On Him who knows my heart have I always relied,
and He has always been my friend, true and tried.
His commandments I have never rejected,
but to His protection have I myself directed.
And before the time of my misfortune,
I had always rejected a heretical fortune.
I did so by the Holy Scriptures,
and following the holy fathers' strictures.
I have remained the faithful son of my faith
and firmly stood for the Eastern Church's Grace.
It was not my wont to debate with the ignorant,
nor did I care for their argument.
By much misfortune have I been accosted,
but by the absence of friends I was sore exhausted.
And no one would fain take a stand for me,
but only the Lord His help granted me.
I have written many words against the enemy
of the faith,

[2] Eighth Council was the first council of the Western Christian Church, which is considered by the Catholics an Ecumenical Council; but it is not recognized by the Eastern Orthodox, who did not take part in its works.

and still I was thrown into such a bitter place.
Many a friend denounced my writing
and launched against me bitter fighting.
They took me from my holy task,
and not a word of thanks could I ask.
As a heretic was I condemned,
and thus my task came to a bitter end.
Look upon their evil doings,
and contrite hearts be not eschewing.
Even my servants became my enemies,
thus depriving me of any serenity.
They took away from me their comfort and support,
and prepared against me the trial in court.
Their lawless hatred was evil,
and they prepared me for burial.
They did so, for they belong to a kind most base,
worse than if they were of a devilish race.
They spewed their poisons at me,
and in their betrayal they agreed.
Their weapons were denunciations,
spreading against me all kind of calumniation.
O Lord, our God, show your might
and judge whether they or I be right.
You alone know of all my devotions
and you will divine the truth in their motions.
They were fed on my bread,
yet they turned my good deed to one of dread.
Yet sweeter than the sweetest flower,
is being in the Lord's power.
Let the work of my slaves be cursed,
let us hope their design will be dispersed.
Don't throw pearls before swine,
for they will be defiled, whether they be yours or mine.
And I underwent many hardships because of my slaves,
and they nearly brought me to the brink of the grave.
They forgot the words of Christ's admonitions
and I could not escape their evil intentions.
Their words were as ensnaring as a spider's web,
and their hatred was like an evil web.
Over them I was placed by my Creator,

by God was I placed over these evil traitors.
I stood alone against this evil horde,
but I was raised above them by my dear Lord.
But they became my bitter enemies,
and they profaned their own souls with their
calumnies.
To win their own freedom,
they wanted to escape their serfdom.
They hurled their words like arrows against their
lord,
and I wonder about those who approve of such
a horde.

46. *The Orderly of Colonel Theodore Zay*
A Love Letter from the Year 1698

THE accidental arrest of a certain Savva Kartsev, who was suspected of participating in political conspiracy, preserved in the archives of the Russian police a love letter written by the orderly of Colonel Theodore Zay. The letter was written for the colonel's son, who had recently married without parental consent, and was to be delivered by Savva Kartsev to the wife of this young man. The intervention of the police prevented its delivery, but preserved the letter for posterity. The rhymed couplets of this letter demonstrate a new poetic vogue, while the metre, epithets, and vocabulary resemble the love songs of Russian folklore.

This poem is translated from the text published by L. Maikov in *Ocherki po istorii russkoi literatury XVII i XVIII stoletii,* St. Petersburg, 1889, page 230.

◆ ◆ ◆

To the most glorious light which has ever appeared
before my eyes,
to the nicest person whom I advise.
May my beloved live for many years,
and not forget the pledge given to me here.
Do not forget our pledge taken before the Lord,
when we exchanged rings of our future concord.

At that time we had our wedding crowns on our
heads,
crowns of gold for the commemoration of the
happy, holy event.
Do not forget me in your prayers,
for I shall forget you never.
And I am so sad without you,
that I could fly from here as if I were a bird,
and I would come to you, my beloved.
We could lock ourselves in our chambers,
and confide in each other's secrets.
O my dear, blue flower, the beloved of my life!
What did I do when I came to my lord-father
and when I saw my lady-mother?
When I looked into their eyes,
I saw that our joy was beshadowed.
I awaited kind words from their graces,
but their words betrayed my faith.
"You can marry
someone with considerable wealth,
but you should marry her that we would care for,
and whom you should love.
You should marry a girl from the house of a
Muscovite nobleman."
But I, my dear nightingale, only thanked them
for their advice,
and now I send you this love letter with my best
regards.

47. *Peter Kvashnin*

AROUND 1680 Peter Kvashnin, a member of an ancient and noble family, wrote about fifty lyric poems, some of which are more than a hundred lines in length. This poetry was first published in 1932 by M. N. Speransky, who thought it was the product of Russian folklore. But the form, vocabulary, and unusual epithets, as well as partially rhymed lines, seem to prove that the poems are instead the personal creations of Kvashnin or of one of his friends. Only in a few aspects do they follow the folklore tradition. The fact, also, that many of them are unfinished would indicate that they are the product of Kvashnin's own poetic creativeness. All the poems have a common topic, that of painful and unrequited love, and are filled with pathos.

The translations of the two poems given here are based on M. N. Speransky's texts published in *Izvestiia Akademii Nauk USSR*, Volume 7, 1932, pages 721–724.

The subject of the first poem is the tender love of a sister for her brother.

✦ ✦ ✦

DEAR BROTHER

It was not a she-turtledove that cooed with a
    turtledove.
It was a sister that spoke with her brother.
And speaking with her brother, the sister
began to praise the darling little brother:
"Oh, my dearest little brother, my fond heart,
my dearest of friends, my beloved.
I cannot cease my enjoyment of looking upon you.
You are my precious darling, beautiful as an apple.
You are handsome, my fair brother, like a poppy
    blossom.
You appear, my young, dear brother, as a cherry.
When I don't see you, my brother,
I could die from sorrow.
And I remember my brother,
but I can only sigh after him.
And I dream steadily of him,
my friendship for him is firm."
The sister speaks with her brother,
and the sister begins to lament:
"Bitter is my life, my brother,
for I hear nonsense and senseless rumors.
Why do those people hate me?
O God, judge those who envy us,
who want to abuse me, a young girl,
and who want to separate me from my brother.
I should rather lose my reputation
than be separated from my brother.
Even if they spread calumnies about me,
I shall never forsake my brother. . . ."

[This poem is unfinished.]

I THOUGHT

I thought, I pondered,
I followed the reasoning of another,
and I said no to my love, straight to his face.
[A hiatus of several lines]
And he decided to take a young wife, a maiden fair.
Oh, come to me, my beloved, on the eve of your wedding!
I shall give you, my beloved, a beautiful linen shirt,
A shirt adorned with muslin.
I waited for my dear friend the whole day until evening.
And my beloved came to me
early in the morning, when a beautiful sun had risen.
And you, my nurses and servants, bring me my trunk with iron bars.
And open this trunk with the iron bars,
and take from it two steel knives
for me and for my friend.
Since I could not keep him with me,
you had better open his white breast.
And then he, my beloved, will belong
neither to me, nor to my sister,
nor to that strumpet who separated us.
But you, my beloved, will belong to our mother, the damp earth.
And only an oaken board will preserve my secret.

A Short Glossary of Some Russian Terms Used in This Anthology

I. Currency and Measures

Grivna An old Russian unit of money equivalent to the old English pound. It was in the form of a silver ingot.

Kuna From the Russian word for marten. A monetary unit, there being twenty-five *kunas* in a *grivna.*

Nogata A unit of money, there being twenty *nogatas* in a *grivna.* It was a vair.

Rezana A vair. There were fifty *rezanas* in a *grivna.*

Ruble A Russian monetary unit since the fifteenth century. Equal to about one English pound at that time.

Versta or *poprishche* Units of measure equal to about ⅔ of a mile.

II. Ranks and Titles

Metropolitan The head of the national Orthodox Church, in particular head of the Russian Church until the end of the sixteenth century. Since the end of the sixteenth century the term has come to denote an archbishop in charge of a large diocese.

Posadnik An elected high official in the cities of early Kievan Russia and in both the Novgorodian and Pskovian republics until the fifteenth century. Similar to rank of commissioner.

Sotnik An officer who commanded a *sotnia,* a company of one hundred men. A centurion.

Stolnik A high official at the tsar's court or of the civil administration.

Strelets (pl. *streltsy*) Professional infantrymen. The corps of *streltsy* was created in the sixteenth century.

Tysiatsky An elected commander of the army in the earlier Kievan period and in the Novgorodian and Pskovian republics.

Voevoda A high-ranking officer either in the civil administration or in the army. A rank equivalent to that of general or governor.

Chronology of Russian History and Culture

Seventh Century B.C. Occupation of the southern prairies of Russia by the Scythians, and the founding of Greek cities on the northern shore of the Black Sea.

Third Century A.D. Goths occupy the southern prairie of Russia.

Fourth Century The Huns penetrate into Europe from Asia, thus causing the Great Migration. The Antes (Slavs?) founded a state in what is present-day southern Russia.

Ninth Century Appearance of the Viking (Varangian) tradesmen in Russia.

862 The legendary founding of the Russian state by Rurik.

907 Oleg's first campaign against Constantinople.

955 Olga travels to Constantinople, and takes baptism there.

988 or 989 The Christianization of Russia by Prince Vladimir.

Early Eleventh Century The Kumans drive out the Pechenegs from the southern prairies of Russia.

Circa 1030 The oldest known Russian literary work, the *Sermon* of Luke Zhidiata.

1019–1054 The reign of Yaroslav the Wise.

Circa 1050 The writing of the *Primary Chronicle* begins.

1113 Monk Nestor ends the writing of the *Primary Chronicle.*

1113–1125 The reign of Vladimir Monomakh, the last great prince of the Kievan Period to be recognized as ruler of all Russia.

1185 Igor's unfortunate campaign against the Kumans.

1186 (?) The writing of the *Lay of Igor's Campaign.*

1223 Russians are defeated by the Mongols at the river Kalka.

1237–1240 The Mongol conquest of Russia.

1283–1304 Daniel, Prince of Moscow, founds the Muscovite state.

1261 The beginning of the Muscovite branch of the Rurik dynasty.

1326 Metropolitan Peter, the head of the Russian Church, moves his office to Moscow.

1328 Ivan Kalita receives the title "Great Prince of All Russia."

1314–1392 St. Sergius of Radoniezh, the founder of monasticism in northern Russia.

1380 Russia defeats the Tatars at the Battle of Kulikovo.

1386 (?) The writing of *Zadonshchina.*

1420 The death of Epiphanius the Wise, author of the lives of St. Sergius and St. Stephen of Perm.

1427 or *1430* Death of the greatest Russian painter of the medieval era, Andrew Rublev.

1462–1505 The reign of Ivan III, the unifier of northern Russia.

1533–1584 The reign of Ivan IV.

1550–1570 The compilation of *Chetii Minei (The Book of the Lives of Saints)*, of the *Book of Grades,* and Nikon's *Illustrated Codex.*

1598 The death of Tsar Fedor, and the consequent end of the Rurik dynasty.

1598–1605 The reign of Tsar Boris Godunov.

1605–1613 The Time of Troubles.

1613–1645 The reign of the first Romanov, Tsar Michael.

1620–1630 Avraamy Palitsyn, M. Katyrev-Rostovsky, and I. Khvorostinin write their works on the Time of Troubles. Probable time of the writing of the *Life of Yuliania Lazarevskaia.*

1645–1676 The reign of Tsar Alexis.

1653 The first reforms of Patriarch Nikon.

1663 Simeon Polotsky comes to Moscow. Beginning of Russian syllabic verse.

1667 The Church Council of Moscow and the consequent schism within the Russian Church.

1672 *Esther,* the first Russian play, is staged in the tsar's theatre.

1673 Avvakum writes his *Life.*

1682–1725 The reign of Peter the First, and the consequent westernization of Russia.

NONE OF THESE DISEASES

S. I. McMillen, M. D.

PILLAR BOOKS NEW YORK

Dedicated to
A MOTHER
A SISTER
A WIFE
A DAUGHTER

Scripture quotations identified as KJV *are from* The King James Version of The Bible.

Scripture quotations identified as ASV *are from* The American Standard Version of The Bible.

Scripture quotations identified as Berkeley *are from* The Holy Bible, The Berkeley Version in Modern English, *Gerrit Verkuyl, Editor, Zondervan Publishing House, Grand Rapids, Michigan, 1960. Used by permission.*

Scripture quotations identified as Moffatt *are from* The Bible: A New Translation, *by James Moffatt, Copyright by James Moffatt, 1954. Used by permission of Harper & Row, Publishers, Incorporated.*

Scripture quotations identified as Phillips *are reprinted with permission of The Macmillan Company from* The New Testament in Modern English, *by J. B. Phillips, Copyright, 1958 by J. B. Phillips.*

Scripture quotations identified as NEB *are from* The New English Bible. *© The Delegates of the Oxford University Press and The Syndics of the Cambridge University Press 1961. Reprinted by permission.*

NONE OF THESE DISEASES

A PILLAR BOOK
Published by arrangement with Fleming H. Revell Company
Second printing, August 1976

ISBN: 0-89129-011-7

Library of Congress Catalog Card Number: 63-13359

Printed in the United States of America

PILLAR BOOKS
Pyramid Publications
(Harcourt Brace Jovanovich, Inc.)
757 Third Avenue, New York, New York 10017, U.S.A.

PREFACE

Peace does not come in capsules! This is regrettable because medical science recognizes that emotions such as fear, sorrow, envy, resentment and hatred are responsible for the majority of our sicknesses. Estimates vary from 60 per cent to nearly 100 per cent.

Emotional stress can cause high blood pressure, toxic goiter, migraine headaches, arthritis, apoplexy, heart trouble, gastrointestinal ulcers, and other serious diseases too numerous to mention. As physicians we can prescribe medicine for the symptoms of these diseases, but we can not do much for the underlying cause—emotional turmoil. *It is lamentable that peace does not come in capsules.*

We need something more than a pill for the disease-producing stresses of the man who has lost his life's savings, the tearful feminine soul who has been jilted, the young father who has an inoperable cancer, the woman whose husband is a philanderer, the distraught teen-ager with a facial birthmark, and the schemer who lies awake at night trying to think of ways to get even with his neighbor.

This book was born as a result of a thousand sighs for the many people who left my office without receiving adequate help. There wasn't time to do much more than prescribe some pills for their complaints, but I knew there was something better than pills for them to take for the rest of their lives. In this book I have written the prescription I would have given to those patients if only I had had the time.

I hasten to add that this counsel is not original with me. When God led the Israelites out of afflicted Egypt, He promised them that if they would obey His statutes, He would put "*none of these diseases*" upon them. God guaranteed a freedom from disease that modern medicine cannot duplicate. Was the divine pledge a hollow assurance? Were the Israelites miraculously freed from these diseases? Would the same regulations save us today?

I am confident that the reader will be intrigued to discover that the Bible's directives can save him from certain infectious diseases, from many lethal cancers, and from a long gauntlet of psychosomatic diseases that are increasing in spite of all efforts of modern medicine.

Debts of gratitude are due many people. First, I owe much to my patients. Although many case histories are given, they are carefully disguised with fictitious names and altered circumstances, and are combined with the histories of other patients.

This book could never have been born without the sympathetic help of Dr. Gustav Prinsell and Dr. J. Myron Stern who took excellent care of my practice for nearly nine months. Another kind of doctor, Ray W. Hazlett, Litt. D., gave me encouragement and help in the first months when I could have given it up so easily.

I am most grateful to Miss Sophie Davis who washed away all the grammatical errors and rubbed it with plenty of commas and marks like that. To Mrs. Muriel Babbitt goes the credit of dressing and redressing the little offspring with neatly typewritten sheets, so that it might look its best for the publisher.

My daughter Linda and her husband, Dr. J. Myron Stern, gave me quite a few stinging "vitamin shots" for which I am now grateful. To Alice Jean, my wife, goes my deepest appreciation for her constant support and encouragement.

Above all, I thank the Lord for His gracious guidance and help manifested to me in many ways.

CONTENTS

CHAPTER 1

Gray Hair and Rattlesnake Oil

"TO PREVENT THE HAIR FROM TURNING GRAY, ANOINT IT with the blood of a black calf which has been boiled in oil, or with the fat of a rattlesnake."[1] This prescription comes from the famous *Papyrus Ebers,* a medical book written in Egypt about 1552 B.C. Since Egypt occupied the dominant position in the ancient medical world, the *Papyrus* is of great importance as a record of the medical knowledge of that day.

The book also contains prescriptions for people who are losing hair: "When it falls out, one remedy is to apply a mixture of six fats, namely those of the horse, the hippopotamus, the crocodile, the cat, the snake, and the ibex. To strengthen it, anoint with the tooth of a donkey crushed in honey."[2] An extra-special hair dressing for the Egyptian Queen Schesch consisted of equal parts of a heel of an Abyssinian greyhound, date blossoms, and asses' hoofs, boiled in oil. The choice preparation was intended to make the royal hair grow.

To save victims bitten by poisonous snakes, physicians of that day gave them "magic water" to drink—water that had been poured over a special idol.[3] To embedded splinters they applied worms' blood and asses' dung. Since dung is loaded with tetanus spores, it is little wonder that lockjaw took a heavy toll of splinter cases.

Several hundred remedies for diseases are advised in the *Papyrus Ebers.* The drugs include "lizards' blood, swines' teeth, putrid meat, stinking fat, moisture from pigs' ears, milk goose grease, asses' hoofs, animal fats from various sources, excreta from animals, including human beings, donkeys, antelopes, dogs, cats, and even flies."[4]

About the time this Egyptian medical book was written, Moses was born in Egypt. Although his parents were

Israelites, he was raised in the royal court and "was learned in all the wisdom of the Egyptians. . . ."[5] There is little doubt that he was well acquainted with the medical knowledge of his time. Many thousands of the Israelites also knew and no doubt had used some of the common remedies mentioned in the *Papyrus Ebers.*

However, when Moses led the great company of Israelites out of Egypt, the Lord gave him a most remarkable promise for the new nation: "If thou wilt diligently hearken to the voice of the Lord thy God, and wilt do that which is right in his sight, and wilt give ear to his commandments, and keep all his statutes, *I will put none of these diseases upon thee,* which I have brought upon the Egyptians: for I am the Lord that healeth thee."[6]

"*. . . none of these diseases . . .*"! What a promise! Had not the Egyptians and Israelites been afflicted with these diseases for ages? The remedies in their medical books had accomplished practically nothing; often they were worse than the diseases. Yet here was the Lord making a fantastic promise to free the Israelites of all the Egyptian diseases.

God proceeded to give Moses a number of commandments, which form part of our Bible today. Because these divinely given medical directions were altogether different from those in the *Papyrus Ebers,* God surely was not copying from the medical authorities of the day. Would Moses, trained in the royal postgraduate universities, have enough faith to accept the divine innovations without adding some of the things he had been taught? From the record we discover that Moses had so much faith in God's regulations that he did not incorporate a single current medical misconception into the inspired instructions. If Moses had yielded to a natural inclination to add even a little of his modern university training, we would be reading such prescriptions as "the heel of an Abyssinian greyhound," or "the tooth of a donkey crushed in honey," not to mention the drugs the leading physicians were compounding out of the bacteria-laden dung of dogs, cats and flies.

The divine instructions were not only devoid of harmful practices, but had many detailed positive recommendations. Let us take a glance at the impact of those positive instructions on the history of prevention of infectious diseases.

For many hundreds of years the dreaded disease leprosy had killed countless millions of people in Europe. The extent of the horrible malady among Europeans is given by Dr. George Rosen, Columbia University professor of public health: "Leprosy cast the greatest blight that threw its shadow over the daily life of medieval humanity. Fear of all other diseases taken together can hardly be compared to the terror spread by leprosy. Not even the Black Death in the fourteenth century or the appearance of syphilis toward the end of the fifteenth century produced a similar state of fright. . . . Early in the Middle Ages, during the sixth and seventh centuries, it began to spread more widely in Europe and became a serious social and health problem. It was endemic particularly among the poor and reached a terrifying peak in the thirteenth and fourteenth centuries."[7]

What did the physicians offer to stop the ever-increasing ravages of leprosy? Some taught that it was "brought on by eating hot food, pepper, garlic and the meat of diseased hogs." Other physicians said it was caused by malign conjunction of the planets. Naturally, their suggestions for prevention were utterly worthless.

Another plague that made the Dark Ages really dark was the Black Death. In the fourteenth century alone, this killer took the lives of one out of four persons, an estimated total of sixty million. It was the greatest disaster ever recorded in human history: "Sweeping everything before it, this plague brought panic and confusion in its train. . . . The dead were hurled pell-mell into huge pits, hastily dug for the purpose, and putrefying bodies lay about everywhere in the houses and streets. The sexton and the physician were cast into the same deep and wide grave; the testator and his heirs and executors were hurled from the same cart into the same hole together."[8]

What brought the major plagues of the Dark Ages under control? George Rosen gives us the answer:

> Leadership was taken by the church, as the physicians had nothing to offer. The church took as its guiding principle the concept of contagion as embodied in the Old Testament. . . . This idea and its practical consequences are defined with great clarity in the book of Leviticus. . . . Once the condition of leprosy had been established, the patient was to be segregated and excluded from the community.

> Following the precepts laid down in Leviticus the church undertook the task of combatting leprosy . . . it accomplished the first great feat . . . in methodical eradication of disease.[9]

The procedures came from Leviticus 13:46: "All the days wherein the plague shall be in him he shall be defiled; he is unclean: he shall dwell alone; without the camp shall his habitation be." Other historians credit the Bible for the dawning of a new era in the effective control of disease: "The laws against leprosy in Leviticus 13 may be regarded as the first model of a sanitary legislation."[10]

As soon as the European nations saw that the application of Scriptural quarantine brought leprosy under control, they applied the same principle against the Black Death. The results were equally spectacular, and millions of lives were saved.

If the lethal plagues had continued unabated, many celebrities of the Renaissance might never have been born, or they might have died untimely deaths. Thus, European history was greatly influenced because men began to practice the words of God to the Israelites: "If thou wilt diligently hearken to the voice of the Lord thy God, . . . I will put none of these diseases upon thee. . . ."

CHAPTER 2

Pride and Prejudice Versus Proof

ALTHOUGH EUROPE BROUGHT ITS MOST DEVASTING PLAGUES under control by obeying the Biblical injunction to isolate the victims, other important diseases continued to decimate mankind because people did not take seriously God's promise that they would be freed from *all* diseases by their obedience to *all* the divine regulations. Hence, intestinal diseases such as cholera, dysentery, and typhoid fever continued to take a heavy toll of lives. Up to the close of the eighteenth century, hygienic provisions, even in the great capitals, were quite primitive. It was the rule for excrement to be dumped into the streets which were unpaved and filthy. Powerful stenches gripped villages and cities. It was a heyday for flies as they bred in the filth and spread intestinal diseases that killed millions.

Such waste of human lives that could have been saved if people had only taken seriously God's provision for freeing man of diseases! With one sentence the Book of books pointed the way to deliverance from the deadly epidemics of typhoid, cholera and dysentery: "You shall set off a place outside the camp and, when you go out to use it, you must carry a spade among your gear and dig a hole, have easement, and turn to cover the excrement."[1]

A medical historian writes that this directive is "certainly a primitive measure, *but an effective one, which indicates advanced ideas of sanitation.*"[2] How could this recommendation, which was given to Moses, possibly offer ideas of sanitation advanced 3,500 years ahead of him? The most logical explanation is that the Bible is what it claims to be: *the inspired Word of God.*

But the pride and prejudices of man are foes too strong for proof. Let me give an example by citing what happened in Vienna in the 1840's, when the Viennese were feasting on the superb waltzes of Johann Strauss and his son.

Vienna was also famous as a medical center. Let us look in on one of the famous teaching hospitals of that day, Allegemeine Krakenhaus. In the maternity wards of this celebrated hospital, one out of every six women died, and this frightening mortality rate was similar in other hospitals around the world. The obstetricians ascribed the deaths to constipation, delayed lactation, fear, and poisonous air.

When the women died, they were wheeled into the autopsy room. The first order of each morning was the entrance of the physicians and medical students into the morgue to perform autopsies on the unfortunate victims who had died during the preceding twenty-four hours. Afterward, without cleansing their hands, the doctors with their retinue of students marched into the maternity wards to make pelvic examinations on the living women. Of course, no rubber gloves were worn.

In the early 1840's, a little over a hundred years ago, a young doctor named Ignaz Semmelweis was given charge over one of the obstetrical wards. He observed that it was particularly the women who were examined by the teachers and students who became sick and died. After watching this heartbreaking situation for three years, he established a rule that, in his ward, every physician and medical student who had participated in the autopsies of the dead must carefully wash his hands before examining the living maternity patients.

In April, 1847, before the new rule went into effect, fifty-seven women had died in Dr. Semmelweis' ward. Then the rule of washing the hands was instituted. In June, only one out of every forty-two women died; in July, only one out of every eighty-four. The statistics strongly indicated that fatal infections had been carried from corpses to living patients.

One day, after performing autopsies and washing their hands, the physicians and students entered the maternity ward and examined a row of beds containing twelve women. Eleven of the twelve women quickly developed temperatures and died.

Another new thought was born in Semmelweis' alert brain: some mysterious element was evidently carried from one living patient to others, and with fatal consequences. Logically, Semmelweis ordered that everybody should wash his hands carefully after examining each living patient. Immediately howls of protest were raised against the "nuisance" of washing, washing, washing—but the mortality rate went further down.

Was Semmelweis acclaimed by his fellows? On the contrary, lazy students, prejudiced obstetricians, and jealous superiors scorned and belittled him so much that his annual contract was not renewed. His successor threw out the wash basins and up shot the mortality rate to the old terrifying figures. Were his colleagues convinced then? Not at all! We mortals might as well face it—the human mind is so warped by pride and prejudice that proof can rarely penetrate it.

For eight months Semmelweis tried to get a respectable position in the hospital again, but to no avail. Shocked and depressed, he left Vienna without saying good-by to his few friends and went to Budapest, his home city. There he obtained a position in a hospital; there too the mortality rate of pregnant women was frightful. Again he instituted the practice of washing the hands before examining the individual patient. At once the grim reaper was halted, but again prejudices and jealousies overpowered the proof and many of Semmelweis' colleagues passed him in the hospital corridors without speaking.

Dr. Semmelweis wrote an excellently documented book on his work, which only spurred his assailants to the bitterest sarcasm. The strain plus the death cries of dying mothers so haunted and weighed on his sensitive nature that his mind finally broke. Ignaz Semmelweis died in a mental institution without ever receiving the recognition he richly deserved.

Many, many centuries before Semmelweis, God gave to Moses detailed instructions on the safest method of cleansing the hands after handling the dead or the infected living.[8] Semmelweis' method of cleansing went a long way in preventing many deaths, but it would not be accepted in any hospital today. In contrast, the Scriptural method specified not merely washing in a basin, but repeated washings in *running water,* with time intervals allowed for drying and exposure to sun to kill bacteria not washed off. Furthermore, the Scriptural method also required contacts to change to clothes that had been washed and dried. The Biblical technique was so different from and so much more effective than anything man ever devised that, again, it is logical to believe the regulations were given, as the Bible claims, from God to Moses.

The spirit of pride and prejudice regarding the washing of hands also existed in surgery. During most of the nineteenth century the preliminaries of major surgery were frightfully simple. The patient came into the operating room, took off his trousers and underwear, and crawled up on the operating table. The surgeon took off his coat, rolled up his shirt sleeves, took some instruments out of a bag or a cupboard, and started to operate. If the surgeon wished his students to examine something inside the opening, he would have them step forward and poke their germ-covered hands into a sterile abdomen.

Of course, the mortality from surgery was frightful. Dr. Roswell Park tells about his own experiences in his book on medical history: "When I began my work, in

1876, as a hospital *interne*, in one of the largest hospitals in this country, it happened that during my first winter's experience, with but one or two exceptions, every patient operated upon in that hospital, and that by men who were esteemed the peers of any one in their day, died of blood poisoning. . . ."[4]

Such mortality would not have occurred if surgeons had only followed the method God gave to Moses regarding the meticulous method of hand washing and changing of clothes after contact with infectious diseases.

Dr. Park states that in the two years following 1876, the antiseptic method of cleansing hands and instruments was introduced, and there was a spectacular drop in the mortality rate. The work of John Tyndall, Louis Pasteur, Robert Koch, and Sir Joseph Lister finally furnished visible proof that slowly dispelled pride and prejudice.

In the twentieth century no surgical procedure is performed without meticulous scrubbing of the hands. However, any failure to wash the hands carefully when treating medical cases has resulted in needless loss of lives. Staphylococcus infections have become disastrous epidemics in some hospital nurseries. In the summer of 1958 an epidemic of a staph infection, caused by improperly washed hands, spread through a large general hospital in the eastern United States. The various antibiotics were of little help, and before the infection was brought under control it snuffed out the lives of eighty-six men, women and children.

The New York State Department of Health became alarmed because these infections could be spread so quickly by a carrier who failed to wash his hands carefully. In 1960 the Department issued a book describing a method of washing the hands, and the procedures closely approximate the Scriptural method given in Numbers 19.

At long last, in the year 1960, man finally muddled through. He learned, after centuries and at a frightful cost, what God gave to Moses by *inspiration*.

CHAPTER 3

Science Arrives —Four Thousand Years Late

"DOCTOR, YOU MUST TELL ME WHETHER I HAVE CANCER or not. I insist. What do the reports from the laboratory show? I must know!" Pretty, thirty-six-year-old Beth Howard sat on the edge of her seat. For over two weeks her doctor had been using delaying tactics in order to condition her somewhat for this moment.

When the truth was given, it crushed her. "But, doctor, you can't let me die! You must save me. I couldn't possibly leave Lorna and Jane now. They are only in their teens. They need me now more than ever. Then Phil and Dick—and Bill—"

Sobbing, she buried her face in the pillow. At such a time many a doctor wishes he had taken up ditchdigging for a living. All he can give are pain killers and tranquilizers. Because Beth's cancer was advanced it was only a question of months before she would die.

Beth had cancer of the cervix. In the year she died, thirteen thousand other funerals went down our American streets with victims of this particular cancer. Many of them were middle-aged women, the peak incidence being between the ages of thirty-one and fifty.[1] Cancer of the cervix is one of the most common cancers in women. It comprises twenty-five per cent of all cancers in women and eighty per cent of all their genital cancers. These statistics are even more pathetic because *the large majority of deaths could have been prevented by following an instruction that God gave to Abraham.*

The history of this recognition is intriguing. In the early 1900's Dr. Hiram N. Wineberg, while studying records of patients in New York's Mount Sinai Hospital, observed that Jewesses were comparatively free from this common cancer.[2] It was an astonishing finding! Here was a group who had suffered far less from the giant killer than had other women.

Following this lead, Dr. Ira I. Kaplan and his associates studied their records at New York's Bellevue Hospital and were also astonished by the scarcity of cervical cancer among Jewish women.[3] In 1949 gynecologists at the Mayo Clinic noted that in 568 consecutive cases of cervical cancer, not a single Jewess was among the victims. Seven per cent of the admissions at Mayo Clinic are Jewish, and one would expect seven per cent of 568, or forty Jewesses, to have had uterine cancer. Instead, *there was not a single case.*[4] In 1954, in a vast study of 86,214 women in Boston, it was observed that cancer of the cervix in non-Jewish women was eight and one half times more frequent than in Jewish women.[5]

Why are Jewish women comparatively free of cervical cancer? Medical researchers now agree *that this spectacular freedom results from the practice of circumcision in Jewish men—which God ordered Abraham to institute four thousand years ago.*

A number of recent studies have borne out the fact that freedom from cancer of the womb is not due to factors such as race or food or environment, but wholly to circumcision. Other convincing studies were made in India. Although the people there have similar racial backgrounds, eat the same types of food, and live in the same climate and environment, the population is divided into two religious groups. Those who worship Mohammed, also a descendant of Abraham, practice circumcision. Among that group there is a much lower incidence of cervical cancer than among other women of the same race who eat the same food and live in the same environment.[6]

An editorial in the *American Journal of Obstetrics and Gynecology,* notes that both Jewish women and Indian Moslem women have a low incidence of cervical cancer, and observes that these two otherwise dissimilar people, have only one pertinent common denominator in their backgrounds—circumcision of the males. The editorial further records that in the Fiji Islands the cervical cancer rate is definitely lower among those people who practice circumcision. The editorial concludes with the advice that all newborn males should be circumcised to prevent this cancer.[7]

Medical science recognizes the fact, but unfortunately the general public is still unaware of the value of circumcision. How can circumcision of the male prevent cancer in women? The human male is cursed with a superabundance of foreskin over the penis. Circumcision (*circum*, "around," and *cision*, "*cutting*") remedies the fault by removing the excess of foreskin. If the tight, unretractable foreskin is not removed, proper cleansing can not be readily performed. As a result many virulent bacteria, including the cancer-producing Smegma bacillus, can grow profusely. During sexual intercourse these bacteria are deposited on the cervix of the uterus, but if the mucous membrane of the cervix is intact, little harm results. However, if lacerations exist, as they frequently do after childbirth, these bacteria can cause considerable irritation. Since any part of the body which is subjected to irritation is susceptible to cancer, it is perfectly understandable why cervical cancer is likely to develop in women whose mates are not circumcised.

These bacteria not only produce cancer in women, but also irritate the male organ and may cause cancer of the penis. The extreme rarity of penile cancer in circumcised men is shown by the fact that in 1955 only the fourth case in medical history was reported.[8] Thus we can say that circumcision is an almost perfect prophylaxis against this deadly cancer. Prevention by circumcision is far more important than treatment, because once a diagnosis of cancer is made, surgical removal of the penis is mandatory.

After many laborious years of study, medical science has at last accepted the best method of preventing two deadly cancers in men and women. Medical science has at last arrived—four thousand years late. Science did not arrive because of any laboratory steam that had been generated; it was carried forward by a long train of statistics—statistics that existed only because down through the years many generations of Jews had been faithful to the command that God gave to their father Abraham.[9]

Some people doubt the miracles by which God protected the Israelites during the plagues of Egypt, and dried up the Red Sea for their escape from bondage. Yet these miracles are small indeed compared to the miraculous, God-given directions that have saved the Israelites and others from plagues, epidemics and cancer for many centuries.

There is one final but remarkably unique fact about the

matter of circumcision. In November, 1946, an article in the *Journal of the American Medical Association* listed the reasons why circumcision of the newborn male is advisable. Three months later a letter from another specialist appeared in the same journal. He agreed heartily with the writer of the article on the advantages of circumcision, but he criticised him for failing to mention the safest time to perform the operation.[10]

This is a point well taken. L. Emmett Holt and Rustin McIntosh report that a newborn infant has "peculiar susceptibility to bleeding between the second and fifth days of life. . . . Hemorrhages at this time, though often inconsequential, are sometimes extensive; they may produce serious damage to internal organs, especially to the brain, and cause death from shock and exsanguination."[11] It is felt that the tendency to hemorrhage is due to the fact that the important blood-clotting element, vitamin K, is not formed in the normal amount until the *fifth* to the *seventh* day of life. If vitamin K is not manufactured in the baby's intestinal tract until the *fifth* to the *seventh* day, it is clear that the first safe day to perform circumcision would be the *eighth* day, the very day that Jehovah commanded Abraham to circumcise Isaac.

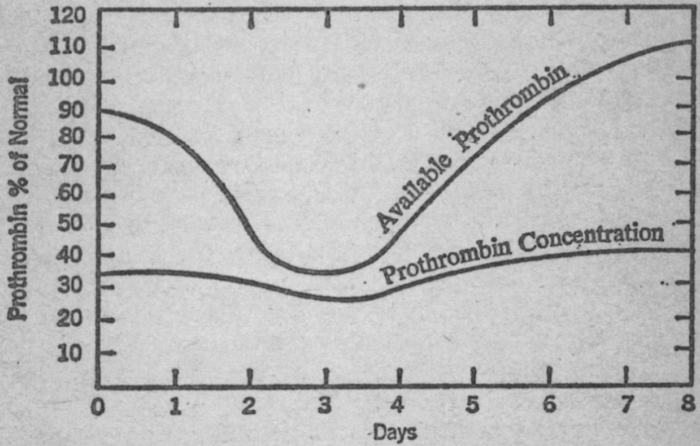

Composite Curves of Normal Infants Showing Concentration of Prothrombin and Available Prothrombin During First Week of Life, from Data of Owen, Hoffman, Ziffren and Smith.

A second element which is also necessary for the normal clotting of blood is prothrombin. A chart based on data discussed in *Holt Pediatrics* reveals that on the third day of a baby's life the available prothrombin is only thirty per cent of normal. Any surgical operation performed on a baby during that time would predispose to serious hemorrhage. From the chart we also see that the prothrombin skyrockets on the eighth day to a level even better than normal—110 per cent. It then levels off to 100 per cent. It appears that an eight-day-old baby has more available prothrombin than on any other day in its entire life. Thus

one observes that from a consideration of vitamin K and prothrombin determinations the perfect day to perform a circumcision is the *eighth* day.

We should commend the many hundreds of workers who labored at great expense over a number of years to discover that the safest day to perform circumcision is the eighth. Yet, as we congratulate medical science for this recent finding, we can almost hear the leaves of the Bible rustling. They would like to remind us that four thousand years ago, when God *initiated* circumcision with Abraham, He said, "And he that is eight days old shall be circumcised. . . ."[12]

Abraham did not pick the eighth day after many centuries of trial-and-error experiments. Neither he nor any of his company from the ancient city of Ur in the Chaldees had ever been circumcised. It was a day picked by the Creator of vitamin K.

The Old Testament circumcision was a symbol or type that looked forward to Christ and the circumcision He performs on the carnal heart:

> In him also you were circumcised, not in a physical sense, but by being divested of the lower nature; this is Christ's way of circumcision.[13]

> Then put to death those parts of you which belong to the earth—fornication, indecency, lust, foul cravings. . . . But now you yourselves must lay aside all anger, passion, malice. . . . now that you have discarded the old nature with its deeds. . . .[14]

As God required physical circumcision of the Jew, so today He requires of us "Christ's way of circumcision," which means "being divested of the lower nature" with its emotions of "anger, passion, malice" and self-centeredness. Such circumcision and such riddance of unlovely emotions are to man's great advantage, since *these emotions are clearly recognized by modern psychiatrists as causes or aggravations of the majority of all diseases.* Carnal emotions produce stress—which some authorities are now questioning as being the cause of all disease.[15]

While *physical* circumcision prevents two fatal cancers, Christ's *spiritual* circumcision of our evil nature prevents a far greater number of important diseases. Circumcision of the *body* looked forward to circumcision of the *spirit.*[16] Bodily circumcision is not required of Christians today because it looked forward to a greater circumcision that Christ now performs on the mind and heart of man.[17] Is it not intriguing and appropriate that both the *type* and the *fulfillment* prevent deadly diseases?

Failure of the Jew to observe the symbol of circumcision made him a spiritual outcast, and it is understandable why God makes Christ's circumcision a requirement of belonging to Him: "And those who belong to Christ Jesus have crucified the lower nature with its passions and desires."[18] Only when this divine surgery has been performed can man enjoy the promise of his heavenly Father—"none of these diseases."

CHAPTER 4

"Robber of Five Million Brains"

WHEN MY PHONE RANG ABOUT MIDNIGHT, I WAS VERY sleepy, but the voice on the other end aroused me instantly: "Say, Doc, can you come out here right away? Two people were killed on the highway, and two others are in desperate shape!"

A crowd was there when I arrived. The driver had hit a bridge abutment, and the steering wheel had flattened his chest. One look at him showed me that he was beyond human help. The other three occupants of the car had been hurtled twenty or thirty feet into a dry creek bed. One of them, a woman, was dead. A second woman was lying on the crumpled windshield that she took with her as she was propelled forward. She was moaning with pain. A semiconscious man was also down there in the mud and gravel of the creek.

What an unforgettable scene of devastation—the telescoped car, two mangled people covered with blood and mud, and two motionless figures who would never breathe again. The horror of the catastrophe was particularly pathetic because it could have been prevented. The brain of the driver had been robbed by a drug.

That ghastly night, I saw the destruction, suffering and death that can result when the brain of even one person is robbed. I confess that my mind is much too small to multiply the scenes of greater and lesser magnitude that occur daily because the brains of five million Americans are thus robbed.

Visualize another drunken driver as his school bus careens crazily over a steep, winding road. Imagine the havoc of twenty-six terrified, wide-eyed children, fearing for their lives, jumping out in ones and twos as the bus slows a bit on the curves.

In the *Journal of the American Medical Association,* Milton Golin summarizes his article, "Robber of Five Million Brains," with the statement: "Drink has taken five million men and women in the United States, taken them as a master takes slaves, and new acquisitions are going on at the rate of 200,000 a year."[1]

How many deaths are caused by partially decerebrated Americans on our highways? A study conducted in Delaware indicates that alcohol figures in about half of our traffic deaths.[2] In New York City a joint study made by the New York State Department of Health and Cornell University revealed that seventy-three per cent of the drivers responsible for the accidents in which they died had been drinking.[3] And in Westchester County, New York, blood tests were done on eighty-three drivers who were killed in single-vehicle accidents. The tests revealed that seventy-nine per cent of these drivers were "under the influence" of liquor.[4]

If one were to estimate that even fifty per cent of our

forty thousand annual automobile deaths were caused by John Barleycorn, it would mean a colossal indictment against the character of the annual mass murderer of twenty thousand American men, women and children. Many a driver has had his license taken away for causing one wanton death on the highway, yet here is one who is *legally* licensed to perpetuate the slaughter of thousands. He is indeed highly privileged to continue with such carnage.

In defense of this massacre, it is argued that our income taxes would be higher if the liquor industry did not exist. However, many studies indicate that a half dozen other costs would be lower. An insurance executive revealed that auto insurance rates could be cut forty per cent "if drinking drivers were not such a problem."[5]

What part do these five million Americans play in other types of violent deaths, such as homocide? I shall never forget the night I entered a house to find a drunken man pressing a cocked revolver against the temple of his wife, the mother of his five children. It was fortunate that I arrived when I did. Perhaps it was my presence that made him release her, but as he did, he said, "If I didn't think I would hang for this, I would blow your brains out."

A statistical study reveals that alcohol plays a prominent part in all kinds of violent deaths: "A résumé of 27 years of autopsy findings in Middlesex County, N.J., showed alcohol was a factor in 41.2 per cent of violent deaths, according to a report by the Chief Medical Examiner of the county, Dr. William C. Wilentz."[6] No drug known to man is more widely used nor more frequently responsible for deaths, injuries, or crimes than is ethyl alcohol.

Also revealing is a quick look at the matter of suicides, the eleventh leading cause of violent death, with an annual total close to twenty thousand. Expert statisticians estimate that alcohol is responsible for five thousand of these deaths.[7]

Alcohol robs brains in a variety of ways. When I was an intern, it was not uncommon to see a man ride into the hospital ward on a pink elephant. At least he thought he was riding one. If it wasn't a pink elephant, the man would be screaming because he was being charged by a herd of orange-colored buffaloes, or clawed by scarlet gorillas.

The large wards of that day became a bedlam as the

man shouted and sought refuge from the ferocious "animals" bent on his destruction. Sometimes he would try to escape from them by breaking a window to make a leap from the top floor. Fortunately the nurses were usually quick enough to grasp the tail of his nightgown and pull him back.

When we had to handcuff these patients to the beds and give them large doses of morphine, some of them died. Even today, under improved techniques, the mortality from delirium tremens is four per cent.[8]

Death results from other forms of alcoholic damage to the brain. Some victims develop disturbances of hearing, which can cause so much fear that they may commit suicide.

Alcohol is one of the most important factors in making mental disease the No. 1 health problem of America. A recent medical text states: "About 10% of the admissions to mental hospitals are officially reported as due to alcoholism, and another 10% have alcoholism of considerable degree noted as an important contributing cause. In addition, general hospitals take care of many of the acutely disturbed alcoholics."[9] In fact, six per cent of chronic alcoholics develop insanity in some form.[10] Because alcohol produces areas of atrophy in the brain, a large percentage of drinkers are actually committing a slow suicide of their personalities.

Alcohol, the licensed robber, every year kills many tens of thousands on our highways; it incites people to murder, homocide and suicide; it places others behind bars as raving maniacs. An amazed Shakespeare in his day exclaimed, "O God! that men should put an enemy in their mouths to steal away their brains. . . ."[11]

Furthermore, the effects of alcohol are certainly not limited to the anatomy above the ears. A drinker who was in my office recently complained that he couldn't raise his hands high enough to shave his beard. Not only does one out of every five alcoholics develop partial paralysis of certain muscles, but many of them complain bitterly about painful neuritis.

Hardening of the liver is a more serious affair because the blood from the gastrointestinal tract is prevented from flowing freely through the hardened liver. As a result of the back pressure in the veins, the lower extremities become badly swollen and the abdominal cavity is so distended with fluid that the victim can scarcely breathe. We can relieve the acute distress of the huge abdomen by inserting a hollow tube through the abdominal wall and drawing off some of the fluid, but unfortunately the fluid builds up in shorter intervals until the patient succumbs. The obstructed liver also can cause back pressure and ballooning of the veins of the esophagus. These thinned-out veins are prone to rupture when food is swallowed and can cause serious or fatal hemorrhage.

Hardening of the liver commonly occurs between the ages of thirty-five and sixty-five. When a physician witnesses the suffering and of men dying at a comparatively young age, he can not help but think of the way life is wasted in pursuit of its so-called pleasures.

I recall a certain New Year's Day. My wife and I arose refreshed and happy, and we thoroughly enjoyed a breakfast of grapefruit, cereal, ham and eggs. At noon we enjoyed to the full a New Year's dinner with all the luscious trimmings. But not so the other two couples who visited us. They had seen the New Year in with drinks and had spent the entire morning holding their heads, swallowing aspirin, and fighting severe nausea. None of the four could eat a bite of the superb feast. My wife and I discovered that life was much more wonderful without certain "pleasures!"

Alcoholics are deprived of the superlatives in life. Enjoyment is blurred or absent in areas of real living, such as recreation, music, art, eating, sex, sight and conversation. Some people hesitate to walk the Christian way because they do not want to give up certain "pleasures." These people need to embrace the promise: ". . . no good thing will he withhold from them that walk uprightly."[12] They need to understand that Biblical regulations have been written so that man might obtain the greatest amount of joy in life.

Food not only ceases to give enjoyment to the alcoholic, but often gives him great discomfort because of a severe inflammation of the lining of his stomach. He may be in torment from an ulcer, or lose many years from his life because of a resulting gastric cancer.

Alcohol not only robs a man of his brains and his health, but it robs his pocketbook. Money that should provide food, clothes, and proper housing for a man and family is far too often tossed over the bar. Many families never know anything of the niceties of living, and frequently their deprivations result in sickness and serious neglect.

The drinker also loses by the days he is not able to work. Statistics show that he loses a month's work every year. Yale University professors have also shown that his efficiency on the job is only fifty per cent.[13] Hence, they aptly refer to the drinker as the "half man," because he lacks discrimination and skill. He is likely to become involved in minor and major disputes with his fellows. His mind has been compared to a man driving a car in a fog, and in the factory he is accident-prone. A study of 340 patients who sustained accidental injuries revealed that forty-eight per cent had a blood level of over 0.5 gm. per liter.[14]

The revenues received from taxing the liquor industry fall far short of paying John Barleycorn's extravagant expenditures. A study made in France is most revealing: "In 1950 the direct cost of alcoholism to the country was about 132 billion francs, while the treasury revenues from alcoholic beverages was only 53 billion francs. There was therefore a loss to the country of nearly 80 billion francs. The loss of productivity caused by alcohol is estimated at about 325 billion francs a year.[15]

A publication of the American Medical Association reports that because of the industrial losses caused by this "half man" in industry, you and I are annually defrauded out of ten billion dollars.[16]

To these billions add the many more millions it costs to take care of the destitute families of alcoholics, to pay the bills of impoverished drinkers in their old age, and to pay for the institutional care of liquor's insane. A fraction of these billions of dollars would do much for medical research and would save mankind from a wide variety of ills.

This colossal waste of life and money is preventable by obedience to the Book of books, and "none of these diseases" is the promise to those who heed the many Scriptural injunctions against drunkenness. Here is one passage that warns in crisp but colorful language of the economic, medical and social aspects of drink, even including a description of delerium tremens:

Listen, my son, and be wise,
  be guided by good sense:
  never sit down with tipsy men or among gluttons;
  the drunkard and the glutton come to poverty,
  and revelling leaves men in rags. . . .
Who shriek? who groan?
Who quarrel and grumble?
Who are bruised for nothing?
Who have bleary eyes?
Those who linger over the bottle,
  those who relish blended wines.
Then look not on the wine so red,
  that sparkles in the cup;
  it glides down smoothly at the first,
  but in the end it bites like any snake,
  it stings you like an adder.
You will be seeing odd things,
  you will be saying queer things;
  you will be like a man asleep at sea,
  asleep in the midst of a storm.[17]

CHAPTER 5

Coronary and Cancer By the Carton

THE MANAGER OF A GROCERY STORE PHONED ME ONE DAY. "Doctor," he said, "I received a note from Mrs. Henderson, which she smuggled out of her house. Her husband is very sick, so sick that he is almost out of his head. He won't allow her to leave the house for fear she will never come back. She is afraid he may kill her. She wants you to go to her house to examine her husband."

Mrs. Henderson's husband was over six feet tall. He had been a strong muscular fellow, but now, his flesh wasted away and his eyes sunk deep in their sockets, he appeared more like a ghost than a man. For months he hadn't slept well because he was coughing up masses of blood. His suffering and misery had been long and horrible. His wife was distracted and afraid of him because he had threatened to kill her if she attempted to leave him.

After I questioned and examined him, a diagnosis of cancer of the lung seemed highly probable. I made application by phone to have him admitted to the hospital and it was a big relief to all concerned when the day of his admission arrived. However, during his first night in the hospital, he had a severe hemorrhage and drowned in his own blood. An autopsy revealed widespread cancer of both lungs.

How often does this sanguinary horror occur in the lives of men and women? Every year thirty-five thousand Americans are strangled to death by lung cancer. This figure proclaims that no cancer statistic ever skyrocketed as high or as rapidly as lung cancer.

Back in 1912, lung cancer was called "the rarest of diseases."[1] Then, in the 1920's, it began to increase. In the 1940's and 1950's, the mortality figures zoomed upward at an unbelievable rate.

In England, between 1924 and 1951, the death rates shot up tenfold while in Holland they soared twentyfold.[2] In New York State, in 1947, the death rate was frightening; yet even that high figure was doubled in 1957.[3] In the country as a whole during the past twenty years the death toll from lung cancer increased five hundred per cent.[4] At the present time more men die from it than from any other cancer; in fact, one out of every seven people who die of cancer has undergone the horrors of lung cancer. Authorities declare that soon every third person who dies of cancer will die of cancer of the lung. That is a far cry from 1912 when it was "the rarest of diseases."

What is the cause of lung cancer? When the statistics shot skyward, surgeons suspected the cause, but it was as late as 1949 that Dr. E. L. Wynder supplied the first statistical evidence of the relationship between smoking and lung cancer. In 1950 Wynder and Graham reported 684 proven cases of lung cancer in men and women. They discovered that of the 605 cases in men *only eight had been nonsmokers.*[5]

From England came a report from a study of 1,357

cases of lung cancer. In this vast group of victims, only seven nonsmokers were found.[6]

By 1958 eighteen scientific studies in five different countries proved that tobacco is undoubtedly the culprit committing yearly mass murder by strangling tens of thousands with the two ugliest words in medicine—lung cancer.[7]

The largest of the eighteen studies into the effects of smoking was made by the American Cancer Society.[8] This organization did follow-up studies on over 187,000 men, aged fifty to sixty-nine years, for a period of forty-four months. These men, comprising both smokers and nonsmokers, were typical Americans living in widely separated segments of the country. First, a careful questionnaire was made of the smoking habits of those who smoked. During these forty-four months, 11,870 men died. Photostatic copies of their death certificates were made and the causes of death were carefully tabulated.

The summary of this vast study not only proved beyond any doubt that smoking is the main cause of cancer of the lung, but it also revealed that smoking is responsible for *many other cancers of the body* and also a surprisingly large number of deaths from other diseases. The study revealed that in smokers there was:

1) an extremely high association for . . . cancer of the lung, cancer of the larynx, cancer of the esophagus, and gastric ulcers
2) a very high association for . . . pneumonia, and influenza, duodenal ulcer, aortic aneurysm, and cancer of the bladder
3) a high association for . . . coronary artery disease, cirrhosis hardening of the liver, and cancer of other sites
4) a moderate association for cerebral vascular lesions, strokes.[9]

While thirty-five thousand men and women currently die from cancer of the lung, smoking is also slaughtering even more from cancer in other sites. The surest way to die a painful and premature death is to buy cancer by the carton.

One wonders how smoking can produce cancer in organs such as the urinary bladder, which is far removed from the cigarette. But scientists have now identified in tobacco smoke eight different chemicals that can cause cancer when injected into animals. They are soluble products that can be spread throughout the body by the blood stream. One of these is 3-, 4-, 9-, 10-dibenspyrene. When it was injected into four thousand mice, every one of them developed cancer and died.[10]

Can filters eliminate these carcinogenics? Are filters a help or a hoax? Filters have been examined in elaborate studies which are summarized by the Surgeon General of the United States Public Health Service: "No method of treating tobacco by filtering the smoke has been demonstrated to be effective in materially reducing or eliminating the hazard of lung cancer."[11]

A few years ago I was called out of bed to treat a man who was experiencing severe pain over his heart. When I arrived, the man's face was ashen gray. His eyes were open, the pupils greatly enlarged, and his eyeballs insensitive to touch. He was not breathing; his heart was not beating. He had died of a heart attack caused by a large clot of the arteries, which supply the heart with its blood. The blocked coronary is the master of all executioners. He squeezed the life out of 474,000 men and women in this country in 1959.[12]

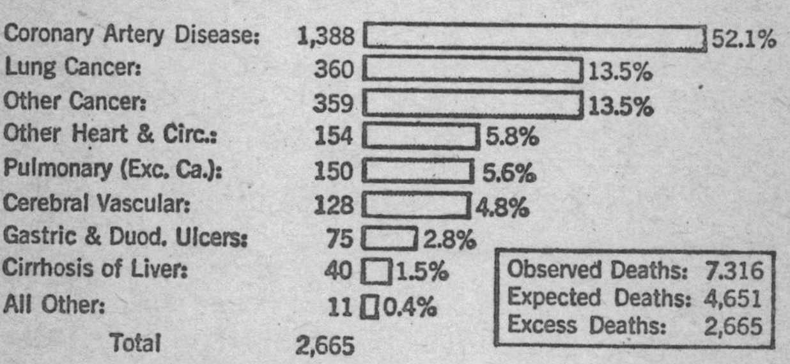

Excess deaths among men with a history of regular cigarette smoking

In my patient's shirt pocket was a partly empty pack of cigarettes. Can smoking cause heart disease? In the American Cancer Society's monumental study of 187,000 men, it was discovered that death from coronary artery disease was seventy per cent higher among smokers than among the comparable group of nonsmokers. This study revealed that the more a man smoked the greater was his liability of dying of heart disease. For those who smoked one half to one pack a day, the death rate was nearly double. For those who smoked two packs, the mortality was even higher.

I would like to call attention to one of the graphs made from the mammoth study by the American Cancer Society and published in the *Journal of the American Medical Association*. During the period of study there were 7,316 deaths among the group who smoked cigarettes. Statisticians figured that only 4,651 deaths would have occurred "if the age-specific death rates of the smokers had been the same as for men who never smoked." Subtracting the latter figure from the total, we see that 2,665 of *these deaths would not have occurred if the victims had not smoked.*[13] *In other words one out of every three of the men studied died because he was a smoker.* How many people would engage passage with an airline if the records showed that one out of every three passengers was doomed to die in a crash? *Yet one out of every three people who start off with cigarettes will experience a nicotine death.*

The metaphor of an airplane has another application. Once you commit yourself to a plane and take off, it is rather difficult to leave the plane, even if you decide you want to get out. Similarly, the individual who commits himself to smoking will soon be locked in by a habit from which he may not be able to escape.

What causes the death of such a huge percentage of smokers? In the graph one observes that *four times as many smokers die of coronary disease as die of lung cancer.* The study revealed that one out of every three coronary deaths is due to smoking. Since over 474,000 Americans died of bad coronaries, smoking is thus responsible for about 155,000 fatal heart cases. The appalling indictment of 70,000 cancer deaths against smoking is dwarfed by the fact that smoking kills 155,000 more with heart disease.

Not only is smoking the greatest single factor in causing lung cancer, but it is also the greatest factor in causing fatal heart attacks. Comparing a cigarette to a coffin nail is far more than a figure of speech.

By what mechanism does smoking cause a fatal heart attack? I recall the first time I saw the machine that measures the amount of blood flowing in the body. It was in 1956 at the Chicago meeting of the American

Medical Association. Doctors were asked to sit down and place one hand under the instrument. A basic reading was made on a revolving drum which recorded the amount of blood flowing in the arteries. After the basic reading was made, the physicians were given cigarettes to smoke. After only a few puffs on a cigarette, the recording needle on the revolving drum dropped rapidly, showing that smoking markedly reduces blood flow. Since coronary heart attacks are precipitated by a lack of blood in the coronary vessels, it is quite evident why smoking is responsible for many fatal heart attacks.

Another reason for these attacks is the fact that nicotine calls forth cholesterol which forms fatty tumors within the blood vessels, markedly reducing the flow of blood and facilitating clotting.

Reduction of blood flow and damage to the arteries can cause serious trouble in other organs. In the brain, the damaged arteries are prone to induce clots, the cause of strokes. A large-scale study revealed that the death rate from apoplexy is thirty per cent higher in smokers.[14] Since 192,980 people died from strokes of apoplexy in 1958,[15] the aforementioned percentage is decidedly startling.

As a result of the decreased blood flow, smokers are also likely to develop gangrene of the legs. After gangrene sets in, amputation of the leg is imperative.

Smoking can cause eye diseases and blindness.[16] It has also been indicted for its part in causing multiple sclerosis[17] and high blood pressure.[18] In pulmonary diseases, such as pneumonia, influenza, tuberculosis and asthma, the death rate is nearly three times as high as that of nonsmokers.[19]

Another common and serious condition caused by smoking is emphysema. This condition results from the "cigarette cough" that breaks down the delicate breathing cells of the lungs. Emphysema is even more common than cancer of the lung, with an outlook about as gloomy. A recent report of nineteen men and six women with this debilitating condition revealed that all of them had been heavy smokers.[20]

The danger of smoking to asthma cases is clearly enunciated in this quotation from the Mayo Clinic: "Smoking is one of the commonest sources of bronchial irritation, and invariably increases cough and asthma. Smoker's tongue, smoker's cough, smoker's throat, and smoker's bronchitis are no figments of the imagination, and when smoking is discontinued, these effects of tobacco smoking clear up in most instances. Smoking also has an irritating effect on the larynx. If a patient has asthma, he should not merely reduce smoking, he should completely stop it."[21]

Tobacco smoke can even affect others in the room. F. L. Rosen and A. Levy reported the case of an infant who had typical asthmatic attacks, which were promptly relieved when his parents stopped smoking and were reproduced when his parents resumed smoking.[22]

I was called out one evening to see a four-year-old boy fighting a life and death struggle to get his breath. He had been in a room in which half a dozen people were smoking. Even after he was taken to his bedroom, and in spite of adrenalin injections and other measures, his difficulty remained and he had to be moved out of the house to a smoke-free hospital room.

Ulcers of the gastrointestinal tract are also caused and aggravated by smoking. Every physician in general practice has a number of patients who are tortured by ulcers and who know that smoking is at the bottom of their trouble. In spite of their misery and the expenditure of hundreds of dollars for treatment, these people often curse heartily the day they began smoking but claim they can not stop it now.

Even duodenal ulcers, which are found beyond the stomach, cause twice as many deaths in smokers as compared to nonsmokers.[23] In the previously mentioned study by the American Cancer Society, there were fifty-one deaths from gastric ulcers. *Every one* of these deaths occured in a smoker.[24] In 1958 10,740 Americans died from duodenal and gastric ulcers. Smoking causes mass murder by the thousands in areas never suspected by the average citizen.

Mention should be made of the effect of smoking on women. The only reason that fewer women are suffering medical tragedies today is that they have not been smoking for as many years as men. Dr. P. Bernhard made studies on 5,458 women. If anything, tobacco has a more widespread effect on women than on men. For instance, he observed that disorders of the thyroid gland were nearly seven times more frequent among women who smoked than among women who did not. Menstrual disturbances were present in over thirty-six per cent of the smokers as compared to thirteen per cent of the nonsmokers. Symptoms of premature aging were observed in sixty-seven per cent of the smokers as compared to less than four per cent of the nonsmokers. Masculinization was more common among smokers. Also, there was an increase of miscarriages and premature births.[25]

If one were to total the deaths from cancer of the lung and other areas of the body, plus the deaths from apoplexy, pneumonia, influenza, tuberculosis, emphysema, asthma, ulcers and coronary heart trouble—deaths in which tobacco plays a major role—the grand total would be between two hundred thousand and three hundred thousand Americans per year.

Our U.S. Public Health Service has power to prevent this mass murder. Its power was demonstrated in October 1959, when the department put strict clamps on the sale of cranberries. There was only a remote chance that the spray used on the cranberries could have caused cancer in people, because a human being would have had to eat fifteen thousand pounds of cranberries to get the equivalent amount of spray used to induce cancer in mice. Because of the very possibility of such trouble, the government forbade the sale of sprayed cranberries—and just before our Thanksgiving dinners. But tobacco is a proven killer of tens of thousands each year and the government seems to close its eyes to the evidence.

Let us face squarely the reason behind this paradox. Any political party that attacked the five-billion-dollar tobacco industry would be committing political suicide. The cranberry companies could be squelched, but not the Goliaths of nicotine. Although the government counts its tobacco killings by the hundreds of thousands, it counts its profit from cigarette taxes by the hundreds of millions of dollars. Yet our government seems as devoid of conscience as an IBM machine. As Nero kept aloof and fiddled while Rome burned, so our government appears to be detached while the nicotine burning of over two hundred thousand American men and women occurs annually. We hope it may take action before tobacco claims multitudes more of American lives.

Why do people ever stick their heads into the noose of the smoking habit? Not because it is a pleasant sensation, since many are nauseated in the beginning. Why do they begin? I recall our arrival in Philadelphia from one of our African terms. While we were shopping in the large stores, our three-year-old daughter kept putting little pieces of paper between her lips and I kept pulling them out. Finally, I said, "Linda, why are you putting these pieces of paper between your lips?"

"Daddy, everybody in America has fire in their mouths. This is my fire."

To pre-teen-agers and teen-agers, smoking is the hallmark of maturity. It is an accreditation to show the world that they have arrived. Why do they continue? Nicotine, whether inhaled or injected with a needle, is a habit-producing drug that calls for more and more.

I remember a young woman who attended a nearby college a number of years ago. She thought it was sophisticated and smart to do a little smoking, under cover. She considered the college standards fanatical, radical and foolish. Because her style was cramped there, she finally went elsewhere.

Quite a few years have rolled by since then. To my surprise, she called me on the phone a few months ago to ask me what she could possibly do to stop smoking. Something had come up and she wanted to get rid of the habit. Was there any drug I could send her to deliver her from her bondage. Now she recognized that the maturity she was proud of a few years ago was actually a most disappointing immaturity. The freedom she sought had enslaved and tortured her.

One of my medical colleagues stopped smoking about six years ago, after having smoked most of his life. I asked him if he had found it difficult to stop. "No," he said, "not after I really made up my mind. When I quit, I got rid of the biggest nuisance in my life."

"What?" I retorted. "What do you mean? I thought people smoked because they derived fun from it."

He replied, "Not at all! I got rid of a grand nuisance. I was always looking for cigarettes, for matches, for places to put the ashes. I burned holes in my suits and the furniture. When I quit, I got rid of the worst nuisance anybody can ever have."

He is only one of many thousands of physicians who decided they were fools to continue smoking. A surprising change in attitude has occurred during the past eight years. The American Medical Association journals now will accept no advertising from cigarette companies, and no tobacco companies are allowed to take booths in AMA conventions.

Only a few years ago the air in our medical meetings was blue with smoke. For a day or two after attending the meetings I smelled like something smoked. In June 1961, in one of the section meetings held in New York City and attended by about two hundred physicians, I was so impressed by the nice clear air I was breathing that I decided to count how many doctors were smoking cigarettes. I only counted three, and a few years before I could have counted perhaps seventy-five. Some contrast!

A change in attitude has occurred because during recent years medical science has discovered and proved that smoking is the greatest single cause of:

Public Killer No. 1—Heart disease
Public Killer No. 2—Cancer.

Everybody should be thankful that medical science has its eyes open to the dangers of smoking. How much more thankful we should be to the Lord because He warned His people and saved countless thousands of His followers from a variety of horrible deaths many years before any scientific studies were done.

I recall the testimony of a man who was converted in an environment where there was no preaching against smoking. He stated that the Spirit of God told him to stop smoking. He said he thought it was very strange that God should make such an odd request of him, but he obeyed. Some time later he came across passages in the Bible that confirmed him in the course he had taken.

Although tobacco was not used when the Bible was written and is therefore not mentioned specifically, the impact of many verses has given sufficient warning to keep millions of Christians from using tobacco in any form. These admonitions, coupled with observations of tobacco users with their spittoons, smells, smoke, and sicknesses, have deterred the Christian from indulging. To a Christian, indulgence would be inconsistent with obedience to such Scriptures as:

What? know ye not that your body is the temple of the Holy Ghost which is in you . . . and ye are not your own? For ye are bought with a price: therefore glorify God in your body, and in your spirit, which are God's.[26]

If any man defile the temple of God, him shall God destroy; for the temple of God is holy, which temple ye are.[27]

Whether therefore ye eat, or drink, or whatsoever ye do, do all to the glory of God.[28]

Obedience to God's Spirit and admonitions allows one to enjoy full-orbed living and His promise, "none of these diseases."

CHAPTER 6

They Have The Devil To Pay

CLICK-I-TY, CLICK, CLICK! IN AFRICA, WHEN WE HEARD THE rapid little clicks of a stick hitting the stony path, we knew it was Saturday, beggar's day. One of the first to arrive was blind Alpha, whose only eyes were on the end of his stick.

Who sinned?—this blind beggar or his parents? Probably his parents, since gonorrhea in the mother is the most common cause of lifelong blindness in the next generation. When the mother is infected with gonorrhea, the eyes of the baby can become infected as it passes through the birth canal. Gonorrheal infection of newborn babies is very severe and scars the eye so that the baby cannot see.

Africa and the East have their multiplied thousands of blind beggars, most of them blinded by gonorrhea. Their only food is the crumbs that seldom fall from the tables of an impoverished people. When they ask for bread, they often are pelted with stones, while a pack of lean, mangy dogs drive them out of town. When night comes, the beggars may carefully feel their way out of the forest to sleep on a porch, which affords some protection against torrential rains and wild jungle animals.

In our country we do not see blind beggars cluttering

our streets. Instead, they tap their way around the black corridors of our institutions. It wasn't many years ago that about ninety per cent of the blind in our institutions were there because of gonorrhea. Today, in countries where silver nitrate for the eyes of the newborn is not available, colossal indeed is the devastation to the eyes, bodies and lives from this venereal scourge. How tragic it is that hundreds of thousands of hopelessly blind people must pay the devil for the sins of their parents!

Syphilis is also the cause for many a baby born macerated and dead. If an infected baby lives, it may have various physical or mental deficiencies. Not only do these handicapped children have to pay a price during their lives, but their parents, as they look daily on their deformed or insane children, must pay dearly and bitterly with lifelong remorse. In 1946 a medical text reported the state of affairs in the United States: "Each year it is estimated that . . . more than 50,000 infants with congenital syphilis are born."[1] No doubt penicillin has reduced this figure a great deal.

Some of these blighted children have offspring, who in their bodies and minds show sad evidences of the blasting character of syphilis. They exemplify the truth of the Scriptural warning of the visitation of "the iniquity of the fathers upon the children, and upon the children's children, unto the third and to the fourth generation."[2] In all, medical science recognizes five venereal diseases with their many scores of debilitating complications.

I shall not soon forget the first case of constriction of the urinary passage that I saw while I was in Africa. The victim was a man in his thirties. He gave a history of being unable to pass any urine from the normal passage for many years. The blocking of the passage was caused by an infection from "a lover." The urine thus obstructed had burrowed other little channels in his groin around the scrotum. He was indeed a pathetic character. He had found it was a costly business, this paying the devil.

Sometimes women have to pay a higher price than men. A few decades ago the opening statement from a professor of female diseases to his students was, "Curse the day when a woman walks into your office with a pelvic inflammatory disease." He made this statement because of the frightful suffering and lifelong invalidism that gonorrhea can produce in women. The gonococcus, after providing a profusely purulent vaginitis, spreads upward through the womb to the tubes, ovaries, and the abdominal cavity. High fever, vomiting, and severe abdominal pain result, because of the localized peritonitis and abscess formation. After several weeks of such misery, a woman has respite for only a short time before recurrences of the same pain and symptoms. The chronic ill health, disability, suffering, sterility, unhappiness, and premature deaths caused by gonorrhea in backward areas of the world are still numbered in countless millions. These people have the devil to pay because they paid no attention to God's Word: "Neither let us commit fornication, as some of them committed, and fell in one day three and twenty thousand."[3]

With the advent of sulfa drugs and penicillin it was thought that venereal disease would be wiped out, because when penicillin was introduced in the early 1940's cases of venereal disease began to drop in civilized countries. This decrease continued until the 1950's when the trend started upward again in the United States.

Similarly, in Sweden there was a decrease in gonorrhea cases from 1946 to 1949. Now we read from there that gonorrhea has jumped "since 1949 by an extraordinary rise." In fact, between 1949 and 1952, gonorrhea actually "doubled in the county of Stockholm." By 1953 the number of gonorrheal cases reported exceeded the total of the ten other leading communicable diseases.[4] These increases occurred in spite of growing emphasis on educational propaganda. The devil surely collects his pay whenever and wherever people do not heed this Biblical warning: "Flee fornication. Every sin that a man doeth is without the body; but he that committeth fornication sinneth against his own body."[5]

American servicemen in Korea discovered that even penicillin did not prevent them from paying the devil. In 1959 Ernst Epstein reported that not only among our troops in Korea, but also among those in Japan, England, and America, studies indicated that strains of gonococcus were now becoming resistant to penicillin. He concludes: "From the clinical standpoint, the emergence of penicillin-resistant strains of N. gonorrhea has grave significance. No longer can acute gonorrhea be considered lightheartedly as a disease with a certain cure. . . . The twin problems of chronic gonorrhea in the male and the asymptomatic carrier . . . have returned. It is probably only a matter of time until penicillin resistance will be met on an increasing scale all over the world."[6] Further studies will be needed before we can accept this conclusion.

From England comes another report: "The fact that, in spite of penicillin and other antibiotics, venereal urethritis in men as well as gonorrhea in women has increased during 1952 should restrain any tendency to complacency about the venereal disease position, or any temptation to exaggerate the impact of antibiotics on these diseases. Sexual promiscuity is still rife and as long as this is the case, the danger of venereal disease remains."[7]

Young people and oldsters the world around are trying to avoid paying the devil, but medical statistics prove they are losing. Figures released from a national survey in 1957 show that "teenage venereal disease is increasing in 11 states; new epidemic outbreaks are reported in 19 states."[8] Comparing 1955 with 1959 figures for syphilis, we discover that in these four years the rate jumped: in Washington, D.C., 208%; Los Angeles, 291%; Houston, 378%; San Francisco, 591%; while New Orleans rates during this short period skyrocketed 818%.[9] The chief cause of the increase is attributable to a decline in moral standards.

There is a myth extant that venereal disease can be prevented if intelligence is used. A girl who had sexual relations with only one boyfriend thought she was safe. She was terribly shocked when her doctor told her she was infected. A "venereal tracer" revealed: the boy had consorted with only one other girl. This girl had had relations with five other men, who in turn had been with nineteen women, some of them prostitutes. The girl who thought her relationship had been limited to one person had had contact, through him, with at least ninety-two others.[10]

Legalized houses of prostitution, whose inmates are medically examined, do not prevent venereal disease, as was once thought. Actually, they increase the spread of these diseases. Dr. Walter Lentino, U.S. Army venereal disease control officer, asserts that in a study made, "80% of all cases of venereal disease came from houses of prostitution." These were all medically inspected houses. Dr. Lentino writes:

> Medical inspection of prostitutes, even when performed with the utmost scrupulousness and honesty, cannot deter-

mine with even reasonable accuracy the infectivity of a prostitute. This being the case, any certification as to freedom from communicability of venereal disease in a prostitute is meaningless and gives a sanctified cloak to this business that is quite misleading. In fact, the unsuspecting tyro, who hears that the prostitutes are "medically O.K.'d" may require just this to remove the brakes of fear that may otherwise have stopped him from going to a house of prostitution and may, therefore, actually encourage venereal disease.[11]

Obedience to God's helpful Guidebook has been and still is the best way to avoid the calamitous effects of venereal disease. Everybody who stubbornly seeks to circumvent his heavenly Father's suggestions will sooner or later have to pay the devil's price.

The failure of penicillin is particularly conspicuous in its inability to treat some of the worst complications of syphilis. These sometimes develop before the individual is aware that he is infected. This is especially true of women, where the first ulcer of syphilis may be internal and pass unnoticed. The outstanding characteristic of syphilis is its tendency to awaken to destructive action many years after the original infection. Twenty or more years after the disease is contracted, it may strike down its victim with a dreaded or fatal complication.

One late manifestation of syphilis is paresis, an insanity caused by syphilis hitting the brain cells. This insanity can develop in a person from five to thirty years after the original infection. People between thirty-five and forty-five years of age are often affected. Little can be done unless treatment is instituted early. Unfortunately, early therapy is often delayed because the condition is similar to epilepsy, neurasthenia, or other insanities.

Another complication that may come on years after the initial infection is locomotor ataxia. Here the spinal nerves and occasionally the cranial nerves are involved. Disturbances of the cranial nerves may produce squints, blindness, or deafness. (Please do not diagnose everybody with squints, blindness, or deafness as having syphilis!) When the spinal cord is affected, the gait is characteristic—the foot is thrown out and then slapped down. Involvement of the bladder muscle can cause an inability to hold the urine.

In the light of the following description of locomotor

ataxia, one would do well to consider whether the illicit pleasure of a few seconds is worth lifelong misery:

At the time of sphincteric involvement, sexual debility and eventual impotence are almost invariable. . . . The most horrible of the tabetic symptoms are the crises which may be peripheral or visceral. Agonizing lightning pains occur in the muscles of the extremities, abdomen and chest. They are described by the patient as burning, gnawing, lancinating, twitching, or resembling a stabbing with a hot knife. The attacks come on with the rapidity of lightning; they may last for hours or days with brief intervals of freedom.[12]

Three thousand years ago our heavenly Father sought to save us from such an end:

My son, attend to wisdom,
bend your ear to knowledge, . . .
that they may save you from the loose woman:
her lips drop honied words,
her talk is smoother than oil itself,
but the end with her is bitter as poison,
sharp as a sword with double edge. . . .
Now listen to me, my son,
hold fast to what I say:
keep clear of her,
never go near her door, lest . . .
you are left at last to moan . . .
'Ah! why did I hate guidance,
why did I despise all warning?'[13]

The Lord not only gives many warnings to help mankind, but Jesus so transforms and fortifies one with the energy and power of His Holy Spirit that man has no valid excuse for falling into sexual sin. The Apostle Paul expresses the matter forcibly in his Epistle to the Thessalonians:

God's plan is to make you holy, and that entails first of all a clean cut with sexual immorality. Every one of you should learn to control his body, keeping it pure and treating it with respect, and never regarding it as an instrument for self-gratification, as do pagans with no knowledge of God. You cannot break this rule without in some way cheating your fellow-men. And you must remember that

God will punish all who do offend in this matter, and we have warned you how we have seen this work out in our experience of life. The calling of God is not to impurity but to the most thorough purity, and anyone who makes light of the matter is not making light of a man's ruling but of God's command. It is not for nothing that the Spirit God gives us is called the *Holy* Spirit.[14]

It must be bitter mockery, indeed, for people who steal a little illicit sexual pleasure to end with "sexual debility and eventual impotence." The type of sin often determines the pattern of the punishment.

Syphilis not only attacks the brain, causing insanity, and the spinal cord, causing the excruciating pains of locomotor ataxia, but it frequently attacks the heart. I remember a patient whose heart was devastated by syphilis. Though at first he denied any sexual safaris, he finally confessed that many years ago he was "kinda bad." And like Shylock of old, the devil wanted his "pound of flesh" right out of the heart. In fact, in the United States during 1945, the death rate from cardiovascular syphilis was reputedly the cause of forty thousand deaths.[15] The advent of penicillin reduced that figure, but we read that in 1953 "The management of cardiovascular syphilis . . . remains unsatisfactory, because the pathologic changes are the result of scarring."[16]

In spite of penicillin, in spite of venereal disease clinics, and in spite of educational programs, the U.S. Public Health Service reports that in 1957 there were one million fresh cases of gonorrhea. If we have these figures in the United States, highly favored with a host of antibiotics, it is staggering to the mind to imagine what the situation is among the great bulk of the world's population, many of whom are deprived of medical care, information, and antibiotics.

Medical science with all its knowledge is inadequate to take care of the world's venereal disease problem. Yet millenniums before the microscope, and before man knew the method of the transmission of venereal diseases, God knew all about them and gave to man the only feasible plan of preventing these universal and blighting killers. Jesus clearly stated that, from the beginning, our Father ordained that one man and one woman should constitute a family unit.[17] This plan of two, and two alone, constituting a family unit is so unique, so different from human plans, and so effective in the prevention of the vast complications of horrible venereal diseases, that again we are forced to recognize another medical evidence of the inspiration of the Bible.

CHAPTER 7

The Enemies of Sexual Happiness

EVERYONE REMEMBERS THE STORY OF THE PIED PIPER OF Hamelin who enticed the younger set to follow the enchanting, irresistible music of his flute. He led the children into a cave in a mountain, and they were never seen again.

Each generation produces a swarm of pied pipers. In the middle of this century one of them swung down the main streets of America, playing the catchy tune of "sex freedom." His sprightly, jazzy jingles promised emancipation from the "traditions" and "horrible confinement of religious inhibitions." There were many who left their homes and loved ones to race down the street after this alluring music. The piper had neither flute nor the waving hips of a rock-and-roll singer. He was a zoologist who gathered certain statistics on the theme of sex, and he shook them and beat upon them like a tambourine.

First, let us look at the statistics he gathered.[1] He and his associates had interviewed 5,940 women, questioning them about the intimate details of their past and present sexual lives. From these reports, our piper figured the percentages of the women engaged in this and that sexual perversion, the percentages of those who had had premarital experiences, and the percentages of those who were guilty of extramarital affairs. From these percentages he drew certain conclusions.

Authorities and specialists have taken exception to this report and to the conclusions that Dr. Alfred C. Kinsey made. In the first place, Kinsey interviewed only one out of every fourteen thousand women in the country. Second, these women were certainly not typical of the average American woman, because in this abnormal sampling the ratio of single women to married women was three times greater than that found in the country at large, and the ratio of college women to noncollege women was ten times greater. Third, the only women in the group were women who had volunteered to lay bare the details of their intimate sexual lives. Such women are rare in more ways than one. Women who would volunteer to reveal such sexual secrets would be women who had, probably as a result of their sexual experiences, lost an inborn feminine reticence. Many of these women stated that they enjoyed being bitten during the sex act, and that trait certainly marks them as being abnormal. It is a neurotic mind that can translate pain into pleasure.

Kinsey's sampling was loaded with atypical and masochistic women. It was the sexual image of this group of women—who were strangely devoid of the natural inhibitions of women—that was superimposed on all other women.

There are a number of other faults in the Kinsey report. First, it is inferred that if the "average woman" is engaged in an act, then that act is advisable. There is a gulf as wide as the Grand Canyon between that which is *advisable* and that which is *average*. The average Hindu drinks filthy water on his pilgrimages, but it is certainly not advisable, since the Hindus die of cholera by the thousands. The faulty implication in the Kinsey report is that it is advisable for women to adjust to that which is average, even to a badly distorted average.

Second, having classified a woman and a hog in the same zoological category, Kinsey could see no reason why a woman's sexual life should not be patterned after that of a hog. A hog has no horrible inhibitions about sex; why should a woman?

Many people thought the reasoning seemed plausible, smacking as it did of science. After all, they asked themselves, had not "certain skilled psychiatrists" told Kinsey that restraints were bad for the mind? Now, if men and women mingled freely in the pen of promiscuity, the ultimate in living could be achieved. There would be no restraints and no frustrations. Here at last was the panacea that could cure all their longings. People could disregard the Biblical warnings against fornication, adultery, homosexuality, and other perversions.[2] They could follow the piper of promiscuity into a Utopia where nary a restriction would be placed on sexual impulses, however wild and bizarre they might be.

This zoologist deplored the fact that the "outdated laws" of the moral code were a great hindrance to the operation of his ideas. But modern pipers feel that these laws will soon be changed. Until they are, they suggest that their followers seek "to avoid open conflict with the law." I suppose rape of little girls and defenseless women should not be attempted if there were the probability of conflict with the law.

Is it not a little strange that a zoologist, a specialist in animals, should set himself up as an authority on the sex life of women? Dealing with the purely animal aspects of the matter, he fails completely to realize the deeply human relationships involved.

What do medical specialists think about putting women and hogs in the same sexual category? Two specialists, a gynecologist and a psychiatrist, resented this bull-in-the-china-shop intrusion so strongly that they wrote a book to refute Kinsey's erroneous statements. Here is a little [illegible] their thought:

> Kinsey argues that inasmuch as all types of sexual behavior occur in subhuman species, these patterns are normal for humans. This kind of logic disregards all the ethical, religious, and moral advances mankind has made. . . . Kinsey also abandons the whole medical concept of perversions and puts heterosexuality on the same level as homosexuality and animal contact. . . . The healthy sex act consists of very complex psychological phenomena. It depends on the spiritual merger of one personality with another. The sex impulse in humans is tied to the deepest emotions. . . . Love simply cannot be measured on an IBM machine. Orgasm per se means nothing.[3]

Kinsey assured his followers that the spread of venereal diseases through premarital intercourse is "a relatively unimportant matter today."[4] This salesman of promiscuity is at variance with the U.S. Public Health Service which recently reported: "We estimate the reservoir of untreated syphilitics today at 1,200,000 cases and that the true annual incidence is 60,000 cases."[5] It has been further estimated that the annual number of new cases of gonorrhea in this country is 1,000,000 cases.

Kinsey is far removed from the best medical opinions when he makes repeated inferences that girls who engage in premarital petting have more successful marriages than those who do not.[6] Medical specialists, who deal with people rather than animals, refute his deduction:

> Such advice is scientifically wrong. There is no premium for premarital petting to orgasm. There are no penalties for not indulging in this manner. Experience proves that neurotic girls are the most persistent petters and that emotionally healthy girls usually reject sex without love. Successful marriage and sexual adjustment are based more on gradually established confidence, liking and mutual respect than on any premarital trial and error sexual process.[7]

A reviewer of a book written by medical experts states in the *Journal of the American Medical Association:*

> The authors justly allege that Kinsey has discussed many difficult medical problems without the medical knowledge and clinical experience necessary to an understanding of the principles involved, that he has vitally overlooked the profound influence of the psychological aspects of sexual behavior, and that, without training and experience in psychiatry, he has exhibited an utter disregard of the sexual neuroses with their multifaceted evil effects.[8]

Dr. J. Irving Sands of the Neurological Institute of New York also disagrees with Dr. Kinsey:

> My own experience in dealing with many neurotic and psychotic people . . . has led me to conclude that premarital sexual activity by females leaves a blight on the emotional part of their personality. Moreover, these activities are a source of emotional conflict.[9]

All of which reminds me of a sign I once saw in a department store: "Slightly Used. Greatly Reduced in Price."

Before any of us are tempted to listen to this pied piper, it might be smart to look at the fate of those who have already followed him. Enough human guinea pigs, geared to the idea that *newness* is synonymous with *superiority,* have already raced down the street after him, so that an honest-to-goodness appraisal can be made.

An outstanding New York City psychoanalyst, Dr. Eugene Eisner, tells of a patient who was certainly not frustrated by any "horrible religious inhibitions," yet in 1950 the patient reported, "I've had six love affairs since 1940, but I can't seem to enjoy any of it. Is there something the matter with me? I feel that I am not getting out of sex what I'm supposed to."[10]

Another psychiatrist states, "For about fifteen years I have been the confidant of Broadway and Hollywood actors and actresses who have opportunities to live a promiscuous sexual life. And some of them live it to the hilt—eight, ten, twelve 'affairs' a year. But when they trust you and let down their hair, they will confess how frustrating and unsatisfying it all is."[11]

Into a health clinic in San Francisco landed two thousand girls who had been enthralled by the flutes, hips and statistics of a variety of pied pipers. These girls were asked if they had obtained even transitory pleasure from their sexual experiences. According to the advocates of sexual freedom, one would expect an enthusiastic affirmative. On the contrary, only a third of the girls reported "some pleasure." The other two thirds described their feelings as those of "doubt, guilt, shame, indifference, or definitely unpleasant."[12]

It should ever be remembered that it is God who created sex urges in men and women, and God put His stamp of approval on marriage. "Marriage is honourable in all, and the bed undefiled: but whoremongers and adulterers God will judge."[13] The restraints in God's Guidebook were never designed to diminish man's sexual enjoyment but rather to enable him to achieve maximal pleasure in this area. Pathetic indeed that many people are like cows who break through a fence surrounding their lush pasturage and then live on starvation rations in a desert of cactus.

Howard Whitman, American journalist who traveled extensively to study the human products of this neosexuality, writes:

New standards of sex freedom have been tried, bringing new highs of illegitimacy, a crushing burden of divorce, and a greater psychiatric caseload than ever. . . . the old formula has been flouted and the "new freedom" has failed. Youth has been hurt badly. There are the kind of hurts we know about, when social agencies and the law step in and file their reports on pregnancies, forced marriages, and venereal disease. There are the hushed-up hurts, when distraught families manage "to keep quiet." And there are the silent hurts, when youth is "lucky," manages to "get away with it." These silent hurts—the remorse, the regrets, the loss of self-respect, the blight upon the individual's future life—can be the greatest hurts of all.[14]

As a physician I have had some experience with these various hurts. Many a young girl has dampened my desk with her tears. The shame, the disgrace, and the ostracism brand her, and the pain often lasts through many years. A great variety of resulting neurotic manifestations can produce any of the many psychosomatic diseases. The community does not know, but the physician knows, that breaking through God's fences around sex is the basic cause of Kathy's toxic goiter, or Helen's arthritis, or Suzanne's commitment to an insane asylum. True, these girls were not bound by the "horrible confinement of religious inhibitions." But they experienced confinements of different sorts—and much, much harder to bear. The promised "sex freedom" turned out to be unbearable slavery of the worst sort.

The real enemies of man's sexual happiness are those who would entice him away from his home, his family, and the Biblical standards. Few people have ever stopped to realize that the blessings of sex and civilization that we enjoy exist because a large proportion of people take heed of the words of Jesus: "But from the beginning of the creation, God made them male and female. For this cause shall a man leave his father and mother, and cleave to his wife; And they twain shall be one flesh: so then they are no more twain, but one flesh."[15]

People who take this Scriptural standard as their model will save themselves from many diseases and a thousand heartaches. It is refreshing to see outstanding specialists recognize that the Biblical standard of marriage surpasses all human plans. Addressing an annual meeting of New York State physicians, Dr. Irving J. Sands said:

It may be well to call attention to the fact that change and progress are not synonymous and all that is new is not necessarily good, nor all that is old necessarily bad. . . . The Ten Commandments are old indeed, and yet they comprise the greatest mental hygiene code and the best set of rules and regulations for ethical human relationships ever produced by mankind. . . . A happy marriage is the result of a harmonious relationship between two mature people. Marriage is the greatest institution of civilized man.[16]

CHAPTER 8

The Superlatives in Sex

"DOCTOR, I CAN'T SLEEP, AND I CAN'T ENJOY ANYTHING any more. I know when my trouble began—when Gil started to play cards with a bunch of fellows. They don't gamble, but they go out one night every single week to an expensive hotel for a big steak dinner. Then they play cards until one or two in the morning. Everything is on the up and up, but—"

Pretty Mrs. Gilbert Steiner choked a bit and then continued. "Oh, I know I'm foolish. But still, here is the way I look at it. With our five children, we have to watch every penny to make ends meet. I've told Gil that I get tired and nervous staying home month in and month out. I've asked him to take me out to the movies or to dinner once in a while, but he always says there is no money for that and a babysitter, too. But he takes the little money we could use for recreation and spends it on himself. As a result there is considerable tension between us, and we aren't enjoying each other at all."

Here was a marriage falling apart because an important cohesive had been lost. The password to a happy marriage is *together*—live together, play together, work together, think together and plan together. Two people can not be held together long unless there is some sort of binding force, and sexuality is a short-lived binder, as the sex marriages of Hollywood have long demonstrated. Because sex is the only cohesive that many couples know anything about, it is not strange that about one out of every three marriages falls apart.

There is one binder that has never failed to hold two people together—love. "Love never fails." This love is not the "puppy love" played up in novels and on TV. What is love, the element so essential to every happy marriage?

Although most people understand the meaning of sexuality, few have a clear conception of what is love. The vagueness concerning love is evidenced by the fact that the dictionary gives eight different definitions. In this chapter I wish to discuss only the meaning of love as *an outward reach of the mind to help and please others. Love in this meaning of the word is not sexual, yet this kind of love must be present if the superlatives are to be obtained from sex.* The superlatives in sex—the best, the most, and for the longest time—are only possible when thoughtfulness, consideration and love for others exist.

Mr. Guy Bullom is continents away from the superlatives when he blatantly asserts that he is going "to look after No. 1," both in his business and his sex life. He perpetually berates his wife for her faults, yet he can't understand why she doesn't exhibit enthusiasm for him and his approaches. Although he has had several "affairs" with his secretaries, he fails to realize why none of them satisfied him. Variety and frequency is a mocking substitute for quality, and Mr. Bullom knows nothing of that superlative—the best.

This highly-sexed, egocentric individual gets practically nothing out of sex for the simple reason that he is sadly lacking in love. As a result he is always disappointed and frustrated sexually. His resentments toward others are largely responsible for boosting his blood pressure to 240/110. Many are the nights the poor fellow sits in a chair, wheezing through the long hours with his asthma, which is often triggered by emotional upsets.

Dr. Carl Jung recognized the underlying reason why many a man like Guy Bullom has such illnesses and such an unhappy existence: "It arises from his having no love, but only sexuality . . . and no understanding, because he has failed to read the meaning of his own existence."[1]

There are countless unhappy marriages, devoid of sexual fulfillment, because the couples do not know the difference between love and sexuality. The only love they know is something pictured in novels, torrid magazines, movies and TV. Because some couples know only "puppy love," it is no wonder they lead "a dog's life."

Yvonne was that kind of a person. She put her head on my desk and sobbed. After awhile she blurted out, "I was only kidding when I said something about Mike's mother. But he got mean and said something awful about my mother. Then I slapped him good and hard across his face. Just what he deserved! But the big brute up and punched me in the face. Look at my eye! I'm moving out! I'm taking my two kids and going back to Mom's. I love Mike, but I can't take this!"

Then, as Yvonne held an ice bag over her left eye and looked at me with the other, I gave her a little marriage counseling, somewhat belated to be sure. I ended my lecture with words something like these: "Yvonne, in every marriage, situations are bound to arise in which one of the partners must give in, out of consideration and love for the other partner. Don't feel sorry for yourself if you discover that you are the one who has to give in most of the time. I have strange but good news for you: when you give in to Mike, you are losing your life in the one and only way to find life and worthwhile happiness. The secret of happiness in married life depends on each partner making small sacrifices, readily and cheerfully.

"You say you have love for Mike. Is it the kind of love that suffers long and is kind? The only love that will stand the acid test of everyday living is that which God describes and gives to those who walk in the light of His commandments: 'Love is patient; love is kind and envies no one. Love is never boastful, nor conceited, nor rude; never selfish, not quick to take offence. Love keeps no scores of wrongs. . . . There is nothing love cannot face; there is no limit to its faith, its hope, and its endurance. Love will never come to an end.' "[2]

Love is a basic necessity, not only for obtaining the superlatives of sex but also for living. Dr. Smiley Blanton, in his recent book *Love or Perish,* says: "For more than forty years I have sat in my office and listened while people of all ages and classes told me of their hopes and fears. . . . As I look back over the long, full years, one truth emerges clearly in my mind—the universal need for love. . . . They cannot survive without love; they must have it or they will perish."[3]

Many couples are not happy. They go through the

motions of sex but have no sexual fulfillment. If they have other affairs, their frustrations only increase. They hardly ever sense that the feelings they long for can only be obtained where love for one another exists. There can be no real ecstasy unless the sex act expresses a love and intense awareness of the needs and desires of the other. Wrangling during the day will make sex lifeless and mechanical, if not repulsive.

Frustrated couples often think there must be something wrong with their sex departments, so they go off to a psychiatrist for help. Fortunate they are if they go to one who gives them advice such as psychoanalyst Erich Fromm offers:

> There is no more convincing proof that the injunction, "Love thy neighbor as thyself," is the most important norm of living and that its violation is the basic cause of unhappiness and mental illness than the evidence gathered by the psychoanalyst. Whatever complaints the . . . patient may have, whatever symptoms he may present, are rooted in his inability to love, if we mean by love a capacity for the experience of concern, responsibility, respect and understanding of another person and an intense desire for that other person's growth. Analytic therapy is essentially an attempt to help the patient gain or regain his capacity for love. If this aim is not fulfilled, nothing but surface changes can be accomplished.[4]

Love is as essential to happiness and mental health as is food to our physical well-being. Men particularly fail to comprehend that sex alone is inadequate nourishment for a happy marriage. Orgasm in men is almost a purely mechanical act, while in women it is much more complex. A woman must be fully aware of the man's thoughtfulness for her, of his fidelity to her, and of his love that puts her pleasure ahead of his own.

Psychiatrist Max Levin recognized that unselfish love is necessary for obtaining the superlatives in sex: "It is obvious, then, that maturity is a prerequisite for a happy marriage. In the immature state of infancy there is no obligation to give. The infant *receives;* he is not expected to do anything else. The success of a marriage will depend in great degree on the extent to which the partners have outgrown their infantile dependency and achieved the capacity to assume responsibility, to wish more to give than to receive."[5]

Centuries quarrel, and atry, the Bible showed turity with love and thus gave a happy marriage: "When I was outlook, and my thoughts were all ch up, I had finished with childish things. . . there are three things that last forever: faith, hope, love; but the greatest of them all is love."[6]

The love that is thoughtful and unselfish makes life's greatest dream come to pass, but sex without love can make of life a horrible nightmare. One of many who discovered this truth the hard way was the prodigal son.[7] His was the voice of immaturity: "Give me." He, like many today, hastened into a country far removed from his father's precepts and there wasted the endowments of money and body "with riotous living." His soul became an empty void inhabited only by haunting echoes. He hit bottom in one of life's pigpens where he yearned to eat the empty husks that the hogs were crunching. He discovered that sex in a country removed from God's will is empty, disappointing and ugly. Self-gratification is ever a one-way street—with a hogpen at the end.

As the young man remembered that his father's house always had "bread enough and to spare," he discovered that "the horrible religious inhibitions" were not as bad as he had been led to believe. He began to sense that there is a close relationship between proper inhibitions and abundant blessings.

When he had left home, his immaturity was evidenced by his attitude of "Give me." When he returned, repenting, the spirit of *"Give me"* was absent. In its place was thoughtfulness for others—*"Make me a servant."*

How important is the matter of sex in the marriage relationship? Dr. Emil Novak, of Johns Hopkins Medical School, states convincingly that "There are many women who are physically and emotionally normal, who love thei husbands devotedly, who have borne children, yet ha never throughout their married lives experienced a great degree of physical satisfaction from the sex Nor do they feel frustrated or cheated."[8]

In fact, some authorities state that less than h married women have ever experienced sexual However, the emotions they derive from the sexua

ithout any need for
are diffused throughout
ving embers of hardwood
quick bright flash of a little

ignorance of these facts, many young
op frustrations and resentments that tragi-
worsen the marital situation. If thoughtfulness for one another predominates, then these same women will experience increasingly greater satisfaction from the marital relationship. Possession of God-given love will prevent frustrations, unhappiness and divorce, with their long trains of mental and physical diseases.

Someone has said: "The cure for all the ills and wrongs, the cares, the sorrows and the crimes of humanity, all lie in one word 'love.' It is the divine vitality that everywhere produces and restores life. To each and every one of us, it gives the power of working miracles if we will."

How is this *summum bonum* obtained and maintained? It is obtained in its fullest measure when God, who is Love, comes to indwell the man or woman who opens the door of the heart. Nothing less than the divine indwelling will suffice when the individual finds himself in the strong current of sexual temptation.

This love is maintained by obediently following the leadings of the Word and the Spirit. There is no valid reason for the Christian to succumb to a host of diseases, for the promise of God is sure: "There hath no temptation taken you but such as is common to man: but God is faithful, who will not suffer you to be tempted above that ye are able; but will with the temptation also make a way to escape, that ye may be able to bear it."[9]

Centuries before Yvonne and Mike had their childish quarrel, and centuries before the birth of modern psychiatry, the Bible showed the necessity of displacing immaturity with love and thus gave a splendid prescription for a happy marriage: "When I was a child, my speech, my outlook, and my thoughts were all childish. When I grew up, I had finished with childish things. . . . In a word, there are three things that last forever: faith, hope, and love; but the greatest of them all is love."[6]

The love that is thoughtful and unselfish makes life's greatest dream come to pass, but sex without love can make of life a horrible nightmare. One of many who discovered this truth the hard way was the prodigal son.[7] His was the voice of immaturity: "Give me." He, like many today, hastened into a country far removed from his father's precepts and there wasted the endowments of money and body "with riotous living." His soul became an empty void inhabited only by haunting echoes. He hit bottom in one of life's pigpens where he yearned to eat the empty husks that the hogs were crunching. He discovered that sex in a country removed from God's will is empty, disappointing and ugly. Self-gratification is ever a one-way street—with a hogpen at the end.

As the young man remembered that his father's house always had "bread enough and to spare," he discovered that "the horrible religious inhibitions" were not as bad as he had been led to believe. He began to sense that there is a close relationship between proper inhibitions and abundant blessings.

When he had left home, his immaturity was evidenced by his attitude of "Give me." When he returned, repenting, the spirit of *"Give me"* was absent. In its place was thoughtfulness for others—*"Make me a servant."*

How important is the matter of sex in the marriage relationship? Dr. Emil Novak, of Johns Hopkins Medical School, states convincingly that "There are many women who are physically and emotionally normal, who love their husbands devotedly, who have borne children, yet have never throughout their married lives experienced any great degree of physical satisfaction from the sex act. Nor do they feel frustrated or cheated."[8]

In fact, some authorities state that less than half of married women have ever experienced sexual orgasm. However, the emotions they derive from the sexual act are

beautiful and completely gratifying without any need for physical climax. Their emotions are diffused throughout their bodies. To them the glowing embers of hardwood are just as satisfying as the quick bright flash of a little gunpowder.

Because of their ignorance of these facts, many young women develop frustrations and resentments that tragically worsen the marital situation. If thoughtfulness for one another predominates, then these same women will experience increasingly greater satisfaction from the marital relationship. Possession of God-given love will prevent frustrations, unhappiness and divorce, with their long trains of mental and physical diseases.

Someone has said: "The cure for all the ills and wrongs, the cares, the sorrows and the crimes of humanity, all lie in one word 'love.' It is the divine vitality that everywhere produces and restores life. To each and every one of us, it gives the power of working miracles if we will."

How is this *summum bonum* obtained and maintained? It is obtained in its fullest measure when God, who is Love, comes to indwell the man or woman who opens the door of the heart. Nothing less than the divine indwelling will suffice when the individual finds himself in the strong current of sexual temptation.

This love is maintained by obediently following the leadings of the Word and the Spirit. There is no valid reason for the Christian to succumb to a host of diseases, for the promise of God is sure: "There hath no temptation taken you but such as is common to man: but God is faithful, who will not suffer you to be tempted above that ye are able; but will with the temptation also make a way to escape, that ye may be able to bear it."[9]

CHAPTER 9

Upset Mind—Sick Body

SIX-YEAR-OLD HELEN SEIBERT, SITTING ON HER MOTHER'S lap, eyed me like a scared rabbit. Her mother answered my inquiring look: "Doctor, Helen has been vomiting every day for six weeks. Nearly everything I give her comes up. She began to vomit the day after Labor Day."

The day after Labor Day was the time Helen began to attend the large central school with its hundreds of new, strange faces. This experience was indeed overwhelming to her because she lived far up Turtle Creek where children were few.

Why was she vomiting? Her fear of the many strangers had sent hurried impulses along nerves from her emotional center to tighten the muscular outlet of her stomach. As a result much of her food could not pass into the intestines and was regurgitated. Little Helen had lost a great deal of weight.

I suggested that she remain home for a week. There was no more vomiting. Then the better-adjusted Helen returned to school and had no further trouble.

Such trouble is not confined to children. On a Saturday night, eighteen-year-old Donna Cole told me she had been vomiting and suffering from severe abdominal cramps and diarrhea for five days. Her trouble had begun about an hour after she had left the dentist's office.

The dentist had told this pretty, popular girl that she must have all of her teeth pulled and be fitted with false ones. Result: a tempest in her emotional center. Nerve impulses from this center quickly initiated and perpetuated vomiting, severe cramps, and diarrhea. Donna was greatly surprised when I told her that the cause of the trouble was not in her abdomen but above her ears.

Equally surprised was Elaine Johnson when she discovered that her headaches came from anxiety about losing her boyfriend. Bill Landry found out that that it was not the professor's assignment that gave him asthma, but his griping about it. Hal Stevens could not understand why his diabetes flared out of control after he took that "stupid test." And the professor who gave the test could not see how his arthritis became so much worse after he corrected the test papers.

These cases illustrate the most intriguing subject in modern medicine. With every passing year, we obtain a wider comprehension of the ability of the mind (*psyche*) to produce varied disturbances in the body (*soma*): hence the term *psychosomatic*. Invisible emotional tension in the mind can produce striking visible changes in the body, changes that can become serious and fatal.

This concept should give us a new perspective on conditions that are often contemptuously referred to as "being in the head." Obviously such conditions as vomiting, diarrhea, asthma, diabetes, and deformed arthritic joints are not "in the head," yet these and scores of other serious diseases are triggered by tension in the mind.

What percentage of a physician's practice is made up of patients whose symptoms and bodily diseases are caused by emotional turmoil? Statistics reported in 1948 indicated that two thirds of the patients who went to a physician had symptoms caused or aggravated by mental stress.[1] In 1955 an article describing the work of a leading authority on stress was published under the questioning title, "Stress the Cause of All Disease?"[2]

At the beginning of this century, bacteria were considered the center of attention. Now, fifty years later, mental stress has taken its place. In fact, experiments with animals indicated that certain bacteria could only cause disease when animals' resistance was lowered by stress.

How can certain emotions cause visible changes in the body, such as strokes of apoplexy, blindness, toxic goiters, fatal clots in the heart, bleeding ulcers of the intestinal tract, kidney diseases, and gangrene of the legs, to mention only a few of the conditions? Dr. O. Spurgeon English published an excellent, illustrated book explaining how emotions can cause debilitating and fatal illnesses.[3] The first picture in this book depicts the emotional center in the brain from which nerve fibers go out to every organ of the body. Because of the intricate nerve connections, it is understandable how any turmoil in the emotional center can send out impulses which can cause anything from a headache to itching in the soles of the feet.

The emotional center produces these widespread changes by means of three principal mechanisms: by changing the amount of blood flowing to an organ; by affecting the secretions of certain glands; and by changing the tension of muscles.

Emotional stress can influence the amount of blood that flows to an organ. Embarrassment can cause the blood vessels of the face and neck to open up to produce blushing, and the emotions of anxiety or hate can so increase the amount of blood within the rigid skull that headaches and vomiting result.

Irritation in the emotional center is also directed toward the glands of the body. Many of us can remember the first time we attempted to speak before an audience and we recall how parched our mouths became. Alarm messages had gone from our emotional centers, which dried up the salivary secretions. It is indeed hard to speak when the mouth is dry. Even experienced speakers may experience emotional strain and consequent drying of the saliva. Perhaps that is why a glass of water is often placed on the speaker's rostrum.

Frequently an emotional tempest sends S.O.S. messages to the thyroid gland for its secretions. When an excess of thyroxin is poured into the blood over a long period, the symptoms of toxic goiter are seen: extreme nervousness, bulging eyes, rapid pulse, and even fatal heart disease.

Emotional tension affects the secretion of the ovaries in a variety of ways. Disturbance of these glands can cause a cessation of the menses, pain at the time of the period, or an upset before the period characterized by irritableness, headaches, and bloating.

The highly important adrenal glands are frequently the target of emotional fire. Their secretions in abnormal amounts can cause high blood pressure, arthritis, kidney disease, and hardening of the arteries—the last killer alone is responsible for the annual slaughter of 800,000 in the United States.

Emotional stress can affect the tone of the muscles. All of us have felt our muscles tightening up when we became frightened or angry. Tightened muscles can produce pain, as one can demonstrate by clenching a fist for a few minutes. Hence, it is understandable why people with chronic anxieties suffer a great deal with severe tension headaches that stem from tightened neck muscles.

The involuntary muscles of the intestines can also be affected. As an example, consider the initial landing of our paratroopers during the invasion of France in World War II. As the men slowly floated down in their parachutes, German bullets screeched all around them. Consider how you would have felt if you had been up there! Consider the rapid messages that went from their emotional centers to the muscles of their intestines.

Emotional turmoil can also manifest itself through pain over the heart. One day I received an urgent call to see a student who was "dying from a heart attack." I found him on the floor, gasping for breath and suffering real pain over his heart. He presented almost the same picture as a person dying from heart trouble, but he was in no danger at all.

He was a freshman at the college and was having difficulty adjusting to the tempo of college life. The pain over his heart was as real as a pain from a broken rib; it was not caused by a diseased heart, but by a troubled emotional center.

During World War I men with such a condition were great liabilities in the army. When World War II came along, special efforts were made to weed out such men. In fact, ten times as many men were rejected for this emotional type of heart pain as for all other heart diseases. Plenty of it was seen too among the civilian population after every bombing of English cities, when tens of thousands were unable to go to work because of chest pains.

Even in peace times, it constitutes one of the most common conditions seen in a physician's office. I think now of a very fine man who, with pain over his heart and gasping for breath, has often been speeded in an ambulance to a hospital. Expensive hospitalization and tests always indicate that his trouble originates in emotional upsets. Frightening and incapacitating as these attacks are, they are not dangerous.

However, fatal heart attacks can be triggered by "anger in all degrees, depression, and anxiety," according to Dr. Roy R. Grinker, one of the medical directors of Michael Reese Hospital in Chicago. This doctor states that anxiety places more stress on the heart than any other stimulus, including physical exercise and fatigue.[4]

The influence of emotional stress on the human body can be demonstrated by a partial listing of diseases it causes or aggravates. Of course it should not be assumed that the emotional factor is the sole cause in any of these cases:

Disorders of the Digestive System
Ulcers of the mouth, stomach, and intestines
Ulcerative and mucous colitis
Loss of appetite
Hiccoughs
Constipation
Diarrhea

Disorders of the Circulatory System
High blood pressure
Soldier's heart
Paroxysmal tachycardia
Arteriosclerosis
Coronary thrombosis
Gangrene of legs
Rheumatic fever
Cerebral strokes of apoplexy

Disorders of the Genito-Urinary System
Painful menstruation
Lack of menstruation
Premenstrual tension and irritability
Frigidity and vaginismus
Painful coitus
Frequent and painful urination
Acute glomerular nephritis (kidney disease)
Menopausal symptoms
Impotence

Disorders of the Nervous System
Headaches of several types
Alcoholism
Epilepsy
Psychoneuroses
Insanities such as schizophrenia
Senile dementia

Disorders of Glands of Internal Secretion
Hyperthyroidism
Diabetes
Obesity

Allergic Disorders
Hives
Hay fever
Asthma

Muscle-Joint Disorders
Backache
Pain and spasm of muscles
Rheumatoid arthritis
Osteoarthritis

Infections
Infectious mononucleosis
Polio
Many, perhaps all, infections

Eye Diseases
Glaucoma
Keratitis

Skin Diseases
Hives
Atopic dermatitis
Neurodermatitis
Raynaud's disease
Scleroderma
Lupus erythematosus disseminata
Psoriasis

CHAPTER 10

It's Not What You Eat —It's What Eats You

BIG BILL BRANDON WAS A VERY LIKABLE FELLOW—WHEN he didn't "go off at the handle." When one of his men at the plant messed up an assignment, Bill would get furious and throw at him the sharpest epithets in his voluminous but unprintable vocabulary. But the abuse he hurled at the other fellow always seemed to boomerang on poor Bill and eventually put him in bed.

Then his wife would call me to the house. It was such an old story that she would merely open the door and

SELF-CENTEREDNESS ENVY JEALOUSY RESENTMENT
HATE WORRY OVERSENSITIVITY GUILT FEELINGS
FEAR SORROW DESIRE FOR APPROVAL FRUSTRATION

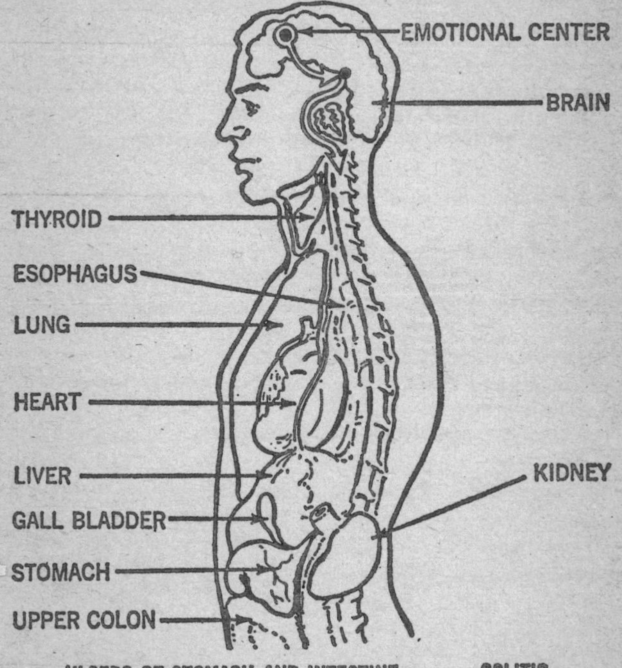

ULCERS OF STOMACH AND INTESTINE COLITIS
HIGH BLOOD PRESSURE HEART TROUBLE STROKES
ARTERIOSCLEROSIS KIDNEY DISEASE HEADACHES
MENTAL DISTURBANCES GOITER DIABETES ARTHRITIS

Effects of Emotions on Physical Health

give a broad sweep of her hand toward Bill's bedroom with a laconic shrug of her shoulders and a forced smile. "Doc, he has been vomiting two weeks straight, but he wouldn't let me call you until this morning."

One couldn't help feeling sorry for big Bill as he lay

on his stomach in bed. His eyes were big, red, desperate and pleading for help. Of course, he had been studied and X rayed in several hospitals, where he had spent a small fortune. His trouble was always brought on by anger, which tightened the outlet of his stomach and caused the intractable vomiting. The occurrences were so frequent and severe that Bill was having a hard time working enough to support his wife and eight children.

Bill's stomach must have had a stainless steel lining, because after such a build-up of acid in the stomach most people develop ulcers, if not cancer. In fact, it is generally agreed in medical circles that ulcers are caused not so much by what the person eats as by "what eats" the person. Of course, after ulcers develop they are aggravated by certain foods and emotional upsets.

Another picture in Dr. English's book portrays the emotions that can cause a tightening of the muscular outlet of the stomach. Fear, love need (need for security), and sorrow will be taken up in later chapters. Also pictured are jealousy, envy, self-centeredness, ambition, frustration, rage, resentment and hatred. Observe that these disease-producing emotions are concerned with protecting and coddling the self, and they could be summarized under one title—*self-centeredness.*

Centuries before modern psychiatry discovered that carnal emotions were important factors in the causation of many psychosomatic diseases, the Bible condemned these emotions and provided a cure for them: "The activities of the lower nature are obvious. Here is a list: sexual immorality, . . . hatred, quarrelling, jealousy, bad temper, rivalry, factions, party-spirit, envy, drunkenness, orgies and things like that . . .";[1] "Those who belong to Christ Jesus have crucified the flesh with its emotions and passions."[2]

Dr. William Sadler was also impressed by the close connection between the sinful "activities of the lower nature" and many diseases. We read:

> No one can appreciate so fully as a doctor the amazingly large percentage of human disease and suffering which is directly traceable to worry, fear, conflict, immorality, dissipation, and ignorance—to unwholesome thinking and unclean living. *The sincere acceptance of the principles and teachings of Christ with respect to the life*

of mental peace and joy, the life of unselfish thought and clean living, would at once wipe out more than half the difficulties, diseases, and sorrows of the human race. In other words, more than one half of the present affliction of mankind could be prevented by the tremendous prophylactic power of actually living up to the personal and practical spirit of the real teachings of Christ.

The teachings of Jesus applied to our modern civilization—understandingly applied, not merely nominally accepted—would so purify, uplift, and vitalize us that the race would immediately stand out as a new order of beings, possessing superior mental power and increased moral force. Irrespective of the future rewards of living, laying aside all discussion of future life, *it would pay any man or woman to live the Christ-life just for the mental and moral rewards it affords here in this present world.* Some day man may awake to the fact that the teachings of Christ are potent and powerful in preventing and curing disease. Some day our boasted scientific development, as regards mental and moral improvement, may indeed catch up with the teachings of this man of Galilee.[3]

Shakespeare knew enough of the Bible and psychiatry to recognize that people can become sick from unconfessed sin. It was the memory of the murder of Duncan that produced psychosomatic overtones in Lady Macbeth. When Macbeth asked the physician about her illness, he replied:

> "No so sick, my lord,
> As she is troubled with thick-coming fancies,
> That keep her from her rest."[4]

The doctor was then asked the same question put to many a physician today:

> Canst thou not minister to mind diseas'd,
> Pluck from the memory a rooted sorrow,
> Raze out the written troubles of the brain,
> And with some sweet oblivious antidote
> Cleanse the stuff'd bosom of that perilous stuff
> Which weighs upon the heart?[5]

A man about forty years of age came into my office one evening. His stomach was bothering him and he could not sleep. It seemed as though he might have to give up his job and would be unable to support his family of three. When he came into my office, I did not detect any bodily ailment, but I recognized that he was on the verge of a serious nervous breakdown.

After telling me about some of the things that he felt had caused his trouble, he said, "Doctor, I have done other things that would put me behind bars."

I recognized that we were dealing with something far beyond the reach of a tranquilizer. I told him so and advised him to bow his head on my desk, confess, and ask his heavenly Father for forgiveness.

He did just that, simply and earnestly. Immediately and miraculously God removed "that perilous stuff, which weighs upon the heart." Several years have passed, and the man has not lost a day from his work. He is happy and buoyant. His trouble had not been caused by anything he was eating; it had stemmed from elements gnawing at his vitals.

Psychiatrist Sadler writes, "A clear conscience is a great step toward barricading the mind against neuroticism." Psychologist Henry C. Link also sees the connection between sin and disease: "The emphasis on sin has largely disappeared from the teachings of religion . . . at the very time when psychology has discovered its importance and extended its meaning."[6]

One may ask, "If an individual is converted and crucifies everything in his life that is contrary to God's Word, will that individual then be free of the diseases caused by jealousy, envy, self-centeredness, resentment and hatred?"

An episode about a person I know might answer that question. The woman was a missionary in India and under great burden for the immoral conditions that existed there. She prayed about them, but spent many an hour lamenting to her husband and others about the deplorable conditions. Let us assume she was justified in resenting the people responsible for the state of affairs; but the point is, *she did resent them.*

Her resentment tightened up the muscular ring at the outlet of her stomach, and she developed an ulcer. One day that ulcer began to bleed and it bled for about six days until that woman was almost exsanguinated. Here was a fine Christian woman who loved the Lord, who had crucified self, and was in full-time service for the Lord. Yet she developed an ulcer and nearly died from hemorrhage.

By changing a few details, the same story could be told of tens of thousands of professed Christians who, instead of bleeding ulcers, come down with one of the psychosomatic diseases already listed. Consecrations made at an altar are not sufficient. There must be a daily crucifixion of self, and obedience to all of God's commandments, if one is to be freed from these diseases.

Furthermore, human beings are not perfect in knowledge. We can still make errors in judgment and in attitudes toward others. Verily, verily, in proportion as we understand and obey the directions in the Guidebook we shall be blessed in mind and body.

Applicable here is an admonition from the Letter to the Hebrews: "Let it be your ambition to live at peace with all men and to achieve holiness 'without which no man shall see the Lord.' Be careful that none of you fails to respond to the grace which God gives, for if he does there can very easily spring up in him a bitter spirit which is not only bad in itself but can also poison the lives of many others."[7]

What a person eats is not as important as the bitter spirit, the hates, and the feelings of guilt that eat at him. A dose of baking soda in the stomach will never reach these acids that destroy body, mind and soul.

The Bible doesn't merely treat the disease-producing factors of envy, self-centeredness, resentment, hatred and immorality, but it strikes at the cause with an effective and curative manner: "Those who belong to Christ have crucified their old nature with all that it loved and lusted for."[8]

CHAPTER 11

"The High Cost of Getting Even"

I RECEIVED MUCH INSPIRATION FOR THIS CHAPTER FROM Dale Carnegie's account of a trip to Yellowstone Park and a visit to the place where the grizzly bears are fed.[1] He did not have to wait long before a grizzly bear came into a clearing where garbage had been dumped to entice him. The guide told the group that the grizzly bear can whip any animal in the West with the possible exceptions of the buffalo and Kadiak bear. That night, as Dale Carnegie sat with the other tourists in the bleachers, he noticed that there was only one animal the grizzly would allow to eat with him—a *skunk*. Of course, the grizzly could have won in any fight with a skunk. He resented the skunk and yearned to get even with him for his brazen impudence. But he didn't. Why? Because he knew there would be *the high cost of getting even.*

Smart grizzly! Certainly much smarter than many human beings who spend weary days and sleepless nights brooding over their resentments and trying to hatch ways to squelch someone. Man doesn't ever seem to learn that the high cost of getting even may be toxic goiter, strokes of apoplexy, and fatal heart attacks.

One day a man came into my office with his fourteen-year-old boy. The father said to me, "I only came to get some more pills for my wife's colitis."

Immediately the youngster asked, "Well, Dad, who has Ma been colliding with now?"

Is there any connection between this distressing diarrhea of blood and mucous and our "colliding" with people and then trying to get even? The preponderance of evidence favors the view that a disordered emotional life is the primary disturbance in cases of colitis. Flare-ups of mucous colitis can often be caused and perpetuated by "collisions" with others. Two authorities on the subject write: "Murray noted that the onset and each exacerbation of the disease occurred during periods of stressful life situations. Many investigators have corroborated his findings. Experimental studies have demonstrated the relationship between life stress and ulceration of the colonic mucosa of man."[2]

A study at one hospital revealed, through personal interviews with patients suffering from mucous colitis, that resentment was the most prominent personality characteristic, occurring in ninety-six per cent of the victims.[3]

The more serious ulcerative colitis also can be caused by emotional turmoil. The ulcers in the colon can truly plague the sufferer, who often gets little help from any medication. The only surgical procedure of any avail is the surgical removal of the colon and entire rectum, a high price to pay for getting even with an enemy.

For centuries scoffers have ridiculed the advice of Jesus, "Love your enemies," as being impractical, idealistic and absurd. Now psychiatrists are recommending it as a panacea for many of man's ills.

When Jesus said, "Forgive seventy-times seven," He was thinking not only of our souls, but of saving our bodies from ulcerative colitis, toxic goiters, high blood pressure, and scores of other diseases. The advice of the Great Physician appears to have percolated even into the hard-boiled bulletin of a Milwaukee police department. "If selfish people try to take advantage of you, cross them off your list, but don't try to get even. When you try to get even, you hurt yourself more than you hurt the other fellow."[4]

Booker T. Washington, who became famous in spite of prejudice against his color, and who was insulted times without number, wrote, "I will not let any man reduce my soul to the level of hatred."

The famous physiologist, John Hunter, knew what anger could do to his heart: "The first scoundrel that gets me angry will kill me." Some time later, at a medical meeting, a speaker made assertions that incensed Hunter. As he stood up and bitterly attacked the speaker, his anger caused such a contraction of the blood vessels in his heart that he fell dead.

In life's frog ponds, perhaps we are able to out-croak our fellows, but it might truthfully be written on many thousands of death certificates that the victims died of "grudgitis." We have heard people say, from between clenched teeth, "I'll get even with that skunk if it's the last thing I ever do!" Too often it is exactly that.

I am reminded of a perky old lady, about eighty years old, who came to me at regular intervals to have her blood pressure checked. It usually hovered around 200, but on one particular day it soared to 230. Inwardly I was startled. However I said, calmly, "Your blood pressure is up today."

With a smile she answered, "I can easily account for that. I just had a heated argument with another patient in your waiting room."

Think of it: that cultured, intelligent woman could well have blown a cerebral "fuse" and suffered a fatal stroke, simply because she wanted to get even verbally with a man noted for his provocative chatter. Her diagnosis of the spectacular rise of her blood pressure was correct. Arguments and verbal duels cause many and aggravate all cases of high blood pressure.

The methods we use in retaliation vary. My one-year-old granddaughter, when peeved, puts out her little hands and claws the air in front of her. Some babies, when frustrated, will beat their heads against the floor. Because a baby can't see his head, it is the last part of the anatomy to be recognized as belonging to him.

Most of us cannot remember when we tried to get even with our parents by pounding our heads on the floor. However, some of us can recall how we tried to spite our parents by refusing to eat our meals. Our parents had to tell us many times that we were spiting nobody but ourselves before that obvious fact penetrated our little numbskulls.

Within the past few years, I have treated three adolescents who tried to get even with their schoolmates by punching them. None of the youngsters on the receiving end of the punches needed any medical attention, but the three boys who did the punching suffered fractures of the bones in their hands.

A few years ago I knew a college student—we shall call him Pierre—who suffered a great deal from a burning sensation and distress in his upper abdomen. I gave him the newest, most effective medication but he obtained only partial and transient relief. Going to several specialists afforded no further relief and extensive X ray studies revealed no pathology. After observing his rather tense personality pattern for several months, I felt that some emotional strain might be at the bottom of his trouble. Of course, he denied most emphatically that he was under any tension.

Pierre was a puzzle until another student told me about hearing him speak in a nearby city. Most of his talk had been devoted to a harangue describing how his grandfather had been wronged and defrauded by some people many years ago. He sought to get even with the offenders by frequent and fiery denunciations. The student who was in the audience said Pierre stood, rigid and tense as a board, and talked for over an hour, the perspiration flowing in streams down his face. Not once did he stop to wipe his face. When he finished, his collar was wilted and his shirt soaked.

When Pierre came to my office the next time I asked him again if he was under any strain or held any grudges against people. All these he denied. Then I reminded him of that talk that had been reported to me. I suggested to him that his intense desire to get even with the enemies of his grandfather was probably causing his stomach trouble. I used pictures to explain how cerebral stress can tighten up the muscular outlet of the stomach to cause indigestion. Pierre's desire for revenge was so intense that he refused to give up his resentments. Paying the price with wretched days and sleepless nights, he fattened his grudges by repeated rehearsals to every available auditor. His only concern was to learn the name of the student who had given me the information. He actually pleaded with me for that name because he wanted to give the boy a tongue lashing.

Finally, Pierre's abdominal distress bothered him so much throughout the year that his grades and personality were hurt and prevented him from returning to college.

Going up in the age scale, I recall a professional man who, when bested in an argument with his wife, would try to get even with her by grinding his teeth together. It is still a mystery to me how he thought he was spiting her by grinding and tearing the fillings out of his own teeth. That wasn't even tooth for tooth.

Many chronological years separated this man from the diaper state, yet in the area of interpersonal relationships he wasn't smarter than the vindictive baby who pounds his own head on the floor. The similarity of the two might be explained, I suppose, on the basis that they each possessed an innate carnal nature.

Most of us do not retaliate against others by pounding our heads on the floor or grinding our teeth together. Neither do we shoot one another or give doses of rat poison. That isn't Scriptural—or legal! The most common way people get even with others is by talking about them. Of course, that isn't Scriptural either, but it has the advantage of keeping us clear of the electric chair.

Running people down does not keep us free from a host of diseases of body and mind. The verbal expression of animosity toward others calls forth certain hormones from the pituitary, adrenal, thyroid, and other glands, an excess of which can cause disease in any part of the body.

Many diseases can develop when we fatten our grudges by rehearsing them in the presence of others.

The moment I start hating a man, I become his slave. I can't enjoy my work any more because he even controls my thoughts. My resentments produce too many stress hormones in my body and I become fatigued after only a few hours of work. The work I formerly enjoyed is now drudgery. Even vacations cease to give me pleasure. It may be a luxurious car that I drive along a lake fringed with the autumnal beauty of maple, oak and birch. As far as my experience of pleasure is concerned, I might as well be driving a wagon in mud and rain.

The man I hate hounds me wherever I go. I can't escape his tyrannical grasp on my mind. When the waiter serves me porterhouse steak with French fries, asparagus, crisp salad, and strawberry shortcake smothered with ice cream, it might as well be stale bread and water. My teeth chew the food and I swallow it, but the man I hate will not permit me to enjoy it.

King Solomon must have had a similar experience, for he wrote: "Better a dish of vegetables, with love, than the best beef served with hatred."[5]

The man I hate may be many miles from my bedroom; but more cruel than any slave driver, he whips my thoughts into such a frenzy that my innerspring mattress becomes a rack of torture. The lowliest of the serfs can sleep, but not I. I really must acknowledge the fact that I am a slave to every man on whom I pour the vials of my wrath.

Is it because human beings are dumber than grizzly bears that they can fill every moment in twenty-four hours with thoughts that fume like nitric acid and corrode as deeply? Or is man controlled far more than he realizes by an inner force that he recognizes and calls "Old Nick"?

I think Jesus gave the answer when James and John wanted Him to call down fire on a Samaritan village because the Samaritans wouldn't give them lodging. These disciples were believers in and followers of Jesus. Yet, mind you, these Christians, smarting from the sting of racial discrimination, were so full of carnality that they besought the Lord to call down fire on the village. The Lord rebuked them by saying, "Ye know not what manner of spirit ye are of."[6]

Before Pentecost, Peter also had an innate evil spirit.

In the Garden of Gethsemane, Peter, convulsed with fiery vengeance, tried to cut off the head of one of the opposition party. He wasn't the first or the last carnal theologian who has retaliated by cutting off heads.

What a complete transformation occurred in James, John and Peter after they crucified self and were filled with the Holy Spirit. The old spirit of getting even was replaced by the Holy Spirit of Christ who, when He was reviled, reviled not again.

The seventh chapter of Acts describes how Stephen, "being full of the Holy Spirit," reacted when he was stoned. Stoning was a horrible and painful way to kill a man, but Stephen was devoid of the spirit of revenge. Bleeding and bruised, he summoned his last bit of energy to get on his knees and pray, "Lord, lay not this sin to their charge."[7] How many of us, stoned by a vicious mob, would be primarily interested in praying with our last breath for their spiritual welfare?

We can partly answer that question by taking a little inventory. Have we been engaged in hurling back the stones that came our way? Have we, in our conversations, been trying to cut off heads or call down fire upon those who have given us a rough time? How have we reacted to some of our associates who either purposely or ignorantly did something we didn't like? Did we slam the door, refuse to go down to eat, sit and pout the rest of the evening, or run them down? An honest appraisal should make it clear whether we truly possess the Holy Spirit of Christ.

Failure to possess His Spirit will make us susceptible to many diseases of body and mind, because when we are shamefully wronged by someone, we can't resist the temptation to get even—although it means paying the high price of a pound of our own flesh. Christ can crucify the carnal spirit if we drive the spikes into everything in our lives that He marks for destruction. Then we are candidates for His baptism with the Holy Spirit.

Paul, who was convicted as he witnessed the stoning of Stephen and heard his prayer, outlines the steps toward getting rid of the disease-producing spirit of retaliation:

> So put to death those members that are on earth. . . . Once you moved among them, when you lived in them; but off with them all now, off with anger, rage, malice,

slander. . . . you have stripped off the old nature with its practices, and put on the new nature. . . . be clothed with compassion, kindliness, humility, gentleness, and good temper—forbear and forgive each other in any case of complaint; as Christ forgave you, so must you forgive. And above all you must be loving, for love is the link of the perfect life.[8]

"None of these diseases" is the promise available to us only if we "have stripped off the old nature with its practices" of getting even.

CHAPTER 12

Eggs—Just Eggs

"DOCTOR, MY WIFE AND I HAVE DRIVEN THIRTY MILES TO talk with you. Neither one of us knew a sick day until a few months ago when we developed insomnia. We both take sleeping capsules now, sometimes two or more a night, but we don't think that is the answer. I began to develop pains in the pit of my stomach, but I had an X ray and there is no trouble there. My wife started to have pains over her heart, but a specialist examined her and said there wasn't anything wrong. We drove over here this afternoon to see if you could help us."

They were a pleasant looking couple in their seventies who had retired from teaching school. I have never seen them before. I was very busy that afternoon and was a little nonplussed about helping them in the short time at my disposal.

After I had asked the woman a few questions and made a superficial examination without finding anything wrong, she pulled a letter out of her pocket. "Doctor, you may think I am foolish, but our troubles seemed to start right after we got this letter. Here it is, read it.'

Dear George,
I understand that you are selling some eggs to Harry Bickerstaff. You people ought to know that I have invested considerable money in the chicken business and am able to supply more eggs to the people of this little hamlet than they can eat. You ought to know that my business is hurt by your dabbling around with a few hens and selling eggs to Harry. I think you ought to stop.

Manning Caspar

Her eyes were wet with tears when I looked up at her. She continued, "We felt we had a right to sell those eggs to Harry because he preferred our Rhode Island brown eggs to the white ones. But from that day Manning Caspar has refused to speak to us when we see him on the street. We feel terrible because we never had an experience like this. We have been upset over the whole matter. I think our whole trouble stems from—eggs—just eggs."

When she suggested that they go home and give up their egg business. I told her it might be worth a trial. Several months later the couple's daughter told me they had done just that and they had never felt so well in their lives. They stopped taking sleeping capsules and did not have an ache or a pain.

Of course, they had a perfect right to continue to sell eggs. Perhaps it was a foolish thing for them to give in to Manning Caspar. Or was it? They had already spent close to two hundred dollars for X rays and other examinations, while their profits from the eggs amounted to only a few dollars. In dollars and cents it wasn't a paying business. Besides, they were losing their peace of mind, the value of which is priceless.

I tell the following story without documentation. A friend was surprised to discover that a minister had given up his pulpit several years before and was practicing medicine. My friend asked the man why he had done it.

"I took up the practice of medicine because I discovered that people will pay more money to care for their bodies than for their souls," he answered.

Some years later the man gave up medicine and became an attorney. Perplexed, my friend again asked for a reason and received this reply: "I took up the practice of law because I discovered that people will pay more money to get their own way than for either body or soul."

How right he was! Countless people today are ruining body, mind and soul because they are bent on having their own selfish ways. Worthwhile is the saying that a man is a fool who can't be angry, but a man is wise who won't be angry.

A man and his wife avoided unhappiness, insomnia and disease because they put the inspired admonitions of God's Bible ahead of their own right to sell eggs: "And whosoever shall compel thee to go one mile, go with him two."[1] Foolish? To walk an extra mile and insure peace of mind and unbroken sleep night after night? Any of us who have done it can testify to the refreshing medical benefits we have experienced in our own bodies. Jesus, in giving this command, must have been thinking of our bodies and minds as well as our souls. "And if any man would go to law with thee, and take away thy coat, let him have thy cloak also."[2]

Such a course is hard on our pride, but it is highly beneficial to our health and happiness. Each of us must decide whether we are going to cater to our pride or to our health.

CHAPTER 13

"Love or Perish"

IN A PREVIOUS CHAPTER WE MENTIONED DR. ENGLISH'S book. In it he listed the following disease-producing emotions: jealousy, envy, self-centeredness, ambition, rage, frustration, resentment and hatred. Nineteen hundred years ago, the Apostle Paul not only warned against these emotions but also gave the antidote—love. It is coincidental, but Dr. English lists these emotions in somewhat the same order that Paul did many centuries before:

Dr. English	*Apostle Paul*[1]
Jealousy and envy	"love envieth not"
self-centeredness	"love vaunteth not itself, is not puffed up"
ambition	"doth not behave itself unseemly, seeketh not its own,"
frustration, rage, resentment, hatred	"is not provoked"

Love is the one and only antidote that can save man from the many diseases produced by the emotions of our evil nature. Psychiatrist Smiley Blanton emphasized this fact in the title of one of his books, *Love or Perish*. Without love—that thoughtfulness and keen consideration of others—man is likely to perish from a variety of diseases of mind and body.

An internationally known psychiatrist, Alfred Adler, writes, "The most important task imposed by religion has always been, 'Love thy neighbor. . . .' It is the individual who is not interested in his fellow man who has the greatest difficulties in life and provides the greatest injury to others. It is from among such individuals that all human failures spring."[2] Dr. Adler based these sweeping conclusions on a careful analysis of thousands of patients. He observed that a lack of love was observed in "all human failures."

This is in line with Biblical teaching. Love was the cornerstone of the Old Testament. Jesus did not disturb that stone but made it the cornerstone of the New Testament when he said, "Thou shalt love the Lord thy God with all thy heart, and with all thy soul, and with all thy mind. This is the great and first commandment. And a second like unto it is this, Thou shalt love thy neighbor as thyself. On these two commandments the whole law hangeth, and the prophets."[3]

When I quote the Bible and Dr. Adler to patients who are suffering physically and mentally from a lack of love, some of them retort that it is very difficult to change one's feelings—to change hate to love. That is true. Psychologists support this view, claiming that the will does not have complete control over the emotions. However, these psychologists also state that the will has good control over our actions. Our wills, therefore, largely do have the power to decide what we do and what we don't do. That is fortunate, because actions, over which we do have power, can change our feelings. Jesus said, "Love your enemies, bless them that curse you, do good to them that hate you. . . ."[4] Do something good for your enemy and it will surprise you to find how much easier it is to love him. This is the Scripturally and psychologically sound method of changing our feelings. It will work as many wonders as were ever ascribed to Aladdin's lamp.

"Do good to them that hate you." Impossible? Not if you follow some easy directions. The first step in the performance of the impossible is to walk out into your kitchen. Now, you *can* do that. You have done it many times and you can walk there again.

Step number two! Make up a lemon meringue pie as delicious as one on a magazine cover. Or make a pecan pie if that is your forte. Actually the kind isn't too important as long as you dress up that pie as though it were going on exhibition. You have made your pie. So far so good! By that time you will begin to feel a little better.

Give your feet the sternest look they ever got, and inform them in a tone of authority, "Feet, you are going to carry me and this pie to Mrs. Quirk's. Yes, I know you haven't been there in many a year, but you are going today."

Off you go. As you begin your adventure to seek the golden fleece of love, you feel strangely different. You feel warm, behind and a little to the left of your wishbone. You sense something wonderful happening inside. It gives you the same anticipation as the sight of icicles melting in the April sun.

Across the railroad tracks you go and down the dingy alley called Depot Street. You begin to understand Mrs. Quirk's attitude a little better as a heavy, noisy freight train passes, shaking houses and sidewalks, as the black soot soils your immaculate white gloves, and as dirty, boisterous children send shivers up your spine with their shrieks and cursing.

"Yes," you say to yourself, "if I had to live here, I think I would be irritable, too."

As you go up the steps, you cannot help smiling at the vastly new role you are playing. You rap on the door and wait. To Mrs. Quirk's truly surprised look, you present your peace offering with a nice smile that you decide to throw in for good measure.

A little chat in the living room, a cordial invitation for her to visit you, then on leaving a mutual hug and kiss—the fervor and spontaneity of it surprises both of you. You sense that a divine miracle has happened inside you because the love of God is truly coursing through your whole being. The impossible has happened! On your way home you feel like skipping along the street, as you did when you were a carefree girl. Inside is the spirit of singing and summer, absent for many a year.

You feel so well you decide you don't need to stop at the doctor's to take that "shot" for your frayed nerves. They aren't frayed any more. You never felt better in your life—even the pain in your back is gone.

> He drew a circle that shut me out—
> Heretic, rebel, a thing to flout.
> But Love and I had the wit to win:
> We drew a circle that took him in.[5]

"Love your enemies, do good to them that hate you." That may be a very bitter tonic to swallow but you will discover that when it reaches the heart, it will be surprisingly invigorating and exhilarating. You can love; you need not perish. By *doing* good you can change hate to love.

Obedience to the Lord in loving others, even the unlovely, will save you from a host of debilitating and serious diseases. Only when such love exists between individuals, between races, and between nations is there any hope for the world.

CHAPTER 14

Cats and Crocodiles

WHEN A CAT UNEXPECTEDLY ENCOUNTERS A DOG, THE hairs on the back of the cat stand on end. Its heart beats much faster, the blood pressure is raised, and breathing is accelerated. Adrenaline and other glandular products are immediately squirted into the blood stream because the emotional center, aroused by fear, sends lightning-quick messages of alarm to all parts of the body. The body's response to these messages is called the *alarm reaction.*

A close relative to the cat is the lion, which we have often seen in the zoo. In his cage he restlessly paces back and forth hundreds of times in a day. He is fearful, fidgety and frustrated. When he stops a moment to peer through the bars, his expression is anxious and there are deep vertical furrows in his forehead—the exact brow and image of a man who is making out his annual income tax return.

In another part of the zoo is the crocodile, quite a contrast to the lion. Mr. Crocodile lies there, motionless as an old log; rarely does he even blink an eye. He is the animalization of tranquility. He certainly doesn't worry about what the Lyons might say about him; neither is he trying to keep up with the Barrs. Bumps and blemishes on his face he has aplenty, but he has never shed any crocodile tears over them.

How long do these two different animals live? In one zoo I saw a lion that was twenty-five years old. His eyes were dim and his gait was unsteady. He was truly decrepit and sorely in need of dentures. At only twenty-five he was ready for the boneyard.

Is the crocodile old at twenty-five? Not at all! He lives long after the bones of the lion are dried and bleached.

Why are these two animals so vastly different in their

life spans? Dr. George Crile gave a group of doctors the answer in his Cleveland Clinic Museum. He had mounted many stuffed animals from all over the world, and by the side of each animal were exact replicas of its adrenal and thyroid glands.

The lion had very large adrenal glands. He had lived a life of great stress and alarm reactions were frequent occurrences. The lion's emotional center was ever calling for plenty of adrenaline for his long hard flights after swift antelope or fierce fights with other lions and African buffaloes. The lion had a large thyroid gland, indicating that he had packed the hours with strenuous activity.

In marked contrast these same glands in the crocodile were very small. His emotional center had not been making rapid demands for their products, and adrenaline had not repeatedly whipped his heart to full-throttle speed. Nor had adrenaline been raising the blood pressure and prematurely hardening the arteries.

In a human being the number of alarms sent out from the emotional center determines the size of stress glands such as the adrenal and thyroid. The New York State Department of Health published photographs of two human adrenal glands. One gland was normal in size, the other hypertrophied and greatly enlarged, "a result of stress."[1] The individual from whom the enlarged gland was removed probably died many years ahead of his time because the increased supply of adrenaline played havoc with one or more of his bodily functions. He not only shortened his days, but his days were likely filled with emotional turmoil.

One also must remember that the adrenal and thyroid glands are normally beneficial and necessary. If one awakes at night to the fact that a burglar is in the house, fear arouses the emotional center to send out messages to these glands for an increased supply of their hormones to enable the individual's heart to beat faster and to give him more energy for either a fight or a flight. This reserve of energy made available by the glands can be lifesaving if one is running from a lion or crossing a busy highway.

However, if a person sits at high noon in the security of his own home and allows his mind to think of burglars and charging bulls, his emotional center will send out identical alarm messages to the glands, heart and blood-pressure centers, as it would if the individual were actually attacked. Although the body needs an excess of hormones for genuine emergency situations, an excessive and frequent production of hormones over weeks and months results in deleterious responses.

The stresses of living are not nearly as responsible for a host of debilitating diseases as are our faulty reactions to those stresses. The office of a physician is filled with people suffering from nearly every disease in the book because their minds are beset by a thousand worries about their finances, their health or their children.

Sometimes it is the doctor who suffers. Recently I was faced with a loss of some money. The loss was on my mind when I went to bed and it awakened me about 4 A.M. The next night I didn't sleep well because I was

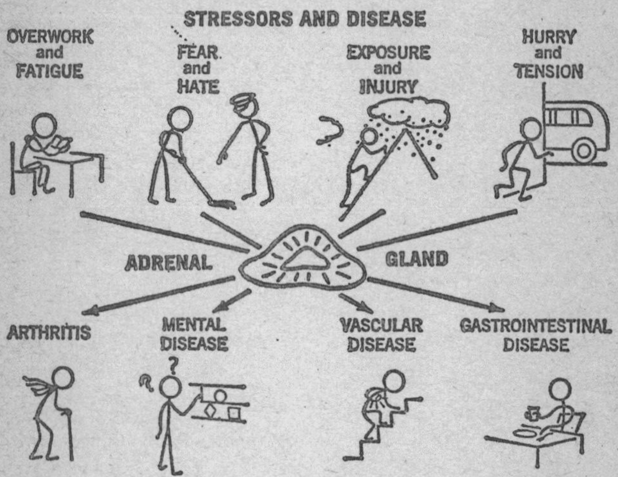

Based on a chart that appeared in *New York State Health News,* February, 1955.

depressed. I am sure my adrenal and other glands were pumping an excess of deleterious hormones into my system. I think my worrying would have continued for a long time, but on the second morning I had immediate relief from my depressed feelings when I began to practice this verse from the Bible: "Be thankful, whatever the circumstances may be."[2] Before I read that verse I was the victim of circumstances; afterwards I was the master of them.

I experienced far more relief than I would have gained from a sedative or a tranquilizer, which can give no inner peace and only temporarily blocks some of the impulses going out from the emotional center. Much more helpful and permanent is another prescription from the Book of books: "Don't worry over anything whatever; tell God every detail of your needs in earnest and thankful prayer, and the peace of God, which transcends human understanding, will keep constant guard over your hearts and minds as they rest in Christ Jesus."[3]

I know some words that are a prescription worth a thousand dollars, and I have prescribed them many times to sick men and women. Actually they are worth far more to anyone who memorizes them and determines that they shall be the standard of what he thinks and talks about: "Finally, brethren, whatsoever things are true, whatsoever things are honest, whatsoever things are just, whatsoever things are pure, whatsoever things are lovely, whatsoever things are of good report; if there be any virtue, and if there be any praise, think on these things."[4]

CHAPTER 15

You're As Old As Your Arteries

IN RUNNING LIFE'S GAUNTLET OF MANY KILLERS, THE runner is offered much help by medical science. He can now get safely past Mr. Diabetes by blinding him with a few squirts of insulin. Often Mr. Cancer can be eliminated by the talents of a surgeon. Even Mr. Pneumonia can now be liquidated by shooting him with penicillin.

But along that line, successfully defying medical weapons and wielding a bigger cutlass with every passing year, stands Mr. Arteriosclerosis. In fact, recent statistics reveal that this one savage alone scalps fifty-four per cent of all gauntlet runners.[1]

One can understand how diseased arteries are responsible for so many deaths when he knows that bad arteries are the basic cause of strokes of apoplexy, of coronary heart attacks, of angina pectoris, of gangrene of the bowel and legs, of certain kidney diseases, as well as other fatal conditions. Arteries cause widespread trouble because their openings become clogged and the blood clots in them. Since living tissue requires blood, dire results and death follow quickly when the body's blood supply is cut off. If the arteries to the vital organs of the body could only be kept open, half of the people who now die would go on living.

Truly a man is as old as his arteries. Arteriosclerosis has properly been called "Everybody's Disease."

What can we do to dodge man's most savage killer? Medical literature abounds with studies showing the importance of reducing a fatty substance called cholesterol. Cholesterol tumors form in the walls of blood vessels and obstruct the openings of the arteries. These tumors are called *atheromas*, hence the term *atherosclerosis* for the most important type of arteriosclerosis.

At this writing great emphasis is being placed on reducing cholesterol in the blood, since there appears to be a close connection between high levels of cholesterol and atherosclerosis. Many [illegible] studies show that the important agents that increase this dangerous cholesterol in the blood are:

1. Eating fat of animals
2. Overweight
3. Smoking
4. Carnal emotions and stress.

In the past few years medical science has awakened to the fact that the eating of animal fat is an important cause of arteriosclerosis. This fat forms the tiny, fatty, cholesterol tumors within the walls of the arteries, which hinder the flow of blood. Now, in this decade, magazines, radio and TV are broadcasting the good news that we can reduce the ravages from man's greatest killer by cutting down our intake of animal fats. Happy as we are with the fact that medical science has arrived, we may be amazed to discover that our ultramodern research is about thirty-five hundred years behind the Book of books:

"And the Lord spake unto Moses, saying, Speak unto the children of Israel, saying, Ye shall eat no manner of fat, of ox, or of sheep, or of goat. And the fat of the beast . . . may be used in any other use: But ye shall in no wise eat of it."[2] Because the Lord wanted to emphasize the tremendous danger of arteriosclerosis, He repeated his previous admonition not to eat animal fat.[3]

Overweight is another important factor in the

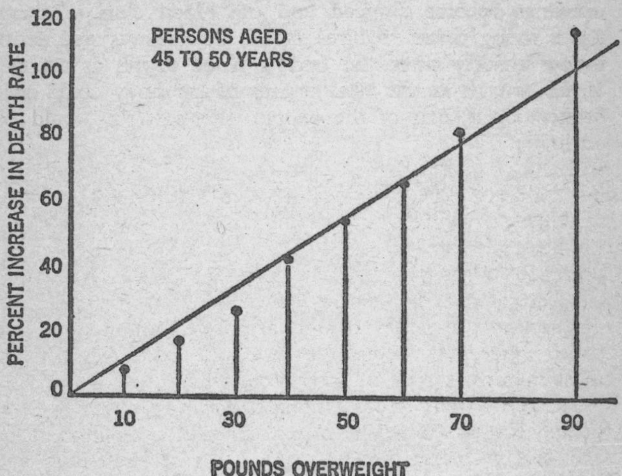

Pounds overweight	Increase in death rate over average, %
10	8
20	18
30	28
40	45
50	56
60	67
70	81
90	116

formation of cholesterol plaques within the arteries. Since overweight is composed of fat, the obese already have plenty of animal fat under their own skins. In a recent textbook we read: "It is no new doctrine that gluttons have a relatively high morbidity and mortality from vascular disease. . . . More recent evidence has strengthened this traditional impression. It is stated with statistical support that the obese have a greater incidence of hypertension (high blood pressure) and that atherosclerotic plaques develop earlier and more abundantly in the overfed."[4]

Centuries before, the inspired Apostle Paul wrote to Titus who was preaching in Crete: "A prophet from their own people said of them, Cretans are . . . lazy gluttons. This testmony is true. For this reason correct them sternly, so they may be sound in the faith. . . ."[5]

The Bible has many other references, direct and indirect, which warn against intemperance in eating. Obedience to the warnings would make for efficiency, pleasant appearance, character building, happiness and longevity.

Smoking also increases the cholesterol in the blood. This fact could well explain why, in a study of 187,000 men over a period of forty-four months, it was discovered that one third of the coronary deaths were attributable to smoking.[6] The United States' vital statistics for 1957 revealed that arteriosclerotic heart disease killed 452,507 people, and one can assume that smoking alone was responsible for about 150,000 of these unfortunate deaths.[7]

How can smoking increase cholesterol in the blood? Philadelphia researchers have recently shown that it is the nicotine which results in the formation of the following substances, in this order: adrenaline, free fatty acids, and cholesterol. They report that both smoking and psychic stress produce adrenaline, and adrenaline calls forth from the fatty deposits of the body the slow but sure killer—cholesterol.[8] Since both smoking and psychic stress can produce adrenaline, which in turn produces cholesterol, we can now understand even the method by which smoking and psychic stress kill human beings.

Now a further word about psychic stress. Although medical science now knows the chemicals stress releases in the body to produce its lethal effects, medical science can offer little help to prevent stress and fear from affecting people.

Political science boldly asserted in 1941 that it would eliminate man's mighty enemy—fear. Former president Franklin D. Roosevelt met with the great leaders of the world and incorporated in the Atlantic Charter the Four Freedoms. This Charter bid fair to be included among the greatest doctrines of all ages because it promised to all nations Four Freedoms, one of them being freedom from fear.

Four short years after this promise of millennial blessedness, the first atomic bomb was dropped, killing thousands and subjecting tens of thousands to excruciating suffering and lingering death. Realizing that women, children and the aged were as vulnerable as the soldier in the front line trench, the world was filled with immeasurable fear such as had never before gripped mankind. H. G. Wells, reflecting the fear of that day, said, "This world is at the end of its tether. The end of everything we call life is at hand."[9]

In the years since that first devastating bomb was dropped, far mightier bombs have been developed. Stress and the diseases from fear are increasing. One authority has said there is only one chance out of five that the world would finish this century without far-reaching devastation.

Speaking before the United Nations on September 26, 1961, President John F. Kennedy said, "Every man, woman and child lives under a nuclear sword of Damocles, hanging by the slenderest of threads, capable of being cut at any moment by accident, miscalculation, or madness."

One Book offers freedom from the fear and stress of this atomic age. One Book can make the statement with confidence because it has proved its value to millions subjected to all types of fears. The Book of books abounds in assurances that have comforted and helped men and women in every walk of life:

> Surely he shall deliver thee from the snare of the fowler,
> and from the noisome pestilence.
> He shall cover thee with his feathers,
> and under his wings shalt thou trust. . . .
> Thou shalt not be afraid for the terror by night;
> nor for the arrow that flieth by day;
> Nor for the pestilence that walketh in darkness;
> nor for the destruction that wasteth at noonday.
> A thousand shall fall at thy side, and
> ten thousand at thy right hand;
> but it shall not come nigh thee.[10]

Scoffers will retort, "Don't you know the atomic bombs are so powerful now that one of them blew a small Pacific island out of the sea?" Perhaps the Lord had the inspired writer record Psalm 46 for us in this atomic day:

God is our refuge and strength,
 a very present help in trouble.
 therefore will not we fear,
Though the earth be removed,
 and though the mountains be carried into the midst
 of the sea;
Though the waters thereof roar and be troubled,
 though the mountains shake with the swelling thereof.[11]

Be still, and know that I am God;
I will be exalted among the nations,
I will be exalted in the earth.
Jehovah of hosts is with us;
The God of Jacob is our refuge.[12]

Today the world outlook is darker than at any previous time in history. Yet to the believing Christian the gloom is only an indication of the imminent and glorious return of Jesus Christ. The believer need not entertain fear. As times grow worse, he has more reason to look up, for his deliverance is close at hand.

CHAPTER 16

David and the Giant—Worry

"DOCTOR, I CAME TO YOU BECAUSE I AM ALL TUCKERED out. Before this thing hit me I could work all day and not be tired. Now, when I start across the field on the tractor, I get so weak that I stop before I get halfway across. I have to get off the tractor and lie down by the fence before I get strength to go on. That's not like me. For the past month I have been completely bushed. I have been losing weight, too."

I stared in amazement at a husky, twenty-year-old farmer. He was the type who was never sick, yet here he was wholly incapacited for work. My first thoughts were of severe anemia, leukemia, or perhaps internal bleeding.

The possibility of cancer and tuberculosis came to my mind. However, a physical examination and laboratory tests showed no organic trouble.

I questioned the young man more carefully. I discovered that his attractive fianceé was doing a little dating with another lad. Also, a man who had promised to give him a good bargain on a used car had now raised the price two hundred dollars. The fear of losing both girl and car had been causing my patient to lose his appetite, his sleep and his strength.

Yes, this unusual fatigue was entirely due to worry and anxiety. Dr. Hans Selye, a world authority on stress, has shown that long and continued stress results in exhaustion. Not work but worry makes us weary. Explaining the situation to my patient and giving him a few sedative tablets did the trick. His normal strength came back and even his appearance improved so much that he won and married the girl of his choice.

Perhaps you have had a similar experience. Some days you work hard from early morning until late at night without experiencing fatigue. Then, another day, you are frayed out by the middle of the day. The next time you have such unusual weariness, pause and think. Often you will be able to remember some emotional upset. It may not be anything more than the boss looking over your sales record and asking, "Is that the best you can do?" Or you may have worn a new dress, one you made yourself, and not a single person in the office made a comment about it.

Patients often tell me that they are just as tired upon arising as when they went to bed. Sleep refreshes our exhaustion from work, but not the weariness that stems from worry. Far too many people take their anxieties to bed with them. The best medicine for that is to count one's blessings and thank the Lord for His gifts and kindnesses.

Anxiety can manifest itself in other ways. A mother brought to me her five-year-old son, who was plastered with hives. She inquired, "Doctor, what causes my Tony to break out like this? He never had hives until the past few months. His diet has not changed."

She hesitated. When I urged her to continue, she laughed and said, "You may think I am foolish, but Tony gets hives only when he stays all day with his aunt. She moved here recently, and keeping her house spic and span has always been her god. It is true Tony is a careless youngster, but his aunt scolds and nags him constantly. Fear of her couldn't possibly—?"

"Oh, yes," I replied. "Not infrequently hives are caused by an emotional upset." I advised her to park Tony elsewhere. He has never had another attack of hives.

Then there was Mrs. Shirley Johnson, who would come into my office with one or both eyes nearly swollen shut. Her lips were swollen to three times their size. She had experienced angioneurotic edema so often that she recognized the cause: emotional stress, such as the fear of driving in city traffic or the fear and bustle of entertaining many people. The name of this condition, angio*neurotic* edema, indicates its association with stress.

Asthma can also be triggered by stress. The difficult breathing of asthma induces fear and tension which aggravate the condition a great deal by establishing a vicious circle.

A psychiatrist told of a patient who developed asthma every time he heard a church bell ring. The cause of these onsets is intriguing. His trouble began several years before, while he was waiting for his bride to arrive at the church. As the church bell was ringing, a messenger arrived with the news that his fiancée had changed her mind, and the emotional shock induced a severe attack of asthma in the man. In the years that followed, every time he heard a church bell he was seized with an attack of asthma.

The Psalmist David had more reasons than most of us to have justifiable fears. Consider his encounters with a lion, a bear, the giant Goliath, and the many times he missed death at the hands of King Saul. David saved himself from a host of psychosomatic diseases because he always put his trust in the Lord: "The Lord is my light and my salvation; whom shall I fear? The Lord is the stronghold of my life; of whom shall I be afraid? . . . Though an army should encamp against me, my heart shall not fear: though war should rise against me, I would still be confident."[1]

High blood pressure can be caused not only by hates, as previously shown, but also by worries. For this reason physicians seek to keep their patients from knowing what the pressure is when it has gone up. That knowledge could induce fear and shoot the pressure still higher, with serious results. One authority advises physicians in such cases to do

joints give a clear-cut history of emotional stress. After the disease becomes established, flare-ups and spreading of the arthritis follow emotional crises and prolonged tensions. Stresses such as breaking an engagement, getting a divorce, having financial tangles, harboring resentments, or losing a loved one, are only a few of the causative agents.

Of course, arthritis can also be caused by fatigue, injury or exposure to wet and cold, which are also properly considered stress factors. Arthritis victims number two million sufferers in the United States alone.

Many a man fears he is going to lose an acre of his farm or even a few inches of a city lot because of the claims of his neighbor. Surveyors give conflicting opinions. Foolish and impractical seem the words of Jesus to a man in this situation: "... if any man will sue thee at the law, and take away thy coat, let him have thy cloak also."[1] The disturbed man considers His advice idealistic and ill suited to a twentieth-century problem. Instead, he decides to fight it out in the courts and hires a lawyer.

During the long months before his case is called, and during the tense days of the trial and the months after the trial, his pituitary gland, his adrenals and his thyroid glands work overtime to pump their products into his system. When the judge hands down the decision, the contesting neighbor takes the man's shirt, his lawyer takes his coat, and the court costs take his trousers. All too often such a man ends up in a wheel chair for the rest of his life with a disabling arthritis—a high price to pay for refusing the Lord's advice.

Any discussion of the effect of fear on the body would not be complete without considering the effect of this emotion on the heart. I recall the case of a prominent Israeli physician who was reading a newspaper account of the murderous persecution of Jews in Russia, where many of his relatives lived. To a friend in the room, he mentioned the great fear he felt for the safety of his loved ones. A moment later he slumped over dead in his chair, a victim of a clot of the coronary artery (the artery that supplies the heart with blood).

Can fear really precipitate clotting of blood such as occurs in that most common heart killer—coronary thrombosis? Dr. David Macht gave the answer at the 1951 annual meeting of the American Medical Association in Atlantic City. In his laboratory he had measured the number of minutes required for the blood of fifty normally happy people to clot, and he compared this clotting time with the clotting time of the blood of a hundred nervous people. Here is a tabulation of his results:

	Clotting Time
50 normally happy people	8 — 12 minutes
50 apprehensive people	4 — 5 minutes
50 highly nervous people	1 — 3 minutes

Dr. Macht concluded, "It was surprising to find that such a profound influence was produced by ordinary acute and transient emotions in healthy persons."[2]

A previous chapter revealed that when arteries become partially obstructed by tiny cholesterol plaques, the flow of blood is slowed and the blood is more likely to form a clot, which completely stops the circulation. Dr. Macht showed that stress is another very important factor in causing blood to clot.

In other words, stress not only narrows the artery and greatly slows the blood flow to facilitate clotting, but it also affects the blood itself so that it is much more likely to clot. Hence, we see the almost unbelievable importance of stress in both setting the stage for and performing the act of clotting. A number of recent medical articles have emphasized the importance of stress in this condition.[3] However, we must not paint a lopsided picture of the importance of stress by ignoring the other factors that play a part in setting the stage for clotting, such as eating animal fat, overeating and smoking.

Dr. Hans Selye's definition of stress embraces not only the emotions of hate, fear and sorrow, but also includes external factors such as cold, light and noise. Many an individual who has set the stage for a fatal heart attack by overeating fatty and other foods, or smoking, or worrying, actually succumbs when he walks against a cold wind or goes out to shovel snow.

Consider the stress that my wife once experienced on our Canadian fishing trip. My wife, daughter and I arrived at Matawan, Ontario, about five o'clock on a Saturday evening. We had to catch some fish for our Sunday meals, so my daughter Linda and I rowed a boat up the treacherous Matawan Rapids, which was new territory to us. My wife stayed in the cabin to unpack and arrange things for the night. Then she sat down to await our return. Eight o'clock came, but no boat came down the swiftly moving river. Then nine o'clock, nine-thirty—still no daughter, no husband, appeared.

If my wife had become excited or hysterical, she might have developed a number of medical conditions. But the Lord reminded her of a verse in Psalm 34 which we had been memorizing on our vacation: "I sought the Lord, and he heard me, and delivered me from all my fears."[4] My wife sought the Lord and He gave her remarkable deliverance from all her fears as she sat alone on the dock in the darkness, the lantern by her side.

At ten o'clock she heard the voice of Linda behind her on the shore: "Daddy sent me by land, because he did not want to bring me down the rapids in the dark. The fish were slow in biting, but once they started they bit like a house afire!"

Still more waiting. Ten-thirty, and no boat. To my wife's calls no answer came from the dark, swirling river. She knew she was doing everything feasible by keeping the lantern on the dock. She had ample reason to fear, but the Lord gave her that peace of mind that passeth understanding. She did not panic or start off with the lantern to search for help. Instead, her faith in the Scriptural promise that the Lord had tailored for this special need gave her restful assurance. Divine strength she needed, since it was not until eleven o'clock that the evidence of her faith arrived safely at the dock.

CHAPTER 18

Cutting Man's Greatest Fear Down to Size

NEARLY EVERYBODY HAS BEEN IN A J. C. PENNEY STORE, one of the world's largest chains of drygoods stores, with seventeen hundred branches in the United States. But few people know about one of the most important events in the life of J. C. Penney, the founder.

In the crash of 1929, J. C. Penney's business was solid but he had made some unwise personal commitments. He became so worried that he couldn't sleep. Then he developed "shingles," a disorder that can cause great annoyance and severe pain. He was hospitalized and given sedatives, but got no relief and tossed all night. A combination of circumstances had broken him so completely, physically and mentally, that he was overwhelmed with a fear of death. He wrote farewell letters to his wife and son, for he did not expect to live until morning.

The next morning the great business tycoon heard singing in the hospital chapel. He pulled himself together and entered as the group was singing "God Will Take Care of You." Then followed a Scripture reading and a prayer. In Mr. Penney's own words, "Suddenly something happened. I can't explain it. I can only call it a miracle. I felt as if I had been instantly lifted out of the darkness of a dungeon into warm, brilliant sunlight. I felt as if I had been transported from hell to paradise. I felt the power of God as I had never felt it before. I realized then that I alone was responsible for all my troubles. I know that God with His love was there to help me. From that day to this, my life has been free from worry. I am seventy-one years old, and the most dramatic and glorious minutes of my life were those I spent in that chapel that morning: 'God Will Take Care of You.' "[1]

Thus, a man has been able to dwarf every fear because he saw a loving, heavenly Father—his Father—anxious and ready to take care of him in life's dilemmas.

William Ewart Gladstone, on being questioned for the secret of the unusual serenity he was able to maintain in spite of situational stresses, replied, "At the foot of my bed, where I can see it on retiring and on arising in the morning, are the words, 'Thou wilt keep him in perfect peace, whose mind is stayed on thee: because he trusteth in thee.' "[2]

Some psychiatrists have given far more than superficial help in the medical textbooks they have written for physicians. William Sadler advises physicians how to get at the cause of people's troubles:

> Prayer is a powerful and effectual worry-remover. Men and women who have learned to pray with childlike sincerity, literally talking to, and communicating with the Heavenly Father, are in possession of the great secret whereby they can cast their care upon God, knowing that He careth for us. A clear conscience is a great step toward barricading the mind against neuroticism.
>
> Many are victims of fear and worry because they fail properly to maintain their spiritual nutrition. . . . The majority of people liberally feed their bodies, and many make generous provision for their mental nourishment; but the vast majority leave the soul to starve, paying very little attention to their spiritual nutrition; and as a result the spiritual nature is so weakened that it is unable to exercise the restraining influence over the mind which would enable it to surmount its difficulties and maintain an atmosphere above conflict and despondency.[3]

He further advises physicians to encourage their patients to engage "in daily, systematic Bible reading." In fact, in his textbook for doctors, Dr. Sadler prints forty-three different verses as examples of the therapeutic value of Bible reading. We shall give only eight of them here. Each of them, if assimilated into the mind, can accomplish more than any sedative or tranquilizer:

> If we confess our sins, he is faithful and just to forgive us our sins, and to cleanse us from all unrighteousness (I John 1:9, KJV).

Come unto me, all ye that labour and are heavy laden, and I will give you rest. Take my yoke upon you, and learn of me; for I am meek and lowly in heart: and ye shall find rest unto your souls (Matthew 11:28-29, KJV).

Behold, I stand at the door, and knock: if any man hear my voice, and open the door, I will come in to him, and will sup with him, and he with me (Revelation 3:20, KJV).

Create in me a clean heart, O God; and renew a right spirit within me (Psalm 51:10, KJV).

Peace I leave with you, my peace I give unto you: not as the world giveth, give I unto you. Let not your heart be troubled, neither let it be afraid (John 14:27, KJV).

Behold, God is my salvation; I will trust, and not be afraid: for the Lord Jehovah is my strength and my song; he also is become my salvation (Isaiah 12:2, KJV).

But my God shall supply all your need according to his riches in glory by Christ Jesus (Philippians 4:19, KJV).

I can do all things through Christ which strengtheneth me (Philippians 4:13, KJV).

For he shall give his angels charge over thee, to keep thee in all thy ways. They shall bear thee up in their hands, lest thou dash thy foot against a stone (Psalm 91:11-12, KJV).

These verses become alive and real only after we have experienced them. The night I asked God, for Christ's sake, to forgive my sins, I was weighed down with a sense of guilt and fear. After a few moments of confession and forsaking of sin, the guilt and fears vanished, and a miraculous, heaven-sent joy filled my mind. Instead of long-continued and expensive trips to a psychiatrist's couch to get rid of a disease-producing *guilt complex,* I made one trip to God's altar and got rid of *guilt itself.*

The Bible says that God removes the guilt "As far as the east is from the west. . . ."[4] From that moment I felt very grateful to God, and love sprang up between us. I experienced what John wrote: "There is no fear in love; but perfect love casteth out fear. . . ."[5] As love increases, fear decreases.

Last summer as I sat in the yard, a chipmunk approached

a hole in the ground only three feet away from me. His cheeks were ballooned with food for his loved ones down in the hole. Because I was so very close, he hesitated, but not for long. His love for the young ones overcame his fear and into the hole he skipped.

Love for Christ and His Word helped Jim Vaus when he needed relief from fear. Before his conversion, Jim had been the wiretapper for the infamous underworld gang of Mickey Cohen in Los Angeles. The morning after his conversion during a Billy Graham meeting, the newspapers blazoned the story about him.

When Jim Vaus read the morning papers, he began to do some serious thinking. What action would the gangsters take about this matter? After all, Jim knew a host of secrets that might send some of the gang to the penitentiary, if not to the gas chamber. From the gang's viewpoint, Jim's conversion meant he had turned traitor to them, and he knew that a desertion with gang secrets called for speedy liquidation.

When he put down the paper, he didn't have long to wait. As he looked out the window, a big limousine stopped in front of his house. Jim recognized the men who emerged as some of the most heartless killers in the underworld. Looking carefully up and down the street, they approached his front door. Did Jim become panicky and make for the back door?

If ever a man had reason to run in fear for his life, he did. If he had been in such danger twenty-four hours earlier, he certainly would have fled—and probably would still be running. But he didn't run, because the love of God filled his being and strengthened him with a verse the Lord had given him that morning when he opened his Bible at random: "When a man's ways please the Lord, he maketh even his enemies to be at peace with him."[6]

Jim opened the door to the gunmen and they told him that a wiretapping job had been assigned to him. He must fly to St. Louis immediately, or else. Jim told them he couldn't go because the Lord had changed his heart. When he described his conversion, his visitors looked bewildered and left. Jim knew that the Lord had fulfilled the verse He had given him.

The "dread of death" is undoubtedly man's greatest fear. However, millions of men and women have gone through the valley of the shadow of death without any apprehension. John Bunyan expressed the attitude of many Christians when he wrote: "Let dissolution come when it will, it can do the Christian no harm, for it be but a passage out of a prison into a palace; out of a sea of troubles into a haven of rest; out of a crowd of enemies, to an innumerable company of true, loving, and faithful friends; out of shame, reproach, and contempt into exceeding great and eternal glory."

The Apostle Paul was able to dwarf the greatest fear of all when he looked death in the face and exultingly exclaimed, "So when this corruptible shall have put on incorruption, and this mortal shall have put on immortality, then shall be brought to pass the saying that is written, Death is swallowed up in victory. O death, where is thy sting? O grave, where is thy victory?"[7]

Truly, in every age the Spirit and Word of God have provided abundant deliverance for Christians from fears and their long trains of diseases. Even the master of all fears, *death,* should hold no terror for the believer who has his eyes on the resurrection and eternal joyful life. Only the Christian is able to heed the advice of William Cullen Bryant:

> So live, that when thy summons comes to join
> The innumerable caravan which moves
> To that mysterious realm, where each shall take
> His chamber in the silent halls of death,
> Thou go not, like the quarry-slave at night,
> Scourged to his dungeon, but, sustained and soothed
> By an unfaltering trust, approach thy grave,
> Like one that wraps the drapery of his couch
> About him, and lies down to pleasant dreams.[8]

CHAPTER 19

"See Farther Through a Tear Than Through a Telescope"

LATE ONE AFTERNOON A HEALTHY YOUNG MARRIED WOMAN received the shocking news that her husband had been instantly killed. Any of us can sympathize with her in the grief, heartache and tears that she experienced during the evening and long hours of the night when she couldn't sleep. The one who meant everything to her had been cruelly snatched away. She was so completely and irreconcilably overwhelmed with grief that she refused to listen to anything her sympathetic friends tried to say.

If chemical tests could have been made of her blood, they would have disclosed the presence of a great increase in hormones and abnormal toxins from the pituitary, thyroid and adrenal glands. That somethng was present in toxic amounts is proved by the fact that the next morning some of her fingers and her wrist joints were stiff, swollen and painful. This was the onset of an arthritis that eventually invalided the young woman.

Thus we see that not only the emotions of hate and fear are capable of causing a variety of serious and fatal diseases. The emotion of sorrow can also damage the body. Grief can trigger onsets of ulcerative colitis, rheumatoid arthritis, asthma, and many other diseases.

To prevent the minor and major diseases resulting from the inundating grief over a loved one's death, the Bible provides the greatest possible barricade. The eleventh chapter of John not only gives clear teaching on this matter but also presents public and highly dramatic proof of the veracity of the assertions made. In the village of Bethany lived Lazarus and his two sisters, Mary and Martha. When Lazarus became sick, word was sent to Jesus for help. But Jesus purposely delayed His going because He wanted to teach the world the transitory character of the state we call death. When Jesus started His trip to Bethany, He told His disciples that He was going to raise Lazarus out of his *sleep.*

The disciples thought it was rather ridiculous to make a hazardous journey to wake a sick man out of sleep. Then Jesus talked to them in the only language that they in their immaturity could understand: "Lazarus is dead."

Arriving in Bethany, Jesus revealed to a sister mourning for her dead brother another important aspect of the state that we erroneously call *death:* ". . . the believer in Me will live even when he dies, and everyone who lives and believes in Me shall never, never die. Do you believe this?"[1]

How could anybody believe that Christians never really die—that they are only asleep? Jesus knew that even His disciples and the others at Bethany would not believe such assertions without proof. A million empty human words never would have convinced anybody, but three words from the Master did: "Lazarus, come forth." Out came Lazarus, a living proof that for the Christians there is no horrible existence that we associate with the word *death.* It is only a sleep that requires His call to awaken us. Quite understandably, Christians changed the names of their graveyards to sleeping chambers (our English word "cemetery" comes from the Greek *koimeterion,* which means "a sleeping chamber").

When Jesus told those who were mourning over the dead body of Jairus' daughter, ". . . she is not dead, but sleepeth,"[2] they ridiculed Him with scornful epithets. Again He wanted to prove false the utterly hopeless view we have about the state we call *death.* So He merely took the cold and motionless girl by the hand and awakened her from the state that He calls *sleep.*

The Apostle Paul understood fully this new concept that Jesus had drilled into His disciples. In I Corinthians 15, Paul elaborates on this matter to show that all who have fallen asleep will be awakened by the trumpet call of the Master on His return to the earth. Paul also wrote to Christians in another church who had suffered the temporary loss of loved ones: "But we do not want to keep you in ignorance, brothers, about those who have fallen asleep, so you may not grieve as others do, who have no hope."[3]

Neither should we grieve today over our children and loved ones who are asleep in their chambers. Of course, we can be excused if we shed some tears over the separation. But Christians who truly believe what Jesus proved about the promise of their awakening should certainly not grieve with such bitter and tumultuous emotion that they bring down upon themselves arthritis and other diseases that the Bible enables them to avoid. It is both a wonderful privilege and a duty for believers to refrain from harboring despair and disease-producing grief when we know that our loved ones, though absent from our immediate presence, are sleeping.

One writer has expressed this temporary separation in another way: "I love to think of my little children whom God has called to Himself as away at school—at the best school in the universe, under the best teachers, learning the best things, in the best possible way."

Some may wonder why God allows His children to experience sorrow at all. Death is not a gift from God but a result of the sin of Adam—". . . death came through a man. . . ."[4] Throughout this book we have repeatedly seen that disease and death are products of sin; we can't blame God for them. Instead, we ought to give God the credit for our deliverance from the tragedy of death: "For just as in Adam all die, so in Christ shall all be made to live."[5] God is not the author of death, but the Giver of eternal life.

Not only in the future, but here in this life and now, the divine Alchemist can miraculously change a sorrowing heart of lead into a golden mellowness that sings praises through tears. A poet said, "Sorrows are our best educators. A man can see farther through a tear than through a telescope."

Is it not remarkable that the sorrows that cause devastating diseases in some people can in others develop character and maturity? Polishing is certainly not a pleasant process for the object being polished but it is a necessary procedure for every stone that becomes a gem. We admire the finished product, but we shrink from the process.

In December 1961, a letter brought sorrow to our home. For over three weeks we had not heard from our daughter who, with her husband, was engaged in missionary work in Southern Rhodesia. Then came a letter from her, written in a hospital where she had been a patient for several weeks. An examination of her spinal fluid revealed an abundance of a deadly fungus, Monilia. The well-trained English physicians had started her on a medication, but only as a gesture, for they were well aware that it had proved utterly worthless in cases of meningitic infection. They were reluctant to use a new and toxic drug because of its serious side effects.

This news from our only child, nine thousand miles away and stricken with a seemingly hopeless cerebrospinal infection, brought keen sorrow to my wife and me. Never before could we fully appreciate and sympathize with those who had lost their children.

Our grief might well have overwhelmed us if it had not been for the comfort and solace of God's Holy Spirit and the Bible. We wondered how people without Christ in their hearts were able to stand up under great sorrow. A thousand times more effective than any tranquilizer, the Lord gave us this Scriptural wonder drug: "For this slight, momentary trouble is producing for us an everlasting weight of glory that exceeds all calculations, granted we do not fasten our eyes on the visible but on the unseen; for the visible things are transitory, but the unseen things are everlasting."[6]

I saw that my crushing load of sorrow need not result in disease. Instead, it could give me "an everlasting weight of glory that exceeds all calculations. . . ." My attitude could determine whether my grief would cause a disease in me or a glorious and everlasting reward. It was my privilege to look through my tears and see farther than through any telescope to the glory of eternal verities.

Observe the condition: ". . . granted we do not fasten our eyes on the visible but on the unseen. . . ." An unreasonable condition? After all, if the Christian truly has the proper sense of proportion between the transitory things of this life, as compared to the eternal value of the life beyond, is it not a confession of doubt for him to mourn *unduly* for the passing of a loved one? Should the visible things and people of this earth assume greater value than eternal issues? Sorrow causes diseases in us because we *grieve over the past*. The Bible erases irreconcilable grief and prevents disease by telling us to *look forward to the future*.

In the weeks that followed the receipt of our daughter's first letter, the Word of God and His Spirit made life bearable for us. We had peace of mind because we had committed everything to Him.

My daughter, her husband, and their two babies were

flown home, and she was studied thoroughly in a Philadelphia hospital. No fungus or bacteria were found in repeated spinal fluid examinations, but her spinal fluid contained pus cells. Although Linda continued to have a low-grade fever, headaches, a stiff neck, and vomiting, the specialists were hesitant about starting her on antibiotics. However, after two months, several antibiotics were tried and one of them, when given in large doses, freed her from the fever and other troublesome symptoms. After a month on the high dosage, a spinal tap showed that the spinal fluid was normal in every respect.

Will Linda's meningeal infection return if the heavy doses of antibiotics are stopped? Someone has said that we do not know what the future holds but we do know who holds the future. Faith in loving Omnipotence allows one to say, with Paul, "Entertain no worry, but under all circumstances let your petitions be made known before God by prayer and pleading along with thanksgiving. So shall the peace of God, that surpasses all understanding, keep guard over your hearts and your thoughts in Christ Jesus."[7]

Linda, her husband, and all of us thank the Lord, not for the sorrow, but that out of our experience in the valley of the shadow of death, He has matured us and given "us an everlasting weight of glory that exceeds all calculations. . . ." As we keep taking our eyes from the visible and the transitory, endearing to us though they are, and look beyond to that which is eternal, we discover that faith can see farther through a tear than through a telescope.

CHAPTER 20

Mud or Stars?

> Two men look out through the same bars:
> One sees the mud, and one the stars.[1]

THIS QUOTATION WAS WRITTEN LONG BEFORE ANY OF US kicked at the slats in our cribs. However, the medical significance of it was not sensed by scientists until the past decade. The two men who looked through the same prison bars reacted in widely different fashions to the stress factors in their confinement: one was frustrated by the bars, whereas the other, subjected to the identical environment, was inspired by the stars. The frustrated man developed stress in his body and thus exposed himself to many serious, even fatal, diseases.

Physicians now recognize the great importance of internal stress in causing and aggravating a host of diseases. Because all of us are subjected to a host of stresses, it behooves us to scrutinize the subject.

Two prisoners were subjected to the same stress factors, but only one developed inner stress and exposed himself to disease. Examination of his blood would have revealed the presence of abnormal chemical compounds that were called forth as a result of his emotions of frustration, resentment, anger, hate, anxiety and fear—the same brood of carnal emotions referred to in previous chapters.

One needs to distinguish between *inner stress,* which one experiences in his body, and external *stress factors.* All of us are subjected to many, many stress factors in our daily lives, but that does not mean we have to develop inner stress with its resultant toxic chemicals and diseases. One of the men subjected to the external stress factors of prison bars was actually inspired by the stars—stars he may never have noticed before.

There are great differences in the ways people react to stress agents such as experiencing an automobile accident, speaking in public, disciplining a child, deciding the brand of refrigerator to buy, chasing the neighbor's dog out of the flower bed, or being awakened at 2 A.M. by a philandering cat. Physicians are kept busy treating people who react poorly to these and other stressful situations. Some patients develop sieges of abdominal distress that last three or four weeks and require a great deal of medication. Others suffer the agonies of severe migraine headaches, with vomiting, which incapacitate them for a day or two. A few succumb to coronary heart attacks.

On the other hand, some people who are subjected to the identical stress factors adapt so well that they experience no ill effects at all. Since we often have little control over the stress factors that daily bombard us, it is of the utmost importance that we learn to adapt properly to them if we are to save our bodies and minds from the ravages of stress and disease.

Three things must be practiced if one is to adapt successfully to life's disease-producing stressors:

1. Diversify the stressful agents
2. Avoid long exposure to such agents by resting
3. Take the proper attitude of mind.

First, it is important to remember that man can not take long or continued exposure to any one stress factor. The carpenter who pounds nails all day should not spend his evenings spading flower beds, mowing the lawn, or working in his carpentry shop. These activities would be ideal for a clerk or a lawyer.

Failure to diversify the stressful agents will sooner or later result in *fatigue,* one of the most important symptoms of stress in the body. A number of years ago I saw a diagram in a medical journal which purported to show how one could avoid fatigue. The article explained that attention should be given to three angles of life:

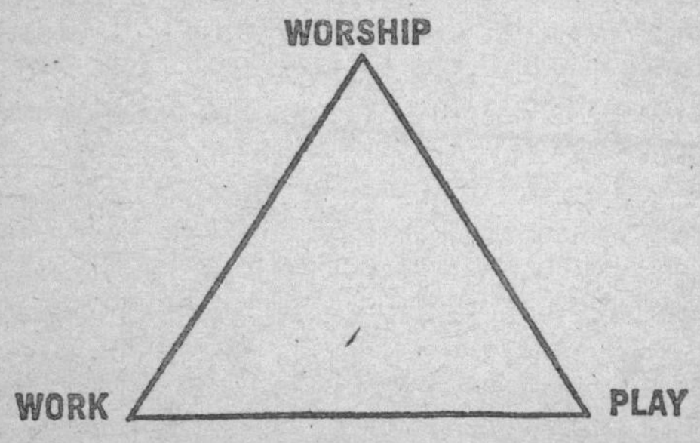

From my experience I can recall times when I worked so hard during the day that I was tempted not to go to prayer meeting because of my fatigue. Before the prayer meeting ended, however, I was surprised to find that not only had my fatigue gone, but I was rested and refreshed. Daily Bible reading, prayer and attendance at church services are of the greatest medicinal value.

Second, our attitude of mind is a most important factor in determining whether we shall suffer from exposure to life's daily stress. Our tendency in the past has been to blame our diseases on the people around us instead of blaming our troubles on our faulty reactions to those people. The sorrows and insults of daily living need not cause much trouble if we take them with the right mental attitude. Chronic brooding over sorrows and insults indicates faulty adaptation, which can cause any condition from itching feet to insanity. *The most common form of faulty reaction is self-pity.*

Actually, one shouldn't blame an unreasonable boss or teacher or marital partner for one's ulcers. Ulcers and high blood pressure are caused by internal resentments which produce toxic reactions within one's body. Take as an example my telephone, which rings dozens of times while I am trying to do a job. After the first dozen calls, I have a tendency to cringe from these repeated interruptions. Yet I know that if I allow myself to react with antagonism, the repeated ringing of a simple thing like a telephone might cause my ulcer to flare up. The stresses that hit me are not as culpable as my reaction to them. *Most of us have been guilty of generating ten dollars' worth of adrenaline over a ten-cent incident.*

In fact, while I was typing the last sentence, my telephone rang. I heard the voice of one of the college infirmary nurses: "Dr. McMillen, I have sent over to your office a girl with a dog. The dog has a fishhook in its ear. I don't know how to take it out, so I am sending her to you."

I can remember a time when my remarks to that nurse might have burned out a wire in the telephone circuit. I also know that if I had reacted with antagonism, I would have experienced a severe, pounding headache, not because of the telephone message but because of my big *reaction* to the insignificant stress—a simple, humanitarian request. A faulty reaction on my part, instead of giving me a pounding headache, could have given me a stroke of apoplexy or a fatal heart attack. Years ago my faulty adaptation to stress nearly caused my death from a bleeding ulcer.

We should remember that stress per se is usually innocent of disease causation. Furthermore, it has been shown that stress can even help to cure certain mild diseases. Dr. Hans Selye injected irritating croton oil under the skins of a large number of rats. This oil formed tender, inflammatory pouches. Selye discovered that when he subjected some of the rats to mild stresses, healing of the inflammations was hastened.[2]

I can recall many times when I had to make house calls on patients when I wasn't feeling well myself. I found out that the stress of making the trip often cured me of my minor aches and pains. However, if I had made the trip in the spirit of antagonism, my faulty reaction might have put me in the hospital for a week.

Is it not a remarkable fact that our reactions to stress determine whether stress is going to cure us or make us sick? Here is an important key to longer and happier living. We hold the key and can decide whether stress is going to work *for* us or *against* us. Our attitude decides whether stress makes us "better or bitter."

The Bible anticipated these findings by centuries. Naturally we are restless when we have to live with thorny people, or in a disagreeable environment, or when we possess aches and pains in our bodies. Thorny people, taken with a wrong attitude, can give the body any disease from boils to gallstones. Thorny people, taken with the right attitude, may free the body of certain chemicals and thus cure an illness.

Paul had a "thorn in the flesh" that gave him stress: "Thrice I invoked the Lord about this, to have it removed from me, and He told me, 'My grace is sufficient for you, for My strength comes to perfection where there is weakness.' So I am happy to take pride rather in my weaknesses, so that the power of Christ may abide upon me. I delight, therefore, in weaknesses, in insults, in needy circumstances, in persecutions and dire calamities, all on account of Christ. For when I am weak, then I am strong."[3]

There is a third factor to remember if we are to adapt successfully to the assaults of daily living: avoidance of long and continued exposure to severe stress agents, without resting. There is a limit to the stress that any person can endure, and every physician sees men and women who pay dearly in body and mind for their excessive application to work without proper rest periods. Many people could be alive today if they had heeded the admonition of Jesus to His laboring disciples: "Come ye yourselves apart into a desert place, and rest a while: for there were many coming and going, and they had no leisure so much as to eat."[4]

Many of some 31,000 Allied soldiers imprisoned in Japan and Korea in the 1940's couldn't see anything except mud. Dr. Harold Wolff states that even though these prisoners were offered enough food, "the prisoner became apathetic, listless, neither ate nor drank, helped himself in no way, stared into space and finally died." Of the 31,000 imprisoned, over 8,000 died. Dr. Wolff states that many of these deaths were caused by "despair and deprivation of human support and affection." Dr. Wolff, who is editor-in-chief of *Archives and Neurology and Psychiatry*, declares that "Hope, like faith and a purpose in life, is medicinal. This is not merely a statement of belief, but a conclusion proved by meticulously controlled scientific experiment."[5]

Another prisoner could see stars. Such a one was my esteemed Japanese friend, Dr. David Tsutada. When Japan entered World War II, the Japanese government put him in prison because of his belief in the return of the Lord to reign on this earth. The government tried to starve him to death and his weight dropped to seventy pounds. He was even confined in a cold, damp hole in a prison that was utterly filthy. As he sat on the floor, he wondered if this was the way the Lord was going to take him home to heaven. If it was, he was perfectly resigned to it. He wasn't frustrated by the bars or the mud or the Lord's apparent lack of care for him. If Dr. Tsutada had not adapted himself and resigned himself, I am convinced that the stress of self-pity, added to the severe stress of starvation, would have killed him.

While he was in prison, the Lord began to reveal to him plans for a Bible School. Dr. Tsutada worked out many details for the school while he sat in the darkness and stench of the death cell. When the war was over, he was released and immediately he put his plans into operation. Today this man has one of the finest Bible training schools in Japan. All of this transpired because he didn't fret about evildoers (Psalm 37) but trusted, committed himself to, and delighted in God's word. Dr. Tsutada created his own environment.

There were others who saw stars through prison bars. Madame Guyon reacted so well to the strain of imprisonment that out of it came writings that have inspired all Christendom.

Few people were ever behind as many bars as Helen Keller—blind, deaf and dumb—yet she became immortal in the annals of fame because she utilized her adversities as steppingstones in climbing out of her dungeon to bless a world with her spirit and love.

We should not unduly fear life's difficulties or go to great lengths to avoid them. Strong contrary winds need not blow us to destruction. In fact, the intelligent mariner can adjust his sails properly so that even adverse winds shall help him reach his goal. Contrary people can help us if we make the necessary adjustments in our mental rigging. On the water they call it *tacking,* but on land they call it *tact*.

John Bunyan forgot about the prison bars, so taken up was he with things beyond this world. He blessed not only his own soul but millions of others with that notable great seller of the centuries, *Pilgrim's Progress.* In one of his other books Bunyan gave excellent advice about preparing the mind for stresses even before they hit. Although his advice was written three hundred years ago, nothing today can surpass it:

> Moreover, it is our wisdom, that while we are at ease, have our comforts about us, let us look for troubles; afflictions *from* God, as well as *for* God, are part of our cross which we must take up daily. Sickness, death of friends, loss of estate, etc., we must look for them that we may not be surprised.
>
> So it must be our care to provide for afflictions; for to prevent them altogether we cannot; but prepare for them we may, and must, as was hinted before; to treasure up God's promises, and store our souls with graces, and spiritual comforts, and firm resolutions in God's strength, to bear up and to hold on: we need be well "shod with the preparation of the gospel of peace," Eph. 6:15.
>
> Most Christians are not mortified and crucified to the world, not acquainted with God and the promises as they ought to be, nor so resolved to follow God fully, as they

ought, and therefore are so dejected and discontented when affliction comes.[6]

Here is solid truth. Since we have shown that our attitudes of mind are more important than the daily insults of life, it is important that we condition our minds before life's major catastrophies hit us. Armies recognize this basic truth and put their troops through rigorous training. If Christians would practice such Biblical admonitions as fasting and disciplining of bodily desires, perhaps we wouldn't have so many "chocolate soldiers" who melt down when they have to undergo the hot and fierce experiences of unexpected sorrow, desertion by a mate, or financial losses.

Jacob looked at mud and grabbed for the things of mud even from the moment of his birth. He came into the world with his little baby fist reaching for the heel of his brother. As soon as he was able to trade, he created a black market on pottage and traded a little of it for his brother's birthright. He even outtricked that past master in knavery—his father-in-law.

How would you expect a character like Jacob to react to stress? When he was told that his favorite son, Joseph, had been killed, there was nothing wrong in the natural sorrow he felt, but his adaptation to the stress was very faulty because Jacob kept weeping long after he should have stopped. To those who sought to comfort him, he said, "I want to go down to the grave mourning for my son."[7] He preferred the warming balm of self-pity to facing the situations of life. The man who never learns to adjust properly to stress never becomes mature.

Jacob insisted on looking at mud instead of believing that even misfortunes can be an important part of God's blueprints, as was certainly the case with him. Jacob's insistence on protracted weeping was entirely out of order because God had actually preserved Joseph. It would appear that Jacob thought God had died, too, for his faith was so deficient that all he could do was groan, ". . . all these things are against me."[8]

He evidently suffered in his own body the results of his maladjustment, for near the close of his life, he grunted, ". . . few and strenuous my life's days and years have been and not equal to the pilgrim years of my father's. . . ."[9]

Now Paul had far more assaults to withstand than

Jacob, but he saw the stars: "Five times I received from the Jews forty lashes minus one; thrice I was cudgeled; once I was stoned; three times I was shipwrecked; for a night and a day I have been adrift at sea. In my many travels I have been in dangers of rivers and of robbers, of Jews and Gentiles, of city, desert, and sea; in dangers among sham brothers; in wearying work and hardship through many a sleepless night; in hunger, thirst, and many fastings; in cold and lack of clothing."[10] In these frightful situations did Paul ever moan, "All these things are against me?" In contrast, he exclaimed, "None of these things move me." He refused to allow self-pity to fill his body with disease-producing hormones. What was the secret of Paul's successful adaptation to these many stressful agents? Where can one obtain adaptation to repeated floggings, stonings, and deprivation of food?

We have already observed that our reactions to the unavoidable stresses of life determine whether they can cure us or kill us. Therefore, it will be highly profitable for us to analyze the *method* used and taught by the Apostle.

After listing the many stress agents that assail mankind, he gives the divine secret for successful adaptation: "Can anything separate us from the love of Christ? Can trouble, pain or persecution? Can lack of clothes and food, danger to life and limb, the threat of force of arms? Indeed some of us know the truth of that ancient text: 'For Thy sake we are killed all the day long; We were accounted as sheep for the slaughter.' No, in all these things we win an overwhelming victory through Him Who has proved His love for us."[11]

Here is the Scriptural secret for victorious adaptation to life's insults. At the beginning of each day consider yourself a sheep that is going to be abused even to the extreme of being slaughtered. If you take that attitude of mind, then nothing that comes up should frustrate or disturb you.

A man awaiting death is not disturbed by many stress factors that upset people. He is not upset because his neighbor's chickens are scratching up his flower bed; his arthritis is not worsened because the taxes on his house have been raised; his blood pressure is not raised because his employer discharged him; he doesn't get a migraine headache because his wife burned his toast; and his ulcerative colitis doesn't flair up because the stock market goes down ten points. The crucified soul is not frustrated. The man who willingly, cheerfully and daily presents himself as a "living sacrifice" can excellently adapt to the severest situations and, with Paul, be "more than conquerors. . . ."[12]

One may ask, "Isn't it foolish to give up our rights?" Perhaps it is not foolish, since in giving up our rights we insure our health and happiness. In giving the other fellow a "piece of our mind," we always lose our peace of heart. To the natural man it is unthinkable that he should give in when he is right. He refuses to sacrifice his pride, but in so doing he sacrifices his health. Not too intelligent a transaction!

It is the spirit of retaliation that calls forth glandular toxins, and man suffers from his strong sense of self-expression and self-pity. If one takes time to analyze the cause of faulty adaptation to life's difficulties, one will often discover a little four letter word—*self*. Stress and disease result because of our unwillingness to sacrifice the big "I."

CHAPTER 21

The Nation's No. 1 Health Problem

ABOUT NINE MILLION AMERICANS SUFFER FROM EMOTIONAL and mental illness. As many hospital beds are filled by the mentally deranged as are occupied by all medical and surgical patients combined. In fact, one out of every twenty Americans will have a psychotic disturbance severe enough to confine him in a hospital for the insane. Mental disease is indeed the nation's No. 1 health problem.

What does it cost to take care of the patients in our

mental hospitals? The annual cost is about one billion dollars. Besides, outside the asylums there are a vast number who do not need confinement but who are incapable of supporting themselves. They work little or not at all and constitute a great burden on the taxpayer.

What is the cause of mental illness? In this chapter we wish to discuss briefly those disturbances in which visible changes occur in the brain. First, an insignificant percentage of these cases are caused by direct injury to the brain in an accident. Second, brain damage may also result from an infection or a toxin. The most common infection responsible for insanity is syphilis. A score of years ago, ten per cent of the inmates of our asylums were put there by syphilis.

By far the most common toxin responsible for insanity is alcohol. From the 1959 edition of *A Textbook of Medicine,* we read: "About 10% of the admissions to mental hospitals are officially reported as due to alcoholism and another 10% have alcoholism of considerable degree reported as an important contributing cause. In addition, general hospitals take care of many of the acutely disturbed alcoholics, and there is an unknown but large number of persons . . . who are ruining their careers and undergoing a sort of gradual personality suicide through addiction to alcohol."[1]

The third common type of insanity that involves visible changes in the brain is arteriosclerosis of the cerebral arteries. In a previous chapter we noted the important factors causing arteriosclerosis, such as heredity, eating of animal fat, overeating, smoking and stress. However, these frequent mental disturbances in the elderly are often due to a combination of arteriosclerosis and a personality factor. Some elderly people may suffer from a frank insanity but often, instead of being considered insane, they are better described as "impossible." The unlovely personality that develops in some senior citizens is not a sudden onset. It is rather the continuation of childhood temper tantrums, the elaboration of teenage assertiveness, the further development of middle-aged orneriness which has now fully developed into the thorny, sour and crabbed frustrations of old age.

Before arteriosclerosis started to clog his cerebral arteries, the peppery outbreaks of this individual were endurable only because they were spread over a variety of contacts and lasted for a short time. Now that arteriosclerosis has radically reduced his physical activities, changed his bluster to obstreperousness and concentrated it within the four walls of one house, he has become impossible.

If we lead cranky, complaining and censorious lives down through the years, then pity our children when the ugliness of our bad personalities is multiplied and aggravated by the clogging of our cerebral arteries. It may be as difficult to change our attitudes as it is to change a deep groove in a phonograph record, and if we are not careful now, we may end up as a two-legged bore.

Dr. Bess Fancher, a keen observer of people, once said to me, "Doctor, we don't have much to say about how we look at sixteen. But we are the ones who determine how we are going to look at sixty." William Wordsworth expressed the same thought in another way: "The child is father of the man."[2]

Typical of the attitude of those who have the care of their elderly parents are the words of Mrs. Sabin: "Doctor, you must tell me what I am going to do with Mom. I simply can't take any more. She had us up most of the night. My husband got about one half hour's sleep and then had to go to work. I find myself yelling at the children and they are upset. After these years of having my mother here, I am completely worn out. Even the sleeping capsules don't help her any more. Doctor, I am bushed. I have had it! You must do something!"

Needless to say, physicians have no easy solution for some of these problems. Hospitals and nursing homes don't want troublesome patients because they disturb others, and relatives are always loathe to put their loved ones in a mental institution. Actually, these cases aren't serious enough for an asylum, but they are too difficult for any other place. If they live long enough many of them do end up there. Some of these people fray the patience and shorten the lives of those who are ministering to them.

Lest I give the wrong impression of old age, I hasten to describe a man in his nineties, one of the grandest men I ever knew. Throughout the many years I knew him, he always displayed kindness, cheerfulness and consideration for everybody. When Reverend D. B. Hampe retired from an active, successful ministry in Akron, Ohio, he was, in his words, "ninety-two years young." For many years he refused to be superannuated because he said he was "superanimated." He was, and he had more vision and energy than some men thirty years younger.

After his retirement, Reverend Hampe and his crippled wife went to live with their married daughter. Some time later, he had a number of "little strokes," the comas lasting a few minutes to a few hours. Then a severe stroke hit him. The coma lasted for several days and deepened. He was not able to swallow. To prolong his days which, even in his illness, seemed to radiate a blessing to those around him, I passed a stomach tube and thus supplied him with nourishment. Once more he became partly conscious. He sensed what we were doing to keep him alive, smiled a bit, and said, "I think it would be better if you would let me go home to be with the Lord."

A day or two later we tried to talk to him in his semicomatose state. He seemed to hear, although he couldn't open his eyes or talk, but he did summon up the last particles of his strength to raise a feeble hand to wave goodby.

Six years have now passed and his wife is still living in their daughter's home. Mrs. Hampe will soon be ninety-four. Though badly crippled and confined largely to a chair, she is always happy and cheerful. When food is brought on her tray, she says, "That looks good," or makes some other complimentary remark. She has plenty of aches and pains but never mentions them.

What is the reason for the contrast between this couple and others even much younger? To my mind the answer is evident. They obeyed Biblical injunctions and saved themselves from many of the factors that cause arteriosclerosis. Not only did they live a long time, but they developed choice personalities because they took the Bible as their guide. For fifty-five years they served the Lord in their unselfish devotion to help others. Often, on small ministerial appointments, they eked out an existence for themselves and their four children. No arteriosclerotic plaques developed in them from overeating, and they always took what the Lord gave them with happy, thankful hearts.

Little wonder that this crippled widow is loved by all who know her. Her daughter and the in-laws with whom she lives never feel burdened with her but thank the Lord for keeping her alive to refresh their own souls.

The Bible has hundreds of helpful suggestions for long, happy and sane living. Here is one of them:

Come, listen to me, my sons,
  I will teach you true religion.
'Tis your desire to live,
  to live long and be happy?
Then keep your tongue from evil,
  keep your lips from deceit;
  shun evil and do good,
  seek to be friendly—aim at that.[3]

In those few lines there is medical therapy that would prevent millions of cases of mental illness. ". . . shun evil . . ."—the perfect prophylaxis against syphilitic paresis, formerly the cause of one out of every ten cases in our asylums. ". . . shun evil . . ."—and avoid alcoholic psychosis, which currently tops the list in admissions to our mental institutions.

"Then keep your tongue from evil, keep your lips from deceit, . . . do good, seek to be friendly . . ."—there you have advice that, if followed, would save one from becoming a censorious whiner. Doing friendly acts to others always develops a personality that is lovely and fragrant. If tens of thousands in our institutions today had developed such Scriptural attitudes, they would not be kicking out their last tantrums in asylums and nursing homes.

CHAPTER 22

Snails and Schizophrenics

ROSEMARY WAS DEMURE, RESERVED, AND GAVE METICULOUS attention to herself and her clothes. She patterned herself after her mother, who was "fluffily feminine." On a summer day one could find Rosemary sitting in the garden, weaving garlands of flowers. She did not go out of her way to mix with others. As a young child she read a great deal, and the knights and ladies of King Arthur's court seemed more real to her than anyone else. As she grew older her ideals were always fictional characters, devoid of faults and much more glamorous than ordinary people who sometimes said nasty things.

When Rosemary went away to college she became unhappy. At home she had had a room of her own, but in the dormitory she shared a room with two other girls—girls far removed from Jane Austen's heroines. Her roommates and classmates sensed Rosemary's unconscious shrinking from them and labeled her "stuckup." She slept poorly, was constipated, did not exercise, and could not take any interest in her environment.

One morning Rosemary did not get up. A little past noon she was still in bed while her breakfast and luncheon trays remained untouched. To the questions of the dormitory dean she gave only a vacant stare. She was as motionless and stiff as a wax figure.

She was taken to the college infirmary, where she required more care than a baby. Food that was placed in her mouth remained there, and liquid nourishment had to be given through a small stomach tube. Previously very immaculate about her hygiene, she now had to be washed and the bedding had to be changed frequently. When her mother arrived, Rosemary did not recognize her.

The most surprising characteristic of Rosemary's affliction was that an attendant could place her body or limbs in any awkward position and they remained fixed. Within a few hours an intelligent girl with good scholastic grades had changed to a motionless, waxy figure incapable of helping herself in any way. Dr. Melvin Thorner presents this case as a typical illustration of schizophrenia.[1]

Schizophrenia is the most common form of insanity, accounting for twenty-three per cent of first admissions to state hospitals. These patients require longer hospitalizations than those with any other mental condition; hence fifty per cent of the half million patients in our mental hospitals are schizophrenic cases. The age of onset is usually between eighteen and thirty-five years of age.

Not all patients come down with this malady as did Rosemary. Psychiatrists divide schizophrenics into four or more different types. Since it is one of the most difficult mental conditions to cure after it is fully developed, and since there is much we can do to prevent it, we should take a closer look at this dreary affliction.

Actually, before Rosemary became frankly insane, her mind was split between a pleasant fictional world of glamorous people and an unpleasant world of reality. Because of these *two* worlds in which she lived, we refer to her condition as *schizophrenia (schizo,* "to split," and *phrenia,* "the mind").

A look at the snail will help one to understand this lamentable form of insanity. A snail has such a timid personality that he never comes completely out of his shell. Even when he has to emerge a little, he is fearful and unhappy. Slowly he raises two little periscopes equipped with eyes on top and looks around very shyly. If things seem favorable, he projects a bit of himself into the fearsome world of reality and then laboriously pulls his stony, spiraled castle after him. If the world becomes threatening in any degree, he retracts every bit of himself into his shell. There he may stay inordinately long, even after the danger has disappeared.

Of course, all of us who glory in our normality must confess that we sometimes retreat into our shells, a reaction which is properly protective. However, we need to be careful lest our retreat inward, to suckle comfort from self-pity, become too frequent an occurrence. Unless we exercise caution, we shall spend too much time daydreaming and lolling in the lovely labyrinths of fantasy. Certainly, if we continue to brood and lick the sores of our wounded pride rather than push ourselves outward to face the realities of a cold, factual world, or if we form the habit of withdrawal every time the going gets hard, our personalities may become as twisted as the spirals of a snail's shell.

Depending on the degree of our withdrawal, people will refer to us as the dreamy type, or an introvert, or a shut-in personality, or a queer soul, or finally a schizophrenic.

Schizophrenia is a specific reaction to severe anxiety arising from inability to meet the demands of adult adjustment.[2] Anxiety in the emotional center can result in various glands being stimulated with the formation of abnormal chemicals. These chemicals, acting on the brain, may be responsible for abnormal mental disturbances. Supporting this view are the changes that occur in a dog when a chemical, bulbocapnine, is injected. These changes are surprisingly similar to those that occurred in Rosemary. An injected dog refuses to eat or drink, does not recognize old friends, and has the same waxy rigidity of the legs. Furthermore, chemists have proved that the injection of other chemicals can cause psychotic hallucinations or feeblemindedness. Dr. Carl Jung was the first to teach that the cause of schizophrenia was a toxin injurious to the brain—said toxin being formed by emotional disturbance, especially anxiety.

In some cases, heredity appears to make some people more likely to develop schizophrenia. However, an individual who has a number of schizophrenics in his background certainly should not be unduly upset. Anyone who has inherited a lot of dynamite in his cerebral attic should remember that this dynamite is dangerous only when it is exposed to the hot sparks of emotional fire. Such a person should know that heredity does not *cause* schizophrenia, but may be a *predisposing* factor. Hence, it would be wise for one who has a schizophrenic heredity to exercise more than average caution to avoid anxiety and stressful situations.

Also very important as a predisposing factor is environment. An individual whose home, community or occupation is loaded with stressful situations should exercise more care. Supporting this view is a study of 263 schizophrenics who improved and were released from asylums. Analysis of the patients who had a recurrence of their insanity revealed that the most common cause of relapse was emotional conflict in the environment.

Parents are big factors in helping their children to adjust smoothly to the outside world, and it is obvious that they too play a role in the development of schizophrenia. The parents of Rosemary had done little to prepare her for entrance to college. Her life was centered in daisy chains and novels. Because other children did not allow her to have her own way, she avoided them, and her parents, instead of training her to give in, had taken her part in her conflicts. Perhaps Rosemary's parents had read that frustrations were bad and had catered to her every whim. She had never been made to work, so her physical activity was almost nil.

We do not understand the chemistry involved, but it is a well-recognized fact that physical work is both a preventive and curative factor in a number of mental disturbances. Many a mother washes the dishes with the excuse, "I would rather do them myself than go through all the fuss of making Milly do them." Such a remark indicates maternal failure and may forecast a personality disturbance for Milly.

Suppose Darlene has been jilted by her high-school boyfriend. The best thing to free her from the deleterious effects of toxic brooding is physical activity. There is no better psychotherapeutic appliance than the common scrub brush.

Pity the youngster who is not required to work. An indulgent father shovels the snow off the walks and driveway because Junior didn't get in until late last night. As a result Dad threatens himself with a coronary attack while six-foot Junior spends the entire morning sleeping. Junior is given all the time he wants to build castles in the air, but he has never been taught to build a woodshed on the ground.

Psychiatry recognizes that laziness is a frequent characteristic of schizophrenics. Dr. William S. Sadler writes, "Many of these cases are youths who are not disposed to accept the social restrictions and the cultural demands of their environments."[3] They are unwilling to put forth constructive efforts to adapt because it is so much easier to get away from work and real people by withdrawing themselves into the twisted spirals of their fantasies.

A boy who is given a program of work is not likely to turn into a hoodlum who goes around chopping up pianos and furniture for "thrills." Neither is he likely to dent the family income to pay for treatment by a psychiatrist. A more effective treatment, if he is not too old, would be a visit to the family woodshed and the warm application of this Biblical wisdom: "Foolishness is bound up in the heart of a child; But the rod of correction shall drive it far from him."[4]

People are still talking about a Houghton College commencement address delivered many years ago by Dr. James S. Luckey on the subject of the neglected command, "Six days shalt thou labor. . . ."[5] I suspect John Smith lessened the possibilities for schizophrenia in the early Jamestown colony because he enforced another Scriptural directive: ". . . this we commanded you, that if any would not work, neither should he eat."[6]

Parental fear of frustrating a youngster often produces an undisciplined teen-ager who is an easy prey for life's frustrations. About ten years ago I was called to a college infirmary to see an eighteen-year-old girl whom I shall call Lorna Henderson. She was partly withdrawn, responded poorly to questioning, and kept fearfully exclaiming, "I am two people, and I don't know which one to listen to!"

From her classmates I discovered that she had lost a great deal of sleep because of studying for midterm examinations and also because she had wanted to participate in a number of social engagements. She was the holder of an excellent scholarship, which meant that her marks had to stay in the upper brackets.

Lorna and her roommate had been arguing. Then, three days before her mental breakdown, she and her fiancè had quarreled. Cumulative anxiety did something inside her and she withdrew from cruel reality.

The next day her parents arrived and came to my office for a conference. With them were two other children about seven and nine years of age. During our interview these two children moved everything that was movable in my office. The refined and educated parents made many verbal remonstrances but nothing more. In return the little boy kicked his mother in the shins and several times the girl spit at her father.

I am reminded of what Dr. Douglas Kelly, University of California professor and chief psychiatrist at the Nuremberg trials, said: "Spare the Freud and save the child." He said the fear of repressing the child has run wild through modern education and child rearing. The result, in his words, is: "A generation of children who have not been taught the discipline required for getting along with the world. . . . We have been overenthusiastic in our refusal to teach control lest we traumatize."[7]

If Lorna did not meet frustration when she was five, ten and fifteen years old at home, it is quite understandable why she was incapable of coping in a strange environment with the frustrations caused by a roommate, by her inability to get high grades, and by her fiancè's desertion. *Children who have never been conditioned by some frustrations during the first fifteen years of life will not be very fit to meet the demands of adult living without experiencing unusual stress, with its abnormal and potent chemicals.*

Finally, the individual himself is a tremendous factor in determining whether schizophrenia develops. True, he has nothing to say about his heredity, often not much more to say about his environment and the type of parental training he receives. If all these have been exceptionally bad, he may have a difficult task trying to change the mold in which he was cast. Yet to a considerable extent he is the captain and can direct his course. Forty years ago I knew a young woman whose heredity, environment and parental training were deplorable. Today she possesses a beautifully integrated personality. Everyone who knows her will affirm that her excellent qualities and transformation have been due to following Christ.

The individual who has Christ in his heart and the Bible in his hand has splendid fortifications against man's greatest mental disturbance—schizophrenia. Why do I make that statement? It is medically recognized that schizophrenia is the result of anxiety stemming from an inability to meet the adjustments of adulthood. In highly predisposed individuals even a little anxiety can tip the scales. Furthermore, it is felt that any individual, if subjected to sufficient stress, could experience the schizophrenic reaction.

Naturally, anything that lessens anxiety is important in the prevention of schizophrenia. In reduction of anxiety, nothing is more important than spiritual conversion and Christian living. Anyone who ever truly repented his sins and asked God to forgive him can never forget the miraculous way in which his mind was immediately freed of "the guilt complex." Whether the offense is trivial or enormous, Christ immediately forgives and brings a peace "which passeth all understanding. . . ."[8] Millions can testify to the veracity of His promise: "Peace I leave with you; my peace I give unto you: not as the world giveth, give I unto you. Let not your heart be troubled, neither let it be fearful."[9]

Since the schizophrenic patient is suffering because his interest and energies are directed inward, it is not surprising to read: "The objective is to . . . detach his emotions from subjective material, redirect his interests to things outside himself, inculcate healthful social habits. . . ."[10] The Bible gave this same advice centuries before: "None of you should think only of his own affairs, but should learn to see things from other people's point of view."[11]

Certainly Lorna had neither been taught nor had she picked up the self-discipline that is necessary for getting along with people in this world. Because she couldn't get along with her fiancè, he had broken their engagement. Consecrated Christians spell disappointments with a capital H—*His appointments.* Actually Lorna was partly to blame, for she had created much of the emotional hurricane that swamped her. She had been unwilling to accept any frustrations from anyone, so intent was she on having her own self-centered way. One cannot help wondering if things would not have been different had she been living out these Scriptural admonitions:

Let there be no more resentment, no more anger or temper, no more violent self-assertiveness, no more slander and no more malicious remarks. Be kind to each other, be understanding. Be as ready to forgive others as God for Christ's sake has forgiven you.[12]

Let us have real warm affection . . . and a willingness to let the other man have the credit.[13]

So let us concentrate on the things which make for harmony, and on the growth of one another's character.[14]

I have seen Christians in their zeal for the Lord become guilty of another fault that Lorna had—they attempt too much. One must have time for rest and relaxation: "And he [Jesus] saith unto them, Come ye yourselves apart into a desert place, and rest a while. For there were many coming and going, and they had not leisure so much as to eat."[15]

Lorna, in her anxiety to keep up her grades, studied seven days a week. She didn't think the Biblical command to rest one day in seven was for her and her generation. She didn't sense that the worth of this regulation has been amply confirmed by modern research workers studying stress. Lorna, like thousands of others, never learned that a loving Father gave these admonitions for the sake of saving His children from physical and mental disturbances.

From the moment man sinned and brought upon himself bodily and mental diseases, the Lord sought to succor him and mitigate the effects of diseases. But man, with his perverted mind, has often brushed aside as worthless the very admonitions that could have saved him. In view of the factors mentioned in the prevention of schizophrenia, we can clearly see a Father's love shining through the commands to work, to rest, to "learn to see things from other people's point of view," to see to it that "there be no more resentment, no more anger or temper, no more violent self-assertiveness," and to open the door of our hearts so that the Holy Comforter may enter. Since we have learned that schizophrenia is "a specific reaction to severe anxiety," we can understand the emphasis Jesus and the Apostles placed on the infilling of man with the Holy Spirit who is the personification of peace. "Peace I leave with you; my peace I give unto you. . . ."

CHAPTER 23

A Lesson From John D.

AS A YOUNG MAN, JOHN D. ROCKEFELLER, SR., WAS AS strong and husky as a farm lad. When he entered business he drove himself harder than any slave was ever driven by the whip of a taskmaster. At the early age of thirty-three, he had made his first million dollars. By consecrating every waking moment to his work, he controlled, at forty-three, the biggest business in the world. When he was fifty-three, he was the richest man on earth and the world's only billionaire.

For this achievement he had bartered his own happiness and health. He developed alopecia, a condition in which not only the hair of the head drops off but also most of the hair from the eyelashes and eyebrows. One of his biographers said that he looked like a "mummy." His weekly income was a million dollars, but his digestion was so bad that he could eat only crackers and milk.

Like Scrooge, John D. was as solitary as an oyster. He once confessed that he "wanted to be loved," but did not sense that people love only those who emanate affection. Lacking in consideration for others, he had often crushed the helpless into the mire in his lust to make bigger profits. So hated was he in the oil fields of Pennsylvania that the men whom he had pauperized hanged him in effigy, and he had bodyguards day and night. The mass of wealth he had accumulated gave him neither peace nor happiness. In fact, as he sought to protect and control it, he discovered that he was being smothered by it. He could not sleep; he enjoyed nothing.

When John D. was only fifty-three, Ida Tarbell wrote of him, "An awful age was in his face. He was the oldest man that I have ever seen." The crackers and milk he glumly swallowed could no longer hold together his skinny body and restless soul. It was generally agreed that he would not live another year, and newspaper writers had his obituary written and ready in their files.

Then John D. began to do some thinking in the long nights when he couldn't sleep. One night he made a startling discovery: *he would not be able to take even one of his thin dimes with him into the next world!* His was the despair and helplessness of the little boy who sees the relentless tide coming in to sweep into oblivion all the sand castles he has been building.

For the first time in his life he recognized that money was not a commodity to be hoarded but something to be shared for the benefit of others. In the morning he, like Scrooge, lost no time in transforming his money into blessings to others. He began to help worthy causes. He established the Rockefeller Foundation so that some of his fortune could be channeled to needed areas. It would require a book to describe the benefits that resulted from the many hundreds of millions of dollars that he showered on universities, hospitals, mission work, and millions of underprivileged people. He was the one who helped rid the South of its greatest economic and physical scourge—hookworm. We can thank John D. every time our lives and the lives of our children are saved by an injection of penicillin because his contributions aided in the discovery of this miracle drug. His money sparked the research that saved and is still saving millions of people from untimely deaths from malaria, tuberculosis, diphtheria and many other diseases.

It is not my purpose to detail the blessings the world received when John D. changed the current of his thinking from *getting* to *giving*. My object is to tell you that when he began to think *outwardly* toward the needs of others, a miracle occurred. He began to sleep, to eat normally, and to enjoy life in general. The bitterness, rancor and the deadness of self-centeredness went out of his life, and into the soul of John D. came refreshing streams of love and gratitude from those whom he was helping. He who had been repulsive and lifeless now teemed with vibrancy and activity.

When Rockefeller was fifty-three, it certainly appeared that he would never celebrate another birthday, but he started to practice one of God's eternal laws, and he reaped its promised benefits: ". . . give, and it shall be given unto you; good measure, pressed down, shaken together, running over, shall they give into your bosom."[1] He proved the value of this promise for he lived not only until his fifty-fourth and fifty-fifth birthdays, but he experienced "the good measure . . . running over"—he lived until he was ninety-eight years old.

Modern psychiatry is also catching up with the numerous and valuable Biblical admonitions to think outwardly in helpfulness toward others. One psychiatrist writes, "Without love, we lose the will to live. Our mental and physical vitality is impaired, our resistance is lowered, and we succumb to illnesses that often prove fatal. We may escape death, but what remains is a meager and barren existence, emotionally so impoverished that we can only be called half alive."[2]

Those well-known observers of human nature, Harry and Bonaro Overstreet, have written, ". . . it is one of the basic facts of human life that the ungiven self is the unfulfilled self."[3]

As human beings we take very good care of our bodies with medicine, physical examinations, vitamins, and with dozens of other aids, but we are sadly ignorant of certain mental exercises that are necessary for full-orbed happy living. Ideally, this training to think outwardly should begin at birth. Unfortunately, a tiny baby is trained to think inwardly and to sense his own importance when his parents and grandparents rush to cuddle him every time he makes the slightest fuss. They rush to the crib, pick him up, give him a bottle or a pacifier, walk the floor, or do something to let him know that sun, moon and stars are ready to answer his every beck and squall. A baby becomes so accustomed to having everything rise and set according to his cry that, with the passing of months and years, he cleverly perfects his technique for keeping the current of interests directly inwardly, *ad nauseam.*

As a first-grader in school, he reports to his parents that a smaller boy called him a "sissy." So when he knocks the boy down and kicks him in the face, the doting father chuckles and applauds, "Good boy!" When the sixth-grader wails, "That old principal punished me just for nothing at all!" doesn't the average parent judge the case on the plea of the juvenile plaintiff? My father never had to judge any of my pleas because I knew that if he heard I was punished at school I would automatically get a whipping at home. My father might be called unreasonable, yet his method did much to prevent my self-centeredness.

Parents who everlastingly throw mud at their neighbors' doorsteps in order to make their own look cleaner are setting a vicious example which their children usually follow. Parents should not blame their children for developing sour personalities if the dining table becomes an autopsy slab on which the neighbors are dissected.

Far too much of our efforts and money are directed inwardly, to build up the egos of our children. We buy eight-year-old Susie more expensive clothes than the family budget can afford, make her "fluffily feminine," á la Rosemary, foster the spirit of selfishness in her, buy a piano and other instruments, give her music lessons, but never make any worthwhile effort to get her to think outwardly toward others.

Positive outward thinking is possible. We can buy Susie a cake mix and have her bake and frost a cake to take to an overworked or sick mother. What better investment can one make with so little money to give Susie happiness and a flying start down the road to joyful living and mental health? Some of the loveliest personalities I know are little children who sacrifice candy-money so that they may give to missions and the underprivileged. Children trained early to be considerate of others are not very likely to cause heartbreak to parents and others in the years ahead.

The parent is really wise who can guide fourteen-year-old Junior to go over to a needy neighbor to mow the lawn, rake the leaves, or shovel snow. There is no better way to inculcate healthful social habits. From where I sit it seems that parents are going the opposite way when they equip three-year-old Keith with gun belt and six shooters to bang-bang at every passing person, and thus accustom him to the idea of getting what he wants by hurting, even killing, other people.

Because we have allowed the six-month-old baby to be *all lungs,* the ten-year-old to be *all play,* the teen-aged boy to be *all competitive sports,* the teen-aged girl to be *all fluffs and frills,* the thirty-five-year-olds *all business or bridge,* the forty-five-year-olds *all middle,* is it any wonder that the fifty-five-year-olds are *all frustrations,* and the sixty-year-olds are *all in*?

John D. Rockefeller proved that healthful, enjoyable living is not obtained by *grabbing* but by *giving* to others. When grateful citizens of Cleveland, Ohio, congratulated him, he spoke from his own experience: "Turn your thoughts upon the higher things of life. Be of service to humanity. Turn your thoughts into channels of usefulness; look forward to a determination that something useful shall come out of your success. Let your question be, 'What shall be the fruitage of my career? Shall it be the endowment of hospitals, churches, schools and asylums?' . . . . *Do everything you can for the betterment of your fellow-men and in doing this you will enjoy life the better.*"[4]

For Rockefeller, it took over a half century of sickly, wretched living and learning the hard way before he found one of the basic secrets to real life. It is pathetic indeed that earlier he did not read and heed the healthful admonitions given in the Book of books:

> One who is not loving remains in death.[5]
>
> Harmonize with others in your thinking. . . .[6]
>
> Don't become snobbish but take a real interest in ordinary people. Don't become set in your own opinions.[7]

It is not easy for anybody to practice these directives in his own strength. Modern psychiatry may be close to the Bible in appreciating the importance of directing the current of thinking outwardly, yet psychiatry ordinarily can not provide sufficient motivating force to get any

senior year she began to feel herself slipping. The thought of being dropped from that list after all those years made her anxious, panicky, and decreased her ability to concentrate on her studies.

Then one day Arlene entered the infirmary because she couldn't read. She could pronounce words but was completely unable to understand what they meant. A week passed, with little improvement. Each day increased her anxiety because it lessened her chances of corraling those elusive A's.

She was sure there was something physically wrong with her. Even though I told her that she needed more relaxation and play as well as a changed viewpoint about striving for the moon, she returned to her home, where she was thoroughly examined in a hospital. She emerged with a large bill and a diagnosis of "somatic conversion symptoms," which means in five-cent words that her inability to read was caused by mental turmoil. Anxiety about her grades had manifested itself by a withdrawal symptom—and inability to read.

Psychic turmoil, arising out of our desires to go to the moon or to attain superiority over our fellows, is very common. An outstanding psychiatrist, Dr. Alfred Adler, taught that most modern nervous and emotional disorders grow out of a definite striving for power.[1] Because the average man in his mad drive for power is in a daily race with others for earthly goals, his day is full of failures, frustrations, banged-up feelings and, often, fenders.

The next time you feel unduly fatigued because life's race has been unusually rough and bumpy, stop and analyze the events and conversation of the foregoing hours. Ninety-nine times out of a hundred you will discover that someone recently let the air out of your ego. We suffer rough going, mental weariness, exhaustion and disease, not because of the work we do, but because we consciously or subconsciously try to prove to ourselves and to our fellows that our ideals are superior, our doctrines are the correct ones, our church is the best, our city is the choicest, our state is the most important, our political concepts and party are necessary to save the world from destruction, our ball team is going to win the world series, and our, our, our—you name it, and we will argue until we are blue in the face that *we* are the people and that at our demise wisdom will surely vanish from the earth. It is a wonder that we don't more often blow a cerebral fuse.

Last week a young man came to my office with a large hemorrhage in his eye. Nobody had punched him. The blood vessel in his eye had broken because he had developed too much blood pressure while playing the high soprano parts on his horn. Remember that young man the next time you are tempted "to toot your horn."

Is it not a pity that we are cursed with an innate urge to be ever madly racing with one another like the participants in a stock car race? In our excitement to be first we become oblivious to the damage we inflict on others and ourselves. The stock cars that are battered, banged, dented, and noisy are no worse off than bruised humanity broken down with many a disease from life's competitions.

Here are only a few of many New Testament admonitions—or, more accurately, prescriptions—that would save millions of crushed and broken hearts if people had enough faith to swallow and assimilate them:

> Don't cherish exaggerated ideas of yourself or your importance, but try to have a sane estimate of your capabilities. . . .[2]

> Let your love be perfectly sincere . . . allowing one another to enjoy preference of honor . . . do not aspire to eminence, but willingly adjust yourselves to humble situations; do not become wise in your own conceits.[3]

> Don't aim at adding to the number of teachers, . . . I beg you! Remember that we who are teachers will be judged by a much higher standard.[4]

> Live together in harmony, live together in love, as though you had only one mind and one spirit between you. Never act from motives of rivalry or personal vanity, but in humility think more of each other than you do of yourselves.[5]

Before the disciples had crucified their urge for power, which Dr. Adler calls the "ego ambition," their main drive had been to sit in places of authority and prominence and to be the greatest in the Kingdom. Speaking of the Pharisees and scribes, Jesus said:

They increase the size of their phylacteries and lengthen the tassels of their robes; they love seats of honour at dinners and front places in the synagogues. They love to be greeted with respect in public places and to have men call them "Rabbi!" Don't you ever be called "Rabbi"—

you have only one Teacher, and all of you are brothers. . . . And you must not let people call you "leaders"—you have only one leader, Christ! The only "superior" among you is the one who serves the others. For every man who promotes himself will be humbled, and every man who learns to be humble will find promotion.[6]

This Scriptural teaching is diametrically opposed to the philosophies of the world. Jesus very forcibly warns us against aspiring to leadership. His teaching does not give us any excuse whatsoever for laziness but rather exhorts that proper motivation and direction be given to the expenditure of our energies. The teaching of Jesus translated into college language is: Don't get your heart set on being a four-pointer or being on the Dean's List. Don't lose sleep over being selected queen, don't try to be the leader of any class, any committee, or anything else. Graduate work is necessary but don't "lengthen the tassels" on your robes. Don't, for the sake of the degrees, "lengthen the tassel" on the end of your name. In God's Book, "The only 'superior' among you is the one who serves the others."

Going back to medical considerations, you may wonder why the individual working to be a four-pointer suffers in his body and mind while another student, working just as hard, is free from such injuries. The student who is striving for the coveted A's and for the pre-eminence they will give him is actually digging a channel to direct the current of interests toward himself. His egocentric life, with no outflow, will be bitter and senseless. He will suffer from self-intoxication. He who refuses the Biblical injunction to adjust himself to "humble situations" will soon discover that his associates will take it upon themselves to make the necessary adjustments to him in a fashion that may be crude and heartless. The stress he then suffers can cause plenty of trouble in mind or body.

In contrast, the individual who practices God's Word is spared many bodily insults. The psalmist wrote, "Great peace have they which love thy law: and nothing shall offend them."[7] Nothing? I can't imagine greater stress than being thrown into a fire. Yet I know people, and you know people, who were thrown in and they emerged without having the smoke of fire on their garments.

Everybody meets frustration every day, but the Christian need never become frustrated. A number of times I have seen Stephen W. Paine face frustrating and personally embarrassing situations as a college president. Each time my soul has been refreshed when he said, "It is perfectly all right. Perhaps the Lord sent it to keep me humble." The man who thus yields quickly to being knocked down is not as likely to be knocked out.

There is another big difference between the individual who is seeking great things for himself and the one whose energies are devoted to God's Kingdom. In our world of business the individual who is self-employed has only his own resources to fall back upon when he meets trouble. But the man who is a vital part of a large corporation has all the resources of a billion-dollar company. Hence, he has a sense of security in knowing that, regardless of what happens, he doesn't have to worry. Doesn't it go without saying that the man or woman who is faithfully devoting his energies to a corporation that owns the cattle on a thousand hills, the oil in a million wells, and the silver, gold, and jewels in a billion solar systems, has a sense of security and freedom from frustration and disease that nothing else in this old world can ever give?

Not only is he free from worries, insults, antagonisms, and disease-producing insults incident to self-seeking, but he is granted a pleasing personality denied to those who shoot for the moon. Some time ago I read about a young woman who wanted to go to college. Her heart sank when she read one question on the application blank: "Are you a leader?" Being a conscientious girl she wrote "No" and sent in the form with a heavy heart. To her surprise she received a letter from one of the college officials which read something like this: "A study of the application blanks reveals that this year our college will have 1452 leaders. Therefore, we are accepting you because we feel it is imperative that they have *one* follower."

We are living in a day when it is not difficult to find people who want to be head cook, but few are available to wash dishes. There are always several hundreds of girls who yearn to ride in the parade as the beautiful queen, but sometimes only a disgruntled half dozen will agree to decorate the float. Organizations have never lacked those who want to be boss carpenters, but they have had to search for men to drive nails and saw boards.

Medical statistics show that it will be the whistling ditchdigger who will be digging the grave for the distraught business manager. Maybe, in our striving for the moon, we aren't too smart, after all. I grant you, it must be a thrill to shoot for the moon in an upholstered space capsule. Yet, that capsule bears an uncanny similarity to an asylum's padded cell.

Jesus said something that few people took seriously because it was as high above our earthly thinking as the heavens are above the earth. He said, ". . . the meek . . . shall inherit the earth."[8] We can believe that the meek will inherit heaven when they die, but Jesus was trying to tell us that the meek are going to inherit the earth here and now. Study the meek people you know, and you will discover that they are actually coming into possession of everything that is worth while on this earth.

With a little reflection you can understand why the meek inherit the earth. They have been thoughtful and considerate of your interests, they have been slow to talk about their great accomplishments and quick to congratulate you on your minor achievements. Down through the years they have always laughed at your "corny" jokes. Yes, you will gladly give them what you possess. The earth belongs to them.

Here is one of their prayers, seasoned with a bit of irony:

Lord, keep me from becoming talkative and possessed with the idea that I must express myself on every subject.

Release me from the craving to straighten out everyone's affairs.

Teach me the glorious lesson that occasionally I may be wrong.

Make me helpful but not bossy.

With my vast store of wisdom and experience, it does seem a pity not to use it all—.
But thou knowest, Lord, that I want a few friends at the end. *Amen.*[9]

Jesus said, ". . . the meek . . . shall inherit the earth." Benito Mussolini and Adolf Hitler didn't believe that, for they attempted to take it by force. No one ever lived unhappier lives or died more despicable deaths than they.

How are we going to take care of this inner power urge, "the ego ambition?" Dr. Adler sought to appease this strong egotistical power urge so that it might work amicably with the widely different feelings of altruism that man also possesses.[10] To this end he urged his patients to follow the Golden Rule: "Thou shalt love thy neighbour as thyself."[11]

The weakness of the Adler plan was that he was looking only at the *power urge,* which is one symptom of our carnal nature, just as Freud centered his attention on another outstanding symptom—man's strong sexual and lustful propensity. The trouble with both Adler and Freud lies in treating merely *symptoms* of the carnal nature instead of directing therapy at the *cause*. When a person is dying of meningitis, it helps little to treat the symptom of headache with some aspirin and fail to attack the evil infection itself.

The Bible focuses therapy on the *cause o*f the symptoms: the *carnal nature:* "And those who belong to Christ Jesus have crucified the lower nature with its passions and desires."[12]

Instead of making frequent, expensive and often futile trips to a psychiatrist's couch, we are invited by the Lord to make one trip to the cross for crucifixion of the troublemaker. When we drive the spikes into everything in our lives that God has marked for destruction, then God, for Christ's sake, executes that old self which ever breathes out "ego ambition" and licentious, lustful living. "And, while Christ was actually taking upon Himself the sins of men, God condemned that sinful nature."[13]

"Wherefore Jesus also, that he might sanctify the people with his own blood, suffered without the gate. Let us go forth therefore unto him without the camp, bearing his reproach."[14] Now, if you go outside the gate, beyond the opinions and doctrines of man, for the crucifixion of that disease-maker, the old self, you will be able to say with Paul, "I am crucified with Christ; nevertheless I live; yet not I, but Christ liveth in me. . . ."[15]

CHAPTER 25

"Two Souls, Alas, Dwell in My Breast Apart"

ONE OF THE MOST BRUTAL MURDERS EVER COMMITTED happened on a summer evening some years ago. Joseph Ransler went to the home of his brother, who was working on a night shift. He visited with his brother's wife who, he later reported, "was dressed in shorts and a bra, like she always was." A few hours later Joseph made a sexual assault on the woman, and to cover up his crime he strangled her and her little daughter. The lifeless victims were found by Joseph's brother when he returned home from work.

After seven hours of questioning by the police, Joseph Ransler confessed and made this statement: "What makes a guy act like I do? I want to pray and everything, and inwardly I feel that I want to be the best Christian in the world. But outwardly I'm a maniac and I can't control the outward part. I don't know why." He hadn't made much headway following the inward voice, for the police had previously arrested him a half-dozen times.

However, his recognition of two forces working within him, one for the good and one for the bad, is worthy of notice. Sigmund Freud recognized the active conflict that occurs in a man's mind because of the presence of these two different forces. In fact, the Freudian school of psychoanalysis believes that this cerebral conflict is the source of most of man's psychic disorders.

In an earlier chapter we mentioned that Dr. Karl Menninger recognizes the existence of these two inner forces and refers to them as the "life instinct" and "death instinct." The life instinct of man seeks to preserve his life while the death instinct seeks to destroy it, as well as the lives of others. Dr. Menninger's book on suicide is aptly titled *Man Against Himself*.[1]

People standing near the brink of a deep canyon often sense an inner agent that wants to push them over the edge. But they also sense and usually heed another agent that causes them to step back.

Because the strong evil agent that dwells in man seeks his destruction, it is not surprising that in the United States there occur annually nineteen thousand suicides, not to mention the many who disguise their suicides successfully as an accident, and the many other thousands who attempt suicide but who fail in one way or another.

Carl Jung, the founder of the school of analytical psychology, was also impressed by the fact that neuroses were caused by the battle between two warring cerebral agents: "What drives people to war with themselves is the intuition or the knowledge that they consist of two persons in opposition to one another. The conflict may be between the sensual and the spiritual man. . . . It is what Faust means when he says, 'Two souls, alas, dwell in my breast.' . . . A neurosis is a dissociation of personality. Healing may be called a religious problem."[2]

Robert Louis Stevenson, in *Dr. Jekyl and Mr. Hyde*, gave a fascinating description of an individual who was swayed one moment by the beneficent Dr. Jekyl in his nature, and then the next minute he was turned into and controlled by his evil and murderous Mr. Hyde nature.

Modern psychologists and psychiatrists can give a clear-cut answer to the question of the sex murderer, Joseph Ransler, "What makes a guy act like I do?" Many other people sense their ambivalence—the presence of two inner forces, one good and one bad. Many individuals also recognize the greater power of the evil agent. Perhaps they haven't had to hang by the neck for their misdeeds, but many times they have had to hang their faces in shame.

With a little introspection, each of us can sense the presence of two opposite forces within; it is especially easy to sense our duality when we have a moral issue to decide. It is not pleasant to have two pugilists battling it out and making a rumpus in our cerebral attics.

Four thousand years before psychiatry awoke to the importance of two forces within man, God described this conflict in a drama recorded in the first book of the Bible.[3] To Abraham and his wife Sarah, God promised a son through whom all the nations of the earth would be blessed. With the passing of many years, Sarah became so old that she thought God had forgotten His promise. She decided to help out a dilatory Jehovah by lending her slave girl Hagar to Abraham so that he might obtain the promised heir whose posterity would bless all the nations of the world. Abraham consented to this human scheme without consulting God. In due time the slave girl bore Abraham a son and called him Ishmael.

Abraham was elated because he had a son and an heir. Now God could use Ishmael to fulfill the divine purpose. Holding Ishmael on his knee and tenderly caring for him from infancy, the aged patriarch felt strong affection for this one and only child. He beamed, doted, and wrapped his heart strings around Ishmael.

When Ishmael was thirteen years old, God shocked the blissful Abraham by telling him that Ishmael, born of the slave girl, was not the one through whom He would bless the world. God told Abraham that his shrunken, ninety-year-old wife Sarah was going to bear him a son through whom the promise would be fulfilled. The idea of setting aside Ishmael, the idol of his heart, greatly disturbed Abraham, who implored God, ". . . oh that Ishmael might live before thee!"[4]

God, knowing the nature of Ishmael and foreseeing the murderous tendencies in him and his posterity, could not grant Abraham's prayer. When Abraham recognized that God would not change, he accepted the divine plan. By faith a son was miraculously born to the aged Abraham and Sarah, and he was called Isaac.

As the years passed the conflict between these two basically different sons of Abraham and their two mothers became intense, bitter and murderous. Abraham's mind was in turmoil—as the mind of unregenerate man is upset by two warring elements under his cerebral roof. Abraham's mind would be pulled one moment by the appeals of the good son Isaac. Then his mind would be torn by the demands of Ishmael, who the angel predicted would be the son of lust and hate. Abraham was very conscious of these two diametrically opposed forces under his roof, just as Ransler the sex murderer sensed both the good and the bad forces within himself.

Because God saw that the hate in Ishmael's heart was

nearing the point of murder, He called Abraham to him and told him to cast Ishmael out of his house. Cast out his firstborn, his seventeen-year-old son, the idol of his heart? Undoubtedly Abraham shed many a tear over this command, but by faith he obeyed God. It was better to shed a few tears over Ishmael's dismissal than to shed many more over the murder of Isaac, the son through whom the Christ was to come. One should remember that the tears Abraham shed over Ishmael were the result of his getting outside of God's will.

Paul tells us that these two sons of Abraham were symbolical of the two natures within carnal man:

Now we, brethren, as Isaac was, are the children of promise. But as then he that was born after the flesh persecuted him that was born after the Spirit, even so it is now. Nevertheless what saith the scripture? Cast out the bondwoman and her son: for the son of the bondwoman shall not be heir with the son of the freewoman. So then, brethren, we are not children of the bondwoman, but of the free.[5]

For the flesh lusteth against the Spirit, and the Spirit against the flesh: and these are contrary the one to the other: so that ye cannot do the things that ye would.[6]

In writing to the Romans, Paul describes two warring forces within his own mind before he was filled with the Holy Spirit. He dramatically describes the greater power of the carnal force nineteen centuries before the birth of psychiatry:

My own behavior baffles me. For I find myself not doing what I really want to do but doing what I really loathe. Yet surely if I do things I really don't want to do it cannot be said that "I" am doing them at all—it must be sin that has made its home in my nature. (And indeed, I know from experience that the carnal side of my being can scarcely be called the home of good!) I often find that I have the will to do good, but not the power. That is, I don't accomplish the good I set out to do, and the evil I don't really want to do I find I am always doing. Yet if I do things that I don't really want to do then it is not, I repeat, "I" who do them, but the sin which has made its home within me. When I come up against the Law [Mosaic Law] I want to do good, but in practice I do evil. My conscious mind whole-heartedly endorses the Law, yet I observe an entirely different principle at work in my nature. This is in continual conflict with my conscious attitude, and makes me an unwilling prisoner to the law of sin and death. In my mind I am God's willing servant, but in my own nature I am bound fast, as I say, to the law of sin and death. It is an agonising situation, and who on earth can set me free from the clutches of my own sinful nature?[7]

Here is the greatest human question of all time. Abraham, the Apostle Paul, and the sex murderer Ransler faced it. Everyone will have some important questions in the tomorrows, but none is as important as this one: ". . . Who on earth can set me free from the clutches of my own sinful nature?" If one fails here he will, in a sense, fail in every day that he lives.

There is no lack of answers. Every school of psychiatric thought has a different one—pretty good evidence that none is truly effective. Furthermore, these various schools concern themselves with merely treating symptoms. But there is a *cure* for mankind's agonizing situation.

CHAPTER 26

Freedom From an Agonizing Situation

"WHO ON EARTH CAN SET ME FREE FROM THE CLUTCHES of my own sinful nature?" This question asked long ago by the Apostle Paul is being asked by millions of people today. It was the question that troubled two psychiatrists—husband and wife—as they held a consultation in their offices in Chicago. They were discussing the best way to free a patient from a serious situation.

Dr. Lena Sadler had asked her husband, Dr. William S. Sadler, to see one of her patients, a "refined, highly educated" woman. The patient still did not respond, even after their combined psychiatric counselings. Dr. William Sadler advised his wife that she need not expect any worthwhile improvement "until her patient's mental life was set in order and numerous psychic slivers were removed." To the question of how long did he think that would take, he replied, "Probably a year or more."

Now let Dr. William Sadler tell in his own words what happened:

> Imagine my surprise when this patient walked into my office a few days later and informed me that her "troubles were over," that the things she had assured me a few days previously she "could never do," had all been done, that everything I had asked her to do as part of her "cure" had been set in operation—she had completely overhauled her social, family, and personal life, had made numerous "confessions," and had accomplished a score of almost impossible mental and "moral" stunts.
>
> In reply to my astonished question, "How in the world did you ever do all this and effect this great change in your mental attitude toward yourself and the world in less than one week?" she smilingly replied, "Dr. Lena taught me to pray."[1]

Without further long, drawn-out and expensive sessions in a psychiatrist's office, the woman had confessed her sins to God and to others. Then she experienced *immediately* the healing and refreshment of the promise of Jesus: "Peace I leave with you, my peace I give unto you: not as the world giveth, give I unto you. Let not your heart be troubled, neither let it be afraid."[2]

Dr. Carl Jung also recognized the importance of God in healing the ills of mankind:

> I should like to call attention to the following facts. During the past thirty years, people from all the civilized countries of the earth have consulted me. I have treated many hundreds of patients. . . . Among all my patients in the second half of life—that is to say, over thirty-five—there has not been *one* whose problem in the last resort was not that of finding a religious outlook on life. . . .
>
> It seems to me, that, side by side with the decline of religious life, the neuroses grow noticeably more frequent. . . .
>
> The patient is looking for something that will take pos-

session of him and give meaning and form to the confusion of his neurotic mind. Is the doctor equal to the task? To begin with, he will probably hand over his patient to the clergyman or the philosopher, or abandon him to that perplexity which is the special note of our day. . . . Human thought cannot conceive any system or final truth that could give the patient what he needs in order to live: that is faith, hope, love, and insight. . . .

There are however persons who, while well aware of the psychic nature of their complaint, nevertheless refuse to turn to the clergyman. They do not believe that he can really help them. Such persons distrust the doctor for the same reason, and they are justified by the fact that both doctor and clergyman *stand before them with empty hands, if not—what is even worse—with empty words*. . . . It is from the clergyman, not from the doctor, that the sufferers should expect such help.[3]

Freud, Adler, and Jung largely agreed that many of man's mental disturbances are due to *conflict* between inner good and evil forces. Freud emphasized the *sexual propensities* of the bad force, Adler stressed the *ruthless drive* of the carnal nature for power and supremacy, while Jung likened the evil part of man to a *wild, ravenous wolf*.

In the 1930's, specialists in psychosomatic medicine began to learn that a host of *physical diseases* were caused by envy, jealousy, self-centeredness, resentment, fear and hatred—*the identical emotions that the Bible lists as attributes of our wolfish nature. Hence, we see that most of the mental and physical ills of man are caused by the activities of an inner evil force*. Understandable is the inefficacy of human agents to free man from an innate evil nature that is tied as tightly to him as a corpse was bound to a condemned criminal in ancient times.

Paul himself answered the question he had raised:

I thank God there *is* a way out through Jesus Christ our Lord.[4]

. . . *while Christ was actually taking upon Himself the sins of men, God condemned that sinful nature*. So that . . . we are living no longer by the dictates of our sinful nature, but in obedience to the promptings of the Spirit.[5]

Now if Christ does live within you His presence means that your sinful nature is dead. . . .[6]

By His death and resurrection Jesus did not automatically deliver every man from the bondage of his lower nature. He made this freedom available through our obedience to these divine conditions:

. . . if . . . you cut the nerve of your instinctive actions by obeying the Spirit, you are on the way to real living.[7]

So that . . . we are living no longer by the dictates of our sinful nature, but in obedience to the promptings of the Spirit.[8]

And those who belong to Christ Jesus have crucified the lower nature with its passions and desires.[9]

Then put to death those parts of you which belong to the earth— fornication, indecency, lust, foul cravings, and the ruthless greed which is nothing less than idolatry.[10]

But now you yourselves must lay aside all anger, passion, malice, cursing, filthy talk—have done with them! Stop lying to one another, now that you have discarded the old nature with its deeds and have put on the new nature, which is being constantly renewed in the image of its Creator and brought to know God.[11]

Billy Graham expresses well the part we must play: "It is only when we come to the *will* that we find the very heart of repentance. There must be that determination to forsake sin—to change one's attitude toward self, toward sin, and God; to change one's feeling: to change one's will, disposition, and purpose. . . . There is not one verse of Scripture that indicates you can be a Christian and live any kind of a life you want to."[12]

Paul tells us that Abraham, with two warring sons under his roof, was a symbol of the two forces within man's mind.[13] But Paul makes the application for us: "Nevertheless what saith the scripture? Cast out the . . . son. . . ."[14] It will give us pain to bid a final farewell to the carnal part of our natures which has given us a large share of life's so-called pleasures. It will mean giving up some of our habits, our friends, our practices, and our ways of thinking. Let us face it squarely—it is a sorrowful experience to bid adieu to every worldly pleasure, friend and habit that God marks for dismissal. Yet it is not a dismissal of worthwhile joys and friends but of those born, like Ishmael, outside of God's will for our lives.

" 'I promise you,' " returned Jesus, 'nobody leaves home or brothers or sisters or mother or father or children or property for my sake or the Gospel's without getting back a hundred times over, now in this present life; . . . and in the next world eternal life.' "[15]

Jesus recognizes that we feel some pain in giving up that which is carnal, but He promises that we will receive here and now one hundred times as much of the worthwhile. His statement is understandable when we realize the vast array of mental and physical diseases from which we are freed when we, with God's help, cast out the innate troublemaker.

We may shed some tears in saying farewell to the old life and its lure, but our grief will seem inconsequential moments later when we experience the exhilaration of His resurrection, life, and power within us: "For if we have grown jointly with Him in experiencing a similar death, then the same must be true of our resurrection with Him, aware of this, that our old self has been jointly crucified with Him, so that the sin-controlled body might be devitalized and we no longer be slaves of sin.[16]

Surrendering one's will to the divine will may seem to be a negative procedure, but it gives positive dividends. Psychologist Wallace Emerson writes, "It is a will that, while giving up the mastery, has finally become something of a master in its own house. . . ."[17] Only when we do our part in crucifying the inner troublemaker, and in opening the door so that Christ may occupy the throne room of the soul, can we experience real living, new strength and vitality, life and inward peace, and the fullness of the promise, ". . . none of these diseases. . . ."

NOTES

CHAPTER 1

1. S. E. Massengill, *A Sketch of Medicine and Pharmacy* (Bristol, Tenn., S. E. Massengill Company, 1943), p. 16.
2. *Ibid.*
3. *Scope* (Summer 1955), p. 13.
4. Massengill, *op. cit.*, pp. 16-17.
5. Acts 7:22, KJV.
6. Exodus 15:26, KJV.
7. George Rosen, *History of Public Health* (New York, MD Publications, 1958), pp. 62-63.
8. Fielding Garrison, *History of Medicine* (Philadelphia, W. B. Saunders Co., 1929), p. 187.
9. Rosen, *op. cit.*, pp. 63-65.
10. Arturo Castiglione, *A History of Medicine* (New York, Alfred A. Knopf, Inc., 1941), p. 71.

CHAPTER 2

1. Deuteronomy 23:12-13, BERKELEY.
2. Arturo Castiglione, *op. cit.*, p. 70.
3. Numbers 19, KJV.
4. *An Epitome of the History of Medicine,* second edition (Philadelphia, F. A. Davis Co., 1901), p. 326.

CHAPTER 3

1. Harold Thomas Hyman, *An Integrated Practice of Medicine* (Philadelphia, W. B. Saunders Co., 1946), p. 2551.
2. Hiram N. Wineberg, "The Rare Occurrence of Cancer of the Womb Among Jewish Women," *Bulletin of Mt. Sinai Hospital* (1919).
3. I. Kaplan, and R. Rosh, *American Journal of Roentgenology* (June 1947), pp. 659-664.
4. "Cancer of Cervix and Non-Jews," *Journal of the American Medical Association* (July 23, 1949), p. 1069.
5. W. B. Ober, and L. Reiner, "Cancer of Cervix in Jewish Women," *New England Journal of Medicine* (November 30, 1954), pp. 555-559.

6. A. Symeonidis, "Acta Union Internationale Contre le Cancer," *Bulletin of U. S. Public Health Service* (Vol. VII, No. 1), p. 127; P. S. Rao, R. S. Reddy, and D. J. Reddy, "A Study of the Etiological Factors in Guntur," *Journal of the American Medical Association* (November 7, 1959), p. 1421.
7. S. L. Israel, "Relative Infrequency of Cervical Carcinoma in Jewish Women: Is the Enigma Solved?" *American Journal of Obstetrics and Gynecology* (March 1955), pp. 358-360.
8. A. J. Paquin, Jr., and J. M. Pearce, *Journal of Urology* (November 1955), pp. 626-627.
9. Genesis 17:10-12.
10. Martin C. Rosenthal, *Journal of the American Medical Association* (February 1947), p. 436.
11. L. Emmett Holt, Jr., and Rustin McIntosh, *Holt Pediatrics*, twelfth edition (New York, Appleton-Century-Crofts, Inc., 1953), pp. 125-126.
12. Genesis 17:12, KJV.
13. Colossians 2:11, NEB.
14. Colossians 3:5-9, NEB.
15. J. D. Ratcliff, "Stress the Cause of All Disease?" *Reader's Digest* (January 1955), pp. 24-28.
16. Deuteronomy 10:12, 16; Jeremiah 4:4; Romans 2:28-29; 4:11; Galatians 6:13-15.
17. Acts 15:22-30.
18. Galatians 5:24, NEB.

CHAPTER 4

1. Milton Golin, "Robber of Five Million Brains," *Journal of the American Medical Association* (July 19, 1958), p. 1496.
2. "Motor-Vehicle Accidents," *Journal of the American Medical Association* (March 30, 1957), p. 1149.
3. *New York State Department of Health Bulletin,* (Vol. XIV, May 29, 1961), p. 85.
4. *Ibid.* (Vol. XI, July 14, 1958), p. 113.
5. William N. Plymat, *Buffalo Evening News* (July 29, 1960), p. 1.
6. "Incidence of Violent Deaths Tied to Alcohol Reported High," *Medical Tribune* (July 25, 1960), p. 4.
7. Eli Robins, "Recognition and Management of the Seriously Suicidal Patient," *Medical Science* (July 25, 1960), p. 78.
8. Russell L. Cecil and Robert F. Loeb, *Textbook of Medicine* (Philadelphia, W. B. Saunders Co., 1959), p. 1653.
9. *Ibid.*

10. Frederick Lemere, "Final Outcome of Alcoholism," *Modern Medicine* (July 15, 1953), p. 110.
11. *Othello,* ii. 3. 293.
12. Psalm 84:11, KJV.
13. "A Problem in Business and Industry," *Yale Center of Alcohol Studies,* p. 251.
14. "Alcoholism," *Journalism of the American Medical Association* (August 7, 1954), p. 1366.
15. *Ibid.*
16. Howard Earle, "They're Helping the Alcoholic Worker," *Today's Health* (December 1960), p. 73.
17. Proverbs 23:19-21, 29-34, MOFFATT.

CHAPTER 5

1. Alton Ochsner, *Smoking and Cancer* (New York, Julian Messner, Inc., 1954), p. 12.
2. *Today's Health* (March 1959), p. 54.
3. Victor H. Handy, "Lung Cancer in Men," *Health News* (November 1958), p. 16.
4. Ochsner, *op. cit.,* p. 18.
5. *Ibid.,* p. 4.
6. *Ibid.,* p. 14.
7. David Rutstein, *Cancer* (March-April 1958), p. 46.
8. E. C. Hammond and Daniel Horn, "Smoking and Death Rates—Report on 44 Months of Follow-Up of 187,783 Men," *Journal of the American Medical Association* (March 15, 1958), pp. 1294-1308.
9. *Ibid.,* p. 1308.
10. *Scope* (February 13, 1957).
11. L. E. Burney, "Smoking and Lung Cancer," *Journal of the American Medical Association* (November 28, 1959), p. 1829; L. M. Miller, and James Monahan, "The Facts Behind Filter-Tip Cigarettes," *Reader's Digest* (July 1957), pp. 33-39.
12. "Mortality From Selected Causes, by Age, Race, and Sex: United States, 1959," *Vital Statistics* (Septem-22, 1961).
13. E. C. Hammond, and Daniel Horn, *op. cit.,* p. 1307.
14. *Ibid.,* p. 1305.
15. *World Almanac and Book of Facts for 1960* (New York, *New York World Telegram and the Sun),* p. 307.
16. H. S. Hedges, "Eye Damage By Alcohol," *Journal of the American Medical Association* (February 18, 1956), p. 604.
17. J. D. Spillane, "Nicotine and the Nervous System," *Journal of the American Medical Association* (February 18, 1956), p. 584.

18. "Cigarette Smoking," *Journal of the American Medical Association* (May 19, 1956), p. 301.
19. E. C. Hammond, and Daniel Horn, *op. cit.*, p. 1296.
20. Francis C. Lowell, William Franklin, Alan L. Michelson, and Irving W. Schiller, *The New England Journal of Medicine* (January 19, 1956).
21. "Smoking and Asthma," *Journal of the American Medical Association* (December 12, 1952), p. 1540.
22. F. L. Rosen, and A. Levy, "Bronchial Asthma Due to Allergy to Tobacco Smoke in an Infant," *Journal of the American Medical Association* (October 21, 1950), pp. 620-621.
23. E. C. Hammond, and Daniel Horn, *op. cit.*, p. 1306.
24. *Ibid.*
25. P. Bernhard, "Injurious Effects of Cigarette Smoking in Women," *Journal of the American Medical Association* (October 15, 1949), p. 492.
26. I Corinthians 6:19-20, KJV.
27. I Corinthians 3:17, KJV.
28. I Corinthians 10:31, KJV.

CHAPTER 6

1. Harold Thomas Hyman, *An Integrated Practice of Medicine* (Philadelphia, W. B. Saunders Co., 1946), p. 332.
2. Exodus 34:7, KJV.
3. I Corinthians 10:8, ASV.
4. Johan Wintzell, *Svenska lakartidningen* (April 2, 1954), abstracted in the *Journal of the American Medical Association* (July 15, 1954), p. 1097.
5. I Corinthians 6:18, ASV.
6. Ernst Epstein, "Failure of Penicillin in Treatment of Acute Gonorrhea in American Troops in Korea," *Journal of the American Medical Association* (March 7, 1959), p. 1054.
7. *Journal of the American Medical Association* (February 13, 1954), p. 608.
8. "Syphilis Again on the Increase," *Journal of the American Medical Association* (April 20, 1957), p. 1545.
9. Howard Whitman, "The Slavery of Sex Freedom," *Better Homes & Gardens* (June 1957), p. 59.
10. Sylvanus M. Duvall, "Fiction and Facts About Sex," *Reader's Digest* (June 1960), p. 128.
11. Walter Lentino, "Evaluation of a System of Legalized Prostitution," *Journal of the American Medical Association* (May 7, 1955), p. 22.
12. Harold Thomas Hyman, *op. cit.*, p. 1465.

13. Proverbs 5:1-12, MOFFATT.
14. I Thessalonians 4:3-8, PHILLIPS.
15. Harold Thomas Hyman, *op. cit.*, p. 332.
16. R. H. Kampmeier, "Management of Syphilis," *Modern Medicine* (July 15, 1953), p. 88.
17. Mark 10:4-9, KJV.

CHAPTER 7

1. Alfred C. Kinsey, Wardell B. Pomeroy, Clyde E. Martin and Paul H. Gebhard, *Sexual Behavior in the Human Female* (Philadelphia, W. B. Saunders Co., 1953).
2. Romans 1:24-32; Mark 7:20-23; Galatians 5:19-21, KJV.
3. Edmund Bergler, and William S. Kroger, "Sexual Behavior," *Journal of the American Medical Association* (January 9, 1954), p. 168.
4. Alfred C. Kinsey, et al, *op. cit.*, p. 327.
5. William J. Brown, "Current Status of Syphilis in the United States," *Erie County Bulletin* (February 1961), p. 10.
6. Alfred C. Kinsey, et al, *op. cit.*, pp. 328-330, 385-390,
7. Edmund Bergler, and William S. Kroger, *op. cit.*, p. 168.
8. Review of *Kinsey's Myth of Female Sexuality: The Medical Facts* (Edmund Bergler and William S. Kroger), in the *Journal of the American Medical Association* (April 17, 1954), p. 1396.
9. Irving J. Sands, "Marriage Counseling as a Medical Responsibility," *New York State Journal of Medicine* (July 15, 1954), p. 2052.
10. Maurice Zolotow, "Love Is Not a Statistic," *Reader's Digest* (April 1954), p. 9.
11. *Ibid.*
12. Howard Whitman, "The Slavery of Sex Freedom," *Better Homes & Gardens* (June 1957), p. 219.
13. Hebrews 13:4, KJV.
14. "Youth and the Natural Urge," *Better Homes & Gardens* (July 1957), p. 43.
15. Mark 10:6-8, ASV.
16. Irving J. Sands, *op. cit.*, pp. 2052-2055.

CHAPTER 8

1. Carl Jung, *Modern Man in Search of a Soul* (New York, Harcourt, Brace and Co., Inc., 1933), p. 260.
2. I Corinthians 13:4-5, 7-8, NEB.
3. New York, Simon and Schuster, Inc., 1956, pp. 3-15.

4. *Psychoanalysis and Religion* (New Haven, Yale University Press, 1950), pp. 86-87.
5. "Sex in Modern Life," *Current Medical Digest* (September 1961), p. 55.
6. I Corinthians 13:11, 13, NEB.
7. Luke 15:11-32.
8. Paul H. Landis, "Don't Expect Too Much of Sex in Marriage," *Reader's Digest* (December 1954), pp. 26-27.
9. I Corinthians 10:13, KJV.

CHAPTER 9

1. *Journal of the American Medical Association* (May 29, 1948), p. 442.
2. J. D. Ratcliff, *Reader's Digest* (January 1955), pp. 24-28.
3. *Personality Manifestations in Psychosomatic Illness* (Philadelphia, Edward Stern & Co., 1953).
4. *Scope* (November 13, 1947).

CHAPTER 10

1. Galatians 5:19-21, PHILLIPS.
2. Galatians 5:24, MOFFATT.
3. *Practice of Psychiatry* (St. Louis, C. V. Mosby Co., 1953), p. 1008.
4. *Macbeth*, v. 3. 38.
5. *Ibid*,, v. 3. 40.
6. *The Way to Security* (Garden City, N. Y., Doubleday & Co., Inc., 1951), p. 52.
7. Hebrews 12:14-15, PHILLIPS.
8. Galatians 5:24, PHILLIPS.

CHAPTER 11

1. Dale Carnegie, *How to Stop Worrying and Start Living* (New York, Simon and Schuster, Inc., 1948), p. 101.
2. William J. Grace, and Harold G. Wolff, "Treatment of Ulcerative Colitis," *Journal of the American Medical Association* (July 14, 1951), p. 981.
3. George W. Gray, "Anxiety and Illness," *Harper's* (May 1939), p. 610.
4. Dale Carnegie, *op. cit.*, p. 101.
5. Proverbs 15:17, MOFFATT.
6. Luke 9:55, KJV.
7. Acts 7:60, KJV.
8. Colossians 3:5, 7-10, 13-14, MOFFATT.

CHAPTER 12

1. Matthew 5:41, ASV.
2. Matthew 5:40 ASV.

CHAPTER 13

1. I Corinthians 13:4-5, ASV.
2. *What Life Should Mean to You* (Boston, Little, Brown and Co., 1931), p. 258.
3. Matthew 22:37-40, ASV.
4. Matthew 5:44, KJV.
5. Edwin Markham, "Outwitted," *Poems of Edwin Markham* (New York, Harper & Brothers, 1950), p. 18. Reprinted by permission of Virgil Markham.

CHAPTER 14

1. *Health News* (February 1955), p. 9.
2. I Thessalonians 5:18, PHILLIPS.
3. Philippians 4:6-7, PHILLIPS.
4. Philippians 4:8, KJV.

CHAPTER 15

1. Paul B. Roen, "Atherosclerosis," *General Practice* (January 1959), p. 11.
2. Leviticus 7:22-24, KJV.
3. Leviticus 3:17.
4. Russell L. Cecil, and Robert F. Loeb, *A Textbook of Medicine* (Philadelphia, W. B. Saunders Co., 1959), p. 645.
5. Titus 1:12-13, BERKELEY.
6. E. C. Hammond, and Daniel Horn, "Smoking and Death Rates," *Journal of the American Medical Association* (March 15, 1958), p. 1304.
7. "Vital Statistics," *National Summaries* (April 24, 1959), p. 130.
8. "Free-Fatty-Acid Rise Tied to Smoking," *Medical News* (June 2, 1961), p. 1.
9. Harold Gretzinger, "No Time to Waste," *Christian Life* (February, 1949).
10. Psalm 91:3-7, KJV.
11. Psalm 46:1-3, KJV.
12. Psalm 46:10-11, ASV.

CHAPTER 16

1. Psalm 27:1-3, BERKELEY.
2. Harold Thomas Hyman, *An Integrated Practice of Medicine* (Philadelphia, W. B. Saunders Co., 1946), p. 909.
3. Psalm 56:3-4, BERKELEY.
4. W. T. Purkiser, *Exploring the Old Testament* (Kansas City, Beacon Hill Press, 1960), p. 25.
5. Psalm 23:1-4, KJV.

CHAPTER 17

1. Matthew 5:40, KJV.

2. "Influence of Some Drugs and Emotions on Blood Coagulation," *Journal of the American Medical Association* (January 26, 1952), p. 269.
3. R. H. Rosenman, and M. Friedman, "Stress Affects Serum Cholesterol and Clotting Time," *Medical Newsletter* (November—December, 1957), p. 1; Stewart Wolf, "Emotional Tension Alone Is Found to Raise Serum Cholesterol Level," *Scope* (January 6, 1960), p. 1; "Stress and Heart Disease," *Modern Concepts of Cardiovascular Disease* (American Heart Association, July 1960), p. 599.
4. Psalm 34:4, KJV.

CHAPTER 18
1. Dale Carnegie, *op. cit.*, pp. 253-254.
2. Isaiah 26:3, KJV.
3. *Practice of Psychiatry* (St. Louis, C. V. Mosby Co., 1953), pp. 1012-1013.
4. Psalm 103:12, KJV.
5. I John 4:18, KJV.
6. Proverbs 16:7, KJV.
7. I Corinthians 15:54-55, KJV.
8. "Thanatopsis."

CHAPTER 19
1. John 11:25-26, BERKELEY.
2. Luke 8:52, ASV.
3. I Thessalonians 4:13, BERKELEY.
4. I Corinthians 15:21, BERKELEY.
5. I Corinthians 15:22, KJV.
6. II Corinthians 4:17-18, BERKELEY.
7. Philippians 4:6-7, BERKELEY.

CHAPTER 20
1. Frederick Langbridge, "A Cluster of Quiet Thoughts" (published by the Religious Tract Society).
2. *The Stress of Life* (New York, McGraw-Hill Book Co., Inc., 1956), p. 154.
3. II Corinthians 12:8-10, BERKELEY.
4. Mark 6:31, KJV.
5. "A Scientific Report on What Hope Does for Man" (New York State Heart Assembly, 105 East 22nd Street, New York, New York).
6. John Bunyan, *Grace Abounding to the Chief of Sinners* (Philadelphia, J. J. Woodward, 1928), p. 148.
7. Genesis 37:35, BERKELEY.
8. Genesis 42:36, KJV.
9. Genesis 47:9, BERKELEY.
10. II Corinthians 11:24-27, BERKELEY.

11. Romans 8:35-37, PHILLIPS.
12. Romans 8:37, KJV.

CHAPTER 21

1. Philadelphia, W. B. Saunders Co., 1959, p. 1653.
2. William Wordsworth, "My Heart Leaps Up."
3. Psalm 34:11-14, MOFFATT.

CHAPTER 22

1. *Psychiatry in General Practice* (Philadelphia, W. B. Saunders Co., 1949), pp. 265-268.
2. S. Arieti, *Interpretation of Schizophrenia* (New York, Robert Brunner, 1955), p. 3.
3. *Practice of Psychiatry* (St. Louis, C. V. Mosby Co., 1953), p. 396.
4. Proverbs 22:15, ASV.
5. Exodus 20:9, ASV.
6. II Thessalonians 3:10, KJV.
7. "Psychiatry At Work," *Time* (July 18, 1955), p. 55.
8. Philippians 4:7, KJV.
9. John 14:27, ASV.
10. *The Merck Manual* (Rahway, N. J., Merck & Co., 1956), p. 1311.
11. Philippians 2:4, PHILLIPS.
12. Ephesians 4:31-32, PHILLIPS.
13. Romans 12:10, PHILLIPS.
14. Romans 14:19, PHILLIPS.
15. Mark 6:31, ASV.

CHAPTER 23

1. Luke 6:38, ASV.
2. Smiley Blanton, *Love or Perish* (New York, Simon and Schuster, Inc., 1956), p. 4.
3. Harry J. Johnson, *Blue Print for Health* (Chicago, Blue Cross Association, Summer 1962), p. 19.
4. John D. Rockefeller, Sr., *Outlook* (October 7, 1905), pp. 300-301.
5. I John 3:14, BERKELEY.
6. Romans 12:16, BERKELEY.
7. Romans 12:16, PHILLIPS.
8. Matthew 16:25, KJV.

CHAPTER 24

1. *Understanding Human Nature* (Garden City, N. Y., Garden City Publishing Co., 1927), pp. 285-286; *Individual Psychology and Social Problems* (London, The C. S. Daniel Co., 1932), pp. 15, 22.
2. Romans 12:3, PHILLIPS.
3. Romans 12:9-10, 16, BERKELEY.
4. James 3:1, PHILLIPS.

5. Philippians 2:2-3, PHILLIPS.
6. Matthew 23:5-12, PHILLIPS.
7. Psalm 119:165, KJV.
8. Matthew 5:5, KJV.
9. Anonymous.
10. *What Life Should Mean to You* (Boston, Little, Brown and Co., 1931), p. 258.
11. Matthew 19:19, KJV.
12. Galatians 5:24, NEB.
13. Romans 8:3, PHILLIPS.
14. Hebrews 13:12-13, KJV.

CHAPTER 25

1. New York, Harcourt, Brace and Co., Inc., 1938, p. 81.
2. *Modern Man in Search of a Soul* (New York, Harcourt, Brace and Co., Inc., 1933), p. 273.
3. Genesis 21, KJV.
4. Genesis 17:18, ASV.
5. Galatians 4:28-31, KJV.
6. Galatians 5:17, KJV.
7. Romans 7:15-24, PHILLIPS.

CHAPTER 26

1. *Theory and Practice of Psychiatry* (St. Louis, C. V. Mosby Co., 1936), p. 1075.
2. John 14:27, KJV.
3. Carl G. Jung, *Modern Man in Search of a Soul* (New York, Harcourt, Brace and Co., Inc., 1933), pp. 260-262.
4. Romans 7:25, PHILLIPS.
5. Romans 8:3-4, PHILLIPS.
6. Romans 8:10, PHILLIPS.
7. Romans 8:13, PHILLIPS.
8. Romans 8:4, PHILLIPS.
9. Galatians 5:24, NEB.
10. Colossians 3:5, NEB.
11. Colossians 3:8-10, NEB.
12. *Peace With God* (New York, Permabooks, 1955), pp. 124-125.
13. Galatians 4:28-31; 5:17, KJV.
14. Galatians 4:30, KJV.
15. Mark 10:30-31, PHILLIPS.
16. Romans 6:5-6, BERKELEY.
17. *Outline of Psychology* (Wheaton, Ill., Van Kampen Press), p. 453.